MW00964932

Chapters 12–26

Accounting

Charles T. Horngren Series in Accounting

Auditing and Assurance Services: An Integrated Approach, 10th ed.
Arens/Elder/Beasley

Essentials of Auditing and Assurance Services, 1st ed.
Arens/Elder/Beasley

Governmental and Nonprofit Accounting: Theory and Practice, 7th ed.
Freeman/Shoulders

Financial Accounting, 5th ed.
Harrison/Horngren

Cases in Financial Reporting, 4th ed.
Hirst/McAnally

Cost Accounting: A Managerial Emphasis, 11th ed.
Horngren/Datar/Foster

Accounting, 6th ed.
Horngren/Harrison/Bamber

Introduction to Financial Accounting, 8th ed.
Horngren/Sundem/Elliott

Introduction to Management Accounting, 13th ed.
Horngren/Sundem/Stratton

Budgeting, 7th ed.
Welsch/Hilton/Gordon

Chapters 12–26

Accounting

Sixth Edition

Charles T. Horngren

Stanford University

Walter T. Harrison Jr.

Baylor University

Linda Smith Bamber

University of Georgia

PEARSON

Prentice Hall

Upper Saddle River, New Jersey 07458

Library of Congress Cataloging-in-Publication Data

Horngren, Charles T.
 Accounting / Charles T. Horngren, Walter T. Harrison, Jr., Linda Smith Bamber.—6th ed.
 1216 p. cm.
 Includes indexes.
 ISBN 0-13-143596-5
 1. Accounting. I. Harrison, Walter T. II. Bamber, Linda S. (Linda Smith), III.
 Title.

HF5635.H8 2003
657—dc22   2003065606

Editor-in-Chief: P.J. Boardman
Assistant Editor: Sam Goffinet
Editorial Assistant: Jane Avery
Director of Development: Stephen Deitmer
Senior Development Editor: Jeannine Ciliotta
Senior Media Project Manager: Nancy Welcher
Executive Marketing Manager: Beth Toland
Managing Editor (Production): Cynthia Regan
Senior Production Editor: Anne Graydon
Production Assistant: Joe DeProspero
Permissions Supervisor: Suzanne Grappi
Associate Director, Manufacturing: Vincent Scelta
Production Manager, Manufacturing: Arnold Vila
Design Manager: Maria Lange

Designer: Steve Frim
Interior Design: Jill Little; Atelier de ZIN
Cover Design: Steve Frim
Cover Photo: David Mager/Pearson Learning Group Photo Studio
Illustrator (Interior): Precision Graphics
Photo Researcher: Julie Tesser; Elaine Soares
Image Permission Coordinator: Michelina Viscusi
Manager, Print Production: Christy Mahon
Composition/Full-Service: UG / GGS Information Services, Inc.
Project Management: UG / GGS Information Services, Inc.
Printer/Binder: R.R. Donnelley, Willard

Credits and acknowledgments borrowed from other sources and reproduced, with permission, in this textbook:
Page 3 AP/Wide World Photos; **7** AP/Wide World Photos; **43** PhotoEdit; **65** Hisham F. Ibrahim/Getty Images, Inc.-Photodisc; **91** It's Just Lunch! Inc.; **95** Laurence Manning/CORBIS BETTMANN; **139** AP/Wide World Photos; **156** Dell Computer Corporation; **139** AP/Wide World Photos; **194** Amazon.com; **247** Raymond Watt/Albuquerque International Balloon Fiesta ®; **261** Athlete's Foot; **281** PriceKubecha, PLLC; **286** TADOnline; **323** James Leynse/Corbis/SABA Press Photos, Inc.; **327** Getty Images, Inc.-Hilton Archive Photos; **361** Marvin Jones/Getty Images, Inc.-Hilton Archive Photos; **371** Index Stock Imagery, Inc.; **399** Lawrence Manning/CORBIS-NY; **418** AP/Wide World Photos; **435** Michael Newman/PhotoEdit; **438** Don Farrall/Getty Images, Inc.-Photodisc; **469** Taxi/Getty Images, Inc.-Taxi; **474** James Nielsen/CORBIS-NY; **505** The Image Works; **514** Alex Farnsworth/The Image Works; **543** John Van Hasselt/CORBIS/Sygma; **551** Deluxe Corporation; **579** Mario Tama/Getty Images Inc.-Hilton Archive Photos; **598** AP/Wide World Photos; **625** Steven Harris/Getty Images Inc.-Hilton Archive Photos; **640** Marty Lederhandler/AP/Wide World Photos; **657** David McNew/Getty Images Inc.-Hilton Archive Photos; **660** Taxi/Getty Images Inc.-Taxi; **705** Robin Laurance/Photo Researchers, Inc.; **724** Expedia.com; **751** Regal Marine Industries, Inc.; **770** The Image Works; **797** Courtesy of Dell Computer Corp.; **806** Intermec Technologies Corporation; **845** Used with permission from Jelly Belly Candy Company; **869** Levi Strauss & Co.; **897** Al Richmond/Grand Canyon Railway; **906** Neeme Frederic/CORBIS BETTMANN; **939** Courtesy of Amazon.com; **956** Fossil, Inc.; **985** Roberto Brosan/Getty Images Time Life Pictures; **998** AP/Wide World Photos; **1033** Dell Computer Corporation; **1054** Texas Instruments Incorporated; **1078** Eric Schramm/Eric Schramm Photography; **1089** Courtesy of International Business Machines Corporation. Unauthorized use not permitted.

Copyright © 2005, 2002, 1999, 1996, 1993 by Pearson Education, Inc., Upper Saddle River, New Jersey, 07458.
Pearson Prentice Hall. All rights reserved. Printed in the United States of America. This publication is protected by Copyright and permission should be obtained from the publisher prior to any prohibited reproduction, storage in a retrieval system, or transmission in any form or by any means, electronic, mechanical, photocopying, recording, or likewise. For information regarding permission(s), write to: Rights and Permissions Department.

Pearson Prentice Hall™ is a trademark of Pearson Education, Inc.
Pearson® is a registered trademark of Pearson plc
Prentice Hall® is a registered trademark of Pearson Education, Inc.

Pearson Education LTD.
Pearson Education Singapore, Pte. Ltd
Pearson Education, Canada, Ltd
Pearson Education–Japan

Pearson Education Australia PTY, Limited
Pearson Education North Asia Ltd
Pearson Educación de Mexico, S.A. de C.V.
Pearson Education Malaysia, Pte. Ltd

10 9 8 7 6 5 4 3 2 1
ISBN: 0-13-143630-9

To Betsy Willis and Becky Jones for their wisdom on learning and teaching over a 15-year period and to Michael Bamber for his insight on business practices and ethical issues in management accounting.

Brief Contents

■ Contents

Professor Harrison has lectured in several foreign countries and published articles in numerous journals, including *The Accounting Review, Journal of Accounting Research, Journal of Accountancy, Journal of Accounting and Public Policy, Economic Consequences of Financial Accounting Standards, Accounting Horizons, Issues in Accounting Education*, and *Journal of Law and Commerce*.

He is co-author of *Financial Accounting*, Fifth Edition, 2004 (with Charles T. Horngren), published by Prentice Hall. Professor Harrison has received scholarships, fellowships, and research grants or awards from PriceWaterhouse Coopers, Deloitte & Touche, the Ernst & Young Foundation, and the KPMG Foundation.

Linda Smith Bamber holds the J.M. Tull Chair of Accounting at the J.M. Tull School of Accounting at the University of Georgia. She graduated summa cum laude from Wake Forest University, where she was a member of Phi Beta Kappa. She is a Certified Public Accountant, and received an Elijah Watt Sells Award as well as the North Carolina Bronze Medal for her performance on the CPA examination. Before returning to graduate school, Professor Bamber gained professional experience working in management accounting at R.J. Reynolds, Inc. She then earned an MBA from Arizona State University, and a Ph.D. from The Ohio State University.

Professor Bamber has received numerous teaching awards from The Ohio State University, the University of Florida, and the University of Georgia.

She has lectured in Canada and Australia, in addition to the U.S., and her research has appeared in numerous journals, including *The Accounting Review, Journal of Accounting Research, Journal of Accounting and Economics, Journal of Finance, Contemporary Accounting Research, Accounting Horizons, Issues in Accounting Education*, and *The CPA Journal*. She also developed the annotations for the *Annotated Instructor's Edition* of Horngren, Foster, and Datar's *Cost Accounting: A Managerial Emphasis*, Seventh, Eighth, and Ninth Editions.

A member of the Institute of Management Accounting, the American Accounting Association (AAA) and the AAA's Management Accounting Section and Financial Accounting and Reporting Section, Professor Bamber has chaired the AAA New Faculty Consortium and the AAA Competitive Manuscript Award Committees, served on the AAA Council, the AAA Research Advisory Committee, the AAA Nominations Committee, and numerous other AAA and section committees. She served as Associate Editor of *Accounting Horizons*, and as editor of *The Accounting Review*.

■ Preface

From The Authors

This new sixth edition of *Accounting* has been tailored to meet instructors' needs and to help students master accounting. We think our efforts have made this revision much easier for instructors to teach and students to learn from. Throughout the text, we have streamlined the presentation and focused the content on the core topics of first-year accounting. To better prepare students for the business world, wherever possible we have used actual documents and real situations.

The text revisions and the new design, combined with an outstanding resource package, provide excellent tools for success in accounting. We hope you agree.

Charles Horngren   **Tom Harrison**   **Linda Bamber**

For The Student

New! A+ Tips leads you to all the learning resources that accompany the text. Follow the A+ Tips to improve your understanding—and your course grade!

Learning Objectives give you an overview of the skills you will learn in the chapter.

Chapter-opening vignettes take you into the real world of accounting—where business decisions affect the future of actual organizations. Each vignette introduces you to the central issues covered in the chapter. Many of the vignettes—on Jelly Belly, Oracle, Dell—are linked to unique, custom-created *On Location!* **Videos** available on the **Student and Instructor Resource CD-ROMs**.

New feature company: Amazon.com Amazon.com's annual report is bound into the book; Amazon is also the feature company in several chapter-opening vignettes, and in end-of-chapter financial statement cases.

Features

New! *Sitemaps* appear at the beginning of each chapter and at main headings throughout the chapter as a roadmap to show you where you are and what is coming next.

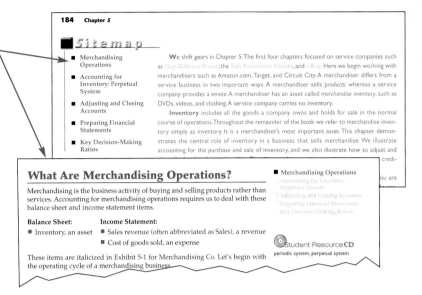

New! An open and reader-friendly **text design** includes many new exhibits and info-graphics.

A Running Glossary provides a full definition when a term is introduced. A list of terms appears at the end of each chapter, and there is a complete Glossary at the end of the book.

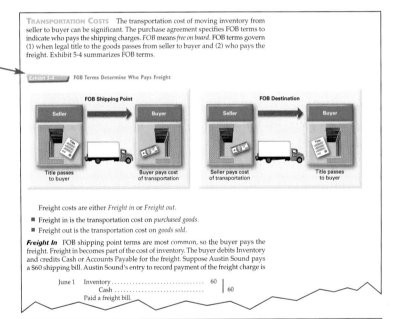

Unique! Concept Links help you remember material learned earlier. Concept links in the side margins point you to relevant topics covered earlier: they provide both a rationale for the material and a chapter and text page cross reference.

Stop & Think

This Stop & Think example is exactly like the preceding one, but with freight in. On September 15, Austin Sound purchased $1,000 of merchandise, with *$80 freight added,* for an invoice total of $1,080. Austin returns $100 of the goods for credit on September 20 and pays the account payable in full on September 25. Journalize these transactions.

Answer

Purchase: Sept. 15	Inventory ($1,000 + $80)......................	1,080	
	Accounts Payable......................		1,080
Return: Sept. 20	Accounts Payable...........................	100	
	Inventory..........................		100
Payment: Sept. 25	Accounts Payable ($1,080 − $100)...............	980	
	Inventory [($1,000 − $100) × 0.02).........		18
	Cash ($1,000 + $80 − $100 − $18).........		962

There is no discount on freight.

Stop & Think exercise boxes appear within the text in every chapter. The exercises encourage you to assess your understanding of concepts by providing immediate practice of what you have just learned.

Accounting.com

Amazon.com: For E-Tailers Free Shipping Isn't Free, But It's Not a Cost, Either

Like most accounting students, Jennifer didn't have time to go Christmas shopping. She cruised the online mall and ended up buying all her presents from Amazon.com, the largest player in online retailing. Jennifer was lured by Amazon.com's huge selection and an offer of free shipping for all orders over $25.

Amazon.com views free shipping as a key factor in boosting its growth—revenue jumped 233% to $851 million in one year. Yet, the company doesn't send packages via eight trusty reindeer. Amazon has to pay freight companies to deliver DVD players, books, and blenders to customers around the world. How does an e-tailer—one that is just barely making a profit—account for these shipping and handling costs?

Fortunately for Amazon and other e-tailers, in the process of revolutionizing business, e-commerce has also bent certain accounting rules. One such rule is that the cost of products sold to customers is usually recorded as Cost of Goods Sold, a merchandiser's major expense. But online powerhouses like Amazon.com and Buy.com count some of this cost as "sales and marketing expenses." By listing these "fulfillment costs" as marketing expenses, both e-tailers and catalog houses such as L. L. Bean don't have to subtract the expense in arriving at gross profit.

Small wonder that this controversial approach came under investigation by the Financial Accounting Standards Board (FASB). The dot-com bubble had burst, and e-tailers were poised to reclassify shipping and handling costs as costs of goods sold. That would restate gross profit downward. However, the Emerging Issues Task Force of the FASB recommended that shipping and handling *revenue* should be included in sales, without giving any guidance about how to account for shipping and handling *costs.* So Amazon and other e-tailers are free to continue including shipping and handling costs under marketing expense. The result: Gross profits are still high.

Based on: Nick Winfield, "Survival Strategy: Amazon Takes Page from Wal-Mart to Prosper on Web—Internet Retailer Cuts Prices and Keeps Eye on Costs in Bid for High Volumes—Betting Big on Free Shipping," *The Wall Street Journal,* November 22, 2002, p. Al. Saul Hansell, "Amazon's Loss in Quarter Shows a Sharp Decrease," *The New York Times,* October 25, 2002, p. 8. Katherine Hobson, "Silver Lining: FASB Spares E-Tailers in Cost Ruling," *The Street.com,* August 8, 2000.

Accounting.com boxes Nothing has changed business more in recent years than the Internet. Horngren/Harrison/Bamber's Accounting.com boxes identify accounting issues affecting companies doing business on the Web.

MID-CHAPTER *Summary Problem*

Suppose Amazon.com engaged in the following transactions during June of the current year:

CHECK YOUR RESOURCES

June 3 Purchased inventory on credit terms of 1/10 net eom (end of month), $1,600.
  9 Returned 40% of the inventory purchased on June 3. It was defective.
  12 Sold goods for cash, $920 (cost, $550).
  15 Purchased goods for $5,000. Credit terms were 3/15 net 30.
  16 Paid a $260 freight bill on goods purchased.
  18 Sold inventory on credit terms of 2/10 n/30, $2,000 (cost, $1,180).
  22 Received returned goods from the customer of the June 18 sale, $800 (cost, $480).
  24 Borrowed money from the bank to take advantage of the discount

Summary Problems This unique Horngren/Harrison/Bamber feature enables you to pause and assess your progress at two locations within each chapter—midway and again at the end of the chapter text. Solutions appear with the problems for immediate feedback.

END-OF-CHAPTER *Summary Problem*

CHECK YOUR RESOURCES

The adjustment data and trial balance of Jan King Distributing Company follow. (*The solution to Requirement 1 is on page 208.*)

Adjustment data at December 31, 20X6:

a. Supplies used during the year, $2,580.
b. Prepaid rent in force, $1,000.
c. Unearned sales revenue still not earned, $2,400.
d. Depreciation. The furniture and fixtures' estimated useful life is 10 years, and they are expected to be worthless when they are retired from service.
e. Accrued salaries, $1,300.
f. Accrued interest expense, $600.
g. Inventory on hand, $65,800.

Required

1. Enter the trial balance on a work sheet and complete the work sheet.
2. Journalize the adjusting and closing entries at December 31. Post to the Income Summary account as an accuracy check on the entries affecting that account. The credit balance closed out of Income Summary should equal net income computed on the work sheet.
3. Prepare the company's multi-step income statement, statement of owner's equity, and balance sheet in account format. Draw arrows linking the statements.
4. Compute the inventory turnover for 20X6. Inventory at December 31, 20X5, was $61,000. Turnover for 20X5 was 2.1 times. Would you expect Jan King Distributing Company to be more profitable or less profitable in 20X6 than in 20X5? Give your reason.

A+ Tips reminders appear with both Mid-Chapter and End-of-Chapter review problems.

Unique! Decision Guidelines show when, why, and how managers—not just accountants—use accounting information to make good business decisions.

Excel Application Exercises Every business professional must know how to use Excel, and Horngren/Harrison/Bamber provides the tools you need to master it. Excel Application Exercises appear in each chapter, with instructions for creating your own spreadsheets. Spreadsheet templates appear on the CD.

Decision Guidelines

MERCHANDISING OPERATIONS AND THE ACCOUNTING CYCLE

Amazon.com and Kinko's Copy Centers are two very different companies. How do Amazon and Kinko's differ? How are they similar? The Decision Guidelines answer these questions.

Decision	Guidelines
How do merchandisers differ from service entities?	• Merchandisers, such as Amazon.com, buy and sell *merchandise inventory*. • Service entities, such as Kinko's, perform a *service*.
How do a merchandiser's financial statements differ from the statements of a service business?	

Income Statement:

Merchandiser

Sales revenue	$XXX
−Cost of goods sold	(X)
= Gross profit	XX
−Operating expenses	(X)
= Net income	$ X

Statements of Owner's Equity:

Which type of inventory system to use?

Balance sheet:
• Merchandiser has *inventory*, an asset.
• Service business has no inventory.

Service Business

Service revenue	$ XX
−Operating expenses	(X)
= Net income	$ X

No difference

• *Perpetual system* shows the amount of *inventory* on hand (the asset) and the cost of goods sold (the expense) at all times.
• *Periodic system* shows the correct balances of inventory and cost of goods sold only after a physical count of the inventory, which occurs at least once each year.

Excel Application Exercise

Goal: Create a spreadsheet to compute Amazon.com's gross profit percentage and inventory turnover for the past three years.

Scenario: You are intrigued by Amazon's ability to sell merchandise via the Internet and would like to invest in such a venture. Before doing so, however, you remember from your accounting course that ratio analysis is an important part of making an investment decision. You decide to calculate two key ratios: gross profit percentage and inventory turnover. (You may need to visit Amazon.com on the Web to find inventory data from past years. Look under Investor Relations at the bottom of the Home page.) When you have completed your worksheet, answer the following questions:

1. What has happened to Amazon's gross profit percentage over the past three years?
2. What can you tell about Amazon's inventory operations from its inventory turnover ratio for the past two years?

Step-by-Step:
1. Open a new Excel spreadsheet.
2. In column 1, create a bold-faced heading as follows:
   a. Chapter 5 Excel Application Exercise
   b. Evaluating Amazon Inventory Operations
   c. Today's Date
3. Two rows down and two columns over, create bold and underlined headings for the most recent three years (e.g., 2002, 2001, and 2000).
4. In column A, enter the following (one per row):
   a. Net Sales (in thousands)
   b. Cost of Goods Sold (Cost of Sales)
   c. Gross Profit
   d. Inventory
   e. Gross Profit Percentage
   f. Inventory Turnover
5. Locate the data for items **a-d** in the Amazon.com annual report (or on the Web) and enter it in the appropriate columns.
6. Calculate gross profit percentage and inventory turnover. To help visualize the data trends, use the Chart Wizard to create a bar graph of performance.
7. Format all columns, rows, and data as needed. Save your work and print a copy for your files.

Assignment Materials

New! Starters Starters serve as warm-ups and confidence builders at the beginning of the assignment material. Try to solve these easy, single-concept exercises. Each Starter is referenced within the chapter so that if you need more guidance, you know exactly what material to review to complete the exercise.

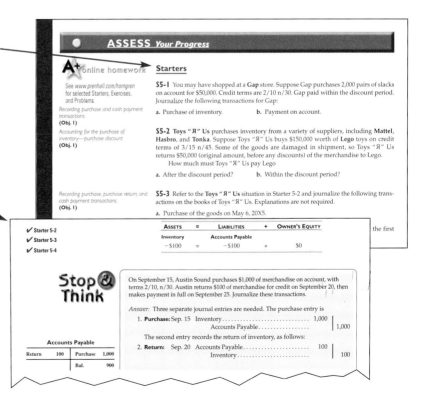

● **ASSESS** *Your Progress*

A+ online homework

See www.prenhall.com/horngren for selected Starters, Exercises, and Problems.

Recording purchase and cash payment transactions
(Obj. 1)

Accounting for the purchase of inventory—purchase discount
(Obj. 1)

Recording purchase, purchase return, and cash payment transactions.
(Obj. 1)

Starters

S5-1 You may have shopped at a **Gap** store. Suppose Gap purchases 2,000 pairs of slacks on account for $50,000. Credit terms are 2/10 n/30. Gap paid within the discount period. Journalize the following transactions for Gap:

a. Purchase of inventory.   b. Payment on account.

S5-2 **Toys "Я" Us** purchases inventory from a variety of suppliers, including **Mattel**, **Hasbro**, and **Tonka**. Suppose Toys "Я" Us buys $150,000 worth of **Lego** toys on credit terms of 3/15 n/45. Some of the goods are damaged in shipment, so Toys "Я" Us returns $50,000 (original amount, before any discounts) of the merchandise to Lego.
   How much must Toys "Я" Us pay Lego

a. After the discount period?   b. Within the discount period?

S5-3 Refer to the **Toys "Я" Us** situation in Starter 5-2 and journalize the following transactions on the books of Toys "Я" Us. Explanations are not required.

a. Purchase of the goods on May 6, 20X5.

✔ Starter 5-2
✔ Starter 5-3
✔ Starter 5-4

ASSETS	=	LIABILITIES	+	OWNER'S EQUITY
Inventory		Accounts Payable		
−$100	=	−$100	+	$0

the first

Stop & Think

On September 15, Austin Sound purchases $1,000 of merchandise on account, with terms 2/10, n/30. Austin returns $100 of merchandise for credit on September 20, then makes payment in full on September 25. Journalize these transactions.

Answer: Three separate journal entries are needed. The purchase entry is

1. **Purchase:** Sep. 15 Inventory 1,000
                              Accounts Payable . . . . | 1,000

The second entry records the return of inventory, as follows:

2. **Return:** Sep. 20 Accounts Payable   100
                              Inventory . . . . | 100

Accounts Payable

Return	100	Purchase	1,000
		Bal.	900

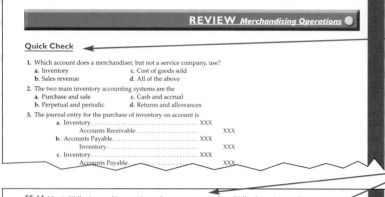

New! Quick Check These new multiple-choice questions appear at the ends of chapters so you can test your understanding of material before taking multiple-choice exams. Answers to Quick Checks appear in Appendix D at the end of the book.

Exercises and Problems Exercises and Problems give you plenty of practice in solving accounting dilemmas and checking your understanding of major concepts in the chapter.

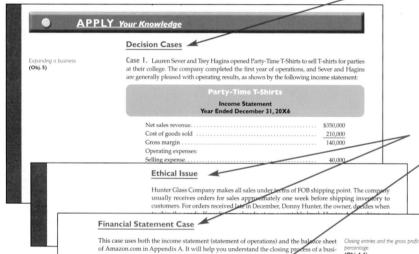

Cases A variety of cases, plus **Team Projects**—and **Comprehensive Problems** at the ends of groups of chapters—give you opportunities to practice decision-making in real business situations. Cases include **Decision Cases**, **Ethical Issues**, and **Financial Statement Cases** that use the **Amazon.com** annual report at the end of the book.

Study Aids And Resources

Throughout the book, margin icons indicate resources available on the **Student Resource CD**. Selected end-of-chapter problems appear in **spreadsheet templates** on the CD, and also in **General Ledger (GL)**, **QuickBooks (QB)**, and **Peachtree (PT)** formats. Other assignments are linked to Prentice Hall's new online homework program that includes a variety of assignments whose results feed directly into the grading program. The program includes algorithm-based problems, to give you extensive practice on a single concept.

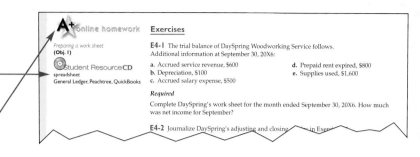

New Student and Instructor Resource CD-ROMs This innovative product includes all resources for the text—Powerpoint files, video clips, spreadsheet templates, tutorial software, General Ledger software, and Peachtree and QuickBooks software. You can access resources by chapter or by keyword (like "LIFO"). The student version of the CD allows you to create your own individualized review program. Free with new texts.

Text Icons

Resources

Writing Assignment

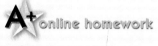

Online homework program

Study Guide This chapter-by-chapter learning aid systematically and effectively helps you study accounting and get the maximum benefit from study time. Each chapter provides a Chapter Overview and Review, a Featured Exercise that covers in a single exercise all of the most important topics in the chapter, and Review Questions and Exercises that test your understanding of the material.

Powerpoint slides help you review concepts by providing a summary of important points. *Remember!* You can choose to review **Powerpoints** by chapter or by keyword.

Video Clips include a series of **tutorial videos** designed to help you review concepts, plus **On Location! Videos** that take you inside companies such as **Jelly Belly** and **It's Just Lunch** to show you how managers use accounting information to make everyday business decisions. *Remember!* You can choose to review **videos** by chapter or by keyword.

Spreadsheet templates Selected end-of-chapter exercises and problems appear on pre-created templates for you to use in solving these assignments. If you need additional help in using Excel, you may opt to review the tutorial segment.

More Study Aids

General Ledger Software enables you to complete homework assignments using a general ledger software package. You may also enter and solve your own problems. E-Working Papers are available for each chapter.

New! Getting Started If your professor has chosen to package one of the Getting Started series manuals with your text, you may access the data files to use with the manuals.

Companion Web site **www.prenhall.com/horngren** Prentice Hall's Learning on the Internet Partnership offers extensive Internet-based support. Our Web sites provide a wealth of free resources for you, including Student Study Hall, Online Tutorial Assistance, Study Guide with Quizzes, Internet Exercises, and much more.

For The Instructor

(A complete list of chapter-by-chapter highlights follows this overview)

Text & Assignment Material

- *New Amazon.com Annual Report & Financial Statement Analysis Cases!* New copies of the text now include the Amazon.com annual report. This is linked to many of the chapter-opening vignettes, and end-of-chapter financial statement analysis cases.

- *New Theme: Show More. Say Less.* Throughout the text, the authors have worked hard to tighten and focus the content on core topics in first year accounting.

- *New, more open and student-friendly design* includes many new exhibits to aid in student understanding.

- *New Chapter Organization.* The chapters on merchandising and inventory (previously Chapters 5 & 9) are now Chapters 5-6 to enable students to link these topics more easily.

- *New A+Tips* at each chapter opening list resources to help students learn key concepts; reminders appear within the chapter.

- *New Quick Check Questions.* New multiple-choice exercises at the ends of chapters enable students to test their understanding before taking multiple-choice examinations. Answers appear in Appendix D.

- *New Starters* (previously called "Daily Exercises") serve as warm-ups/confidence builders at the beginning of the assignment material. Students solve these easy, single-concept exercises (many using real companies). Each problem is referenced to material within the chapter so that if students need more guidance, they know exactly what to review to complete the exercise.

- *New Excel Application Exercises*, now for each chapter in the book, with spreadsheet solutions.

Grading & Practice

- *New Peachtree, QuickBooks, and General Ledger Assignments.* Selected end-of-chapter problems are available on templates for Peachtree, QuickBooks, and General Ledger software. In addition, instructors may opt to package a brief introductory manual on the latest release of Peachtree or QuickBooks at no charge with new texts.

- *New Manual and Computerized Practice Sets* include optional exercises using Peachtree and QuickBooks. Package any Practice Set at 50% off with new texts.

- *New Automatic Homework Grading!* Prentice Hall's online homework program includes a variety of in-text assignments for students to complete online—and results feed directly into the grading program. The program includes *algorithm-based problems* that enable students to have extensive practice on a single concept. They *reduce cheating* because two students sitting next to one another could see different versions of the problem (the instructor determines whether the problem is viewed in static or algorithm-based format). Students get extensive feedback to help them understand where they went wrong.

The New CD

- *New Instructor and Student Resource CD-ROMs:* This innovative CD-ROM includes all resources for the text and allows instructors to create custom multi-media lectures in less than 5 minutes! Access the resources by chapter or keyword (e.g., "LIFO"). A student version of the CD enables students to create individualized review programs. Free with new texts.

Chapter-by-Chapter Highlights

CHAPTER 1 Accounting and the Business Environment

- New chapter opener focuses on **Amazon.com**, the feature company for this edition.
- Discussion of ethics in accounting features **Enron**, **WorldCom**, and **Xerox**.
- New illustration of the effects of transactions on balance sheet and income statement.

CHAPTER 2 Recording Business Transactions

- New chapter opener features **Frito-Lay**.
- New notations for journal entries clarify the rules of debit and credit.
- New roadmap shows how accounts, ledgers, journals, and the trial balance fit together.

CHAPTER 3 The Adjusting Process

- New notations for adjusting entries clarify the rules of debit and credit.
- New graphic shows the difference between the accrual basis and the cash basis.

CHAPTER 4 Completing the Accounting Cycle

- New chapter opener features the **Chicago Cubs** baseball team.
- New exhibit illustrates the closing process.
- Dell Computer's balance sheet illustrates the accounts covered to date.

CHAPTER 5 Merchandising Operations

- New chapter opener features **Amazon.com**.
- This completely revised chapter begins with purchase of merchandise, then moves to sales, all based on the perpetual system.

- Appendix on the periodic system.

CHAPTER 6 Merchandise Inventory

- New chapter opener features **Columbia Sportswear** and the **International Balloon Festival**.
- New exhibits! One shows the effect of merchandising on the financial statements; another shows FIFO, LIFO, and average costing; and others show the relationship between transactions in a perpetual system and related journal entries.
- New, streamlined coverage of accounting for inventory in a periodic system.

CHAPTER 7 Accounting Information Systems

- New discussion of Enterprise Resource Planning (ERP) systems.
- New explanation of the relationship between manual and computerized systems.

CHAPTER 8 Internal Control and Cash

- Discussion of the Sarbanes-Oxley Act and internal controls.
- Streamlined discussion of the bank reconciliation.
- New graphics: internal controls for cash receipts and cash payments.
- New: Enron examples to illustrate ethics in accounting.

CHAPTER 9 Receivables

- Simplified examples to illustrate accounting for uncollectibles.
- New graphics: integration of order entry, shipping, and billing of receivables.

CHAPTER 10 Plant Assets and Intangible Assets

- New chapter opener features airlines and their assets.
- New exhibit: relationship between plant assets and related expenses.
- New graphic: relative-sales-value method.
- Streamlined coverage of Depreciation and Income Taxes.
- Simplified coverage of Partial-Year Depreciation.
- Updated accounting for goodwill.

CHAPTER 11 Current Liabilities and Payroll

- New chapter opener features General Motors, Sony, and Goodyear.
- New graphic: how to allocate interest expense to the appropriate period.
- Streamlined accounting for sales tax payable.
- Beefed up—and streamlined—coverage of accounting for contingencies.
- Simplified payroll illustrations.
- Added Form 941, Employer's Quarterly Federal Tax Return.

CHAPTER 12 Partnerships

- New chapter opener on the fragility of partnerships, featuring the Arthur Andersen debacle.
- New graphics illustrate the various ways to start a partnership.

CHAPTER 13 Corporations: Paid-in Capital and the Balance Sheet

- New discussion of closing net income for a corporation.
- Streamlined accounting for income tax by a corporation.

CHAPTER 14 Retained Earnings, Treasury Stock, and the Income Statement

- New chapter opener features Coca-Cola, Dell Computer, and Pier 1 Imports.
- New graphic: retained earnings are not cash.
- New coverage of stock dividends.
- Scaled-down treatment of the corporate income statement.
- Simplified treatment of earnings per share.

CHAPTER 15 Long-term Liabilities

- Revised chapter opener features Amazon.com.

- New roadmap guides students through issuing bonds payable to borrow money.
- Deleted sections on Leases and Pensions.

CHAPTER 16 Investments and International Operations

- New chapter opener features McDonald's, Panasonic, and Nokia.
- Scaled-down coverage of accounting for international operations.

CHAPTER 17 The Statement of Cash Flows

- New chapter opener features eBay.
- Completely revised chapter: Two distinct sections for the indirect method and the direct method. Each section features step-by-step preparation of the statement.
- Scaled-down level of complexity for both methods—fewer accounts to analyze.
- New graphics: how cash is affected by changes in the other current accounts.

CHAPTER 18 Financial Statement Analysis

- New chapter opener features Bristol-Myers Squibb.
- Revised chapter organized around decisions and the need for financial statement analysis.
- New graphics illustrate horizontal analysis and vertical analysis.
- Scaled-down financial statements—fewer accounts to analyze.
- Revised discussions of the ratios—shorter paragraphs, fewer words.
- New section on Red Flags in Financial Statement Analysis.
- New section on Analyzing Nonfinancial Data.

CHAPTER 19 Introduction to Management Accounting

- New chapter opener and **On Location!** video on Regal Marine.
- New infographics.
- New exhibit simplifies and clarifies the distinction between merchandisers' and manufacturers' income statements.
- Simplified discussion of cost of goods manufactured, linking the flow of activities.
- Brief new discussion of ERP systems.

CHAPTER 20 Job Costing

- Updated chapter opener: why and how Dell figures the cost of a built-to-order computer.

- Emphasis on why all managers need to know how much it costs to produce a product or to serve a customer.

- Reorganized and simplified discussion of accounting for materials and labor.

- Exciting new team project asks students to compare the cost (and profits) of regular airlines' versus budget airlines' flights, using real-world data.

CHAPTER 21 Process Costing

- New chapter opener and **On Location!** video feature Jelly Belly.

- Text discussion uses Jelly Belly to illustrate key process costing principles.

- *First half* of chapter enables students to grasp the basics of process costing without complications caused by the presence of beginning work in process inventory. Instructors who prefer to introduce the basics of process costing can assign just the first half of the chapter. There is plenty of relevant assignment material.

- The *second half* of the chapter allows for beginning inventories. Scaled-back coverage focuses on the process costing method students find easiest to grasp—weighted average.

- Full and self-contained coverage of the more complex FIFO method appears in a new appendix. Instructors can add—or substitute—the FIFO-based appendix for the second half of the chapter.

- Several new Decision Guidelines emphasize the big picture—job versus process costing, the checks and balances in the 5-step process costing approach illustrated in the chapter, the goal of process costing, and how managers use the production cost report.

CHAPTER 22 Cost-Volume-Profit Analysis

- Streamlined presentation of variable, fixed, and mixed costs.

- Significantly reorganized chapter: Illustrations proceed from cost behavior, to basic CVP analysis, to using CVP analysis for profit planning, to conducting sensitivity analyses with CVP.

- Chapter midpoint now follows basic CVP analysis. This speed bump prompts students to reinforce their understanding of the basics.

- Significantly revised discussion of sensitivity analyses includes realistic business decision contexts for changing various components of the CVP analysis, covers the margin of safety, and explains how managers use information technology.

CHAPTER 23 The Master Budget and Responsibility Accounting

- New chapter opener features Amazon.com CEO Jeff Bezos' use of budgets to control costs.

- Focus on Amazon.com throughout chapter, including new Decision Guidelines contexts, new end-of-chapter multiple-choice questions, and several new infographics.

- New pedagogy moves from students' personal budgets, to a simple budget for a small company, to the main example featuring a retail store's budget, to how large companies use software to roll up individual unit budgets into the companywide budget.

- Emphasizes how managers *use* the budget to plan and control, and also considers behavioral issues such as tips for increasing employees' acceptance of the budget.

- New infographic organization chart coupled with a new exhibit showing a responsibility performance report illustrate how responsibility accounting works in a real-world context.

CHAPTER 24 The Flexible Budget and Standard Costs

- New introductory example based on students' daily life shows why variances are important guides to future action.

- Mid-chapter Decision Guidelines and new Excel exercise show how students can use flexible budgets and variances to plan and control costs in start-up businesses.

- New discussion of how managers set price and quantity standards.

- Significantly streamlined discussion of allocating manufacturing overhead in a standard costing system

- Streamlined explanation of overhead variances: more visuals, fewer words.

CHAPTER 25 Activity Based Costing and Other Cost Management Tools

- Streamlined and updated discussion of how managers use activity-based management in pricing, product mix, and cost-cutting decisions.

(continued)

(*Chapter 25 continued*)

- Streamlined discussion of when ABC passes the cost-benefit test.
- Simplified discussion of the just-in-time philosophy and total quality management.
- New Financial Statement Case highlights Amazon.com's unique activities as an e-tailer.

CHAPTER 26 Special Business Decisions and Capital Budgeting

- New graphics: decision rules for special short-term decisions such as special orders, product mix, and sell or process further.
- Simplified coverage of special sales orders.

- Discussion and new examples of the trend toward outsourcing all kinds of business functions.
- Simplified illustration of opportunity costs in the context of decisions on best use of facilities and outsourcing.
- New graphics: decision rules for long-term capital budgeting decisions.
- Simplified coverage of net present value.
- New Financial Statement Case asks students to apply payback, accounting rate of return, and discounted cash flow techniques to Amazon.com's investments.

Instructor Resources

Everything you need where you need it. The Prentice Hall Instructor Resource Center/CD-ROM increases your effectiveness and saves you time and effort. Harness the power of having all of your resources in one well-organized place. Because resources should simplify, not overwhelm.

Technology Resources: How Horngren Makes It Easier for You to Test and Grade

NEW! INSTRUCTOR AND STUDENT RESOURCE CD-ROMs

These CD's are powerful teaching and learning tools. They first serve as a roadmap through the chapters to identify key concepts and then guide students to other resources on the CD-ROM, where they can further develop their skills.

- Available in separate versions for faculty and students, this unique tool enables faculty to **save time** and **quickly prepare highly effective and interactive multimedia classroom presentations**.
- Using a **highly accessible menu**, students and faculty can easily customize study programs or presentations. By simply clicking on a chapter or keyword, they can access an interactive library of resources.
- Instructor's CD-ROM contains all ancillaries. Student CD-ROM contains tutorial software, On Location! video clips, PowerPoints, General Ledger software, Excel tutorial, spreadsheet templates, and much more.

These CD-ROMs also contain a special option for instructors who wish to build their own online courses! Faculty can pick and choose from the various supplements (organized by chapter and topic), and export them to their hard drive in HTML. From hard drive to online course is an easy step!

The IRCD contains all print and technology (e.g., spreadsheets, videos) supplements on a single CD-ROM. Enjoy the freedom to transport the entire package from office, to home, to classroom. This enables you to customize any of the ancillaries, print only the chapters or materials you wish to use, or access any item from the package within the classroom!

NEW! COMPUTERIZED ACCOUNTING PRACTICE SETS

Containing lots of simulated real-world examples, the **A-1 Photography** and **Runners Corporation** practice sets are available complete with data files for Peachtree, QuickBooks, and PH General Ledger. Each practice set also includes business stationery for manual entry work.

NEW! PRENTICE HALL AUTOMATIC HOMEWORK GRADING!

An outstanding Web-based homework solution. Students can work end-of-chapter problems at their own pace online. In addition, the algorithmically generated numbers ensure that problems are never repetitive.

NEW! GETTING STARTED SERIES

Upon request, faculty may package their choice of one of these approximately 70-page manuals on the latest professional accounting software packages with **Accounting, 6th ed.**, at no charge. Each manual introduces students to the concepts of Excel, Peachtree, QuickBooks, or PH General Ledger.

NEW! SPECIAL OFFERS – PROFESSIONAL ACCOUNTING SOFTWARE PACKAGES

Package your choice of the latest software releases of Peachtree or QuickBooks, for less than $15, with new text purchases.

- *General Ledger Software*   General Ledger software enables students to complete homework assignments using a general ledger software package. Students may also enter and solve their own problems. Available on the Student CD-ROM, Instructor CD-ROM, and downloadable from Companion Web site.

- *Working Papers and e-Working Papers*   Working Papers contain tailormade spreadsheets for all end-of-chapter Excel problems. A sample set of working papers is packaged free with every Student Resource CD-ROM.

- *INNOVATION! Standard Online Courses in WebCT, CourseCompass, and BlackBoard*   Teach a complete online course or a Web-enhanced course. Add your own course materials, take advantage of online testing and Gradebook opportunities, and utilize the bulletin board and discussion board functions. Free upon request. This is an excellent time to build your own course using our CD-ROMs with your choice of platform.

- *Companion Web site* **www.prenhall.com/horngren**   Prentice Hall's Learning on the Internet Partnership offers extensive Internet-based support. Our Web site provides a wealth of resources for students and faculty including: Student Study Hall, Online Tutorial Assistance, Study Guide with Quizzes, Internet Exercises, and much more.

More Instructor Resources: Horngren makes it easier for you to prepare your classes!

- **Annotated Instructor's Edition** Replete with teaching tips, real-world examples, short exercises, ethical insights, and discussion, this annotated edition is ideal for instructors wishing to augment their classroom discussions.

- **Instructor's Resource Manual** Each chapter of this comprehensive resource consists of a list of the student learning objectives, a narrative overview of main topics, and an outline with teaching tips interspersed.

- **Test Item File** The printed Test Item File consists of over 2,900 questions, including true/false questions, conceptual and quantitative multiple-choice questions, critical thinking problems, and exercises. Each question identifies the difficulty level and the corresponding learning objective. Prentice Hall TestGenEQ can create exams, and evaluate and track student results. New to this edition are algorithmically generated conceptual questions integrated throughout the TestGen.

- **Solutions Manual** In addition to fully worked-out and accuracy-checked solutions for every question, exercise, problem, and case in the text, this manual provides a categorization of assignment material. In addition, every page of the Solutions Manual has been reproduced in acetate form for use on the overhead projector.

- **On Location! Videos** These brief videos take students "on location" to real companies where real accounting situations are discussed and explained.

Acknowledgments

Special Thanks to:

Professor Michael Bamber of the University of Georgia for his substantive contributions to the ethics cases and team projects in Chapters 19–26.

Professor Lynn Mazzola of Nassau Community College for her help in checking assignment material and reading the text of Chapters 19–26.

Professors Becky Jones and Betsy Willis for writing the Instructor's Manual and Professor Jones for coordinating the accuracy checking of the Solutions Manual.

Professor Robert Bauman of Allan Hancock College for providing the annotations for the Instructor's Edition.

Pradeep Nagar at the University of Georgia for helping ensure the clarity and accuracy of all the assignments in Chapters 19–26.

Writer Nancy Brandwein for the Accounting.com boxes.

We also want to thank the reviewers of the Sixth Edition and the Focus Group participants, who gave of their time and talents to help us streamline the new edition and focus on the essentials. We especially want to thank the reviewers of Chapters 5 and 6, who provided so many useful comments and suggestions.

Finally, we want to thank the hard-working members of our Prentice Hall team, all of whom contributed so much to this edition: P. J. Boardman, editor-in-chief; Jeannine Ciliotta, senior development editor; Beth Toland, executive marketing manager; Sam Goffinet, assistant editor; Jane Avery, senior editorial assistant; Melene Kubat, administrative assistant; Steve Frim, designer; Anne Graydon, production editor; Arnold Vila, production manager; Christy Mahon, manager, multimedia production; and Nancy Welcher, media project manager.

Reviewers of Accounting, 6th ed.

[alphabetized by school]

Jenny Davis *Angelo State University*
Paulette Ratliff *Arkansas State University*
Frank Marino *Assumption College*
Terry Willyard *Baker College*
Charles Birnberg *Bergen Community College*
Robert D. Collmier *Bloomfield College*
Bonnie Giraldi *Cecil Community College*
Jeffrey Jones *Community College of Southern Nevada*
Kimberly Smith *County College of Morris*
Patty Holmes
Tom Turner *DesMoines Area Community College*
Rachel Ezelle *East Mississippi Community College*
John L. Stancil *Florida Southern College*
Rebecca Floor *Greenville Tech*
Linda Tarrago *Hillsborough Community College*
Judy Isonhood *Hinds Community College*
Cynthia Beier-Greeson
Warren Smock
Cynthia Vanoosterum *Ivy Tech State College*
Suzie Cordes *Johnson County Community College*
Tara Laken *Joliet Junior College*
Ron Carlin *Lamar University-Pt. Arthur*
Susan Logorda *Lehigh Carbon Community College*
Fred R. Jex *Macomb Community College*
David Grooms *Maui Community College*
Bruce Swindle *McNeese State University*
Josie Mathias *Mercer County Community College*

Judith Garcia *Miami Dade Community College—ESL*
Pamela Bogart *University of Michigan—ESL*
Joe Flynn *Moraine Valley Community College*
Cheryl McKay *Monroe County Community College*
Laura Prosser *National American University*
Laura Ilcisin *University of Nebraska*
Toni Clegg *Palm Beach Community College*
Randy Kidd *Penn Valley*
Shifei Chung
Stephanie Weidman *Rowan Community College*
Merrily Hoffman
Jeff Jackson
Randall Whitmore *San Jacinto College Central*
Patricia Halliday *Santa Monica College*
Ann Gregory *South Plains College*
Patricia Novak *Southeast Community College*
Gloria Worthy *Southwest Tennessee Community College*
Jack Fatica *Terra Community College*
Tracy Burdis *Sylvan Learning Center*
Julie Dailey *Tidewater Community College*
Michael Stemkoski *Utah Valley State College*
Chuck Bunn *Wake Tech*
Clyde Galbraith *West Chester University*
Jerry Kreuze *Western Michigan University*
Jim Murray *Western Wisconsin Technical College*
Rajeev Parikh *Wilmington College*

Focus Group Participants

Sheila Arnouts
Thomas Badley *Baker College*
Janet Grange *Chicago State University*
William Harvey *Henry Ford Community College*
Linda Tarrago *Hillsborough Community College*
Dennis Valenti *Hudson County Community College*
Shirley Glass
Fred R. Jex *Macomb Community College*

Cheryl McKay *Monroe County Community College*
Nashwa George *Montclair State University*
Zach Holmes
Meg Costello Lambert *Oakland Community College*
Daniel Clark *Owens Community College*
Patricia Halliday *Santa Monica College*
Ruth Henderson *Union County College*
Michael Stemkoski *Utah Valley State College*

Resource Authors and Technical Reviewers

Instructor's Manual
Becky Jones, *Baylor University*
Betsy Willis, *Baylor University*
Alice Sineath, *Forsyth Technical Community College*

Solutions Manual & Solutions Transparencies
Charles T. Horngren, *Stanford University*
Walter T. Harrison, *Baylor University*
Linda Smith Bamber, *University of Georgia*

Working Papers
Ellen Sweatt, *Georgia Perimeter College*

Test Item File
Alice Sineath, *Forsyth Technical Community College*

Study Guide
Ann B. DeCapite

A1 Photography & Runner's Corporation Practice Sets
Jean Insinga, *Middlesex Community College*

On Location! Videos
Beverly Amer, *Northern Arizona University*

Companion Web site Online Student Self-Tests
Timothy Carse

Online Courses (WebCT, Blackboard, CourseCompass)
PowerPoints by Timothy Carse, with audio developed and created by Beverly Amer, *Northern Arizona University*. Original course content by Tony Fortini, *Camden Community College*, revised by Beverly Amer

Prentice Hall's Online Homework Program
Larry Kallio of the *Universtiy of Minnesota at Mankato*, with many thanks to Nancy Welcher of PH Business Publishing for extensive project coordination and support.

TestGenEQ Software
Alice B. Sineath, with algorithms selected and created by Alfonse Oddo of *Niagara University*. Software by Tamarack Software, Inc.

Student Resource CD-ROM
Instructor's Resource CD-ROM
PowerPoint Presentations by Olga Quintana of the *University of Miami*.
PH General Ledger by Jean Insinga and Carol Goetters. Spreadsheet Templates by Al Fisher of the *Community College of Southern Nevada*. Instructions to the templates provided by Diane Fisher & Associates.

Technical Reviewers
Lynn Mazzola, *Nassau Community College*; Robert Bauman, *Allan Hancock College*; Carolyn Stroebel; Becky Jones, *Baylor University*; Timothy Carse; Tom How; Pradeep Nagar, *University of Georgia*

CHAPTER 12

Partnerships

TIPS CHECK YOUR RESOURCES

- Visit the www.prenhall.com/horngren **Web site** for self-study quizzes, video clips, and other resources

- Try the **Quick Check** exercise at the end of the chapter to test your knowledge

- Learn the **key terms**

- Do the **Starter** exercises keyed in the margins

- Work the **mid-** and **end-of-chapter summary problems**

- Use the **Concept Links** to review material in other chapters

- Search the **CD** for review materials by chapter or by key word

- Watch the **tutorial videos** to review key concepts

LEARNING OBJECTIVES

1. Identify the characteristics of a partnership

2. Account for the partners' investments in a partnership

3. Allocate profits and losses to the partners

4. Account for the admission of a new partner

5. Account for a partner's withdrawal from the firm

6. Account for the liquidation of a partnership

7. Prepare partnership financial statements

Arthur Andersen LLP

Partnerships are very fragile indeed. Unlike corporations, which continue regardless of who owns the company, a partnership lives and dies with its owners: the partners. A case in point is Arthur Andersen LLP, the once-famous accounting firm. The previous edition of this book featured Arthur Andersen as a "profit-making machine," with "each partner's profit [averaging] well over half a million dollars a year." Now the firm is dead.

Arthur Andersen unraveled during 2002 and 2003. One of the world's largest—and most respected—accounting firms went from international star to has-been in a matter of months. What could cause such a rapid fall from grace?

The short answer is that the firm performed a few high-profile audits that proved to be flawed. Arthur Andersen's auditors okayed the financial statements of several companies that had been overstating their profits and their assets. The final blow came when the government indicted Andersen on the charge that a partner in the firm destroyed legal evidence. Immediately, hundreds of Andersen's clients began announcing that they were switching to other certified public accountants.

The partnership form of business organization contributed to the swiftness of Andersen's death. Why? Because a single partner can commit an entire firm to a legal liability. For this and other reasons, you should enter a business partnership very carefully. ■

■ S i t e m a p

The partnership form of business introduces some complexities that a proprietorship avoids. How much cash should a new partner contribute to the business? How should the partners divide profits and losses? How should a partner who leaves the firm be compensated for his or her share of the business? These issues were important to the partners of Arthur Andersen LLP (LLP is the abbreviation for limited liability partnership).

A **partnership** is an association of two or more persons who co-own a business for profit. This definition comes from the Uniform Partnership Act, which nearly every state in the United States has adopted to regulate partnership practice.

Forming a partnership is easy. It requires no permission from the government and no legal procedures. When two persons decide to go into business together, a partnership is automatically formed. A partnership brings together the assets and the experience of the partners. Business opportunities may open up to a partnership as two or more individuals pool their talents and resources. Their partnership may offer a fuller range of goods and services than any one person can offer alone.

Partnerships come in all sizes. Many have one or two partners, but some medical and law firms have 20 or more. The largest accounting firms have over 2,000 partners. Exhibit 12-1 lists the seven largest accounting firms in the United States and their revenues in 2002.

| Exhibit 12-1 | The Seven Largest Accounting Partnerships in the United States |

Revenue Rank (2002)	Firm Name and Location	Accounting/Auditing Revenue (In millions)
1	PricewaterhouseCoopers, New York	$ 3,001
2	Ernst & Young, New York	2,664
3	Deloitte & Touche, Wilton, Connecticut	2,137
4	KPMG, New York	1,496
5	RSM McGladrey, Bloomington, Minnesota	205
6	Grant Thornton, Chicago	200
7	BDO Seidman, Chicago	145

Source: Adapted from *Accounting Today* (March 17–April 6, 2003).

Characteristics of a Partnership

A person cannot be forced to join a partnership, and partners cannot be forced to accept another person as a partner. The following characteristics distinguish partnerships from sole proprietorships and corporations.

The Written Agreement

A business partnership is like a marriage. To be successful, the partners must cooperate. But business partners don't vow to remain together for life. To lower the chances that any partner might misunderstand how the business is run, partners may draw up a **partnership agreement,** which is also called the **articles of partnership**. This agreement is a contract between the partners, so transactions involving the agreement are governed by contract law. The articles of partnership should make the following points clear:

1. Name, location, and nature of the business
2. Name, capital investment, and duties of each partner
3. Method of sharing profits and losses among the partners
4. Withdrawals of assets by the partners
5. Procedures for admitting new partners
6. Procedures for settling up with a partner who withdraws from the firm
7. Procedures for liquidating the partnership—selling the assets, paying the liabilities, and disbursing remaining cash to the partners

Limited Life

A partnership has a life limited by the length of time that all partners continue to own the business. If a partner withdraws, the old partnership ceases to exist. A new partnership may emerge to continue the same business, but the old partnership is dissolved. **Dissolution** is the ending of a partnership. The addition of a new partner dissolves the old partnership and creates a new partnership. Large partnerships such as PricewaterhouseCoopers retain the firm name even after partners resign from the firm.

Mutual Agency

Mutual agency in a partnership means that every partner can bind the business to a contract within the scope of the partnership's regular business operations. If Jana Jones, a partner in the firm of Willis & Jones, enters into a contract to provide legal service, then the firm of Willis & Jones—not just Jones—is bound to provide that service. If Jones signs a contract to construct her home, however, the partnership will not be bound to pay because that is a personal matter for Jones. It is not a transaction of the partnership.

Unlimited Liability

Each partner has an **unlimited personal liability** for the debts of the partnership. When a partnership cannot pay its debts, the partners must use their personal assets to meet the debt.

Suppose the Willis & Jones firm has had an unsuccessful year and the partnership's liabilities exceed its assets by $20,000. Willis and Jones must pay this amount with their personal assets. Because each partner has unlimited liability, if

### Sidebar

■ **Partnership Characteristics**
☐ Types of Partnerships
☐ Partnership Start-Up
☐ Profits and Losses, Drawings
☐ Admission of a Partner
☐ Withdrawal of a Partner
☐ Liquidation
☐ Financial Statements

 Identify the characteristics of a partnership

Partnership
An association of two or more persons who co-own a business for profit.

Partnership Agreement
The contract between partners that specifies such items as the name, location, and nature of the business; the name, capital investment, and duties of each partner; and the method of sharing profits and losses among the partners. Also called **articles of partnership**.

Dissolution
Ending of a partnership.

Mutual Agency
Every partner can bind the business to a contract within the scope of the partnership's regular business operations.

Unlimited Personal Liability
When a partnership (or a proprietorship) cannot pay its debts with business assets, the partners (or the proprietor) must use personal assets to meet the debt.

a partner is unable to pay his or her part of the debt, the other partner (or partners) must pay. If Jones can pay only $5,000 of the liability, Willis must pay $15,000.

Partners can avoid unlimited personal liability for partnership debts by forming a *limited partnership*. Ernst & Young LLP is a limited liability partnership, as are the other large accounting firms in Exhibit 12-1. In a limited partnership, the partners have limited liability similar to that of the stockholders in a corporation.

Co-Ownership of Property

Any asset—cash, inventory, computer software, and so on—that a partner invests in the partnership becomes the joint property of all the partners. The partner who invested the asset is no longer its sole owner.

No Partnership Income Taxes

✔ **Starter 12-1**

A partnership pays no income tax on its business income. Instead, the net income of the partnership becomes the taxable income of the partners. Suppose Willis & Jones, Attorneys, earned net income of $200,000, shared equally by the partners. The firm would pay no income tax *as a business entity*. But Willis and Jones would each pay personal income tax on $100,000 of partnership income.

Partners' Owner's Equity Accounts

Accounting for a partnership is much like accounting for a proprietorship. But a partnership has more than one owner, so it needs more than one owner's equity account.

Every partner in the business has an individual capital account. For example, the owner's equity account for Blake Willis would read "Willis, Capital." Similarly, each partner has a withdrawal account. If the number of partners is large, the general ledger may contain the single account Partners' Capital, or Owners' Equity. A subsidiary ledger can be used for individual partner accounts.

Exhibit 12-2 lists the advantages and disadvantages of partnerships (compared with proprietorships and corporations). A partnership is really a "multiple proprietorship." Most features of a proprietorship also apply to a partnership—in particular, limited life and unlimited liability.

Exhibit 12-2

Advantages and Disadvantages of Partnerships

Partnership Advantages	Partnership Disadvantages
Versus Proprietorships: 1. Can raise more capital. 2. Brings together the expertise of more than one person. 3. 1 + 1 > 2 in a good partnership. If the partners work well together, they can add more value than by working alone. *Versus Corporations:* 1. Less expensive to organize than a corporation, which requires a charter from the state. 2. No taxation of partnership income, which is taxed to the partners as individuals.	1. Partnership agreement may be difficult to formulate. Each time a new partner is admitted or a partner withdraws, the business needs a new partnership agreement. 2. Relationships among partners may be fragile. 3. Mutual agency and unlimited personal liability create personal obligations for each partner.

Types of Partnerships

There are two basic types of partnerships: general and limited.

Student Resource**CD**

general partnership, limited partnership,
limited liability partnership,
S corporation

General Partnerships

A **general partnership** is the basic form of partnership organization. Each partner is an owner of the business with all the privileges and risks of ownership. The profits and losses of the partnership pass through to the partners, who then pay personal income tax on their income.

General Partnership
A form of partnership in which each partner is an owner of the business, with all the privileges and risks of ownership.

Limited Partnerships

A **limited partnership** has at least two classes of partners. There must be at least one *general partner*, who takes primary responsibility for the business. The general partner also takes the bulk of the risk in the event the partnership goes bankrupt (liabilities exceed assets). Usually, the general partner is the last owner to receive a share of profits and losses. But the general partner may earn all excess profits after satisfying the limited partners' demands for income.

The *limited partners* are so named because their liability for the partnership's debts is limited to their investment in the business. Limited partners usually have first claim to partnership profits and losses, but only up to a specified limit. In exchange for their limited liability, their potential for profits is also limited.

Most of the large accounting firms are organized as **limited liability partnerships**, or **LLPs**, which means that each partner's personal liability for the business's debts is limited to a certain amount. The LLP must carry a large insurance policy to protect the public in case the partnership is found guilty of malpractice. Medical, legal, and other firms of professionals can also be organized as LLPs.

Limited Partnership
A partnership with at least two classes of partners: a general partner and limited partners.

Limited Liability Partnership
A form of partnership in which each partner's personal liability for the business's debts is limited to a certain amount. Also called **LLPs**.

S Corporations

An **S Corporation** is a corporation that is taxed the same as a partnership. This form of business organization derives its name from Subchapter S of the U.S. Internal Revenue Code.

An S corporation offers its owners the benefits of a corporation—no personal liability for business debts—and of a partnership—no double taxation. An ordinary (Subchapter C) corporation is subject to double taxation. First, the corporation pays corporate income tax on its income. Then, when the corporation pays dividends to the stockholders, they pay personal income tax on their dividend income.[1]

An S corporation pays no corporate income tax. Instead, the corporation's income flows directly to the stockholders (the owners), who pay personal income tax on their share of the S corporation's income. The one-time taxation of an S corporation's income is an important advantage over an ordinary corporation. From a tax standpoint, an S corporation operates like a partnership.

To qualify as an S corporation, a company can have no more than 75 stockholders, all of whom must be citizens or residents of the United States. Accounting for an S corporation resembles accounting for a partnership because the allocation of corporate income follows the same procedure used by partnerships.

S Corporation
A corporation taxed in the same way as a partnership.

---

[1]From time to time, U.S. presidents and congressmen propose eliminating the tax on dividends received by individuals.

⭐ *Account for the partners' investments in a partnership*

Let's go into business together. I have a computer network.

Okay, I've got some software.

Benz   Hanna

The Partnership Start-Up

Let's examine the start-up of a partnership. Partners in a new business may invest assets and liabilities. These contributions are entered in the books in the same way that a proprietor's assets and liabilities are recorded—debit the assets and credit the liabilities. Subtraction of liabilities from assets yields the amount of each partner's capital. Often, the partners hire an independent firm to appraise their assets and liabilities at current market value at the time a partnership is formed. This outside evaluation assures an objective accounting of assets, liabilities, and capital.

Assume that Dave Benz and Joan Hanna form a partnership to sell computer software. The partners agree on the following values:

Benz's Contributions

- Cash, $10,000; inventory, $70,000; and accounts payable, $85,000 (The appraiser believes that the current market values for these items equal Benz's values.)
- Accounts receivable, $30,000, less allowance for doubtful accounts of $5,000
- Computer equipment—cost, $800,000; accumulated depreciation, $200,000; current market value, $450,000

Hanna's Contributions

- Cash, $5,000
- Computer software: cost, $18,000; market value, $100,000

(continued on page 475)

Accounting.com

From Respected Partnership to Dead Duck: The Fall of Arthur Andersen

If you were considering an accounting career a few years ago, the respected firm of Arthur Andersen might have been your top choice. As of June 2001, Andersen Worldwide was a $9.3 billion global partnership with 85,000 employees in 84 countries. By late 2002, Andersen's payroll had dwindled to 3,000 and almost all 1,300 clients had switched to other accounting firms. Why? Because a few partners okayed the failed audits that Andersen performed for a handful of companies including Enron, WorldCom, Adelphia, and Global Crossing. The moral of the story is this: An accountant's good reputation attracts clients, and a bad reputation can kill you.

Cracks in the Arthur Andersen partnership began forming in the 1980s, when the firm shifted resources toward management consulting and away from auditing. Ill will between the auditing and consulting sides of the Andersen partnership resulted in a bitter divorce. Andersen Consulting, renamed Accenture, broke free from the accounting firm. "There is no question in my mind that Andersen took its eye off the ball," said Paul A. Volker, former Federal Reserve Board chairman. "Their compensation practices were based on how much revenue [they] could generate."

The death knell for the firm came with a criminal indictment. Andersen Worldwide could survive a few botched audits but not a criminal indictment. On October 16, 2002, the firm that once stood for "integrity" was sentenced for obstructing justice related to its work for Enron.

Based on: John A. Byrne, "Fall from Grace," *Business Week,* August 12, 2002, pp. 50–56. Carrie Johnson, "Arthur Andersen To Be Sentenced Today," *Washington Post,* October 16, 2002, p. E4. Robert Lea, "End of Andersen," *Management Today,* October 2002, pp. 46–53.

The partnership records the partners' investments at current market value because the partnership is buying the assets and assuming the liabilities at their current market values. The partnership entries are as follows:

Benz's Investment

June 1	Cash	10,000	
	Accounts Receivable................	30,000	
	Inventory	70,000	
	Computer Equipment	450,000	
	Allowance for Doubtful Accounts..		5,000
	Accounts Payable................		85,000
	Benz, Capital ($560,000 – $90,000)..		470,000
	To record Benz's investment in the partnership.		

Hanna's Investment

June 1	Cash	5,000	
	Computer Software	100,000	
	Hanna, Capital		105,000
	To record Hanna's investment in the partnership.		

The initial partnership balance sheet appears in Exhibit 12-3. The assets and liabilities are the same for a proprietorship and a partnership.

✔ Starter 12-2

✔ Starter 12-3

Benz and Hanna

Balance Sheet
June 1, 20X5

Assets			Liabilities		
Cash.................		$ 15,000	Accounts payable.............		$ 85,000
Accounts receivable....	$30,000				
Less Allowance					
for doubtful					
accounts.........	(5,000)	25,000	**Capital**		
Inventory.............		70,000	Benz, capital		470,000
Computer equipment ..		450,000	Hanna, capital		105,000
Computer software		100,000	Total liabilities		
Total assets		$660,000	and capital.................		$660,000

Exhibit 12-3

Partnership Balance Sheet

☐ Partnership Characteristics
☐ Types of Partnerships
☐ Partnership Start-Up
■ **Profits and Losses, Drawings**
☐ Admission of a Partner
☐ Withdrawal of a Partner
☐ Liquidation
☐ Financial Statements

Student ResourceCD

allocation of profit and loss, partnership, partnership agreement, sharing profit and loss

⭐3 *Allocate profits and losses to the partners*

Sharing Profits and Losses, and Partner Drawings

Allocating profits and losses among partners is one of the most challenging aspects of managing a partnership. If the partners have not drawn up an agreement or if the agreement does not state how the partners will divide profits and losses, then they share equally. If the agreement specifies a method for dividing profits but not losses, then losses are shared in the same proportion as profits. For example, a partner who gets 75% of the profits likewise absorbs 75% of any losses. Partners may agree to any profit-and-loss-sharing method they desire.

Typical arrangements for dividing profits and losses among the partners include the following:

1. Sharing based on a stated fraction for each partner, such as 50/50 or 2/3 and 1/3 or 4:3:3 (which means 40% to Partner A, 30% to Partner B, and 30% to Partner C)

2. Sharing based on each partner's capital contribution

3. Sharing based on each partner's service to the partnership

4. Sharing based on a combination of each partner's stated fraction, capital contribution, and service

The sections that follow illustrate some of these profit-and-loss-sharing plans.

Sharing Based on a Stated Fraction

Partners may state a particular fraction of the total profits and losses each individual partner will share. Suppose the partnership agreement of Lou Cagle and Justin Dean allocates 2/3 of the business profits and losses to Cagle and 1/3 to Dean. This sharing rule can also be expressed as 2:1. If net income for the year is $90,000 and all revenue and expense accounts have been closed, the Income Summary account has a credit balance of $90,000:

Income Summary	
	Bal. 90,000

The entry to close the profit to the partners' capital accounts is

Dec. 31	Income Summary	90,000	
	Cagle, Capital ($90,000 × 2/3). .		60,000
	Dean, Capital ($90,000 × 1/3) . .		30,000
	To allocate net income to partners.		

Consider the effect of this entry. Does Cagle get $60,000 cash and Dean $30,000 cash? No. The increase in the partners' capital accounts cannot be linked to any particular asset, including cash. Instead, the entry indicates that Cagle's ownership in *all* the assets of the business increased by $60,000 and Dean's by $30,000.

If the year's operations resulted in a net loss of $66,000, the Income Summary account would have a debit balance of $66,000. In that case, the entry to close the loss to the partners' capital accounts would be

✔ **Starter 12-4**

Dec. 31	Cagle, Capital ($66,000 × 2/3)	44,000	
	Dean, Capital ($66,000 × 1/3)	22,000	
	Income Summary		66,000
	To allocate net loss to partners.		

Sharing Based on Capital Contributions and on Service

One partner may contribute more capital. Another partner may put more work into the business. Even among partners who log equal time, one person's experience may command a greater share of income. To reward the harder-working or the more-valuable person, the profits and losses may be divided based on a combination of contributed capital *and* service to the business. The Chicago-based law firm Baker & McKenzie, for example, has about 500 partners. Baker & McKenzie takes seniority into account in determining partner compensation.

Assume that Debbie Randolph and Nancy Scott formed a partnership in which Randolph invested $60,000 and Scott $40,000, for a total of $100,000. But Scott devotes more time to the partnership and earns the larger salary. Accordingly, the two partners have agreed to share profits as follows:

1. The first $50,000 of partnership profits is allocated on the basis of the partners' capital contributions.

2. The next $60,000 is allocated on the basis of service, with Randolph receiving $24,000 and Scott $36,000.

3. Any remaining amount will be allocated equally.

The partnership's net income for the first year is $125,000, and the partners share this profit as follows:

	Randolph	Scott	Total
Total net income			$125,000
Sharing of first $50,000 of net income, based on capital contributions:			
Randolph ($60,000/$100,000 × $50,000).....	$30,000		
Scott ($40,000/$100,000 × $50,000)		$20,000	
Total.................................			50,000
Net income remaining for allocation			75,000
Sharing of next $60,000, based on service:			
Randolph	24,000		
Scott.................................		36,000	
Total.................................			60,000
Net income remaining for allocation			15,000
Remainder shared equally:			
Randolph ($15,000 × 1/2).................	7,500		
Scott ($15,000 × 1/2)		7,500	
Total.................................			15,000
Net income remaining for allocation			$ 0
Net income allocated to the partners........	$61,500	$63,500	$125,000

For this allocation, the closing entry is

Dec. 31	Income Summary................	125,000	
	Randolph, Capital		61,500
	Scott, Capital..............		63,500
	To allocate net income to partners.		

✔ Starter 12-5

Partner Drawings of Cash and Other Assets

Like anyone else, partners need cash for personal expenses. Partnership agreements usually allow partners to withdraw assets from the business. Drawings from a partnership are recorded exactly as for a proprietorship. Assume that both Randy Lewis and Gerald Clark get monthly withdrawals of $3,500. The partnership records the March withdrawals with this entry:

Mar. 31	Lewis, Drawing..................	3,500	
	Clark, Drawing	3,500	
	Cash		7,000
	Monthly partner withdrawals of cash.		

During the year, each partner gets 12 monthly withdrawals, a total of $42,000 ($3,500 × 12). At the end of the period, the general ledger shows the following balances for the partners' drawing accounts:

Lewis, Drawing		Clark, Drawing	
Dec. 31 Bal. 42,000		Dec. 31 Bal. 42,000	

The drawing accounts are closed at the end of the period, exactly as for a proprietorship: Credit the partner's drawing account and debit his or her capital account.

Admission of a Partner

The addition of a new partner or the withdrawal of a partner dissolves the old partnership. We now discuss how partnerships dissolve—and how new partnerships arise.

Student ResourceCD

book value, partnership

4 Account for the admission of a new partner

Often, a new partnership is formed to carry on the old partnership's business. In fact, the new firm may retain the dissolved partnership's name. PricewaterhouseCoopers LLP, for example, is an accounting firm that adds new partners and retires old ones each year. Thus, the old partnership may dissolve and a new partnership begin many times during a year. But the business retains its name and continues operating. Other partnerships may dissolve and then re-form under a new name. Let's look at the ways a new member may be admitted into an existing partnership.

Admission by Purchasing a Partner's Interest

A person may become a member of a partnership by gaining the approval of the other partner (or partners) for entrance into the firm *and* by purchasing a present partner's interest in the business. Let's assume that Roberta Fisher and Benitez Garcia have a partnership that carries these figures:

Garcia   Fisher   Holt

Cash	$ 40,000	Total liabilities	$120,000
Other assets	360,000	Fisher, capital	110,000
		Garcia, capital	170,000
Total assets	$400,000	Total liabilities and capital	$400,000

Suppose Fisher receives an offer from Barry Holt, an outside party, to buy her $110,000 interest in the business for $150,000. Fisher agrees to sell out to Holt, and Garcia approves Holt as a new partner. The firm records the transfer of capital interest in the business with this entry:

Apr. 16	Fisher, Capital	110,000	
	Holt, Capital		110,000
	To transfer Fisher's equity in the business to Holt.		

The debit entry closes Fisher's capital account because she is no longer a partner in the firm. The credit side opens Holt's capital account. The entry amount is Fisher's capital balance ($110,000) and not the $150,000 that Holt paid Fisher to buy into the business. The full $150,000 goes to Fisher. In this example, the partnership receives no cash because the transaction was between Holt and Fisher, not between Holt and the partnership. Suppose Holt pays Fisher less than Fisher's capital balance. The entry on the partnership books is not affected. Fisher's equity is transferred to Holt at book value ($110,000).

✔ **Starter 12-6**

The old partnership has dissolved. Garcia and Holt draw up a new partnership agreement with a new profit-and-loss-sharing ratio and continue in business. If Garcia does not accept Holt as a partner, Holt gets no voice in management of the firm. However, under the Uniform Partnership Act, the purchaser shares in the profits and losses of the firm and in its assets at liquidation.

Admission by Investing in the Partnership

A person may be admitted as a partner by investing directly in the partnership rather than by buying an existing partner's interest. The new partner contributes assets—for example, cash or equipment—to the business. Assume that the partnership of Robin Ingel and Michael Jay has the following assets, liabilities, and capital:

Cash	$ 20,000	Total liabilities	$ 60,000
Other assets	200,000	Ingel, capital	70,000
		Jay, capital	90,000
Total assets	$220,000	Total liabilities and capital	$220,000

Laura Kahn offers to invest equipment and land (labeled Other Assets) with a market value of $80,000. Ingel and Jay agree to dissolve the existing partnership and to start up a new business, giving Kahn 1/3 interest [$80,000/($70,000 + $90,000 + $80,000) = 1/3] in exchange for the assets. Notice that Kahn is buying into the partnership at book value because her 1/3 investment ($80,000) equals 1/3 of the new partnership's total capital ($240,000). The entry to record Kahn's investment is

July 18	Other Assets.	80,000	
	Kahn, Capital.		80,000
	To admit L. Kahn as a partner with a one-third interest in the business.		

After this entry, the partnership books show

Cash	$ 20,000	Total liabilities.	$ 60,000
Other assets.		Ingel, capital	70,000
($200,000 + $80,000)	280,000	Jay, capital	90,000
		Kahn, capital	80,000
Total assets	$300,000	Total liabilities and capital. . . .	$300,000

Kahn's 1/3 interest in the partnership does not necessarily entitle her to 1/3 of the profits. The sharing of profits and losses is a separate element in the partnership agreement.

✔ **Starter 12-7**

ADMISSION BY INVESTING IN THE PARTNERSHIP—BONUS TO THE OLD PARTNERS The more successful a partnership, the higher the payment demanded from a new partner. Partners in a business that is doing quite well might require an incoming person to pay them a bonus. The bonus increases the current partners' capital accounts.

Suppose that Hiro Nagasawa and Ralph Osburn's partnership has earned above-average profits for 10 years. The two partners share profits and losses equally. The partnership balance sheet carries these figures:

Cash	$ 40,000	Total liabilities.	$100,000
Other assets.	210,000	Nagasawa, capital.	70,000
		Osburn, capital	80,000
Total assets	$250,000	Total liabilities and capital. . . .	$250,000

The partners agree to admit Glen Parker to a 1/4 interest with his cash investment of $90,000. Parker's capital balance on the partnership books is only $60,000, computed as follows:

Partnership capital before Parker is admitted ($70,000 + $80,000). . .	$150,000
Parker's investment in the partnership	90,000
Partnership capital after Parker is admitted	$240,000
Parker's capital in the partnership ($240,000 × 1/4)	$ 60,000
Bonus to the old partners ($90,000 − $60,000)	$ 30,000

In effect, Parker had to buy into the partnership at a price ($90,000) above the book value of his 1/4 interest ($60,000). Parker's investment of an extra $30,000 creates a *bonus* for the existing partners. The entry to record the receipt of Parker's investment is

Mar. 1	Cash 90,000		
	Parker, Capital.		60,000
	Nagasawa, Capital ($30,000 × 1/2). .		15,000
	Osburn, Capital ($30,000 × 1/2)		15,000
	To admit G. Parker as a partner with a one-fourth interest in the business.		

✔ **Starter 12-8**

Parker's capital account is credited for his 1/4 interest in the partnership. The *bonus* is allocated to the partners on the basis of their profit-and-loss ratio.

The new partnership's balance sheet reports these amounts:

Cash ($40,000 + $90,000) . .	$130,000	Total liabilities	$100,000
Other assets	210,000	Nagasawa, capital	
		($70,000 + $15,000)	85,000
		Osburn, capital	
		($80,000 + $15,000)	95,000
		Parker, capital	60,000
Total assets	$340,000	Total liabilities and capital . . .	$340,000

Mia and Susan are partners with capital balances of $25,000 and $75,000, respectively. They share profits and losses in a 30:70 ratio. Mia and Susan admit Tab to a 10% interest in a new partnership when Tab invests $20,000 in the business.

1. Journalize the partnership's receipt of cash from Tab.

2. What is each partner's capital in the new partnership?

Answers.

1. Cash	20,000	
Tab, Capital		12,000
Mia, Capital ($8,000 × 0.30)		2,400
Susan, Capital ($8,000 × 0.70)		5,600
To admit Tab with a 10% interest in the business.		

Partnership capital before Tab is admitted ($25,000 + $75,000)	$100,000
Tab's investment in the partnership	20,000
Partnership capital after Tab is admitted	$120,000
Tab's capital in the partnership ($120,000 × 1/10)	$ 12,000
Bonus to the old partners ($20,000 − $12,000)	$ 8,000

2. Partners' capital balances:

Mia, capital ($25,000 + 30% of $8,000)	$ 27,400
Susan, capital ($75,000 + 70% of $8,000) . . .	80,600
Tab, capital	12,000
Total partnership capital	$120,000

ADMISSION BY INVESTING IN THE PARTNERSHIP—BONUS TO THE NEW PARTNER A new partner may be so important that the existing partners offer him or her a partnership share that includes a bonus. A law firm may want a former governor or other official as a partner because of the person's reputation and connections. A restaurant owner may want to go into partnership with a famous sports personality or a movie star. For example, Planet Hollywood opened its first restaurant in New York City with the help of celebrity partners Sylvester Stallone, Arnold Schwarzenegger, Bruce Willis, and Don Johnson.

Suppose Allan Page and Olivia Franco have a law partnership. The firm's balance sheet appears as follows:

Cash	$140,000	Total liabilities	$120,000
Other assets	360,000	Page, capital	230,000
		Franco, capital	150,000
Total assets	$500,000	Total liabilities and capital . . .	$500,000

Page and Franco admit Martin Schiller, a former attorney general, as a partner with a 1/3 interest in exchange for his cash investment of $100,000. Page and Franco share profits and losses in the ratio of 2/3 to Page and 1/3 to Franco. The computation of Schiller's equity in the partnership is

What they're thinking

We need Schiller: He's got lots of good connections.

What they say to Schiller

We'd like to offer you a deal.

Schiller   Franco   Page

Partnership capital before Schiller is admitted ($230,000 + $150,000)..	$380,000
Schiller's investment in the partnership	100,000
Partnership capital after Schiller is admitted	$480,000
Schiller's capital in the partnership ($480,000 × 1/3).............	$160,000
Bonus to the new partner ($160,000 − $100,000).................	$ 60,000

In this case, Schiller bought into the partnership at a price ($100,000) below the book value of his interest ($160,000). The bonus of $60,000 went to Schiller from the other partners. The capital accounts of Page and Franco are debited for the $60,000 difference between the new partner's equity ($160,000) and his investment ($100,000). The existing partners share this decrease in capital as though it were a loss, on the basis of their profit-and-loss ratio. The entry to record Schiller's investment is

Aug. 24	Cash	100,000	
	Page, Capital ($60,000 × 2/3)......	40,000	
	Franco, Capital ($60,000 × 1/3)....	20,000	
	Schiller, Capital		160,000
	To admit M. Schiller as a partner with a one-third interest in the business.		

The new partnership's balance sheet reports these amounts:

Cash			Total liabilities	$120,000
($140,000 + $100,000)...	$240,000		Page, capital	
Other assets.............	360,000		($230,000 − $40,000)	190,000
			Franco, capital	
			($150,000 − $20,000)	130,000
			Schiller, capital.............	160,000
Total assets	$600,000		Total liabilities and capital...	$600,000

John and Ron are partners with capital balances of $30,000 and $40,000, respectively. They share profits and losses in a 25:75 ratio. John and Ron admit Lou to a 20% interest in a new partnership when Lou invests $10,000 in the business.

1. Journalize the partnership's receipt of cash from Lou.

2. What is each partner's capital in the new partnership?

Answers:

1. Cash	....	10,000	
	John, Capital ($6,000 × 0.25)	1,500	
	Ron, Capital ($6,000 × 0.75)........................	4,500	
	Lou, Capital................................		16,000
	To admit Lou with a 20% interest in the business.		

Partnership capital before Lou is admitted ($30,000 + $40,000)	$70,000
Lou's investment in the partnership...........................	10,000
Partnership capital after Lou is admitted.......................	$80,000
Lou's capital in the partnership ($80,000 × 0.20).................	$16,000
Bonus to the new partner ($16,000 − $10,000)	$ 6,000

(continued)

Student ResourceCD

allocation of profit and loss, book value, partnership

Account for a partner's withdrawal from the firm

I need to retire and leave the partnership.

We hate to see you go, but we understand.

Isaac   Green   Henry

2. Partners' capital balances:

John, capital ($30,000 − $1,500)	$28,500
Ron, capital ($40,000 − $4,500)	35,500
Lou, capital	16,000
Total partnership capital	$80,000

Withdrawal of a Partner

A partner may withdraw from the business for many reasons, including retirement, or a dispute. The resignation of a partner dissolves the old partnership. The partnership agreement should contain a provision to govern how to settle with a withdrawing partner. In the simplest case, a partner may resign and sell his or her interest to another partner in a personal transaction. The only entry needed to record this transfer of equity debits the withdrawing partner's capital account and credits the purchaser's capital account. The dollar amount of the entry is the capital balance of the withdrawing partner, regardless of the price paid by the purchaser. This situation is illustrated for Fisher and Holt on page 478.

The withdrawing partner may receive his or her share of the business in partnership assets other than cash. Then the question is what value to assign the partnership assets—book value or current market value? The settlement procedure may specify an independent appraisal to determine current market value. If market values have changed, the appraisal will result in revaluing the partnership assets. The partners share in any market-value changes their efforts caused.

Suppose Keith Isaac is retiring from the partnership of Green, Henry, and Isaac. Before any asset appraisal, the partnership balance sheet reports the following:

Cash		$ 69,000	Total liabilities	$ 80,000
Inventory		44,000	Green, capital	54,000
Land		55,000	Henry, capital	43,000
Building	$95,000		Isaac, capital	21,000
Less Accum. depr. . . .	(65,000)	30,000	Total liabilities and	
Total assets		$198,000	capital	$198,000

An independent appraiser revalues the inventory at $38,000 (down from $44,000) and the land at $101,000 (up from $55,000). The partners share the differences between these assets' market values and their prior book values on the basis of their profit-and-loss ratio.

The partnership agreement has allocated 1/4 of the profits to Susan Green, 1/2 to Charles Henry, and 1/4 to Keith Isaac. (This ratio may be written 1:2:1 for one part to Green, two parts to Henry, and one part to Isaac.) For each share that Green or Isaac has, Henry has two. The entries to record the revaluation of the inventory and land are

July 31	Green, Capital ($6,000 × 1/4)		1,500	
	Henry, Capital ($6,000 × 1/2)		3,000	
	Isaac, Capital ($6,000 × 1/4)		1,500	
	Inventory ($44,000 − $38,000)			6,000
	To revalue the inventory and allocate the loss to the partners.			
31	Land ($101,000 − $55,000)		46,000	
	Green, Capital ($46,000 × 1/4)			11,500
	Henry, Capital ($46,000 × 1/2)			23,000
	Isaac, Capital ($46,000 × 1/4)			11,500
	To revalue the land and allocate the gain to the partners.			

After the revaluations, the partnership balance sheet reports the following:

Cash	$ 69,000		Total liabilities	$80,000
Inventory	38,000		Green, capital ($54,000 − $1,500 + $11,500)	64,000
Land	101,000		Henry, capital ($43,000 − $3,000 + $23,000)	63,000
Building	$95,000		Isaac, capital ($21,000 − $1,500 + $11,500)	31,000
Less Accum. depr.	(65,000)	30,000		
Total assets		$238,000	Total liabilities and capital	$238,000

The books now carry the assets at current market value, which becomes the new book value, and the capital accounts are adjusted accordingly. As the balance sheet shows, Isaac has a claim to $31,000 in partnership assets. Now we can account for Keith Isaac's withdrawal from the business.

Withdrawal at Book Value

If Keith Isaac withdraws by receiving cash equal to the book value of his owner's equity, the entry will be

July 31	Isaac, Capital	31,000	
	Cash		31,000
	To record withdrawal of K. Isaac from the business.		

This entry records the payment of cash to Isaac and the closing of his capital account.

✔ **Starter 12-9**

Withdrawal at Less Than Book Value

The withdrawing partner may be so eager to leave the business that he or she is willing to take less than his or her equity. Assume that Keith Isaac withdraws from the business and agrees to receive partnership cash of $10,000 and the new partnership's note for $15,000. This $25,000 settlement is $6,000 less than Isaac's $31,000 equity in the business. The remaining partners share this $6,000 difference—which is a bonus to them—according to their profit-and-loss ratio.

Because Isaac has withdrawn from the partnership, a new agreement—and a new profit-and-loss ratio—must be drawn up. In forming a new partnership, Henry and Green may decide on any ratio that they see fit. Let's assume they agree that Henry will earn 2/3 of partnership profits and losses and Green 1/3. The entry to record Isaac's withdrawal at less than his book value is

July 31	Isaac, Capital	31,000	
	Cash		10,000
	Note Payable to K. Isaac		15,000
	Green, Capital ($6,000 × 1/3)		2,000
	Henry, Capital ($6,000 × 2/3)		4,000
	To record withdrawal of K. Isaac from the business.		

Isaac's account is closed, and Henry and Green may or may not continue the business as a new partnership.

Withdrawal at More Than Book Value

The settlement with a withdrawing partner may allow him or her to take assets of greater value than the book value of that partner's capital. Also, the remaining partners may be so eager for the withdrawing partner to leave that they pay him or her a bonus to withdraw from the business. In either case, the partner's withdrawal causes a decrease in the book equity of the remaining partners. This decrease is allocated to the partners on the basis of their profit-and-loss ratio.

The accounting for this situation follows the pattern illustrated for withdrawal at less than book value—with one exception. The remaining partners' capital accounts are debited because the withdrawing partner receives more than his or her book equity.

> Matt is withdrawing from the partnership of Matt, Lee, and Karla. The partners share profits and losses in a 1:2:3 ratio for Matt, Lee, and Karla, respectively. After the revaluation of assets, Matt's capital balance is $50,000, and the other partners agree to pay him $60,000. Journalize the payment to Matt and his withdrawal from the partnership.
>
> *Answer:*
>
> | | | |
> |---|---|---|
> | Matt, Capital .... | 50,000 | |
> | Lee, Capital [($60,000 − $50,000) × 2/5] .... | 4,000 | |
> | Karla, Capital [($60,000 − $50,000) × 3/5] .... | 6,000 | |
> | Cash .... | | 60,000 |
> | To record withdrawal of Matt from the business. | | |

✔ **Starter 12-10**

6 Account for the liquidation of a partnership

Death of a Partner

The death of a partner dissolves a partnership. The partnership accounts are adjusted to measure net income or loss for the fraction of the year up to the date of death. Then they are closed to determine all partners' capital balances on that date. Settlement with the deceased partner's estate is based on the partnership agreement. The estate commonly receives partnership assets equal to the partner's capital balance. The partnership closes the deceased partner's capital account with a debit. This entry credits a payable to the estate.

Suppose Susan Green (of the partnership at the top of page 483) dies, and her capital balance is $64,000. Green's estate may request cash for her final share of the partnership's assets. At this time the business has only $39,000 of cash, so it must borrow. Let's assume the partnership borrows $50,000 and then pays Green's estate. The partnership's journal entries are

Aug. 1	Cash	50,000		
	Note Payable		50,000	
	To borrow money.			
Aug. 1	Green, Capital	64,000		
	Cash		64,000	
	To record withdrawal of Green from the business.			

Alternatively, a remaining partner may purchase the deceased partner's equity. The deceased partner's equity is debited, and the purchaser's equity is credited. The journal entry to record this transaction follows the pattern given on page 478 for the transfer of Fisher's equity to Holt. The amount of this entry is the ending credit balance in the deceased partner's capital account.

☐ Partnership Characteristics
☐ Types of Partnerships
☐ Partnership Start-Up
☐ Profits and Losses, Drawings
☐ Admission of a Partner
☐ Withdrawal of a Partner
■ **Liquidation**
☐ Financial Statements

Student ResourceCD
liquidation, partnership

Liquidation
The process of going out of business by selling the entity's assets and paying its liabilities. The final step in liquidation is the distribution of any remaining cash to the owner(s).

Liquidation of a Partnership

Admission of a new partner or withdrawal or death of an existing partner dissolves the partnership. However, the business may continue operating with no apparent change to outsiders, such as customers and creditors. In contrast, **liquidation** is the process of going out of business by selling an entity's assets and paying its liabilities. The final step in liquidation is the *distribution of the remaining cash to the owners.*

Before a business is liquidated, its books should be adjusted and closed. After closing, only asset, liability, and partners' capital accounts remain open.

Liquidation includes three steps:

1. Sell the assets. Allocate the gain or loss to the partners' capital accounts on the basis of the profit-and-loss ratio.

2. Pay the partnership liabilities.

3. Disburse the remaining cash to the partners on the basis of their capital balances.

In practice, the liquidation of a business can stretch over weeks or months. Selling every asset and paying every liability takes time. After the partners of Shea & Gould, one of New York's best-known law firms, voted to dissolve their partnership, the firm remained open for an extra year to collect bills and pay off liabilities.

To avoid excessive detail in our illustrations, we include only two asset categories—Cash and Noncash Assets—and a single liability category—Liabilities. Our examples assume that the business sells the noncash assets in a single transaction and then pays the liabilities in another single transaction.

Assume that Jane Akers, Elaine Bloch, and Mark Crane have shared profits and losses in the ratio of 3:1:1. (This ratio is equal to 3/5, 1/5, 1/5, or a 60%, 20%, 20% sharing ratio.) They decide to liquidate their partnership. After the books are adjusted and closed, the general ledger contains the following balances:

Cash	$ 10,000	Liabilities	$ 30,000
Noncash assets	90,000	Akers, capital..............	40,000
		Bloch, capital	20,000
		Crane, capital.............	10,000
Total assets............	$100,000	Total liabilities and capital...	$100,000

Sale of Noncash Assets at a Gain

Assume that the Akers, Bloch, and Crane partnership sells its noncash assets (shown on the balance sheet as $90,000) for cash of $150,000. The partnership realizes a gain of $60,000, which is allocated to the partners on the basis of their profit-and-loss-sharing ratio. The entry to record this sale and allocation of the gain is

Oct. 31	Cash	150,000	
	Noncash Assets................		90,000
	Akers, Capital ($60,000 × 0.60)...		36,000
	Bloch, Capital ($60,000 × 0.20) ...		12,000
	Crane, Capital ($60,000 × 0.20)...		12,000
	To sell noncash assets at a gain.		

The partnership next must pay off its liabilities:

Oct. 31	Liabilities	30,000	
	Cash		30,000
	To pay liabilities.		

In the final liquidation transaction, the remaining cash is disbursed to the partners. *The partners share in the cash according to their capital balances.* (*Gains and losses* on the sale of assets are shared by the partners on the basis of their profit-and-loss-sharing ratio.) The amount of cash left in the partnership is $130,000— the $10,000 beginning balance plus the $150,000 cash sale of assets minus the

$30,000 cash payment of liabilities. The partners divide the remaining cash according to their capital balances:

Oct. 31	Akers, Capital ($40,000 + $36,000) ...	76,000
	Bloch, Capital ($20,000 + $12,000)....	32,000
	Crane, Capital ($10,000 + $12,000) ...	22,000
	Cash........................	130,000
	To pay cash in liquidation.	

A convenient way to summarize the transactions in a partnership liquidation is given in Exhibit 12-4. Remember: Upon liquidation, gains on the sale of assets are divided according to the *profit-and-loss ratio*. The final cash payment to the partners is based on *capital balances*.

Exhibit 12-4   **Partnership Liquidation—Sale of Assets at a Gain**

						Capital		
	Cash	+	Noncash Assets	=	Liabilities +	Akers (60%) +	Bloch (20%) +	Crane (20%)
Balance before sale of assets...............	$ 10,000		$90,000		$30,000	$40,000	$20,000	$10,000
Sale of assets and sharing of gain	150,000		(90,000)			36,000	12,000	12,000
Balances................................	160,000		0		30,000	76,000	32,000	22,000
Payment of liabilities....................	(30,000)				(30,000)			
Balances................................	130,000		0		0	76,000	32,000	22,000
Payment of cash to partners..............	(130,000)					(76,000)	(32,000)	(22,000)
Balances................................	$ 0		$ 0		$ 0	$ 0	$ 0	$ 0

After the payment of cash to the partners, the business has no assets, liabilities, or owners' equity. All the balances are zero. By the accounting equation, partnership assets always *must* equal partnership liabilities plus partnership capital.

Sale of Noncash Assets at a Loss

✔ **Starter 12-11**

✔ **Starter 12-12**

Liquidation of a business often includes the sale of noncash assets at a loss. When this occurs, the partners' capital accounts are debited as they share the loss in their profit-and-loss-sharing ratio. Otherwise, the accounting follows the pattern illustrated for the sale of noncash assets at a gain.

Stop & Think

☐ Partnership Characteristics
☐ Types of Partnerships
☐ Partnership Start-Up
☐ Profits and Losses, Drawings
☐ Admission of a Partner
☐ Withdrawal of a Partner
☐ Liquidation
■ **Financial Statements**

Student ResourceCD

allocation of profit and loss, financial statements, partnership

⭐ *Prepare partnership financial statements*

The liquidation of the Dirk & Cross partnership included the sale of assets at a $150,000 loss. Lorraine Dirk's capital balance of $45,000 was less than her $60,000 share of the loss. Allocation of losses to the partners created a $15,000 deficit (debit balance) in Dirk's capital account. Identify ways that the partnership could deal with the negative balance (a capital deficiency) in Dirk's capital account.

Answer: Two possibilities are

1. Dirk could contribute assets to the partnership in an amount equal to her capital deficiency.
2. Joseph Cross could absorb Dirk's capital deficiency by decreasing his own capital balance.

Partnership Financial Statements

Partnership financial statements are much like those of a proprietorship. However, a partnership income statement includes a section showing the division of net income to the partners. For example, the partnership of Leslie Gray and Wayne Hayward might report its statements for the year ended December 31, 20X3, as shown in Exhibit 12-5. All amounts are assumed.

Exhibit 12-5

Financial Statements of a Partnership

Gray & Hayward Consulting

Income Statement
Year Ended December 31, 20X3

		Thousands
Revenues		$460
Expenses		(270)
Net income		$190
Allocation of net income:		
To Gray	$114	
To Hayward	76	$190

Gray & Hayward Consulting

Statement of Owners' Equity
Year Ended December 31, 20X3

	Thousands	
	Gray	Hayward
Capital, December 31, 20X2	$ 50	$ 40
Additional investments	10	—
Net income	114	76
Subtotal	174	116
Drawings	(72)	(48)
Capital, December 31, 20X3	$102	$ 68

Gray & Hayward Consulting

Balance Sheet
December 31, 20X3

Assets	Thousands
Cash and other assets	$170
Owners' Equity	
Gray, capital	$102
Hayward, capital	68
Total capital	$170

Large partnerships may not find it feasible to report the net income of every partner. Instead, the firm may report average earnings per partner, as shown in Exhibit 12-6 for a small firm.

Exhibit 12-6

Reporting Net Income for an Accounting Partnership

Price & Young

Income Statement
Year Ended August 31, 20X4

Fees for professional services	$1,500,000
Earnings for the year	$ 600,000
Average earnings per partner (2 partners)	$ 300,000

✔ Starter 12-13

✔ Starter 12-14

Decision Guidelines

ACCOUNTING FOR PARTNERSHIPS

Suppose you have a friend who's a biology major. Your friend has achieved amazing success growing plants hydroponically (in water). Your friend knows plants but has no sense for business, so the two of you form a partnership to take advantage of your respective skills. How do you organize? What decisions must you make? Consider these decision guidelines.

Decision	Guidelines
How to organize the business?	A partnership offers both advantages and disadvantages in comparison with proprietorships and corporations. (See Exhibit 12-2).
On what matters should the partners agree?	See "The Written Agreement" on page 471.
At what value does the partnership record assets and liabilities?	Current market value on the date of acquisition, because the partnership is buying its assets at their current market value.

How are partnership profits and losses shared among the partners?	• Equally if there is no profit-and-loss-sharing agreement.
	• As provided in the partnership agreement. Can be based on the partners'
	  a. Stated fractions
	  b. Capital contributions
	  c. Service to the partnership
	  d. Any combination of the above.

What happens when a partner withdraws from the firm?	The old partnership ceases to exist. The remaining partners may or may not form a new partnership.
How are new partners admitted to the partnership?	• *Purchase a partner's interest.* The old partnership is dissolved. The remaining partners may admit the new partner to the partnership. If not, the new partner gets no voice in management but shares in the profits and losses. Close the withdrawing partner's Capital account, and open a Capital account for the new partner. Carry over the old partner's Capital balance to the Capital account of the new partner. • *Invest in the partnership.* Buying in at book value creates no bonus to any partner. Buying in at a price above book value creates a bonus to the old partners. Buying in at a price below book value creates a bonus for the new partner.

How to account for the withdrawal of a partner from the business?	• First, adjust and close the books up to the date of the partner's withdrawal from the business.
	• Second, appraise the assets and the liabilities at their current market value.
	• Third, account for the partner's withdrawal.
	  a. At book value (no change in remaining partners' Capital balances)
	  b. At less than book value (increase the remaining partners' Capital balances)
	  c. At more than book value (decrease the remaining partners' Capital balances)

What happens if the partnership goes out of business?	Liquidate the partnership, as follows:
	  a. Adjust and close the partnership books up to the date of liquidation.
	  b. Sell the partnership's assets. Allocate gain or loss to the partners' Capital accounts based on their profit-and-loss ratio.
	  c. Pay the partnership liabilities.
	  d. Pay any remaining cash to the partners based on their Capital balances.

Excel Application Exercise

Goal: Create a simple spreadsheet to prepare the financial statements of a partnership.

Scenario: Joey Ginsberg and Tommy Wong have decided to become partners and launch Hydro-Gro Partners, their hydroponic plant business. At the end of the year, Ginsberg prepares the new partnership's financial statements in Excel. The statements include an income statement, a statement of owners' equity, and a balance sheet. Revenues for the year were $8,000 and expenses were $4,500. Ginsberg had an initial investment of $700; Wong contributed $300. Ginsberg drew $630 from the business and Wong drew $440. Ginsberg and Wong agree to share profits and losses in proportion to their capital contributions.

When you have completed your work sheet, answer the following questions:

1. How much net income is allocated to Ginsberg? To Wong?
2. How much total capital does each partner have at year end?
3. What amount does the balance sheet report for the partnership's total capital at year-end?

Step-by-Step:

1. Open a new Excel spreadsheet.
2. In column 1, create a bold-faced heading as follows:
   a. Chapter 12 Excel Application Exercise
   b. Hydro-Gro Partners
   c. Today's Date
3. Two rows down, enter the bold-faced title, "Partnership Financial Statements." Then, enter individual rows for revenues, expenses, investment by Ginsberg, investment by Wong, drawings by Ginsberg, and drawings by Wong. Enter the amounts in column B.
4. Using Exhibit 12-5 as your guide, create Hydro-Gro Partners' income statement and statement of owners' equity for the year ended December 31, 20X5, and the balance sheet on that date. Be sure all statements contain formulas based on the data supplied in the problem. (*Hint 1:* The allocation of net income is based on the relative proportion of the investment by each partner. Your formula needs to reflect this proportion. *Hint 2:* "Cash and other assets" must equal the total capital at year-end in the balance sheet.)
5. Save your work sheet and print a copy for your files.

END-OF-CHAPTER *Summary Problem*

The partnership of Taylor & Uvalde is considering admitting Steven Vaughn as a partner on January 1, 20X5. The partnership general ledger includes the following balances on that date:

CHECK YOUR RESOURCES

Cash	$ 9,000	Total liabilities	$ 50,000
Other assets	110,000	Taylor, capital	45,000
		Uvalde, capital	24,000
Total assets	$119,000	Total liabilities and capital . .	$119,000

Ross Taylor's share of profits and losses is 60%, and Thomas Uvalde's share is 40%.

Required (Items 1 and 2 Are Independent)

1. Suppose that Vaughn pays Uvalde $31,000 to acquire Uvalde's interest in the business. Taylor approves Vaughn as a partner.
   a. Record the transfer of owner's equity on the partnership books.
   b. Prepare the partnership balance sheet immediately after Vaughn is admitted as a partner.
2. Suppose that Vaughn becomes a partner by investing $31,000 cash to acquire a one-fourth interest in the business.
   a. Compute Vaughn's capital balance, and record his investment in the business.
   b. Prepare the partnership balance sheet immediately after Vaughn is admitted as a partner. Include the heading.

Solution

Requirement 1

a.

Jan. 1	Uvalde, Capital	24,000	
	Vaughn, Capital		24,000
	To transfer Uvalde's equity in the partnership to Vaughn.		

b. The balance sheet for the partnership of Taylor and Vaughn is identical to the balance sheet given for Taylor and Uvalde in the problem, except that Vaughn's name replaces Uvalde's name in the title and in the listing of Capital accounts.

Requirement 2

a. Computations of Vaughn's capital balance:

Partnership capital before Vaughn is admitted ($45,000 + $24,000)	$ 69,000
Vaughn's investment in the partnership........................	31,000
Partnership capital after Vaughn is admitted....................	$100,000
Vaughn's capital in the partnership ($100,000 × 1/4)	$ 25,000

Jan. 1	Cash	31,000	
	Vaughn, Capital		25,000
	Taylor, Capital [($31,000 − $25,000) × 0.60] ..		3,600
	Uvalde, Capital [($31,000 − $25,000) × 0.40] ..		2,400
	To admit Vaughn as a partner with a one-fourth interest in the business.		

b.

Taylor, Uvalde, & Vaughn

Balance Sheet
January 1, 20X5

Cash ($9,000 + $31,000) ..	$ 40,000	Total liabilities.............	$ 50,000
Other assets............	110,000	Taylor, capital	
		($45,000 + $3,600)	48,600
		Uvalde, capital	
		($24,000 + $2,400)	26,400
		Vaughn, capital............	25,000
Total assets	$150,000	Total liabilities and capital ..	$150,000

●REVIEW *Partnerships*

Quick Check

1. How does a partnership get started?
   a. The partners get a charter from the state.
   b. The partners reach an agreement and simply begin operations.
   c. The partners register with the Better Business Bureau.
   d. All of the above.

2. Which characteristic identifies a partnership?
   a. Limited life
   b. No business income tax
   c. Unlimited personal liability
   d. All of the above

3. An S Corporation is taxed like a
   a. Corporation
   b. Partnership
   c. Either of the above, depending on the partners' decision
   d. None of the above

4. The partnership of Abbot and Brown splits profits in the ratio of 2/3 to Abbot and 1/3 to Brown. The partnership has a net loss of $450,000. What is Brown's share of the loss?
   a. $150,000
   b. $225,000
   c. $300,000
   d. Cannot be determined from the data given

5. Partner drawings
   a. Decrease partnership liabilities
   b. Increase partnership capital
   c. Decrease partnership capital
   d. Decrease partnership net income

6. Malcolm pays $100,000 to Lloyd to acquire Lloyd's $75,000 interest in a partnership. The journal entry to record this transaction is

   a. Lloyd, Capital 100,000
       Malcolm, Capital . .   100,000

   b. Lloyd, Capital 75,000
       Malcolm, Capital . .   75,000

   c. Lloyd, Capital 25,000
       Malcolm, Capital . .   25,000

   d. Malcolm, Capital 75,000
       Lloyd, Capital   75,000

7. Clark and Douglas admit Evans to their partnership, with Evans paying $50,000 more than the book value of her equity in the new partnership. Clark and Douglas have no formal profit-and-loss-sharing agreement. What effect does admission of Evans into the partnership have on the capital balances of Clark and Douglas?
   a. Cannot be determined from the data given
   b. Debit the Clark and Douglas capital accounts for $25,000 each
   c. Credit the Clark and Douglas capital accounts for $50,000 each
   d. Credit the Clark and Douglas capital accounts for $25,000 each

8. Tate retires from the partnership of Roberts, Smith, and Tate. The partners share profits and losses in the ratio of 3:3:4. Tate's capital balance is $40,000, and he receives $50,000 in final settlement. What is the effect on the capital accounts of Roberts and Smith?
   a. Roberts' capital decreases by $5,000.
   b. Smith's capital decreases by $5,000.
   c. Both *a* and *b*.
   d. None of the above.

9. The book value of the assets of the KLM partnership is $100,000. In liquidation, the partnership sells the assets for $130,000. How should the partnership account for the sale of the assets?
   a. Credit the assets for $100,000
   b. Debit cash for $130,000
   c. Increase the partners' capital accounts
   d. All of the above

10. Partnership financial statements report
    a. Revenues on the income statement
    b. Liabilities on the income statement
    c. Net income on the balance sheet
    d. Expenses on the balance sheet

Accounting Vocabulary

articles of partnership (p. 471)	limited partnership (p. 473)	partnership (p. 471)
dissolution (p. 471)	liquidation (p. 484)	partnership agreement (p. 471)
general partnership (p. 473)	LLPs (p. 473)	S Corporation (p. 473)
limited liability partnership (p. 473)	mutual agency (p. 471)	unlimited personal liability (p. 471)

●ASSESS *Your Progress*

online homework

See *www.prenhall.com/horngren*
for selected Starters, Exercises,
and Problems.

Partnership characteristics
(Obj. 1)

A partner's investment in a partnership
(Obj. 2)

Investments by partners
(Obj. 2)

*Partners' profits, losses, and capital
balances*
(Obj. 3)

*Dividing partnership profits based on
capital contributions and service*
(Obj. 3)

*Admitting a partner who purchases an
existing partner's interest*
(Obj. 4)

Starters

S12-1 After studying the characteristics of a partnership, write two short paragraphs, as follows:

1. Explain the *advantages* of a partnership over a proprietorship and a corporation.
2. Explain the *disadvantages* of a partnership over a proprietorship and a corporation.

S12-2 Dean Hahn invests land in a partnership with Margo Klem. Hahn purchased the land in 20X1 for $300,000. A real estate appraiser now values the land at $400,000. Hahn wants $400,000 capital in the new partnership, but Klem objects. Klem believes that Hahn's capital contribution should be measured by the book value of his land.

Klem and Hahn seek your advice. Which value of the building is appropriate for measuring Hahn's capital—book value or current market value? State the reason for your answer. Give the partnership's journal entry to record Hahn's investment in the business.

S12-3 Seth Green and Nate Smith are forming the partnership Sun Development to develop a theme park near Panama City, Florida. Green contributes cash of $4 million and land valued at $10 million. When Green purchased the land in 20X1, its cost was $8 million. The partnership will assume Green's $3 million note payable on the land. Smith invests cash of $5 million and equipment worth $7 million.

1. Compute the partnership's total assets, total liabilities, and total owners' equity immediately after organizing.
2. Journalize the partnership's receipt of assets and liabilities from Green and from Smith. Record each asset at its current market value.

S12-4 Examine the Benz and Hanna balance sheet in Exhibit 12-3, page 475. Note that Benz invested far more in the partnership than Hanna. Suppose the two partners fail to agree on a profit-and-loss-sharing ratio. For the first month (June 20X5), the partnership lost $20,000.

1. How much of this loss goes to Benz? How much goes to Hanna?
2. The partners withdrew no assets during June. What is each partner's capital balance at June 30? Prepare a T-account for each partner's capital to answer this question.

S12-5 Lawson, Martinez, and Norris have capital balances of $20,000, $30,000, and $50,000, respectively. The partners share profits and losses as follows:

a. The first $40,000 is divided based on the partners' capital balances.
b. The next $40,000 is based on service, shared equally by Lawson and Norris.
c. The remainder is divided equally.

Compute each partner's share of the business's $110,000 net income for the year.

S12-6 Study the Ingel and Jay partnership balance sheet at the bottom of page 478. Claire Reynaldo pays $100,000 to purchase Michael Jay's interest in the partnership.

1. Journalize the partnership's transaction to admit Reynaldo to the partnership. What happens to the $10,000 difference between Reynaldo's payment and Jay's capital balance?
2. Must Robin Ingel accept Claire Reynaldo as a full partner? What right does Reynaldo have after purchasing Jay's interest in the partnership?

S12-7 Return to the partnership balance sheet of Ingel and Jay near the bottom of page 478. Suppose Ann Teal invests cash of $80,000 to acquire a 1/3 interest in the partnership.

1. Does Teal's investment provide a bonus to the partners? Show calculations to support your answer.
2. Journalize the partnership's receipt of the $80,000 from Teal.

Admitting a partner who invests in the business
(Obj. 4)

S12-8 Refer to the partnership balance sheet of Page and Franco near the bottom of page 480. Page gets 2/3 of profits and losses, and Franco gets 1/3. Assume Neely invests $140,000 to acquire a 25% interest in the new partnership of Page, Franco, and Neely. Journalize the partnership's receipt of cash from Neely.

Admitting a new partner; bonus to the old partners
(Obj. 4)

S12-9 Examine the Green, Henry, and Isaac balance sheet in the middle of page 482. The partners share profits and losses as follows: 25% to Green, 50% to Henry, and 25% to Isaac. Suppose Susan Green is withdrawing from the business, and the partners agree that no appraisal of assets is needed. How much in assets can Green take from the partnership? Give the reason for your answer, including an explanation of why the profit-and-loss-sharing ratio is not used for this determination.

Withdrawal of a partner
(Obj. 5)

S12-10 Refer to the Green, Henry, and Isaac partnership balance sheet in the middle of page 482. Suppose Henry is retiring from the business and the partners agree to revalue the assets at current market value. A real-estate appraiser values the land at $95,000. The book values of all other assets approximate their current market value. The profit-and-loss ratio is 1:2:1.

Journalize (a) the revaluation of the land and (b) payment of $63,000 to Henry upon his retirement July 31.

Withdrawal of a partner; asset revaluation
(Obj. 5)

S12-11 Use the data in Exhibit 12-4. Suppose the partnership of Akers, Bloch, and Crane liquidates by selling all noncash assets for $85,000. Complete the liquidation schedule as shown in Exhibit 12-4.

Liquidation of a partnership at a loss
(Obj. 6)

S12-12 This Starter builds on the solution to Starter 12-11. After completing the liquidation schedule in Starter 12-11, journalize the partnership's (a) sale of noncash assets for $85,000 (use a single account for Noncash Assets), (b) payment of liabilities, and (c) payment of cash to the partners. Include an explanation with each entry.

Liquidation of a partnership
(Obj. 6)

S12-13 This Starter uses the Green, Henry, and Isaac balance sheet, after revaluation of inventory and land, given at the top of page 483. Assume Isaac has withdrawn from the partnership at his book value, receiving cash. Prepare the balance sheet of the new partnership of Green and Henry on July 31.

Partnership balance sheet
(Obj. 7)

S12-14 The partnership of Frost and Martin had these balances at September 30, 20X4:

Partnership income statement
(Obj. 7)

Cash	$20,000	Service revenue	$140,000
Liabilities	40,000	Frost, capital	30,000
Martin, capital	10,000	Total expenses	35,000
Other assets	60,000		

Frost gets 60% of profits and losses, and Martin 40%. Prepare the partnership's income statement for the year ended September 30, 20X4.

Exercises

E12-1 Ryan Amman, a friend from college, approaches you about forming a partnership to export software. Since graduating, Amman has worked for the International Trade Bank, developing important contacts among government officials and business leaders in South America. Amman believes he is in a unique position to capitalize on growing markets. With expertise in finance, you would have responsibility for the partnership's accounting and finance.

Organizing a partnership
(Obj. 1)

Required

Discuss the advantages and disadvantages of organizing the export business as a partnership rather than a proprietorship. Comment on how partnership income is taxed and how your taxes would change if you organized as an S corporation.

Recording a partner's investment
(Obj. 2)

E12-2 Vivien Monteros has been operating an apartment-locator service as a proprietorship. She and Barrett Schraeder have decided to reorganize the business as a partnership. Monteros's investment in the partnership consists of cash, $8,000; accounts receivable, $10,600; office furniture, $1,600; a small building, $55,000; accounts payable, $3,300; and a note payable to the bank, $10,000.

To determine Monteros's equity in the partnership, she and Schraeder hire an independent appraiser. The appraiser values all the assets and liabilities at their book value except the building, which has a current market value of $71,000. Also there are accrued expenses payable of $1,200.

Required

Make the entry on the partnership books to record Monteros's investment.

Computing partners' shares of net income and net loss
(Obj. 3)

Student ResourceCD

spreadsheet

E12-3 David Coe and Jen Price form a partnership, investing $40,000 and $80,000, respectively. Determine their shares of net income or net loss for each of the following situations:

a. Net loss is $60,000 and the partners have no written partnership agreement.
b. Net income is $90,000, and the partnership agreement states that the partners share profits and losses on the basis of their capital contributions.
c. Net income is $98,000. The first $60,000 is shared on the basis of partner capital contributions. The next $30,000 is based on partner service, with Coe receiving 30% and Price receiving 70%. The remainder is shared equally.

Computing partners' capital balances
(Obj. 3)

E12-4 David Coe withdrew cash of $50,000 for personal use, and Jen Price withdrew cash of $40,000 during the year. Using the data from situation (c) in Exercise 12-3, journalize the entries to close (1) the income summary account and (2) the partners' drawing accounts. Explanations are not required. What was the overall effect on partnership capital?

Admitting a new partner
(Obj. 4)

E12-5 Adam Tse is admitted to a partnership. Prior to his admission, the partnership books show Sean Graham's capital balance at $100,000 and Kelly Ott's capital balance at $60,000. Compute each partner's equity on the books of the new partnership under the following plans:

a. Tse pays $90,000 for Ott's equity. Tse's payment goes directly to Ott.
b. Tse invests $40,000 to acquire a 1/5 interest in the partnership.
c. Tse invests $60,000 to acquire a 1/5 interest in the partnership.

Admitting a new partner
(Obj. 4)

E12-6 Make the partnership journal entry to record the admission of Tse under plans (a), (b), and (c) in Exercise 12-5. Explanations are not required.

Withdrawal of a partner
(Obj. 5)

E12-7 After the books are closed, Echols & Schaeffer's partnership balance sheet reports capital of $60,000 for Echols and $90,000 for Schaeffer. Echols is withdrawing from the firm. The partners agree to write down partnership assets by $40,000. They have shared profits and losses in the ratio of 1/4 to Echols and 3/4 to Schaeffer. The partnership agreement states that a withdrawing partner will receive assets equal to the book value of his owner's equity.

1. How much will Echols receive? Schaeffer will continue to operate the business as a proprietorship.
2. What is Schaeffer's beginning capital on the books of his new proprietorship?

E12-8 Lon Augustine is retiring from the partnership of Augustine, Rye, and Bermuda on May 31. The partner capital balances are Augustine, $36,000; Rye, $51,000; and Bermuda, $22,000. The partners agree to have the partnership assets revalued to current market values. The independent appraiser reports that the book value of the inventory should be decreased by $12,000, and the book value of the land should be increased by $32,000. The partners agree to these revaluations. The profit-and-loss ratio has been 5:3:2 for Augustine, Rye, and Bermuda, respectively. In retiring from the firm, Augustine receives $30,000 cash and a $30,000 note from the partnership.

Withdrawal of a partner
(Obj. 5)

Required

Journalize (a) the asset revaluations and (b) Augustine's withdrawal from the firm.

E12-9 Grant, Harris, and Isbell are liquidating their partnership. Before selling the noncash assets and paying the liabilities, the capital balances are Grant $23,000; Harris, $20,000; and Isbell, $11,000. The partnership agreement specifies no division of profits and losses.

Liquidation of a partnership
(Obj. 6)

Required

1. After selling the noncash assets and paying the liabilities, the partnership has cash of $54,000. How much cash will each partner receive in final liquidation?
2. After selling the noncash assets and paying the liabilities, the partnership has cash of $45,000. How much cash will each partner receive in final liquidation?

E12-10 Prior to liquidation, the accounting records of Park, Quade, and Ross included the following balances and profit-and-loss-sharing percentages:

Liquidation of a partnership
(Obj. 6)

| | Cash | + | Noncash Assets | = Liabilities + | Capital | | |
					Park (40%) +	Quade (30%) +	Ross (30%)
Balances before sale of assets..............	$ 8,000		$57,000	$19,000	$20,000	$15,000	$11,000

The partnership sold the noncash assets for $72,000, paid the liabilities, and gave the remaining cash to the partners. Complete the summary of transactions in the liquidation of the partnership. Use the format illustrated in Exhibit 12-4.

E12-11 The partnership of West, Young, and Zeno is dissolving. Business assets, liabilities, and partners' capital balances prior to dissolution follow at the top of page 496. The partners share profits and losses as follows: West, 25%; Young, 45%; and Zeno, 30%.

Liquidation of a partnership
(Obj. 6)

Required

Create a spreadsheet or solve manually (see the top of page 496)—as directed by your instructor—to compute the ending balances in all accounts after the noncash assets are sold for $140,000 and for $90,000. Determine the unknown amounts. Identify two ways the partners can deal with the negative ending balance in Zeno's capital account.

E12-12 On December 31, 20X5, Cindy Dougherty and Marla Pehacek agree to combine their proprietorships as a partnership. Their balance sheets on December 31 are shown in the lower part of page 496.

Partnership balance sheet
(Obj. 7)

Required

Prepare the partnership balance sheet at December 31, 20X5.

Exercise 12-11 West, Young, and Zeno

	A	B	C	D	E	F
1			**West, Young & Zeno**			
2			**Sale of Noncash Assets**			
3			**(For $140,000)**			
4						
5		Noncash		West	Young	Zeno
6	Cash	Assets	Liabilities	Capital	Capital	Capital
7	$ 6,000	$126,000	$77,000	$12,000	$37,000	$6,000
8	140,000	(126,000)		?	?	?
9						
10	$146,000	$ 0	$77,000	$?	$?	$?
11						
12				=($A8–$B7) * .25		
13						
14						
15			**(For $90,000)**			
16		Noncash		West	Young	Zeno
17	Cash	Assets	Liabilities	Capital	Capital	Capital
18	$ 6,000	$126,000	$77,000	$12,000	$37,000	$6,000
19	90,000	(126,000)		?	?	?
20						
21	$96,000	$ 0	$77,000	$?	$?	$?
22						
23				=($A19–$B18) * .25		
24						

Exercise 12-12

Dougherty and Pehacek

	Dougherty's Business		Pehacek's Business	
	Book Value	Current Market Value	Book Value	Current Market Value
Assets				
Cash	$ 10,700	$ 10,700	$ 4,000	$ 4,000
Accounts receivable (net)	22,000	20,200	8,000	6,300
Inventory...............................	51,000	46,000	34,000	35,100
Plant assets (net)........................	121,800	103,500	53,500	57,400
Total assets	$205,500	$180,400	$99,500	$102,800
Liabilities and Capital				
Accounts payable........................	$ 25,500	$ 25,500	$ 8,300	$ 8,300
Accrued expenses payable	9,200	9,200	1,400	1,400
Notes payable...........................	55,000	55,000		
Dougherty, capital	115,800	?		
Pehacek, capital			89,800	?
Total liabilities and capital	$205,500	$180,400	$99,500	$102,800

Problems

(Group A)

Writing a partnership agreement
(Obj. 1)

P12-1A Ron Jaworski and Lori Miller are forming a partnership, Compass Web Designs, to maintain Web sites for clients. Jaworski is skilled at systems design, and his designs can draw large sales volumes. Miller is a super salesperson and has already lined up several clients.

Required

Write a partnership agreement to cover all elements essential for Compass Web Designs to operate smoothly. Make up names, amounts, profit-and-loss percentages, and so on as needed.

P12-2A On June 30, Alice Ogden and Dan Croyle formed a partnership. The partners agree to invest equal amounts of capital. Ogden invests her proprietorship's assets and liabilities (credit balances in parentheses), as follows:

Investments by partners
(Obj. 2, 7)

	Ogden's Book Values	Current Market Values
Accounts receivable	$ 7,200	$ 7,200
Inventory	22,340	24,100
Prepaid expenses..................	1,700	1,700
Office equipment..................	45,900	27,600
Accumulated depreciation..........	(15,300)	0
Accounts payable	(19,100)	(19,100)

On June 30, Croyle invests cash in an amount equal to the current market value of Ogden's partnership capital. The partners decide that Ogden will earn two-thirds of partnership profits because she will manage the business. Croyle agrees to accept one-third of the profits. During the remainder of the year, the partnership earns net income of $90,000. Ogden's drawings are $39,000, and Croyle's drawings are $31,000.

Required

1. Journalize the partners' initial investments.
2. Prepare the partnership balance sheet immediately after its formation on June 30.
3. Journalize the December 31 entries to close the Income Summary account and the partners' drawing accounts.

P12-3A The owners of NBC partnership are considering admitting Sue Carter as a new partner. On March 31 of the current year, the capital accounts of the three existing partners and their shares of profits and losses are as follows:

Admitting a new partner
(Obj. 4)

	Capital	Profit-and-Loss Share
Nick Nelson.....................	$ 40,000	15%
Luke Bright	100,000	30%
Lisa Clapton....................	160,000	55%

Required

Journalize the admission of Carter as a partner on March 31 for each of the following independent situations:

1. Carter pays Clapton $200,000 cash to purchase Clapton's interest in the partnership.
2. Carter invests $60,000 in the partnership, acquiring a one-sixth interest in the business.
3. Carter invests $80,000 in the partnership, acquiring a one-fourth interest in the business.

P12-4A Charles Lake, Liz Wood, and Hal Parks have formed a partnership. Lake invested $15,000, Wood $18,000, and Parks $27,000. Lake will manage the store; Wood will work in the store half-time; and Parks will not work in the business.

Computing partners' shares of net income and net loss; preparing the partnership income statement
(Obj. 3, 7)

⊙ Student ResourceCD

General Ledger, Peachtree, QuickBooks

Required

1. Compute the partners' shares of profits and losses under each of the following plans:
   a. Net loss is $60,000, and the partnership agreement allocates 40% of profits to Lake, 25% to Wood, and 35% to Parks. The agreement does not specify the sharing of losses.

b. Net income for the year ended January 31, 20X4, is $210,000. The first $75,000 is allocated on the basis of partner capital contributions, and the next $36,000 is based on service, with Lake receiving $28,000 and Wood receiving $8,000. Any remainder is shared equally.

2. Revenues for the year ended January 31, 20X4, were $540,000, and expenses were $330,000. Under plan (b), prepare the partnership income statement for the year.

Withdrawal of a partner
(Obj. 4, 5)

P12-5A Priority Financial Planners is a partnership owned by three individuals. The partners share profits and losses in the ratio of 28% to Cary Black, 38% to Dick McNut, and 34% to Jen Tate. At December 31, 20X6, the firm has the following balance sheet:

Cash		$ 12,000	Total liabilities...........		$ 75,000
Accounts receivable......	$ 22,000				
Less allowance for					
uncollectibles........	(4,000)	18,000			
Building	$310,000		Black, capital.............		83,000
Less accumulated			McNut, capital		50,000
depreciation.........	(70,000)	240,000	Tate, capital.............		62,000
			Total liabilities and		
Total assets.............		$270,000	capital...............		$270,000

McNut withdraws from the partnership on December 31, 20X6, to establish his own consulting practice.

Required

Record McNut's withdrawal from the partnership under the following plans:

1. In personal transactions, McNut sells his equity in the partnership to Ashley Napper and Jim Lucks, who each pay McNut $40,000 for half his interest. Black and Tate agree to accept Napper and Lucks as partners.

2. The partnership pays McNut cash of $20,000 and gives him a note payable for the remainder of his book equity in settlement of his partnership interest.

3. McNut receives cash of $10,000 and a note for $70,000 from the partnership.

4. The partners agree that the building is worth only $250,000 and that its accumulated depreciation should remain at $70,000. After the revaluation, the partnership settles with McNut by giving him cash of $10,000 and a note payable for the remainder of his book equity.

Liquidation of a partnership
(Obj. 6)

P12-6A The partnership of Parr, Johnston, & Rake has experienced operating losses for three consecutive years. The partners—who have shared profits and losses in the ratio of Parr, 10%; Johnston, 30%; and Rake, 60%—are liquidating the business. They ask you to analyze the effects of liquidation and present the following partnership balance sheet at December 31, end of the current year:

Cash	$ 27,000	Liabilities	$131,000
Noncash assets	202,000	Parr, capital	21,000
		Johnston, capital	39,000
		Rake, capital.................	38,000
Total assets..................	$229,000	Total liabilities and capital.....	$229,000

Required

1. Prepare a summary of liquidation transactions (as illustrated in Exhibit 12-4). The noncash assets are sold for $189,000.

2. Make the journal entries to record the liquidation transactions.

P12-7A ← *Link Back to Chapter 4 (Closing Entries).* VT&P is a partnership owned by Vela, Thomas, and Prago, who share profits and losses in the ratio of 5:3:2. The adjusted trial balance of the partnership at September 30, end of the current fiscal year, follows.

Capital amounts for the balance sheet of a partnership
(Obj. 7)

VT&P		
Adjusted Trial Balance		
September 30, 20XX		
Cash	$ 10,000	
Noncash assets	177,000	
Liabilities		$135,000
Vela, capital		57,000
Thomas, capital		44,000
Prago, capital		21,000
Vela, drawing	45,000	
Thomas, drawing	37,000	
Prago, drawing	18,000	
Revenues		211,000
Expenses	181,000	
Totals	$468,000	$468,000

Required

1. Prepare the September 30 entries to close the revenue, expense, income summary, and drawing accounts.

2. Insert the opening capital balances in the partner capital accounts, post the closing entries to the capital accounts, and determine each partner's ending capital balance.

Problems

(Group B)

P12-1B Anna Frank and Sara Gilbert are forming a partnership, Taxco Silver Co., to import silver jewelry from Mexico. Frank is especially artistic and will travel to Mexico to buy merchandise. Gilbert is a super salesperson and has already lined up several department stores to sell the jewelry.

Writing a partnership agreement
(Obj. 1)

Required

Write a partnership agreement to cover all elements essential for the business to operate smoothly. Make up names, amounts, profit-and-loss percentages, and so on as needed.

P12-2B Beth Dalton and Kim Sperry formed a partnership on March 15. The partners agreed to invest equal amounts of capital. Sperry invested his proprietorship's assets and liabilities (credit balances in parentheses). See the table that follows.

Investments by partners
(Obj. 2, 7)

	Sperry's Book Values	Current Market Values
Accounts receivable	$12,000	$12,000
Inventory	43,850	31,220
Prepaid expenses	3,700	3,700
Store equipment	36,700	26,600
Accumulated depreciation	(9,200)	(0)
Accounts payable	(22,300)	(22,300)

On March 15, Dalton invested cash in an amount equal to the current market value of Sperry's partnership capital. The partners decided that Sperry will earn 70% of partnership profits because he will manage the business. Dalton agreed to accept 30% of profits. During the period ended December 31, the partnership earned net income of $70,000. Dalton's drawings were $27,000, and Sperry's drawings totaled $41,000.

Required

1. Journalize the partners' initial investments.
2. Prepare the partnership balance sheet immediately after its formation on March 15.
3. Journalize the December 31 entries to close the Income Summary account and the partners' drawing accounts.

Admitting a new partner
(Obj. 4)

P12-3B Lost Pines Escape is a partnership, and its owners are considering admitting Duane Milano as a new partner. On July 31 of the current year, the capital accounts of the three existing partners and their shares of profits and losses are as follows:

	Capital	Profit-and-Loss Ratio
Eric Runyan...................	$48,000	1/6
Sara Braden	64,000	1/3
Ken Maness	88,000	1/2

Required

Journalize the admission of Milano as a partner on July 31 for each of the following independent situations:

1. Milano pays Maness $114,000 cash to purchase Maness's interest.
2. Milano invests $50,000 in the partnership, acquiring a one-fifth interest in the business.
3. Milano invests $50,000 in the partnership, acquiring a one-eighth interest in the business.

Computing partners' shares of net income and net loss; preparing the partnership income statement
(Obj. 3, 7)

Student ResourceCD
GL, PT, QB

P12-4B Rudy Trump, Monica Rivers, and Courtney Jetta have formed a partnership. Trump invested $20,000; Rivers, $40,000; and Jetta, $60,000. Trump will manage the store; Rivers will work in the store three-quarters of the time; and Jetta will not work.

Required

1. Compute the partners' shares of profits and losses under each of the following plans:
   a. Net loss is $47,000, and the partnership agreement allocates 45% of profits to Trump, 35% to Rivers, and 20% to Jetta. The agreement does not discuss the sharing of losses.
   b. Net income for the year ended September 30, 20X4, is $86,000. The first $30,000 is allocated on the basis of partner capital contributions. The next $30,000 is based on service, with $20,000 going to Trump and $10,000 going to Rivers. Any remainder is shared equally.
2. Revenues for the year ended September 30, 20X4, were $572,000, and expenses were $486,000. Under plan (b), prepare the partnership income statement for the year.

Withdrawal of a partner
(Obj. 4, 5)

P12-5B TMB Design is a partnership owned by three individuals. The partners share profits and losses in the ratio of 30% to Pam Tracy, 40% to Bill Mertz, and 30% to Cameron Brucks. At December 31, 20X3, the firm has the balance sheet that follows.

Cash		$ 25,000	Total liabilities.........	$103,000
Accounts receivable......	$ 16,000			
Less allowance for				
uncollectibles........	(1,000)	15,000		
Inventory...............		92,000	Tracy, capital	38,000
Equipment..............	130,000		Mertz, capital..........	49,000
Less accumulated			Brucks, capital.........	42,000
depreciation.........	(30,000)	100,000	Total liabilities and	
Total assets..............		$232,000	capital..............	$232,000

Tracy withdraws from the partnership on this date.

Required

Record Tracy's withdrawal from the partnership under the following plans:

1. In personal transactions, Tracy sells her equity in the partnership to Walt Fair and Beverly Holtz, who each pay Tracy $35,000 for half her interest. Mertz and Brucks agree to accept Fair and Holtz as partners.

2. The partnership pays Tracy cash of $10,000 and gives her a note payable for the remainder of her book equity in settlement of her partnership interest.

3. Tracy receives cash of $6,000 and a note payable for $34,000 from the partnership.

4. The partners agree that the equipment is worth $160,000 and that accumulated depreciation should remain at $30,000. After the revaluation, the partnership settles with Tracy by giving her cash of $15,000 and inventory for the remainder of her book equity.

P12-6B The partnership of Jackson, Pierce, & Fenner has experienced operating losses for three consecutive years. The partners—who have shared profits and losses in the ratio of Leigh Jackson, 15%; Trent Pierce, 60%; and Bruce Fenner, 25%—are liquidating the business. They ask you to analyze the effects of liquidation. They present the following condensed partnership balance sheet at December 31, end of the current year:

Liquidation of a partnership
(Obj. 6)

Cash	$ 7,000	Liabilities	$ 63,000
Noncash assets	163,000	Jackson, capital	24,000
		Pierce, capital................	66,000
		Fenner, capital	17,000
		Total liabilities and	
Total assets...................	$170,000	capital	$170,000

Required

1. Prepare a summary of liquidation transactions (as illustrated in Exhibit 12-4). The noncash assets are sold for $141,000.

2. Make the journal entries to record the liquidation transactions.

P12-7B ← *Link Back to Chapter 4 (Closing Entries).* ABS Company is a partnership owned by Alberts, Beech, and Sumner, who share profits and losses in the ratio of 1:3:4. The adjusted trial balance of the partnership at June 30, end of the current fiscal year, follows.

Capital amounts for the balance sheet of a partnership
(Obj. 7)

ABS Company		
Adjusted Trial Balance		
June 30, 20XX		
Cash	$ 24,000	
Noncash assets	116,000	
Liabilities.........................		$100,000
Alberts, capital		22,000
Beech, capital		41,000
Sumner, capital.....................		62,000
Alberts, drawing	14,000	
Beech, drawing.....................	35,000	
Sumner, drawing	54,000	
Revenues..........................		108,000
Expenses	90,000	
Totals	$333,000	$333,000

Required

1. Prepare the June 30 entries to close the revenue, expense, income summary, and drawing accounts.

2. Insert the opening capital balances in the partners' capital accounts, post the closing entries to the capital accounts, and determine each partner's ending capital balance.

●APPLY *Your Knowledge*

Decision Cases

Settling disagreements among partners
(Obj. 3)

Case 1. Kimberly Gardner invested $20,000 and Leah Johanssen invested $10,000 in a public relations firm that has operated for 10 years. Neither partner has made an additional investment. Gardner and Johanssen have shared profits and losses in the ratio of 2:1, which is the ratio of their investments in the business. Gardner manages the office, supervises the employees, and does the accounting. Johanssen, the moderator of a television talk show, is responsible for marketing. Her high profile generates important revenue for the business. During the year ended December 20X4, the partnership earned net income of $87,000, shared in the 2:1 ratio. On December 31, 20X4, Gardner's capital balance was $150,000, and Johanssen's capital balance was $100,000.

Required

Respond to each of the following situations.

1. During January 20X5, Gardner learned that revenues of $18,000 were omitted from the reported 20X4 income. She brings this omission to Johanssen's attention, pointing out that Gardner's share of this added income is two-thirds, or $12,000, and Johanssen's share is one-third, or $6,000. Johanssen believes that they should share this added income on the basis of their capital balances—60%, or $10,800, to Gardner and 40%, or $7,200, to herself. Which partner is correct? Why?

2. Assume that the 20X4 $18,000 omission was an account payable for an operating expense. On what basis would the partners share this amount?

Partnership issues
(Obj. 1, 5)

Case 2. The following questions relate to issues faced by partnerships.

1. The text states that a written partnership agreement should be drawn up between the partners in a partnership. One benefit of an agreement is that it provides a mechanism for resolving disputes between the partners. List five areas of dispute that might be resolved by a partnership agreement.

2. The statement has been made that "if you must take on a partner, make sure the partner is richer than you are." Why is this statement valid?

3. Corwin & Corwin is a law partnership. Natalie Corwin is planning to retire from the partnership and move to Israel. What options are available to Corwin to enable her to convert her share of the partnership assets to cash?

Ethical Issue

Tom Crenshaw and Lee Spitz operate Northern Engraving in Toledo, Ohio. The partners split profits and losses equally, and each takes an annual salary of $80,000. To even out the workload, Spitz does the buying and Crenshaw serves as the accountant. From time to time, they use small amounts of store merchandise for personal use. In preparing for a large party, Crenshaw took engraved invitations and other goods that cost $5,000. He recorded the transaction as follows:

Cost of Goods Sold	5,000	
Inventory		5,000

1. How should Crenshaw have recorded this transaction?
2. Discuss the ethical aspects of Crenshaw's action.

Team Project

Visit a business partnership in your area and interview one or more of the partners. Obtain answers to the following questions and ask your instructor for directions. As directed by your instructor, either (a) prepare a written report of your findings or (b) make a presentation to your class.

Required

1. Why did you organize the business as a partnership? What advantages does the partnership form of organization offer the business? What are the disadvantages of the partnership form of organization?

2. Is the business a general partnership or a limited partnership?

3. Do the partners have a written partnership agreement? What does the agreement cover? Obtain a copy if possible.

4. Who manages the business? Do all partners participate in day-to-day management, or is management the responsibility of only certain partners?

5. If there is no written agreement, what is the mechanism for making key decisions?

6. Has the business ever admitted a new partner? If so, when? What are the partnership's procedures for admitting a new partner?

7. Has a partner ever withdrawn from the business? If so, when? What are the partnership's procedures for settling up with a withdrawing partner?

8. If possible, learn how the partnership divides profits and losses among the partners.

9. Ask for any additional insights the partner you interview can provide about the business.

For Internet Exercises, go to the Web site www.prenhall.com/horngren.

CHAPTER 13

Corporations: Paid-in Capital and the Balance Sheet

A+ TIPS CHECK YOUR RESOURCES

- Visit the www.prenhall.com/horngren **Web site** for self-study quizzes, video clips, and other resources

- Try the **Quick Check** exercise at the end of the chapter to test your knowledge

- Learn the **key terms**

- Do the **Starter** exercises keyed in the margins

- Work the **mid-** and **end-of-chapter summary problems**

- Use the **Concept Links** to review material in other chapters

- Search the **CD** for review materials by chapter or by key word

- Watch the **tutorial videos** to review key concepts

- Watch the **Amy's Ice Creams On Location** video for a review of forms of business ownership

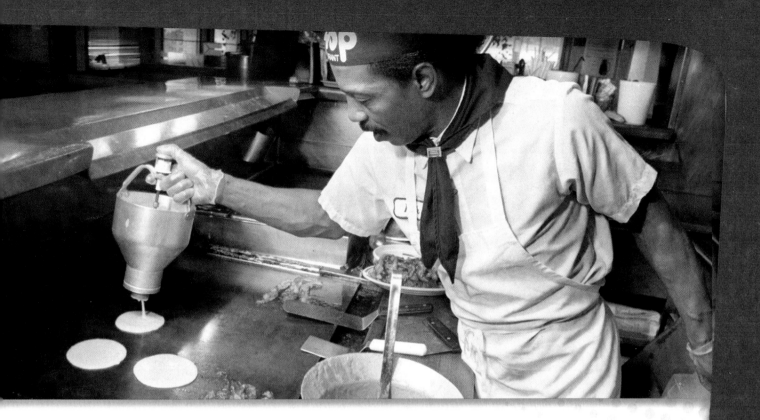

LEARNING OBJECTIVES

1 Identify the characteristics of a corporation

2 Record the issuance of stock

3 Prepare the stockholders' equity section of a corporation balance sheet

4 Account for cash dividends

5 Use different stock values in decision making

6 Evaluate return on assets and return on stockholders' equity

7 Account for the income tax of a corporation

Get on any interstate highway, and you'll see the distinctive shape of an IHOP (International House of Pancakes) building. We've all stopped at an IHOP for pancakes— or a sandwich. The restaurants are clean, the food is good, and the prices are right. Ever think about how IHOP swept across the country?

IHOP Corporation began as a small operation in Glendale, California. To grow the company, IHOP *went public*. This means IHOP offered its stock to anyone who would buy it. The initial public offering of IHOP stock was pretty successful: The company offered 6.2 million shares for $10 a share. As it turned out, investors bought 3.2 million shares. The $32 million (3.2 million × $10) IHOP received was used to open new restaurants and upgrade old ones.

IHOP

Today, IHOP operates restaurants throughout the United States and in several foreign countries. The restaurants serve pancakes, sandwiches, and other casual food mainly to college students and families, which is the target market. Thanks to the sale of its stock, IHOP has become a large, well-known corporation. ■

■Sitemap

 Identify the characteristics of a corporation

 Student Resource**CD**

corporation, limited liability, capital stock, stock

Charter
Document that gives the state's permission to form a corporation.

Stockholder
A person who owns the stock of a corporation. Also called **shareholder**.

Stock
Shares into which the owners' equity of a corporation is divided.

We introduced the idea of mutual agency for partnerships in Chapter 12, page 471.

This chapter covers the issuance of stock by corporations such as IHOP. Any company—large or small—can sell (issue) its stock to investors. All companies issue stock for the same reasons: to raise money, obtain assets, or pay off debt. Now let's explore how corporations differ from the proprietorships and partnerships we have been studying.

Corporations: An Overview

The corporation is the dominant form of business organization in the United States. IHOP is one example. Proprietorships and partnerships are more numerous, but corporations do much more business and are far larger. Most well-known companies, such as Amazon.com and Intel, are corporations. Their full names include *Corporation* or *Incorporated* (abbreviated *Corp.* and *Inc.*) to show that they are corporations—for example, Intel Corporation and Nike, Inc.

Characteristics of a Corporation

What makes the corporate form of organization so attractive? Several things. We now examine the features of corporations and their advantages and disadvantages.

SEPARATE LEGAL ENTITY   A corporation is a business entity formed under the laws of a particular state. For example, the state of New York may grant a **charter**, a document that gives a business the state's permission to form a corporation. Neither a proprietorship nor a partnership requires a charter, because in the eyes of the law those businesses are the same as their owner(s).

A corporation is totally separate from its owners, who are called **stockholders** or **shareholders**. A corporation has many of the rights of a person. For example, a corporation may buy, own, and sell property. The assets and liabilities of IHOP belong to the corporation, not to its owners. The corporation may enter into contracts, sue, and be sued, just like an individual.

CONTINUOUS LIFE AND TRANSFERABILITY OF OWNERSHIP   The owners' equity of a corporation is divided into shares of **stock**. Corporations have *continuous lives* regardless of who owns the stock. Stockholders may sell or trade stock to another person, give it away, or bequeath it in a will. Transfer of the stock does not affect the continuity of the corporation. By contrast, proprietorships and partnerships end when their ownership changes.

NO MUTUAL AGENCY   *Mutual agency* means that all owners act as agents of the business. A contract signed by one owner is binding for the whole company. Mutual agency operates in partnerships but *not* in corporations. ← A stockholder of IHOP Corp. cannot commit IHOP to a contract (unless the person is also an officer in the business).

LIMITED STOCKHOLDER LIABILITY   Stockholders have **limited liability** for corporation debts. That means they have no personal obligation for the corporation's liabilities. The most that a stockholder can lose on an investment in a corporation is the amount invested. In contrast, proprietors and partners are personally liable for all the debts of their businesses, unless the partnership is a limited liability partnership (LLP).

The combination of limited liability and no mutual agency means that persons can invest in a corporation without fear of losing all their personal wealth if the business fails. This feature enables a corporation to raise more money than proprietorships and partnerships.

SEPARATION OF OWNERSHIP AND MANAGEMENT   Stockholders own a corporation, but a *board of directors*—elected by the stockholders—appoints the officers to manage the business. Stockholders may invest $1,000 or $1 million without having to manage the business.

Management's goal is to maximize the firm's value for the benefit of the stockholders. The separation of stockholders and management can create problems. Corporate officers may manage the business for their own benefit. The distance between the stockholders and management may make it difficult for stockholders to overturn bad management. How can stockholders protest? They can vote their shares on matters that come before them. In the extreme, they can sell their stock.

CORPORATE TAXATION   Corporations are separate taxable entities. They pay several taxes not borne by proprietorships or partnerships, including an annual franchise tax levied by the state. The franchise tax keeps the corporate charter in force and enables the corporation to continue doing business. Corporations also pay federal and state income taxes just as individuals do.

Corporate earnings are subject to **double taxation**. First, corporations pay income taxes on corporate income. Then, stockholders pay personal income tax on the cash dividends they receive from corporations. Proprietorships and partnerships pay no business income tax. Instead, the tax falls solely on the owners.

GOVERNMENT REGULATION   Because stockholders have only limited liability for corporation debts, outsiders can look no further than the corporation for payment of its debts. To protect persons who do business with corporations, government agencies monitor corporations. This *government regulation* creates some expenses not borne by proprietorships or partnerships.

Exhibit 13-1 summarizes the advantages and disadvantages of corporations.

Limited Liability
No personal obligation of a stockholder for corporation debts. A stockholder can lose no more on an investment in a corporation's stock than the cost of the investment.

Double Taxation
Corporations pay their own income taxes on corporate income. Then, the stockholders pay personal income tax on the cash dividends they receive from corporations.

Advantages	Disadvantages
1. Can raise more money than a proprietorship or partnership	1. Separation of ownership and management
2. Continuous life	2. Corporate taxation
3. Easy transfer of ownership	3. Government regulation
4. No mutual agency of the stockholders	
5. Limited liability of the stockholders	

Exhibit 13-1

Advantages and Disadvantages of a Corporation

Organizing a Corporation

The process of organizing a corporation begins when the *incorporators* obtain a charter from the state. The charter **authorizes** the corporation to issue a certain number of shares of stock. The incorporators pay fees, sign the charter, and file documents with the state. The corporation then becomes a legal entity. The stockholders agree to a set of **bylaws**, which act as their constitution.

Authorization of Stock
Provision in a corporate charter that gives the state's permission for the corporation to issue—that is, to sell—a certain number of shares of stock.
Bylaws
Constitution for governing a corporation.

Board of Directors
Group elected by the stockholders to set policy and to appoint the officers.

Chairperson
Elected by a corporation's board of directors, the most powerful person in the corporation.

Ultimate control of the corporation rests with the stockholders as they vote their shares of stock. For example, the stockholders elect the **board of directors**, which sets policy and appoints the officers. The board elects a **chairperson**, who is the most powerful person in the company. The board appoints the **president**, who is in charge of day-to-day operations. Most corporations also have a number of vice presidents. Exhibit 13-2 shows the authority structure in a corporation.

Exhibit 13-2 Structure of a Corporation

President
Chief operating officer in charge of managing the day-to-day operations of a corporation.

✔ Starter 13-1

Exhibit 13-3

Stock Certificate

Capital Stock

A corporation issues *stock certificates* to the stockholders when they invest in the business. The stock represents the corporation's capital, so it is called *capital stock*. The basic unit of stock is a *share*. A corporation may issue a stock certificate for any number of shares. Exhibit 13-3 shows a stock certificate for 288 shares of

Company's name ——

Stockholder's name ——

Number of shares held by the stockholder ——

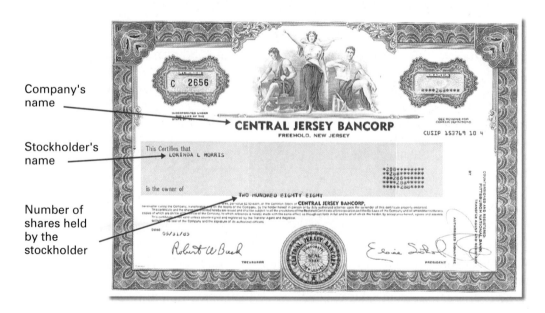

Central Jersey Bancorp common stock. The certificate shows the company's name, the stockholder's name, and the number of shares.

Stock that is held by the stockholders is said to be **outstanding**. The total shares of stock outstanding represent 100% ownership of the corporation.

Stockholders' Equity: The Basics

The balance sheet of a corporation reports assets and liabilities in the same way as for a proprietorship or a partnership. But the owners' equity of a corporation—called **stockholders' equity**—is reported differently. State laws require corporations to report the sources of their capital. There are two basic sources of capital:

- **Paid-in capital** (also called **contributed capital**) represents amounts received from the stockholders.
- **Retained earnings** is capital earned by profitable operations.

Exhibit 13-4 outlines a summarized version of the stockholders' equity of IHOP Corporation.

Stockholders' Equity	
Paid-in capital:	
Common stock	$ 89
Retained earnings	275
Total stockholders' equity	364

Paid-In Capital Comes from the Stockholders

Common stock is paid-in capital because it comes from the stockholders. Suppose IHOP is issuing common stock. IHOP's entry to record the receipt of $20,000 cash and the issuance of stock is

Oct. 20	Cash		20,000	
	Common Stock			20,000
	Issued stock.			

This entry shows that issuing stock increases both the assets and the stockholders' equity of a corporation.

Retained Earnings Come from Profitable Operations

Profitable operations generate income, which increases stockholders' equity through a separate account called Retained Earnings. As we've just seen, a corporation needs more capital accounts than a proprietorship: A corporation uses a Common Stock account and a Retained Earnings account. Corporations close their revenues and expenses into Income Summary, and then they close net income to Retained Earnings. To illustrate, assume IHOP's revenues were $500,000 and expenses totaled $400,000 for December. The closing entries would be

Dec. 31	Sales Revenue		500,000	
	Income Summary			500,000
	To close sales revenue.			
31	Income Summary		400,000	
	Expenses (detailed)			400,000
	To close expenses.			

Outstanding Stock
Stock in the hands of stockholders.

☐ Overview
■ **Stockholders' Equity**
☐ Issuing Stock
☐ Dividends
☐ Stock Values
☐ Evaluating Operations
☐ Income Taxes

Stockholders' Equity
Owners' equity of a corporation.

Paid-in Capital
Capital from investments by the stockholders. Also called **contributed capital**.

Retained Earnings
Capital earned through profitable operation of the business.

Exhibit 13-4

Summarized Stockholders' Equity Sheet of IHOP Corporation (Amounts in Millions)

Student Resource CD

common stock, dividends, paid-in capital, preferred stock, retained earnings, share, stockholders' equity

✔ **Starter 13-2**

Common Stock
The basic form of capital stock. In a corporation, the common stockholders are the owners of the business.

Now, the Income Summary account holds revenues, expenses, and net income.

Income Summary			
Expenses	400,000	Revenues	500,000
		Balance	
		(net income)	100,000

Finally, Income Summary's balance is closed to Retained Earnings.

Dec. 31	Income Summary..............	100,000	
	Retained Earnings........		100,000
	To close net income to Retained Earnings.		

This closing entry completes the closing process. Income Summary is zeroed out, and Retained Earnings now holds net income, as follows:

Income Summary					Retained Earnings	
Expenses	400,000	Revenues	500,000		Closing	
Closing	100,000	Net income	100,000		(net income)	100,000

If IHOP has a net *loss*, Income Summary will have a debit balance. To close a $60,000 loss, the final closing entry credits Income Summary and debits Retained Earnings as follows:

Dec. 31	Retained Earnings..............	60,000	
	Income Summary.........		60,000
	To close *net loss* to Retained Earnings.		

Deficit
Debit balance in the Retained Earnings account.

A loss may cause a debit balance in the Retained Earnings account. This condition—called a Retained Earnings **deficit**—is reported on the balance sheet as a negative amount in stockholders' equity. HAL, Inc., which owns Hawaiian Airlines, Inc., reported this deficit:

Stockholders' Equity	(In millions)
Paid-in capital: Common stock	$ 50
Deficit	(193)
Total stockholders' equity	$ (143)

Corporations May Pay Dividends to the Stockholders

If the corporation has been profitable and has sufficient cash, it may distribute cash to the stockholders. Such distributions are called **dividends**. Dividends are similar to the withdrawals made by a proprietor. Dividends decrease both the assets and the retained earnings of the corporation. Most states prohibit using paid-in capital for dividends. Accountants use the term *legal capital* to refer to the portion of stockholders' equity that cannot be used for dividends.

Dividends
Distributions by a corporation to its stockholders.

Some people think of Retained Earnings as a fund of cash. It is not, because Retained Earnings is an element of stockholders' equity. Retained earnings has no particular relationship to cash or any other asset. *Remember that cash dividends are paid out of assets, not out of retained earnings.*

Stockholders' Rights

The ownership of stock entitles a stockholder to four basic rights, unless specific rights are withheld by contract:

1. *Vote.* Stockholders participate in management by voting on matters that come before them. This is a stockholder's sole right to manage the corporation. Each share of stock carries one vote.

2. *Dividends.* Stockholders receive a proportionate part of any dividend. Each share of stock receives an equal dividend with every other share of the same class.

3. *Liquidation.* Stockholders receive their proportionate share of any assets remaining after the corporation pays its liabilities in liquidation (goes out of business).

4. *Preemption.* Stockholders can maintain their proportionate ownership in the corporation. Suppose you own 5% of a corporation's stock. If the corporation issues 100,000 new shares of stock, it must offer you the opportunity to buy 5% (5,000) of the new shares. This right, called the *preemptive right*, is usually withheld from the stockholders.

Classes of Stock

Corporations issue different types of stock. The stock of a corporation may be either common or preferred and either par or no-par.

COMMON AND PREFERRED STOCK   Every corporation issues *common stock*, the basic form of capital stock. The owners of a corporation are the common stockholders. Some companies issue Class A common stock, which carries the right to vote. They may also issue Class B common stock, which may be nonvoting. (Classes of stock may also be designated Series A, Series B, and so on.) There is a separate account for each class of stock.

Preferred stock gives its owners certain advantages over the common stockholders. Preferred stockholders receive dividends before the common stockholders, and they receive assets before the common stockholders if the corporation liquidates. Corporations pay a fixed amount of dividends on preferred stock. Investors usually buy preferred stock to earn those fixed dividends.

Owners of preferred stock also have the four basic stockholder rights, unless a right is specifically denied. The right to vote is sometimes withheld from preferred stockholders. Companies may issue different classes of preferred stock (Class A and Class B, or Series A and Series B, for example). Each class of stock is recorded in a separate account. Preferred stock is rarer than you might think. A recent survey of 600 corporations revealed that only 86 of them (14%) had some preferred stock outstanding (Exhibit 13-5).

PAR VALUE, STATED VALUE, AND NO-PAR STOCK   Stock may be par-value stock or no-par stock. **Par value** is an arbitrary amount assigned by a company to a share of its stock. Most companies set par value quite low to avoid legal difficulties from issuing their stock below par. Companies maintain a minimum amount of stockholders' equity for the protection of creditors, and this minimum represents the corporation's legal capital. For corporations with par-value stock, **legal capital** is usually the par value of the shares issued.

The common stock par value of Oracle Corporation, the software giant, is $0.01 (1 cent) per share. Pier 1 Imports' common carries a par value of $1 per share. Par value of preferred stock is often higher; some preferred stocks have par values of $25 or $100. Par value is used to compute dividends on preferred stock, as we shall see.

No-par stock does not have par value. Kimberly Clark, the paper company, has preferred stock with no par value. But some no-par stock has a **stated value**, which makes it similar to par-value stock. The stated value is an arbitrary amount that is similar to par value.

Preferred Stock
Stock that gives its owners certain advantages over common stockholders, such as the right to receive dividends before the common stockholders and the right to receive assets before the common stockholders if the corporation liquidates.

Exhibit 13-5

Preferred Stock

14% Corporations with preferred stock

86% Corporations with no preferred stock

Par Value
Arbitrary amount assigned to a share of stock.

Legal Capital
The portion of stockholders' equity that cannot be used for dividends.

Stated Value
An arbitrary amount that accountants treat as though it were par value.

⭐*2 Record the issuance of stock*

◉ Student ResourceCD

common stock, initial public offering, preferred stock

Issuing Stock

Large corporations such as Hewlett-Packard and Coca-Cola use huge quantities of money. They cannot finance all their operations through borrowing, so they raise capital by issuing stock. Corporations may sell the stock directly to stockholders or use the services of an *underwriter*, such as the brokerage firms Merrill Lynch and Morgan Stanley, Dean Witter. An underwriter agrees to buy all the stock it cannot sell to its clients.

The price that the corporation receives from issuing stock is called the *issue price*. Usually, the issue price exceeds the stock's par value because par value is quite low. In the following sections, we show how to account for the issuance of stock.

Issuing Common Stock

The Wall Street Journal is the most popular medium for advertising stock to attract investors. The ads are called *tombstones*. Exhibit 13-6 reproduces IHOP's tombstone, which appeared in *The Wall Street Journal*.

Exhibit 13-6

Announcement of Public Offering of IHOP Stock (Adapted)

The lead underwriter of IHOP's public offering was The First Boston Corporation. Other brokerage firms and investment bankers also sold IHOP's stock to clients. IHOP's tombstone shows that IHOP hoped to raise approximately $62 million of capital. But in the final analysis, IHOP issued only 3.2 million of the shares and received cash of approximately $32 million.

COMMON STOCK AT PAR Suppose IHOP's common stock carried a par value of $10 per share. The stock issuance entry of 3.2 million shares would be

Jan. 31	Cash (3,200,000 × $10)	32,000,000	
	Common Stock		32,000,000
	Issued common stock at par.		

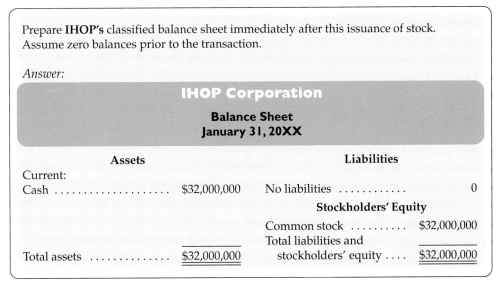

Prepare **IHOP's** classified balance sheet immediately after this issuance of stock. Assume zero balances prior to the transaction.

Answer:

IHOP Corporation

Balance Sheet
January 31, 20XX

Assets		Liabilities	
Current:			
Cash	$32,000,000	No liabilities	0
		Stockholders' Equity	
		Common stock	$32,000,000
		Total liabilities and	
Total assets	$32,000,000	stockholders' equity	$32,000,000

COMMON STOCK AT A PREMIUM Most corporations set par value low and issue common stock for a price above par. The amount above par is called a *premium*. IHOP's common stock has an actual par value of $0.01 (1 cent) per share. The $9.99 difference between issue price ($10) and par ($0.01) is a premium. This sale of stock increases the corporation's paid-in capital by the full $10, total issue price of the stock. Let's see how to account for the premium.

A premium on the sale of stock is not a gain, income, or profit because the entity is dealing with its own stockholders. This situation illustrates one of the fundamentals of accounting: *A company can have no profits or losses when buying or selling its own stock.*

With a par value of $0.01, IHOP's entry to record the issuance of the stock is

July 31	Cash (3,200,000 × $10)	32,000,000	
	Common Stock (3,200,000 × $0.01)		32,000
	Paid-In Capital in Excess of Par—		
	Common (3,200,000 × $9.99)		31,968,000
	Issued common stock at a premium.		

✔ **Starter 13-3**

Paid-In Capital in Excess of Par—Common is also called *Additional Paid-In Capital—Common*. Because both par value and premium amounts increase the corporation's capital, they appear in the stockholders' equity section of the balance sheet.

IHOP Corp. would report stockholders' equity on its balance sheet as follows, assuming that the corporate charter authorizes 40,000,000 shares of common stock and the balance of retained earnings is $26,000,000.

Stockholders' Equity	
Paid-in capital:	
Common stock, $0.01 par, 40 million shares	
authorized, 3.2 million shares issued	$ 32,000
Paid-in capital in excess of par	31,968,000
Total paid-in capital	32,000,000
Retained earnings	26,000,000
Total stockholders' equity	$58,000,000

Common stock equals the total number of shares *issued* (3.2 million) multiplied by the par value per share ($0.01). The stock *authorization* reports the maximum number of shares the company may issue under its charter.

All transactions recorded in this section include the receipt of cash by the corporation for new stock issued to stockholders. These transactions are different from the vast majority of stock transactions reported each day in the financial press. In those transactions, stockholders are buying and selling stock to each other. The corporation doesn't journalize these transactions because its paid-in capital is unchanged.

NO-PAR COMMON STOCK   When a company issues stock that has no par value, there can be no premium. A recent survey of 600 companies revealed 57 issues of no-par stock.

When a company issues no-par stock, it debits the asset received and credits the stock account. Rocky Mountain Corporation, which manufactures ski equipment, issues 4,000 shares of no-par common stock for $20 per share. The stock-issuance entry is

Aug. 14	Cash (4,000 × $20)	80,000	
	Common Stock		80,000
	Issued no-par common stock.		

Regardless of the stock's price, Cash is debited and Common Stock is credited for the cash received. There is no Paid-In Capital in Excess of Par for no-par stock.

Rocky Mountain's charter authorizes 10,000 shares of no-par stock, and the company has $151,000 in retained earnings. Rocky Mountain reports stockholders' equity on the balance sheet as follows:

Stockholders' Equity	
Paid-in capital:	
Common stock, no par, 10,000 shares authorized, 4,000 shares issued	$ 80,000
Retained earnings.	151,000
Total stockholders' equity	$231,000

Accounting.com

UPS Delivers the Dough at Record-Breaking IPO

If you want stock in a company that operates in the global electronic marketplace, what comes to mind? Pioneering dot.coms like Amazon.com or eBay? Think again. There's a 97-year-old business whose workers drive old-fashioned brown trucks and run parcels up to your door. UPS is a business as traditional as apple pie. UPS raised a record-breaking $5.5 billion at its IPO (initial public offering) when it went public. All this money came from investors who saw UPS as a sign of the new economy.

Why would UPS sell its stock to the public? To build a cross-border, USA / European infrastructure, UPS figured it would need to acquire and merge with foreign firms. That required a lot of money. During the first hours of trading in UPS stock, the company's share price soared 40%. By the end of a week, the UPS workforce included 10,000 new millionaires.

Source: Based on Avital Louria Hahn, "Men in Brown: A Growth Story—UPS Recasts Itself for IPO," *The Investment Dealers' Digest: IDD*, December 13, 1999, p. 35. Elise Ackerman, "UPS Delivers as IPO Investors Give the World's No. 1 Package-Delivery Company Full Dot-Com Treatment," *U.S. News & World Report*, November 22, 1999, p. 53. Jenny Anderson, "Up, UPS and Away," *Institutional Investor*, January 2000, pp. 96–98.

NO-PAR COMMON STOCK WITH A STATED VALUE Accounting for no-par stock with a stated value is identical to accounting for par-value stock. No-par common stock with a stated value uses an account titled Paid-In Capital in Excess of *Stated* Value—Common.

COMMON STOCK FOR ASSETS OTHER THAN CASH A corporation may issue stock and receive assets other than cash. It records the assets received at their current market value and credits the capital accounts accordingly. The assets' prior book value is irrelevant because the stockholder will demand stock equal to the market value of the asset given. Kahn Corporation issued 15,000 shares of its $1 par common stock for equipment worth $4,000 and a building worth $120,000. Kahn's entry is

Nov. 30	Equipment...........................	4,000	
	Building..............................	120,000	
	Common Stock (15,000 × $1)...........		15,000
	Paid-In Capital in Excess of Par—		
	Common ($124,000 – $15,000)........		109,000
	Issued common stock in exchange for equipment and a building.		

✔ **Starter 13-4**

Prepare the stockholders' equity section of Kahn's balance sheet immediately after this transaction. Before this issuance of stock, Kahn already had outstanding 10,000 shares of common stock that the company had issued for $8 per share. Kahn's charter authorizes the issuance of 100,000 shares of common stock. Retained earnings is $500,000.

Answer:

Stockholders' Equity	
Paid-in capital:	
Common stock, $1 par, 100,000 shares authorized,	
25,000 (10,000 + 15,000) shares issued	$ 25,000
Paid-in capital in excess of par ($70,000* + $109,000)	179,000
Total paid-in capital	204,000
Retained earnings	500,000
Total stockholders' equity	$704,000
*10,000 shares × ($8 – $1 par) = $70,000	

✔ **Starter 13-5**

✔ **Starter 13-6**

Issuing Preferred Stock

Accounting for preferred stock follows the pattern illustrated for common stock. Chiquita Brands International, Inc., famous for its bananas, has some preferred stock outstanding. Assume Chiquita issued 100,000 shares of preferred stock at par value of $1 per share. The issuance entry is

July 31	Cash	100,000	
	Preferred Stock		
	(100,000 shares × $1).................		100,000
	Issued preferred stock at par.		

✔ **Starter 13-7**

Most preferred stock is issued at par value. Therefore, Paid-In Capital in Excess of Par is rare for preferred stock. For this reason, we do not cover it in this book.

Ethical Considerations

Issuance of stock for *cash* poses no ethical challenge. The company receives cash and issues stock, giving the stockholders certificates as evidence of their ownership.

Issuing stock for assets other than cash can pose an ethical challenge. The company issuing the stock often wishes to record a large amount for the asset received (such as land or a building) and for the stock being issued. Why? Because large asset and equity amounts make the business look successful. The desire to look good can motivate a company to record a high amount for the assets.

A company is supposed to record an asset received at its current market value. But one person's evaluation of a building can differ from another's. One person may appraise the building at a market value of $4 million. Another may honestly believe it is worth only $3 million. A company receiving the building in exchange for its stock must decide whether to record the building at $3 million, $4 million, or some other amount.

The ethical course of action is to record the asset at its current market value, as determined by independent appraisers. Public corporations are rarely found guilty of *understating* the asset values on their balance sheets but companies have been embarrassed by *overstating* asset values.

⭐ *Prepare the stockholders' equity section of a corporation balance sheet*

Review of Accounting for Paid-In Capital

Let's review the first half of this chapter by showing the stockholders' equity section of MedTech.com Corporation's balance sheet in Exhibit 13-7.

Exhibit 13-7

Part of MedTech.com Corporation's Balance Sheet

Stockholders' Equity	
Paid-in capital:	
Preferred stock, 5%, $100 par, 5,000 shares authorized, 400 shares issued..................	$ 40,000
Common stock, $10 par, 20,000 shares authorized, 5,000 shares issued	50,000
Paid-in capital in excess of par—common	70,000
Total paid-in capital..........................	160,000
Retained earnings	90,000
Total stockholders' equity.........................	$250,000

✔ **Starter 13-8**

✔ **Starter 13-9**

Note the two sections of stockholders' equity: paid-in capital and retained earnings. Also observe the order of the equity accounts:

- Preferred stock
- Common stock at par value
- Paid-in capital in excess of par—common
- Retained earnings (after the paid-in capital accounts)

Additional Paid-In Capital
The paid-in capital in excess of par, common plus other accounts combined for reporting on the balance sheet.

Many companies label Paid-In Capital in Excess of Par—Common as **Additional Paid-In Capital** on the balance sheet. However, they are careful not to include preferred stock because that paid-in capital belongs to the preferred stockholders.

Review the Decision Guidelines feature to solidify your understanding of stockholders' equity as it is reported on the balance sheet.

Decision Guidelines

STOCKHOLDERS' EQUITY OF A CORPORATION

Suppose you are interested in investing in stock. The following guidelines will help you sort out some of the relevant factors for your decision.

Decision	Guidelines
What are the two main segments of stockholders' equity?	• Paid-in capital • Retained earnings

Decision Guidelines (*continued*)

Decision	Guidelines
Which is more permanent, paid-in capital or retained earnings?	Paid-in capital is more permanent because corporations can use their retained earnings for dividends.
How are paid-in capital and retained earnings	
• Similar?	• Both represent the stockholders' equity (ownership) in the assets of the corporation.
• Different?	• Paid-in capital and retained earnings come from different sources:
	a. *Paid-in capital* comes from the corporation's stockholders, who invested in the company.
	b. *Retained earnings* comes from profitable operations.
What are the main categories of paid-in capital?	• Preferred stock
	• Common stock, plus paid-in capital in excess of par

MID-CHAPTER *Summary Problem*

1. Test your understanding of the first half of this chapter: Is each of the following statements true or false?
   a. Issuance of 1,000 shares of $5 par-value stock at $12 increases contributed capital by $7,000.
   b. The issuance of no-par stock with a stated value is fundamentally different from issuing par-value stock.
   c. A corporation issues its preferred stock in exchange for land and a building with a combined market value of $200,000. This transaction increases the corporation's owners' equity by $200,000 regardless of the assets' prior book value.
   d. A stockholder may bind the corporation to a contract.
   e. The policy-making body in a corporation is called the board of directors.
   f. The owner of 100 shares of preferred stock has greater voting rights than the owner of 100 shares of common stock.
   g. Par-value stock is worth more than no-par stock.
2. The brewery **Adolph Coors Company** has two classes of common stock. The company's balance sheet included the following (adapted):

TIPS

CHECK YOUR RESOURCES

Stockholders' Equity	
Capital stock	
Class A common stock, voting, $1 par value,	
authorized and issued 1,260,000 shares	$ 1,260,000
Additional paid-in capital—Class A common.	2,011,000
Class B common stock, nonvoting, no par value,	
authorized and issued 46,200,000 shares	11,000,000
Retained earnings	872,403,000
	$886,674,000

Required

a. Record the issuance of the Class A common stock. The additional paid-in capital is related to the Class A common stock. Use the Coors account titles.
b. Record the issuance of the Class B common stock. Use the Coors account titles.
c. What is the total paid-in capital of the company?

Solutions

1. Answers to true/false statements:
   a. False   c. True   e. True   g. False
   b. False   d. False   f. False

2. Adolph Coors Company:

a. Cash 3,271,000
     Class A Common Stock   1,260,000
     Additional Paid-In Capital   2,011,000
     To record issuance of Class A common stock.

b. Cash 11,000,000
     Class B Common Stock   11,000,000
     To record issuance of Class B common stock.

c. Total paid-in capital is $14,271,000 ($1,260,000 + $2,011,000 + $11,000,000).

dividends

Account for cash dividends

Accounting for Cash Dividends

Corporations share their wealth with the stockholders through dividends. Corporations declare dividends from retained earnings and then pay with cash. The corporation must have enough *retained earnings* to declare the dividend and also have enough *cash* to pay the dividend.

Dividend Dates

A corporation declares a dividend before paying it. The board of directors declares the dividend. The corporation has no obligation to pay a dividend until the board declares one. However, once the dividend is declared, it becomes a legal liability. Three relevant dates for dividends are

1. *Declaration date.* On the declaration date, the board of directors announces the intention to pay the dividend. The declaration creates a liability for the corporation.

2. *Date of record.* Those stockholders holding the stock on the date of record—a week or two after declaration—will receive the dividend when it's paid.

3. *Payment date.* Payment of the dividend usually follows the record date by a week or two.

Dividends on Preferred and Common Stock

Declaration of a cash dividend is recorded by debiting Retained Earnings and crediting Dividends Payable, as follows:[1]

May 1	Retained Earnings....................	XXX	
	Dividends Payable..............		XXX
	Declared a cash dividend.		

Payment of the dividend usually follows declaration by a few weeks. Payment is recorded by debiting Dividends Payable and crediting Cash:

May 30	Dividends Payable....................	XXX	
	Cash...........................		XXX
	Paid the cash dividend.		

Dividends Payable is a current liability. When a company has issued both preferred stock and common stock, the preferred stockholders receive their dividends first. The common stockholders receive dividends only if the total dividend is large enough to satisfy the preferred requirement.

✔ Starter 13-10

---

[1]Some accountants debit a Dividends account, which is closed to Retained Earnings. But most businesses debit Retained Earnings, as shown here.

Pine Industries, Inc., has 10,000 shares of preferred stock outstanding, plus common stock. Preferred dividends are paid at the annual rate of $1.50 per share. Exhibit 13-8 shows the division of dividends between preferred and common for two situations.

Exhibit 13-8

Dividing a Dividend Between Preferred Stock and Common Stock

Case A: Total dividend of $8,000:
  Preferred dividend (the full $8,000 goes to preferred
    because the annual preferred dividend is $15,000:
    10,000 shares × $1.50) . . . . $ 8,000
  Common dividend (none because the total dividend
    did not cover the preferred dividend for the year)   0
  Total dividend . . . . $ 8,000

Case B: Total dividend of $50,000:
  Preferred dividend (10,000 shares × $1.50 per share). $15,000
  Common dividend ($50,000 – $15,000)   35,000
  Total dividend $50,000

✔ **Starter 13-11**

If Pine Industries' annual dividend is large enough to cover the preferred dividend for the year (Case B), the preferred stockholders receive their regular dividend, and the common stockholders receive the remainder. But if the year's dividend falls below the amount of the annual preferred dividend (Case A), the preferred stockholders receive the entire dividend, and the common stockholders get nothing that year.

The preferred-stock dividend preference can be stated as a percentage rate or a dollar amount. For example, preferred stock may be "6% preferred," which means that owners of the preferred stock receive an annual dividend of 6% of the par value of the stock. If par value is $100 per share, then the preferred stockholders get an annual dividend of $6 per share (6% of $100). The preferred stock may be "$3 preferred," which means that stockholders get an annual dividend of $3 per share regardless of the preferred stock's par value. The dividend rate on no-par preferred stock is stated in a dollar amount per share.

Dividends on Cumulative and Noncumulative Preferred

The allocation of dividends may be complex if the preferred stock is *cumulative*. Corporations sometimes fail to pay a dividend to their preferred stockholders. This is called *passing the dividend,* and the passed dividends are said to be *in arrears.* The owners of **cumulative preferred stock** must receive all dividends in arrears plus the current year's dividend before the common stockholders get a dividend.

The preferred stock of Pine Industries is cumulative. Suppose the company passed the 20X4 preferred dividend of $15,000. Before paying dividends to its common stockholders in 20X5, the company must first pay preferred dividends of $15,000 for both 20X4 and 20X5, a total of $30,000. *Preferred stock is cumulative in the eyes of the law unless it is labeled as noncumulative.* Most preferred stock is cumulative.

Assume that Pine Industries passes its 20X4 preferred dividend. In 20X5, the company declares a $50,000 dividend. The entry to record the declaration of this dividend is

Cumulative Preferred Stock
Preferred stock whose owners must receive all dividends in arrears before the corporation pays dividends to the common stockholders.

Sep. 6   Retained Earnings.   50,000
             Dividends Payable, Preferred
                ($15,000 × 2).   30,000
             Dividends Payable, Common
                ($50,000 – $30,000)   20,000
           Declared a cash dividend.

If the preferred stock is *noncumulative*, the corporation need not pay dividends in arrears. Suppose Pine Industries' preferred stock was noncumulative and the company passed the 20X4 preferred dividend. The preferred stockholders would lose the 20X4 dividend forever. Of course, the common stockholders would not receive a 20X4 dividend either. Before paying any common dividends in 20X5, the company would have to pay the 20X5 preferred dividend of $15,000.

Dividends in arrears are *not* a liability for the corporation. A liability for dividends arises only after the board of directors declares the dividend. Nevertheless, a corporation must report cumulative preferred dividends in arrears. This information alerts common stockholders about how much must be paid before the common stockholders will receive any dividends.

Different Values of Stock

There are several different *stock values* in addition to par value. Market value and book value are used for various investor decisions.

Market Value

A stock's **market value**, or *market price*, is the price for which a person could buy or sell a share of the stock. The corporation's net income, future prospects, and general economic conditions affect market value. The Internet and most newspapers report the market price of many stocks. Log on to any company's Web site to track its stock price. *In almost all cases, stockholders are more concerned about the market value of a stock than about any other value.*

In the chapter-opening story, IHOP's stock had a market price of $10 when it was issued. Shortly thereafter, IHOP's stock shot up to $36, which means that the stock could be bought for $36 per share. The purchase of 100 shares of IHOP stock at $36 would cost $3,600 ($36 × 100), plus a commission. If you were selling 100 shares of IHOP stock, you would receive cash of $3,600 less a commission. The commission is the fee a stockbroker charges for buying or selling the stock. The price of a share of IHOP stock has fluctuated from $10 at issuance to a recent high of $26.

Book Value

The **book value** of a stock is the amount of owners' equity on the company's books for each share of its stock. If the company has only common stock outstanding, divide total stockholders' equity by the number of shares *outstanding*. A company with stockholders' equity of $180,000 and 5,000 shares of common stock has a book value of $36 per share ($180,000/5,000 shares).

If the company has both preferred stock and common stock outstanding, the preferred stockholders have the first claim to owners' equity. Therefore, we subtract preferred equity from total equity to compute book value per share of the common stock. To illustrate, Lille Corporation reports the following amounts:

Stockholders' Equity	
Paid-in capital:	
Preferred stock, 6%, $10 par, 5,000 shares issued.......	$ 50,000
Common stock, $1 par, 20,000 shares authorized, 10,000 shares issued...........................	10,000
Paid-in capital in excess of par—common..........	170,000
Total paid-in capital........................	230,000
Retained earnings.................................	420,000
Total stockholders' equity........................	$650,000

 Use different stock values in decision making

Market Value
Price for which a person could buy or sell a share of stock.

Student Resource**CD**
book value, market value

Book Value
Amount of owners' equity on the company's books for each share of its stock.

The book-value-per-share computation of common stock follows.

Common	
Total stockholders' equity	$650,000
Less stockholders' equity allocated to preferred	(50,000)
Stockholders' equity allocated to common	$600,000
Book value per share ($600,000/10,000 shares)	$ 60.00

✔ Starter 13-12

Book value is used in decision making. Book value may figure into the price to pay for a closely-held corporation, whose stock is not publicly traded. Also, a company may buy out a stockholder by agreeing to pay the book value of the person's stock.

Some investors compare the book value of a stock with its market value. The idea is that a stock selling below book value is underpriced and thus a good buy. But the relationship between book value and market value is far from clear. Other investors believe that if a stock sells below book value, the company must be experiencing difficulty. Exhibit 13-9 contrasts the book values and market prices for the stocks of three well-known companies. In all three cases, the stock price, which is the market value, exceeds book value—a sign of success. Dell Computer's stock price far exceeds its book value.

✔ Starter 13-13

Exhibit 13-9

Book Value and Market Value for Three Well-Known Companies

	Book Value Per Share	Recent Stock Price
IHOP Corp.	$17.12	$26.00
Fossil	7.34	18.13
Dell Computer	1.80	28.88

Evaluating Operations

Investors and creditors are constantly comparing companies' profits. IHOP's net income may not be comparable with the net income of a new company because IHOP is an established company and the other company is just getting started. IHOP's profits run into the millions, which far exceed a new company's net income. To compare companies, investors use standard profitability ratios. Two key measures are the rate of return on total assets and rate of return on common stockholders' equity.

- Overview
- Stockholders' Equity
- Issuing Stock
- Dividends
- Stock Values
- ■ **Evaluating Operations**
- Income Taxes

Evaluate return on assets and return on stockholders' equity

Student ResourceCD

rate of return, stockholders' equity

Rate of Return on Total Assets

The **rate of return on total assets**, or simply **return on assets**, measures a company's success in using assets to earn income for those who are financing the business.

- Stockholders hold the stock and therefore earn the *net income*.
- Creditors have loaned money to the corporation and thus earn *interest*.

Interest expense and net income are the returns to the two groups that have financed the corporation. The sum of net income plus interest expense is the numerator of the return-on-assets ratio. The denominator is average total assets. Return on assets is computed as follows, using data from the 2002 annual report of IHOP Corp. (dollar amounts in millions):

Rate of Return on Total Assets
The sum of net income plus interest expense divided by average total assets. Measures the success a company has in using its assets to earn income for those financing the business. Also called **return on assets**.

$$\text{RATE OF RETURN ON TOTAL ASSETS} = \frac{\text{NET INCOME} + \text{INTEREST EXPENSE}}{\text{AVERAGE TOTAL ASSETS}}$$

$$= \frac{\$41 + \$22}{(\$641 + \$820)/2} = \frac{\$63}{\$730.5} = 0.086$$

Net income and interest expense are taken from the income statement. Average total assets comes from the beginning and ending balance sheets.

What is a good rate of return on total assets? There is no single answer because rates of return vary widely by industry. For example, high-tech companies such as Intel and Microsoft earn higher returns than utility companies and manufacturers of consumer goods. In most industries, a return on assets of 10% is considered good.

Rate of Return on Common Stockholders' Equity

Rate of return on common stockholders' equity, often called **return on equity**, shows the relationship between net income available to the common stockholders and average common equity. The numerator is net income minus preferred dividends. Preferred dividends are subtracted because the preferred stockholders have the first claim to dividends from net income. The denominator is average *common stockholders' equity*—total equity minus preferred equity. IHOP's rate of return on common stockholders' equity for 2002 is computed as follows (amounts in millions):

✔ Starter 13-14

✔ Starter 13-15

$$\text{RATE OF RETURN ON COMMON STOCKHOLDERS' EQUITY} = \frac{\text{NET INCOME} - \text{PREFERRED DIVIDENDS}}{\text{AVERAGE COMMON STOCKHOLDERS' EQUITY}}$$

$$= \frac{\$41 - \$0}{(\$312 + \$364)/2} = \frac{\$41}{\$338} = 0.121$$

IHOP has no preferred stock, so preferred dividends are zero.

IHOP's return on equity (12.1%) is higher than its return on assets (8.6%). This indicates a healthy company because IHOP is earning more for its stockholders than it is paying for interest expense. Companies borrow at one rate (say, 7%) and try to earn a higher rate (12%) on investments. This is what IHOP did. Borrowing at a lower rate than the return on equity is called *using leverage*.

If a company's return on assets exceeds its return on equity, the company is in trouble. Why?Because interest expense is greater than return on equity. Interest expense should always be lower than the return on equity. Investors and creditors use return on equity in much the same way they use return on total assets—to compare companies. The higher the rate of return, the more successful the company. IHOP's 12% return on common stockholders' equity would be considered fairly good in many industries.

Account for the income tax of a corporation

Accounting for Income Taxes by Corporations

Corporations pay income tax just as individuals do, but not at the same rates. At this writing, the federal tax rate on most corporate income is 35%. Most states also levy a corporate income tax, so most corporations have a combined federal and state income tax rate of approximately 40%.

To account for income tax, the corporation measures

■ Income tax expense, an expense on the income statement

■ Income tax payable, a liability on the balance sheet

Let's illustrate accounting for income tax with a realistic example. In general, income tax expense and income tax payable can be computed as follows:[2]

Income tax expense	=	Income before tax— from the income statement	×	Income tax rate		Income tax payable	=	Taxable income— from the tax return filed with the IRS	×	Income tax rate

[2]The authors thank Jean Marie Hudson for suggesting this presentation.

The income statement and the income tax return are entirely separate documents. The income statement is the financial statement you've been studying throughout this course. The tax return is used only to report taxes to the IRS.

For most companies, income tax expense and income tax payable differ. The most important difference occurs when a corporation uses straight-line depreciation for the income statement and accelerated depreciation → for the tax return.

Continuing with the IHOP illustration, suppose for 20X6 that IHOP Corp. has

We learned in Chapter 10 that the MACRS depreciation method is used for tax purposes.

- Income before income tax of $70 million (This comes from the income statement.)
- Taxable income of $50 million (This comes from the tax return.)

IHOP will record income tax for 20X6 as follows (dollar amounts in millions and an income tax rate of 40%):

```
20X6
Dec. 31  Income Tax Expense ($70 × 0.40) . . . . . . . . . . . .  28
              Income Tax Payable ($50 × 0.40). . . . . . . .       20
              Deferred Tax Liability . . . . . . . . . . . . . . .   8
         Recorded income tax for the year.
```

IHOP will pay the $20 million of Income Tax Payable within a few months. The Deferred Tax Liability account is long-term, so IHOP will pay this debt over a number of years. IHOP's 20X6 financial statements would report these figures (adapted, in millions):

✔ Starter 13-16

Income Statement		Balance Sheet	
Income before income tax	$70	Current liabilities:	
Income tax expense	(28)	Income tax payable	$20
Net income	$42	Long-term liabilities:	
		Deferred tax liability	8*

*The beginning balance of Deferred tax liability was zero.

Decision Guidelines

DIVIDENDS, STOCK VALUES, EVALUATING OPERATIONS, & CORPORATE INCOME TAX

Suppose you operate an **IHOP** restaurant near your college. You are naturally interested in how well the company as a whole is doing. Does IHOP pay dividends? What are IHOP's stock values? What are the rates of return on IHOP's assets and equity? The Decision Guidelines will help you evaluate the company.

Decision	Guidelines
Dividends	
Whether to declare a cash dividend?	• Must have enough retained earnings to declare the dividend. • Must have enough cash to pay the dividend.
What happens with a dividend?	• The corporation's board of directors declares the dividend. Then the dividend becomes a liability of the corporation. • The date of record fixes who will receive the dividend. • Payment of the dividend occurs later.
Who receives the dividend?	• Preferred stockholders receive their dividends first. Preferred dividends have a specified rate. • Common stockholders receive the remainder.

Decision Guidelines (*continued*)

Decision	Guidelines
Stock Values	
How much to pay for a stock?	Its market value.
How is book value used in decision making?	Sometimes used to help determine the market value of a stock that is not traded on a stock exchange.
Evaluating Operations	
How to evaluate the operations of a corporation?	Two measures that relate earnings to the amount stockholders have invested include: • Rate of return on assets • Rate of return on common stockholders' equity For a healthy company, return on stockholders' equity should exceed return on assets.
Accounting for Income Tax	
What are the three main tax accounts?	• Income tax expense • Income tax payable, a current liability • Deferred tax liability, usually a long-term liability
How to measure	
• Income tax expense?	Income before income tax (from the income statement) × Income tax rate
• Income tax payable?	Taxable income (from the income tax return filed with the Internal Revenue Service) × Income tax rate
• Deferred tax liability?	Difference between income tax expense and income tax payable for any one year

Excel Application Exercise

Goal: To create an Excel worksheet that compares the financial performances of two publicly traded stocks in the restaurant industry.

Scenario: Your task is to create an Excel worksheet that compares the historical performance of **IHOP** and **Cracker Barrel** on two key financial measures. Embedded graphs of each financial dimension also must be created. All data used in your spreadsheet will come from **Morningstar's** Web site.

When finished, answer these questions:

1. Which company has earned a consistently higher return on equity?
2. Which company has earned a consistently higher return on assets?

Step-by-Step:

1. Locate www.morningstar.com on the Web.
2. Under the "Morningstar Quicktake Reports" section, enter the ticker symbol for each company. IHOP's symbol is IHP, and Cracker Barrel's symbol is CBRL. To locate the required information, look under "Financial Statements." (Note: If the Web site differs from these headings, you may have to search

other areas of the Web site.) Print out the pages used for each company.
3. Open a new Excel worksheet.
4. Create a bold-faced heading for your spreadsheet that contains the following:
   a. Chapter 13 Excel Application Exercise
   b. Investing in Stock
   c. Stock Performance Analysis
   d. Today's Date
5. Under the heading, create a bold-faced, underlined section titled "Return on Equity %." Move down one row. Create one column each for the past four years (for example, "2001," "2000," and so on). Create one row each for IHOP and Cracker Barrel.
6. Enter the "Return on Equity %" data for the past five years for each company.
7. Repeat steps 5 and 6 for "Return on Assets %."
8. Using the Excel Chart Wizard, create separate graphs for Return on Equity % and Return on Assets %. Resize and position each graph to the right of the data so that everything appears on one page when you print.
9. Save your work, and print your work sheet in landscape mode (with graphs) for your files.

END-OF-CHAPTER *Summary Problem*

Use the following accounts and related balances to prepare the classified balance sheet of Whitehall, Inc., at September 30, 20X4. Use the account format of the balance sheet.

CHECK YOUR RESOURCES

Common stock, $1 par,			Long-term note payable	$ 73,000
50,000 shares authorized,			Inventory.....................	85,000
25,000 shares issued	$25,000		Property, plant, and	
Dividends payable	4,000		equipment, net	225,000
Cash	15,000		Accounts receivable, net	23,000
Accounts payable	28,000		Preferred stock, $3.50, no-par,	
Retained earnings..............	80,000		10,000 shares authorized,	
Paid-in capital in excess of			2,000 shares issued.........	20,000
par—common	115,000		Accrued liabilities	3,000

Compute the book value per share of Whitehall's common stock. No prior-year preferred dividends are in arrears, but Whitehall has not declared the current-year dividend.

Solution

Whitehall, Inc.

Balance Sheet
September 30, 20X4

Assets		Liabilities	
Current:		Current:	
Cash	$ 15,000	Accounts payable.........................	$ 28,000
Accounts receivable, net	23,000	Dividends payable........................	4,000
Inventory.................................	85,000	Accrued liabilities	3,000
Total current assets......................	123,000	Total current liabilities...................	35,000
Property, plant, and equipment, net	225,000	Long-term note payable	73,000
		Total liabilities...........................	108,000

Stockholders' Equity	
Paid-in capital:	
Preferred stock, $3.50, no-par,	
10,000 shares authorized,	
2,000 shares issued	$ 20,000
Common stock, $1 par, 50,000	
shares authorized, 25,000	
shares issued	25,000
Paid-in capital in excess of	
par—common	115,000
Total paid-in capital	160,000
Retained earnings.................	80,000
Total stockholders' equity	240,000

Total assets	$348,000	Total liabilities and stockholders' equity.............	$348,000

Preferred equity:	
Carrying value..	$ 20,000
Cumulative dividend for current year (2,000 shares × $3.50)	7,000
Stockholders' equity allocated to preferred..................	$ 27,000
Common:	
Total stockholders' equity	$240,000
Less stockholders' equity allocated to preferred	(27,000)
Stockholders' equity allocated to common	$213,000
Book value per share ($213,000/25,000 shares)...............	$8.52

REVIEW *Corporations: Paid-In Capital and the Balance Sheet*

Quick Check

1. Which characteristic of a corporation differs from a proprietorship and a partnership?
   a. Separate legal entity
   b. Double taxation
   c. Limited stockholder liability
   d. All of the above

2. Among the corporate characteristics listed in question 1, which is a disadvantage?
   a. Separate legal entity
   b. Double taxation
   c. Limited stockholder liability
   d. None of the above

3. The two basic sources of corporate capital are
   a. Paid-in capital and retained earnings
   b. Stock and bonds
   c. Common stock and preferred stock
   d. Retained earnings and dividends

4. Which class of stockholders takes the greater risk?
   a. Preferred
   b. Common
   c. Neither; bondholders take the most risk
   d. Both preferred and common take equal risk

5. Suppose **IHOP** issued 100,000 shares of its $0.05 par common stock at $1 per share. Which journal entry correctly records the issuance of this stock?

   a. Cash. 100,000
          Common Stock. . | 100,000
   b. Common Stock 100,000
          Cash . . . . | 5,000
          Paid-In Capital
            in Excess of Par | 95,000
   c. Cash. 100,000
          Common Stock. . | 5,000
          Paid-In Capital
            in Excess of Par | 95,000
   d. Common Stock 100,000
          Cash . . . . | 100,000

6. Suppose IHOP issues common stock to purchase a building. IHOP should record the building at
   a. Its market value
   b. Its book value
   c. The par value of the stock given
   d. A value assigned by the board of directors

7. Chewning Corporation has 10,000 shares of 5%, $10 par preferred stock and 50,000 shares of common stock outstanding. Chewning declared no dividends in 20X5. In 20X6, Chewning declares a total dividend of $25,000. How much of the dividends go to the common stockholders?
   a. $5,000
   b. $10,000
   c. $15,000
   d. None; it all goes to preferred

8. Techster Company has 10,000 shares of $1 par common stock outstanding, which Techster issued at $5 per share. Techster also has retained earnings of $80,000. How much is Techster's total stockholders' equity?
   a. $50,000
   b. $80,000
   c. $90,000
   d. $130,000

9. Dale Corporation has the following data:

Net income.	$22,000	Average total assets	$300,000
Interest expense	8,000	Average common equity . . .	100,000
Preferred dividends	10,000		

   Dale's return on common stockholders' equity is
   a. 4%
   b. 10%
   c. 12%
   d. 15%

10. A corporation's income tax expense is computed as follows:
    a. Income before tax × Income tax rate
    b. Taxable income × Income tax rate
    c. Net income × Income tax rate
    d. Return on equity × Income tax rate

Accounting Vocabulary

additional paid-in capital (p. 516)
authorization of stock (p. 507)
board of directors (p. 508)
book value (p. 520)
bylaws (p. 507)
chairperson (p. 508)
charter (p. 506)
common stock (p. 509)
contributed capital (p. 509)
cumulative preferred stock (p. 519)
deficit (p. 510)
dividends (p. 510)

double taxation (p. 507)
legal capital (p. 511)
limited liability (p. 507)
market value (p. 520)
outstanding stock (p. 509)
paid-in capital (p. 509)
par value (p. 511)
preferred stock (p. 511)
president (p. 508)
rate of return on common stockholders' equity (p. 522)

rate of return on total assets (p. 521)
retained earnings (p. 509)
return on assets (p. 521)
return on equity (p. 522)
shareholder (p. 506)
stated value (p. 511)
stock (p. 506)
stockholder (p. 506)
stockholders' equity (p. 509)

ASSESS *Your Progress*

Starters

A⁺ online homework

See *www.prenhall.com/horngren* for selected Starters, Exercises, and Problems.

S13-1 Consider the authority structure in a corporation, as diagrammed in Exhibit 13-2.

1. Who is in charge of day-to-day operations?
2. Who is in charge of accounting?
3. What group holds the ultimate power in a corporation?
4. Who is the most powerful person in the corporation?

Authority structure in a corporation
(Obj. 1)

S13-2 Examine the stockholders' equity of **IHOP Corporation** in Exhibit 13-4. Suppose IHOP were a proprietorship owned by Joe Hopper. How would the IHOP proprietorship balance sheet differ from the one given in Exhibit 13-4? How would the proprietorship balance sheet be similar to the one given in Exhibit 13-4?

The balance sheets of a corporation and a proprietorship
(Obj. 1)

S13-3 Study **IHOP's** July 31 stock issuance entry at a premium on page 513, and answer these questions about the IHOP transaction.

Effect of a stock issuance on net income
(Obj. 2)

1. IHOP received $32,000,000 for the issuance of its stock. The par value of the IHOP stock was only $32,000. Was the excess amount of $31,968,000 a profit to IHOP? Did the excess affect net income? If not, what was it?
2. Suppose the par value of the IHOP stock had been $1 per share, $5 per share, or $10 per share. Would a change in the par value of the company's stock affect IHOP's total paid-in capital? What does affect total paid-in capital?

S13-4 This exercise shows the similarity and the difference between two ways to acquire plant assets.

Issuing stock to finance the purchase of assets
(Obj. 2)

Case A—Issue stock and buy the assets in separate transactions:
  Avisa, Inc., issued 10,000 shares of its $10 par common stock for cash of $700,000. In a separate transaction, Avisa purchased a building for $500,000 and equipment for $200,000. Journalize the two transactions.
Case B—Issue stock to acquire the assets:
  Avisa issued 10,000 shares of its $10 par common stock to acquire a building valued at $500,000 and equipment worth $200,000. Journalize this single transaction.

Compare the balances in all accounts after making both sets of entries. Are the account balances similar or different?

Issuing stock and interpreting
stockholders' equity
(Obj. 2)

S13-5 The **Coca-Cola Company** reported the following on its balance sheet at December 31, 2002 (adapted, with amounts in millions, except for par value per share):

Common stock, $0.25 par value	
Authorized: 5,600 shares	
Issued: 3,500 shares	$ 875
Paid-in capital in excess of par......................	3,855
Retained earnings..................................	24,506

1. Assume Coca-Cola issued all of its stock during 2002. Journalize the company's issuance of the stock for cash.
2. Was Coca-Cola's main source of stockholders' equity paid-in capital or profitable operations? How can you tell?

Issuing stock and analyzing retained
earnings
(Obj. 2)

S13-6 At December 31, 2002, **The Coca-Cola Company** reported the following on its comparative balance sheet, which included 2001 amounts for comparison (adapted, with all amounts in millions except par value per share):

	December 31,	
	2002	2001
Common stock, $0.25 par value		
Authorized: 5,600 shares		
Issued: 3,500 shares in 2002	$ 875	
3,490 shares in 2001		$ 873
Paid-in capital in excess of par	3,855	3,520
Retained earnings	24,506	23,443

1. How much did Coca-Cola's total paid-in capital increase during 2002? What caused total paid-in capital to increase? How can you tell?
2. Did Coca-Cola have a profit or a loss for 2002? How can you tell?

Issuing stock
(Obj. 2)

S13-7 Bruner Corporation has two classes of stock: Common, $1 par: Preferred, $10 par. Journalize Bruner's issuance of

a. 1,000 shares of common stock for $50 per share
b. 1,000 shares of preferred stock for a total of $32,000

Explanations are not required.

Preparing the stockholders' equity section
of a balance sheet
(Obj. 3)

S13-8 The financial statements of Manatee Corporation reported the following accounts (in thousands except for par value):

Paid-in capital in excess of par......	$170	Net sales	$1,080
Cost of goods sold	588	Accounts payable..............	60
Common stock, $1 par,		Retained earnings	166
400 shares issued	400	Other current liabilities.........	52
Cash	240	Operating expenses............	412
Long-term debt..................	76	Total assets	?

Prepare the stockholders' equity section of the Manatee balance sheet. Net income has already been closed to Retained Earnings.

Using stockholders' equity data
(Obj. 3)

S13-9 → *Link Back to Chapter 1 (Accounting Equation, Income Statement).* Use the Manatee Corporation data in Starter 13-8 to compute Manatee's

a. Net income   **b.** Total liabilities   **c.** Total assets

S13-10 Colombia Coffee Company earned net income of $85,000 during the year ended December 31, 20X8. On December 15, Colombia declared the annual cash dividend on its 6% preferred stock (par value, $100,000) and a $0.50 per share cash dividend on its common stock (50,000 shares). Colombia then paid the dividends on January 4, 20X9.

Accounting for cash dividends **(Obj. 4)**

Journalize for Colombia Company:

a. Declaring the cash dividends on December 15
b. Paying the cash dividends on January 4, 20X9

S13-11 Refer to the stockholders' equity of MedTech.com Corporation in Exhibit 13-7. Answer these questions about MedTech.com's dividends.

Dividing cash dividends between preferred and common stock **(Obj. 4)**

1. How much in dividends must MedTech.com declare each year before the common stockholders get any cash dividends for the year?
2. Suppose MedTech.com declares cash dividends of $20,000 for 20X5. How much of the dividends goes to preferred? How much goes to common?
3. Is MedTech.com's preferred stock cumulative or noncumulative? How can you tell?
4. Suppose MedTech.com passed the preferred dividend in 20X6 and 20X7. In 20X8, the company declares cash dividends of $9,000. How much of the dividends goes to preferred? How much goes to common?

S13-12 Refer to the stockholders' equity of MedTech.com Corporation in Exhibit 13-7. MedTech.com has not declared preferred dividends for three years (including the current year). Compute the book value per share of MedTech.com's common stock.

Book value per share of common stock **(Obj. 5)**

S13-13 Answer the following questions about various stock values.

Explaining the use of different stock values for decision making **(Obj. 5)**

1. Suppose you are an investor considering the purchase of **Intel** common stock as an investment. You have called your stockbroker to inquire about the stock. Which stock value are you most concerned about? Explain your reasoning.
2. How is the book value of a stock used in decision making?

S13-14 Answer these questions about two rates of return.

1. Give the formula for computing (a) rate of return on common stockholders' equity and (b) rate of return on total assets.

Computing and explaining return on assets and return on equity **(Obj. 6)**

2. Why are preferred dividends subtracted from net income to compute return on common stockholders' equity?
3. Why is interest expense added to net income to compute return on assets?

S13-15 **Coca-Cola's** 2002 financial statements reported the following items—with 2001 figures given for comparison (adapted, in millions):

Computing return on assets and return on equity for a leading company **(Obj. 6)**

	2002	2001
Balance sheet		
Total assets	$24,501	$22,417
Total liabilities	$12,701	$11,051
Total stockholders' equity (all common)	11,800	11,366
Total liabilities and equity	$24,501	$22,417
Income statement		
Net sales	$19,564	
Cost of goods sold	7,105	
Gross profit	12,459	
Selling, administrative, and general expenses	7,001	
Interest expense	199	
All other expenses, net	2,209	
Net income	$ 3,050	

Compute Coca-Cola's rate of return on total assets and rate of return on common stockholders' equity for 2002. Do these rates of return look high or low?

Accounting for a corporation's income tax
(Obj. 7)

S13-16 Harry's Hot Dogs had income before income tax of $100,000 and taxable income of $80,000 for 20X4, the company's first year of operations. The income tax rate is 40%.

1. Make the entry to record Harry's income taxes for 20X4.
2. Show what Harry's Hot Dogs will report on its 20X4 income statement, starting with income before income tax.

Exercises

Organizing a corporation
(Obj. 1)

E13-1 Kyle Dietz and Joe Phipps are opening a limousine service to be named Good Times Limo. They need outside capital, so they plan to organize the business as a corporation. They come to you for advice. Write a memorandum informing them of the steps in forming a corporation. Identify specific documents used in this process, and name the different parties involved in the ownership and management of a corporation.

Issuing stock
(Obj. 2)

Student Resource CD

General Ledger (GL), QuickBooks (QB), Peachtree (PT)

E13-2 Carolina Systems completed the following stock issuance transactions:

April 19	Issued 1,000 shares of $1 par common stock for cash of $10.50 per share.
May 3	Sold 300 shares of $4.50, no-par preferred stock for $15,000 cash.
11	Received inventory valued at $23,000 and equipment with market value of $11,000. Issued 3,000 shares of the $1 par common stock.

Required

1. Journalize the transactions. Explanations are not required.
2. How much paid-in capital did these transactions generate for Carolina Systems?

Issuing stock and preparing the stockholders' equity section of the balance sheet
(Obj. 2, 3)

Student Resource CD

GL, QB, PT

E13-3 The charter for Mohammed Rugs, Inc., authorizes the company to issue 100,000 shares of $3, no-par preferred stock and 500,000 shares of common stock with $1 par value. During its start-up phase, Mohammed completed the following transactions:

Aug. 6	Issued 500 shares of common stock to the promoters who organized the corporation, receiving cash of $15,000.
12	Issued 300 shares of preferred stock for cash of $20,000.
14	Issued 1,000 shares of common stock in exchange for land valued at $26,000.
31	Closed net income of $25,000 into Retained Earnings.

Required

1. Record the transactions in the general journal.
2. Prepare the stockholders' equity section of the Mohammed Rugs balance sheet at August 31.

Recording issuance of no-par stock
(Obj. 2)

E13-4 Amalfi Furniture Co., located in Chicago, imports Mediterranean furniture. The corporation issued 5,000 shares of no-par common stock for $10 per share. Record issuance of the stock if the stock (a) is true no-par stock and (b) has stated value of $2 per share. Which type of stock results in more total paid-in capital?

Stockholders' equity section of a balance sheet
(Obj. 3)

Student Resource CD

GL, QB, PT

E13-5 The charter of Big Bear Corporation authorizes the issuance of 5,000 shares of Class A preferred stock, 1,000 shares of Class B preferred stock, and 10,000 shares of common stock. During a two-month period, Big Bear completed these stock-issuance transactions:

Nov. 23	Issued 2,000 shares of $1 par common stock for cash of $12.50 per share.	
Dec. 2	Sold 300 shares of $4.50, no-par Class A preferred stock for $20,000 cash.	
12	Received inventory valued at $25,000 and equipment with market value of $16,000 for 3,000 shares of the $1 par common stock.	
17	Issued 1,000 shares of 5%, no-par Class B preferred stock with stated value of $50 per share. The issue price was stated value.	

Required

Prepare the stockholders' equity section of the Big Bear Corporation balance sheet for the transactions given in this exercise. Retained Earnings has a balance of $70,000.

E13-6 ReadyTech Co. recently organized. The company issued common stock to an attorney in exchange for his patent with a market value of $40,000. In addition, ReadyTech received cash both for 2,000 shares of its $50 par preferred stock at par value and for 26,000 shares of its no-par common stock at $10 per share. Retained Earnings at the end of the first year was $70,000. Without making journal entries, determine the total paid-in capital created by these transactions.

Paid-in capital for a corporation
(Obj. 2)

E13-7 Liston Fry Co. has the following selected account balances at June 30, 20X2. Prepare the stockholders' equity section of the company's balance sheet.

Stockholders' equity section of a balance sheet
(Obj. 3)

Student ResourceCD
spreadsheet

Common stock, no par with $1 stated value, 100,000 shares authorized and issued..................	$100,000	Inventory....................	$112,000
		Machinery and equipment	109,000
		Preferred stock, 5%, $20 par, 20,000 shares authorized,	
Accumulated depreciation— machinery and		5,000 shares issued..........	100,000
		Paid-in capital in excess of	
equipment..................	62,000	stated value—common	90,000
Retained earnings	110,000	Cost of goods sold	81,000

E13-8 Qualcomm Communications has the following stockholders' equity:

Dividing dividends between preferred and common stock
(Obj. 4)

Preferred stock, 8%, $10 par, 100,000 shares authorized, 20,000 shares issued.................	$ 200,000
Common stock, $0.50 par, 500,000 shares authorized, 300,000 shares issued................	150,000
Paid-in capital in excess of par—common...........	600,000
Total paid-in capital	950,000
Retained earnings	150,000
Total stockholders' equity	$1,100,000

First, determine whether preferred stock is cumulative or noncumulative. Then compute the amount of dividends to preferred and to common for 20X1 and 20X2 if total dividends are $15,000 in 20X1 and $50,000 in 20X2.

E13-9 The following elements of stockholders' equity are adapted from the balance sheet of Bullock Corporation.

Computing dividends on preferred and common stock
(Obj. 4)

Stockholders' Equity	$ Thousands
Preferred stock, cumulative, $2 par (Note 7), 50,000 shares issued..	$100
Common stock, $0.10 par, 9,000,000 shares issued	900

Note 7. Preferred Stock:
Designated Annual Cash Dividend Per Share—$0.40.

Bullock paid no preferred dividends in 20X3.

Required

Compute the dividends to preferred and common for 20X4 if total dividends are $150,000 in 20X4.

Book value per share of common stock
(Obj. 5)

E13-10 The balance sheet of Westview Landscaping reported the following:

Preferred stock, $50 par value, 6%,	
100 shares issued and outstanding	$ 5,000
Common stockholders' equity, 10,000 shares issued	
and outstanding.	222,000
Total stockholders' equity	$227,000

Assume that Westview has paid preferred dividends for the current year and all prior years (no dividends in arrears). Compute the book value per share of the common stock.

Book value per share of common stock;
preferred dividends in arrears
(Obj. 5)

E13-11 Refer to Exercise 13-10. Compute the book value per share of the common stock if three years' preferred dividends (including dividends for the current year) are in arrears. Round book value to the nearest cent.

Evaluating profitability
(Obj. 6)

E13-12 Columbus Furniture, Inc., reported these figures for 20X8 and 20X7:

	20X8	20X7
Income statement:		
Interest expense	$ 2,400,000	$ 7,100,000
Net income	18,000,000	18,700,000
Balance sheet:		
Total assets.	326,000,000	317,000,000
Preferred stock, $1.30, no-par,		
100,000 shares issued and		
outstanding	2,500,000	2,500,000
Common stockholders' equity	164,000,000	157,000,000
Total stockholders' equity	166,500,000	159,500,000

Compute rate of return on total assets and rate of return on common stockholders' equity for 20X8. Do these rates of return suggest strength or weakness? Give your reason.

Accounting for income tax by a
corporation
(Obj. 7)

E13-13 The income statement of **Pier 1 Imports, Inc.**, reported income before income tax of $160 million during a recent year. Assume Pier 1's taxable income for the year was $100 million. The company's income tax rate was close to 40%.

1. Journalize Pier 1's entry to record income tax for the year.

2. Show how Pier 1 would report income tax on its income statement and on its balance sheet. Complete the income statement, starting with income before tax. For the balance sheet, assume all beginning balances were zero.

Accounting for an actual company's
transactions
(Obj. 2, 4)

E13-14 **Wal-Mart Stores, Inc.**, completed many transactions during 20X2, including the following (adapted in billions):

a. Sales revenue—assume all for cash, $218.
b. Total expenses—90% paid in cash; 10% on account, $210.
c. Closing entries for sales revenue and total expenses.
d. Closing entry for net income to Retained Earnings.
e. Total cash dividends declared and then paid later, $1.

Required

Journalize these 20X2 transactions.

Problems

(Group A)

P13-1A Del Chesser and Mark Bailes are opening a **Pier 1 Imports** store in a shopping center in Taos, New Mexico. The area is growing, and no competitors are located nearby. Their basic decision is how to organize the business. Chesser thinks the partnership form is best. Bailes favors the corporate form of organization. They seek your advice.

Organizing a corporation
(Obj. 1)

Required

Write a memo to Chesser and Bailes to make them aware of the advantages and disadvantages of organizing the business as a corporation. Use the following format for your memo:

> **Date:** _____
>
>   **To:** Del Chesser and Mark Bailes
>
> **From:** Student Name
>
> **Subject:** Advantages and disadvantages of the corporate form of business organization

P13-2A Partners Craven and Thames wish to avoid the unlimited personal liability of the partnership form of business, so they are incorporating the company as C & T Services, Inc. The charter from the state of Arizona authorizes the corporation to issue 10,000 shares of 6%, $100 par preferred stock and 250,000 shares of no-par common stock. In its first month, C & T Services completed the following transactions:

Journalizing corporation transactions and preparing the stockholders' equity section of the balance sheet
(Obj. 2, 3)

GL, QB, PT

Jan. 3	Issued 6,300 shares of common stock to Craven and 3,800 shares to Thames, both for cash of $10 per share.
12	Issued 1,100 shares of preferred stock to acquire a patent with a market value of $110,000.
22	Issued 1,500 shares of common stock to other investors for $10 cash per share.

Required

1. Record the transactions in the general journal.
2. Prepare the stockholders' equity section of the C & T Services, Inc., balance sheet at January 31. The ending balance of Retained Earnings is $40,000.

P13-3A Delta Corporation was organized in 20X4. At December 31, 20X4, Delta's balance sheet reported the following stockholders' equity:

Issuing stock and preparing the stockholders' equity section of the balance sheet
(Obj. 2, 3)

Preferred stock, 5%, $10 par, 50,000 shares authorized, none issued .. $ —	
Common stock, $2 par, 100,000 shares authorized,	
10,000 shares issued	20,000
Paid-in capital in excess of par—common	30,000
Retained earnings (Deficit)	(5,000)
Total stockholders' equity	$45,000

Required

Answer the following questions, making journal entries as needed.

1. What does the 5% mean for the preferred stock? After Delta issues preferred stock, how much in annual cash dividends will Delta expect to pay on 1,000 shares?
2. At what price per share did Delta issue the common stock during 20X4?
3. Were first-year operations profitable? Give your reason.
4. During 20X5, the company completed the following selected transactions. Journalize each transaction. Explanations are not required.
   a. Issued for cash 5,000 shares of preferred stock at par value.
   b. Issued for cash 1,000 shares of common stock at a price of $7 per share.
   c. Net income for the year was $50,000, and the company declared no dividends. Make the closing entry for net income.

(continued)

5. Prepare the stockholders' equity section of the Delta Corporation balance sheet at December 31, 20X5.

Stockholders' equity section of the balance sheet
(Obj. 3)

P13-4A Stockholders' equity information for two independent companies, Seville Enterprises, Inc., and Madrid Corp., is as follows:

- *Seville Enterprises, Inc.* Seville is authorized to issue 60,000 shares of $5 par common stock. All the stock was issued at $12 per share. The company incurred a net loss of $41,000 in 20X6. It earned net income of $30,000 in 20X7 and $90,000 in 20X8. The company declared no dividends during the three-year period.
- *Madrid Corp.* Madrid's charter authorizes the company to issue 10,000 shares of $2.50 preferred stock with par value of $50 and 120,000 shares of no-par common stock. Madrid issued 1,000 shares of the preferred stock at par. It issued 40,000 shares of the common stock for a total of $220,000. The company's Retained Earnings balance at the beginning of 20X8 was $64,000, and net income for the year was $90,000. During 20X8, the company declared the specified dividend on preferred and a $0.50 per share dividend on common. Preferred dividends for 20X7 were in arrears.

Required

For each company, prepare the stockholders' equity section of its balance sheet at December 31, 20X8. Show the computation of all amounts. Entries are not required.

Analyzing the stockholders' equity of an actual corporation
(Obj. 3, 4)

P13-5A **Radioshack Corp.** operates Radio Shack stores. Radioshack included the following stockholders' equity on its year-end balance sheet at December 31, 20X1, with all dollar amounts, except par value per share, adapted, and in millions:

Stockholders' Equity	($ Millions)
Preferred stock, 6% cumulative	$ 65
Common stock—par value $1 per share; 650,000,000	
shares authorized, 236,000,000 shares issued	236
Paid-in capital in excess of par—common	70
Retained earnings	2,003
Other	(1,646)
Total	$ 728

Required

1. Identify the different issues of stock Radioshack has outstanding.
2. Give two summary entries to record issuance of all the Radioshack stock. Assume that all the stock was issued for cash. Explanations are not required.
3. Assume that preferred dividends are in arrears for 20X0 and 20X1. Record the declaration of a $50 million cash dividend on December 30, 20X2. Use separate Dividends Payable accounts for Preferred and Common. Round to the nearest $1 million. An explanation is not required.

Preparing a corporation balance sheet; measuring profitability
(Obj. 3, 6)

P13-6A → *Link Back to Chapter 1 (Accounting Equation).* The following accounts and June 30, 20X5, balances of Witt, Inc., are arranged in no particular order:

Property, plant, and		Accounts receivable, net	$ 46,000
equipment, net	$ 231,000	Paid-in capital in excess of	
Common stock, $1 par,		par—common	19,000
500,000 shares authorized,		Accrued liabilities	26,000
236,000 shares issued	236,000	Long-term note payable	12,000
Dividends payable	9,000	Inventory	81,000
Retained earnings	29,000	Prepaid expenses	10,000
Preferred stock, $0.10, no-par,		Cash	10,000
10,000 shares authorized and		Accounts payable	31,000
issued	25,000	Trademark, net	9,000

Required

1. Prepare the company's classified balance sheet in the account format at June 30, 20X5.

2. Compute Witt's rate of return on total assets and rate of return on common stockholders' equity for the year ended June 30, 20X5. For the rates of return, you will need these data:

Total assets, June 30, 20X4	$404,000
Common equity, June 30, 20X4	222,000
Net income, 20X5	51,000
Interest expense, 20X5	6,000

3. Do these rates of return suggest strength or weakness? Give your reason.

P13-7A OnPoint Consulting, Inc., has 10,000 shares of $4.50, no-par preferred stock and 50,000 shares of no-par common stock outstanding. OnPoint declared and paid the following dividends during a three-year period: 20X1, $20,000; 20X2, $100,000; and 20X3, $200,000.

Computing dividends on preferred and common stock
(Obj. 4)

spreadsheet

Required

1. Compute the total dividends to preferred stock and to common stock for each of the three years if
   a. Preferred is noncumulative.   **b.** Preferred is cumulative.

2. For case (1b), journalize the declaration of the 20X3 dividends on December 28, 20X3, and the payment of the dividends on January 17, 20X4. Use separate Dividends Payable accounts for Preferred and Common.

P13-8A The balance sheet of The Lopez Group reported the following:

Analyzing the stockholders' equity of a corporation
(Obj. 4, 5)

Stockholders' Equity	
Nonvoting preferred stock, no-par	$320,000
Common stock, $1.50 par value, authorized	
75,000 shares; issued 30,000 shares	45,000
Additional paid-in capital—common.	240,000
Retained earnings	141,000
Total stockholders' equity.	$746,000

Notes to the financial statements indicate that 8,000 shares of $3.00 preferred stock with a stated value of $40 per share are issued and outstanding. Preferred dividends are in arrears for three years, including the current year. On the balance sheet date, the market value of the Lopez common stock is $10 per share.

Required

1. Is the preferred stock cumulative or noncumulative? How can you tell?

2. What is the amount of the annual preferred dividend?

3. Which class of stockholders controls the company? Give your reason.

4. What is the total paid-in capital of the company?

5. What was the total market value of the common stock?

6. Compute the book value per share of the common stock.

P13-9A The accounting (not the income tax) records of Wolf Security Systems, Inc., provide the income statement for 20X8.

Computing and recording a corporation's income tax
(Obj. 7)

Total revenue	$680,000
Expenses:	
Cost of goods sold.	$290,000
Operating expenses.	180,000
Total expenses before tax	470,000
Income before income tax	$210,000

The operating expenses include depreciation of $50,000 computed under the straight-line method. In calculating taxable income on the tax return, Wolf uses MACRS. MACRS depreciation was $70,000 for 20X8. The corporate income tax rate is 40%.

Required

1. Compute Wolf's taxable income for the year.

2. Journalize the corporation's income tax for 20X8.

3. Prepare the corporation's single-step income statement for 20X8.

Problems

(Group B)

Organizing a corporation
(Obj. 1)

P13-1B Megan Thomas and Ann Kraft are opening a **Cracker Barrel Restaurant** in Durango, Colorado. There are no competing family restaurants in the immediate vicinity. Their fundamental decision is how to organize the business. Thomas thinks the partnership form is best for their business. Kraft favors the corporate form of organization. They seek your advice.

Required

Write a memo to Thomas and Kraft to make them aware of the advantages and disadvantages of organizing the business as a corporation. Use the following format:

Date: _____
To: Megan Thomas and Ann Kraft
From: Student Name
Subject: Advantages and disadvantages of the corporate form of business organization

Journalizing corporation transactions and preparing the stockholders' equity section of the balance sheet
(Obj. 2, 3)

GL, QB, PT

P13-2B The partnership of Duran & Nueces needed additional capital to expand into new markets, so the business incorporated as Ventura, Inc. The charter from the state of Texas authorizes Ventura to issue 50,000 shares of 6%, $100-par preferred stock and 100,000 shares of no-par common stock. To start, Ventura completed the following transactions:

Dec. 2	Issued 9,000 shares of common stock to Duran and 12,000 shares to Nueces, both for cash of $5 per share.
10	Issued 500 shares of preferred stock to acquire a patent with a market value of $50,000.
27	Issued 12,000 shares of common stock to other investors for cash of $60,000.

Required

1. Record the transactions in the general journal.

2. Prepare the stockholders' equity section of the Ventura, Inc., balance sheet at December 31. The ending balance of Retained Earnings is $57,000.

Issuing stock and preparing the stockholders' equity section of the balance sheet
(Obj. 2, 3)

P13-3B Hudson Corporation was organized in 20X8. At December 31, 20X8, Hudson's balance sheet reported the following stockholders' equity:

Preferred stock, 6%, $50 par,	
100,000 shares authorized, none issued	$ —
Common stock, $1 par, 500,000 shares authorized,	
60,000 shares issued	60,000
Paid-in capital in excess of par—common	40,000
Retained earnings.	25,000
Total stockholders' equity	$125,000

Required

Answer the following questions, making journal entries as needed.

1. What does the 6% mean for the preferred stock? After Hudson issues preferred stock, how much in annual cash dividends will Hudson expect to pay on 1,000 shares?
2. At what price per share did Hudson issue the common stock during 20X8?
3. Were first-year operations profitable? Give your reason.
4. During 20X9, the company completed the following selected transactions. Journalize each transaction. Explanations are not required.
   a. Issued for cash 1,000 shares of preferred stock at par value.
   b. Issued for cash 2,000 shares of common stock at a price of $3 per share.
   c. Net income for the year was $82,000, and the company declared no dividends. Make the closing entry for net income.
5. Prepare the stockholders' equity section of the Hudson Corporation balance sheet at December 31, 20X9.

P13-4B The following summaries for Yurman Jewelry, Inc., and Northern Insurance Company provide the information needed to prepare the stockholders' equity section of each company's balance sheet. The two companies are independent.

Stockholders' equity section of the balance sheet
(Obj. 3)

- *Yurman Jewelry, Inc.* Yurman Jewelry is authorized to issue 40,000 shares of $1 par common stock. All the stock was issued at $10 per share. The company incurred net losses of $50,000 in 20X1 and $14,000 in 20X2. It earned net income of $23,000 in 20X3 and $71,000 in 20X4. The company declared no dividends during the four-year period.

- *Northern Insurance Company.* Northern's charter authorizes the issuance of 50,000 shares of 7%, $15 par preferred stock and 500,000 shares of no-par common stock. Northern issued 1,000 shares of the preferred stock at $15 per share. It issued 100,000 shares of the common stock for $400,000. The company's retained earnings balance at the beginning of 20X4 was $120,000. Net income for 20X4 was $90,000, and the company declared the specified preferred dividend for 20X4. Preferred dividends for 20X3 were in arrears.

Required

For each company, prepare the stockholders' equity section of its balance sheet at December 31, 20X4. Show the computation of all amounts. Entries are not required.

P13-5B The **Procter & Gamble Company** reported the following stockholders' equity, as adapted, on its balance sheet at June 30, 20X3:

Analyzing the stockholders' equity of an actual corporation
(Obj. 3, 4)

Stockholders' Equity	$ Millions
Preferred stock, 6.125%—	
Authorized 600,000,000 shares; issued 1,634,000 shares	$ 1,634
Common stock—$1 stated value—	
Authorized 5,000,000,000 shares; issued 1,301,000,000	1,301
Additional paid-in capital, common.	2,490
Retained earnings	11,980
Other	(3,699)
Total	$13,706

Required

1. Identify the different issues of stock Procter & Gamble has outstanding.
2. Make two summary journal entries to record issuance of all the Procter & Gamble stock. Assume all the stock was issued for cash. Explanations are not required.
3. Assume no preferred dividends are in arrears. Journalize the declaration of a $500 million dividend at June 30, 20X3. Use separate Dividends Payable accounts for Preferred and Common. Round to the nearest $1 million. An explanation is not required.

Preparing a corporation balance sheet; measuring profitability
(Obj. 3, 6)

P13-6B → *Link Back to Chapter 1 (Accounting Equation).* The following accounts and November 30, 20X6, balances of Omaha Mutual, Inc., are arranged in no particular order.

Common stock, $5 par,		Retained earnings.............	$132,000
100,000 shares authorized,		Inventory	101,000
22,000 shares issued........	$110,000	Property, plant, and	
Dividends payable...........	3,000	equipment, net..............	278,000
Additional paid-in capital—		Prepaid expenses..............	13,000
common..................	140,000	Goodwill.....................	37,000
Accounts payable............	31,000	Accrued liabilities.............	17,000
Preferred stock, 4%, $10 par,		Long-term note payable........	104,000
25,000 shares authorized,		Accounts receivable, net	102,000
3,700 shares issued.........	37,000	Cash.........................	43,000

Required

1. Prepare the company's classified balance sheet in the account format at November 30, 20X6.

2. Compute Omaha Mutual's rate of return on total assets and rate of return on common stockholders' equity for the year ended November 30, 20X6. For the rates of return, you will need these data:

Total assets, Nov. 30, 20X5.........................	$581,000
Common equity, Nov. 30, 20X5.....................	383,000
Net income, 20X5	47,200
Interest expense, 20X5	12,800

3. Do these rates of return suggest strength or weakness? Give your reason.

Computing dividends on preferred and common stock
(Obj. 4)

Student ResourceCD

spreadsheet

P13-7B Eastern Airlines has 5,000 shares of 5%, $10 par value preferred stock and 100,000 shares of $1.50 par common stock outstanding. During a three-year period, Eastern declared and paid cash dividends as follows: 20X1, $1,500; 20X2, $15,000; and 20X3, $23,000.

Required

1. Compute the total dividends to preferred stock and to common stock for each of the three years if
   a. Preferred is noncumulative.
   b. Preferred is cumulative.
2. For case (1b), journalize the declaration of the 20X3 dividends on December 22, 20X3, and the payment of the dividends on January 14, 20X4. Use separate Dividends Payable accounts for Preferred and Common.

Analyzing the stockholders' equity of a corporation
(Obj. 4, 5)

P13-8B The balance sheet of Maple Furniture, Inc., reported the following:

Stockholders' Equity	($ Thousands)
Cumulative preferred stock	$ 45
Common stock, $1 par, authorized 40,000,000 shares;	
issued 16,000,000 shares	16,000
Additional paid-in capital	217,000
Retained earnings (Deficit)............................	(77,165)
Total stockholders' equity.............................	$155,880

Notes to the financial statements indicate that 9,000 shares of $1.50 preferred stock with a stated value of $5 per share are issued and outstanding. Preferred dividends are in arrears for two years, including the current year. On the balance sheet date, the market value of the Maple Furniture common stock was $9.50 per share.

Required

1. Is the preferred stock cumulative or noncumulative? How can you tell?

2. What is the amount of the annual preferred dividend?

3. What is the total paid-in capital of the company?

4. What was the total market value of the common stock?

5. Compute the book value per share of the common stock.

P13-9B The accounting (not the income tax) records of Solarex Energy Corporation provide the income statement for 20X4.

Computing and recording a corporation's income tax
(Obj. 7)

Total revenue	$930,000
Expenses:	
Cost of goods sold	$430,000
Operating expenses	270,000
Total expenses before tax	700,000
Income before income tax	$230,000

The operating expenses include depreciation of $50,000 computed on the straight-line method. In calculating taxable income on the tax return, Solarex uses the modified accelerated cost recovery system (MACRS). MACRS depreciation was $80,000 for 20X4. The corporate income tax rate is 35%.

Required

1. Compute taxable income for the year.

2. Journalize the corporation's income tax for 20X4.

3. Prepare the corporation's single-step income statement for 20X4.

APPLY *Your Knowledge*

Decision Cases

Case 1. Ray Link and Sam Chain have written a spreadsheet program (Link Chain) to rival Excel. They need additional capital to market the product, and they plan to incorporate the business. They are considering the capital structure for the corporation. Their primary goal is to raise as much capital as possible without giving up control of the business. Link and Chain plan to invest the software program in the company and receive 100,000 shares of the corporation's common stock. The partners have been offered $100,000 for the rights to the software program.

Evaluating alternative ways to raise capital
(Obj. 2, 3)

    The corporation's plans for a charter include an authorization to issue 5,000 shares of preferred stock and 500,000 shares of $1 par common stock. Link and Chain are uncertain about the most desirable features for the preferred stock. Prior to incorporating, the partners are discussing their plans with two investment groups. The corporation can obtain capital from outside investors under either of the following plans:

- *Plan 1.* Group 1 will invest $100,000 to acquire 1,000 shares of $5, no-par preferred stock and $70,000 to acquire 70,000 shares of common stock. Each preferred share receives 50 votes on matters that come before the stockholders.

- *Plan 2.* Group 2 will invest $150,000 to acquire 1,500 shares of 6%, $100 par nonvoting, noncumulative preferred stock.

Required

Assume that the corporation is chartered.

1. Journalize the issuance of common stock to Link and Chain. Explanations are not required.
2. Journalize the issuance of stock to the outsiders under both plans. Explanations are not required.
3. Net income for the first year is $180,000 and total dividends are $30,000. Prepare the stockholders' equity section of the corporation's balance sheet under both plans.
4. Recommend one of the plans to Link and Chain. Give your reasons.

Characteristics of corporations' capital stock
(Obj. 2, 5)

Case 2. Answering the following questions will enhance your understanding of the capital stock of corporations. Consider each question independently of the others.

1. Preferred shares have advantages with respect to dividends and corporate liquidation. Why would investors buy common stock when preferred stock is available?
2. Why are capital stock and retained earnings shown separately in the shareholders' equity section of the balance sheet?
3. Chiu Wang, major shareholder of C-W, Inc., proposes to sell some land she owns to the company for common shares in C-W. What problem does C-W, Inc., face in recording the transaction?
4. If you owned 100 shares of stock in **Dell Computer Corporation** and someone offered to buy the stock for its book value, would you accept the offer? Why or why not?

Ethical Issue

Note: This case is based on an actual situation.

Jeremy Copeland paid $50,000 for a franchise that entitled him to market Success Associates software programs in the countries of the European Union. Copeland intended to sell individual franchises for the major language groups of western Europe—German, French, English, Spanish, and Italian. Naturally, investors considering buying a franchise from Copeland asked to see the financial statements of his business.

Believing the value of the franchise to be greater than $50,000, Copeland sought to capitalize his own franchise at $500,000. The law firm of St. Charles & LaDue helped Copeland form a corporation chartered to issue 500,000 shares of common stock with par value of $1 per share. Attorneys suggested the following chain of transactions:

a. A third party borrows $500,000 and purchases the franchise from Copeland.
b. Copeland pays the corporation $500,000 to acquire all its stock.
c. The corporation buys the franchise from the third party, who repays the loan.

In the final analysis, the third party is debt-free and out of the picture. Copeland owns all the corporation's stock, and the corporation owns the franchise. The corporation's balance sheet lists a franchise acquired at a cost of $500,000. This balance sheet is Copeland's most valuable marketing tool.

Required

1. What is unethical about this situation?
2. Who can be harmed? How can they be harmed? What role does accounting play?

Analyzing stockholders' equity
(Obj. 2, 6, 7)

Financial Statement Case

The **Amazon.com** financial statements appear in Appendix A. Answer the following questions about Amazon's stock.

Required

1. How much of Amazon's preferred stock was outstanding at December 31, 2002? How can you tell?
2. Examine Amazon.com's balance sheet. Which stockholders' equity account increased the most during 2002? What caused this increase? The statement of cash flows answers this question under Financing Activities.
3. Show how to compute the balances in Amazon.com's Common Stock account at the end of both 2002 and 2001.
4. Would it be meaningful to compute Amazon.com's return on equity? Explain your answer.

Team Project

Competitive pressures are the norm in business. **Lexus** automobiles (made in Japan) have cut into the sales of **Mercedes Benz** (a German company), Jaguar (now a division of Ford), **General Motors'** Cadillac Division, and **Ford's** Lincoln Division. **Dell, Gateway**, and **Compaq** computers have siphoned business away from **IBM**. Foreign steelmakers have reduced the once-massive U.S. steel industry to a fraction of its former size.

Indeed, corporate downsizing has occurred on a massive scale. During the past few years, each company or industry mentioned here has pared down plant and equipment, laid off employees, or restructured operations.

Required

1. Identify all the stakeholders of a corporation and the stake each group has in the company. A *stakeholder* is a person or a group who has an interest (that is, a stake) in the success of the organization.
2. Identify several measures by which a corporation may be considered deficient and which may indicate the need for downsizing. How can downsizing help to solve this problem? Discuss how each measure can indicate the need for downsizing.
3. Debate the downsizing issue. One group of students takes the perspective of the company and its stockholders, and another group of students takes the perspective of other stakeholders of the company.

For Internet exercises, go to the Web site www.prenhall.com/horngren.

CHAPTER 14

Retained Earnings, Treasury Stock, and the Income Statement

A+ TIPS — CHECK YOUR RESOURCES

- Visit the www.prenhall.com/horngren **Web site** for self-study quizzes, video clips, and other resources
- Try the **Quick Check** exercise at the end of the chapter to test your knowledge
- Learn the **key terms**
- Do the **Starter** exercises keyed in the margins
- Work the **mid-** and **end-of-chapter summary problems**
- Use the **Concept Links** to review material in other chapters
- Search the **CD** for review materials by chapter or by key word
- Watch the **tutorial videos** to review key concepts

LEARNING OBJECTIVES

1 Account for stock dividends

2 Distinguish stock splits from stock dividends

3 Account for treasury stock

4 Report restrictions on retained earnings

5 Analyze a complex income statement

6 Prepare a statement of stockholders' equity

Coca-Cola/ Dell/ Pier 1

Coca-Cola, Dell Computer, and Pier 1 Imports are all leaders in their respective industries. What do these three companies have in common? A lot, including the fact that all three have bought back large amounts of their own stock. In Chapter 13 we saw how corporations raise capital by issuing their stock. Stock issuance increases stockholders' equity.

Companies also buy their own stock back from the stockholders. A stock repurchase decreases both corporate assets and equity. A company's own stock that it has repurchased is called treasury stock, because the company holds the stock in the corporate treasury. Coca-Cola, Dell, and Pier 1 have spent large sums to buy back their own stock. Coca-Cola's stock buybacks have totaled more than $14 billion—more than the company's total equity. Dell has spent over $2 billion—almost half of its total equity—to reacquire its own stock. ■

Student Resource CD

common stock, dividends, stock
dividend, stock split

Why do companies repurchase their own stock? This chapter covers the topic of treasury stock, along with retained earnings, stock dividends, and the corporate income statement. Let's begin with retained earnings.

Retained Earnings, Stock Dividends, and Stock Splits

We have seen that the owners' equity of a corporation is called *stockholders' equity* or *shareholders' equity*. The paid-in capital accounts and retained earnings make up stockholders' equity.

Retained Earnings

Retained Earnings carries the balance of the business's net income less all net losses and less all dividends accumulated over the corporation's lifetime. *Retained* means "held onto." Retained Earnings is the shareholders' stake in total assets that come from profits. A debit balance in Retained Earnings is called a *deficit*. Retained earnings deficits are rare because they can lead to corporate failure and bankruptcy.

When you see a balance sheet, remember these facts about Retained Earnings:

1. *Credits to the Retained Earnings account arise only from net income.*
   Retained Earnings shows how much net income a corporation has earned and retained in the business. Its balance is the cumulative, lifetime earnings of the company minus all net losses and all dividends.

2. *The Retained Earnings account is not a reservoir of cash.* Retained Earnings represents no asset in particular. In fact, the corporation may have a large balance in Retained Earnings but too little cash to pay a dividend.

Cash is an Asset. ≠ Retained Earnings is Stockholders' Equity.

Cash and Retained Earnings are two very
different accounts, unrelated to each other.

Stop & Think

Assume that the beginning balance of Retained Earnings was $70,000. The net loss for the year was $80,000. What will the Retained Earnings balance be after this net loss?

Answer:

		Retained Earnings	
		Dec. 31, 20X0 Balance	70,000
Dec. 31, 20X1 Net loss	80,000		
Dec. 31, 20X1 Balance	10,000		

 Account for stock dividends

Stock Dividend
A distribution by a corporation of its
own stock to its stockholders.

Stock Dividends

A **stock dividend** is a distribution by a corporation of its own stock to its stockholders. Unlike cash dividends, stock dividends do not give any assets to the stockholders. Stock dividends

- Affect *only* stockholders' equity accounts (including Retained Earnings and Common Stock)

- Have *no* effect on total stockholders' equity

As Exhibit 14-1 shows, a stock dividend decreases Retained Earnings and increases Common Stock. Both accounts are stockholders' equity, so total equity is unchanged. This is a transfer from Retained Earnings to Common Stock. No asset or liability is affected by a stock dividend.

Exhibit 14-1

Effects of a Stock Dividend

The corporation distributes stock dividends to stockholders in proportion to the number of shares they already own. Suppose you own 300 shares of Pier 1 Imports' common stock. If Pier 1 distributes a 10% common stock dividend, you would receive 30 (300 × 0.10) additional shares. You would now own 330 shares of the stock. All other Pier 1 stockholders would also receive additional shares equal to 10% of their prior holdings. You and all the other Pier 1 stockholders would be in the same relative position after the dividend as before it.

WHY ISSUE STOCK DIVIDENDS? A company issues stock dividends for several reasons:

1. *To continue dividends but conserve cash.* A company may want to keep cash in the business. Yet it may also wish to continue dividends in some form.

2. *To reduce the market price of its stock.* A stock dividend may cause the market price of the company's stock to fall because of the increased supply of the stock. A share of Pier 1 Imports stock has traded at $20 recently. Doubling the shares outstanding by issuing a stock dividend would drop the stock's market price by approximately half, to $10 per share. The objective is to make the stock less expensive and thus more attractive to investors.

RECORDING STOCK DIVIDENDS The board of directors announces stock dividends on the declaration date. The date of record and the distribution date then follow. (These are the same dates used for a cash dividend.) The declaration of a stock dividend does *not* create a liability because the corporation is not obligated to pay assets. (Recall that a liability is a claim on *assets*.) Instead, the corporation has declared its intention to distribute its stock. Assume that Pier 1 Imports has the following stockholders' equity prior to a stock dividend:

Pier 1 Imports
Stockholders' Equity (Adapted)

Paid-in capital:	
Common stock, $1 par, 500,000 shares authorized,	
100,000 shares issued..........................	$100,000
Paid-in capital in excess of par....................	60,000
Total paid-in capital..........................	160,000
Retained earnings	430,000
Total stockholders' equity.......................	$590,000

The entry to record a stock dividend depends on its size. Generally accepted accounting principles distinguish between

- A *small* stock dividend (less than 20% to 25% of issued stock)
- A *large* stock dividend (25% or more of issued stock)

Stock dividends between 20% and 25% are rare.

Small Stock Dividends—Less Than 20% to 25% Small stock dividends are accounted for at their market value. Retained Earnings is decreased for the market value of the dividend shares, Common Stock is credited for the stock's par value, and Paid-In Capital in Excess of Par is credited for the remainder.

Assume Pier 1 Imports distributes a stock dividend when the market value of the company's common stock is $20 per share. Exhibit 14-2 illustrates the accounting for a 10% stock dividend.[1]

Exhibit 14-2

Accounting for Stock Dividends—
Pier 1 Imports

Small Stock Dividend—For Example, 10% (Accounted for at *market* value)		
Retained Earnings		
(100,000 × 0.10 × $20 market value)	200,000	
Common Stock		
(100,000 × 0.10 × $1 par)		10,000
Paid-In Capital in Excess of Par		190,000

A stock dividend does not affect assets, liabilities, or total stockholders' equity. A stock dividend merely rearranges the stockholders' equity accounts, leaving total equity unchanged.

✔ **Starter 14-1**

✔ **Starter 14-2**

Large Stock Dividends—25% or More Large stock dividends are rare, so we do not illustrate them. Instead of large stock dividends, companies split their stock, as we illustrate in the next section.

Stock Splits

Stock Split
An increase in the number of outstanding shares of stock coupled with a proportionate reduction in the par value of the stock.

A **stock split** is fundamentally different from a stock dividend. A stock split increases the number of authorized, issued, and outstanding shares of stock. A stock split is also coupled with a proportionate reduction in the stock's par value. For example, if the company splits its stock 2 for 1, the number of outstanding shares is doubled and each share's par value is cut in half. A stock split decreases the market price of the stock—with the intention of making the stock more affordable. Most leading companies in the United States—General Electric, IBM, and many others—have split their stock.

The market price of a share of Pier 1 Imports common stock has been approximately $20. Assume that Pier 1 wishes to decrease the market price to approximately $10. Suppose Pier 1 decides to split the common stock 2 for 1, and the stock's market price drops from $20 to $10. A 2-for-1 stock split means that Pier 1 will have twice as many shares of stock outstanding after the split as before, and each share's par value is cut in half. Assume that Pier 1 had issued 100,000 shares of $1 par common stock before the split. The following table shows how a 2-for-1 split affects Pier 1 Imports' stockholders' equity.

---

[1]A stock dividend can be recorded with two journal entries—for (1) the declaration and (2) the stock distribution. But most companies record stock dividends with a single entry on the date of distribution, as we illustrate here.

Pier 1 Imports' Stockholders' Equity (Adapted)		After 2-for-1 Stock Split	
Before 2-for-1 Stock Split			
Common stock, $1.00 par,		Common stock, $0.50 par,	
500,000 shares authorized,		1,000,000 shares authorized,	
100,000 shares issued......................	$100,000	200,000 shares issued......................	$100,000
Paid-in capital in excess of par................	60,000	Paid-in capital in excess of par...............	60,000
Retained earnings...........................	430,000	Retained earnings...........................	430,000
Total stockholders' equity...................	$590,000	Total stockholders' equity...................	$590,000

After the 2-for-1 stock split, Pier 1 Imports would have 1 million shares authorized and 200,000 shares (100,000 shares × 2) of $0.50 (50 cents) par ($1.00/2) common stock outstanding. Total stockholders' equity would be exactly as before. Indeed, the balance in the Common Stock account does not even change. Only the par value of the stock and the number of shares change.

Because the stock split affects no account balances, no formal journal entry is needed. Instead, the split is recorded in a *memorandum entry* such as the following:

✔ **Starter 14-3**

Aug. 19	Split the common stock 2 for 1. Called in the $1 par common stock and distributed two shares of $0.50 par common stock for each old share previously outstanding.

Stock Dividends and Stock Splits Compared

2 Distinguish stock splits from stock dividends

Both stock dividends and stock splits increase the number of shares of stock owned by each stockholder. Neither stock dividends nor stock splits change investors' cost of the stock they own.

SIMILARITIES Consider Dell Computer Corporation, the leader in personal computers. Assume you own 100 shares of Dell stock.

- If Dell distributes a stock dividend or a stock split, your 100 shares increase, but your total cost is unchanged.
- Neither a stock dividend nor a stock split creates taxable income for the investor.

DIFFERENCES Stock dividends and stock splits differ in that

- A stock *dividend* shifts an amount from retained earnings to the stock account. Par value per share is unchanged.
- A stock *split* increases the number of shares of stock authorized, issued, and outstanding. Par value per share decreases.

Exhibit 14-3 summarizes the effects of dividends and stock splits on total stockholders' equity.

Exhibit 14-3

Effects of Dividends and Stock Splits on Total Stockholders' Equity

Event	Effect on Total Stockholders' Equity
Declaration of *cash* dividend	Decreases total equity
Payment of *cash* dividend	No effect on equity
Distribution of *stock* dividend	No effect on equity
Stock split	No effect on equity

Source: Adapted from material provided by Beverly Terry.

Account for treasury stock

Treasury Stock
A corporation's own stock that it has
issued and later reacquired.

Student ResourceCD

treasury stock

Treasury Stock

A company's own stock that it has issued and later reacquired is called **treasury stock.**[2] In effect, the corporation holds the stock in its treasury. Corporations such as Coca-Cola, Dell Computer, and Pier 1 Imports may purchase their own stock for several reasons:

1. The business is trying to increase net assets by buying its shares low and hoping to sell them for a higher price later.

2. The purchase supports the stock's market price by decreasing the supply of stock available.

3. Management wants to avoid a takeover by an outside party.

When a company buys its own stock back, the company gives up cash and becomes a smaller entity as a result. Now let's see how companies account for their treasury stock.

Purchase of Treasury Stock

We record the purchase of treasury stock by debiting Treasury Stock and crediting Cash. Suppose that Jupiter Cable Company had the following stockholders' equity before purchasing treasury stock:

Jupiter Cable Company
Stockholders' Equity [*Before Purchase of Treasury Stock*]

Common stock, $1 par, 10,000 shares authorized,	
9,000 shares issued.	$ 9,000
Paid-in capital in excess of par—common.	12,000
Retained earnings	14,000
Total stockholders' equity.	$35,000

On March 31, Jupiter purchases 1,000 shares of its common as treasury stock, paying cash of $5 per share. Jupiter records the purchase of treasury stock as follows:

Treasury Stock—Common

5,000	

Mar. 31	Treasury Stock—Common (1,000 × $5). .	5,000	
	Cash		5,000
	Purchased treasury stock.		

The Treasury Stock account has a debit balance, which is the opposite of the other owners' equity accounts. Therefore, *Treasury Stock is a contra equity account.* Treasury stock is recorded at cost, without reference to par value. The Treasury Stock account is reported beneath Retained Earnings on the balance sheet. Treasury Stock's balance is subtracted from the sum of total paid-in capital and retained earnings, as follows:

Jupiter Cable Company
Stockholders' Equity [*After Purchase of Treasury Stock*]

Common stock, $1 par, 10,000 shares authorized,	
9,000 shares issued.	$ 9,000
Paid-in capital in excess of par—common.	12,000
Retained earnings	14,000
Subtotal.	35,000
Less: Treasury stock, 1,000 shares at cost	(5,000)
Total stockholders' equity.	$30,000

---

[2]We illustrate the *cost* method of accounting for treasury stock because it is used most widely. Intermediate accounting courses also cover an alternative method.

Total stockholders' equity decreases by $5,000, the cost of the treasury stock. Also, the stock *outstanding* decreases. *Outstanding* shares are computed as follows:

Shares of stock *issued*	9,000
Less: Shares of treasury stock	(1,000)
Shares of stock *outstanding*	8,000

Outstanding shares are important because only outstanding shares have voting rights, receive cash dividends, and receive assets if the corporation liquidates. Treasury stock doesn't carry a vote, receive dividends, or have a claim on assets in liquidation.

Ethical Issue: Treasury stock transactions have a serious ethical and legal dimension. A company such as **Dell Computer** buying its own shares as treasury stock must be careful that its information releases are accurate. What will happen if Dell purchases treasury stock at $17 per share and one day later announces a technological breakthrough that will generate millions of dollars in new business?

Answer: Dell's stock price would likely rise in response to the new information. If it could be proved that Dell management withheld the information, a shareholder selling stock back to Dell could file a lawsuit against the company. The stockholder would claim that with the new information, he would have been able to sell the Dell stock at a higher price.

Sale of Treasury Stock

A company may sell its treasury stock at its cost, above cost, or below cost.

SALE AT COST   If the stock is sold for cost—the same price the corporation paid to reacquire it—the entry debits Cash and credits Treasury Stock for the same amount.

SALE ABOVE COST   If treasury stock is sold for more than its cost, the difference is credited to a new account, Paid-In Capital from Treasury Stock Transactions, because the excess came from the company's stockholders. Suppose Jupiter Cable Company resold its treasury shares for $9 per share (cost was $5). The entry is

Dec. 7 Cash (1,000 × $9)	9,000	
Treasury Stock—Common (1,000 × $5 cost)		5,000
Paid-In Capital from Treasury Stock Transactions..		4,000
Sold treasury stock.		

Treasury Stock—Common	
5,000	5,000
0	

✔ Starter 14-4

Paid-In Capital from Treasury Stock Transactions is reported with the other paid-in capital accounts on the balance sheet, beneath the Common Stock and Paid-In Capital in Excess of Par accounts, as shown here:

Jupiter Cable Company
Stockholders' Equity [*After* Purchase and Sale of Treasury Stock]

Paid-in capital:	
Common stock, $1 par, 10,000 shares authorized,	
9,000 shares issued	$ 9,000
Paid-in capital in excess of par—common	12,000
Paid-in capital from treasury stock transactions	4,000
Retained earnings	14,000
Total stockholders' equity	$39,000

Exhibit 14-4 tracks the stockholders' equity of Jupiter Cable Company to show how treasury stock transactions affect corporate equity.

Exhibit 14-4

Jupiter Cable Stockholders' Equity

SALE BELOW COST The resale price of treasury stock can be less than cost. The shortfall is debited first to Paid-In Capital from Treasury Stock Transactions. If this account's balance is too small, then debit Retained Earnings for the remaining amount.

Reporting Issues

□ Retained Earnings, Stock
   Dividends & Splits
□ Treasury Stock
■ **Reporting Issues**
□ Corporate Income Statement

Student ResourceCD

retained earnings, stock buyback

Companies may retire their stock, restrict retained earnings, and vary the way they report stockholders' equity. This section covers these reporting issues.

Retirement of Stock

A corporation may purchase its own stock and *retire* it by canceling the stock certificates. Retirements of preferred stock are common because companies wish to avoid paying dividends on the preferred stock. The retired stock cannot be reissued.

Retiring stock decreases both the stock issued and the stock outstanding. In retiring stock, the corporation removes all the stock and the paid-in capital accounts related to the retired shares, such as Preferred Stock and Capital in Excess of Par.

Report restrictions on retained earnings

Restrictions on Retained Earnings

Dividends, purchases of treasury stock, and retirements of stock require a cash payment. These outlays decrease assets, so the corporation has fewer resources to pay liabilities. A bank may agree to loan $500,000 only if Jupiter Cable Company limits dividend payments and the purchase of treasury stock.

LIMITS ON DIVIDENDS AND TREASURY STOCK PURCHASES To ensure that corporations maintain a minimum level of stockholders' equity, state laws restrict the amount of treasury stock a corporation may purchase. The restriction often focuses on the balance of retained earnings. Companies usually report their retained earnings restrictions in notes to the financial statements. The following disclosure by RTE Corporation, a manufacturer of electronic transformers, is typical:

Notes to Consolidated Financial Statements

Note F—Long-Term Debt The . . . Company's loan agreements . . . restrict cash dividends and similar payments to shareholders. Under the most restrictive of these provisions, retained earnings of $4,000,000 were unrestricted as of December 31, 20X6.

With this restriction, the maximum dividend that RTE Corporation can pay its stockholders is $4,000,000.

Are Stock Buybacks a Value Booster or a PR Gimmick?

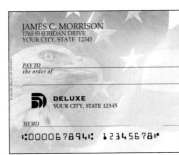

What could signal more confidence than a company buying back lots of its own stock? Stock buybacks were a strategy for investing spare cash in the 1990s. Now the buyback has become a strategy for propping up a company's stock prices. For example, the stock of Tenet Healthcare Corporation plunged by 50% in a week, and the health-care giant paid $140 million to buy its own stock. The strategy worked because two weeks later, the stock had risen by 13%.

Purchases of a company's own shares reduce the number of outstanding shares, and earnings per share go up. A dramatic example of this occurred when Deluxe, the country's leading check printer, purchased 19 million of its own shares. Deluxe's stock price soared 116% after the buyback.

When the market falls, boosting stock prices becomes a priority, and there's a rush of buyback activity. In the second quarter of 2002, for instance, U.S. companies announced plans to repurchase $24 billion of their own stock. The key words here are "*announced plans.*" Skeptical shareholders point out that buyback announcements aren't always followed by actual stock repurchases. Columnist John Ellis says, "Nothing so perfectly captures the fiber of today's whimpering CEOs than the stock buyback announcement." Ellis complains that CEOs don't always carry through on their buyback announcements: "While many have been announced, probably 6 out of 10 [buybacks] are nothing more than public relations gimmicks."

Dividend announcements are different. Unlike a buyback announcement, a cash dividend, once declared, becomes a real liability. The joke on Wall Street is this: Stock buybacks are like dating. A dividend is more like getting married.

Based on: Tom Petruno, "Stock Buybacks Face Increasing Scrutiny," *Los Angeles Times*, November 24, 2002, p. C.13. Shaheen Pasha, "Stock Buybacks Have Increased as Equities Fall," *The Wall Street Journal*, July 18, 2002, p. C9. John Ellis, "Strategy," *Fast Company*, October 2002, p. 74.

APPROPRIATIONS OF RETAINED EARNINGS **Appropriations** are restrictions on Retained Earnings that are recorded by formal journal entries. A corporation may *appropriate*—segregate in a separate account—a portion of Retained Earnings for a specific use. For example, the board of directors may appropriate part of Retained Earnings for expansion. Appropriated Retained Earnings can be reported as shown near the bottom of Exhibit 14-5.

Retained earnings appropriations are rare. Most companies report any retained earnings restrictions in the notes to the financial statements, as illustrated for RTE Corporation and in the real-world format of Exhibit 14-5.

Appropriation of Retained Earnings
Restriction of retained earnings that is recorded by a formal journal entry.

✔ Starter 14-5

Variations in Reporting Stockholders' Equity

Accountants sometimes report stockholders' equity in ways that differ from our examples. We use a detailed format to help you learn the components of stockholders' equity. Companies assume that investors and creditors understand the details.

One of the most important skills you will learn in this course is how to read the financial statements of real companies. In Exhibit 14-5, we present a side-by-side comparison of our general teaching format and the format you are likely to encounter in actual balance sheets. Note the following points in the real-world format:

1. The heading Paid-In Capital does not appear. It is commonly understood that Preferred Stock, Common Stock, and Additional Paid-In Capital are elements of paid-in capital.

2. Preferred stock is often reported in a single amount that combines par value and premium.

3. For presentation in the financial statements, all additional paid-in capital appears as a single amount labeled Additional Paid-In Capital. Additional Paid-In Capital belongs to the common stockholders; therefore it follows Common Stock in the real-world format.

4. Often, total stockholders' equity ($4,000,000 in Exhibit 14-5) is not specifically labeled.

Exhibit 14-5 **Formats for Reporting Stockholders' Equity**

General Teaching Format		Real-World Format	
Stockholders' equity		**Stockholders' equity**	
Paid-in capital:			
Preferred stock, 8%, $10 par,		Preferred stock, 8%, $10 par,	
30,000 shares authorized and issued	$ 300,000	30,000 shares authorized	
Paid-in capital in excess of par—preferred	10,000	and issued	$ 310,000
Common stock, $1 par, 100,000 shares		Common stock, $1 par,	
authorized, 60,000 shares issued	60,000	100,000 shares authorized,	
Paid-in capital in excess of par—common	2,140,000	60,000 shares issued	60,000
Paid-in capital from treasury stock		Additional paid-in capital	2,160,000
transactions, common	9,000	Retained earnings (Note 7)	1,500,000
Paid-in capital from retirement of		Less: Treasury stock, common	
preferred stock	11,000	(1,000 shares at cost)	(30,000)
Total paid-in capital	2,530,000		$4,000,000
Retained earnings appropriated for		*Note 7—Restriction on retained earnings.*	
contingencies	400,000	At December 31, 20XX, $400,000 of retained	
Retained earnings—unappropriated	1,100,000	earnings is restricted for contingencies	
Total retained earnings	1,500,000	by the company's board of directors.	
Subtotal	4,030,000	Accordingly, dividends are restricted to a	
Less: Treasury stock, common		maximum of $1,100,000.	
(1,000 shares at cost)	(30,000)		
Total stockholders' equity	$4,000,000		

Review the first half of the chapter by studying the following Decision Guidelines feature.

Decision Guidelines

ACCOUNTING FOR RETAINED EARNINGS, DIVIDENDS, AND TREASURY STOCK

Retained earnings, dividends, and treasury stock transactions are unique because they can affect a corporation's equity. The Decision Guidelines provide a foundation for you to understand their effects.

Decision

How to record:

- Distribution of a small stock dividend (20% to 25%)?

- Stock split?

What are the effects of stock dividends and stock splits on:

- Number of shares issued?
- Shares outstanding?
- Par value per share?
- Total assets and total liabilities?
- Total stockholders' equity?
- Common Stock?
- Retained Earnings?

How to record:

- Purchase of treasury stock?
- Sale of treasury stock?

At cost? (Amount received = Cost)

Above cost?

Below cost?

What are the effects of the purchase and sale of treasury stock on:

- Total assets?

- Total stockholders' equity?

Guidelines

Retained Earnings. . . . .   Market value |
    Common Stock . . . . | Par value
    Paid-In Capital in Excess of Par . . | Excess

Memorandum only: Split the common stock 2 for 1. Called in the outstanding $10 par common stock and distributed two shares of $5 par for each old share outstanding (amounts assumed).

Effects of Stock

Dividend	Split
Increase	Increase
Increase	Increase
No effect	Decrease
No effect	No effect
No effect	No effect
Increase	No effect
Decrease	No effect

Treasury Stock	Cost	
Cash		Cost
Cash	Amt received	
Treasury Stock		Cost
Cash	Amt received	
Treasury Stock		Cost
Paid-In Capital from Treasury		
Stock Transactions		Excess
Cash	Amt received	
Paid-In Capital from Treasury		
Stock Transactions	Amt up to prior bal	
Retained Earnings	Excess	
Treasury Stock		Cost

Effects of

Purchase	Sale
Decrease by full amount of payment	Increase by full amount of cash receipt
Decrease by full amount of payment	Increase by full amount of cash receipt

---

MID-CHAPTER *Summary Problem*

Simplicity Graphics, creator of magazine designs, reported shareholders' equity:

Shareholders' Equity	
Preferred stock, $1.00 par value	
Authorized—10,000 shares; Issued—None	$ —
Common Stock, $0.80 par value	
Authorized, 30,000 shares; Issued 14,000 shares	11,200
Capital in excess of par value	48,000
Earnings retained in business	89,000
	148,200
Less: Treasury stock, at cost (1,900 common shares)	(15,200)
	$133,000

TIPS
CHECK YOUR RESOURCES

Required

1. What was the average issue price per share of the common stock?
2. Journalize the issuance of 1,000 shares of common stock at $4 per share. Use Simplicity's account titles.
3. How many shares of Simplicity's common stock are outstanding?
4. How many shares of common stock would be outstanding after Simplicity split its common stock 3 for 1?
5. Using Simplicity account titles, journalize the distribution of a 10% stock dividend when the market price of Simplicity common stock is $5 per share. Simplicity distributes the common stock dividend on the shares outstanding, which were computed in requirement 3.
6. Journalize the following treasury stock transactions, which occur in the order given:
   a. Simplicity purchases 500 shares of treasury stock at $8 per share.
   b. Simplicity sells 100 shares of treasury stock for $9 per share.

Solution

1. Average issue price of common stock was $4.23 per share
   [($11,200 + $48,000)/14,000 shares = $4.23]
2. Cash (1,000 × $4) 4,000
         Common Stock (1,000 × $0.80) . . . . | 800
         Capital in Excess of Par Value . . . . | 3,200
   Issued common stock.

3. Shares outstanding = 12,100 (14,000 shares issued minus 1,900 shares of treasury stock).
4. Shares outstanding after a 3-for-1 stock split = 36,300 (12,100 shares outstanding × 3).
5. Earnings Retained in Business (12,100 × 0.10 × $5) 6,050
         Common Stock (12,100 × 0.10 × $0.80) . . . . | 968
         Capital in Excess of Par Value . . . . | 5,082
   Distributed a 10% common stock dividend.

6. a. Treasury Stock (500 × $8) 4,000
         Cash . . . . | 4,000
      Purchased treasury stock.
   b. Cash (100 × $9) 900
         Treasury Stock (100 × $8) . . . . | 800
         Paid-In Capital from Treasury Stock Transactions . . | 100
      Sold treasury stock.

 Analyze a complex income statement

 Student ResourceCD

comprehensive income, discontinued operations, earnings per share, extraordinary items, income statement, preferred stock, statement of shareholders' equity

The Corporate Income Statement: Analyzing Earnings

Now that we have covered stockholders' equity in detail, we turn to the corporate income statement. Net income (revenues plus gains minus expenses and losses) receives more attention than any other item in the financial statements. In fact, net income is probably the most important piece of information about a company. Net income measures how successfully the company has operated.

Suppose you are considering investing in the stock of Coca-Cola, Dell Computer, or Pier 1 Imports. You would examine these companies' income statements. Of particular interest is the amount of net income they can expect to earn year after year. To understand net income, let's examine Exhibit 14-6, which presents the income statement of Allied Electronics Corporation, a small manufacturer of precision instruments.

Continuing Operations

In Exhibit 14-6, the topmost section reports income from continuing operations. This part of the business should continue from period to period. Income from continuing operations, therefore, helps investors make predictions about future

Exhibit 14-6 Income Statement of Allied Electronics Corporation

Allied Electronics Corporation

Income Statement
Year Ended December 31, 20X5

Continuing operations	
Net sales revenue	$500,000
Cost of goods sold	240,000
Gross profit	260,000
Operating expenses (detailed)	181,000
Operating income	79,000
Other gains (losses):	
Gain on sale of machinery	11,000
Income from continuing operations before income tax	90,000
Income tax expense	36,000
Income from continuing operations	54,000
Special items	
Discontinued operations, income of $35,000, less income tax of $14,000	21,000
Income before extraordinary item and cumulative effect of accounting change	75,000
Extraordinary flood loss, $20,000, less income tax saving of $8,000	(12,000)
Cumulative effect of accounting change, $10,000, less income tax of $4,000	6,000
Net income	$ 69,000
Earnings per share	
Earnings per share of common stock (20,000 shares outstanding):	
Income from continuing operations	$2.70
Income from discontinued operations	1.05
Income before extraordinary item and cumulative effect of accounting change	3.75
Extraordinary loss	(0.60)
Cumulative effect of accounting change	0.30
Net income	$3.45

earnings. We may use this information to predict that Allied Electronics Corporation will earn approximately $54,000 next year. The continuing operations of Allied Electronics include two items needing explanation.

First, Allied had a gain on the sale of machinery, which is outside the company's core business activity of selling electronics products. This explains why the gain is reported separately from Allied's sales revenue, cost of goods sold, and gross profit.

Second, income tax expense is subtracted to arrive at income from continuing operations. Allied Electronics' income tax rate is 40% ($90,000 × 0.40 = $36,000).

Special Items

After continuing operations, an income statement may include three types of special gains and losses:

✔ **Starter 14-6**

✔ **Starter 14-7**

- Discontinued operations
- Extraordinary gains and losses
- Cumulative effect of an accounting change

DISCONTINUED OPERATIONS Most large corporations engage in several lines of business. For example, Sears, Roebuck & Co. is best known for its retail stores, but it also has a real-estate development company (Homart) and an insurance company (Allstate). Each identifiable division of a company is called a **segment of the business**. Allstate is the insurance segment of Sears.

Segment of the Business
One of various separate divisions of a company.

A company may sell a segment of its business. For example, May Department Stores, the chain that operates Lord & Taylor and Foley's, sold Payless, its chain of shoe stores. Financial analysts typically do not include discontinued operations to predict a company's future income because the discontinued segments will generate no income in the future.

The income statement reports information on the discontinued segment under the heading Discontinued operations. Income from discontinued operations ($35,000) is taxed at 40% and reported by Allied Electronics Corporation, as shown in Exhibit 14-6. A loss on discontinued operations is reported similarly, with a subtraction for the income tax *savings* on the loss.

Companies dispose of old plant and equipment all the time. Gains and losses on these asset dispositions are *not* reported as discontinued operations. Gains and losses on normal asset dispositions are reported as "Other gains (losses)" up among continuing operations.

EXTRAORDINARY GAINS AND LOSSES (EXTRAORDINARY ITEMS)

Extraordinary Gains and Losses
A gain or loss that is both unusual for the company and infrequent. Also called **extraordinary items**.

Extraordinary gains and losses, also called **extraordinary items**, are both unusual and infrequent. Losses from natural disasters (floods, earthquakes, and tornadoes) and the taking of company assets by a foreign government (expropriation) are extraordinary.

Extraordinary items are reported along with their income tax effect. During 20X5, Allied Electronics Corporation lost $20,000 of inventory in a flood. This flood loss reduced income and also reduced Allied's income tax. The tax effect decreases the net amount of the loss in the same way that the income tax reduces net income. An extraordinary loss can be reported along with its tax effect, as follows:

Extraordinary flood loss..........................	$(20,000)
Less: Income tax saving........................	8,000
Extraordinary flood loss, net of tax	(12,000)

Trace this item to the income statement in Exhibit 14-6. An extraordinary gain is reported in the same way as a loss, net of the income tax.

Gains and losses due to employee strikes, lawsuits, and the sale of plant assets are *not* extraordinary. These are normal business events. But they are outside the business's central operations, so they are reported on the income statement as other gains and losses. Examples include the gain on sale of machinery reported up in the Other gains (losses) section of Exhibit 14-6.

For a review of depreciation methods, ➡ *see Chapter 10. For a review of inventory methods, see Chapter 6.*

Cumulative Effect of a Change in Accounting Principle

Companies sometimes change accounting methods, such as from double-declining-balance (DDB) to straight-line depreciation, or from first-in, first-out (FIFO) to average cost for inventory. ⬅ An accounting change makes it difficult to compare one period's financial statements with the statements of earlier periods.

Investors and creditors can be misled into thinking that the current year is better when in fact the only difference is a change in accounting method. Investors must separate the effects of business operations from the effects created by accounting. Companies, therefore, report the effect of the accounting change in a special section of the income statement. This section appears after extraordinary items.

Allied Electronics Corporation has changed its method of accounting for depreciation from DDB to straight-line at the beginning of 20X5. If the company had been using straight-line depreciation every year, depreciation expense would have been less in prior years, and net income would have been higher. Exhibit 14-6 reports the $6,000 cumulative effect of this accounting change. A change from straight-line to double-declining-balance depreciation usually produces a negative cumulative effect.

✔ Starter 14-8

Examine all the income tax amounts in Exhibit 14-6. How much was Allied Electronics' *total* income tax expense during 20X5?

Answer: $46,000 = $36,000 + $14,000 − $8,000 + $4,000

Note that $36,000 is the company's income tax expense from continuing operations: $46,000 is *total* income tax expense.

Earnings per Share

The final segment of a corporate income statement presents the company's earnings per share, abbreviated as EPS. EPS is the most widely used of all accounting statistics. **Earnings per share (EPS)** reports the amount of net income for each share of the company's *outstanding common stock*. It is a key measure of success in business. EPS is computed as follows:

Earnings Per Share (EPS)
Amount of a company's net income for each share of its outstanding common stock.

$$\text{Earnings per Share} = \frac{\text{Net income − Preferred dividends}}{\text{Average number of Common shares outstanding}}$$

Just as the corporation lists its different sources of income separately—from continuing operations, discontinued operations, and so on—it also shows a separate EPS figure for each element of income. Allied Electronics Corporation's EPS calculations are as follows:

Earnings per share of common stock (20,000 shares outstanding):	
Income from continuing operations ($54,000/20,000)	$2.70
Income from discontinued operations ($21,000/20,000)	1.05
Income before extraordinary item and cumulative effect of	
accounting change ($75,000/20,000)	3.75
Extraordinary loss ($12,000/20,000)	(0.60)
Cumulative effect of accounting change ($6,000/20,000)	0.30
Net income ($69,000/20,000)	$3.45

✔ **Starter 14-9**

The final section of Exhibit 14-6 reports the EPS figures for Allied Electronics.

EFFECT OF PREFERRED DIVIDENDS ON EARNINGS PER SHARE
Preferred dividends also affect EPS. Recall that EPS is earnings per share of *common* stock. Recall also that dividends on preferred stock are paid first. → Therefore, preferred dividends must be subtracted from income to compute EPS. Suppose Allied Electronics had 10,000 shares of preferred stock outstanding, each paying a $1.00 dividend. The annual preferred dividend would be $10,000 (10,000 × $1.00). The $10,000 would be subtracted from each of the income subtotals (lines 1, 3, and 6), resulting in the following EPS computations for the company:

← *Chapter 13, p. 511, provides detailed information on preferred stock.*

	Earnings per share of common stock (20,000 shares outstanding):	
1	Income from continuing operations ($54,000 − $10,000)/20,000 . . .	$2.20
2	Income from discontinued operations ($21,000/20,000)	1.05
3	Income before extraordinary item and cumulative	
	effect of accounting change ($75,000 − $10,000)/20,000	3.25
4	Extraordinary loss ($12,000/20,000)	(0.60)
5	Cumulative effect of accounting change ($6,000/20,000)	0.30
6	Net income ($69,000 − $10,000)/20,000	$2.95

✔ **Starter 14-10**

BASIC AND DILUTED EARNINGS PER SHARE Some corporations must report two sets of EPS figures, as follows:

- EPS based on outstanding common shares (*basic* EPS).
- EPS based on outstanding common shares plus the additional common shares that would arise from conversion of the preferred stock into common stock (*diluted* EPS). Diluted EPS is always lower than basic EPS.

> What makes earnings per share so useful as a business statistic?
>
> *Answer:* Earnings per share is useful because it relates a company's income to one share of stock. Stock prices are quoted at an amount per share, and investors usually consider how much they must pay for a certain number of shares. Earnings per share is used to help determine the value of a share of stock.

Combined Statement of Income and Retained Earnings

Companies can report income and retained earnings on a single statement. Exhibit 14-7 illustrates how Allied Electronics would combine its income statement and its statement of retained earnings.

Exhibit 14-7

Combined Statement of Income and Retained Earnings

Allied Electronics Corporation		
Summarized Statement of Income and Retained Earnings **Year Ended December 31, 20X5**		
Income statement	Sales revenue........................	$500,000
	Cost of goods sold	240,000
	Gross profit	260,000
	Expenses (listed individually)	191,000
	Net income for 20X5.................	$ 69,000
Statement of retained earnings	Retained earnings, December 31, 20X4...	130,000
		199,000
	Dividends for 20X5..................	(54,000)
	Retained earnings, December 31, 20X5...	$145,000

Reporting Comprehensive Income

As we have seen, all companies report net income or net loss on the income statement. There is another income figure. **Comprehensive income** is the company's change in total stockholders' equity from all sources other than from its owners. Comprehensive income includes net income plus some specific gains and losses, as follows:

Comprehensive Income
Company's change in total stockholders' equity from all sources other than from the owners.

- Unrealized gains or losses on certain investments
- Foreign-currency translation adjustments

These items do not enter into the determination of net income but instead are reported as other comprehensive income, as shown in Exhibit 14-8. Assumed figures are used for all items.

✔ **Starter 14-11**

Earnings per share applies only to net income and its components, as discussed earlier. Earnings per share is *not* reported for other comprehensive income.

Exhibit 14-8

Reporting Comprehensive Income

National Express Company
Income Statement
Year Ended December 31, 20X2

Revenues	$10,000
Expenses (summarized)	6,000
Net income	4,000
Other comprehensive income:	
Unrealized gain on investments.	1,000
Comprehensive income.	$ 5,000

Prior-Period Adjustments

A company may make an error in recording revenues or expenses. After the revenue and expense accounts are closed, Retained Earnings holds the error. The balance of Retained Earnings is wrong until corrected. Corrections to Retained Earnings for errors of an earlier period are called **prior-period adjustments**. The prior-period adjustment (correction) either increases or decreases the beginning balance of Retained Earnings and appears on that statement.

Prior-Period Adjustment
A correction to retained earnings for an error of an earlier period.

The year 2003 saw more prior-period adjustments than in the 20 previous years combined. Enron, Worldcom, Xerox, and many other companies restated their net income to correct accounting errors made in earlier years. To illustrate, assume De Graff Corporation recorded $30,000 of income tax expense for 20X7. The correct amount was $40,000. This error

- Understated expenses by $10,000
- Overstated net income by $10,000

In 20X8, the government required De Graff to pay the additional $10,000 in taxes for the prior year. De Graff's prior-period adjustment will decrease retained earnings as follows.

De Graff Corporation
Statement of Retained Earnings
Year Ended December 31, 20X8

✔ Starter 14-12

Retained earnings, December 31, 20X7, as originally reported	$390,000
Prior-period adjustment—To correct error in 20X7	(10,000)
Retained earnings, December 31, 20X7, as adjusted	380,000
Net income for 20X8	100,000
	480,000
Dividends for 20X8	(40,000)
Retained earnings, December 31, 20X8	$440,000

Statement of Stockholders' Equity

Prepare a statement of stockholders' equity

Most companies report a statement of stockholders' equity, which includes retained earnings. The statement of stockholders' equity is formatted exactly like a statement of retained earnings but with columns for each element of equity. The **statement of stockholders' equity** reports the changes in all categories of equity during the period:

Statement of Stockholders' Equity
Reports the changes in all categories of stockholders' equity during the period.

- Common stock
- Additional paid-in capital
- Retained earnings
- Treasury stock

Exhibit 14-9 uses assumed figures for Allied Electronics Corporation to illustrate the statement of stockholders' equity. Negative amounts—debits—appear in parentheses. If the company has preferred stock, the statement includes a column for Preferred Stock.

| Exhibit 14-9 | Statement of Stockholders' Equity |

Allied Electronics Corporation

Statement of Stockholders' Equity
Year Ended December 31, 20X5

	Common Stock	Additional Paid-in Capital	Retained Earnings	Treasury Stock	Total
Balance, December 31, 20X4...............	$ 80,000	$160,000	$130,000	$(25,000)	$345,000
Issuance of stock.........................	20,000	60,000			80,000
Net income			69,000		69,000
Cash dividends...........................			(20,000)		(20,000)
Stock dividends—8%.....................	8,000	26,000	(34,000)		0
Purchase of treasury stock				(10,000)	(10,000)
Sale of treasury stock....................		10,000		5,000	15,000
Balance, December 31, 20X5..............	$108,000	$256,000	$145,000	$(30,000)	$479,000

✔ Starter 14-13

Decision Guidelines

ANALYZING A CORPORATE INCOME STATEMENT

Three years out of college, you've saved $5,000 and are ready to start investing. Where do you start? You might begin by analyzing the income statements of **Coca-Cola, Dell Computer**, and **Pier 1 Imports**. These Decision Guidelines will help you understand a corporate income statement.

Decision	Guidelines
What are the main sections of the income statement? See Exhibit 14-6 for an example.	Continuing operations $\big\{$ • Continuing operations, including other gains and losses and less income tax expense
	Special items $\big\{$ • Discontinued operations—gain or loss—less the income tax effect • Extraordinary gain or loss, less the income tax effect • Cumulative effect of an accounting change, less the income tax effect
	• Net income (or net loss) • Other comprehensive income (Exhibit 14-8)
What earnings-per-share (EPS) figures must a corporation report?	• Earnings per share—applies only to net income (or net loss), not to other comprehensive income Separate EPS figures for
	Earnings per share $\big\{$ • Income from continuing operations • Discontinued operations • Income before extraordinary item and cumulative effect of accounting change • Extraordinary gain or loss • Cumulative effect of accounting change • Net income (or net loss)
How to compute EPS for net income?	$$\text{EPS} = \frac{\text{Net income} - \text{Preferred dividends}}{\text{Average number of common shares outstanding}}$$

Excel Application Exercise

Goal: Create an Excel worksheet that charts the earnings-per-share (EPS) trend of a company with extraordinary items and/or changes in accounting principle.

Scenario: You are considering investing $5,000 in your favorite soft drink company, **Coca-Cola**. After taking a financial accounting class, you remember that smart investors investigate the financial performance of companies before investing. One measure of financial performance is earnings (net income) per share of common stock. When finished with your spreadsheet, answer these questions:

1. Why is EPS such a useful business statistic?
2. What is the trend in basic EPS (net income) for Coca-Cola?
3. List the EPS components given in the chapter. Fill in the amounts for Coca-Cola for the most recent year, and calculate EPS. Explain any difference between the amount you calculate and the one reported in the financial statements.
4. Besides EPS, what other financial measures should you examine prior to making an investment decision?

Step-by-Step:

1. Obtain a copy of the most recent annual report for Coca-Cola (online, try www.cocacola.com). Locate the Consolidated Statements of Income and Consolidated Balance Sheets.
2. Open a new Excel worksheet.
3. Create a bold-faced heading for your spreadsheet that contains the following:
   a. Chapter 14 Excel Application Exercise
   b. Coca-Cola Earnings-per-Share Analysis
   c. Today's Date

4. Move down two rows and enter the following title:
   Coca-Cola Company
   Income Statement
   Year Ended December 31, 2002 (or the most recent year)
   (In millions)
5. Copy the Consolidated Statements of Income, following the format used by Coca-Cola (leave out the description "Year Ended . . ."). Include all line items, using formulas where appropriate.
6. Starting with the row containing the three years' titles, highlight all rows of the income statement.
7. Click on the Chart Wizard. Select the line chart type with line markers displayed at each data value. Click next and select "Series in: rows." Then, click on the "Series" tab.
8. Remove from the series all line items except basic net income per share "before accounting change." You'll see lines disappear from your chart as you do this.
9. Then, click the "Add" button. Give the new series the name "EPS, net of changes." Click in the "Values" box, deleting any existing values. On the income statement, select the three amounts underneath the earnings-per-share line item "cumulative effect of accounting change" (these amounts do not have a name in the statement). The cell references should now be in the "Values" box. Click next.
10. Click on the "Titles" tab. For the chart title, enter "Earnings per Share." For the category X axis, enter "Year," and for the category Y axis, enter "EPS."
11. Click on the "Legend" tab, and click to move the legend to the bottom of the chart. Then, click on the "Data Labels" tab. Check "Value," then click "Finish." Position your chart to the right or bottom of your income statement.
12. Save your work, and print your work sheet in landscape mode (with graphs) for your files.

END-OF-CHAPTER *Summary Problem*

The following information was taken from the ledger of **Kraft Corporation** at December 31, 20X6.

Common stock, no-par, 45,000 shares issued	$180,000	Discontinued operations, income	$ 20,000
Sales revenue	620,000	Prior-period adjustment—credit to Retained Earnings	5,000
Extraordinary gain	26,000	Gain on sale of plant assets	21,000
Loss due to lawsuit	11,000	Cost of goods sold	380,000
General expenses	62,000	Income tax expense (saving):	
Preferred stock 8%	50,000	Continuing operations	32,000
Selling expenses	108,000	Discontinued operations	8,000
Retained earnings, beginning, as originally reported	103,000	Extraordinary gain	10,000
Cumulative effect of change in inventory method (debit)	(10,000)	Cumulative effect of change in inventory method	(4,000)
Dividends	16,000	Treasury stock, common (5,000 shares)	25,000

Required

Prepare a single-step income statement and a statement of retained earnings for Kraft Corporation for the year ended December 31, 20X6. Include the EPS presentation and show your computations. Kraft had no changes in its stock accounts during the year.

Solution

Kraft Corporation
Income Statement
Year Ended December 31, 20X6

Revenue and gains:		
Sales revenue		$620,000
Gain on sale of plant assets		21,000
Total revenues and gains		641,000
Expenses and losses:		
Cost of goods sold.	$380,000	
Selling expenses.	108,000	
General expenses.	62,000	
Loss due to lawsuit	11,000	
Income tax expense.	32,000	
Total expenses and losses.		593,000
Income from continuing operations.		48,000
Discontinued operations, income of $20,000, less income tax of $8,000		12,000
Income before extraordinary item and cumulative effect of change in inventory method		60,000
Extraordinary gain, $26,000, less income tax, $10,000		16,000
Cumulative effect of change in inventory method, $10,000, less income tax saving, $4,000. . . .		(6,000)
Net income.		$ 70,000
Earnings per share:		
Income from continuing operations [($48,000 – $4,000)/40,000 shares].		$1.10
Income from discontinued operations ($12,000/40,000 shares).		0.30
Income before extraordinary item and cumulative effect of change in inventory method [($60,000 – $4,000)/40,000 shares]		1.40
Extraordinary gain ($16,000/40,000 shares)		0.40
Cumulative effect of change in inventory method ($6,000/40,000)		(0.15)
Net income [($70,000 – $4,000)/40,000 shares].		$1.65

Computations:

$$\text{EPS} = \frac{\text{Income} - \text{Preferred dividends}}{\text{Common shares outstanding}}$$

Preferred dividends: $50,000 × 0.08 = $4,000

Common shares outstanding:
45,000 shares issued − 5,000 treasury shares = 40,000 shares outstanding

Kraft Corporation
Statement of Retained Earnings
Year Ended December 31, 20X6

Retained earnings balance, beginning, as originally reported.	$103,000
Prior-period adjustment—credit	5,000
Retained earnings balance, beginning, as adjusted.	108,000
Net income for current year	70,000
	178,000
Dividends for current year	(16,000)
Retained earnings balance, ending	$162,000

REVIEW *Retained Earnings, Treasury Stock, and the Income Statement*

Quick Check

1. A company's own stock that it has issued and repurchased is called
    a. Issued stock
    b. Outstanding stock
    c. Stock dividend
    d. Treasury stock

2. A stock dividend
    a. Increases Common Stock
    b. Decreases Retained Earnings
    c. Has no effect on total equity
    d. All of the above

3. In a small stock dividend,
    a. Retained Earnings is debited for the market value of the shares issued.
    b. Common stock is debited for the par value of the shares issued.
    c. Paid-In Capital in Excess of Par is debited for the difference between the debits to Retained Earnings and to Common Stock.
    d. Net income is always decreased.

4. Stock splits
    a. Increase the number of shares of stock issued
    b. Decrease the par value of the stock
    c. Both a and b
    d. None of the above

5. Assume that **Pier 1 Imports** paid $10 per share to purchase 1,000 of its $1 par common as treasury stock. The purchase of treasury stock
    a. Decreased total equity by $1,000
    b. Increased total equity by $1,000
    c. Decreased total equity by $10,000
    d. Increased total equity by $10,000

6. Assume that Pier 1 Imports sold all 1,000 shares of its treasury stock for $15 per share. The sale of treasury stock
    a. Decreased total equity by $15,000
    b. Increased total equity by $15,000
    c. Decreased total equity by $5,000
    d. Increased total equity by $5,000

7. Analyze the income statement of Allied Electronics in Exhibit 14-6, page 555. Suppose you are predicting next year's net income. Allied is most likely to earn net income of $x next year. How much is $x?
    a. $54,000
    b. $75,000
    c. $79,000
    d. $90,000

8. Which of the following events would be an extraordinary loss?
    a. Loss on the sale of equipment
    b. Loss due to an earthquake
    c. Loss on discontinued operations
    d. All of the above are extraordinary items

9. What is the most widely followed statistic in accounting?
    a. Earnings per share
    b. Total assets
    c. Retained earnings
    d. Dividends

10. Earnings per share is *not* computed for
    a. Net income
    b. Discontinued operations
    c. Comprehensive income
    d. Extraordinary items

Accounting Vocabulary

appropriation of retained earnings (p. 551)

comprehensive income (p. 558)

earnings per share (EPS) (p. 557)

extraordinary gains and losses (p. 556)

extraordinary item (p. 556)

prior-period adjustment (p. 559)

segment of the business (p. 555)

statement of stockholders' equity (p. 559)

stock dividend (p. 544)

stock split (p. 546)

treasury stock (p. 548)

●ASSESS *Your Progress*

online homework

See *www.prenhall.com/horngren* for selected Starters, Exercises, and Problems.

Recording a small stock dividend
(Obj. 1)

Comparing and contrasting cash dividends and stock dividends
(Obj. 1)

Accounting for a stock split
(Obj. 2)

Accounting for the purchase and sale of treasury stock (above cost)
(Obj. 3)

Interpreting a restriction of retained earnings
(Obj. 4)

Preparing a corporate income statement
(Obj. 5)

Starters

S14-1 Benetech, Inc., has 200,000 shares of $2.50 par common stock outstanding. Benetech distributes a 5% stock dividend when the market value of its stock is $10 per share.

1. Journalize Benetech's distribution of the stock dividend on September 30. An explanation is not required.
2. What is the overall effect of the stock dividend on Benetech's total assets? On total stockholders' equity?

S14-2 → *Link Back to Chapter 13 (Cash Dividends)*. Compare and contrast the accounting for cash dividends and stock dividends. In the space provided, insert either "Cash dividends," "Stock dividends," or "Both cash dividends and stock dividends" to complete each of the following statements:

1. _____ increase paid-in capital by the same amount that they decrease Retained Earnings.
2. _____ decrease both total assets and total stockholders' equity, resulting in a decrease in the size of the company.
3. _____ decrease Retained Earnings.
4. _____ have no effect on a liability.

S14-3 Examine **Pier 1 Imports'** stockholders' equity on page 545. Suppose Pier 1 split its common stock 2 for 1 in order to decrease the market price of its stock. The company's stock was trading at $20 immediately before the split.

1. Prepare the stockholders' equity section of Pier 1 Imports' balance sheet after the stock split.
2. Which account balances changed after the stock split? Which account balances were unchanged?

S14-4 Celine Corporation began operations in 20X8. After issuing its common stock to the public, Celine completed the following treasury stock transactions:

a. Purchased 2,000 shares of the company's $1 par common stock as treasury stock, paying cash of $5 per share.
b. Sold 1,000 shares of the treasury stock for cash of $8 per share.

   Journalize these transactions. Explanations are not required. Show how Celine will report treasury stock on its December 31, 20X8, balance sheet after completing the two transactions. In reporting the treasury stock, focus solely on the Treasury Stock account. You may ignore all other accounts.

S14-5 Study Exhibit 14-5, page 552. The company's board of directors is preparing to declare a cash dividend.

1. The company has plenty of cash. What is the maximum amount of cash dividends the board of directors can declare? Explain how you arrived at your answer.
2. What is the nature of the retained earnings restriction in the exhibit? Why did the company restrict (appropriate) its retained earnings? Explain.

S14-6 List the major parts of a complex corporate income statement for IMAX Corporation for the year ended December 31, 20X4. Include all the major parts of the income statement, starting with net sales revenue and ending with net income (net loss). You may ignore dollar amounts and earnings per share. Use Exhibit 14-6, page 555, as a guide.

S14-7 Study the income statement of Allied Electronics Corporation in Exhibit 14-6, page 555. Answer these questions about the company's operations:

Explaining the items on a complex corporate income statement
(Obj. 5)

1. How much total gross profit did Allied earn on the sale of its products—before deducting any operating expenses? Name this item and give its amount.
2. Why is the gain on sale of machinery reported as Other gains (losses)?
3. What dollar amount of net income would most sophisticated investors predict for Allied Electronics to earn during 20X6 and beyond? Name this item, give its amount, and state your reason.

S14-8 H&R Young Corporation accounting records include the following items, listed in no particular order, at December 31, 20X3.

Preparing a corporate income statement
(Obj. 5)

Extraordinary gain	$ 5,000	Other gains (losses)	$ (2,000)
Cost of goods sold	71,000	Net sales revenue	182,000
Operating expenses	64,000	Loss on discontinued	
Accounts receivable	19,000	operations	(15,000)

Income tax of 40% applies to all items.

Prepare H&R Young Corporation's income statement for the year ended December 31, 20X3. Use Exhibit 14-6, page 555, as a guide. Omit earnings per share.

S14-9 Return to the H&R Young Corporation data in Starter 14-8. H&R Young had 10,000 shares of common stock outstanding during 20X3. H&R Young declared and paid preferred dividends of $3,000 during 20X3.

Show how H&R Young reported EPS data on its 20X3 income statement.

Reporting earnings per share
(Obj. 5)

S14-10 The **Procter & Gamble Company** has preferred stock outstanding, and the corporation issued additional common stock during the year.

Interpreting earnings-per-share data
(Obj. 5)

1. Give the basic equation to compute earnings per share of common stock for net income.
2. List all the income items for which Procter & Gamble must report EPS data.

S14-11 Use the H&R Young Corporation data in Starter 14-8. In addition, H&R Young had unrealized losses of $4,000 on investments during 20X3. Start with H&R Young's net income from Starter 14-8 and show how the company could report other comprehensive income on its 20X3 income statement.

Should H&R Young report EPS data for other comprehensive income?

Reporting comprehensive income
(Obj. 5)

S14-12 Examine De Graff Corporation's statement of retained earnings on page 559. Suppose instead that De Graff had overpaid 20X7 income tax expense by $10,000. Show how De Graff would report this prior-period adjustment on the statement of retained earnings for 20X8.

Reporting a prior-period adjustment
(Obj. 6)

S14-13 ← *Link Back to Chapter 1 (Accounting Equation).* Use the statement of stockholders' equity in Exhibit 14-9, page 560, to answer the following questions about Allied Electronics Corporation.

Using the statement of stockholders' equity
(Obj. 6)

1. Make a single journal entry to record Allied's declaration and payment of cash dividends during 20X5.
2. How much cash did the issuance of common stock bring in during 20X5?
3. What was the cost of the treasury stock that Allied purchased during 20X5? What was Allied's cost of the treasury stock that Allied sold during the year? For how much did Allied sell the treasury stock during 20X5?

Journalizing a stock dividend and reporting stockholders' equity
(Obj. 1)

Exercises

E14-1 The stockholders' equity for Clifton, Inc., on December 31, 20X4, follows:

Stockholders' Equity	
Common stock, $1 par, 100,000 shares authorized,	
50,000 shares issued............................	$ 50,000
Paid-in capital in excess of par.....................	400,000
Retained earnings	120,000
Total stockholders' equity.........................	$570,000

On April 30, 20X5, the market price of Clifton's common stock was $16 per share and the company distributed a 10% stock dividend.

Required

1. Journalize the distribution of the stock dividend.
2. Prepare the stockholders' equity section of the balance sheet after the stock dividend.

Journalizing cash and stock dividends
(Obj. 1)

E14-2 Hunter Racing Motors is authorized to issue 500,000 shares of $1 par common stock. The company issued 80,000 shares at $4 per share, and all 80,000 shares are outstanding. When the market price of common stock was $5 per share, Hunter distributed a 10% stock dividend. Later, Hunter declared and paid a $0.50 per share cash dividend.

Required

1. Journalize the distribution of the stock dividend.
2. Journalize both the declaration and the payment of the cash dividend.

Reporting stockholders' equity after a stock split
(Obj. 2)

E14-3 Harwood Travel, Inc., had the following stockholders' equity at May 31:

Common stock, $10 par, 200,000 shares authorized,	
50,000 shares issued............................	$500,000
Paid-in capital in excess of par.....................	100,000
Retained earnings	200,000
Total stockholders' equity.........................	$800,000

On June 30, Harwood split its common stock 2 for 1. Make the necessary entry to record the stock split, and prepare the stockholders' equity section of the balance sheet immediately after the split.

Effects of stock issuance, dividends, and treasury stock transactions
(Obj. 1, 2, 3)

E14-4 Identify the effects of the following transactions on total stockholders' equity. Each transaction is independent.

a. Issuance of 50,000 shares of $10 par common at $15.
b. Purchase of 1,000 shares of treasury stock (par value $0.50) at $5 per share.
c. A 10% stock dividend. Before the dividend, 500,000 shares of $1 par common stock were outstanding; market value was $7 at the time of the dividend.
d. Sale of 600 shares of $1 par treasury stock for $5 per share. Cost of the treasury stock was $2 per share.
e. A 3-for-1 stock split. Prior to the split, 60,000 shares of $4 par common were outstanding.

Journalizing treasury stock transactions
(Obj. 3)

E14-5 Journalize the following transactions of **Foot Locker**, a chain of sports stores:

Feb.	4	Issued 20,000 shares of no-par common stock at $15 per share.
Apr.	22	Purchased 1,000 shares of treasury stock at $14 per share.
Aug.	22	Sold 600 shares of treasury stock at $20 per share.

E14-6 Far Side, Inc., had the following stockholders' equity on November 30:

Journalizing treasury stock transactions and reporting stockholders' equity
(Obj. 3)

Stockholders' Equity	
Common stock, $5 par, 500,000 shares authorized, 50,000 shares issued................................	$250,000
Paid-in capital in excess of par......................	150,000
Retained earnings	520,000
Total stockholders' equity..........................	$920,000

On December 30, Far Side purchased 5,000 shares of treasury stock at $10 per share. Journalize the purchase of the treasury stock, and prepare the stockholders' equity section of the balance sheet at December 31.

E14-7 The agreement under which Patterson, Inc., issued its long-term debt requires the restriction of $200,000 of the company's retained earnings balance. Total retained earnings is $250,000, and total paid-in capital is $500,000.

Reporting a retained earnings restriction
(Obj. 4)

Required

Show how to report stockholders' equity on Patterson's balance sheet, assuming the following:

a. Patterson discloses the restriction in a note. Write the note.
b. Patterson appropriates retained earnings in the amount of the restriction and includes no note in its statements.
c. Patterson's cash balance is $100,000. What is the maximum amount of dividends Patterson can declare?

E14-8 Schindler Corporation's accounting records include the following for 20X8:

Preparing a multistep income statement
(Obj. 5)

spreadsheet

Sales revenue...................	$410,000	Income tax expense— extraordinary gain.............	$ 6,000
Operating expenses (including income tax).........	106,000	Income tax expense—change in depreciation method.........	3,000
Cumulative effect of change in depreciation method, a credit...	7,000	Income tax saving—loss on discontinued operations.....	20,000
Cost of goods sold	245,000	Extraordinary gain	15,000
Loss on discontinued operations..	50,000		

Required

Prepare a multistep income statement for 20X8. Omit earnings per share.

E14-9 Tyler, Inc. earned net income of $74,000 for 20X6. The ledger reveals the following figures:

Computing earnings per share
(Obj. 5)

Preferred stock, $4.00 per year, no-par, 1,000 shares issued and outstanding.........................	$ 50,000
Common stock, $10 par, 52,000 shares issued.........	520,000
Treasury stock, common, 2,000 shares at cost	36,000

Required

Compute Tyler's EPS for the year.

E14-10 San Marcos, Inc., had 50,000 shares of common stock and 10,000 shares of 5%, $10 par preferred stock outstanding through December 31, 20X5. Income from continuing operations of 20X5 was $110,000, and loss on discontinued operations (net of income tax saving) was $8,000. The company had an extraordinary gain (net of tax) of $50,000.

Computing earnings per share
(Obj. 5)

Required

Compute San Marcos's EPS amounts for 20X5, starting with income from continuing operations.

Preparing a statement of retained earnings with a prior-period adjustment
(Obj. 6)

spreadsheet

E14-11 The French Bakery reported a prior-period adjustment in 20X3. An accounting error caused net income of prior years to be understated by $5 million. Retained earnings at December 31, 20X2, as previously reported, stood at $395 million. Net income for 20X3 was $110 million, and dividends totaled $40 million.

Required

Prepare the company's statement of retained earnings for the year ended December 31, 20X3.

Preparing a combined statement of income and retained earnings
(Obj. 5, 6)

spreadsheet

E14-12 The Ritz Hotel Company, a large hotel chain, had retained earnings of $410 million at December 31, 20X6. The company reported these figures for 20X7:

	($ Millions)
Net income	$140
Cash dividends—preferred	2
common	88

Required

Beginning with net income, prepare a combined statement of income and retained earnings for The Ritz Hotel Company for the year ended December 31, 20X7.

Computing comprehensive income
(Obj. 5)

E14-13 During 20X6, BMW Group earned income from continuing operations of $95,000. The company also sold its land-development segment (discontinued operations) at a gain of $30,000 and had an extraordinary loss of $8,000. At year-end, BMW had an unrealized loss on investments of $3,000.

1. Compute BMW's net income and comprehensive income for 20X6. All amounts are net of income taxes.

2. What would be the final EPS figure that BMW would report for 20X6? Show the amount. BMW had 20,000 shares of common stock (and no preferred stock) outstanding.

Preparing a statement of stockholders' equity
(Obj. 6)

E14-14 At December 31, 20X6, Labrador Corp. reported the following stockholders' equity.

Common stock, $5 par, 200,000 shares authorized,	
120,000 shares issued.........................	$ 600,000
Additional paid-in capital	100,000
Retained earnings	700,000
Treasury stock, 2,500 shares at cost	(80,000)
	$1,320,000

During 20X7, Labrador completed these transactions and events (listed in chronological order):

a. Sold 1,000 shares of treasury stock for $35 per share (cost of these shares was $30 per share).

b. Issued 500 shares of common stock at $20 per share.

c. Net income for the year was $200,000.

d. Declared and paid cash dividends of $100,000.

Required

Prepare Labrador Corp.'s statement of stockholders' equity for 20X7.

Recording a stock dividend and preparing a statement of stockholders' equity
(Obj. 1, 6)

E14-15 Omni Communications, Inc., began 20X5 with 2.9 million shares of $1 par common stock issued and outstanding. Beginning paid-in capital in excess of par was $6 million, and retained earnings was $7 million. In February 20X5, Omni issued 100,000 shares of stock at $11 per share. In September, when the stock's market price was $12 per share, the board of directors distributed a 10% stock dividend.

Required

1. Make the journal entries for the issuance of stock for cash and for the distribution of the 10% stock dividend.

2. Prepare the company's statement of stockholders' equity for the year ended December 31, 20X5.

Problems

(Group A)

P14-1A **Titleist Sports Corporation** completed the following selected transactions during 20X6:

Journalizing stockholders' equity transactions
(Obj. 1, 3)

*Student Resource**CD***
General Ledger (GL), QuickBooks (QB), Peachtree (PT)

Jan.	6	Declared a cash dividend on the 10,000 shares of $2.25, no-par preferred stock. Declared a $0.20 per share dividend on the 10,000 shares of common stock outstanding. The date of record is January 17, and the payment date is January 20.
Jan.	20	Paid the cash dividends.
Mar.	21	Split common stock 2 for 1 by calling in the 10,000 shares of $10 par common and issuing new stock in its place.
Apr.	18	Distributed a 10% stock dividend on the common stock. The market value of the common stock was $27 per share.
June	18	Purchased 2,000 shares of treasury common stock at $25 per share.
Dec.	22	Sold 1,000 shares of treasury common stock for $26 per share.

Required

Record the transactions in the general journal.

P14-2A The balance sheet of Quartz, Inc., at December 31, 20X5, reported 500,000 shares of $1 par common stock authorized with 100,000 shares issued. Paid-In Capital in Excess of Par had a balance of $300,000. Retained Earnings had a balance of $101,000. During 20X6, the company completed the following selected transactions:

Journalizing dividend and treasury stock transactions and reporting stockholders' equity
(Obj. 1, 2, 3)

*Student Resource**CD***
GL, QB, PT

Feb.	15	Purchased 5,000 shares of the treasury stock at $4 per share.
Mar.	8	Sold 2,000 shares of treasury stock for $7 per share.
Sep.	28	Distributed a 10% stock dividend on the 97,000 shares of *outstanding* common stock. The market value of Quartz's common stock was $5 per share.
Dec.	31	Earned net income of $73,000 during the year. Closed net income to Retained Earnings.

Required

1. Record the transactions in the general journal. Explanations are not required.

2. Prepare the stockholders' equity section of the balance sheet at December 31, 20X6.

P14-3A Monahans Corporation is well positioned. Located in Tucson, Arizona, Monahans is the only company between Texas and California with reliable sources for its imported gifts. The company does a brisk business with specialty stores such as **Pier 1 Imports**. Monahans' recent success has made the company a prime target for a takeover. An investment group from Hong Kong is attempting to buy 51% of Monahans' outstanding stock against the wishes of Monahans' board of directors. Board members are convinced that the Hong Kong investors would sell the most desirable pieces of the business and leave little of value.

Purchasing treasury stock to fight off a takeover of the corporation
(Obj. 3)

At the most recent board meeting, several suggestions were advanced to fight off the hostile takeover bid. The suggestion with the most promise is to purchase a huge quantity of treasury stock. Monahans has the cash to carry out this plan.

Required

1. As a significant stockholder of Monahans Corporation, write a memorandum to explain to the board how the purchase of treasury stock would make it difficult for the Hong Kong group to take over Monahans. Include a discussion of the effect that purchasing treasury stock would have on stock outstanding and on the size of the corporation.

2. Suppose Monahans' management is successful in fighting off the takeover bid and later sells the treasury stock at prices greater than the purchase price. Explain what effect these sales will have on assets, stockholders' equity, and net income.

Journalizing dividend and treasury stock transactions; reporting retained earnings and stockholders' equity
(Obj. 1, 3)

GL, QB, PT

P14-4A The balance sheet of Swingline, Inc., at December 31, 20X8, presented the following stockholders' equity:

Paid-in capital:	
Common stock, $1 par, 250,000 shares authorized,	
50,000 shares issued	$ 50,000
Paid-in capital in excess of par—common	350,000
Total paid-in capital	400,000
Retained earnings.	99,000
Total stockholders' equity	$499,000

During 20X9, Swingline completed the following selected transactions:

Mar. 29	Distributed a 5% stock dividend on the common stock. The market value of Swingline common stock was $8 per share.
July 13	Purchased 2,000 shares of treasury stock at $8 per share.
Oct. 4	Sold 1,000 shares of treasury common stock for $9 per share.
Dec. 10	Declared a $0.20 per share cash dividend on the 51,500 shares of common stock outstanding. The date of record is December 17, and the payment date is January 2.
31	Closed the $71,000 net income to Retained Earnings.

Required

1. Record the transactions in the general journal.
2. Prepare the retained earnings statement at December 31, 20X9.
3. Prepare the stockholders' equity section of the balance sheet at December 31, 20X9.

Preparing a detailed income statement
(Obj. 5)

P14-5A The following information was taken from the records of Jeffries Corporation at June 30, 20X5:

Common stock, no-par, 22,000		Selling expenses	$ 120,000
shares authorized and issued	$350,000	General expenses	71,000
Preferred stock, 6%, $25 par,		Gain on discontinued operations.	1,000
4,000 shares issued	100,000	Cost of goods sold	279,000
Retained earnings, beginning	63,000	Dividend revenue	19,000
Income tax expense (tax saving):		Treasury stock, common (2,000 shares). . . .	28,000
Continuing operations	28,000	Extraordinary loss	42,000
Gain on discontinued operations	400	Net sales revenue	567,000
Extraordinary loss (tax saving)	(15,400)		

Required

Prepare a single-step income statement, including earnings per share, for Jeffries Corporation for the fiscal year ended June 30, 20X5.

Preparing a corrected combined statement of income and retained earnings
(Obj. 5)

P14-6A Eloy Santos, accountant for Airstream, Inc., was injured in an auto accident. Another employee prepared the following income statement for the fiscal year ended June 30, 20X4:

Airstream, Inc.
Income Statement
June 30, 20X4

Revenues and gains:		
Sales		$733,000
Paid-in capital in excess of par—common		111,000
Total revenues and gains.		844,000
Expenses and losses:		
Cost of goods sold	$383,000	
Selling expenses	103,000	
General expenses	91,000	
Sales returns	22,000	
Sales discounts	10,000	
Dividends	15,000	
Income tax expense—continuing operations.	32,000	
Total expenses and losses		656,000
Income from operations		188,000
Other gains and losses:		
Loss on discontinued operations.		(15,000)
Net income		$173,000
Earnings per share		$8.65

The individual *amounts* listed on the income statement are correct. However, some accounts are reported incorrectly, and one doesn't belong on the income statement at all. Also, income tax has not been applied to all appropriate figures. The income tax rate on discontinued operations is 40%. Airstream issued 24,000 shares of common stock in 20X1 and held 4,000 shares as treasury stock during fiscal year 20X4. Retained earnings at June 30, 20X3, was $209,000.

Required

Prepare a corrected combined statement of income and retained earnings for the fiscal year ended June 30, 20X4. Prepare the income statement in single-step format, and include earnings per share.

Computing earnings per share and reporting a retained earnings restriction
(Obj. 4, 5)

P14-7A The capital structure of Avian Company at December 31, 20X7, included 5,000 shares of $2 preferred stock and 120,000 shares of common stock. Common shares outstanding during 20X8 were 120,000. Income from continuing operations during 20X8 was $370,000. The company discontinued a segment of the business at a gain of $60,000 and also had an extraordinary loss of $48,000. Avian's board of directors has restricted $300,000 of retained earnings for expansion of the company's office facilities.

Required

1. Compute Avian's earnings per share for 20X8. Start with income from continuing operations. Income and loss amounts are net of income tax.

2. Show two ways of reporting Avian's retained earnings restriction. Retained earnings at December 31, 20X7, was $120,000, and Avian declared cash dividends of $100,000 during 20X8.

Using a statement of stockholders' equity
(Obj. 6)

P14-8A Business Analysts, Inc., reported the following statement of stockholders' equity for the year ended September 30, 20X9:

Business Analysts, Inc.					
Statement of Stockholders' Equity **Year Ended September 30, 20X9**					
(Dollar amounts in thousands)	Common Stock	Additional Paid-in Capital	Retained Earnings	Treasury Stock	Total
Balance, September 30, 20X8	$173	$2,118	$1,706	$(18)	$3,979
Net income			520		520
Cash dividends........................			(117)		(117)
Issuance of stock (5,000 shares)	9	46			55
Stock dividend	18	92	(110)		—
Sale of treasury stock....................		5		11	16
Balance, September 30, 20X9	$200	$2,261	$1,999	$ (7)	$4,453

Required

1. What is the par value of the company's common stock?
2. At what price per share did the company issue its common stock during the year?
3. What was the cost of treasury stock sold during the year? What was the selling price of the treasury stock sold? What was the increase in total stockholders' equity from selling the treasury stock?
4. What overall effect did the stock dividend have on total stockholders' equity?

Problems

(Group B)

Journalizing stockholders' equity transactions
(Obj. 1,3)

GL, QB, PT

P14-1B Alan Cook Corp. completed the following transactions during 20X9:

Feb. 2	Declared a cash dividend on the 5%, $100 par preferred stock (1,000 shares outstanding). Declared a $0.20 per share dividend on the 100,000 shares of common stock outstanding. The date of record is February 15 and the payment date is February 23.
Feb. 23	Paid the cash dividends.
June 10	Split common stock 2 for 1 by calling in the 100,000 shares of $10 par common and issuing new stock in its place.
July 30	Distributed a 10% stock dividend on the common stock. The market value of the common stock was $15 per share.
Oct. 26	Purchased 2,500 shares of treasury common stock at $14 per share.
Nov. 8	Sold 1,000 shares of treasury common stock for $17 per share.

Required

Record the transactions in Allen Cook's general journal.

Journalizing dividend and treasury stock transactions and reporting stockholders' equity
(Obj. 1, 2, 3)

GL, QB, PT

P14-2B The balance sheet of Recreation Concepts, Inc., at December 31, 20X6, reported 100,000 shares of no-par common stock authorized, with 30,000 shares issued and a Common Stock balance of $180,000. Retained Earnings had a balance of $140,000. During 20X7, the company completed the following selected transactions:

Mar. 15	Purchased 5,000 shares of treasury stock at $8 per share.
Apr. 30	Distributed a 20% stock dividend on the 25,000 shares of *outstanding* common stock. The market value of Recreation Concepts common stock was $10 per share.
Oct. 8	Sold 2,000 shares of treasury stock for $12 per share.
31	Earned net income of $110,000 during the year. Closed net income to Retained Earnings.

Required

1. Record the transactions in the general journal. Explanations are not required.

2. Prepare the stockholders' equity section of Recreation Concepts' balance sheet at December 31, 20X7.

P14-3B Cooper Fashions is ideally positioned in the clothing business. Located in Toledo, Ohio, Cooper is the only company with a distribution network for its imported goods. The company does a brisk business with specialty stores such as **Neiman Marcus, Saks Fifth Avenue**, and **Nordstrom**. Cooper's recent success has made the company a prime target for a takeover. Against the wishes of Cooper's board of directors, an investment group from Canada is attempting to buy 51% of Cooper's outstanding stock. Board members are convinced that the Canadian investors would sell off the most desirable pieces of the business and leave little of value.

Increasing dividends to fight off a takeover of the corporation
(Obj. 1)

At the most recent board meeting, several suggestions were advanced to fight off the hostile takeover bid. One suggestion is to increase the stock outstanding by distributing a 100% stock dividend. The intent is to spread the company's ownership in order to make it harder for the Canadian group to buy a controlling interest.

Required

As a significant stockholder of Cooper Fashions, write a short memo to explain to the board whether distributing the stock dividend would make it more difficult for the investor group to take over Cooper. Include in your memo a discussion of the effect that the stock dividend would have on assets, liabilities, and total stockholders' equity—that is, the dividend's effect on the size of the corporation.

P14-4B The balance sheet of Beta Concepts, Inc., at December 31, 20X6, reported the following stockholders' equity:

Journalizing dividend and treasury stock transactions; reporting retained earnings and stockholders' equity
(Obj. 1, 3)

Student ResourceCD

GL, QB, PT

Paid-in capital:	
Common stock, $10 par, 100,000 shares authorized,	
20,000 shares issued	$200,000
Paid-in capital in excess of par—common	300,000
Total paid-in capital	500,000
Retained earnings	180,000
Total stockholders' equity	$680,000

During 20X7, Beta Concepts completed the following selected transactions:

Feb.	6	Distributed a 10% stock dividend on the common stock. The market value of Beta Concepts' stock was $24 per share.
July	29	Purchased 2,000 shares of treasury stock at $21 per share.
Nov.	13	Sold 400 shares of treasury stock for $22 per share.
	27	Declared a $0.30 per share cash dividend on the 20,400 shares of common stock outstanding. The date of record is December 17, and the payment date is January 7, 20X8.
Dec.	31	Closed the $70,000 net income to Retained Earnings.

Required

1. Record the transactions in the general journal.

2. Prepare a retained earnings statement at December 31, 20X7.

3. Prepare the stockholders' equity section of the balance sheet at December 31, 20X7.

Preparing a detailed income statement
(Obj. 5)

P14-5B The following information was taken from the records of Courtyard Classics, Inc., at September 30, 20X8.

Cost of goods sold.	$435,000		General expenses	$133,000
Retained earnings, beginning	88,000		Preferred stock, $2, no-par,	
Selling expenses	121,000		5,000 shares issued	200,000
Income from discontinued operations	8,000		Common stock, $10 par, 25,000	
Income tax expense (tax saving):			shares authorized and issued	250,000
Continuing operations	72,000		Net sales revenue	837,000
Income from discontinued operations	2,000		Treasury stock, common (1,000 shares)	11,000
Extraordinary loss (tax saving)	(12,000)		Extraordinary loss	30,000

Required

Prepare a single-step income statement, including earnings per share, for Courtyard Classics, Inc., for the fiscal year ended September 30, 20X8.

Preparing a corrected combined statement of income and retained earnings
(Obj. 5)

P14-6B Quincy Caldwell, accountant for Brooks Furniture Company, was injured in a boating accident. Another employee prepared the accompanying income statement for the year ended December 31, 20X3.

The individual *amounts* listed on the income statement are correct. However, some accounts are reported incorrectly, and one doesn't belong on the income statement at all. Also, income tax has not been applied to all appropriate figures. The income tax rate on discontinued operations was 40%. Brooks Furniture Company issued 52,000 shares of common stock in 20X1 and held 2,000 shares as treasury stock during 20X3. Retained earnings at December 31, 20X2, was $361,000.

Brooks Furniture Company
Income Statement
Year Ended December 31, 20X3

Revenue and gains:		
Sales		$362,000
Paid-in capital in excess of par—common		90,000
Total revenues and gains		452,000
Expenses and losses:		
Cost of goods sold	$105,000	
Selling expenses	67,000	
General expenses	61,000	
Sales returns	11,000	
Sales discounts	6,000	
Dividends	7,000	
Income tax expense	20,000	
Total expenses and losses		277,000
Income from operations		175,000
Other gains and losses:		
Loss on discontinued operations		(3,000)
Net income		$172,000
Earnings per share		$3.44

Required

Prepare a corrected combined statement of income and retained earnings for 20X3; include earnings per share. Prepare the income statement in single-step format.

Computing earnings per share and reporting a retained earnings restriction
(Obj. 4, 5)

P14-7B The capital structure of Smirnoff, Inc., at December 31, 20X6, included 20,000 shares of $1.25 preferred stock and 46,000 shares of common stock. Common stock outstanding during 20X7 totaled 46,000 shares. Income from continuing operations during 20X7 was $94,000. The company discontinued a segment of the business at a gain of $23,000, and also had an extraordinary gain of $11,500. Smirnoff's board of directors restricts $60,000 of retained earnings for contingencies.

Required

1. Compute Smirnoff's earnings per share for 20X7. Start with income from continuing operations. All income and loss amounts are net of income tax.

2. Show two ways of reporting Smirnoff's retained earnings restriction. Retained earnings at December 31, 20X6, was $100,000, and Smirnoff declared cash dividends of $20,000 during 20X7.

P14-8B Public Trust, Inc., reported the following statement of stockholders' equity for the year ended October 31, 20X4:

Using a statement of stockholders' equity
(Obj. 6)

Public Trust, Inc.
Statement of Stockholders' Equity
Year Ended October 31, 20X4

(Dollar amounts in thousands)	Common Stock	Additional Paid-In Capital	Retained Earnings	Treasury Stock	Total
Balance, Oct. 31, 20X3	$427	$1,622	$904	$(117)	$2,836
Net income			336		336
Cash dividends.			(194)		(194)
Issuance of stock (60,000 shares)	120	264			384
Stock dividend	22	48	(70)		—
Sale of treasury stock.		9		19	28
Balance, Oct. 31, 20X4	$569	$1,943	$976	$ (98)	$3,390

Required

Answer these questions about Public Trust's stockholders' equity transactions.

1. What is the par value of the company's common stock?

2. At what price per share did Public Trust issue its common stock during the year?

3. What was the cost of treasury stock sold during the year? What was the selling price of the treasury stock sold? What was the increase in total stockholders' equity from selling the treasury stock?

4. What effect did the stock dividend have on total stockholders' equity?

APPLY *Your Knowledge*

Decision Cases

Case 1. Modem Transmission, Inc., had the following stockholders' equity amounts on June 30, 20X2:

Analyzing cash dividends and stock dividends
(Obj. 1)

Common stock, no-par, 100,000 shares issued	$ 750,000
Retained earnings	790,000
Total stockholders' equity	$1,540,000

In the past, Modem has paid an annual cash dividend of $1 per share. Despite the large retained earnings balance, the board of directors wished to conserve cash for expansion. The board delayed the payment of cash dividends and in July distributed a 10% stock dividend. During August, the company's cash position improved. The board declared and paid a cash dividend of $0.9091 per share in September.

Suppose you owned 5,000 shares of Modem common stock, acquired three years ago, prior to the 10% stock dividend. The market price of the stock was $30 per share before any of these dividends.

Required

1. What amount of cash dividends did you receive last year—before the stock dividend? What amount of cash dividends will you receive after the stock dividend?

2. How does the stock dividend affect your proportionate ownership in Modem Transmission, Inc.? Explain.

3. Immediately after the stock dividend was distributed, the market value of Modem stock decreased from $30 per share to $27.273 per share. Does this decrease represent a loss to you? Explain.

Reporting special items
(Obj. 3, 5)

Case 2. The following accounting issues have arisen at T-Shirts Plus, Inc.:

1. T-Shirts Plus earned a significant profit in the year ended November 30, 20X6, because land that it held was purchased by the State of North Carolina for a new highway. The company proposes to treat the sale of land as operating revenue. Why do you think the company is proposing this plan? Is this disclosure appropriate?

2. Corporations sometimes purchase their own stock. When asked why they do so, T-Shirts Plus management responds that the stock is undervalued. What advantage would T-Shirts Plus gain by buying and selling its own undervalued stock?

3. The treasurer of T-Shirts Plus wants to report a large loss as an extraordinary item because the company produced too much product and cannot sell it. Why do you think the treasurer wants to report the loss as extraordinary? Would that be acceptable?

Ethical Issue

← *Link Back to Chapter 6 (Accounting Principles)*. High Plains Production Company is an independent oil producer in Midland, Texas. In February, geologists discovered a pool of oil that tripled the company's proven reserves. Prior to disclosing the new oil to the public, top managers of the company quietly bought most of High Plains' stock for themselves. After the discovery was announced, the High Plains' stock price rose from $7 to $52.

Required

1. Did High Plains managers behave ethically? Explain your answer.

2. Identify the accounting principle relevant to this situation. Review Chapter 6 if necessary.

3. Who was helped and who was harmed by management's action?

Financial Statement Case

Complex income statement, earnings per share
(Obj. 5)

Use the **Amazon.com** financial statements in Appendix A to answer the following questions.

Required

1. Study Amazon.com's income statement, which the company labels "consolidated statement of operations." *Consolidated* means that Amazon owns other companies. Amazon reported one "special" item of income on its income statement. What was the special item, and what was its amount for 2002? Was this special item a gain or a loss? How can you tell?

2. Show how Amazon.com computed earnings per share of $(0.39) for 2002.

3. Prepare a T-account to show the beginning and ending balances and all activity in Retained Earnings (Accumulated Deficit) for 2002.

Team Project

Required

Obtain the annual reports (or annual report data) of five well-known companies. You can get the reports either from your college library or by mailing a request directly to the company (allow two weeks for delivery). Or you can visit the Web site for this book (http://www.prenhall.com/horngren) or the SEC EDGAR database, which includes the financial reports of most well-known companies.

1. After selecting five companies, examine their income statements to search for the following items:
   a. Income from continuing operations
   b. Discontinued operations
   c. Extraordinary gains and losses
   d. Cumulative effects of accounting changes
   e. Net income or net loss
   f. Earnings-per-share data
2. Study the companies' balance sheets to see
   a. What classes of stock each company has issued.
   b. Which item carries a larger balance—the Common Stock account, or Paid-In Capital in Excess of Par (also labeled Additional Paid-In Capital).
   c. What percentage of each company's total stockholders' equity is made up of retained earnings.
   d. Whether the company has treasury stock. If so, how many shares and how much is the cost?
3. Examine each company's statement of stockholders' equity for evidence of
   a. Cash dividends
   b. Stock dividends (Some companies use the term *stock split* to refer to a large stock dividend.)
   c. Treasury stock purchases and sales
4. As directed by your instructor, either write a report or present your findings to your class. You may be unable to understand *everything* you find, but neither can the Wall Street analysts! You will be amazed at how much you have learned.

For Internet exercises, go to the Web site www.prenhall.com/horngren.

CHAPTER **15**

Long-Term Liabilities

 TIPS CHECK YOUR RESOURCES

- Visit the www.prenhall.com/horngren **Web site** for self-study quizzes, video clips, and other resources
- Try the **Quick Check** exercise at the end of the chapter to test your knowledge
- Learn the **key terms**
- Do the **Starter** exercises keyed in the margins
- Work the **mid-** and **end-of-chapter summary problems**
- Use the **Concept Links** to review material in other chapters
- Search the **CD** for review materials by chapter or by key word
- Watch the **tutorial videos** to review key concepts

LEARNING OBJECTIVES

⭐1 Account for bonds payable transactions

⭐2 Measure interest expense by the effective-interest method

⭐3 Account for retirement and conversion of bonds payable

⭐4 Report liabilities on the balance sheet

⭐5 Show the advantages and disadvantages of borrowing

What's the best way to finance a company—issue stock or borrow the money? When the stock market declines, companies find it hard to sell their stock. They have to look to the bond market for cash to expand. For example, Amazon.com has borrowed by issuing convertible notes payable. Convertible bonds offer advantages for companies that need to borrow and for individuals with money to invest. By issuing convertible bonds, companies can borrow at lower interest rates than if they issued straight bonds. Then if a company's stock goes up, investors can swap the bonds for stock. Amazon gets a lower interest rate and investors can benefit if Amazon's stock price rises. They can convert the bonds into stock.

Amazon.com

Accessing bond information has never been easier. You can log on to www.investinginbonds.com for topics such as What Are Bonds? Also,

<u>www.convertbond.com</u> provides data on convertible bonds plus chat rooms and search functions. These information sources make it easier for companies to borrow and for people to make informed investment decisions.

Sources: Forbes, May 22, 2000, "Best of the Web," p. 86; Jennifer Ablan, "Volume of Convertible Bond Offerings Continues to Rise with Big Deals by Technology Concerns," *The Wall Street Journal*, July 13, 2000, p. C25. ■

■ Sitemap

Chapters 13 and 14 showed two ways to finance operations. Chapter 13 covered the stock accounts and additional paid-in capital, and Chapter 14 discussed profitable operations and retained earnings. This chapter shows the third way to finance a company: borrowing on long-term liabilities. The chapter appendix on the time value of money provides background on the valuation of long-term liabilities.

Before launching into accounting for bonds payable, let's compare stocks and bonds. The following chart shows how stocks and bonds differ.

Stocks	Bonds
1. Stock represents the *ownership* (equity) of the corporation.	1. Bonds represent a *liability* of the corporation.
2. Each shareholder is an *owner* of the corporation.	2. Each bondholder is a *creditor* of the corporation.
3. The corporation *may or may not* pay dividends.	3. The corporation *must* pay interest.
4. Dividends are *not* an expense of the corporation.	4. Interest is a *tax-deductible* expense of the corporation.
5. Corporation is *not* obligated to repay stock amounts to the shareholders.	5. Corporation *must* repay the bonds payable at maturity.

Bonds Payable
Groups of notes payable issued to multiple lenders called bondholders.

◉ Student Resource CD

bonds payable, bond pricing, market interest rate, present value, stated interest rate

Bonds: An Introduction

Well-known companies such as Amazon.com, Inc., and eBay cannot borrow billions from a single lender because no bank will loan that much to a single company. Then how do corporations borrow the huge amounts they need to expand? They issue bonds payable to the public. **Bonds payable** are groups of notes issued to multiple lenders, called bondholders. Amazon can borrow millions of dollars from thousands of individual investors. Each investor buys a modest amount of Amazon bonds.

Purchasers of the bonds each receive a bond certificate, which shows the borrower's name, exactly like a note payable. The certificate states the *principal*, which is the amount the company has borrowed. This figure, typically stated in units of $1,000, is also called the bond's maturity value, or par value. The bond obligates the issuing company to pay the holder the principal amount at a specific future date, called the maturity date.

Bondholders lend their money to earn interest. The bond certificate states the interest rate that the issuer will pay and the dates the interest payments are due (generally twice a year). Exhibit 15-1 shows an actual bond certificate issued by Washington Public Power Supply System (WPPSS).

Exhibit 15-1   Bond Certificate (Adapted)

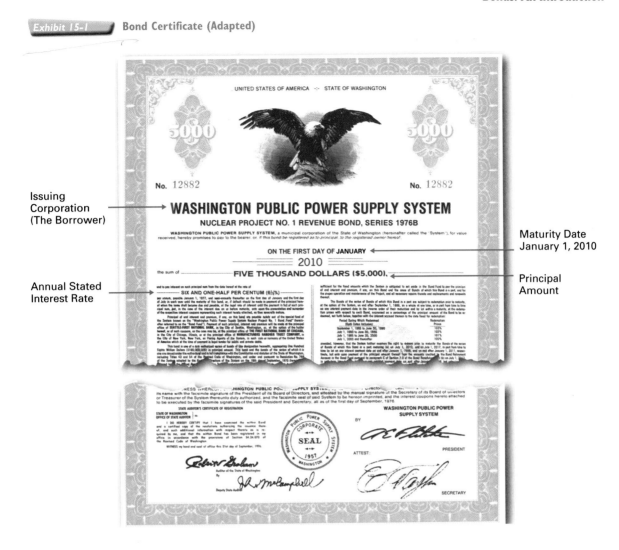

Issuing Corporation (The Borrower)

Maturity Date January 1, 2010

Annual Stated Interest Rate

Principal Amount

Review these bond fundamentals in Exhibit 15-1.

- **Principal amount** (also called maturity value, or par value). The amount the borrower must pay back to the lender.
- **Maturity date** The date on which the borrower must pay the principal amount to the lender.
- **Stated interest rate** The annual rate of interest that the borrower pays the lender.

Types of Bonds

All the bonds in a particular issue may mature at a specified time **(term bonds)**, or they may mature in installments **(serial bonds)**. Serial bonds are like installment notes payable.

Secured, or mortgage, bonds give the bondholder the right to take specified assets of the issuer (called *collateral*) if the company fails to pay interest or principal. A **mortgage** is an example of a secured note or bond. Unsecured bonds, called **debentures**, are backed only by the good faith of the borrower.

Bond Prices

A bond issued at a price above its maturity value is said to be issued at a **premium**, and a bond issued at a price below maturity value has a **discount**. As a bond nears maturity, its market price moves toward maturity value. On the

Term Bonds
Bonds that all mature at the same time for a particular issue.

Serial Bonds
Bonds that mature in installments over a period of time.

Mortgage
Borrower's promise to transfer the legal title to certain assets to the lender if the debt is not paid on schedule.

Debentures
Unsecured bonds backed only by the good faith of the borrower.

Premium
Excess of a bond's issue price over its maturity value. Also called **bond premium**.

Discount (on a Bond)
Excess of a bond's maturity value over its issue price. Also called a **bond discount**.

maturity date, the market value of a bond exactly equals its maturity value because the company pays that amount to retire the bond.

After a bond is issued, investors may buy and sell it through the bond market just as they buy and sell stocks through the stock market. The most famous bond market is the New York Exchange, which lists several thousand bonds. Bond prices are quoted at a percentage of their maturity value. For example, a $1,000 bond quoted at 100 is bought or sold for $1,000, which is 100% of its maturity value. The same bond quoted at 101.5 has a market price of $1,015 (101.5% of maturity value, or $1,000 × 1.015). A $1,000 bond quoted at 88.375 means 88.375% of $1,000, and it is priced at $883.75 ($1,000 × 0.88375).

Exhibit 15-2 contains price information for the bonds of Ohio Edison Company, taken from *The Wall Street Journal*. On this particular day, 12 of Ohio Edison's 9 1/2% bonds maturing in 2006 (indicated by 06) were traded. The bonds' highest price on this day was $795 ($1,000 × 0.795). The lowest price of the day was $784.50 ($1,000 × 0.7845). The closing price (last sale of the day) was $795.

✔ **Starter 15-1**

Exhibit 15-2

Bond Price Information for Ohio Edison Company (OhEd)

Bonds	Volume	High	Low	Close
OhEd 9 1/2 of 06	12	79.5	78.45	79.5

Present Value

The appendix to this chapter covers the time value of money in detail. →

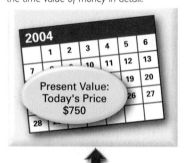

Present Value:
Today's Price
$750

Future Value:
Maturity Value
$1,000

Present value is always less than future value.

Present Value
Amount a person would invest now to receive a greater amount in the future.

Stated Interest Rate
Interest rate that determines the amount of cash interest the borrower pays and the investor receives each year.

Market Interest Rate
Interest rate that investors demand in order to loan their money. Also called the **effective interest rate**.

Money earns income over time, a fact called the *time value of money*. ← Let's examine how the time value of money affects bond prices. Assume that a bond with a face value of $1,000 reaches maturity three years from today and carries no interest. As an investor, would you pay $1,000 to purchase the bond? No, because paying $1,000 today to receive the same amount later provides you with no income on the investment. How much would you pay today in order to receive $1,000 in three years? The answer is some amount *less* than $1,000. Suppose $750 is a fair price. By investing $750 now to receive $1,000 later, you will earn $250 over the three years. The company that issued the bonds sees the transaction this way: It pays you $250 interest for the use of your $750 for three years.

The amount that a person would invest *at the present time* to receive a greater amount in the future is called the **present value**. In our example, $750 is the present value, and the $1,000 to be received in three years is the future amount.

Present value is always less than future value. The difference between present value and future value is interest. We show how to compute present value in the chapter appendix. If your instructor so directs you, study the appendix now.

Bond Interest Rates

Bonds are sold at market price, which is the maximum amount an investor will pay for a bond. Market price is the bond's present value, which is the sum of the present value of the principal payment plus the present value of all the stated interest payments, which may be semiannual, annual, or quarterly.

Two interest rates work together to set the price of a bond:

- The **stated interest rate** is the interest rate that determines the amount of cash interest the borrower pays each year. The stated rate is printed on the bond and *does not change*. For example, Amazon.com's 10% notes payable have a stated interest rate of 10%. Thus, Amazon pays $1,000 of interest annually on each $10,000 bond. Each semiannual interest payment is $500 ($10,000 × 0.10 × 1/2).

- The **market interest rate** is the rate investors demand for loaning their money. The market interest rate *varies* daily. A company may issue bonds with a stated interest rate that differs from the market interest rate.

Amazon.com may issue its 10% notes when the market rate has risen to 11%. Will the Amazon notes attract investors in this market? No, because investors can earn 11% on other bonds and notes. Therefore, investors will purchase Amazon notes only at a price less than maturity value. The difference between the lower price and the notes' maturity value is a *discount*.

✔ Starter 15-2

Conversely, if the market interest rate is 8%, Amazon's 10% notes will be so attractive that investors will pay more than maturity value for them. The difference between the higher price and maturity value is a *premium*. Exhibit 15-3 shows how the stated interest rate and the market interest rate work together to determine the price of a bond.

Example: Bond with a Stated Interest Rate of 8%			
Bond's Stated Interest Rate*	Market Interest Rate**		Issue Price of Bonds Payable
8%	=	8% ⇒	Maturity (par) value
8%	<	10% ⇒	Discount [price below maturity (par) value]
8%	>	6% ⇒	Premium [price above maturity (par) value]

*Determines the amount of each cash interest payment.
**Used to set the bond's market price.

Exhibit 15-3

Interaction of the Stated Interest Rate and the Market Interest Rate to Determine the Price of a Bond

✔ Starter 15-3

✔ Starter 15-4

☐ Bonds: Introduction
■ Issuing Bonds Payable
☐ Effective-Interest Method
☐ Additional Bond Topics
☐ Bonds versus Stock
☐ Lease Liabilities
☐ Appendix: Time Value of Money

Issuing Bonds Payable to Borrow Money

The basic entry to record issuing bonds payable debits Cash and credits Bonds Payable. The company may issue bonds for three different bond prices:

- At *maturity (par)* value
- At a *discount*
- At a *premium*

We begin with the simplest case: issuing bonds at maturity (par) value.

Issuing Bonds Payable at Maturity (Par) Value

Account for bonds payable transactions

Student ResourceCD

amortizing bonds, bonds payable, bond discount, bond premium, stated interest rate

Suppose Amazon.com, Inc., has $50,000 of 8% bonds payable that mature in 5 years. Assume that Amazon issues these bonds at maturity (par) value on January 1, 2002. The issuance entry is

```
2002
Jan. 1   Cash ........................... 50,000
             Bonds Payable...............         50,000
         Issued bonds payable.
```

Amazon, the borrower, makes this one-time journal entry to record the receipt of cash and the issuance of bonds payable. Interest payments occur each January 1 and July 1. Amazon's entry to record the first semiannual interest payment is

```
2002
July 1   Interest Expense ($50,000 × 0.08 × 6/12)   2,000
             Cash .......................              2,000
         Paid semiannual interest.
```

At maturity, Amazon.com will record payment of the bonds as follows:

✔ Starter 15-5

```
2007
Jan. 1   Bonds Payable.................... 50,000
             Cash .......................         50,000
         Paid off bonds payable at maturity.
```

How much interest expense will **Amazon.com** record for each year on these bonds?

Answer: $4,000 ($50,000 × 0.08)

Now we turn to the issuance of bonds payable at a discount.

Issuing Bonds Payable at a Discount

Bonds are often issued at a discount. We know that market conditions may force the issuing corporation to accept a discount price for its bonds. Suppose Amazon.com, Inc., issues $100,000 of its 9%, five-year bonds when the market interest rate is 9 1/2%. The market price of the bonds drops to 98, which means 98% of par value. Amazon receives $98,000 ($100,000 × 0.98) at issuance and makes the following journal entry:

```
2002
Jan. 1   Cash  ($100,000 × 0.98) . . . . . . . . . . . . .   98,000
         Discount on Bonds Payable . . . . . . . . .    2,000
              Bonds Payable . . . . . . . . . . . . . . .           100,000
         Issued bonds payable at a discount.
```

After posting, the bond accounts have these balances:

Bonds Payable		Discount on Bonds Payable	
	100,000	2,000	

Discount on Bonds Payable is a contra account to Bonds Payable. Bonds Payable minus the discount gives the carrying amount of the bonds. The relationship between Bonds Payable and the Discount account is similar to the relationship between Equipment and Accumulated Depreciation. Amazon would report these bonds payable as follows:

Long-term liabilities:
  Bonds payable $100,000
  Less: Discount on bonds payable . . . .   (2,000) $98,000

INTEREST EXPENSE ON BONDS PAYABLE ISSUED AT A DISCOUNT   We saw that the stated interest rate and the market interest rate may differ. The market interest rate was 9 1/2% when Amazon.com issued its 9% bonds. The 1/2% interest-rate difference created the $2,000 discount on the bonds. Investors were willing to pay only $98,000 for a $100,000, 9% bond when they could purchase similar bonds and earn 9 1/2% on them. Amazon thus borrowed $98,000 cash but must pay $100,000 cash when the bonds mature five years later.

What happens to the $2,000 discount? The discount is additional interest expense to Amazon. It raises Amazon's interest expense on the bonds to the market interest rate of 9 1/2%. For each accounting period over the life of the bonds, the discount is accounted for as interest expense through a process called *amortization*. Amortization is the gradual reduction of an item over time.

STRAIGHT-LINE AMORTIZATION OF BOND DISCOUNT   We can amortize a bond discount by dividing it into equal amounts for each interest period. This method is called *straight-line amortization*. In our example, the initial discount is $2,000, and there are 10 semiannual interest periods during the bonds' 5-year life.

Therefore, 1/10 of the $2,000 ($200) of bond discount is amortized each interest period. Amazon.com's first semiannual interest entry is[1]

2002
July 1   Interest Expense   4,700
   Cash ($100,000 × 0.09 × 6/12) ...   4,500
   Discount on Bonds Payable
    ($2,000/10)................   200
  Paid semiannual interest and amortized bond discount.

Interest expense of $4,700 for the six-month period is the sum of

- The stated interest ($4,500, which is paid in cash)
- *Plus* the amortization of discount ($200)

✔ Starter 15-6

Discount on Bonds Payable is credited to amortize its balance. Ten amortization entries will decrease the discount to zero, and the carrying amount of the bonds payable will increase to the maturity value of $100,000.
 Finally, the entry to pay off the bonds at maturity is

2007
Jan. 1   Bonds Payable....................   100,000
   Cash   100,000
  Paid off bonds payable at maturity.

Bond discount decreases — Bond carrying amount increases

How much interest expense will **Amazon** record each year on these bonds? How much cash interest will Amazon pay each year? What causes the difference?

Answer: Interest expense each year: $9,400 ($4,700 × 2)
    Cash interest paid each year: $9,000 ($4,500 × 2)

The difference is caused by amortization of the bond discount.

Issuing Bonds Payable at a Premium

The issuance of bonds at a premium is rare because companies don't like to pay a stated interest rate higher than the market rate. To illustrate a bond premium, let's change the Amazon.com example. Assume that the market interest rate is 8% when Amazon issues its 9%, five-year bonds. Because 9% bonds are attractive in this market, investors will pay a premium to acquire them. Suppose the bonds are priced at 104 (104% of maturity value). In that case, Amazon receives $104,000 cash upon issuance. The entry to borrow money and issue bonds is

2002
Jan. 1   Cash ($100,000 × 1.04)   104,000
   Bonds Payable   100,000
   Premium on Bonds Payable ...   4,000
  Issued bonds payable at a premium.

---

[1]Some accountants record the payment of interest and the amortization of bond discount in two separate entries, as follows:

2002
July 1 Interest Expense................................ 4,500
     Cash ($100,000 × 0.09 × 6/12)................   4,500
   Paid semiannual interest.
July 1 Interest Expense............................... 200
     Discount on Bonds Payable ($2,000/10).......   200
   Amortized discount on bonds payable.

After posting, the bond accounts have the following balances:

Bonds Payable		Premium on Bonds Payable	
	100,000		4,000

Premium on Bonds Payable is added to Bonds Payable to determine the carrying amount of the bonds. Amazon.com would report these bonds payable as follows:

Long-term liabilities:		
Bonds payable	$100,000	
Plus: Premium on bonds payable	4,000	$104,000

INTEREST EXPENSE ON BONDS PAYABLE ISSUED AT A PREMIUM The 1% difference between the 9% stated interest rate on the bonds and the 8% market interest rate creates the $4,000 premium. Amazon borrows $104,000 cash but must pay only $100,000 at maturity. The premium is like a savings of interest expense to Amazon. The premium cuts Amazon's cost of borrowing and reduces interest expense to 8%, the market rate. We amortize the bond premium as a decrease in interest expense over the life of the bonds.

STRAIGHT-LINE AMORTIZATION OF BOND PREMIUM In our example, the beginning premium is $4,000, and there are 10 semiannual interest periods during the bonds' 5-year life. Therefore, 1/10 of the $4,000 ($400) of bond premium is amortized each interest period. Amazon.com's first semiannual interest entry is[2]

2002			
July 1	Interest Expense	4,100	
	Premium on Bonds Payable ($4,000/10)..	400	
	Cash ($100,000 × 0.09 × 6/12)		4,500
	Paid semiannual interest and amortized bond premium.		

✔ Starter 15-7

Interest expense of $4,100 is

- The stated interest ($4,500, which is paid in cash)
- *Minus* the amortization of the premium

Consider bonds issued at a discount. Which will be greater, the cash interest paid per period or the amount of interest expense? Answer the same question for bonds issued at a premium.

Answer: Discount: Interest expense > Stated interest paid
Premium: Stated interest paid > Interest expense

---

[2]The payment of interest and the amortization of bond premium can be recorded in separate entries as follows:

2002			
July 1	Interest Expense.................................	4,500	
	Cash ($100,000 × 0.09 × 6/12)................		4,500
	Paid semiannual interest.		
July 1	Premium on Bonds Payable ($4,000/10)	400	
	Interest Expense...........................		400
	Amortized premium on bonds payable.		

Reporting Bonds Payable

Bonds payable are reported on the balance sheet at maturity value plus bond premium or minus bond discount. For example, in the preceding example of a bond premium, Amazon.com would report the following on its balance sheet at December 31, 2002:

Long-term liabilities:
　Bonds payable.................................... $100,000
　　Plus: Premium on bonds payable [$4,000 − (2 × $400)]...　3,200　$103,200

Over the life of the bonds, 10 amortization entries will decrease the premium to zero. The payment at maturity will debit Bonds Payable and credit cash for $100,000.

Adjusting Entries for Interest Expense

Companies issue bonds when they need cash. The interest payments seldom occur on December 31 (or the end of the fiscal year). So interest expense must be accrued at the end of the period to measure income accurately. → The accrual entry should include the amortization of any bond discount or premium.

Xenon Corporation issued $100,000 of 8%, 10-year bonds at a $2,000 discount on October 1, 2006. The interest payments occur on March 31 and September 30 each year. On December 31, Xenon records interest for three months (October, November, and December) as follows:

← The adjusting entry for bond interest expense follows the pattern for the adjusting entries for other accrued liabilities, as in Chapters 3 (p. 105) and 11 (p. 450), except for the addition of the amortization of the premium or discount.

2006
Dec. 31　Interest Expense 2,050
　　　　　　Interest Payable ($100,000 × 0.08 × 3/12)........　2,000
　　　　　　Discount on Bonds Payable ($2,000/10 × 3/12) ..　50
　　　　　Accrued three months' interest and amortized bond discount.

Interest Payable is credited for three months (October, November, and December). Discount on Bonds Payable must also be amortized for these three months.

Xenon's balance sheet at December 31, 2006, reports Interest Payable of $2,000 as a current liability. Bonds Payable are shown as follows:

Long-term liabilities:
　Bonds payable.................................... $100,000
　　Less: Discount on bonds payable ($2,000 − $50) ....　(1,950)　$98,050

Observe that the bonds' carrying amount increases by $50. The bonds' carrying amount continues to increase until it reaches $100,000 at maturity, when the discount will be fully amortized.

The next semiannual interest payment occurs on March 31, 2007:

✔ **Starter 15-8**

2007
Mar. 31　Interest Expense 2,050
　　　　　Interest Payable................................ 2,000
　　　　　　Cash ($100,000 × 0.08 × 6/12) ....　4,000
　　　　　　Discount on Bonds Payable ($2,000/10 × 3/12) ..　50
　　　　　Paid semiannual interest and amortized bond discount.

✔ **Starter 15-9**

Amortization of a bond premium is similar except that Premium on Bonds Payable is debited.

Decision Guidelines

LONG-TERM LIABILITIES—PART A

Amazon.com has borrowed some money by issuing bonds payable. What type of bonds did Amazon issue? How much cash must Amazon pay each interest period? At maturity? The Decision Guidelines address these and other questions.

Decision	Guidelines
When will you pay off the bonds • At maturity? • In installments?	Type of bond to issue: • Term bonds • Serial bonds
Are the bonds secured? • Yes • No	Then they are • Mortgage or secured bonds • Debenture or unsecured bonds
How are bond prices • Quoted? • Determined? What are the two interest rates used for bonds?	 • As a percentage of maturity value (Example: A $500,000 bond priced at $510,000 would be quoted at 102 ($510,000 ÷ $500,000 = 1.02) • Present value of the future principal amount to pay plus present value of the future interest payments (see chapter appendix) • The *stated interest rate* determines the amount of cash interest the borrower pays. This interest rate does not change. • The *market interest rate* is the rate investors demand for loaning their money. The market interest rate determines the borrower's true rate of interest expense. This rate varies daily.
What causes a bond to be priced at • Maturity (par) value? • A premium? • A discount?	When the bonds are issued, • The *stated* interest rate on the bond *equals* the *market* interest rate • The *stated* interest rate on the bond is *greater than* the *market* interest rate • The *stated* interest rate on the bond is *less than* the *market* interest rate
What is the relationship between interest expense and interest payments when bonds are issued at • Maturity (par) value? • A premium? • A discount?	 • Interest expense *equals* Interest payment • Interest expense is *less than* Interest payment • Interest expense is *greater than* Interest payment
How to report bonds payable on the balance sheet?	Maturity (par) value $\begin{cases} + \text{Premium on bonds payable} \\ \text{or} \\ - \text{Discount on bonds payable} \end{cases}$

● MID-CHAPTER *Summary Problem*

CHECK YOUR RESOURCES

Assume that Alabama Power Company has an issue of 9% bonds payable that mature on May 1, 2028. The bonds are dated May 1, 2008, and Alabama Power pays interest each April 30 and October 31.

Required

1. Will the bonds be issued at par, at a premium, or at a discount if the market interest rate on the date of issuance is 8%? If the market interest rate is 10%?

2. Assume that Alabama Power issued $1,000,000 of the bonds at 104 on May 1, 2008.
  a. Record issuance of the bonds.
  b. Record the interest payment and amortization of the premium on October 31, 2008. Use the straight-line method of amortization.
  c. Accrue interest and amortize premium on December 31, 2008.
  d. Show how the company would report the bonds on the balance sheet at December 31, 2008.
  e. Record the interest payment and amortization of premium on April 30, 2009.

Solution

Requirement 1

Market Interest Rate	Bond Price
8%	Premium
10%	Discount

Requirement 2

2008

a. May 1   Cash ($1,000,000 × 1.04) $1,040,000
           Bonds Payable.   1,000,000
           Premium on Bonds Payable   40,000
         Issued bonds at a premium.

b. Oct. 31   Interest Expense   44,000
         Premium on Bonds Payable ($40,000/40).   1,000
           Cash ($1,000,000 × 0.09 × 6/12)   45,000
         Paid semiannual interest and amortized bond premium.

c. Dec. 31   Interest Expense   14,667
         Premium on Bonds Payable
           ($40,000/40 × 2/6)   333
           Interest Payable
             ($1,000,000 × 0.09 × 2/12)   15,000
         Accrued interest and amortized bond premium.

d. Long-term liabilities:
         Bonds payable, 9% $1,000,000
         Premium on bonds payable
           ($40,000 − $1,000 − $333) 38,667 $1,038,667

2009

e. Apr. 30   Interest Expense   29,333
         Interest Payable   15,000
         Premium on Bonds Payable ($40,000/40 × 4/6)   667
           Cash ($1,000,000 × 0.09 × 6/12)   45,000
         Paid semiannual interest and amortized bond premium.

Effective-Interest Method of Amortization

We began with the straight-line amortization method to introduce the concept of amortizing bonds. However, that method has a theoretical weakness. Under the straight-line method, each period's interest expense is the same dollar amount. But over their life, the bonds' carrying amount moves toward maturity. The amount of interest expense should also increase or decrease as the bonds move toward maturity.

⭐ *Measure interest expense by the effective-interest method*

Student ResourceCD

bond discount, bond premium, effective-interest method

Generally accepted accounting principles require that interest expense be measured using the *effective-interest method* unless the straight-line amounts are similar. In that case, either method is permitted. Total interest expense over the life of the bonds is the same under both methods. We now show how the effective-interest method works.

Effective-Interest Method for a Bond Discount

Assume that eBay Inc. issues $100,000 of 9% bonds at a time when the market rate of interest is 10%. These bonds mature in 5 years and pay interest semiannually, so there are 10 semiannual interest payments. The issue price of the bonds is $96,149,[3] and the discount on these bonds is $3,851 ($100,000 − $96,149). Exhibit 15-4 shows how to measure interest expense by the effective-interest method. (You will need an amortization table to account for bonds by the effective-interest method.)

Exhibit 15-4 Effective-Interest Method for a Bond Discount

PANEL A—Bond Data
Maturity value—$100,000
Stated interest rate—9%
Interest paid—4 1/2% semiannually, $4,500 ($100,000 × 0.045)
Market interest rate at time of issue—10% annually, 5% semiannually
Issue price—$96,149 on January 1, 2005

PANEL B—Amortization Table

End of Semiannual Interest Period	A Interest Payment (4 1/2% of maturity value)	B Interest *Expense* (5% of preceding bond carrying amount)	C Discount Amortization (B − A)	D Discount Balance (D − C)	E Bond Carrying Amount ($100,000 − D)
Jan. 1, 2005				$3,851	$ 96,149
July 1	$4,500	$4,807	$307	3,544	96,456
Jan. 1, 2006	4,500	4,823	323	3,221	96,779
July 1	4,500	4,839	339	2,882	97,118
Jan. 1, 2007	4,500	4,856	356	2,526	97,474
July 1	4,500	4,874	374	2,152	97,848
Jan. 1, 2008	4,500	4,892	392	1,760	98,240
July 1	4,500	4,912	412	1,348	98,652
Jan. 1, 2009	4,500	4,933	433	915	99,085
July 1	4,500	4,954	454	461	99,539
Jan. 1, 2010	4,500	4,961*	461	0	100,000

*Adjusted for effect of rounding.

Notes

• *Column A* The interest payments are constant—fixed by the stated interest rate and the bonds' maturity value.

• *Column B* The interest expense each period is the preceding bond carrying amount multiplied by the market interest rate. Interest expense increases as the bond carrying amount (E) increases.

• *Column C* The excess of interest expense (B) over interest payment (A) is the discount amortization.

• *Column D* The discount decreases by the amount of amortization for the period (C). Balance of discount + Bonds' carrying amount = Bonds' maturity value ($100,000) at all times.

• *Column E* The bonds' carrying amount increases from $96,149 at issuance to $100,000 at maturity.

---

[3]We compute this present value in the chapter appendix.

The *accounts* debited and credited under the effective-interest method and the straight-line method are the same. Only the *amounts* differ.

Exhibit 15-4 gives the amounts for all the bond transactions of eBay. Let's begin with issuance of the bonds payable on January 1, 2005, and the first interest payment on July 1. Entries follow, using amounts from the respective lines of Exhibit 15-4.

```
2005
Jan. 1   Cash (column E)......................  96,149
            Discount on Bonds Payable (column D)..   3,851
                Bonds Payable (maturity value).....              100,000
         Issued bonds at a discount.
```

```
2005
July 1   Interest Expense (column B)............  4,807
            Discount on Bonds Payable
                (column C)......................                307
            Cash (column A)...................                4,500
         Paid semiannual interest and amortized bond discount.
```

✔ **Starter 15-10**

How much interest expense will **eBay** record for 2005 on these bonds? How much cash interest will eBay pay each year? What causes the difference?

Answer: Interest expense for 2005: $9,630 ($4,807 + $4,823)

Cash interest paid each year: $9,000 ($4,500 × 2)

The difference is caused by amortization of the bond discount.

Stop & Think

Exhibit 15-5 diagrams the carrying amount of bonds issued at a discount. Observe how it rises to maturity. All amounts are taken from Exhibit 15-4.

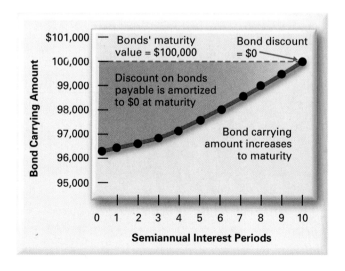

Exhibit 15-5

Carrying Amount for Bonds Payable Issued at a Discount

Effective-Interest Method for a Bond Premium

eBay may issue its bonds payable at a premium. Assume that eBay issues $100,000 of 5-year, 9% bonds when the market interest rate is 8%. The bonds' issue price is $104,100,[4] and the premium is $4,100.

---

[4]Again, we compute the present value of the bonds in the chapter appendix.

Exhibit 15-6 provides the data for all the bond transactions of eBay. Let's begin with issuance of the bonds on January 1, 2005, and the first interest payment on July 1. These entries follow.

```
2005
Jan. 1   Cash (column E)................    $104,100
              Bonds Payable (maturity value)..              100,000
              Premium on Bonds Payable
                  (column D)..................                 4,100
         Issued bonds at a premium.


2005
July 1   Interest Expense (column B) ........      4,164
         Premium on Bonds Payable (column C)        336
                  Cash (column A)..............                4,500
         Paid semiannual interest and amortized bond premium.
```

Exhibit 15-6 / Effective-Interest Method for a Bond Premium

PANEL A—Bond Data
Maturity value—$100,000
Stated interest rate—9%
Interest paid—4 1/2% semiannually, $4,500 ($100,000 × 0.045)
Market interest rate at time of issue—8% annually, 4% semiannually
Issue price—$104,100 on January 1, 2005

PANEL B—Amortization Table

	A	B	C	D	E
End of Semiannual Interest Period	Interest Payment (4 1/2% of maturity value)	Interest *Expense* (4% of preceding bond carrying amount)	Premium Amortization (A – B)	Premium Balance (D – C)	Bond Carrying Amount ($100,000 + D)
Jan. 1, 2005				$4,100	$104,100
July 1	$4,500	$4,164	$336	3,764	103,764
Jan. 1, 2006	4,500	4,151	349	3,415	103,415
July 1	4,500	4,137	363	3,052	103,052
Jan. 1, 2007	4,500	4,122	378	2,674	102,674
July 1	4,500	4,107	393	2,281	102,281
Jan. 1, 2008	4,500	4,091	409	1,872	101,872
July 1	4,500	4,075	425	1,447	101,447
Jan. 1, 2009	4,500	4,058	442	1,005	101,005
July 1	4,500	4,040	460	545	100,545
Jan. 1, 2010	4,500	3,955*	545	0	100,000

*Adjusted for effect of rounding.

Notes

- *Column A* The interest payments are constant—fixed by the stated interest rate and the bonds' maturity value.
- *Column B* The interest expense each period is the preceding bond carrying amount multiplied by the market interest rate. Interest expense decreases as the bond carrying amount decreases.
- *Column C* The excess of interest payment (A) over interest expense (B) is the premium amortization.
- *Column D* The premium balance decreases by the amount of amortization for the period. Bonds' carrying amount – Premium balance = Bonds' maturity value ($100,000) at all times.
- *Column E* The bonds' carrying amount decreases from $104,100 at issuance to $100,000 at maturity.

How much interest expense will **eBay** record for 2005 on these bonds? How much cash interest will eBay pay each year? What causes the difference?

Answer: Interest expense for 2005: $8,315 ($4,164 + $4,151)

　　　　 Cash interest paid each year: $9,000 ($4,500 × 2)

The difference is caused by amortization of the bond premium.

✔ **Starter 15-11**

Exhibit 15-7 diagrams the carrying amount of the bonds issued at a premium. Observe how it falls to maturity. All amounts are taken from Exhibit 15-6.

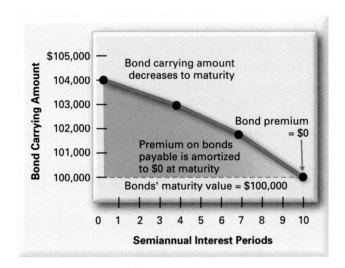

Exhibit 15-7

Carrying Amount for Bonds Payable Issued at a Premium

☐ Bonds: Introduction
☐ Issuing Bonds Payable
☐ Effective-Interest Method
■ **Additional Bond Topics**
☐ Bonds versus Stock
☐ Lease Liabilities
☐ Appendix: Time Value of Money

 Account for retirement and conversion of bonds payable

 Student ResourceCD

callable bonds, convertible bonds, debenture

Additional Bond Topics

Companies that issue bonds payable face additional issues, such as

- Issuance of bonds payable between interest dates
- Retirement of bonds payable
- Convertible bonds payable
- Advantages and disadvantages of issuing bonds versus stock

Issuing Bonds Payable Between Interest Dates

In all the examples we've seen thus far, companies have issued bonds payable on an interest date, such as January 1. Corporations can also issue bonds between interest dates. That creates a complication.

Suppose Intel Corporation has $100,000 of 8% bonds payable that are dated January 1. That means the interest starts accruing on January 1. Suppose Intel issues these bonds on April 1. How should we account for the interest for January, February, and March? At issuance on April 1, Intel collects three months' accrued interest from the bondholder and records the issuance of bonds payable as follows:

```
2005
April 1  Cash.........................    102,000
             Bonds Payable ..............            100,000
             Interest Payable
                ($100,000 × 0.08 × 3/12)......            2,000
         Issued bonds two months after the date of the bonds.
```

On the next interest date, Intel will pay six months' interest to whoever owns the bonds at that time. But Intel will record interest expense only for the three months the bonds have been outstanding (April, May, and June). To allocate interest expense to the correct months, Intel makes this entry on July 1 for the customary six-month interest payment:

✔ **Starter 15-12**

```
2005
July 1    Interest Payable (see entry on April 1) . . .   2,000
          Interest Expense (for April, May, June). . .   2,000
              Cash ($100,000 × 0.08 × 6/12) . . . . . . .            4,000
          Paid six months' interest.
```

Retirement of Bonds Payable

Normally, companies wait until maturity to pay off, or *retire*, their bonds payable. The retirement entry debits Bonds Payable and credits Cash for the maturity value. But companies sometimes retire their bonds payable prior to maturity. The main reason for retiring bonds early is to relieve the pressure of paying interest.

Callable Bonds
Bonds that the issuer may call or pay off at a specified price whenever the issuer wants.

Some bonds are **callable**, which means that the corporation may *call*, or pay off, those bonds at a specified price whenever it chooses. The call price is usually 100 or a few percentage points above par value, perhaps 101 or 102. Callable bonds give the issuer the flexibility to pay off the bonds whenever it is beneficial. An alternative to calling the bonds is to purchase them in the open market at their current market price. Whether the bonds are called or purchased in the open market, the journal entry is the same.

ETrade Associates has $700,000 of bonds payable outstanding with a discount of $30,000. Lower interest rates have convinced management to pay off these bonds now. Assume that the bonds are callable at 103. If the market price of the bonds is 95, will ETrade call the bonds or purchase them in the open market? The market price is lower than the call price, so ETrade will pay off the bonds at their market price. Retiring the bonds at 95 results in a gain of $5,000, computed as follows:

Maturity value of bonds being retired	$700,000
Less: Discount	(30,000)
Carrying amount of bonds payable	670,000
Market price ($700,000 × 0.95)	665,000
Gain on retirement of bonds payable	$ 5,000

The following entry records retirement of the bonds, immediately after an interest date:

```
June 30   Bonds Payable . . . . . . . . . . . . . . . . . .   700,000
              Discount on Bonds Payable . . .                30,000
              Cash ($700,000 × 0.95) . . . . . . . .         665,000
              Gain on Retirement
                  of Bonds Payable . . . . . . . . . .        5,000
          Retired bonds payable.
```

✔ **Starter 15-13**

The entry removes the bonds payable and the related discount from the accounts and records a gain on retirement. Any existing premium would be removed with a debit. If ETrade Associates retired only half of these bonds, the accountant would remove only half the discount or premium.

When retiring bonds before maturity, follow these steps: (1) Record partial-period amortization of discount or premium if the retirement date does not fall on an interest date. (2) Write off the portion of Discount or Premium that relates to the bonds being retired. (3) Compute gain or loss on retirement.

Convertible Bonds Payable

As the chapter-opening story indicates, convertible bonds and notes are popular. **Convertible bonds** and notes payable may be converted into the common stock of the issuing company at the option of the investor. These bonds, called convertible bonds, combine the benefits of interest and principal on the bonds with the opportunity for a gain on the stock. The conversion feature is so attractive that investors accept a lower interest rate than they would on non-convertible bonds. For example, Amazon.com's convertible bonds payable carry an interest rate of only 4 3/4%. The low cash interest payments benefit Amazon.com.

Convertible Bonds
Bonds that may be converted into the common stock of the issuing company at the option of the investor.

The issuance of convertible bonds payable is recorded like any other debt: Debit Cash and credit Convertible Bonds Payable. Then, if the market price of Amazon's stock gets above the market value of the bonds, the bondholders will convert the bonds into stock. The corporation records conversion by removing the bond accounts and crediting the stock accounts. The carrying amount of the bonds becomes the book value of the newly issued stock. There is no gain or loss.

Assume the Amazon bondholders convert $100,000 of the bonds into 2,000 shares of Amazon's common stock, which has a par value of $0.01 (1 cent) per share. Assume further that the carrying amount of the Amazon bonds is $90,000; thus, there is a discount of $10,000. To record the conversion, Amazon would make this journal entry:

May 14	Bonds Payable...................	100,000	
	Discount on Bonds Payable		
	($100,000 − $90,000).........		10,000
	Common Stock (2,000 × $0.01)...		20
	Paid-in Capital in Excess of		
	Par—Common..............		89,980
	Recorded conversion of bonds payable.		

The entry closes the bonds payable account and its related discount. The carrying amount of the notes ($90,000) becomes the amount of new stockholders' equity ($89,980 + $20).

✔ Starter 15-14

Reporting Liabilities on the Balance Sheet

As we have seen, bonds come in all varieties. Companies report their bonds and notes payable among the liabilities on the balance sheet, divided between the current and long-term categories.

 Report liabilities on the balance sheet

Serial bonds are payable in installments. The portion payable within one year is a current liability, and the remaining debt is long-term. For example, assume that Toys "Я" Us has $500,000 of notes payable maturing in various amounts in future years. Assume that the portion payable next year is $200,000. This amount is a current liability, and the remaining $300,000 is a long-term liability. Toys "Я" Us would report the following among its liabilities:

Current liabilities:	
Notes payable, current	$200,000
Long-term liabilities:	
Note payable, long-term.	300,000

Bonds payable are reported in a similar fashion.

Advantages and Disadvantages: Bonds versus Stock

Borrowing by issuing bonds payable carries a risk: The company may be unable to pay off the bonds. Why then do companies borrow so heavily? Because bonds are a cheaper source of money than stock. Borrowing can help a company increase its earnings per share of common stock. Companies thus face this decision: How shall we finance the expansion of the company?

Exhibit 15-8 shows the earnings-per-share (EPS) advantage of borrowing. Suppose that Vista.com, an Internet startup, has net income of $300,000 and 100,000 shares of common stock outstanding. Earnings per share of common stock is $3.00 ($300,000/100,000 shares). Vista needs $500,000 for expansion and the company is considering two finance plans:

- Plan 1 is to borrow $500,000 at 10% (issue $500,000 of 10% bonds payable).
- Plan 2 is to issue 50,000 shares of common stock for $500,000.

Vista management believes the new cash can be used to earn income of $200,000 before interest and taxes.

EPS is higher if Vista.com borrows. If all goes well, Vista can earn more on the investment ($90,000) than the interest it pays on the bonds ($50,000). Earning more income on borrowed money than the related interest expense increases the earnings for common stockholders and is called using **leverage**. It is widely used to increase earnings per share of common stock.

⭐ *Show the advantages and disadvantages of borrowing*

Earnings per share (EPS) is a company's ➡ net income for each share of outstanding common stock (Chapter 14, p. 557). EPS may be the most important figure on the income statement.

Borrow the money. Take a risk in hopes of increasing earnings per share.

Issue stock. It's safer, but earnings per share will drop.

Exhibit 15-8

Earnings-per-Share Advantage of Borrowing versus Issuing Stock

	Plan 1 Borrow $500,000 at 10%	Plan 2 Issue $500,000 of Common Stock
Net income before expansion.		$300,000		$300,000
Expected income on the new project before interest and income tax expenses	$200,000		$200,000	
Less: Interest expense ($500,000 × 0.10)	(50,000)		0	
Project income before income tax	150,000		200,000	
Less: Income tax expense (40%).	(60,000)		(80,000)	
Project net income		90,000		120,000
Total company net income		$390,000		$420,000
Earnings per share after expansion:				
Plan 1 ($390,000/100,000 shares).		$3.90		
Plan 2 ($420,000/150,000 shares).				$2.80

Leverage
Earning more income on borrowed money than the related interest expense, thereby increasing the earnings for the owners of the business.

Borrowing can increase EPS, but borrowing has its disadvantages. Interest expense may be high enough to eliminate net income and lead to a cash shortage or even bankruptcy. This happens to lots of ambitious companies. Borrowing creates liabilities that must be paid during bad years as well as good years.

Lease Liabilities

A **lease** is a rental agreement in which the tenant (**lessee**) obtains the use of an asset by paying rent to the property owner (**lessor**). Leasing can avoid having to make a large initial cash down payment. Accountants divide leases into two types: operating leases and capital leases.

Operating Leases

Operating leases include many apartment leases and car-rental agreements. An operating lease gives the lessee use of an asset but no continuing right to the asset. The lessor keeps the usual rewards and risks of owning the leased asset. To account for an operating lease, the lessee debits Rent Expense and credits Cash for the amount of each lease payment. The lessee's books report no leased asset and no lease liability. This is why lessees prefer operating leases over capital leases. They report no liability.

Lease
Rental agreement in which the tenant (lessee) agrees to make rent payments to the property owner (lessor) to obtain the use of the asset.

Lessee
Tenant in a lease agreement.

Lessor
Property owner in a lease agreement.

Operating Lease
Usually a short-term or cancelable rental agreement.

Capital Leases

A capital lease requires the lessee to record both an asset and a lease liability. Capital leases are both long-term and noncancelable. A **capital lease** meets any *one* of the following criteria:

1. The lease transfers title of the leased asset to the lessee at the end of the lease term. Thus, the lessee becomes the legal owner of the leased asset.

2. The lease contains a *bargain purchase option*. The lessee can be expected to purchase the leased asset and become its legal owner.

3. The lease term is 75% or more of the estimated useful life of the leased asset. The lessee therefore uses up most of the leased asset's service potential.

4. The present value of the lease payments is 90% or more of the market value of the leased asset. In effect, the lease payments operate as installment payments for the leased asset.

Only those leases that meet *none* of these criteria are accounted for as operating leases.

Capital Lease
Lease agreement that meets any one of four criteria: (1) The lease transfers title of the leased asset to the lessee. (2) The lease contains a bargain purchase option. (3) The lease term is 75% or more of the estimated useful life of the leased asset. (4) The present value of the lease payments is 90% or more of the market value of the leased asset.

Accounting for a Capital Lease

Accounting for a capital lease is like accounting for a purchase of a long-term asset. The lessee records an asset and a lease liability even though the lessee may never actually own the property.

Safeway, the grocery chain, leases buildings for its stores. Suppose Safeway leases a store building for a 20-year period. This lease is similar to purchasing the building on an installment plan.

Suppose Safeway's liability under this capital lease totals $1,000,000. The lease liability measures Safeway's cost of the building. Safeway makes this entry at the beginning of the lease:

```
2006
Jan. 1   Building ...................   1,000,000
               Lease Liability...........              1,000,000
         Acquired building under a capital lease.
```

During the lease period, Safeway will report both the building and the lease liability on its balance sheet.

Accounting.com

Qwest: Swapping Bonds to Cut Debt Leaves Bondholders Wary

In the summer of 1998, Baby Bell phone company USWest made corporate history with the largest long-term bond issue: $1.5 billion in 30-year bonds. With the company's solid, investment-grade rating and a yield of 6.9 percent for 30 years, the bonds seemed the ideal investment vehicle. Yet individuals and large institutional investors alike are now unsure whether the bonds issued in 1998 will be paid in full at maturity.

USWest was bought by Qwest Communications, which sought to create the telecom company of the future. Old-economy USWest and new-economy Qwest never did mesh, and Qwest took on an enormous amount of debt to finance its fiber-optic dreams. Furthermore, the company's attempt to inflate revenue via illegal telecom-capacity swaps and other accounting shenanigans have landed former executives in jail, sunk the stock price, and sparked rumors of impending bankruptcy.

Qwest's capacity swaps were illegal, but a U.S. District judge decided that the company could go ahead with a bond swap to pare down its total debt of $24.5 billion. Qwest came up with a debt-for-debt swap for its institutional investors. It works like this: If a bondholder has a $100 face-value bond now trading at $80, Qwest will issue that holder an $80 face-value bond. In return for giving up the $20 difference, the bondholder gets a better rank among Qwest's creditors—in other words, it's more likely that they will get repaid. Qwest then gets to wipe that $20 off its balance sheet.

For those who bought Qwest's bonds at a discount as the company's troubles mounted, the deal is good. They can exchange bonds they bought at distressed values for little or no loss, get a better interest rate and higher standing among creditors. Those who bought the bonds at full face value are not so happy. In fact, bondholders owning about $4 billion of Qwest's bonds sued to stop the exchange, because those who abstain will be punished. They lost their case. Individual investors aren't even given the option to swap.

But who knows? Those who hold on to their Qwest bonds might benefit in the long run. If Qwest can cut its long-term debt, it becomes less likely that the company will go into bankruptcy, thus boosting the value of its bonds.

Based on: Stephanie N. Mehta, "Joe Nacchio's Dream Has Unraveled," *Fortune,* April 29, 2002, pp. 78–82. Kris Hudson, "Qwest Set to Shuffle Bond Debt," *Denver Post,* November 21, 2002, p. C1. Floyd Norris, "A Bond Swap Available Only to Big Players," *The New York Times,* December 18, 2002, p. C1. Kris Hudson, "Qwest Can Proceed on Bond Plan," *Denver Post,* December 19, 2002, p. C2.

Decision Guidelines

LONG-TERM LIABILITIES—PART B

Suppose **American Airlines** needs $500 million for new **Boeing** aircraft. American issues bonds payable to finance the purchase and now must account for the bonds payable. The Decision Guidelines outline some of the issues American must decide.

Decision

What happens to the bonds' carrying amount when bonds payable are issued at

- Maturity (par) value?
- A premium?
- A discount?

How to account for the retirement of bonds payable?

How to account for the conversion of convertible bonds payable into common stock?

What are the advantages of financing operations with

- Stock

- Bonds (or notes) payable?

Guidelines

- Carrying amount *stays* at maturity (par) value.
- Carrying amount *falls* gradually to maturity value.
- Carrying amount *rises* gradually to maturity value.

At maturity date:

Bonds Payable	Maturity value	
Cash		Maturity value

Before maturity date (assume a discount on the bonds and a gain on retirement):

Bonds Payable	Maturity value	
Discount on Bonds Payable . .		Balance
Cash		Amount Paid
Gain on Retirement of Bonds Payable		Excess

Remove the bonds payable (and related premium or discount) and credit Common Stock at par, plus any excess to Paid-In Capital in Excess of Par.

- Creates no liability or interest expense. Less risky to the issuing corporation.
- Results in higher earnings per share—under normal conditions.

Excel Application Exercise

Goal: Create an Excel worksheet to compare earnings per share under two financing scenarios: borrowing and issuing stock.

Scenario: Suppose **American Airlines** is building a new warehouse to serve its central hub operations. To finance construction of the warehouse, managers must decide whether to borrow the $5 million or issue stock. If borrowing is chosen, long-term bonds payable will be issued at 8%. If stock is chosen, 80,000 shares will be issued. Managers expect sales to increase by $700,000. Income tax expense is 40%. Net income before construction is $4 million, and shares outstanding before construction total 500,000.

Your task is to create a spreadsheet that compares earnings per share under the two scenarios described above. After completing the spreadsheet, answer these questions:

1. Which plan generates the higher earnings per share? Why?
2. Under what circumstances would American consider using debt to finance its new warehouse?
3. Under what circumstances would American consider the use of equity to finance its new warehouse?
4. Which option do you recommend? Why? Does your recommendation change if the bond interest rate is 10% rather than 8%?

Step-by-Step:

1. Open a new Excel worksheet.
2. Create a heading for your work sheet that contains the following:
   a. Chapter 15 Excel Application Exercise
   b. Financing with Debt or Stock
   c. American Airlines
   d. Today's date
3. Use Exhibit 15-8 in your textbook as a model for the layout of your spreadsheet. Label the long-term bonds as "Plan 1," and the issuance of common stock as "Plan 2." Be sure to set up the spreadsheet so that you can change variables, such as the interest rate on the bonds, without retyping any formulas in the body of the spreadsheet.
4. When finished, your spreadsheet should show earnings per share under both plans, and be capable of recomputing earnings per share simply by changing the interest rate on the bonds.
5. Save your work and print a copy of the work sheet (in landscape mode) for your files.

END-OF-CHAPTER *Summary Problem*

Trademark, Inc., has outstanding an issue of 8% convertible bonds payable that mature in 2020. Suppose the bonds were dated October 1, 2006, and pay interest each April 1 and October 1.

Required

1. With the bond data below, complete the following effective-interest amortization table through October 1, 2008:
   - Maturity value—$100,000
   - Stated interest rate—8%
   - Interest paid—4% semiannually, $4,000 ($100,000 × 0.04)
   - Market interest rate—9% annually, 4 1/2% semiannually
   - Issue price—90.75 on October 1, 2006

Semiannual Interest Date	A Interest Payment (4% of maturity amount)	B Interest Expense (4 1/2% of preceding bond carrying amount)	C Discount Amortization (B – A)	D Discount Balance (D – C)	E Bond Carrying Amount ($100,000 – D)
10-1-06					
4-1-07					
10-1-07					
4-1-08					
10-1-08					

2. Using the amortization table, record the following transactions:

   a. Issuance of the bonds on October 1, 2006.
   b. Accrual of interest and amortization of discount on December 31, 2006.
   c. Payment of interest and amortization of discount on April 1, 2007.
   d. Conversion of one-third of the bonds payable into no-par common stock on October 2, 2008.
   e. Retirement of two-thirds of the bonds payable on October 2, 2008. Purchase price of the bonds was 102.

Solution

Requirement 1

Semiannual Interest Date	A Interest Payment (4% of maturity amount)	B Interest Expense (4 1/2% of preceding bond carrying amount)	C Discount Amortization (B – A)	D Discount Balance (D – C)	E Bond Carrying Amount ($100,000 – D)
10-1-06				$9,250	$90,750
4-1-07	$4,000	$4,084	$84	9,166	90,834
10-1-07	4,000	4,088	88	9,078	90,922
4-1-08	4,000	4,091	91	8,987	91,013
10-1-08	4,000	4,096	96	8,891	91,109

Requirement 2

```
        2006
    a. Oct. 1    Cash ($100,000 × 0.9075). . . . . . . . . . . .  90,750
                 Discount on Bonds Payable. . . . . . . . .   9,250
                         Bonds Payable . . . . . . . . . . . . . . .        | 100,000
                 Issued bonds payable at a discount.

    b. Dec. 31   Interest Expense ($4,084 × 3/6). . . . . . .   2,042
                 Discount on Bonds Payable
                     ($84 × 3/6) . . . . . . . . . . . . . . . .            |      42
                 Interest Payable ($4,000 × 3/6) . . .               | 2,000
                 Accrued interest and amortized bond discount.

        2007
    c. Apr. 1    Interest Expense  . . . . . . . . . . . . . . . . . .   2,042
                 Interest Payable. . . . . . . . . . . . . . . . . . .   2,000
                 Discount on Bonds Payable
                     ($84 × 3/6) . . . . . . . . . . . . . . . .            |      42
                 Cash. . . . . . . . . . . . . . . . . . . . . . . . .         | 4,000
                 Paid semiannual interest and amortized bond discount.

        2008
    d. Oct. 2    Bonds Payable ($100,000 × 1/3) . . . . . .  33,333
                 Discount on Bonds Payable
                     ($8,891 × 1/3). . . . . . . . . . . . . . .             | 2,964
                 Common Stock ($91,109 × 1/3). .               | 30,369
                 Recorded conversion of bonds payable.

    e. Oct. 2    Bonds Payable ($100,000 × 2/3) . . . . . .  66,667
                 Loss on Retirement Bonds . . . . . . . . . .   7,260
                 Discount on Bonds Payable
                     ($8,891 × 2/3). . . . . . . . . . . . . . .             | 5,927
                 Cash ($100,000 × 2/3 × 1.02) . . . .              | 68,000
                 Retired bonds payable before maturity.
```

REVIEW *Long-Term Liabilities*

Quick Check

1. Which type of bond is unsecured?
   a. Debenture bond   **c.** Serial bond
   b. Mortgage bond   **d.** Common bond

2. A $100,000 bond priced at 103.5 can be bought or sold for
   a. $100,000 + interest   **c.** $103,500
   b. $3,500   **d.** $103,000 + $500 of interest

3. Which interest rate on a bond determines the amount of the semiannual interest payment?
   a. Market rate   **c.** Semiannual rate
   b. Effective rate   **d.** Stated rate

4. The final journal entry to record for bonds payable is

```
    a. Interest Expense. . . .   xxx |                c. Bonds Payable. . . . . . . . . . . . . .  xxx |
              Cash. . . . . . . . .       | xxx                Cash . . . . . . . . . . . . . . . .         | xxx
    b. Cash . . . . . . . . . . . .   xxx |                d. Discount on Bonds Payable . .  xxx |
              Bonds Payable          | xxx                        Interest Expense . . . . . . .       | xxx
```

5. Lafferty Corporation's bonds payable carry a stated interest rate of 7%, and the market rate of interest is 8%. The price of the Lafferty bonds will be at
   a. Premium
   b. Discount
   c. Par value
   d. Maturity value

6. Bonds issued at a premium always have
   a. Interest expense less than the interest payments
   b. Interest expense greater than the interest payments
   c. Interest expense equal to the interest payments
   d. None of the above

7. Imported Cars of Sarasota has $500,000 of 10-year bonds payable outstanding. These bonds had a discount of $40,000 at issuance, which was 5 years ago. The company uses the straight-line amortization method. The carrying amount of Imported Cars' bonds payable is
   a. $460,000
   b. $480,000
   c. $500,000
   d. $520,000

8. Imported Cars issued its 8% bonds payable at a price of $440,000 (maturity value is $500,000). The market interest rate was 10% when Imported Cars issued its bonds. The company uses the effective-interest method for the bonds. Interest expense for the first year is
   a. $35,200
   b. $40,000
   c. $44,000
   d. $50,000

9. Milton Corporation issued bonds payable on August 1. Milton's bonds were dated July 1. Which statement is true of Milton's journal entry to record issuance of the bonds payable?
   a. Milton must pay one month's accrued interest.
   b. Milton will collect one month's accrued interest in advance.
   c. Milton will collect five months' accrued interest in advance.
   d. Milton will pay five months' interest on the next interest date.

10. Bull & Bear, Inc., retired $100,000 of its bonds payable, paying cash of $103,000. On the retirement date, the bonds payable had a discount of $2,000. The bond retirement created a
    a. Gain of $3,000
    b. Loss of $3,000
    c. Gain of $5,000
    d. Loss of $5,000

Accounting Vocabulary

bond discount (p. 581)
bond premium (p. 581)
bonds payable (p. 580)
callable bonds (p. 594)
capital lease (p. 597)
convertible bonds (p. 595)
debentures (p. 581)

discount (on a bond) (p. 581)
effective interest rate (p. 582)
lease (p. 597)
lessee (p. 597)
lessor (p. 597)
leverage (p. 596)
market interest rate (p. 582)

mortgage (p. 581)
operating lease (p. 597)
premium (p. 581)
present value (p. 582)
serial bonds (p. 581)
stated interest rate (p. 582)
term bonds (p. 581)

ASSESS *Your Progress*

See www.prenhall.com/horngren for selected Starters, Exercises, and Problems.

Pricing bonds
(Obj. 1)

Starters

S15-1 Compute the price of the following 8% bonds:
a. $100,000 quoted at 92.6
b. $100,000 quoted at 102.5
c. $100,000 quoted at 77.75
d. $100,000 quoted at 110.375

Which bond will have the least interest expense over its life?
Which bond will have the most interest expense? Explain.

S15-2 **Washington Public Power Supply System (WPPSS)** borrowed money by issuing the bond payable in Exhibit 15-1. Assume the issue price was 96.5.

Determining bonds payable amounts
(Obj. 1)

1. How much cash did WPPSS receive when it issued the bond payable?
2. How much must WPPSS pay back at maturity? When is the maturity date?
3. How much cash interest will WPPSS pay each six months? Carry the interest amount to the nearest cent.

S15-3 Assume the **WPPSS** bond in Exhibit 15-1 was issued at a price of 96.5. Was the market interest rate at the date of issuance 6 1/2%, above 6 1/2%, or below 6 1/2%? Explain.

Bond interest rates
(Obj. 1)

S15-4 Determine whether the following bonds payable will be issued at maturity value, at a premium, or at a discount:

Determining bond prices at par, discount, or premium
(Obj. 1)

a. The market interest rate is 7%. Chicago Corp. issues bonds payable with a stated rate of 8 1/2%.
b. Phoenix, Inc., issued 7% bonds payable when the market rate was 7 1/2%.
c. Tallahassee Corporation issued 8% bonds when the market interest rate was 8%.
d. Seattle Company issued bonds payable that pay cash interest at the stated rate of 7%. At the date of issuance, the market interest rate was 8 1/4%.

S15-5 Suppose **WPPSS** issued the 10-year bond in Exhibit 15-1 when the market interest rate was 6 1/2%. Assume that the fiscal year of WPPSS ends on December 31. Journalize the following transactions for WPPSS. Include an explanation for each entry.

Journalizing basic bond payable transactions
(Obj. 1)

a. Issuance of the bond payable at par on January 1, 2000.
b. Payment of semiannual cash interest on July 1, 2000. (Round to the nearest dollar.)
c. Payment of the bonds payable at maturity. (Give the date.)

S15-6 Assume **WPPSS** issued the 10-year bond in Exhibit 15-1 at a price of 90 on January 1, 2000. Also assume that the WPPSS fiscal year ends on June 30. Journalize the following transactions for WPPSS. Include an explanation for each entry.

Issuing bonds payable at a discount; paying interest and amortizing discount by the straight-line method
(Obj. 1)

a. Issuance of the bond payable on July 1, 2000.
b. Payment of semiannual interest and amortization of bond discount on July 1, 2000. (Use the straight-line method to amortize the discount. Round interest to the nearest dollar.)

S15-7 Assume **WPPSS** issued the 10-year bond payable in Exhibit 15-1 at a price of 110 on January 1, 2000. Also assume that the WPPSS fiscal year ends on December 31. Journalize the following transactions for WPPSS. Include an explanation for each entry.

Issuing bonds payable at a premium; paying interest and amortizing premium by the straight-line method
(Obj. 1)

a. Issuance of the bond payable on January 1, 2000.
b. Payment of semiannual interest and amortization of bond premium on July 1, 2000. (Use the straight-line method to amortize the premium. Round interest to the nearest dollar.)

S15-8 Return to the **WPPSS** bond in Exhibit 15-1. Assume that WPPSS issued the 10-year bond payable on January 1, 2000, at a price of 90. Also assume that the WPPSS accounting year ends on December 31. Journalize the following transactions for WPPSS. Include an explanation for each entry.

Issuing bonds payable, accruing interest, and amortizing bond discount
(Obj. 1)

a. Issuance of the bonds on July 1, 2000.
b. Accrual of semiannual interest expense and amortization of bond discount on December 31, 2000. Interest will be paid tomorrow, on January 1. (Use the straight-line amortization method, and round interest to the nearest dollar.)
c. Payment of the first semiannual interest amount on January 1, 2001.

Reporting interest payable and bonds payable on the balance sheet
(Obj. 5)

S15-9 Use the situation in Starter 15-8, and show how **WPPSS** would report interest payable and the bond payable on its balance sheet at December 31, 2000.

Issuing bonds payable and amortizing discount by the effective-interest method
(Obj. 2)

S15-10 Clever Path Information Systems issued $600,000 of 7%, 10-year bonds payable at a price of 90 on March 31, 20X3. The market interest rate at the date of issuance was 9%, and the bonds pay interest semiannually.

1. How much cash did Clever Path receive upon issuance of the bonds payable?
2. Prepare an effective-interest amortization table for the bond discount, through the first two interest payments. Use Exhibit 15-4 as a guide, and round amounts to the nearest dollar.
3. Record Clever Path's issuance of the bonds on March 31, 20X3, and on September 30, 20X3, payment of the first semiannual interest amount and amortization of the bond discount. Explanations are not required.

Issuing bonds payable and amortizing premium by the effective-interest method
(Obj. 2)

S15-11 Sandals, Inc., issued $200,000 of 8%, 10-year bonds payable at a price of 110 on May 31, 20X5. The market interest rate at the date of issuance was 6%, and the Sandals bonds pay interest semiannually.

1. How much cash did Sandals receive upon issuance of the bonds payable?
2. Prepare an effective-interest amortization table for the bond premium, through the first two interest payments. Use Exhibit 15-6 as a guide, and round amounts to the nearest dollar.
3. Record Sandals' issuance of the bonds on May 31, 20X5, and, on November 30, 20X5, payment of the first semiannual interest amount and amortization of the bond premium. Explanations are not required.

Issuing bonds payable between interest dates and then paying the interest
(Obj. 1)

S15-12 Assume **WPPSS** issued the 10-year bond in Exhibit 15-1 at par value on May 1, 2000, four months after the bond's original issue date of January 1, 2000. Assume that the fiscal year of WPPSS ends on December 31. Journalize the following transactions for WPPSS. Include an explanation for each entry.

a. Issuance of the bonds payable on May 1, 2000. (Carry amounts to the nearest cent.)
b. Payment of the first semiannual interest amount on July 1, 2000. (Carry amounts to the nearest cent.)

Accounting for the retirement of bonds payable
(Obj. 3)

S15-13 Assume that Pacifica, Inc., issued the bonds payable in Exhibit 15-6. Pacifica has extra cash and wishes to retire the bonds payable on January 1, 2008, immediately after making the sixth semiannual interest payment. The bonds are quoted in the market at a price of 95.

1. What is Pacifica's carrying amount of the bonds payable on the retirement date?
2. How much cash must Pacifica pay to retire the bonds payable?
3. Compute Pacifica's gain or loss on the retirement of the bonds payable.
4. Journalize Pacifica's transaction to retire the bonds payable.

Accounting for the conversion of bonds payable
(Obj. 3)

S15-14 ← *Link Back to Chapter 4 (Debt Ratio).* New Blue Corp. has $1,000,000 of convertible bonds payable outstanding, with a bond premium of $20,000 also on the books. The bondholders have notified New Blue that they wish to convert the bonds into stock. Specifically, the bonds may be converted into 200,000 shares of New Blue's $1 par common stock.

1. What is New Blue's carrying amount of its convertible bonds payable prior to the conversion?
2. Journalize New Blue's conversion of the bonds payable into common stock. No explanation is required.
3. How will the conversion affect New Blue's debt ratio?

Reporting liabilities
(Obj. 4)

S15-15 Suburban Magazine, Inc., includes the following selected accounts in its general ledger at December 31, 20X8:

Notes payable, long-term........	$100,000	Accounts payable...............	$19,000
Bonds payable.................	350,000	Discount on bonds	
Interest payable (due next year)..	7,000	payable (all long-term)	6,000

Prepare the liabilities section of Suburban Magazine, Inc.'s balance sheet at December 31, 20X8, to show how the company would report these items. Report a total for current liabilities.

S15-16 Leather Products, Inc. (LPI), needs to raise $1 million to expand company operations. LPI's president is considering two plans:

Earnings-per-share effects of financing with bonds versus stock
(Obj. 5)

- Plan A: $1,000,000 of 8% bonds payable to borrow the money
- Plan B: 100,000 shares of common stock at $10 per share

Before any new financing, LPI expects to earn net income of $500,000, and the company already has 100,000 shares of common stock outstanding. LPI believes the expansion will increase income before interest and income tax by $200,000. LPI's income tax rate is 35%.

    Prepare an analysis similar to Exhibit 15-8 to determine which plan is likely to result in the higher earnings per share. Which financing plan would you recommend for LPI?

Exercises

E15-1 Neptune Corporation issued 8%, 20-year bonds payable with a maturity value of $500,000 on March 31. The bonds were issued at 100 and pay interest on March 31 and September 30. Record (a) issuance of the bonds on March 31, (b) payment of interest on September 30, and (c) accrual of interest on December 31.

Issuing bonds payable, paying and accruing interest
(Obj. 1)

E15-2 On January 1, Quest Corp. issues 8%, 20-year bonds payable with a maturity value of $100,000. The bonds sell at 98 and pay interest on January 1 and July 1. Quest amortizes bond discount by the straight-line method. Record (a) issuance of the bonds on January 1, and (b) the semiannual interest payment on July 1.

Issuing bonds payable, paying interest, and amortizing discount by the straight-line method
(Obj. 1)

E15-3 Sandia, Inc., issued $100,000 of 10-year, 6% bonds payable on January 1, 20X6. Sandia pays interest each January 1 and July 1 and amortizes discount or premium by the straight-line method. The company can issue its bonds payable under various conditions:

Bond transactions at par, at a discount, and at a premium
(Obj. 1)

a. Issuance at par (maturity) value
b. Issuance at a price of 95
c. Issuance at a price of 105

Required

1. Journalize Sandia's issuance of the bonds and first semiannual interest payment for each situation. Explanations are not required.
2. Which method results in the most interest expense for Sandia? Explain in detail.

E15-4 All Star Productions is planning to issue long-term bonds payable to borrow for a major expansion. The chief executive, Marty Boyd, asks your advice on some related matters, as follows:

Determining whether the bond price will be at par, at a discount, or at a premium
(Obj. 1)

a. The stated interest rate on the bonds is 7%, and the market interest rate is 8%. What type of price can All Star expect for the bonds?
b. All Star could raise the stated interest rate on the bonds to 9% (market rate is 8%). In that case, what type of price can All Star expect for the bonds?
c. At what type of bond price will All Star have total interest expense equal to the cash interest payments?
d. Under which type of price will All Star's total interest expense be less than the cash interest payments?
e. Under which type of price will All Star's total interest expense be greater than the cash interest payments?

Effective-interest method for bond discount; recording interest payments and interest expense
(Obj. 2)

tudent Resource**CD**

spreadsheet

E15-5 Autorama Corp. is authorized to issue 7%, 10-year bonds payable. On January 2, 20X4, when the market interest rate is 8%, the company issues $300,000 of the bonds and receives cash of $279,600. Autorama amortizes bond discount by the effective-interest method. Interest dates are January 2 and July 2.

Required

1. Prepare an amortization table for the first two semiannual interest periods. Follow the format of Exhibit 15-4.
2. Record issuance of the bonds payable and the first semiannual interest payment on July 2.

Effective-interest method for bond premium; recording interest accrual and payment and the related interest expense
(Obj. 2)

tudent Resource**CD**

spreadsheet

E15-6 On March 31, 20X2, the market interest rate is 7%. First Federal Bank issues $200,000 of 8%, 20-year bonds payable at 110. The bonds pay interest on March 31 and September 30. First Federal measures interest expense by the effective-interest method.

Required

1. Prepare an amortization table for the first two semiannual interest periods. Follow the format of Exhibit 15-6, Panel B.
2. Record issuance of the bonds on March 31, 20X2, and the semiannual interest payment on September 30.

Debt payment and discount amortization schedule
(Obj. 2)

tudent Resource**CD**

spreadsheet

E15-7 Einstein Productions issued $500,000 of 8 3/8% (0.08375), five-year bonds payable when the market interest rate was 9 1/2% (0.095). Einstein pays interest annually at year-end. The issue price of the bonds was $478,402.

Required

Create a spreadsheet model to prepare a schedule to measure interest expense on these bonds. Use the effective-interest method of amortization. Round to the nearest dollar, and format your answer as follows:

	A	B	C	D	E	F
1						
2						**Bond**
3		**Interest**	**Interest**	**Discount**	**Discount**	**Carrying**
4	**Date**	**Payment**	**Expense**	**Amortization**	**Balance**	**Amount**
5	1-1-X1				$	$478,402
6	12-31-X1	$	$	$		
7	12-31-X2					
8	12-31-X3					
9	12-31-X4					
10	12-31-X5					
		500000*.08375	+F5*.095	+C6–B6	500000–F5	+F5+D6

Issuing bonds between interest dates
(Obj. 1)

E15-8 Refer to the data for Neptune Corporation in Exercise 15-1. If Neptune issued the bonds payable on June 30, how much cash would Neptune receive upon issuance of the bonds?

Issuing bonds between interest dates and paying interest
(Obj. 1)

E15-9 Newton, Inc., issues $400,000 of 6%, 20-year bonds payable that are dated April 30. Record (a) issuance of bonds at par on May 31 and (b) the next semiannual interest payment on October 31.

Recording retirement of bonds payable
(Obj. 3)

E15-10 Microdot Printing issued $600,000 of 8% bonds payable at 97 on October 1, 20X0. These bonds mature on October 1, 20X8, and are callable at 102. Microdot pays interest each April 1 and October 1. On October 1, 20X5, when the bonds' market price is 101, Microdot retires the bonds in the most economical way available.

Required

Record the payment of the interest and amortization of bond discount at October 1, 20X5, and the retirement of the bonds on that date. Microdot uses the straight-line amortization method.

E15-11 Jacobs-Cathey Company issued $700,000 of 15-year, 8 1/2% bonds payable on July 31, 20X3, at a price of 98. The bonds may be converted into the company's common stock. Each $1,000 maturity amount of the bonds is convertible into 40 shares of $20 par stock. On July 31, 20X9, bondholders converted bonds into common stock.

Recording conversion of bonds payable **(Obj. 3)**

Required

1. What would cause the bondholders to convert their bonds into common stock?
2. Without making journal entries, compute the carrying amount of the bonds payable at July 31, 20X9. Jacobs-Cathey uses the straight-line method to amortize bond discount.
3. All amortization has been recorded properly. Journalize the conversion transaction at July 31, 20X9. No explanation is required.

E15-12 Shaker Village Food Industries reported the following at September 30:

Recording early retirement and conversion of bonds payable **(Obj. 3)**

Long-term liabilities:		
Convertible bonds payable	$400,000	
Less: Discount on bonds payable	(12,000)	$388,000

Required

1. Record retirement of half of the bonds on October 1 at the call price of 101.
2. Record conversion of the remainder of the bonds into 10,000 shares of Shaker Village's $5 par common stock on October 1. What would cause the bondholders to convert their bonds into stock?

E15-13 At December 31, Crestview Carpets owes $50,000 on accounts payable, plus salary payable of $14,000 and income tax payable of $8,000. Crestview also has $300,000 of bonds payable that require payment of a $30,000 installment next year and the remainder in later years. The bonds payable also require an interest payment of $7,000 at the end of each year.

Reporting liabilities **(Obj. 4)**

  Report Crestview's liabilities on its year-end classified balance sheet. List liabilities in descending order (largest first, and so on).

E15-14 OK Copiers is considering two plans for raising $1,000,000 to expand operations. Plan A is to borrow at 9%, and plan B is to issue 100,000 shares of common stock. Before any new financing, OK has net income of $600,000 and 100,000 shares of common stock outstanding. Management believes the company can use the new funds to earn additional income of $420,000 before interest and taxes. The income tax rate is 40%.

Analyzing alternative plans for raising money **(Obj. 5)**

Required

Analyze OK Copiers' situation to determine which plan will result in higher earnings per share. Use Exhibit 15-8 as a guide.

E15-15 This (partial and adapted) advertisement appeared in *The Wall Street Journal.*

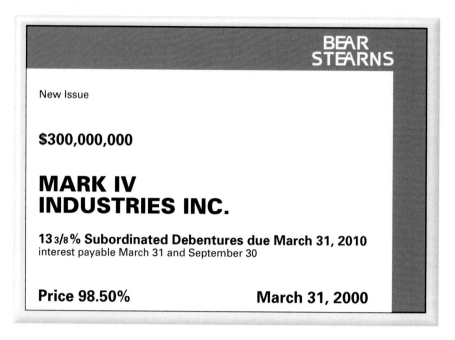

New Issue

$300,000,000

MARK IV
INDUSTRIES INC.

13 3/8% Subordinated Debentures due March 31, 2010
interest payable March 31 and September 30

Price 98.50%   **March 31, 2000**

A *subordinated* debenture gives rights to the bondholder that are more restricted than the rights of other bondholders.

Required

Answer these questions about **Mark IV Industries'** debenture bonds payable:

1. Suppose Mark IV Industries issued these bonds payable at their offering price on March 31, 2000. Describe the transaction in detail, indicating who received cash, who paid cash, and how much.
2. Why is the stated interest rate on these bonds so high?
3. Compute Mark IV Industries' annual cash interest payment on the bonds.
4. Compute Mark IV Industries' annual interest expense under the straight-line amortization method.
5. Prepare an effective-interest amortization table for Mark IV Industries' first two interest payments on September 30, 2000, and March 31, 2001. Use Exhibit 15-4 as a guide and show all amounts in thousands. The market rate of interest on the bonds is 13.65% per year.
6. Compute Mark IV Industries interest expense for the first full year ended March 31, 2001, under the effective-interest method. Use the amortization table you prepared for requirement 5.

E15-16 Refer to the bond situation of **Mark IV Industries** in Exercise 15-15. Assume Mark IV Industries issued the bonds at the advertised price and that the company uses the straight-line amortization method and reports financial statements on a calendar-year basis.

Required

1. Journalize the following bond transactions of Mark IV Industries. Show all amounts in thousands of dollars. Explanations are not required.

2000	
Mar. 31	Issuance of the bonds.
Sep. 30	Payment of interest expense and amortization of discount on bonds payable.

2. What is Mark IV Industries' carrying amount of the bonds payable at
   a. September 30, 2000?   b. March 31, 2001?

Problems

(Group A)

P15-1A Mill Creek Golf Club issued $600,000 of 20-year, 9% bonds payable at maturity (par) value on February 1, 20X3. The bonds pay interest each January 31 and July 31, and the company ends its accounting year on December 31.

Analyzing bonds, recording bond transactions at par, and reporting on the financial statements
(Obj. 1, 4)

Student ResourceCD
General Ledger, Peachtree, QuickBooks

1. Fill in the blanks to complete these statements:
   a. Mill Creek's bonds are priced at (express the price as a percentage) ____.
   b. When Mill Creek issued its bonds, the market interest rate was ____%.
   c. The amount of bond discount or premium for Mill Creek to account for is $____ because the bonds were issued at ____.
2. Journalize for Mill Creek
   a. Issuance of the bonds payable on February 1, 20X3.
   b. Payment of interest on July 31, 20X3.
   c. Accrual of interest at December 31, 20X3.
   d. Payment of interest on January 31, 20X4.
   Explanations are not required.
3. Show what Mill Creek Golf Club will report on its income statement for the year ended December 31, 20X3, and on its balance sheet at December 31, 20X3.

P15-2A Assume that on April 1, 20X6, **Goretex Corp.** issues 8%, 10-year notes payable with maturity value of $400,000. The notes pay interest on March 31 and September 30, and Goretex amortizes premium and discount by the straight-line method.

Issuing notes payable and amortizing premium by the straight-line method
(Obj. 1)

Required

1. If the market interest rate is 7 1/2% when Goretex issues its notes, will the notes be priced at maturity (par) value, at a premium, or at a discount? Explain.
2. If the market interest rate is 9% when Goretex issues its notes, will the notes be priced at par, at a premium, or at a discount? Explain.
3. Assume that the issue price of the notes is 101. Journalize the following note payable transactions:
   a. Issuance of the notes on April 1, 20X6.
   b. Payment of interest and amortization of premium on September 30, 20X6.
   c. Accrual of interest and amortization of premium on December 31, 20X6.
   d. Payment of interest and amortization of premium on March 31, 20X7.

P15-3A Global Positioning System (GPS) finances operations with both bonds and stock. Suppose GPS issued $200,000 of 10-year, 8% bonds payable under various market conditions. Match each market interest rate with the appropriate bond price, as follows:

Determining bond price; recording bond transactions by the straight-line amortization method
(Obj. 1, 3)

Market Interest Rate	Bond Price
7%	?
8%	?
9%	?

The three possible bond prices are $187,000; $200,000; and $214,000. GPS pays annual interest each December 31.

After determining the respective bond prices, make the following journal entries for the bond premium situation (explanations are not required):

Dec. 31, 2008	Issuance of the bonds at a premium.
Dec. 31, 2009	Payment of interest and amortization of bond premium by the straight-line method.
Dec. 31, 2018	Payment of interest and amortization of bond premium by the straight-line method.
Dec. 31, 2018	Final payment of the bonds payable.

How much total interest expense will GPS have during the 10-year life of these bonds?

Analyzing a company's long-term debt and journalizing its transactions
(Obj. 2)

P15-4A The balance sheet of Cellular Tracking Company reported the following data on September 30, Year 1, end of the fiscal year:

Long-Term Debt	
5% bonds payable, net of	
discount of $55,200 (market interest rate of 8%)	$144,800

Cellular Tracking uses the effective-interest amortization method.

Required

1. Answer the following questions about Cellular Tracking's bonds payable:
   a. What is the maturity value of the 5% bonds?
   b. What is the carrying amount of the 5% bonds at September 30, Year 1?
   c. What is Cellular Tracking's annual cash interest payment on the 5% bonds?
2. Prepare an amortization table through September 30, Year 3, for the 5% bonds. Cellular Tracking pays interest annually on September 30.
3. Record the September 30, Year 3, interest payment and amortization of the discount on the 5% bonds.
4. What is the carrying amount of the 5% bonds at September 30, Year 3, immediately after the interest payment?

Recording bonds (at par) and reporting bonds payable on the balance sheet—bonds issued between interest dates
(Obj. 1)

⊙ Student Resource**CD**

GL, PT, QB

P15-5A The board of directors of Alpha Communications authorizes the issuance of $3 million of 9%, 20-year bonds payable. The semiannual interest dates are March 31 and September 30. The bonds are issued on April 30, 20X4, at par plus accrued interest.

Required

1. Journalize the following transactions:
   a. Issuance of the bonds on April 30, 20X4.
   b. Payment of interest on September 30, 20X4.
   c. Accrual of interest on December 31, 20X4.
   d. Payment of interest on March 31, 20X5.
2. Report interest payable and bonds payable as they would appear on the Alpha balance sheet at December 31, 20X4.

Issuing convertible bonds at a discount, using the effective-interest method, retiring bonds early, and reporting on the balance sheet
(Obj. 2, 3, 4)

⊙ Student Resource**CD**

GL, PT, QB

P15-6A On December 31, 20X7, Bible Distributing Company issues 8%, 10-year convertible bonds with a maturity value of $700,000. The semiannual interest dates are June 30 and December 31. The market interest rate is 9%, and the issue price of the bonds is 94. Bible Distributing Company amortizes bond premium and discount by the effective-interest method.

Required

1. Prepare an effective-interest-method amortization table for the first four semiannual interest periods.
2. Journalize the following transactions:
   a. Issuance of the bonds on December 31, 20X7. Credit Convertible Bonds Payable.
   b. Payment of interest on June 30, 20X8.
   c. Payment of interest on December 31, 20X8.
   d. Retirement of bonds with maturity value of $100,000 on December 31, 20X9. Bible Distributing Company purchases the bonds at 98 in the open market.
3. Prepare a balance sheet presentation of the bonds payable that are outstanding at December 31, 20X9.

Reporting liabilities on the balance sheet
(Obj. 4)

P15-7A The accounting records of Far Side Productions, Inc., include the following items:

Salary payable	$32,000	Accounts payable	$ 60,000
Bonds payable, current		Mortgage note payable—	
portion	25,000	long-term	90,000
Discount on bonds payable		Interest payable	19,000
(all long-term)	7,000	Bonds payable, long-term . .	300,000
Income tax payable	16,000		

Required

Report these liabilities on Far Side Productions' balance sheet, including headings and totals for current liabilities and long-term liabilities.

P15-8A Market surveys show that consumers prefer upscale restaurants. To capitalize on this trend, Palomino, Inc., is embarking on a massive expansion. Plans call for opening 20 new restaurants within the next two years. Each restaurant is scheduled to be 30% larger than the company's existing locations and feature upgraded menus. Management estimates that company operations will provide $3 million of the cash needed for expansion. Palomino must raise the remaining $1.5 million from outsiders. The board of directors is considering obtaining the $1.5 million either through borrowing or by issuing common stock.

Financing operations with debt or with stock
(Obj. 5)

Required

1. Write a memo to company management. Discuss the advantages and disadvantages of borrowing and of issuing common stock to raise the needed cash. Use the following format for your memo:

Date: _____	
To: Management of Palomino, Inc.	
From: <u>Student Name</u>	
Subject: Advantages and disadvantages of borrowing versus issuing stock to raise $1.5 million for expansion	
Advantages and disadvantages of borrowing:	
Advantages and disadvantages of issuing stock:	

2. How will what you learned in this problem help you manage a business?

Problems

(Group B)

P15-1B McLaren Ford Sales issued $500,000 of 10-year, 8% bonds payable at maturity (par) value on May 1, 20X5. The bonds pay interest each April 30 and October 31, and the company ends its accounting year on December 31.

Analyzing bonds, recording bonds at par, and reporting on the financial statements
(Obj. 1, 4)

Student Resource **CD**
GL, PT, QB

Required

1. Fill in the blanks to complete these statements:
   a. McLaren's bonds are priced at (express the price as a percentage) _____.
   b. When McLaren issued its bonds, the market interest rate was _____%.
   c. The amount of bond discount or premium for McLaren to account for is $ _____ because the bonds were issued at _____.

2. Journalize for McLaren
   a. Issuance of the bonds payable on May 1, 20X5.
   b. Payment of interest on October 31, 20X5.
   c. Accrual of interest at December 31, 20X5.
   d. Payment of interest on April 30, 20X6.
   Explanations are not required.

3. Show what McLaren will report on its income statement for 20X5 and on its balance sheet at December 31, 20X5.

Issuing bonds and amortizing discount by the straight-line method
(Obj. 1)

P15-2B On March 1, 20X4, CD Warehouse issues 8 1/4%, 20-year bonds payable with maturity value of $400,000. The bonds pay interest on February 28 and August 31. CD Warehouse amortizes premium and discount by the straight-line method.

Required

1. If the market interest rate is 7 3/8% when CD Warehouse issues its bonds, will the bonds be priced at maturity (par) value, at a premium, or at a discount? Explain.

2. If the market interest rate is 8 7/8% when CD Warehouse issues its bonds, will the bonds be priced at par, at a premium, or at a discount? Explain.

3. The issue price of the bonds is 96. Journalize the following bond transactions:
   a. Issuance of the bonds on March 1, 20X4.
   b. Payment of interest and amortization of discount on August 31, 20X4.
   c. Accrual of interest and amortization of discount on December 31, 20X4.
   d. Payment of interest and amortization of discount on February 28, 20X5.

Determining bond price, recording bond transactions by the straight-line amortization method
(Obj. 1, 3)

P15-3B **UPS** finances operations with both bonds and stock. Suppose UPS issued $500,000 of 10-year, 7% bonds payable under various market conditions. Match each market interest rate with the appropriate bond price, as follows:

Market Interest Rate	Bond Price
6%	?
7%	?
8%	?

The three possible bond prices are $500,000; $537,000; and $466,000. Assume that UPS pays annual interest each December 31.

After determining the respective bond prices, make the following journal entries for the bond discount situation (explanations are not required):

Dec. 31, 2004	Issuance of the bonds at a discount.
Dec. 31, 2005	Payment of interest and amortization of bond discount by the straight-line method.
Dec. 31, 2014	Payment of interest and amortization of bond discount by the straight-line method.
Dec. 31, 2014	Final payment of the bonds payable.

How much total interest expense will UPS have during the 10-year life of these bonds?

Analyzing a company's long-term debt and journalizing its transactions
(Obj. 2)

P15-4B **MUNY** Digital's balance sheet reported the following data on September 30, Year 1, end of the fiscal year:

Long-Term Debt:
6.00% bonds payable with a
market interest rate of 8.00%, net of discount of $35,200 .... $164,800

MUNY Digital uses the effective-interest amortization method.

Required

1. Answer the following questions about MUNY Digital's bonds payable:
   a. What is the maturity value of the 6.00% bonds?
   b. What is the carrying amount of the 6.00% bonds at September 30, Year 1?
   c. What is MUNY's annual cash interest payment on the 6.00% bonds?

2. Prepare an amortization table through September 30, Year 3, for the 6.00% bonds. MUNY pays interest annually on September 30.

3. Record the September 30, Year 3 interest payment and amortization of the discount on the 6.00% bonds.

4. What is the carrying amount of the 6% bonds at September 30, Year 3, immediately after the interest payment?

P15-5B The board of directors of Galaxy Production Company authorizes the issuance of $8 million of 7%, 10-year bonds payable. The semiannual interest dates are May 31 and November 30. The bonds are issued on August 31, 20X5, at par plus accrued interest.

Recording bonds (at par) and reporting bonds payable on the balance sheet—bond issued between interest dates
(Obj. 1)

GL, PT, QB

Required

1. Journalize the following transactions:
   a. Issuance of the bonds on August 31, 20X5.
   b. Payment of interest on November 30, 20X5.
   c. Accrual of interest on December 31, 20X5.
   d. Payment of interest on May 31, 20X6.
2. Report interest payable and bonds payable as they would appear on the Galaxy balance sheet at December 31, 20X5.

P15-6B On December 31, 20X7, Early Bird Wireless, Inc., issues 9%, 10-year convertible bonds with a maturity value of $500,000. The semiannual interest dates are June 30 and December 31. The market interest rate is 8%, and the issue price of the bonds is 106.8. Early Bird measures interest expense by the effective-interest method.

Issuing convertible bonds at a premium, using the effective-interest method, retiring bonds early, and reporting on the balance sheet
(Obj. 2, 3, 4)

GL, PT, QB

Required

1. Prepare an effective-interest-method amortization table for the first four semiannual interest periods.
2. Journalize the following transactions:
   a. Issuance of the bonds on December 31, 20X7. Credit Convertible Bonds Payable.
   b. Payment of interest on June 30, 20X8.
   c. Payment of interest on December 31, 20X8.
   d. Retirement of bonds with maturity value of $100,000 on December 31, 20X9. Early Bird pays the call price of 102.
3. Prepare the balance sheet presentation of the bonds payable that are outstanding at December 31, 20X9.

P15-7B The accounting records of Modern Language Associates include the following items:

Reporting liabilities on the balance sheet
(Obj. 4)

Salary payable	$ 9,000	Mortgage note payable,	
Bonds payable, long-term	160,000	long-term	$116,000
Premium on bonds payable		Accounts payable	54,000
(all long-term)	13,000	Bonds payable, current	
Unearned sales revenue	3,000	installment	20,000
		Interest payable	14,000

Required

Report these liabilities on Modern Language Associates' balance sheet, including headings and totals for current liabilities and long-term liabilities.

P15-8B Two businesses are considering how to raise $10 million.

Jefferson Corporation is having its best year since it began operations in 1980. For each of the past 10 years, earnings per share have increased by at least 15%. The outlook for the future is equally bright, with new markets opening up and competitors unable to manufacture products of Jefferson's quality. Jefferson Corporation is planning a large-scale expansion.

Madison Company has fallen on hard times. Net income has been flat for the last six years, with this year falling by 10% from last year's level of profits. Top management has experienced turnover, and the company lacks leadership. To become competitive again, Madison Company desperately needs $10 million for expansion.

Financing operations with debt or with stock
(Obj. 5)

Required

1. Propose a plan for each company to raise the needed cash. Which company should borrow? Which company should issue stock? Consider the advantages and the disadvantages of raising money by borrowing and by issuing stock, and discuss them in your answer. Use the following memorandum headings to report your plans for the two companies:
   - Plan for Madison Company to raise $10 million
   - Plan for Jefferson Corporation to raise $10 million

2. How will what you learned in this problem help you manage a business?

APPLY *Your Knowledge*

Decision Cases

Analyzing alternative ways of raising
$4 million
(Obj. 5)

Case 1. Business is going well for Email Designers. The board of directors of this family-owned company believes that Email Designers could earn an additional $1,000,000 income before interest and taxes by expanding into new markets. However, the $4,000,000 the business needs for growth cannot be raised within the family. The directors, who strongly wish to retain family control of the company, must issue securities to outsiders. They are considering three financing plans.

Plan A is to borrow at 6%. Plan B is to issue 100,000 shares of common stock. Plan C is to issue 100,000 shares of nonvoting, $2.50 preferred stock ($2.50 is the annual cash dividend for each share of preferred stock). Email Designers currently has net income of $2,000,000 and 400,000 shares of common stock outstanding. The company's income tax rate is 35%.

Required

1. Prepare an analysis similar to Exhibit 15-8 to determine which plan will result in the highest earnings per share of common stock.

2. Recommend one plan to the board of directors. Give your reasons.

Questions about long-term debt
(Obj. 1, 4 and Appendix to Chapter 15)

Case 2. → *Link Back to Chapter 4 (Debt Ratio).* The following questions are not related.

1. **IMAX Theater Corp.** needs to borrow $2 million to open new theaters. IMAX can borrow $2 million by issuing 8%, 20-year bonds at a price of 96. How much will IMAX actually be borrowing under this arrangement? How much must IMAX pay back at maturity? How will IMAX account for the difference between the amount borrowed and the amount paid back?

2. IMAX Corporation likes to borrow for longer periods when interest rates are low and for shorter periods when interest rates are high. Why is this a good business strategy?

Ethical Issue

Python.com owes $6 million on notes payable that will come due for payment in $1.5 million annual installments. The company has used its cash to advertise heavily in the competitive dotcom business environment. The result is that cash is scarce, and Python.com's management doesn't know where next year's note payment will come from. Python.com has prepared its balance sheet at December 31, 20X4, and it reports the following:

Liabilities	
Current:	
Accounts payable	$1,900,000
Salary payable and other accrued liabilities	300,000
Unearned revenue collected in advance	500,000
Income tax payable	200,000
Total current liabilities	2,900,000
Long-term:	
Notes payable	6,000,000

What is wrong with the way Python.com reported its liabilities? Why did Python.com report its liabilities this way? What is unethical about this way of reporting *these* liabilities? Who can be harmed as a result?

Financial Statement Case

The **Amazon.com** balance sheet, income statement (statement of operation's), and Note 6 in Appendix A provide details about the company's long-term debt. Use those data to answer the following questions.

Analyzing long-term debt
(Obj. 1, 2)

Required

1. How much did Amazon.com owe on long-term debt at December 31, 2002? How much of this debt was payable in the coming year?

2. Journalize in a single entry Amazon's interest expense for 2002. Amazon paid cash of $139,896 thousand for interest.

3. Refer to Note 6 and compute the annual interest on Amazon's 4.75% convertible subordinated notes. Round to the nearest $1 thousand.

Team Project

Note: This project uses the chapter appendix.

Bermuda Corporation leases the equipment that it uses in operations. Bermuda prefers operating leases (versus capital leases) in order to keep the lease liability off its balance sheet and maintain a low debt ratio.

Bermuda is negotiating a 10-year lease on equipment with an expected useful life of 15 years. The lease requires Bermuda to make 10 annual lease payments of $20,000 each, due at the end of each year, plus a down payment that is due at the beginning of the lease term. The interest rate in the lease agreement is 10%. The leased asset has a market value of $160,000. The lease agreement specifies no transfer to title to the lessee and includes no bargain purchase option.

Write a report for Bermuda's management to explain how Bermuda should account for this lease—as an operating lease or as a capital lease. Use the following format for your report:

Date: _____	
To: Bermuda Management	
From: Student Names	
Subject: Accounting for the company's equipment lease	

For Internet exercises, go to the Web site www.prenhall.com/horngren.

APPENDIX *to Chapter 15*

Time Value of Money: Future Value and Present Value

This discussion of future value lays the foundation for present value but is not essential. For the valuation of long-term liabilities, some instructors may wish to begin in the middle of page 619.

The term *time value of money* refers to the fact that money earns interest over time. Interest is the cost of using money. To borrowers, interest is the expense of renting money. To lenders, interest is the revenue earned from lending. We must recognize the interest. Otherwise we overlook an important part of the transaction.

Suppose you invest $4,545 in corporate bonds that pay 10% interest each year. After one year, the value of your investment has grown to $5,000. The difference between your original investment ($4,545) and its future value ($5,000) is the amount of interest revenue you will earn ($455). Interest becomes more important as the time period lengthens because the amount of interest depends on how long the money is invested.

Let's consider a second example, but from the borrower's perspective. Suppose you purchase a machine for your business. The cash price of the machine is $8,000, but you cannot pay cash now. To finance the purchase, you sign an $8,000 note payable. The note requires you to pay the $8,000 plus 10% interest one year from the date of purchase. Is your cost of the machine $8,000, or is it $8,800 [$8,000 plus interest of $800 ($8,000 × 0.10)]? The cost is $8,000. The additional $800 is interest expense, which is not part of the cost of the machine.

Future Value

The main application of future value is the accumulated balance of an investment at a future date. In our first example, the investment earned 10% per year. After one year, $4,545 grew to $5,000, as shown in Exhibit 15A-1.

Exhibit 15A-1

Future Value

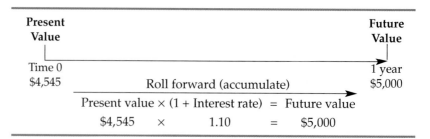

Present Value		Future Value
Time 0		1 year
$4,545	Roll forward (accumulate)	$5,000

Present value × (1 + Interest rate) = Future value
$4,545 × 1.10 = $5,000

If the money were invested for five years, you would have to perform five such calculations. You would also have to consider the compound interest your investment is earning. *Compound interest* is the interest you earn not only on your principal amount, but also on the interest to date. Most business applications include compound interest. The following table shows the interest revenue earned each year at 10%:

End of Year	Interest	Future Value
0	—	$4,545
1	$4,545 × 0.10 = $455	5,000
2	5,000 × 0.10 = 500	5,500

Earning 10%, a $4,545 investment grows to $5,000 at the end of one year, to $5,500 at the end of two years, and so on. (Throughout this discussion, we round dollar amounts to the nearest dollar.)

Future-Value Tables The process of computing a future value is called *accumulating* because the future value is *more* than the present value. Mathematical tables ease the computational burden. Exhibit 15A-2, Future Value of $1, gives the future value for a single sum (a present value), $1, invested to earn a particular interest rate for a specific number of periods. Future value depends on three factors: (1) the amount of the investment, (2) the length of time between investment and future accumulation, and (3) the interest rate.

Exhibit 15A-2   Future Value of $1

					Future Value of $1					
Period	4%	5%	6%	7%	8%	9%	10%	12%	14%	16%
1	1.040	1.050	1.060	1.070	1.080	1.090	1.100	1.120	1.140	1.160
2	1.082	1.103	1.124	1.145	1.166	1.188	1.210	1.254	1.300	1.346
3	1.125	1.158	1.191	1.225	1.260	1.295	1.331	1.405	1.482	1.561
4	1.170	1.216	1.262	1.311	1.360	1.412	1.464	1.574	1.689	1.811
5	1.217	1.276	1.338	1.403	1.469	1.539	1.611	1.762	1.925	2.100
6	1.265	1.340	1.419	1.501	1.587	1.677	1.772	1.974	2.195	2.436
7	1.316	1.407	1.504	1.606	1.714	1.828	1.949	2.211	2.502	2.826
8	1.369	1.477	1.594	1.718	1.851	1.993	2.144	2.476	2.853	3.278
9	1.423	1.551	1.689	1.838	1.999	2.172	2.358	2.773	3.252	3.803
10	1.480	1.629	1.791	1.967	2.159	2.367	2.594	3.106	3.707	4.411
11	1.539	1.710	1.898	2.105	2.332	2.580	2.853	3.479	4.226	5.117
12	1.601	1.796	2.012	2.252	2.518	2.813	3.138	3.896	4.818	5.936
13	1.665	1.886	2.133	2.410	2.720	3.066	3.452	4.363	5.492	6.886
14	1.732	1.980	2.261	2.579	2.937	3.342	3.797	4.887	6.261	7.988
15	1.801	2.079	2.397	2.759	3.172	3.642	4.177	5.474	7.138	9.266
16	1.873	2.183	2.540	2.952	3.426	3.970	4.595	6.130	8.137	10.748
17	1.948	2.292	2.693	3.159	3.700	4.328	5.054	6.866	9.276	12.468
18	2.026	2.407	2.854	3.380	3.996	4.717	5.560	7.690	10.575	14.463
19	2.107	2.527	3.026	3.617	4.316	5.142	6.116	8.613	12.056	16.777
20	2.191	2.653	3.207	3.870	4.661	5.604	6.727	9.646	13.743	19.461

The heading in Exhibit 15A-2 states $1. Future-value and present-value tables are based on $1 because unity (the value 1) is so easy to work with. Look at the Period column and the interest-rate columns 4–16%. In business applications, interest rates are always stated for the annual period of one year unless specified otherwise. In fact, an interest rate can be stated for any period, such as 3% per quarter or 5% for a six-month period. The length of the period is arbitrary.

An investment may promise a return (income) of 3% per quarter for six months (two quarters). In that case, you would be working with 3% interest for two periods. It would be incorrect to use 6% for one period because the interest is 3% compounded quarterly, and that amount differs from 6% compounded semi-annually. Take care in studying future-value and present-value problems to align the interest rate with the appropriate number of periods.

Let's use Exhibit 15A-2. The future value of $1.00 invested at 8% for one year is $1.08 ($1.00 × 1.080, which appears at the junction under the 8% column and across from 1 in the Period column). The figure 1.080 includes both the principal (1.000) and the compound interest for one period (0.080).

Suppose you deposit $5,000 in a savings account that pays annual interest of 8%. The account balance at the end of one year will be $5,400. To compute the future value of $5,000 at 8% for one year, multiply $5,000 by 1.080 to get $5,400. Now suppose you invest in a 10-year, 8% certificate of deposit (CD). What will be the future value of the CD at maturity? To compute the future value of $5,000 at 8% for 10 periods, multiply $5,000 by 2.159 (from Exhibit 15A-2) to get $10,795.

This future value of $10,795 indicates that $5,000 earning 8% interest compounded annually grows to $10,795 at the end of 10 years. You can find any present amount's future value at a particular future date.

Future Value of an Annuity In the preceding example, we made an investment of a single amount. Other investments, called annuities, include multiple investments of an equal periodic amount at fixed intervals over the duration of the investment. Consider a family investing for a child's education. The Dietrichs can invest $4,000 annually to accumulate a college fund for 15-year-old Helen. The investment can earn 7% annually until Helen turns 18—a three-year investment. How much will be available for Helen on the date of the last investment? Exhibit 15A-3 shows the accumulation—a total future value of $12,860.

Exhibit 15A-3

Future Value of an Annuity

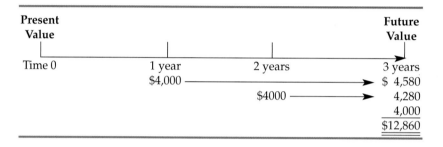

The first $4,000 invested by the Dietrichs grows to $4,580 over the investment period. The second amount grows to $4,280, and the third amount stays at $4,000 because it has no time to earn interest. The sum of the three future values ($4,580 + $4,280 + $4,000) is the future value of the annuity ($12,860), which can be computed as follows:

End of Year	Annual Investment	+	Interest	=	Increase for the Year	Future Value of Annuity
0	—		—		—	0
1	$4,000		—		$4,000	$ 4,000
2	4,000	+	($4,000 × 0.07 = $280)	=	4,280	8,280
3	4,000	+	($8,280 × 0.07 = $580)	=	4,580	12,860

As with the Future Value of $1 table (a lump sum), mathematical tables ease the strain of calculating annuities. Exhibit 15A-4, Future Value of Annuity of $1, gives the future value of a series of investments, each of equal amount, at regular intervals.

What is the future value of an annuity of three investments of $1 each that earn 7%? The answer 3.215 can be found in the 7% column and across from 3 in the Period column of Exhibit 15A-4. This amount can be used to compute the future value of the investment for Helen's education, as follows:

AMOUNT OF EACH PERIODIC INVESTMENT	×	FUTURE VALUE OF ANNUITY OF $1 (EXHIBIT 15A-4)	=	FUTURE VALUE OF INVESTMENT
$4,000	×	3.215	=	$12,860

This one-step calculation is much easier than computing the future value of each annual investment and then summing the individual future values. You can compute the future value of any investment consisting of equal periodic amounts at regular intervals. Businesses make periodic investments to accumulate funds for plant expansion and other uses—an application of the future value of an annuity.

Exhibit 15A-4   Future Value of Annuity of $1

Future Value of Annuity of $1

Period	4%	5%	6%	7%	8%	9%	10%	12%	14%	16%
1	1.000	1.000	1.000	1.000	1.000	1.000	1.000	1.000	1.000	1.000
2	2.040	2.050	2.060	2.070	2.080	2.090	2.100	2.120	2.140	2.160
3	3.122	3.153	3.184	3.215	3.246	3.278	3.310	3.374	3.440	3.506
4	4.246	4.310	4.375	4.440	4.506	4.573	4.641	4.779	4.921	5.066
5	5.416	5.526	5.637	5.751	5.867	5.985	6.105	6.353	6.610	6.877
6	6.633	6.802	6.975	7.153	7.336	7.523	7.716	8.115	8.536	8.977
7	7.898	8.142	8.394	8.654	8.923	9.200	9.487	10.089	10.730	11.414
8	9.214	9.549	9.897	10.260	10.637	11.028	11.436	12.300	13.233	14.240
9	10.583	11.027	11.491	11.978	12.488	13.021	13.579	14.776	16.085	17.519
10	12.006	12.578	13.181	13.816	14.487	15.193	15.937	17.549	19.337	21.321
11	13.486	14.207	14.972	15.784	16.645	17.560	18.531	20.655	23.045	25.733
12	15.026	15.917	16.870	17.888	18.977	20.141	21.384	24.133	27.271	30.850
13	16.627	17.713	18.882	20.141	21.495	22.953	24.523	28.029	32.089	36.786
14	18.292	19.599	21.015	22.550	24.215	26.019	27.975	32.393	37.581	43.672
15	20.024	21.579	23.276	25.129	27.152	29.361	31.772	37.280	43.842	51.660
16	21.825	23.657	25.673	27.888	30.324	33.003	35.950	42.753	50.980	60.925
17	23.698	25.840	28.213	30.840	33.750	36.974	40.545	48.884	59.118	71.673
18	25.645	28.132	30.906	33.999	37.450	41.301	45.599	55.750	68.394	84.141
19	27.671	30.539	33.760	37.379	41.446	46.018	51.159	63.440	78.969	98.603
20	29.778	33.066	36.786	40.995	45.762	51.160	57.275	72.052	91.025	115.380

Present Value

Often a person knows a future amount and needs to know the related present value. Recall Exhibit 15A-1, in which present value and future value are on opposite ends of the same time line. Suppose an investment promises to pay you $5,000 at the *end* of one year. How much would you pay *now* to acquire this investment? You would be willing to pay the present value of the $5,000 future amount.

Present value also depends on three factors: (1) the amount of the future payment (or receipt), (2) the time span between investment and future receipt (or payment), and (3) the interest rate. Computing a present value is called *discounting* because the present value is *always less* than the future value.

In our example, the future receipt is $5,000. The investment period is one year. Assume that you demand an annual interest rate of 10% on your investment. With all three factors specified, you can compute the present value of $5,000 at 10% for one year.

$$\frac{\text{Future value}}{(1 + \text{Interest rate})} = \frac{\$5,000}{1.10} = \$4,545$$

By turning the data around into a future-value problem, we verify the present-value computation:

Amount invested (present value)......................	$4,545
Expected earnings ($4,545 × 0.10)......................	455
Amount to be received one year from now (future value)..	$5,000

This example illustrates that present value and future value are based on the same equation:

$$\text{Present value} \times (1 + \text{Interest rate}) = \text{Future value}$$

$$\frac{\text{Future value}}{(1 + \text{Interest rate})} = \text{Present value}$$

If the $5,000 is to be received two years from now, you will pay only $4,132 for the investment, as shown in Exhibit 15A-5.

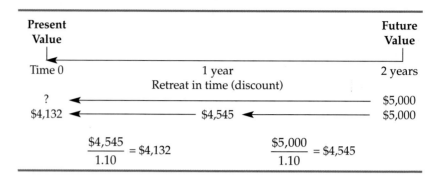

By turning the data around, we verify that $4,132 accumulates to $5,000 at 10% for two years:

Amount invested (present value)...............................	$4,132
Expected earnings for first year ($4,132 × 0.10)	413
Value of investment after one year.............................	4,545
Expected earnings for second year ($4,545 × 0.10).................	455
Amount to be received two years from now (future value).........	$5,000

You would pay $4,132—the present value of $5,000—to receive the $5,000 future amount at the end of two years at 10% per year. The $868 difference between the amount invested ($4,132) and the amount to be received ($5,000) is the return on the investment, the sum of the two interest receipts: $413 + $455 = $868.

Present-Value Tables We have shown the simple formula for computing present value. However, figuring present value "by hand" for investments spanning many years is burdensome. Present-value tables ease our work. Let's reexamine our examples of present value by using Exhibit 15A-6, Present Value of $1.

				Present Value of $1					
Period	**4%**	**5%**	**6%**	**7%**	**8%**	**10%**	**12%**	**14%**	**16%**
1	0.962	0.952	0.943	0.935	0.926	0.909	0.893	0.877	0.862
2	0.925	0.907	0.890	0.873	0.857	0.826	0.797	0.769	0.743
3	0.889	0.864	0.840	0.816	0.794	0.751	0.712	0.675	0.641
4	0.855	0.823	0.792	0.763	0.735	0.683	0.636	0.592	0.552
5	0.822	0.784	0.747	0.713	0.681	0.621	0.567	0.519	0.476
6	0.790	0.746	0.705	0.666	0.630	0.564	0.507	0.456	0.410
7	0.760	0.711	0.665	0.623	0.583	0.513	0.452	0.400	0.354
8	0.731	0.677	0.627	0.582	0.540	0.467	0.404	0.351	0.305
9	0.703	0.645	0.592	0.544	0.500	0.424	0.361	0.308	0.263
10	0.676	0.614	0.558	0.508	0.463	0.386	0.322	0.270	0.227
11	0.650	0.585	0.527	0.475	0.429	0.350	0.287	0.237	0.195
12	0.625	0.557	0.497	0.444	0.397	0.319	0.257	0.208	0.168
13	0.601	0.530	0.469	0.415	0.368	0.290	0.229	0.182	0.145
14	0.577	0.505	0.442	0.388	0.340	0.263	0.205	0.160	0.125
15	0.555	0.481	0.417	0.362	0.315	0.239	0.183	0.140	0.108
16	0.534	0.458	0.394	0.339	0.292	0.218	0.163	0.123	0.093
17	0.513	0.436	0.371	0.317	0.270	0.198	0.146	0.108	0.080
18	0.494	0.416	0.350	0.296	0.250	0.180	0.130	0.095	0.069
19	0.475	0.396	0.331	0.277	0.232	0.164	0.116	0.083	0.060
20	0.456	0.377	0.312	0.258	0.215	0.149	0.104	0.073	0.051

For the 10% investment for one year, we find the junction in the 10% column and across from 1 in the Period column. The figure 0.909 is computed as follows: $1/1.10 = 0.909$. This work has been done for us, and only the present values are given in the table. The heading in Exhibit 15A-6 states $1. To figure present value for $5,000, we multiply $5,000 by 0.909. The result is $4,545, which matches the result we obtained by hand.

For the two-year investment, we read down the 10% column and across the Period 2 row. We multiply 0.826 (computed as $0.909/1.10 = 0.826$) by $5,000 and get $4,130, which confirms our earlier computation of $4,132 (the difference is due to rounding in the present-value table). Using the table, we can compute the present value of any single future amount.

Present Value of an Annuity Let's return to the investment example that provided the investor with only a single future receipt ($5,000 at the end of two years). Annuity investments provide multiple receipts of an equal amount at fixed intervals over the investment's duration.

Consider an investment that promises *annual* cash receipts of $10,000 to be received at the end of each of three years. Assume that you demand a 12% return on your investment. What is the investment's present value? What would you pay today to acquire the investment? The investment spans three periods, and you would pay the sum of three present values. The computation follows.

The present value of this annuity is $24,020. By paying this amount today, you will receive $10,000 at the end of each of the three years while earning 12% on your investment.

Year	Annual Cash Receipt	×	Present Value of $1 at 12% (Exhibit 15A-6)	=	Present Value of Annual Cash Receipt
1	$10,000	×	0.893	=	$ 8,930
2	10,000	×	0.797	=	7,970
3	10,000	×	0.712	=	7,120
		Total present value of investment		=	$24,020

The example illustrates repetitive computations of the three future amounts. One way to ease the computational burden is to add the three present values of $1 (0.893 + 0.797 + 0.712) and multiply their sum (2.402) by the annual cash receipt ($10,000) to obtain the present value of the annuity ($10,000 × 2.402 = $24,020).

An easier approach is to use a present value of an annuity table. Exhibit 15A-7 on the next page shows the present value of $1 to be received at the end of each period for a given number of periods. The present value of a three-period annuity at 12% is 2.402 (the junction of the Period 3 row and the 12% column). Thus, $10,000 received annually at the end of each of three years, discounted at 12%, is $24,020 ($10,000 × 2.402), which is the present value.

Present Value of Bonds Payable The present value of a bond—its market price—is the present value of the future principal amount at maturity plus the present value of the future stated interest payments. The principal is a single amount to be paid at maturity. The interest is an annuity because it occurs periodically.

Let's compute the present value of the 9%, five-year bonds of **eBay Inc.** The maturity value of the bonds is $100,000, and they pay 4 1/2% stated (cash) interest semiannually. At issuance, the market interest rate is expressed as 10%, but it is computed at 5% semiannually. Therefore, the market interest rate for each of the 10 semi-

Exhibit 15A-7 | Present Value of Annuity of $1

Present Value of Annuity of $1

Period	4%	5%	6%	7%	8%	10%	12%	14%	16%
1	0.962	0.952	0.943	0.935	0.926	0.909	0.893	0.877	0.862
2	1.886	1.859	1.833	1.808	1.783	1.736	1.690	1.647	1.605
3	2.775	2.723	2.673	2.624	2.577	2.487	2.402	2.322	2.246
4	3.630	3.546	3.465	3.387	3.312	3.170	3.037	2.914	2.798
5	4.452	4.329	4.212	4.100	3.993	3.791	3.605	3.433	3.274
6	5.242	5.076	4.917	4.767	4.623	4.355	4.111	3.889	3.685
7	6.002	5.786	5.582	5.389	5.206	4.868	4.564	4.288	4.039
8	6.733	6.463	6.210	5.971	5.747	5.335	4.968	4.639	4.344
9	7.435	7.108	6.802	6.515	6.247	5.759	5.328	4.946	4.607
10	8.111	7.722	7.360	7.024	6.710	6.145	5.650	5.216	4.833
11	8.760	8.306	7.887	7.499	7.139	6.495	5.938	5.453	5.029
12	9.385	8.863	8.384	7.943	7.536	6.814	6.194	5.660	5.197
13	9.986	9.394	8.853	8.358	7.904	7.103	6.424	5.842	5.342
14	10.563	9.899	9.295	8.745	8.244	7.367	6.628	6.002	5.468
15	11.118	10.380	9.712	9.108	8.559	7.606	6.811	6.142	5.575
16	11.652	10.838	10.106	9.447	8.851	7.824	6.974	6.265	5.669
17	12.166	11.274	10.477	9.763	9.122	8.022	7.120	6.373	5.749
18	12.659	11.690	10.828	10.059	9.372	8.201	7.250	6.467	5.818
19	13.134	12.085	11.158	10.336	9.604	8.365	7.366	6.550	5.877
20	13.590	12.462	11.470	10.594	9.818	8.514	7.469	6.623	5.929

annual periods is 5%. We use 5% in computing the present value (PV) of the maturity and of the stated interest. The market price of these bonds is $96,149, as follows:

	Effective Annual Interest Rate ÷ 2	Number of Semiannual Interest Payments	
PV of principal:			
$100,000 × PV of single amount at 5%		for 10 periods	
($100,000 × 0.614—Exhibit 15A-6)			$61,400
PV of stated interest:			
($100,000 × 0.045) × PV of annuity at 5%		for 10 periods	
($4,500 × 7.722—Exhibit 15A-7)			34,749
PV (market price) of bonds			$96,149

The market price of the eBay bonds show a discount because the stated interest rate on the bonds (9%) is less than the market interest rate (10%). We discuss these bonds in more detail on pages 590–591.

Let's consider a premium price for the eBay bonds. Assume that the market interest rate is 8% at issuance. The market rate is 4% for each of the 10 semiannual periods:

	Effective Annual Interest Rate ÷ 2	Number of Semiannual Interest Periods	
PV of principal:			
$100,000 × PV of single amount at 4%		for 10 periods	
($100,000 × 0.676—Exhibit 15A-6)			$ 67,600
PV of stated interest:			
($100,000 × 0.045) × PV of annuity at 4%		for 10 periods	
($4,500 × 8.111—Exhibit 15A-7)			36,500
PV (market price) of bonds			$104,100

We discuss accounting for these bonds on page 591–592.

Appendix Assignments
Problems

P15A-1 Gordon Riley is considering two plans for building an education fund for his children.

Computing future values of investments

Plan A—Invest $2,000 each year to earn 10% annually for six years.

Plan B—Invest $10,000 now, to earn 8% annually for six years.

Which plan provides the larger amount at the end of six years? At the outset, which plan would you expect to provide the larger future amount?

P15A-2 Georgia-Atlantic Corp. needs new manufacturing equipment. Two companies can provide similar equipment but under different payment plans:

Computing present-value amounts

a. **General Electric (GE)** offers to let Georgia-Atlantic pay $60,000 each year for five years. The payments include interest at 12% per year. What is the present value of the payments?

b. **Westinghouse** will let Georgia-Atlantic make a single payment of $400,000 at the end of five years. This payment includes both principal and interest at 12%. What is the present value of this payment?

c. Georgia-Atlantic will purchase the equipment that costs the least, as measured by present value. Which equipment should Georgia-Atlantic select? Why?

P15A-3 This problem demonstrates the relationship between the future value of 1 and the present value of 1.

Relating future-value and present-value amounts

1. Rocky Tanner will need $10,000 at the end of 10 years to cover a business expense due at that time. To meet this future expense, Tanner can invest a sum today. His investment will earn 6% each year over the 10-year period. How much must Tanner invest today (present value)?

2. Now, let's turn this present-value situation around and view it in terms of a future value: Tanner has $5,580 to invest today. He can earn 6% each year over a 10-year period. How much will his investment be worth at the end of 10 years (future value)?

P15A-4 Determine the present value of the following notes and bonds:

Computing the present values of various notes and bonds

a. Ten-year bonds payable with maturity value of $88,000 and stated interest rate of 12%, paid semiannually. The market rate of interest is 12% at issuance.

b. Same bonds payable as in a, but the market interest rate is 14%.

c. Same bonds payable as in a, but the market interest rate is 10%.

P15A-5 For each bond in Problem 15A-4, journalize issuance of the bond and the first semiannual interest payment. The company amortizes bond premium and discount by the straight-line method. Explanations are not required.

Recording bond transactions

P15A-6 On December 31, 20X1, when the market interest rate is 8%, Willis Realty Co. issues $400,000 of 7.25%, 10-year bonds payable. The bonds pay interest semiannually.

Computing a bond's present value, recording its issuance, interest payments, and amortization by the effective-interest method

Required

1. Determine the present value of the bonds at issuance.

2. Assume that the bonds are issued at the price computed in requirement 1. Prepare an effective-interest method amortization table for the first two semiannual interest periods.

3. Using the amortization table prepared in requirement 2, journalize issuance of the bonds and the first two interest payments.

Investments and International Operations

TIPS CHECK YOUR RESOURCES

- Visit the www.prenhall.com/horngren **Web site** for self-study quizzes, video clips, and other resources
- Try the **Quick Check** exercise at the end of the chapter to test your knowledge
- Learn the **Key terms**
- Do the **Starter** exercises keyed in the margins
- Work the **mid-** and **end-of-chapter summary problems**
- Use the **Concept Links** to review material in other chapters
- Search the **CD** for review materials by chapter or by key word
- Watch the **tutorial videos** to review key concepts
- Watch the **On Location McDonald's International** video on consolidation accounting

★1 Account for trading investments

★2 Account for available-for-sale investments

★3 Use the equity method for investments

★4 Understand consolidated financial statements

★5 Account for long-term investments in bonds

★6 Account for transactions stated in a foreign currency

Have you ever invested in a stock? What type of company would interest you? McDonald's? Panasonic? Nokia? If you have some cash, you can invest in these companies' stocks. McDonald's is an American company, Panasonic is Japanese, and Nokia is headquartered in Finland. In a global economy, we do business with companies around the world as though they were next door.

Take McDonald's, for example. McDonald's recently invaded Disneyland-Paris and also entered Azerbaijan and Gibraltar. With restaurants in over 100 countries, McDonald's Corporation is one of the world's best-known companies.

McDonald's

McDonald's annual report featured a Chinese boy eating French fries. McDonald's bought those potatoes in China and must pay in Chinese currency, rather than dollars. In Russia, McDonald's pays for potatoes in rubles, and in France, in euros. Where does McDonald's get rubles and euros? That brings up accounting for international operations, the second topic of this chapter.

McDonald's has split its stock and has increased cash dividends over the years. Investors like rising stock prices and dividend increases. These topics bring up accounting for investments, the beginning topic of this chapter. ▪

■ Sitemap

■ **Stock Investments**

■ **Investments in Bonds and Notes**

■ **International Operations**

■ Stock Investments
☐ Investments in Bonds and Notes
☐ International Operations

available-for-sale investment, consolidation accounting, controlling interest, equity method, long-term investment, market-value method, minority interest, short-term investment, trading investment

✔ **Starter 16-1**

Exhibit 16-1

Stock Price Information for McDonald's Corporation

Short-Term Investment
A current asset; an investment that is readily convertible to cash and that the investor intends either to convert to cash within one year or use to pay a current liability. Also called a **marketable security**.

Long-Term Investment
A noncurrent asset; a separate asset category reported on the balance sheet between current assets and plant assets.

Investments can be a few shares of stock or the acquisition of an entire company. In earlier chapters, we discussed the stocks and bonds that IHOP and Amazon.com issued. Here we examine stocks and bonds for the investor who bought them. We begin with stock investments and then move to bonds. As you study investments, picture yourself as the investor. Your investment decisions would be similar to those of McDonald's or Amazon.com.

Stock Investments: An Overview

Some Basics

STOCK PRICES Stock prices are quoted as the market price per share—in dollars and cents. Newspapers and Internet news services such as nyse.com and nasdaq.com carry daily information on the stocks of thousands of corporations.

Exhibit 16-1 presents information for the common stock of McDonald's Corporation as it appeared in the media. During the previous 52 weeks, McDonald's stock reached a high price of $30.72 and a low of $12.12 per share. The annual cash dividend is $0.24 (24 cents) per share. On the previous day, McDonald's common stock closed at a price of $15.92 per share, which was $0.07 higher than the price of the preceding day.

52 weeks					
High	Low	Stock Symbol	Dividend	Close	Net Change
30.72	12.12	MCD	.24	15.92	.07

The owner of the stock in a corporation is the *investor*. The corporation that issued the stock is the *investee*. If you own shares of McDonald's stock, you are an investor and McDonald's is the investee.

CLASSIFYING INVESTMENTS An investment is an asset to the investor. The investment may be short-term or long-term. **Short-term investments**—sometimes called **marketable securities**—are current assets. Short-term investments are liquid (readily convertible to cash), and the investor intends to convert them to cash within one year.

Investments that are not short-term are classified as **long-term investments** on the balance sheet. Long-term investments include stocks and bonds that the investor expects to hold longer than one year or that are not readily marketable—for instance, real estate held for sale. Exhibit 16-2 shows the positions of short-term and long-term investments on the balance sheet.

The balance sheet reports assets by order of liquidity, starting with cash. Short-term investments are the second-most-liquid asset. Long-term investments are less liquid than current assets but more liquid than property, plant, and equipment.

ASSETS
Current Assets
  Cash... $X
  Short-term investments...................................... X
  Accounts receivable X
  Inventories X
  Prepaid expenses....................................... X
    Total current assets .... $X
  Long-term investments (or simply Investments).............. X
  Property, plant, and equipment X
  Intangible assets X
  Other assets X

Exhibit 16-2

Reporting Investments on the Balance Sheet

TRADING AND AVAILABLE-FOR-SALE INVESTMENTS We begin stock investments with situations in which the investor owns less than 20% of the investee company. These investments in stock are classified as trading investments or as available-for-sale investments. **Trading investments** are to be sold in the very near future—days, weeks, or only a few months—with the intent of generating a profit on a quick sale. Trading investments are short-term.

Available-for-sale investments are all less-than-20% investments other than trading investments. Available-for-sale investments are current assets if the business expects to sell them within the next year or within the operating cycle if longer than a year. All other available-for-sale investments are long-term.

The investor accounts for trading investments and available-for-sale investments separately. We begin with trading investments.

Trading Investments
Investments that are to be sold in the very near future with the intent of generating profits on price changes.

Available-for-Sale Investments
All less-than-20% investments other than trading securities.

Accounting for Trading Investments

The **market-value method** is used to account for trading investments because they will be sold in the near future at their current market value. Cost is the initial amount for a trading investment. Assume McDonald's Corporation has excess cash to invest. Suppose McDonald's buys 500 shares of Ford Motor Company stock for $50 per share on October 23, 20X5. Assume further that McDonald's management plans to sell this stock within three months. This is a trading investment, which McDonald's records as follows:

✔ **Starter 16-2**

⭐ *Account for trading investments*

Market-Value Method
Used to account for all trading investments. These investments are reported at their current market value.

20X5			
Oct. 23	Short-Term Investment (500 × $50) ..	25,000	
	Cash		25,000
	Purchased investment.		

Short-Term Investment

25,000 |

Ford pays a cash dividend of $2 per share, so McDonald's would receive a dividend on the investment. McDonald's entry to record receipt of a cash dividend is

20X5			
Nov. 14	Cash (500 × $2.00).................	1,000	
	Dividend Revenue...........		1,000
	Received cash dividend		

Trading investments are reported on the balance sheet at current market value, not at cost. This requires a year-end adjustment of the trading investment to current market value on the balance-sheet date. Assume that the Ford stock has decreased in value, and at December 31, 20X5, McDonald's investment in Ford stock is worth $20,000 ($5,000 less than the purchase price). At year-end, McDonald's would make the following adjustment:

Short-Term Investment

25,000	5,000
20,000	

20X5

Dec. 31 Loss on Trading Investment
($25,000 – $20,000)   5,000
        Short-Term Investment   5,000
Adjusted trading investment to market value.

The T-account shows the $20,000 ($25,000 – $5,000) balance of Short-Term Investment. McDonald's would report its trading investment on the balance sheet at December 31, 20X5, and the loss on trading investment on the 20X5 income statement, as follows:

Balance Sheet (Partial):	**Income Statement (Partial):**
ASSETS	Other gains and losses:
Current assets:	Gain (loss) on trading investment . . . . $(5,000)
Short-term investments, at market value $20,000	

If the investment's market value had risen above $25,000, McDonald's would have debited Short-Term Investment and credited Gain on Trading Investment.

When a company sells a trading investment, the gain or loss on the sale is the difference between the sale proceeds and the last carrying amount. Suppose McDonald's sells the Ford stock for $18,000 on January 19, 20X6. McDonald's would record the sale as follows:

Short-Term Investment

25,000	5,000
20,000	20,000

20X6

Jan. 19 Cash   18,000
        Loss on Sale of Investment   2,000
            Short-Term Investment   20,000
        Sold investment.

✔ Starter 16-3

✔ Starter 16-4

For reporting on the income statement, McDonald's could combine all gains and losses ($5,000 + $2,000) on short-term investments and report a single net amount under Other gains (losses). . . . $(7,000).

Account for available-for-sale investments

Accounting for Long-Term Available-for-Sale Investments

The **market-value method** is used to account for available-for-sale investments because the company expects to resell the stock at its market value. Available-for-sale investments therefore are reported on the balance sheet at their *current market value*, just like trading investments.

Suppose Dell Corporation purchases 1,000 shares of Hewlett-Packard Company (HP) common stock at the market price of $33. Dell plans to hold this stock for longer than a year and classifies it as a long-term available-for-sale investment. Dell's entry to record the investment is

20X1

Feb. 23 Long-Term Available-for-Sale
        Investment (1,000 × $33)   33,000
            Cash   33,000
        Purchased investment.

Dell receives a $0.60 per share cash dividend on the Hewlett-Packard stock. Dell's entry for receipt of the dividend is

```
20X1
July 14   Cash (1,000 × $0.60) .....................  600
                Dividend Revenue................         | 600
          Received dividend.
```

STOCK DIVIDEND VERSUS A CASH DIVIDEND   A *stock* dividend is different from a cash dividend. → For a stock dividend, the investor records no dividend revenue. Instead, he makes a memorandum entry in the accounting records to show the new number of shares of stock held. The shares have increased, so the investor's cost per share decreases. For example, suppose Dell Corporation receives a 10% stock dividend from Hewlett-Packard. Dell would receive 100 shares (10% of 1,000 shares previously held) and make this memorandum entry:

For a review of stock dividends, see Chapter 14, page 544.

✔ **Starter 16-5**

> MEMORANDUM—Receipt of stock dividend: Received 100 shares of Hewlett-Packard common stock in a 10% stock dividend. New cost per share is $30 (cost of $33,000 ÷ 1,100 shares).

For all future Hewlett-Packard investment transactions, Dell will use the new cost per share of $30.

REPORTING AVAILABLE-FOR-SALE INVESTMENTS   Available-for-sale investments are reported on the balance sheet at market value. This requires an adjustment to current market value on the balance-sheet date. Assume that the market value of Dell's investment in Hewlett-Packard common stock is $36,000 on December 31, 20X1. In this case, Dell makes the following adjustment:

```
20X1
Dec. 31   Allowance to Adjust Investment to
             Market ($36,000 – $33,000) .............. 3,000
                   Unrealized Gain on Investment. . . . .       | 3,000
             Adjusted investment to market value.
```

✔ **Starter 16-6**

Allowance to Adjust Investment to Market is a companion account to Long-Term Investment. The Allowance account brings the investment to current market value. Cost ($33,000) plus the Allowance ($3,000) equals the investment carrying amount ($36,000).

Long-Term Available-for-Sale Investment	Allowance to Adjust Investment to Market
33,000	3,000

Investment carrying amount = Market value of $36,000

Here the Allowance has a debit balance because the investment has increased in value. If the investment's value declines, the Allowance is credited. In that case, the investment carrying amount is cost *minus* the Allowance. The Allowance with a credit balance becomes a contra account. →

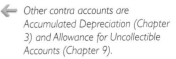

Other contra accounts are Accumulated Depreciation (Chapter 3) and Allowance for Uncollectible Accounts (Chapter 9).

    The other side of the December 31 adjustment credits Unrealized Gain on Investment. If the investment declines, the company debits an Unrealized Loss. *Unrealized* means that the gain or loss resulted from a change in market value, not a sale. A gain or loss on the sale of an investment is said to be *realized* because the company receives cash. *Cash* turns a gain or loss into a realized gain or loss. For available-for-sale investments, the Unrealized Gain (or Loss) account is reported on the balance sheet as part of stockholders' equity, as shown here.

Balance Sheet (Partial)			
ASSETS		**STOCKHOLDERS' EQUITY**	
Total current assets	$ XXX	Common stock	$ XXX
Long-term available-for-sale		Retained earnings	XXX
investments—at market value.	36,000	Unrealized gain on investments	3,000
Property, plant, and equipment, net.	XXX		

SELLING AN AVAILABLE-FOR-SALE INVESTMENT   The sale of an available-for-sale investment can result in a *realized* gain or loss. Suppose Dell Corporation sells its investment in Hewlett-Packard stock for $32,000 during 20X2. Dell would record the sale as follows:

```
20X2
May 19  Cash  . . . . . . . . . . . . . . . . . . . . . . . . . . . . .    32,000
            Loss on Sale of Investment  . . . . . . . . . .    1,000
                Long-Term Available-for-
                Sale Investment (cost). . . . . . . . .                    33,000
            Sold investment.
```

Dell would report the Loss on Sale of Investment as an "Other gain or loss" on the income statement.[1]

✔ Starter 16-7

Suppose Xenon Corporation holds the following long-term available-for-sale investments at December 31, 20X3:

Stock	Cost	Current Market Value
The Coca-Cola Company	$ 85,000	$ 71,000
Eastman Kodak Company	16,000	12,000
Scott Paper Company	122,000	136,000
	$223,000	$219,000

Show how Xenon will report long-term investments and the unrealized loss on its December 31, 20X3, balance sheet.

Answer:

Assets

Long-term available-for-sale investments, at market value $219,000

Stockholders' Equity

Unrealized gain (loss) on investments
($223,000 – $219,000) . . . .$ (4,000)

 3 Use the equity method for investments

Accounting for Equity-Method Investments

An investor with a stock holding between 20% and 50% of the investee's voting stock owns a sizeable portion of the investee. With a 20% to 50% investment, the investor can *significantly influence* the investee's decisions on dividends and product lines. For this reason, investments in the range of 20% to 50% of another company are common. For example, General Motors owns nearly 40% of Isuzu Motors Overseas Distribution Corporation, and Dow Jones & Company, publisher of *The Wall Street Journal*, owns 50% of Smart Money, the magazine company.

---

[1]We omit the complex journal entry to adjust the Allowance account at year-end. That topic is covered in intermediate accounting courses.

We use the **equity method** to account for 20% to 50% investments. A recent survey of 600 companies by *Accounting Trends & Techniques* showed that 43% of the companies held investments accounted for by the equity method. Investee companies are often called *affiliates* or *affiliated companies*.

Equity Method
Method used to account for investments in which the investor has 20% to 50% of the investee's voting stock and can significantly influence the decisions of the investee.

RECORDING THE INITIAL INVESTMENT Investments accounted for by the equity method are recorded initially at cost. Suppose Amazon.com pays $400,000 for 20% of the common stock of Drugstore.com. Amazon may refer to Drugstore.com as an *affiliated company*. Amazon's entry to record the purchase of this investment follows.

20X8			
Jan. 6	Long-Term Equity-Method Investment	400,000	
	Cash		400,000
	Purchased equity-method investment.		

ADJUSTING THE INVESTMENT ACCOUNT FOR INVESTEE NET INCOME Under the equity method, the investor applies its percentage of ownership to record its share of the investee's net income and dividends. Suppose Drugstore.com reported net income of $250,000 for the year. Amazon would record 20% of this amount as an increase in the investment account and as equity-method investment revenue, as follows:

Dec. 31	Long-Term Equity-Method Investment		
	($250,000 × 0.20)	50,000	
	Equity-Method Investment Revenue		50,000
	Recorded investment revenue.		

The Investment Revenue account carries the Equity-Method label to identify its source. This labeling is similar to distinguishing Sales Revenue from Service Revenue.

The investor increases the Investment account and records Investment Revenue when the investee reports income. As the investee's equity increases, so does the Investment account on the investor's books.

RECEIVING DIVIDENDS ON AN EQUITY-METHOD INVESTMENT Amazon records its proportionate part of cash dividends received from Drugstore.com. Suppose Drugstore.com declares and pays a cash dividend of $100,000. Amazon receives 20% of this dividend and makes this journal entry:

20X9			
Jan. 17	Cash ($100,000 × 0.20)	20,000	
	Long-Term Equity-Method Investment . .		20,000
	Received dividend on equity-method investment.		

The Investment account is credited for the receipt of a dividend on an equity-method investment. Why? Because the dividend decreases both the investee's equity and the investor's investment.

After the preceding entries are posted, Amazon.com's Investment account reflects its equity in the net assets of Drugstore.com:

✔ **Starter 16-8**

Long-Term Equity-Method Investment

20X8			20X9		
Jan. 6	Purchase	400,000	Jan. 17	Dividends received	20,000
Dec. 31	Net income	50,000			
20X9					
Jan. 17	Balance	430,000			

Amazon.com can report the long-term investment on the balance sheet and the revenue on the income statement as follows:

Balance Sheet (Partial):			Income Statement (Partial):		
ASSETS			Income from operations	$	XXX
Total current assets.	$	XXX	Other revenue:		
Long-term equity-method			Equity-method investment		
investments		430,000	revenue		50,000
Property, plant, and equipment, net		XXX	Net income	$	XXX

SELLING AN EQUITY-METHOD INVESTMENT   There may be a gain or a loss on the sale of an equity-method investment. The gain or loss is the difference between the sale proceeds and the investment carrying amount. Suppose Amazon.com sells one-tenth of the Drugstore.com common stock for $40,000. The sale is recorded as follows:

Feb. 13	Cash	40,000		
	Loss on Sale of Investment	3,000		
	Long-Term Equity-Method Investment			
	($430,000 × 1/10).		43,000	
	Sold investment.			

4 *Understand consolidated financial statements*

Controlling Interest
Ownership of more than 50% of an investee company's voting stock. Also called **majority interest**.

Parent Company
An investor company that owns more than 50% of the voting stock of a subsidiary company.

Subsidiary Company
A company in which a parent company owns more than 50% of the voting stock.

Exhibit 16-3

Ownership Structure of General Motors Corporation and Saturn Corporation

The following T-account summarizes the accounting for equity-method investments:

Long-Term Equity-Method Investment	
Cost	**Share of losses**
Share of income	**Share of dividend received**

JOINT VENTURES   A *joint venture* is a separate entity owned by a group of companies. Joint ventures are used for risky endeavors such as oil exploration and the construction of nuclear power plants. Aramco, which stands for Arabian American Oil Company, is a joint venture half-owned by Saudi Arabia. Several multinational oil companies (ExxonMobil, ChevronTexaco, and others) own the remaining 50%.

A participant in a joint venture accounts for its investment by the equity method. Joint ventures are common in international business. Companies such as British Telecom, Total (of France) and Toyota partner with companies in other countries.

Accounting for Consolidated Subsidiaries

Most large corporations own controlling interests in other companies. A **controlling** (or **majority**) **interest** is the ownership of more than 50% of the investee's voting stock. A greater-than-50% investment enables the investor to elect a majority of the investee's board of directors and thereby control the investee. The corporation that controls the other company is called the **parent company**, and the company that is controlled by another corporation is called the **subsidiary**. A well-known example is Saturn Corporation, which is a subsidiary of General Motors, the parent company. Because GM owns Saturn Corporation, the stockholders of GM control Saturn, as diagrammed in Exhibit 16-3.

Why have subsidiaries? Why not have the corporation operate as a single legal entity? A subsidiary arrangement may save on income taxes, limit the parent's liabilities, and ease expansion into foreign countries. For example, McDonald's Corporation finds it easier to operate in France through a French subsidiary than through the U.S. parent company. Exhibit 16-4 shows some of the subsidiaries of three large automakers.

Parent Company	Selected Subsidiaries
General Motors Corporation	Saturn Corporation
	Hughes Aircraft Company
Ford Motor Company	Ford Aerospace Corporation
	Jaguar, Ltd.
DaimlerChrysler Corporation	Jeep/Eagle Corporation
	DaimlerChrysler Rail Systems

Exhibit 16-4

Selected Subsidiaries of Three
Large Automobile Manufacturers

MAJORITY-OWNED SUBSIDIARIES *Consolidation accounting* is a way to combine the financial statements of two or more companies that have the same owners. Most published financial reports include consolidated statements. To understand real financial statements, you need to know the basics of consolidation accounting. **Consolidated statements** combine the balance sheets, income statements, and cash-flow statements of the parent company plus those of its majority-owned subsidiaries. The final outcome is a single set of statements as if the parent and its subsidiaries were the same entity.

In consolidation accounting, the assets, liabilities, revenues, and expenses of each subsidiary are added to the parent's accounts. The consolidated financial statements report the combined account balances. For example, Saturn's cash balance is added to the cash balance of General Motors, and the overall sum is reported on GM's balance sheet. The consolidated financial statements bear only the name of the parent company, in this case, General Motors Corporation.

Exhibit 16-5 shows which accounting method should be used for each type of stock investment.

GOODWILL AND MINORITY INTEREST Goodwill is an intangible asset that is recorded in the consolidation process and reported on the parent company's consolidated balance sheet. As we have seen, *goodwill* is the excess of the cost to acquire another company over the sum of the market value of its net assets. →

A parent company may purchase less than 100% of a subsidiary company. For example, Nokia, the cellular telephone company, has a minority interest (owns less than 100% of) several other companies. **Minority interest** is the portion (less than 50%) of a subsidiary's stock that is owned by outside stockholders. Nokia Corporation, the parent company, therefore reports on its consolidated balance sheet an account titled Minority Interest. Most analysts treat Minority Interest as a liability.

INCOME OF A CONSOLIDATED ENTITY The income of a consolidated entity is the sum of

- Net income of the parent company, plus
- Parent's portion of the subsidiaries' net income

Suppose Parent Company owns all the stock of Subsidiary S-1 and 60% of the stock of Subsidiary S-2. During 20X8, Parent earned net income of $330,000, S-1 earned $150,000, and S-2 had a net loss of $100,000. Parent Company would report consolidated net income of $420,000, computed as follows:

Consolidated Statements
Financial statements of the parent company plus those of majority-owned subsidiaries as if the combination were a single legal entity.

← *Chapter 10 discusses how to account for goodwill.*

✔ **Starter 16-9**

Exhibit 16-5

Accounting Methods for
Investments by Percentage
of Ownership

Minority Interest
A subsidiary company's equity that is held by stockholders other than the parent company.

	Net Income (Net Loss)	×	Parent Stockholders' Ownership	=	Parent's Consolidated Net Income (Net Loss)
Parent Company	$ 330,000	×	100%	=	$330,000
Subsidiary S-1	150,000	×	100%	=	150,000
Subsidiary S-2	(100,000)	×	60%	=	(60,000)
Consolidated net income					$420,000

Answer these questions about consolidated financial statements:

1. Whose name appears on the consolidated statements—the parent company, the subsidiary company, or both?

2. Company A owns 90% of Company B. What is the remaining 10% of Company B's stock called, and where does it appear in Company A's financial statements?

3. Company C paid $1 million to acquire Company D, whose stockholders' equity (same as net assets) totaled $700,000. What is the $300,000 excess called? Which company reports the excess? Where in the financial statements is the excess reported?

Answers:

1. Parent company only

2. Minority interest—reported on (Parent) Company A's balance sheet among the liabilities

3. Goodwill—reported on (Parent) Company C's balance sheet as an intangible asset

☐ Stock Investments

■ **Investments in Bonds and Notes**

☐ International Operations

5 Account for long-term investments in bonds

bond investment, long-term investment, short-term investment

Held-to-Maturity Investments
Investment in bonds, notes, and other debt securities that the investor expects to hold until their maturity date.

See Chapter 15, pages 584–587 for ➡ discussion of bonds payable.

Straight-line amortization of premium ➡ or discount on a bond investment is calculated the same way as for bonds payable (see Chapter 15, page 584).

Accounting for Long-Term Investments in Bonds and Notes

Most companies invest far more in stocks than in bonds. The major holders of bonds are investment companies. The relationship between the issuing corporation and bondholders may be diagrammed as follows:

Issuing Corporation Has	Bondholder Has
Bonds payable ⟷	Investment in bonds
Interest expense ⟷	Interest revenue

The dollar amount of a bond transaction is the same for both the issuing corporation and the bondholder because money passes from one to the other. However, the accounts debited and credited differ. For example, the corporation has bonds payable; the bondholder has an investment. The corporation has interest expense, and the bondholder has interest revenue. Chapter 15 covered bonds payable. ⟵

An investment in bonds is classified as short-term (a current asset) or as long-term. *Short-term investments in bonds are rare.* Therefore, we focus on long-term investments in bonds. These are called **held-to-maturity investments**.

Bond investments are recorded at cost. At maturity, the investor will receive the bonds' full face value. We must amortize any discount or premium, as we did for bonds payable in Chapter 15. Held-to-maturity investments are reported at their *amortized cost.*

Suppose an investor purchases $10,000 of 6% CBS bonds at a price of 94 (94% of maturity value) on July 1, 20X2. The investor intends to hold the bonds as a long-term investment until their maturity. Interest dates are June 30 and December 31. These bonds mature on July 1, 20X7, so they will be outstanding for 60 months. Let's amortize the discount by the straight-line method. ⟵ The following are the bondholder's entries for this investment:

20X2			
July 1	Long-Term Investment in Bonds		
	($10,000 × 0.94)...............	9,400	
	Cash.....................		9,400
	Purchased bond investment.		

At December 31, the year-end entries are

✔ Starter 16-10

Dec. 31	Cash ($10,000 × 0.06 × 6/12)	300	
	Interest Revenue		300
	Received interest.		
Dec. 31	Long-Term Investment in Bonds [($10,000 − $9,400)/5 × 6/12]..........	60	
	Interest Revenue		60
	Amortized discount on bond investment.		

The financial statements at December 31, 20X2, report the following for this investment in bonds:

Balance sheet at December 31, 20X2:	
Long-term investments in bonds ($9,400 + $ 60)	$9,460
Income statement for 20X2:	
Other revenues:	
Interest revenue ($300 + $60)	$ 360

✔ Starter 16-11

Decision Guidelines

ACCOUNTING FOR LONG-TERM INVESTMENTS

Suppose you work for **Bank of America**. Your duties include accounting for the bank's investments. The following Decision Guidelines can serve as your checklist for using the appropriate method to account for each type of investment.

Decision	Guidelines
Investment Type	*Accounting Method*
Short-Term Investment	
Trading investment	Market value—report all gains (losses) on the income statement
Long-Term Investment	
Investor owns less than 20% of investee stock (available-for-sale investment)	Market value—report *unrealized* gains (losses) on the balance sheet
	—report *realized* gains (losses) from sale of the investment on the income statement
Investor owns between 20% and 50% of investee stock	Equity
Investment in a joint venture	Equity
Investor owns more than 50% of investee stock	Consolidation
Long-term investment in bonds (held-to-maturity investment)	Amortized cost

Excel Application Exercise

Goal: Create an Excel work sheet to chart foreign currency exchange rates.

Scenario: Your clothing boutique is expanding to offer merchandise made in other countries. In order to manage your company's foreign exchange rates, you are creating a spreadsheet to track currencies over the past 3 months for countries where you'll be doing business. The currencies you want to track against U.S. dollars are Canada dollars, euros, Australia dollars, and Swiss francs. When done, answer these questions:

1. Which currencies have strengthened, relative to the U.S. dollar, during the past 3 months? Which have weakened?
2. Which accounts are affected by foreign currency rate fluctuations?
3. What actions might a business take to manage its risk of a foreign exchange loss?

Step-by-Step:

1. Open a new Excel work sheet.
2. Create a heading for your work sheet that contains the following:
   a. Chapter 16 Excel Application Exercise
   b. Foreign Exchange Rates
   c. Today's Date
3. Launch your Web browser and go to www.xe.com/ict. This Web site specializes in reporting foreign-currency exchange rates. Under "Show me a currency table," choose "Based on USD (United States Currency)." Then, under "as of this date," click "the following date" and enter the current

month, day 1 (the first day of the month), for the current year (e.g., 2003). Next, click on the button to generate a currency table.

4. On the table just created, locate the currencies listed in the exercise. You will be using the values listed under "USD per Unit." This is how much you'd need in US dollars to buy one unit of the foreign currency. For example, $1.60 USD equals 1 United Kingdom (British) pound.
5. Repeat the table creation process in steps 4 and 5 for the past 3 months. When done, you will have 3 data points for each currency.
6. Two rows down from your heading in your Excel spreadsheet in column A, enter the heading "Foreign Currency (USD per unit)." Starting in column B, set up 3 columns, one for each month of data with labels (Jan 1 2003, Feb 1 2003, etc.). Start with the oldest month first.
7. Return to column A. Under the "Foreign Currency" heading, list the names of the currencies, one per row (for example, Canada Dollars). Enter the monthly rate data collected for each currency in the appropriate columns.
8. Highlight all rows and columns, including titles. Click the Chart Wizard button. Select the "line" chart with markers displayed at each data value. Click next. Click next again.
9. Enter the chart title, "Foreign Currency Rates." Leave the **x** axis title blank. Enter the title, "USD per Unit" for the **y** axis. Click next.
10. Save your chart as an object in your spreadsheet and click finish. Size the chart to fit below your data.
11. When finished, save your work and print a copy for your files.

◯ MID-CHAPTER *Summary Problem*

CHECK YOUR RESOURCES

Required

1. Identify the appropriate accounting method for each of the following situations:
   a. Investment in 25% of investee company's stock.
   b. Available-for-sale investment in stock.
   c. Investment in more than 50% of investee company's stock.
2. At what amount should the following available-for-sale investment portfolio be reported on the December 31 balance sheet? All the investments are less than 5% of the investee's stock.

Stock	Investment Cost	Current Market Value
Amazon.com	$ 5,000	$ 5,500
Intelysis	61,200	53,000
Procter & Gamble	3,680	6,230

Journalize any adjusting entry required by these data.

3. Investor paid $67,900 to acquire a 40% equity-method investment in the common stock of Investee. At the end of the first year, Investee's net income was $80,000, and Investee declared and paid cash dividends of $55,000. Journalize Investor's (a) purchase of the investment, (b) share of Investee's net income, (c) receipt of dividends from Investee, and (d) sale of Investee stock for $80,100.

Solution

1. **(a)** Equity   **(b)** Market value   **(c)** Consolidation
2. Report the investments at market value, $64,730, as follows:

Stock	Investment Cost	Current Market Value
Amazon.com	$ 5,000	$ 5,500
Intelysis	61,200	53,000
Procter & Gamble	3,680	6,230
Totals	$69,880	$64,730

Adjusting entry:

Unrealized Loss on Investments ($69,880 – $64,730)	5,150	
Allowance to Adjust Investment to Market		5,150
To adjust investments to current market value.		

3. **a.**

Long-Term Equity-Method Investment	67,900	
Cash		67,900
Purchased equity-method investment.		

b.

Long-Term Equity-Method Investment ($80,000 × 0.40) . .	32,000	
Equity-Method Investment Revenue		32,000
Recorded investment revenue.		

c.

Cash ($55,000 × 0.40)	22,000	
Long-Term Equity-Method Investment		22,000
Received dividend on equity-method investment.		

d.

Cash	80,100	
Long-Term Equity-Method Investment		
($67,900 + $32,000 – $22,000)		77,900
Gain on Sale of Investment		2,200
Sold investment.		

☐ Stock Investments
☐ Investments in Bonds and Notes
■ International Operations

Student Resource**CD**

exchange rate, exchange rate risk, foreign currency gains and losses, hedging

Accounting for International Operations

Accounting for business activities across national boundaries is called *international accounting*. Did you know that Coca-Cola, IBM, and Bank of America earn most of their revenue outside the United States? It is common for U.S. companies to do a large part of their business abroad. McDonald's and AMR (American Airlines) are also very active in other countries. Exhibit 16-6 shows the percentages of international sales for these companies.

Exhibit 16-6

Extent of International Business

Company	Percentage of International Sales
McDonald's	65%
IBM	60
AMR (American Airlines)	28

Foreign Currencies and Foreign-Currency Exchange Rates

If Boeing, a U.S. company, sells a 747 jet to Air France, will Boeing receive U.S. dollars or euros? If the transaction is stated in dollars, Air France must buy dollars to pay Boeing in U.S. currency. If the transaction is in euros, Boeing must sell euros. In either case, a step has been added to the transaction: One company must convert domestic currency into foreign currency, or vice versa.

Foreign-Currency Exchange Rate
The measure of one currency against another currency.

One nation's currency can be stated in terms of another country's monetary unit. The price of a foreign currency is called the **foreign-currency exchange rate**. In Exhibit 16-7, the U.S. dollar value of a European euro is $1.10. This means that one euro can be bought for $1.10. Other currencies are also listed in Exhibit 16-7.

Exhibit 16-7 Foreign-Currency Exchange Rates

Country	Monetary Unit	U.S. Dollar Value	Country	Monetary Unit	U.S. Dollar Value
Canada	Dollar	$0.69	Japan	Yen	$0.008
European Common Market	European currency unit	1.10	Mexico	Peso	0.096
Great Britain	Pound	1.59	Russia	Ruble	0.03

Source: The Wall Street Journal, April 29, 2003, p. C14.

Strong Currency
A currency that is rising relative to other nations' currencies.

Weak Currency
A currency that is falling relative to other nations' currencies.

We use the exchange rate to convert the price of an item stated in one currency to its price in a second currency. We call this conversion a *translation*. Suppose an item costs 200 Canadian dollars. To compute its cost in U.S. dollars, we multiply the amount in Canadian dollars by the conversion rate: 200 Canadian dollars × $0.69 = $138.

Currencies are described as "strong" or "weak." The exchange rate of a **strong currency** is rising relative to other nations' currencies. The exchange rate of a **weak currency** is falling relative to other currencies.

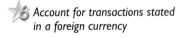 Account for transactions stated in a foreign currency

Foreign-Currency Transactions

More and more companies conduct transactions in foreign currencies. D. E. Shipp Belting of Waco, Texas, provides an example. Shipp makes conveyor belts for several industries, including M&M Mars, which makes Snickers candy bars in Waco. Farmers along the Texas–Mexico border use Shipp conveyor belts to process vegetables. Some of these customers are Mexican, so Shipp Belting conducts some of its business in pesos, the Mexican monetary unit.

COLLECTING CASH IN A FOREIGN CURRENCY   Consider Shipp Belting's sale of conveyor belts to Artes de Mexico, a vegetable grower in Matamoros. The sale can be conducted in dollars or pesos. If Artes agrees to pay in dollars, the transaction is the same as selling to M&M Mars across town. But suppose Artes orders conveyor belts valued at 1,000 pesos (approximately $96). Further suppose that Artes demands to pay in pesos.

Shipp will need to convert the pesos to dollars. What if the peso strengthens (gains value) or weakens (loses value) before Shipp collects from Artes? Shipp will earn more or less than expected. Let's see how to account for this transaction.

Shipp Belting sells goods to Artes de Mexico for a price of 1,000 pesos on June 2. On that date, a peso was worth $0.096. One month later, on July 2, the peso has strengthened against the dollar and a peso is worth $0.100. Shipp still receives 1,000 pesos from Artes because that was the agreed price. Now the dollar value of Shipp's cash receipt is $4 more than the original amount, so Shipp ends up earning $4 more than expected. The following journal entries account for these transactions of Shipp Belting:

June 2	Accounts Receivable—Artes		
	(1,000 pesos × $0.096)	96	
	Sales Revenue		96
	Sale on account.		

✔ **Starter 16-12**

July 2	Cash (1,000 pesos × $0.100).	100	
	Accounts Receivable—Artes.		96
	Foreign-Currency Gain.		4
	Collection on account.		

If Shipp had required Artes to pay at the time of the sale, Shipp would have received pesos worth $96. But during the 30-day credit period, Shipp was exposed to *foreign-currency exchange risk*, the risk of loss in an international transaction. In this case, Shipp experienced a $4 foreign-currency gain and received $4 more than expected, as shown in the collection entry on July 2.

PAYING CASH IN A FOREIGN CURRENCY Purchasing from a foreign company can create foreign-currency risk. Shipp Belting buys inventory from Gesellschaft Ltd., a Swiss company. The two companies decide on a price of 10,000 Swiss francs. On August 10, when Shipp receives the goods, the Swiss franc is priced at $0.72. When Shipp pays two weeks later, the Swiss franc has strengthened against the dollar and is now worth $0.78. This works to Shipp's disadvantage. Shipp would record the purchase of and payment for the inventory as follows:

Aug. 10	Inventory (10,000 Swiss francs × $0.72). . . .	7,200	
	Accounts Payable—Gesellschaft Ltd.. .		7,200
	Purchase on account.		
Aug. 24	Accounts Payable—Gesellschaft Ltd..	7,200	
	Foreign-Currency Loss	600	
	Cash (10,000 Swiss francs × $0.78)		7,800
	Payment on account.		

In this case, the Swiss franc strengthened against the dollar (the dollar weakened), and that gave Shipp a foreign-currency loss. A company with a payable stated in a foreign currency hopes that the dollar gets stronger. The company can then use fewer dollars to pay the debt. But the dollar may weaken and force the company to pay more dollars for the foreign currency, as in the case of Shipp Belting.

REPORTING FOREIGN-CURRENCY GAINS AND LOSSES ON THE INCOME STATEMENT The Foreign-Currency Gain (Loss) account reports gains and losses on transactions in a currency other than the dollar. The company reports the *net amount* of these two accounts on the income statement as Other gains (losses). For example, Shipp Belting would combine a $600 foreign-currency loss and the $4 gain and report the net loss of $596 on the income statement, as follows:

Other gains (losses):
    Foreign-currency gain (loss), net ($600 – $4) . . . . $(596)

These gains and losses fall into the "Other" category because they arise from outside activities. Buying and selling foreign currencies are not Shipp Belting's main business.

Managers examine these gains and losses to see how well the company is doing in foreign-currency transactions. The gains and losses may offset each other, with a small overall effect. But if losses grow large, managers will take action. One possible action is hedging.

HEDGING TO AVOID FOREIGN-CURRENCY LOSSES U.S. companies can avoid foreign-currency losses by requiring international transactions to be settled in dollars. But that strategy may alienate customers. Another protection is called hedging.

Hedging
Protecting oneself from losing money
in one transaction by engaging in a
counterbalancing transaction.

Hedging means to protect oneself from losing money by engaging in a counterbalancing transaction. Suppose Intel is selling goods to be collected in Japanese yen. Intel will receive a fixed number of yen in the future. If yen are losing value, they will be worth fewer dollars than the amount of Intel's receivable. Intel can expect a loss.

In other international transactions, Intel may have accumulated payables stated in another foreign currency, say euros. Losses on the yen may be offset by gains on the euros. This is a natural foreign-currency hedge. It is inexpensive because Intel has to take no special action to protect against foreign-currency loss.

Most companies do not have equal amounts of receivables and payables in foreign currency, so exactly offsetting receivables and payables is unlikely. To obtain a more-precise hedge, companies buy *futures contracts*, which are agreements for foreign currencies to be received in the future. Futures contracts can create a payable to exactly offset a receivable, and vice versa. Many companies use hedging to avoid losses.

Accounting.com

Avon Products Inc.: Staying Up When the Currency Goes Down

Cosmetics giant Avon Products often faces foreign-currency crises because a lot of the company's sales occur outside the United States. In fact, 39% of Avon's operating income comes from South America, so Avon is hit hard when the South American economy falters. CEO Andrea Jung once promised investors that Avon would earn $2.30 for each share of its stock. She then learned that the Argentine peso had devalued and the country's economy was reeling. In one moment, Argentina wiped out 5 cents of Avon's earnings. The company would face more bad news when Brazil went through a similar crisis.

Amazingly, Avon's profits and stock price keep climbing because the company is good at managing risk. To protect against volatile currencies, Avon buys raw materials and makes its products close to the markets where they are sold. Avon recently closed a British facility and moved it to Poland to be nearer Eastern and Central Europe because that part of the world is now the company's fastest-growing market.

Another key strategy is to sacrifice quick profits to grow market share. Avon is willing to take short-term losses to get long-term gains. In Mexico, for example, Avon sets prices low on brands aimed at the poor and the middle class. To keep profits high, the company raises prices on its premium brands.

Avon's main strength is keeping costs low. The company has cut 10 days off of inventory turnover. That saves on expenses. Avon also has reduced product-development cycles by more than 40%. That gets products to market and starts revenues flowing faster. Overall, Avon has trimmed total costs by $230 million. Lower costs mean higher profits.

Based on: Anonymous, "Susan Kropf & Andrea Jung: Avon Products," *Business Week,* January 13, 2003, p. 60. Allison Krampf, "Makeover Magic," *Barron's,* November 4, 2002, p. T6. Subrata N. Chakravarty, "Andrea Calling," *Institutional Investor,* August 2002, pp. 22–24. David Whitford, "A Currency Drowns—Can You Stay Afloat?" *Fortune,* March 1, 1999, pp. 229–235. Mel Mandell, "Asia: Converting Crisis to Opportunity," *World Trade,* April 1998, pp. 36–39. Fred R. Bleakley, "How U.S. Firm Copes with Asia Crisis—Avon Moves to Protect Against Volatile Currencies," *The Wall Street Journal,* December 26, 1997, p. A2.

International Accounting Standards

In this text, we focus on accounting principles that are generally accepted in the United States. Most accounting methods are consistent throughout the world. Double-entry, the accrual system, and the basic financial statements (balance sheet, income statement, and so on) are used worldwide. But some differences exist among countries, as shown in Exhibit 16-8.

Exhibit 16-8 Some International Accounting Differences

Country	Inventories	Goodwill	Research and Development Costs
United States	Specific unit cost, FIFO, LIFO, weighted-average.	Written down when current value decreases.	Expensed as incurred.
Germany	LIFO is unacceptable for tax purposes and is not widely used.	Amortized over 5 years.	Expensed as incurred.
Japan	Similar to U.S.	Amortized over 5 years.	May be capitalized and amortized over 5 years.
United Kingdom (Great Britain)	LIFO is unacceptable for tax purposes and is not widely used.	Amortized over useful life or not amortized if life is indefinite.*	Expense research costs. Some development costs may be capitalized.

* Proposal being considered.

Several organizations seek worldwide harmony of accounting standards. The International Accounting Standards Committee (IASC) is headquartered in London and operates much as the Financial Accounting Standards Board in the United States. It has the support of the accounting professions in the United States, most of the British Commonwealth countries, Japan, France, Germany, the Netherlands, and Mexico. However, the IASC has no authority to require compliance and must rely on cooperation by the various national accounting professions.

Decision Guidelines

FOREIGN-CURRENCY TRANSACTIONS

You've just opened a boutique to import clothing manufactured in China. Should you transact business in Chinese *renminbi* (the official currency unit), or in U.S. dollars? What foreign-currency gains or losses might occur? The Decision Guidelines will help you address these questions.

Decision	Guidelines
When to record a	
• Foreign-currency gain?	• When you receive foreign currency worth *more* U.S. dollars than the receivable on your books • When you pay foreign currency that costs *fewer* U.S. dollars than the payable on your books
• Foreign-currency loss?	• When you receive foreign currency worth *fewer* U.S. dollars than the receivable on your books • When you pay foreign currency that costs *more* U.S. dollars than the payable on your books

CHECK YOUR RESOURCES

END-OF-CHAPTER *Summary Problem*

Required

1. Journalize the following transactions of American Corp. Explanations are not required.

20X5

Nov. 16 Purchased equipment on account for 40,000 Swiss francs when the exchange rate was $0.73 per Swiss franc.

27 Sold merchandise on account to a Belgian company for 7,000 euros. Each euro is worth $1.10.

Dec. 22 Paid the Swiss company when the franc's exchange rate was $0.725.

31 Adjusted for the change in the exchange rate of the euro. Its current exchange rate is $1.08.

20X6

Jan. 4 Collected from the Belgian company. The exchange rate is $1.12.

---

2. In the 20X5 transactions, identify each of the following currencies as strong or weak:
   a. Swiss franc   **b.** Euro   **c.** U.S. dollar
   Which currency strengthened during 20X6? Which currency weakened during 20X6?

Solution

1. Entries for transactions stated in foreign currencies:

20X5

Nov. 16	Equipment (40,000 × $0.73)...........	29,200	
	Accounts Payable..............		29,200
27	Accounts Receivable (7,000 × $1.10) ...	7,700	
	Sales Revenue.................		7,700
Dec. 22	Accounts Payable...................	29,200	
	Cash (40,000 × $0.725)..........		29,000
	Foreign-Currency Gain.........		200
31	Foreign-Currency Loss [7,000 × ($1.10 – $1.08)]..............	140	
	Accounts Receivable...........		140

20X6

Jan. 4	Cash (7,000 × $1.12).................	7,840	
	Accounts Receivable ($7,700 – $140)		7,560
	Foreign-Currency Gain.........		280

2. During 20X5,
   a. Swiss franc—weak   **b.** Euro—weak   **c.** U.S. dollar—strong
   During 20X6, the euro strengthened and the U.S. dollar weakened.

REVIEW *Investments and International Operations*

Quick Check

1. Suppose you are buying 100 shares of **McDonald's** stock. Use the data in Exhibit 16-1, page 626, to determine how much you must pay.
   a. $1,592   **c.** $1,212
   b. $3,072   **d.** $24

2. The two categories of stock investments in less than 20% of the investee's stock are
   a. Current and long-term
   b. Equity and consolidated
   c. Trading and available-for-sale
   d. Majority interest and minority interest

3. Suppose you hold 1,000 shares of **Intel** common stock as a trading investment. The stock cost you a total of $18,000, and you receive $80 in annual cash dividends. At December 31, your investment in Intel common stock is quoted at $19 per share. What will your *balance sheet* report for this investment?
   a. Short-term investment of $18,000
   b. Short-term investment of $19,000
   c. Unrealized gain of $1,000
   d. Dividend revenue of $80

4. Suppose you hold 1,000 shares of Intel common stock as a trading investment. The stock cost you a total of $18,000, and you receive $80 in annual cash dividends. At December 31, your investment in Intel common stock is quoted at $19 per share. What will your *income statement* report for this investment?
   a. Short-term investment of $18,000
   b. Short-term investment of $19,000
   c. Unrealized gain of $1,000
   d. Dividend revenue of $80 and Unrealized gain of $1,000

5. Suppose you hold 1,000 shares of Intel common stock as a long-term *available-for-sale* investment. The stock cost you a total of $18,000, and you receive $80 in annual cash dividends. At December 31, your investment in Intel common stock is quoted at $19 per share. What will your balance sheet report for this investment?
   a. Long-term investment of $18,000
   b. Long-term investment of $19,000
   c. Long-term investment of $19,000 and Unrealized gain of $1,000
   d. Dividend revenue of $80

6. Suppose you hold 20% of the common shares of Griffin Company as an equity-method investment. The stock cost you $18,000, and you receive no cash dividends. At December 31, Griffin reports net income of $15,000. What is the carrying amount of your investment for the December 31 balance sheet?
   a. $18,000
   b. $20,000
   c. $21,000
   d. $22,000

7. What is the minimum percentage ownership for a parent company to consolidate the financial statements of a subsidiary company?
   a. 50%
   b. > 50%
   c. 50.1%
   d. 100%

8. The journal entry to record the final transaction for a bond investment is

   a. Cash.................. XXX
          Investment in Bonds..   XXX
   b. Cash.................. XXX
          Interest Revenue   XXX

   c. Investment in Bonds.... XXX
          Cash   XXX
   d. Cash.................. XXX
          Bonds Payable.......   XXX

9. What causes a foreign-currency gain or loss?
   a. Buying a foreign currency
   b. Paying debts and collecting receivables in amounts that differ from the carrying amounts on your books
   c. Hedging activities
   d. Accounting differences in foreign countries

10. **IBM** purchased silicon chips on account from a Japanese supplier at a cost of 1,000,000 yen, with each yen valued at $0.008. One month later, when IBM paid the account, a yen was quoted at $0.009. Which journal entry records IBM's payment?

    a. Accounts Payable 8,000
           Cash................   8,000
    b. Accounts Payable 9,000
           Foreign-Currency Loss   1,000
           Cash................   8,000

    c. Cash.................. 9,000
           Accounts Payable   9,000
    d. Accounts Payable 8,000
           Foreign-Currency Loss .. 1,000
           Cash   9,000

Accounting Vocabulary

available-for-sale investments (p. 627)	held-to-maturity investments (p. 634)	parent company (p. 632)
consolidated statements (p. 633)	long-term investment (p. 626)	short-term investment (p. 626)
controlling interest (p. 632)	majority interest (p. 632)	strong currency (p. 638)
equity method (p. 631)	marketable security (p. 626)	subsidiary company (p. 632)
foreign-currency exchange rate (p. 638)	market-value method (p. 627)	trading investments (p. 627)
hedging (p. 640)	minority interest (p. 633)	weak currency (p. 638)

○ASSESS *Your Progress*

online homework

See *www.prenhall.com/horngren* for selected Starters, Exercises, and Problems.

Computing the cost of a stock investment
(Obj. 1, 2)

Classifying investments as trading or available-for-sale
(Obj. 1, 2)

Accounting for a trading investment loss
(Obj. 1)

Accounting for a trading investment gain
(Obj. 1)

Starters

S16-1 Compute the cost of each investment. Round to the nearest dollar.

a. 200 shares of **Nokia** stock at 16.57.
b. 450 shares of **IBM** stock at 85.12. IBM pays a cash dividend of $0.60 per year.
c. 1,000 shares of **Nike** stock at 53.97.
d. 70 shares of **Target** stock at 33.12.

S16-2 Milwaukee Corp. purchased 100 shares of stock in each of three companies:

a. Investment in **Intel Corporation** to be sold within the next 9 to 12 months
b. Investment in **AMR (American Airlines)** to be sold within the next 90 days
c. Investment in **Amazon.com** to be sold within the next two years

Classify each investment as (1) a current asset or a long-term asset and as (2) a trading investment or an available-for-sale investment.

S16-3 Frost Bank completed the following transactions during 20X4 and 20X5:

20X4	
Dec. 6	Purchased 1,000 shares of **Nissan** stock at a price of $52.25 per share, intending to sell the investment next week.
23	Received a cash dividend of $1.12 per share on the Nissan stock.
31	Adjusted the investment to its market value of $51 per share.
20X5	
Jan. 27	Sold the Nissan stock for $48 per share.

1. Classify Frost Bank's investment as trading or available-for-sale.
2. Journalize Frost Bank's investment transactions. Explanations are not required.

S16-4 Spitzer Electronics completed the following investment transactions during 20X6 and 20X7:

20X6	
Dec. 12	Purchased 500 shares of **Fedex** stock at a price of $59 per share, intending to sell the investment next week.
21	Received a cash dividend of $0.23 per share on the Fedex stock.
31	Adjusted the investment to its market value of $61 per share.
20X7	
Jan. 16	Sold the Fedex stock for $64.50 per share.

1. Classify Spitzer's investment as trading or available-for-sale.
2. Journalize Spitzer's investment transactions. Explanations are not required.

S16-5 **BankOne** buys 500 shares of **ChevronTexaco** stock, paying $64 per share. Suppose ChevronTexaco distributes a 10% stock dividend. Later, BankOne sells the ChevronTexaco stock for $60 per share.

Measuring gain or loss on the sale of an investment after receiving a stock dividend
(Obj. 2)

1. Compute BankOne's new cost per share after receiving the stock dividend.
2. Compute BankOne's gain or loss on the sale of this available-for-sale investment.

S16-6 Brookstone Financial, Inc., completed these long-term available-for-sale investment transactions during 20X7:

Accounting for an available-for-sale investment: unrealized loss
(Obj. 2)

20X7		
Jan. 14	Purchased 300 shares of **PepsiCo** stock, paying $43.45 per share. Brookstone intends to hold the investment for the indefinite future.
Aug. 22	Received a cash dividend of $0.60 per share on the PepsiCo stock.
Dec. 31	Adjusted the PepsiCo investment to its current market value of $12,600.

1. Journalize Brookstone's investment transactions. Explanations are not required.
2. Show how to report the investment and any unrealized gain or loss on Brookstone's balance sheet at December 31, 20X7.

S16-7 Use the data given in Starter 16-6. On August 4, 20X8, Brookstone Financial, Inc., sold its investment in **PepsiCo** stock for $45.15 per share.

Accounting for the sale of an available-for-sale investment
(Obj. 2)

1. Journalize the sale. No explanation is required.
2. How does the gain or loss that you recorded differ from the gain or loss that was recorded at December 31, 20X7 (in Starter 16-6)?

S16-8 Suppose on January 6, 20X5, **General Motors** paid $100 million for its 40% investment in **Isuzu**. Assume Isuzu earned net income of $20 million and paid cash dividends of $10 million during 20X5.

Accounting for a 40% investment in another company
(Obj. 3)

1. What method should General Motors use to account for the investment in Isuzu? Give your reason.
2. Journalize these three transactions on the books of General Motors. Show all amounts in millions of dollars and include an explanation for each entry.
3. Post to the Long-Term Equity-Method Investment T-account. What is its balance after all the transactions are posted?

S16-9 Answer these questions about consolidation accounting:

Understanding consolidated financial statements
(Obj. 4)

1. Define a parent company. Define a subsidiary company.
2. Which company's name appears on the consolidated financial statements? How much of the subsidiary's stock must the parent own before reporting consolidated statements?
3. How do consolidated financial statements differ from the financial statements of a single company?

S16-10 **Edward Jones Co.** owns vast amounts of corporate bonds. Suppose Edward Jones buys $1,000,000 of **Dow Jones & Co.** bonds at a price of 96. The Dow Jones bonds pay cash interest at the annual rate of 7% and mature within five years.

Working with a bond investment
(Obj. 5)

1. How much did Edward Jones pay to purchase the bond investment? How much will Edward Jones collect when the bond investment matures?
2. How much cash interest will Edward Jones receive each year from Dow Jones & Co.?
3. Will Edward Jones' annual *interest revenue* on the bond investment be more or less than the amount of *cash interest received* each year? Give your reason.
4. Compute Edward Jones' annual interest revenue on this bond investment. Use the straight-line method to amortize the discount on the investment.

Recording bond investment transactions
(Obj. 5)

S16-11 Return to Starter 16-10, the Edward Jones investment in Dow Jones & Co. bonds. Journalize on Edward Jones' books, along with an explanation for each entry:

a. Purchase of the bond investment on January 2, 20X4. Edward Jones expects to hold the investment to maturity.
b. Receipt of annual cash interest on December 31, 20X4.
c. Amortization of discount on December 31, 20X4.
d. Collection of the investment's face value at its maturity date on January 2, 20X9. (Assume the receipt of 20X8 interest and amortization of discount for 20X8 have already been recorded, so you may ignore these entries.)

Accounting for transactions stated in a foreign currency
(Obj. 6)

S16-12 Suppose **Nike Inc.** sells athletic shoes to a Russian company on March 14. Nike agrees to accept 2,000,000 Russian rubles. On the date of sale, the ruble is quoted at $0.036. Nike collects half the receivable on April 19, when the ruble is worth $0.034. Then, on May 10, when the price of the ruble is $0.039, Nike collects the final amount.

Journalize these three transactions for Nike; include an explanation. Overall, how well did Nike come out in terms of a net foreign-currency gain or loss?

online homework

Exercises

Accounting for a trading investment
(Obj. 1)

E16-1 BankOne, headquartered in Columbus, Ohio, holds huge portfolios of investments. Suppose BankOne completed the following investment transactions:

20X8
Dec. 6   Purchased 1,000 shares of **Goodyear Tire & Rubber Co.** stock for $70,000. BankOne plans to sell the stock within a week or two.
30   Received a quarterly cash dividend of $0.85 per share on the Goodyear stock.
31   Adjusted the investment in Goodyear stock. Current market value is $65,000, and BankOne plans to sell the stock early in 20X9.
20X9
Jan. 14   Sold the Goodyear stock for $71,000.

Required

1. Journalize the BankOne investment transactions. Explanations are not required.
2. Show how BankOne would report its investment in the Goodyear stock on the balance sheet at December 31, 20X8.

Journalizing transactions for an available-for-sale investment
(Obj. 2)

E16-2 Journalize the following long-term available-for-sale investment transactions of Cordant Communications. Explanations are not required.

a. Purchased 400 shares (8%) of Marcor Corporation common stock at $38 per share, with the intent of holding the stock for the indefinite future.
b. Received cash dividend of $1 per share on the Marcor investment.
c. At year-end, adjusted the investment account to current market value of $45 per share.
d. Sold the Marcor stock for the market price of $40 per share.

Journalizing transactions for an available-for-sale investment
(Obj. 2)

E16-3 Journalize the following investment transactions of **NEC Corporation**.

Aug. 1   Purchased 500 shares (2%) of Vardaman Corporation common stock as a long-term available-for-sale investment, paying $44 per share.
Sep. 12   Received cash dividend of $1 per share on the Vardaman investment.
Nov. 23   Received 50 shares of Vardaman common stock in a 10% stock dividend.
Dec. 4   Unexpectedly sold the Vardaman stock for $39 per share.

E16-4 Late in the current year, Micron Instruments bought 1,000 shares of **National Geographic** common stock at $81.88, 600 shares of **AT&T Corp.** stock at $46.75, and 1,400 shares of **Hitachi** stock at $79—all as available-for-sale investments. At December 31, *The Wall Street Journal* reports National Geographic stock at $80.38, AT&T at $48.50, and Hitachi at $68.25.

Accounting for long-term investment transactions
(Obj. 2)

Required

1. Determine the cost and the market value of the long-term investment portfolio at December 31.
2. Record any adjusting entry needed at December 31.
3. What two items would Micron Instruments report on its balance sheet for the information given? Make the necessary disclosures.

E16-5 Newbold, Inc., owns equity-method investments in several other department-store companies. Newbold paid $2 million to acquire a 20% investment in Italian Imports Company. Italian Imports reported net income of $780,000 for the first year and declared and paid cash dividends of $500,000. Record the following in Newbold's journal: (a) purchase of the investment, (b) its proportion of Italian Imports' net income, and (c) receipt of the cash dividends.

Accounting for transactions under the equity method
(Obj. 3)

E16-6 Without making journal entries, record the transactions of Exercise 16-5 directly in the Newbold account, Long-Term Equity-Method Investment in Italian Imports. Assume that after all the noted transactions took place, Newbold sold its entire investment in Italian Imports for cash of $2,500,000. How much is Newbold's gain or loss on the sale of the investment?

Measuring gain or loss on the sale of an equity-method investment
(Obj. 3)

E16-7 Nasdaq, Inc., paid $145,000 for a 40% investment in the common stock of Auto Chief, Inc. For the first year, Auto Chief reported net income of $80,000 and at year-end declared and paid cash dividends of $20,000. On the balance sheet date, the market value of Nasdaq's investment in Auto Chief stock was $134,000.

Applying the appropriate accounting method for investments
(Obj. 3)

Required

1. Which method is appropriate for Nasdaq to use in accounting for its investment in Auto Chief? Why?
2. Show everything that Nasdaq would report for the investment and any investment revenue in its year-end financial statements.
3. What role does the market value of the investment play in this situation?

E16-8 On June 30, 20X3, Greenbrier Corp. paid 92 for 6% bonds of **Dean Witter Financial Services** as a long-term held-to-maturity investment. The maturity value of the bonds will be $30,000 on June 30, 20X8. The bonds pay interest on June 30 and December 31.

Recording bond investment transactions
(Obj. 5)

Required

1. What method should Greenbrier Corporation use to account for its investment in the Dean Witter bonds?
2. Using the straight-line method of amortizing the discount, journalize all of Greenbrier's transactions on the bonds for 20X3.
3. Show how Greenbrier would report the bond investment on its balance sheet at December 31, 20X3.

E16-9 Journalize the following foreign-currency transactions. Explanations are not required.

Managing and accounting for foreign-currency transactions
(Obj. 6)

Nov. 17	Purchased inventory on account from a Japanese company. The price was 200,000 yen, and the exchange rate of the yen was $0.0083.
Dec. 16	Paid the Japanese supplier when the exchange rate was $0.0091.
19	Sold merchandise on account to a French company at a price of 60,000 euros. The exchange rate of the euro was $1.10.
30	Collected from the French company when the exchange rate was $1.14.

(*continued*)

On November 18, immediately after your purchase, which currency did you want to strengthen? Which currency did in fact strengthen? Explain your reasoning in detail.

Analyzing available-for-sale investments
(Obj. 2)

E16-10 MAP Incorporated, which makes electronic connection devices, reported the stockholders' equity on its balance sheet, as adapted, at December 31, 20X8.

MAP Incorporated	
Balance Sheet (Partial, adapted)	
December 31, 20X8	
Millions	**20X8**
Shareholders' Equity:	
Common stock...	$ 226
Retained earnings	2,330
Treasury stock, at cost.......................................	(243)
Unrealized gains on available-for-sale investments	14
Total shareholders' equity	$2,327

Required

1. MAP's balance sheet also reports available-for-sale investments at $288 million. What was MAP's cost of the investments? What was the market value of the investments on December 31, 20X8?
2. Suppose MAP sold its available-for-sale investments in 20X9 for $259 million. Determine the gain or loss on the sale of the investments.

Problems

(Group A)

Accounting for trading investments
(Obj. 1)

Student ResourceCD

General Ledger, Peachtree, QuickBooks

P16-1A During the second half of 20X2, the operations of Hercules Steel generated excess cash, which the company invested in securities, as follows:

July 3	Purchased 3,000 shares of common stock as a trading investment, paying $9.25 per share.
Aug. 14	Received cash dividend of $0.32 per share on the trading investment.
Sep. 15	Sold the trading investment for $10.50 per share.
Nov. 24	Purchased trading investments for $226,000.
Dec. 31	Adjusted the trading securities to their market value of $222,500.

Required

1. Record the transactions in the journal of Hercules Steel. Explanations are not required.
2. Post to the Short-Term Investment account. Then show how to report the short-term investment on the Hercules balance sheet at December 31, 20X2.

Accounting for available-for-sale and equity-method investments
(Obj. 2, 3)

Student ResourceCD

GL, PT, QB

P16-2A The beginning balance sheet of TalkNET, Inc., included the following:

Long-Term Equity-Method Investments $300,000

During the year, TalkNET completed the following investment transactions:

Mar. 2	Purchased 2,000 shares of DLV Inc., common stock as a long-term available-for-sale investment, paying $12.25 per share.
Apr. 21	Received cash dividend of $0.75 per share on the DLV investment.
Oct. 17	Received cash dividend of $50,000 from the equity-method investments.
Dec. 31	Received annual reports from the equity-method investee companies. Their total net income for the year was $550,000. Of this amount, TalkNET's proportion is 33%.
31	Adjusted the available-for-sale investment to market value. The market value of TalkNET's investment in DLV is $26,800.

Required

1. Record the transactions in the journal of TalkNET, Inc.

2. Post entries to the Long-Term Equity-Method Investments T-account, and determine its balance at December 31. Do likewise for the Long-Term Available-for-Sale Investment T-account and the Allowance to Adjust Investments to Market T-account.

3. Show how to report the Long-Term Available-for-Sale Investment and the Long-Term Equity-Method Investments accounts on TalkNET's balance sheet at December 31.

P16-3A Baldwin Company owns numerous investments in the stock of other companies. Assume that Baldwin completed the following long-term investment transactions:

Reporting investments on the balance sheet and the related revenue on the income statement
(Obj. 2, 3)

20X2	
Feb. 12	Purchased 20,000 shares, which exceeds 20% of the common stock of Growtech, Inc., at total cost of $700,000.
Aug. 9	Received cash dividend of $0.90 per share on the Growtech investment.
Oct. 16	Purchased 1,000 shares of Varnix Company common stock as an available-for-sale investment, paying $40 per share.
Dec. 31	Received annual report from Growtech, Inc. Net income for the year was $500,000. Of this amount, Baldwin's proportion is 30%.
31	Adjusted the available-for-sale investment in Varnix to current market value of $41,100.

Required

Show what Baldwin Company would report on its year-end balance sheet for these investments. It is helpful to use a T-account for the investment in Growtech stock.

P16-4A Financial institutions such as insurance companies hold large quantities of bond investments. Suppose Liberty Insurance Co. purchases $400,000 of 9% bonds of Inwood Corporation for 103 on January 1, 20X8. These bonds pay interest on June 30 and December 31 each year and mature in five years.

Accounting for a bond investment; straight-line amortization of premium
(Obj. 5)

Required

1. Journalize Liberty's purchase of the bonds as a long-term investment on January 1, 20X8 (to be held to maturity). Then record Liberty's receipt of cash interest and amortization of premium at June 30 and December 31, 20X8. The straight-line method is appropriate for amortizing premium.

2. Show how to report this long-term bond investment on Liberty Insurance Co.'s balance sheet at December 31, 20X8.

P16-5A ← *Link Back to Chapter 15 (Effective-Interest Amortization of Discount).* On December 31, 20X5, when the market interest is 8%, ChaseBank purchases $500,000 of **Michelin Corp.**, 7.4%, six-year bonds. The cost of this long-term bond investment is $486,123, and ChaseBank expects to hold the investment to maturity.

Accounting for a bond investment; effective-interest amortization of discount
(Obj. 5)

Required

Journalize the purchase on December 31, 20X5, the first semiannual interest receipt on June 30, 20X6, and the year-end interest receipt on December 31, 20X6. ChaseBank uses the effective-interest amortization method. Prepare a schedule for amortizing the discount on bond investment through December 31, 20X6. Use Exhibit 15-4 as a guide.

Recording foreign-currency transactions and reporting the transaction gain or loss
(Obj. 6)

Student ResourceCD

GL, PT, QB

P16-6A DVD Burner Company completed the following transactions:

May 1 Sold inventory on account to Marconi Telegraph, an Italian public utility, for $20,000. The exchange rate of the euro is $1.06, and Marconi agrees to pay in dollars.

10 Purchased supplies on account from a Canadian company at a price of Canadian $30,000. The exchange rate of the Canadian dollar is $0.70, and payment will be in Canadian dollars.

17 Sold inventory on account to an English firm for 110,000 British pounds. Payment will be in pounds, and the exchange rate of the pound is $1.60.

22 Collected from Marconi Telegraph.

June 18 Paid the Canadian company. The exchange rate of the Canadian dollar is $0.67.

24 Collected from the English firm. The exchange rate of the British pound is $1.57.

Required

1. Record these transactions in DVD Burner's journal, and show how to report the net foreign-currency gain or loss on the income statement. Explanations are not required.

2. How will what you learned in this problem help you structure international transactions?

Problems

(Group B)

Accounting for trading investments
(Obj. 1)

Student ResourceCD

GL, PT, QB

P16-1B During the second half of 20X4, the operations of Pilot Corporation generated excess cash, which the company invested in securities, as follows:

July 2 Purchased 3,500 shares of common stock as a trading investment, paying $12.75 per share.

Aug. 21 Received cash dividend of $0.45 per share on the trading investment.

Sep. 16 Sold the trading investment for $13.50 per share.

Oct. 8 Purchased trading investments for $136,000.

Dec. 31 Adjusted the trading securities to their market value of $131,500.

Required

1. Record the transactions in the journal of Pilot Corporation. Explanations are not required.

2. Post to the Short-Term Investments account, and show how to report the short-term investments on Pilot's balance sheet at December 31, 20X4.

Accounting for available-for-sale and equity-method investments
(Obj. 2, 3)

Student ResourceCD

GL, PT, QB

P16-2B The beginning balance sheet of Parr Investments Co. included the following:

Long-Term Equity-Method Investments $600,000

During the year Parr completed the following investment transactions:

Mar. 3 Purchased 5,000 shares of LBO Software common stock as a long-term available-for-sale investment, paying $9.25 per share.

May 14 Received cash dividend of $0.82 per share on the LBO investment.

Dec. 15 Received cash dividend of $31,000 from equity-method investments.

31 Received annual reports from equity-method investee companies. Their total net income for the year was $620,000. Of this amount, Parr's proportion is 25%.

31 Adjusted the available-for-sale investment to market value. The market value of Parr's investment in LBO is $44,100.

Required

1. Record the transactions in the journal of Parr Investments.

2. Post entries to the Long-Term Equity-Method Investments T-account, and determine its balance at December 31. Do likewise for the Long-Term Available-for-Sale Investment T-account and the Allowance to Adjust Investment to Market T-account.

3. Show how to report the Long-Term Available-for-Sale Investment and the Long-Term Equity-Method Investments on Parr's balance sheet at December 31.

P16-3B Ambassador Hotel Company owns stock in other companies. During 20X4, Ambassador completed the following long-term investment transactions:

Reporting investments on the balance sheet and the related revenue on the income statement
(Obj. 2, 3)

20X4	
May 1	Purchased 10,000 shares, which exceeds 20%, of the common stock of DeGaulle Company at total cost of $860,000.
Sep. 15	Received cash dividend of $6 per share on the DeGaulle investment.
Oct. 12	Purchased 1,000 shares of Cola Beverage Corporation common stock as an available-for-sale investment, paying $22.50 per share.
Dec. 31	Received annual report from DeGaulle Company. Net income for the year was $360,000. Of this amount, Ambassador's proportion is one third.
31	Adjusted the available-for-sale investment in Cola Beverage to current market value of $20,000.

Required

Show what Ambassador Hotel Company would report on its year-end balance sheet for these investments. (It is helpful to use a T-account for the investment in DeGaulle stock.)

P16-4B Financial institutions hold large quantities of bond investments. Suppose **Goldman Sachs** purchases $800,000 of 8% bonds of **Xerox Corporation** for 92 on January 1, 20X0. These bonds pay interest on June 30 and December 31 each year. They mature on January 1, 20X8.

Accounting for a bond investment; amortizing discount by the straight-line method
(Obj. 5)

Required

1. Journalize Goldman Sachs' purchase of the bonds as a long-term investment on January 1, 20X0 (to be held to maturity). Then record the receipt of cash interest and amortization of discount on June 30 and December 31, 20X0. The straight-line method is appropriate for amortizing discount.

2. Show how to report this long-term bond investment on Goldman Sachs' balance sheet at December 31, 20X0.

P16-5B ← *Link Back to Chapter 15 (Effective-Interest Amortization of Discount).* On December 31, 20X6, when the market interest rate is 10%, First Federal Bank purchases $400,000 of Yuma Inc., 9.5%, 10-year bonds. The cost of this bond investment was $387,578 and the investor expects to hold the investment to maturity.

Accounting for a bond investment; amortizing discount by the effective-interest method
(Obj. 5)

Required

Journalize First Federal's purchase on December 31, 20X6, the first semiannual interest receipt on June 30, 20X7, and the year-end interest receipt on December 31, 20X7. The investor uses the effective-interest amortization method. Prepare a schedule for amortizing the discount on the bond investment through December 31, 20X7. Use Exhibit 15-4 as a guide.

Recording foreign-currency transactions
and reporting the transaction gain or loss
(Obj. 6)

P16-6B Suppose **Ralph Lauren** completed the following transactions:

Student ResourceCD

GL, PT, QB

May 4	Sold clothing on account to a Mexican department store for $71,000. The exchange rate of the Mexican peso is $0.10, and the customer agrees to pay in dollars.
13	Purchased inventory on account from a Canadian company at a price of Canadian $60,000. The exchange rate of the Canadian dollar is $0.75, and payment will be in Canadian dollars.
20	Sold goods on account to an English firm for 80,000 British pounds. Payment will be in pounds, and the exchange rate of the pound is $1.50.
27	Collected from the Mexican company.
June 21	Paid the Canadian company. The exchange rate of the Canadian dollar is $0.72.
July 17	Collected from the English firm. The exchange rate of the British pound is $1.47.

Required

1. Record these transactions in Ralph Lauren's journal, and show how to report the net foreign-currency gain or loss on the income statement. Explanations are not required.
2. How will what you learned in this problem help you structure international transactions?

APPLY *Your Knowledge*

Decision Cases

Explaining the market value and equity
methods of accounting for investments
(Obj. 1, 2)

Case 1. Carla Allman is the manager of Stagg Corp., whose year-end is December 31. The company made two investments during the first week of January 20X2. Both investments are to be held for the indefinite future. Information about the investments follows:

a. Stagg purchased 30% of the common stock of Frontenac Mfg. Co. for its book value of $250,000. During the year ended December 31, 20X2, Frontenac earned $146,000 and paid dividends totaling $53,000. At year-end, the market value of the Frontenac investment is $261,000.
b. One thousand shares of the common stock of St. John Medical Corporation were purchased as an available-for-sale investment for $95,000. During the year ended December 31, 20X2, St. John paid Stagg a dividend of $3,000. St. John earned a profit of $317,000 for that period, and at year-end, the market value of Stagg's investment in St. John stock was $92,000.

Allman has come to you to ask how to account for the investments. Stagg has never had such investments before. Explain the proper accounting to her by indicating that different accounting methods apply to different situations.

Required

Help Allman understand by writing a memo to

1. Describe the methods of accounting applicable to these investments.
2. Identify which method should be used to account for the investments in Frontenac Mfg. Co. and St. John Medical Corporation. Also indicate the dollar amount to report for each investment on the year-end balance sheet.

Case 2. Caesar Saled inherited some investments, and he has received the annual reports of the companies. The financial statements of the companies are puzzling to Saled, and he asks you the following questions:

Understanding the consolidation method for investments
(Obj. 4)

1. The companies label their financial statements as *consolidated* balance sheet, *consolidated* income statement, and so on. What are consolidated financial statements?
2. The consolidated balance sheet lists the asset Goodwill. What is goodwill? Does the presence of goodwill mean that the company's stock has increased in value?

Write a memo to answer each of Saled's questions.

Ethical Issue

Blaze Utilities owns 18% of the voting stock of Southwest Electric Power Company. The remainder of the Southwest stock is held by numerous investors with small holdings. Dee Falco, president of Blaze Utilities and a member of Southwest's board of directors, heavily influences Southwest Electric Power Company's policies.

Under the market-value method of accounting for investments, Blaze's net income increases as it receives dividend revenue from Southwest Power. Blaze Utilities pays President Falco a bonus computed as a percentage of Blaze's net income. Therefore, Falco can control her personal bonus to a certain extent by influencing Southwest's dividends.

A recession occurs in 20X0 and Blaze Utilities' income is low. Falco uses her power as a board member to have Southwest pay a large cash dividend. The action requires Southwest to borrow in order to pay the dividend.

Required

1. In getting Southwest to pay the large cash dividend, is Falco acting within her authority as a member of the Southwest board of directors? Are Falco's actions ethical? Whom can her actions harm?
2. Discuss how using the equity method of accounting for investments would decrease Falco's potential for manipulating her bonus.

Financial Statement Case

Refer to **Amazon.com's** financial statements in Appendix A. Answer the following questions about Amazon's investments.

Accounting for investments
(Obj. 2, 3)

1. Amazon.com reports Marketable Securities on the balance sheet. Amazon accounts for these investments as available-for-sale securities.
   a. What amount is reported for Amazon's marketable securities at December 31, 2002? Does this amount represent cost or market value?
   b. During 2002, Amazon's marketable securities increased in value by $20,294 thousand. Journalize this increase in value, dated December 31, 2002.
2. Amazon.com also reports Other Equity Investments among its long-term assets.

   a. Which accounting method is used for these investments?
   b. The income statement reports the results of operations by these investee companies. Were the investee companies' operations successful or unsuccessful during 2002? How can you tell? In your answer, give the dollar amount to prove your point.

Team Project

Pick a stock from *The Wall Street Journal* or other database or publication. Assume that your group purchases 1,000 shares of the stock as a short-term trading investment. Research the stock in *Value Line, Moody's Investor Record*, or other source to determine whether the company pays cash dividends and, if so, how much and at what intervals.

1. Track the stock for a period assigned by your professor. Over the specified period, keep a daily record of the price of the stock to see how well your investment has performed. Each day, search the Corporate Dividend News in *The Wall Street Journal* to keep a record of any dividends you've received. End the period of your analysis with a month end, such as September 30 or December 31.

2. Journalize all transactions that you have experienced, including the investment purchase, dividends received (both cash dividends and stock dividends), any year-end adjustment required by the accounting method that is appropriate for your investment, and the sale of your investment two ways: at a gain; and at a loss. Assume you will prepare financial statements on the ending date of your study.

3. Show what you will report on your company's balance sheet and income statement as a result of your investment transactions.

For Internet exercises, go to the Web site www.prenhall.com/horngren.

Comprehensive Problem for Chapters 13 to 16

GATEWAY INTERNATIONAL'S CORPORATE TRANSACTIONS

Gateway International's corporate charter authorizes the company to issue 1 million shares of $1 par-value common stock and 200,000 shares of 5%, $10 par-value preferred stock. During the first quarter of operations, Gateway completed the following selected transactions:

Oct.	1	Issued 75,000 shares of common stock for cash of $6 per share.
	5	Issued 2,000 shares of preferred stock, receiving cash of $22,000.
	30	Purchased 5,000 shares (20%) of the outstanding common stock of Newbold Corp. as a long-term equity-method investment, $85,000.
Nov.	1	Issued $200,000 of 9%, 10-year bonds payable at 94.
	14	Purchased long-term available-for-sale investments in the common stocks of **PepsiCo**, $22,000, and Data General, $31,000.
	19	Experienced a $13,000 extraordinary flood loss of inventory that cost $21,000. Cash received from the insurance company was $8,000. There is no income tax effect from this loss.
	30	Purchased 10,000 shares of Gateway common stock for the treasury at $5 per share.
Dec.	1	Received cash dividends of $1,100 on the PepsiCo investment.
	1	Sold 1,000 shares of the treasury stock for cash of $6.25 per share.
	29	Received a report from Newbold Corp. indicating that net income for November and December was $70,000.
	30	Sold merchandise on account, $716,000. Cost of the goods was $439,000. Operating expenses totaled $174,000, with $166,000 of this amount paid in cash. Gateway uses a perpetual inventory system.
	31	Accrued interest and amortized discount (straight-line method) on the bonds payable issued on November 1.
	31	Adjusted the available-for-sale investments to current market value. Market values of the available-for-sale investments: PepsiCo stock, $24,000, and the Data General stock, $30,000.
	31	Accrued income tax expense of $36,000.
	31	Closed all revenues, expenses, and losses to Retained Earnings in a single closing entry.
	31	Declared a quarterly cash dividend of $0.125 per share on the preferred stock. Record date is January 11, with payment scheduled for January 19.

Required

1. Record these transactions in the general journal. Explanations are not required.

2. Prepare a single-step income statement, including earnings per share, for the quarter ended December 31. Gateway had 72,000 shares of common stock outstanding. Remember to compute the preferred dividends for only 1/4 of the year.

CHAPTER 17

The Statement of Cash Flows

TIPS CHECK YOUR RESOURCES

- Visit the www.prenhall.com/horngren **Web site** for self-study quizzes, video clips, and other resources
- Try the **Quick Check** exercise at the end of the chapter to test your knowledge
- Learn the **key terms**
- Do the **Starter** exercises keyed in the margins
- Work the **mid-** and **end-of-chapter summary problems**
- Use the **Concept Links** to review material in other chapters
- Search the **CD** for review materials by chapter or by key word
- Watch the **tutorial videos** to review key concepts

LEARNING OBJECTIVES

⭐ **1** Identify the purposes of the statement of cash flows

⭐ **2** Distinguish among operating, investing, and financing cash flows

⭐ **3** Prepare a statement of cash flows by the indirect method

⭐ **4** Prepare a statement of cash flows by the direct method

Why is cash flow so important? You can probably begin to answer that question from your own experience: It takes cash to pay the bills. You have a certain amount of income, and you have certain expenses: food, gas, entertainment, car insurance, and credit cards. The two have to match in quantity and in timing. You may borrow money for a large purchase, like a car, but if you have to borrow money for everyday living expenses, you are in trouble.

Businesses, including e-businesses, work the same way: They need enough cash flowing in to pay the bills and run their operations. Take eBay, a company that has revolutionized commerce. Lots of dot.coms have come and gone, but eBay is still going strong. One reason is that the company is both profitable and cash-rich. In 2001, eBay's operations provided more than $250 million of cash. In 2002, cash flow almost doubled—to $479 million—

eBay

quite an accomplishment for such a young company. Being cash-rich allows eBay to plan for expansion:

> *eBay Inc. Outlines Global Business Strategy*
>
> *eBay Inc., . . . the world's online marketplace, [recently] outlined its strategy for growth. . . . eBay executives highlighted key areas of growth, both domestically and abroad. "The . . . potential of our business gives us great confidence in the future," said Meg Whitman, President and CEO of eBay. "The eBay marketplace is thriving. . . . "*
> [eBay press release] ■

▊*Sitemap*

- ■ **Basic Concepts**
- ■ **The Indirect Method**
- ■ **The Direct Method**
- ■ **Appendix: Work Sheet Approach**

This chapter is devoted to analyzing cash flows because understanding cash flows is vital for making good business decisions. We will see how to prepare the statement of cash flows, which is the basis for the analysis, and how to interpret cash-flow information.

We begin by explaining the statement format, called the indirect approach, that is used by the vast majority of companies. We end the chapter with the alternate format of the statement of cash flows, the direct approach. This chapter will prepare you to analyze the cash flows of any company you encounter. It has three distinct sections:

- ■ Introduction
- ■ Preparing the Statement of Cash Flows by the Indirect Method, which begins on page 661
- ■ Preparing the Statement of Cash Flows by the Direct Method, which begins on page 671

The introduction applies to all the cash-flow topics. To cover only the indirect method, instructors can assign the first two parts of the chapter. Those interested only in the direct method can cover the Introduction and proceed to the direct method on page 671.

■ Basic Concepts
☐ The Indirect Method
☐ The Direct Method
☐ Appendix: Work Sheet Approach

Student Resource **CD**

direct method, financing activities, indirect method, investing activities, operating activities, statement of cash flows

Statement of Cash Flows
Reports cash receipts and cash payments during the period.

Cash Flows
Cash receipts and cash payments.

Basic Concepts: Statement of Cash Flows

A balance sheet reports financial position, and balance sheets for two periods show whether cash increased or decreased. For example, Anchor Corporation's comparative balance sheet reported the following:

	20X5	20X4	Increase (Decrease)
Cash	$22,000	$42,000	$(20,000)

You can see that Anchor's cash decreased by $20,000 during 20X5. But the balance sheet doesn't show *why* cash decreased. We need the cash-flow statement for that.

The **statement of cash flows** reports **cash flows**—cash receipts and cash payments—during the period. It shows where cash came from and how it was spent. It explains the *causes* of the change in cash during any given time period. The statement of cash flows covers a span of time and therefore is dated "Year Ended December 31, 20X5" or "Month Ended June 30, 20X5." Exhibit 17-1 illustrates the time element of each financial statement.

Exhibit 17-1
Timing of the Financial Statements

The statement of cash flows serves several purposes:

1. **_Predicts future cash flows._** Past cash receipts and payments are good predictors of future cash flows.

2. **_Evaluates management decisions._** If managers make wise investment decisions, the business prospers. If they make unwise investments, the business suffers. The statement of cash flows reports cash flows from operations and also the investments the company is making. Investors and creditors use cash-flow information to evaluate managers' decisions.

3. **_Predicts ability to make debt payments to lenders and to pay dividends to stockholders._** Lenders want to collect interest and principal on their loans. Stockholders want dividends on their investments. The statement of cash flows helps predict whether the business can make these payments.

On a statement of cash flows, _Cash_ means more than just cash on hand and cash in the bank. It includes **cash equivalents**, which are highly liquid short-term investments that can be readily converted into cash. Examples of cash equivalents are money-market investments and investments in U.S. government securities. Businesses invest cash in liquid assets rather than let the cash remain idle. Throughout this chapter, the term _cash_ refers to cash and cash equivalents.

⭐ _Identify the purposes of the statement of cash flows_

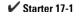 **Starter 17-1**

Cash Equivalents
Highly liquid short-term investments that can be readily converted into cash.

Operating, Investing, and Financing Activities

A business engages in three types of business activities:

- Operating activities
- Investing activities
- Financing activities

Operating activities create revenues, expenses, gains, and losses. They affect _net income_ on the income statement, which is a product of accrual accounting. The statement of cash flows reports the cash effects of operating activities. Operating activities also affect _current assets_ and _current liabilities_ on the balance sheet. Operating activities are the most important of the three categories. A successful business must generate most of its cash from day-to-day operations.

Investing activities increase and decrease _long-term assets_, such as computers and software, land, buildings, and equipment. The purchases and sales of

 Distinguish among operating, investing, and financing cash flows

Operating Activities
Activities that create revenue or expense in the entity's major line of business; a section of the statement of cash flows. Operating activities affect the income statement.

Investing Activities
Activities that increase or decrease long-term assets; a section of the statement of cash flows.

these assets are investing activities. Loans to others and collections of loans are also investing activities. Investing activities are less critical than operating activities.

Financing activities obtain cash to launch a business and keep it running. Financing includes issuing stock, borrowing money, buying and selling treasury stock, and paying dividends. Paying off a loan is another financing activity. Financing cash flows relate to *long-term liabilities* and *owners' equity*. They are the least important of the three categories of cash flows, and that's why they are reported last.

Exhibit 17-2 shows the relationship between operating, investing, and financing activities and the various parts of the balance sheet.

Financing Activities
Activities that obtain the cash needed to launch and sustain the business; a section of the statement of cash flows.

Exhibit 17-2

Operating, Investing, and Financing Cash Flows and the Balance-Sheet Accounts

Cash and Kisses Meet at Match.com

Who says "Money Can't Buy Me Love"? Match.com, the Internet dating service, is proving that money *can* buy at least the potential for love. Cash flow at the online dating service has surged as it has collected over $15 million a month from clients. For their fees, clients can post photos, contact other members, and receive alerts when potential matches show up.

Ticketmaster, Match.com's parent company, is delighted. Ticketmaster posted its first positive cash flow in 2001, thanks largely to Match.com. Analysts are not surprised: "Online dating [...] is one of the few [things] people will [pay] for online, [and...] companies are actually upping their prices."

Match.com's only big operating expense is advertising. The company has stayed on top by spending $50 million a year on TV ads. Yet, boasts the Ticketmaster chief executive, 30% to 70% of Match.com's advertising dollars are "instantly recouped."

Cash-rich Internet companies like Match.com can offer vital lessons about what works online. In general, these companies provide services that are information-intensive and require no physical transport of goods. There are no returned goods or other fulfillment costs to deal with.

For Match.com, fulfillment occurs off-screen: To date, the company boasts 1,300 marriages, hundreds of thousands of relationships, and more than 50 babies born of Match.com unions.

Based on: Robert Barker, "Is Ticketmaster Your Perfect Date?" *Business Week*, April 22, 2002, p. 108. Bob Tedeschi, "Online Matchmakers Are Helping to Bolster the Finances of Their Corporate Parents as They Raise the Romantic Hopes of Clients," *The New York Times*, February 4, 2002, p. C6. Julia Angwin, "Net Income: Latest Dot-Com Fad Is a Bit Old-Fashioned: It's Called 'Profitability,'" *The Wall Street Journal*, August 14, 2002, p. A1. Dennis McCafferty, "Hosting in the Name of Love," Hostingtech.com, October 2002.

Accounting.com

Two Formats for Operating Activities

There are two ways to format operating activities on the statement of cash flows:

- **Indirect method**, which reconciles from net income to net cash provided by operating activities
- **Direct method**, which reports all cash receipts and cash payments from operating activities

The two methods use different computations but produce the same amount of cash from operations. The indirect and direct methods have no effect on investing or financing activities. The following table summarizes the differences between these approaches for operating activities (all dollar amounts are assumed for the illustration).

Indirect Method		Direct Method	
Net income	$ 300	Collections from customers	$ 900
Adjustments:		*Deductions:*	
Depreciation, etc.	100	Payments to suppliers, etc.. . . .	(500)
Net cash provided by		Net cash provided by	
operating activities. . . .	$ 400	operating activities	$ 400

Let's begin with the indirect method because most companies use it.

Indirect Method
Format of the operating activities section of the statement of cash flows; starts with net income and reconciles to net cash provided by operating activities.

Direct Method
Format of the operating activities section of the statement of cash flows; lists the major categories of operating cash receipts and cash payments.

✔ Starter 17-2

Preparing the Statement of Cash Flows by the Indirect Method

To prepare the statement of cash flows, you need data from the income statement and the balance sheet. Consider Anchor Corporation, a dealer in older British sports cars such as MG, Triumph, and Austin Healey. To prepare the statement of cash flows by the indirect method,

STEP 1 Lay out the template as shown in Exhibit 17-3. The exhibit is comprehensive. Steps 2 to 4 will complete the statement of cash flows.

STEP 2 Use the comparative balance sheet to determine the increase or decrease in cash. The change in cash is the "check figure" for the statement of cash flows. Exhibit 17-4 gives the comparative balance sheet of Anchor Corporation at December 31, 20X5 and 20X4, with cash highlighted. Anchor's cash decreased by $20,000 during 20X5.

STEP 3 From the income statement, take net income, depreciation, depletion, and amortization expense, and any gains or losses on the sale of assets. Exhibit 17-5 gives the income statement of Anchor Corporation for the year ended December 31, 20X5, with relevant items highlighted.

STEP 4 Use data from the income statement and balance sheet to complete the statement of cash flows. The statement is complete only after you have explained year-to-year changes in all balance-sheet accounts.

Let's apply these steps to prepare the operating activities section of Anchor Corporation's statement of cash flows. Exhibit 17-6 gives the operating activities section of the statement of cash flows.

☐ Basic Concepts
■ The Indirect Method
☐ The Direct Method
☐ Appendix: Work Sheet Approach

Student ResourceCD

indirect method, financing activities, investing activities, operating activities, financing cash flows, investing cash flows, operating cash flows

Prepare a statement of cash flows by the indirect method

Exhibit 17-3

Template of the Statement of Cash Flows: Indirect Method

✔ **Starter 17-3**

Anchor Corporation

Statement of Cash Flows
Year Ended December 31, 20X5

Cash flows from operating activities:
  Net income
  Adjustments to reconcile net income to net cash provided by
    operating activities:
    + Depreciation / amortization expense
    + Loss on sale of long-term assets
    – Gain on sale of long-term assets
    – Increases in current assets other than cash
    + Decreases in current assets other than cash
    + Increases in current liabilities
    – Decreases in current liabilities
  Net cash provided by operating activities

Cash flows from investing activities:
    Sales of long-term assets (investments, land, building, equipment,
      and so on)
    – Purchases of long-term assets
  Net cash provided by (used for) investing activities

Cash flows from financing activities:
    Issuance of stock
    + Sale of treasury stock
    – Purchase of treasury stock
    + Issuance of notes or bonds payable (borrowing)
    – Payment of notes or bonds payable
    – Payment of dividends
  Net cash provided by (used for) financing activities

Net increase (decrease) in cash during the year
    + Cash at December 31, 20X4
    = Cash at December 31, 20X5

Exhibit 17-4 **Comparative Balance Sheet**

Anchor Corporation

Comparative Balance Sheet
December 31, 20X5 and 20X4

(In thousands)	20X5	20X4	Increase (Decrease)	
Assets				
Current:				
Cash..................................	$ 22	$ 42	$ (20)	Changes in current assets—Operating
Accounts receivable	96	81	15	
Inventory	143	145	(2)	
Plant assets, net of depreciation	464	219	245	Changes in noncurrent assets—Investing
Total......................	$725	$487	$238	
Liabilities				
Current:				
Accounts payable	$ 91	$ 57	$ 34	Changes in current liabilities—Operating
Accrued liabilities	5	9	(4)	
Long-term notes payable.................	160	77	83	Changes in long-term liabilities and common stock—Financing
Stockholders' Equity				
Common stock..........................	359	258	101	
Retained earnings	110	86	24	Change due to net income—Operating / Change due to dividends—Financing
Total.....................	$725	$487	$238	

Anchor Corporation

Income Statement
Year Ended December 31, 20X5

Exhibit 17-5

Income Statement

	(In thousands)	
Revenues and gains:		
Sales revenue	$284	
Interest revenue	12	
Dividend revenue	9	
Gain on sale of plant assets	8	
Total revenues and gains		$313
Expenses:		
Cost of goods sold	$150	
Salary and wage expense	56	
Depreciation expense	18	
Other operating expense	17	
Interest expense	16	
Income tax expense	15	
Total expenses		272
Net income		$ 41

Anchor Corporation

Statement of Cash Flows
Operating Activities Only
For the Year Ended December 31, 20X5

		(In thousands)	
Cash flows from operating activities:			
Net income			$41
Adjustments to reconcile net income to net cash provided by operating activities:			
Ⓐ	Depreciation	$ 18	
Ⓑ	Gain on sale of plant assets	(8)	
	Increase in accounts receivable	(15)	
	Decrease in inventory	2	
Ⓒ	Increase in accounts payable	34	
	Decrease in accrued liabilities	(4)	27
	Net cash provided by operating activities		$68

Cash Flows from Operating Activities

The operating section of the cash-flow statement begins with net income, taken from the income statement (Exhibit 17-5). Additions and subtractions, which follow, are labeled "Adjustments to reconcile net income to net cash provided by operating activities."

Operating Activities Are Related to the Transactions That Make Up Net Income
(Revenues, Expenses, Gains, and Losses).[1]

---

[1]The authors thank Alfonso Oddo for suggesting this summary.

Ⓐ **DEPRECIATION, DEPLETION, AND AMORTIZATION EXPENSES** These expenses are added back to net income to reconcile from net income to cash flow. Let's see why. Depreciation is recorded as follows:

Depreciation Expense	18,000	
Accumulated Depreciation		18,000

You can see that depreciation does not affect cash. However, depreciation, like all other expenses, decreases net income. Therefore, in going from net income to cash flows, we add depreciation back to net income. The add-back cancels the earlier deduction.

Example: Suppose you had only two transactions during the period, a $1,000 cash sale and depreciation expense of $300. Net income is $700 ($1,000 − $300). But cash flow from operations is $1,000. To reconcile from net income ($700) to cash flow ($1,000), add back depreciation ($300). Also add back depletion and amortization.

Ⓑ **GAINS AND LOSSES ON THE SALE OF ASSETS** Sales of long-term assets are *investing* activities. A gain or loss on the sale is included in net income and therefore must be adjusted out of net income on the statement of cash flows. Exhibit 17-6 includes an adjustment for a gain. During 20X5, Anchor sold equipment for $62,000. The equipment's book value was $54,000, so there was a gain of $8,000.

The $62,000 sale is an investing cash flow, and the $8,000 gain on the sale must be removed from operating cash flow. We explain investing activities in the next section.

A loss on the sale of plant assets would be *added back* to net income. The cash received from selling the plant assets is then reported under investing activities.

Ⓒ **CHANGES IN THE CURRENT ASSET AND CURRENT LIABILITY ACCOUNTS** Most current assets and current liabilities result from operating activities. For example, accounts receivable result from sales, inventory relates to cost of goods sold, and so on. Changes in the current accounts are reported as adjustments to net income on the cash-flow statement. The reasoning follows:

↑ Current assets ⇒ ↓ Cash

1. *An increase in a current asset other than cash means a decrease in cash.* The reason is because it takes cash to acquire assets. If Accounts Receivable, Inventory, or Prepaid Expenses increase during the period, subtract the increase from net income to measure cash flow from operations.

↓ Current assets ⇒ ↑ Cash

2. *A decrease in a current asset other than cash means an increase in cash.* Suppose Anchor's Accounts Receivable decreased by $4,000. Anchor must have collected on the Accounts Receivable. Therefore, add decreases in Accounts Receivable and the other current assets to net income.

↓ Current liabilities ⇒ ↓ Cash

3. *A decrease in a current liability means a decrease in cash.* The payment of a current liability causes cash to decrease. Therefore, subtract decreases in current liabilities from net income.

↑ Current liabilities ⇒ ↑ Cash

4. *An increase in a current liability means an increase in cash.* Anchor's Accounts Payable increased. This means that cash was *not* spent to pay this liability, so Anchor has more cash on hand. Thus, increases in current liabilities are *added* to net income.

EVALUATING CASH FLOWS FROM OPERATING ACTIVITIES During 20X5, Anchor Corporation's operations provided net cash flow of $68,000. This amount exceeds net income, as it should because of the add-back of depreciation. However, to fully evaluate a company's cash flows, you must also examine its investing and financing activities. Let's see how to report those cash flows, as shown in Exhibit 17-7, which gives Anchor's full-blown statement of cash flows.

Exhibit 17-7

Statement of Cash Flows—
Indirect Method

Anchor Corporation

Statement of Cash Flows
For the Year Ended December 31, 20X5

		(In thousands)	
Cash flows from operating activities:			
Net income....................................			$ 41
Adjustments to reconcile net income to net cash provided by operating activities:			
Ⓐ Depreciation		$ 18	
Ⓑ Gain on sale of plant assets...................		(8)	
Increase in accounts receivable...............		(15)	
Decrease in inventory........................		2	
Ⓒ Increase in accounts payable.................		34	
Decrease in accrued liabilities................		(4)	27
Net cash provided by operating activities			68
Cash flows from investing activities:			
Acquisition of plant assets.......................		$ (317)	
Proceeds from sale of plant assets		62	
Net cash used for investing activities			(255)
Cash flows from financing activities:			
Proceeds from issuance of common stock...........		$ 101	
Proceeds from issuance of long-term notes payable ..		94	
Payment of long-term notes payable...............		(11)	
Payment of dividends		(17)	
Net cash provided by financing activities.........			167
Net decrease in cash			$ (20)
Cash balance, December 31, 20X4			42
Cash balance, December 31, 20X5			$ 22

✔ Starter 17-4

✔ Starter 17-5

✔ Starter 17-6

Cash Flows from Investing Activities

Investing activities affect long-term asset accounts, such as Plant Assets and Investments. Let's see how to compute the investing cash flows.

COMPUTING ACQUISITIONS AND SALES OF PLANT ASSETS Companies keep separate accounts for Land, Buildings, Equipment, and other plant assets. But for computing investing cash flows, it is helpful to combine these accounts into a single Plant Assets account. Also, we subtract accumulated depreciation from the assets' cost and work with a single net figure for plant assets. This simplifies the computations.

To illustrate, observe that Anchor Corporation's

- Balance sheet reports beginning plant assets, net of depreciation, of $219,000 and an ending net amount of $464,000 (Exhibit 17-4).

- Income statement shows depreciation expense of $18,000 and an $8,000 gain on sale of plant assets (Exhibit 17-5).

Further, the acquisitions of plant assets total $317,000 (see Exhibit 17-7). How much, then, are the proceeds from the sale of plant assets? First, we must determine the book value of plant assets sold, as follows:

Plant Assets (Net)

Beginning balance	+	Acquisitions	−	Depreciation	−	Book value of assets sold	=	Ending balance
$219,000	+	$317,000	−	$18,000	−	− X	=	$464,000
						− X	=	$464,000 − $219,000 − $317,000 + $18,000
						X	=	$54,000

Now we can compute the sale proceeds:

Sale proceeds	=	Book value of assets sold	+	Gain	−	Loss
	=	$54,000	+	$8,000	−	$0
	=	$62,000				

Trace the sale proceeds of $62,000 to the statement of cash flows in Exhibit 17-7. If the sale resulted in a loss of $3,000, the sale proceeds would be $51,000 ($54,000 − $3,000), and the statement of cash flows would report $51,000 as a cash receipt from this investing activity.

The Plant Assets T-account provides another look at the computation of the book value of the assets sold.

Plant Assets (Net)

Beginning balance	219,000	Depreciation		18,000
Acquisitions	317,000	Book value of assets sold		54,000
Ending balance	464,000			

✔ **Starter 17-7**

Proceeds from the sale of an asset can be computed as follows:

Proceeds = Book value sold + Gain, or − Loss

The book-value information comes from the balance sheet; the gain or loss comes from the income statement. Exhibit 17-8 summarizes the computation of the investing cash flows.

Exhibit 17-8 Computing Cash Flows from Investing Activities

Receipts

From sale of plant assets	Beginning plant assets (net)	+	Acquisition cost	−	Depreciation	−	Book value of assets sold	=	Ending plant assets (net)
	Cash received	=	Book value of assets sold	+ or −	Gain on sale / Loss on sale				

Payments

For acquisition of plant assets	Beginning plant assets (net)	+	Acquisition cost	−	Depreciation	−	Book value of assets sold	=	Ending plant assets (net)

Cash Flows from Financing Activities

Financing activities affect the liability and stockholders' equity accounts, such as Long-Term Notes Payable, Bonds Payable, Common Stock, and Retained Earnings.

COMPUTING ISSUANCES AND PAYMENTS OF LONG-TERM NOTES PAYABLE
The beginning and ending balances of Long-Term Notes Payable or Bonds Payable are taken from the balance sheet. If either the amount of new issuances or the payments is known, the other amount can be computed. For Anchor Corporation, new issuances of notes payable total $94,000 (Exhibit 17-7). The computation of debt payments uses the Long-Term Notes Payable account, with amounts from Anchor Corporation's balance sheet in Exhibit 17-4:

Long-Term Notes Payable

Beginning balance	+	Issuance of new notes payable	−	Payment of notes payable	=	Ending balance
$77,000	+	$94,000		−X	=	$160,000
				−X	=	$160,000 − $77,000 − $94,000
				X	=	$11,000

Another view:

Long-Term Notes Payable

		Beginning balance	77,000
Payments	11,000	Issuance of new notes payable	94,000
		Ending balance	160,000

COMPUTING ISSUANCES OF STOCK AND PURCHASES OF TREASURY STOCK

Cash flows for these financing activities can be determined by analyzing the stock accounts. For example, the amount of a new issuance of common stock is determined from Common Stock. Using data from Exhibits 17-4 and 17-7:

Common Stock

Beginning balance	+	Issuance of new stock	=	Ending balance
$ 258,000	+	$101,000	=	$359,000

Another view:

Common Stock

	Beginning balance	258,000
	Issuance of new stock	101,000
	Ending balance	359,000

Apart from the Anchor Corporation example, cash flows affecting Treasury Stock can be analyzed as follows:

Treasury Stock (Amounts assumed for illustration only)

Beginning balance	+	Purchase of treasury stock	=	Ending balance
$16,000	+	$3,000	=	$19,000

Another view:

Treasury Stock

Beginning balance	16,000
Purchases of treasury stock	3,000
Ending balance	19,000

COMPUTING DIVIDEND PAYMENTS   The amount of dividend payments can be computed by analyzing Retained Earnings. The T-accounts below provide another view.

Retained Earnings

Beginning balance	+	Net income	−	Dividends	=	Ending balance
$86,000	+	$41,000		−X	=	$110,000
				−X	=	$110,000 − $86,000 − $41,000
				X	=	$17,000

Retained Earnings

		Beginning balance	86,000
Dividends	17,000	Net income	41,000
		Ending balance	110,000

✔ **Starter 17-8**

A stock dividend has *no* effect on Cash and is *not* reported on the cash-flow statement. Exhibit 17-9 summarizes the computation of cash flows from financing activities, highlighted in color.

Exhibit 17-9 Computing Cash Flows from Financing Activities

Receipts

| From issuance of long-term notes payable | Beginning notes payable | + | Issuance of notes payable | − | Payment of notes payable | = | Ending long-term notes payable |

| From issuance of stock | Beginning stock | + | Issuance of new stock | = | Ending stock |

Payments

| Of long-term notes payable | Beginning notes payable | + | Issuance of notes payable | − | Payment of notes payable | = | Ending long-term notes payable |

| To purchase treasury stock | Beginning treasury stock | + | Cost of treasury stock | = | Ending treasury stock |

| Of dividends | Beginning retained earnings | + | Net income | − | Dividends | = | Ending retained earnings |

Classify each of the following as an operating activity, an investing activity, or a financing activity:

a. Issuance of stock
b. Borrowing
c. Sales revenue
d. Payment of dividends
e. Purchase of land
f. Purchase of treasury stock

g. Paying bonds payable
h. Interest expense
i. Sale of equipment
j. Cost of goods sold
k. Purchase of another company
l. Making a loan

Answer:

a. Financing
b. Financing
c. Operating
d. Financing

e. Investing
f. Financing
g. Financing
h. Operating

i. Investing
j. Operating
k. Investing
l. Investing

Noncash Investing and Financing Activities

Companies make investments that do not require cash. They also obtain financing other than cash. Our examples thus far have included none of these transactions. Now suppose Anchor Corporation issued common stock of $320,000 to acquire a building. Anchor would journalize this transaction as follows:

| Building .... | 320,000 | |
| Common Stock .... | | 320,000 |

This transaction would not be reported on the cash-flow statement because Anchor paid no cash. But the building and the common stock are important. *Noncash investing and financing activities* can be reported in a separate schedule that accompanies the statement of cash flows. Exhibit 17-10 illustrates noncash investing and financing activities (all amounts are assumed). This information follows the cash-flow statement or can be disclosed in a note.

Exhibit 17-10

Noncash Investing and Financing Activities (All amounts assumed)

	Thousands
Noncash Investing and Financing Activities:	
Acquisition of building by issuing common stock..............	$320
Acquisition of land by issuing note payable..................	70
Payment of note payable by issuing common stock	100
Total noncash investing and financing activities	$490

Now let's put into practice what you have learned about the statement of cash flows prepared by the indirect method.

MID-CHAPTER *Summary Problem*

Robins Corporation reported the following income statement and comparative balance sheet for 20X5, along with transaction data for 20X5:

CHECK YOUR RESOURCES

Robins Corporation
Income Statement
Year Ended December 31, 20X5

Sales revenue		$662,000
Cost of goods sold		560,000
Gross profit		102,000
Operating expenses:		
Salary expense	$46,000	
Depreciation expense	10,000	
Rent expense	2,000	
Total operating expenses		58,000
Income from operations		44,000
Other items:		
Loss on sale of equipment		(2,000)
Income before income tax		42,000
Income tax expense		16,000
Net income		$ 26,000

Robins Corporation
Balance Sheet
December 31, 20X5 and 20X4

Assets	20X5	20X4	Liabilities	20X5	20X4
Current:			Current:		
Cash and equivalents	$ 22,000	$ 3,000	Accounts payable	$ 35,000	$ 26,000
Accounts receivable	22,000	23,000	Accrued liabilities	7,000	9,000
Inventories	35,000	34,000	Income tax payable	10,000	10,000
Total current assets	79,000	60,000	Total current liabilities	52,000	45,000
Equipment, net	126,000	72,000	Bonds payable	84,000	53,000
			Owners' Equity		
			Common stock	52,000	20,000
			Retained earnings	27,000	19,000
			Less: Treasury stock	(10,000)	(5,000)
Total assets	$205,000	$132,000	Total liabilities and equity	$205,000	$132,000

Transaction Data for 20X5:

Purchase of equipment	$140,000
Payment of dividends	18,000
Issuance of common stock to retire bonds payable	13,000
Issuance of bonds payable to borrow cash	44,000
Issuance of common stock	19,000
Sale of equipment (book value, $76,000)	74,000
Purchase of treasury stock	5,000

Required

Prepare Robins Corporation's statement of cash flows for the year ended December 31, 20X5. Format operating cash flows by the indirect method. Follow the four steps outlined below.

Requirement 1

STEP 1 Lay out the template of the statement of cash flows.

STEP 2 From the comparative balance sheet, determine the increase in cash during the year, $19,000.

STEP 3 From the income statement, take net income, depreciation, and the loss on sale of equipment to the statement of cash flows.

STEP 4 Complete the statement of cash flows. Account for the year-to-year change in each balance sheet account. Prepare a T-account to show the transaction activity in each long-term balance-sheet account.

Solution

Robins Corporation
Statement of Cash Flows
Year Ended December 31, 20X5

Cash flows from operating activities:		
Net income		$26,000
Adjustments to reconcile net income to		
net cash provided by operating activities:		
Depreciation	$ 10,000	
Loss on sale of equipment	2,000	
Decrease in accounts receivable	1,000	
Increase in inventories	(1,000)	
Increase in accounts payable	9,000	
Decrease in accrued liabilities	(2,000)	19,000
Net cash provided by operating activities		45,000
Cash flows from investing activities:		
Purchase of equipment	$(140,000)	
Sale of equipment	74,000	
Net cash used for investing activities		(66,000)
Cash flows from financing activities:		
Issuance of common stock	$ 19,000	
Payment of dividends	(18,000)	
Issuance of bonds payable	44,000	
Purchase of treasury stock	(5,000)	
Net cash provided by financing activities		40,000
Net increase in cash		$19,000
Cash balance, December 31, 20X4		3,000
Cash balance, December 31, 20X5		$22,000
Noncash investing and financing activities:		
Issuance of common stock to retire bonds payable		$13,000
Total noncash investing and financing activities		$13,000

Equipment, Net			
Bal.	72,000		
	140,000	10,000	
		76,000	
Bal.	126,000		

Bonds Payable			
		Bal.	53,000
		13,000	44,000
		Bal.	84,000

Common Stock		
	Bal.	20,000
		13,000
		19,000
	Bal.	52,000

Retained Earnings		
	Bal.	19,000
18,000		26,000
	Bal.	27,000

Treasury Stock		
Bal.	5,000	
5,000		
Bal.	10,000	

Excel Application Exercise

Goal: To create an Excel work sheet that computes cash flows from operating activities using the indirect method.

Scenario: As an accountant at Ochoa, Inc., you have been asked to compute the net cash provided by operating activities using the indirect method for the month of March. Accounting records for the company reveal the following:

Cash sales	$ 9,000
Loss on sale of land	5,000
Net income	33,000
Depreciation	12,000
Increase in current assets other than cash	17,000
Acquisition of land	37,000
Decrease in current liabilities	9,000

Using the information provided in this exercise, determine the net cash flows from operating activities. When done, answer these questions:

1. Does Ochoa have net cash provided by (or used by) operating activities?
2. Evaluate Ochoa's operating cash flow as either strong or weak.
3. Based on the Application Exercise for this chapter, what decisions might investors make with this information?

Step-by-Step:
1. Open a new Excel work sheet.
2. Create a heading for your work sheet that contains:
   a. Chapter 17 Excel Application Exercise
   b. Ochoa, Inc.
   c. Statement of Cash Flows - Operating Activities
   d. For the Month Ended March 31, 20X5
3. Follow the statement of cash flows format in Exhibit 17-3 and use formulas for all computations.
4. Save your work and print a copy for your files.

Preparing the Statement of Cash Flows by the Direct Method

☐ Basic Concepts
☐ The Indirect Method
■ **The Direct Method**
☐ Appendix: Work Sheet Approach

Student Resource **CD**

direct method, financing activities, investing activities, operating activities, financing cash flows, investing cash flows, operating cash flows

Prepare a statement of cash flows by the direct method

The Financial Accounting Standards Board (FASB) has expressed a preference for the direct method of reporting cash flows from operating activities. Unfortunately, very few companies use this method because it takes more computations than the indirect method. But the direct method provides clearer information about the sources and uses of cash. Investing and financing cash flows are unaffected by operating cash flows.

To illustrate the statement of cash flows, we will be using Anchor Corporation, a dealer in older British sports cars such as MG, Triumph, and Austin Healey. To prepare the statement of cash flows by the direct method, proceed as follows:

STEP 1 Lay out the template of the statement of cash flows by the direct method, as shown in Exhibit 17-11.

Exhibit 17-11

Template of the Statement
of Cash Flows: Direct Method

Anchor Corporation

Statement of Cash Flows
Year Ended December 31, 20X5

Cash flows from operating activities:
Receipts:
  Collections from customers
  Interest received
  Dividends received on investments
    Total cash receipts
Payments:
  To suppliers
  To employees
  For interest and income tax
    Total cash payments
Net cash provided by operating activities

Cash flows from investing activities:
  Sales of long-term assets (investments, land, building, equipment,
    and so on)
 − Purchases of long-term assets
Net cash provided by (used for) investing activities

Cash flows from financing activities:
  Issuance of stock
 + Sale of treasury stock
 − Purchase of treasury stock
 + Issuance of notes or bonds payable (borrowing)
 − Payment of notes or bonds payable
 − Payment of dividends
Net cash provided by (used for) financing activities

Net increase (decrease) in cash during the year
 + Cash at December 31, 20X4
 = Cash at December 31, 20X5

STEP 2 Use the comparative balance sheet to determine the increase or decrease in cash during the period. The change in cash is the "check figure" for the statement of cash flows. The comparative balance sheet of Anchor Corporation at December 31, 20X5 and 20X4 shows that Anchor's cash decreased by $20,000 during 20X5. See Exhibit 17-4.

STEP 3 Use the available data to prepare the statement of cash flows. Suppose Anchor has assembled the summary of 20X5 transactions in Exhibit 17-12. These transactions give the data for both the income statement (Exhibit 17-5) and the statement of cash flows. Some transactions affect one statement and some, the other. For example, sales (item 1) are reported on the income statement, and cash collections (item 2) on the statement of cash flows. Other transactions, such as the cash receipt of dividend revenue (item 4) affect both statements. *The statement of cash flows reports only those transactions with cash effects* (those with an asterisk in Exhibit 17-12). Exhibit 17-13 gives Anchor Corporation's statement of cash flows for 20X5.

Cash Flows from Operating Activities

Operating cash flows are listed first because they are the most important source of cash. Exhibit 17-13 shows that Anchor is sound; its operating activities were the largest source of cash receipts, $290,000. Let's examine the operating cash flows (see page 674).

Operating Activities

1. Sales on account, $284,000
*2. Collections from customers, $269,000
*3. Cash receipt of interest revenue, $12,000
*4. Cash receipt of dividend revenue, $9,000
5. Cost of goods sold, $150,000
* 6. Payments to suppliers, $135,000
* 7. Salary expense and payments, $56,000
8. Depreciation expense, $18,000
9. Other operating expense, $17,000
* 10. Interest expense and payments, $16,000
* 11. Income tax expense and payments, $15,000

Investing Activities

* 12. Cash payments to acquire plant assets, $317,000
* 13. Proceeds from sale of plant assets, $62,000, including $8,000 gain

Financing Activities

* 14. Proceeds from issuance of common stock, $101,000
* 15. Proceeds from issuance of long-term note payable, $94,000
* 16. Payment of long-term note payable, $11,000
* 17. Payment of cash dividends, $17,000

* Indicates a cash flow to be reported on the statement of cash flows
Note: Income statement data are used to prepare Exhibit 17-16, page 676.

Exhibit 17-12

Summary of Anchor Corporation's
20X5 Transactions

Anchor Corporation

Statement of Cash Flows
Year Ended December 31, 20X5

Exhibit 17-13

Statement of Cash Flows—
Direct Method

	(In thousands)	
Cash flows from operating activities:		
Receipts:		
Collections from customers......................	$ 269	
Interest received	12	
Dividends received.............................	9	
Total cash receipts............................		$290
Payments:		
To suppliers	$(135)	
To employees..................................	(56)	
For interest...................................	(16)	
For income tax................................	(15)	
Total cash payments...........................		(222)
Net cash provided by operating activities		68
Cash flows from investing activities:		
Acquisition of plant assets.........................	$(317)	
Proceeds from sale of plant assets	62	
Net cash used for investing activities		(255)
Cash flows from financing activities:		
Proceeds from issuance of common stock..............	$ 101	
Proceeds from issuance of long-term notes payable	94	
Payment of long-term note payable..................	(11)	
Payment of dividends	(17)	
Net cash provided by financing activities...........		167
Net decrease in cash		$ (20)
Cash balance, December 31, 20X4.....................		42
Cash balance, December 31, 20X5.....................		$ 22

✔ **Starter 17-9**

CASH COLLECTIONS FROM CUSTOMERS   Cash sales bring in cash immediately; collections of accounts receivable take longer. Both are reported on the statement of cash flows as "Collections from customers . . . $269,000" in Exhibit 17-13.

CASH RECEIPTS OF INTEREST   The income statement reports interest revenue. Only the cash receipts of interest appear on the statement of cash flows—$12,000 in Exhibit 17-13.

CASH RECEIPTS OF DIVIDENDS   Dividend revenue is reported on the income statement, and this cash receipt is reported on the statement of cash flows—$9,000 in Exhibit 17-13. (Dividends *received* are part of operating activities, but dividends *paid* are a financing activity.)

PAYMENTS TO SUPPLIERS   Payments to suppliers include all payments for inventory and operating expenses except employee compensation, interest, and income taxes. *Suppliers* are those entities that provide the business with its inventory and essential services. In Exhibit 17-13, Anchor Corporation reports payments to suppliers of $135,000.

PAYMENTS TO EMPLOYEES   This category includes payments for salaries and wages. Accrued amounts are not cash flows because they have not yet been paid. The statement of cash flows in Exhibit 17-13 reports only the cash payments ($56,000).

PAYMENTS FOR INTEREST EXPENSE AND INCOME TAX EXPENSE   These cash payments are reported separately from the other expenses. In the Anchor Corporation example, interest ($16,000) and income tax expenses ($15,000) equal their cash payments amounts. Therefore, the same amount appears on the income statement and the statement of cash flows.

DEPRECIATION, DEPLETION, AND AMORTIZATION EXPENSE   These expenses are *not* listed on the statement of cash flows because they do not affect cash.

Cash Flows from Investing Activities

Investing is critical because a company's investments determine its future course. Large purchases of plant assets signal expansion. Low levels of investing over a lengthy period indicate that the business is not replenishing assets.

PURCHASES OF PLANT ASSETS AND INVESTMENTS IN OTHER COMPANIES These cash payments acquire a long-term asset. The first investing activity reported by Anchor Corporation in Exhibit 17-13 is the purchase of plant assets ($317,000).

PROCEEDS FROM THE SALE OF PLANT ASSETS AND INVESTMENTS   These cash receipts are also investing activities. The sale of plant assets needs explanation. Exhibit 17-13 reports that Anchor Corporation received $62,000 cash from the sale of plant assets. The income statement shows an $8,000 gain on this transaction. What is the appropriate amount to show on the cash-flow statement? Report only the cash proceeds from the sale ($62,000), not the $8,000 gain. Investors and creditors are often critical of a company that sells large amounts of its plant assets. The sale may signal an emergency.

Cash Flows from Financing Activities

Cash flows from financing activities include the following:

PROCEEDS FROM ISSUANCE OF STOCK AND NOTES PAYABLE Readers of financial statements want to know how the entity obtains its financing. Issuing stock and borrowing money are two ways to finance a business. In Exhibit 17-13, Anchor Corporation issued common stock and received cash of $101,000. Anchor also issued long-term notes payable to borrow $94,000.

PAYMENT OF NOTES PAYABLE AND PURCHASES OF TREASURY STOCK The payment of notes payable decreases cash, which is the opposite of borrowing. Anchor Corporation reports long-term note payments of $11,000. Other transactions in this category include the purchase of treasury stock.

PAYMENT OF CASH DIVIDENDS The payment of dividends decreases cash and is therefore a financing activity, as shown by Anchor's $17,000 payment in Exhibit 17-13. A stock dividend has *no* effect on cash and is *not* reported on the cash-flow statement.

✔ Starter 17-10

✔ Starter 17-11

✔ Starter 17-12

Noncash Investing and Financing Activities

Companies make investments that do not require cash. They also obtain financing other than cash. Our examples thus far have included none of these transactions. Now suppose that Anchor Corporation issued common stock of $320,000 to acquire a building. Anchor would journalize this transaction as follows:

Building	320,000	
Common Stock		320,000

This transaction would not be reported on the cash-flow statement because Anchor paid no cash. But the building and the common stock are important. Noncash investing and financing activities can be reported in a separate schedule that accompanies the statement of cash flows, as Exhibit 17-14 illustrates (all amounts are assumed). This information follows the cash-flow statement or can be disclosed in a note.

	Thousands
Noncash Investing and Financing Activities:	
Acquisition of building by issuing common stock	$320
Acquisition of land by issuing note payable	70
Payment of note payable by issuing common stock	100
Total noncash investing and financing activities	$490

Exhibit 17-14

Noncash Investing and Financing Activities (All amounts assumed)

Classify each of the following as an operating activity, an investing activity, or a financing activity. Also identify those items that are not reported on the statement of cash flows prepared by the direct method.

a. Net income

b. Payment of dividends

c. Borrowing

d. Payment of cash to suppliers

e. Making a loan

f. Sale of treasury stock

g. Depreciation expense

h. Purchase of equipment

i. Issuance of stock

j. Purchase of another company

k. Payment of a note payable

l. Payment of income taxes

m. Collections from customers

n. Accrual of interest revenue

o. Expiration of prepaid expense

p. Receipt of cash dividends

Answer:

a. Not reported	e. Investing	i. Financing	m. Operating
b. Financing	f. Financing	j. Investing	n. Not reported
c. Financing	g. Not reported	k. Financing	o. Not reported
d. Operating	h. Investing	l. Operating	p. Operating

Now let's see how to compute the operating cash flows for the direct method.

Computing Operating Cash Flows by the Direct Method

How do we compute the operating cash flows for the direct method? We can use the income statement and the *changes* in the related balance sheet accounts, as diagrammed in Exhibit 17-15.

Exhibit 17-15 **Direct Method: Computing Cash Flows from Operating Activities**

Receipts/ Payments	From Income Statement Account	Change in Related Balance Sheet Account	
Receipts:			
From customers	Sales Revenue	+ Decrease in Accounts Receivable – Increase in Accounts Receivable	
Payments:			
To suppliers	Cost of Goods Sold	+ Increase in Inventory – Decrease in Inventory	+ Decrease in Accounts Payable – Increase in Accounts Payable
	Operating Expense	+ Increase in Prepaids – Decrease in Prepaids	+ Decrease in Accrued Liabilities – Increase in Accrued Liabilities

We thank Barbara Gerrity for suggesting this exhibit.

Data for computing Anchor Corporation's operating cash flows come from the income statement (Exhibit 17-16) and comparative balance sheet (Exhibit 17-17).

Exhibit 17-16

Income Statement

Anchor Corporation

Income Statement
Year Ended December 31, 20X5

	(In thousands)	
Revenues and gains:		
Sales revenue	$284	
Interest revenue	12	
Dividend revenue	9	
Gain on sale of plant assets.	8	
Total revenues and gains.		$313
Expenses:		
Cost of goods sold	$150	
Salary and wage expense	56	
Depreciation expense.	18	
Other operating expense.	17	
Interest expense	16	
Income tax expense	15	
Total expenses.		272
Net income		$ 41

Exhibit 17-17 | Comparative Balance Sheet

Anchor Corporation
Comparative Balance Sheet
December 31, 20X5 and 20X4

(In thousands)	20X5	20X4	Increase (Decrease)	
Assets				
Current:				
Cash	$ 22	$ 42	$ (20)	
Accounts receivable	96	81	15	} *Changes in current assets—Operating*
Inventory	143	145	(2)	
Plant assets, net of depreciation	464	219	245	} *Changes in noncurrent assets—Investing*
Total.	$725	$487	$238	
Liabilities				
Current:				
Accounts payable	$ 91	$ 57	$ 34	} *Changes in current liabilities—Operating*
Accrued liabilities	5	9	(4)	
Long-term notes payable	160	77	83	}
Stockholders' Equity				*Changes in long-term liabilities and common stock—Financing*
Common stock.	359	258	101	}
Retained earnings	110	86	24	} *Change due to net income—Operating*
Total.	$725	$487	$238	*Change due to dividends—Financing*

COMPUTING CASH COLLECTIONS FROM CUSTOMERS   Collections can be computed by converting sales revenue (an accrual-basis amount) to the cash basis. Anchor Corporation's income statement (Exhibit 17-16) reports sales of $284,000. But cash collections are different. Exhibit 17-17 shows that Accounts Receivable increased from $81,000 at the beginning of the year to $96,000 at year-end, a $15,000 increase. Based on those amounts, Cash Collections equal $269,000.

Collections from Customers	=	Sales Revenue	−	Increase in Accounts Receivable
$269,000	=	$284,000	−	$15,000

COMPUTING PAYMENTS TO SUPPLIERS   This computation includes two parts:

- Payments for inventory
- Payments for operating expenses (other than interest and income tax)

Payments for inventory are computed by converting cost of goods sold to the cash basis. We must analyze Cost of Goods Sold from the income statement and Inventory and Accounts Payable from the balance sheet. Payments for operating expenses (other than depreciation) use other operating expenses from the income statement and accrued liabilities from the balance sheet. Throughout, all amounts come from Exhibits 17-16 and 17-17.

Payments for Inventory	=	Cost of Goods Sold	−	Decrease in Inventory	−	Increase in Accounts Payable
$114,000	=	$150,000	−	$2,000	−	$34,000

Payments for Operating Expenses	=	Other Operating Expense	+	Decrease in Accrued Liabilities
$21,000	=	$17,000	+	$4,000

Payments to Suppliers	=	Payments for Inventory	+	Payments for Operating Expenses
$135,000	=	$114,000	+	$21,000

Computing Investing and Financing Cash Flows

The computations of investing and financing cash flows are given on pages 665–668.

Viacom, Inc., the company that owns Paramount Pictures, Blockbuster Video, and MTV Music Television, reported the following for 2001 and 2000 (adapted, in millions):

At December 31,	2001	2000
Receivables, net	$ 3,582	$ 3,964
Inventory	5,224	5,035
Accounts payable	945	1,261

Year Ended December 31,	2001	2000
Revenues........................	$23,223	$20,044
Cost of goods sold	14,137	11,707

Based on these figures, how much cash did Viacom collect from customers during 2001? How much cash did Viacom pay for inventory during 2001?

Answer (In millions):

Collections from customers	= $23,605	Beginning Receivables	+	Revenues	−	Collections	=	Ending Receivables
		$3,964	+	$23,223	−	$23,605	=	$3,582

Payments for inventory and related services	= $14,642	Cost of Goods Sold	+	Increase in Inventory	+	Decrease in Accounts Payable	=	Payments
		$14,137	+	($5,224 − $5,035)	+	($1,261 − $945)	=	$14,642

Decision Guidelines

USING CASH-FLOW AND RELATED INFORMATION TO EVALUATE INVESTMENTS

Ann Browning is a private investor. Through the years, she has devised some guidelines for evaluating investments. Here are some of her guidelines.

Question	Financial Statement	What to Look For
Where is most of the company's cash coming from?	Statement of cash flows	Operating activities → Good sign Investing activities → Bad sign Financing activities → Okay sign
Do high sales and profits translate into more cash?	Statement of cash flows	Usually, but cash flows from *operating* activities must be the main source of cash for long-term success.
If sales and profits are low, how is the company generating cash?	Statement of cash flows	If *investing* activities are generating the cash, the business may be in trouble because it is selling off its long-term assets. If *financing* activities are generating the cash, that cannot go on forever. Sooner or later, investors will demand cash flow from operating activities.
Is the cash balance large enough to provide for expansion?	Balance sheet	The cash balance should be growing over time. If not, the company may be in trouble.
Can the business pay its debts?	Income statement	Increasing trend of net income.
	Statement of cash flows	Cash flows from operating activities should be the main source of cash.
	Balance sheet	Current ratio, debt ratio.

END-OF-CHAPTER *Summary Problem* ●

Granite Shoals Corporation reported the following comparative balance sheet and income statement for 20X6.

A+
TIPS
CHECK YOUR RESOURCES

Granite Shoals Corporation

Balance Sheet
December 31, 20X6 and 20X5

	20X6	20X5
Cash	$ 19,000	$ 3,000
Accounts receivable	22,000	23,000
Inventories	34,000	31,000
Prepaid expenses	1,000	3,000
Equipment (net)	90,000	79,000
Intangible assets	9,000	9,000
	$175,000	$148,000
Accounts payable	$ 14,000	$ 9,000
Accrued liabilities	16,000	19,000
Income tax payable	14,000	12,000
Long-term debt	45,000	50,000
Common stock	31,000	20,000
Retained earnings	64,000	40,000
Treasury stock	(9,000)	(2,000)
	$175,000	$148,000

Granite Shoals Corporation

Income Statement
Year Ended December 31, 20X6

Sales revenue	$190,000
Gain on sale of equipment	6,000
Total revenue and gains	196,000
Cost of goods sold	$ 85,000
Depreciation expense	19,000
Other operating expenses	36,000
Total expenses	140,000
Income before income tax	56,000
Income tax expense	18,000
Net income	$ 38,000

Required

Assume that **Berkshire Hathaway** is considering buying Granite Shoals Corporation. Berkshire Hathaway analysts need the following Granite Shoals cash-flow data for 20X6. There were no noncash investing and financing activities.

a. Collections from customers
b. Payments for inventory
c. Issuance of common stock
d. Payment of dividends

Solution

a.

Collections from customers	=	Sales revenue	+	Decrease in Accounts Receivables
$191,000	=	$190,000	+	$1,000

b.

Payments for inventory	=	Cost of goods sold	+	Increase in inventory	−	Increase in Accounts Payable
$83,000	=	$85,000	+	$3,000	−	$5,000

c. Analyze Common Stock (let X = issuance)

Beginning	+	Issuance	=	Ending	
$20,000	+	X	=	$31,000	
		X	=		$11,000

d. Analyze Retained Earnings (let X = dividends)

Beginning	+	Net Income	−	Dividends	=	Ending	
$40,000	+	$38,000	−	X	=	$64,000	
				X	=		$14,000

● REVIEW *the Statement of Cash Flows*

Quick Check

1. The three main categories of cash-flow activities are
   a. Direct and indirect
   b. Operating, investing, and financing
   c. Noncash investing and financing
   d. Current and long-term

2. The purposes of the cash-flow statement are to
   a. Predict future cash flows
   b. Evaluate management decisions
   c. Determine ability to pay liabilities and dividends
   d. All of the above

3. Financing activities are most closely related to
   a. Current assets and current liabilities
   b. Long-term assets
   c. Long-term liabilities and owners' equity
   d. Net income and dividends

4. Which item does *not* appear on a statement of cash flows prepared by the indirect method?
   a. Collections from customers
   b. Net income
   c. Depreciation
   d. Gain on sale of land

5. Euro Bistro earned net income of $60,000 after deducting depreciation of $4,000 and all other expenses. Current assets increased by $3,000, and current liabilities decreased by $5,000. How much was Euro Bistro's cash provided by operations (indirect method)?
   a. $48,000
   b. $50,000
   c. $52,000
   d. $56,000

6. The Plant Assets account of Canyon Corp. shows the following:

Plant Assets, Net

Beg.	100,000	Depr.	30,000
Purchase	400,000	Sale	?
End.	420,000		

Canyon sold plant assets at a $10,000 gain. Where on the statement of cash flows should Canyon report the sale of plant assets? How much should Canyon report for the sale?
   a. Investing cash flows—sale of $40,000
   b. Investing cash flows—sale of $50,000
   c. Investing cash flows—sale of $60,000
   d. Financing cash flows—sale of $60,000

7. Columbia, Inc., borrowed $15,000, issued common stock of $10,000, and paid dividends of $25,000. What was Columbia's net cash provided (used) by financing activities?

a. $0

b. $25,000

c. $(25,000)

d. $50,000

8. Which item does *not* appear on a statement of cash flows prepared by the direct method?

a. Net income

b. Collections from customers

c. Payments to suppliers

d. Payments of income tax

9. Peppertree Copy Center had accounts receivable of $20,000 at the beginning of the year and $50,000 at year-end. Revenue for the year totaled $100,000. How much cash did Peppertree collect from customers?

a. $170,000

b. $150,000

c. $120,000

d. $70,000

10. Greenlawn Service had operating expense of $40,000. At the beginning of the year, Greenlawn owed $5,000 on accrued liabilities. At year-end, accrued liabilities were $8,000. How much cash did Greenlawn pay for operating expenses?

a. $35,000

b. $37,000

c. $43,000

d. $45,000

Accounting Vocabulary

cash equivalents (p. 659)

cash flows (p. 658)

direct method (p. 661)

financing activities (p. 660)

indirect method (p. 661)

investing activities (p. 659)

operating activities (p. 659)

statement of cash flows (p. 658)

ASSESS *Your Progress*

Starters

online homework

See *www.prenhall.com/horngren* for selected Starters, Exercises, and Problems.

S17-1 Describe how the statement of cash flows helps investors and creditors perform each of the following functions:

1. Predict future cash flows

2. Evaluate management decisions

3. Predict the ability to make debt payments to lenders and pay dividends to stockholders

Purposes of the statement of cash flows
(Obj. 1)

S17-2 Answer these questions about the statement of cash flows:

a. What is the "check figure" for the statement of cash flows? Where do you get this check figure?

b. List the categories of cash flows in order of importance.

c. What is the first dollar amount to report for the indirect method?

d. What is the first dollar amount to report for the direct method?

Classifying cash-flow items
(Obj. 1)

S17-3 Post Corporation is preparing its statement of cash flows by the *indirect* method. Post has the following items for you to consider in preparing the statement. Identify each item as

Identifying items for reporting cash flows from operations—indirect method
(Obj. 2)

• Operating activity—addition to net income (O+), or subtraction from net income (O–)

• Investing activity (I)

• Financing activity (F)

• Activity that is not used to prepare the cash-flow statement (N)

Answer by placing the appropriate symbol in the blank space.

_____	**a.** Loss on sale of land		_____	**f.** Increase in accounts
_____	**b.** Depreciation expense			payable
_____	**c.** Increase in inventory		_____	**g.** Payment of dividends
_____	**d.** Decrease in accounts		_____	**h.** Decrease in accrued
	receivable			liabilities
_____	**e.** Purchase of equipment		_____	**i.** Issuance of common stock
			_____	**j.** Gain on sale of building

Computing cash flows from operating activities—indirect method
(Obj. 3)

S17-4 Vis-à-Vis Printers reported these data for 20X7:

Income Statement	
Net income	$50,000
Depreciation	8,000
Balance sheet	
Increase in Accounts Receivable	6,000
Decrease in Accounts Payable	4,000

Compute Vis-à-Vis Printers' net cash provided by operations—indirect method.

Computing operating cash flows—indirect method
(Obj. 3)

S17-5 (Starter 17-6 is an alternate.) Mid-America Resources, Inc., accountants have assembled the following data for the year ended June 30, 20X5.

Payment of dividends	$ 6,000	Net income	$60,000
Proceeds from issuance		Purchase of equipment..........	40,000
of common stock.............	20,000	Decrease in current liabilities.....	5,000
Increase in current		Payment of note payable	30,000
assets other than cash.........	30,000	Proceeds from sale of land.......	60,000
Purchase of treasury stock.......	5,000	Depreciation expense	15,000

Prepare the *operating* activities section of Mid-America's statement of cash flows for the year ended June 30, 20X5. Mid-America uses the *indirect* method for operating cash flows.

Preparing a statement of cash flows—indirect method
(Obj. 3)

S17-6 Use the data in Starter 17-5 to prepare Mid-America's statement of cash flows for the year ended June 30, 20X5. Mid-America uses the *indirect* method for operating activities. Use Exhibit 17-7 as a guide, but you may stop after determining the net increase (or decrease) in cash.

Computing investing cash flows
(Obj. 3)

S17-7 Grace Chemical Company reported the following financial statements for 20X6:

Grace Chemical Company
Income Statement
Year Ended December 31, 20X6

	(In thousands)
Sales revenue	$710
Cost of goods sold	$340
Depreciation expense..........................	60
Other expenses.................................	200
Total expenses.................................	600
Net income	$110

Grace Chemical Company

Comparative Balance Sheet
December 31, 20X6 and 20X5

(In thousands)

Assets	20X6	20X5	Liabilities	20X6	20X5
Current			Current		
Cash	$ 19	$ 16	Accounts payable	$ 47	$ 42
Accounts receivable	54	48	Salary payable	23	21
Inventory	80	84	Accrued liabilities	8	11
Prepaid expenses	3	2	Long-term notes payable ..	66	68
Long-term investments ...	75	90	**Stockholders' Equity**		
Plant assets, net	225	185	Common stock	40	37
			Retained earnings	272	246
Total	$456	$425	Total	$456	$425

Compute the amount of Grace Chemical's acquisition of plant assets, with Grace selling no plant assets.

S17-8 Use the Grace Chemical Company data in Starter 17-7 to compute

Computing financing cash flows
(Obj. 3)

a. New borrowing or payment of long-term notes payable, with Grace having only one long-term note payable transaction during the year

b. Issuance of common stock, with Grace having only one common stock transaction during the year

c. Payment of cash dividends

S17-9 Wellness Health Laboratories began 20X4 with cash of $104,000. During the year, Wellness earned service revenue of $600,000 and collected $590,000 from customers. Expenses for the year totaled $420,000, of which Wellness paid $410,000 in cash to suppliers and employees. Wellness also paid $140,000 to purchase equipment and a cash dividend of $50,000 to its stockholders during 20X4.

Preparing a statement of cash flows—direct method
(Obj. 4)

Prepare the company's statement of cash flows for the year ended December 31, 20X4. Format operating activities by the direct method.

S17-10 (Starter 17-11 is an alternate.) Mid-America Resources, Inc., has assembled the following data for the year ended June 30, 20X5.

Computing operating cash flows—direct method
(Obj. 4)

Payment of dividends.............................	$ 6,000
Proceeds from issuance of stock	20,000
Collections from customers	200,000
Proceeds from sale of land	60,000
Payments to suppliers............................	80,000
Purchase of equipment...........................	40,000
Payments to employees	70,000
Payment of note payable	30,000

Prepare the *operating* activities section of Mid-America's statement of cash flows for the year ended June 30, 20X5. Mid-America uses the direct method for operating cash flows.

S17-11 Use the data in Starter 17-10 to prepare Mid-America's statement of cash flows for the year ended June 30, 20X5. Mid-America uses the *direct* method for operating activities. Use Exhibit 17-13, page 673, as a guide, but you may stop after determining the net increase (or decrease) in cash.

Preparing a statement of cash flows—direct method
(Obj. 4)

S17-12 Use the Grace Chemical Company data in Starter 17-7 to compute the following:

Computing operating cash flows—direct method
(Obj. 4)

a. Collections from customers

b. Payments for inventory

online homework

Identifying the purposes of the statement of cash flows
(Obj. 1)

Exercises

E17-1 Biz Mart Stores, Inc., has experienced an unbroken string of 10 years of growth in net income. Nevertheless, the business is facing bankruptcy. Creditors are calling all of Biz Mart's outstanding loans for immediate payment, and the cash is simply not available. Attempts to explain where Biz Mart went wrong make it clear that managers placed undue emphasis on net income and gave too little attention to cash flows.

Required

Write a brief memo, in your own words, to explain to the managers of Biz Mart Stores the purposes of the statement of cash flows.

Identifying activities for the statement of cash flows—indirect method
(Obj. 2)

E17-2 Identify each of the following transactions as

- Operating activity (O)
- Investing activity (I)
- Financing activity (F)
- Noncash investing and financing activity (NIF)
- Transaction that is not reported on the statement of cash flows (N)

For each cash flow, indicate whether the item increases (+) or decreases (–) cash. The indirect method is used to report cash flows from operating activities.

___ a.	Cash sale of land	___ j.	Loss on sale of land
___ b.	Issuance of long-term note payable to borrow cash	___ k.	Acquisition of equipment by issuance of note payable
___ c.	Depreciation of equipment	___ l.	Payment of long-term debt
___ d.	Purchase of treasury stock	___ m.	Acquisition of building by issuance of common stock
___ e.	Issuance of common stock		
___ f.	Increase in accounts payable	___ n.	Accrual of salary expense
___ g.	Net income	___ o.	Decrease in inventory
___ h.	Payment of cash dividend	___ p.	Increase in prepaid expenses
___ i.	Decrease in accrued liabilities		

Classifying transactions for the statement of cash flows—indirect method
(Obj. 2, 3)

E17-3 Indicate whether each of the following transactions would result in an operating activity, an investing activity, or a financing activity for a statement of cash flows prepared by the *indirect* method and the accompanying schedule of noncash investing and financing activities.

a. Equipment........	18,000		g. Cash	81,000	
Cash		18,000	Common Stock........		81,000
b. Cash	7,200		h. Treasury Stock	13,000	
Long-Term Investment		7,200	Cash........		13,000
c. Bonds Payable........	45,000		i. Cash	60,000	
Cash		45,000	Sales Revenue........		60,000
d. Building........	164,000		j. Land	87,700	
Note Payable, Long-Term...		164,000	Cash........		87,700
e. Loss on Disposal of Equipment...	1,400		k. Depreciation Expense........	9,000	
Equipment Net........		1,400	Accumulated Depreciation..		9,000
f. Dividends Payable........	16,500				
Cash		16,500			

Computing cash flows from operating activities—indirect method
(Obj. 3)

E17-4 The accounting records of Auto Chef Corporation reveal the following:

Net income........	$22,000	Depreciation	$12,000
Sales revenue........	9,000	Decrease in current liabilities..	20,000
Loss on sale of land....	5,000	Increase in current assets	
Acquisition of land	37,000	other than cash	27,000

Required

Compute cash flows from operating activities by the indirect method. Use the format of the operating activities section of Exhibit 17-7. Also evaluate the operating cash flow of Auto Chef Corporation. Give the reason for your evaluation.

E17-5 The accounting records of Ochoa, Inc.; include these accounts:

Computing cash flows from operating activities—indirect method
(Obj. 3)

Cash

Mar. 1	5,000		
Receipts	447,000	Payments	448,000
Mar. 31	4,000		

Accounts Receivable

Mar. 1	18,000		
Sales	443,000	Collections	447,000
Mar. 31	14,000		

Inventory

Mar. 1	19,000		
Purchases	337,000	Cost of sales	335,000
Mar. 31	21,000		

Accounts Payable

		Mar. 1	14,000
Payments	332,000	Purchases	337,000
		Mar. 31	19,000

Accumulated Depreciation—Equipment

		Mar. 1	52,000
		Depreciation	3,000
		Mar. 31	55,000

Retained Earnings

		Mar. 1	64,000
Dividend	18,000	Net income	69,000
		Mar. 31	115,000

Compute Ochoa's net cash provided by (used for) operating activities during March. Use the indirect method.

E17-6 The income statement and additional data of Crawford Properties, Inc., follow:

Preparing the statement of cash flows—indirect method
(Obj. 3)

Crawford Properties, Inc.

Income Statement
Year Ended June 30, 20X6

Revenues:		
Sales revenue		$237,000
Expenses:		
Cost of goods sold	$103,000	
Salary expense	58,000	
Depreciation expense	29,000	
Income tax expense	9,000	199,000
Net income		$ 38,000

Additional data:

a. Acquisition of plant assets is $116,000. Of this amount, $101,000 is paid in cash and $15,000 by signing a note payable.
b. Proceeds from sale of land total $24,000.
c. Proceeds from issuance of common stock total $30,000.
d. Payment of long-term note payable is $15,000.
e. Payment of dividends is $11,000.
f. From the balance sheet:

	June 30,	
	20X6	20X5
Current Assets:		
Cash	$27,000	$20,000
Accounts receivable	43,000	58,000
Inventory	92,000	85,000
Current Liabilities:		
Accounts payable	$35,000	$22,000
Accrued liabilities	13,000	21,000

Required

1. Prepare Crawford Properties, Inc.'s statement of cash flows for the year ended June 30, 20X6, using the indirect method. Include a separate section for noncash investing and financing activities.

2. Evaluate Crawford Properties' cash flows for the year. In your evaluation, mention all three categories of cash flows and give the reason for your evaluation.

Computing investing and financing amounts for the statement of cash flows
(Obj. 3)

E17-7 Compute the following items for the statement of cash flows:

a. Beginning and ending Retained Earnings are $45,000 and $73,000, respectively. Net income for the period is $62,000. How much are cash dividends?

b. Beginning and ending Plant Assets, net, are $103,000 and $107,000, respectively. Depreciation for the period is $16,000, and acquisitions of new plant assets total $27,000. Plant assets were sold at a $1,000 loss. What were the cash proceeds of the sale?

Identifying activities for the statement of cash flows—direct method
(Obj. 4)

E17-8 Identify each of the following transactions as

- Operating activity (O)
- Investing activity (I)
- Financing activity (F)
- Noncash investing and financing activity (NIF)
- Transaction that is not reported on the statement of cash flows (N)

For each cash flow, indicate whether the item increases (+) or decreases (–) cash. The direct method is used for cash flows from operating activities.

_____ **a.** Collection of account receivable	_____ **i.** Sale of land
_____ **b.** Issuance of long-term note payable to borrow cash	_____ **j.** Acquisition of equipment by issuance of note payable
_____ **c.** Depreciation of equipment	_____ **k.** Payment of long-term debt
_____ **d.** Purchase of treasury stock	_____ **l.** Acquisition of building by issuance of common stock
_____ **e.** Issuance of common stock for cash	_____ **m.** Purchase of equipment
_____ **f.** Payment of account payable	_____ **n.** Payment of wages to employees
_____ **g.** Issuance of preferred stock for cash	_____ **o.** Collection of cash interest
_____ **h.** Payment of cash dividend	_____ **p.** Sale of building

Classifying transactions for the statement of cash flows—direct method
(Obj. 4)

E17-9 Indicate where, if at all, each of the following transactions would be reported on a statement of cash flows prepared by the *direct* method and the accompanying schedule of noncash investing and financing activities.

a. Equipment	18,000		**g.** Salary Expense	4,300	
Cash		18,000	Cash		4,300
b. Cash	7,200		**h.** Cash	81,000	
Long-Term Investment		7,200	Common Stock		81,000
c. Bonds Payable	45,000		**i.** Treasury Stock	13,000	
Cash		45,000	Cash		13,000
d. Building	164,000		**j.** Cash	2,000	
Note Payable, Long-Term		164,000	Interest Revenue		2,000
e. Cash	1,400		**k.** Land	87,700	
Accounts Receivable		1,400	Cash		87,700
f. Dividends Payable	16,500		**l.** Accounts Payable	8,300	
Cash		16,500	Cash		8,300

E17-10 The accounting records of Auto Chef Corporation reveal the following:

Computing cash flows from operating activities—direct method
(Obj. 4)

Net income	$22,000	Payment of salaries and wages. .	$ 34,000
Payment of income tax . .	13,000	Depreciation	12,000
Collection of dividend		Payment of interest.	16,000
revenue	7,000	Payment of dividends	7,000
Payment to suppliers. . . .	54,000	Collections from customers.	102,000

Required

Compute cash flows from operating activities by the direct method. Use the format of the operating activities section of Exhibit 17-13. Also evaluate the operating cash flow of Auto Chef Corporation. Give the reason for your evaluation.

E17-11 Selected accounts of Crossroads Clinic, Inc., show the following:

Identifying items for the statement of cash flows—direct method
(Obj. 4)

Dividends Receivable

Beginning balance	9,000		
Dividend revenue	40,000	Cash receipts of dividends	38,000
Ending balance	11,000		

Land

Beginning balance	90,000		
Acquisition	18,000		
Ending balance	108,000		

Long-Term Notes Payable

		Beginning balance	273,000
Payments	69,000	Issuance for cash	83,000
		Ending balance	287,000

Required

For each account, identify the item or items that should appear on a statement of cash flows prepared by the direct method. State where to report the item.

E17-12 The income statement and additional data of Crawford Properties, Inc., follow:

Preparing the statement of cash flows—direct method
(Obj. 4)

Crawford Properties, Inc.

Income Statement
Year Ended June 30, 20X6

Revenues:		
Sales revenue	$229,000	
Dividend revenue	8,000	$237,000
Expenses:		
Cost of goods sold	$103,000	
Salary expense	45,000	
Depreciation expense	28,000	
Advertising expense	12,000	
Interest expense	2,000	
Income tax expense	9,000	199,000
Net income		$ 38,000

Additional data:

a. Collections from customers are $15,000 more than sales.

b. Payments to suppliers are the sum of cost of goods sold plus advertising expense.

c. Payments to employees are $1,000 more than salary expense.

d. Dividend revenue, interest expense, and income tax expense equal their cash amounts.

e. Acquisition of plant assets is $101,000.

f. Proceeds from sale of land total $24,000.

g. Proceeds from issuance of common stock total $30,000.

h. Payment of long-term note payable is $15,000.

i. Payment of dividends is $11,000.

j. Cash balance, June 30, 20X5, was $20,000.

Required

1. Prepare Crawford Properties' statement of cash flows for the year ended June 30, 20X6. Use the *direct* method.

2. Evaluate Crawford's cash flows for the year. In your evaluation, mention all three categories of cash flows and give the reason for your evaluation.

Computing amounts for the statement of cash flows—direct method
(Obj. 4)

E17-13 Compute the following items for the statement of cash flows:

a. Beginning and ending Accounts Receivable are $22,000 and $18,000, respectively. Credit sales for the period total $81,000. How much are cash collections?

b. Cost of goods sold is $90,000. Beginning Inventory balance is $25,000, and ending Inventory balance is $21,000. Beginning and ending Accounts Payable are $11,000 and $8,000, respectively. How much are cash payments for inventory?

Computing cash-flow amounts
(Obj. 3, 4)

E17-14 **Walgreen Company**, the nationwide pharmacy chain, reported the following in its financial statements for the year ended August 31, 20X1 (adapted, in millions):

	20X1	20X0
Income Statement		
Net sales	$24,623	$21,207
Cost of sales	18,048	15,466
Depreciation........................	269	230
Other operating expenses..............	4,883	4,248
Income tax expense	537	486
Net income	$ 886	$ 777
Balance Sheet		
Cash and equivalents	$ 17	$ 13
Accounts receivable...................	798	615
Inventories	3,482	2,831
Property and equipment, net...........	4,345	3,428
Accounts payable.....................	1,547	1,364
Accrued liabilities	938	848
Long-term liabilities	478	464
Common stock.......................	676	446
Retained earnings	4,531	3,788

Determine the following for Walgreen during 20X1:

a. Collections from customers

b. Payments for inventory

c. Payments of operating expenses

d. Acquisitions of property and equipment (no sales during 20X1)

e. Borrowing, with Walgreen paying no long-term liabilities

f. Proceeds from issuance of common stock

g. Payment of cash dividends

For operating cash flows, follow the approach outlined in Exhibit 17-15.

Problems

(Group A)

P17-1A Top managers of Oasis Water, Inc., are reviewing company performance for 20X7. The income statement reports a 20% increase in net income over 20X6. However, most of the increase resulted from an extraordinary gain on insurance proceeds from storm damage to a building. The balance sheet shows a large increase in receivables. The cash-flow statement, in summarized form, reports the following:

Using cash-flow information to evaluate performance
(Obj. 1, 2)

Net cash used for operating activities	$(80,000)
Net cash provided by investing activities	40,000
Net cash provided by financing activities	50,000
Increase in cash during 20X7	$ 10,000

Required

Write a memo giving Oasis Water managers your assessment of 20X7 operations and your outlook for the future. Focus on the information content of the cash-flow data.

P17-2A Scott Corporation, a furniture store, was formed on January 1, 20X8, when Scott issued common stock for $500,000. Early in January, Scott made the following cash payments:

Preparing an income statement, balance sheet, and statement of cash flows—indirect method
(Obj. 2, 3)

a. $150,000 for equipment
b. $260,000 for inventory (2,000 pieces of furniture)
c. $20,000 for 20X8 rent on a store building

Later in the year, Scott purchased 1,000 units of furniture inventory on account. Cost of this inventory was $120,000. Before year-end, Scott paid $60,000 of this debt. Scott uses the FIFO method to account for inventory.

During 20X8, Scott sold 2,000 units of inventory for $200 each. Before year end, Scott collected 80% of this amount.

The store employs a salesperson whose annual pay is $45,000, of which Scott owes $4,000 at year-end. At the end of the year, Scott paid income tax of $10,000.

Late in 20X8, Scott paid cash dividends of $11,000.

For equipment, Scott uses the straight-line depreciation method, over 5 years, with zero residual value.

Required

1. Prepare Scott Corporation's income statement for the year ended December 31, 20X8. Use the single-step format, with all revenues listed together and all expenses together.
2. Prepare Scott's balance sheet at December 31, 20X8.
3. Prepare Scott's statement of cash flows for the year ended December 31, 20X8. Format cash flows from operating activities by the indirect method.

P17-3A Datex Corporation accountants have assembled the following data for the year ended December 31, 20X7.

Preparing the statement of cash flows—indirect method
(Obj. 2, 3)

Required

Prepare Datex Corporation's statement of cash flows using the *indirect* method to report operating activities. Include an accompanying schedule of noncash investing and financing activities.

Datex Corporation

	December 31,	
	20X7	**20X6**
Current Accounts:		
Current assets:		
Cash and cash equivalents....................	$85,000	$22,000
Accounts receivable	69,200	64,200
Inventories....................................	80,000	83,000
Current liabilities:		
Accounts payable	$57,800	$55,800
Income tax payable............................	14,700	16,700

Transaction Data for 20X7:

Net income....................	$ 57,000	Purchase of treasury stock........	$14,000
Issuance of common stock		Loss on sale of equipment........	11,000
for cash....................	41,000	Payment of cash dividends.......	18,000
Depreciation expense...........	21,000	Issuance of long-term note	
Purchase of building	125,000	payable to borrow cash	34,000
Retirement of bonds payable		Sale of equipment	58,000
by issuing common stock	65,000		

Preparing the statement of cash flows—indirect method
(Obj. 2, 3)

Student ResourceCD

spreadsheet

P17-4A The comparative balance sheet of Southern Bell Company at March 31, 20X9, reported the following:

	March 31,	
	20X9	**20X8**
Current Assets:		
Cash and cash equivalents.......................	$ 6,200	$ 4,000
Accounts receivable	14,900	21,700
Inventories....................................	63,200	60,600
Current Liabilities:		
Accounts payable	$30,100	$27,600
Accrued liabilities............................	10,700	11,100
Income tax payable............................	8,000	4,700

Southern Bell's transactions during the year ended March 31, 20X9, included the following:

Payment of cash dividend........	$30,000	Depreciation expense	$ 17,300
Purchase of equipment	78,700	Purchase of building.............	47,000
Issuance of long-term note		Net income.....................	70,000
payable to borrow cash	50,000	Issuance of common stock........	11,000

Required

1. Prepare Southern Bell's statement of cash flows for the year ended March 31, 20X9, using the *indirect* method to report cash flows from operating activities.
2. Evaluate Southern Bell's cash flows for the year. Mention all three categories of cash flows and give the reason for your evaluation.

Preparing the statement of cash flows—indirect method
(Obj. 2, 3)

Student ResourceCD

spreadsheet

P17-5A The 20X5 comparative balance sheet and income statement of Town East Press follow.

Town East had no noncash investing and financing transactions during 20X5. During the year, there were no sales of land or equipment, no issuances of notes payable, no retirements of stock, and no treasury stock transactions.

Required

1. Prepare the 20X5 statement of cash flows, formatting operating activities by the indirect method.
2. How will what you learned in this problem help you evaluate an investment?

Town East Press
Comparative Balance Sheet

	December 31, 20X5	December 31, 20X4	Increase (Decrease)
Current assets:			
Cash and cash equivalents	$ 6,700	$ 5,300	$ 1,400
Accounts receivable	25,300	26,900	(1,600)
Inventories	91,800	89,800	2,000
Plant assets:			
Land	89,000	60,000	29,000
Equipment, net	53,500	49,400	4,100
Total assets	$266,300	$231,400	$34,900
Current liabilities:			
Accounts payable	$ 30,900	$ 35,400	$(4,500)
Accrued liabilities	30,600	28,600	2,000
Long-term liabilities:			
Notes payable	75,000	100,000	(25,000)
Stockholders' equity:			
Common stock	88,300	64,700	23,600
Retained earnings	41,500	2,700	38,800
Total liabilities and stockholders' equity	$266,300	$231,400	$34,900

Town East Press
Income Statement
Year Ended December 31, 20X5

Revenues:		
Sales revenue		$213,000
Interest revenue		8,600
Total revenues		221,600
Expenses:		
Cost of goods sold	$70,600	
Salary expense	27,800	
Depreciation expense	4,000	
Other operating expense	10,500	
Interest expense	11,600	
Income tax expense	29,100	
Total expenses		153,600
Net income		$ 68,000

P17-6A Accountants for Triad Associates, Inc., have developed the following data from the company's accounting records for the year ended April 30, 20X5:

Preparing the statement of cash flows—direct method
(Obj. 2, 4)

a. Purchase of plant assets, $59,400
b. Proceeds from issuance of common stock, $8,000
c. Payment of dividends, $48,400
d. Collection of interest, $4,400
e. Payments of salaries, $93,600
f. Proceeds from sale of plant assets, $22,400
g. Collections from customers, $620,500
h. Cash receipt of dividend revenue, $4,100
i. Payments to suppliers, $368,500
j. Depreciation expense, $59,900
k. Proceeds from issuance of notes payable, $19,600
l. Payments of notes payable, $50,000
m. Interest expense and payments, $13,300
n. Income tax expense and payments, $37,900
o. Cash balance: April 30, 20X4, $39,300; April 30, 20X5, $47,200

Required

Prepare Triad Associates' statement of cash flows for the year ended April 30, 20X5. Use the direct method for cash flows from operating activities. Follow the format of Exhibit 17-13, but do *not* show amounts in thousands.

Preparing an income statement, balance sheet, and statement of cash flows— direct method
(Obj. 2, 4)

P17-7A Use the Scott Corporation data from Problem 17-2A.

Required

1. Prepare Scott Corporation's income statement for the year ended December 31, 20X8. Use the single-step format, with all revenues listed together and all expenses together.

2. Prepare Scott's balance sheet at December 31, 20X8.

3. Prepare Scott's statement of cash flows for the year ended December 31, 20X8. Format cash flows from operating activities by the direct method.

Preparing the statement of cash flows— direct method
(Obj. 2, 4)

Student ResourceCD

spreadsheet

P17-8A Use the Town East Press data from Problem 17-5A.

Required

1. Prepare the 20X5 statement of cash flows by the direct method.

2. How will what you learned in this problem help you evaluate an investment?

Preparing the statement of cash flows— direct method
(Obj. 3, 4)

P17-9A To prepare the statement of cash flows, accountants for Internet Guide, Inc., have summarized 20X8 activity in the Cash account as follows:

Cash

Beginning balance	53,600	**Payments on accounts**	
Receipts of interest	17,100	payable	399,100
Collections from		Payments of dividends	27,200
customers	673,700	Payments of salaries	
Issuance of common stock	47,300	and wages	143,800
		Payments of interest	26,900
		Purchase of equipment	10,200
		Payments of operating	
		expenses	34,300
		Payment of note payable	67,700
		Payment of income tax	18,900
Ending balance	63,600		

Required

Prepare the statement of cash flows of Internet Guide, Inc., for the year ended December 31, 20X8, using the *direct* method for operating activities.

Problems

(Group B)

Using cash-flow information to evaluate performance
(Obj. 1, 2)

P17-1B Top managers of Internet Solutions, Inc., are reviewing company performance for 20X4. The income statement reports a 15% increase in net income, the fifth consecutive year with an income increase above 10%. The income statement includes a nonrecurring loss without which net income would have increased by 16%. The balance sheet shows modest increases in assets, liabilities, and stockholders' equity. The assets posting the largest increases are plant and equipment because the company is halfway through a 5-year expansion program. No other assets and no liabilities are increasing dramatically. A summarized version of the cash-flow statement reports the following:

Net cash provided by operating activities............	$310,000
Net cash used for investing activities................	(290,000)
Net cash provided by financing activities	70,000
Increase in cash during 20X4	$ 90,000

Required

Write a memo giving top managers of Internet Solutions your assessment of 20X4 operations and your outlook for the future. Focus on the information content of the cash-flow data.

P17-2B Dohn Corporation, a discounter of men's suits, was formed on January 1, 20X6, when Dohn issued its common stock for $200,000. Early in January, Dohn made the following cash payments:

Preparing an income statement, balance sheet, and statement of cash flows—indirect method
(Obj. 2, 3)

a. For store fixtures, $50,000
b. For inventory (1,000 men's suits), $100,000
c. For rent on a store building, $10,000

Later in the year, Dohn purchased 2,000 men's suits on account. Cost of each suit was $120, for a total of $240,000. Before year-end, Dohn paid $140,000 of this account payable. Dohn uses the FIFO method to account for inventory.

During 20X6, Dohn sold 2,500 units of inventory for $200 each. Before year end, Dohn collected 90% of this amount.

The store employs three people. The combined annual payroll is $90,000, of which Dohn owes $5,000 at year-end. At the end of the year, Dohn paid income tax of $30,000.

Late in 20X6, Dohn declared and paid cash dividends of $40,000.

For equipment, Dohn uses the straight-line depreciation method, over 5 years, with zero residual value.

amortization

Required

1. Prepare Dohn Corporation's income statement for the year ended December 31, 20X6. Use the single-step format, with all revenues listed together and all expenses together.
2. Prepare Dohn's balance sheet at December 31, 20X6.
3. Prepare Dohn's statement of cash flows for the year ended December 31, 20X6. Format cash flows from operating activities by the indirect method.

P17-3B Accountants for WWW.Smart, Inc., have assembled the following data for the year ended December 31, 20X4:

Preparing the statement of cash flows—indirect method
(Obj. 2, 3)

	December 31,	
	20X4	**20X3**
Current Accounts:		
Current assets:		
Cash and cash equivalents.	$56,000	$34,000
Accounts receivable	70,100	73,700
Inventories	90,600	86,600
Current liabilities:		
Accounts payable	71,600	67,500
Income tax payable.	5,900	6,800

Transaction Data for 20X4:

Depreciation expense.	$30,200	Payment of cash dividends	$48,300
Purchase of equipment	69,000	Issuance of note payable	
Acquisition of land by issuing		to borrow cash	71,000
long-term note payable	118,000	Net income.	50,500
Payment of note payable.	47,900	Issuance of preferred stock	
Gain on sale of equipment	3,500	for cash	36,200

Required

Prepare WWW.Smart's statement of cash flows using the *indirect* method to report operating activities. Include an accompanying schedule of noncash investing and financing activities.

P17-4B The comparative balance sheet of CNA Leasing, Inc., at December 31, 20X5, reported the following:

*Preparing the statement of cash flows—
indirect method*
(Obj. 2, 3)

	December 31,	
	20X5	**20X4**
Current Assets:		
Cash and cash equivalents....................	$12,500	$22,500
Accounts receivable	26,600	29,300
Inventories................................	54,600	53,000
Current Liabilities:		
Accounts payable	$29,100	$28,000
Accrued liabilities........................	14,300	16,800

CNA's transactions during 20X5 included the following:

Payment of cash dividends	$17,000	Purchase of building	$124,000
Purchase of equipment..........	55,000	Net income	31,600
Issuance of long-term note		Issuance of common stock	
payable to borrow cash........	32,000	for cash	105,000
		Depreciation expense	17,700

Required

1. Prepare the statement of cash flows of CNA Leasing, Inc., for the year ended December 31, 20X5. Use the *indirect* method to report cash flows from operating activities.

2. Evaluate CNA's cash flows for the year. Mention all three categories of cash flows and give the reason for your evaluation.

*Preparing the statement of cash flows—
indirect method*
(Obj. 2, 3)

P17-5B The 20X8 comparative balance sheet and income statement of Genie Marketing, Inc., follow.

    Genie had no noncash investing and financing transactions during 20X8. During the year, there were no sales of land or equipment, no issuances of notes payable, no retirements of stock, and no treasury stock transactions.

Required

1. Prepare the 20X8 statement of cash flows, formatting operating activities by the indirect method.

2. How will what you learned in this problem help you evaluate an investment?

Genie Marketing, Inc.		
Comparative Balance Sheet		

	December 31,		Increase
	20X8	**20X7**	**(Decrease)**
Current assets:			
Cash and cash equivalents	$ 21,000	$ 18,700	$ 2,300
Accounts receivable	46,500	43,100	3,400
Inventories........................	84,300	89,900	(5,600)
Plant assets:			
Land	35,100	10,000	25,100
Equipment, net	100,900	93,700	7,200
Total assets.........................	$287,800	$255,400	$ 32,400
Current liabilities:			
Accounts payable	$ 31,100	$ 29,800	$ 1,300
Accrued liabilities...................	18,100	18,700	(600)
Long-term liabilities:			
Notes payable	55,000	65,000	(10,000)
Stockholders' equity:			
Common stock	131,100	122,300	8,800
Retained earnings...................	52,500	19,600	32,900
Total liabilities and stockholders' equity ..	$287,800	$255,400	$ 32,400

Genie Marketing, Inc.

Income Statement
Year Ended December 31, 20X8

Revenues:

Sales revenue		$438,000
Interest revenue		11,700
Total revenues.		449,700

Expenses:

Cost of goods sold	$205,200	
Salary expense	76,400	
Depreciation expense.	15,300	
Other operating expense.	49,700	
Interest expense	24,600	
Income tax expense	16,900	
Total expenses.		388,100
Net income		$ 61,600

P17-6B Data Solutions, Inc., accountants have developed the following data from the company's accounting records for the year ended July 31, 20X5:

Preparing the statement of cash flows—direct method
(Obj. 2, 4)

a. Purchase of plant assets, $100,000
b. Proceeds from issuance of notes payable, $44,100
c. Payments of notes payable, $18,800
d. Proceeds from sale of plant assets, $59,700
e. Cash receipt of dividends, $2,700
f. Payments to suppliers, $673,300
g. Interest expense and payments, $37,800
h. Collection of interest revenue, $11,700
i. Payments of salaries, $104,000
j. Income tax expense and payments, $56,400
k. Depreciation expense, $27,700
l. Collections from customers, $827,100
m. Proceeds from issuance of common stock, $116,900
n. Payment of cash dividends, $50,500
o. Cash balance: July 31, 20X4—$53,800; July 31, 20X5—$75,200

Required

Prepare Data Solutions' statement of cash flows for the year ended July 31, 20X5. Use the direct method for cash flows from operating activities. Follow the format of Exhibit 17-13, but do *not* show amounts in thousands.

P17-7B Use the Dohn Corporation data from Problem 17-2B.

Preparing an income statement, balance sheet, and statement of cash flows—direct method
(Obj. 2, 4)

Required

1. Prepare Dohn Corporation's income statement for the year ended December 31, 20X6. Use the single-step format, with all revenues listed together and all expenses together.
2. Prepare Dohn's balance sheet at December 31, 20X6.
3. Prepare Dohn's statement of cash flows for the year ended December 31, 20X6. Format cash flows from operating activities by the direct method.

P17-8B Use the Genie Marketing, Inc., data from Problem 17-5B.

Preparing the statement of cash flows—direct method
(Obj. 2, 4)

Required

1. Prepare the 20X8 statement of cash flows by the direct method.
2. How will what you learned in this problem help you evaluate an investment?

P17-9B To prepare the statement of cash flows, accountants for Rolex Paper Company have summarized 20X8 activity in the cash account as follows:

Cash

Beginning balance	87,100	Payments of operating expenses	46,100
Issuance of common stock	60,800	Payment of note payable	89,300
Receipts of interest revenue	14,100	Payment of income tax	8,000
Collections from customers	308,100	Payments on accounts payable	101,600
		Payment of dividends	1,800
		Payments of salaries and wages	67,500
		Payments of interest	21,800
		Purchase of equipment	51,500
Ending balance	82,500		

Required

Prepare Rolex's statement of cash flows for the year ended December 31, 20X8, using the *direct* method to report operating activities.

APPLY *Your Knowledge*

Decision Cases

Preparing and using the statement of
cash flows to evaluate operations
(Obj. 3)

Case 1. The 20X6 comparative income statement and the 20X6 comparative balance sheet of Tennis, Tennis, Tennis! Inc., have just been distributed at a meeting of the company's board of directors. The members of the board of directors raise a fundamental question: Why is the cash balance so low? This question is especially troublesome to the board members because 20X6 showed record profits. As the controller of the company, you must answer the question.

Tennis, Tennis, Tennis! Inc.

Comparative Income Statement
Years Ended December 31, 20X6 and 20X5

(In thousands)	20X6	20X5
Revenues and gains:		
Sales revenue	$444	$310
Gain on sale of equipment (sale price, $33).	—	18
Total revenues and gains	$444	$328
Expenses and losses:		
Cost of goods sold	$221	$162
Salary expense	48	28
Depreciation expense	46	22
Interest expense	13	20
Amortization expense on patent.	11	11
Loss on sale of land (sale price, $61).	—	35
Total expenses and losses	339	278
Net income	$105	$ 50

Tennis, Tennis, Tennis! Inc.
Comparative Balance Sheet
December 31, 20X6 and 20X5

(In thousands)	20X6	20X5
Assets		
Cash	$ 25	$ 63
Accounts receivable, net	72	61
Inventories	194	181
Long-term investments	31	0
Property, plant, and equipment	369	259
Accumulated depreciation	(244)	(198)
Patents	177	188
Totals	$624	$554
Liabilities and Owners' Equity		
Accounts payable	$ 63	$ 56
Accrued liabilities	12	17
Notes payable, long-term	179	264
Common stock	149	61
Retained earnings	221	156
Totals	$624	$554

Required

1. Prepare a statement of cash flows for 20X6 in the format that best shows the relationship between net income and operating cash flow. The company sold no plant assets or long-term investments and issued no notes payable during 20X6. There were *no* noncash investing and financing transactions during the year. Show all amounts in thousands.

2. Answer the board members' question: Why is the cash balance so low? In explaining the business's cash flows, identify two significant cash receipts that occurred during 20X5 but not in 20X6. Also point out the two largest cash payments during 20X6.

3. Considering net income and the company's cash flows during 20X6, was it a good year or a bad year? Give your reasons.

Case 2. Carolina Technology, Inc., and Northwest Electric Power Corporation are asking you to recommend their stock to your clients. Because Carolina and Northwest earn about the same net income and have similar financial positions, your decision depends on their cash-flow statements, summarized as follows:

Using cash-flow data to evaluate an investment
(Obj. 1, 2)

	Carolina		Northwest	
Net cash provided by operating activities:		$ 70,000		$ 30,000
Cash provided by (used for) investing activities:				
Purchase of plant assets	$(100,000)		$(20,000)	
Sale of plant assets	10,000	(90,000)	40,000	20,000
Cash provided by (used for) financing activities:				
Issuance of common stock		30,000		—
Paying off long-term debt		—		(40,000)
Net increase in cash		$10,000		$ 10,000

Based on their cash flows, which company looks better? Give your reasons.

Ethical Issue

Victoria British Auto Parts is having a bad year. Net income is only $37,000. Also, two important overseas customers are falling behind in their payments to Victoria, and Victoria's accounts receivable are ballooning. The company desperately needs a loan. The Victoria board of directors is considering ways to put the best face on the company's financial statements. Victoria's bank closely examines cash flow from operations. Daniel Peavey, Victoria's controller, suggests reclassifying as long-term the receivables from the slow-paying clients. He explains to the board that removing the $80,000 rise in accounts receivable from current assets will increase net cash provided by operations. This approach may help Victoria get the loan.

Required

1. Using only the amounts given, compute net cash provided by operations, both without and with the reclassification of the receivables. Which reporting makes Victoria look better?
2. Under what condition would the reclassification of the receivables be ethical? Unethical?

Financial Statement Case

Using the statement of cash flows
(Obj. 2, 3, 4)

Use the **Amazon.com** statement of cash flows along with the company's other financial statements, all in Appendix A, to answer the following questions.

Required

1. Which method does Amazon use to report net cash flows from *operating* activities? How can you tell?
2. Amazon suffered a net loss during 2002. Did operations *provide* cash or *use* cash during 2002? Give the amount. How did operating cash during 2002 compare with 2001? Be specific, and state the reason for your answer.
3. Suppose Amazon reported net cash flows from operating activities by the direct method. Compute these amounts for the year ended December 31, 2002.
   a. Collections from customers (Assume that other current assets are zero)
   b. Payments for inventory
4. Evaluate 2002 in terms of net income, cash flows, balance sheet position, and overall results. Be specific.

Team Projects

Project 1. Each member of the team should obtain the annual report of a different company. Select companies in different industries. Evaluate each company's trend of cash flows for the most recent two years. In your evaluation of the companies' cash flows, you may use any other information that is publicly available—for example, the other financial statements (income statement, balance sheet, statement of stockholders' equity, and the related notes) and news stories from magazines and newspapers. Rank the companies' cash flows from best to worst and write a two-page report on your findings.

Project 2. Select a company and obtain its annual report, including all the financial statements. Focus on the statement of cash flows and, in particular, the cash flows from operating activities. Specify whether the company uses the direct method or the indirect method to report operating cash flows. As necessary, use the other financial statements (income statement, balance sheet, and statement of stockholders' equity) and the notes to prepare the company's cash flows from operating activities by the *other* method.

The Work Sheet Approach to Preparing the Statement of Cash Flows

The body of this chapter discusses the uses of the statement of cash flows in decision making and shows how to prepare the statement using T-accounts. The T-account approach works well as a learning device. In practice, however, most companies face complex situations. In these cases, a work sheet can help in preparing the statement of cash flows. This appendix shows how to prepare the statement using a specially designed work sheet.

The work sheet starts with the beginning balance sheet and concludes with the ending balance sheet. Two middle columns—one for debit amounts and the other for credit amounts—complete the work sheet. These columns, labeled Transaction Analysis, hold the data for the statement of cash flows. Accountants can prepare the statement directly from the lower part of the work sheet. This appendix is based on the Anchor Corporation data used in the chapter. We begin with the indirect method for operating activities.

Preparing the Work Sheet—Indirect Method for Operating Activities

The indirect method reconciles net income to net cash provided by operating activities. Exhibit 17A-1 is the work sheet for preparing the statement of cash flows by the indirect method. Panel A shows the transaction analysis, and Panel B gives the statement of cash flows.

Transaction Analysis on the Work Sheet—Indirect Method Net income, transaction (a), is the first operating cash inflow. Net income is entered on the work sheet (Panel B) as a debit to Net Income under Cash flows from operating activities and as a credit to Retained Earnings. Next come the adjustments to net income, starting with depreciation—transaction (b)—which is debited to Depreciation and credited to Plant Assets, Net. Transaction (c) is the sale of plant assets. The $8,000 gain on the sale is entered as a credit to Gain on Sale of Plant Assets—a subtraction from net income—under operating cash flows. This credit removes the $8,000 gain from operations because the cash proceeds from the sale were $62,000, not $8,000. The $62,000 sale amount is then entered on the work sheet under investing activities. Entry (c) is completed by crediting the plant assets' book value of $54,000 to the Plant Assets, Net account.

Entries (d) through (g) reconcile net income to cash flows from operations for increases and decreases in the other current assets and for increases and decreases in the current liabilities. Entry (d) debits Accounts Receivable for its $15,000 increase during the year. This amount is credited to Increase in Accounts Receivable under operating cash flows. Entries (e), (f), and (g) adjust for the other current accounts.

Entries (h) through (l) account for the investing and financing transactions. Entry (h) debits Plant Assets, Net for their purchase and credits Purchase of plant assets under investing cash flows. Entry (i) debits Proceeds from issuance of common stock under financing cash flows. The offsetting debit is to Common Stock.

The final item in Exhibit 17A-1 is the Net decrease in cash—transaction (m) on the work sheet—a credit to Cash and a debit to Net decrease in cash. To prepare the statement of cash flows, the accountant can rewrite Panel B of the work sheet, adding subtotals for the three categories of activities.

| Exhibit 17A-1 | Work Sheet for Statement of Cash Flows—Indirect Method |

Anchor Corporation
Work Sheet for Statement of Cash Flows (Indirect Method)
Year Ended December 31, 20X5

		In thousands			
		Transaction Analysis			
	Balances				Balances
	Dec. 31, 20X4	Debit		Credit	Dec. 31, 20X5
PANEL A—Balance-Sheet Accounts					
Cash..........	42			(m) 20	22
Accounts receivable.....................	81	(d) 15			96
Inventory......................	145			(e) 2	143
Plant assets, net	219	(h) 317		(b) 18	
				(c) 54	464
Totals	487				725
Accounts payable.........................	57			(f) 34	91
Accrued liabilities	9	(g) 4			5
Long-term notes payable	77	(k) 11		(j) 94	160
Common stock..........................	258			(i) 101	359
Retained earnings	86	(l) 17		(a) 41	110
Totals	487	364		364	725
PANEL B—Statement of Cash Flows					
Cash flows from operating activities:					
Net income		(a) 41			
Add (subtract) items that affect net income and cash flow differently:					
Depreciation..........................		(b) 18			
Gain on sale of plant assets				(c) 8	
Increase in accounts receivable				(d) 15	
Decrease in inventory		(e) 2			
Increase in accounts payable		(f) 34			
Decrease in accured liabilities				(g) 4	
Cash flows from investing activities:					
Purchase of plant assets				(h) 317	
Proceeds from sale of plant assets......................		(c) 62			
Cash flows from financing activities:					
Proceeds from issuance of common stock		(i) 101			
Proceeds from issuance of note payable...................		(j) 94			
Payment of note payable				(k) 11	
Payment of dividends................................				(l) 17	
		352		372	
Net decrease in cash		(m) 20			
Totals		372		372	

Noncash Investing and Financing Activities on the Work Sheet Noncash investing and financing activities can be analyzed on the work sheet. These transactions include both an investing activity and a financing activity, so they require two work-sheet entries. Suppose Anchor Corporation purchased a building by issuing common stock of $300,000. Exhibit 17A-2 illustrates the analysis of this transaction. Cash is unaffected. Work-sheet entry (a) records the purchase of the building, and entry (b) records the issuance of the stock.

Exhibit 17A-2 Noncash Investing and Financing Activities on the Work Sheet

Anchor Corporation
Work Sheet for Statement of Cash Flows
Year Ended December 31, 20X5

	Balances Dec. 31, 20X4	Transaction Analysis		Balances Dec. 31, 20X5
		Debit	Credit	
PANEL A—Balance-Sheet Accounts				
Cash				
Building	600,000	(a) 300,000		900,000
Common stock	400,000		(b) 300,000	700,000
PANEL B—Statement of Cash Flows				
Noncash investing and financing transactions:				
Purchase of building by issuing common stock		(b) 300,000	(a) 300,000	

Preparing the Work Sheet—Direct Method for Operating Activities

The direct method separates operating activities into cash receipts and cash payments. Exhibit 17A-3 is the work sheet for the preparation of the statement of cash flows by the direct method.

Transaction Analysis on the Work Sheet—Direct Method For your convenience, we repeat the Anchor Corporation transaction data here.

Operating Activities:
 a. Sales on account, $284,000
*b. Collections from customers, $269,000
*c. Cash receipt of interest revenue, $12,000
*d. Cash receipt of dividend revenue, $9,000
 e. Purchase of inventory on account, $148,000
 f. Cost of goods sold, $150,000

*g. Payments for inventory on account, $114,000
*h. Salary expense and payments, $56,000
 i. Depreciation expense, $18,000
 j. Accrual of other operating expense, $17,000
*k. Interest expense and payments, $16,000
*l. Income tax expense and payments, $15,000
*m. Payment of accrued liabilities, $21,000

Investing Activities:
*n. Cash payments to acquire plant assets, $317,000

*o. Proceeds from sale of plant assets, $62,000, including $8,000 gain

Financing Activities:
*p. Proceeds from issuance of common stock, $101,000
*q. Proceeds from issuance of long-term note payable, $94,000

*r. Payment of long-term note payable, $11,000
*s. Declaration and payment of cash dividends, $17,000

*Indicates a cash flow to be reported on the statement of cash flows.

The transaction analysis on the work sheet includes journal entries. Only balance-sheet accounts are used on the work sheet. Therefore, revenues are entered as credits to Retained Earnings, and expenses are entered as debits to Retained Earnings. For example, in transaction (a), sales on account are debited to Accounts Receivable and credited to Retained Earnings. Cash is neither debited nor credited because credit sales do not affect cash. But all transactions should be entered on the work sheet to identify all the cash effects of the period's transactions. In transaction (c), the collection of cash for interest revenue is entered by debiting Cash and crediting Retained Earnings.

| Exhibit 17A-3 | Work Sheet for Statement of Cash Flows—Direct Method |

Anchor Corporation
Work Sheet for Statement of Cash Flows (Direct Method)
Year Ended December 31, 20X5

(in thousands)

	Balances	Transaction Analysis		Balances
	Dec. 31, 20X4	Debit	Credit	Dec. 31, 20X5
PANEL A—Balance-Sheet Accounts				
Cash..................................	42		(t) 20	22
Accounts receivable.....................	81	(a) 284	(b) 269	96
Inventory............................	145	(e) 148	(f) 150	143
Equipment, net........................	219	(n) 317	(i) 18	
			(o) 54	464
Totals	487			725
Accounts payable.......................	57	(g) 114	(e) 148	91
Accrued liabilities	9	(m) 21	(j) 17	5
Long-term notes payable	77	(r) 11	(q) 94	160
Common stock........................	258		(p) 101	359
Retained earnings	86	(f) 150	(a) 284	110
		(h) 56	(c) 12	
		(i) 18	(d) 9	
		(j) 17	(o) 8	
		(k) 16		
		(l) 15		
		(s) 17		
Totals	487	1,184	1,184	725
PANEL B—Statement of Cash Flows				
Cash flows from operating activities:				
Receipts:				
Collections from customers		(b) 269		
Interest received.....................		(c) 12		
Dividends received		(d) 9		
Payments:				
To suppliers			(g) 114	
			(m) 21	
To employees			(h) 56	
For interest			(k) 16	
For income tax			(l) 15	
Cash flows from investing activities:				
Purchase of plant assets			(n) 317	
Proceeds from sale of plant assets.......		(o) 62		
Cash flows from financing activities:				
Proceeds from issuance of common stock ...		(p) 101		
Proceeds from issuance of note payable....		(q) 94		
Payment of note payable			(r) 11	
Payment of dividends..................			(s) 17	
		547	567	
Net decrease in cash		(t) 20		
Totals		567	567	

Entries (n) through (s) account for the investing and financing transactions. Entry (n) debits Equipment, Net for their purchase and credits Purchase of plant assets under investing cash flows. Entry (p) debits Proceeds from issuance of common stock under financing cash flows. The offsetting credit is to Common stock.

The final item in Exhibit 17A-3 is the Net decrease in cash—transaction (t) on the work sheet—a credit to cash and a debit to Net decrease in cash. To prepare the statement of cash flows, you can rewrite Panel B of the work sheet, adding subtotals for the three categories of activities.

Appendix Assignments
Problems

P17A-1 The 20X8 comparative balance sheet and income statement of Alden Group, Inc., follow. Alden had no noncash investing and financing transactions during 20X8.

Preparing the work sheet for the statement of cash flows—indirect method

Alden Group, Inc.
Comparative Balance Sheet

	December 31, 20X8	December 31, 20X7	Increase (Decrease)
Current assets:			
Cash and cash equivalents	$ 13,700	$ 15,600	$ (1,900)
Accounts receivable	41,500	43,100	(1,600)
Inventories....................	96,600	93,000	3,600
Plant assets:			
Land	35,100	10,000	25,100
Equipment, net	100,900	93,700	7,200
Total assets....................	$287,800	$255,400	$32,400
Current liabilities:			
Accounts payable..............	$ 24,800	$ 26,000	$ (1,200)
Accrued liabilities.............	24,400	22,500	1,900
Long-term liabilities:			
Notes payable	55,000	65,000	(10,000)
Stockholders' equity:			
Common stock	131,100	122,300	8,800
Retained earnings..............	52,500	19,600	32,900
Total liabilities and stockholders' equity	$287,800	$255,400	$32,400

Alden Group, Inc.
Income Statement for Year Ended December 31, 20X8

Revenues:		
Sales revenue....................		$438,000
Interest revenue.................		11,700
Total revenues		449,700
Expenses:		
Cost of goods sold	$205,200	
Salary expense...............	76,400	
Depreciation expense..........	15,300	
Other operating expense	49,700	
Interest expense..............	24,600	
Income tax expense	16,900	
Total expenses...............		388,100
Net income		$ 61,600

Required

Prepare the work sheet for the 20X8 statement of cash flows. Format cash flows from operating activities by the *indirect* method.

Preparing the work sheet for the statement of cash flows—direct method

P17A-2 Using the Alden Group, Inc., data from Problem 17A-1, prepare the work sheet for Alden's 20X8 statement of cash flows. Format cash flows from operating activities by the *direct* method.

CHAPTER 18

Financial Statement Analysis

TIPS CHECK YOUR RESOURCES

- Visit the www.prenhall.com/horngren **Web site** for self-study quizzes, video clips, and other resources
- Try the **Quick Check** exercise at the end of the chapter to test your knowledge
- Learn the **key terms**
- Do the **Starter** exercises keyed in the margins
- Work the **mid-** and **end-of-chapter summary problems**
- Use the **Concept Links** to review material in other chapters
- Search the **CD** for review materials by chapter or by key word
- Watch the **tutorial videos** to review key concepts
- Watch the **On Location Financial Statement Analysis** video, in which people from three companies talk about how they use financial statements for decision making

LEARNING OBJECTIVES

1. Perform a horizontal analysis of comparative financial statements

2. Perform a vertical analysis of financial statements

3. Prepare and use common-size financial statements

4. Compute the standard financial ratios

5. Measure economic value added

You, or people you know, probably invest in stocks. How do you choose those investments? Do you pick large, established companies, or do you look for a new highflier? What kind of information do you use?

Some of the most important information about a company comes from its financial statements. To make an informed decision, you need to be able to analyze those statements, even if the company has been around a long time and is a household name. Take a look at what happened to health-care giant Bristol-Myers Squibb (BMS). Study BMS's 2002 income statement:

Bristol-Myers Squibb

Bristol-Myers Squibb Company
Income Statement (Adapted)

(In millions)	Year Ended December 31,	
	2002	2001
Earnings		
1 **Net sales**	$18,119	$17,987
2 **Expenses:**		
3 Cost of goods sold	6,388	5,453
4 Marketing, selling, and administrative	3,923	3,894
5 Advertising and product promotion	1,295	1,299
6 Research and development	2,218	2,183
7 Other expense, net*	1,794	251
8 **Income before income tax**	2,501	4,907
9 Income taxes	435	73
10 **Net income**	$ 2,066	$ 4,834

*Includes discontinued operations.

You can see that 2002 was a tough year for the company. Net income (line 10) was down from 2001, and Wall Street wasn't happy.

Companies have to satisfy lots of people, from individual investors like you and me to Wall Street analysts. What analytical tools do people use to make decisions about a company like Bristol-Myers Squibb? They use many of the techniques we cover in this book. ■

■Sitemap

- ■ Horizontal Analysis
- ■ Vertical Analysis
- ■ Benchmarking
- ■ Using Ratios
- ■ Other Evaluation Tools

Investors and creditors can't evaluate a company by examining only one year's data. This is why most financial statements cover at least two periods, like the Bristol-Myers Squibb (BMS) income statement. In fact, most financial analysis covers trends of three to five years. This chapter illustrates some of the analytical tools for charting a company's progress through time.

The graphs in Exhibit 18-1 show some important data about BMS. They depict a three-year trend of net sales and research and development (R&D). Sales and R&D are important drivers of profits.

Exhibit 18-1 Financial Data of Bristol-Myers Squibb Company (Adapted)

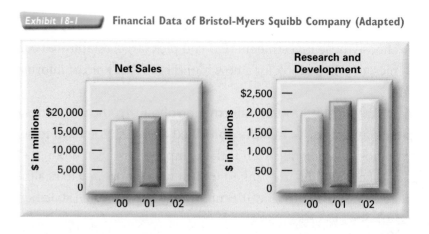

For BMS, both sales and research and development barely grew during 2002. These are not good signs for the future. How can we decide what we really think about BMS's performance in 2002? We need some way to compare that performance

- From one year to another
- With the performance of a competing company, like Procter & Gamble
- With the pharmaceuticals (health-care) industry

Then we will have a better idea of how to judge BMS's situation now and predict what might happen in the near future.

Horizontal analysis provides a direct year-to-year comparison of BMS's performance in 2002 and 2001. Another technique, vertical analysis, is the standard way to compare different companies. Let's begin with horizontal analysis.

Horizontal Analysis

Many decisions hinge on whether the numbers—in sales, income, and expenses—are increasing or decreasing. Have sales risen from last year? By how much? We may find that sales have increased by $20,000. But considered alone, this fact is not very helpful. The *percentage change* in sales over time aids our understanding. It is more useful to know that sales have increased by 20% than to know that the increase is $20,000.

The study of percentage changes in comparative statements is called **horizontal analysis**. Computing a percentage change in comparative statements requires two steps:

1. Compute the dollar amount of the change from the earlier base period to the later period.
2. Divide the dollar amount of change by the base-period amount.

Illustration: Bristol-Myers Squibb

Horizontal analysis is illustrated for Bristol-Myers Squibb as follows (dollar amounts in millions):

	2002	2001	Increase (Decrease)	
			Amount	Percentage
Net sales	$18,119	$17,987	$132	0.7%

Sales increased by only 7/10 of 1% (0.007) during 2002, computed as follows:

STEP 1 Compute the dollar amount of change in sales from 2001 to 2002:

2002	2001	Increase
$18,119	− $17,987 =	$132

STEP 2 Divide the dollar amount of change by the base-period amount. This computes the percentage change for the period:

$$\text{Percentage change} = \frac{\text{Dollar amount of change}}{\text{Base-year amount}}$$

$$= \frac{\$132}{\$17,987} = 0.007 = 0.7\%$$

Detailed horizontal analyses are shown in the two right-hand columns of Exhibits 18-2 and 18-3, the financial statements of BMS Company. The income statements reveal that net sales increased by 0.7% during 2002. But cost of goods sold grew by 17.1%, so gross profit fell by 6.4%. Net income was down by 57.3%. These results are not encouraging.

■ **Horizontal Analysis**
☐ Vertical Analysis
☐ Benchmarking
☐ Using Ratios
☐ Other Evaluation Tools

Student Resource **CD**

horizontal analysis, trend analysis

Perform a horizontal analysis of comparative financial statements

Horizontal Analysis
Study of percentage changes in comparative financial statements.

✔ **Starter 18-1**

Exhibit 18-2

Comparative Income Statement—
Horizontal Analysis

Bristol-Myers Squibb Company
Income Statement (Adapted)
Years Ended December 31, 2002 and 2001

(Dollar amounts in millions)	2002	2001	Increase (Decrease) Amount	Increase (Decrease) Percentage
Net sales	$18,119	$17,987	$ 132	0.7%
Cost of goods sold	6,388	5,453	935	17.1
Gross profit.	11,731	12,534	(803)	(6.4)
Operating expenses:				
Marketing, selling, and administrative....	3,923	3,894	29	0.7
Advertising and product promotion......	1,295	1,299	(4)	(0.3)
Research and development..............	2,218	2,183	35	1.6
Other expense, net	1,794	251	1,543	614.7
Income before income tax	2,501	4,907	(2,406)	(49.0)
Income tax expense	435	73	362	495.9
Net income	**$ 2,066**	**$ 4,834**	$(2,768)	(57.3)

The comparative balance sheet in Exhibit 18-3 shows that 2002 was not a growth year for BMS. Total assets fell by 10.6%. Fortunately, liabilities decreased by 15.1%, so the drop in stockholders' equity was only 1.2%.

Exhibit 18-3

Comparative Balance Sheet—
Horizontal Analysis

Bristol-Myers Squibb Company
Balance Sheet (Adapted)
December 31, 2002 and 2001

(Dollar amounts in millions)	2002	2001	Increase (Decrease) Amount	Increase (Decrease) Percentage
Assets				
Current Assets:				
Cash and cash equivalents	$ 3,978	$ 5,500	$(1,522)	(27.7)%
Other current assets	5,997	7,749	(1,752)	(22.6)
Total current assets......................	9,975	13,249	(3,274)	(24.7)
Property, plant, and equipment, net	5,321	4,887	434	8.9
Intangible assets, net	6,768	7,203	(435)	(6.0)
Other assets.............................	2,810	2,473	337	13.6
Total assets	**$24,874**	**$27,812**	$(2,938)	(10.6)
Liabilities				
Current Liabilities:				
Accounts payable........................	$ 1,553	$ 1,478	$ 75	5.1%
Other current liabilities	6,667	9,631	(2,964)	(30.8)
Total current liabilities..................	8,220	11,109	(2,889)	(26.0)
Long-term liabilities......................	7,687	7,628	59	0.8
Total liabilities	**15,907**	**18,737**	(2,830)	(15.1)
Stockholders' Equity				
Common stock	2,711	2,623	88	3.4
Retained earnings and				
other equity..........................	6,256	6,452	(196)	(3.0)
Total stockholders' equity	**8,967**	**9,075**	(108)	(1.2)
Total liabilities and equity	**$24,874**	**$27,812**	$(2,938)	(10.6)

Trend Percentages

Trend percentages are a form of horizontal analysis. Trends indicate the direction a business is taking. How have sales changed over a five-year period? What trend does net income show? These questions can be answered by trend percentages over a representative period, such as the most recent three to five years.

Trend percentages are computed by selecting a base year whose amounts are set equal to 100%. The amounts for each following year are expressed as a percentage of the base amount. To compute trend percentages, divide each item for following years by the corresponding amount during the base year:

$$\text{Trend \%} = \frac{\text{Any year \$}}{\text{Base year \$}}$$

BMS Company showed the following net sales for the past 6 years:

(In millions)	2002	2001	2000	1999	1998	1997
Net sales	$18,119	$17,987	$17,538	$16,502	$15,007	$13,698
Trend percentages	132%	131%	128%	120%	110%	100%

✔ Starter 18-2

We want trend percentages for the five-year period 1998 to 2002. The base year is 1997. Trend percentages are computed by dividing each year's amount by the 1997 amount. The trend percentages follow net sales (1997, the base year = 100%).

Net sales increased rapidly through 1999. The rate of growth slowed in 2000 and became a trickle in 2001 and 2002.

You can perform a trend analysis on any item you consider important. We selected net sales because sales drive profits. Trend analysis is widely used to predict the future.

Vertical Analysis

Horizontal analysis highlights changes in an item over time. However, no single technique gives a complete picture of a business.

Vertical analysis of a financial statement shows the relationship of each item to its base amount, which is the 100% figure. Every other item on the statement is then reported as a percentage of that base. For an income statement, net sales is the base. Suppose under normal conditions a company's gross profit is 70% of net sales. A drop to 60% may cause the company to suffer a loss. Investors view a large decline in gross profit with alarm.

Illustration: Bristol-Myers Squibb

Exhibit 18-4 shows the vertical analysis of BMS's income statement. In this case,

$$\text{Vertical analysis \%} = \frac{\text{Each income statement item}}{\text{Net sales}}$$

For example, the vertical-analysis percentage for Cost of goods sold for 2002 is 35.3% ($6,388/$18,119 = 0.353). Unfortunately for BMS, this percentage increased during 2002. Look further. Other expenses' percentages also increased. Consequently, the percentage for net income was down from 2001.

Exhibit 18-5 shows the vertical analysis of BMS's balance sheet. The base amount (100%) is total assets.

Trend Percentages
A form of horizontal analysis in which percentages are computed by selecting a base year as 100% and expressing amounts for following years as a percentage of the base amount.

☐ Horizontal Analysis
■ Vertical Analysis
☐ Benchmarking
☐ Using Ratios
☐ Other Evaluation Tools

Student ResourceCD
common-size statement, vertical analysis

2 Perform a vertical analysis of financial statements

Vertical Analysis
Analysis of a financial statement that reveals the relationship of each statement item to a specified base, which is the 100% figure.

Exhibit 18-4

Comparative Income Statement—
Vertical Analysis

Bristol-Myers Squibb Company

Income Statement (Adapted)
Years Ended December 31, 2002 and 2001

	2002		2001	
(Dollar amounts in millions)	Amount	Percent of Total	Amount	Percent of Total
Net sales	$18,119	100.0%	$17,987	100.0%
Cost of goods sold	6,388	35.3	5,453	30.3
Gross profit	11,731	64.7	12,534	69.7
Operating expenses:				
Marketing, selling, and administrative ..	3,923	21.7	3,894	21.7
Advertising and product promotion.....	1,295	7.1	1,299	7.2
Research and development	2,218	12.2	2,183	12.1
Other expense, net....................	1,794	9.9	251	1.4
Income before income tax................	2,501	13.8	4,907	27.3
Income tax expense	435	2.4	73	0.4
Net income...........................	$ 2,066	11.4%	$ 4,834	26.9%

Note: Percentage may contain slight rounding error.

Exhibit 18-5

Comparative Balance Sheet—
Vertical Analysis

Bristol-Myers Squibb Company

Balance Sheet (Adapted)
December 31, 2002 and 2001

	2002		2001	
(Dollar amounts in millions)	Amount	Percent of Total	Amount	Percent of Total
Assets				
Current Assets:				
Cash and cash equivalents	$ 3,978	16.0%	$ 5,500	19.8%
Other current assets.....................	5,997	24.1	7,749	27.8
Total current assets	9,975	40.1	13,249	47.6
Property, plant, and equipment, net	5,321	21.4	4,887	17.6
Intangible assets, net	6,768	27.2	7,203	25.9
Other assets...........................	2,810	11.3	2,473	8.9
Total assets	**$24,874**	100.0%	**$27,812**	100.0%
Liabilities				
Current Liabilities:				
Accounts payable.......................	$ 1,553	6.2%	$ 1,478	5.3%
Other current liabilities..................	6,667	26.8	9,631	34.7
Total current liabilities................	8,220	33.0	11,109	40.0
Long-term liabilities	7,687	30.9	7,628	27.4
Total liabilities.	**15,907**	63.9	**18,737**	67.4
Stockholders' Equity				
Common stock	2,711	10.9	2,623	9.4
Retained earnings and				
other equity.........................	6,256	25.2	6,452	23.2
Total stockholders' equity...............	8,967	36.1	9,075	32.6
Total liabilities and equity	$24,874	100.0%	$27,812	100.0%

Note: Percentages may contain slight rounding error.

The vertical analysis of BMS's balance sheet reveals several things about the company's financial position:

✔ Starter 18-3

- Current assets make up 40.1% of total assets, compared to 47.6% in 2001. A high percentage of current assets can be bad because current assets earn a low rate of return.

- Intangibles make up 27.2% of total assets. This percentage is high because of the nature of the pharmaceutical business. Lenders dislike a high percentage of intangibles because, in a liquidation of the company, intangibles are often worthless. But in today's technology-driven economy, intangible assets are important.

- Total liabilities dropped to 63.9%, and stockholders' equity increased to 36.1% of total assets. Overall, BMS's creditworthiness improved a bit in 2002.

How Do We Compare One Company with Another?

The percentages in Exhibits 18-4 and 18-5 can be presented as a separate statement that reports only percentages (no dollar amounts). Such a statement is called a **common-size statement**.

On a common-size income statement, each item is expressed as a percentage of net sales. Net sales is the *common size* to which we relate the other amounts. In the balance sheet, the common size is total assets. A common-size statement eases the comparison of different companies because amounts are stated in percentages.

Common-size statements may identify the need for corrective action. Exhibit 18-6 gives an example. In 2001, BMS had almost half of its resources tied up in current assets. As we have mentioned, cash, receivables, and inventories earn low rates of return, as compared with long-term assets. It appears that the top management of BMS made a serious shift during 2002. BMS invested in plant and equipment, and the company's long-term assets grew to 59.9% of total resources in 2002.

⭐ *Prepare and use common-size financial statements*

Common-Size Statement
A financial statement that reports only percentages (no dollar amounts).

Bristol-Myers Squibb Company

Common-Size Analysis of Current and Long-Term Assets
December 31, 2002 and 2001

	Percent of Total Assets	
	2002	2001
Current assets	40.1%	47.6%
Long-term assets	59.9	52.4
Total assets	100.0%	100.0%

Exhibit 18-6

Common-Size Analysis of Current Assets

Bristol–Myers Squibb Company
Percent of Total Assets

2002	2001
Current Assets 40.1%	Current Assets 47.6%
Long-Term Assets 59.9%	Long-Term Assets 52.4%

benchmarking

Benchmarking
The practice of comparing a company
with other companies that are leaders.

Benchmarking

Benchmarking is the practice of comparing a company with other companies that are leaders.

Calculate the common-size percentages for the following income statement:

Net sales	$150,000
Cost of goods sold	60,000
Gross profit	90,000
Operating expense	40,000
Operating income	50,000
Income tax expense	15,000
Net income	$ 35,000

Answer:

Net sales	100%	(= $150,000 ÷ $150,000)
Cost of goods sold	40	(= $ 60,000 ÷ $150,000)
Gross profit	60	(= $ 90,000 ÷ $150,000)
Operating expense	27	(= $ 40,000 ÷ $150,000)
Operating income	33	(= $ 50,000 ÷ $150,000)
Income tax expense	10	(= $ 15,000 ÷ $150,000)
Net income	23%	(= $ 35,000 ÷ $150,000)

Benchmarking Against the Industry Average

We study a company to gain insight into past results and future performance. Still, that knowledge is limited to the one company. We may learn that gross profit and net income have increased. This information is helpful, but it does not consider how other companies have fared over the same period. Have competitors profited even more? Investors need to know how a company compares with others in the same line of business. For example, during 2002, Johnson & Johnson and Procter & Gamble increased both sales and profits, while BMS's net income decreased.

Exhibit 18-7 gives the common-size income statement of BMS compared with the average for the pharmaceuticals (health-care) industry. The industry averages were adapted from Risk Management Association's *Annual Statement Studies.* Analysts at Merrill Lynch and Edward Jones & Co. specialize in a particular industry. For example, Merrill Lynch has health-care specialists, airline-industry specialists, and so on. They compare a company with others in the same industry. Exhibit 18-7 shows that BMS compares favorably with competing companies in its industry. BMS's gross profit percentage is much higher than the industry average. Even though 2002 was not a good year, BMS's percentage of net income is still higher than the industry average.

Benchmarking Against a Key Competitor

Common-size statements are also used to compare two or more companies. Suppose you are a financial analyst for Edward Jones & Company. You are considering an investment in the stock of a health-care company, and you are choosing between BMS and P&G. A direct comparison of their financial statements in dollar amounts is not meaningful because the amounts are so different. However, you can convert the two companies' income statements to common size and compare the percentages. Exhibit 18-8 compares the common-size income statements of Bristol-Myers Squibb and Procter & Gamble. The two companies earn similar percentages of net income to sales.

Bristol-Myers Squibb Company

Common-Size Income Statement for Comparison with Industry Average
Year Ended December 31, 2002

	Bristol-Myers Squibb	Industry Average
Net sales	100.0%	100.0%
Cost of goods sold	35.3	51.6
Gross profit	64.7	48.4
Operating and other expenses...............	50.9	40.5
Income before income tax..................	13.8	7.9
Income tax expense	2.4	2.8
Net income...............................	11.4%	5.1%

Exhibit 18-7

Common-Size Income Statement Compared with the Industry Average

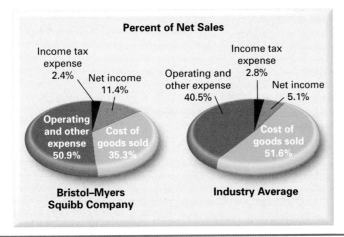

Percent of Net Sales

Bristol–Myers Squibb Company

Industry Average

✔ Starter 18-4

Bristol-Myers Squibb Company

Common-Size Income Statement for Comparison with Key Competitor
Year Ended December 31, 2002

	Bristol-Myers Squibb	Procter & Gamble
Net sales	100.0%	100.0%
Cost of goods sold	35.3	52.2
Gross profit	64.7	47.8
Operating and other expenses...............	50.9	32.0
Income before income tax..................	13.8	15.8
Income tax expense	2.4	5.0
Net income...............................	11.4%	10.8%

Exhibit 18-8

Common-Size Income Statement Compared with a Key Competitor

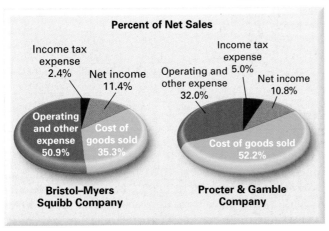

Percent of Net Sales

Bristol–Myers Squibb Company

Procter & Gamble Company

Now let's put your learning to practice. Work the mid-chapter summary problem, which reviews the concepts in the first half of this chapter.

● MID-CHAPTER *Summary Problem*

CHECK YOUR RESOURCES

Perform a horizontal analysis and a vertical analysis of the comparative income statement of TRE Corporation, which makes metal detectors. State whether 20X3 was a good year or a bad year, and give your reasons.

TRE Corporation
Comparative Income Statement
Months Ended December 31, 20X3 and 20X2

	20X3	20X2
Total revenues	$275,000	$225,000
Expenses:		
Cost of products sold	$194,000	$165,000
Engineering, selling, and administrative expenses ..	54,000	48,000
Interest expense	5,000	5,000
Income tax expense	9,000	3,000
Other expense (income)	1,000	(1,000)
Total expenses	263,000	220,000
Net earnings	$ 12,000	$ 5,000

Solution

The horizontal analysis shows that total revenues increased 22.2%. This was greater than the 19.5% increase in total expenses, resulting in a 140% increase in net earnings.

TRE Corporation
Horizontal Analysis of Comparative Income Statement
Months Ended December 31, 20X3 and 20X2

			Increase (Decrease)	
	20X3	20X2	Amount	Percent
Total revenues.................	$275,000	$225,000	$50,000	22.2%
Expenses:				
Cost of products sold.........	$194,000	$165,000	$29,000	17.6
Engineering, selling, and administrative expenses	54,000	48,000	6,000	12.5
Interest expense	5,000	5,000	—	—
Income tax expense	9,000	3,000	6,000	200.0
Other expense (income)	1,000	(1,000)	2,000	—*
Total expenses.............	263,000	220,000	43,000	19.5
Net earnings	$ 12,000	$ 5,000	$ 7,000	140.0%

*Percentage changes are typically not computed for shifts from a negative to a positive amount, and vice versa.

The vertical analysis shows decreases in the percentages of net sales consumed by the cost of products sold (from 73.3% to 70.5%) and by the engineering, selling, and administrative expenses (from 21.3% to 19.6%). Because these two items are TRE's largest dollar expenses, their percentage decreases are quite important. The relative reduction in expenses raised December 20X3 net earnings to 4.4% of sales, compared with 2.2% the preceding December. The overall analysis indicates that December 20X3 was significantly better than December 20X2.

	20X3		20X2	
	Amount	Percent	Amount	Percent
TRE Corporation **Vertical Analysis of Comparative Income Statement** **Months Ended December 31, 20X3 and 20X2**				
Total revenues................	$275,000	100.0%	$225,000	100.0%
Expenses:				
Cost of products sold.........	$194,000	70.5	$165,000	73.3
Engineering, selling, and				
administrative expenses	54,000	19.6	48,000	21.3
Interest expense	5,000	1.8	5,000	2.2
Income tax expense	9,000	3.3	3,000	1.4**
Other expense (income)	1,000	0.4	(1,000)	(0.4)
Total expenses.............	263,000	95.6	220,000	97.8
Net earnings	$ 12,000	4.4%	$ 5,000	2.2%

**Number rounded up.

Using Ratios to Make Decisions

☐ Horizontal Analysis
☐ Vertical Analysis
☐ Benchmarking
■ **Using Ratios**
☐ Other Evaluation Tools

Online financial databases, such as Lexis/Nexis and the Dow Jones News Retrieval Service, provide financial data on thousands of corporations. Assume that you want to compare some companies' recent earnings histories. You might have the computer compare the companies on the basis of return on stockholders' equity. The computer could then give you the names of the 20 companies with the highest return on equity. A manager, lender, or financial analyst may use any ratio that is relevant to a particular decision.

Student ResourceCD

accounts receivable turnover, acid-test ratio, current ratio, day's sales in receivables, debt ratio, dividend yield, earnings per share, inventory turnover ratio, P/E ratio, profitability ratio, return on net sales, return on stockholders' equity, return on total assets, times-interest-earned ratio

The ratios we discuss in this chapter may be classified as follows:

1. Measuring ability to pay current liabilities
2. Measuring ability to sell inventory and collect receivables
3. Measuring ability to pay long-term debt
4. Measuring profitability
5. Analyzing stock as an investment

Measuring Ability to Pay Current Liabilities

Working capital is defined as

$$\text{Working capital} = \text{Current assets} - \text{Current liabilities}$$

Working capital measures the ability to meet short-term obligations with current assets. To use working-capital data in decision making, analysts develop ratios. Two decision tools based on working-capital data are the *current ratio* and the *acid-test ratio*.

CURRENT RATIO The most widely used ratio is the **current ratio**, which is current assets divided by current liabilities. A company's current assets and current liabilities represent the core of day-to-day operations. The current ratio measures ability to pay current liabilities with current assets.

Compute the standard financial ratios

Working Capital
Current assets minus current liabilities; measures a business's ability to meet its short-term obligations with its current assets.

Current Ratio
Current assets divided by current liabilities. Measures ability to pay current liabilities with current assets.

Exhibit 18-9 gives the comparative income statement and balance sheet of Palisades Furniture, Inc. The current ratios of Palisades Furniture, Inc., at December 31, 20X5 and 20X4, follow, along with the average for the retail furniture industry:

	Formula	Palisades' Current Ratio		Industry Average
		20X5	20X4	
Current ratio =	$\dfrac{\text{Current assets}}{\text{Current liabilities}}$	$\dfrac{\$262,000}{\$142,000} = 1.85$	$\dfrac{\$236,000}{\$126,000} = 1.87$	1.50

Exhibit 18-9 Comparative Financial Statements

Palisades Furniture, Inc.
Comparative Income Statement
Years Ended December 31, 20X5 and 20X4

	20X5	20X4
Net sales	$858,000	$803,000
Cost of goods sold	513,000	509,000
Gross profit	345,000	294,000
Operating expenses:		
Selling expenses	126,000	114,000
General expenses	118,000	123,000
Total operating expenses	244,000	237,000
Income from operations	101,000	57,000
Interest revenue	4,000	—
Interest expense	24,000	14,000
Income before income taxes	81,000	43,000
Income tax expense	33,000	17,000
Net income	$ 48,000	$ 26,000

Palisades Furniture, Inc.
Comparative Balance Sheet
December 31, 20X5 and 20X4

	20X5	20X4
Assets		
Current Assets:		
Cash	$ 29,000	$ 32,000
Accounts receivable, net	114,000	85,000
Inventories	113,000	111,000
Prepaid expenses	6,000	8,000
Total current assets	262,000	236,000
Long-term investments	18,000	9,000
Property, plant, and equipment, net	507,000	399,000
Total assets	$787,000	$644,000
Liabilities		
Current Liabilities:		
Notes payable	$ 42,000	$ 27,000
Accounts payable	73,000	68,000
Accrued liabilities	27,000	31,000
Total current liabilities	142,000	126,000
Long-term debt	289,000	198,000
Total liabilities	431,000	324,000
Stockholders' Equity		
Common stock, no par	186,000	186,000
Retained earnings	170,000	134,000
Total stockholders' equity	356,000	320,000
Total liabilities and equity	$787,000	$644,000

✔ **Starter 18-5**

A high current ratio indicates a strong financial position and that the business has sufficient liquid assets to maintain normal business operations. Compare Palisades Furniture's current ratio of 1.85 with the industry average of 1.50 and with the current ratios of some well-known companies:

Company	Current Ratio
Chesebrough-Pond's Inc.	2.50
Wal-Mart Stores, Inc.	1.51
General Mills, Inc.	1.05

What is an acceptable current ratio? The answer depends on the industry. The norm for companies in most industries is around 1.50, as reported by the Risk Management Association. Palisades Furniture's current ratio of 1.85 is strong. In most industries, a current ratio of 2.0 is very strong.

ACID-TEST RATIO   The **acid-test** (or **quick) ratio** tells us whether the entity could pay all its current liabilities if they came due immediately. That is, could the company pass this *acid test*?

To compute the acid-test ratio, we add cash, short-term investments, and net current receivables (accounts and notes receivable, net of allowances) and divide this sum by current liabilities. Inventory and prepaid expenses are the two current assets *not* included in the acid test because they are the least-liquid current assets. Palisades Furniture's acid-test ratios for 20X5 and 20X4 follow.

Acid-Test Ratio

Ratio of the sum of cash plus short-term investments plus net current receivables to total current liabilities. Tells whether the entity can pay all its current liabilities if they come due immediately. Also called the **quick ratio**.

	Formula	Palisades' Acid-Test Ratio		Industry Average
		20X5	**20X4**	
Acid-test ratio =	Cash + Short-term investments + Net current receivables / Current liabilities	$\dfrac{\$29,000 + \$0 + \$114,000}{\$142,000} = 1.01$	$\dfrac{\$32,000 + \$0 + \$85,000}{\$126,000} = 0.93$	0.40

The company's acid-test ratio improved considerably during 20X5 and is significantly better than the industry average. Palisades' 1.01 acid-test ratio also compares favorably with the acid-test values of some well-known companies.

Company	Acid-Test Ratio
Chesebrough-Pond's Inc..	1.25
Wal-Mart Stores, Inc.	0.15
General Motors, Inc..	0.91

The norm for the acid-test ratio ranges from 0.20 for shoe retailers to 1.00 for manufacturers of equipment, as reported by the Risk Management Association. An acid-test ratio of 0.90 to 1.00 is acceptable in most industries.

Schlotzky, Inc., has a current ratio of 2.00 and an acid-test ratio of only 0.70. Which account explains the big difference between these two measures of ability to pay current liabilities? Explain.

Answer: Inventory explains the difference. Inventory is included in the current ratio but not in the acid-test ratio. Prepaid expenses may also explain part of the difference, but inventory is more important.

Stop & Think

Measuring Ability to Sell Inventory and Collect Receivables

The ability to sell inventory and collect receivables is fundamental to business success. Recall the operating cycle of a merchandiser: cash to inventory to receivables and back to cash. In this section, we discuss three ratios that measure the company's ability to sell inventory and collect receivables.

INVENTORY TURNOVER   **Inventory turnover** measures the number of times a company sells its average level of inventory during a year. → A high rate of turnover indicates ease in selling inventory; a low rate indicates difficulty in selling. A value of 6 means that the company's average level of inventory has been sold six times during the year.

Inventory Turnover

Ratio of cost of goods sold to average inventory. Indicates how rapidly inventory is sold.

 We introduced inventory turnover in Chapter 6, page 203.

To compute inventory turnover, we divide cost of goods sold by the average inventory for the period. We use the cost of goods sold—not sales—because both cost of goods sold and inventory are stated *at cost*. Sales are stated at the sales value of inventory, which is not comparable with inventory cost.

Palisades Furniture's inventory turnover for 20X5 is

Formula	Palisades' Inventory Turnover	Industry Average
Inventory turnover = $\dfrac{\text{Cost of goods sold}}{\text{Average inventory}}$	$\dfrac{\$513,000}{\$112,000} = 4.6$	3.4

Cost of goods sold comes from the income statement (Exhibit 18-9). Average inventory is figured by averaging the beginning inventory ($111,000) and ending inventory ($113,000). (See the balance sheet, Exhibit 18-9.)

Inventory turnover varies widely with the nature of the business. For example, most manufacturers of farm machinery have an inventory turnover close to three times a year. In contrast, companies that remove natural gas from the ground hold their inventory for a very short period of time and have an average turnover of 30. Palisades Furniture's turnover of 4.6 times a year is high for its industry, which has an average turnover of 3.4.

Accounts Receivable Turnover
Measures a company's ability to collect cash from credit customers. To compute accounts receivable turnover, divide net credit sales by average net accounts receivable.

ACCOUNTS RECEIVABLE TURNOVER **Accounts receivable turnover** measures the ability to collect cash from credit customers. The higher the ratio, the more successfully the business collects cash. However, a receivable turnover that is too high may indicate that credit is too tight, causing the loss of sales to good customers.

To compute the accounts receivable turnover, we divide net credit sales by average net accounts receivable. Palisades Furniture's accounts receivable turnover ratio for 20X5 is computed as follows:

Formula	Palisades' Accounts Receivable Turnover	Industry Average
$\dfrac{\text{Accounts receivable}}{\text{turnover}} = \dfrac{\text{Net credit sales}}{\text{Average net accounts receivable}}$	$\dfrac{\$858,000}{\$99,500} = 8.6$	51.0

Average net accounts receivable is figured by adding the beginning accounts receivable balance ($85,000) and the ending balance ($114,000), then dividing by 2.

Palisades' receivable turnover of 8.6 times per year is much slower than the industry average. Why the difference? Palisades is a hometown store that sells to local people who tend to pay their bills over time. Many larger furniture stores sell their receivables to other companies called *factors*, a practice that keeps receivables low and receivable turnover high. Palisades Furniture follows a different strategy.

Days' Sales in Receivables
Ratio of average net accounts receivable to one day's sale. Indicates how many days' sales remain in Accounts Receivable awaiting collection. Also called the **collection period**.

Recall from Chapter 9 (page 378) that days' sales in receivables indicates how many days it takes to collect the average level of receivables.

DAYS' SALES IN RECEIVABLES The **days'-sales-in-receivables** ratio also measures the ability to collect receivables. This ratio tells us how many days' sales remain in Accounts Receivable. ← To compute the ratio, we follow a two-step process:

First, divide net sales by 365 days to figure average sales for one day.

Second, divide this average day's sales amount into average net accounts receivable.

The data to compute this ratio for Palisades Furniture, Inc., for 20X5 are taken from the income statement and the balance sheet (Exhibit 18-9):

	Formula	Palisades' Days' Sales in Accounts Receivable	Industry Average
Days' Sales in *average* Accounts Receivable:			
1. One day's sales $= \dfrac{\text{Net sales}}{365 \text{ days}}$		$\dfrac{\$858,000}{365 \text{ days}} = \$2,351$	
2. Days' sales in average accounts receivable $= \dfrac{\text{Average net accounts receivable}}{\text{One day's sales}}$		$\dfrac{\$99,500}{\$2,351} = 42 \text{ days}$	7 days

Average accounts receivable of $99,500 = ($85,000 + $114,000)/2.

Palisades' ratio tells us that 42 average days' sales remain in accounts receivable and need to be collected. Palisades' days' sales in receivables is much higher (worse) than the industry average because Palisades collects its own receivables. Palisades Furniture remains competitive because of its personal relationship with customers. Without their good paying habits, the company's cash flow would suffer.

✔ **Starter 18-6**

Measuring Ability to Pay Long-Term Debt

The ratios discussed so far yield insight into current assets and current liabilities. They help us measure ability to sell inventory, collect receivables, and pay current liabilities. Most businesses also have long-term debt. Two key indicators of a business's ability to pay long-term liabilities are the *debt ratio* and the *times-interest-earned ratio*.

DEBT RATIO   Suppose you are a loan officer at a bank and you are evaluating loan applications from two companies with equal sales and total assets. Both companies have asked to borrow $500,000 and have agreed to repay the loan over a 10-year period. The first firm already owes $600,000 to another bank. The second owes only $250,000. Other things being equal, you are more likely to lend money to Company 2 because that company owes less than Company 1.

This relationship between total liabilities and total assets—called the **debt ratio**—shows the proportion of assets financed with debt. → If the debt ratio is 1, then debt has been used to finance all the assets. A debt ratio of 0.50 means that the company has borrowed to finance half its assets; the owners of the business have financed the other half. The higher the debt ratio, the higher the strain of paying off loans.

The debt ratios for Palisades Furniture at the end of 20X5 and 20X4 follow:

Debt Ratio
Ratio of total liabilities to total assets. Shows the proportion of a company's assets that is financed with debt.

← *We introduced the debt ratio in Chapter 4, page 155.*

		Palisades' Debt Ratio		Industry Average
	Formula	20X5	20X4	
Debt ratio $= \dfrac{\text{Total liabilities}}{\text{Total assets}}$		$\dfrac{\$431,000}{\$787,000} = 0.55$	$\dfrac{\$324,000}{\$644,000} = 0.50$	0.64

Palisades Furniture's debt ratio of 0.55 is not very high. Risk Management Association reports that the average debt ratio for most companies ranges from 0.57 to 0.67, with relatively little variation from company to company. Palisades' debt ratio indicates a fairly low-risk position compared with the industry average debt ratio of 0.64.

✔ **Starter 18-7**

Times-Interest-Earned Ratio
Ratio of income from operations to interest expense. Measures the number of times that operating income can cover interest expense. Also called the **interest-coverage ratio**.

TIMES-INTEREST-EARNED RATIO   The debt ratio says nothing about ability to pay interest expense. Analysts use the **times-interest-earned ratio** to relate income to interest expense. This ratio is also called the **interest-coverage ratio**. It measures the number of times operating income can cover interest expense. A high interest-coverage ratio indicates ease in paying interest expense; a low ratio suggests difficulty.

To compute this ratio, we divide income from operations (operating income) by interest expense. Calculation of Palisades' times-interest-earned ratio follows.

Formula	Palisades' Times-Interest-Earned Ratio		Industry Average
	20X5	**20X4**	
Times-interest-earned ratio $= \dfrac{\text{Income from operations}}{\text{Interest expense}}$	$\dfrac{\$101{,}000}{\$24{,}000} = 4.21$	$\dfrac{\$57{,}000}{\$14{,}000} = 4.07$	2.80

The company's times-interest-earned ratio of around 4.00 is significantly better than the average for furniture retailers. The norm for U.S. business, as reported by Risk Management Association, falls in the range of 2.0 to 3.0. Based on its debt ratio and its times-interest-earned ratio, Palisades Furniture appears to have little difficulty *servicing its debt*, that is, paying liabilities.

Measuring Profitability

The fundamental goal of business is to earn a profit. Ratios that measure profitability are reported in the business press and discussed on Money Line. We examine four profitability measures.

Rate of Return on Net Sales
Ratio of net income to net sales. A measure of profitability. Also called **return on sales**.

RATE OF RETURN ON NET SALES   In business, the term *return* is used broadly as a measure of profitability. Consider a ratio called the **rate of return on net sales**, or simply **return on sales**. (The word *net* is usually omitted for convenience, even though net sales is used to compute the ratio.) This ratio shows the percentage of each sales dollar earned as net income. Palisades Furniture's rate of return on sales follows.

Formula	Palisades' Rate of Return on Sales		Industry Average
	20X5	**20X4**	
Rate of return on sales $= \dfrac{\text{Net income}}{\text{Net sales}}$	$\dfrac{\$48{,}000}{\$858{,}000} = 0.056$	$\dfrac{\$26{,}000}{\$803{,}000} = 0.032$	0.008

Companies strive for a high rate of return on sales. The higher the rate of return, the more sales dollars are providing profit. The increase in Palisades Furniture's return on sales is significant and identifies the company as more successful than the average furniture store. Compare Palisades' rate of return on sales to the rates earned by some leading companies in other industries:

Company	Rate of Return on Sales
eBay..	0.121
Bristol-Myers Squibb	0.114
Wal-Mart..	0.031

RATE OF RETURN ON TOTAL ASSETS   The **rate of return on total assets**, or simply **return on assets**, measures success in using assets to earn a profit. → Two groups finance a company's assets. Creditors have loaned money to the company, and they earn interest. Shareholders have invested in stock, and their return is the company's net income.

We first discussed the rate of return on total assets in Chapter 13, page 521.

The sum of interest expense and net income is thus the return to the two groups that have financed the company's assets. Computation of the return-on-assets ratio for Palisades Furniture follows.

Rate of Return on Total Assets
Net income plus interest expense, divided by average total assets. This ratio measures a company's success in using its assets to earn income for the persons who finance the business. Also called **return on assets**.

Formula	Palisades' 20X5 Rate of Return on Total Assets	Industry Average
$\text{Rate of return on assets} = \dfrac{\text{Net income} + \text{Interest expense}}{\text{Average total assets}}$	$\dfrac{\$48,000 + \$24,000}{\$715,500} = 0.101$	0.078

Average total assets is the average of beginning and ending total assets from the comparative balance sheet: ($644,000 + $787,000)/2 = $715,500. Compare Palisades Furniture's rate of return on assets with the rates of some other companies:

Company	Rate of Return on Assets
General Electric	0.029
Procter & Gamble	0.116
Dell Computer	0.127

RATE OF RETURN ON COMMON STOCKHOLDERS' EQUITY   A popular measure of profitability is **rate of return on common stockholders' equity**, often shortened to **return on equity**. → This ratio shows the relationship between net income and common stockholders' equity—how much income is earned for every $1 invested by the common shareholders.

We examined this ratio in detail in Chapter 13. For a review, see page 522.

To compute this ratio, we first subtract preferred dividends from net income to get net income available to the common stockholders. We then divide net income available to common stockholders by average common equity during the year. Common equity is total stockholders' equity minus preferred equity. The 20X5 rate of return on common stockholders' equity for Palisades Furniture follows.

Rate of Return on Common Stockholders' Equity
Net income minus preferred dividends, divided by average common stockholders' equity. A measure of profitability. Also called **return on equity**.

Formula	Palisades' 20X5 Rate of Return on Common Stockholders' Equity	Industry Average
$\text{Rate of return on common stockholders' equity} = \dfrac{\text{Net income} - \text{Preferred dividends}}{\text{Average common stockholders' equity}}$	$\dfrac{\$48,000 - \$0}{\$338,000} = 0.142$	0.121

Average equity is the average of the beginning and ending balances [($356,000 + $320,000)/2 = $338,000]. Observe that Palisades' return on equity (0.142) is higher than its return on assets (0.101). This difference results from borrowing at one rate—say, 8%—and investing the funds to earn a higher rate, such as the firm's 14.2% return on equity. This practice is called **trading on the equity**, or using **leverage**. It is directly related to the debt ratio. The higher the debt ratio, the higher the leverage. Companies that finance operations with debt are said to *leverage* their positions.

Trading on the Equity
Earning more income on borrowed money than the related interest expense, thereby increasing the earnings for the owners of the business. Also called **leverage**.

Leverage usually increases profitability, but not always. Leverage can have a negative impact on profitability. Therefore, leverage is a double-edged sword, increasing profits during good times but compounding losses during bad times. Compare Palisades Furniture's rate of return on common stockholders' equity with the rates of some leading companies.

✔ **Starter 18-8**

Company	Rate of Return on Common Equity
General Electric (GE)	0.26
Procter & Gamble (P&G)	0.65
Dell Computer	0.35

Palisades Furniture is not as profitable as these leading companies. A return on equity of 15% to 20% year after year is considered good in most industries. GE, P&G, and Dell are exceptional performers. Palisades Furniture is okay.

> For an average company, rank the three rates of return from highest to lowest. Palisades Furniture is typical.
>
> *Answer:*
>   1. Rate of return on common stockholders' equity
>   2. Rate of return on assets
>   3. Rate of return on net sales

Chapter 14 provides detailed treatment of EPS.

Earnings per Share (EPS)
Amount of a company's net income for each share of its outstanding common stock.

EARNINGS PER SHARE OF COMMON STOCK   *Earnings per share of common stock*, or simply ← **earnings per share (EPS)**, is perhaps the most widely quoted of all financial statistics. EPS is the only ratio that must appear on the face of the income statement. EPS is the amount of net income earned for each share of the company's outstanding *common* stock.

Earnings per share is computed by dividing net income available to common stockholders by the number of common shares outstanding during the year. Preferred dividends are subtracted from net income because the preferred stockholders have a prior claim to dividends. Palisades Furniture, Inc., has no preferred stock outstanding and no preferred dividends. The firm's EPS for 20X5 and 20X4 follow (Palisades had 10,000 shares of common stock outstanding throughout 20X4 and 20X5).

	Formula	Palisades' Earnings per Share	
		20X5	**20X4**
Earnings per share of common stock	$=\dfrac{\text{Net income} - \text{Preferred dividends}}{\text{Number of shares of common stock outstanding}}$	$\dfrac{\$48{,}000 - \$0}{10{,}000} = \$4.80$	$\dfrac{\$26{,}000 - \$0}{10{,}000} = \$2.60$

Palisades Furniture's EPS increased 85%. Its stockholders should not expect this big a boost in EPS every year. Most companies strive to increase EPS by 10% to 15% annually, and leading companies do so. But even the most successful companies have an occasional bad year.

Analyzing Stock Investments

Investors purchase stock to earn a return on their investment. This return consists of two parts: (1) gains (or losses) from selling the stock at a price above or below purchase price and (2) dividends. The ratios we examine in this section help analysts evaluate stock in terms of market price or dividends.

PRICE/EARNINGS RATIO   The **price/earnings ratio** is the ratio of the market price of a share of common stock to the company's earnings per share. It shows the market price of $1 of earnings. This ratio, abbreviated P/E, appears in *The Wall Street Journal* stock listings. P/E ratios play an important part in decisions to buy, hold, and sell stocks.

Calculations for the P/E ratios of Palisades Furniture, Inc., follow. The market price of its common stock was $60 at the end of 20X5 and $35 at the end of 20X4. These prices can be obtained from a financial publication, a stockbroker, or the company's Web site.

Price/Earnings Ratio
Ratio of the market price of a share of common stock to the company's earnings per share. Measures the value that the stock market places on $1 of a company's earnings.

	Palisades' Price/Earnings Ratio	
Formula	20X5	20X4
P/E ratio = $\dfrac{\text{Market price per share of common stock}}{\text{Earnings per share}}$	$\dfrac{\$60.00}{\$4.80} = 12.5$	$\dfrac{\$35.00}{\$2.60} = 13.5$

Palisades Furniture's P/E ratio of 12.5 means that the company's stock is selling at 12.5 times earnings. The decline from the 20X4 P/E ratio of 13.5 is no cause for alarm because the market price of the stock is not under Palisades Furniture's control. Net income is more controllable, and net income increased during 20X5.

✔ Starter 18-9

DIVIDEND YIELD   **Dividend yield** is the ratio of dividends per share to the stock's market price per share. This ratio measures the percentage of a stock's market value that is returned annually as dividends. *Preferred* stockholders, who invest primarily to receive dividends, pay special attention to dividend yield.

Palisades Furniture paid annual cash dividends of $1.20 per share of common stock in 20X5 and $1.00 in 20X4, and market prices of the company's common stock were $60 in 20X5 and $35 in 20X4. The firm's dividend yields on common stock follow.

Dividend Yield
Ratio of dividends per share of stock to the stock's market price per share. Tells the percentage of a stock's market value that the company returns to stockholders annually as dividends.

	Dividend Yield on Palisades' Common Stock	
Formula	20X5	20X4
Dividend yield on common stock* = $\dfrac{\text{Dividend per share of common stock}}{\text{Market price per share of common stock}}$	$\dfrac{\$1.20}{\$60.00} = .020$	$\dfrac{\$1.00}{\$35.00} = .029$

*Dividend yields may also be calculated for preferred stock.

An investor who buys Palisades Furniture common stock for $60 can expect to receive 2% of the investment annually in the form of cash dividends.

Expedia.com: Making Investors Happy and Rivals Scared

 For an online travel stock, you might turn to the financial pages of a newspaper. The price/earnings (P/E) ratio of online travel giant Expedia was 67 in the first quarter of 2003. That means that one share of Expedia stock, valued at $63, was selling at 67 times its earnings per share. A P/E ratio of 67 is very high indeed. By contrast, the P/E ratio of competitor Sabre Holdings, Travelocity's owner, was only 10. Why the big difference between these similar companies?

Expedia is doing 55% more business than Travelocity. Why is Expedia so far ahead? Consider the story behind the company's financials: "Our big fat hairy dream is to be the largest seller of travel in the world. . . ," said Richard Barton, Expedia's former CEO.

Profit margins on airline tickets are razor-thin. So, unlike rivals, Expedia doesn't rely on airline bookings. It has expanded into hotel reservations and custom vacation packages, which earn higher profits. In the hotel market, Expedia was not content with the usual 10% commission on reservations. Barton bought hotel rooms at wholesale prices, marked them up as much as 26%, and then sold the rooms to consumers. A 26% markup beats a 10% markup any day.

Based on: Timothy J. Mullaney, "Expedia: Changing Pilots in Mid-Climb," *Business Week*, February 24, 2003, pp. 120–124. Kathy Bergen, "Air-Only Emphasis Trips Up Travel Sites: Online Firms Find Package Deals More Profitable," *Chicago Tribune*, December 1, 2002, p. 5-1. Andrew Chaikivsky, "The Best & Brightest: Business—Richard Barton, CEO, Expedia," *Esquire*, December 2002, p. 177.

Book Value per Share of Common Stock
Common stockholders' equity divided by the number of shares of common stock outstanding. The recorded amount for each share of common stock outstanding.

BOOK VALUE PER SHARE OF COMMON STOCK   **Book value per share of common stock** is simply common equity divided by the number of common shares outstanding. Common equity equals total stockholders' equity less preferred equity. Palisades Furniture has no preferred stock outstanding. Its book-value-per-share-of-common-stock ratios follow (10,000 shares of common stock were outstanding).

	Formula	Book Value per Share of Palisades' Common Stock	
		20X5	**20X4**
Book value per share of common stock	$= \dfrac{\text{Total stockholders' equity} - \text{Preferred equity}}{\text{Number of shares of common stock outstanding}}$	$\dfrac{\$356{,}000 - \$0}{10{,}000} = \$35.60$	$\dfrac{\$320{,}000 - \$0}{10{,}000} = \$32.00$

✔ **Starter 18-10**

✔ **Starter 18-11**

See Chapter 13, page 520, for a discussion of market value and book value.   Many experts argue that book value is not useful for investment analysis. It bears no relationship to market value and provides little information beyond stockholders' equity reported on the balance sheet. But some investors base their investment decisions on book value. For example, some investors rank stocks on the basis of the ratio of market price to book value. To these investors, the lower the ratio, the more attractive the stock.

Other Evaluation Tools

Economic Value Added

☐ Horizontal Analysis
☐ Vertical Analysis
☐ Benchmarking
☐ Using Ratios
■ **Other Evaluation Tools**

EVA

⭐5 *Measure economic value added*

Coca-Cola, Quaker Oats, and other leading companies use **economic value added (EVA®)** to evaluate performance. EVA® measures whether operations have increased stockholder wealth. EVA® can be computed as follows:

$$\text{EVA}^{\circledR} = \text{Net income} + \text{Interest expense} - \text{Capital charge}$$

where

$$\text{Capital charge} = \left(\begin{array}{c} \text{Notes} \\ \text{payable} \end{array} + \begin{array}{c} \text{Bonds} \\ \text{payable} \end{array} + \begin{array}{c} \text{Stockholders'} \\ \text{equity} \end{array} \right) \times \begin{array}{c} \text{Cost of} \\ \text{capital} \end{array}$$

Economic Value Added (EVA®)
EVA = Net income + Interest expense − Capital charge. Used to evaluate a company's operating performance.

Cost of Capital
A weighted average of the returns demanded by the company's stockholders and lenders.

All amounts for the EVA® computation, except the cost of capital, are taken from the financial statements. The **cost of capital** is a weighted average of the returns demanded by the company's stockholders and lenders. The cost of capital varies with the company's level of risk. For example, stockholders and lenders would demand a higher return from a start-up company than from Coca-Cola because the new company is more risky. A new company would thus have a higher cost of capital than Coca-Cola. In the following discussions we assume a value for the cost of capital (such as 10%, 12%, or 15%).

The idea behind EVA® is that the returns to the company's stockholders (net income) and to its creditors (interest expense) should exceed the company's capital charge. The **capital charge** is the amount that investors *charge* for the use of their money. A positive EVA® amount suggests an increase in stockholder wealth, and the company's stock should remain attractive. If EVA® goes negative, stockholders probably will be unhappy and sell the stock, resulting in a decrease in the stock price.

Capital Charge
The amount that stockholders and lenders charge a company for the use of their money. Calculated as (Notes payable + Loans payable + Long-term debt + Stockholders' equity) × Cost of capital.

The Coca-Cola Company is a leading user of EVA.® Coca-Cola's EVA® for 2002 can be computed as follows, assuming a 10% cost of capital for the company (dollar amounts in millions):

	Net income	+	Interest expense	−	(Loans and notes payable	+	Long-term debt	+	Stockholders' equity)	×	Cost of capital
Cola-Cola's EVA® =											
=	$3,050	+	$199	−	[($2,475	+	$2,701	+	$11,800)	×	0.10]
=	$3,249			−			$16,976			×	0.10
=	$3,249			−					$1,698		
=					$1,551						

By this measure, Coca-Cola's operations during 2002 added $1.551 billion ($1,551 million) of value to its stockholders' wealth after meeting the company's capital charge. This performance is outstanding.

✔ **Starter 18-12**

Red Flags in Financial Statement Analysis

Another way to analyze a company's situation is to look for *red flags* that may signal financial trouble. Recent accounting scandals highlight the importance of these red flags. If the following conditions are present, the company may be too risky.

■ *Earnings Problems.* Have income from continuing operations and net income decreased significantly for several years in a row? Has income turned into a loss? Most companies cannot survive consecutive loss years.

■ *Decreased Cash Flow.* Cash flow validates earnings. Is cash flow from operations consistently lower than net income? Are the sales of plant assets a major source of cash? If so, the company may face a cash shortage.

- *Too Much Debt.* How does the company's debt ratio compare to that of major competitors and to the industry average? If the debt ratio is much higher than average, the company may be unable to pay its debts.

- *Inability to Collect Receivables.* Are days' sales in receivables growing faster than for other companies in the industry? A cash shortage may be looming.

- *Buildup of Inventories.* Is inventory turnover slowing down? If so, the company may be unable to sell goods, or it may be overstating inventory. Recall from the cost-of-goods-sold model that one of the easiest ways to overstate net income is to overstate ending inventory.

- *Movement of Sales, Inventory, and Receivables.* Sales, receivables, and inventory generally move together. Increased sales lead to higher receivables and require more inventory to meet demand. Strange movements among these items may spell trouble.

Do these red flags reveal significant difficulties at Bristol-Myers Squibb (BMS)? Maybe so. Net income took a sharp downturn in 2002. Cash flow from operations was also down a lot. But receivables and inventories weren't up too much, and BMS's debt ratio isn't too high. Overall, we get mixed signals about BMS's financial health. Wall Street doesn't like mixed signals about a company. That's probably why the stock market didn't go for the company's performance in 2002.

Analyzing Nonfinancial Data

There is more to analyzing financial statements than performing horizontal and vertical analysis and computing the standard ratios. The nonquantitative parts of the annual report may hold more important information than the financial statements. For example, the president's letter may describe a turnover of top managers. The management discussion and analysis will reveal management's opinion of the year's results. And the auditor's report may indicate a major problem with the company. Let's consider each of these parts of a corporate annual report.

PRESIDENT'S LETTER TO THE STOCKHOLDERS   The president of the company gives his or her view of the year's results and outlines the direction top management is charting for the company. The most recent annual report of Procter & Gamble described the retirement of the company's chairman of the board and the election of a new chairman. A shift in top management or a major change in the company's direction is important to investors.

MANAGEMENT DISCUSSION AND ANALYSIS (MD&A)   The people who know the most about a company are its executives. For this reason, stockholders want to know what management thinks about the company's net income (or net loss), cash flows, and financial position. The MD&A section of the annual report discusses *why* net income was up or down, how the company invested the stockholders' money, and plans for future spending. Through the MD&A, investors may learn of the company's plan to discontinue a product line or to expand into new markets. These forward-looking data are not permitted in the historical financial statements, which are based on past transactions.

AUDITOR REPORT   Both the president's letter and the MD&A express the views of corporate insiders. The financial statements are also produced by the management of the company. These people naturally want to describe the company in a favorable light. Therefore, all the information coming out of the company could be slanted to make the company look good.

Investors are aware of the possibility for management bias in the financial statements. For this reason, the Securities & Exchange Commission, a federal agency, requires that all financial statements of public corporations be audited by independent accountants. The auditors are not employees of the companies they audit. After auditing the Bristol-Myers Squibb (BMS) financial statements, PricewaterhouseCoopers (PwC), an international accounting firm, issued its professional opinion on the BMS statements. PwC stated that the BMS statements agreed with generally accepted accounting principles. This is how investors in the United States and in other developed countries gain assurance that they can rely on a company's financial statements. If the survival of BMS were in doubt, PwC's audit report would alert investors to the difficulty.

The Decision Guidelines summarize the most widely used ratios. The Excel Application Exercise provides an opportunity to apply your understanding of the ratios.

Decision Guidelines

USING RATIOS IN FINANCIAL STATEMENT ANALYSIS

Lane and Kay Collins operate a financial-services firm. They manage other people's money and do most of their own financial-statement analysis. How do they measure companies' ability to pay bills, sell inventory, collect receivables, and so on? They use the standard ratios we have covered throughout this book.

Ratio	Computation	Information Provided
Measuring ability to pay current liabilities:		
1. Current ratio	$\dfrac{\text{Current assets}}{\text{Current liabilities}}$	Measures ability to pay current liabilities with current assets
2. Acid-test (quick) ratio	$\dfrac{\text{Cash} + \dfrac{\text{Short-term}}{\text{investments}} + \dfrac{\text{Net current}}{\text{receivables}}}{\text{Current liabilities}}$	Shows ability to pay all current liabilities if they come due immediately
Measuring ability to sell inventory and collect receivables:		
3. Inventory turnover	$\dfrac{\text{Cost of goods sold}}{\text{Average inventory}}$	Indicates saleability of inventory— the number of times a company sells its average inventory during a year
4. Accounts receivable turnover	$\dfrac{\text{Net credit sales}}{\text{Average net accounts receivable}}$	Measures ability to collect cash from customers
5. Days' sales in receivables	$\dfrac{\text{Average net accounts receivable}}{\text{One day's sales}}$	Shows how many days' sales remain in Accounts Receivable— how many days it takes to collect the average level of receivables
Measuring ability to pay long-term debt:		
6. Debt ratio	$\dfrac{\text{Total liabilities}}{\text{Total assets}}$	Indicates percentage of assets financed with debt
7. Times-interest-earned ratio	$\dfrac{\text{Income from operations}}{\text{Interest expense}}$	Measures the number of times operating income can cover interest expense
Measuring profitability:		
8. Rate of return on net sales	$\dfrac{\text{Net income}}{\text{Net sales}}$	Shows the percentage of each sales dollar earned as net income
9. Rate of return on total assets	$\dfrac{\text{Net income} + \text{Interest expense}}{\text{Average total assets}}$	Measures how profitably a company uses its assets

Decision Guidelines   *(continued)*

Ratio	Computation	Information Provided
10. Rate of return on common stockholders' equity	$$\frac{\text{Net income} - \text{Preferred dividends}}{\text{Average common stockholders' equity}}$$	Gauges how much income is earned for each dollar invested by common shareholders
11. Earnings per share of common stock	$$\frac{\text{Net income} - \text{Preferred dividends}}{\text{Number of shares of common stock outstanding}}$$	Gives the amount of net income earned for each share of the company's common stock

Analyzing stock as an investment:

Ratio	Computation	Information Provided
12. Price/earnings ratio	$$\frac{\text{Market price per share of common stock}}{\text{Earnings per share}}$$	Indicates the market price of $1 of earnings
13. Dividend yield	$$\frac{\text{Annual dividend per share of common (or preferred) stock}}{\text{Market price per share of common (or preferred) stock}}$$	Shows the percentage of a stock's market value returned as dividends to stockholders each year
14. Book value per share of common stock	$$\frac{\text{Total stockholders' equity} - \text{Preferred equity}}{\text{Number of shares of common stock outstanding}}$$	Indicates the recorded accounting amount for each share of common stock outstanding

Excel Application Exercise

Goal: Create an Excel work sheet that calculates financial ratios to compare PepsiCo and Coca-Cola. Then use the results to determine which company has the stronger financial performance.

Scenario: You've saved $5,000 from your summer internship at PepsiCo. You'd like to invest your savings in the stock of your employer, but your parents think the better investment would be stock in Coca-Cola, their favorite brand of soft drink. Before making your purchase, you decide to create an Excel work sheet that compares both companies on several key financial ratios.

Your task is to create an Excel spreadsheet to compare the following ratios for PepsiCo and Coca-Cola.

1. Acid-test (quick) ratio
2. Inventory turnover
3. Debt ratio
4. Return on net sales
5. Price/earnings ratio

When done with the work sheet, answer the following questions:

1. Which company is in a better position to pay all current liabilities if they come due immediately?
2. Which company's inventory is more "saleable"?
3. Which company is financing more of its assets with debt?
4. Which company earned more profit, as a percentage, on each sales dollar?
5. Which company's earnings have a higher market price per dollar of earnings?

Step-by-Step:

1. Locate the data required for each ratio in the annual reports of PepsiCo (www.pepsico.com) and Coca-Cola (www.cocacola.com). *Note:* For fiscal year-end stock prices, go to www.yahoo.com, and then select "Finance." Enter the ticker symbol (PEP for PepsiCo and KO for Coca-Cola), then select "Performance." You should be able to click on "historical prices" to enter the dates for each fiscal year-end.
2. Open a new Excel work sheet.
3. Create a bold-faced heading for your spreadsheet that contains the following:
   a. Chapter 18 Excel Application Exercise
   b. Using Ratios in Financial Statement Analysis
   c. PepsiCo and Coca-Cola Comparison
   d. Today's date
4. In the first column, enter the names of all five ratios. Skip a row between each ratio name.
5. Create bold-faced, underlined column headings for PepsiCo and Coca-Cola. Underneath, enter the "As of" date for the financial statements used in the analysis. (Fiscal year-ends may not match exactly.)
6. Enter the data located in step 1, using the correct ratio formulas found in the Decision Guidelines. For the P/E ratio, use basic EPS in the denominator. Format all cells as necessary.
7. Save your work, and print a copy for your files.

END-OF-CHAPTER *Summary Problem*

The following financial data are adapted from the annual reports of **Gap Inc.**, which operates Gap, Banana Republic, and Old Navy clothing stores:

CHECK YOUR RESOURCES

Gap Inc.
Five-Year Selected Financial Data (adapted)
Years Ended January 31,

Operating Results*	2002	2001	2000	1999
Net sales	$13,848	$13,673	$11,635	$9,054
Cost of goods sold	9,704	8,599	6,775	5,318
Interest expense	109	75	45	46
Income from operations	338	1,455	1,817	1,333
Net earnings (net loss)	(8)	877	1,127	824
Cash dividends	76	75	76	77
Financial Position				
Merchandise inventory.	1,677	1,904	1,462	1,056
Total assets	7,591	7,012	5,189	3,963
Current ratio.	1.48:1	0.95:1	1.25:1	1.20:1
Stockholders' equity	3,010	2,928	2,630	1,574
Average number of shares of common stock outstanding (in thousands).	860	879	895	576

*Dollar amounts are in thousands.

Required

Compute the following ratios for 2000 through 2002, and evaluate Gap's operating results. Are operating results strong or weak? Did they improve or deteriorate during the four-year period? Your analysis will reveal a clear trend.

1. Gross profit percentage
2. Net income as a percentage of sales
3. Earnings per share
4. Inventory turnover
5. Times-interest-earned ratio
6. Rate of return on stockholders' equity

Solution

	2002	2001	2000
1. Gross profit percentage	$\dfrac{\$13{,}848 - \$9{,}704}{\$13{,}848} = 29.9\%$	$\dfrac{\$13{,}673 - \$8{,}599}{\$13{,}673} = 37.1\%$	$\dfrac{\$11{,}635 - \$6{,}775}{\$11{,}635} = 41.8\%$
2. Net income as a percentage of sales	$\dfrac{\$(8)}{\$13{,}848} = (.06\%)$	$\dfrac{\$877}{\$13{,}673} = 6.4\%$	$\dfrac{\$1{,}127}{\$11{,}635} = 9.7\%$
3. Earnings per share	$\dfrac{\$(8)}{860} = \$(0.01)$	$\dfrac{\$877}{879} = \$1.00$	$\dfrac{\$1{,}127}{895} = \$1.26$
4. Inventory turnover	$\dfrac{\$9{,}704}{(\$1{,}677 + \$1{,}904)/2} = 5.4$ times	$\dfrac{\$8{,}599}{(\$1{,}904 + \$1{,}462)/2} = 5.1$ times	$\dfrac{\$6{,}775}{(\$1{,}462 + \$1{,}056)/2} = 5.4$ times
5. Times-interest-earned ratio	$\dfrac{\$338}{\$109} = 3.1$ times	$\dfrac{\$1{,}455}{\$75} = 19.4$ times	$\dfrac{\$1{,}817}{\$45} = 40.4$ times
6. Rate of return on stockholders' equity	$\dfrac{\$(8)}{(\$3{,}010 + \$2{,}928)/2} = (0.3\%)$	$\dfrac{\$877}{(\$2{,}928 + \$2{,}630)/2} = 31.6\%$	$\dfrac{\$1{,}127}{(\$2{,}630 + \$1{,}574)/2} = 53.6\%$

Evaluation: During this period, Gap's operating results deteriorated on all these measures except inventory turnover. The gross profit percentage is down sharply, as are the times-interest-earned ratio and all the return measures. From these data it is clear that Gap could sell its merchandise, but not at the markups the company enjoyed in the past. The final result, in 2002, was a net loss for the year.

●REVIEW *Financial Statement Analysis*

Quick Check

The **Coca-Cola Company** reported these figures (adapted and in millions):

	2002	2001		2002
Cash and equivalents	$ 2,345	$ 1,934	Sales	$19,564
Receivables.	2,097	1,882	Cost of sales	7,105
Inventory	1,294	1,055	Operating expenses	7,001
Prepaid expenses.	1,616	2,300	Operating income	5,458
Total current assets	7,352	7,171	Interest expense	199
Other assets	17,149	15,246	Other expense.	2,209
Total assets	$24,501	$22,417	Net income	$ 3,050
Total current liabilities	$ 7,341	$ 8,429		
Long-term liabilities	5,360	2,622		
Common equity.	11,800	11,366		
Total liabilities and equity	$24,501	$22,417		

1. Horizontal analysis of Coca-Cola's balance sheet for 2002 would report
   a. 21% increase in Cash
   b. Cash as 9.6% of total assets
   c. Current ratio of 1.00
   d. Inventory turnover of 6 times

2. Vertical analysis of Coca-Cola's balance sheet for 2002 would report
   a. 21% increase in Cash
   b. Cash as 9.6% of total assets
   c. Current ratio of 1.00
   d. Inventory turnover of 6 times

3. A common-size income statement for Coca-Cola would report (amounts rounded)
   a. Sales of 100%
   b. Cost of sales at 36%
   c. Net income of 16%
   d. All the above

4. Which statement best describes Coca-Cola's acid-test ratio?
   a. Greater than 1
   b. Equal to 1
   c. Less than 1
   d. None of the above

5. Coca-Cola's inventory turnover during 2002 was
   a. 5 times
   b. 6 times
   c. 7 times
   d. Not determinable from the data given

6. During 2002, Coca-Cola's days' sales in receivables ratio was
   a. 30 days
   b. 35 days
   c. 37 days
   d. 39 days

7. Which measure expresses Coca-Cola's times-interest-earned ratio?
   a. 15 times
   b. 20 times
   c. 27 times
   d. 51.8%

8. Coca-Cola's return on common stockholders' equity can be described as
   a. Strong
   b. Good
   c. Average
   d. Weak

9. The company has 2,500 million shares of common stock outstanding. What is Coca-Cola's earnings per share?
   a. 2.04
   b. 3.6 times
   c. $3.05
   d. $1.22

10. Coca-Cola's stock has traded recently around $44 per share. Use your answer to question 9 to measure the company's price/earnings ratio.
    a. 69
    b. 44
    c. 1.00
    d. 36

Accounting Vocabulary

accounts receivable turnover (p. 718)
acid-test ratio (p. 717)
benchmarking (p. 712)
book value per share of common stock (p. 724)
capital charge (p. 725)
collection period (p. 718)
common-size statement (p. 711)
cost of capital (p. 725)
current ratio (p. 715)
days' sales in receivables (p. 718)
debt ratio (p. 719)

dividend yield (p. 723)
earnings per share (EPS) (p. 722)
economic value added (EVA)® (p. 725)
horizontal analysis (p. 707)
interest-coverage ratio (p. 720)
inventory turnover (p. 717)
leverage (p. 721)
price/earnings ratio (p. 723)
quick ratio (p. 717)
rate of return on common stockholders' equity (p. 721)
rate of return on net sales (p. 720)

return on assets (p. 721)
return on equity (p. 721)
return on sales (p. 720)
rate of return on total assets (p. 721)
return on stockholders' equity (p. 721)
times-interest-earned ratio (p. 720)
trading on the equity (p. 721)
trend percentages (p. 709)
vertical analysis (p. 709)
working capital (p. 715)

ASSESS *Your Progress*

Starters

online homework

S18-1 **Nike, Inc.**, reported the following on its 2002 comparative income statement:

(in millions)	2002	2001	2000
Revenues	$9,893	$9,489	$8,995
Cost of sales	6,005	5,785	5,404

Perform a horizontal analysis of revenues and gross profit—both in dollar amounts and in percentages—for 2002 and 2001.

See *www.prenhall.com/horngren* for selected Starters, Exercises, and Problems.

Horizontal analysis of revenues and gross profit
(Obj. 1)

S18-2 **Nike, Inc.**, reported the following revenues and net income amounts:

(in millions)	2002	2001	2000	1999
Revenues	$9,893	$9,489	$8,995	$8,777
Net income	664	590	579	451

1. Show Nike's trend percentages for revenues and net income. Use 1999 as the base year.
2. Which measure increased faster during 2000–2002?

Trend analysis of revenues and net income
(Obj. 1)

S18-3 Perfect 10 Sporting Goods reported the following amounts on its balance sheets at December 31, 20X6, 20X5, and 20X4:

	20X6	20X5	20X4
Cash and receivables	$ 38,000	$ 30,000	$ 25,000
Inventory	48,000	36,000	24,000
Property, plant, and equipment, net	96,000	88,000	87,000
Total assets	$182,000	$154,000	$136,000

Vertical analysis to correct a cash shortage
(Obj. 2)

Sales and profits are high. Nevertheless, the company is experiencing a cash shortage. Perform a vertical analysis of Perfect 10 assets at the end of years 20X6, 20X5, and 20X4. Use the analysis to explain the reason for the cash shortage.

Common-size income statements of two leading companies
(Obj. 3)

S18-4 **Nike, Inc.,** and **Home Depot** are leaders in their respective industries. Compare the two companies by converting their income statements (adapted) to common size.

(in millions)	Nike	Home Depot
Net sales	$9,489	$19,536
Cost of goods sold	5,785	14,101
Other expense	3,114	4,497
Net income	$ 590	$ 938

Which company earns more net income? Which company's net income is a higher percentage of its net sales? Which company is more profitable? Explain your answer.

Evaluating a company's current ratio
(Obj. 4)

S18-5 Use the **Bristol-Myers Squibb** balance sheet data in Exhibit 18-3, page 708.

1. Compute the company's current ratio at December 31, 2002 and 2001.
2. Did Bristol-Myers Squibb's current ratio value improve, deteriorate, or hold steady during 2002?

Computing inventory turnover and days' sales in receivables
(Obj. 4)

S18-6 Use the **Bristol-Myers Squibb** 2002 income statement (page 708) and balance sheet (page 708) to compute the following (amounts in millions):

a. The rate of inventory turnover for 2002. Inventory was $1,573 at the end of 2002 and $1,699 at the end of 2001.
b. Days' sales in average receivables during 2002. All sales are made on account. Receivables were $2,968 at the end of 2002 and $3,992 at the end of 2001. (Round dollar amounts to one decimal place.)

Measuring ability to pay liabilities
(Obj. 4)

S18-7 Use the financial statements of **Bristol-Myers Squibb Company** (page 708).

1. Compute the debt ratio at December 31, 2002.
2. Is Bristol-Myers Squibb's ability to pay its liabilities strong or weak? Explain your reasoning.

Measuring profitability
(Obj. 4)

S18-8 Use the financial statements of **Bristol-Myers Squibb Company** (page 710) to determine or, if necessary, to compute these profitability measures for 2002.

a. Rate of return on net sales.
b. Rate of return on total assets. Interest expense for 2002 was $410 million.
c. Rate of return on common stockholders' equity.

Are these rates of return strong or weak? Explain.

Computing EPS and the price/earnings ratio
(Obj. 4)

S18-9 The annual report of **Dell Computer Corporation** for fiscal year 2002 included the following items (in millions):

Preferred stock outstanding	$0
Net income	$1,246
Number of shares of common stock outstanding	2,602

1. Compute earnings per share (EPS) for Dell. Round to the nearest cent.
2. Compute Dell's price/earnings ratio. The price of a share of Dell stock is $26.85.

S18-10 A skeleton of **Campbell Soup Company's** income statement (as adapted) appears as follows (amounts in millions):

Using ratio data to reconstruct an income statement
(Obj. 4)

Income Statement	
Net sales...	$7,278
Cost of goods sold	(a)
Selling and administrative expenses...................	1,716
Interest expense	(b)
Other expenses	151
Income before taxes	1,042
Income tax expense	(c)
Net income...	$ (d)

Use the following ratio data to complete Campbell Soup's income statement:

a. Inventory turnover was 5.53 (beginning inventory was $787; ending inventory was $755).
b. Rate of return on sales is 0.0959.

S18-11 A skeleton of **Campbell Soup Company's** balance sheet (as adapted) appears as follows (amounts in millions):

Using ratio data to reconstruct a balance sheet
(Obj. 4)

Balance Sheet			
Cash....................	$ 53	Total current liabilities	$2,164
Receivables.............	(a)	Long-term debt	(e)
Inventories	755	Other long-term liabilities ..	826
Prepaid expenses.........	(b)		
Total current assets	(c)		
Plant assets, net	(d)		
Other assets	2,150	Stockholders' equity.......	2,468
Total assets	$6,315	Total liabilities and equity ..	$ (f)

Use the following ratio data to complete Campbell Soup's balance sheet:

a. Current ratio is 0.7306. **b.** Acid-test ratio is 0.3161.

S18-12 Use the financial statements of **Bristol-Myers Squibb** (page 710).

Measuring economic value added
(Obj. 5)

1. Compute economic value added (EVA®) by the company's operations during 2002. Use beginning-of-year amounts to compute the capital charge. Interest expense was $410 million, and interest-bearing debt totaled $6,411 million. Assume that the company's cost of capital is 12%. Round all amounts to the nearest million dollars.
2. Should the company's stockholders be happy with the EVA® for 2002?

Exercises

E18-1 What were the dollar amount of change and the percentage of change in Micron Electronics' working capital during 2005 and 2006? Is this trend favorable or unfavorable?

Computing year-to-year changes in working capital
(Obj. 1)

	2006	2005	2004
Total current assets..................	$302,000	$290,000	$280,000
Total current liabilities...............	150,000	157,000	140,000

Horizontal analysis of an income statement
(Obj. I)

spreadsheet

E18-2 Prepare a horizontal analysis of the following comparative income statement of Newsletter E-Mail, Inc. Round percentage changes to the nearest one-tenth percent (three decimal places):

Newsletter E-Mail, Inc.
Comparative Income Statement
Years Ended December 31, 2005 and 2004

	2005	2004
Total revenue	$430,000	$373,000
Expenses:		
Cost of goods sold	$202,000	$188,000
Selling and general expenses	98,000	93,000
Interest expense	7,000	4,000
Income tax expense	42,000	37,000
Total expenses	349,000	322,000
Net income	$ 81,000	$ 51,000

Why did net income increase by a higher percentage than total revenues during 2005?

Computing trend percentages
(Obj. I)

E18-3 Compute trend percentages for Metro Graphics' net revenues and net income for the following 5-year period, using year 1 as the base year. Round to the nearest full percent.

(in thousands)	Year 5	Year 4	Year 3	Year 2	Year 1
Total revenue	$1,418	$1,187	$1,106	$1,009	$1,043
Net income	132	114	83	71	85

Which grew faster during the period, total revenue or net income?

Vertical analysis of a balance sheet
(Obj. 2)

E18-4 Consolidated Water System of Sierra, Nevada, has requested that you perform a vertical analysis of its balance sheet to determine the component percentages of its assets, liabilities, and stockholders' equity.

Consolidated Water System of Sierra, Nevada
Balance Sheet
December 31, 20X5

Amount percentages

Assets		
Total current assets	$ 42,000	13%
Property, plant, and equipment, net	247,000	76.2
Other assets	35,000	10.8
Total assets	$324,000	100.0%
Liabilities		
Total current liabilities	$ 48,000	14.8%
Long-term debt	108,000	33.3%
Total liabilities	156,000	48.1%
Stockholders' Equity		
Total stockholders' equity	168,000	51.9
Total liabilities and stockholders' equity	$324,000	100.0%

Preparing a common-size income statement
(Obj. 3)

spreadsheet

E18-5 Prepare a comparative common-size income statement for Newsletter E-Mail, Inc., using the 2005 and 2004 data of Exercise 18-2 and rounding percentages to one-tenth percent (three decimal places). To an investor, how does 2005 compare with 2004? Explain your reasoning.

E18-6 The financial statements of Cunningham Financial Group include the following items:

Computing five ratios
(Obj. 4)

Student ResourceCD

spreadsheet

	Current Year	Preceding Year
Balance sheet:		
Cash	$ 17,000	$ 22,000
Short-term investments.	11,000	26,000
Net receivables	64,000	73,000
Inventory.	77,000	71,000
Prepaid expenses	16,000	8,000
Total current assets.	$185,000	$200,000
Total current liabilities.	$131,000	$ 91,000
Income statement:		
Net credit sales	$454,000	
Cost of goods sold	297,000	

Required

Compute the following ratios for the current year:

a. Current ratio   **c.** Inventory turnover

b. Acid-test ratio   **d.** Days' sales in average receivables

E18-7 Pinnacle Market Research Corporation has asked you to determine whether the company's ability to pay current liabilities and long-term debts improved or deteriorated during 20X4. To answer this question, compute ratios for 20X4 and 20X3:

Analyzing the ability to pay current liabilities
(Obj. 4)

Student ResourceCD

spreadsheet

a. Current ratio   **c.** Debt ratio

b. Acid-test ratio   **d.** Times-interest-earned ratio

Summarize the results of your analysis in a written report.

	20X4	20X3
Cash	$ 61,000	$ 47,000
Short-term investments	28,000	—
Net receivables	102,000	116,000
Inventory	237,000	272,000
Total assets.	543,000	489,000
Total current liabilities	275,000	221,000
Long-term debt	46,000	52,000
Income from operations.	165,000	158,000
Interest expense.	48,000	39,000

E18-8 Compute four ratios that measure ability to earn profits for Save the Planet's Air, Inc., whose comparative income statement follows:

Analyzing profitability
(Obj. 4)

Save the Planet's Air, Inc.		
Comparative Income Statement		
Years Ended December 31, 20X6 and 20X5		
Dollars in Thousands	**20X6**	**20X5**
Net sales.	$174,000	$158,000
Cost of goods sold	93,000	86,000
Gross profit	81,000	72,000
Selling and general expenses	46,000	41,000
Income from operations.	35,000	31,000
Interest expense.	9,000	10,000
Income before income tax	26,000	21,000
Income tax expense	8,000	8,000
Net income.	$ 18,000	$ 13,000

(continued)

Additional data:

	20X6	20X5	20X4
Total assets......................	$204,000	$191,000	$171,000
Common stockholders' equity	$ 96,000	$ 89,000	$ 79,000
Preferred dividends	$ 3,000	$ 3,000	$ 0
Common shares outstanding during the year	20,000	20,000	18,000

Did the company's operating performance improve or deteriorate during 20X6?

Evaluating a stock as an investment
(Obj. 4)

E18-9 Evaluate the common stock of Friedman Energy Company as an investment. Specifically, use the three stock ratios to determine whether the common stock has increased or decreased in attractiveness during the past year.

	20X4	20X3
Net income.....................................	$ 58,000	$ 55,000
Dividends—common.............................	20,000	20,000
Dividends—preferred	12,000	12,000
Total stockholders' equity at year-end (includes 80,000 shares of common stock)	580,000	500,000
Preferred stock, 6%.............................	200,000	200,000
Market price per share of common stock	$ 11.50	$ 7.75

Using economic value added to measure corporate performance
(Obj. 5)

E18-10 Two companies with very different economic-value-added (EVA®) profiles are **Oracle Corporation**, the world's second-largest software company, and **Wells Fargo & Company**, the nationwide banking conglomerate. Adapted versions of the two companies' financial statements are presented here (in millions):

	Oracle	Wells Fargo
Balance sheet data:		
Total assets	$11,030	$307,569
Interest-bearing debt	$ 304	$195,781
All other liabilities	4,448	84,574
Stockholders' equity	6,278	27,214
Total liabilities and equity	$11,030	$307,569
Income statement data:		
Total revenue	$10,860	$ 26,891
Interest expense	24	6,741
All other expenses	8,275	16,727
Net income	$ 2,561	$ 3,423

Required

Compute the EVA® for each company and then decide which company's stock you would rather hold as an investment. Assume Oracle's cost of capital is 15%, and Wells Fargo's is 5%. Round to the nearest $1 million.

Using ratio data to reconstruct a company's balance sheet
(Obj. 4)

E18-11 The following data (dollar amounts in millions) are adapted from the financial statements of **Wal-Mart Stores, Inc.**

Total current assets................................	$ 10,196
Accumulated depreciation	$ 1,448
Total liabilities....................................	$ 11,806
Preferred stock	$ 0
Debt ratio..	60.342%
Current ratio	1.51

Required

Complete the following condensed balance sheet. Report amounts to the nearest $1 million.

Current assets.		$?
Property, plant, and equipment.	$?	
Less Accumulated depreciation.	(?)	?
Total assets		$?
Current liabilities.		$?
Long-term liabilities		?
Stockholders' equity		?
Total liabilities and stockholders' equity		$?

Problems

(Group A)

P18-1A Net sales, net income, and total assets for XT Communications, Inc., for a four-year period follow:

Trend percentages, return on sales, and comparison with the industry
(Obj. 1, 4)

(in thousands)	20X8	20X7	20X6	20X5
Net sales.	$357	$313	$266	$281
Net income	29	21	11	18
Total assets.	286	254	209	197

Required

1. Compute trend percentages for each item for 20X6 through 20X8. Use 20X5 as the base year and round to the nearest percentage.
2. Compute the rate of return on net sales for 20X6 through 20X8, rounding to three decimal places. In the telecommunications industry, rates above 5% are considered good, and rates above 7% are outstanding.
3. How does XT Communications' return on net sales compare with that of the industry?

P18-2A Top managers of Escalade Technology Corporation have asked your help in comparing the company's profit performance and financial position with the average for the cell phone industry. The accountant has given you the company's income statement and balance sheet and also the following data for the industry:

Common-size statements, analysis of profitability, and comparison with the industry
(Obj. 2, 3, 4)

Escalade Technology Corporation
Income Statement Compared with Industry Average
Year Ended December 31, 20X5

	Escalade	Industry Average
Net sales	$957,000	100.0%
Cost of goods sold	652,000	65.9
Gross profit	305,000	34.1
Operating expenses	204,000	28.1
Operating income	101,000	6.0
Other expenses	13,000	0.4
Net income	$ 88,000	5.6%

Escalade Technology Corporation
Balance Sheet Compared with Industry Average
December 31, 20X5

	Escalade	Industry Average
Current assets	$486,000	74.4%
Fixed assets, net	117,000	20.0
Intangible assets, net	24,000	0.6
Other assets	3,000	5.0
Total	$630,000	100.0%
Current liabilities	$246,000	45.6%
Long-term liabilities	136,000	19.0
Stockholders' equity	248,000	35.4
Total	$630,000	100.0%

Required

1. Prepare a common-size income statement and balance sheet for Escalade. The first column of each statement should present Escalade's common-size statement, and the second column should show the industry averages.

2. For the profitability analysis, compute Escalade's (a) ratio of gross profit to net sales, (b) ratio of operating income to net sales, and (c) ratio of net income to net sales. Compare these figures with the industry averages. Is Escalade's profit performance better or worse than the average for the industry?

3. For the analysis of financial position, compute Escalade's (a) ratios of current assets and current liabilities to total assets and (b) ratio of stockholders' equity to total assets. Compare these ratios with the industry averages. Is Escalade's financial position better or worse than average for the industry?

Effects of business transactions on selected ratios
(Obj. 4)

P18-3A Financial statement data on Thunderbird Medical Supply include the following:

Cash	$ 47,000	Accounts payable	$ 96,000
Accounts receivable, net	123,000	Accrued liabilities.............	50,000
Inventories..................	289,000	Long-term liabilities...........	224,000
Total assets.................	933,000	Net income..................	119,000
Short-term notes payable.......	72,000	Common shares outstanding...	22,000

Required

1. Compute Thunderbird's current ratio, debt ratio, and earnings per share. Use the following format for your answer:

Requirement 1

Current Ratio	Debt Ratio	Earnings per Share

2. Compute the three ratios after evaluating the effect of each transaction that follows. Consider each transaction *separately*.
   a. Borrowed $27,000 on a long-term note payable.
   b. Issued 10,000 shares of common stock, receiving cash of $108,000.
   c. Purchased merchandise of $48,000 on account, debiting Inventory.
   d. Received cash on account, $6,000.
   Format your answer as follows:

Requirement 2

Transaction Letter	Current Ratio	Debt Ratio	Earnings per Share

Using ratios to evaluate a stock investment
(Obj. 4)

P18-4A Comparative financial statement data of Advanced Automotive Company follow:

Advanced Automotive Company		
Comparative Income Statement		
Years Ended December 31, 20X6 and 20X5		
	20X6	20X5
Net sales......................................	$667,000	$599,000
Cost of goods sold	378,000	283,000
Gross profit	289,000	316,000
Operating expenses	129,000	147,000
Income from operations	160,000	169,000
Interest expense	57,000	41,000
Income before income tax......................	103,000	128,000
Income tax expense	34,000	53,000
Net income	$ 69,000	$ 75,000

Advanced Automotive Company			
Comparative Balance Sheet			
December 31, 20X6 and 20X5			

	20X6	20X5	20X4*
Current assets:			
Cash..	$ 37,000	$ 40,000	
Current receivables, net	208,000	151,000	$138,000
Inventories	352,000	286,000	184,000
Prepaid expenses...............................	5,000	20,000	
Total current assets	602,000	497,000	
Property, plant, and equipment, net.................	287,000	276,000	
Total assets	$889,000	$773,000	707,000
Total current liabilities	$286,000	$267,000	
Long-term liabilities	245,000	235,000	
Total liabilities	531,000	502,000	
Preferred stockholders' equity, 4%, $20 par............	50,000	50,000	
Common stockholders' equity, no par	308,000	221,000	148,000
Total liabilities and stockholders' equity	$889,000	$773,000	

*Selected 20X4 amounts.

Other Information:

1. Market price of Advanced Automotive's common stock: $36.75 at December 31, 20X6, and $50.50 at December 31, 20X5.

2. Common shares outstanding: 15,000 during 20X6 and 14,000 during 20X5.

3. All sales on credit.

Required

1. Compute the following ratios for 20X6 and 20X5:
   a. Current ratio
   b. Inventory turnover
   c. Times-interest-earned ratio
   d. Return on common stockholders' equity
   e. Earnings per share of common stock
   f. Price/earnings ratio

2. Decide whether (a) Advanced's financial position improved or deteriorated during 20X6 and (b) the investment attractiveness of its common stock appears to have increased or decreased.

3. How will what you learned in this problem help you evaluate an investment?

P18-5A Assume that you are considering purchasing stock in a company in the music industry. You have narrowed the choice to Blues, Inc., and Sonic Sound Corporation and have assembled the following data:

Using ratios to decide between two stock investments; measuring economic value added

(Obj. 4, 5)

Selected income-statement data for the current year:

	Blues	Sonic
Net sales (all on credit)	$603,000	$519,000
Cost of goods sold	484,000	387,000
Interest expense	—	8,000
Net income	56,000	38,000

Selected balance-sheet and market-price data at the *end* of the current year:

	Blues	Sonic
Current assets:		
Cash.....................................	$ 45,000	$ 39,000
Short-term investments	6,000	13,000
Current receivables, net	169,000	164,000
Inventories	211,000	183,000
Prepaid expenses...........................	19,000	15,000
Total current assets	450,000	414,000
Total assets	974,000	938,000
Total current liabilities	366,000	338,000
Total liabilities	667,000*	691,000*
Common stock, $1 par (150,000 shares)	150,000	
$5 par (20,000 shares)		100,000
Total stockholders' equity	307,000	247,000
Market price per share of common stock..........	$ 8	$ 47.50

*Includes bonds payable: Blues, $3,000, and Sonic, $303,000.

Selected balance-sheet data at the *beginning* of the current year:

	Blues	Sonic
Current receivables, net.........................	$142,000	$193,000
Inventories.....................................	209,000	197,000
Total assets....................................	842,000	909,000
Common stock, $1 par (150,000 shares)	150,000	
$5 par (20,000 shares).........................		100,000

Your strategy is to invest in companies that have low price/earnings ratios but appear to be in good shape financially. Assume that you have analyzed all other factors and that your decision depends on the results of ratio analysis.

Required

1. Compute the following ratios for both companies for the current year and decide which company's stock better fits your investment strategy.
   a. Acid-test ratio
   b. Inventory turnover
   c. Days' sales in average receivables
   d. Debt ratio
   e. Earnings per share of common stock
   f. Price/earnings ratio

2. Compute each company's economic-value-added (EVA®) measure and determine whether their EVA®s confirm or alter your investment decision. Each company's cost of capital is 10%. Round all amounts to the nearest $1,000.

Analyzing a company based on its ratios **(Obj. 4)**

P18-6A Take the role of an investment analyst at **Edward Jones Company**. It is your job to recommend investments for your client. The only information you have are the ratio values for two companies in the graphics software industry.

Ratio	GraphTech, Inc.	Core Software Company
Days' sales in receivables	51	43
Inventory turnover	9	7
Gross profit percentage.........	62%	71%
Net income as a percent of sales .	16%	14%
Times-interest earned	12	18
Return on equity...............	29%	36%
Return on assets...............	19%	14%

Write a report to the Edward Jones investment committee. Recommend one company's stock over the other. State the reasons for your recommendation.

Problems

(Group B)

P18-1B Net revenues, net income, and common stockholders' equity for xCel Corporation, a manufacturer of contact lenses, for a four-year period follow.

Trend percentages, return on common equity, and comparison with the industry
(Obj. 1, 4)

(in thousands)	2008	2007	2006	2005
Net revenues........................	$781	$714	$641	$662
Net income	51	45	32	48
Ending common stockholders' equity................	366	354	330	296

Required

1. Compute trend percentages for each item for 2006 through 2008. Use 2005 as the base year. Round to the nearest percent.

2. Compute the rate of return on common stockholders' equity for 2006 through 2008, rounding to three decimal places. In the contact lens industry, rates of 13% are average, rates above 16% are good, and rates above 20% are outstanding. xCel has no preferred stock outstanding.

3. How does xCel's return on common stockholders' equity compare with the industry?

P18-2B Bose Stereo Shops has asked you to compare the company's profit performance and financial position with the average for the stereo industry. The proprietor has given you the company's income statement and balance sheet, as well as the industry average data for retailers.

Common-size statements, analysis of profitability, and comparison with the industry
(Obj. 2, 3, 4)

Bose Stereo Shops
Income Statement Compared with Industry Average
Year Ended December 31, 20X6

	Bose	Industry Average
Net sales	$781,000	100.0%
Cost of goods sold	497,000	65.8
Gross profit	284,000	34.2
Operating expenses	163,000	19.7
Operating income	121,000	14.5
Other expenses	6,000	0.4
Net income	$115,000	14.1%

Bose Stereo Shops
Balance Sheet Compared with Industry Average
December 31, 20X6

	Bose	Industry Average
Current assets	$350,000	70.9%
Fixed assets, net	74,000	23.6
Intangible assets, net	4,000	0.8
Other assets	22,000	4.7
Total	$450,000	100.0%
Current liabilities	$207,000	48.1%
Long-term liabilities	62,000	16.6
Stockholders' equity	181,000	35.3
Total	$450,000	100.0%

Required

1. Prepare a common-size income statement and balance sheet for Bose. The first column of each statement should present Bose's common-size statement, and the second column, the industry averages.

2. For the profitability analysis, compute Bose's (a) ratio of gross profit to net sales, (b) ratio of operating income to net sales, and (c) ratio of net income to net sales. Compare these figures with the industry averages. Is Bose's profit performance better or worse than the industry average?

3. For the analysis of financial position, compute Bose's (a) ratio of current assets to total assets and (b) ratio of stockholders' equity to total assets. Compare these ratios with the industry averages. Is Bose's financial position better or worse than the industry averages?

Effects of business transactions on selected ratios
(Obj. 4)

P18-3B Financial statement data of Biz Mart Discount Center include the following items (dollars in thousands):

Cash	$ 22,000
Accounts receivable, net	102,000
Inventories	149,000
Total assets	657,000
Short-term notes payable	49,000
Accounts payable..............................	103,000
Accrued liabilities	38,000
Long-term liabilities	191,000
Net income	71,000
Common shares outstanding.....................	40,000

Required

1. Compute Biz Mart's current ratio, debt ratio, and earnings per share. Use the following format for your answer:

Requirement 1

Current Ratio	Debt Ratio	Earnings per Share

2. Compute the three ratios after evaluating the effect of each transaction that follows. Consider each transaction *separately*.
   a. Purchased store supplies of $46,000 on account.
   b. Borrowed $125,000 on a long-term note payable.
   c. Issued 5,000 shares of common stock, receiving cash of $120,000.
   d. Received cash on account, $19,000.
   Format your answer as follows:

Requirement 2

Transaction (Letter)	Current Ratio	Debt Ratio	Earnings per Share

Using ratios to evaluate a stock investment
(Obj. 4)

P18-4B Comparative financial-statement data of i2 Networks, Inc., follow.

i2 Networks, Inc.		
Comparative Income Statement		
Years Ended December 31, 20X9 and 20X8		
	20X9	20X8
Net sales...	$462,000	$427,000
Cost of goods sold	229,000	218,000
Gross profit	233,000	209,000
Operating expenses	136,000	134,000
Income from operations	97,000	75,000
Interest expense	11,000	12,000
Income before income tax........................	86,000	63,000
Income tax expense	30,000	27,000
Net income	$ 56,000	$ 36,000

i2 Networks, Inc.
Comparative Balance Sheet
December 31, 20X9 and 20X8

	20X9	20X8	20X7*
Current assets:			
Cash...	$ 96,000	$ 97,000	
Current receivables, net	112,000	116,000	$103,000
Inventories	147,000	162,000	207,000
Prepaid expenses................................	16,000	7,000	
Total current assets	371,000	382,000	
Property, plant, and equipment, net..................	214,000	178,000	
Total assets	$585,000	$560,000	598,000
Total current liabilities	$206,000	$223,000	
Long-term liabilities	119,000	117,000	
Total liabilities	325,000	340,000	
Preferred stockholders'			
equity, 6%, $100 par............................	100,000	100,000	
Common stockholders' equity, no par	160,000	120,000	90,000
Total liabilities and stockholders' equity	$585,000	$560,000	

*Selected 20X7 amounts.

Other information:

1. Market price of i2 Networks' common stock: $53 at December 31, 20X9, and $32.50 at December 31, 20X8.

2. Common shares outstanding: 10,000 during 20X9 and 9,000 during 20X8.

3. All sales on credit.

Required

1. Compute the following ratios for 20X9 and 20X8:
   a. Current ratio
   b. Inventory turnover
   c. Times-interest-earned ratio
   d. Return on common stockholders' equity
   e. Earnings per share of common stock
   f. Price/earnings ratio

2. Decide (a) whether i2 Networks' financial position improved or deteriorated during 20X9 and (b) whether the investment attractiveness of its common stock appears to have increased or decreased.

3. How will what you learned in this problem help you evaluate an investment?

P18-5B Assume that you are purchasing an investment and have decided to invest in a company in the air-conditioning/heating business. You have narrowed the choice to Caremark Laboratories and AmeriCorp, Inc., and have assembled the following data:

Using ratios to decide between two stock investments; measuring economic value added
(Obj. 4, 5)

Selected income-statement data for the current year:

	Caremark	AmeriCorp
Net sales (all on credit)	$371,000	$497,000
Cost of goods sold	209,000	258,000
Interest expense	—	19,000
Net income	48,000	72,000

Selected balance-sheet data at the *beginning* of the current year:

	Caremark	AmeriCorp
Current receivables, net	$ 40,000	$ 48,000
Inventories	93,000	88,000
Total assets	259,000	270,000
Common stock, $1 par (10,000 shares)	10,000	
$2.50 par (5,000 shares).....................		12,500

Selected balance-sheet and market-price data at the *end* of the current year:

	Caremark	AmeriCorp
Current assets:		
Cash	$ 22,000	$ 19,000
Short-term investments	20,000	18,000
Current receivables, net	42,000	46,000
Inventories	87,000	100,000
Prepaid expenses	2,000	3,000
Total current assets	173,000	186,000
Total assets	265,000	328,000
Total current liabilities	108,000	98,000
Total liabilities	108,000*	131,000*
Common stock, $1 par (10,000 shares)	10,000	
$2.50 par (5,000 shares)		12,500
Total stockholders' equity	157,000	197,000
Market price per share of common stock	$ 51	$ 112

*Includes notes payable: Caremark, $1,000, and AmeriCorp, $86,000.

Your strategy is to invest in companies that have low price/earnings ratios but appear to be in good shape financially. Assume that you have analyzed all other factors and that your decision depends on the results of ratio analysis.

Required

1. Compute the following ratios for both companies for the current year, and decide which company's stock better fits your investment strategy.
   a. Acid-test ratio
   b. Inventory turnover
   c. Days' sales in average receivables
   d. Debt ratio
   e. Earnings per share of common stock
   f. Price/earnings ratio

2. Compute each company's economic-value-added (EVA®) measure and determine whether their EVA®s confirm or alter your investment decision. Each company's cost of capital is 12%. Round all amounts to the nearest $1,000.

Analyzing a company based on its ratios
(Obj. 4)

P18-6B Take the role of an investment analyst at **Goldman Sachs**. It is your job to recommend investments for your clients. The only information you have are ratio values for two companies in the pharmaceuticals industry.

Ratio	Pratt Corp.	Jacobs, Inc.
Days' sales in receivables.	36	42
Inventory turnover	6	8
Gross profit percentage	49%	51%
Net income as a percentage of sales	7.2%	8.3%
Times-interest-earned	16	9
Return on equity	32.3%	21.5%
Return on assets	12.1%	16.4%

Write a report to Goldman Sachs' investment committee. Recommend one company's stock over the other. State the reasons for your recommendation.

● APPLY *Your Knowledge*

Decision Cases

Assessing the effects of transactions on a company
(Obj. 4)

Case 1. **AOL Time Warner, Inc.,** had a bad year in 2001; the company suffered a net loss. The loss pushed most of the return measures into the negative column, and the current ratio dropped below 1.0. The company's debt ratio is still only 0.27. Assume top management of AOL Time Warner is pondering ways to improve the company's ratios. In particular, management is considering the following transactions:

1. Borrow $100 million of long-term debt.
2. Purchase treasury stock for $500 million cash.
3. Expense one-fourth of goodwill carried on the books at $128 million.
4. Sell advertising, and the advertisements will run immediately.
5. Purchase trademarks from **NBC**, paying $20 million cash.

Required

Top management wants to know the effects of these transactions (increase, decrease, or no effect) on the following ratios of AOL Time Warner:

a. Current ratio **b.** Debt ratio **c.** Return on equity

Case 2. Consider the following business situations:

Understanding the components of accounting ratios
(Obj. 4)

a. Pinehurst Corporation's owners are concerned because the number of days' sales in receivables has increased over the previous two years. Explain why the ratio might have increased.
b. Sara Fulton has asked you about the stock of a particular company. She finds it attractive because it has a high dividend yield relative to another stock she is also considering. Explain to her the meaning of the ratio and the danger of making a decision based on dividend yield alone. Suggest other information (ratios) Sara should consider as she makes her investment decision.
c. Nathanael Smith is the controller of Saturn Ltd., a dance club whose year-end is December 31. Smith prepares checks for suppliers in December and posts them to the appropriate accounts in that month. However, he holds on to the checks and mails them to the suppliers in January. What financial ratio(s) are most affected by the action? What is Smith's purpose in undertaking this activity?

Ethical Issue

Balmoral Golf Corporation's long-term debt agreements make certain demands on the business. For example, Balmoral may not purchase treasury stock in excess of the balance of retained earnings. Also, long-term debt may not exceed stockholders' equity, and the current ratio may not fall below 1.50. If Balmoral fails to meet any of these requirements, the company's lenders have the authority to take over management of the company.

Changes in consumer demand have made it hard for Balmoral to attract customers. Current liabilities have mounted faster than current assets, causing the current ratio to fall to 1.47. Before releasing financial statements, Balmoral management is scrambling to improve the current ratio. The controller points out that an investment can be classified as either long-term or short-term, depending on management's intention. By deciding to convert an investment to cash within one year, Balmoral can classify the investment as short-term—a current asset. On the controller's recommendation, Balmoral's board of directors votes to reclassify long-term investments as short-term.

Required

1. What effect will reclassifying the investments have on the current ratio? Is Balmoral's true financial position stronger as a result of reclassifying the investments?
2. Shortly after the financial statements are released, sales improve; so, too, does the current ratio. As a result, Balmoral management decides not to sell the investments it had reclassified as short-term. Accordingly, the company reclassifies the investments as long-term. Has management behaved unethically? Give the reasoning underlying your answer.

Financial Statement Case

Amazon.com's financial statements in Appendix A reveal some unusual relationships for a company with a bright future. Answer these questions about Amazon.com.

Measuring profitability and analyzing stock as an investment
(Obj. 4)

1. What is most unusual about the balance sheet?
2. What is most unusual about the income statement (statement of operations)?

3. Consider Amazon's profitability ratios, ratios that measure the ability to pay long-term debt, and ratios for analyzing stock as an investment. What about Amazon makes these ratios meaningless? How can Amazon.com continue as a going business? The statement of cash flows helps to answer this critical question.

Team Projects

Project 1. Select an industry you are interested in, and use the leading company in that industry as the benchmark. Then select two other companies in the same industry. For each category of ratios in the Decision Guidelines on pages 727 and 728, compute at least two ratios for all three companies. Write a two-page report that compares the two companies with the benchmark company.

Project 2. Select a company and obtain its financial statements. Convert the income statement and the balance sheet to common size, and compare the company you selected to the industry average. Risk Management Association's *Annual Statement Studies*, **Dun & Bradstreet's** *Industry Norms & Key Business Ratios*, and Prentice Hall's *Almanac of Business and Industrial Financial Ratios*, by Leo Troy, publish common-size statements for most industries.

For Internet exercises, go to the Web site <u>www.prenhall.com/horngren</u>.

Comprehensive Problem for Chapters 17 and 18

ANALYZING A COMPANY FOR ITS INVESTMENT POTENTIAL

In its 2003 annual report, **Wal-Mart Stores, Inc.**, includes an 11-year financial summary (see pp. 748–749). Analyze the company's financial summary for the fiscal years 1999 to 2003 to decide whether to invest in the common stock of Wal-Mart. Include the following sections in your analysis, and fully explain your final decision.

1. Trend analysis for net sales and net income (use 1999 as the base year)
2. Profitability analysis
3. Measuring ability to sell inventory (Wal-Mart uses the LIFO method)
4. Measuring ability to pay debts
5. Measuring dividends

Wal-Mart Stores, Inc.

11-Year Financial Summary (Partial; adapted)

(Dollar Amounts in Millions Except per Share Data)	2003	2002	2001
Net sales	$244,524	$217,799	$191,329
Net sales increase	12%	14%	16%
Domestic comparative store sales increase	5%	6%	5%
Other income—net	2,001	1,873	1,787
Cost of sales	191,838	171,562	150,255
Operating, selling, and general and administrative expenses	41,043	36,173	31,550
Interest costs:			
Debt	803	1,083	1,104
Capital leases	260	274	279
Interest income	(138)	(171)	(188)
Provision for income taxes	4,487	3,897	3,692
Minority interest and equity in unconsolidated subsidiaries	(193)	(183)	(129)
Cumulative effect of accounting change, net of tax	—	—	—
Net income	8,039	6,671	6,295
Per share of common stock:			
Basic net income	1.81	1.49	1.41
Diluted net income	1.81	1.49	1.40
Dividends	0.30	0.28	0.24
Financial Position			
Current assets	$ 30,483	$ 27,878	$ 26,555
Inventories at LIFO cost	24,891	22,614	21,442
Net property, plant, and equipment and capital leases	51,904	45,750	40,934
Total assets	94,685	83,527	78,130
Current liabilities	32,617	27,282	28,949
Long-term debt	16,607	15,687	12,501
Long-term obligations under capital leases	3,001	3,045	3,154
Shareholders' equity	39,337	35,102	31,343
Financial Ratios			
Current ratio	0.9	1.0	0.9
Inventories/working capital	(11.7)	38.2	(9.0)
Return on assets	9.2%	8.5%	8.7%
Return on shareholders' equity	21.6%	20.1%	22.0%

2000	1999	1998	1997	1996	1995	1994	1993
$165,013	$137,634	$117,958	$104,859	$93,627	$82,494	$67,344	$55,484
20%	17%	12%	12%	13%	22%	21%	26%
8%	9%	6%	5%	4%	7%	6%	11%
1,615	1,391	1,290	1,293	1,138	904	633	490
129,664	108,725	93,438	83,510	74,505	65,586	53,444	44,175
27,040	22,363	19,358	16,946	15,021	12,858	10,333	8,321
779	535	558	629	693	520	331	143
266	268	229	216	196	186	186	180
(204)	(189)	(54)	(26)	(9)	(10)	(12)	(7)
3,338	2,740	2,115	1,794	1,606	1,581	1,358	1,171
(170)	(153)	(78)	(27)	(13)	4	(4)	4
(198)	—	—	—	—	—	—	—
5,377	4,430	3,526	3,056	2,740	2,681	2,333	1,995
1.21	0.99	0.78	0.67	0.60	0.59	0.51	0.44
1.20	0.99	0.78	0.67	0.60	0.59	0.51	0.44
0.20	0.16	0.14	0.11	0.10	0.09	0.07	0.05
$ 24,356	$ 21,132	$ 19,352	$ 17,993	$17,331	$15,338	$12,114	$10,198
19,793	17,076	16,497	15,897	15,989	14,064	11,014	9,268
35,969	25,973	23,606	20,324	18,894	15,874	13,176	9,793
70,349	49,996	45,384	39,604	37,541	32,819	26,441	20,565
25,803	16,762	14,460	10,957	11,454	9,973	7,406	6,754
13,672	6,908	7,191	7,709	8,508	7,871	6,156	3,073
3,002	2,699	2,483	2,307	2,092	1,838	1,804	1,772
25,834	21,112	18,503	17,143	14,756	12,726	10,753	8,759
0.9	1.3	1.3	1.6	1.5	1.5	1.6	1.5
(13.7)	3.9	3.4	2.3	2.7	2.6	2.3	2.7
9.5%	9.6%	8.5%	7.9%	7.8%	9.0%	9.9%	11.1%
22.9%	22.4%	19.8%	19.2%	19.9%	22.8%	23.9%	25.3%

Introduction to Management Accounting

TIPS CHECK YOUR RESOURCES

- Visit the www.prenhall.com/horngren **Web site** for self-study quizzes, video clips, other resources

- Try the **Quick Check** exercise at end of chapter to test your knowledge

- Learn the **key terms**

- Do the **Starter** exercises keyed in the margins

- Work the **mid-** and **end-of-chapter summary problems**

- Use the **Concept Links** to review material in other chapters

- Search the **CD** for review materials by chapter or by key word

- Watch the **tutorial videos** to review **key concepts**

- Watch the **On Location Regal Marine** video for an overview of management accounting in a real setting.

LEARNING OBJECTIVES

1. Distinguish financial accounting from management accounting

2. Describe service, merchandising, and manufacturing companies, and classify their costs by value-chain element

3. Distinguish among (a) direct costs and indirect costs; and (b) full product costs, inventoriable product costs, and period costs

4. Prepare the financial statements of a manufacturing company

5. Identify trends in the business environment and use cost-benefit analysis to make business decisions

6. Use reasonable standards to make ethical judgments

You are relaxing in your new 1800 LSR Regal sport boat after a day on the lake. As you sit there, you ask yourself how Regal Marine can make a profit selling these boats at such low prices.

The answer: Regal's managers use management accounting information. It enables them to give you the best-performing boat for your hard-earned dollar. Regal's engineers pioneered the FasTrac hull, which maximizes performance and fuel efficiency while holding down costs. Scientists identified the most durable fiberglass, gelcoats, and upholstery fabrics. Then Regal's purchasing managers worked closely with the makers of

Regal Marine

these materials to keep prices down. The goal is to ensure that suppliers can deliver "just in time" to Regal's plant, so Regal does not have to hold a large inventory. Expert craftsmen cut materials to minimize waste. Others assemble the parts with precision and speed. The efficiency reduces Regal's cost, and Regal passes the savings on to customers.

In addition to controlling production costs, Regal Marine uses accounting information to make other strategic decisions:

- **Which products to emphasize:** Which of Regal's 22 boat models are the most profitable and deserve the most sales emphasis?

- **Which new products to launch:** Would a proposed new jet boat be profitable?

- **Which customers are most important:** Which of Regal's worldwide network of dealers contribute the most to the company's profitability and thus deserve the most attention and support?

- **What marketing strategy to use:** Should Regal continue selling only through its dealer network, or should it also sell direct to consumers?

By using management accounting information to help run its business, Orlando-based Regal Marine has become one of the most successful companies in the marine industry, with more than $100 million in sales each year. ■

■Sitemap

So far, we have focused on reporting accounting information for decision makers outside the organization: investors, creditors, and government authorities. We analyzed *financial accounting* reports—the income statement, the balance sheet, and the statement of cash flows—that report *past* performance and financial position.

Now we shift our focus to how accounting information helps managers shape the company's future. You'll see how managers such as those at Regal Marine use *management accounting* reports to make business decisions that increase profits and, in turn, shareholder value.

✫ *Distinguish financial accounting from management accounting*

How Is Management Accounting Different?

Financial and management accounting both use the accrual basis, and both reflect the same underlying economic transactions. However, their focus differs. Financial accounting leads to financial statements that allow stockholders and creditors to make investment decisions. These highly summarized reports are constrained by GAAP and focus on past performance. What you will learn in management accounting is very different from what you learned in financial accounting, because company managers need detailed and timely information to run the company efficiently and effectively day by day.

To understand the kind of information managers need to carry out these responsibilities, let's look first at their main responsibilities.

Newsletter E-mail, Inc.

Horizontal Analysis of Comparative Income Statement

Years Ended December 31, 2005 and 2004

	2005	2004	Increase (Decrease) Amount	Percent
Total revenues	$430,000	$373,000	$57,000	15.3%
Expenses:				
Cost of goods sold	$202,000	$188,000	$14,000	7.4
Selling and general expenses	98,000	93,000	5,000	5.4
Interest expense	7,000	4,000	3,000	75.0
Income tax expense	42,000	37,000	5,000	13.5
Total expenses	349,000	322,000	27,000	8.4
Net income	$81,000	$51,000	$30,000	58.8

Net income increased by a much higher percentage
than total revenues during 2005 because
revenues increased at a higher rate (15.3%)
than did total expenses (8.4%)

E 18-3

Trend percentages:

	Year 5	Year 4	Year 3	Year 2	Year 1
Total revenue	136%	114%	106%	92%	100%
Net income	155	134	98	84	100

Net income grew by 55% during the period,
compared to 36% for total revenue

E 18-6

a. Current ratio $= \dfrac{\$185,000}{\$131,000} = 1.41$

b. Acid-test (quick) ratio $= \dfrac{\$17,000 + \$11,000 + \$64,000}{\$131,000} = 0.70$

c. Inventory turnover $= \dfrac{\$297,000}{(\$77,000 + \$71,000)/2} = 4.01 \text{ times}$

d. Days' sales in average receivables

$= \dfrac{(\$64,000 + \$73,000)/2}{\$454,000/365} = 55 \text{ days}$

E 18-7

a. Current ratio:

20X4: $$\frac{\$61,000 + \$28,000 + \$102,000 + \$237,000}{\$275,000} = 1.56$$

20X3: $$\frac{\$47,000 + \$116,000 + \$272,000}{\$221,000} = 1.97$$

b. Acid +test ratio:

20X4: $$\frac{\$61,000 + \$28,000 + \$102,000}{\$275,000} = 0.69$$

20X3: $$\frac{\$47,000 + \$116,000}{\$221,000} = 0.74$$

c. Debt ratio:

20X4: $$\frac{\$321,000}{\$543,000} = 0.59$$ ＊ $$\$275,000 + \$46,000 = \$321,000$$

20X3: $$\frac{\$273,000}{\$489,00} = 0.56$$ ＊ $$221,000 + \$52,000 = 273,000.$$

d. Times - interest -earned ratio:

20X4: $$\frac{\$165,000}{\$48,000} = 3.44 \text{ times}$$

20X3: $$\frac{\$158,000}{\$39,000} = 4.05 \text{ times}$$

Summary: The company's ability to pay its current liabilities, long-term debt, and interest expense deteriorated during 20X4, as shown by the worsening of all four ratios.

Managers' Main Responsibilities

Managers have two main responsibilities: planning and controlling (Exhibit 19-1). **Planning** means choosing goals and deciding how to achieve them. For example, one of Regal Marine's goals is to increase operating income. The company's managers could

1. Raise sales prices
2. Increase advertising to stimulate sales
3. Redesign the boats for faster production and servicing

Suppose Regal's managers choose alternative 3. Regal's engineers, purchasing officer, and production, marketing, and service managers work together to redesign the 1800 LSR 18-foot sport boat to speed assembly and servicing. Managers use the new design to budget the cost of the 1800 LSR, considering both the cost per boat and the number they expect to sell. The **budget** is a quantitative expression of a plan that helps managers coordinate and implement the plan.

Regal's purchasing officer uses the new design and the number of boats Regal expects to sell to decide how many component parts to order. The production manager alerts plant workers to the design changes before they begin assembling the new model. After they implement the plan, controlling begins. **Controlling** means evaluating the results of business operations by comparing the actual results to the plan. Regal's accounting system records the number of boats produced and the purchase prices and number of components used to assemble them.

Student ResourceCD
budget, management accounting

planning
Choosing goals and deciding how to achieve them.

budget
Quantitative expression of a plan that helps managers coordinate and implement the plan.

controlling
Evaluating the results of business operations by comparing the actual results to the plan.

Exhibit 19-1   Managers' Main Responsibilities

Feedback

After completing production, managers can compare actual to budgeted costs to evaluate employees' performance. If actual costs fall below budgeted costs, that is good news. But if actual costs exceed the budget, managers may need to act. Costs provide feedback that helps managers decide whether their decision to redesign the 1800 LSR increased or decreased profits.

Management versus Financial Accounting

✔ **Starter 19-1**

Exhibit 19-2 summarizes the differences between

- What you'll learn in management accounting—to help managers plan and control business operations
- What you already learned in financial accounting—to help external users make investment decisions

Exhibit 19-2

Management Accounting versus
Financial Accounting

	Management Accounting	Financial Accounting
1. Primary users	Internal—the company's managers	External—investors, creditors, and government authorities such as the IRS and SEC
2. Purpose of information	Help managers plan and control business operations	Help investors, creditors, and others make investment, credit, and other decisions
3. Focus and time dimension	Relevance and focus on the future—example: 2007 budget prepared in 2006	Reliability, objectivity, and focus on the past—example: 2004 actual performance reported in 2005.
4. Type of report	Internal reports not restricted by GAAP— determined by cost-benefit analysis	Financial statements restricted by GAAP
5. Verification	No independent audit	Annual independent audit by certified public accountant
6. Scope of information	Detailed reports on parts of the company (products, departments, territories), often on a daily or weekly basis	Summary reports primarily on the company as a whole, usually on a quarterly or annual basis
7. Behavioral implications	Concern about how reports will affect employee behavior	Concern about adequacy of disclosure; behavioral implications are secondary

Let's apply points 1, 2, and 3 to Regal. Deciding whether to build a new production plant in Michigan relates to Regal Marine's future, and its managers are the decision makers. Regal will budget (predict) the plant's future income and cash inflows. Its managers then will compare these inflows against the costs of operating the plant. Even if the result is a net inflow, Regal will compare it to net inflows from other investments, like developing a new jet boat. Management accounting helps Regal executives identify which investment has the greatest expected net benefit.

Both management accounting reports and financial accounting reports share the same foundation—the accrual basis of accounting. But managers enjoy more leeway in preparing management accounting reports. Point 4 of Exhibit 19-2 shows that there are no GAAP-type standards for the information managers need to run the business. Managers tailor the company's management accounting system to provide the information they need to help them make better decisions. Managers weigh the *benefits* of the system (information that helps managers make decisions that increase profits) against the *costs* to develop and run the system.

cost-benefit analysis
Weighing costs against benefits to help make decisions.

Weighing the costs against benefits is called **cost-benefit analysis**. The costs and benefits of any particular management accounting system differ from one company to another. Different companies create different systems. In contrast, *all* companies follow GAAP for external reporting. Point 5 of Exhibit 19-2 shows that independent certified public accountants audit the company's financial statements each year, but not the internal management accounting reports.

Point 6 indicates that management accounting provides more detailed and timely information than does financial accounting. Managers use this information to identify ways to cut costs, set prices that will be competitive and yet yield profits, identify the most profitable products and customers so the sales force can focus on key profitmakers, and evaluate employees' job performance. Technology, from Web-based company Intranets to handheld computers, lets managers access this information with the click of a mouse.

Point 7 reminds us that management accounting reports affect employees' behavior. "You get what you measure," because employees try to perform well on the parts of their jobs that the accounting system measures. If the manager of a Regal Marine production plant is evaluated only on her ability to control costs, she may use cheaper raw materials or hire less experienced workers. Although these actions cut costs, they can hurt profits if the quality of the product drops and sales decline as a result.

service company
A company that sells intangible services, rather than tangible products.

merchandising company
A company that resells products previously bought from suppliers.

manufacturing company
A company that uses labor, plant, and equipment to convert raw materials into new finished products.

☐ What Is Management
   Accounting?
■ **The Value Chain**
☐ Determining Costs
☐ Costs in Financial Statements
☐ Today's Business Environment
☐ Ethical Standards

Service, Merchandising, and Manufacturing Companies, and the Value Chain

Service companies, such as eBay (online auction), H&R Block (tax return preparation), and Randstad (temporary personnel services), sell intangible services, so labor often makes up 70% of their costs. Service companies incur other costs to develop new services, for marketing, and for customer service such as dispute resolution.

Merchandisers and manufacturers sell tangible products. **Merchandising companies**, such as Amazon.com, Wal-Mart, and Footlocker, resell products they buy from suppliers. Amazon.com, for example, buys goods such as books, CDs, and DVDs for resale to customers. Amazon's cost in inventory is simply the price it pays for an item plus freight-in costs. → Because all of the inventory is ready for sale, a merchandiser's balance sheet usually reports just one category of inventory. Of course, merchandisers also incur other costs to research new products and locations for new stores, to market their products, and to provide customer service.

Manufacturing companies use labor, plant, and equipment to convert raw materials into new finished products. For example, Regal Marine's production workers use the company's plant and equipment to transform raw materials such as plywood and fiberglass into high-performance powerboats.

Because of their broader range of activities, manufacturers have three kinds of inventory:

Describe service, merchandising, and manufacturing companies, and classify their costs by value-chain element.

Student ResourceCD

direct materials inventory, finished goods inventory, supply chain management, value chain, work in progress inventory

← See Chapter 5, pages 186–187, for a review of inventory in merchandising firms.

1. **Materials inventory**: *Raw materials used in manufacturing.* Regal Marine's materials include plywood, fiberglass, engines, wiring, glass, carpeting, and upholstery fabric.

2. **Work in process inventory**: *Goods that are partway through the manufacturing process but not yet complete.* At Regal Marine, partly completed boats are the work in process inventory.

3. **Finished goods inventory**: *Completed goods that have not yet been sold.* Finished goods are what the manufacturer sells to a merchandiser (or to other customers). Regal Marine sells its completed boats to retail dealers/distributors such as The Boat Tree. Regal's finished goods inventory becomes the inventory of The Boat Tree, which then sells the boats to individual customers.

Exhibit 19-3 summarizes the differences among service, merchandising, and manufacturing companies.

Materials inventory

Work in process inventory

Finished goods inventory

| Exhibit 19-3 | Service, Merchandising, and Manufacturing Companies |

	Service Companies	Merchandising Companies	Manufacturing Companies
Examples	Advertising agencies eBay Law firms Merrill Lynch	Amazon.com Kroger Wal-Mart Wholesalers	Procter & Gamble DaimlerChrysler Dell Computer Regal Marine
Primary Output	Intangible services (auctions or advice)	Tangible products purchased from suppliers	New tangible products made as workers and equipment convert raw materials into new finished products
Type(s) of Inventory	None	Inventory	Materials inventory Work in process inventory Finished goods inventory

materials inventory
Raw materials for use in manufacturing.

work in process inventory
Goods that are partway through the manufacturing process but not yet complete.

finished goods inventory
Completed goods that have not yet been sold.

value chain
The activities that add value to a firm's products and services. Includes R&D, design, production or purchases, marketing, distribution, and customer service.

Which Business Activities Make Up the Value Chain?

Many people describe Regal Marine, Dell Computer, and General Motors as manufacturing companies. But it would be more accurate to say these are companies that do manufacturing. Why? Because companies that do manufacturing also do many other things. Regal Marine also conducts research to determine how to improve next year's models. Regal designs the new models based on its research and then produces, markets, and distributes the boats. These activities form Regal's **value chain**—the activities that add value to its products and services.

To set a selling price or to determine how profitable the 1800 LSR sport boat is, Regal must know how much it costs to develop, produce, market, distribute, and service the product. To figure the full cost of the 1800 LSR, Regal totals the costs incurred across all six elements of the value chain in Exhibit 19-4.

| Exhibit 19-4 | The Value Chain |

✔ **Starter 19-2**

✔ **Starter 19-3**

Value chain

Research and development · Design · Production or purchases · Marketing · Distribution · Customer service

research and development (R&D)
Researching and developing new or improved products or services, or the processes for producing them.

design
Detailed engineering of products and services, or processes for producing them.

production or purchases
Resources used to produce a product or service, or to purchase finished merchandise.

- **Research and development (R&D)**: Researching and developing new or improved products or services, or the processes for producing them. Regal Marine invested heavily to create its unique FasTrac Hull, which maximizes performance and fuel efficiency.

- **Design**: Detailed engineering of products and services, or the processes for producing them. Regal's engineers transformed the FasTrac Hull concept into reality by designing hull molds to use in production.

- **Production or purchases**: Resources used to produce a product or service, or to purchase finished merchandise. For a manufacturer such as Regal Marine, this category includes the actual costs incurred to make the products, including materials, labor, and the cost of the equipment. For a merchandiser like The Boat Tree, this category includes the purchase cost of inventory, such as boats and jet skis (and their freight in), that The Boat Tree buys to resell to customers.

- **Marketing:** Promotion of products or services, such as the costs of Regal's print ads and the costs of attending boat shows.
- **Distribution:** Delivery of products or services to customers. For Regal, this category includes the costs of trucking its finished boats to retailers like The Boat Tree.
- **Customer service:** Support provided for customers after the sale. This includes warranty service work.

marketing
Promotion of products or services.

distribution
Delivery of products or services to customers.

customer service
Support provided for customers after the sale.

Managers do not proceed step by step in this exact order through the value chain. Instead, a project team works on R&D, design, production, marketing, and customer service simultaneously.

Controlling Costs Through the Value Chain

The value chain in Exhibit 19-4 also reminds managers to control costs over the value chain as a whole. For example, Regal Marine spends more in R&D and product design to increase the quality of its boats, which in turn reduces customer service costs. Even though R&D and design costs are higher, the total cost of the boat—as measured throughout the entire value chain—is lower as a result of this tradeoff.

The value chain applies to service and merchandising firms, as well as manufacturing firms. For example, an advertising agency such as Saatchi & Saatchi incurs

- *Marketing* costs to obtain a new client
- *Design* costs to develop the client's ad campaign
- *Customer service* costs to address the new client's concerns
- *Distribution* costs to get the ads to the media

Determining the Costs to Serve a Customer or to Make a Product

How do companies like eBay, Amazon.com, and Regal Marine determine how much it costs to serve a customer, fill an order, or produce a sport boat? Before we can answer this question, let's first consider the specialized language accountants use when referring to costs.

Cost Objects, Direct Costs, and Indirect Costs

A **cost object** is anything for which managers want a separate measurement of costs. Regal Marine's cost objects may include:

- Individual products (the 1800 LSR sport boat or the Commodore 4260 yacht)
- Alternative marketing strategies (sales through retailers versus direct-to-customer sales)
- Geographic segments of the business (United States, Europe, the Middle East)
- Departments (personnel, accounting, production)

Suppose the manager of a Regal Marine plant wants to know how much it costs to produce a product—an 1800 LSR sport boat. We can trace the engine directly to the cost object—a particular 1800 LSR boat—so the cost of the engine

3 *Distinguish among (a) direct costs and indirect costs; and (b) full product costs, inventoriable product costs, and period costs.*

Student ResourceCD

direct costs, direct materials inventory, indirect costs, inventoriable product cost, manufacturing overhead

cost object
Anything for which managers want a separate measurement of costs.

direct cost
A cost that can be specifically traced to a cost object.

indirect cost
A cost that cannot be specifically traced to a cost object.

is a **direct cost**. We cannot trace the plant manager's salary to any individual boat, so the salary is an **indirect cost**.

Now let's look more carefully at how companies determine the costs of one of the most common cost objects: products.

Product Costs

As a manager, you'll want to focus on the products that are most profitable. But which products are these? To determine the profit a product provides, you start with its selling price and then subtract the cost of the product. But how do you figure the cost of the product? The rest of this section explains how you do it.

Most companies use two different definitions of product costs: (1) full product costs for internal decision-making, and (2) inventoriable product costs for external reporting. Let's see what they are and how managers use each type of cost.

full product costs
The costs of all resources used throughout the value chain for a product.

FULL PRODUCT COSTS **Full product costs** are the costs of all resources used throughout the value chain. For Regal Marine, the full product cost of a particular boat model is the total cost to research, design, manufacture, market, and distribute the model, as well as to service the customers who buy it. Before launching a new model, managers predict the full product costs of the boat to set a selling price that will cover all costs plus return a profit. Regal also compares each model's sale price to its full cost to determine which models are the most profitable. Marketing can then focus on selling the more profitable models.

inventoriable product costs
All costs of a product that GAAP requires companies to treat as an asset for external financial reporting. These costs are not expensed until the product is sold.

INVENTORIABLE PRODUCT COSTS FOR EXTERNAL REPORTING GAAP does not regulate the product costs companies use for internal reporting. But for *external* reporting, GAAP requires companies to treat **inventoriable product costs** as an asset until the product is sold, at which time the costs are expensed. GAAP requires specific inventoriable product costs that include only a *portion* of full product costs. Thus, inventoriable costs do not include costs from all elements of the value chain.

Which costs are inventoriable under GAAP? The answer depends on whether the company is a merchandiser or a manufacturer.

Chapter 6 explains how merchandisers compute inventoriable costs.

MERCHANDISING COMPANIES' INVENTORIABLE PRODUCT COSTS Merchandising companies' inventoriable costs include *only* the cost of purchasing the inventory from suppliers (for example, the price The Boat Tree pays Regal Marine for boats) plus freight in. These are the costs in the third element of the value chain in Exhibit 19-4. ← The Boat Tree's inventoriable cost (purchase price plus freight in) of boats is an asset—Inventory—in its accounting records. This inventoriable cost remains an asset (Inventory) until the boats are *sold*. Then it becomes an expense—Cost of Goods Sold.

Costs incurred in other elements of the value chain—such as The Boat Tree's employee salaries, commissions paid to sales staff, and distribution costs—are not inventoriable product costs. Instead, these are **period costs**, operating costs that are always expensed in the period in which they are incurred. Period costs are never part of the Inventory asset account.

period costs
Operating costs that are expensed in the period in which they are incurred.

Exhibit 19-5 shows the difference between full product costs and the inventoriable product costs GAAP requires for external reporting. Study the exhibit carefully to make sure you understand how the two components of full product costs—inventoriable product costs and period costs—affect the income statement and balance sheet.

Exhibit 19-5 Full Product Costs, Inventoriable Product Costs, and Period Costs

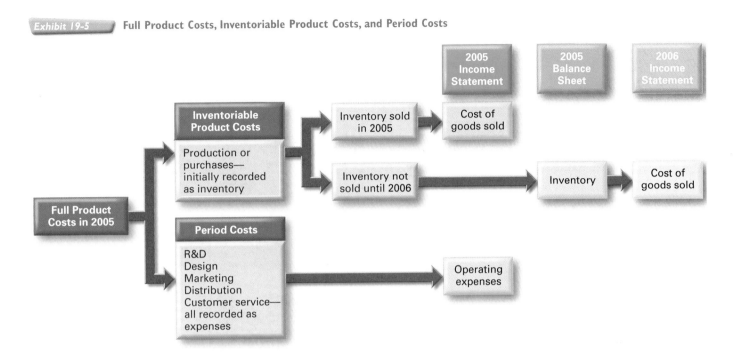

What are the inventoriable costs for a service firm such as **H&R Block**?

Answer: Service firms like H&R Block have no inventory of products for sale. Services cannot be produced today and stored up to sell later. Because service firms have no inventory, they have no inventoriable costs. Instead, they have only period costs that are expensed as incurred.

MANUFACTURING COMPANIES' INVENTORIABLE PRODUCT COSTS

✓ Starter 19-4

Manufacturing companies like Regal Marine figure their inventoriable product costs by totaling three components of manufacturing costs: direct materials, direct labor, and manufacturing overhead.

Direct Materials Direct materials (1) must become a physical part of the finished product, and (2) their costs (invoice cost plus freight in) must be traceable to the finished product. For Regal Marine's 1800 LSR, direct materials include the wood used to fashion the hull, the gel coat that creates a waterproof seal throughout the exterior, the engine, and dashboard instruments like the speedometer and the depth finder.

direct materials
Materials that become a physical part of a finished product and whose costs are traceable to the finished product.

Direct Labor Direct labor is the compensation of employees who physically convert materials into the company's products. For Regal, direct labor includes the wages of different craftsmen who build the hulls, apply the gel coat sealant, and sew the seat cushions; the wages of technicians who wire the electronics; and the wages of workers who assemble the parts to build the completed boat. Their effort can be traced *directly* to the finished products.

direct labor
The compensation of employees who physically convert materials into the company's products; labor costs that are directly traceable to finished products.

Manufacturing Overhead Manufacturing overhead includes all manufacturing costs other than direct materials and direct labor. Examples include indirect materials; indirect labor; plant repairs and maintenance; plant utilities, rent, insurance, and property taxes; and depreciation on plant buildings and equipment. Manufacturing overhead also is called **factory overhead** or **indirect manufacturing cost**.

Exhibit 19-6 summarizes Regal's inventoriable product costs.

manufacturing overhead
All manufacturing costs other than direct materials and direct labor. Also called **factory overhead** or **indirect manufacturing cost**.

Exhibit 19-6   A Manufacturer's Inventoriable Product Costs

Direct Materials

+

Direct Labor

+

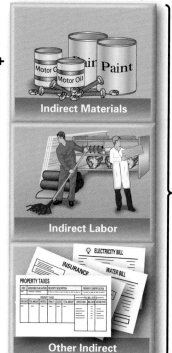
Indirect Materials

Indirect Labor

Other Indirect Manufacturing Costs

=

Inventoriable Product Cost

▶ **Manufacturing overhead**

Now look back at Exhibit 19-5. Regal Marine's 2005 income statement reports as Cost of Goods Sold the inventoriable costs of the boats the company sold during 2005. Regal's 2005 balance sheet reports the inventoriable costs of the finished boats still on hand at the end of 2005 (direct materials, direct labor, and manufacturing overhead) as an asset—inventory. If Regal sells the boats in this inventory in 2006, the costs will be included as part of Cost of Goods Sold on Regal's 2006 income statement.

✔ **Starter 19-5**

A CLOSER LOOK AT MANUFACTURING OVERHEAD *Manufacturing overhead includes only those indirect costs that are related to the manufacturing plant.* Insurance and depreciation on the *plant's* building and equipment are indirect manufacturing costs, so they are part of manufacturing overhead. In contrast, depreciation on *delivery trucks* is not a manufacturing cost. Delivery is part of the distribution element of the value chain (see Exhibit 19-4), so its cost is part of distribution expense (a period expense), not manufacturing overhead. Similarly, auto insurance for the sales force is part of the marketing element of the value chain, so it is part of marketing expense (a period expense), not manufacturing overhead.

Manufacturing overhead also includes indirect materials and indirect labor. The bolts and screws used to build the boat become physical parts of the finished product. But, compared with the engine and hull, the costs of bolts and screws are minor. It is hard to measure the costs of those low-priced materials in a particular boat. Materials whose costs cannot conveniently be directly traced to particular finished products are called **indirect materials** and are part of manufacturing overhead.

indirect materials
Materials whose costs cannot conveniently be directly traced to particular finished products.

indirect labor
Labor costs that are difficult to trace to specific products.

Like indirect materials, **indirect labor** is difficult to trace to specific products so it is part of manufacturing overhead. Examples include the pay of forklift operators in the plant, plant janitors, and plant managers.

Inventoriable Product Costs or Period Costs?

Exhibit 19-7 summarizes the differences between inventoriable and period costs for service, merchandising, and manufacturing companies. Study this exhibit carefully. When are costs like depreciation, insurance, utilities, and property taxes inventoriable product costs? *Only* when those costs are related to the manufacturing plant. When those costs are related to nonmanufacturing activities like R&D or marketing, they are treated as period costs. Service companies and merchandisers do no manufacturing, so they always treat depreciation, insurance, utilities, and property taxes as period costs.

Exhibit 19-7	Inventoriable Product Costs and Period Costs for Service, Merchandising, and Manufacturing Companies	
Type of Company	**Inventoriable Product Costs—** Initially an asset (Inventory), and not expensed (Cost of Goods Sold) until inventory is sold	**Period Costs—** Expensed in period incurred; never considered an asset
Service company	None	Salaries, depreciation expense, utilities, insurance, property taxes, advertising
Merchandising company	Purchases plus freight in	Salaries, depreciation expense, utilities, insurance, property taxes, advertising, freight out
Manufacturing company	Direct materials, plus direct labor, plus manufacturing overhead (including indirect materials; indirect labor; depreciation on plant and equipment; plant insurance, utilities, and property taxes)	R&D; freight out; depreciation expense, utilities, insurance, and property taxes on executive headquarters (separate from plant); advertising; CEO's salary

Inventoriable Product Costs and Period Costs in Financial Statements

The difference between inventoriable product costs and period costs is important because they are treated differently in the financial statements. We begin with a short review to help you see how a manufacturer's financial statements differ from those of service and merchandising companies.

Prepare the financial statements of a manufacturing company

Student ResourceCD
cost of goods sold, cost of goods manufactured, inventoriable product cost

Chapter 1, p. 6, introduced income statements for service companies.

Service Companies

Service companies have the simplest accounting. Exhibit 19-8 (on page 762) shows the income statement of eNow!, a group of e-commerce consultants. The firm has no inventory and thus no inventoriable costs, so eNow!'s income statement has no Cost of Goods Sold. The statement groups all expenses (period costs) together. eNow!'s largest expense is for the salaries of employees who perform the services.

Merchandising Companies

In contrast with service companies, merchandisers' income statements feature Cost of Goods Sold as the major expense. Consider Apex Showrooms, a

Exhibit 19-8

Service Company Income
Statement

eNow!
Income Statement
Month Ended December 31, 20X5

Revenues..		$160,000
Expenses:		
Salary expense	$106,000	
Office rent expense	18,000	
Depreciation expense—furniture and equipment ...	3,500	
Marketing expense	2,500	(130,000)
Operating Income		$ 30,000

merchandiser of lighting fixtures. Apex's *only* inventoriable costs are for the purchase of chandeliers and track lights that it buys to resell, plus freight in. Merchandisers like Apex compute the Cost of Goods Sold as follows: [1]

Beginning inventory	$ 9,500	What Apex had at the beginning of the period
+ Purchases and freight in	110,000	What Apex bought during the period
= Cost of goods available for sale	119,500	Total available for sale during the period
− Ending inventory	13,000	What Apex had left at the end of the period
= Cost of goods sold	$106,500	What Apex sold

Panel A of Exhibit 19-9 shows Apex's complete income statement.

Manufacturing Companies

Panel B of Exhibit 19-9 shows the income statement of Top-Flight, a manufacturer of golf equipment and athletic shoes. Compare its income statement with the merchandiser's income statement in Panel A. The only difference is that the merchandiser (Apex) uses *purchases* in computing cost of goods sold, while the manufacturer (Top-Flight) uses the *cost of goods manufactured*. Notice that the term **cost of goods manufactured** is in the past tense. It is the manufacturing (or plant-related) cost of the goods that Top-Flight *finished producing during 20X5*. This is the manufacturer's cost to obtain new *finished goods* that are ready to sell (only finished goods are sold), so it is the manufacturer's counterpart to the merchandiser's *purchases*.

cost of goods manufactured
The manufacturing (or plant-related) cost of the goods that *finished* the production process this period.

CALCULATING THE COST OF GOODS MANUFACTURED   The cost of goods manufactured summarizes the activities that take place in a manufacturing plant over the period (and their associated costs). Let's begin by reviewing these activities. Exhibit 19-10 reminds us that the manufacturer starts by buying materials. Then it uses direct labor and plant and equipment (whose costs are part of manufacturing overhead) to transform these materials into work in process inventory. When the work in process inventory is completed, it becomes finished goods inventory. These are all inventoriable product costs because they are plant-related.

---

[1]To highlight the roles of beginning inventory, purchases, and ending inventory, we assume that Apex uses a periodic inventory system. However, the concepts in this chapter apply equally to companies that use perpetual inventory systems.

PANEL A: Merchandiser's Income Statement

Exhibit 19-9

Comparing a Merchandiser's and a Manufacturer's Income Statements

✔ Starter 19-6

Apex Showrooms
Income Statement
Month Ended December 31, 20X5

Sales revenue.		$150,000
Cost of goods sold:		
Beginning inventory	$ 9,500	
Purchases and freight in	110,000	
Cost of goods available for sale	119,500	
Ending inventory	(13,000)	
Cost of goods sold		106,500
Gross profit		43,500
Operating expenses:		
Showroom rent expense	5,000	
Sales salary expense	4,000	9,000
Operating income.		$ 34,500

PANEL B: Manufacturer's Income Statement

Top-Flight
Income Statement
Year Ended December 31, 20X5

Sales revenue.		$65,000
Cost of goods sold:		
Beginning finished goods inventory	$ 6,000	
Cost of goods manufactured*	42,000	
Cost of goods available for sale	48,000	
Ending finished goods inventory	(8,000)	
Cost of goods sold		40,000
Gross profit		25,000
Operating expenses:		
Sales salary expense	3,000	
Delivery expense	7,000	10,000
Operating income.		$15,000

*From the Schedule of Cost of Goods Manufactured in Exhibit 19-11.

Finished goods are the only inventory that is ready to sell. The cost of the finished goods that the manufacturer sells becomes its Cost of Goods Sold on the income statement. Costs the manufacturer incurs in other (nonmanufacturing) elements of the value chain are operating expenses, or period costs that are expensed in the period incurred. Exhibit 19-10 shows that these operating costs are deducted from gross profit to obtain operating income.

Exhibit 19-10 Manufacturing Company: Inventoriable Costs and Period Costs

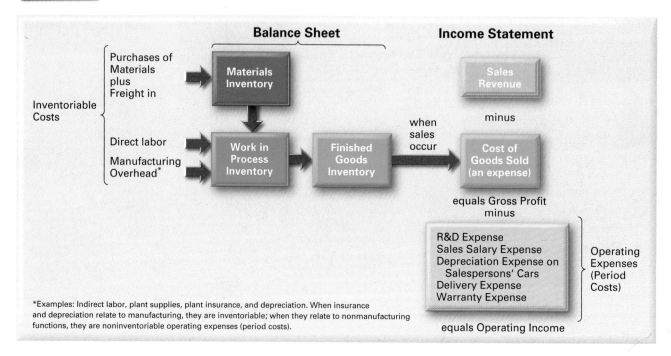

You now have a clear understanding of the flow of activities and costs in the plant, and you're ready to figure the cost of goods manufactured. Exhibit 19-11 shows how Top-Flight computes its cost of goods manufactured—the cost of the goods the plant *finished* during 20X5.

Exhibit 19-11

Schedule of Cost of Goods Manufactured

Top-Flight			
Schedule of Cost of Goods Manufactured			
Year Ended December 31, 20X5			
Beginning work in process inventory			$ 2,000
Add: Direct materials used			
Beginning materials inventory	$ 9,000		
Purchases of direct materials			
plus freight in	27,000		
Available for use	36,000		
Ending materials inventory	(22,000)		
Direct materials used		$14,000	
Direct labor		19,000	
Manufacturing overhead:			
Indirect materials	$ 1,500		
Indirect labor	3,500		
Depreciation—plant and equipment	3,000		
Plant utilities, insurance, and			
property taxes	4,000	12,000	
Total manufacturing costs incurred			
during year			45,000
Total manufacturing costs to account for			47,000
Less: Ending work in process inventory			(5,000)
Costs of goods manufactured			$42,000

✔ Starter 19-7

✔ Starter 19-8

✔ Starter 19-9

The computation of the cost of goods manufactured summarizes the activities and related costs incurred on Top-Flight's plant floor throughout 20X5. By the end of 20X4, Top-Flight had spent a total of $2,000 to partially complete the golf clubs and shoes that remained on the plant floor at the close of business on December 31, 20X4. This ending work in process inventory for 20X4 is Top-Flight's beginning work in process inventory for 20X5.

Exhibit 19-11 shows that during 20X5, Top-Flight's production plant used $14,000 of direct materials, $19,000 of direct labor, and $12,000 of manufacturing overhead. Adding the sum of these three costs ($45,000) to the beginning Work in Process Inventory balance of $2,000 gives the total cost assigned to goods the plant worked on during the year: $47,000. The plant finished most of these goods and sent them to Finished Goods Inventory, but some were not finished. By the close of business on December 31, 20X5, Top-Flight had spent $5,000 on ending work in process inventory that lay partially complete on the plant floor.

The final step is to figure the *cost of goods manufactured during 20X5*—that is, the cost of the goods that Top-Flight *finished* during 20X5. Take the $47,000 total cost of goods worked on during the year and subtract the $5,000 cost of the goods that were not finished (the ending work in process inventory at December 31, 20X5). Top-Flight's cost of goods manufactured for 20X5 is $42,000 ($47,000 – $5,000).

FLOW OF COSTS THROUGH INVENTORY ACCOUNTS Exhibit 19-12 diagrams the flow of costs through Top-Flight's inventory accounts. The format is the same for all three stages: direct materials, work in process, and finished goods. The final amount at each stage flows into the next stage. Take time to see how the schedule of cost of goods manufactured in Exhibit 19-11 uses the flows of the direct materials and work in process stages, while the income statement in Panel B of Exhibit 19-9 uses the flows for the finished goods inventory.

Exhibit 19-12 Flow of Costs Through a Manufacturer's Inventory Accounts

Direct Materials Inventory		Work in Process Inventory		Finished Goods Inventory	
Beginning inventory	$ 9,000	Beginning inventory	$ 2,000	Beginning inventory	$ 6,000
+ Purchases and freight in.............	27,000	+ Direct materials used ..... $14,000 + Direct labor 19,000		+ Cost of goods manufactured	42,000
		+ Manufacturing overhead	12,000		
		Total manufacturing costs incurred during the year	45,000		
= Direct materials available for use	36,000	= Total manufacturing costs to account for.......	47,000	= Cost of goods available for sale.....	48,000
− Ending inventory	(22,000)	− Ending inventory	(5,000)	− Ending inventory	(8,000)
= Direct materials used	$14,000	= Cost of goods manufactured	$42,000	= Cost of goods sold ...	$40,000

Source: The authors are indebted to Judith Cassidy for this presentation.

Effects on the Balance Sheet

The only difference in the balance sheets of service, merchandising, and manufacturing companies relates to inventories. Exhibit 19-13 shows how the current asset sections of eNOW! (service company), Apex Showrooms (merchandising company), and Top-Flight (manufacturing company) might differ at the end of 20X5. eNOW! has no inventory at all, Apex has a single category of inventory, and Top-Flight has three categories of inventory (materials, work in process, and finished goods). ✔ Starter 19-10

Exhibit 19-13 Current Asset Sections of Balance Sheets

eNOW! (Service Company)		Apex Showrooms (Merchandising Company)		Top-Flight (Manufacturing Company)		
Cash........................	$ 4,000	Cash	$ 4,000	Cash......................		$ 4,000
Accounts receivable	5,000	Accounts receivable	5,000	Accounts receivable		5,000
		Inventory (Exhibit 19-9, Panel A).........	13,000	Materials inventory (Exhibit 19-11)	$22,000	
				Work in process inventory (Exhibit 19-11)	5,000	
				Finished goods inventory (Exhibit 19-9, Panel B)....	8,000	35,000
Prepaid expenses...........	1,000	Prepaid expenses	1,000	Prepaid expenses		1,000
Total current assets	$10,000	Total current assets	$23,000	Total current assets		$45,000

Take time to review the following Decision Guidelines. Make sure you have a solid understanding of all these concepts before you read further.

Decision Guidelines

BUILDING BLOCKS OF MANAGEMENT ACCOUNTING

HP engages in *manufacturing* when it assembles its computers, *merchandising* when it sells them on its Web site, and support *services* such as start-up and implementation services. HP had to make the following decisions in designing its management accounting system to provide managers with the information they need to run the manufacturing, merchandising, and service operations efficiently and effectively.

Decision	Guidelines
What information should management accountants provide? What is the primary focus of management accounting?	Management accounting provides information that helps managers make better decisions; it has a • *Future* orientation • Focus on *relevance* to business decisions
How do you decide on a company's management accounting system, which is not regulated by GAAP?	Use cost-benefit analysis: Design the management accounting system so that benefits (from helping managers make wiser decisions) outweigh the costs of the system.

How do you distinguish among service, merchandising, and manufacturing companies? How do their balance sheets differ?	*Service companies:*
	
	• Provide customers with intangible services
	• Have no inventories on the balance sheet
	
	Merchandising companies:
	
	• Resell tangible products purchased ready-made from suppliers
	• Have only one category of inventory
	
	Manufacturing companies:
	
	• Use labor, plant, and equipment to transform raw materials into new finished products
	• Have three categories of inventory:
	    Materials inventory
	    Work in process inventory
	    Finished goods inventory

Decision Guidelines *(continued)*

Decision	Guidelines

How do you compute cost of goods sold?	• *Service companies:* No cost of goods sold, because they don't sell tangible goods
	
	• *Merchandising companies:*
	
	   Beginning inventory
	   + Purchases and freight in
	   − Ending inventory
	   = Cost of goods sold
	
	• *Manufacturing companies:*
	
	   Beginning finished goods inventory
	   + Cost of goods manufactured
	   − Ending finished goods inventory
	   = Cost of goods sold

How do you compute the cost of goods manufactured for a manufacturer?	Beginning work in process inventory + Current period manufacturing costs (direct materials used + direct labor + manufacturing overhead) − Ending work in process inventory = Cost of goods manufactured
Which costs are initially treated as assets for external reporting? When are these costs expensed?	*Inventoriable product costs* are initially treated as assets (Inventory); these costs are not expensed (as Cost of Goods Sold) until the products are sold.
What costs are inventoriable under GAAP?	• *Service companies:* No inventoriable product costs • *Merchandising companies:* Purchases and freight in • *Manufacturing companies:* Direct materials used, direct labor, and manufacturing overhead

MID-CHAPTER *Summary Problem*

1. Show how to compute cost of goods manufactured. Use the following amounts: direct materials used ($24,000); direct labor ($9,000); manufacturing overhead ($17,000); beginning work in process inventory ($5,000); and ending work in process inventory ($4,000).
2. For a manufacturing company, identify the following as either an inventoriable product cost or a period cost:
   a. Depreciation on plant equipment
   b. Depreciation on salespersons' automobiles
   c. Insurance on plant building
   d. Marketing manager's salary

CHECK YOUR RESOURCES

Solution

Requirement 1

Cost of goods manufactured:

Beginning work in process inventory.....................		$ 5,000
Add: Direct materials used.............................	$24,000	
Direct labor	9,000	
Manufacturing overhead	17,000	
Total manufacturing costs incurred during the period .		50,000
Total manufacturing costs to account for.................		55,000
Less: Ending work in process inventory		(4,000)
Cost of goods manufactured		$51,000

Requirement 2

(a) Inventoriable product cost; (b) Period cost; (c) Inventoriable product cost; (d) Period cost

⭐5 *Identify trends in the business environment and use cost-benefit analysis to make business decisions*

Student Resource CD

enterprise resource planning, JIT, total quality management

Today's Business Environment

The following chapters describe management accounting tools that managers use to make business decisions. Before we turn to these tools, let's first consider recent trends that affect managers' decisions and the management accounting systems that support them. These trends include the shift toward a service economy; the rise of the global marketplace; time-based competition (including changes in information systems, electronic commerce, and just-in-time management); and total quality management.

Shift Toward a Service Economy

Service companies provide health care, communication, transportation, banking, and other important benefits to society. In the last century, North American economies shifted focus from manufacturing to service. Service companies now make up the largest sector of the U.S. economy and employ 55% of the workforce. The U.S. Bureau of the Census expects services, especially technology and health-care services, to be among the fastest growing industries over the next decade. Even companies that do manufacturing, such as General Electric (GE), are shifting to selling more services. It's easy to see why. In GE's jet engine business, services contribute only 30% of the revenues but generate two-thirds of the profit.

Service company managers need cost information to make decisions. For example, banks must include the cost of servicing checking and savings accounts in the fees they charge customers. Hospitals need to know the cost of performing appendectomies to justify reimbursement from insurance companies and from Medicare.

Competing in the Global Marketplace

The costs of international trade have plummeted over the last decade, allowing foreign companies to compete with local firms. Firms that are not world-class competitors will vanish from the global market. However, global markets provide competitive companies with great potential: Foreign operations account for over 25% of Regal Marine's and Amazon.com's revenues, and over 40% of General Electric's revenues. McDonald's has expanded in Russia and China, two countries with billions of consumers.

Manufacturers often move operations to other countries to be closer to new markets and less expensive labor. For example, Thomson SA, maker of GE television sets, closed the world's largest TV factory in Bloomington, Indiana, and moved the work to Mexico to save an estimated $75 million a year in labor costs. Ford, General Motors, and DaimlerChrysler all built plants in Brazil to feed Brazil's car-hungry middle class. The same week Alcoa announced it was closing two plants in the United States, it spelled out plans to build a $1 billion plant in Iceland. Alcoa will go ahead with the plan if the benefits (less expensive energy and labor) outweigh the costs of building the new plant.

Globalization has several implications for management accounting:

1. Stiffer competition means managers need more accurate information to make wise decisions. If Nokia overestimates the cost of its new cell phone, it may set prices too high and lose business to competitors.

2. Companies must decide whether to expand sales and/or production into foreign countries. Managers need estimates of the costs and benefits of international expansion.

3. Globalization fosters the transfer of management philosophy across international borders. Many U.S. companies now follow the just-in-time philosophy developed in Japan.

Time-Based Competition

Question: When did you need that order?
Response: Yesterday, of course!

The Internet, electronic commerce (e-commerce), e-mail, and express delivery speed the pace of business. Customers who surf the Web and Instant Message with people all over the world will not wait four weeks to receive their purchases. Time is the latest competitive turf for world-class business.

Dell Computer commits to delivering your desktop computer within a week of receiving your order. Toyota says it can make a car within five days of receiving a custom order. Sweden's Ericsson Radio Systems has increased on-time delivery from 20% to 99.98%—nearly perfect. How do they do it? By using advanced information systems, e-commerce, and just-in-time management.

ADVANCED INFORMATION SYSTEMS   Many small businesses use QuickBooks or Peachtree software to track their costs and develop the information owners and managers need to run the business. But large companies such as Fujitsu and Allstate Insurance are turning to **enterprise resource planning (ERP) systems** that can integrate all of a company's worldwide functions, departments, and data. ERP systems such as SAP, Oracle, and Peoplesoft gather company data into a centralized data warehouse. The system feeds these data into software for all of the company's business activities, from budgeting and purchasing to production and customer service.

ERP
Software systems that can integrate all of a company's worldwide functions, departments, and data into a single system.

Advantages of ERP systems include:

- Companies streamline their operations before mapping them into ERP software. Streamlining operations saves money.

- ERP helps companies respond to changes. A change in sales instantly ripples through the ERP's purchases, production, shipping, and accounting systems.

■ An ERP system can replace hundreds of separate software systems, such as different software in different regions, or different payroll, shipping, and production software.

ERP is expensive: Major installations cost Fujitsu and Allstate over $40 million. ERP also requires a large commitment of time and people. For example, Hershey Foods tried to shrink a four-year ERP project into two and a half years. The result? The software did not map into Hershey's operations, and disrupted deliveries hurt profits in the critical Halloween season.

E-COMMERCE To survive in a competitive globally wired economy, companies use the Internet in everyday operations such as budgeting, planning, selling, and customer service. Imagine a sales clerk who can sell to thousands of customers at once. This clerk instantly provides every product, option, and price the company offers. It works 24 hours a day, 365 days a year, and never takes a break or vacation. This sales clerk is an e-commerce Web site!

Business-to-business e-commerce takes this speed and efficiency to new levels. Imagine sitting in your office, anywhere in the world. You enter Dell's Web site and customize the new computer you're buying. After you fill your virtual shopping cart, business-to-business software automates ordering, approval, and delivery.

Electronic purchases below specified dollar limits are often untouched by human hands, generate little if any paper, and avoid the time and cost of

Refining Dining with Data Mining

As chefs in the kitchen slice and dice meat and veggies, managers back at headquarters are asking accountants to "slice and dice" the data. Using the latest in data mining

technology from Digital Equipment Corp. and Informix, large restaurant operators now analyze a dizzying amount of data that extend well beyond sales, cash management, and inventory.

- **AFC**, operator and franchiser of more than 3,300 Church's, Popeye's Chicken & Biscuits, Seattle Coffee Company, and Torrefazione Italia outlets worldwide, collects customer-purchase data by item, item combination, day, and location. Sophisticated data mining software ferrets out patterns, trends, and even challenges and problems. Managers get information on how factors such as location affect the profitability of sales promotions and which patrons respond to which offers.
- **Red Robin International**, a 135-unit casual-dining chain based in Englewood, Colorado, relies on patterns revealed by its data warehouse to hone menus. "We do a lot of menu changes, with new items and specials," explains Howard Jenkins, Red Robin's Vice President of Information Systems. "With data mining in place, we can ask ourselves, 'If we put the items with the high margin in the middle of the menu, do we sell more versus putting [them] at the top or bottom . . . ?'"
- **Pizzeria Uno** uses a more economical decision-support system to define and analyze data in response to specific queries, such as take-out versus eat-in pizza sales. A nifty tool called "80/20" identifies the 20% of customers who contribute 80% of sales, so management can adjust menus and promos to suit top patrons' preferences.

Source: Based on "Mining the data of dining," *Nation's Restaurant News*, May 22, 2000, pp. S22–S24.

Accounting.com

processing this paperwork. Even the federal government is on the e-bandwagon. An electronic marketplace, E-Mall, allows buyers in the Department of Defense and other federal agencies access to 17 million items online. Orders on E-Mall cost about $11 to process, while those placed by hand cost around $150.

Electronically billing customers is also becoming more popular. Analysts estimate that

1. Companies save $7 per invoice by billing customers electronically
2. The average large company issues 800,000 invoices a year
3. The average cost of installing an e-billing system is $500,000

Should companies that issue 800,000 invoices a year consider e-billing?

Answer: Yes, these companies should consider e-billing. Comparing expected benefits to costs reveals significant expected net benefits from e-billing:

Expected benefits:	
800,000 invoices × $7 savings per invoice	$5,600,000
Expected costs:	
Installation of e-billing system	(500,000)
Net expected benefits	$5,100,000

Managers of Krispy Kreme stores use the company's customized Web portal to plan production and order supplies. Weather news appears on the opening screen. Why? Because Krispy Kreme found that people buy more coffee and donuts when the weather is bad. This simple innovation helps managers forecast how many donuts to make. "I've seen a good 2 to 3 percent increase in profitability just from the portal," says the manager of a Miami-based store.[2]

Firms also use the Internet to tap into other companies' business processes. Companies that supply component parts to Dell use the Internet to look into Dell's production process through a customized virtual window. Each supplier sees the current demand for, and inventory levels of, the parts it supplies Dell. Access to real-time information that lets suppliers automate the size of the next day's order helps Dell cut order-to-delivery times and control costs.

E-commerce is thus an important means of **supply-chain management**, where companies exchange information with suppliers and customers to reduce costs, improve quality, and speed delivery of goods and services from suppliers, through the company itself, and on to customers. E-commerce also increases firms' ability (and need) to use just-in-time management.

JUST-IN-TIME MANAGEMENT   Costs of holding inventory can add up to 25% of the inventory's value. Money tied up in inventory cannot be used for other purposes. Inventory held too long becomes obsolete. Storing inventory takes space that could be used to increase production. The just-in-time philosophy helps managers cut these costs by speeding the transformation of raw materials into new finished products. Let's see how.

Toyota generally gets credit for pioneering the **just-in-time (JIT)** philosophy, which means producing *just in time* to satisfy needs. Ideally, suppliers deliver materials for today's production in exactly the right quantities *just in time* to begin production, and finished units are completed *just in time* for delivery to customers.

Firms adopting JIT report sharp reductions in inventory. Reducing inventory and speeding the production process reduce **throughput time**, the time between

supply-chain management
Exchange of information with suppliers and customers to reduce costs, improve quality, and speed delivery of goods and services from suppliers, through the company itself, and on to customers.

✔ **Starter 19-11**

just-in-time (JIT)
A system in which a company produces just in time to satisfy needs. Suppliers deliver materials just in time to begin production, and finished units are completed just in time for delivery to customers.

throughput time
The time between buying raw materials and selling finished products.

[2]Catherine Skip, "Hot Bytes, by the Dozen," *Newsweek*, April 28, 2003, page 42.

buying raw materials and selling finished products. For example, Dell Computer recently cut its throughput time from 17 to fewer than 5 days. Why is this important? *The Wall Street Journal* estimates that new technologies reduce the value of a completed PC by 1% *per week.*[3] Moving inventory quickly means that Dell can cut prices immediately when component part costs decline. Less inventory means that Dell can quickly incorporate new technologies and that more plant space is available for production.

Manufacturers adopting just-in-time have limited safety stock of raw materials, so they depend on their suppliers to make on-time deliveries of perfect-quality materials. As we noted earlier, Dell designed special Web pages for its major suppliers that give them a "virtual window" into the Dell operations they supply. Suppliers use these windows to decide when and how much raw material to deliver to Dell. As another example, one of Regal Marine's suppliers goes to Regal's production floor, takes orders from Regal's assembly-line workers, and then delivers the materials directly to the production floor two days later.

Companies that adopt JIT strive for perfect quality because defects stop production lines. Firms that adopt JIT also commit to total quality management.

Total Quality Management

total quality management (TQM)
A philosophy of delighting customers by providing them with superior products and services. Requires improving quality and eliminating defects and waste throughout the value chain.

Companies must deliver high-quality goods and services to remain competitive. Hewlett-Packard and Ford in the United States, British Telecom in the United Kingdom, and Toyota in Japan view **total quality management (TQM)** as key to succeeding in the global economy. The goal of total quality management is to delight customers by providing them with superior products and services. Companies achieve this goal by improving quality and eliminating defects and waste throughout the value chain.

In TQM, each business function examines its own activities and works to improve performance by setting higher and higher goals. For example, Motorola wanted to reduce the time required to issue a purchase order. Motorola's purchasing department TQM team reduced the number of steps in handling a purchase order from 17 to 6, slashing average processing time from 30 minutes to 3. Service organizations also strive to improve quality. For example, the American Institute of Certified Public Accountants was the first professional membership organization in the United States to earn the ISO 9001 international certification for quality management and assurance.

The Appendix to Chapter 15 ➡
discusses present-value computations; we cover this subject in more detail in Chapter 26.

Quality improvement programs cost money today, but the benefits accrue over time. In deciding whether to undertake such projects, managers compare the project's cost to the present value today of the project's future benefits. (This is called *discounting* the future amounts to their *present values.*) ⬅ Also, because no one can foresee the future, the exact amount of the future benefits is not known. Let's see how managers adjust for this uncertainty.

GE recently started nearly 3,000 quality-related projects at a cost of more than $200 million. The first-year cost savings from these projects totaled only $170 million. Does this mean that GE made a bad decision? Not necessarily. GE expects these projects to continue yielding benefits in the future.

 Starter 19-12

Suppose GE managers predict these projects will be either moderately successful or extremely successful. Assume that if the projects are moderately successful, they will yield additional benefits (cost savings) with a present value of $20 million. If the projects are extremely successful, they will yield extra benefits with a present value of $100 million. GE managers think the projects are more likely to be extremely successful. Suppose they estimate a 60% chance that the

---

[3] "Compaq Stumbles as PCs Weather New Blow," *Wall Street Journal*, March 9, 1998, page B1.

projects will be extremely successful and a 40% chance that they will be moderately successful.

In an uncertain environment, managers make decisions based on expected values. We compute expected values by multiplying the dollar value of each possible outcome by the probability of that outcome, and then adding the results:

Outcome	Benefit	×	Probability	=	Expected Value (of Additional Benefit)
Extremely successful	$100 million	×	60% chance	=	$60 million
Moderately successful	20 million	×	40% chance	=	8 million
Total expected value of benefits					$68 million

What does this $68 million mean? If GE faced this exact situation ten times, it would expect to get $100 million in extra benefits six times and only $20 million of additional benefits four times. The *average* extra benefits across the ten situations is $68 million.

Thus, the total benefits expected from GE's quality projects ($238 million—calculated as $170 million initial benefits + $68 million additional expected benefits) exceed the $200 million cost of the projects. This analysis suggests that GE's quality initiative was worthwhile.

Even after adopting quality programs, companies cannot rest on their laurels. TQM requires that companies (and individual employees) continually look for ways to improve performance. This is the **continuous improvement** philosophy.

How do companies improve? Many businesses find that investments in higher quality earlier in the value chain (R&D and design) generate savings in later stages (production, marketing, and customer service). Successful companies design and build quality into their products and services rather than depending on finding and fixing defects later. For example, by increasing the proportion of vehicles built right the first time from 50% to 70%, General Motors cut average warranty costs from roughly $1,600 to $1,000 per vehicle, in addition to reducing costs of rework and inspections.

continuous improvement
A philosophy requiring employees to continually look for ways to improve performance.

 Use reasonable standards to make ethical judgments.

Ethical Standards

As is evident from the accounting scandals that felled multinational giants like Enron and WorldCom, ethical behavior is a critical component of quality. Unfortunately, the ethical path is not always clear. You may want to act ethically and do the right thing, but the consequences can make it difficult to decide what to do. Consider the following examples:

■ Sarah Baker is examining the expense reports of her staff, who counted inventory at Top-Flight's warehouses in Arizona. She discovers that Mike Flinders has claimed but not included hotel receipts for over $1,000 of accommodation expenses. Other staff, who also claimed $1,000, did attach hotel receipts. When asked about the receipt, Mike admits that he stayed with an old friend, not in the hotel, but he believes he deserves the money he saved. After all, the company would have paid his hotel bill.

■ As the accountant of Entreé Computer Co., you are aware of your company's weak financial condition. Entreé is close to signing a lucrative contract that should ensure its future. To do so, the controller states that the company *must* report a profit this year (ending December 31). He suggests: "Two customers have placed orders that are really not supposed to be shipped until early January. Ask production to fill and ship those orders on December 31, so we can record them in this year's sales."

The Institute of Management Accountants (IMA) has developed standards to help management accountants deal with these situations. The standards remind us that society expects professional accountants to exhibit the highest level of ethical behavior. An excerpt from the *Standards of Ethical Conduct for Management Accountants* appears in Exhibit 19-14. These standards require management accountants to

- Maintain their professional competence
- Preserve the confidentiality of the information they handle
- Act with integrity and objectivity

Exhibit 19-14

IMA Standards of Ethical Conduct for Management Accountants (excerpt)

✔ **Starter 19-13**

✔ **Starter 19-14**

Management accountants have an obligation to maintain the highest standards of ethical conduct. These standards include

Competence

- Maintain professional competence by ongoing development of knowledge and skills.
- Perform professional duties in accordance with relevant laws, regulations, and technical standards.

Confidentiality

- Refrain from disclosing confidential information acquired in the course of work except when authorized, unless legally obligated to do so.

Integrity

- Avoid actual or apparent conflicts of interest and advise all appropriate parties of any potential conflict.
- Refuse any gift, favor, or hospitality that would influence or would appear to influence actions.
- Communicate unfavorable as well as favorable information and professional judgments or opinions.

Objectivity

- Communicate information fairly and objectively.

Source: Adapted from Institute of Management Accountants, *Standards of Ethical Conduct for Management Accountants* (Montvale, N.J.).

To resolve ethical dilemmas, the IMA also suggests discussing ethical situations with your immediate supervisor, or with an objective adviser.

Let's return to the two ethical dilemmas. By asking to be reimbursed for hotel expenses he did not incur, Mike Flinders violated the IMA's integrity standards (conflict of interest in which he tried to enrich himself at company expense). Because Sarah Baker discovered the inflated expense report, she would not be fulfilling her ethical responsibilities (integrity and objectivity) if she allowed the reimbursement and did not take disciplinary action.

The second dilemma, in which the controller asked you to accelerate the shipments, is less clear-cut. You should discuss the available alternatives and their consequences with others. Many people believe that following the controllers' suggestion to manipulate the company's income would violate the standards of competence, integrity, and objectivity. Others would argue that because Entreé Computer already has the customer order, shipping the goods and recording the sale in December is still ethical behavior. If you refuse to ship the goods in December and you simply resign without attempting to find an alternative solution, you might only hurt yourself and your family.

Weighing costs against benefits to make the best decision comes up again and again in management accounting. Study the Cost-Benefit Analysis Decision Guidelines to make sure you understand this important concept.

Decision Guidelines

COST-BENEFIT ANALYSIS

The company in the chapter-opening story, **Regal Marine**, has responded to changes in the business environment by developing a worldwide network of dealers and a stunning Web site, and by using supply-chain management, JIT, and TQM. Here are some of the key decisions Regal's managers considered to ensure that the company thrives in the future.

Decision	Guidelines
How to compete in a globally wired economy?	Update information systems, embrace e-commerce, and use supply-chain management, JIT, and TQM to compete more effectively.
How to decide whether to undertake new projects such as international expansion, ERP, JIT, and TQM?	Cost-benefit analysis: Compute the benefits of the project and compare with the costs. Undertake the project if benefits exceed costs. Abandon the project if costs exceed benefits.
How to adjust the cost-benefit analysis if the exact amount of the benefit (or cost) is not known?	Compute the *expected value* of the benefits (or costs) of each outcome as follows: $$\text{Estimated amount} \times \text{Probability of occurrence} = \text{Expected value}$$ Then add the expected values across all possible outcomes.
How to resolve an ethical dilemma?	Weigh the costs and benefits of alternative courses of action. Consult the IMA's *Standards of Ethical Conduct for Management Accountants* (Exhibit 19-14). Also consult the Framework for Ethical Judgments in Chapter 8.

Excel Application Exercise

Goal: Create a spreadsheet to assess the costs and benefits of a new project, and use the results to answer questions about the decision.

Scenario: Dennis Popper of EZ-Rider Motorcycles has asked you to prepare an Excel spreadsheet that calculates the net benefits (expected value of benefits minus total costs) of expansion into Germany. The background data for EZ-Rider's expansion project appears in the End-of-Chapter Summary Problem, which follows.

When you have completed your worksheet, answer the following questions:

1. What is the expected value of the benefits of the expansion project? What are the total costs? Does the expected value of the benefits exceed the total costs? If so, what is the expected value of the net benefits?

2. What is the minimum probability of a gas price increase that would justify the expansion? What is the expected value of the net benefits at this point?

(continued on the next page)

Excel Application Exercise *(continued)*

Step-by-Step:

1. Open a new Excel spreadsheet.
2. Create a boldfaced heading as follows:
   a. Chapter 19 Excel Application Exercise
   b. Cost-Benefit Analysis
   c. EZ-Rider Motorcycles
   d. Today's Date
3. Two rows down, enter the heading "Cost Data" in column A. Under the heading, enter the data (with descriptions) needed to calculate total costs. Compute total costs. (For help in formatting currency in euros, click "Help," then search for "euro symbol.")
4. Move down three rows. In the first column, enter the bold-faced and underlined heading "PV If Stable Gas Price."
5. Under this heading, enter the present value of the project if gas prices remain stable. Copy the cell contents down 10 more rows.
6. In the next column, enter the boldfaced and underlined heading, "Probability of Stable Gas Price." Spread the heading over two rows.
7. Under this heading, enter a probability of 100%. In the next 10 rows, decrement 100% by 10% each row, so that the probability is zero at the bottom.
8. In the next column, enter the boldfaced and underlined heading, "PV If Gas Price Increases."
9. Under this heading, enter the present value of the project if gas prices increase. Copy the cell contents down 10 more rows.
10. In the next column, enter the boldfaced and underlined heading, "Probability of Gas Price Increase." Spread the heading over two rows.
11. Under this heading, enter a probability of 0%. In the next 10 rows, increment the percentage by 10% each row, so that the probability is 100% at the bottom.
12. In the next column, enter the boldfaced and underlined heading, "Expected Value of Benefits." Spread the heading over two rows. Compute the expected value for all combinations of percentages for each row.
13. In the last column, enter the boldfaced and underlined heading, "Expected Value of Net Benefits." Spread the heading over two rows. Compute the net benefits for all rows.
14. Save your file to disk and print a copy for your files.

● END-OF-CHAPTER *Summary Problem*

CHECK YOUR RESOURCES

This summary review problem shows how you can apply cost-benefit analysis to a decision about international expansion.

EZ-Rider Motorcycles is considering whether to expand into Germany. If gas prices increase, EZ-Rider expects more interest in fuel-efficient transportation such as motorcycles. EZ-Rider is considering setting up a motorcycle-assembly plant on the outskirts of Berlin.

EZ-Rider estimates it will cost €850,000 (850,000 euros) to convert an existing building to motorcycle production. Workers will need training, at a total cost of €65,000. The CEO of EZ-Rider, Dennis Popper, would have to spend a month in Berlin to organize the business and to establish relationships. He estimates the cost of this travel at €43,000.

Popper sees a 60% chance that the price of gasoline in Germany will increase significantly. If this increase occurs, he believes EZ-Rider can earn profits (before considering the costs in the preceding paragraph) with a present value of €1,624,000. However, if gas prices remain stable, Popper expects to earn profits of only about €812,000. He believes there is a 40% chance that gas prices will remain stable.

Required

1. What are the total costs of EZ-Rider's proposed expansion into Germany?
2. Compute the *expected value* of the benefits if EZ-Rider expands into Germany.
3. Do the benefits outweigh the costs of expanding into Germany?

Solution

Requirement 1

The total costs are as follows:

Conversion of manufacturing plant...............	€850,000
Workforce training.............................	65,000
Popper's trip to Berlin	43,000
Total costs	€958,000

Requirement 2

Expected value of the benefits is computed as follows:

Benefit	×	Probability	=	Expected Value
€1,624,000	×	0.60	=	€ 974,400
812,000	×	0.40	=	324,800
				€1,299,200

The *expected value* of the benefits, or profits is €1,299,200. This means that should EZ-Rider find itself in this exact situation many times, its average profits across all the situations would be €1,299,200.

Requirement 3

Yes, the total expected benefits outweigh the costs of the expansion:

Total expected benefits of expansion (from requirement 2)	€1,299,200
Total costs of expansion (from requirement 1)	958,000
Net benefits of expansion	€ 341,200

●REVIEW *Introduction to Management Accounting*

Quick Check

1. Which is *not* a characteristic of management accounting information?
   a. Emphasizes relevance
   b. Focuses on the future
   c. Provides detailed information about parts of the company, not just the company as a whole
   d. Emphasizes reliability

2. Which is *not* an element of **Regal Marine's** value chain?
   a. Administrative costs
   b. Cost of trucking boats to customers
   c. Salaries of engineers who update boat design
   d. Cost of print ads and attending boat shows

3. For Regal, which is a direct cost with respect to the LSR 1800 sportboat?
   a. Depreciation on plant and equipment
   b. Cost of boat engine
   c. Salary of engineer who rearranges plant layout
   d. Cost of customer hotline

4. Which of the following is *not* part of Regal Marine's manufacturing overhead?
   a. Insurance on plant and equipment
   b. Depreciation on delivery trucks
   c. Plant property taxes
   d. Plant utilities

5. In computing cost of goods sold, which of the following is the manufacturer's counterpart to the merchandiser's purchases?
   a. Direct materials used
   b. Total manufacturing costs incurred during the period
   c. Total manufacturing costs to account for
   d. Cost of goods manufactured

Questions 6, 7, and 8 refer to the list that follows. Suppose Regal Marine reports this information (in hundreds of thousands of dollars):

Beginning materials inventory........................	$ 6
Ending materials inventory	5
Beginning work in process inventory..................	2
Ending work in process inventory	1
Beginning finished goods inventory...................	3
Ending finished goods inventory	5
Direct labor	30
Purchases of direct materials	100
Manufacturing overhead	20

6. What is the cost of the direct materials that Regal used?
   a. $99
   b. $100
   c. $101
   d. $106

7. What is the cost of goods manufactured?
   a. $149
   b. $150
   c. $151
   d. $152

8. What is the cost of goods sold?
   a. $150
   b. $152
   c. $153
   d. $154

9. Suppose Regal Marine is considering buying an ERP system for $800,000. Regal would spend another $600,000 implementing the system. Management estimates there is a 40% chance that Regal could implement the system on its own, but a 60% chance that it will have to purchase assistance from **Accenture** at an additional cost of $500,000. Regal expects the ERP system to lead to savings with a present value of $1,800,000. What is the net benefit (or cost) of implementing the ERP system?
   a. $100,000 net benefit
   b. $400,000 net benefit
   c. $100,000 net cost
   d. $300,000 net cost

10. A management accountant who refuses an expensive gift from a software salesman meets the ethical standard of
    a. Objectivity
    b. Confidentiality
    c. Integrity
    d. Competence

Accounting Vocabulary

budget (p. 753)
continuous improvement (p. 773)
controlling (p. 753)
cost-benefit analysis (p. 754)
cost object (p. 757)
cost of goods manufactured (p. 762)
customer service (p. 757)
design (p. 756)
direct cost (p. 758)
direct labor (p. 759)
direct materials (p. 759)
distribution (p. 757)
enterprise resource planning (ERP) (p. 769)

factory overhead (p. 759)
finished goods inventory (p. 756)
full product costs (p. 758)
indirect cost (p. 758)
indirect labor (p. 760)
indirect manufacturing cost (p. 759)
indirect materials (p. 760)
inventoriable product costs (p. 758)
just-in-time (JIT) (p. 771)
manufacturing company (p. 755)
manufacturing overhead (p. 759)
marketing (p. 757)
materials inventory (p. 756)

merchandising company (p. 755)
period costs (p. 758)
planning (p. 753)
production or purchases (p. 756)
research and development (R&D) (p. 756)
service company (p. 755)
supply-chain management (p. 771)
throughput time (p. 771)
total quality management (TQM) (p. 772)
value chain (p. 756)
work in process inventory (p. 756)

●ASSESS *Your Progress*

Starters

See *www.prenhall.com/horngren* for selected Starters, Exercises, and Problems.

S19-1 Your roommate, who plans to specialize in international business, is considering whether to enroll in the second principles of accounting course. She says, "I don't want to be an accountant, so why do I need a second accounting course? I just spent a whole term on financial accounting. Most of this second course focuses on management accounting, but how can that be so different from what I already learned in financial accounting?" Respond.

Distinguishing financial from management accounting
(Obj. 1)

S19-2 Give an example of costs that **E*TRADE** (an online brokerage firm) might incur in each of the six business functions in the value chain. Provide another example that shows how E*TRADE might deliberately decide to spend more money on one of the six business functions in order to reduce the costs in other business functions.

Classifying costs by value-chain function
(Obj. 2)

S19-3 Classify each of **Hewlett-Packard's** costs as one of the six business functions in the value chain.

Classifying costs by value-chain function
(Obj. 2)

a. Depreciation on Roseville, California, plant.
b. Costs of a customer support center Web site.
c. Transportation costs to deliver laser printers to retailers, like **Best Buy**.
d. Depreciation on research lab.
e. Cost of a prime-time TV ad featuring the new Hewlett-Packard logo.
f. Salary of scientists at Hewlett-Packard Laboratories who are developing new printer technologies.
g. Purchase of plastic used in printer casings.
h. Salary of engineers who are redesigning the printer's on–off switch.
i. Depreciation on delivery vehicles.
j. Plant manager's salary.

S19-4 Consider **Marvin Windows'** manufacturing plant. Give two examples of

Distinguishing between direct and indirect costs
(Obj. 3)

a. Direct materials   **d.** Indirect labor
b. Direct labor   **e.** Other manufacturing overhead
c. Indirect materials

S19-5 Classify each of **Georgia-Pacific's** costs as either inventoriable or period costs:

Inventoriable vs. period costs
(Obj. 3)

a. Depreciation on the gypsum board plant.
b. Purchase of lumber to be cut into boards.
c. Life insurance on CEO.
d. Salaries of scientists studying ways to speed forest growth.
e. Cost of a new software package to track inventory.
f. Cost of electricity at one of Georgia-Pacific's paper mills.
g. Salaries of Georgia-Pacific's top executives.
h. Cost of mold inhibitor applied to treated lumber.
i. Cost of TV ads promoting environmental awareness.

S19-6 ← *Link Back to Chapter 5.* Given the following information for Circuits Plus, an electronics e-tailer, compute the cost of goods sold.

Preparing the cost-of-goods-sold section of a merchandiser's income statement
(Obj. 4)

Web site maintenance	$7,000
Delivery expenses	1,000
Freight in	3,000
Purchases	40,000
Ending inventory	5,500
Revenues	60,000
Marketing expenses	10,000
Beginning inventory	3,500

Computing the cost of goods manufactured
(Obj. 4)

S19-7 Turn to Exhibit 19-11 (page 764). If direct material purchases were $20,000 rather than $27,000, what would be the cost of direct materials used and the cost of goods manufactured? (Other costs remain the same as in Exhibit 19-11.)

Computing manufacturing overhead
(Obj. 4)

S19-8 Snap's manufactures disposable cameras. Suppose the company's March records include the following items. What is Snap's total manufacturing overhead cost in March?

Glue for camera frames	$ 250	Company president's salary ..	$25,000
Depreciation expense on company cars used by sales force	3,000	Plant foreman's salary	4,000
		Plant janitor's salary.........	1,000
		Oil for manufacturing equipment	25
Plant depreciation expense ..	10,000		
Interest expense..........	2,000	Flash bulbs................	50,000

Computing direct materials used
(Obj. 4)

S19-9 You are a new accounting intern at Sunny's Bikes, Inc. Your boss gives you the following information and asks you to compute direct materials used.

Purchases of direct materials.......................	$17,000
Freight in..	200
Freight out	1,000
Ending inventory of direct materials	1,500
Beginning inventory of direct materials.............	4,000

Differences among service, merchandising, and manufacturing companies' balance sheets
(Obj. 4)

S19-10 The current asset sections of the balance sheets of three companies follow. Which company is a service company? Which is a merchandiser? Which is a manufacturer? How can you tell?

X-Treme		Y-Not?		Zesto	
Cash	$ 2,500	Cash	$3,000	Cash....................	$ 2,000
Accounts receivable.......	5,500	Accounts receivable	6,000	Accounts receivable.......	5,000
Inventory................	8,000	Prepaid expenses	500	Materials inventory.......	1,000
Prepaid expenses	300	Total	$9,500	Work in process inventory .	800
Total	$16,300			Finished goods inventory..	4,000
				Total....................	$12,800

Understanding JIT
(Obj. 5)

S19-11 Is JIT more appropriate for **Amazon.com**, a book, music, and electronics e-tailer, or **Mouton-Rothschild**, a French winemaker specializing in fine red wines? Explain.

Expected value of the benefits of a quality program
(Obj. 5)

S19-12 Consider the cost-benefit analysis for the **GE** quality program discussed on pages 772 and 773. Suppose GE's managers now estimate an 85% chance that the projects will yield an extra $20 million in benefits, and a 15% chance that the projects will yield an extra $80 million. What is the expected value of the additional benefits *now*? Assuming total costs remain $200 million, does this change your mind about whether the quality program was a worthwhile investment? (Hint: Remember the initial cost savings given on page 772.)

Understanding ethics
(Obj. 6)

S19-13 Explain why each of the four broad ethical standards in the Institute of Management Accountants' *Standards of Ethical Conduct for Management Accountants* (Exhibit 19-14, page 774) is necessary.

S19-14 The Institute of Management Accountants' *Standards of Ethical Conduct for Management Accountants* (Exhibit 19-14, page 774) require management accountants to meet standards regarding

Making ethical decisions
(Obj. 6)

- Competence
- Confidentiality
- Integrity
- Objectivity

Consider the following situations. Which guidelines are violated in each situation?

a. You tell your brother that your company will report earnings significantly above financial analysts' estimates.

b. You see that others take home office supplies for personal use. As an intern, you do the same thing, assuming that this is a "perk."

c. At a conference on e-commerce, you skip the afternoon session and go sightseeing.

d. You failed to read the detailed specifications of a new general ledger package that you asked your company to purchase. After it is installed, you are surprised that it is incompatible with some of your company's older accounting software.

e. You do not provide top management with the detailed job descriptions they requested because you fear they may use this information to cut a position from your department.

Exercises

A⁺ online homework

E19-1 Complete the following statements with one of the terms listed here. You may use a term more than once, and some terms may not be used at all.

Management vs. financial accounting and managers' use of information
(Obj. 1)

Budget	Creditors	Managers	Planning
Controlling	Financial accounting	Management accounting	Shareholders

a. Companies must follow GAAP in their _____ systems.

b. Financial accounting develops reports for external parties, such as _____ and _____.

c. When managers evaluate the company's performance compared to the plan, they are performing the _____ role of management.

d. _____ are decision makers inside a company.

e. _____ provides information on a company's past performance.

f. _____ systems are not restricted by GAAP but are chosen by comparing the costs versus the benefits of the system.

g. Choosing goals and the means to achieve them is the _____ function of management.

E19-2 Suppose the cell phone manufacturer **Samsung Electronics** provides the following information for its costs last month (in hundreds of thousands):

Value chain, direct and indirect costs, inventoriable costs
(Obj. 2, 3)

Salaries of telephone salespeople . . $ 5	Transmitters $61
Depreciation on plant and equipment 65	Rearrange production process to accommodate new robot 2
Exterior case for phone 6	Assembly-line workers' wages . . 10
Salaries of scientists who developed new model 12	Technical customer-support hotline 3
Delivery expense via **Airborne Express** 7	1-800 (toll-free) line for customer orders 1

(continued on next page)

Required

1. Use the following format to classify each cost according to its place in the value chain. (*Hint:* You should have at least one cost in each value-chain function.)

R&D	Design of Products, Services, or Processes	Production			Marketing	Distribution	Customer Service
		Direct Materials	Direct Labor	Manufacturing Overhead			

2. Compute the total costs for each value-chain category.

3. How much are the total inventoriable product costs?

Value chain, inventoriable costs
(Obj. 2, 3)

E19-3 Suppose **Radio Shack** incurred the following costs at its Charleston, South Carolina, store.

Research on whether store should sell satellite radio service...... $	400	Payment to consultant for advice on location of new store....................	$2,500
Purchases of merchandise ...	30,000	Freight in	3,000
Rearranging store layout	750	Salespersons' salaries	4,000
Newspaper advertisements	5,000	Customer complaint department.............	800
Depreciation expense on delivery trucks...........	1,000		

Required

1. Use the following format to classify each cost according to its place in the value chain.

R&D	Design of Products, Services, or Processes	Purchases of Merchandise Inventory	Marketing	Distribution	Customer Service

2. Compute the total costs for each value-chain category.

3. How much are the total inventoriable product costs?

Service, merchandising, and manufacturing companies and their inventories
(Obj. 4)

E19-4 Complete the following statements with one of the terms listed here. You may use a term more than once, and some terms may not be used at all.

Finished goods inventory	Inventory (merchandise)	Service companies
Manufacturing companies	Merchandising companies	Work in process inventory
Materials inventory		

a. _____ produce their own inventory.

b. _____ typically have a single category of inventory.

c. _____ do not have tangible products intended for sale.

d. _____ resell products they previously purchased ready-made from suppliers.

e. _____ use their workforce and equipment to transform raw materials into new finished products.

(continued on next page)

f. Swaim, a company based in North Carolina, makes furniture. Partially completed sofas are _____. Completed sofas that remain unsold in the warehouse are _____. Fabric and wood are _____.

g. For **Kellogg's,** corn, cardboard boxes, and waxed-paper liners are classified as _____.

E19-5 Consider the following selected amounts and account balances of Lords:

Reporting current assets
(Obj. 4)

Cost of goods sold	$104,000	Prepaid expenses	$ 6,000
Direct labor	47,000	Marketing expense	30,000
Direct materials used	20,000	Work in process inventory	40,000
Accounts receivable	80,000	Manufacturing overhead	26,000
Cash	15,000	Finished goods inventory	63,000
Cost of goods manufactured	94,000	Materials inventory	10,000

Show how Lords reports current assets on the balance sheet. Not all data are used. Is Lords a service company, a merchandiser, or a manufacturer? How do you know?

E19-6 Compute the 20X5 cost of goods manufactured and cost of goods sold for Strike Marine Company using the following amounts: *Computing CGM and CGS* **(Obj. 3, 4)**

Student ResourceCD
spreadsheet

	Beginning of Year	End of Year		End of Year
Materials inventory	$25,000	$28,000	Insurance on plant	$ 9,000
Work in process inventory	50,000	35,000	Depreciation—plant building and equipment	13,000
Finished goods inventory	18,000	25,000	Repairs and maintenance—plant	4,000
Purchases of raw materials		78,000	Marketing expenses	77,000
Direct labor		82,000	General and administrative expenses	29,000
Indirect labor		15,000	Income tax expense	23,000

E19-7 Prepare the 20X5 income statement for the Strike Marine Company in Exercise 19-6. Assume that it sold 32,000 units of its product at a price of $12 during 20X5. *Preparing a manufacturer's I/S* **(Obj.4)**

E19-8 Smooth Sounds manufactures and sells a new line of MP-3 players. Unfortunately, Smooth Sounds suffered serious fire damage at its home office. As a result, the accounting records for October were partially destroyed—and completely jumbled. Smooth Sounds has hired you to help figure out the missing pieces of the accounting puzzle.

Student ResourceCD
spreadsheet

Flow of costs through manufacturing companies
(Obj. 3, 4)

Work in process inventory, October 31	$ 1,500	Accounts payable, October 1	$3,000
Finished goods inventory, October 1	4,300	Direct materials used in October	8,000
Direct labor in October	3,000	Accounts payable, October 31	5,200
Purchases of direct materials in October	9,000	Accounts receivable, October 31	6,500
Work in process inventory, October 1	0	Direct materials inventory, October 31	3,000
Revenues in October	27,000		
Accounts receivable, October 1	2,000	Manufacturing overhead in October	6,300
Gross profit in October	12,000		

(continued on next page)

Required Find the following amounts:

a. Cost of goods sold in October
b. Beginning direct materials inventory
c. Ending finished goods inventory

    (*Hint:* You may find Exhibit 19-12 helpful.)

Understanding today's business environment
(Obj. 5)

E19-9 Complete the following statements with one of the terms listed here. You may use a term more than once, and some terms may not be used at all.

E-commerce	Future value	Shift to service economy
ERP	JIT	Throughput time
Expected value	Present	TQM
Future	Present value	

a. To account for uncertainty in the amounts of future costs and benefits, we compute the _____ by multiplying the probability of each outcome by the dollar value of that outcome.
b. To make a cost-benefit decision today, we must find the _____ of the costs and benefits that are incurred in the future.
c. The goal of _____ is to delight customers by providing them with superior products and services by eliminating defects and waste throughout the value chain.
d. Most of the costs of adopting ERP, JIT, expanding into a foreign market, or improving quality are incurred in the _____, but most of the benefits occur in the _____.
e. _____ is the time between buying raw materials and selling the finished products.
f. _____ serves the information needs of people in accounting, as well as people in marketing and in the warehouse.
g. Firms adopt _____ to conduct business on the Internet.

Comparing costs and benefits of adopting JIT
(Obj. 5)

E19-10 Wild Rides manufactures snowboards. Shawn Mobbs, the CEO, is trying to decide whether to adopt just-in-time (JIT). He expects that in present-value terms, adopting JIT would save $97,000 in warehousing expenses and $46,000 in spoilage costs.

    Adopting JIT will require several one-time up-front expenditures: (1) $13,500 for an employee training program, (2) $37,000 to streamline the plant's production process, and (3) $8,000 to identify suppliers that will guarantee zero defects and on-time delivery.

Required

1. What are the total costs of adopting JIT?
2. What are the total benefits of adopting JIT?
3. Should Wild Rides adopt JIT? Why or why not?

Making ethical decisions
(Obj. 6)

E19-11 Mary Gonzales is the controller at Automax, a car dealership. Cory Loftus has recently been hired as bookkeeper. Cory wanted to attend a class on Excel spreadsheets, so Mary temporarily took over Cory's duties, including overseeing a fund for topping up a car's gas before a test drive. Mary found a shortage in this fund and confronted Cory when he returned to work. Cory admitted that he occasionally uses this fund to pay for his own gas. Mary estimated that the amount involved is close to $300.

Required

1. What should Mary Gonzales do?
2. Would you change your answer to the previous question if Mary Gonzales was the one recently hired as controller and Cory Loftus was a well-liked longtime employee who indicated that he always eventually repaid the fund?

Problems

(Group A)

P19-1A ShaZam Cola produces a lemon-lime soda. The production process starts with workers mixing the lemon syrup and lime flavors in a secret recipe. The combined syrup is enhanced with caffeine. Finally, the mixture is diluted with carbonated water.

ShaZam Cola incurs the following costs (in thousands):

Value chain, direct vs. indirect costs, inventoriable costs
(Obj. 2, 3)

Plant utilities	$ 750	Production costs of "cents-off" store coupons for customers....	$ 600
Depreciation on plant and equipment	3,000	Delivery-truck drivers' wages	250
Payment for new recipe.	1,000	Bottles	1,300
Salt	25	Sales commissions.	400
Replace products with expired dates upon customer complaint.	50	Plant janitors' wages.	1,000
Rearranging plant layout	1,100	Wages of workers who mix syrup	8,000
Lemon syrup	18,000	Customer hotline.	200
Lime flavoring.	1,000	Depreciation on delivery trucks	150
		Freight in.	1,500
		Total	$38,325

Required

1. Use the following format to classify each of these costs according to its place in the value chain. (*Hint:* You should have at least one cost in each value-chain function.)

	Design of Products or	Production					
R&D	Processes	Direct Materials	Direct Labor	Manufacturing Overhead	Marketing	Distribution	Customer Service

2. Compute the total costs for each value-chain category.
3. How much are the total inventoriable product costs?
4. Suppose the managers of the R&D and design functions receive year-end bonuses based on meeting their own unit's target cost reductions. What are they likely to do? How might this affect costs incurred in other elements of the value chain?

P19-2A *Part One:* In 20X7, Hannah Summit opened Hannah's Pets, a small retail shop selling pet supplies. On December 31, 20X7, her accounting records show the following:

Preparing financial statements for merchandising and manufacturing companies
(Obj. 3, 4)

Inventory on December 31, 20X7	$10,250
Inventory on January 1, 20X7	15,000
Sales revenue.	54,000
Utilities for shop.	2,450
Rent for shop.	4,000
Sales commissions	2,300
Purchases of merchandise.	27,000

Required Prepare an income statement for Hannah's Pets, a merchandiser, for the year ended December 31, 20X7.

(continued on next page)

Part Two: Hannah's Pets succeeded so well that Hannah decided to manufacture her own brand of pet toys—Best Friends. At the end of December 20X8, her accounting records show the following:

Work in process inventory, December 31, 20X8	$ 720	Plant janitorial services	$ 1,250
Finished goods inventory, December 31, 20X7	0	Direct labor	18,300
Finished goods inventory, December 31, 20X8	5,700	Direct material purchases	31,000
Sales revenue	105,000	Rent on manufacturing plant	9,000
Customer service hotline expense	1,000	Direct materials inventory, December 31, 20X7.....	13,500
Utilities for plant	4,600	Direct materials inventory, December 31, 20X8.....	9,275
Delivery expense................................	1,500	Work in process inventory, December 31, 20X7. ...	0
Sales salaries expense	5,000		

Required

1. Prepare a schedule of cost of goods manufactured for Best Friends Manufacturing for the year ended December 31, 20X8.

2. Prepare an income statement for Best Friends Manufacturing for the year ended December 31, 20X8.

3. How does the format of the income statement for Best Friends Manufacturing differ from the income statement of Hannah's Pets?

Part Three: Show the ending inventories that would appear on these balance sheets:

1. Hannah's Pets at December 31, 20X7.
2. Best Friends Manufacturing at December 31, 20X8.

Preparing financial statements for a manufacturer
(Obj. 4)

P19-3A Certain item descriptions and amounts are missing from the monthly schedule of cost of goods manufactured and the income statement of Tretinik Manufacturing Company. Fill in the missing items.

_____ Manufacturing Company		
_____ June 30, 20X6		
Beginning _____		$21,000
Direct _____ :		
Beginning materials inventory	$ X	
Purchases of materials	51,000	
_____	78,000	
Ending materials inventory	(23,000)	
Direct _____		$ X
Direct _____		X
Manufacturing overhead.................		40,000
Total _____ costs _____		166,000
Total _____ costs _____		X
Ending _____		(25,000)
_____		$ X

(continued on next page)

_____ Manufacturing Company

_____ June 30, 20X6

Sales revenue	$ X	
Cost of goods sold:		
Beginning _____	$115,000	
_____	X	
Cost of goods _____	X	
Ending _____	X	
Cost of goods sold.		209,000
Gross profit.		254,000
_____ expenses:		
Marketing expense	99,000	
Administrative expense	X	154,000
_____ income		$ X

P19-4A As CEO of SeaSpray Marine, Ron Greenwood knows it is important to control costs and to respond quickly to changes in the highly competitive boat-building industry. When IDG Consulting proposes that SeaSpray invest in an ERP system, he forms a team to evaluate the proposal: the plant engineer, the plant foreman, the systems specialist, the human resources director, the marketing director, and the management accountant.

Using cost-benefit analysis to compute the expected value of an ERP installation **(Obj. 5)**

A month later, management accountant Mike Cobalt reports that the team and IDG estimate that if SeaSpray implements the ERP system, it will incur the following costs:

a. $350,000 in software costs
b. $80,000 to customize the ERP software and load SeaSpray's data into the new ERP system
c. $125,000 for employee training

The team estimates that the ERP system should provide several benefits:

a. More-efficient order processing should lead to savings with a present value of $185,000.
b. Streamlining the manufacturing process so that it maps into the ERP system will create savings with a present value of $275,000.
c. Integrating purchasing, production, marketing, and distribution into a single system will allow SeaSpray to reduce inventories, saving $220,000.
d. Higher customer satisfaction should increase sales, which in turn should increase the present value of profits by $150,000.

The team knows that because of complexity, some ERP installations are not successful. If SeaSpray's fails, there will be no cost savings and no additional sales. The team predicts that there is an 80% chance that the ERP installation will succeed and a 20% chance that it will fail.

Required

1. If the ERP installation succeeds, what is the dollar amount of the benefits?
2. Should SeaSpray install the ERP system? Why or why not? Show your calculations.

P19-5A Problem 19-4A asked you to perform a quantitative analysis to help SeaSpray's managers decide whether to install an ERP system. Now consider some qualitative factors.

ERP, expected value **(Obj. 5)**

Required

1. Why did Ron Greenwood create a team to evaluate IDG's proposal? Consider each piece of cost-benefit information that management accountant Mike Cobalt reported. Which person on the team is most likely to have contributed each item? (_Hint:_ Which team member is likely to have the most information about each cost or benefit?)

(_continued on next page_)

2. Quantifying ERP benefits can be difficult. After further discussion, the team predicts that there is a 60% chance that the ERP installation will succeed and a 40% chance that it will fail. Should SeaSpray still install the new ERP system?

Using cost-benefit analysis to evaluate an e-commerce project
(Obj. 5)

P19-6A Sun Gas Corporation wants to move its sales-order system to the Web. Under the proposed system, gas stations and other merchants will use a Web browser and, after typing in a password for the Sun Gas Web page, will be able to check the availability and current price of various products and place an order. Currently, customer service representatives take dealers' orders over the phone; they record the information on a paper form, then manually enter it into the firm's computer system.

CFO Carrie Smith believes that dealers will not adopt the new Web system unless Sun Gas provides financial assistance to help them purchase or upgrade their PCs. Smith estimates this one-time cost at $750,000. Sun Gas will also have to invest $150,000 in upgrading its own computer hardware. The cost of the software and the consulting fee for installing the system will be $230,000. The Web system will enable Sun Gas to eliminate 25 clerical positions. Smith estimates that the benefits of the new system's lower labor costs will have a present value of $1,357,000.

Required

Use a cost-benefit analysis to recommend to Carrie Smith whether Sun Gas should proceed with the Web-based ordering system. Give your reasons, showing supporting calculations.

Using cost-benefit analysis to compute the expected value of an e-commerce project
(Obj. 5)

P19-7A Consider the Sun Gas proposed entry into e-commerce in Problem 19-6A. Carrie Smith revises her estimates of the benefits from the new system's lower labor costs. She now thinks there is a 40% chance of receiving the $1,357,000 in benefits and a 60% chance the benefits will only be $933,000.

Required

1. Compute the expected benefits of the Web-based ordering system.
2. Would you recommend Sun Gas accept the proposal?
3. Before Carrie Smith makes a final decision, what other factors should she consider?

Making ethical decisions
(Obj. 6)

P19-8A Kate Royer is the new controller for ED Software, Inc., which develops and sells education software. Shortly before the December 31 fiscal year-end, Matt Adams, the company president, asks Royer how things look for the year-end numbers. He is not happy to learn that earnings growth may be below 15% for the first time in the company's five-year history. Adams explains that financial analysts have again predicted a 15% earnings growth for the company and that he does not intend to disappoint them. He suggests that Royer talk to the assistant controller, who can explain how the previous controller dealt with this situation. The assistant controller suggests the following strategies:

a. Persuade suppliers to postpone billing until January 1.
b. Record as sales certain software awaiting sale that is held in a public warehouse.
c. Delay the year-end closing a few days into January of the next year, so that some of next year's sales are included as this year's sales.
d. Reduce the allowance for bad debts (and bad debts expense), given the company's continued strong performance.
e. Postpone routine monthly maintenance expenditures from December to January.

Which of these suggested strategies are inconsistent with IMA standards? What should Royer do if Adams insists that she follow all of these suggestions?

Problems

(Group B)

P19-1B Suppose Apple Computer reported the following costs last month. (All costs are in millions.)

(continued on next page)

Payment to UPS for delivering PCs to customers	$ 300
Cost of hard drives used.....................................	4,700
Cost of Internet banner ads	650
Plant janitors' wages..	10
Wages of workers who assemble the PCs	1,500
Cost of customer hotline for troubleshooting problems	40
Wages of forklift drivers on the plant floor	25
Plant utilities...	35
Cost of software loaded on computers.........................	30
Depreciation on plant and equipment	300
Salaries of scientists working on next generation laptops..........	45
Insurance and taxes on plant property.........................	40
Cost of oil used for conveyor belt and other plant equipment	5
Payment to engineers redesigning the exterior case	20
Wages of sales associates taking phone orders	50
Cost of circuit boards used..................................	5,500
Total...	$13,250

Value chain, direct vs. indirect costs, inventoriable costs
(Obj. 2, 3)

Required

1. Use the following format to classify each of these costs according to its place in the value chain. (*Hint:* You should have at least one cost in each value-chain function.)

	Design of Products or	Production					
R&D	Processes	Direct Materials	Direct Labor	Manufacturing Overhead	Marketing	Distribution	Customer Service

2. Compute the total costs for each category.

3. How much are the total inventoriable product costs?

4. Suppose the managers of the R&D and design departments receive year-end bonuses based on meeting their own department's target cost reductions. What are they likely to do? How might this affect costs incurred in other elements of the value chain?

P19-2B *Part One:* On January 1, 2005, Terri Shaw opened Precious Memories, a small retail store dedicated to selling picture frames, crafts, and art. On December 31, 2005, her accounting records show the following:

Preparing financial statements for merchandising and manufacturing companies
(Obj. 3, 4)

Store rent................	$7,000	Sales revenue...............	$90,000
Sales salaries.............	4,500	Store utilities	1,950
Freight in................	550	Purchases of merchandise	36,000
Inventory on December 31, 2005	8,750	Inventory on January 1, 2005..	12,700
		Advertising expense.........	2,300

(*continued on next page*)

Required

Prepare an income statement for Precious Memories, a merchandiser, for the year ended December 31, 20X5.

Part Two: Precious Memories succeeded so well that Terri Shaw decided to manufacture her own special brand of picture frames, to be called Forever. At the end of December 20X7, her accounting records show the following:

Finished goods inventory, December 31, 20X7	$ 2,000	Rent on plant	$ 11,000
Work in process inventory, December 31, 20X7	1,750	Finished goods inventory, December 31, 20X6	0
Direct materials inventory, December 31, 20X7	7,750	Depreciation expense on delivery truck	2,500
R&D for graphic designs	3,700	Depreciation expense on plant	
Sales commissions	4,000	equipment	3,500
Utilities for plant	2,000	Work in process inventory, December 31, 20X6	0
Plant janitorial services	750	Sales revenue	126,450
Direct labor	20,000	Customer warranty refunds	1,500
Direct material purchases	32,000	Direct materials inventory, December 31, 20X6	13,000

Required

1. Prepare a schedule of cost of goods manufactured for Forever Manufacturing, for the year ended December 31, 20X7.
2. Prepare an income statement for Forever Manufacturing, for the year ended December 31, 20X7.
3. How does the format of the income statement for Forever Manufacturing differ from the income statement of Precious Memories?

Part Three: Show the ending inventories that would appear on these balance sheets:

1. Precious Memories at December 31, 2005.
2. Forever Manufacturing at December 31, 20X7.

Preparing financial statements for a manufacturer
(Obj. 4)

P19-3B Certain item descriptions and amounts are missing from the monthly schedule of cost of goods manufactured and income statement of Pacific Manufacturing Company. Fill in the missing items in the financial statement here and at the top of the next page.

_____ Manufacturing Company			
_____ April 30, 20X6			
_____ work in process inventory			$ 15,000
Direct materials used:			
_____ materials _____	$ X		
_____ of materials	65,000		
_____	75,000		
_____ materials _____	(23,000)		
Direct _____		$ X	
Direct _____		68,000	
Manufacturing overhead		X	
Total _____ costs _____			X
Total _____ costs _____			175,000
_____ work in process inventory			X
_____			$150,000

_____ Manufacturing Company		
_____ April 30, 20X6		
_____ revenue		$450,000
_____:		
Beginning _____	$ X	
_____	X	
Cost of goods _____	X	
Ending _____	(67,000)	
Cost of goods sold		X
_____		243,000
_____ expenses:		
Marketing expenses	X	
Administrative expenses	$64,000	X
_____		$ 76,000

P19-4B CRM, Inc., manufactures computer disk drives. It sells these disk drives to other manufacturers, which use them in assembling computers. CRM is having trouble with its new DVD drive. About half the time, CRM employees find defects while the disk drive is still on the production line. These drives are immediately reworked in the plant. Otherwise, CRM's customers do not identify the problem until they install the disk drives they've purchased. Customers return defective drives for replacement under warranty, and they have also complained that after they install the disk drive, the drive's connector (which plugs into the computer system board) often shakes loose while the computer is being assembled. The customer must then reassemble the computer after fixing the loose connection.

Using cost-benefit analysis to compute the expected value of a TQM program **(Obj. 5)**

CRM CEO Jay Rich has just returned from a seminar on total quality management (TQM). He forms a team to address these quality problems. The team includes the plant engineer, the production foreman, a customer service representative, the marketing director, and the management accountant.

Three months later, the team proposes a major project to *prevent* these quality problems. CRM's accountant Anna Crowe reports that implementing the team's proposal will require CRM to incur the following costs over the next three months:

- $180,500 for CRM scientists to develop a completely new disk drive.
- $70,000 for company engineers to redesign the connector so that it better tolerates rough treatment.

The project team is unsure whether this investment will pay off. If the effort fixes the problem, Crowe expects that

- A reputation for higher quality will increase sales, which in turn will increase the present value of profits by $200,000.
- Fewer disk drives will fail. The present value of the savings from fewer warranty repairs is $170,300.
- The plant will have fewer defective disk drives to rework. The present value of this savings is $100,200.

However, if this project is not successful, there will be no cost savings and no additional sales. The team predicts a 70% chance that the project will succeed and a 30% chance that it will fail.

Required

1. If the quality improvement project succeeds, what is the dollar amount of the benefits?
2. Should CRM undertake this project? Why or why not? Show supporting calculations.

Value chain, TQM
(Obj. 2, 5)

P19-5B Problem 19-4B asked you to perform a *quantitative* analysis to help CRM's managers decide whether to embark on the project. Now consider some *qualitative* factors in CRM's quality improvement project.

Required

1. Why did Jay Rich create a team to address this quality problem, rather than assigning the task to one person? Consider each piece of cost/benefit information reported by management accountant Anna Crowe. Which person on the team is most likely to have contributed each item? (*Hint:* Which team member is likely to have the most information about each cost or benefit?)

2. Classify the following amounts into one of the six value-chain business functions.
   a. $180,500 cost to develop the new disk drive
   b. $70,000 cost to redesign the connector
   c. $170,300 for warranty repairs on disk drives
   d. $100,200 to rework disk drives identified as defective while still in the factory

3. This problem illustrates how CRM can make trade-offs across business functions in the value chain. Which of the six value-chain functions are involved in the trade-offs proposed by the quality improvement team? What specific trade-offs do they propose?

Using cost-benefit analysis to evaluate an e-commerce project
(Obj. 5)

P19-6B Smart Bank processes checks for smaller banks and insurance companies. When a customer complains that a check was not deposited to its account, a Smart Bank clerk takes the complaint over the phone and fills out a paper form. The complaint form triggers a long search through piles of canceled checks in a warehouse to find the check in question. Smart Bank then compares this check to its computer and paper records.

Smart Bank is considering moving this process to the Web. When a customer has a question, an employee simply uses a Web browser and a password to access Smart Bank's databases. The customer's employee pulls up a computerized image of the check in question to verify the amount and then queries Smart Bank's databases to locate the mistake. If required, a credit to the customer's account can be issued immediately.

The Web-based system will require the bank to invest $83,000 in a new server and check-scanning equipment. eNow! consultants will charge $110,000 for the software and consulting fees to get the system running. The system will also require increasing the bank's Internet capacity. The present value of this cost is $20,000.

Smart Bank has identified two benefits of this project. First, several bank clerks freed from searching through stacks of canceled checks will be reassigned, which will lead to cost savings with a present value of $173,000. Second, the new system's additional capacity will enable Smart Bank to accept more check-processing business, which should lead to additional profits with a present value of $43,200.

Required

Does a cost-benefit analysis justify the Web-based system? Explain why, showing supporting calculations.

Using cost-benefit analysis to compute the expected value of an e-commerce project
(Obj. 5)

P19-7B Consider the Smart Bank project described in Problem 19-6B. Smart Bank has revised its estimates of additional profits the bank is likely to earn. There is an 80% chance that the bank will earn $43,200 in extra profits, but also a 20% chance the bank will earn $75,000.

Required

1. Compute the expected value of the benefits from the additional business.

2. Would you recommend that Smart Bank accept the proposal? Give your reason, showing supporting calculations.

3. Are there other potential benefits not listed in Problems 19-6B or 19-7B that may make the proposal more attractive to Smart Bank?

P19-8B Kara Williams is the new controller for Colors, a designer and manufacturer of sportswear. Shortly before the December 31 fiscal year-end, Lashea Lucas (the company president) asks Kara how things look for the year-end numbers. Lashea is not happy to learn that earnings growth may be below 10% for the first time in the company's five-year history. Lashea explains that financial analysts have again predicted a 12% earnings growth for the company and that she does not intend to disappoint them. She suggests that Kara talk to the assistant controller, who can explain how the previous controller dealt with this situation. The assistant controller suggests the following strategies:

Making ethical decisions
(Obj. 6)

a. Postpone planned advertising expenditures from December to January.
b. Do not record sales returns and allowances on the basis that they are individually immaterial.
c. Persuade retail customers to accelerate January orders to December.
d. Reduce the allowance for bad debts, given the company's continued strong performance.
e. Colors ships finished goods to public warehouses across the country for temporary storage, until it receives firm orders from customers. As Colors receives orders, it directs the warehouse to ship the goods to the nearby customer. The assistant controller suggests recording goods sent to the public warehouses as sales.

Which of these suggested strategies are inconsistent with IMA standards? What should Kara Williams do if Lashea Lucas insists that she follow all of these suggestions?

●APPLY *Your Knowledge*

Decision Cases

Case 1. PowerBox, Inc., designs and manufactures switches used in telecommunications. Serious flooding throughout North Carolina affected PowerBox's facilities. Inventory was completely ruined, and the company's computer system, including all accounting records, was destroyed.

Working backward, using the flow of costs through manufacturing companies to file an insurance claim
(Obj. 4)

Before the disaster recovery specialists clean the buildings, Annette Plum, the company controller, is anxious to salvage whatever records she can to support an insurance claim for the destroyed inventory. She is standing in what is left of the accounting department with Paul Lopez, the cost accountant.

"I didn't know mud could smell so bad," Paul says. "What should I be looking for?"

"Don't worry about beginning inventory numbers," responds Annette, "we'll get them from last year's annual report. We need first-quarter cost data."

"I was working on the first-quarter results just before the storm hit," Paul says. "Look, my report's still in my desk drawer. But all I can make out is that for the first quarter, material purchases were $476,000 and that direct labor, manufacturing overhead, and total manufacturing costs to account for were $505,000, $245,000, and $1,425,000, respectively. Wait, and cost of goods available for sale was $1,340,000."

"Great," says Annette. "I remember that sales for the period were approximately $1.7 million. Given our gross profit of 30%, that's all you should need."

Paul is not sure about that, but decides to see what he can do with this information. The beginning inventory numbers are

- Direct materials, $113,000
- Work in process, $229,000
- Finished goods, $154,000

He remembers a schedule he learned in college that may help him get started.

(continued on next page)

Required

1. Exhibit 19-12 resembles the schedule Paul has in mind. Use it to determine the ending inventories of direct materials, work in process, and finished goods.

2. Draft an insurance claim letter for the controller, seeking reimbursement for the flood damage to inventory. PowerBox's insurance representative is Gary Streer, at Industrial Insurance Co., 1122 Main Street, Hartford, CT 06268. The policy number is #3454340-23. PowerBox's address is 5 Research Triangle Way, Raleigh, NC 27698.

Applying ethical standards in daily life
(Obj. 6)

Case 2. The IMA's *Standards of Ethical Conduct for Management Accountants* can be applied to more than just management accounting. They are also relevant to college students. Explain at least one situation that shows how each IMA standard in Exhibit 19-14 is relevant to your experiences as a student. For example, the ethical standard of competence would suggest not cutting classes!

Ethical Issue

Making ethical decisions
(Obj. 6)

← *Link Back to Chapter 8.* Ricardo Valencia recently resigned his position as controller for Tom White Automotive, a small, struggling foreign car dealer in Austin, Texas. Ricardo has just started a new job as controller for Mueller Imports, a much larger dealer for the same car manufacturer. Demand for this particular make of car is exploding, and the manufacturer cannot produce enough to satisfy demand. The manufacturer's regional sales managers are each given a certain number of cars. Each sales manager then decides how to divide the cars among the independently owned dealerships in the region. Because most dealerships can sell every car they receive, the key is getting a large number of cars from the manufacturer's regional sales manager.

Ricardo's former employer, White Automotive, received only about 25 cars a month. Consequently, the dealership was not very profitable.

Ricardo is surprised to learn that his new employer, Mueller Imports, receives over 200 cars a month. Ricardo soon gets another surprise. Every couple of months, a local jeweler bills the dealer $5,000 for "miscellaneous services." Franz Mueller, the owner of the dealership, personally approves payment of these invoices, noting that each invoice is a "selling expense." From casual conversations with a salesperson, Ricardo learns that Mueller frequently gives Rolex watches to the manufacturer's regional sales manager and other sales executives. Before talking to anyone about this, Ricardo decides to work through his ethical dilemma using the framework from Chapter 8. Put yourself in Ricardo's place and complete the framework.

1. What is the ethical issue?
2. What are my options?
3. What are the possible consequences?
4. What shall I do?

Financial Statement Case

Identifying type of company and its cost objects, and analyzing its response to time-based competition
(Obj. 3, 5)

To help determine whether current profits will continue and grow in the future, investors need information on management's plans. Investors are especially interested in how management plans to compete in today's business environment. Let's use **Amazon.com's** annual report to consider the company's operations and management's plans. To answer the following questions, refer to the CEO's letter to shareholders in the company's 2002 annual report, the financial statements, and the notes to the financial statements.

Required

1. Is Amazon.com a service company, a merchandiser, or a manufacturer? What financial statement information supports your answer? What information outside the financial statements supports your answer?

(continued on next page)

2. What costs would Amazon.com classify as inventoriable?

3. Use notes 1 and 15 to the financial statements to identify some of the company's cost objects.

4. Does Amazon.com's management see time-based competition as critical to the company's success? What specific steps is it taking to meet this challenge? Identify an example of how Amazon.com uses advanced information systems, e-commerce, and JIT management to engage in time-based competition. (*Hint:* see the CEOs letter to shareholders.)

Team Project

Search the Internet for a nearby company that also has a Web page. Arrange an interview with a management accountant, a controller, or other accounting/finance officer of the company. Before you conduct the interview, answer the following questions:

Investigating management accounting, e-commerce, and information systems in the real world
(Obj. 1, 5)

1. Is this a service, merchandising, or manufacturing company? What is its primary product or service?

2. Is the primary purpose of the company's Web site to provide information about the company and its products, to sell online, or to provide financial information for investors?

3. Are parts of the company's Web site restricted so that you need password authorization to enter? What appears to be the purpose of limiting access?

4. Does the Web site provide an e-mail link for contacting the company?

At the interview, begin by clarifying your answers to questions 1 through 4, and ask the following additional questions:

5. If the company sells over the Web, what benefits has the company derived? Did the company perform a cost-benefit analysis before deciding to begin Web sales?

Or

If the company does not sell over the Web, why not? Has the company performed a cost-benefit analysis and decided not to sell over the Web?

6. What is the biggest cost of operating the Web site?

7. Does the company make any purchases over the Internet? What percentage?

8. How has e-commerce affected the company's management accounting system? Have the management accountant's responsibilities become more or less complex? More or less interesting?

9. Does the company use Web-based accounting applications, such as accounts receivable or accounts payable?

10. Does the company use an ERP system? If so, do they view the system as a success? What have been the benefits? The costs?

Prepare a report describing the results of your interview.

For an Internet Exercise, go to the Web site www.prenhall.com/horngren.

CHAPTER 20

Job Costing

TIPS CHECK YOUR RESOURCES

- Visit the www.prenhall.com/horngren **Web site** for self-study quizzes, video clips, other resources

- Try the **Quick Check** exercise at end of chapter to test your knowledge

- Learn the **key terms**

- Do the **Starter** exercises keyed in the margins

- Work the **mid-** and **end-of-chapter summary problems**

- Use the **Concept Links** to review material in other chapters

- Search the **CD** for review materials by chapter or by key word

- Watch the **tutorial videos** to review key concepts

- Watch the **On Location Dell Computer** video to see how Dell handles job costing

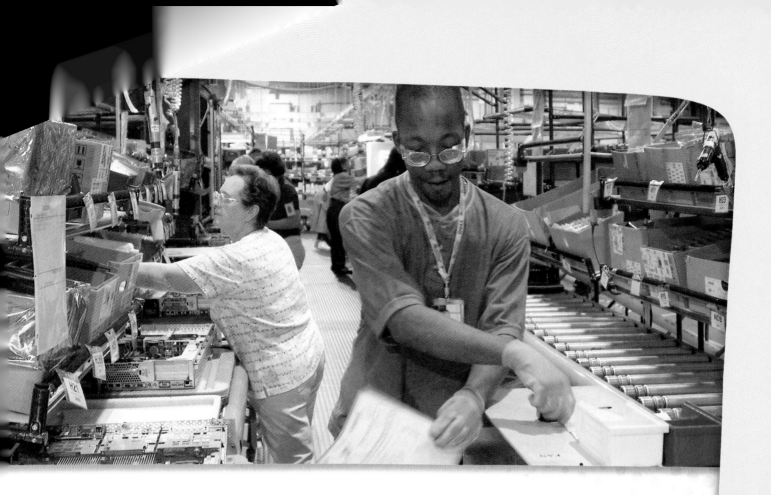

LEARNING OBJECTIVES

1 Distinguish between job costing and process costing

2 Trace materials and labor in a manufacturer's job costing system

3 Allocate manufacturing overhead in a manufacturer's job costing system

4 Account for completion and sales of finished goods and adjust for under- or overallocated manufacturing overhead

5 Assign noninventoriable costs in job costing

Despite intense competition in the technology sector, Dell Computer continues to gain market share and increase profits while rivals like IBM struggle. How does Dell do it? Cutting costs is one way. Using management accounting information to decide how to cut costs gives Dell a 10% to 15% cost advantage over its competitors.

To pinpoint cost-cutting opportunities, Dell first figures out how much it costs to assemble a computer. Dell's workers build each computer to a specific customer order, which is called a *job*. Dell's *job costing* system traces direct materials (such as CD-ROMs and hard drives) and direct labor (such as assembly-line labor) to each job. Then Dell allocates indirect manufacturing overhead costs (such as depreciation on the plant) to each job. The sum of the job's direct materials, direct labor, and overhead is its total manufacturing cost.

Dell Computer

Dell compiles this cost information for each product into a *cost package* spreadsheet that is available online to all Dell managers. Managers throughout the company need to know how much it costs to assemble desktops, laptops, and servers to make vital business decisions, such as:

- Identifying opportunities to cut costs of different products
- Setting selling prices that will lead to profits for each product
- Determining which products are the most profitable, and therefore, deserve the most sales emphasis

They also need costs to prepare Dell's financial statements:

- Cost of goods manufactured and cost of goods sold for the income statement
- Inventory for the balance sheet

Sources: Lohr, S. "Dell's Results Match Those of a Year Ago," *The New York Times*, May 17, 2002, p. C5; McWilliams, G. "Lean Machine: How Dell Fine-Tunes Its PC Pricing to Gain Edge in Slow Market," *The Wall Street Journal*, June 8, 2001, p. A1; and McWilliams, G. "Mimicking Dell, Compaq to Sell Its PCs Directly," *The Wall Street Journal*, November 11, 1998, p. B1.

∎ Sitemap

For a review of the value chain, see → *Chapter 19.*

Student Resource**CD**

inventoriable product costs,
noninventoriable product costs

The Dell story shows why you need to know how much it costs to produce a product, whether you plan a career in marketing, engineering, production, general management, or finance. Dell's marketing team needs to know how much it costs to assemble a computer to set the selling price high enough to cover costs. Engineers study the materials, labor, and overhead that go into each computer to pinpoint new cost-cutting opportunities. Production managers who know how much it costs to assemble a motherboard can decide whether it is more profitable for Dell to assemble motherboards itself or to *outsource* (or buy) them from a supplier. General managers who know Dell's cost to make desktops, laptops, and servers can identify the most profitable products and guide marketing to boost sales of those products. And the finance department uses product costs to figure the cost of goods sold and inventory for the financial statements.

Because it is so important for managers in all areas of the business to know how much it costs to make each product, in this chapter and the next we show you how to figure these costs.

Full Product Costs: A Brief Overview

First, though, let's review some key points about product costs. In Chapter 19, you learned that managers make certain decisions (like setting sale prices) based on *full product costs* from all elements of the value chain: R&D, design, production, marketing, distribution, and customer service.

Recall that full product costs have two components: inventoriable product costs and period costs (also called noninventoriable costs). Inventoriable product costs are from the third element of the value chain in Exhibit 20-1: production for manufacturers and purchases for merchandisers. ← They are called inventoriable costs because in addition to serving as one of the six building blocks for computing full product costs, these are the costs GAAP requires companies to use in computing inventory and cost of goods sold for the balance sheet and income

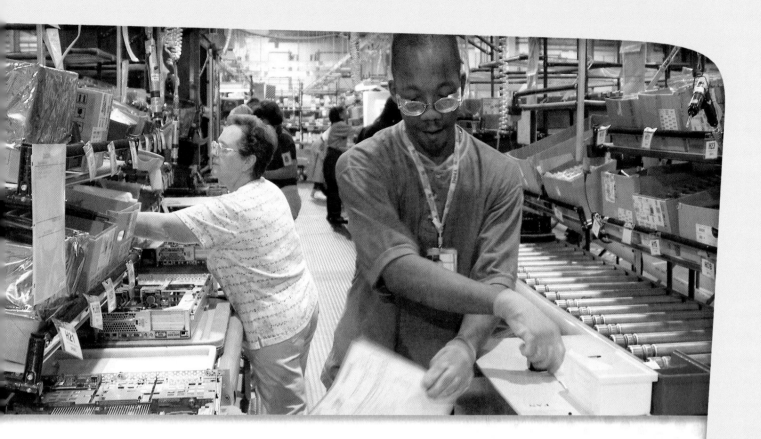

LEARNING OBJECTIVES

1. Distinguish between job costing and process costing

2. Trace materials and labor in a manufacturer's job costing system

3. Allocate manufacturing overhead in a manufacturer's job costing system

4. Account for completion and sales of finished goods and adjust for under- or overallocated manufacturing overhead

5. Assign noninventoriable costs in job costing

Despite intense competition in the technology sector, Dell Computer continues to gain market share and increase profits while rivals like IBM struggle. How does Dell do it? Cutting costs is one way. Using management accounting information to decide how to cut costs gives Dell a 10% to 15% cost advantage over its competitors.

To pinpoint cost-cutting opportunities, Dell first figures out how much it costs to assemble a computer. Dell's workers build each computer to a specific customer order, which is called a *job*. Dell's *job costing* system traces direct materials (such as CD-ROMs and hard drives) and direct labor (such as assembly-line labor) to each job. Then Dell allocates indirect manufacturing overhead costs (such as depreciation on the plant) to each job. The sum of the job's direct materials, direct labor, and overhead is its total manufacturing cost.

Dell Computer

Dell compiles this cost information for each product into a *cost package* spreadsheet that is available online to all Dell managers. Managers throughout the company need to know how much it costs to assemble desktops, laptops, and servers to make vital business decisions, such as:

- Identifying opportunities to cut costs of different products

- Setting selling prices that will lead to profits for each product

- Determining which products are the most profitable, and therefore, deserve the most sales emphasis

They also need costs to prepare Dell's financial statements:

- Cost of goods manufactured and cost of goods sold for the income statement

- Inventory for the balance sheet

Sources: Lohr, S. "Dell's Results Match Those of a Year Ago," *The New York Times*, May 17, 2002, p. C5; McWilliams, G. "Lean Machine: How Dell Fine-Tunes Its PC Pricing to Gain Edge in Slow Market," *The Wall Street Journal*, June 8, 2001, p. A1; and McWilliams, G. "Mimicking Dell, Compaq to Sell Its PCs Directly," *The Wall Street Journal*, November 11, 1998, p. B1.

■ Sitemap

- **Full Product Costs**

- **Costing a Product**

- **Accounting for Materials and Labor**

- **Allocating Manufacturing Overhead**

- **Accounting for Finished Goods**

- **Assigning Noninventoriable Costs**

■ **Full Product Costs**
  □ Costing a Product
  □ Accounting for Materials and Labor
  □ Allocating Manufacturing Overhead
  □ Accounting for Finished Goods
  □ Assigning Noninventoriable Costs

For a review of the value chain, see ➡ *Chapter 19.*

● Student ResourceCD

inventoriable product costs, noninventoriable product costs

The Dell story shows why you need to know how much it costs to produce a product, whether you plan a career in marketing, engineering, production, general management, or finance. Dell's marketing team needs to know how much it costs to assemble a computer to set the selling price high enough to cover costs. Engineers study the materials, labor, and overhead that go into each computer to pinpoint new cost-cutting opportunities. Production managers who know how much it costs to assemble a motherboard can decide whether it is more profitable for Dell to assemble motherboards itself or to *outsource* (or buy) them from a supplier. General managers who know Dell's cost to make desktops, laptops, and servers can identify the most profitable products and guide marketing to boost sales of those products. And the finance department uses product costs to figure the cost of goods sold and inventory for the financial statements.

Because it is so important for managers in all areas of the business to know how much it costs to make each product, in this chapter and the next we show you how to figure these costs.

Full Product Costs: A Brief Overview

First, though, let's review some key points about product costs. In Chapter 19, you learned that managers make certain decisions (like setting sale prices) based on *full product costs* from all elements of the value chain: R&D, design, production, marketing, distribution, and customer service.

Recall that full product costs have two components: inventoriable product costs and period costs (also called noninventoriable costs). Inventoriable product costs are from the third element of the value chain in Exhibit 20-1: production for manufacturers and purchases for merchandisers. ← They are called inventoriable costs because in addition to serving as one of the six building blocks for computing full product costs, these are the costs GAAP requires companies to use in computing inventory and cost of goods sold for the balance sheet and income statement. Most of Chapter 20 focuses on how companies determine these inventoriable product costs. The chapter concludes with a discussion of assigning noninventoriable costs (period costs from the other five elements of the value chain) to products and services. By adding noninventoriable costs to inventoriable costs, managers can build up full product costs to make their internal decisions.

| Exhibit 20-1 | The Value Chain, Inventoriable Costs, and Noninventoriable Costs |

Inventoriable
Product Costs

With this big picture in mind, let's see how companies like Dell, Boeing, and Kellogg's figure the costs of making computers, airplanes, and cornflakes.

How Much Does It Cost to Make a Product? Two Approaches

Dell traces the cost of direct materials like hard drives to the computers in which they are installed. But indirect costs such as depreciation on the plant cannot be traced directly to an individual computer because Dell cannot determine exactly how much depreciation a particular computer "caused." → The existence of these indirect costs means that we cannot determine the precise cost of a specific product. Instead, companies use one of two product costing systems that *average* costs across products:

- Process costing
- Job costing

As the name suggests, *process costing* focuses on accumulating costs for each production process. *Job costing* accumulates costs for each individual job. Let's see how each works.

Process Costing

Process costing is used by companies that produce large numbers of identical units in a continuous fashion through a series of uniform production steps or processes. For example, Pace Foods uses two processes to make picante sauce: (1) chopping vegetables and (2) mixing and bottling. Pace separately accumulates the costs for each of the two processes. Next, the company averages the costs of the chopping process over all units passing through the process. Then it _____ of the mixing and bottling process over all units passing

☐ Full Product Costs
■ **Costing a Product**
☐ Accounting for Materials and Labor
☐ Allocating Manufacturing Overhead
☐ Accounting for Finished Goods
☐ Assigning Noninventoriable Costs

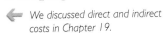 We discussed direct and indirect costs in Chapter 19.

Student Resource**CD**

job costing, process costing

 Distinguish between job costing and process costing

process costing
System for assigning costs to large numbers of identical units that usually proceed in a continuous fashion through a series of uniform production steps or processes.

through that process. If Pace spent $50,000 to mix and bottle 100,000 bottles of picante sauce, the mixing and bottling cost per bottle would be

$$\text{Cost per bottle of mixing and bottling picante sauce} = \frac{\$50,000}{100,000 \text{ bottles}} = \$0.50$$

✔ Starter 20-1

To get the total manufacturing cost of a bottle of picante sauce, Pace would add the $0.50 mixing and bottling cost to the cost per bottle of vegetables and the chopping process. Each bottle of picante sauce is identical to every other bottle, so each bears the same average cost.

Other companies that use process costing include:

- Oil refining—Texaco
- Food and beverages—Kellogg's
- Pharmaceuticals—Bayer

Exhibit 20-2 shows that process costing is not limited to manufacturers. Service companies like banks use it to determine the cost of processing customer transactions. Merchandisers such as granaries use process costing to determine the storage cost for each bushel of grain. We consider process costing in detail in Chapter 21.

Exhibit 20-2

Job and Process Costing in Service, Merchandising, and Manufacturing Companies

	Service	Merchandising	Manufacturing
Job Costing	Law firms (cases) Health care (diagnoses, procedures, or patients) Public relations (campaigns)	E-Tailers such as Amazon.com Mail-order catalog companies such as L.L. Bean	Commercial building construction Custom furniture Aircraft manufacturers
Process Costing	Banks (processing customer deposit transactions)	Granaries (distribute tons of identical grains)	Paper mills Mining operations Textile mills

Job Costing

job costing
System for assigning costs to a specific unit or to a small batch of products or services that (1) pass through production steps as a distinct identifiable job and (2) can vary considerably in materials, labor, and overhead costs.

Job costing assigns costs to a specific unit or to a small batch of products or services that passes through production steps as a distinct identifiable job. Different jobs can vary considerably in materials, labor, and overhead costs, so job costing accumulates costs separately for each individual job. We focus on job costing in this chapter.

Job costing is common in industries that produce goods to meet customer specifications. Dell Computer's assembly process is one example. Another is contract manufacturing, in which manufacturing plants (often in Mexico and Asia) produce electronic goods for a variety of customers, including Cisco Systems, HP, and Sony. For example, Singapore-based Flextronics International makes X-box game consoles for Microsoft, cell phones for Sony-Ericsson and Siemens, and printers for HP and Epson. Clearly, Flextronics must carefully track the costs of each of these separate jobs.

Job costing is not confined to manufacturers. Exhibit 20-2 shows that service organizations such as hospitals and physicians also use job costing. A hospital might consider each medical procedure a different job, while a doctor consid vidual patient a job. Architects, accountants, and attor determine the cost of jobs for individual clients. Merchandisers like Amazon.com use job costing to determine the cost of meeting each customer order.

Companies use job costing when different jobs vary widely in:

- The resources and time required
- The complexity of the production process

Because the jobs are so different, it would not be reasonable to assign them equal costs. It is worth the trouble to compile the costs for each job.

Exhibit 20-3 summarizes key differences between job and process costing.

	Job Costing	Process Costing
Cost object	Job	Process
Outputs	Single units or small batches, with large differences between jobs	Large quantities of identical units
Extent of averaging	Less averaging—costs are averaged over the small number of units in a batch (often 1 unit)	More averaging—costs are averaged over the many identical units in the large batch

Exhibit 20-3

Differences Between Job and Process Costing

HOW JOB COSTS FLOW THROUGH THE ACCOUNTS: AN OVERVIEW

Let's consider how a manufacturer, E-Z-Boy Furniture, uses job costing. For E-Z-Boy, each customer order is a separate job. E-Z-Boy uses a **job cost record** to accumulate the direct materials, direct labor, and manufacturing overhead costs assigned to each individual job. The company starts the job cost record when work begins on the job.

As E-Z-Boy incurs costs for the job, it adds them to the job cost record. For jobs that the company has started but not yet finished, the job cost records form the subsidiary ledger for the general ledger account Work in Process Inventory. →

When E-Z-Boy finishes the job, it totals the costs and transfers them out of Work in Process Inventory and into Finished Goods Inventory.

When the job's units are sold, E-Z-Boy's job costing system moves the costs of the job out of Finished Goods Inventory and into Cost of Goods Sold. Exhibit 20-4 summarizes how the costs of the jobs flow from Work in Process Inventory into Finished Goods Inventory and finally into Cost of Goods Sold.

job cost record
Document that accumulates the direct materials, direct labor, and manufacturing overhead costs assigned to each individual job.

← *For a review of ledgers and subsidiary ledgers, see Chapter 7.*

Exhibit 20-4   Flow of Costs Through the Accounts in a Job Costing System

INFORMATION FOR E-Z-BOY JOB COSTING ILLUSTRATION

Let's look at E-Z-Boy's job costing system in more detail. We'll see how E-Z-Boy:

✔ **Starter 20-2**

1. *Accumulates* total direct material costs, direct labor costs, and manufacturing overhead costs incurred during the period for all jobs.
2. *Assigns* appropriate amounts of these costs to individual jobs.

On December 31, 20X8, E-Z-Boy reports the following inventories:

Materials inventory (many kinds)	$20,000
Work in process inventory (5 jobs)	29,000
Finished goods inventory (unsold recliners from 2 completed jobs) ...	12,000

The following data summarize transactions for 20X9. We will explain the accounting for these transactions, step by step. (For simplicity, we will show summary journal entries for the entire year 20X9. In practice, however, companies record these transactions much more frequently.)

1. Materials purchased on account...........................	$320,000
2. Direct materials used for manufacturing	285,000
Indirect materials used for manufacturing....................	40,000
3. Manufacturing wages incurred	335,000
4. Direct labor on jobs......................................	250,000
Indirect labor to support manufacturing	85,000
5. Depreciation on plant and equipment......................	50,000
6. Plant utilities	20,000
7. Plant insurance	5,000
8. Property taxes—plant	10,000
9. Manufacturing overhead allocated to jobs..................	200,000
10. Cost of goods manufactured..............................	740,000
11. Sales on account	996,000
Cost of goods sold.......................................	734,000

Student Resource**CD**

cost assignment, labor costs, materials costs

⭐ 2 *Trace materials and labor in a manufacturer's job costing system*

cost tracing
Assigning direct costs (such as direct materials and direct labor) to cost objects (such as jobs or production processes) that used those costs.

cost allocation
Assigning indirect costs (such as manufacturing overhead) to cost objects (such as jobs or production processes).

cost assignment
A general term that refers to both tracing direct costs and allocating indirect costs to cost objects.

Job Costing: Accounting for Materials and Labor

Managers want to know the costs incurred in each job. There are two steps to obtaining this information.

STEP 1 *Accumulate the costs the plant incurred for all jobs.* Accumulate total purchases of materials, labor, and overhead items such as utilities, depreciation on the plant and equipment, and so on.

STEP 2 *Assign the costs incurred in the plant to the individual cost objects (the individual jobs).* This step assigns the costs the plant incurred to the specific jobs that used those costs. Accountants use **cost tracing** to assign direct costs (such as direct material and direct labor) to jobs that *use* those costs. They use **cost allocation** to assign manufacturing overhead and other indirect costs to jobs. **Cost assignment** is a general term that refers to *both* (1) tracing direct costs and (2) allocating indirect costs to cost objects (jobs, in a job costing system).

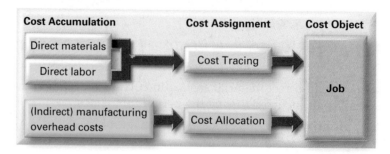

Accounting for Materials

PURCHASING MATERIALS   The job costing system *accumulates* the total material costs and then *traces* or *assigns* the costs to each individual job based on its usage of the materials. We begin by making the journal entry to *accumulate* the costs of all the materials E-Z-Boy purchased (data from page 802):

(1) Materials Inventory...................	320,000		
Accounts Payable		320,000	

Entry (1) is similar to the way a merchandiser like Amazon.com records purchases (under the perpetual method). The entry *accumulates* materials costs but does not *assign* them. E-Z-Boy cannot assign the costs to specific jobs until it *uses* the materials on those jobs.

Materials Inventory is a general ledger account. The subsidiary materials ledger includes a separate record for each type of material. The lumber record in Exhibit 20-5 shows that E-Z-Boy received 20 units of lumber at $9 each on July 23.

Exhibit 20-5

Subsidiary Materials Ledger Record

SUBSIDIARY MATERIALS LEDGER RECORD   **E-Z-Boy**

Item No. B–220   Description Lumber / Recliner chairs

	Received			Used				Balance		
Date	Units	Cost	Total Cost	Mat. Req. No.	Units	Cost	Total Cost	Units	Cost	Total Cost
20X9										
7–20								30	$9.00	$270
7–23	20	$9.00	$180					50	9.00	450
7–24				334	10	$9.00	$90	40	9.00	360

Exhibit 20-6 shows the Materials Inventory general ledger account and the subsidiary ledger for all the materials E-Z-Boy uses. The balance of Materials Inventory in the general ledger ($1,170) equals the sum of the balances in the subsidiary materials ledger.

Exhibit 20-6   Materials Inventory Subsidary Ledger and General Ledger

materials requisition
Request for the transfer of materials to the production floor, prepared by the production team.

USING MATERIALS   Now that you've seen how to *accumulate* the total cost of all the direct and indirect materials that E-Z-Boy purchased, let's see how to *assign* the cost of the materials E-Z-Boy actually used. For both direct and indirect materials, the production team completes a **materials requisition** to request the transfer of materials to the production floor so work can begin. Exhibit 20-7 shows E-Z-Boy's materials requisition for the 10 units of lumber needed to make 10 recliner chairs for Job 293.

Exhibit 20-7

Materials Requisition

To assign, or trace, the cost of the direct material (lumber) to Job 293, Exhibit 20-8 shows how E-Z-Boy posts the costs of lumber used from the materials requisition to the "Direct Materials" section of the job cost record for Job 293. Follow the $90 cost of the lumber from the materials inventory subsidiary ledger record (Exhibit 20-5), to the materials requisition (Exhibit 20-7), to the job cost record in Exhibit 20-8. Of course, all the dollar amounts in these exhibits show E-Z-Boy's *costs*—not the prices at which E-Z-Boy sells its products.

Exhibit 20-8

Direct Materials Entry on Job Cost Record

JOB COST RECORD   **E-Z-Boy**

Job No. 293
Customer Name and Address Macy's New York City
Job Description 10 Recliner Chairs

Date Promised		7–31	Date Started	7–24	Date Completed		
Date	Direct Materials		Direct Labor		Manufacturing Overhead Allocated		
	Requisition Numbers	Amount	Labor Time Record Numbers	Amount	Date	Rate	Amount
7–24	334	$90					
					Overall Cost Summary		
					Direct Materials ....$		
					Direct Labor		
					Manufacturing Overhead Allocated		
Totals					Total Job Cost ....$		

Technology simplifies both the *accumulation* and the *assignment* of materials costs. As explained in Chapter 19, Dell creates specialized Web pages for each of its key suppliers. Suppliers use these pages, which contain information on Dell's production schedule, to decide how much material to deliver to Dell's production floor. Upon receipt of the materials, Dell's information system can trigger the *accumulation* of material costs. Dell's workers then scan electronic bar codes on materials to *assign* individual computers the cost of materials such as hard drives and CD-ROMs as they are installed.

DIRECT AND INDIRECT MATERIALS   Journal entry (1) debited Materials Inventory for the costs of all materials E-Z-Boy purchased—whether direct or indirect. Thus, when E-Z-Boy *uses* materials (whether direct or indirect), it credits Materials Inventory.

But what account does E-Z-Boy debit? The answer depends on the type of material used. To *assign* the cost of *direct materials* used, such as lumber and upholstery fabric, E-Z-Boy:

- Debits Work in Process Inventory in the general ledger for the total cost of the direct materials used
- Records the total cost of the direct materials used on the specific job cost records in the subsidiary ledger, as shown in Exhibit 20-8

However, E-Z-Boy cannot trace the costs of *indirect materials* like nails and thread to a specific job (otherwise, these would be *direct* materials). This means that E-Z-Boy cannot record indirect materials on any of the specific job cost records in the subsidiary ledger that underlies the general ledger Work in Process Inventory account. So it cannot debit Work in Process Inventory. Instead, it debits indirect materials costs to a separate account, Manufacturing Overhead, in the general ledger. (Recall from Chapter 19 that manufacturing overhead includes all manufacturing costs *other than* direct materials and direct labor.)

Keep this distinction in mind: *Indirect manufacturing costs, such as indirect materials used, are not debited directly to Work in Process Inventory. Instead, they are accumulated in the (separate) Manufacturing Overhead account.*

E-Z-Boy works on many jobs during the year. The summary entry to assign the cost of the direct and indirect materials that E-Z-Boy used in all of its jobs during 20X9 is (data from page 802):

(2) Work in Process Inventory (for direct materials)	285,000		✔ **Starter 20-3**
Manufacturing Overhead (for indirect materials)	40,000		
Materials Inventory		325,000	

We can summarize the flow of materials costs through the T-accounts as follows:

✔ **Starter 20-4**

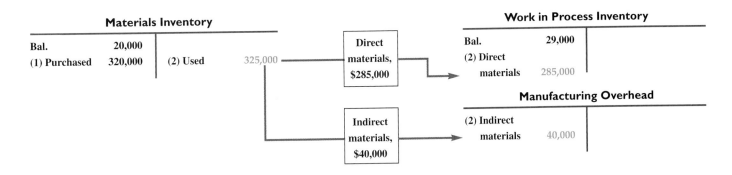

Accounting·com

Beyond the Bar Code: Radio-Frequency Identification Systems

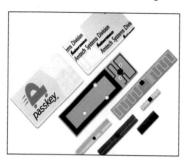

For the past 25 years, companies have used bar codes to identify and follow components in the factory. But if the contents or the destination of an industrial part or product change, someone must print and attach a new bar code label. Even in automated identification systems, as many as 60% of warehouse workers spend time checking bar codes and lining up each item for scanning.

Now there is a better method. Radio-frequency identification (RFID), uses electromagnetic waves to identify, track, and sort objects. An RFID system has two major components: the reader and the card/tag. Radio-frequency waves between the two make the identification. The plastic tag has a memory chip the size of a pinhead, yet it contains far more information than a bar code. And because it relies on radio waves, workers don't have to waste time aligning tagged products for scanning. The Gap uses RFID to trace each item of merchandise from the point of manufacture to the point of sale. Coca-Cola uses RFID to improve the efficiency of workers who refill and maintain vending machines. In the United Kingdom, Marks & Spencer uses RFID to track frozen foods.

The sophisticated "read–write" version of RFID has even more advantages. Employees can change tag information without touching the tag. They can change the route of a component on the factory floor or the destination of a shipment. The read–write tag is a small database that the company can synchronize with its other databases—and now with customers who have RFID technology. The fashion house Prada, for instance, gives customers RFID identification cards which, when combined with tagged merchandise, provide them with product information, videos of the clothing being shown on the runway, and even size and color options.

Based on: Gene Bylinsky, "Hot New Technologies for American Factories," *Fortune*, June 26, 2000, pp. 288A–288K. John Mesenbrink, "Shopping for RFID," *Security*, October 2002, pp. 10–16. Anonymous, "Top 100 2002: Top 10 Companies," *Frontline Solutions*, November 2002, pp. 17–30.

Accounting for Labor

Chapter 11 defined the payroll record as a special journal that lists each employee and the data to record payroll amounts. →

Using the payroll record, E-Z-Boy *accumulates* the actual labor costs incurred during 20X9 (data from page 802): ←

(3) Manufacturing Wages	335,000	
Wages Payable		335,000

This entry *accumulates* the costs of both direct and indirect labor.

How does E-Z-Boy *assign* labor costs to individual jobs? Each employee whose work is considered direct labor fills out a labor time record for each job he or she works on. The **labor time record** in Exhibit 20-9 identifies the employee (Jay Barlow), the amount of time he spent on Job 293 (7 hours and 30 minutes), and the labor cost charged to the job ($60 = 7½ hours × $8 per hour).

For each job, E-Z-Boy totals the labor time records to trace, or *assign*, the direct labor cost to that job. Exhibit 20-10 shows how E-Z-Boy adds the direct labor cost to the job cost record. The "labor time record numbers" show that on July 24, three employees worked on Job 293. Labor time record 251 is Jay

labor time record
Identifies the employee, the amount of time spent on a particular job, and the labor cost charged to the job; a record used to assign direct labor cost to specific jobs.

Exhibit 20-9

Labor Time Record

```
                        LABOR TIME RECORD              No.  251
     Employee  Jay Barlow                              Date  7–24
     Job  293

     TIME:
        Started    1:00          Rate     $8.00
        Stopped    8:30          Cost of Labor
        Elapsed    7:30          Charged to Job   $60.00

        Employee  JB          Supervisor  GDC
```

Barlow's, from Exhibit 20-9. Labor time records 236 and 258 (not shown) indicate that two other employees also worked on Job 293. The job cost record shows that E-Z-Boy assigned Job 293 a total of $150 of direct labor costs for the three employees' work ($60 from Jay Barlow's labor time record and the remainder from the other two employees' records).

Exhibit 20-10

Direct Labor Entry on Job Cost Record

JOB COST RECORD   E-Z-Boy

Job No. 293
Customer Name and Address Macy's New York City
Job Description 10 Recliner Chairs

Date Promised		7–31	Date Started	7–24	Date Completed		
	Direct Materials		Direct Labor		Manufacturing Overhead Allocated		
Date	Requisition Numbers	Amount	Labor Time Record Numbers	Amount	Date	Rate	Amount
7–24	334	$90	236, 251, 258	$150			
					Overall Cost Summary		
					Direct Materials.................$		
					Direct Labor.......................		
					Manufacturing Overhead Allocated...................		
Totals					Total Job Cost...................$		

Recall that the job cost records form the subsidiary ledger for the general ledger account Work in Process Inventory. Therefore, the total direct labor costs traced to all the individual jobs E-Z-Boy worked on during the period (as recorded on job cost records like Exhibit 20-10) must equal the total direct labor debits to Work in Process Inventory.

The rest of the labor cost is for indirect labor, such as maintenance and janitorial services. Indirect labor cannot be traced to any specific job. Therefore, indirect labor, like indirect materials, is debited to Manufacturing Overhead.

The entry to *assign* total direct and indirect labor costs that E-Z-Boy incurred during 20X9 (data from page 802) is:

✔ Starter 20-5

(4) Work in Process Inventory (for direct labor)............. 250,000
    Manufacturing Overhead (for indirect labor)............. 85,000
        Manufacturing Wages   335,000

This entry brings the balance in Manufacturing Wages to zero, because its transferred balance is now divided between Work in Process Inventory (direct labor) and Manufacturing Overhead (indirect labor), as shown in the following T-accounts:

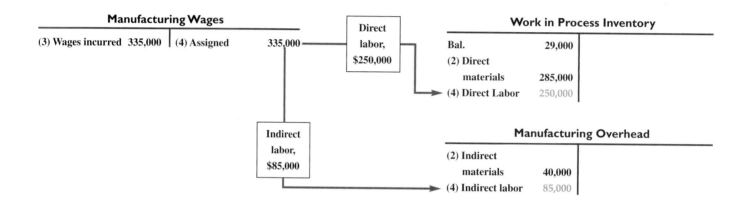

E-Z-Boy uses traditional source documents like the labor time record in Exhibit 20-9 to identify the direct labor cost of each specific job. But many companies have automated this process. For example, at various stages in the production of Saturn automobiles, employees insert their identification cards into computer terminals set up on the plant floor. This system captures direct labor time and cost without using documents.

How can E-Z-Boy managers use the materials inventory subsidiary ledger (Exhibit 20-6), labor time records (Exhibit 20-9), and job cost records (Exhibit 20-10) to run the company more effectively and efficiently?

Answer: Managers can use the *materials inventory subsidiary ledger* to see when lumber, nails, thread, and other materials are running low, so they can reorder.

  Managers use *labor time records* to control labor costs. Suppose E-Z-Boy pays an employee for 7½ hours of work per day. Summing the time recorded on all her labor time records for the day should yield a total of 7½ hours worked. If not, the manager should find out how the employee spent any time unaccounted for. By showing how much time employees spend on each job, labor time records and job cost records help managers determine whether employees are working efficiently. If they spend longer than expected on a job, that job may not yield a profit.

  Engineers study the detailed materials and labor charges on the *job cost records* to see if they can use materials and labor more efficiently. If a job's costs exceed its budget, E-Z-Boy may be able to use the job cost record to negotiate a price increase with the customer. E-Z-Boy's managers must do a better job controlling costs on future jobs, or raise the sale price on similar jobs, to ensure that the company remains profitable.

Decision Guidelines

JOB COSTING: TRACING DIRECT MATERIALS AND DIRECT LABOR

Dell Computer uses a job costing system that assigns manufacturing costs to each individual computer Dell assembles. These guidelines explain some of the decisions Dell made in designing its system to trace direct materials and labor.

Decision	Guidelines
Should we use job or process costing?	Dell uses *job costing* because the company produces unique products (custom-tailored computers) in small batches (usually a "batch" contains one computer). Dell does not use *process costing*, because that is appropriate for companies like oil refineries, which produce identical products in large batches, often in a continuous flow.

How to record:

• Purchase and use of materials?

Purchase:
Materials Inventory XX
      Accounts Payable (or Cash). XX

Use:
Work in Process Inventory (direct materials). XX
Manufacturing Overhead (indirect materials) XX
      Materials Inventory XX

• Incurrence and assignment of labor?

Incurred:
Manufacturing Wages. XX
      Wages Payable (or Cash). XX

Assigned:
Work in Process Inventory (direct labor). XX
Manufacturing Overhead (indirect labor) XX
      Manufacturing Wages. XX

MID-CHAPTER *Summary Problem*

Ecosphere Associates, Ltd. in Tucson, Arizona, produces ecospheres—self-sustaining enclosed glass spheres that include water, algae, tiny shrimp, and snails. Suppose Ecosphere has the following transactions:

a. Purchased raw materials on account, $35,000.
b. Materials costing $30,000 were requisitioned for production. Of this total, $3,000 were indirect materials.
c. Labor time records show that direct labor of $22,000 and indirect labor of $4,000 were incurred (but not yet paid).

Required

Prepare journal entries for each transaction.

CHECK YOUR RESOURCES

Solution

a. Materials Inventory. 35,000
     Accounts Payable 35,000

When materials are purchased on account:

- Debit (increase) Materials Inventory for the *cost* of the materials
- Credit (increase) Accounts Payable to record the liability for the cost of the materials

b. Work in Process Inventory   27,000
     Manufacturing Overhead   3,000
          Materials Inventory . . . . | 30,000

When materials are requisitioned (used) in production, we record the movement of materials out of materials inventory and into production:

- Debit (increase) Work in Process Inventory for the cost of the *direct* materials (in this case, $27,000—the $30,000 total materials requisitioned less the $3,000 indirect materials)
- Debit (increase) Manufacturing Overhead for the cost of the *indirect* materials
- Credit (decrease) Materials Inventory for the cost of both direct and indirect materials moved out of the materials storage area and into production

c. Manufacturing Wages   26,000
     Wages Payable . . . . | 26,000

To record total labor costs actually incurred ($22,000 + 4,000):

- Debit (increase) Manufacturing Wages
- Credit (increase) Wages Payable to record the liability for wages incurred, but not paid

     Work in Process Inventory   22,000
     Manufacturing Overhead   4,000
          Manufacturing Wages . . . . | 26,000

To assign the labor costs:

- Debit (increase) Work in Process Inventory for the cost of the *direct* labor
- Debit (increase) Manufacturing Overhead for the cost of the *indirect* labor
- Credit (decrease) Manufacturing Wages for the cost of both direct and indirect labor

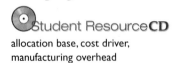

Student Resource**CD**

allocation base, cost driver, manufacturing overhead

⭐3 *Allocate manufacturing overhead in a manufacturer's job costing system*

✔ **Starter 20-6**

Job Costing: Allocating Manufacturing Overhead

All manufacturing overhead costs are *accumulated* as debits to a single general ledger account—Manufacturing Overhead. We have already recorded the indirect materials (entry 2) and indirect labor (entry 4) manufacturing overhead costs. Entries 5 through 8 record the other manufacturing overhead costs E-Z-Boy incurred, as given on page 802. The account titles in parentheses indicate the specific records debited in the overhead subsidiary ledger.

(5) Manufacturing Overhead (Depreciation—Plant and Equipment) 50,000
     Accumulated Depreciation—Plant and Equipment . . . . | 50,000
(6) Manufacturing Overhead (Plant Utilities) 20,000
     Cash . . . . | 20,000
(7) Manufacturing Overhead (Plant Insurance) 5,000
     Prepaid Insurance—Plant . . . . | 5,000
(8) Manufacturing Overhead (Property Taxes—Plant) 10,000
     Property Taxes Payable . . . . | 10,000

The actual manufacturing overhead costs (such as indirect materials, indirect labor, and depreciation, utilities, insurance and property taxes related to the plant) are debited to Manufacturing Overhead as they occur throughout the year. By the end of the year, the Manufacturing Overhead account has accumulated all the actual overhead costs as debits:

Manufacturing Overhead

(2) Indirect materials	40,000
(4) Indirect labor	85,000
(5) Depreciation—plant and equipment	50,000
(6) Plant utilities	20,000
(7) Plant insurance	5,000
(8) Property taxes—plant	10,000
Total overhead cost	210,000

How can E-Z-Boy's managers use the Manufacturing Overhead subsidiary ledger to control overhead costs?

Answer: Managers plan the amount of each manufacturing overhead item, such as plant-related depreciation, utilities, and insurance. If actual costs differ from planned costs, they find out why. For example, why are plant utilities higher than expected? Did utility rates increase? Did workers waste electricity or water? Was there a delay in installing more energy-efficient machinery? Answers to these questions may help managers control (reduce) utility costs. On the other hand, if utility costs have increased for reasons beyond the company's control, management may have to increase selling prices to cover the higher utility costs.

Now you have seen how E-Z-Boy *accumulates* overhead costs in the accounting records. But how does it *assign* overhead costs to individual jobs? As you can see from the manufacturing overhead T-account, overhead includes a variety of costs that E-Z-Boy cannot trace to individual jobs. For example, it is impossible to say how much of the cost incurred to cool the plant is related to Job 293. Yet manufacturing overhead costs are as essential as direct materials and direct labor, so E-Z-Boy must find some way to assign these costs to specific jobs.

Allocating Manufacturing Overhead to Jobs

E-Z-Boy traces direct material and direct labor costs directly to each job, as we've seen. Now let's see how it allocates each job its share of the wide variety of indirect manufacturing costs like depreciation and insurance on plant and equipment, indirect materials, and indirect labor.

HOW TO CHOOSE AN ALLOCATION BASE   The key to assigning indirect manufacturing costs to jobs is to identify a manufacturing overhead allocation base. The **allocation base** is a common denominator that links indirect manufacturing overhead costs to the cost objects. Ideally, the allocation base is the primary cost driver of manufacturing overhead costs. As the phrase implies, a **cost driver** is the primary factor that causes a cost. For example, in many companies, manufacturing overhead costs rise and fall with direct labor costs. In this case, accountants use direct labor costs or direct labor hours as the allocation base. The more direct labor a job uses, the more manufacturing overhead cost the job is allocated.

But labor is less important in companies that use automated production, like Saturn. Equipment depreciation, maintenance, and utilities change with the number of machine hours used. These companies often use machine hours as the

allocation base
A common denominator that links indirect costs to cost objects. Ideally, the allocation base is the primary cost driver of the indirect cost.

cost driver
The primary factor that causes a cost.

allocation base. The important point is that the cost allocation base should be the primary driver of the manufacturing overhead costs.

For simplicity, we'll assume E-Z-Boy uses only one allocation base to assign manufacturing overhead costs to jobs. Chapter 25 relaxes this assumption. There, we'll see how companies use a method called *activity-based costing* to identify different allocation bases that more accurately link indirect costs with the jobs that caused those costs. Because activity-based costing is a straightforward extension of the single allocation base method, it is important to develop a solid understanding of the simpler system we describe here.

HOW TO ESTIMATE A MANUFACTURING OVERHEAD RATE The most accurate allocation can be made only when the total amount of the manufacturing overhead cost is known, at the end of the year. But managers making decisions today cannot wait that long for product cost information. So E-Z-Boy develops an estimated manufacturing overhead allocation rate at the beginning of the year. This **predetermined manufacturing overhead rate** (sometimes called the **budgeted manufacturing overhead rate**) is computed as follows:

predetermined manufacturing overhead rate
Estimated manufacturing overhead allocation rate computed at the beginning of the year, calculated as the total estimated manufacturing overhead costs divided by the total estimated quantity of the manufacturing overhead allocation base. Also called the **budgeted manufacturing overhead rate**.

$$\text{Predetermined manufacturing overhead rate} = \frac{\text{Total estimated manufacturing overhead costs}}{\text{Total estimated quantity of the manufacturing overhead allocation base}}$$

A key point is that both the numerator and the denominator are estimated *before* the year begins. (Actual overhead costs and the actual quantity of the allocation base are not known until after the end of the period.) Throughout the year, companies use this predetermined rate to allocate overhead to individual jobs.

Six Steps in Allocating Manufacturing Overhead

Companies follow six steps in allocating manufacturing overhead cost to jobs:

1. Estimate the total overhead cost for the planning period, which is usually a year. In 20X8, E-Z-Boy predicted overhead costs for 20X9 of $220,000.

2. Identify the manufacturing overhead (cost) allocation base. E-Z-Boy uses direct labor cost as the allocation base.

3. Estimate the total quantity of the overhead allocation base. E-Z-Boy expects to incur $275,000 of direct labor cost during 20X9.

4. Compute the predetermined manufacturing overhead rate as follows:

$$\text{Predetermined manufacturing overhead rate} = \frac{\text{Total estimated manufacturing overhead costs (from Step 1)}}{\text{Total estimated quantity of the manufacturing overhead allocation base (from Step 3)}}$$

$$= \frac{\text{Total estimated manufacturing overhead costs (from Step 1)}}{\text{Total estimated direct labor costs (from Step 3)}}$$

$$= \frac{\$220,000}{\$275,000} = 0.80, \text{ or } 80\%$$

This overhead rate is *predetermined* because the numerator and the denominator are both *estimated before* the year starts.

5. Obtain *actual* quantities of the overhead allocation base used by individual jobs as the year unfolds. The total actual direct labor cost of Job 293 is $400, as Exhibit 20-11 shows.

6. Allocate manufacturing overhead cost to jobs by multiplying the *predetermined* manufacturing overhead rate (computed in step 4) by the *actual* quantity of the allocation base used by each job (from step 5). E-Z-Boy uses the same predeter-

mined rate (80% of direct labor cost) to allocate manufacturing overhead to all jobs worked on throughout the year. Because the total direct labor cost for Job 293 is $400 and the predetermined overhead allocation rate is 80% of direct labor cost, E-Z-Boy allocates $320 ($400 × 0.80) of manufacturing overhead to Job 293.

The completed job cost record for Macy's order of 10 recliner chairs (Exhibit 20-11) shows that the job cost E-Z-Boy a total of $1,220: $500 in direct materials, $400 in direct labor, and $320 of allocated manufacturing overhead. The job cost record also shows that a job can include more than a single unit of product. In this case, the Macy's job includes 10 recliners, so E-Z-Boy's cost per recliner is $122 ($1,220 ÷ 10).

Exhibit 20-11

Manufacturing Overhead Entry on Job Cost Record

✔ Starter 20-7

JOB COST RECORD   **E-Z-Boy**

Job No. 293
Customer Name and Address Macy's New York City
Job Description 10 Recliner Chairs

Date Promised	7–31	Date Started	7–24	Date Completed	7-29

Date	Direct Materials		Direct Labor		Manufacturing Overhead Allocated		
	Requisition Numbers	Amount	Labor Time Record Numbers	Amount	Date	Rate	Amount
7–24	334	$ 90	236, 251, 258	$150	7-29	80% of Direct Labor Cost	$320
25	338	180	264, 269, 273, 291	200			
28	347	230	305	50	Overall Cost Summary		
					Direct Materials...........$ 500		
					Direct Labor....................400		
					Manufacturing Overhead Allocated...............320		
Totals		$500		$400	Total Job Cost $1,220		

Knowing that the manufacturing cost is $122 per recliner can help E-Z-Boy's management make what kinds of decisions?

Answer

1. *Pricing*—Marketing must price the recliners considerably above the $122 manufacturing cost to cover R&D, design, marketing, distribution, and customer service costs, as well as profits.

2. *Product emphasis*—Using profit calculations (selling price minus cost), E-Z-Boy's top management can design operations and marketing strategy to focus on the most profitable products.

3. *Cost control*—Engineers can study the detailed cost information to identify opportunities to cut costs below $122. Production managers can compare the $122 cost per recliner with the budgeted cost to evaluate worker efficiency.

4. *Outsourcing*—Management can compare the $122 cost to make the recliner versus the cost of buying a similar recliner from a subcontractor. (For example, **Teva** outsources production of its footwear to companies in China; Teva's management focuses on design and marketing.)

5. *Valuing inventory*—Finance and accounting can use the $122 per recliner to value the job as inventory (before it is sold) and as cost of goods sold (after the sale).

Stop & Think

Of course, E-Z-Boy also allocated manufacturing overhead to each of the other jobs worked on during 20X9. The total overhead allocated to all jobs is 80% of the total $250,000 direct labor cost, or $200,000 (data from page 802). The journal entry to allocate manufacturing overhead costs to Work in Process Inventory is

(9) Work in Process Inventory 200,000
    Manufacturing Overhead . . . . | 200,000

The flow of manufacturing overhead though the T-accounts follows:

Manufacturing Overhead				**Work in Process Inventory**		
(2) Indirect materials	40,000	**(9) Allocated**	200,000	**Bal.**	29,000	
(4) Indirect labor	85,000			**(2) Direct materials**	285,000	
(5) Depreciation—plant				**(4) Direct labor**	250,000	
and equipment	50,000		Manufacturing overhead allocated			
(6) Plant utilities	20,000			**(9) Manufacturing**		
(7) Plant insurance	5,000		→	overhead		
(8) Property taxes—				allocated	200,000	
plant	10,000					
Actual overhead cost	210,000					
Bal.	10,000					

✔ **Starter 20-9**

☐ Full Product Costs
☐ Costing a Product
☐ Accounting for Materials and Labor
☐ Allocating Manufacturing Overhead
■ **Accounting for Finished Goods**
☐ Assigning Noninventoriable Costs

Student Resource**CD**

labor costs, manufacturing overhead, materials costs

★ *Account for completion and sales of finished goods and adjust for under- or overallocated manufacturing overhead*

After allocation, a $10,000 debit balance remains in the Manufacturing Overhead account. This means that E-Z-Boy's actual overhead costs exceed the overhead allocated to Work in Process Inventory. We say that E-Z-Boy's Manufacturing Overhead is *underallocated*. We'll discuss how to correct this problem on pages 815 and 816.

Accounting for Completion and Sale of Finished Goods and Adjusting Manufacturing Overhead

Now you know how to accumulate and assign direct materials, direct labor, and manufacturing overhead to jobs. To complete the process, we must account for the completion and sale of finished goods and then adjust manufacturing overhead at the end of the period.

Accounting for Completion and Sale of Finished Goods

Look at Exhibit 20-4 on page 801 to review the flow of costs as a job goes from work in process, to finished goods, to cost of goods sold. For E-Z-Boy, the $740,000 cost of goods manufactured (from the data on page 802) is the cost of the jobs E-Z-Boy finished this year. E-Z-Boy credits Work in Process Inventory as the jobs leave the plant floor. The debit is to Finished Goods Inventory because the completed products move into the finished goods storage area. A summary entry for E-Z-Boy's goods completed in 20X9 is as follows:

(10) Finished Goods Inventory 740,000
    Work in Process Inventory . . . . | 740,000

In turn, E-Z-Boy makes the usual entries for sales and cost of goods sold (data from page 802):

(11)	Accounts Receivable................	996,000	
	Sales Revenue.................		996,000
	Cost of Goods Sold	734,000	
	Finished Goods Inventory		734,000

The key T-accounts for E-Z-Boy's manufacturing costs now show

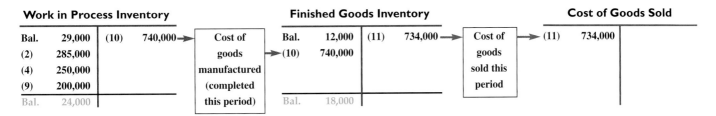

The Work in Process Inventory T-account summarizes what happens on the man-ufacturing plant floor. Notice that the Work in Process T-account also summarizes the Schedule of Cost of Goods Manufactured: →E-Z-Boy starts the period with beginning inventory of jobs that were started but not finished last period ($29,000). During the current period, the plant uses direct materials ($285,000) and direct labor ($250,000) and manufacturing overhead is allocated to the jobs pass-ing through the plant floor ($200,000). Some jobs are completed, and their costs are transferred out to Finished Goods Inventory ($740,000). We end the period with other jobs started but not finished during this period ($24,000).

✔ **Starter 20-8**

⬅ *See Exhibit 19-11 to review the schedule of Cost of Goods Manufactured. Compare the schedule to the entries in the Work in Process Inventory T-account.*

Adjusting Underallocated or Overallocated Manufacturing Overhead at Period's End

During the year, E-Z-Boy debits Manufacturing Overhead for the overhead costs the company actually incurred and credits Manufacturing Overhead for amounts allocated to Work in Process Inventory. The total debits rarely equal the total credits. Why? Because E-Z-Boy allocates overhead to jobs using a *predetermined* allocation rate that represents the *expected* relation between over-head costs and the allocation base. In our example, the $10,000 debit balance of Manufacturing Overhead shown on page 814 is called **underallocated manufac-turing overhead** (or simply **underallocated overhead**) because the manufactur-ing overhead allocated to Work in Process Inventory is *less* than the amount actu-ally incurred. (**Overallocated manufacturing overhead** is just the opposite.)

Accountants adjust underallocated and overallocated overhead at year-end, when closing the Manufacturing Overhead account. When overhead is underal-located, as in our example, a credit to Manufacturing Overhead brings the account balance to zero. What account is debited?

To see the answer you need to understand why E-Z-Boy underallocated manufacturing overhead. E-Z-Boy *expected* to incur 20X9 manufacturing over-head at the predetermined rate of

underallocated (manufacturing) overhead
The manufacturing overhead allocated to Work in Process Inventory is *less* than the amount of manufacturing overhead costs actually incurred.

overallocated (manufacturing) overhead
The manufacturing overhead allocated to Work in Process Inventory is *more* than the amount of manufacturing overhead costs actually incurred.

$$\frac{\$220,000 \text{ } expected \text{ manufacturing overhead costs}}{\$275,000 \text{ } expected \text{ direct labor cost}} = 80\%$$

Without a crystal ball to tell the future, it would be surprising indeed if *actual* costs and *actual* quantities of the allocation base—which are not known until the end of the year—exactly match the expected amounts that E-Z-Boy used to compute the predetermined rate at the beginning of the year. At the end of 20X9, E-Z-Boy's actual manufacturing overhead rate turns out to be

$$\frac{\$210,000 \text{ } actual \text{ manufacturing overhead costs}}{\$250,000 \text{ } actual \text{ direct labor cost}} = 84\%$$

At the beginning of the year, E-Z-Boy *underestimated* the manufacturing overhead rate, expecting it to be only 80%.

Because the predetermined rate was *less* than the actual rate, E-Z-Boy allocated too *little* manufacturing overhead to every job. In other words, every job worked on in 20X9 was *undercosted*. To correct this error, E-Z-Boy should *increase* the cost of these jobs.

Many companies use software that automatically corrects each job at the end of the year. In companies without such software, accountants usually close the balance in the Manufacturing Overhead account to Cost of Goods Sold, because most of the jobs have been sold.

Because E-Z-Boy *undercosted* jobs during the year, the correction should increase (debit) Cost of Goods Sold:

✔ **Starter 20-10**

✔ **Starter 20-11**

(12) Cost of Goods Sold	10,000	
Manufacturing Overhead..........		10,000

The T-accounts show that the Manufacturing Overhead balance is now zero:

Manufacturing Overhead				Cost of Goods Sold	
Actual	210,000	Allocated	200,000	734,000	
		Closed	10,000 →	10,000	

Exhibit 20-12 summarizes the accounting for manufacturing overhead:

- Before the period
- During the period
- At the end of the period

Exhibit 20-12

Summary of Accounting for Manufacturing Overhead

Before the Period

$$\frac{\text{Compute predetermined}}{\text{manufacturing overhead rate}} = \frac{\text{Total estimated manufacturing overhead cost}}{\text{Total estimated quantity of allocation base}}$$

During the Period

$$\text{Allocate the overhead} = \begin{array}{c}\text{Actual quantity of}\\\text{the manufacturing}\\\text{overhead allocation}\\\text{base}\end{array} \times \begin{array}{c}\text{Predetermined}\\\text{manufacturing}\\\text{overhead rate}\end{array}$$

At the End of the Period

Close the Manufacturing Overhead account:

Jobs are **undercosted**	If actual > allocated → *Underallocated* manufacturing overhead
	Need to *increase* Cost of Goods Sold

Cost of Goods Sold	xxx	
Manufacturing Overhead....................		xxx

Jobs are **overcosted**	If actual < allocated → *Overallocated* manufacturing overhead
	Need to *reduce* Cost of Goods Sold

Manufacturing Overhead.........................	xxx	
Cost of Goods Sold		xxx

Suppose E-Z-Boy's actual manufacturing overhead costs were $180,000 rather than $210,000.

Questions

1. What would the actual overhead rate have been?
2. Would manufacturing overhead have been underallocated or overallocated?
3. What journal entry would you make to close the Manufacturing Overhead account?

Answers

1. The actual manufacturing overhead rate would have been

$$\frac{\$180,000 \ actual \ \text{manufacturing overhead costs}}{\$250,000 \ actual \ \text{direct labor cost}} = 72\%$$

2. The predetermined manufacturing overhead rate (80%) is *higher* than the actual manufacturing overhead rate (72%). In this case, each job would be *overcosted*. And Manufacturing Overhead would be *overallocated* by $20,000, as shown in this T-account:

Manufacturing Overhead

Actual	180,000	Allocated	200,000

3. The jobs E-Z-Boy worked on during the year were allocated too much manufacturing overhead. Accordingly, jobs in Cost of Goods Sold were *overcosted*, so the correction should decrease (credit) Cost of Goods Sold, as shown in the following journal entry:

Manufacturing Overhead	20,000	
Cost of Goods Sold		20,000

Overview of Job Costing in a Manufacturing Company

Exhibit 20-13 provides an overview of E-Z-Boy's job costing system. Each entry is keyed to 1 of the 12 transactions described on pages 803–816 (amounts in thousands). Study this exhibit carefully.

Review the flow of costs through the general ledger accounts:

- Material and labor costs are split between direct costs (traced directly to specific jobs in Work in Process Inventory) and indirect costs (accumulated in Manufacturing Overhead and then allocated to Work in Process Inventory).

- The Work in Process Inventory account summarizes the transactions that occurred on the floor of the manufacturing plant.

- The $740,000 credit to Work in Process Inventory (debit to Finished Goods Inventory) is the cost of goods manufactured—the cost of goods completed and ready for sale—which is the manufacturer's counterpart to merchandise purchases.

In the Manufacturing Overhead account, actual overhead costs are recorded as debits as they occur throughout the period. Credits to the account represent allocated overhead. E-Z-Boy also closed the $10,000 underallocated Manufacturing Overhead to Cost of Goods Sold.

The T-accounts shown in Exhibit 20-13 are general ledger control accounts. Behind each general ledger account appears three examples of subsidiary accounts that underlie the general ledger control account.

We discussed control accounts in Chapter 6.

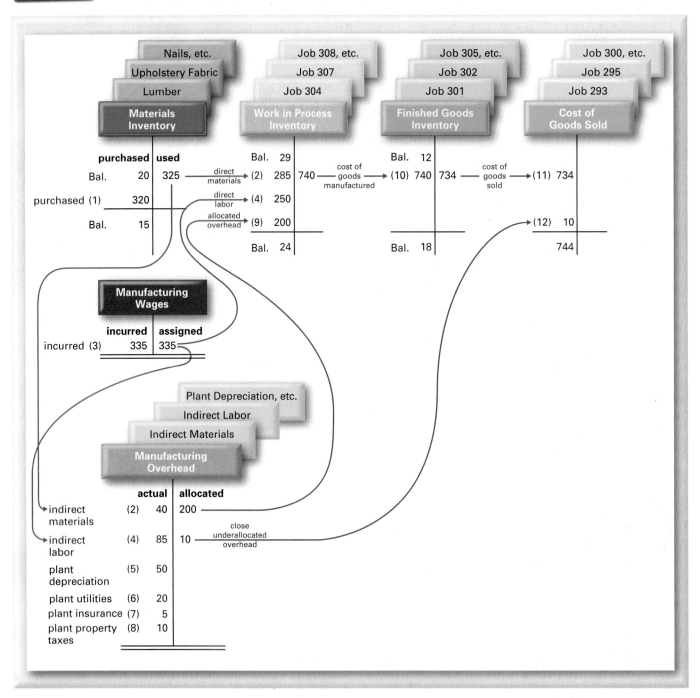

How Information Technology Has Changed Job Costing

The flow of costs through the T-accounts and the journal entries applies to systems ranging from simple manual costing to sophisticated ERP systems. The main difference is the source of data. In traditional systems, sources include material requisitions, labor time records, and job cost records like those we have described. These documents can be paper-based or automated.

In contrast, highly automated systems may have no physical source documents. Employees use bar codes to record materials used and scan identification cards to record their labor time. The software immediately tracks these material and labor costs to the specific job and updates the general ledger accounts (for example, Materials Inventory, Work in Process Inventory, Manufacturing Wages, and Manufacturing Overhead). ERP systems may not store data in the form of separate job cost records. But when employees enter the job number, the system quickly tallies costs assigned to the job so far. Even in sophisticated ERP systems, however, the cost flows and journal entries are identical to those we've described for E-Z-Boy.

Assigning Noninventoriable Costs

So far, we've explained how companies assign inventoriable costs to jobs. But for internal decision-making, many companies also assign noninventoriable costs (R&D, design, marketing, distribution, and customer service) to jobs. Let's see why and how.

Noninventoriable Costs in Manufacturing Companies

Job costing in manufacturing companies has traditionally focused on assigning *manufacturing* costs (*inventoriable* costs) to jobs. This is why our E-Z-Boy illustration focuses on assigning only manufacturing costs. The focus on manufacturing costs arises because generally accepted accounting principles require that the accounting records treat only inventoriable costs (manufacturing costs, for a manufacturer) as assets. Costs incurred in other elements of the value chain are not assigned to products for external reporting, but instead are treated as expenses (or period costs).

As we noted in Chapter 19, managers often want to know the full (total) cost of a product or a job, not just the inventoriable cost. The same principles of tracing direct costs and allocating indirect costs (using predetermined allocation rates) apply to noninventoriable period costs incurred in other elements of the value chain: R&D, design, marketing, distribution, and customer service. Managers can add these noninventoriable (period) costs to inventoriable costs to build the full cost of the product or job to guide internal decisions, such as setting long-run average sale prices. However, these noninventoriable costs are assigned to products (or jobs) *only for internal decision making*. Noninventoriable costs are not assigned to products for external reporting.

Noninventoriable Costs and Job Costing in Nonmanufacturing Companies

Because they have no inventory, service firms incur only noninventoriable costs. But their managers still need to know the costs of different jobs to make decisions. We now illustrate how service firms assign noninventoriable costs to jobs. (A manufacturer such as E-Z-Boy or a merchandiser such as Amazon.com could use the same approach to assign noninventoriable costs to individual jobs.)

The law firm of Barnett Associates considers each client a separate job. Barnett's most significant cost is direct labor—attorney time spent on clients' cases. How do service firms trace direct labor to individual jobs?

For automated services like Web site design, information technology consulting, and external auditing, employees simply enter the client number when they start on the client's job. Software records the time elapsed until the employee signs off that job. When the service is not automated, employees typically fill out a weekly **time record**. Software tallies the weekly total time spent on each job. Attorney Teresa Fox's time record in Exhibit 20-14 shows that she devoted 14 hours to client 367 during the week of June 10, 20X9.

Student Resource **CD**

inventoriable costs, noninventoriable costs

5 Assign noninventoriable costs in job costing

time record
Source document used to trace direct labor to specific jobs.

Exhibit 20-14

Employee Time Record

Barnett Associates	M	T	W	Th	F
Name __Teresa Fox__ 8:00 – 8:30	367	520	415	367	415
8:30 – 9:00					
Employee Time Record 9:00 – 9:30					
Week of __6/10/X9__ 9:30 – 10:00					
10:00 – 10:30			367		
Weekly Summary 10:30 – 11:00					
Client # Total hours 11:00 – 11:30	520				
367 14 11:30 – 12:00	520				
415 13 12:00 – 1:00					
520 13 1:00 – 1:30	520	367	367	520	415
1:30 – 2:00			367		
2:00 – 2:30			415		
2:30 – 3:00					
3:00 – 3:30					
3:30 – 4:00					
4:00 – 4:30					
4:30 – 5:00					

✔ **Starter 20-12**

Fox's salary and benefits total $100,000 per year. Assuming a 40-hour work-week and 50 workweeks in each year, Fox has 2,000 available work hours per year (50 weeks × 40 hours per week). Barnett Associates' hourly cost rate of employing Teresa Fox is

$$\text{Hourly cost rate to the employer} = \frac{\$100,000 \text{ per year}}{2,000 \text{ hours per year}} = \$50 \text{ per hour}$$

Fox is the only attorney who served client 367, so the direct labor cost traced to the client is 14 hours × $50 per hour = $700.

Founding partner John Barnett wants to know the total costs of serving clients, not just the direct labor cost. Barnett Associates also allocates indirect costs to individual jobs (clients). The law firm develops a predetermined indirect cost allocation rate, following the same six-step approach that E-Z-Boy (pages 812–813) used.

1. ***Estimate the total indirect costs.*** In December 20X8, Barnett estimates that the following indirect costs will be incurred in 20X9:

Office rent...	$200,000
Office support staff.......................................	70,000
Maintaining and updating law library for case research	25,000
Advertisements in the yellow pages	3,000
Sponsorship of the symphony............................	2,000
Total indirect costs.....................................	$300,000

2. ***Identify a cost allocation base.*** Barnett uses direct labor hours as the allocation base, because the number of hours that attorneys work on clients' cases is the main driver of indirect costs.

3. **Estimate the total quantity of the indirect cost allocation base.** Barnett estimates that its attorneys will work 10,000 direct labor hours in 20X9.

4. **Compute the predetermined indirect cost allocation rate. (Divide step 1 by step 3.)**

$$\text{Predetermined indirect cost allocation rate} = \frac{\$300,000 \text{ expected indirect costs}}{10,000 \text{ expected direct labor hours}}$$

$$= \$30 \text{ per direct labor hour}$$

✔ **Starter 20-13**

5. **Obtain the actual quantity of the indirect cost allocation base used by individual jobs as the year unfolds.** Exhibit 20-14 shows that client 367 required 14 direct labor hours.

6. **Allocate indirect costs to jobs by multiplying the predetermined indirect cost rate (step 4) by the actual quantity of the allocation base used by each job (step 5).** Client 367 is allocated indirect costs as follows:

$$14 \text{ direct labor hours} \times \$30/\text{hour} = \$420$$

To summarize, the total costs assigned to client 367 are

Direct labor: 14 hours × $50/hour.....................	$ 700
Indirect costs: 14 hours × $30/hour....................	420
Total costs	$1,120

You have learned how to use a job cost system to assign costs to jobs. Review the Job Costing Decision Guidelines to solidify your understanding.

Decision Guidelines

JOB COSTING

Dell Computer pioneered the assemble-to-order PC production process. To figure the cost of its computers, Dell uses a job costing system that treats each individual computer as a separate cost object. In designing its job costing system, Dell made decisions like these, in addition to those listed in the mid-chapter Decision Guidelines on page 809:

Decision	Guidelines
Who should have access to product cost information?	All Dell's managers have access to product cost information. *Marketing* uses it to set selling prices that cover costs and contribute to profits. *Top management* uses it to identify the most profitable products, so it can focus on increasing sales of those products. *Engineers* study product costs to identify opportunities for further cost cuts. *Production* managers use product cost information to evaluate how efficiently assembly-line employees are working. *Finance and accounting* use product costs to figure inventory for the balance sheet and cost of goods sold for the income statement.

Decision Guidelines *(continued)*

Decision	Guidelines
Are utilities, insurance, property taxes, and depreciation • Manufacturing overhead?	These costs are part of manufacturing overhead *only* if they are incurred in the manufacturing plant.
• Or operating expenses?	If not related to manufacturing, they are operating expenses. For example, if related to the research lab, they are R&D expenses. If related to executive headquarters, they are administrative expenses. If related to distribution centers, they are distribution expenses. These are all operating expenses, not manufacturing overhead.

How to record *actual* manufacturing overhead costs?

Manufacturing Overhead	XXX
Accumulated Depreciation— Plant and Equipment	XX
Prepaid Insurance—Plant and Equipment. .	XX
Utilities Payable (or Cash)	XX
and so on	XX

How to compute a predetermined manufacturing overhead rate?

$$\frac{\text{Total estimated manufacturing overhead cost}}{\text{Total estimated quantity of allocation base}}$$

How to record allocation of manufacturing overhead?

Work in Process Inventory	XX
Manufacturing Overhead	XX

What is the *amount* of the allocated manufacturing overhead?

$$\begin{array}{c}\text{Actual quantity}\\\text{of the manufacturing}\\\text{overhead allocation base}\end{array} \times \begin{array}{c}\text{Predetermined}\\\text{manufacturing}\\\text{overhead rate}\end{array}$$

How to close Manufacturing Overhead at the end of the period?

Close directly to Cost of Goods Sold.

When providing services, how to trace employees' direct labor to individual jobs?

Either automated software directly captures time employees spend on a client's job, or employees fill out a time record.

Why allocate noninventoriable costs to jobs?

Managers need total product costs for internal decisions (such as setting selling prices). For external reporting, assign only inventoriable costs to jobs.

Excel Application Exercise

Goal: Create a spreadsheet to compute a predetermined manufacturing overhead rate and to allocate manufacturing overhead.

Scenario: You've just signed on as one of Dell Computer's new accounting interns. The plant manager is working on next year's budget and asks you to answer some key questions about the plant's manufacturing overhead:

1. What is the plant's predetermined manufacturing overhead rate?
2. What is the total amount of allocated manufacturing overhead?
3. What is the total actual overhead?

4. How much is left in the manufacturing overhead account at year-end? Is overhead under- or overallocated?

To get started, you have some figures available: total estimated manufacturing overhead cost, $500,000; total estimated quantity of allocation base, 200,000 direct labor hours; and actual quantity of allocation base, 195,000 direct labor hours. You've also gathered actual overhead costs: depreciation on plant and equipment, $240,000; insurance on plant and equipment, $24,000; plant utilities, $22,000; property taxes on plant and equipment, $20,000; production manager's salary, $90,000; and maintenance and repair costs for plant and equipment, $85,000.

Step-by-Step:

1. Open a new Excel spreadsheet.
2. In column I, create a bold-faced heading as follows:
   a. Chapter 20 Excel Application Exercise
   b. Dell Computer Manufacturing Overhead
   c. Today's date
3. Two rows down, create a bold-faced heading, "Estimated and Actual Data for 200X."
4. In the next three rows, enter labels and values for total estimated manufacturing overhead cost, total estimated quantity of allocation base, and actual quantity of allocation base.

5. Two rows down, create a bold-faced heading, "Actual Overhead Costs."
6. Underneath the heading, enter labels and values for the remaining data (six rows total).
7. Two rows down, create a bold-faced heading, "Calculations for 200X."
8. Underneath the heading, enter labels for the four items to be calculated. Then, use formulas to compute the values.
9. Format all cells appropriately, save your work, and print a copy for your files.

END-OF-CHAPTER *Summary Problem*

StarZ, Ltd., manufactures skateboards. The company has a highly automated production process, so it allocates manufacturing overhead based on machine hours. StarZ expects to incur $240,000 of manufacturing overhead costs and to use 4,000 machine hours during 20X9.

At the end of 20X8, StarZ reported the following inventories:

CHECK YOUR RESOURCES

Materials Inventory.	$20,000
Work in Process Inventory.	17,000
Finished Goods Inventory.	11,000

During January 20X9, StarZ actually used 300 machine hours and recorded the following transactions:

a. Purchased materials on account, $31,000.
b. Used direct materials, $39,000.
c. Manufacturing labor cost incurred was $40,000.
d. Manufacturing labor was 90% direct labor and 10% indirect labor.
e. Used indirect materials, $3,000.
f. Incurred other manufacturing overhead, $13,000 (credit Accounts Payable).
g. Allocated manufacturing overhead for January 20X9.
h. Cost of completed skateboards, $99,000.
i. Sold skateboards on account, $172,000; cost of skateboards sold, $91,400.

Required

1. Compute StarZ's predetermined manufacturing overhead rate for 20X9.
2. Record the transactions in the general journal.
3. Post the transactions and inventory balances to the following accounts:

Materials Inventory	**Work in Process Inventory**	**Finished Goods Inventory**	**Cost of Goods Sold**

Manufacturing Wages	**Manufacturing Overhead**

4. Record the journal entry to close the ending balance of Manufacturing Overhead. Post your entry to the T-accounts.
5. What are the ending balances in the three inventory accounts and Cost of Goods Sold?

Solution

Requirement 1

$$\text{Predetermined manufacturing overhead rate} = \frac{\text{Total estimated manufacturing overhead cost}}{\text{Total estimated quantity of allocation base}}$$

$$= \frac{\$240,000}{4,000 \text{ machine hours}}$$

$$= \$60/\text{machine hour}$$

Requirement 2

Journal entries:

a. Materials Inventory......................	31,000	
Accounts Payable		31,000
b. Work in Process Inventory................	39,000	
Materials Inventory.................		39,000
c. Manufacturing Wages....................	40,000	
Wages Payable....................		40,000
d. Work in Process Inventory ($40,000 × 0.90)..	36,000	
Manufacturing Overhead ($40,000 × 0.10)....	4,000	
Manufacturing Wages...............		40,000
e. Manufacturing Overhead..................	3,000	
Materials Inventory.................		3,000
f. Manufacturing Overhead..................	13,000	
Accounts Payable		13,000
g. Work in Process Inventory (300 × $60)......	18,000	
Manufacturing Overhead............		18,000
h. Finished Goods Inventory	99,000	
Work in Process Inventory...........		99,000
i. Accounts Receivable.....................	172,000	
Sales Revenue.....................		172,000
Cost of Goods Sold	91,400	
Finished Goods Inventory		91,400

Requirement 3

Post the transactions:

Materials Inventory			
Bal.	20,000	(b)	39,000
(a)	31,000	(e)	3,000
Bal.	9,000		

Work in Process Inventory			
Bal.	17,000	(h)	99,000
(b)	39,000		
(d)	36,000		
(g)	18,000		
Bal.	11,000		

Finished Goods Inventory			
Bal.	11,000	(i)	91,400
(h)	99,000		
Bal.	18,600		

Cost of Goods Sold			
(i)	91,400		

Manufacturing Wages			
(c)	40,000	(d)	40,000

Manufacturing Overhead			
(d)	4,000	(g)	18,000
(e)	3,000		
(f)	13,000		
Bal.	2,000		

Requirement 4

Close Manufacturing Overhead:		
Cost of Goods Sold	2,000	
Manufacturing Overhead............		2,000

Manufacturing Overhead				Cost of Goods Sold		
(d)	4,000	(g)	18,000	(i)	91,400	
(e)	3,000		2,000		2,000	
(f)	13,000					
				Bal.	93,400	

Requirement 5

Ending Balances:

Materials Inventory (from requirement 3)	$ 9,000
Work in Process Inventory (from requirement 3)	11,000
Finished Goods Inventory (from requirement 3)..........	18,600
Cost of Goods Sold (from requirement 4)................	93,400

●REVIEW *Job Costing*

Quick Check

1. Would the advertising agency **Saatchi and Saatchi** use job or process costing? What about a **Georgia-Pacific** paper mill?
   a. Saatchi and Saatchi—job costing
      Georgia-Pacific—job costing
   b. Saatchi and Saatchi—job costing
      Georgia-Pacific—process costing
   c. Saatchi and Saatchi—process costing
      Georgia-Pacific—job costing
   d. Saatchi and Saatchi—process costing
      Georgia-Pacific—process costing

2. When **Dell Computer** *uses* direct materials, it *traces* the cost by debiting:
   a. Materials Inventory
   b. Direct Materials
   c. Manufacturing Overhead
   d. Work in Process Inventory

3. When Dell Computer *uses* indirect materials, it *assigns* the cost by debiting:
   a. Materials Inventory
   b. Indirect Materials
   c. Manufacturing Overhead
   d. Work in Process Inventory

4. When Dell Computer *uses* direct labor, it *traces* the cost by debiting:
   a. Direct Labor
   b. Manufacturing Wages
   c. Manufacturing Overhead
   d. Work in Process Inventory

Questions 5, 6, 7, and 8 are based on the following information. Assume that Dell's Austin, Texas, plant allocates manufacturing overhead based on machine hours. Suppose Dell budgeted 10 million machine hours and $90 million of manufacturing overhead costs. Finally, assume that Dell actually used 12 million machine hours and incurred the following actual costs (in millions):

Indirect labor	$10
Depreciation on plant.................................	47
Machinery repair.....................................	15
Direct labor...	75
Plant supplies..	5
Plant utilities	8
Advertising..	35
Sales commissions....................................	25

(continued)

5. What is Dell's predetermined manufacturing overhead rate?
   a. $9.00/machine hour   **c.** $0.13/machine hour
   b. $7.50/machine hour   **d.** $0.11/machine hour

6. What is Dell's actual manufacturing overhead cost?
   a. $85   **c.** $160
   b. $120   **d.** $220

7. How much manufacturing overhead would Dell allocate?
   a. $85   **c.** $108
   b. $90   **d.** $220

8. What entry would Dell make to close the manufacturing overhead account?

a. Manufacturing Overhead	5	
Cost of Goods Sold		5
b. Manufacturing Overhead	23	
Cost of Goods Sold		23
c. Cost of Goods Sold	5	
Manufacturing Overhead		5
d. Cost of Goods Sold	23	
Manufacturing Overhead		23

9. Dell's management uses product cost information to:
   a. Set prices of its products   **c.** Identify ways to cut production costs
   b. Decide which products to emphasize   **d.** All of the above

10. For which of the following reasons would John Barnett, owner of the Barnett Associates law firm, want to know the total costs of a job (serving a particular client)?
    a. To determine the fees charged to the client
    b. For inventory valuation
    c. For external reporting
    d. For all of the above

Accounting Vocabulary

allocation base (p. 811)
budgeted manufacturing overhead rate (p. 812)
cost allocation (p. 802)
cost assignment (p. 802)
cost driver (p. 811)
cost tracing (p. 802)

job cost record (p. 801)
job costing (p. 800)
labor time record (p. 806)
materials requisition (p. 804)
overallocated (manufacturing) overhead (p. 815)

predetermined manufacturing overhead rate (p. 812)
process costing (p. 799)
time record (p. 819)
underallocated (manufacturing) overhead (p. 815)

● ASSESS *Your Progress*

See *www.prenhall.com/horngren* for selected Starters, Exercises, and Problems.

Distinguishing between job and process costing
(Obj. 1)

Flow of costs in job costing
(Obj. 2, 3, 4)

Starters

S20-1 Would the following companies use job costing or process costing?

A manufacturer of plywood
A manufacturer of wakeboards
A manufacturer of luxury yachts
A professional services firm
A landscape garden contractor

S20-2 For a manufacturer that uses job costing, diagram the flow of costs through the accounts. Label each transaction. Include the following accounts in your diagram: Finished Goods Inventory, Manufacturing Wages, Cost of Goods Sold, Work in Process Inventory, Materials Inventory, and Manufacturing Overhead.

S20-3 Trekker manufactures backpacks. Its plant records include the following materials-related transactions:

Purchases of canvas (on account).....................	$70,000
Purchases of thread (on account).....................	1,100
Material requisitions:	
Canvas	63,000
Thread	280

What journal entries record these transactions? Post these transactions to the Materials Inventory account. If the company had $35,680 of Materials Inventory at the beginning of the period, what is the ending balance of Materials Inventory?

S20-4 Use the following T-accounts to determine direct materials used and indirect materials used.

Materials Inventory			
Bal.	16		
Purchases	230	X	
Bal.	24		

Work in Process Inventory			
Bal.	32		
Direct materials	Y	Cost of goods	
Direct labor	320	manufactured	744
Manufacturing			
overhead	200		
Bal.	8		

S20-5 Art Glass reports the following labor-related transactions at its plant in Seattle, Washington.

Plant janitor's wages	600
Furnace operator's wages..........................	900
Glass blowers' wages..............................	76,000

Record the journal entries for the incurrence and assignment of these wages.

S20-6 Classic Outdoor Furniture manufactures wood patio furniture. The company reports the following costs for June 20X7. What is the balance in the Manufacturing Overhead account?

Wood...	$230,000
Nails and glue....................................	12,000
Wood preserving stain.............................	9,000
Depreciation on saws..............................	5,000
Depreciation on delivery truck......................	2,200
Assembly-line workers' wages......................	56,000
Salesman's auto lease..............................	1,400
Indirect manufacturing labor	39,000

S20-7 In the E-Z-Boy job cost record (Exhibit 20-11), how much manufacturing overhead cost would be allocated to Job 293 if the predetermined manufacturing overhead allocation rate is 70% of direct labor cost rather than 80%? What would be the total cost assigned to Job 293?

Accounting for materials, labor, and completed goods
(Obj. 2, 4)

S20-8 Touch Enterprises produces LCD touch screen products. The company reports the following information at December 31, 20X6. Touch began operations on January 30, 20X6.

Work in Process Inventory		Manufacturing Wages		Manufacturing Overhead		Finished Goods Inventory		Materials Inventory	
30,000	123,000	70,000	70,000	2,000	48,000	123,000	111,000	52,000	32,000
60,000				10,000					
48,000				37,000					

1. What is the cost of direct materials used? The cost of indirect materials used?
2. What is the cost of direct labor? The cost of indirect labor?
3. What is the cost of goods manufactured?
4. What is cost of goods sold (before adjusting for any under- or overallocated manufacturing overhead)?

Allocating overhead
(Obj. 3)

S20-9 Refer to S20-8.

1. What is the actual manufacturing overhead? Allocated manufacturing overhead?
2. What is the predetermined manufacturing overhead rate as a percentage of direct labor cost?
3. Is manufacturing overhead underallocated or overallocated? By how much?

Under/overallocated overhead
(Obj. 4)

S20-10 In the E-Z-Boy illustration on pages 810–817, actual manufacturing overhead was $210,000. Suppose instead that the actual manufacturing overhead was $225,000.

1. What would be the actual manufacturing overhead rate?
2. Is manufacturing overhead underallocated or overallocated? By how much?
3. Is Cost of Goods Sold too high or too low?

Closing out under/overallocated overhead
(Obj. 4)

S20-11 Refer to S20-10. Make the journal entry to close out E-Z-Boy's Manufacturing Overhead account.

Job costing in a service company
(Obj. 5)

S20-12 In the Barnett Associates example on page 819–821, suppose Teresa Fox's annual salary is $110,000 rather than $100,000.

1. What would be the hourly (cost) rate to Barnett Associates of employing Fox?
2. What direct labor cost would be traced to client 367?

Job costing in a service company
(Obj. 5)

S20-13 Return to the original data in the Barnett Associates example on pages 819–821. Suppose the Barnett attorneys expected to work a total of 12,000 direct labor hours rather than 10,000 direct labor hours.

1. What is the indirect cost allocation rate?
2. What indirect costs will be allocated to client 367?

online homework

Exercises

Distinguishing job and process costing
(Obj. 1)

E20-1 Listed below are several terms. Complete the following statements with one of these terms. You may use a term more than once, and some terms may not be used at all.

Cost allocation	Cost driver	Job costing	Process costing
Cost tracing	Job cost record	Materials requisition	

a. A _____ accumulates the costs of an individual job.
b. _____ is used by companies that produce small quantities of many different products.

(continued)

c. A _____ is any factor that affects costs.

d. **Georgia-Pacific** pulverizes wood into pulp to manufacture cardboard. The company would use a _____ system.

e. To record costs of maintaining thousands of identical mortgage files, financial institutions like **Money Tree** would use a _____ system.

f. _____ is assigning direct costs to cost objects.

g. Companies that produce large numbers of identical products use _____ systems for product costing.

h. The computer repair service that visits your home and repairs your computer would use a _____ system.

i. A _____ is manufacturing personnel's request that materials be moved to the production floor.

j. _____ is assigning indirect costs to cost objects.

E20-2 Thrifty Trailers' job cost records yielded the following information:

Accounting for job costs
(Obj. 2, 3, 4)

Job No.	Date Started	Date Finished	Date Sold	Total Cost of Job at March 31
1	February 21	March 16	March 17	$ 3,800
2	February 29	March 21	March 26	13,000
3	March 3	April 11	April 13	6,400
4	March 7	March 29	April 1	4,000
5	March 9	March 30	April 2	7,120
6	March 22	April 11	April 13	2,000

Required

Compute Thrifty's cost of (a) work in process inventory at March 31, (b) finished goods inventory at March 31, and (c) cost of goods sold for March.

E20-3 Record the following transactions in Micro Speakers' general journal.

Job costing journal entries
(Obj. 2, 3, 4)

a. Incurred and paid Web site expenses, $3,400.

b. Incurred and paid manufacturing wages, $16,000.

c. Purchased materials on account, $14,750.

d. Used in production: direct materials, $7,000; indirect materials, $3,000.

e. Assigned $15,000 of manufacturing labor to jobs, 70% of which was direct labor and 30% of which was indirect labor.

f. Recorded manufacturing overhead: depreciation on plant, $13,000; plant insurance, $1,700; plant property tax, $4,200 (credit Property Tax Payable).

g. Allocated manufacturing overhead to jobs, 200% of direct labor costs.

h. Completed production, $33,000.

i. Sold inventory on account, $23,000; cost of goods sold, $11,000.

E20-4 Describe the lettered transactions in the following manufacturing accounts:

Identifying job costing journal entries
(Obj. 2, 3, 4)

Manufacturing Wages		Manufacturing Overhead		Cost of Goods Sold	
(a)	(b)	(b)	(e)	(g)	
		(c)	(f)	(f)	
		(d)			

Materials Inventory		Work in Process Inventory		Finished Goods Inventory	
(h)	(i)	(i)	(j)	(j)	(g)
	(c)	(b)			
		(e)			

E20-5 September production generated the following activity in Digital Connection's Work in Process Inventory:

Work in Process Inventory

September 1 Bal.	16,000
Direct materials used	29,000
Direct labor assigned to jobs	32,000
Manufacturing overhead	
allocated to jobs	12,000

Completed production, not yet recorded, consists of Jobs B-78 and G-65, with total costs of $41,000 and $37,000, respectively.

Required

1. Compute the cost of work in process at September 30.
2. Prepare the journal entry for production completed in September.
3. Prepare the journal entry to record the sale (on credit) of Job G-65 for $45,000. Also make the cost-of-goods-sold entry.
4. What is the gross profit of Job G-65? What other costs must this gross profit cover?

E20-6 Selected cost data for Star Poster Co. are as follows:

Expected manufacturing overhead cost for the year ...	$ 97,800
Expected direct labor cost for the year	61,125
Actual manufacturing overhead cost for the year......	104,600
Actual direct labor cost for the year	63,900

Required

1. Compute the predetermined manufacturing overhead rate per direct labor dollar.
2. Prepare the journal entry to allocate overhead cost for the year.
3. Use a T-account to determine the amount of overallocated or underallocated manufacturing overhead.
4. Prepare the journal entry to close the balance of the manufacturing overhead account.

E20-7 Freeman Foundry in Charleston, South Carolina, uses a predetermined manufacturing overhead rate to allocate overhead to individual jobs, based on the machine hours required. At the beginning of 20X6, the company expected to incur the following:

Manufacturing overhead costs......................	$ 600,000
Direct labor cost	1,500,000
Machine hours	75,000

At the end of 20X6, the company had actually incurred:

Direct labor cost	$1,210,000
Depreciation on manufacturing property, plant,	
and equipment	480,000
Property taxes on plant	20,000
Sales salaries	25,000
Delivery drivers' wages.....................	15,000
Plant janitors' wages	10,000
Machine hours	55,000 hours

(*continued*)

Required

1. Compute Freeman's predetermined manufacturing overhead rate.
2. Record the summary journal entry for *allocating* manufacturing overhead.
3. Post the manufacturing overhead transactions to the Manufacturing Overhead T-account. Is manufacturing overhead underallocated or overallocated? By how much?
4. Close the Manufacturing Overhead account to Cost of Goods Sold. Does your entry increase or decrease cost of goods sold?

E20-8 Refer to the data in Exercise 20-7. Freeman's accountant found an error in her 20X6 expense records. Depreciation on manufacturing property, plant, and equipment was actually $400,000, not the $480,000 she had originally reported. Unadjusted balances at the end of 20X6 include

Allocating manufacturing overhead **(Obj. 3, 4)**

Finished Goods Inventory.	$130,000
Cost of Goods Sold.	600,000

Required

1. Use a T-account to determine whether manufacturing overhead is underallocated or overallocated, and by how much.
2. Record the entry to close out the underallocated or overallocated manufacturing overhead.
3. What is the adjusted ending balance of Cost of Goods Sold?

E20-9 Land Resources, a real estate consulting firm, specializes in advising companies on potential new plant sites. Land Resources uses a job cost system with a predetermined indirect cost allocation rate, computed as a percentage of expected direct labor costs.

At the beginning of 20X5, managing partner Tony Black prepared the following plan, or budget, for 20X5:

Job costing in a service company **(Obj. 5)**

Student Resource CD
spreadsheet

Direct labor hours (professionals)	17,000 hours
Direct labor costs (professionals)	$2,669,000
Office rent	350,000
Support staff salaries	1,194,300
Utilities	324,000

Auto Supplies, Inc., is inviting several consultants to bid for work. Tony Black estimates that this job will require about 220 direct labor hours.

Required

1. Compute Land Resources' (a) hourly direct labor cost rate and (b) indirect cost allocation rate.
2. Compute the predicted cost of the Auto Supplies job.
3. If Black wants to earn a profit that equals 50% of the job's cost, how much should he bid for the Auto Supplies job?

Allocating manufacturing overhead
(Obj. 3)

Student Resource **CD**
spreadsheet

E20-10 At the end of the 20X7 fiscal year, Rave Kayaks' manufacturing records show the following unadjusted ending account balances:

	Work in Process Inventory	Finished Goods Inventory	Cost of Goods Sold
Direct materials	$100,000	$170,000	$ 360,000
Direct labor	80,000	250,000	600,000
Manufacturing overhead . .	70,000	300,000	440,000
Total	$250,000	720,000	$1,400,000

Rave's accountants allocated overhead during the year using a predetermined rate of $40 per machine hour. At year-end, they computed the actual rate of $52 per machine hour. The beginning balances of both Work in Process Inventory and Finished Goods Inventory were zero.

Required

1. How many machine hours did Rave Kayaks use in 20X7?
2. Was manufacturing overhead over- or underallocated for the year? By how much?
3. Record the entry to close out the over- or underallocated overhead.

A+ online homework

Problems

(Group A)

Analyzing job cost data
(Obj. 2, 3, 4)

P20-1A CarNut, Inc., reconditions engines. Its job cost records yield the following information. CarNut uses a perpetual inventory system.

Job No.	Date Started	Date Finished	Sold	Total Cost of Job at March 31	Total Manufacturing Cost Added in April
1	2/26	3/7	3/9	$1,400	
2	2/3	3/12	3/13	1,600	
3	3/29	3/31	4/3	1,300	
4	3/31	4/1	4/1	500	$ 400
5	4/8	4/12	4/14		700
6	4/23	5/6	5/9		1,200

Required

1. Compute CarNut's cost of (a) work in process inventory at March 31 and April 30, (b) finished goods inventory at March 31 and April 30, and (c) cost of goods sold for March and April.
2. Make summary journal entries to record the transfer of completed jobs from work in process to finished goods for March and April.
3. Record the sale of Job 5 for $1,600.
4. Compute the gross profit for Job 5. What costs must the gross profit cover?

Accounting for manufacturing transactions
(Obj. 2, 3, 4)

P20-2A Getaway Homes manufactures prefabricated chalets in Colorado. The company uses a perpetual inventory system and a job cost system in which each chalet is a job. The following events occurred during May.

a. Purchased materials on account, $405,000.
b. Incurred manufacturing wages of $111,600. Requisitioned direct materials and used direct labor in manufacturing:

	Direct Materials	Direct Labor
Chalet 13	$41,100	$14,800
Chalet 14	56,800	28,500
Chalet 15	62,100	19,200
Chalet 16	66,000	21,000

c. Depreciation of manufacturing equipment used on different chalets, $20,000.
d. Other overhead costs incurred on chalets 13 through 16:

Indirect labor......................................	$28,100
Equipment rentals paid in cash	10,400
Plant insurance expired............................	6,000

e. Allocated overhead to jobs at the predetermined rate of 60% of direct labor cost.
f. Chalets completed: 13, 15, 16.
g. Chalets sold: 13 for $99,000; 16 for $141,900.

Required

1. Record the preceding events in the general journal.
2. Open T-accounts for Work in Process Inventory and Finished Goods Inventory. Post the appropriate entries to these accounts, identifying each entry by letter. Determine the ending account balances, assuming that the beginning balances were zero.
3. Add the costs of the unfinished chalet, and show that this equals the ending balance in Work in Process Inventory.
4. Add the cost of the completed chalet that has not yet been sold, and show that this equals the ending balance in Finished Goods Inventory.
5. Compute the gross profit on each chalet that was sold. What costs must the gross profit cover for Getaway Homes?

P20-3A Geolander Co. manufactures tires for all-terrain vehicles. Geolander uses job costing and has a perpetual inventory system.

Preparing and using a job cost record
(Obj. 2, 3, 4)

On September 22, Geolander received an order for 100 TX tires from ATV Corporation at a price of $55 each. The job, assigned number 298, was promised for October 10. After purchasing the materials, Geolander began production on September 30 and incurred the following costs in completing the order:

Date	Labor Time Record No.	Description	Amount
9/30	1896	12 hours @ $20	$240
10/3	1904	30 hours @ $19	570

Date	Materials Requisition No.	Description	Amount
9/30	437	60 lb. rubber @ $18	$1,080
10/2	439	40 meters polyester fabric @ $12	480
10/3	501	100 meters steel cord @ $10	1,000

(continued)

Geolander allocates manufacturing overhead to jobs on the basis of the relation between expected overhead ($420,000) and expected direct labor cost ($300,000). Job 298 was completed on October 3 and shipped to ATV on October 5.

Required

1. Prepare a job cost record similar to Exhibit 20-8 for Job 298.
2. Journalize in summary form the requisition of direct materials and the assignment of direct labor and manufacturing overhead to Job 298.
3. Journalize completion of the job and sale of the goods.

Accounting for manufacturing overhead
(Obj. 3, 4)

P20-4A Suit Up produces uniforms. The company allocates manufacturing overhead based on the machine hours each job uses. Suit Up reports the following cost data for 20X6:

	Budget	Actual
Direct labor hours	7,000 hours	6,200 hours
Machine hours	6,920 hours	6,400 hours
Depreciation on salespersons' autos	$22,000	$22,000
Indirect materials	50,000	52,000
Depreciation on trucks used to deliver uniforms to customers	14,000	12,000
Depreciation on plant and equipment	65,000	67,000
Indirect manufacturing labor	40,000	43,000
Customer service hotline	19,000	21,000
Plant utilities	18,000	20,000
Direct labor cost	70,000	85,000

Required

1. Compute the predetermined manufacturing overhead rate.
2. Post actual and allocated manufacturing overhead to the Manufacturing Overhead T-account.
3. Close the under- or overallocated overhead to cost of goods sold.
4. How can managers use accounting information to help control manufacturing overhead costs?

Comprehensive accounting for manufacturing transactions
(Obj. 2, 3, 4)

P20-5A ← *Link Back to Chapters 2 and 19.* UbiquiTel manufactures specialized parts used in wireless communication. Initially, the company manufactured the parts for its own use, but it gradually began selling them to wireless companies as well. The trial balance of UbiquiTel's manufacturing operations on January 1 is as follows:

UbiquiTel—Manufacturing Operations		
Trial Balance		
January 1, 20XX		
Cash...	$146,550	
Accounts receivable	87,880	
Inventories:		
Materials....................................	16,680	
Work in process	44,480	
Finished goods..............................	60,550	
Plant assets...................................	352,890	
Accumulated depreciation......................		$157,070

(continued)

Accounts payable		84,120
Wages payable..............................		5,600
Common stock..............................		225,000
Retained earnings		237,240
Sales revenues		—
Cost of goods sold..........................	—	
Manufacturing wages........................	—	
Manufacturing overhead	—	
Marketing and general expenses	—	
	709,030	709,030

January 1 balances in the subsidiary ledgers were

- Materials ledger: amplifiers, $6,280; electronic parts, $8,800; indirect materials, $1,600.
- Work in process ledger: Job 86, $44,480.
- Finished goods ledger: transmitters, $37,800; power supplies, $22,750.

January transactions are summarized as follows:

a. Payments on account, $81,430.
b. Marketing and general expenses incurred and paid, $22,400.
c. Collections on account, $194,880.
d. Materials purchased on credit: amplifiers, $20,160; electronic parts, $28,930; indirect materials, $6,690.
e. Materials used in production (requisitioned):
  - Job 86: amplifiers, $4,200.
  - Job 88: amplifiers, $8,080; electronic parts, $30,290.
  - Indirect materials, $6,940.
f. Manufacturing wages incurred during January, $54,060, of which $50,490 was paid. Wages payable at December 31 were paid during January, $5,600.
g. Labor time records for the month: Job 86, $6,600; Job 88, $27,600; indirect labor, $19,860.
h. Depreciation on manufacturing plant and equipment, $7,610.
i. Manufacturing overhead was allocated at the predetermined rate of 120% of direct labor cost.
j. Jobs completed during the month: Job 86, 1,000 transmitters at total cost of $63,200.
k. Credit sales on account: All of Job 86 for $124,690 (cost $63,200).
l. Close Manufacturing Overhead account to Cost of Goods Sold.

Required

1. Open T-accounts for the general ledger, the materials ledger, the work in process ledger, and the finished goods ledger. Insert each account balance as given, and use the reference *Bal.*
2. Record the January transactions directly in the accounts, using the letters as references. UbiquiTel uses a perpetual inventory system.
3. Prepare a trial balance at January 31.
4. Use the work in process T-account to prepare a schedule of cost of goods manufactured for the month of January. (You may want to review Exhibit 19-11.)
5. Prepare an income statement for the month of January. To calculate cost of goods sold, you may want to review Exhibit 19-9. (*Hint:* In transaction l, you closed any under/overallocated manufacturing overhead to Cost of Goods Sold. In the income statement, show this correction as an adjustment to Cost of Goods Sold. If manufacturing overhead is underallocated, the adjustment will increase Cost of Goods Sold. If overhead is overallocated, the adjustment will reduce Cost of Goods Sold.)

Job costing in a service company
(Obj. 5)

Student Resource**CD**

spreadsheet

P20-6A Adnet.com is an Internet advertising agency. The firm uses a job cost system in which each client is a different "job." Adnet.com traces direct labor, software licensing costs, and travel costs directly to each job (client). The company allocates indirect costs to jobs based on a predetermined indirect cost allocation rate, computed as a percentage of direct labor costs.

At the beginning of 20X5, managing partner Ricky Buena prepared a budget:

Direct labor hours (professional)............	17,500 hours
Direct labor costs (professional).............	$1,750,000
Support staff salaries......................	305,000
Rent and utilities	95,000
Supplies..................................	15,000
Leased computer hardware	285,000

In January 20X5, Adnet.com served several clients. Records for two clients appear here:

	GoVacation.com	Port Armour Golf Resort
Direct labor hours	460 hours	32 hours
Software licensing costs	$1,490	$280
Travel costs	9,000	—

Required

1. Compute Adnet.com's predetermined indirect cost allocation rate for 20X5.
2. Compute the total cost of each job.
3. If Adnet.com wants to earn profits equal to 20% of sales revenue, how much (what total fee) should it charge each of these two clients?
4. Why does Adnet.com assign costs to jobs?

Problems

(Group B)

Analyzing job cost data
(Obj. 2, 3, 4)

P20-1B Serenity Manufacturing makes headphones for portable electronic devices. Its job cost records yield the following information.

Job No.	Date Started	Date Finished	Sold	Total Cost of Job at November 30	Total Manufacturing Costs Added in December
1	11/3	11/12	11/13	$1,400	
2	11/3	11/30	12/1	1,900	
3	11/17	12/24	12/27	300	$ 700
4	11/29	12/29	1/3	500	1,600
5	12/8	12/12	12/14		750
6	12/23	1/6	1/9		500

Required

1. Compute Serenity's cost of (a) work in process inventory at November 30 and December 31, (b) finished goods inventory at November 30 and December 31, and (c) cost of goods sold for November and December.

2. Record summary journal entries for the transfer of completed units from work in process to finished goods for November and December.

3. Record the sale of Job 3 for $1,400.

4. What is the gross profit for Job 3? What other costs must this gross profit cover?

P20-2B Aloha Construction, Inc., is a home builder in Hawaii. Aloha uses a perpetual inventory system and a job cost system in which each house is a job. Because it constructs houses, the company uses accounts titled Construction Wages and Construction Overhead. The following events occurred during August:

Accounting for construction transactions
(Obj. 2, 3, 4)

a. Purchased materials on account, $480,400.

b. Incurred construction wages of $219,800. Requisitioned direct materials and used direct labor in construction:

	Direct Materials	Direct Labor
House 302...............................	$58,400	$42,300
House 303...............................	69,000	32,800
House 304...............................	67,600	50,400
House 305...............................	84,200	52,700

c. Depreciation of construction equipment, $6,400.

d. Other construction overhead costs incurred on houses 302 through 305:

Indirect labor......................................	$41,600
Equipment rentals paid in cash.....................	37,300
Worker liability insurance expired	7,100

e. Allocated overhead to jobs at the predetermined overhead rate of 40% of direct labor cost.

f. Houses completed: 302, 304.

g. House sold: 304 for $189,500.

Required

1. Record the events in the general journal.

2. Open T-accounts for Work in Process Inventory and Finished Goods Inventory. Post the appropriate entries to these accounts, identifying each entry by letter. Determine the ending account balances, assuming that the beginning balances were zero.

3. Add the costs of the unfinished houses, and show that this total amount equals the ending balance in the Work in Process Inventory account.

4. Add the cost of the completed house that has not yet been sold, and show that this equals the ending balance in Finished Goods Inventory.

5. Compute gross profit on the house that was sold. What costs must gross profit cover for Aloha Construction?

P20-3B Guandong Technology Co. manufactures CDs and DVDs for computer software and entertainment companies. Guandong uses job costing and has a perpetual inventory system.

Preparing and using a job cost record
(Obj. 2, 3, 4)

On November 2, Guandong began production of 5,000 DVDs, Job 423, for Lion Pictures for $1.10 each. Guandong promised to deliver the DVDs to Lion by November 5. Guandong incurred the following costs:

(continued)

Date	Labor Time Record No.	Description	Amount
11-2	655	10 hours @ $22	$220
11-3	656	20 hours @ $16	320

Date	Materials Requisition No.	Description	Amount
11-2	63	31 lb. polycarbonate plastic @ $11	$341
11-2	64	25 lb. acrylic plastic @ $28	700
11-3	74	3 lb. refined aluminum @ $48	144

Guandong Technology allocates manufacturing overhead to jobs based on the relation between expected overhead ($537,600) and expected direct labor costs ($448,000). Job 423 was completed and shipped on November 3.

Required

1. Prepare a job cost record similar to Exhibit 20-8 for Job 423.
2. Journalize in summary form the requisition of direct materials and the assignment of direct labor and manufacturing overhead to Job 423.
3. Journalize completion of the job and the sale of the 5,000 DVDs.

Accounting for manufacturing overhead
(Obj. 3, 4)

P20-4B Precious Treasures manufactures jewelry boxes. The primary materials (wood, brass, and glass) and direct labor are traced directly to the products. Manufacturing overhead costs are allocated based on machine hours. Data for 20X7 follow:

	Budget	Actual
Machine hours	28,000 hours	32,800 hours
Direct labor hours	42,000 hours	40,000 hours
Wood	$150,000	$148,000
Maintenance labor (repairs to equipment)	9,000	22,500
Plant supervisor's wages	40,000	44,000
Screws, nails, and glue	20,400	41,000
Plant utilities	45,600	90,850
Brass	75,000	70,500
Glass	125,000	126,275
Freight out	35,000	44,500
Direct labor	65,000	63,000
Depreciation on plant and equipment	81,000	81,000
Advertising expenses	40,000	55,000

Required

1. Compute the predetermined manufacturing overhead rate.
2. Post actual and allocated manufacturing overhead to the Manufacturing Overhead T-account.
3. Close the under- or overallocated overhead to cost of goods sold.
4. The predetermined manufacturing overhead rate usually turns out to be inaccurate. Why don't accountants just use the actual manufacturing overhead rate?

P20-5B → *Link Back to Chapters 2 and 19.* Flextronix produces components for telecommunication systems. Initially the company manufactured the parts for its own networks, but it gradually began selling them to other companies as well. Flextronix's trial balance on April 1 follows.

Comprehensive accounting for manufacturing transactions **(Obj. 2, 3, 4)**

Flextronix		
Trial Balance		
April 1, 20XX		
Cash	$ 17,980	
Accounts receivable.	170,360	
Inventories:		
Materials	5,290	
Work in process	41,280	
Finished goods	21,280	
Plant assets	249,570	
Accumulated depreciation		$ 68,400
Accounts payable.		129,360
Wages payable		2,800
Common stock		140,000
Retained earnings.		165,200
Sales revenues.		—
Cost of goods sold	—	
Manufacturing wages	—	
Manufacturing overhead	—	
Marketing and general expenses.	—	
	$505,760	$505,760

April 1 balances in the subsidiary ledgers were

- Materials ledger: glass substrate, $2,080; multiplexers, $2,660; indirect materials, $550.
- Work in process ledger: Job 145, $41,280.
- Finished goods ledger: fiber optic cable, $9,010; laser diodes, $12,270.

April transactions are summarized as follows:

a. Collections on account, $148,270.
b. Marketing and general expenses incurred and paid, $25,740.
c. Payments on account, $37,890.
d. Materials purchased on credit: glass substrate, $7,640; multiplexers, $16,980; indirect materials, $4,600.
e. Materials used in production (requisitioned):
   - Job 145: glass substrate, $740.
   - Job 146: glass substrate, $2,180; multiplexers, $5,640.
   - Indirect materials, $2,010.
f. Manufacturing wages incurred during April, $38,420, of which $36,200 was paid. Wages payable at March 31 were paid during April, $2,800.
g. Labor time records for the month: Job 145, $4,200; Job 146, $17,800; indirect labor, $16,420.
h. Depreciation on plant and equipment, $2,340.

(*continued*)

i. Manufacturing overhead was allocated at the predetermined rate of 70% of direct labor cost.

j. Jobs completed during the month: Job 145, 400 fiber optic cables at total cost of $49,160.

k. Credit sales on account: all of Job 145 for $110,460 (cost $49,160).

l. Closed the Manufacturing Overhead account to Cost of Goods Sold.

Required

1. Open T-accounts for the general ledger, the materials ledger, the work in process ledger, and the finished goods ledger. Insert each account balance as given, and use the reference *Bal.*

2. Record the April transactions directly in the accounts, using the letters as references. Flextronix uses a perpetual inventory system.

3. Prepare a trial balance at April 30.

4. Use the work in process T-account to prepare a schedule of cost of goods manufactured for the month of April. (You may want to review Exhibit 19-11.)

5. Prepare an income statement for the month of April. To calculate cost of goods sold, you may want to review Exhibit 19-9. (*Hint:* In transaction l you closed any under/overallocated manufacturing overhead to Cost of Goods Sold. In the income statement, show this correction as an adjustment to Cost of Goods Sold. If manufacturing overhead is underallocated, the adjustment will increase Cost of Goods Sold. If overhead is overallocated, the adjustment will reduce Cost of Goods Sold.)

Job costing in a service company
(Obj. 5)

Student Resource**CD**

spreadsheet

P20-6B WB Design, Inc., is a Web site design and consulting firm. The firm uses a job cost system, in which each client is a different "job." WB Design traces direct labor, licensing costs, and travel costs directly to each job (client). It allocates indirect costs to jobs based on a predetermined indirect cost allocation rate, computed as a percentage of direct labor costs.

At the beginning of 20X7, managing partner Mary Milici prepared the following budget:

Direct labor hours (professional).	8,000 hours
Direct labor costs (professional)	$1,000,000
Support staff salaries.	80,000
Computer leases.	46,000
Office supplies	25,000
Office rent	49,000

In November 20X7, WB Design served several clients. Records for two clients appear here:

	Organic Foods	SunNow.com
Direct labor hours	750 hours	50 hours
Licensing costs	$ 1,850	$160
Travel costs	14,150	—

Required

1. Compute WB Design's predetermined indirect cost allocation rate for 20X7.

2. Compute the total cost of each job.

3. If Milici wants to earn profits equal to 20% of sales revenue, how much (what total fee) should she charge each of these two clients?

4. Why does WB Design assign costs to jobs?

APPLY *Your Knowledge*

Decision Cases

Case 1. Hegy Chocolate Ltd. is located in Cleveland. The company prepares gift boxes of chocolates for private parties and corporate promotions. Each order contains a selection of chocolates determined by the customer, and the box is designed to the customer's specifications. Accordingly, Hegy uses a job cost system and allocates manufacturing overhead based on direct labor cost.

Costing and pricing identical products **(Obj. 2, 3)**

One of Hegy's largest customers is the Bailey and Choi law firm. This organization sends chocolates to its clients each Christmas and also provides them to employees at the firm's gatherings. The law firm's managing partner, Peter Bailey, placed the client gift order in September for 500 boxes of cream-filled dark chocolates. But Bailey and Choi did not place its December staff-party order until the last week of November. This order was for an additional 100 boxes of chocolates identical to the ones to be distributed to clients.

Hegy budgeted the cost per box for the original 500-box order as follows:

Chocolate, filling, wrappers, box	$14.00
Employee time to fill and wrap the box (10 min.)	2.00
Manufacturing overhead	1.00
Total manufacturing cost	$17.00

Ben Hegy, president of Hegy Chocolate Ltd., priced the order at $20 per box.

In the past few months, Hegy Chocolate Ltd. has experienced price increases for both dark chocolate and direct labor. *All other costs have remained the same.* Hegy budgeted the cost per box for the second order as:

Chocolate, filling, wrappers, box	$15.00
Employee time to fill and wrap the box (10 min.)	2.20
Manufacturing overhead	1.10
Total manufacturing cost	$18.30

1. Do you agree with the cost analysis for the second order? Explain your answer.
2. Should the two orders be accounted for as one job or two in Hegy's system?
3. What sale price per box should Ben Hegy set for the second order? What are the advantages and disadvantages of this price?

Case 2. All Natural manufactures organic fruit preserves sold primarily through health food stores and on the Web. The company closes for two weeks each December to allow employees to spend time with their families over the holiday season. All Natural's manufacturing overhead is mostly straight-line depreciation on its plant and air-conditioning costs for keeping the berries cool during the summer months. The company uses direct labor hours as the allocation base. President Kara Wise has just approved new accounting software and is telling Controller Melissa Powers about her decision.

Accounting for manufacturing overhead **(Obj. 3)**

"I think this new software will be great," Wise says. "It will save you time in preparing all those reports."

"Yes, and having so much more information just a click away will help us make better decisions and help control costs," replies Powers. "We need to consider how we can use the new system to improve our business practices."

"And I know just where to start," says Wise. "You complain each year about having to predict the weather months in advance for estimating air-conditioning costs and direct labor hours for the denominator of the predetermined manufacturing overhead rate, when professional meteorologists can't even get tomorrow's forecast right! I think we should calculate the predetermined overhead rate on a monthly basis."

Controller Powers is not so sure this is a good idea.

Required

1. What are the advantages and disadvantages of Wise's proposal?
2. Should All Natural compute its predetermined manufacturing overhead rate on an annual basis or monthly basis? Explain.

Ethical Issue

Ethics
(Obj. 4, 5)

← *Link back to Chapter 19.* Micro Tek is a contract manufacturer that produces customized computer components for several well-known computer-assembly companies. Micro Tek's latest contract with CompNow.com calls for Micro Tek to deliver sound cards that simulate surround sound from two speakers. Micro Tek spent several hundred thousand dollars to design the sound card to meet CompNow.com's specifications.

Micro Tek's president, Isabel Wang, has stipulated a pricing policy that requires bids (selling prices) for new contracts to be based on Micro Tek's estimated full product cost from all elements of the value chain, plus a profit margin. Upon reviewing the contract figures, Micro Tek's controller, Pennie Bagley, was startled to find that the cost estimates developed by Micro Tek's cost accountant, Anthony Haywood, for the CompNow.com bid were based on only the *inventoriable* costs. Bagley is upset with Haywood. She is not sure what to do next.

Required

1. How did using inventoriable cost rather than full product cost affect the amount of Micro Tek's bid for the CompNow.com job?
2. Identify the parties involved in Pennie Bagley's ethical dilemma. What are her alternatives? How would each party be affected by each alternative? What should Bagley do next?

Team Project

Comparing job costs across airlines, evaluating strategic alternatives
(Obj. 2, 3)

Major airlines like **American**, **Delta**, and **Continental** are struggling to meet the challenges of budget carriers such as **Southwest** and **JetBlue**. Suppose Delta CFO M. Michele Burns has just returned from a meeting on strategies for responding to competition from budget carriers. The vice-president of operations suggested doing nothing: "We just need to wait until these new airlines run out of money. They cannot be making money with their low fares." In contrast, the vice-president of marketing, not wanting to lose marketing share, suggests cutting Delta's fares to match the competition. "If JetBlue charges only $75 for that flight from New York, so must we!" Others, including CFO Burns, emphasized the potential for cutting costs. Another possibility is starting a new budget airline within Delta. Imagine that CEO Leo Mullin cut the meeting short, and directed Burns to "get some hard data."

As a start, Burns decides to collect cost and revenue data for a typical Delta flight, and then compare it to the data for a competitor. Assume she prepares the following schedule:

	Delta	**JetBlue**
Route: New York to Tampa	Flight 1247	Flight 53
Distance	1,011 miles	1,011 miles
Seats per plane.	142	162
One-way ticket price.	$80–$621*	$75
Food and beverage	Meal	Snack

*The highest price is first class airfare

Excluding food and beverage, Burns estimates that the cost per available seat mile is 8.4 cents for Delta, compared to 5.3 cents for JetBlue. (That is, the cost of flying a seat for one mile—whether or not the seat is occupied—is 8.4 cents for Delta, and 5.3 cents for JetBlue.) Assume the average cost of food and beverage is $5 per passenger for snacks and $10 for a meal.

Split your team into two groups. Group 1 should prepare its response to Requirement 1 and group 2 should prepare its response to Requirement 2 before the entire team meets to consider Requirements 3 through 6.

Required

1. Group 1 uses the data to determine for Delta:
   a. the total cost of Flight 1247, assuming a full plane (100% load factor)
   b. the revenue generated by Flight 1247, assuming a 100% load factor and average revenue per one-way ticket of $102
   c. the profit per Flight 1247, given the responses to a. and b.

2. Group 2 uses the data to determine for JetBlue:
   a. the total cost of Flight 53, assuming a full plane (100% load factor)
   b. the revenue generated by Flight 53, assuming a 100% load factor
   c. the profit per Flight 53, given the responses to a. and b.

3. The entire team meets, and both groups combine their analyses. Based on the responses to Requirements 1 and 2, carefully evaluate each of the four alternative strategies discussed in Delta's executive meeting.

4. CFO Burns wants additional data before she meets again with Delta's CEO. Each group should repeat the analyses in *both* Requirements 1 and 2, using another Delta route in Requirement 1, and a budget airline other than JetBlue in Requirement 2 (other budget airlines include **America West**, with a cost per available seat mile of about 6.5 cents, or **Southwest Airlines**, with a cost per available seat mile of about 6.3 cents). Information on flights, available seats, airfares, and mileage are available on airline Web sites.

5. The analysis in this project is based on several simplifying assumptions. As a team, brainstorm factors that your quantitative evaluation does not include, but that may affect a comparison of Delta's operations against budget carriers.

6. Prepare a memo from CFO Burns addressed to Delta CEO Mullin, summarizing the results of your analyses. Be sure to include the limitations of your analyses identified in Requirement 5. Use the following format for your memo.

Date:	_____
To:	CEO Leo F. Mullin
From:	CFO M. Michele Burns
Subject:	Delta's Response to Competition from Budget Airlines

For Internet Exercises, go to the Web site www.prenhall.com/horngren.

CHAPTER 21

Process Costing

TIPS CHECK YOUR RESOURCES

- Visit the www.prenhall.com/horngren **Web site** for self-study quizzes, video clips, and other resources

- Try the **Quick Check** exercise at the end of the chapter to test your knowledge

- Learn the **key terms**

- Do the **Starter** exercises keyed in the margins

- Work the **mid-** and **end-of-chapter summary problems**

- Use the **Concept Links** to review material in other chapters

- Search the **CD** for review materials by chapter or by key word

- Watch the **On Location Jelly Belly** video to review process costing

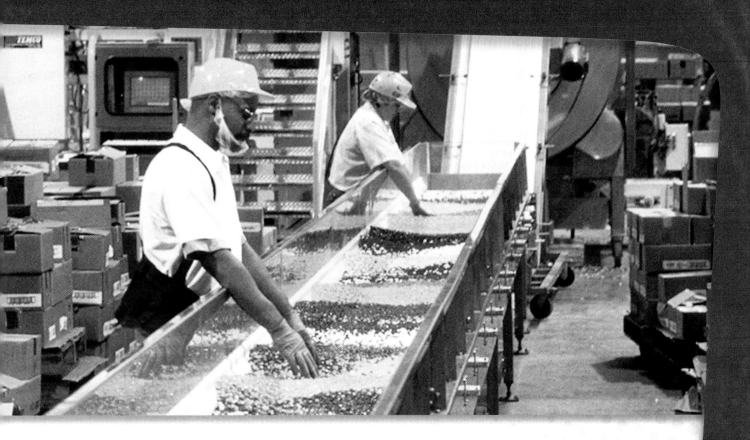

LEARNING OBJECTIVES

1. Distinguish between the flow of costs in process costing and job costing

2. Compute equivalent units

3. Use process costing to assign costs to units completed and to units in ending work in process inventory

4. Use the weighted-average method to assign costs to units completed and to units in ending work in process inventory in a second department

What's your favorite Jelly Belly flavor? Chocolate Pudding? Very Cherry? Lemon Drop? Peanut Butter? Or maybe Piña Colada? Have you ever wondered how they make these tasty gems?

Each tiny Jelly Belly jelly bean spends 7 to 10 days going through eight different processes:

- Cooking the centers
- Shaping hot liquid centers into jelly beans
- Drying
- Sugar shower
- Shell-building
- Polishing
- Stamping (name of the company on each bean)
- Packaging

Jelly Belly Jelly Beans

The family that owns Jelly Belly needs to know how much it costs to make each batch. That helps them set selling prices and measure profits. They also want to know how efficiently each process is operating. That helps them control costs. The owners use accounting information to answer these questions.

Jelly Belly mass produces its jelly beans in a sequence of processes and accumulates costs for each *process*. Then the company spreads these costs over the pounds of jelly beans passing through each process. This *process costing* approach differs from the job costing approach that Dell Computer uses for its computers. Why the difference? Because Jelly Belly mass produces its products, while Dell custom builds each computer to a specific order. It certainly would not be practical to use job cost records to compile the cost of individual jelly beans! ■

■Sitemap

Student ResourceCD

job costing, process costing, work in process inventory

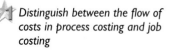

Distinguish between the flow of costs in process costing and job costing

As the chapter-opening story explains, managers need to know how much it costs to make their products. Why? So they can control costs, set selling prices, and identify their most profitable products.

Process Costing: An Overview

Let's start by contrasting the two basic types of costing systems: *job costing* and *process costing*.

Two Basic Costing Systems: Job Costing and Process Costing

We saw in Chapter 20 that Dell Computer, Boeing, and PricewaterhouseCoopers use job costing to determine the cost of producing custom goods and services. Job cost records accumulate the cost of each individual job, like each computer Dell custom-builds to a customer order. In contrast, companies like Jelly Belly, Shell Oil, and Sony use a series of steps (called *processes*) to make large quantities of similar products. These companies typically use *process costing* systems.

For the rest of our discussion, we'll simplify Jelly Belly's processes. We'll combine cooking, shaping, and drying the jelly bean centers into a single process called Centers. We'll also combine the sugar shower, shell-building, polishing, and stamping steps into a second process called Shells. The third process is Packaging.

Jelly Belly *accumulates* the costs of each process and then *assigns* these costs to the units (pounds of jelly beans) passing through that process.

Suppose the Centers process incurs $1,350,000 of costs to produce centers for 1,000,000 pounds of jelly beans, the Shells process incurs $800,000, and Packaging incurs $700,000. The total cost to produce a pound of jelly beans is the sum of the cost per pound for each of the three processes:

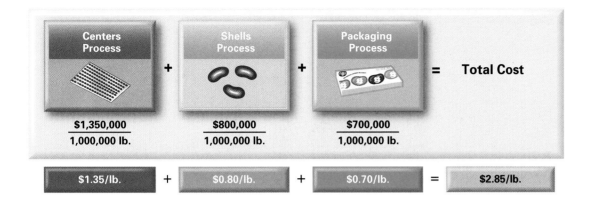

Jelly Belly's owners use the cost per unit of each process to help control costs. For example, they can compare the actual cost of producing centers for a pound of jelly beans (assumed to be $1.35 in our example) to the budget or plan. If the actual cost of the Centers process exceeds the budget, they can look for ways to cut costs in that process. Jelly Belly's owners also consider the total cost of making a pound of jelly beans (assumed to be $2.85 in our example) when setting selling prices. Of course, the price should be high enough to cover costs *and* to return a profit. Jelly Belly also uses the total cost of making a pound of jelly beans for financial reporting:

- To value the ending inventory of jelly beans for the balance sheet
- To value cost of goods sold for the income statement

The simple computation of the cost to make a pound of jelly beans is correct only if there are no work in process inventories. But it takes 7 to 10 days to complete all the processes. So Jelly Belly does have inventories of partially complete jelly beans. These inventories make the costing more complicated. In the rest of this chapter, you'll learn how to do process costing when there are work in process inventories.

How Does the Flow of Costs Differ Between Job and Process Costing?

Exhibit 21-1 compares the flow of costs in

- A job costing system for **Dell Computer**
- A process costing system for **Jelly Belly**

Panel A shows that Dell's job costing system has a single Work in Process Inventory control account, supported by individual subsidiary job cost records for each job in process (that is, each custom-built computer). Dell assigns direct materials, direct labor, and manufacturing overhead to individual jobs, as explained in Chapter 20. When a job is finished, its costs flow directly into Finished Goods Inventory, *not* from one Work in Process Inventory account into another.

In contrast to Dell's individual jobs, Jelly Belly uses a series of *manufacturing processes* to produce jelly beans. Exhibit 21-2 shows that in the Centers process, Jelly Belly uses labor and equipment to cook flavorings and sugar into jelly bean centers. In the Shells process, Jelly Belly uses labor and equipment to coat the centers with syrup and glaze to form the crunchy shells. Finally, the Packaging process uses labor and other equipment to package the finished jelly beans into various boxes and bags.

✔ Starter 21-1

Exhibit 21-1   Comparison of Job Costing and Process Costing

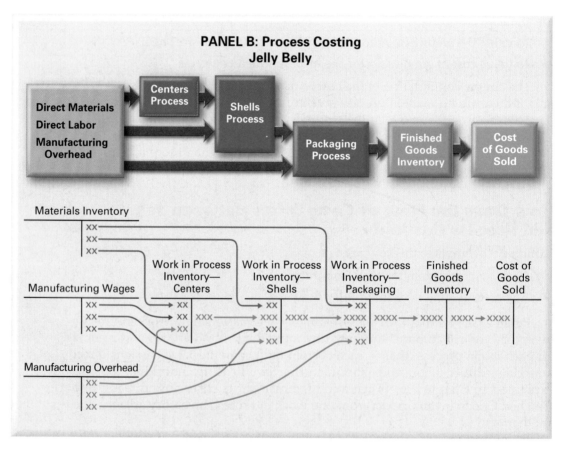

Exhibit 21-2   Flow of Costs in Production of Jelly Beans

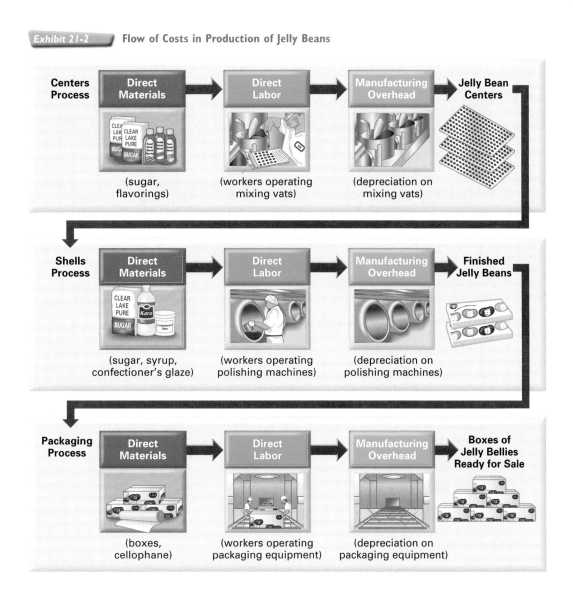

Panel B of Exhibit 21-1 summarizes the flow of costs through this process costing system. Study the exhibit carefully, paying particular attention to the following key points.

1. Each process (Centers, Shells, and Packaging) has its own separate Work in Process Inventory account.
2. Direct materials, direct labor, and manufacturing overhead are assigned to the Work in Process Inventory accounts for each process. For example:

	Work in Process Inventory—Centers	Work in Process Inventory—Shells	Work in Process Inventory—Packaging
Direct materials	Sugar, flavorings	Sugar, syrup, confectioners' glaze	Boxes, cellophane
Direct labor	Mixing-vat operators' wages	Polishing-machine operators' wages	Packaging-equipment operators' wages
Manufacturing overhead	Depreciation on mixing vat	Depreciation on polishing machine	Depreciation on packaging equipment

3. When the Centers process is complete, the jelly bean centers move out of this process and into the Shells process. The cost of the centers is also transferred out of Work in Process Inventory—Centers into Work in Process Inventory—Shells.

4. When the Shells process is complete, the finished jelly beans move out of this process and into the Packaging process. The cost of the jelly beans flows out of Work in Process Inventory—Shells into Work in Process Inventory—Packaging.

5. When the Packaging process is complete, the finished packages of Jelly Bellies go into finished goods storage. The combined costs from the Centers, Shells, and Packaging processes flow into Finished Goods Inventory. In process costing *costs flow into Finished Goods Inventory only from the Work in Process Inventory of the **last** manufacturing process.*

Building Blocks of Process Costing

In Panel B of Exhibit 21-1, how much of the total costs incurred in the Centers process should we assign to:

- The centers transferred out to the Shells process versus
- The ending inventory in the Centers process?

To answer this key question, we must first learn about two building blocks of process costing: conversion costs and equivalent units.

Conversion Costs

Chapter 19 introduced three kinds of manufacturing costs: direct materials, direct labor, and manufacturing overhead. Companies like **HP** and **Harley-Davidson** that use automated production processes often find that direct labor is only a small part of total manufacturing costs. Such companies often use only two categories:

- Direct materials
- **Conversion costs** (direct labor plus manufacturing overhead)

Combining direct labor and manufacturing overhead in a single category simplifies the accounting. We call this category *conversion costs* because it is the cost (direct labor plus manufacturing overhead) to *convert* raw materials into new finished products.

Equivalent Units

When a company has work in process inventories of partially completed goods, we use equivalent units to measure the amount of work done during a period. **Equivalent units** express the amount of work done during a period in terms of fully complete units of output. Assume **Calloway's** golf ball production plant has 5,000 balls in ending work in process inventory. Each ball is 80% of the way through the production process. If conversion costs are incurred evenly throughout the process, then getting 5,000 balls each 80% of the way through the process takes about the same amount of work as getting 4,000 balls (5,000 × 80%) all the way through. Thus, ending work in process inventory has 4,000 equivalent units.

For costs that are incurred evenly throughout the production process:

NUMBER OF PARTIALLY COMPLETE UNITS	×	PERCENTAGE OF PROCESS COMPLETED	=	NUMBER OF EQUIVALENT UNITS
5,000	×	80%	=	4,000

This formula holds only for costs that are incurred evenly throughout production. This is usually true for conversion costs (direct labor and manufacturing overhead). However, direct materials are often added at a particular point in the process. Rubber is added at the beginning of the production process, and packaging materials are not added until the end. How many equivalent units of rubber and packaging materials are in the ending inventory of 5,000 balls?

Student Resource**CD**

conversion costs, cost assignment, equivalent unit costs

2 Compute equivalent units

Conversion Costs
Direct labor plus manufacturing overhead.

Equivalent Units
Express the amount of work done during a period in terms of fully complete units of output.

Look at the time line in Exhibit 21-3:

✔ Starter 21-2

Exhibit 21-3 Calloway Production Plant Time Line

All 5,000 balls are 80% complete, so they all have passed the point at which rubber is added. Each ball has its full share of rubber, so the balls have 5,000 equivalent units of rubber. In contrast, the time line shows that *none* of the 5,000 balls has made it to the end of the process, where the packaging materials are added. The ending inventory therefore has *zero* equivalent units of packaging materials.

To summarize, the 5,000 balls in ending work in process inventory have

- 5,000 equivalent units of rubber
- 0 equivalent units of packaging materials
- 4,000 equivalent units of conversion costs

Be careful to distinguish the *end of the production process* from the *end of the accounting period*. Goods at the end of the production process are transferred to the next process or to finished goods. For example, Calloway's completed golf balls proceed to the finished goods warehouse. By contrast, at the end of the accounting period, goods that are only partway through the production process are the ending work in process inventory. Calloway's ending work in process inventory includes 5,000 golf balls that have their rubber cores but no packaging.

Colleges and universities use the equivalent-unit concept to describe the number of faculty as well as the number of students. The **University of Georgia** has about 2,000 full-time faculty and 400 part-time faculty. Assume the following:

1. A full-time faculty member teaches six courses per year
2. 100 part-time faculty teach three courses per year
3. 300 part-time faculty teach two courses per year

What is the "full-time equivalent" faculty—the number of equivalent units of faculty?

Answer: Compute the full-time equivalent faculty as follows:

Full-time faculty	$2{,}000 \times 6/6 = 2{,}000$
Half-time faculty	$100 \times 3/6 = 50$
One-third time faculty	$300 \times 2/6 = \underline{100}$
Full-time equivalent faculty	$\underline{2{,}150}$

Illustrating Process Costing

Let's see how SeaView, a sporting goods company, uses process costing to measure (1) its cost of producing swim masks and (2) the cost of the two major processes it uses to make the masks. Exhibit 21-4 illustrates SeaView's production process. The Shaping Department begins with direct materials (including

☐ Overview
☐ Building Blocks
■ Illustrating Process Costing
☐ Costing in a Second Department
☐ Appendix: FIFO

Student Resource CD

conversion costs, cost assignment, equivalent unit costs, transferred-in costs, work in process inventory

Use process costing to assign costs to units completed and to units in ending work in process inventory

plastic) that labor and equipment transform into shaped masks. The direct materials are added at the beginning but conversion costs are incurred evenly throughout the process. After shaping, the partially completed masks move to the Insertion Department, where the clear faceplates are inserted.

Flow of Costs in Producing Swim Masks

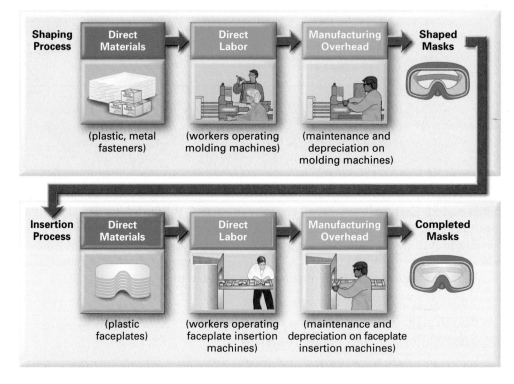

During October, the Shaping Department incurs the following costs for 50,000 masks:

Direct materials		$140,000
Conversion costs:		
Direct labor	$21,250	
Manufacturing overhead	46,750	68,000
Costs to account for		$208,000

If shaping is complete for all 50,000 masks, the costs transferred to Work in Process Inventory—Insertion are the full $208,000. The unit cost is $4.16 ($208,000/50,000 masks).

But what if only 40,000 masks are completely through the shaping process? At October 31, the Shaping Department still has 10,000 masks that are only one-quarter of the way through. How do we split the $208,000 between

- 40,000 completely shaped masks transferred to the Insertion Department
- 10,000 partially shaped masks remaining in the Shaping Department's ending work in process inventory

The answer lies in a five-step process costing procedure.

Step 1: Summarize the Flow of Physical Units

Exhibit 21-5 tracks the movement of swim masks into and out of the Shaping Department. We assume work began October 1, so Work in Process Inventory had a zero balance at September 30. This simplifies the computations so you can more easily learn basic process costing. But the simplification is realistic for firms that have little or no work in process inventory, such as food processors, and financial institutions that clear transactions daily. In the second half of the chapter, you'll see how beginning work in process inventory affects the analysis.

Of the 50,000 masks started in October, 40,000 were completed and transferred out to the Insertion Department during the month. The remaining 10,000 partially shaped masks are the Shaping Department's ending work in process inventory on October 31.

Exhibit 21-5   Step 1: Summarize the Flow of Physical Units; Step 2: Compute Output in Terms of Equivalent Units

SeaView Shaping Department
Month Ended October 31, 20XX

	Step 1	Step 2: Equivalent Units	
Flow of Production	Flow of Physical Units	Direct Materials	Conversion Costs
Units to account for:			
Beginning work in process, September 30	—		
Started in production during October	50,000		
Total physical units to account for	50,000		
Units accounted for:			
Completed and transferred out during October	40,000	40,000	40,000
Ending work in process, October 31	10,000	10,000	2,500*
Total physical units accounted for	50,000		
Equivalent units		50,000	42,500

*10,000 units each 25% complete = 2,500 equivalent units

Step 2: Compute Output in Terms of Equivalent Units

The Shaping Department time line in Exhibit 21-6 shows that all direct materials are added at the beginning of the process. In contrast, conversion costs are incurred evenly throughout the process. Thus, we must compute equivalent units separately for direct materials and conversion costs.

✔ **Starter 21-3**

✔ **Starter 21-4**

Exhibit 21-6   SeaView's Shaping Department Time Line

As Exhibit 21-6 shows, 40,000 masks are complete as to both materials and conversion costs. These completed masks have incurred 40,000 equivalent units of direct materials and 40,000 equivalent units of conversion costs.

The Shaping Department has another 10,000 masks that are only 25% of the way through the process on October 31. The time line shows that all the direct materials have been added to these 10,000 masks. The total equivalent units of direct materials include the 40,000 finished masks plus the 10,000 masks in ending (work in process) inventory that are complete as to direct materials, as shown in step 2 of Exhibit 21-5.

Shaping Department conversion costs are incurred evenly throughout the process. The time line shows that for each of the 10,000 partially completed masks, 25% of the conversion costs have been incurred by October 31. The equivalent units of conversion costs are:

$$10,000 \times 25\% = 2,500 \text{ equivalent units}$$

The total equivalent units of conversion costs include the 40,000 finished masks plus the 2,500 equivalent units of conversion costs from the masks in ending work in process inventory that are only partially completed on October 31. See step 2 of Exhibit 21-5.

Suppose that direct materials were added at the *end* of SeaView's shaping process rather than at the beginning.

1. Draw a new time line similar to Exhibit 21-6.
2. Use the time line to determine the number of equivalent units of direct materials.

Answers

1. Conversion costs added evenly throughout process

2. The time line shows that the 10,000 masks in ending work in process inventory have not made it to the end of the shaping process where materials are added. Materials have been added *only* to the 40,000 masks completed and transferred out. Thus, there are 40,000 equivalent units of direct materials.

Step 3: Summarize Total Costs to Account For

Exhibit 21-7 summarizes the total costs to account for in the Shaping Department (cost data are from page 852). These costs are the total debits in Work in Process Inventory—Shaping, because the beginning balance is zero.

Exhibit 21-7

Step 3: Summarize Total Costs
to Account For

SeaView Shaping Department
Month Ended October 31, 20XX

Work in Process Inventory—Shaping

	Physical Units	Dollars		Physical Units	Dollars
Beginning inventory, September 30	-0-	$ -0-	Transferred out	40,000	$?
Production started:	50,000				
Direct materials		140,000			
Conversion costs:					
Direct labor		21,250			
Manufacturing overhead		46,750			
Total to account for	50,000	$208,000			
Ending inventory, October 31	10,000	$?			

The Shaping Department has 50,000 physical units and $208,000 of costs to account for. Our next task is to split these costs between the 40,000 shaped masks transferred out to the Insertion Department and the 10,000 masks that remain in the Shaping Department's ending work in process inventory.

Step 4: Compute the Cost per Equivalent Unit

In step 2, we computed the total number of equivalent units for direct materials (50,000) and conversion costs (42,500). Because the equivalent units differ, we must compute a separate cost per unit for each category. Exhibit 21-7 shows that the direct materials cost is $140,000. Conversion cost is $68,000, which is the sum of direct labor ($21,250) and manufacturing overhead ($46,750).

To compute the cost per equivalent unit, remember that the word *per* means "divided by." So the cost *per* equivalent unit is the cost *divided by* the number of equivalent units, as shown in Exhibit 21-8.

✔ Starter 21-5

✔ Starter 21-6

Exhibit 21-8

Step 4: Compute the Cost per
Equivalent Unit

SeaView Shaping Department
Month Ended October 31, 20XX

	Direct Materials	Conversion Costs
Beginning work in process, September 30	$ 0	$ 0
Costs added during October (from Exhibit 21-7) . .	$140,000	$68,000
Divide by equivalent units (from Exhibit 21-5)	÷ 50,000	÷42,500
Cost per equivalent unit	$2.80	$1.60

In addition to using the cost per equivalent unit in the five-step process costing procedure, managers also use this information to determine how well they have controlled costs. If the cost per equivalent unit of conversion (or direct materials) meets or beats the budgeted target cost per equivalent unit, the manager has successfully controlled the conversion (or direct materials) costs.

Step 5: Assign Costs to Units Completed and to Units in Ending Work in Process Inventory

Exhibit 21-9 shows how the equivalent units computed in step 2 (Exhibit 21-5) are costed at the cost per equivalent unit computed in step 4 (Exhibit 21-8). The goal of Exhibit 21-9 is to determine how much of the $208,000 total costs incurred by the Shaping Department should be assigned to (1) the 40,000 completely shaped masks that have been transferred out to the Insertion Department and (2) the 10,000 partially shaped masks remaining in Shaping's ending work in process inventory.

✔ Starter 21-7

Exhibit 21-9   Step 5: Assign Costs to Units Completed and to Units in Ending Work in Process Inventory

SeaView Shaping Department
Month Ended October 31, 20XX

	Direct Materials	Conversion Costs	Total
Completed and transferred out (40,000)	[40,000 × ($2.80 + $1.60)]		= $176,000
Ending work in process inventory (10,000):			
Direct materials	[10,000 × $2.80]		= $ 28,000
Conversion costs		[2,500 × $1.60]	= 4,000
Total cost of ending work in process inventory			$ 32,000
Total costs accounted for			$208,000

First consider the 40,000 masks completed and transferred out. Exhibit 21-5 reveals 40,000 equivalent units of work for both direct materials and conversion costs. Thus, the total cost of these completed masks is 40,000 × ($2.80 + $1.60) = $176,000, as shown in Exhibit 21-9.

Next consider the 10,000 masks still being shaped at the end of the month. These masks have 10,000 equivalent units of direct materials (at $2.80 per unit), so the direct material cost is 10,000 × $2.80 = $28,000. The 2,500 equivalent units of conversion work in the ending inventory at $1.60 per equivalent unit yields conversion costs of $4,000 (2,500 × $1.60). As Exhibit 21-9 shows, the total cost of the 10,000 partially completed masks in Shaping's ending (work in process) inventory is the sum of these direct material and conversion costs: $28,000 + $4,000 = $32,000.

Exhibit 21-9 has accomplished our goal of splitting the $208,000 total cost identified in step 3 (Exhibit 21-7) between

The 40,000 masks completed and transferred out to the Insertion Department.	$176,000
The 10,000 masks remaining in the Shaping Department's ending work in process inventory on October 31	32,000
Total costs of the Shaping Department	$208,000

Journal entries to record October production in the Shaping Department follow (data from Exhibit 21-7):

Work in Process Inventory—Shaping.......	208,000	
Materials Inventory.............		140,000
Manufacturing Wages...........		21,250
Manufacturing Overhead........		46,750

To requisition materials and assign labor and overhead cost to the Shaping Department.

The entry to transfer the cost of the 40,000 completed masks out of the Shaping
Department and into the Insertion Department is as follows (data from Exhibit 21-9):

Work in Process Inventory—Insertion	176,000	
Work in Process Inventory—Shaping ..		176,000

After these entries are posted, the Work in Process Inventory—Shaping account
appears as follows:

Work in Process Inventory—Shaping

Balance, September 30	—	Transferred to Insertion	176,000
Direct materials	140,000		
Direct labor	21,250		
Manufacturing overhead	46,750		
Balance, October 31	32,000		

✔ Starter 21-8

What is the shaping cost per mask for each of the 40,000 masks completed and transferred out of the Shaping Department and into the Insertion Department? Why would
SeaView's managers want this information?

Answer: Shaping's cost per mask is $4.40 ($2.80 + $1.60)—the $176,000 total
Shaping Department cost assigned to the masks completed and transferred out
(from Exhibit 21-9) divided by the total number of masks completed and
transferred out of Shaping and into Insertion (40,000).
    SeaView's managers would compare the cost per mask of the shaping process in
October against the planned cost per mask to evaluate the efficiency of the Shaping
Department's October operations. Also, the costs of the shaped masks will flow into the
Insertion Department and will become part of the total cost of the completed masks.
Management can use the total cost of the masks to set selling prices and to determine
which products are most profitable.

Before continuing, review the Process Costing Decision Guidelines to make sure
you understand equivalent units and the flow of costs in process costing.

Decision Guidelines

PROCESS COSTING—FIRST PROCESS (NO BEGINNING INVENTORY)

Here are some of the key decisions SeaView made in setting up its process costing system.

Decision	Guidelines
Should SeaView use job or process costing?	SeaView mass-produces large quantities of identical swim masks using two production processes: shaping and insertion. It uses *process costing* to:
	1. *Accumulate* the cost of each process
	2. *Assign* these costs to the masks passing through that process

Decision Guidelines *(continued)*

Decision	Guidelines
How do costs flow from Work in Process Inventory to Finished Goods Inventory in SeaView's process costing system?	In SeaView's process costing system, costs flow from: Work in Process Inventory—Shaping ↓ Work in Process Inventory—Insertion ↓ Finished Goods Inventory More generally, costs flow from one Work in Process Inventory account to the next until the last process, after which they flow into Finished Goods Inventory.
How many Work in Process Inventory accounts does SeaView's process costing system have?	SeaView uses a separate Work in Process Inventory account for each of its two major processes: Shaping and Insertion.
How to account for partially completed products?	Use equivalent units.
Which costs require separate equivalent-unit computations?	Compute equivalent units separately for each input added at a different point in the production process. SeaView computes equivalent units separately for materials and conversion costs because materials are added at a particular point in the production process, but conversion costs are added evenly throughout the process.
How to compute equivalent units?	SeaView's *conversion costs* are incurred evenly throughout the production process, so the equivalent units are computed as follows: $$\text{Equivalent units} = \begin{array}{c}\text{Number of}\\\text{partially}\\\text{complete}\\\text{units}\end{array} \times \begin{array}{c}\text{Percentage}\\\text{of}\\\text{process}\\\text{completed}\end{array}$$ SeaView's *materials* are added at specific points in the production process, so the equivalent units are computed as follows: • If physical units have passed the point at which materials are added → units are complete with respect to materials, so equivalent units of materials = physical units • If physical units have *not* passed the point at which materials are added → units have not incurred any materials, so equivalent units of materials = 0
How to compute the cost per equivalent unit?	Divide the cost by the number of equivalent units.
How to split the costs of the shaping process between • Swim masks completed and transferred out? • Partially complete swim masks in ending work in process inventory?	Multiply the cost per equivalent unit by • Number of equivalent units of work in the physical units completed and transferred out • Number of equivalent units of work in the ending work in process inventory
How well did the manager of the Shaping Department control the department's costs?	If direct material and conversion cost per equivalent unit meets or beats target unit costs, the manager has done a good job controlling costs.

MID-CHAPTER *Summary Problem*

CHECK YOUR RESOURCES

Use the five steps of process costing to identify the missing amounts X and Y in the following report prepared by Florida Tile Industries for May.

Tile-Forming Department
Month Ended May 31, 20XX

	Physical Units	Total Costs
Beginning work in process, April 30	—	$ —
Started in production during May	20,000	43,200*
Total to account for	20,000	$43,200
Completed and transferred to Finishing Department during May	16,000	$ X
Ending work in process, May 31 (25% complete as to direct materials, 55% complete as to conversion cost)	4,000	Y
Total accounted for	20,000	$43,200

*Includes direct materials of $6,800 and conversion costs of $36,400

Solution

STEP 1 Summarize the flow of physical units.

STEP 2 Compute output in terms of equivalent units.

Tile-Forming Department
Month Ended May 31, 20XX

	Step 1	Step 2: Equivalent Units	
Flow of Production	Flow of Physical Units	Direct Materials	Conversion Costs
Units to account for:			
Beginning work in process, April 30	—		
Started in production during May	20,000		
Total physical units to account for	20,000		
Units accounted for:			
Completed and transferred out in May	16,000	16,000	16,000
Ending work in process, May 31	4,000	1,000*	2,200*
Total physical units accounted for	20,000		
Equivalent units		17,000	18,200

*Direct materials: 4,000 units each 25% complete = 1,000 equivalent units
Conversion costs: 4,000 units each 55% complete = 2,200 equivalent units

STEP 3 Summarize total costs to account for.

Tile-Forming Department
Month Ended May 31, 20XX

	Direct Materials	Conversion Costs	Total
Beginning work in process, April 30...	$ 0	$ 0	$ 0
Costs added during May*	6,800	36,400	43,200
Total costs to account for	$6,800	$36,400	$43,200

*From the first report in the Mid-Chapter Summary Problem.

STEP 4 Compute the cost per equivalent unit.

Tile-Forming Department
Month Ended May 31, 20XX

	Direct Materials	Conversion Costs
Beginning work in process, April 30	$ 0	$ 0
Costs added during May	$ 6,800	$36,400
Divide by equivalent units	÷17,000	÷18,200
Cost per equivalent unit	$0.40	$2.00

STEP 5 Assign costs to units completed and to units in ending work in process inventory.

Tile-Forming Department
Month Ended May 31, 20XX

	Direct Materials	Conversion Costs	Total
X: Units completed and transferred out (16,000)	[16,000 × ($0.40 + $2.00)]		= $38,400
Units in ending work in process inventory (4,000):			
Direct materials.............	[1,000 × $0.40]		= 400
Conversion costs...........		[2,200 × $2.00]	= 4,400
Y: Total cost of ending work in process inventory			4,800
Total costs accounted for			$43,200

Student ResourceCD

conversion costs, cost assignment, equivalent unit costs, weighted-average costing method

 Use the weighted-average method to assign costs to units completed and to units in ending work in process inventory in a second department.

Process Costing in a Second Department

Most products require a series of processing steps. In this section, we consider a second department—SeaView's Insertion Department—to complete the picture of process costing.

The Insertion Department receives the shaped masks and polishes them before inserting the faceplates at the end of the process. Exhibit 21-10 shows that

■ Shaped masks are transferred in from Shaping at the beginning of Insertion's process.

■ Insertion's conversion costs are added evenly throughout the process.

■ Insertion's direct materials (faceplates) are not added until the end of the process.

Keep in mind that *direct materials* in the Insertion Department refers to the faceplates added *in that department* and not to the materials (the plastic) added in the Shaping Department. Likewise, *conversion cost* in the Insertion Department refers to all manufacturing costs (other than direct materials) incurred only in Insertion.

Exhibit 21-10 SeaView's Insertion Department Time Line (Weighted-Average)

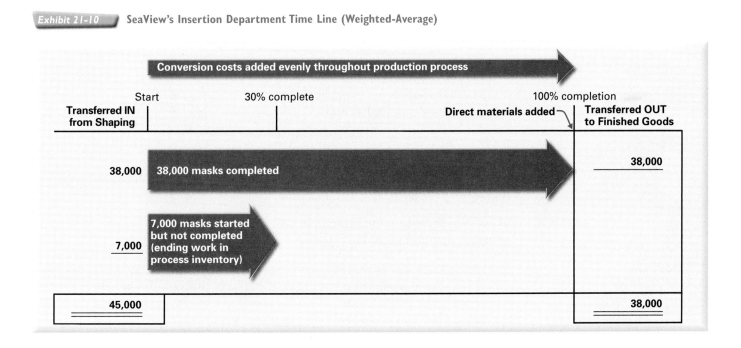

The Weighted-Average Process Costing Method

Here we consider the weighted-average method of accounting for process costs. → The appendix to this chapter covers the FIFO method. Both the weighted-average and the FIFO methods rely on the five-step process costing procedure. The only difference between the two methods lies in how they treat beginning inventory. We focus on the weighted-average method because

Chapter 6 introduced the weighted-average method of inventory costing.

■ It is simpler.

■ Differences between the two methods' results are usually insignificant.

Because SeaView's Shaping Department had no beginning work in process inventory, we did not need to specify whether that department used the weighted-average or FIFO method. By contrast, SeaView's Insertion Department does have beginning work in process inventory. Let's see how this beginning inventory affects the process costing computations.

Exhibit 21-11 lists October information for SeaView's Insertion Department. Study this information carefully and think about what each item means.

Exhibit 21-11

SeaView's Insertion Department
Data for October

Units:	
Beginning work in process, September 30	
(0% complete as to direct materials,	
60% complete as to conversion work).......	5,000 masks
Transferred in from Shaping Department	
during October (Exhibit 21-6).............	40,000 masks
Completed and transferred out to Finished	
Goods Inventory during October...........	38,000 masks
Ending work in process, October 31	
(0% complete as to direct materials,	
30% complete as to conversion work).......	7,000 masks
Costs:	
Beginning work in process, September 30	
(transferred-in costs, $22,900;	
conversion costs, $1,100)	$ 24,000
Transferred in from Shaping Department	
during October (from Exhibit 21-9)	176,000
Direct materials added during October in	
Insertion Department....................	19,000
Conversion costs added during October in	
Insertion Department:	
Direct labor .... $ 3,710	
Manufacturing overhead................. 11,130	14,840

Remember that work in process inventory at the close of business on September 30 is both:

- Ending inventory for September *and*
- Beginning inventory for October

Exhibit 21-11 shows that SeaView's Insertion Department started the October period with 5,000 masks that had made it partway through the insertion process in September. During October, the Insertion Department started work on 40,000 additional masks received from the Shaping Department.

The weighted-average method combines the Insertion Department's:

- Work done in September to start the insertion process on the 5,000 masks in the department's October beginning work in process inventory
- Work done in October to complete the 5,000 masks in beginning inventory and to work on the 40,000 additional masks transferred in from the Shaping Department during October.

Weighted-Average Process Costing Method
A process costing method that costs all equivalent units of work with a weighted average of the previous period's and the current period's cost per equivalent unit.

Thus, the **weighted-average process costing method** costs all of the Insertion Department's equivalent units of work on these 45,000 masks (5,000 beginning work in process inventory + 40,000 transferred in) with a weighted average of the previous period's and the current period's cost per equivalent unit.

Just as we did for the Shaping Department, our goal is to split the total cost in the Insertion Department between:

- The 38,000 masks that the department completed and transferred out to finished goods inventory, and
- The 7,000 partially complete masks remaining in the department's ending work in process inventory at the end of October.

We use the same five-step process costing procedure that we used for the Shaping Department.

Steps 1 and 2: Summarize the Flow of Physical Units and Compute Output in Terms of Equivalent Units

SUMMARIZE THE FLOW OF PHYSICAL UNITS   Exhibit 21-11 shows that the Insertion Department had a beginning work in process inventory of 5,000 masks that were partway through the insertion process at the start of the period. Exhibits 21-6 and 21-11 show that during October, the Shaping Department finished 40,000 masks and transferred them into the Insertion Department. Thus, Exhibit 21-12 shows that the Insertion Department has 45,000 masks to account for (5,000 + 40,000).

✔ Starter 21-9

Exhibit 21-12 Step 1: Summarize the Flow of Physical Units; Step 2: Compute Output in Terms of Equivalent Units

SeaView Insertion Department
Month Ended October 31, 20XX

Flow of Production	Step 1: Flow of Physical Units	Step 2: Transferred In	Step 2: Direct Materials	Step 2: Conversion Costs
Units to account for:				
Beginning work in process, September 30	5,000			
Transferred in during October	40,000			
Total physical units to account for	45,000			
Units accounted for:				
Completed and transferred out during October	38,000	38,000	38,000*	38,000*
Ending work in process, October 31	7,000	7,000	—†	2,100†
Total physical units accounted for	45,000			
Equivalent units		45,000	38,000	40,100

In the Insertion Department:
*Units completed and transferred out
Direct materials: 38,000 units each 100% completed = 38,000 equivalent units
Conversion costs: 38,000 units each 100% completed = 38,000 equivalent units

†Ending inventory
Direct materials: 7,000 units each 0% completed = 0 equivalent units
Conversion costs: 7,000 units each 30% completed = 2,100 equivalent units

Where did these masks go? Exhibits 21-10 and 21-11 show that the Insertion Department completed and transferred 38,000 masks out to finished goods inventory (the 5,000 masks from beginning work in process inventory, plus another 33,000 masks started and completed this period). The Insertion Department's ending work in process inventory consists of 7,000 masks that were partway through the insertion process at the close of business on October 31. Thus, Exhibit 21-12 shows that the department has accounted for all 45,000 masks (38,000 completed and transferred out + 7,000 in ending work in process inventory).

COMPUTE EQUIVALENT UNITS   Exhibit 21-12 uses the flow of physical units from step 1 and the time line in Exhibit 21-10 to compute the Insertion Department's equivalent units of work. Under the weighted-average method, SeaView computes the equivalent units for the total work done to date. This includes all the work done in the current period (October), plus the work done in the prior period (September) to start the insertion process on the masks in the current period's beginning work in process inventory.

The Insertion Department has three categories of equivalent units. In addition to direct materials (faceplates) and conversion costs added in the Insertion

Department, SeaView must also compute equivalent units for the shaped swim masks that are *transferred in* from the Shaping Department. All second and later departments must account for units (and costs) transferred in from preceding departments.

Let's see how to compute the equivalent units for the Insertion Department. This will include all the work ever done on the 45,000 masks that were in process during October, for each of the three categories of costs.

EQUIVALENT UNITS TRANSFERRED IN   After the Shaping Department completes its work on the masks and transfers them out, the Insertion Department receives those masks (and their accumulated costs) for final processing. Exhibit 21-10 shows that transferred-in costs (from Shaping) act like costs that are added at the very beginning of the insertion process.

The time line in Exhibit 21-10 shows that the Insertion Department completed and transferred out 38,000 masks to finished goods inventory. Of course, these masks are complete with respect to transferred-in (shaping) costs; masks must be completely shaped before they can begin the insertion process. Similarly, the 7,000 masks partway through the insertion process at the end of the period are also complete with respect to the transferred-in (shaping) costs. Why? Because the insertion process cannot begin until the shaping process is complete. Exhibit 21-12 shows that the total transferred-in equivalent units sum to 45,000 (38,000 + 7,000).

EQUIVALENT UNITS OF DIRECT MATERIALS   Now turn to the direct materials added in the Insertion Department. Workers insert the faceplates at the *end* of the process, as shown in Exhibit 21-10. Exhibit 21-10 also shows that during October, 38,000 masks passed the end of the insertion process. So workers inserted faceplates in all of these 38,000 completed masks. However, the time line shows that ending work in process inventory is only 30% of the way through the process, so it has not yet reached the point at which workers insert the faceplates. Thus, the ending work in process inventory has no faceplates—that is, no Insertion Department direct materials. Exhibit 21-12 summarizes the results, showing that the Insertion Department incurred 38,000 equivalent units of direct materials.

EQUIVALENT UNITS OF CONVERSION COSTS   Finally, consider conversion costs. The time line in Exhibit 21-10 shows that the 38,000 masks completed and transferred out of the Insertion Department are 100% complete with respect to the Insertion Department's conversion costs. Any swim mask transferred to finished goods inventory must have all of the Insertion Department's conversion work completed.

By contrast, the 7,000 masks in the Insertion Department's ending work in process inventory are only 30% of the way through the insertion process on October 31. The Insertion Department has performed $7,000 \times 30\% = 2,100$ equivalent units of conversion work on this ending inventory.

The conversion costs column of Exhibit 21-12 shows that total equivalent units of conversion work include:

38,000	units for the swim masks completed and transferred out to finished goods inventory
2,100	units for the swim masks in the Insertion Department's ending work in process inventory
40,100	total equivalent units of conversion costs

Steps 3 and 4: Summarize Total Costs to Account For and Compute the Cost per Equivalent Unit

Exhibit 21-13 accumulates the Insertion Department's total costs to account for, based on the data in Exhibit 21-11.

Exhibit 21-13 Step 3: Summarize Total Costs to Account For; Step 4: Compute the Cost per Equivalent Unit

SeaView Insertion Department
Month Ended October 31, 20XX

	Transferred In	Direct Materials	Conversion Costs	Total
Beginning work in process, September 30 (from Exhibit 21-11).	$ 22,900	$ —	$ 1,100	$ 24,000
Costs added during October (from Exhibit 21-11)	176,000	19,000	14,840	209,840
Total costs	$198,900	$19,000	$15,940	
Divide by equivalent units (from Exhibit 21-12).	÷ 45,000	÷38,000	÷40,100	
Cost per equivalent unit	$4.42	$0.50	$0.3975*	
Total costs to account for.				$233,840

*Rounded.

In addition to direct material and conversion costs, the Insertion Department must account for transferred-in costs. **Transferred-in costs** are incurred in a previous process (the Shaping Department, in the SeaView example) and are carried forward as part of the product's cost when it moves to the next process.

Transferred-in Costs
Costs incurred in a previous process that are carried forward as part of the product's cost when it moves to the next process.

Transferred-in costs from a previous process are a special category of costs incurred in second (and later) processes. The Insertion Department can view the masks coming in from the Shaping Department as raw materials introduced at the beginning of the Insertion Department's process. If the Insertion Department had bought these shaped masks from an outside supplier, it would have to account for the costs of purchasing the masks. In this case, Insertion receives the masks from an *internal* supplier—the Shaping Department. Thus, Insertion must account for the costs Shaping incurred to provide the shaped masks (Insertion's transferred-in costs) as well as Insertion's own direct materials (faceplates) and conversion costs (labor and overhead to insert the faceplates).

Exhibit 21-13 shows that in step 3, the Insertion Department's total cost to account for ($233,840) is the sum of:

- The cost incurred in September to start the insertion process on the 5,000 masks in Insertion's beginning work in process inventory ($24,000)

- The costs added to Work in Process Inventory—Insertion during October ($209,840 = $176,000 transferred in from the Shaping Department + $19,000 direct materials incurred in the Insertion Department + $14,840 conversion costs incurred in the Insertion Department)

Exhibit 21-13 also shows the results of step 4—the cost per equivalent unit. For each of the three cost categories, simply divide the total cost of that category by the number of equivalent units of work in that category. Perform this computation for each of the three categories: transferred-in costs, direct materials, and conversion costs.

✔ **Starter 21-10**

Step 5: Assign Total Costs to Units Completed and to Units in Ending Work in Process Inventory

Exhibit 21-14 shows how SeaView assigns the total Insertion Department costs ($233,840, from Exhibit 21-13) to (1) units completed and transferred out to finished goods inventory and (2) units remaining in the Insertion Department's ending work in process inventory. Use the same approach as we used for the Shaping Department in Exhibit 21-9. Multiply the number of equivalent units from step 2 (Exhibit 21-12) by the cost per equivalent unit from step 4 (Exhibit 21-13).

✔ **Starter 21-11**

Exhibit 21-14 | Step 5: Assign Total Costs to Units Completed and to Units in Ending Work in Process Inventory

SeaView Insertion Department
Month Ended October 31, 20XX

	Transferred In	Direct Materials	Conversion Costs	Total
Units completed and transferred out to Finished Goods Inventory	[38,000 × ($4.42 + $0.50 + $0.3975)]			202,065
Ending work in process, October 31:				
Transferred-in costs	[7,000 × $4.42]			30,940
Direct materials		—		—
Conversion costs			[2,100 × $0.3975]	835*
Total ending work in process, October 31				31,775
Total costs accounted for.				$233,840

*Rounded.

Exhibit 21-15 shows how Exhibit 21-14 assigns the Insertion Department's costs.

Exhibit 21-15

Assigning Insertion Department's Costs to Units Completed and Transferred Out and to Ending Work in Process Inventory

The Insertion Department's journal entries are similar to those of the Shaping Department. First, recall the entry previously made to transfer the cost of shaped swim masks into the Insertion Department (page 857):

```
Work in Process Inventory—Insertion . . . . .    176,000
     Work in Process Inventory—Shaping                         176,000
```

The following entry records other costs the Insertion Department incurred during October (data from Exhibit 21-11):

```
Work in Process Inventory—Insertion . . . . .     33,840
     Materials Inventory. . . . . . . . . . . . . . .              19,000
     Manufacturing Wages. . . . . . . . . . . . . .               3,710
     Manufacturing Overhead. . . . . . . . . . .                 11,130
To requisition materials and assign conversion costs to the
Insertion Department.
```

The entry to transfer the cost of completed masks out of the Insertion Department and into Finished Goods Inventory is based on the dollar amount in Exhibit 21-14:

```
Finished Goods Inventory . . . . . . . . . . . . . .   202,065
     Work in Process Inventory—Insertion                         202,065
```

After posting, the key accounts appear as follows:

✔ **Starter 21-12**

Work in Process Inventory—Shaping

(Exhibit 21-7)		(Exhibit 21-9)	
Balance, September 30	—	Transferred to Insertion	176,000
Direct materials	140,000		
Direct labor	21,250		
Manufacturing overhead	46,750		
Balance, October 31	32,000		

Work in Process Inventory—Insertion

(Exhibit 21-11)		(Exhibit 21-14)	
Balance, September 30	24,000	Transferred to Finished	
Transferred in from Shaping	176,000	Goods Inventory	202,065
Direct materials	19,000		
Direct labor	3,710		
Manufacturing overhead	11,130		
Balance, October 31	31,775		

Finished Goods Inventory

Balance, September 30	—		
Transferred in from Insertion	202,065		

How Managers Use a Production Cost Report

The **production cost report** in Exhibit 21-16 summarizes SeaView's Insertion Department's operations during October. The report combines Exhibit 21-13 and 21-14. It shows the beginning work in process inventory, the cost transferred in from the Shaping Department during October, and the direct material and conversion costs added in the Insertion Department during October.

Production Cost Report
Summarizes a processing department's operations for a period.

Exhibit 21-16 | Production Cost Report (Weighted-Average)

SeaView Insertion Department
Production Cost Report (Weighted-Average Method)
Month Ended October 31, 20XX

	Transferred In	Direct Materials	Conversion Costs	Total
Beginning work in process, September 30..........	$ 22,900	$ —	$ 1,100	$ 24,000
Costs added during October	176,000	19,000	14,840	209,840
Total costs to account for........................	$198,900	$19,000	$15,940	$233,840
Equivalent units................................	÷ 45,000	÷38,000	÷40,100	
Cost per equivalent unit	$4.42	$0.50	$0.3975	
Assignment of total costs:				
Units completed during October.................	[38,000 × ($4.42 + $0.50 + $0.3975)]			$202,065
Ending work in process, October 31:				
Transferred-in costs..........................	[7,000 × $4.42]			30,940
Direct materials		—		—
Conversion costs			[2,100 × $0.3975*]	835*
Total ending work in process, October 31				31,775
Total costs accounted for........................				$233,840

*Rounded.

The report also shows that the costs of the masks completed and transferred out of the Insertion Department in October ($202,065) and the cost assigned to the Insertion Department's ending work in process inventory ($31,775) sum to the Insertion Department's total costs to account for ($233,840).

How do managers use the production cost report? When faced with economic uncertainty and falling prices for their products, managers carefully monitor product costs to see what they can cut. For example, as the selling prices for its tools continued to decline, Connecticut-based toolmaker Stanley Works decided to use fewer raw material suppliers. By purchasing more from its remaining suppliers, Stanley had the leverage to negotiate better prices.

Similarly, SeaView's managers monitor production costs by comparing the actual direct materials and conversion costs—particularly the equivalent unit costs in Exhibit 21-16—with expected amounts. If actual unit costs are too high, managers look for ways to cut. If actual costs are less than expected (and assuming quality is maintained), the Insertion Department's managers will likely receive good performance evaluations.

SeaView can use these unit costs for making other decisions. Sales managers must set the mask's selling price high enough to cover the unit manufacturing costs shown in Exhibit 21-16 ($5.3175 = $4.42 + $0.50 + $0.3975) plus nonmanufacturing costs from the other elements of the value chain, such as marketing and distribution. Armed with selling price and cost information for each of their many products, SeaView's managers can figure out which products are most profitable. Then they can design sales campaigns to promote those products. Finally, the production cost report supports financial reporting. It provides information for valuing inventory on the balance sheet and cost of goods sold on the income statement.

Overseas Production Cuts Labor Costs

Once it was a matter of pride that our clothing would sport a "Made in the U.S.A." label. Now our clothes are made overseas—wherever labor is cheap and willing.

In the process costing equation, lower manufacturing wages reduce unit costs and increase profit margins. The opportunity to cut costs fueled the exodus of U.S. apparel jobs to low-cost production areas in Asia, Mexico, and Latin America. In 1950, 1.2 million Americans worked in apparel manufacturing. By 2001, that figure had fallen to 566,000, even though the U.S. population had doubled. Consider Levi Strauss & Co., a brand as American as apple pie.

In 2003, Levi's closed its last two U.S. plants, Levi's said it would become a "marketing company" and that future production would be done by contract manufacturers in 50 countries, including Bangladesh and Mexico.

Companies are shifting operations to countries with the lowest costs. Toy maker Hasbro closed its Monterrey, Mexico, plant in 2001 and moved to China. Mexico's workers earn $1.47 an hour, compared to the 28 cents a worker makes in China. Labor activists have dubbed this shift to low-cost overseas production a "race to the bottom." However, many major companies now have codes of conduct and monitoring programs to improve working conditions in manufacturing facilities worldwide. In 1991, Levi Strauss & Co. was the first multinational to develop such a code for its contract manufacturers. Called "terms of engagement," it is based on international labor standards.

Based on: Fred Dickey, "Cover Story, Levi Strauss and the Price We Pay," *Los Angeles Times*, December 1, 2002, p. MAG.14. Evelyn Iritani and Richard Boudreux, "Mexico's Factories Shift Gears to Survive," *Los Angeles Times*, January 5, 2003, p. C1. Michael Riley, "High-Tech Industries Meet Low-Cost Labor," *Houston Chronicle*, February 12, 2000, p. C1.

Decision Guidelines

PROCESS COSTING—SECOND PROCESS (WITH BEGINNING INVENTORY)

Beginning work in process inventory makes process costing a bit more complicated, and second (or later) departments must account for units and costs transferred in from previous departments. Let's use SeaView's Insertion Department to review some of the key process costing decisions that arise in a second (or later) process that has beginning inventory.

Decision	Guidelines
At what point in the insertion process are transferred-in costs (from the shaping process) incurred?	Transferred-in costs are incurred at the *beginning* of the insertion process. The masks must be completely shaped before the insertion process begins.
How to compute equivalent units using the weighted-average method?	Weighted-average equivalent units equal • All work done on units completed and transferred out this period (whether work was done this period or last period), plus • Work done to *start* the ending inventory

Decision Guidelines *(continued)*

Decision	Guidelines
What checks and balances does the five-step process costing procedure provide?	The five-step procedure provides two important checks: **1.** The units to account for (beginning inventory + units started or transferred in) must equal the units accounted for (units completed and transferred out + units in ending inventory). **2.** The total costs to account for (cost of beginning inventory + costs incurred in the current period) must equal the costs accounted for (cost of units completed and transferred out + cost of ending inventory).
What is the main goal of the Insertion Department's process costing?	The main goal is to split total costs between swim masks completed and transferred out to finished goods inventory and the masks that remain in the Insertion Department's ending work in process inventory.
For what kinds of decisions do SeaView's managers use the Insertion Department's production cost report?	Managers use the cost per equivalent unit to control material and conversion costs and to evaluate the performance of the Insertion Department's managers. If actual costs per equivalent unit are higher than the budget, managers try to cut costs. If actual costs are lower than the budget while quality is maintained, Insertion Department managers likely will receive a favorable performance evaluation. SeaView's managers also use the cost per equivalent unit to build the cost of producing a swim mask. These costs provide a basis for setting selling prices, profitability analysis to decide which products to emphasize, and so on. These costs are also the basis for valuing inventory on the balance sheet and cost of goods sold on the income statement.

Excel Application Exercise

Goal: Create an Excel worksheet containing all five steps of the process costing procedure.

Scenario: As assistant to the production manager at work, you are asked to create the production cost report for the Tile-Forming Department for the month ended May 31, 20XX. Using Excel, your worksheet must calculate (1) the total cost of the units completed and transferred out, and (2) the total cost of the units in ending work in process inventory in the last step. When done with your spreadsheet, answer these questions:

1. What are the equivalent units of direct materials and conversion costs for: the units completed and transferred out in May, and ending work in process for May?
2. What is the total cost of units completed and transferred out during the month?

3. What is the total cost of ending work in process inventory for the month?

Step-by-Step:

1. Open a new Excel worksheet.
2. Create a bold-faced heading for your spreadsheet that contains the following:
   a. Chapter 21 Excel Application Exercise
   b. Production Cost Report
   c. Today's date
3. Using the Mid-Chapter Summary Problem on pages 859–860 as your guide, prepare the reports for the five-step process costing procedure. You are re-creating the solution to the Mid-Chapter Summary Problem. Start by creating a data section with the following heading format:

Tile-Forming Department Month Ended May 31, 20XX	Physical Units	Total Costs Direct Materials	Conversion
Beginning work in process, April 30	—	—	—
Started in production during May	20,000	$6,800	$36,400
Total to account for	20,000	$6,800	$36,400
Completed and transferred to Finishing Department during May	16,000		
Ending work in process, May 31 (units):	4,000		
Percentage complete as to:		25%	55%
Total accounted for	20,000		

This data section differs slightly from the way the same information is presented at the beginning of the Mid-Chapter Summary Problem. Your spreadsheet separates Total Costs into the direct materials and conversion components. Separating these two items will allow you to reference these values later.

4. Once finished with the data section, move down two rows and enter the Tile-Forming Department heading as follows:

Tile-Forming Department
Month Ended May 31, 20XX

Format this section as illustrated in the Mid-Chapter Summary Problem report for steps 1 and 2 of the 5-step

process costing procedure (page 859). Use formulas and data section cell references as appropriate.

5. Now re-create the two reports for steps 3 and 4 of the five-step process costing procedure. Use the Mid-Chapter Summary Problem reports on page 860 as your guide. Use formulas and data section cell references as appropriate.

6. Finally, re-create the report for the fifth and final step of the process costing procedure (use the report on page 860 as a guide). Be sure to use formulas instead of the calculations shown in the body of the report on page 860.

7. Save your work, and print a copy for your files.

END-OF-CHAPTER *Summary Problem*

This problem extends the Mid-Chapter Summary problem to a second department. During May, Florida Tile Industries reports the following in its Finishing Department:

CHECK YOUR RESOURCES

Finishing Department Data for May

Units:
Beginning work in process, April 30 (20% complete as to
direct materials, 70% complete as to conversion work). . . . 4,000 units
Transferred in from Tile-Forming Department during May . . 16,000 units
Completed and transferred out to Finished Goods Inventory
during May. . . . . 15,000 units
Ending work in process, May 31 (36% complete as to direct
materials, 80% complete as to conversion work) . . . . 5,000 units

Costs:
Work in process, April 30 (transferred-in costs, $11,982;
direct materials costs, $488; conversion costs, $5,530) $18,000
Transferred in from Tile-Forming Department during May
(page 860) 38,400
Finishing direct materials added during May. 6,400
Finishing conversion costs added during May. 24,300

Required

Assign the Finishing Department's May total costs to units completed and to units in ending work in process inventory, using the weighted-average method.

Hint: Don't confuse the Finishing Department with finished goods inventory. The Finishing Department is Florida Tile's second process. The tiles do not become part of finished goods inventory until they have completed the second process, which happens to be called the Finishing Department.

Solution

STEPS 1 AND 2 Summarize the flow of physical units; compute output in terms of equivalent units.

Finishing Department
Month Ended May 31, 20XX

Flow of Production	Step 1 Flow of Physical Units	Step 2: Equivalent Units Transferred In	Direct Materials	Conversion Costs
Units to account for:				
Beginning work in process, April 30...........	4,000			
Transferred in from Tile-Forming during May ..	16,000			
Total physical units to account for.............	20,000			
Units accounted for:				
Completed and transferred out during May....	15,000	15,000	15,000	15,000
Ending work in process, May 31..............	5,000	5,000	1,800*	4,000*
Total physical units accounted for.............	20,000			
Equivalent units.............................		20,000	16,800	19,000

*Start ending inventory

Direct materials: 5,000 units each 36% completed = 1,800 equivalent units
Conversion costs: 5,000 units each 80% completed = 4,000 equivalent units

STEPS 3 AND 4 Summarize total costs to account for; compute the cost per equivalent unit.

Finishing Department
Month Ended May 31, 20XX

	Transferred In	Direct Materials	Conversion Costs	Total
Beginning work in process, April 30 ..	$11,982	$ 488	$ 5,530	$18,000
Costs added during May	38,400	6,400	24,300	69,100
Total costs......................	$50,382	$ 6,888	$29,830	
Divide by equivalent units..........	÷20,000	÷16,800	÷19,000	
Cost per equivalent unit............	$2.5191	$ 0.41	$ 1.57	
Total costs to account for				$87,100

STEP 5 Assign costs to units completed and to units in ending work in process inventory.

Finishing Department
Month Ended May 31, 20XX

	Transferred In	Direct Materials	Conversion Costs	Total
Units completed and transferred out to Finished Goods Inventory:................	[15,000 × ($2.5191 + $0.41 + $1.57)]			$67,486*
Ending work in process, May 31:				
Transferred-in costs......................	[5,000 × $2.5191]			12,596*
Direct materials		[1,800 × $0.41]		738
Conversion costs			[4,000 × $1.57]	6,280
Total ending work in process, May 31				19,614
Total costs accounted for...................				$87,100

*Rounded

●REVIEW *Process Costing*

Quick Check

1. Which of these companies would use process costing?
   a. **Saatchi & Saatchi** advertising firm
   b. **Pace Foods**, producer of Pace picante sauce
   c. **Accenture** management consultants
   d. **Amazon.com**

2. Which of the following statements describes **Jelly Belly's** process costing system?
   a. Direct materials and direct labor are traced to each specific order.
   b. Costs flow directly from a single Work in Process Inventory account to Finished Goods Inventory.
   c. Costs flow through a sequence of Work in Process Inventory accounts and then into Finished Goods Inventory from the final Work in Process Inventory account.
   d. The subsidiary Work in Process Inventory accounts consist of separate records for each individual order, detailing the materials, labor, and overhead assigned to that order.

Use the following data to answer questions 3 through 7. Suppose Jelly Belly's Centers process adds sugar at the beginning of the process and flavorings 75% of the way through the process, and conversion costs are incurred evenly throughout the process. Assume there are no beginning inventories, the company started making centers for 10,000 pounds of jelly beans, and the 2,000 pounds in the Centers ending work in process inventory are 65% through the Centers process.

3. Compute the equivalent units of *sugar* used.
   a. 8,000   c. 9,300
   b. 8,700   d. 10,000

4. How many equivalent units of *flavorings* did Jelly Belly use?
   a. 8,000   c. 9,300
   b. 8,700   d. 10,000

5. What are the equivalent units of *conversion costs*?
   a. 8,000   c. 9,300
   b. 8,700   d. 10,000

6. If the cost per equivalent unit is $0.50 for sugar, $1.00 for flavorings, and $0.40 for conversion costs, what is the cost assigned to the Centers ending work in process inventory?
   a. $1,520   c. $2,520
   b. $1,800   d. $3,800

7. Suppose Jelly Belly's second process, Shells, starts out with 3,000 pounds of jelly beans in its beginning work in process inventory. Assume that the Shells process has 1,500 pounds of jelly beans 70% through the process at the end of the period. Start by using the information preceding question 3 to determine how many pounds of jelly beans started in the Shells process this period. Then use this result to compute the number of equivalent units of transferred-in costs that the Shells process will use in computing its weighted-average cost per equivalent unit.
   a. 6,500   c. 9,500
   b. 8,000   d. 11,000

8. In general, transferred-in costs include:
   a. Costs incurred in the previous period
   b. Costs incurred in all prior periods
   c. Costs incurred in only the previous process
   d. Costs incurred in all prior processes

To answer questions 9 and 10, look at the computation of cost per equivalent unit in SeaView's Insertion Department in Exhibit 21-13.

9. Which of the following describes the $22,900 transferred-in costs in beginning inventory?
   a. Costs incurred in October in the Shaping Department
   b. Costs incurred in September in the Shaping Department
   c. Costs incurred in October in the Insertion Department
   d. Costs incurred in September in the Insertion Department

10. Which of the following best describes the swim masks associated with the $22,900 transferred-in costs in the Insertion Department's beginning work in process inventory?
    a. Masks that are partway through the shaping process and have not begun the insertion process by the beginning of October
    b. Masks that moved from the Shaping Department into the Insertion Department in September but have not yet begun the insertion process by the beginning of October
    c. Masks that moved from the Shaping Department into the Insertion Department during October
    d. Masks that moved from the Shaping Department to the Insertion Department in September and are partway through insertion by the beginning of October

Accounting Vocabulary

conversion costs (p. 850)

equivalent units (p. 850)

production cost report (p. 867)

transferred-in costs (p. 865)

weighted-average process costing
method (p. 862)

● ASSESS *Your Progress*

online homework

See *www.prenhall.com/horngren*
for selected Starters, Exercises,
and Problems.

*Distinguishing between the flow of costs
in job costing and process costing*
(Obj. 1)

*Flow of costs in process costing, cost per
equivalent unit*
(Obj. 1, 2)

Starters

S21-1 Use Exhibit 21-1 to help you describe, in your own words, the major difference in the flow of costs between a job costing system and a process costing system.

S21-2 Polar Spring produces premium bottled water. Polar Spring purchases artesian water, stores the water in large tanks, and then runs the water through two processes:

- Filtration, where workers microfilter *and* ozonate the water
- Bottling, where workers bottle and package the filtered water

During February, the filtration process incurs the following costs in processing 200,000 liters:

Wages of workers operating the filtration equipment..	$ 11,100
Wages of workers operating ozonation equipment....	12,850
Manufacturing overhead allocated to filtration	24,050
Water..	120,000

Polar Spring has no beginning inventory in the Filtration Department.

1. Compute the February conversion costs in the Filtration Department.
2. If the Filtration Department completely processed 200,000 liters, what is the *total* filtration cost per liter?
3. Now assume that the total costs of the filtration process listed in the chart above yield 160,000 liters that are completely filtered and ozonated, while the remaining 40,000 are only partway through the process at the end of February. Is the cost per completely filtered and ozonated liter higher, lower, or the same as in requirement 2? Why?

S21-3 Refer to Starter 21-2. At Polar Spring, water is added at the beginning of the filtration process. Conversion costs are added evenly throughout the process, and in February 160,000 liters have been completed and transferred out of the Filtration Department into the Bottling Department. The 40,000 units remaining in Filtration's ending work in process inventory are 80% of the way through the filtration process. Recall that Polar Spring has no beginning inventories.

1. Draw a time line for the filtration process, similar to the one in Exhibit 21-6.
2. Compute the equivalent units of direct materials and conversion costs for the Filtration Department. (Refer to Exhibit 21-5 if necessary.)

Drawing a time line, computing equivalent units
(Obj. 2)

S21-4 Look at SeaView Shaping Department's equivalent-unit computation in Exhibit 21-5. Suppose the ending work in process inventory is 30% of the way through the shaping process, rather than 25% of the way through. Compute the total equivalent units of direct materials and conversion costs.

Computing equivalent units
(Obj. 2)

S21-5 Return to the original SeaView example. Suppose direct labor is $34,000 rather than $21,250. Now what is the conversion cost per equivalent unit? (Use Exhibit 21-8 to format your answer.)

Computing the cost per equivalent unit
(Obj. 3)

S21-6 Return to Polar Spring's Filtration Department described in Starters 21-2 and 21-3. Using your answers to those exercises, compute the cost per equivalent unit for direct materials and for conversion costs in the Filtration Department. (Recall that there were no beginning inventories.)

Computing the cost per equivalent unit
(Obj. 3)

S21-7 Return to Polar Spring's Filtration Department. Use the information in Starters 21-2, 21-3, and 21-6 to answer the following questions:

1. What is the cost of the 160,000 liters completed and transferred out of Polar Spring's Filtration Department?
2. What is the cost of 40,000 liters remaining in Filtration's ending work in process inventory?

Assigning costs to units completed and ending inventory
(Obj. 3)

S21-8 Use the information in Starters 21-2 and 21-7 to

1. Record the journal entry to transfer the cost of the 160,000 liters completed and transferred out of Filtration and into the Bottling Department.
2. Record all the transactions in the Work in Process Inventory—Filtration T-account. (*Hint:* Use SeaView's Work in Process Inventory—Shaping T-account on page 857 as a guide.)

Preparing a journal entry and posting to a T-account
(Obj. 3)

S21-9 Polar Spring produces premium bottled water. Preceding Starters considered Polar Spring's first process—filtration. We now consider Polar Spring's second process—bottling. In the Bottling Department, workers bottle the filtered water and pack the bottles into boxes. Conversion costs are incurred evenly throughout the bottling process, but packaging materials are not added until the end of the process.
    February data from the Bottling Department follow:

Drawing a time line; computing equivalent units; second department; weighted-average method
(Obj. 1, 4)

Beginning work in process inventory (40% of the way through the process)	8,000 liters
Transferred in from Filtration*	160,000 liters
Completed and transferred out to Finished Goods Inventory in February	154,000 liters
Ending work in process inventory (70% of the way through the bottling process).	14,000 liters

(continued)

Costs in beginning work in process inventory		Costs added during February	
Transferred in	$1,760	Transferred in*	$136,000
Direct materials	0	Direct materials	30,800
Direct labor	600	Direct labor	33,726
Manufacturing overhead . . .	520	Manufacturing overhead . .	22,484
Total beginning work in process inventory as of February 1 . .	$2,880	Total costs added during February	$223,010

*Starter 21-7 showed that Polar Spring's Filtration Department completed and transferred out 160,000 liters at a total cost of $136,000.

1. Draw a time line similar to the one in Exhibit 21-10 using the weighted-average method.
2. Use the time line to help you compute the Bottling Department equivalent units for the month of February, using the weighted-average method.

Computing costs per equivalent unit; second department; weighted average
(Obj. 4)

S21-10 Using data from Polar Spring's Bottling Department and the equivalent units computed in Starter 21-9, compute the cost per equivalent unit for February, using the weighted-average method.

Assigning costs to units completed and ending inventory; second department; weighted-average method
(Obj. 4)

S21-11 Refer to the information on Polar Spring's Bottling Department and the equivalent units and cost per equivalent unit you computed in Starters 21-9 and 21-10. Use these to assign the costs to units completed and transferred out and to ending inventory, using the weighted-average method.

Preparing a journal entry and posting to a T-account; second department; weighted-average method
(Obj. 1, 4)

S21-12 Using data from Polar Spring's Bottling Department in Starter 21-9 and the cost assignments in Starter 21-11:

1. Prepare the journal entry to record the cost of units completed and transferred out under the weighted-average method.
2. Post all transactions from Starters 21-9 and 21-11 to the Work in Process Inventory— Bottling Department T-account. What is the ending balance?

Exercises

Diagramming flows through a process costing system
(Obj. 1)

E21-1 Pule produces kitchen cabinets in a three-stage process that includes milling, assembling, and finishing, in that order. Direct materials are added in the Milling and Finishing Departments. Direct labor and overhead are incurred in all three departments. The company's general ledger includes the following accounts:

Cost of Goods Sold	Work in Process Inventory—Finishing
Manufacturing Wages	Materials Inventory
Work in Process Inventory—Milling	Finished Goods Inventory
Work in Process Inventory—Assembling	Manufacturing Overhead

Outline the flow of costs through the company's accounts, including a brief description of each flow. Include a T-account for each account title given.

Journalizing process costing transactions
(Obj. 1, 3)

E21-2 Record the following process costing transactions in the general journal:

a. Purchase of raw materials on account, $9,000
b. Requisition of direct materials to
   Assembly Department, $4,000
   Finishing Department, $2,000
c. Incurrence and payment of manufacturing labor, $10,800.

(continued)

d. Incurrence of manufacturing overhead costs:
Property taxes—plant, $1,900
Utilities—plant, $4,500
Insurance—plant, $1,100
Depreciation—plant, $3,400

e. Assignment of conversion costs to the Assembly Department:
Direct labor, $4,700
Manufacturing overhead, $2,900

f. Assignment of conversion costs to the Finishing Department:
Direct labor, $4,400
Manufacturing overhead, $6,200

g. Cost of goods completed and transferred out of Assembly and into Finishing, $10,250.

h. Cost of goods completed and transferred out of the Finishing Department into Finished Goods Inventory, $15,600.

E21-3 Color World prepares and packages paint products. Color World has two departments: (1) Blending and (2) Packaging. Direct materials are added at the beginning of the blending process (dyes) and at the end of the packaging process (cans). Conversion costs are added evenly throughout each process. Data from the month of May for the Blending Department are as follows:

Drawing a time line; computing equivalent units and assigning cost to completed units and ending work in process; no beginning inventory or cost transferred in
(Obj. 2, 3)

Gallons:	
Beginning work in process inventory	0
Started production	8,000 gallons
Completed and transferred out to Packaging in May	6,000 gallons
Ending work in process inventory (30% of the way through the blending process)	2,000 gallons
Costs:	
Beginning work in process inventory	$ 0
Costs added during May:	
Direct materials (dyes)	4,800
Direct labor	800
Manufacturing overhead	1,840
Total costs added during May	$7,440

Required

1. Draw a time line for the Blending Department, similar to Exhibit 21-6.

2. Use the time line to help you compute the Blending Department's equivalent units for direct materials and for conversion costs.

3. Compute the total costs of the units (gallons)
  a. Completed and transferred out to the Packaging Department
  b. In the Blending Department ending work in process inventory

E21-4 Return to the Blending Department for Color World in Exercise 21-3.

Preparing journal entries and posting to work in process T-account
(Obj. 1, 3)

Required

1. Present the journal entries to record the use of direct materials and direct labor and the allocation of manufacturing overhead to the Blending Department. Also, give the journal entry to record the costs of the gallons completed and transferred out to the Packaging Department.

2. Post the journal entries to the Work in Process Inventory—Blending T-account. What is the ending balance?

3. What is the average cost per gallon transferred out of Blending into Packaging? Why would Color World's managers want to know this cost?

E21-5 The Assembly Department of ZAP Surge Protectors began September with no work in process inventory. During the month, production that cost $39,860 (direct materials, $9,900, and conversion costs, $29,960) was started on 23,000 units. ZAP completed and transferred to the Testing Department a total of 15,000 units. The ending work in process inventory was 37.5% complete as to direct materials and 80% complete as to conversion work.

Required

1. Compute the equivalent units for direct materials and conversion costs.
2. Compute the cost per equivalent unit.
3. Assign the costs to units completed and transferred out and ending work in process inventory.
4. Record the journal entry for the costs transferred out of Assembly into Testing.
5. Post all the transactions in the Work in Process Inventory—Assembly Department T-account. What is the ending balance?

E21-6 Royal Vine Winery in Kingston, New York, has two departments: Fermenting and Packaging. Direct materials are added at the beginning of the fermenting process (grapes) and at the end of the packaging process (bottles). Conversion costs are added evenly throughout each process. Data from the month of March for the Fermenting Department are as follows:

Gallons:	
Beginning work in process inventory	0
Started production	8,000 gallons
Completed and transferred out to Packaging in March	6,550 gallons
Ending work in process inventory (80% of the way	
through the fermenting process)	1,450 gallons
Costs:	
Beginning work in process inventory	$ 0
Costs added during March:	
Direct materials.	11,600
Direct labor	2,400
Manufacturing overhead.	4,539
Total costs added during May	$18,539

Required

1. Draw a time line for the Fermenting Department, similar to Exhibit 21-6.
2. Use the time line to help you compute the equivalent units for direct materials and for conversion costs.
3. Compute the total costs of the units (gallons)
   a. Completed and transferred out to the Packaging Department
   b. In the Fermenting Department ending work in process inventory

E21-7 Return to the Fermenting Department for Royal Vine Winery in Exercise 21-6.

Required

1. Present the journal entries to record the use of direct materials and direct labor, and the allocation of manufacturing overhead to the Fermenting Department. Also give the journal entry to record the cost of the gallons completed and transferred out to the Packaging Department.
2. Post the journal entries to the Work in Process Inventory—Fermenting T-account. What is the ending balance?

(continued)

3. What is the average cost per gallon transferred out of Fermenting into Packaging? Why would Royal Vine's managers want to know this cost?

E21-8 The following information was taken from the ledger of Denver Roping. Ending inventory is 60% complete as to direct materials but 20% complete as to conversion work.

Computing equivalent units; assigning costs to goods completed and ending work in process inventory; first department, no beginning inventory (**Obj. 2, 3**)

Work in Process—Forming

	Physical Units	Dollars		Physical Units	Dollars
Beginning inventory,					
September 30	-0-	$ -0-	Transferred to		
Production started:	80,000		Finishing	72,000	$?
Direct materials		215,040			
Conversion costs		195,040			
Ending Inventory	8,000	?			

Required

Journalize the transfer of costs to the Finishing Department. (*Hint:* First compute the number of equivalent units and the cost per equivalent unit.)

E21-9 Selected production and cost data of Martha's Fudge Co. follow for May 20X6.

Computing equivalent units, 2 departments, WA method (**Obj. 4**)

	Flow of Physical Units	
Flow of Production	Mixing Department	Heating Department
Units to account for:		
Beginning work in process, April 30	20,000	6,000
Transferred in during May.................	70,000	80,000
Total physical units to account for	90,000	86,000
Units accounted for:		
Completed and transferred out during May..	80,000	76,000
Ending work in process, May 31.............	10,000	10,000
Total physical units accounted for	90,000	86,000

Martha uses weighted-average costing.

Required

1. Fill in the blanks:
   a. On May 31, the Mixing Department ending work in process inventory was 70% complete as to materials and 20% complete as to conversion costs. This means that for the ending inventory _____% of the materials and _____% of the conversion costs were added during May.
   b. On May 31, the Heating Department ending work in process inventory was 65% complete as to materials and 55% complete as to conversion costs. This means that for the ending inventory _____% of the materials and _____% of the conversion costs were added during May.

Computing equivalent units and assigning costs to completed units and to ending work in process inventory; second department, weighted average (**Obj. 4**)

2. Use the information in the Flow of Production table and the information in Requirement 1 to compute the equivalent units for transferred-in costs, direct materials, and conversion costs for both the Mixing and the Heating Departments.

E21-10 Alpha Semiconductors, Inc., experienced the following activity in its Photolithography Department during December. Materials are added at the beginning of the photolithography process.

⊙Student ResourceCD

spreadsheet

(continued)

Units:	
Work in process, November 30	
(80% of the way through the process)	8,000 units
Transferred in from the Polishing and Cutting Department	
during December.....................................	27,000 units
Completed during December	26,000 units
Work in process, December 31	
(70% of the way through the process)	9,000 units
Costs:	
Work in process, November 30 (transferred-in costs,	
$20,050; direct materials costs, $20,250; and	
conversion costs, $19,816)	$60,116
Transferred in from the Polishing and Cutting Department	
during December.....................................	97,200
Direct materials added during December	74,250
Conversion costs added during December	90,650

Required

1. Draw a time line for the Photolithography Department using the weighted-average method. (See Exhibit 21-10.)

2. Use the time line to help you compute the number of equivalent units of work for the Photolithography Department in December. Use the weighted-average method.

3. Compute the cost per equivalent unit, and assign total costs to (a) units completed and transferred to Finished Goods Inventory, and (b) units in December 31 work in process inventory.

Problems

(Group A)

Computing equivalent units and assigning costs to completed units and ending work in process; no beginning inventory or cost transferred in
(Obj. 1, 2, 3)

P21-1A Winter Lips produces a lip balm used for cold-weather sports. The balm is manufactured in a single processing department. No lip balm was in process on May 31, and Winter Lips started production on 20,400 lip balm tubes during June. Direct materials are added at the beginning of the process, but conversion costs are incurred evenly throughout the process. Completed production for June totaled 15,200 units. The June 30 work in process was 40% of the way through the production process. Direct materials costing $4,080 were placed in production during June, and direct labor of $3,315 and manufacturing overhead of $1,005 were assigned to the process.

Required

1. Draw a time line for Winter Lips that is similar to Exhibit 21-6.

2. Use the time line to help you compute the number of equivalent units and the cost per equivalent unit for June.

3. Assign total costs to (a) units completed and transferred to finished goods and (b) units still in process at June 30.

4. Prepare a T-account for Work in Process Inventory to show activity during June, including the June 30 balance.

Computing equivalent units; assigning costs to completed units and ending work in process; journalizing transactions; no beginning inventory or cost transferred in
(Obj. 2, 3)

P21-2A The New England Furniture Company produces dining tables in a three-stage process: sawing, assembly, and staining. Costs incurred in the Sawing Department during September are summarized as follows:

(continued)

Work in Process Inventory—Sawing

Sep. 1 balance	0
Direct materials	1,860,000
Direct labor	139,100
Manufacturing overhead	153,400

Direct materials (lumber) are added at the beginning of the sawing process, while conversion costs are incurred evenly throughout the process. September activity in the Sawing Department included sawing of 11,000 meters of lumber, which were transferred to the Assembly Department. Also, work began on 1,000 meters of lumber, which on September 30 were 70% of the way through the sawing process.

Required

1. Draw a time line for the Sawing Department, similar to Exhibit 21-6.
2. Use the time line to help you compute the number of equivalent units and the cost per equivalent unit in the Sawing Department for September.
3. Show that the sum of (a) cost of goods transferred out of the Sawing Department and (b) ending Work in Process Inventory—Sawing equals the total cost accumulated in the department during September.
4. Journalize all transactions affecting the company's sawing process during September, including those already posted.

EU and assigning costs to completed units and ending WIP; materials added at different points in the production process; no beginning inventory or costs transferred in
(Obj. 1, 2, 3)

P21-3A Kun Pow produces canned chicken à la king. The chicken à la king passes through three departments: (1) Mixing, (2) Retort (sterilization), and (3) Packing. In the Mixing Department, chicken and cream are added at the beginning of the process, the mixture is partly cooked, then chopped green peppers and mushrooms are added at the end of the process. Conversion costs are added evenly throughout the mixing process. November data from the Mixing Department are as follows:

Gallons		Costs	
Beginning work in process inventory........	0 gallons	Beginning work in process inventory	$ 0
Started production.......................	15,000 gallons	Costs added during November:	
Completed and transferred out to		Chicken.....................................	12,500
Retort in November....................	12,900 gallons	Cream	4,000
		Green peppers and mushrooms	11,610
Ending work in process inventory		Direct labor..................................	11,108
(60% of the way through the		Manufacturing overhead	3,052
mixing process)	2,100 gallons	Total costs	$42,270

Required

1. Draw a time line for the Mixing Department, similar to Exhibit 21-6.
2. Use the time line to help you compute the equivalent units. (*Hint:* Each direct material added at a different point in the production process requires its own equivalent-unit computation.)
3. Compute the total costs of the units (gallons)
   a. Completed and transferred out to the Retort Department
   b. In the Mixing Department's ending work in process inventory
4. Prepare the journal entry to record the cost of the gallons completed and transferred out to the Retort Department.
5. Post the transactions to the Work in Process Inventory—Mixing T-account. What is the ending balance?
6. What is the primary purpose of the work required in steps 1 through 3?

Computing equivalent units for a second department with beginning inventory; preparing a production cost report and recording transactions based on the report; WA method
(Obj. 2, 3, 4)

Student Resource**CD**

spreadsheet

P21-4A Off Road, Inc., manufactures auto roof racks in a two-stage process that includes shaping and plating. Steel alloy is the basic raw material of the shaping process. The steel is molded according to the design specifications of automobile manufacturers (**Ford** and **General Motors**). The Plating Department then adds an anodized finish.

At March 31, before recording the transfer of cost from the Plating Department to Finished Goods Inventory, the Off Road general ledger included the following account:

Work in Process Inventory—Plating

Feb. 28 balance	30,480
Transferred in from Shaping	36,000
Direct materials	24,200
Direct labor	21,732
Manufacturing overhead	35,388

The direct materials (rubber pads) are added at the end of the plating process. Conversion costs are incurred evenly throughout the process. Work in process of the Plating Department on February 28 consisted of 600 racks. The $30,480 beginning balance of Work in Process—Plating includes $18,000 of transferred-in cost and $12,480 of conversion cost. During March, 3,000 racks were transferred in from the Shaping Department. The Plating Department transferred 2,200 racks to Finished Goods Inventory in March, and 1,400 were still in process on March 31. This ending inventory was 50% of the way through the plating process. Off Road uses weighted-average process costing.

Required

1. Draw a time line for the Plating Department, similar to Exhibit 21-10.

2. Use the time line to help you compute the equivalent units, cost per equivalent unit, and total costs to account for in the Plating Department for March.

3. Prepare the March production cost report for the Plating Department.

4. Journalize all transactions affecting the Plating Department during March, including the entries that have already been posted.

Computing EU for a second department with BI; assigning cost to completed units and ending WIP; WA method
(Obj. 2, 3, 4)

P21-5A Sidcrome uses three departments to produce plastic handles for screwdrivers. Forming the handles requires mixing the raw materials, molding, and drying.

Sidcrome's Drying Department requires no direct materials. Conversion costs are incurred evenly throughout the drying process. Other process costing information follows:

Units:	
Beginning work in process	7,000 units
Transferred in from the Molding Department during the period	28,000 units
Completed during the period	16,000 units
Ending work in process (20% complete as to conversion work)	19,000 units
Costs:	
Beginning work in process (transferred-in cost, $140; conversion cost, $231)	$ 371
Transferred in from the Molding Department during the period	4,760
Conversion costs added during the period	1,947

After the drying process, the screwdrivers are completed by assembling the handles and shanks and packaging for shipment to retail outlets. Sidcrome uses weighted-average process costing.

Required

1. Draw a time line of the Drying Department's process, similar to the one in Exhibit 21-10.

2. Use the time line to compute the number of equivalent units of work performed by the Drying Department during the period, the cost per equivalent unit, and the total costs to account for.

(continued)

3. Assign total costs to (a) units completed and transferred to the assembly operation and (b) units in the Drying Department's ending work in process inventory.

Problems

(Group B)

P21-1B E-Z Solutions, Inc., makes electronic personal data assistants (PDAs) in three processes: assembly, programming, and packaging. The Assembly Department had no work in process on May 31. In mid-June, E-Z Solutions started production on 100,000 PDAs. Of this number, 76,400 PDAs were assembled during June. Direct materials are added at the beginning of the assembly process. Conversion costs are incurred evenly throughout the process. The June 30 work in process in the Assembly Department was 60% of the way through the assembly process. Direct materials costing $375,000 were placed in production in Assembly during June, and direct labor of $157,248 and manufacturing overhead of $118,960 were assigned to that department.

Computing equivalent units and assigning costs to completed units and ending work in process; no beginning inventory or cost transferred in **(Obj. 1, 2, 3)**

Required

1. Draw a time line for the Assembly Department, similar to Exhibit 21-6.
2. Use the time line to help you compute the number of equivalent units and the cost per equivalent unit in the Assembly Department for June.
3. Assign total costs in the Assembly Department to (a) units completed and transferred to Programming during June and (b) units still in process at June 30.
4. Prepare a T-account for Work in Process Inventory—Assembly to show its activity during June, including the June 30 balance.

P21-2B Papyrus Co. produces the paper used by wallpaper manufacturers. Papyrus's four-stage process includes mixing, cooking, rolling, and cutting. In the Mixing Department, wood pulp and chemicals are blended. The resulting mix is heated in the Cooking Department in much the same way as food is prepared. Then the cooked mix is rolled to produce sheets. The final process, cutting, divides the sheets into large rolled units. The Mixing Department incurred the following costs during August:

Computing equivalent units; assigning costs to completed units and ending work in process; journalizing transactions; no beginning inventory or cost transferred in **(Obj. 2, 3)**

Work in Process Inventory—Mixing		
Aug. 1 balance	0	
Direct materials	5,520	
Direct labor	580	
Manufacturing overhead	3,560	

During August, the Mixing Department started and completed mixing for 4,500 rolls of paper. The department started but did not finish the mixing for an additional 500 rolls, which were 20% complete with respect to both direct materials and conversion work at the end of August. Direct materials and conversion costs are incurred evenly throughout the mixing process.

Required

1. Draw a time line for the Mixing Department, similar to Exhibit 21-6.
2. Use the time line to help you compute the number of equivalent units and the cost per equivalent unit in the Mixing Department for August.
3. Show that the sum of (a) cost of goods transferred out of the Mixing Department and (b) ending Work in Process Inventory—Mixing equals the total cost accumulated in the department during August.
4. Journalize all transactions affecting the company's mixing process during August, including those already posted.

EU and assigning costs to completed units and ending WIP inventory; materials added at different points; no beginning inventory or cost transferred in
(Obj. 1, 2, 3)

P21-3B Ply-Wall produces exterior siding for homes. The Preparation Department begins with wood, which is chopped into small bits. At the end of the process, an adhesive is added. Then the wood/adhesive mixture goes on to the Compression Department, where the wood is compressed into sheets. Assume conversion costs are added evenly throughout the preparation process. Suppose that April data for the Preparation Department are as follows (in millions):

Sheets		Costs		
Beginning work in process inventory........	0 sheets	Beginning work in process inventory	$	0
Started production........................	3,000 sheets	Costs added during April:		
Completed and transferred out to		Wood		2,700
Compression in April	1,950 sheets	Adhesives...................................		1,365
Ending work in process inventory		Direct labor................................		629
(40% of the way through the		Manufacturing overhead		1,267
preparation process)	1,050 sheets	Total costs		$5,961

Required

1. Draw a time line for the Preparation Department, similar to Exhibit 21-6.
2. Use the time line to help you compute the equivalent units for direct materials and for conversion costs. (*Hint:* Each direct material added at a different point in the production process requires its own equivalent-unit computation.)
3. Compute the total costs of the units (sheets)
   a. Completed and transferred out to the Compression Department
   b. In the Preparation Department's ending work in process inventory
4. Prepare the journal entry to record the cost of the sheets completed and transferred out to the Compression Department.
5. Post the journal entries to the Work in Process Inventory—Preparation T-account. What is the ending balance?

Computing equivalent units for a second department with beginning inventory; preparing a production cost report and recording transactions on the basis of the report's information; WA method
(Obj. 2, 3, 4)

Student Resource CD
spreadsheet

P21-4B Athena Carpeting manufactures broadloom carpet in seven processes: spinning, dyeing, plying, spooling, tufting, latexing, and shearing. First, fluff nylon purchased from a company such as **DuPont** or **Monsanto** is spun into yarn that is dyed the desired color. Then threads of the yarn are joined together, or plied, for added strength. The plied yarn is spooled for carpet making. Tufting is the process by which yarn is added to burlap backing. After the backing is latexed to hold it together and make it skid-resistant, the carpet is sheared to give it an even appearance and feel.

At March 31, before recording the transfer of costs out of the Dyeing Department, the Athena Carpeting general ledger included the following account for one of its lines of carpet:

Work in Process Inventory—Dyeing

Feb. 28 Balance	11,174
Transferred in from Spinning	21,000
Direct materials	11,760
Direct labor	8,445
Manufacturing overhead	42,900

In the Dyeing Department, direct materials (dye) are added at the beginning of the process. Conversion costs are incurred evenly throughout the process. Work in process inventory of the Dyeing Department on February 28 consisted of 75 rolls. The $11,174 beginning balance of Work in Process—Dyeing includes $4,400 of transferred-in cost, $1,575 of direct materials cost, and $5,199 of conversion cost. During March, 560 rolls were transferred in from the Spinning Department. The Dyeing Department completed and transferred 500 rolls to the Plying Department in March, and 135 rolls were still in process on March 31. The ending inventory was 80% of the way through the dyeing process. Athena uses weighted-average process costing.

(*continued*)

Required

1. Prepare a time line for the Dyeing Department, similar to Exhibit 21-10.

2. Use the time line to help you compute the equivalent units, cost per equivalent unit, and total costs to account for in the Dyeing Department for March.

3. Prepare the March production cost report for Athena's Dyeing Department.

4. Journalize all transactions affecting the Dyeing Department during March, including the entries that have already been posted.

P21-5B Waterwise uses three processes to manufacture lifts for personal watercraft: forming a lift's parts from galvanized steel, assembling the lift, and testing the completed lifts. The lifts are transferred to finished goods before shipment to marinas across the country.

Computing equivalent units for a second department with beginning inventory; assigning costs to completed units and ending work in process; WA method
(Obj. 2, 3, 4)

Waterwise's Testing Department requires no direct materials. Conversion costs are incurred evenly throughout the testing process. Other information follows:

Units:	
Beginning work in process...	2,000 units
Transferred in from the Assembling Department during the period...	7,000 units
Completed during the period	4,000 units
Ending work in process (40% complete as to conversion work)	5,000 units
Costs:	
Beginning work in process (transferred-in costs, $93,000;	
conversion costs, $18,000)......................................	$111,000
Transferred in from the Assembling Department during the period...	672,000
Conversion costs added during the period	48,000

The cost transferred into Finished Goods Inventory is the cost of the lifts transferred out of the Testing Department. Waterwise uses weighted-average process costing.

Required

1. Draw a time line for the Testing Department, similar to the one in Exhibit 21-10.

2. Use the time line to compute the number of equivalent units of work performed by the Testing Department during the period, the cost per equivalent unit, and total costs to account for.

3. Assign total costs to (a) units completed and transferred out of Testing and (b) units in Testing's ending work in process inventory.

4. Compute the cost per unit for lifts completed and transferred out to Finished Goods Inventory. Why would management be interested in this cost?

●APPLY *Your Knowledge*

Decision Case

Jimmy Jones operates Jimmy's Cricket Farm in Eatonton, Georgia. Jimmy's raises about 18 million crickets a month. Most are sold to pet stores at $12.60 for a box of 1,000 crickets. Pet stores sell the crickets for 5 to 10 cents each as live feed for reptiles.

Using WA process cost information to evaluate production performance
(Obj. 4)

Raising crickets requires a two-step process: incubation and brooding. In the first process, incubation employees place cricket eggs on mounds of peat moss to hatch. In the second process, employees move the newly hatched crickets into large boxes filled with cardboard dividers. Depending on the desired size, the crickets spend approximately

(continued)

two weeks in Brooding before shipment to pet stores. In the brooding process, Jimmy's crickets consume about 16 tons of food and produce 12 tons of manure.

Jones has invested $400,000 in the cricket farm and he had hoped to earn a 24% annual rate of return, which works out to a 2% monthly return on his investment. After looking at the farm's bank balance, Jones fears he is not achieving this return. To get more-accurate information on the farm's performance, Jones bought new accounting software that provides weighted-average process cost information. After Jones input data, the software provided the following reports. However, Jones needs help interpreting these reports.

Jones does know that a unit of production is a box of 1,000 crickets. For example, in June's report, the 7,000 physical units of beginning work in process inventory are 7,000 boxes (each one of the 7,000 boxes contains 1,000 immature crickets). The finished goods inventory is zero because the crickets ship out as soon as they reach the required size. Monthly operating expenses total $2,000 (in addition to the costs below).

Jimmy's Cricket Farm
Brooding Department
Month Ended June 30, 20XX

| | | Equivalent Units | | |
Flow of Production	Flow of Physical Units	Transferred In	Direct Materials	Conversion Costs
Units to account for:				
Beginning work in process inventory......	7,000			
Transferred in during June...............	21,000			
Total units to account for................	28,000			
Units accounted for:				
Completed and shipped out during June...	19,000	19,000	19,000	19,000
Ending work in process, June 30..........	9,000	9,000	7,200	3,600
Total physical units accounted for........	28,000			
Equivalent units..........................		28,000	26,200	22,600

Jimmy's Cricket Farm
Brooding Department
Production Cost Report (Weighted-Average Method)
Month Ended June 30, 20XX

	Transferred In	Direct Materials	Conversion Costs	Total
Unit costs:				
Beginning work in process, May 31	$21,000	$39,940	$ 5,020	$ 65,960
Costs added during June	46,200	156,560	51,480	254,240
Total costs to account for	$67,200	$196,500	$56,500	$320,200
Divide by equivalent units....................	÷28,000	÷26,200	÷22,600	
Cost per equivalent unit.....................	$2.40	$7.50	$2.50	
Assignment of total cost:				
Units completed and shipped out during June...	[19,000 × ($2.40 + $7.50 + $2.50)]			$235,600
Ending work in process, June 30:				
Transferred-in costs.......................	[9,000 × $2.40]			21,600
Direct materials		[7,200 × $7.50]		54,000
Conversion costs			[3,600 × $2.50]	9,000
Total ending work in process, June 30				84,600
Total cost accounted for				$320,200

Required

Jimmy Jones has the following questions about the farm's performance during June.

1. What is the cost per box of crickets sold? (*Hint:* This is the cost of the boxes completed and shipped out of brooding.)
2. What is the gross profit per box?
3. How much operating income did Jimmy's Cricket Farm make in June?
4. What is the return on Jones' investment of $400,000 for the month of June? (Compute this as June's operating income divided by Jones' $400,000 investment, expressed as a percentage.)
5. What monthly operating income would provide a 2% monthly rate of return? What price per box would Jimmy's Cricket Farm have had to charge in June to achieve a 2% monthly rate of return?

Ethical Issue

Rick Penn and Joe Lopus are the plant managers for Pacific Lumber's particle board division. Pacific Lumber has adopted a just-in-time management philosophy. Each plant combines wood chips with chemical adhesives to produce particle board to order, and all production is sold as soon as it is completed. Laura Green is Pacific Lumber's regional controller. All of Pacific Lumber's plants and divisions send Green their production and cost information. While reviewing the numbers of the two particle board plants, she is surprised that both plants estimate their ending work in process inventories at 80% complete, which is higher than usual. Green calls Lopus, whom she has known for some time. He admits that to ensure their division met its profit goal and that both he and Penn would make their bonus (which is based on division profit), he and Penn agreed to inflate the percentage completion. Lopus explains, "Determining the percent complete always requires judgment. Whatever the percent complete, we'll finish the work in process inventory first thing next year."

Effect of percentage completion of ending inventory on financial results
(Obj. 1, 2, 3)

Required

1. How would inflating the percentage completion of ending Work in Process Inventory help Penn and Lopus get their bonus?
2. The particle board division is the largest of Pacific Lumber's divisions. If Green does not correct the percentage completion of this year's ending work in process inventory, how will the misstatement affect Pacific Lumber's financial statements?
3. Evaluate Lopus' justification, including the effect, if any, on next year's financial statements.
4. → *Link Back to Chapter 8.* Apply the ethical framework from Chapter 8 (page 342) in considering what Green should do.

Team Project

Hermiston Food Processors in Hermiston, Oregon, processes potatoes into french fries. Production requires two processes: cutting and cooking. The cutting process begins as scalding steam explodes the potatoes' brown skins. Workers using paring knives gouge out black spots before high pressure water blasts potatoes through a pipe and into blades arranged in a quarter-inch grid. In the cooking process, the raw shoestring fries are cooked in a bleacher, dried, partially fried at 380°F and immediately flash frozen at minus 75°F before being dropped into 5-pound bags. Direct materials are added at the beginning of the cutting process (potatoes) and at the end of the cooking process (bags). Conversion costs are incurred evenly throughout each process. Hermiston uses the weighted-average method of process costing.

Computing allowable cost per unit; computing cost per equivalent unit; second process; WA method
(Obj. 3, 4)

    Assume that **McDonald's** offers Hermiston $0.40 per pound to supply restaurants in the Far East. If Hermiston accepts McDonald's offer, the cost (per equivalent unit) that Hermiston will incur to fill the McDonald's order equals the April cost per equivalent

(continued)

unit. J. R. Simlott, manager of the cooking process, must prepare a report explaining whether Hermiston should accept the offer. Simlott gathers the following information from April's cooking operations:

Hermiston Food Processors
Cooking Department
April 20XX Activity and Costs

Beginning work in process inventory	12,000 pounds
Raw shoestring fries started in April.	129,000 pounds
French fries completed and transferred out	130,000 pounds
Ending work in process inventory (30% of way through process).	11,000 pounds
Costs incurred *within* the Cooking Dept. to start the 12,000 pounds of beginning work in process inventory in March.	$ 576
Costs added during April:	
Direct materials.	6,500
Conversion costs.	15,420

Lola Mendez manages the cutting process. She reports the following data for her department's April operations.

Hermiston Food Processors
Cutting Department
April 20XX Activity and Costs

Beginning work in process inventory	21,000 pounds
Potatoes started in April	121,000 pounds
Raw shoestring fries completed and transferred out	129,000 pounds
Ending work in process inventory (60% of way through process).	13,000 pounds
Costs to start the 21,000 pounds of beginning work in process inventory in March ($1,260 for direct materials and $840 for conversion costs).	$ 2,100
Costs added during April:	
Direct materials.	8,680
Conversion costs.	12,840

Split your team into two groups. Each group should meet separately before a meeting of the entire team.

Required

1. The first group takes the role of J. R. Simlott, manager of the cooking production process. Before meeting with the entire team, determine the maximum transferred-in cost per pound of raw shoestring fries the Cooking Department can incur from the Cutting Department if Hermiston is to make a profit on the McDonald's order. (*Hint:* You may find it helpful to prepare a time line and to use Exhibits 21-10 through 21-13 as a guide to your analysis.)

2. The second group takes the role of Lola Mendez, manager of the cutting process. Before meeting with the entire team, determine the April cost per pound of raw shoestring fries in the cutting process. (*Hint:* You may find it helpful to prepare a time line and to use Exhibits 21-10 through 21-13 as a guide to your analysis.)

3. After each group meets, the entire team should meet to decide whether Hermiston should accept or reject McDonald's offer.

For Internet Exercises, go to the Web site **www.prenhall.com/horngren**.

APPENDIX *to Chapter 21*

The FIFO Process Costing Method

The cost per equivalent unit often changes over time. In the second half of the chapter, we used the weighted-average process costing method in SeaView's Insertion Department. The weighted-average method values both beginning inventory and current production at the same cost per equivalent unit, but that cost is a weighted average of last period's and this period's costs.

In contrast, the **first-in, first-out (FIFO) method** of process costing values each equivalent unit of work at the cost per equivalent unit in effect during the period the work is done. Therefore, FIFO requires us to keep the beginning inventory units and costs (which were incurred *last period*) completely separate from current-period production and costs.[1]

Let's see how SeaView could use FIFO process costing in its Insertion Department. Consider a batch of swim masks transferred out of the Shaping Department and into Insertion at the end of September. These masks did not make it completely through the Insertion Department during September, so the masks are in the Insertion Department's ending (work in process) inventory at the end of September. The masks are not completed until October. Under FIFO, when these masks are completed in October, the total Insertion Department cost of these masks is the sum of

- September's equivalent units of Insertion's work on these masks, costed at September's cost per equivalent unit, *plus*
- October's equivalent units of Insertion's work on these masks, costed at October's cost per equivalent unit

Steps 1 and 2: Summarize the Flow of Physical Units and Compute Output in Terms of Equivalent Units

Summarize the Flow of Physical Units Review the October data for SeaView's Insertion Department in Exhibit 21-11. The time line in Exhibit 21A-1 shows that shaped masks are transferred in from Shaping at the beginning of Insertion's process, but Insertion's direct materials (faceplates) are not added until the end of the process.

The FIFO time line that diagrams the Insertion Department's flow of physical units (step 1) is more complex than the weighted-average time line in Exhibit 21-10. Why? Because FIFO costs each equivalent unit of work at the cost per equivalent unit in effect at the time the work was done. Under FIFO, we must separate the work done last period (September) from the work done this period (October). Exhibit 21A-1 identifies work Insertion performed during *October*.

Start with the 38,000 swim masks completed and transferred out of the Insertion Department and into finished goods inventory during October. The time line in Exhibit 21A-1 shows that these include:

□ Overview
□ Building Blocks
□ Illustrating Process Costing
□ Costing in a Second Department
■ Appendix: FIFO

tudent Resource**CD**

cost assignment, equivalent unit costs, FIFO costing method, transferred-in costs, work in process inventory

First-In, First-Out (FIFO) Process Costing Method
A process costing method that values each equivalent unit of work at the cost per equivalent unit in effect during the period the work is done.

---

[1] The FIFO and weighted-average process costing methods differ only in how they treat beginning inventory. Because SeaView's first department, Shaping, had no beginning work in process inventory, we did not need to specify which method that department used.

Exhibit *21A-1* SeaView's Insertion Department Time Line (FIFO)

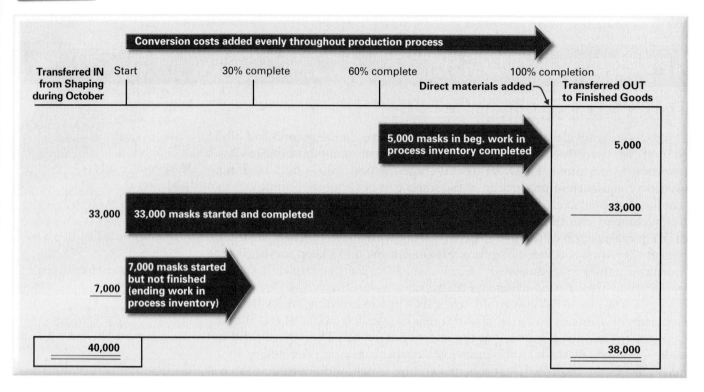

- 5,000 masks that were the Insertion Department's beginning work in process inventory. These masks were *completed* (but not started) in October.
- 33,000 masks that Insertion both *started* and *completed* during October. This number is computed as

38,000	masks completed and transferred out of the Insertion Department in October
(5,000)	masks completed from Insertion's beginning inventory
33,000	masks *started and completed during October*

The time line also shows that the 40,000 masks *transferred into* Insertion from Shaping during October (see Exhibits 21-5 and 21-6) also fall into two categories: (1) 33,000 masks *started and completed* in the Insertion Department during October, plus (2) 7,000 masks *started* in Insertion but not completed in October

Exhibit 21A-2 summarizes the flow of physical units diagrammed in the time line. The Insertion Department starts October with 5,000 masks in beginning inventory and begins work on 40,000 more transferred in from Shaping during the month. Insertion thus must account for 45,000 masks (5,000 + 40,000). Where did these 45,000 masks go? Exhibit 21A-2 shows that 38,000 were completed and transferred out to finished goods inventory (the 5,000 from beginning inventory + 33,000 started and completed during October). The remaining 7,000 masks are still in the Insertion Department's ending inventory.

✔ Starter 21A-1

Compute Equivalent Units The Insertion Department has three categories of equivalent units. In addition to direct materials (faceplates) and conversion costs added in the Insertion Department, SeaView must also compute equivalent units for the shaped swim masks that are *transferred in* from the Shaping Department. (All second and later departments must account for units (and costs) transferred in from preceding departments.) Exhibit 21A-1 shows that these transferred-in costs (from Shaping) act like costs that are added at the very beginning of the insertion process.

Exhibit 21A-2   FIFO, Step 1: Summarize the Flow of Physical Units; Step 2: Compute Output in Terms of Equivalent Units

SeaView Insertion Department
Month Ended October 31, 20XX

Flow of Production	Step 1 Flow of Physical Units	Transferred In	Direct Materials	Conversion Costs
		Step 2: Equivalent Units		
Units to account for:				
Beginning work in process, September 30	5,000			
Transferred in during October	40,000			
Total physical units to account for.	45,000			
Units accounted for:				
Completed and transferred out during October:				
From beginning work in process inventory.	5,000	—	5,000*	2,000*
Started and completed during October				
(38,000 − 5,000)	33,000	33,000	33,000	33,000
Ending work in process, October 31	7,000	7,000	— †	2,100†
Total physical units accounted for.	45,000			
Equivalent units.		40,000	38,000	37,100

During October in the Insertion Department:
*Finish beginning inventory
    Direct materials: 5,000 units each 100% completed = 5,000 equivalent units
    Conversion costs: 5,000 units each 40% completed = 2,000 equivalent units
†Start ending inventory
    Direct materials: 7,000 units each 0% completed   = 0 equivalent units
    Conversion costs: 7,000 units each 30% completed = 2,100 equivalent units

To figure out how many equivalent units of work the Insertion Department completed *during October*, look at the time line in Exhibit 21A-1 and add the number of equivalent units of work performed to:

- *Complete* the 5,000 masks in beginning inventory that were started in September,
- *Start and complete* an additional 33,000 masks, and
- *Start* (but not complete) the 7,000 masks that make up the department's work in process inventory at the end of October.

Repeat these computations for each of the three cost categories.

Equivalent Units Transferred In.   Keep in mind that our goal is to figure the number of equivalent units of work performed *during October*. Also recall that transferred-in costs (from Shaping) act like costs that are added at the very beginning of the insertion process. The time line in Exhibit 21A-1 shows that the 5,000 units in Insertion's beginning inventory were *not* transferred in from Shaping *this* month.

Look at the time line again—it shows that the 33,000 masks Insertion started and completed during October and the 7,000 masks in Insertion's ending inventory *were* transferred in during October. Exhibit 21A-2 shows that the total transferred-in equivalent units during October is 40,000 (33,000 + 7,000).

Equivalent Units of Direct Materials.   The time line in Exhibit 21A-1 shows that the Insertion Department's direct materials (faceplates) are not added until the end of the process. Exhibit 21A-1 shows that during October the 5,000 units in beginning inventory were completed, so they reached the end of the production process, where the faceplates are added. The 33,000 units started and completed also reached the end of the process. However, ending inventory has not yet reached the point where workers insert faceplates. Thus, Exhibit 21A-2 shows that Insertion added 5,000 + 33,000 = 38,000 equivalent units of materials (faceplates) during October.

Equivalent Units of Conversion Costs. The time line shows that beginning inventory was 60% complete at the beginning of October. This means that during October these 5,000 masks from the Insertion Department's beginning inventory went through the final 40% of the insertion process. This yields $5,000 \times 0.40 = 2,000$ equivalent units of conversion work during October. The 33,000 masks started and completed during October went through the entire process during October. Finally, the time line shows that the 7,000 masks in ending inventory that were *started* in Insertion during October made it 30% of the way through the process by October 31. Insertion performed $7,000 \times 0.30 = 2,100$ equivalent units of conversion work on this ending inventory during October. Thus, Exhibit 21A-2 shows that the total conversion work performed in Insertion during October includes:

2,000 units to *complete* the beginning inventory
33,000 units from masks started *and* completed during October
2,100 units to *start* the ending inventory
37,100 total equivalent units of conversion costs during October

Steps 3 and 4: Summarize Total Costs to Account For and Compute the Cost per Equivalent Unit

✔ Starter 21A-2

Exhibit 21A-3 accumulates the Insertion Department's October costs from Exhibit 21-11. *Under FIFO, the October cost per equivalent unit equals the costs incurred in October divided by the equivalent units of work performed in October.* The $24,000 cost of the beginning inventory is kept separate and is not included in the cost per equivalent unit for work done in October. Why? Because Insertion incurred this $24,000 in *September* to start the 5,000 masks in process on October 1.

Exhibit 21A-3 FIFO, Steps 3 and 4: Summarize Total Costs to Account for and Compute the Cost per Equivalent Unit

SeaView Insertion Department
Month Ended October 31, 20XX

	Transferred In	Direct Materials	Conversion Costs	Total
Beginning work in process, September 30 (Exhibit 21-11)				$ 24,000
Costs added during October (Exhibit 21-11)	$176,000	$ 19,000	$ 14,840	209,840
Divide by equivalent units (Exhibit 21A-2)	÷ 40,000	÷ 38,000	÷ 37,100	
Cost per equivalent unit	$4.40	$0.50	$0.40	
Total cost to account for				$233,840

Step 5: Assign Total Costs to Units Completed and to Units in Ending Work in Process Inventory

✔ Starter 21A-3

Exhibit 21A-4 shows that the Insertion Department uses the same approach as we have used previously to assign its total cost ($233,840 from Exhibit 21A-3) to:

- Units completed and transferred out to Finished Goods Inventory
- Units still in Insertion's ending work in process inventory

Multiply the number of equivalent units from step 2 (Exhibit 21A-2) by the cost per equivalent unit from step 4 (Exhibit 21A-3).

Exhibit 21A-4 shows that when computing the cost of masks completed and transferred out of Insertion, we must remember to include the costs of the beginning inventory:

- $24,000 of Insertion Department beginning inventory costs (incurred in September)
- $3,300 of costs to complete that beginning inventory in October [(5,000 equivalent units of materials added × $0.50) + (2,000 equivalent units of conversion costs added × $0.40)]

Exhibit 21A-4   FIFO, Step 5: Assign Total Costs to Units Completed and to Units in Ending Work in Process Inventory

SeaView Insertion Department
Month Ended October 31, 20XX

	Transferred In	Direct Materials	Conversion Costs	Total
Units completed and transferred out to Finished Goods Inventory:				
From beginning work in process, Sept. 30				$ 24,000
Costs added during October:				
Direct materials		[5,000 × $0.50]		2,500
Conversion costs			[2,000 × $0.40]	800
Total completed from beginning inventory				27,300
Units started and completed during October	[33,000 × ($4.40 + $0.50 + $0.40)]			174,900
Total costs transferred out				202,200
Ending work in process, October 31:				
Transferred-in costs	[7,000 × $4.40]			30,800
Direct materials		—		—
Conversion costs			[2,100 × $0.40]	840
Total ending work in process, October 31				31,640
Total costs accounted for.				$233,840

The entry to transfer the cost of completed masks out of the Insertion Department and into Finished Goods Inventory is based on the dollar amount computed in Exhibit 21A-4:

Finished Goods Inventory.	202,200	
Work in Process Inventory—Insertion . .		202,200

Many companies combine Exhibits 21A-3 and 21A-4 to form a FIFO-based production cost report. (This report is the FIFO-based counterpart to the weighted-average-based production cost report in Exhibit 21-16.)

When will FIFO and weighted average give different results?

Answer: FIFO and weighted average give different results when

1. There is beginning inventory. If there is no beginning inventory, FIFO and weighted average yield identical results. This is why we did not need to specify whether SeaView's Shaping Department used FIFO or weighted average—Shaping had no beginning inventory.

2. The cost per unit changes from one period to the next. If the cost per unit in the current period is the same as in the prior period, then FIFO and weighted average yield identical results.

FIFO and weighted average yield significantly different results only when there are large beginning inventories *and* costs change dramatically from one period to the next. This could happen, for example, in the wine-making industry, in which there are significant work in process inventories and the cost of grapes fluctuates.

Appendix Assignments
Starters

Computing equivalent units under FIFO

S21A-1 Refer to the Polar Spring Bottling process in Starter 21-9.

1. Draw a time line for the Bottling Department under FIFO process costing. Your time line should be similar to Exhibit 21A-1.
2. Use the time line to help you compute the Bottling Department's equivalent units using the FIFO method.

Cost per equivalent unit, FIFO; second department

S21A-2 Consider Polar Spring's Bottling Department, as described in Starter 21-9, and your solution to Starter 21-A1. Compute the cost per equivalent unit using FIFO.

Assigning costs FIFO; second department

S21-A3 Use the information about Polar Spring's Bottling Department in Starters 21-9, 21-A1, and 21-A2 to assign the costs to units completed and transferred out and to ending inventory under FIFO.

Exercises

Computing equivalent units; 2 departments, FIFO method

E21A-1 Zee's Candy uses FIFO process costing. Selected production and cost data follow for May 20X6.

	Flow of Physical Units	
Flow of Production	**Mixing Department**	**Cooking Department**
Units to account for:		
Beginning work in process, April 30..........	20,000	6,000
Transferred in during May..................	70,000	80,000
Total physical units to account for............	90,000	86,000
Units accounted for:		
Completed and transferred out during May		
From beginning work in process inventory..	20,000	6,000
Started and completed during May	60,000	70,000
Ending work in process, May 31.............	10,000	10,000
Total physical units accounted for.............	90,000	86,000

Required

1. **a.** On April 30, the Mixing Department beginning work in process inventory was 60% complete as to materials and 75% complete as to conversion costs. This means that for the beginning inventory _____% of the materials and _____% of the conversion costs were added during May.
    b. On May 31, the Mixing Department ending work in process inventory was 70% complete as to materials and 20% complete as to conversion costs. This means that for the ending inventory _____% of the materials and _____% of the conversion costs were added during May.
    c. On April 30, the Cooking Department beginning work in process inventory was 60% complete as to materials and 80% complete as to conversion costs. This means that for the beginning inventory _____% of the materials and _____% of the conversion costs were added during May.
    d. On May 31, the Cooking Department ending work in process inventory was 65% complete as to materials and 55% complete as to conversion costs. This means that for the ending inventory _____% of the materials and _____% of the conversion costs were added during May.
2. Use the information in the Flow of Production table and the information in requirement 1 to compute the equivalent units for transferred-in costs, direct materials, and conversion costs for both the Mixing and the Cooking Departments.

E21A-2 Refer to the Alpha Semiconductors, Inc. information in E21-10.

Computing equivalent units and assigning costs to completed units and to ending work in process inventory; second department, FIFO

1. Draw a time line for the Photolithography Department using the FIFO method. (See Exhibit 21A-1.)

2. Use the time line to help you compute the number of equivalent units of work performed by the Photolithography Department during December. Use the FIFO method.

3. Compute the cost per equivalent unit, and assign total costs to (a) units completed and transferred to Finished Goods Inventory and (b) units in December 31 work in process inventory.

Appendix Problems

P21A-1 Tuff, Inc., manufactures tire tubes in a two-stage process that includes shaping and sealing. The Sealing Department tests the tubes and adds a puncture-resistant coating to each tube to prevent air leaks.

Computing equivalent units for a second department with beginning inventory; assigning costs to completed units and ending work in process; recording transactions, FIFO method

At March 31, before recording the transfer of costs from the Sealing Department to Finished Goods Inventory, the Tuff general ledger included the following account:

Work in Process Inventory—Sealing

Feb. 28 balance	28,100
Transferred in from Shaping	36,000
Direct materials	24,800
Direct labor	23,595
Manufacturing overhead	32,245

The direct materials (coating) are added at the end of the sealing process. Conversion costs are incurred evenly throughout the process. Work in process of the Sealing Department on February 28 consisted of 700 tubes that were 30% of the way through the production process. During March, 3,600 tubes were transferred in from the Shaping Department. The Sealing Department transferred 3,100 tubes to Finished Goods Inventory in March, and 1,200 were still in process on March 31. This ending inventory was 50% of the way through the sealing process. Tuff uses FIFO process costing.

Required

1. Draw a time line for the Sealing Department, similar to Exhibit 21A-1.

2. Use the time line to help you compute the equivalent units, cost per equivalent unit, and total costs to account for in the Sealing Department for March.

3. Assign total Sealing Department costs to (a) goods transferred out of the Sealing Department and (b) Work in Process Inventory—Sealing on March 31.

4. Journalize all transactions affecting the Sealing Department during March, including the entries that have already been posted.

Computing EU for a second department with BI; assigning costs to completed units and ending WIP; FIFO

P21A-2 Do P21-5A using the FIFO method. The Drying Department beginning work in process of 7,000 units is 30% complete as to conversion costs. For requirement 1, use the time line in Exhibit 21A-1 as a guide.

P21A-3 Do P21-4A using the FIFO method. The Plating Department beginning work in process of 600 racks is 30% complete as to conversion costs. For requirement 1, use the time line in Exhibit 21A-1 as a guide. In Requirement 3, prepare a cost assignment report similar to Exhibit 21A-4, instead of a full production cost report.

Computing EU for a second department with BI; assigning costs to completed units and ending WIP; recording transactions; FIFO

CHAPTER 22

Cost-Volume-Profit Analysis

TIPS CHECK YOUR RESOURCES

- Visit the www.prenhall.com/horngren **Web site** for self-study quizzes, video clips, and other resources

- Try the **Quick Check** exercise at the end of the chapter to test your knowledge

- Learn the **key terms**

- Do the **Starter** exercises keyed in the margins

- Work the **mid-** and **end-of-chapter summary problems**

- Use the **Concept Links** to review material in other chapters

- Search the **CD** for review materials by chapter or by key word

- Watch the **tutorial videos** to review key concepts

- Watch the **Grand Canyon Railway On Location video** to review CVP analysis

LEARNING OBJECTIVES

⭐**1** Identify how changes in volume affect costs

⭐**2** Use CVP analysis to compute breakeven points

⭐**3** Use CVP analysis for profit planning, and graph the cost-volume-profit relations

⭐**4** Use CVP methods to perform sensitivity analyses

⭐**5** Compute income using variable costing and absorption costing

"**A**ll aboard!" shouts the conductor of the Grand Canyon Railway as the train departs from the Williams, Arizona, depot. The restored turn-of-the-century train features musicians in period costumes. Passengers have breakfast on the morning trip to the canyon and nibble appetizers on the afternoon trip back to Williams.

Few of the railway's costs vary with the number of passengers because most costs are *fixed*. Track maintenance, insurance, the costs to operate the depot's railway museum, and depreciation on the locomotive and cars stay the same whether 1 or 1,000 passengers travel the scenic 65-mile route. But food and beverage costs are *variable*. They rise and fall with the number of passengers on board.

Grand Canyon Railway

The Railway's managers must set ticket prices high enough to cover costs and earn a profit, but low enough to fill seats. Most costs are fixed, so the extra costs to serve each additional passenger are low. Once fixed costs are covered, most of the revenue from extra guests goes toward profits. ■

Student Resource CD

CVP analysis, fixed costs, mixed costs, variable costs

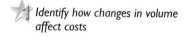

Identify how changes in volume affect costs

Cost-Volume-Profit (CVP) Analysis
Expresses the relationships among costs, volume, and profit or loss.

Cost Behavior
Describes how costs change as volume changes.

Total Variable Costs
Costs that change in total in direct proportion to changes in volume.

Total Fixed Costs
Costs that do not change in total despite wide changes in volume.

How do the railway's managers ensure that revenues cover costs and provide profits? How many seats must the railway fill to cover costs? Grand Canyon's managers perform cost-volume-profit analysis to answer these questions.

Cost-volume-profit (CVP) analysis expresses the relationships among costs, volume, and profit or loss. That is, you use CVP analysis to estimate how changes in volume affect costs and profits. To do this, you first need to understand **cost behavior**: how costs change—if they change at all—as volume changes.

How Do Changes in Volume Affect Costs?

We consider two types of cost behavior:

- **Total variable costs** change in direct proportion to changes in volume. For Grand Canyon Railway, breakfast pastries and afternoon snacks are variable costs because total food costs increase with the number of passengers.

- **Total fixed costs** do not change despite wide changes in volume. For Grand Canyon, depreciation on the tracks and locomotive are fixed costs that will be the same, regardless of the number of passengers carried.

Variable Costs

On the morning trip from Williams, Grand Canyon's passengers enjoy pastries, orange juice, and coffee. Let's assume this breakfast costs the railway $3 per person. On the afternoon return trip, passengers snack on appetizers and sip champagne and soft drinks. Say this costs Grand Canyon $10 per person. Exhibit 22-1 graphs Grand Canyon's $3-per-person breakfast cost and the $10-per-person afternoon snack cost. The vertical axis shows total variable costs, while the horizontal axis plots total volume (thousands of passengers, in this case).

Look at the total variable breakfast costs in Exhibit 22-1(a). If there are no passengers, Grand Canyon incurs no breakfast costs, so the total variable cost line begins at the bottom left corner. This point is called the *origin*, and it represents zero volume and zero cost. The *slope* of the total variable cost line is the change in total variable cost (on the vertical axis) divided by the change in the total volume (on the horizontal axis). This equals the variable cost per unit. In Exhibit 22-1(a), the slope of the breakfast total variable cost line is $3 because the railway spends an additional $3 on breakfast for each additional passenger. If the railroad carries 2,000 passengers, it will spend a total of $6,000 (2,000 passengers × $3 each) for breakfast service. Follow this total variable cost line to the right to see that doubling the number of passengers to 4,000 likewise doubles the total variable cost to $12,000 (4,000 × $3 = $12,000).

Now look at Exhibit 22-1(b), the total variable costs for afternoon snacks and beverages. The slope of the total variable cost line is the $10 cost of providing

Exhibit 22-1

Variable Costs

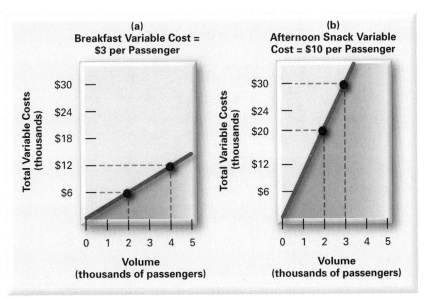

afternoon refreshments for each passenger. The total cost of afternoon snacks for 2,000 passengers is $20,000 (2,000 × $10). This is much higher than the breakfast cost for 2,000 passengers ($6,000), so the slope of the afternoon snack's total variable cost line is much steeper than that for breakfast.

The **key point** is

The higher the variable cost per unit, the steeper the slope of the total variable cost line.

Exhibit 22-1 shows how *total variable costs* vary with the number of passengers. *But note that the per-person cost remains constant.* That is, Grand Canyon incurs $3 in breakfast costs and $10 in afternoon snack costs for each passenger, no matter how many passengers the railway carries. The **key point** is

---

Total variable costs fluctuate with changes in volume, but the variable cost per unit remains constant.

Fixed Costs

In contrast to total variable costs, total fixed costs do not change over wide ranges of volume. Most of Grand Canyon's costs are fixed, because the train makes one round-trip each day, regardless of the number of passengers. The railway's fixed costs include

- Salaries of conductors
- Depreciation and maintenance on the track, the locomotive, and the museum
- Entertainment costs (salaries of the strolling musicians)
- Administrative expenses (salaries of managers and accountants)

Suppose Grand Canyon incurs $200,000 of fixed costs each month. Exhibit 22-2 graphs total fixed costs as a flat line that intersects the cost axis at $200,000, because Grand Canyon will incur the same $200,000 of fixed costs regardless of the number of passengers.

Exhibit 22-2

Fixed Costs

✔ **Starter 22-1**

In contrast to the *total fixed costs* shown in Exhibit 22-2, the *fixed cost per passenger* depends on the number of passengers. If the railway carries 2,000 passengers, the fixed cost per passenger is $100 ($200,000 ÷ 2,000 passengers). If the number of passengers doubles to 4,000, the fixed cost per passenger is cut in half to $50 ($200,000 ÷ 4,000 passengers). Thus, the fixed cost per passenger is *inversely* proportional to the number of passengers. The **key point** is

---

Total fixed costs remain constant, but fixed cost per unit is inversely proportional to volume.

World class companies capitalize on this principle to maximize profits. For example, the founder of Europe's budget airline easyJet credits the company's success to keeping planes full and flying them hard. "If you have a very expensive fixed asset, you need to make it work for you," he said.[1]

Mixed Costs

Mixed Costs
Costs that have both variable and fixed components.

Costs that have both variable and fixed components are called **mixed costs**. For example, your cell phone company may charge $10 a month to provide the service and $0.15 for each minute you talk. If you talk for 100 minutes, the company will bill you $25 [$10 + (100 × $0.15)].

Exhibit 22-3 shows how you can separate your cell phone bill into fixed and variable components. The $10 monthly charge is a fixed cost because it is the

Exhibit 22-3

Mixed Costs

✔ **Starter 22-2**

---

[1]Scott Kirsner, "Stelios Makes Growth Look Easy," *Fast Company*, November 2002, pp. 98–104.

same no matter how many minutes you use. The $0.15 a minute charge is a variable cost that increases in direct proportion to the number of minutes you talk. If you talk for 100 minutes, your total variable cost is $15, because each minute costs $0.15. If you double your talking to 200 minutes, total variable cost also doubles to $30 (200 × $0.15), and your total bill is $40 ($10 + $30).

If you double your talk time from 100 to 200 minutes, does your total cell phone bill double? Explain.

Answer: No, your total cell phone bill increases by less than double [($40 − $25) ÷ $25 = 60% increase]. Variable costs double from $15 to $30, but the $10 fixed cost does not change.

Relevant Range

The **relevant range** is the band of volume where total fixed costs remain constant and the variable cost *per unit* remains constant. To estimate costs, managers need to know the relevant range. Why? Because

- Total "fixed" costs can differ in different relevant ranges, and
- The variable cost *per unit* can differ in different relevant ranges

Exhibit 22-4 shows *fixed costs* for a Footlocker store over three different relevant ranges. If the store expects to sell 15,000 pairs of shoes next year, the relevant range is between 10,000 and 20,000 pairs, and managers budget fixed costs of $80,000.

To sell 22,000 pairs of shoes, Footlocker will have to expand the store. This will increase rent expense. Exhibit 22-4 shows that total fixed costs increase to $120,000 as the relevant range shifts to this higher band of volume. Conversely, if the store expects to sell only 8,000 pairs of shoes, Exhibit 22-4 shows that the store will budget only $40,000 of fixed costs. Managers will have to cut operating hours, lay off employees, or take other actions to cut fixed costs.

Variable cost per unit also can change outside the relevant range. For example, Footlocker may receive a quantity discount (a lower purchase cost per pair of shoes) if it can sell more than 20,000 pairs of Reeboks.

Basic CVP Analysis: What Must We Sell to Break Even?

Now let's use your understanding of how changes in volume affect costs. Kay Pak is considering starting an e-tail business selling art posters on the Internet. Pak plans to be a "virtual retailer" and carry no inventory. Pak's software will

Relevant Range
The band of volume where total fixed costs remain constant and the variable cost *per unit* remains constant.

Exhibit 22-4

Relevant Range

☐ Changes in Volume and Costs
■ **Basic CVP Analysis**
☐ Using CVP to Plan Profits
☐ Using CVP for Sensitivity Analysis
☐ Variable Costing, Absorption Costing

tudent ResourceCD

breakeven point, contribution margin, income statement approach

⭐ 2 *Use CVP analysis to compute breakeven points*

Exhibit 22-5

Components of CVP Analysis

Posters

Volume of Units

$35.00

Sale Price per Unit

Variable Cost per Unit

INVOICE
Simplified Servers
Service | Price
Server leasing | $4,000

+

INVOICE
Software House
Product | Price
software | $1,000

+

INVOICE
T.K.Realtors
Rental | Price
Office space | $2,000

= $7,000

Total Fixed Costs

INCOME STATEMENT
Sales .... $XXX
-Variable costs.... (XX)
-Fixed costs....... (XX)
Operating income ...$XX

Operating Income (or loss)

tabulate all customer orders each day and then automatically place Pak's order to buy posters from a wholesaler. Pak buys only what she needs to fulfill the prior day's sales orders. The posters will cost Pak $21 each, and she plans to sell them for $35 each. Monthly fixed costs for server leasing and maintenance, software, and office rental total $7,000.

Armed with this information about the components of CVP analysis, which is illustrated in Exhibit 22-5, you can use CVP analysis to help Kay answer questions such as these: How many posters must she sell to break even? What will profits be if sales double? How will changes in selling price, variable costs, or fixed costs affect profits? Before getting started, we review the assumptions required for CVP analysis to be accurate.

Assumptions

CVP analysis assumes that

1. The only factor that affects costs is change in volume.
2. Managers can classify each cost (or the components of mixed costs) as either variable or fixed.
3. Both costs and revenues are linear throughout the relevant range of volume.
4. Inventory levels will not change.
5. The sales mix of products will not change. **Sales mix** is the combination of products that make up total sales. For example, in 2002, Amazon.com's U.S. retail sales mix was 75% books and music products and 25% electronics and other products. If profits differ across products, then changes in sales mix affect CVP analysis. (The appendix to this chapter covers the technical details of how changes in sales mix affect CVP analysis.)

Pak's business meets these assumptions. Sales volume is the only factor that affects her costs. The $21 purchase cost for each poster is a variable cost. Thus, Pak's *total variable cost* increases directly with the number of posters she sells (an extra $21 in cost for each extra poster she sells). The $7,000 monthly server leasing and maintenance, software, and office rental costs are fixed and do not change no matter how many posters she sells. Pak has no inventory. She sells just one type of poster, so her sales mix is constant at 100% art posters.

Pak's business meets all five assumptions, so her CVP analysis is accurate. Because most business conditions do not perfectly meet these assumptions, managers regard CVP analysis as approximate, not exact.

How Much Must We Sell to Break Even? Three Approaches

The **breakeven point** is the sales level at which operating income is zero: Total revenues equal total expenses. Sales below the breakeven point result in a loss. Sales above the breakeven point provide a profit. Pak does not want to start her business unless it can make a profit, so she wants to know how many posters she must sell to break even.

There are several ways to figure the breakeven point. We start with the most versatile and easiest-to-remember method, which is based on the income statement.

THE INCOME STATEMENT APPROACH   Start by expressing income in equation form:

Sales revenue −	Total expenses	= Operating income

Sales revenue − Variable expenses − Fixed expenses = Operating income

Sales Mix
Combination of products that make up total sales.

Sales revenue equals the unit sale price ($35 per poster in this case) multiplied by the number of units (posters) sold. Variable expenses equal variable cost per unit ($21 in this case) times the number of units sold. Pak's fixed expenses total $7,000. At the breakeven point, operating income is zero. We use this information to solve the income statement equation for the number of posters Pak must sell to break even.

Breakeven Point
The sales level at which operating income is zero: Total revenues equal total expenses.

SALES REVENUE	–	VARIABLE EXPENSES		– FIXED EXPENSES	= OPERATING INCOME
$\left(\dfrac{\text{Sale price}}{\text{per unit}} \times \text{Units sold}\right)$ –		$\left(\dfrac{\text{Variable cost}}{\text{per unit}} \times \text{Units sold}\right)$		– Fixed expenses	= Operating income
($35	× Units sold) –	($21	× Units sold) –	$7,000	= $0
($35	–	$21)	× Units sold) –	$7,000	= $0
		$14	× Units sold		= $7,000
			Units sold		= $7,000/$14
		Breakeven sales in units			= 500 posters

Kay Pak must sell 500 posters to break even. Her breakeven sales level in dollars is $17,500 (500 posters × $35).

Be sure to check your calculations. "Prove" the breakeven point by substituting the breakeven number of units into the income statement equation and checking that this level of sales results in zero profit.

$$(\$35 \times 500) - (\$21 \times 500) - \$7,000 = \$0$$
$$\$17,500 - \$10,500 - \$7,000 = \$0$$

THE CONTRIBUTION MARGIN APPROACH: A SHORTCUT   To use this shortcut method of computing the breakeven point, we first must know Pak's contribution margin. **Contribution margin** is sales revenue minus variable expenses. It is called the *contribution margin* because the excess of sales revenue over variable costs contributes to covering fixed expenses and then to providing operating income. We can refer to contribution margin on a total basis or on a per-unit basis:

Contribution Margin
Sales revenue minus variable expenses.

$$\text{Total contribution margin} = \text{Total sales revenue} - \text{Total variable expenses}$$
$$\text{Contribution margin per unit} = \text{Sales revenue per unit} - \text{Variable expense per unit}$$

✔ **Starter 22-3**

Now let's rearrange the income statement equation and use the contribution margin to develop a shortcut method for finding the number of posters Pak must sell to break even.

$$\text{Sales revenue} - \text{Variable expenses} - \text{Fixed expenses} = \text{Operating income}$$
$$\left(\dfrac{\text{Sale price}}{\text{per unit}} \times \text{Units sold}\right) - \left(\dfrac{\text{Variable cost}}{\text{per unit}} \times \text{Units sold}\right) - \text{Fixed expenses} = \text{Operating income}$$
$$\underbrace{\left(\dfrac{\text{Sale price}}{\text{per unit}} - \dfrac{\text{Variable cost}}{\text{per unit}}\right)}_{\text{Contribution margin per unit}} \times \text{Units sold} = \dfrac{\text{Fixed}}{\text{expenses}} + \dfrac{\text{Operating}}{\text{income}}$$
$$\text{Contribution margin per unit} \times \text{Units sold} = \dfrac{\text{Fixed}}{\text{expenses}} + \dfrac{\text{Operating}}{\text{income}}$$

Dividing both sides of the equation by contribution margin per unit yields

$$\text{Units sold} = \dfrac{\text{Fixed expenses} + \text{Operating income}}{\text{Contribution margin per unit}}$$

Kay Pak can use this contribution margin approach to find her breakeven point. Her fixed expenses total $7,000. Operating income is zero at the breakeven point. Her contribution margin per poster is $14 ($35 sale price − $21 variable cost). Pak's breakeven computation is

$$= \frac{\$7,000 + \$0}{\$14}$$
$$= 500 \text{ posters}$$

Why does this shortcut method work? Each poster Pak sells provides $14 of contribution margin. To break even, Pak must generate enough contribution margin to cover $7,000 of fixed expenses. At the rate of $14 per poster, Pak must sell 500 posters ($7,000/$14) to cover her $7,000 of fixed expenses. Because the contribution margin approach simply rearranges the income statement equation, the breakeven point is the same under both methods (500 posters).

✔ **Starter 22-4**

USING THE CONTRIBUTION MARGIN RATIO TO COMPUTE THE BREAKEVEN POINT IN SALES DOLLARS It's easy to compute the breakeven point for a simple business like Kay Pak's that has only one product. The sale price and variable cost per poster are available, as are the fixed costs necessary for the business. But what about companies that have thousands of products, like Amazon.com or Sony?

If they don't have detailed information on individual products, companies use the contribution margin ratio to compute breakeven points in terms of *sales dollars*. The **contribution margin ratio** is the ratio of contribution margin to sales revenue. For Kay Pak's poster business, we have:

Contribution Margin Ratio
Ratio of contribution margin to sales revenue.

$$\text{Contribution margin ratio} = \frac{\text{Contribution margin}}{\text{Sales revenue}} = \frac{\$14}{\$35} = 40\%$$

The 40% contribution margin ratio means that each dollar of sales revenue contributes $0.40 toward fixed costs and profit, as shown in Exhibit 22-6.

Exhibit 22-6

Breakdown of $1 of Revenue into Variable Costs and Contribution Margin

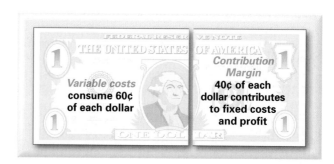

The contribution margin *ratio* approach differs from the shortcut contribution margin approach we've just seen in only one way: fixed expenses plus operating income are divided by the contribution margin *ratio* to yield sales in *dollars*:

$$\text{Sales in dollars} = \frac{\text{Fixed expenses} + \text{Operating income}}{\text{Contribution margin ratio}}$$

Using this ratio formula, Kay Pak's breakeven point in sales dollars is

$$\text{Sales in dollars} = \frac{\$7,000 + \$0}{0.40}$$
$$= \$17,500$$

This is the same breakeven sales revenue as shown in the proof on page 903.

Why does the contribution margin ratio formula work? Each dollar of Kay Pak's sales contributes $0.40 to fixed expenses and profit. To break even, she must generate enough contribution margin at the rate of $0.40 per sales dollar to cover the $7,000 fixed expenses ($7,000 ÷ 0.40 = $17,500).

Suppose that **Amazon.com**'s total revenues are $4.5 billion, its variable costs are $3.15 billion, and its fixed costs are $1.1 billion. What is the breakeven point in sales dollars?

Answer: The contribution margin ratio is 30% [($4.5 − $3.15) ÷ $4.5].

$$\text{Sales in dollars} = \frac{\text{Fixed expenses + Operating income}}{\text{Contribution margin ratio}}$$

$$= \frac{\$1.1 \text{ billion} + \$0}{0.30}$$

$$= \$3.667 \text{ billion (rounded)}$$

We've seen how companies use *contribution margin* to estimate breakeven points in CVP analysis. But managers use the contribution margin for other purposes too, such as motivating the sales force. Salespeople who know the contribution margin of each product can generate more profit by emphasizing high-margin products. This is why many companies base sales commissions on the contribution margins produced by sales rather than on sales revenue alone.

Using CVP to Plan Profits

For established products and services, managers are more interested in the sales level needed to earn a target profit than in the breakeven point. Managers of new business ventures are also interested in the profits they can expect to earn. For example, now that she knows she must sell 500 posters to break even, Kay Pak wants to know how many more posters she must sell to earn $4,900 a month in profit.

Student ResourceCD
breakeven point, income statement approach

3 *Use CVP analysis for profit planning, and graph the cost-volume-profit relations*

How Much Must We Sell to Earn a Profit?

The only difference from our prior analysis is that instead of determining the sales level needed for zero profit, Pak now wants to know how many posters she must sell to earn a $4,900 profit. We can use the income statement approach or the shortcut contribution margin approach to find the answer. Let's use the income statement approach.

✔ Starter 22-5

SALES REVENUE	−	VARIABLE EXPENSES	−	FIXED EXPENSES	=	OPERATING INCOME
($35 × Units sold)	−	($21 × Units sold)	−	$7,000	=	$4,900
($35	−	$21) × Units sold	−	$7,000	=	$4,900
		$14 × Units sold			=	$11,900
				Units sold	=	$11,900/$14
				Units sold	=	850 posters

Proof:

($35 × 850)	−	($21 × 850)	−	$7,000	=	$4,900
$29,750	−	$17,850	−	$7,000	=	$4,900

This analysis shows that Pak must sell 850 posters each month to earn profits of $4,900 a month. This is 850 − 500 = 350 more posters than the breakeven sales level (500 posters).

Accounting.com

Webvan.com: How Fixed Costs Kept It from Delivering the Goods

When online grocer Webvan.com opened its virtual doors in April 1999, it seemed to have all the ingredients for an e-commerce success story: financial backing of high-profile financiers and public funding totaling $1.2 billion, an experienced management team led by former Andersen Consulting CEO George Shaheen, and a service custom-made for today's busy professionals.

Shaheen expected the start-up to eventually deliver not just groceries, but everything from CDs to dry cleaning. To handle the huge demand he expected for Webvan's services, Shaheen built 26 state-of-the-art distribution centers in seven cities. They cost the company $25 million each. Each warehouse was equipped with 1,000 expensive servers, 16 employees, and a fleet of top-of-the-line trucks.

Alas, the company's business model turned out to be its undoing. Webvan, like eToys and other failed e-businesses, racked up enormous fixed costs by insourcing distribution. It tanked when the huge sales needed to cover those fixed costs never materialized (Webvan needed 4,000 orders per day at *each* distribution center to break even!). Then, instead of reducing fixed costs by cutting the costs of warehouses and tech support, the company lowered the quality of its produce, further reducing customer demand.

Webvan's approach stands in direct contrast to Amazon.com, which started with more of a variable cost structure. Amazon sold books from its Web site without investing in warehouses or inventory. It did not acquire the books it sold until after it received a customer order. Without warehousing and inventory, Amazon avoided fixed costs if business was slow. Later, as demand grew, it took on more fixed costs—building its own warehouses, for instance.

In 2002, Amazon was finally turning an operating profit, while Webvan was auctioning off its vans and trucks.

Based on: Carrie Kirby, "NEWS ANALYSIS: Webvan's Swan Song: Crash, Burn Calls E-Commerce into Serious Question," *San Francisco Chronicle*, July 10, 2001, p. B.1. Justin Rock, "The Inevitable Crash of Webvan," *Weekly Corporate Growth Report*, July 30, 2001, pp. 11453, 11464. Anonymous, "Digits," *The Wall Street Journal*, May 9, 2002, p. B5. Information about Amazon is from Amazon.com financial statements, stock-analyst reports, and conversations with company management.

The proof shows that Pak needs sales revenues of $29,750 to earn a profit of $4,900. Alternatively, we can compute the dollar sales necessary to earn a $4,900 profit directly, using the contribution margin ratio form of the CVP formula:

$$\textbf{SALES IN DOLLARS} = \frac{\textbf{Fixed expenses + Operating income}}{\textbf{Contribution margin ratio}}$$

$$= \frac{\$7,000 + \$4,900}{0.40}$$

$$= \frac{\$11,900}{0.40}$$

$$= \$29,750$$

Graphing Cost-Volume-Profit Relations

By graphing the cost-volume-profit relations for her proposed business, Kay Pak can see at a glance how changes in the levels of sales will affect profits. As in the variable-, fixed-, and mixed-cost graphs in Exhibits 22-1 through 22-3, she places the volume of units (posters) on the horizontal axis and dollars on the vertical axis. Then she follows five steps to graph the CVP relations for her business, as illustrated in Exhibit 22-7:

Exhibit 22-7

Cost-Volume-Profit Graph

✔ Starter 22-6

✔ Starter 22-7

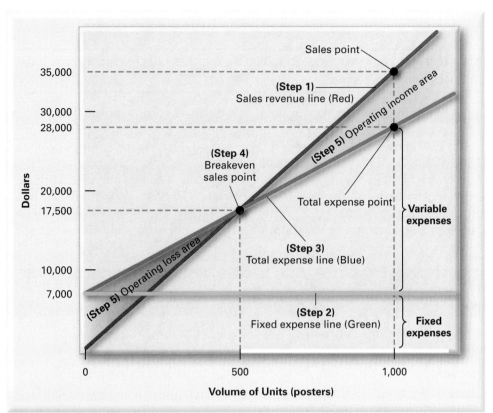

STEP 1 Choose a sales volume, such as 1,000 posters. Plot the point for total sales revenue at that volume: 1,000 posters × $35 per poster = sales of $35,000. Draw the *sales revenue line* from the origin (0) through the $35,000 point. Why does the sales revenue line start at the origin? If Pak does not sell any posters, there is no sales revenue.

STEP 2 Draw the *fixed expense line*, a horizontal line that intersects the dollars axis at $7,000. Why is the fixed expense line flat? Because fixed expenses are the same ($7,000) no matter how many posters Pak sells.

STEP 3 Draw the *total expense line*. Total expense is the sum of variable expense plus fixed expense. Thus, total expense is a *mixed* cost. So the total expense line follows the form of the mixed cost line in Exhibit 22-3. Begin by computing variable expense at the chosen sales volume: 1,000 posters × $21 per poster = variable expense of $21,000. Add variable expense to fixed expense: $21,000 + $7,000 = $28,000. Plot the total expense point ($28,000) for 1,000 units. Then draw a line through this point from the $7,000 fixed expense intercept on the dollars axis. This is the *total expense line*. Why does the total expense line start at the fixed expense line? If Pak sells no posters, she still incurs the $7,000 fixed cost for the server leasing, software, and office rental, but she incurs no variable costs.

STEP 4 Identify the *breakeven point*. The breakeven point is the point where the sales revenue line intersects the total expense line. This is the point where sales revenue exactly equals total expenses. Our previous analyses told us that Pak's breakeven point is 500 posters, or $17,500 in sales. The graph shows this information visually.

STEP 5 Mark the *operating income* and the *operating loss* areas on the graph. To the left of the breakeven point, the total expense line lies above the sales revenue line. Expenses exceed sales revenue, leading to an operating loss. If Pak sells only 300 posters, she incurs an operating loss. The amount of the loss is the vertical distance between the total expense line and the sales revenue line:

SALES REVENUE − VARIABLE EXPENSES − FIXED EXPENSES = OPERATING INCOME (LOSS)
$(300 \times \$35)$ − $(300 \times \$21)$ − $\$7,000$ = $\$(2,800)$

To the right of the breakeven point, the business earns a profit. The vertical distance between the sales revenue line and the total expense line equals income. Exhibit 22-7 shows that if Pak sells 1,000 posters, she earns operating income of $7,000 ($35,000 sales revenue − $28,000 total expenses).

Why bother with a graph? Why not just use the income statement approach or the shortcut contribution margin approach? Graphs like Exhibit 22-7 help managers quickly estimate the profit or loss earned at different levels of sales. The income statement and contribution margin approaches indicate income or loss for only a single sales amount.

MID-CHAPTER *Summary Problem*

TIPS

CHECK YOUR RESOURCES

Fleet Foot buys hiking socks for $6 a pair and sells them for $10. Management budgets monthly fixed costs of $10,000 for sales volumes between 0 and 12,000 pairs.

Required

1. Use both the income statement approach and the shortcut contribution margin approach to compute the company's monthly breakeven sales in units.
2. Use the contribution margin ratio approach to compute the breakeven point in sales dollars.
3. Compute the monthly sales level (in units) required to earn a target operating income of $14,000. Use either the income statement approach or the shortcut contribution margin approach.
4. Prepare a graph of Fleet Foot's CVP relationships, similar to Exhibit 22-7. Draw the sales revenue line, the fixed expense line, and the total expense line. Label the axes, the breakeven point, the operating income area, and the operating loss area.

Solution

Requirement 1

Income statement approach:

$$
\text{Sales revenue} \quad - \quad \text{Variable expenses} \quad - \quad \begin{matrix}\text{Fixed}\\\text{expenses}\end{matrix} \quad = \quad \begin{matrix}\text{Operating}\\\text{income}\end{matrix}
$$

$$
\left(\begin{matrix}\text{Sale price}\\\text{per unit}\end{matrix} \times \begin{matrix}\text{Units}\\\text{sold}\end{matrix}\right) - \left(\begin{matrix}\text{Variable}\\\text{cost per unit}\end{matrix} \times \begin{matrix}\text{Units}\\\text{sold}\end{matrix}\right) - \begin{matrix}\text{Fixed}\\\text{expenses}\end{matrix} = \begin{matrix}\text{Operating}\\\text{income}\end{matrix}
$$

$(\$10 \times \text{Units sold})$ −	$(\$6 \times \text{Units sold})$ −	$\$10,000$	= \$0
$(\$10$ −	$\$6) \times \text{Units sold}$		= \$10,000
	$\$4 \times \text{Units sold}$		= \$10,000
	Units sold		= \$10,000 ÷ \$4
	Breakeven sales in units		= 2,500 units

Shortcut contribution margin approach:

$$
\text{Units sold} = \frac{\text{Fixed expenses} + \text{Operating income}}{\text{Contribution margin per unit}}
$$

$$
\text{Breakeven sales in units} = \frac{\$10,000 + \$0}{\$10 - \$6}
$$

$$
= \frac{\$10,000}{\$4}
$$

$$
= 2,500 \text{ units}
$$

Requirement 2

$$\text{Breakeven sales in dollars} = \frac{\text{Fixed expenses} + \text{Operating income}}{\text{Contribution margin ratio}}$$

$$= \frac{\$10,000 + \$0}{0.40^*}$$

$$= \$25,000$$

$$^* \text{Contribution margin ratio} = \frac{\text{Contribution margin per unit}}{\text{Sale price per unit}} = \frac{\$4}{\$10} = 0.40$$

Requirement 3

Income statement equation approach:

$$\text{Sales revenue} \quad - \quad \text{Variable expenses} \quad - \quad \begin{array}{c}\text{Fixed}\\\text{expenses}\end{array} = \begin{array}{c}\text{Operating}\\\text{income}\end{array}$$

$$\left(\begin{array}{c}\text{Sale price}\\\text{per unit}\end{array} \times \begin{array}{c}\text{Units}\\\text{sold}\end{array}\right) - \left(\begin{array}{c}\text{Variable}\\\text{cost per unit}\end{array} \times \begin{array}{c}\text{Units}\\\text{sold}\end{array}\right) - \begin{array}{c}\text{Fixed}\\\text{expenses}\end{array} = \begin{array}{c}\text{Operating}\\\text{income}\end{array}$$

$$
\begin{aligned}
(\$10 \times \text{Units sold}) \quad - \quad (\$6 \times \text{Units sold}) \quad - \quad \$10,000 &= \$14,000 \\
(\$10 \quad - \quad \$6) \times \text{Units sold} &= \$10,000 + \$14,000 \\
\$4 \times \text{Units sold} &= \$24,000 \\
\text{Units sold} &= \$24,000 \div \$4 \\
\text{Units sold} &= 6,000 \text{ units}
\end{aligned}
$$

Shortcut contribution margin approach:

$$\text{Units sold} = \frac{\text{Fixed expenses} + \text{Operating income}}{\text{Contribution margin per unit}}$$

$$= \frac{\$10,000 + \$14,000}{(\$10 - \$6)}$$

$$= \frac{\$24,000}{\$4}$$

$$= 6,000 \text{ units}$$

Requirement 4

Student ResourceCD

breakeven point, fixed costs, margin of safety, sensitivity analysis, variable costs

Use CVP methods to perform sensitivity analyses

Sensitivity Analysis
A "what if" technique that asks what results will be if actual prices or costs change, or if an underlying assumption changes.

Using CVP for Sensitivity Analysis

In today's fast-changing business world, managers need to quickly estimate how changes in sale price, costs, or volume affect profits. In a recent drive to increase profitability, Starbucks analyzed the profitability of each product at the store level. Then it realigned prices. For example, coffee mugs and CDs had been money-losers, so it raised the prices of these items.

To predict how raising or lowering prices will affect profits, managers use CVP to conduct **sensitivity analysis**. Sensitivity analysis is a "what if" technique that asks what results will be if actual prices or costs change, or if an underlying assumption changes. Let's see how Kay Pak uses CVP to estimate the effects of important changes in her business environment.

Changing the Sale Price

Competition in the art poster business is so fierce that Kay Pak believes she must cut the sale price to $31 per poster to maintain her market share. If her variable costs remain $21 per poster and her fixed costs stay at $7,000, how will this lower sale price affect her breakeven point?

Using the income statement approach:

SALES REVENUE	– VARIABLE EXPENSES	– FIXED EXPENSES	= OPERATING INCOME
($31 × Units sold) –	($21 × Units sold) –	$7,000	= $0
($31 –	$21) × Units sold –	$7,000	= $0
	$10 × Units sold		= $7,000
		Units sold	= $7,000/$10
		Units sold	= 700 posters

Proof:

Sales revenue (700 × $31)		$ 21,700
Less: Variable expenses (700 × $21)	$14,700	
Fixed expenses	7,000	(21,700)
Operating income		$ 0

With the original $35 sale price, Pak's breakeven point is 500 posters (page 903). With the new lower sale price of $31 per poster, her breakeven point increases to 700 posters. The lower sale price means that each poster contributes less toward fixed expenses, so Pak must sell 200 more posters to break even.

Stop & Think

> Kay Pak believes she could dominate the e-commerce art poster business if she cut the sale price to $20. Is this a good idea?
>
> *Answer:* No. The variable cost per poster is $21. If Pak sells posters for $20 each, she loses $1 on each poster. There can be no profit if the sale price does not even cover variable expenses.

Changing Variable Costs

Return to Kay Pak's original data on page 902. Pak's supplier raises his prices, which increases her purchase cost for each poster to $23.80 (instead of the original $21). Pak does not want to pass this increase on to her customers, so she holds her sale price at the original $35 per poster. Her fixed costs remain at $7,000. How many posters must she sell to break even after her supplier raises his prices?

Using the income statement approach:

SALES REVENUE –	VARIABLE EXPENSES –	FIXED EXPENSES	= OPERATING INCOME
($35 × Units sold) –	($23.80 × Units sold) –	$7,000	= $0
($35 –	$23.80) × Units sold –	$7,000	= $0
	$11.20 × Units sold		= $7,000
		Units sold	= $7,000/$11.20
		Units sold	= 625 posters

✔ Starter 22-8

Higher variable expenses per poster reduce Pak's per-unit contribution margin from $14 per poster to $11.20 per poster. As a result, Pak must sell more posters to break even—625 rather than the original 500 posters. This analysis shows why managers are particularly concerned with controlling costs during an economic downturn. Increases in cost increase the breakeven point, and a higher breakeven point could lead to serious problems if demand falls due to a recession.

Of course, a decrease in variable costs would have just the opposite effect. Lower variable costs increase the contribution each poster provides and, therefore, lower the breakeven point.

Changing Fixed Costs

Return to Kay Pak's original data on page 902. Kay is considering spending an additional $3,500 on Web site banner ads. This would increase her fixed costs from $7,000 to $10,500. If she sells the posters at the original price of $35 each and her variable costs are the original $21 per poster, what is her new breakeven point?

Using the income statement approach:

SALES REVENUE –	VARIABLE EXPENSES –	FIXED EXPENSES	= OPERATING INCOME
($35 × Units sold) –	($21 × Units sold) –	$10,500	= $0
($35 –	$21) × Units sold –	$10,500	= $0
	$14 × Units sold		= $10,500
		Units sold	= $10,500/$14
		Units sold	= 750 posters

✔ Starter 22-9

Higher fixed costs increase the total contribution margin required to break even. In this case, increasing the fixed costs from $7,000 to $10,500 increases the breakeven point to 750 posters (from the original 500 posters).

Managers usually prefer a lower breakeven point to a higher one. But don't overemphasize this one aspect of CVP analysis. Even though investing in the Web banner ads increases her breakeven point, Kay Pak may be willing to pay the extra $3,500 if she expects the ads to stimulate enough extra sales and profits to more than cover the additional advertising expense.

Margin of Safety

The **margin of safety** is the excess of expected sales over breakeven sales. This is the "cushion" or drop in sales the company can absorb without incurring a loss. The higher the margin of safety, the greater the cushion against loss and the less risky the business plan. Managers use the margin of safety to evaluate the risk of current operations, as well as the risk of new plans.

Margin of Safety
Excess of expected sales over breakeven sales. Drop in sales a company can absorb without incurring an operating loss.

Kay Pak's breakeven point in our original data is 500 posters. Suppose she expects to sell 950 posters. Her margin of safety is

✔ **Starter 22-10**

✔ **Starter 22-11**

MARGIN OF SAFETY IN UNITS = EXPECTED SALES IN UNITS − BREAKEVEN SALES IN UNITS

= 950 posters   − 500 posters

= 450 posters

MARGIN OF SAFETY IN DOLLARS = MARGIN OF SAFETY IN UNITS × SALE PRICE PER UNIT

= 450 posters   × $35

= $15,750

Sales can drop by 450 posters, or $15,750, before Pak incurs a loss. This is a comfortable margin.

Managers can also compute the margin of safety as a percentage for any level of sales. Simply divide the margin of safety by sales. We obtain the same percentage whether we use units or dollars.

In units:

$$\text{MARGIN OF SAFETY AS A PERCENTAGE} = \frac{\text{Margin of safety in units}}{\text{Expected sales in units}}$$

$$= \frac{450 \text{ posters}}{950 \text{ posters}}$$

$$= 47.4\% \text{ (rounded)}$$

In dollars:

$$\text{MARGIN OF SAFETY AS A PERCENTAGE} = \frac{\text{Margin of safety in dollars}}{\text{Expected sales in dollars}}$$

$$= \frac{450 \text{ units} \times \$35}{950 \text{ units} \times \$35}$$

$$= \frac{\$15,750}{\$33,250}$$

$$= 47.4\% \text{ (rounded)}$$

Knowing that she will not incur a loss unless sales fall short of expectations by more than 47.4% should tell Kay Pak that her business plan is not unduly risky.

Information Technology and Sensitivity Analysis

Information technology allows managers to perform a wide array of sensitivity analyses before committing to decisions. Managers of small- to medium-sized companies use Excel spreadsheets to perform sensitivity analyses like those we just did for Kay Pak. Spreadsheets allow managers to estimate how one change (or several changes simultaneously) affects business operations. Managers also use the information the spreadsheets store on basic CVP components (sale price, variable cost, and fixed costs) to display profit-planning graphs similar to Exhibit 22-7.

Many large companies use sophisticated enterprise resource planning software like SAP, Oracle, and Peoplesoft to provide detailed data for CVP analysis. For example, after Sears stores lock their doors at 9:00 P.M., records for each individual transaction flow into a massive database. From a Diehard battery sold in Texas to a Trader Bay polo shirt sold in New Hampshire, the system compiles an average of 1.5 million transactions a day. With the click of a mouse, managers access sale price, variable cost, and sales volume for individual products to conduct breakeven or profit planning analyses.

The next section uses the building blocks of CVP analysis (contribution margin and the distinction between variable and fixed costs) to explain a costing approach many managers use for internal decisions. Before continuing, review the CVP Analysis Decision Guidelines to make sure you understand these basic concepts.

Decision Guidelines

COST-VOLUME-PROFIT ANALYSIS

Take on the role of general manager of **Grand Canyon Railways**, from the chapter opening story. How can you use CVP analysis to make key decisions for the Railway?

Decision	Guidelines
How do changes in the number of passengers affect	
• total costs?	Total variable costs → Change in proportion to changes in volume (number of passengers)
	Total fixed costs → No change
• cost per passenger?	Variable cost per passenger → No change
	Fixed cost per passenger:
	Increases when volume drops (Fixed costs are spread over fewer passengers)
	Decreases when volume rises (Fixed costs are spread over more passengers)
How to compute sales needed to break even or earn a target operating income	
• in passengers?	*Income Statement Method:*

$$\text{Sales revenue} - \text{Variable expenses} - \frac{\text{Total fixed}}{\text{expenses}} = \frac{\text{Operating}}{\text{income}}$$

$$\left(\begin{array}{l}\text{Sale price per passenger} \\ \times \text{Number of passengers}\end{array}\right) - \left(\begin{array}{l}\text{Variable cost per passenger} \\ \times \text{Number of passengers}\end{array}\right) - \frac{\text{Total fixed}}{\text{expenses}} = \frac{\text{Operating}}{\text{income}}$$

Shortcut Contribution Margin Method:

$$\frac{\text{Fixed expense} + \text{Operating income}}{\text{Contribution margin per passenger}}$$

• in dollars?	*Shortcut Contribution Margin Ratio Method:*

$$\frac{\text{Fixed expense} + \text{Operating income}}{\text{Contribution margin ratio}}$$

How to estimate the effects of changes in sale price, costs, or volume of passengers?	Use CVP methods to perform sensitivity analyses. For example, enter the new sale price, cost, or volume of passengers in the income statement equation:

$$\left(\begin{array}{l}\text{Sale price per passenger} \\ \times \text{Number of passengers}\end{array}\right) - \left(\begin{array}{l}\text{Variable cost per passenger} \\ \times \text{Number of passengers}\end{array}\right) - \frac{\text{Total fixed}}{\text{expenses}} = \frac{\text{Operating}}{\text{income}}$$

How to use CVP analysis to measure risk?	Margin of safety = Expected sales − Breakeven sales

Excel Application Exercise

Goal: Create a spreadsheet and graph to show the relationship between costs, volume, and profit and to discover the breakeven point.

Scenario: Phonetronix, Inc., makes telephone and communications devices. Recently, management decided to investigate the profitability of producing cellular phones. The proposed new phone would sell for $99.00. Variable cost per unit is $55.00, and total fixed costs are $110,000.

When you have completed your worksheet, answer the following questions:

Excel Application Exercise *(continued)*

1. How many phones must Phonetronix sell to break even? On the graph in the spreadsheet, point the cursor at the breakeven point. Does the "pop up" value for Total Costs match Total Revenue?

2. What is the breakeven point if Phonetronix raises the price per phone to $129? Note the changes in the graph. Which direction did the breakeven point move?

3. What is the breakeven point if the selling price per phone is $99 but Phonetronix slashes the variable costs per phone to $49? Note the changes in the graph. Which direction did the breakeven point move?

Step-by-Step:

1. Open a new Excel spreadsheet.
2. In column A, create a bold-faced heading as follows:
   a. Chapter 22 Excel Application Exercise
   b. Cost-Volume-Profit Analysis
   c. Phonetronix, Inc.
   d. Today's Date
3. Two rows down, enter the bold-faced and underlined heading, "Data Section" in column A.

4. Move down one row. Starting in column A, enter three rows of data, with these descriptions: price, variable cost per unit, and total fixed costs. Format cells as needed as you work.

5. Move down two rows. Enter the following bold-faced and underlined column headings, in order:
   a. # Units Sold   d. Total Fixed Costs
   b. Total Revenue   e. Total Costs
   c. Total Variable Costs f. Total Profit

6. Enter # Units Sold, in 200-unit increments, starting at 100 units and going up to 3,500 units. (Hint: Use a formula.)

7. Enter the formulas for the remaining five columns.

8. Create your graph by selecting one row of titles and all data except the "Total Profit" column. Then, click on the Chart Wizard. Select the basic line graph without data values or 3D effects.

9. Title your graph "CVP Analysis." Label the x-axis "# Units Sold" and y-axis "Dollars." Click to finish the graph. (Your x-axis values will range from "1" to "17," not the actual unit values. To see the actual values, position your cursor over the x-axis to see a pop-up box containing the values.)

10. Position the graph at the bottom of your data in the spreadsheet and size to fit if necessary.

11. Save your file to disk, and print a copy (in color, if possible) for your files after each scenario change.

- ☐ Changes in Volume and Costs
- ☐ Basic CVP Analysis
- ☐ Using CVP to Plan Profits
- ☐ Using CVP for Sensitivity Analysis
- ■ **Variable Costing, Absorption Costing**

 Student Resource CD

absorption costing, contribution margin, fixed costs, variable costs

 Compute income using variable costing and absorption costing

Variable Costing
The costing method that assigns only variable manufacturing costs to products.

Absorption Costing
The costing method that assigns both variable and fixed manufacturing costs to products.

Variable Costing and Absorption Costing

In this chapter, you have seen how managers use contribution margin and CVP analysis to make decisions. Managers often extend this approach to use **variable costing**, which assigns only variable manufacturing costs to products—for internal reporting. Then they use variable costing to prepare special income statements for *internal management decisions*. These variable costing income statements group costs by behavior—variable costs or fixed costs—and highlight the contribution margin. Before we delve into variable costing and how managers use its income statement format to make decisions, let's first review the fundamentals of costing for *external reporting*.

Up to this point, you have focused on the income statements that companies prepare for external reporting under GAAP. GAAP requires that we assign both variable and fixed manufacturing costs to products. This approach is called **absorption costing** because products absorb fixed manufacturing costs as well as variable manufacturing costs. Supporters of absorption costing argue that companies cannot produce products without fixed manufacturing costs, so these costs are an important part of product costs.

For planning and decision making, many managers prefer a different approach. Variable costing assigns only variable manufacturing costs to products. Under variable costing, fixed manufacturing costs are considered period costs and are expensed in the period when they are incurred. Supporters of variable costing argue that fixed manufacturing costs (such as depreciation on the plant) provide the capacity to produce during a period. Because the company incurs these fixed expenses whether or not it produces any products or services, they are period costs, not product costs.

The key difference between absorption costing and variable costing is that absorption costing considers fixed manufacturing costs as inventoriable product costs, while variable costing considers fixed manufacturing costs as period costs (expenses).

All other costs are treated the same way under both absorption and variable costing:

- Variable manufacturing costs are inventoriable products costs.
- All nonmanufacturing costs are period costs.

Exhibit 22-8 summarizes the difference between variable and absorption costing.

Differences Between Absorption Costing and Variable Costing

	Absorption Costing	Variable Costing
Product Costs (Capitalized as Inventory until expensed as Cost of Goods Sold)	Direct materials Direct labor Variable manufacturing overhead Fixed manufacturing overhead	Direct materials Direct labor Variable manufacturing overhead
Period Costs (Expensed in period incurred)	Variable nonmanufacturing costs Fixed nonmanufacturing costs	Fixed manufacturing overhead Variable nonmanufacturing costs Fixed nonmanufacturing costs
Focus	External reporting— required by GAAP	Internal reporting only
Income Statement Format	Conventional income statement, as in Chapters 1–19	Contribution margin statement

Variable versus Absorption Costing: Sportade

To see how absorption costing and variable costing differ, let's consider the following example. Sportade incurs the following costs for its powdered sports beverage mix in March 20X5.

Direct material cost per case	$ 6.00
Direct labor cost per case	3.00
Variable manufacturing overhead cost per case	2.00
Sales commission per case	2.50
Total fixed manufacturing overhead expenses	50,000
Total fixed marketing and administrative expenses.....	25,000

Sportade produced 10,000 cases of powdered mix as planned but sold only 8,000 cases, at a price of $30 per case. There were no beginning inventories, so Sportade has 2,000 cases of powdered mix in ending finished goods inventory (10,000 cases produced – 8,000 cases sold).

What is Sportade's inventoriable product cost per case under absorption costing and variable costing?

	Absorption Costing	Variable Costing
Direct materials	$ 6.00	$ 6.00
Direct labor.....................................	3.00	3.00
Variable manufacturing overhead	2.00	2.00
Fixed manufacturing overhead	5.00*	
Total cost per case...............................	$16.00	$11.00

* $\dfrac{\$50{,}000 \text{ fixed manufacturing overhead}}{10{,}000 \text{ cases}} = \$5 \text{ per case}$

The only difference between absorption and variable costing is that fixed manufacturing overhead is a product cost under absorption costing, but a period cost under variable costing. This is why the cost per case is $5 higher under absorption (total cost of $16) than under variable costing ($11).

Exhibit 22-9 shows that absorption costing income statements use the format we have used in Chapters 1 through 19: Sales minus cost of goods sold equals gross profit.

Exhibit 22-9

Absorption Costing Income Statement

Sportade		
Income Statement (Absorption Costing)		
Month Ended March 31, 20X5		
Sales revenue (8,000 × $30)		$240,000
Deduct: Cost of goods sold:		
Beginning finished goods inventory	$ 0	
Cost of goods manufactured		
(10,000 × $16).............................	160,000	
Cost of goods available for sale	160,000	
Ending finished goods inventory (2,000 × $16) ...	(32,000)	
Cost of goods sold		(128,000)
Gross profit		112,000
Deduct: Operating expenses		
[(8,000 × $2.50) + $25,000]		(45,000)
Operating income		$ 67,000

Notice that:

- The absorption costing income statement in Exhibit 22-9 groups costs by *function*: manufacturing costs or nonmanufacturing costs. *We subtract manufacturing costs of goods sold **before** gross profit, whereas we subtract all nonmanufacturing costs (operating expenses) **after** gross profit.*

- Total cost of goods manufactured is the number of cases *produced* multiplied by the $16 total manufacturing cost per case. In contrast, total variable marketing expense (for sales commissions) equals the number of cases *sold* times the sales commission per case.

- Absorption costing holds back as an asset (ending inventory) $32,000 of the manufacturing cost Sportade incurred this period (2,000 cases × $16 total manufacturing cost per case). This $32,000 is not expensed in the month when Sportade incurred these manufacturing costs. Instead, these manufacturing costs are held back as the asset *Inventory* until the related 2,000 cases are sold.

- The absorption costing income statement does not distinguish between variable and fixed costs. This limits the statement's usefulness for managerial decisions. If the CEO of Sportade wants to predict how a 10% increase in sales will affect operating income, the absorption costing income statement is of little help: It does not separate variable costs (which increase with sales) from fixed costs (which will not change).

Contribution Margin Income Statement
Income statement that groups costs by behavior—variable costs or fixed costs—and highlights the contribution margin.

The limitations of absorption costing–based income statements lead many managers to prefer variable costing and contribution margin income statements *for internal reporting and decision making*. Exhibit 22-10 recasts the Sportade information using variable costing and a **contribution margin income statement** that groups costs by behavior—variable costs or fixed costs—and highlights the contribution margin.

Exhibit 22-10

Variable Costing Contribution
Margin Income Statement

Sportade
Contribution Margin Income Statement (Variable Costing)
Month Ended March 31, 20X5

Sales revenue (8,000 × $30)		$240,000
Deduct: Variable expenses:		
Variable cost of goods sold:		
Beginning finished goods inventory	$ 0	
Variable cost of goods manufactured (10,000 × $11)...	110,000	
Variable cost of goods available for sale	110,000	
Ending finished goods inventory (2,000 × $11)	(22,000)	
Variable cost of goods sold	88,000	
Sales commission expense (8,000 × $2.50)............	20,000	(108,000)
Contribution margin................................		132,000
Deduct: Fixed expenses:		
Fixed manufacturing overhead....................	50,000	
Fixed marketing and administrative expenses........	25,000	(75,000)
Operating income		$ 57,000

Compare the general format of the absorption costing income statement in Exhibit 22-9 with the variable costing contribution margin income statement in Exhibit 22-10. The conventional absorption costing income statement subtracts cost of goods sold (including both variable and fixed manufacturing costs) from sales to obtain *gross profit*. In contrast, the contribution margin income statement subtracts all variable costs (both manufacturing and nonmanufacturing) to obtain *contribution margin*. The following chart highlights the differences between gross profit and contribution margin:

✔ Starter 22-12

✔ Starter 22-13

Conventional Income Statement	Contribution Margin Income Statement
Sales revenue	Sales revenue
deduct Cost of Goods Sold:	deduct Variable Expenses:
Variable manufacturing cost of goods sold	Variable manufacturing cost of goods sold
Fixed manufacturing cost of goods sold	Variable nonmanufacturing expenses
= Gross profit	= Contribution margin

The two major differences are

- Fixed manufacturing cost of goods sold is subtracted from sales to compute gross profit, but not to compute contribution margin.
- Variable nonmanufacturing expenses are subtracted from sales to calculate contribution margin, but not to compute gross profit.

Now let's look more closely at the variable costing contribution margin income statement in Exhibit 22-10. First, notice that the details of the (variable) cost of goods sold computation in Exhibit 22-10 parallel those in the absorption costing income statement, *except that we use the $11 variable costing product cost per case rather than the $16 absorption cost per case*. Second, variable costing holds back as an asset (ending inventory) only $22,000 (2,000 cases × $11 variable manufacturing cost per case). Third, the variable costing contribution margin income statement subtracts *all* of the variable costs (*both* the $88,000 manufacturing variable cost of goods sold *and* the $20,000 variable sales commission expense) from sales to get contribution margin. Finally, we subtract fixed costs (both the $50,000 fixed manufacturing overhead and the $25,000 fixed marketing and administrative costs) from contribution margin to get operating income. To summarize, the variable costing contribution margin income statement subtracts all variable costs *before* contribution margin and all fixed costs *after* contribution margin.

By separating variable and fixed costs, the variable costing contribution margin income statement (Exhibit 22-10) allows managers to estimate how changes in sales, costs, or volume will affect profits.

Suppose Sportade can increase the number of cases sold by 10%, using its existing capacity. Compute the likely effect on operating income.

Answer: Because Sportade can accommodate the increased production using existing capacity, fixed costs will be unaffected. Thus, the entire increase in contribution margin flows through to operating income.

A 10% increase in sales is an extra 800 cases (10% × 8,000).

Increase in sales revenue (800 cases × $30/case)	$ 24,000
Increase in variable costs (800 cases × $13.50/case*)	(10,800)
Increase in contribution margin	$ 13,200
Increase in fixed costs	(0)
Increase in operating income	$ 13,200

---

*Total variable costs per case = $6.00 direct materials + $3.00 direct labor + $2.00 variable manufacturing overhead + $2.50 sales commission. (All variable costs, including the sales commission as well as variable manufacturing costs, must be considered to estimate how the sales increase will affect contribution margin and operating profit.)

Reconciling the Difference in Income

Exhibit 22-9 shows that Sportade's absorption costing operating income is $67,000. Exhibit 22-10 shows that variable costing yields only $57,000 of operating income. Why? To answer this question, we need to understand what happened to the $160,000 ($110,000 variable + $50,000 fixed) total manufacturing costs under each costing method.

Manufacturing costs incurred in March are either

- Expensed in March, or
- Held back in inventory (an asset)

Exhibit 22-11 shows that of the $160,000 total manufacturing costs incurred during March, absorption costing holds back $32,000 (2,000 × $16) as inventory. This $32,000 assigned to inventory is not expensed until next month, when the units are sold. Thus, only $160,000 – $32,000 = $128,000 of the manufacturing costs are expensed as cost of goods sold during March.

Variable costing holds back in ending inventory only $22,000 (2,000 × $11) of the total manufacturing costs. This is $10,000 ($22,000 – $32,000) *less* than absorption costing holds back. The difference arises because absorption costing assigns the $5 per case fixed manufacturing overhead costs to the 2,000 cases in ending inventory. In contrast, variable costing does not—it expenses all the fixed manufacturing overhead in the current month.

Costs that are not held back in inventory are expensed in the current period, so variable costing expenses $138,000 ($160,000 – $22,000) of manufacturing costs in March. (This $138,000 also equals the $88,000 variable cost of goods sold plus the $50,000 fixed manufacturing overhead.) This is $10,000 *more* than the $128,000 absorption costing manufacturing expenses during March. *Variable costing has $10,000 more expense in March, so its income is $10,000 lower than absorption costing income.*

Exhibit 22-11 Inventory versus Expenses Under Absorption and Variable Costing

 Starter 22-14

Suppose Sportade has no inventory at the end of the next month, April. Will absorption costing report higher or lower operating income than variable costing for the month of April?

Answer: Absorption costing will report lower income than variable costing during April. Ending inventory in March becomes the beginning inventory of April. Absorption costing assigns a higher value to beginning inventory in April. When that beginning inventory is sold, the higher beginning inventory costs increase cost of goods sold for April, which in turn reduces income.

Absorption Costing and Manager's Incentives

The general rule is this: When inventories increase (more units are produced than sold), absorption costing income is higher than variable costing income. When inventories decline (when fewer units are produced than sold), absorption costing income is lower than variable costing income. Suppose the Sportade manager receives a bonus based on absorption costing income. Will the manager want to increase or decrease production?

The manager knows that absorption costing assigns each case of Sportade $5 of fixed manufacturing overhead.

■ For every case that is produced but not sold, absorption costing "hides" $5 of fixed overhead in ending inventory (an asset).

■ The more cases added to inventory, the more fixed overhead is "hidden" in ending inventory at the end of the month.

■ The more fixed overhead in ending inventory, the smaller the cost of goods sold and the higher the operating income.

To maximize the bonus under absorption costing, the manager may try to increase production to build up inventory.

Chapter 19 introduced the just-in-time philosophy.

This incentive directly conflicts with the just-in-time philosophy, which emphasizes minimal inventory levels. ← Companies that have adopted just-in-time should either (1) evaluate their managers based on variable costing income or (2) use strict controls to prevent inventory buildup.

Decision Guidelines

ABSORPTION AND VARIABLE COSTING

Suppose you are the CEO of Sportade. You are considering whether to use variable costing. Here are some decisions you will have to make.

Decision	Guideline
When to use absorption costing? Variable costing?	Sportade must use absorption costing for external reporting. Sportade can use variable costing only for internal reporting.
What is the difference between absorption and variable costing?	Fixed manufacturing costs are treated as • inventoriable product costs under absorption costing • period costs under variable costing

How to compute product costs under absorption costing and variable costing?	*Absorption Costing*	*Variable Costing*
	Direct materials	Direct materials
	+ Direct labor	+ Direct labor
	+ Variable overhead	+ Variable overhead
	+ Fixed overhead	
	= Product cost	= Product cost

Decision	Guideline
Will absorption costing income be higher, lower, or the same as variable costing income?	If units produced > units sold: Absorption costing income > Variable costing income If units produced < units sold: Absorption costing income < Variable costing income If units produced = units sold: Absorption costing income = Variable costing income
Why should Sportade use variable costing for internal reporting?	• Sportade managers can use variable costing contribution margin income statements to estimate how changes in sales or costs will affect profits. • Variable costing does not give Sportade's managers incentives to build up inventory.

● END-OF-CHAPTER *Summary Problem*

CHECK YOUR RESOURCES

Continue the Sportade illustration from pages 915–919. In April 20X5, Sportade produces 10,000 cases of the powdered sports beverage and sells 12,000 cases (the 2,000 cases of inventory on March 31, 20X5, plus the 10,000 cases produced during April). The variable costs per case and the total fixed costs are the same as in March.

Required:

1. Prepare an income statement for the month ended April 30, 20X5, using absorption costing.
2. Prepare an income statement for the month ended April 30, 20X5, using variable costing.

(continued)

3. Reconcile (explain the difference between) operating income under absorption versus variable costing.

Solutions

Requirement 1

Sportade
Income Statement (Absorption Costing) **Month Ended April 30, 20X5**

Sales revenue (12,000 × $30)......................		$360,000
Deduct: Cost of goods sold		
Beginning finished goods inventory	$ 32,000[1]	
Cost of goods manufactured (10,000 × $16)........	160,000[2]	
Cost of goods available for sale.................	192,000	
Ending finished goods inventory	(0)	
Cost of goods sold............................		192,000
Gross profit.....................................		168,000
Deduct: Operating expenses		
[(12,000 × $2.50) + $25,000].....................		(55,000)
Operating income		$113,000

[1]Ending inventory from March 31, 20X5 (Exhibit 22-9).
[2]Absorption costing cost per case = $6.00 + $3.00 + $2.00 + $5.00.

Requirement 2

Sportade
Contribution Margin Income Statement (Variable Costing) **Month Ended April 30, 20X5**

Sales revenue (12,000 × $30)......................		$360,000
Deduct: Variable expenses		
Variable cost of goods sold		
Beginning finished goods inventory..............	$ 22,000[3]	
Variable cost of goods manufactured (10,000 × $11)..	110,000[4]	
Variable cost of goods available for sale............	132,000	
Ending finished goods inventory	(0)	
Variable cost of goods sold......................	132,000	
Sales commission expense (12,000 × $2.50)	30,000	(162,000)
Contribution margin		198,000
Deduct: Fixed expenses		
Fixed manufacturing overhead	50,000	
Fixed marketing and administrative expenses	25,000	(75,000)
Operating income		$123,000

[3]Ending inventory from March 31, 20X5 (Exhibit 22-10).
[4]Variable costing cost per case = $6.00 + $3.00 + $2.00.

Requirement 3

April 20X5 operating income is $10,000 higher under variable costing than under absorption costing. Why? Both methods expense all of April's $160,000 manufacturing costs ($110,000 variable + $50,000 fixed) during April. However, the two methods differ in the amount of *March* manufacturing cost expensed in April. Absorption costing holds $32,000 of March manufacturing costs in inventory and expenses them in April when the goods are sold. Variable costing holds only $22,000 of March manufacturing costs in inventory and expenses them in April.

Thus, absorption costing operating income is

- $10,000 higher than variable costing income in March (because absorption costing defers $10,000 more of March cost to April).
- $10,000 lower than variable costing income in April (because absorption costing expenses $10,000 more of March costs in April).

●REVIEW *CVP Analysis*

Quick Check

1. For **Grand Canyon Railway** in the chapter opening story, straight-line depreciation on the train cars is a:
   a. Variable cost
   b. Fixed cost
   c. Mixed cost

2. Assume **Grand Canyon Railway** is considering hiring a reservations agency to handle its passenger reservations. The agency would charge a flat fee of $10,000 per month, plus $1 per passenger reservation. What is the total reservation cost if 100,000 passengers take the trip next month?
   a. $1.10
   b. $10,000
   c. $100,000
   d. $110,000

3. If **Grand Canyon Railway's** fixed costs total $50,000 per month, the variable cost per passenger is $10, and tickets sell for $60, what is the breakeven point?
   a. 1,000 passengers
   b. 833 passengers
   c. 714 passengers
   d. 100 passengers

4. Suppose **Amazon.com's** total revenues are $5 billion, its variable costs are $3 billion, and its fixed costs are $1 billion. Compute the breakeven point in dollars.
   a. $0.4 billion
   b. $2.5 billion
   c. $4.0 billion
   d. $5.0 billion

5. Assume the same facts about **Grand Canyon Railway** as in Question 3, except that Grand Canyon wants to know how many passengers must buy tickets for the Railway to earn $100,000 in profit per month. The answer is
   a. 1,000 passengers
   b. 3,000 passengers
   c. 30,000 passengers
   d. 31,000 passengers

6. On a CVP graph, the total cost line intersects the vertical (dollars) axis at:
   a. The level of the fixed costs
   b. The level of the variable costs
   c. The breakeven point
   d. The origin

7. Assume the same facts about **Grand Canyon Railway** as in Question 3, except that the Railway is considering cutting its ticket price to $50 per passenger. The new breakeven point is
   a. 100 more passengers than with the original $60 ticket price
   b. 250 more passengers than with the original $60 ticket price
   c. 100 fewer passengers than with the original $60 ticket price
   d. 250 fewer passengers than with the original $60 ticket price

8. Assume the same facts about **Grand Canyon Railway** as in Question 3. If the Railway expects to serve 1,200 passengers next month, what is the margin of safety?
   a. 200 passengers
   b. 1,000 passengers
   c. 1,200 passengers
   d. 2,200 passengers

9. The only difference between variable costing and absorption costing lies in the treatment of:
   a. Fixed manufacturing overhead costs
   b. Variable manufacturing overhead costs
   c. Direct materials and direct labor costs
   d. Variable nonmanufacturing costs

10. When inventories decline, operating income under variable costing is
   a. Lower than operating income under absorption costing
   b. The same as operating income under absorption costing
   c. Higher than operating income under absorption costing

Accounting Vocabulary

absorption costing (p. 914)
breakeven point (p. 903)
contribution margin (p. 903)
contribution margin income statement (p. 916)
contribution margin ratio (p. 904)

cost behavior (p. 898)
cost-volume-profit (CVP) analysis (p. 898)
margin of safety (p. 911)
mixed costs (p. 900)
relevant range (p. 901)

sales mix (p. 902)
sensitivity analysis (p. 910)
total fixed costs (p. 898)
total variable costs (p. 898)
variable costing (p. 914)

ASSESS *Your Progress*

Starters

online homework

See *www.prenhall.com/horngren* for selected Starters, Exercises, and Problems.

S22-1 Ariel builds innovative loudspeakers for music and home theater. Identify the following costs as variable or fixed:

a. Depreciation on routers used to cut wood enclosures
b. Wood for speaker enclosures
c. Patents on crossover relays
d. Crossover relays

e. Grill cloth
f. Glue
g. Quality inspector's salary

Variable and fixed costs
(Obj. 1)

S22-2 Suppose World-Link offers an international calling plan that charges $5.00 per month plus $0.35 per minute for calls outside the United States.

Mixed costs
(Obj. 1)

1. Under this plan, what is your monthly international long-distance cost if you call Europe for
   a. 20 minutes?   b. 40 minutes?   c. 80 minutes?
2. Draw a graph illustrating your total cost under this plan. Label the axes, and show your costs at 20, 40, and 80 minutes.

S22-3 Consider the **Grand Canyon Railway** example from the chapter opening story. Suppose the Railway decides to offer Coach class service at an all-inclusive round-trip ticket price of $60 per passenger. Assume variable expenses of $20 per passenger. If Grand Canyon has $275,000 of fixed expenses per month, compute the number of round-trip tickets it must sell to break even:

Computing breakeven point in units
(Obj. 2)

a. Using the income statement equation approach
b. Using the shortcut contribution margin CVP formula

Perform a numerical proof to ensure that your answer is correct.

S22-4 Refer to the information in Starter 22-3.

Computing breakeven point in sales dollars
(Obj. 2)

1. Compute Grand Canyon Railway's contribution margin ratio. Carry your computation to five decimal places.
2. Use the contribution margin ratio CVP formula to determine the sales revenue Grand Canyon Railway needs to break even.

S22-5 If Grand Canyon Railway has a target operating income of $40,000 per month, how many round-trip tickets must the company sell? Use the original data given in Starter 22-3.

Sales needed to earn target income
(Obj. 3)

Graphing cost-volume-profit relationships
(Obj. 3)

S22-6 Using the original information in Starter 22-3, draw a graph of Grand Canyon Railway's cost-volume-profit relationships. Include the sales revenue line, the fixed expense line, and the total expense line. Label the axes, the breakeven point, the income area, and the loss area.

Interpreting a CVP graph
(Obj. 3)

S22-7 Describe what each letter stands for in the cost-volume-profit graph.

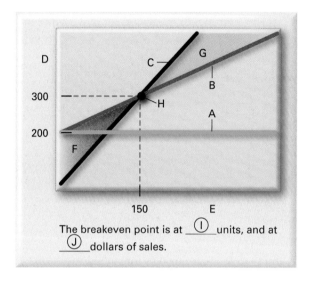

The breakeven point is at ___Ⓘ___ units, and at ___Ⓙ___ dollars of sales.

Sensitivity analysis of changing sale price and variable expense on breakeven point
(Obj. 4)

S22-8 Refer to the information in Starter 22-3.

1. Suppose the Railway cuts its round-trip ticket price from $60 to $50 to increase the number of passengers. Compute the new breakeven point in units (passenger round-trips) and in sales dollars. Carry your computations to five decimal places.
2. Return to Starter 22-3. The Railway could reduce its variable costs by cutting champagne from the afternoon beverages. Suppose this reduces the variable expense from $20 to $15 per passenger. Compute the new breakeven point in units (passenger round-trips), and in dollars. Carry your computations to five decimal places.

Sensitivity analysis of changing fixed cost on breakeven point
(Obj. 4)

S22-9 Consider the original Grand Canyon Railway information in Starter 22-3. Suppose Grand Canyon embarks on a cost reduction drive and slashes fixed expenses from $275,000 per month to $200,000 per month.

1. Compute the new breakeven point in units (passenger round-trips) and in sales dollars.
2. Is the breakeven point higher or lower than in Starter 22-3? Explain.

Computing margin of safety
(Obj. 4)

S22-10 Consider the original Grand Canyon Railway information in Starter 22-3. If Grand Canyon expects to sell 7,000 round-trip tickets, compute the margin of safety.

a. In units (round-trip tickets) b. In sales dollars c. As a percentage of expected sales

Computing margin of safety
(Obj. 4)

S22-11 Consider Kay Pak's e-tail poster business. Suppose Pak expects to sell 800 posters. Use the original data on page 902 to compute her margin of safety:

a. In units (posters) b. In sales dollars c. As a percentage of expected sales

Computing variable costing income
(Obj. 5)

S22-12 Consider the Sportade example on pages 915–919. Suppose that during April, the company produces 10,000 cases of powdered drink mix and sells 11,000 cases. Sale price, variable cost per case, and total fixed expenses remain the same as in March. Prepare the April income statement using variable costing.

Comparing variable and absorption costing income
(Obj. 5)

S22-13 Refer to the Sportade example on pages 915–919 and the data and your answer to Starter 22-12.

1. Prepare the April income statement under absorption costing.
2. Is absorption costing income higher or lower than variable costing income? Explain why.

S22-14 For a service company like Grand Canyon Railway, will absorption and variable costing give different operating income figures? Explain.

Absorption and variable costing
(Obj. 5)

Exercises

E22-1 Graph these cost behavior patterns over a relevant range of 0–10,000 units:

a. Variable expenses of $8 per unit
b. Mixed expenses made up of fixed costs of $20,000 and variable costs of $3 per unit
c. Fixed expenses of $15,000

Graphing cost behavior
(Obj. 1)

E22-2 For its top managers, Aussie Travel formats its income statement as follows:

Computing breakeven sales using a contribution margin income statement
(Obj. 2, 5)

spreadsheet

Aussie Travel	
Contribution Margin Income Statement **Three Months Ended March 31, 20XX**	
Sales revenue..	$312,500
Variable expenses	125,000
Contribution margin	187,500
Fixed expenses	170,000
Operating income..	$ 17,500

Aussie's relevant range is between sales of $250,000 and $360,000. Prepare contribution margin income statements at those volume levels. (*Hint*: The proportion of each sales dollar that goes toward variable costs is constant within the relevant range. The proportion of each sales dollar that goes toward contribution margin is also constant within the relevant range.) Also, compute breakeven sales in dollars.

E22-3 Big Foot Co. produces sports socks. The company has fixed expenses of $85,000, and variable expenses of $0.85 per package. Each package sells for $1.70.

Computing breakeven sales by the contribution margin approach
(Obj. 2)

Required

1. Compute the contribution margin per package and the contribution margin ratio.
2. Find the breakeven point in units and in dollars, using the contribution margin approach.

spreadsheet

E22-4 Owner Shan Lo is considering franchising her Happy Wok restaurant concept. She believes people will pay $5 for a large bowl of noodles. Variable costs are $1.50 a bowl. Lo estimates monthly fixed costs for franchisees at $8,400.

Computing a change in breakeven sales
(Obj. 2)

Required

1. Use the contribution margin ratio approach to find a franchise's breakeven sales ($).
2. Is franchising a good idea for Lo if franchisees will want a minimum monthly operating income of $8,750, and Lo believes most locations could generate $25,000 in monthly sales?

E22-5 Dave's Steel Parts produces parts for the automobile industry. The company has monthly fixed expenses of $640,000 and a contribution margin of 80% of revenues.

Computing breakeven sales and operating income or loss under different conditions
(Obj. 2, 3, 5)

Required

1. Compute Dave's monthly breakeven sales in dollars. Use the contribution margin ratio approach.
2. Use contribution margin income statements to compute Dave's monthly operating income or operating loss if revenues are $500,000 and if they are $1,000,000.
3. Do the results in Requirement 2 make sense given the breakeven sales you computed in Requirement 1? Explain.

Analyzing a cost-volume-profit graph
(Obj. 3)

E22-6 Chad Brown is considering starting a Web-based educational business, e-Prep MBA. He plans to offer a short-course review of accounting for students entering MBA programs. The materials would be available on a password-protected Web site and students would complete the course through self-study. Brown would have to grade the course assignments, but most of the work is in developing the course materials, setting up the site, and marketing. Unfortunately, Brown's hard drive crashed before he finished his financial analysis. However, he did recover the following partial CVP chart:

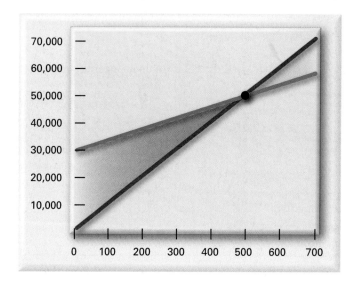

Required

1. Label each axis, sales revenue line, total expenses line, fixed expenses line, operating income area, and operating loss area.
2. If Brown attracts 400 students to take the course, will the venture be profitable?
3. What are the breakeven sales in students and dollars?

Graphing cost-volume-profit relationships
(Obj. 3)

E22-7 Suppose that Turner Field, the home of the Atlanta Braves, earns total revenue that averages $24 for every ticket sold. Assume that annual fixed expenses are $24 million, and variable expenses are $4 per ticket.

Required

1. Prepare the ballpark's CVP graph under these assumptions. Label the axes, sales revenue line, fixed expense line, total expense line, the operating loss area, and the operating income area on the graph.
2. Show the breakeven point in dollars and in tickets.

Computing breakeven and a margin of safety
(Obj. 2, 4)

E22-8 Ronnie's Repair Shop has a monthly target operating income of $12,000. Variable expenses are 70% of sales, and monthly fixed expenses are $9,000.

Required

1. Compute the monthly margin of safety in dollars if the shop achieves its income goal.
2. Express Ronnie's margin of safety as a percentage of target sales.

Preparing absorption costing and variable costing income statements; business decision
(Obj. 5)

E22-9 The 20X6 data that follow pertain to Rays, a manufacturer of swimming goggles. (Rays has no beginning inventories in January 20X6.)

Sale price.........................	$35	Fixed manufacturing	
Variable manufacturing		overhead	$2,000,000
expense per unit	15	Fixed operating expense.......	250,000
Sales commission		Number of goggles produced ..	200,000
expense per unit	5	Number of goggles sold	185,000

(continued)

Required

1. Prepare both conventional (absorption costing) and contribution margin (variable costing) income statements for Rays, for the year ended December 31, 20X6.

2. Which statement shows the higher operating income? Why?

3. Rays' marketing vice president believes a new sales promotion that costs $150,000 would increase sales to 200,000 goggles. Should the company go ahead with the promotion? Give your reason.

Problems

(Group A)

P22-1A Custom Kitchens is opening early next year. Kate Royer, the owner, is considering two plans for obtaining the assets and the sales force needed for operations. Plan 1 calls for purchasing all equipment and paying the sales force straight salaries. Under plan 2, Custom Kitchens would lease equipment month by month and pay the sales force low salaries but give them a big part of their pay in commissions. Discuss the effects of the two plans on variable expenses, fixed expenses, breakeven sales, and likely profits for a new business in the start-up stage. Indicate which plan you favor for Custom Kitchens.

Explaining the effects of different cost behavior patterns on the breakeven point and on likely profits
(Obj. 1)

P22-2A The budgets of four companies yield the following information:

Using CVP analysis to compute contribution margin and breakeven sales
(Obj. 2, 5)

	Company			
	Q	R	S	T
Target sales	$720,000	$300,000	$190,000	$
Variable expenses.	216,000			260,000
Fixed expenses		156,000	100,000	
Operating income (loss)	$ 30,000	$	$	$ 80,000
Units sold		112,000	12,000	16,000
Contribution margin per unit . . .	$ 6		$ 9.50	$ 40
Contribution margin ratio		0.60		

Fill in the blanks for each company. Which company has the lowest breakeven point in sales dollars? What causes the low breakeven point?

P22-3A A traveling production of *The Phantom of the Opera* performs each year. The average show sells 800 tickets at $50 a ticket. There are 100 shows each year. The show has a cast of 40, each earning an average of $260 per show. The cast is paid only after each show. The other variable expense is program printing costs of $6 per guest. Annual fixed expenses total $942,400.

BE sales and sales to earn a target Op. Inc.; CM/IS
(Obj. 2, 3, 5)

Student Resource CD
spreadsheet

Required

1. Compute revenue and variable expenses for each show.

2. Use the income statement equation approach to compute the number of shows needed annually to break even.

3. Use the shortcut contribution margin approach to compute the number of shows needed annually to earn a profit of $1,438,400. Is this goal realistic? Give your reason.

4. Prepare *The Phantom of the Opera's* contribution margin income statement for 100 shows each year. Report only two categories of expenses: variable and fixed.

P22-4A Team Spirit imprints calendars with college names. The company has fixed expenses of $1,035,000 each month plus variable expenses of $3.60 per carton of calendars. Team Spirit sells each carton of calendars for $10.50.

Analyzing CVP relationships
(Obj. 2, 3, 4)

(continued)

Required

1. Use the income statement equation approach to compute the number of cartons of calendars Team Spirit must sell each month to break even.

2. Use the contribution margin ratio CVP formula to compute the dollar amount of monthly sales Team Spirit needs to earn $285,000 in operating income. (Round the contribution margin ratio to 2 decimal places.)

3. Prepare Team Spirit's contribution margin income statement for June for sales of 450,000 cartons of calendars. Cost of goods sold is 70% of variable expenses. Operating expenses make up the rest of the variable expenses and all of the fixed expenses.

4. The company is considering an expansion that will increase fixed expenses by 40% and variable expenses by one-fourth. Compute the new breakeven point in units and in dollars. How would this expansion affect Team Spirit's risk? Should Team Spirit expand?

Computing breakeven sales and sales needed to earn a target operating income; graphing CVP relationships
(Obj. 1, 2, 3, 4)

P22-5A Personal Investors is opening an office in Lexington, Kentucky. Fixed monthly expenses are office rent ($2,500), depreciation on office furniture ($260), utilities ($280), special telephone lines ($600), a connection with an online brokerage service ($640), and the salary of a financial planner ($3,400). Variable expenses include payments to the financial planner (10% of revenue), advertising (5% of revenue), supplies and postage (2% of revenue), and usage fees for the telephone lines and computerized brokerage service (3% of revenue).

Required

1. Use the contribution margin ratio CVP formula to compute the investment firm's breakeven revenue in dollars. If the average trade leads to $400 in revenue for Personal Investors, how many trades must be made to break even?

2. Use the income statement equation approach to compute dollar revenues needed to earn monthly operating income of $3,840.

3. Graph Personal Investors' CVP relationships. Assume that an average trade leads to $400 in revenue for Personal Investors. Show the breakeven point, sales revenue line, fixed expense line, total expense line, operating loss area, operating income area, and the sales in units (trades) and dollars when monthly operating income of $3,840 is earned. The graph should range from 0 to 40 units (trades).

4. Assume that the average revenue Personal Investors earns decreases to $300 per trade. How does this affect the breakeven point in number of trades?

Preparing absorption and variable costing income statements and explaining the difference in income
(Obj. 5)

P22-6A ← *Link Back to Chapter 19 (Manufacturing Company Income Statement) and Chapter 20 (Manufacturing Overhead).* Mario's Foods produces frozen meals, which it sells for $7 each. The company uses the FIFO inventory costing method, and it computes a new monthly fixed manufacturing overhead rate based on the actual number of meals produced that month. All costs and production levels are exactly as planned. The following data are from Mario's Foods' first two months in business.

	January 20X7	February 20X7
Sales	1,000 meals	1,200 meals
Production.	1,400 meals	1,000 meals
Variable manufacturing expense per meal.	$4	$4
Sales commission expense per meal	$1	$1
Total fixed manufacturing overhead.	$700	$700
Total fixed marketing and administrative expenses . .	$600	$600

Required

1. Compute the product cost per meal produced under absorption costing and under variable costing. Do this first for January and then for February.

(continued)

2. Prepare separate monthly income statements for January and for February, using
   a. Absorption costing
   b. Variable costing
3. Is operating income higher under absorption costing or variable costing in January? In February? Explain the pattern of differences in operating income based on absorption costing versus variable costing.

Problems

(Group B)

P22-1B Brooke Miller is in charge of the New York Regional Head Start program. Legislators have just cut the program's funding by 15%. Miller cannot cut total fixed costs like the rent for the program's offices or salaries of the administrative staff. The other main costs are salaries for teachers ($30,000/yr) and teachers' aides ($12,000/yr). Miller cannot cut the salary paid per teacher or teacher's aide.

Explaining the effects of different cost behavior patterns
(Obj. 1)

What alternatives does Miller have to meet the budget? Will the 15% funding cut reduce services provided by more than 15%, less than 15%, or close to 15%? Explain your reasoning.

P22-2B The budgets of four companies yield the following information:

Use CVP analysis to compute contribution margin and breakeven sales
(Obj. 2, 5)

	Company			
	A	B	C	D
Target sales	$680,000	$ ____	$550,000	$ ____
Variable expenses.	_____	150,000	280,000	156,000
Fixed expenses	_____	123,000	138,000	
Operating income (loss)	$120,000	$ ____	$ ____	$ 35,000
Units sold	187,000	10,000	_____	_____
Contribution margin per unit . . .	$ 2	$ ____	$ 100	$ 12
Contribution margin ratio	_____	0.20	_____	0.20

Fill in the blanks for each company. Which company has the lowest breakeven point in sales dollars? What causes the low breakeven point?

P22-3B International Productions performs *Cats*, the play. The average show sells 1,000 tickets at $60 a ticket. There are 120 shows a year. *Cats* has a cast of 60, each earning an average of $320 a show. The cast is paid only after each show. The other variable expense is program printing costs of $8 per guest. Annual fixed expenses total $295,200.

BE and sales to earn a target Op. Inc.; CM/IS
(Obj. 2, 3, 5)

Student Resource**CD**

spreadsheet

Required

1. Compute revenue and variable expenses for each show.
2. Use the income statement equation approach to compute the number of shows *Cats* must perform each year to break even.
3. Use the shortcut contribution margin approach to compute the number of shows needed each year to earn a profit of $4,264,000. Is this profit goal realistic? Give your reason.
4. Prepare the *Cats* contribution margin income statement for 120 shows for the year. Report only two categories of expenses: variable and fixed.

P22-4B Fanfare sells flags with team logos. Fanfare has fixed expenses of $678,600 per year plus variable expenses of $4.20 per flag. Each flag sells for $12.00.

Analyzing CVP relationships
(Obj. 2, 3, 4)

(continued)

Required

1. Use the income statement equation approach to compute the number of flags Fanfare must sell each year to break even.

2. Use the contribution margin ratio CVP formula to compute the dollar sales Fanfare needs to earn $32,500 in operating income.

3. Prepare Fanfare's contribution margin income statement for the year ended December 31, 20X7, for sales of 70,000 flags. Cost of goods sold is 60% of variable expenses. Operating expenses make up the rest of variable expenses and all of fixed expenses.

4. The company is considering an expansion that will increase fixed expenses by 20% and variable expenses by 30 cents per flag. Compute the new breakeven point in units and in dollars. Should Fanfare undertake the expansion? Give your reason.

Computing breakeven sales and sales needed to earn a target operating income; graphing CVP relationships
(Obj. 1, 2, 3, 4)

P22-5B Money Maker Investment Group is opening an office in Atlanta. Fixed monthly expenses are office rent ($9,100), depreciation on office furniture ($700), utilities ($1,400), special telephone lines ($1,600), a connection with an online brokerage service ($2,000), and the salary of a financial planner ($4,800). Variable expenses include payments to the financial planner (8% of revenue), advertising (12% of revenue), supplies and postage (4% of revenue), and usage fees for the telephone lines and computerized brokerage service (6% of revenue).

Required

1. Use the contribution margin ratio CVP formula to compute Money Maker's breakeven revenue in dollars. If the average trade leads to $700 in revenue for Money Maker, how many trades must be made to break even?

2. Use the income statement equation approach to compute the dollar revenues needed to earn a target monthly operating income of $9,800.

3. Graph Money Maker's CVP relationships. Assume that an average trade leads to $700 in revenue for Money Maker. Show the breakeven point, sales revenue line, fixed expense line, total expense line, operating loss area, operating income area, and the sales in units (trades) and dollars when monthly operating income of $9,800 is earned. The graph should range from 0 to 80 units (trades).

4. Assume that the average revenue Money Maker earns decreases to $560 per trade. Compute the new breakeven point in trades. How does this affect the breakeven point?

Preparing absorption and variable costing income statements and explaining the difference in income
(Obj. 5)

P22-6B ← *Link Back to Chapter 19 (Manufacturing Company Income Statement) and Chapter 20 (Manufacturing Overhead).* Game Source manufactures video games, which it sells for $40 each. The company uses the FIFO inventory costing method, and it computes a new monthly fixed manufacturing overhead rate based on the actual number of games produced that month. All costs and production levels are exactly as planned. The following data are from Game Source's first two months in business during 20X7:

	October	November
Sales......................................	2,000 units	2,200 units
Production	2,500 units	2,000 units
Variable manufacturing expense per game........	$15	$15
Sales commission per game....................	$8	$8
Total fixed manufacturing overhead	$10,000	$10,000
Total fixed marketing and administrative expenses..	$ 9,000	$ 9,000

Required

1. Compute the product cost per game produced under absorption costing and under variable costing. Do this first for October and then for November.

(continued)

2. Prepare separate monthly income statements for October and for November, using
   a. Absorption costing   **b.** Variable costing

3. Is operating income higher under absorption costing or variable costing in October? In November? Explain the pattern of differences in operating income based on absorption costing versus variable costing.

APPLY *Your Knowledge*

Decision Cases

Case 1. Brian and Nui Soon live in Macon, Georgia. Two years ago, they visited Thailand. Nui, a professional chef, was impressed with the cooking methods and the spices used in the Thai food. Macon does not have a Thai restaurant, and the Soons are contemplating opening one. Nui would supervise the cooking, and Brian would leave his current job to be the maitre d'. The restaurant would serve dinner Tuesday through Saturday.

Using CVP analysis to make business decisions
(Obj. 2, 4)

    Brian has noticed a restaurant for lease. The restaurant has seven tables, each of which can seat four. Tables can be moved together for a large party. Nui is planning two seatings per evening, and the restaurant will be open 50 weeks per year.

    The Soons have drawn up the following estimates:

Average revenue, including beverages and dessert	$40 per meal
Average cost of the food	$12 per meal
Chef's and dishwasher's salaries	$50,400 per *year*
Rent (premises, equipment)	$4,000 per month
Cleaning (linen and premises)	$800 per month
Replacement of dishes, cutlery, glasses	$300 per month
Utilities, advertising, telephone	$1,900 per month

Required

Compute *annual* breakeven number of meals and sales revenue for the restaurant. Also compute the number of meals and the amount of sales revenue needed to earn operating income of $75,600 for the year. How many meals must the Soons serve each night to earn their target income of $75,600? Should the couple open the restaurant?

Case 2. ← *Link Back to Chapter 19 (Just-in-Time Philosophy).* Suppose you serve on the board of directors of American Faucet, a manufacturer of bathroom fixtures that recently adopted just-in-time production. Part of your responsibility is to develop a compensation contract for Toni Moen, the vice president of manufacturing. To give her the incentive to make decisions that will increase the company's profits, the board decides to give Moen a year-end bonus if American Faucet meets a target operating income.

Absorption and variable cost incentives
(Obj. 5)

    Write a memo to the Chairman of the Board, Herbert Kohler, explaining whether the bonus contract should be based on absorption costing or variable costing. Use the following format:

Date:	_____
To:	_____
From:	_____
Subject:	_____

Effect of error on cost-volume-profit analysis
(Obj. 2, 4)

Ethical Issue

You have just begun your summer internship at Tmedic. The company supplies sterilized surgical instruments for physicians. To expand sales, Tmedic is considering paying a commission to its sales force. The controller, Jane Hewitt, asks you to compute (1) the new breakeven sales figure and (2) the operating profit if sales increase 15% under the new sales commission plan. She thinks you can handle this task because you learned CVP analysis in your accounting class.

You spend the next day collecting information from the accounting records, performing the analysis, and writing a memo to explain the results. The company president is pleased with your memo. You report that the new sales commission plan will lead to a significant increase in operating income and only a small increase in breakeven sales.

The following week, you realize that you made an error in the CVP analysis. You overlooked the sales personnel's $2,500 monthly salaries and you did not include this fixed marketing expense in your computations. You are not sure what to do. If you tell Jane Hewitt of your mistake, she will have to tell the president. In this case, you are afraid Tmedic might not offer you permanent employment after your internship.

Required

1. How would your error affect breakeven sales and operating income under the proposed sales commission plan? Could this cause the president to reject the sales commission proposal?

2. Consider your ethical responsibilities. Is there a difference between (a) initially making an error and (b) subsequently failing to inform the controller?

3. Suppose you tell Jane Hewitt of the error in your analysis. Why might the consequences not be as bad as you fear? Should Hewitt take any responsibility for your error? What could Hewitt have done differently?

4. After considering all the factors, should you inform Jane Hewitt or simply keep quiet?

Financial Statement Case

Identifying cost behavior patterns and computing and analyzing breakeven sales
(Obj. 1, 2, 4)

Refer to **Amazon.com's** Consolidated Statements of Operations, and to CEO Jeff Bezos' 2002 letter to shareholders. (Both are included in the financial statements in Appendix A.)

1. Is Amazon.com's cost of sales a fixed cost or a variable cost? Is technology and content a fixed cost or a variable cost? Explain.

2. Look at CEO Jeff Bezos' letter to shareholders. How does the structure of Amazon.com's fixed and variable costs support Bezos' objective to offer both world-leading customer experience and the lowest possible prices?

3. Assume that 90% of Amazon.com's operating expenses are fixed costs. Calculate the contribution margin for each of the last three years.

4. What is the contribution margin ratio for each of the last three years? (Carry your computations to five decimal places.)

5. What is the breakeven sales in dollars for *operations* for each of the last three years? Ignore all items below Income (Loss) from Operations.

6. Refer to your answers to Requirements 3 through 5. Look at the trend in contribution margin, costs, and breakeven sales. Amazon's management has emphasized cost control over the last three years. Has it been successful? Explain.

Team Project

Variable and absorption costing, bonus contract incentives, using contribution margin statements to make decisions
(Obj. 2, 5)

EZPAK Manufacturing produces filament packaging tape. In 20X6, EZPAK produced and sold 15 million rolls of tape. The company has recently expanded its capacity, so it can now produce up to 30 million rolls per year. EZPAK's accounting records show the following results from 20X6:

(continued)

Sale price per roll	$3.00
Variable manufacturing expenses per roll	$2.00
Variable marketing and administrative expenses per roll. . . .	$0.50
Total fixed manufacturing overhead costs	$8,400,000
Total fixed marketing and administrative expenses.	$600,000
Sales	15 million rolls
Production.	15 million rolls

There were no beginning or ending inventories in 20X6.

In January 20X7, EZPAK hired a new president, Kevin McDaniel. McDaniel has a one-year contract that specifies he will be paid 10% of EZPAK's 20X7 absorption costing operating income, instead of a salary. In 20X7, McDaniel must make two major decisions:

- Should EZPAK undertake a major advertising campaign? This campaign would raise sales to 25 million rolls. This is the maximum level of sales EZPAK can expect to make in the near future. The ad campaign would add an additional $3.5 million in marketing and administrative costs. Without the campaign, sales will be 15 million rolls.
- How many rolls of tape will EZPAK produce?

At the end of the year, EZPAK Manufacturing's Board of Directors will evaluate McDaniel's performance and decide whether to offer him a contract for the following year.

Required

Within your group, form two subgroups. The first subgroup assumes the role of Kevin McDaniel, EZPAK Manufacturing's new president. The second subgroup assumes the role of EZPAK Manufacturing's Board of Directors. McDaniel will meet with the Board of Directors shortly after the end of 20X7 to decide whether he will remain at EZPAK. Most of your effort should be devoted to advance preparation for this meeting. Each subgroup should meet separately to prepare for the meeting between the Board and McDaniel. [*Hint*: Keep computations (other than per-unit amounts) in millions.]

Kevin McDaniel should:

1. Compute EZPAK Manufacturing's 20X6 operating income.
2. Decide whether to adopt the advertising campaign. Prepare a memo to the Board of Directors explaining this decision. Use the memo format outlined in Decision Case 2. Give this memo to the Board of Directors as soon as possible (before the joint meeting).
3. Assume EZPAK adopts the advertising campaign. Decide how many rolls of tape to produce in 20X7.
4. Given your response to Requirement 3, prepare an absorption costing income statement for the year ended December 31, 20X7, ending with operating income before bonus. Then compute your bonus separately. The variable cost per unit and the total fixed expenses (with the exception of the advertising campaign) remain the same as in 20X6. Give this income statement and your bonus computation to the Board of Directors as soon as possible (before your meeting with the Board).
5. Decide whether you wish to remain at EZPAK for another year. You currently have an offer from another company. The contract with the other company is identical to the one you currently have with EZPAK—you will be paid 10% of absorption costing operating income instead of a salary.

The Board of Directors should:

1. Compute EZPAK's 20X6 operating income.
2. Determine whether EZPAK should adopt the advertising campaign.
3. Determine how many rolls of tape EZPAK should produce in 20X7.
4. Evaluate McDaniel's performance, based on his decisions and the information he provided the Board. (*Hint:* You may want to prepare a variable costing income statement.)
5. Evaluate the contract's bonus provision. Are you satisfied with this provision? If so, explain why. If not, recommend how it should be changed.

(*continued*)

After McDaniel has given the Board his memo and income statement, and after the Board has had a chance to evaluate McDaniel's performance, McDaniel and the Board should meet. The purpose of the meeting is to decide whether it is in their mutual interest for McDaniel to remain with EZPAK, and if so, the terms of the contract EZPAK will offer McDaniel.

For Internet Exercises, go to the Web site, www.prenhall.com/horngren.

APPENDIX *to Chapter 22*

Effect of Sales Mix on CVP Analysis

Our CVP example focused on Kay Pak's e-tail business, which had a single product: art posters. Companies that sell more than one product must consider *sales mix* in figuring CVP relationships. A company earns more income by selling high-margin products than by selling an equal number of low-margin items.

For example, Continental Airlines has focused on attracting more business-people. Business travelers generally pay more for the same flight than leisure travelers. By increasing the proportion of higher-paying business fliers, Continental boosted its sales revenue per available seat-mile (available seats × miles flown) from $0.074 to $0.09. Improving sales mix by selling more high-margin tickets reduced Continental's breakeven point. Before the change, Continental had to fill 63% of its seats to break even. By attracting more business travelers, Continental only has to fill 61%.

We can use the same CVP formulas we used for a company with a single product to perform CVP analysis for a company that sells more than one product. But first, we must compute the *weighted-average contribution margin* of all products. The sales mix provides the weights. ←

We saw another weighted-average procedure—for inventory costing—in Chapter 6, where it was called the average-cost method, and for process costing in Chapter 21.

Continuing the Kay Pak e-tail illustration from the chapter, suppose Pak plans to sell two types of posters. Recall that the regular poster costs $21 and sells for $35. Its contribution margin is $14 ($35 − $21). The second, larger poster costs $40 and sells for $70. Its contribution margin is $30 ($70 − $40). Pak's fixed expenses remain $7,000.

Pak expects to sell 500 regular posters and 300 large posters. This is a 5 : 3 sales mix. For every 5 regular posters, Pak expects to sell 3 large posters, so she expects 5/8 of the sales to be regular posters and 3/8 to be large posters. To compute breakeven sales in units, Pak first computes the weighted-average contribution margin, as follows:

✔ Starter 22A-1

	Regular Posters	Large Posters	Total
Sale price per unit..........................	$ 35	$ 70	
Deduct: Variable expense per unit............	(21)	(40)	
Contribution margin per unit................	$ 14	$ 30	
Sales mix in units	× 5	× 3	8
Contribution margin	$ 70	$ 90	$160
Weighted-average contribution margin per unit ($160/8).................			$ 20

$$\text{SALES IN TOTAL UNITS} = \frac{\text{Fixed expenses} + \text{Operating income}}{\text{Weighted-average contribution margin per unit}}$$

$$= \frac{\$7,000 + \$0}{\$20}$$

$$= 350 \text{ posters}$$

Breakeven sales of regular posters $(350 \times 5/8)$	218.75 regular posters
Breakeven sales of large posters $(350 \times 3/8)$	131.25 large posters

✔ Starter 22A-2

As is often the case in real situations, these computations don't yield round numbers. Since Pak cannot sell partial posters, she must sell 219 regular posters and 132 large posters to avoid a loss. Using these rounded numbers would lead to a small rounding error in our check figures, however, so the rest of our computations will use the exact results: 218.75 regular posters and 131.25 large posters.

The overall breakeven point in sales dollars is $16,844 (amounts rounded to the nearest dollar):

218.75 regular posters at $35 each	$ 7,656
131.25 large posters at $70 each	9,188
Total revenues....................	$16,844

We can prove this breakeven point by preparing a contribution margin income statement (amounts rounded to the nearest dollar):

	Regular	Large	Total
Sales revenue:			
Regular posters $(218.75 \times \$35)$	$7,656		
Large posters $(131.25 \times \$70)$		$9,188	$16,844
Variable expenses:			
Regular posters $(218.75 \times \$21)$	4,594		
Large posters $(131.25 \times \$40)$		5,250	9,844
Contribution margin	$3,062	$3,938	$ 7,000
Fixed expenses			(7,000)
Operating income........................			$ 0

The breakeven proof shows that Pak's breakeven sales are $16,844. Pak could also use the contribution margin ratio approach shown in the chapter body to estimate breakeven sales in dollars. But first, she must estimate her contribution margin ratio:

Total expected contribution margin:		
Regular posters $(500 \times \$14)$	$ 7,000	
Large posters $(300 \times \$30)$	9,000	$ 16,000
Divided by total expected sales:		
Regular posters $(500 \times \$35)$	$17,500	
Large posters $(300 \times \$70)$	21,000	÷38,500
Contribution margin ratio.....................		41.558%

Then, Pak uses the contribution margin ratio approach to estimate breakeven sales in dollars:

$$\text{SALES IN DOLLARS} = \frac{\textbf{Fixed expenses + Operating income}}{\textbf{Contribution margin ratio}}$$

$$= \frac{\$7,000 + \$0}{0.41558}$$

$$= \$16,844 \text{ (rounded)}$$

If Pak's actual sales mix is not 5 regular posters to 3 large posters, her actual operating income will differ from the planned amount, even if she sells exactly 800 total posters. For each total number of posters sold, there are as many different operating incomes as there are sales mixes. Similarly, there are as many different breakeven points—in total units and in sales dollars—as there are sales mixes.

> Suppose Kay Pak plans to sell 800 total posters in the 5 : 3 sales mix (5 regular posters sold for every 3 large posters). She *actually* sells 800 posters—375 regular and 425 large. The unit sale prices and variable expenses are exactly as predicted, and the fixed expense is the budgeted $7,000. Can you tell, without computations, whether Pak's actual operating income is greater than, less than, or equal to her expected income?
>
> *Answer:* Pak sold more of the higher-margin large posters. This favorable change in the sales mix increased her operating income.

Appendix Assignments

Starters

Sales mix and weighted-average contribution margin
(Appendix)

S22A-1 Consider the **Grand Canyon Railway** example from the chapter opening story. Suppose Grand Canyon decides to offer two classes of service: Coach class and Chief class. Assume Grand Canyon incurs $250,000 of fixed expenses per month and that it has the following ticket prices and variable expenses:

	Coach Class	Chief Class
Sale price per ticket.	$60.00	$120.00
Variable expense per passenger	12.00	20.00

If Grand Canyon Railway expects to sell seven tickets in Coach class for every four tickets in Chief class, compute the weighted-average contribution margin per unit (round-trip ticket).

Breakeven point and sales mix
(Appendix)

S22A-2 Refer to the Grand Canyon Railway data in Starter 22A-1 and your answer. Compute:

a. The total number of tickets Grand Canyon must sell to break even.
b. The number of Coach class tickets and the number of Chief class tickets the company must sell to break even.

Exercises

CVP analysis with a sales mix
(Appendix)

E22A-1 Racer Scooters plans to sell a standard scooter for $54 and a chrome scooter for $78. Racer purchases the standard scooter for $36, and the chrome scooter for $50. Racer expects to sell two chrome scooters for every three standard scooters. Racer's monthly fixed expenses are $9,680. How many of each type of scooter must Racer sell monthly to break even? To earn $6,600?

Computing contribution margin for one of two products
(Appendix)

E22A-2 Kenisha, Inc., manufactures two styles of watches—the Digital and the Classic. The following data pertain to the Digital:

Variable manufacturing cost.	$120
Variable operating cost	30
Sale price	200

(continued)

Kenisha's monthly fixed expenses total $190,000. When Digitals and Classics are sold in the mix of 7 : 3, respectively, the sale of 2,000 total watches results in an operating income of $60,000. Compute the contribution margin per watch for the Classic.

Problems

P22A-1 The contribution margin income statement of Extreme Coffee for February 20XX follows:

Using a contribution margin income statement for breakeven analysis; sales mix, margin of safety, and changes in CVP relationships

(Obj. 2, 3, 4, Appendix)

Extreme Coffee		
Contribution Margin Income Statement **For the Month of February 20XX**		
Sales revenue		$90,000
Variable expenses:		
Cost of goods sold.	$32,000	
Marketing expense	10,000	
General and administrative expense	3,000	45,000
Contribution margin.		45,000
Fixed expenses:		
Marketing expense	16,500	
General and administrative expense	3,500	20,000
Operating income		$25,000

Extreme Coffee sells three small coffees for every large coffee. A small coffee sells for $2, with a variable expense of $1. A large coffee sells for $4, with a variable expense of $2.

Required

1. Determine Extreme Coffee's monthly breakeven point in the numbers of small coffees and large coffees. Prove your answer by preparing a summary contribution margin income statement at the breakeven level of sales. Show only two categories of expenses: variable and fixed.

2. Compute Extreme Coffee's margin of safety in dollars.

3. If Extreme Coffee can increase monthly sales volume by 15%, what will operating income be? (The sales mix remains unchanged.)

CHAPTER 23

The Master Budget and Responsibility Accounting

TIPS CHECK YOUR RESOURCES

- Visit the www.prenhall.com/horngren **Web site** for self-study quizzes, video clips, and other resources

- Try the **Quick Check** exercise at the end of the chapter to test your knowledge

- Learn the **key terms**

- Do the **Starter** exercises keyed in the margins

- Work the **mid-** and **end-of-chapter summary problems**

- Use the **Concept Links** to review material in other chapters

- Search the **CD** for review materials by chapter or by key word

LEARNING OBJECTIVES

★1 Learn why managers use budgets

★2 Prepare an operating budget

★3 Prepare a financial budget

★4 Use sensitivity analysis in budgeting

★5 Prepare performance reports for responsibility centers

Over 20% of sales of books, music, and electronics occur online. If you're one of the millions of customers worldwide who point and click to buy your books and CDs on Amazon.com, then you're part of Amazon's strategy to "get big fast." This strategy increased Amazon's sales, but at a cost. Spending was out of control. There was no budget, and managers spared no expense to help the company grow. As a result, Amazon lost more than half a billion dollars in the fourth quarter of 2000.

Founder and CEO Jeff Bezos had to turn this sea of red ink into income. Bezos set up a *budget* for Amazon's plan of action. Now each division budgets both sales and expenses. In weekly meetings, managers compare actual results to the budget, which helps them correct problems quickly.

Amazon.com

The result? Between 2000 and 2002, Amazon.com's sales increased 42%. With such an increase in sales, you'd expect expenses to also increase. But Amazon's new budget helped managers *cut* operating expenses. How did they decrease expenses when sales are increasing so dramatically? The budget helped Amazon reduce order-filling and distribution costs by 5%. Switching to lower-cost computer systems reduced "technical and content" operating costs by 20%. The result? Amazon.com reported its first-ever income from operations in 2002.

Sources: Katrina Brooker, "Beautiful Dreamer," *Fortune*, December 18, 2000, pp. 234–239. Fred Vogelstein, "Bezos," *Fortune*, September 2, 2002, pp. 186–187. Fred Vogelstein, "What Went Right 2002," *Fortune*, December 30, 2002, p. 166. Nick Wingfield, "Survival Strategy: Amazon Takes Page from Wal-Mart to Prosper on Web," *The Wall Street Journal*, November 22, 2002, A1. Fred Vogelstein, "Mighty Amazon," *Fortune*, May 26, 2003, pp. 60–74. ■

▪Sitemap

Chapter 19 defined a budget as a quantitative expression of a plan that helps managers coordinate and implement the plan.

◉Student ResourceCD

benchmarking, budget

☆ *Learn why managers use budgets*

Perhaps, like Amazon.com, you've prepared a budget to ensure that you have enough cash to pay your expenses. ← The budget forces you to plan. If your budgeted cash inflow falls short of expenses, you can:

- Increase your cash inflow (by taking on a job or a student loan), or
- Cut your expenses

In addition to planning, your personal budget can help you control expenses. To stay within your grocery budget, you may buy macaroni and cheese instead of shrimp. At the end of the month, if your bank balance is less than expected, you can compare your actual cash inflows and expenses to your budget to see why. You need to know whether cash inflows are lower than expected or expenses are higher than expected to know what corrective action to take.

As Amazon.com learned, it's easy for spending to get out of control if you don't have a budget. That's why everyone, from individuals like you to complex international organizations like Amazon.com, uses budgets. Careful budgeting helps both individuals and businesses stay out of trouble by reducing the risk that they will spend more than they earn.

Why Managers Use Budgets

Let's continue our study of budgets by moving from your personal budget to see how a small service business develops a simple budget. Assume you begin an online service that provides travel itineraries for leisure travelers. You want to earn $550 a month to help with your college expenses. You expect to sell 20 itineraries per month at a price of $30 each. Over the past six months, you paid your Internet service provider an average of $18 a month, and you spent an additional $20 per month on reference materials. You expect these monthly costs to remain about the same. Finally, you spend 5% of your sales revenues for banner ads on other travel Web sites.

Exhibit 23-1 shows how to compute budgeted revenues and then subtract budgeted expenses to arrive at budgeted operating income.

If business goes according to plan, you will not meet your $550 per month operating income goal. You will have to increase revenue (perhaps through word-of-mouth advertising) or cut expenses (perhaps by finding a less-expensive Internet access provider).

Custom Travel Itineraries		
Budget for May 20X9		
Budgeted sales revenue (20 × $30)		$600
Less budgeted expenses:		
Internet-access expense	$18	
Reference-materials expense	20	
Advertising expense (5% × $600)	30	68
Budgeted operating income...............................		$532

Exhibit 23-1

Service Company Budget

Using Budgets to Plan and Control

Large international for-profit companies like Amazon.com and nonprofit organizations like Habitat for Humanity use budgets for the same reasons as you do in your personal life or in your small business—to plan and control actions and the related revenues and expenses. Exhibit 23-2 shows how managers use budgets in fulfilling their major responsibilities. First, they develop strategies—overall business goals like Amazon.com's goal to expand its international operations, or Gateway's to be a value leader in the personal computer market, while diversifying into other markets. Then companies plan and budget for specific actions to achieve those goals. The next step is to act. For example, Amazon.com recently planned for and then added the Marketplace auction feature to its Web sites for the United Kingdom, Germany, and Japan. And Gateway is leaning on its suppliers to cut costs, while at the same time it is pumping out new products like plasma TVs and audio and video gear.

Exhibit 23-2

Managers Use Budgets to Plan and Control Business Activities

After acting, managers compare actual results with the budget. This feedback allows them to determine what, if any, corrective action to take. If Amazon spent more than expected to add the Marketplace to its international Web sites, managers must cut other costs or increase revenues. These decisions affect the company's future strategies and plans.

Amazon.com has a number of budgets. Its managers develop budgets for their own divisions. Software then "rolls up" the division budgets to create an organization-wide budget for the company as a whole. Managers also prepare both long-term and short-term budgets. Boeing's long-term budget forecasts demand for planes for the next 20 years.

On the other hand, most companies (including Boeing) budget their cash flows monthly, weekly, and even daily to ensure that they have enough cash. They also budget revenues and expenses—and thus operating income—for months, quarters, and years. This chapter focuses on short-term budgets of one year or less. Chapter 26 explains how companies prepare long-term budgets for major capital expenditures on property, plant, and equipment.

Benefits of Budgeting

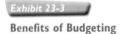

Exhibit 23-3 summarizes three key benefits of budgeting. Budgeting forces managers to plan, promotes coordination and communication, and provides a benchmark for evaluating actual performance.

Exhibit 23-3

Benefits of Budgeting

Budgets force managers to plan.

Budgets promote coordination and communication.

Budgets provide a benchmark that motivates employees and helps managers evaluate performance.

PLANNING Exhibit 23-1 shows that your expected income from the online travel itinerary business falls short of the target. The sooner you learn of the expected shortfall, the more time you have to plan how to increase revenues or cut expenses. The better your plan, and the more time you have to act on the plan, the more likely you will find a way to meet your target. Amazon.com's budget required that managers plan the expansion of the Web sites tailored for customers in Germany, France, and Japan.

COORDINATION AND COMMUNICATION The master budget coordinates a company's activities. It forces managers to consider relations among operations across the entire value chain. For example, Amazon.com stimulates sales by offering free shipping on orders over a specified dollar amount. The budget encourages managers to ensure that the extra profits from increased sales outweigh the revenue lost from not charging for shipping.

Budgets also communicate a consistent set of plans throughout the company. For example, the initial Amazon.com budget communicated the message that all employees should help control costs.

BENCHMARKING Budgets provide a benchmark that motivates employees and helps managers evaluate performance. In most companies, part of the manager's performance evaluation depends on how actual results compare to the budget. So, for example, the budgeted expenses for international expansion encourage Amazon.com's employees to increase the efficiency of international warehousing operations and to find less-expensive technology to support the Web sites.

Let's return to your online travel business. Suppose that comparing actual results to the budget in Exhibit 23-1 leads to the performance report in Exhibit 23-4.

	Actual	Budget	Variance (Actual − Budget)
Sales revenue	$550	$600	$(50)
Total expenses	90	68	(22)
Net income	$460	$532	$(72)

Exhibit 23-4

Summary Performance Report

This report should prompt you to investigate why actual sales are $50 less than budgeted ($550 − $600). There are three possibilities:

- The budget was unrealistic.
- You did a poor selling job.
- Uncontrollable factors (such as a sluggish economy) reduced sales.

Of course, all three may have contributed to the poor results.

You will also want to know why expenses are $22 higher than expected ($90 − $68). Did your Internet service provider increase rates? Did you have to buy more reference materials than planned? Did you spend more than 5% of your revenue on Web banner ads? You need to know the answers to these kinds of questions to decide how to get your business back on track.

Preparing the Master Budget

Now that you know *why* managers go to the trouble of developing budgets, let's consider the steps they take to prepare a budget.

Components of the Master Budget

The **master budget** is the set of budgeted financial statements and supporting schedules for the entire organization. Exhibit 23-5 shows the order in which managers prepare the components of the master budget for a merchandiser such as Amazon.com.

Student Resource **CD**
budget, budgeted financial statements, capital expenditures budget, financial budget, master budget, operating budget

Exhibit 23-5

Master Budget for a Merchandising Company

✔ **Starter 23-2**

Master Budget
The set of budgeted financial statements and supporting schedules for the entire organization. Includes the operating budget, the capital expenditures budget, and the financial budget.

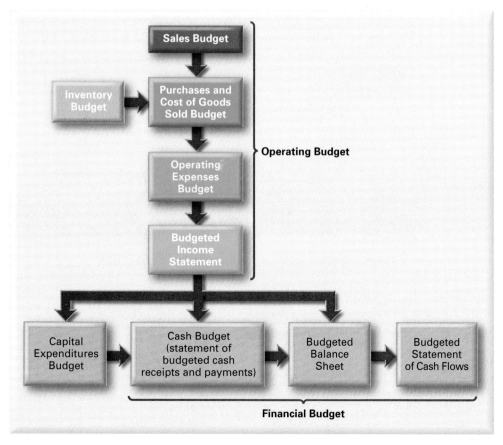

The exhibit shows that the master budget includes three types of budgets:

- The operating budget
- The capital expenditures budget
- The financial budget

Let's consider each in turn.

Operating Budget

Projects sales revenue, cost of goods sold, and operating expenses, leading to the budgeted income statement that projects operating income for the period.

The first component of the **operating budget** is the sales budget, the cornerstone of the master budget. Why? Because sales affect most other components of the master budget. After projecting sales revenue, cost of goods sold, and operating expenses, management prepares the end result of the operating budget: the budgeted income statement that projects operating income for the period.

Capital Expenditures Budget

A company's plan for purchases of property, plant, equipment, and other long-term assets.

The second type of budget is the **capital expenditures budget**. This budget presents the company's plan for purchases of property, plant, equipment, and other long-term assets.

Financial Budget

The cash budget (cash inflows and outflows), the budgeted period-end balance sheet, and the budgeted statement of cash flows.

The third type is the **financial budget**. Prior components of the master budget, including the budgeted income statement and the capital expenditures budget, along with plans for raising cash and paying debts, provide information for the first element of the financial budget: the cash budget. The cash budget, which projects cash inflows and outflows, feeds into the budgeted period-end balance sheet, which in turn feeds into the budgeted statement of cash flows. These budgeted financial statements look exactly like ordinary statements. The only difference is that they list budgeted (projected) rather than actual amounts.

Data for Whitewater Sporting Goods' Master Budget

We'll use Whitewater Sporting Goods Store No. 18 to see how managers prepare operating and financial budgets. (Chapter 26 will explain how to develop the capital expenditures budget.) Here is the information you have.

1. *You manage Whitewater Sporting Goods Store No. 18, which carries a complete line of outdoor recreation gear.* You are to prepare the store's master budget for April, May, June, and July, the main selling season. The division manager and the head of the Accounting Department will arrive from headquarters next week to review the budget with you.

2. *Cash collections follow sales because the company sells on account.*

3. *Your store's balance sheet at March 31, 20X6, the beginning of the budget period, appears in Exhibit 23-6.* ←

We examined the balance sheet in Chapter 5, pages 198–200. →

Exhibit 23-6

Balance Sheet

Whitewater Sporting Goods Store No. 18

**Balance Sheet
March 31, 20X6**

Assets		Liabilities	
Current assets:		**Current liabilities:**	
Cash	$ 15,000	Accounts payable	$ 16,800
Accounts receivable	16,000	Salary and commissions	
Inventory	48,000	payable	4,250
Prepaid insurance	1,800	Total liabilities	21,050
Total current assets	80,800		
Plant assets:		**Owners' Equity**	
Equipment and fixtures	32,000	Owners' equity	78,950
Accumulated depreciation	(12,800)		
Total plant assets	19,200	Total liabilities	
Total assets	$100,000	and owners' equity	$100,000

4. *Sales in March were $40,000. The sales force predicts these future monthly sales:*

April	$50,000
May	80,000
June	60,000
July	50,000

Sales are 60% cash and 40% on credit. Whitewater collects all credit sales the month after the sale. The $16,000 of accounts receivable at March 31 arose from credit sales in March (40% of $40,000). Uncollectible accounts are insignificant.

5. *Whitewater maintains inventory equal to $20,000 plus 80% of the budgeted cost of goods sold for the following month.* Target ending inventory on July 31 is $42,400. Cost of goods sold averages 70% of sales. Inventory on March 31 is $48,000:

$$\text{March 31 inventory} = \$20,000 + 0.80 \times (0.70 \times \text{April sales of } \$50,000)$$
$$= \$20,000 + (0.80 \times \$35,000)$$
$$= \$20,000 + \$28,000 = \$48,000$$

Whitewater pays for inventory as follows: 50% during the month of purchase and 50% during the next month. Accounts payable consists of inventory purchases only. March purchases were $33,600, so accounts payable at the end of March totals $16,800 ($33,600 × 0.50).

6. *Monthly payroll has two parts: a salary of $2,500 plus sales commissions equal to 15% of sales.* The company pays half this amount during the month and half early in the following month. Therefore, at the end of each month Whitewater reports salary and commissions payable equal to half the month's payroll. The $4,250 liability on the March 31 balance sheet is half the March payroll of $8,500:

$$\text{March payroll} = \text{Salary of } \$2,500$$
$$+ \text{Sales commissions of } \$6,000 \ (0.15 \times \$40,000)$$
$$= \$8,500$$
$$\text{March 31 salary and commissions payable} = 0.50 \times \$8,500 = \$4,250$$

7. *Other monthly expenses are as follows:*

Rent expense	$2,000, paid as incurred
Depreciation expense, including truck	500
Insurance expense	200 expiration of prepaid amount
Miscellaneous expenses	5% of sales, paid as incurred

8. *Whitewater plans to purchase a used delivery truck in April for $3,000 cash.*

9. *Whitewater requires each store to maintain a minimum cash balance of $10,000 at the end of each month.* The store can borrow money on six-month notes payable of $1,000 each at an annual interest rate of 12%. Management borrows no more than the amount needed to maintain the $10,000 minimum. Notes payable require six equal monthly payments of principal, plus monthly interest on the entire unpaid principal. Borrowing and all principal and interest payments occur at the end of the month.

10. *Income taxes are the responsibility of corporate headquarters, so you can ignore tax.*

Student Resource CD

budgeted financial statements, operating budget

Prepare an operating budget.

✔ Starter 23-3

✔ Starter 23-5

As you prepare the master budget, remember that you are developing the store's operating and financial plan for the next four months. The steps in this process may seem mechanical, but you must think carefully about pricing, product lines, job assignments, needs for additional equipment, and negotiations with banks. Successful managers use this opportunity to make decisions that affect the future course of business.

Preparing the Operating Budget

The first three components of the operating budget as shown in Exhibit 23-5, are:

■ Sales budget (Exhibit 23-7)
■ Inventory, purchases, and cost of goods sold budget (Exhibit 23-8)
■ Operating expenses budget (Exhibit 23-9)

The results of these three budgets feed into the fourth element of the operating budget: the budgeted income statement (Exhibit 23-10). We consider each in turn.

The Sales Budget

The forecast of sales revenue is the cornerstone of the master budget because the level of sales affects expenses and almost all other elements of the master budget. Budgeted total sales for each product is the sale price multiplied by the expected number of units sold. The overall sales budget in Exhibit 23-7 is the sum of the budgets for the individual products. Trace the April through July total sales ($240,000) to the budgeted income statement in Exhibit 23-10.

Exhibit 23-7

Sales Budget

					April–July
Whitewater Sporting Goods Store No. 18					
Sales Budget					
	April	May	June	July	Total
Cash sales, 60%	$30,000	$48,000	$36,000	$30,000	
Credit sales, 40%	20,000	32,000	24,000	20,000	
Total sales, 100%	$50,000	$80,000	$60,000	$50,000	$240,000

The Inventory, Purchases, and Cost of Goods Sold Budget

This budget determines cost of goods sold for the budgeted income statement, ending inventory for the budgeted balance sheet, and purchases for the cash budget. The familiar cost-of-goods-sold computation specifies the relations among these items:

$$\text{Beginning inventory} + \text{Purchases} - \text{Ending inventory} = \text{Cost of goods sold}$$

Beginning inventory is known from last month's balance sheet; budgeted cost of goods sold is 70% of sales; and budgeted ending inventory is a computed amount. You must solve for the budgeted purchases figure. To do this, rearrange the previous equation to isolate purchases on the left side:

$$\text{Purchases} = \text{Cost of goods sold} + \text{Ending inventory} - \text{Beginning inventory}$$

This equation makes sense. How much does Whitewater have to purchase? Enough to cover sales and desired ending inventory, less the amount of beginning inventory already on hand at the start of the period. Exhibit 23-8 shows Whitewater's inventory, purchases, and cost of goods sold budget.

✔ Starter 23-4

✔ Starter 23-6

Exhibit 23-8 | Inventory, Purchases, and Cost of Goods Sold Budget

Whitewater Sporting Goods Store No. 18
Inventory, Purchases, and Cost of Goods Sold Budget

	April	May	June	July	April–July Total
Cost of goods sold (0.70 × sales, from Sales Budget in Exhibit 23-7)	$35,000	$ 56,000	$42,000	$35,000	$168,000
+ Desired ending inventory ($20,000 + 0.80 × Cost of goods sold for the next month)	64,800*	53,600	48,000	42,400‡	
= Total inventory required	99,800	109,600	90,000	77,400	
− Beginning inventory	(48,000)†	(64,800)	(53,600)	(48,000)	
= Purchases	$51,800	$ 44,800	$36,400	$29,400	

* $20,000 + (0.80 × $56,000) = $64,800.
† Balance at March 31 (Exhibit 23-6).
‡ Given in item 5 on page 945.

Trace the total budgeted cost of goods sold from Exhibit 23-8 ($168,000) to the budgeted income statement in Exhibit 23-10. We will use the budgeted inventory and purchases amounts later.

The Operating Expenses Budget

Exhibit 23-9 shows the operating expense budget. Study each expense to make sure you know how it is computed. For example, sales commissions fluctuate with sales. Other expenses, such as rent and insurance, are the same each month (fixed).

Trace the April through July totals from the operating expenses budget in Exhibit 23-9 (salary and commissions of $46,000, rent expense of $8,000, and so on) to the budgeted income statement in Exhibit 23-10.

Exhibit 23-9 | Operating Expenses Budget

Whitewater Sporting Goods Store No. 18
Operating Expenses Budget

	April	May	June	July	April–July Total
Salary, fixed amount (item 6, page 945)	$ 2,500	$ 2,500	$ 2,500	$ 2,500	
Commission, 15% of sales from Sales Budget (item 6, page 945 and Exhibit 23-7)	7,500	12,000	9,000	7,500	
Total salary and commissions	10,000	14,500	11,500	10,000	$46,000
Rent expense, fixed amount (item 7, page 945)	2,000	2,000	2,000	2,000	8,000
Depreciation expense, fixed amount (item 7, page 945)	500	500	500	500	2,000
Insurance expense, fixed amount (item 7, page 945)	200	200	200	200	800
Miscellaneous expenses, 5% of sales from Sales Budget (item 7, page 945 and Exhibit 23-7)	2,500	4,000	3,000	2,500	12,000
Total operating expenses	$15,200	$21,200	$17,200	$15,200	$68,800

The Budgeted Income Statement

Use the sales budget (Exhibit 23-7); the inventory, purchases, and cost of goods sold budget (Exhibit 23-8); and the operating expenses budget (Exhibit 23-9) to prepare the budgeted income statement in Exhibit 23-10. (We explain the computation of interest expense as part of the cash budget in the next section.)

Exhibit 23-10 Budgeted Income Statement

Whitewater Sporting Goods Store No. 18

Budgeted Income Statement
Four Months Ending July 31, 20X6

	Amount	Source
Sales revenue	$240,000	Sales Budget (Exhibit 23-7)
Cost of goods sold	168,000	Inventory, Purchases, and Cost of Goods Sold
Gross profit	72,000	Budget (Exhibit 23-8)
Operating expenses:		
Salary and commissions $46,000		Operating Expenses Budget (Exhibit 23-9)
Rent expense 8,000		Operating Expenses Budget (Exhibit 23-9)
Depreciation expense 2,000		Operating Expenses Budget (Exhibit 23-9)
Insurance expense 800		Operating Expenses Budget (Exhibit 23-9)
Miscellaneous expenses 12,000	68,800	Operating Expenses Budget (Exhibit 23-9)
Operating income	3,200	
Interest expense	225*	Cash Budget (Exhibit 23-14)
Net income	$ 2,975	

* $90 + $75 + $60

Take this opportunity to solidify your understanding of operating budgets by carefully working the Mid-Chapter Summary Problem.

● MID-CHAPTER *Summary Problem*

CHECK YOUR RESOURCES

Review the Whitewater Sporting Goods example. You now think July sales might be $40,000 instead of the projected $50,000 in Exhibit 23-7. You want to see how this change in sales affects the budget.

Required

Revise the sales budget (Exhibit 23-7), the inventory, purchases, and cost of goods sold budget (Exhibit 23-8), and the operating expenses budget (Exhibit 23-9). Prepare a revised budgeted income statement for the four months ended July 31, 20X6.
  Note: You need not repeat the parts of the revised schedules that do not change.

Solution

Although not required, this solution repeats the budgeted amounts for April, May, and June. Revised figures appear in color for emphasis.

Whitewater Sporting Goods Store No. 18

Revised—Sales Budget

	April	May	June	July	Total
Cash sales, 60%	$30,000	$48,000	$36,000	$24,000	
Credit sales, 40%	20,000	32,000	24,000	16,000	
Total sales, 100%	$50,000	$80,000	$60,000	$40,000	$230,000

Whitewater Sporting Goods Store No. 18
Revised—Inventory, Purchases, and Cost of Goods Sold Budget

	April	May	June	July	Total
Cost of goods sold (0.70 × sales, from Revised Sales Budget)	$35,000	$56,000	$42,000	$28,000	$161,000
+ Desired ending inventory ($20,000 + 0.80 × cost of goods sold for next month)	64,800	53,600	42,400	42,400†	
= Total inventory required	99,800	109,600	84,400	70,400	
− Beginning inventory	(48,000)*	(64,800)	(53,600)	(42,400)	
= Purchases	$51,800	$44,800	$30,800	$28,000	

* Balance at March 31, Exhibit 23-6.
† Given in item 5 on page 945.

Whitewater Sporting Goods Store No. 18
Revised—Operating Expenses Budget

	April	May	June	July	Total
Salary, fixed amount	$ 2,500	$ 2,500	$ 2,500	$ 2,500	
Commission, 15% of sales from Revised Sales Budget	7,500	12,000	9,000	6,000	
Total salary and commissions	10,000	14,500	11,500	8,500	$44,500
Rent expense, fixed amount	2,000	2,000	2,000	2,000	8,000
Depreciation expense, fixed amount	500	500	500	500	2,000
Insurance expense, fixed amount	200	200	200	200	800
Miscellaneous expenses, 5% of sales from Revised Sales Budget	2,500	4,000	3,000	2,000	11,500
Total operating expenses	$15,200	$21,200	$17,200	$13,200	$66,800

Whitewater Sporting Goods Store No. 18
Revised Budgeted Income Statement
Four Months Ending July 31, 20X6

	Amount		Source
Sales revenue		$230,000	Revised Sales Budget
Cost of goods sold		161,000	Revised Inventory, Purchases, and Cost of Goods Sold Budget
Gross profit		69,000	
Operating expenses:			
Salary and commissions	$44,500		Revised Operating Expenses Budget
Rent expense	8,000		Revised Operating Expenses Budget
Depreciation expense	2,000		Revised Operating Expenses Budget
Insurance expense	800		Revised Operating Expenses Budget
Miscellaneous expenses	11,500	66,800	Revised Operating Expenses Budget
Operating income		2,200	
Interest expense		225	Revised Cash Budget (page 964)
Net income		$ 1,975	

Preparing the Financial Budget

Armed with a clear understanding of Whitewater's operating budget, you're now ready to prepare the financial budget. Exhibit 23-5 shows that the financial budget includes the cash budget, the budgeted balance sheet, and the budgeted statement of cash flows. We start with the cash budget.

 Prepare a financial budget

Student ResourceCD

budgeted financial statements, cash
budget, financial budget

Cash Budget
Details how the business expects to go
from the beginning cash balance to the
desired ending balance. Also called the
**statement of budgeted cash receipts
and payments.**

Preparing the Cash Budget

The **cash budget**, or **statement of budgeted cash receipts and payments**, details how the business expects to go from the beginning cash balance to the desired ending balance. The cash budget has four major parts:

- Cash collections from customers (Exhibit 23-11)
- Cash payments for purchases (Exhibit 23-12)
- Cash payments for operating expenses (Exhibit 23-13)
- Cash payments for capital expenditures (for example, the $3,000 capital expenditure to acquire the delivery truck)

Cash collections and payments depend on revenues and expenses, which appear in the operating budget. This is why you cannot prepare the cash budget until you have finished the operating budget.

✔ Starter 23-7

✔ Starter 23-9

BUDGETED CASH COLLECTIONS FROM CUSTOMERS   Exhibit 23-11 shows that April's budgeted cash collections consist of two parts: (1) April's cash sales from the sales budget in Exhibit 23-7 ($30,000) plus (2) collections of March's credit sales ($16,000 from the March 31 balance sheet, Exhibit 23-6). Trace April's $46,000 ($30,000 + $16,000) total cash collections to the cash budget in Exhibit 23-14.

Exhibit 23-11   Budgeted Cash Collections

Whitewater Sporting Goods Store No. 18
Budgeted Cash Collections from Customers

	April	May	June	July	April–July Total
Cash sales from Sales Budget (Exhibit 23-7)	$30,000	$48,000	$36,000	$30,000	
Collections of last month's credit sales, from Sales Budget (Exhibit 23-7).....................................	16,000*	20,000	32,000	24,000	
Total collections	$46,000	$68,000	$68,000	$54,000	$236,000

* March 31 accounts receivable, Exhibit 23-6.

BUDGETED CASH PAYMENTS FOR PURCHASES   Exhibit 23-12 uses the inventory, purchases, and cost of goods sold budget from Exhibit 23-8 and payment information from item 5 to compute budgeted cash payments for purchases of inventory. April's cash payments for purchases consist of two parts: (1) payment of 50% of March's purchases ($16,800 accounts payable balance from the March 31 balance sheet, Exhibit 23-6) plus (2) payment for 50% of April's purchases ($25,900 = 50% × $51,800 from Exhibit 23-8). Trace April's $42,700 ($16,800 + $25,900) cash outlay for purchases to the cash budget in Exhibit 23-14.

✔ Starter 23-8

Exhibit 23-12   Budgeted Cash Payments for Purchases

Whitewater Sporting Goods Store No. 18
Budgeted Cash Payments for Purchases

	April	May	June	July	April–July Total
50% of last month's purchases from Inventory, Purchases, and Cost of Goods Sold Budget (Exhibit 23-8)	$16,800*	$25,900	$22,400	$18,200	
50% of this month's purchases from Inventory, Purchases, and Cost of Goods Sold Budget (Exhibit 23-8)	25,900	22,400	18,200	14,700	
Total payments for purchases......................................	$42,700	$48,300	$40,600	$32,900	$164,500

*March 31 accounts payable, Exhibit 23-6.

BUDGETED CASH PAYMENTS FOR OPERATING EXPENSES Exhibit 23-13 uses items 6 and 7 and the operating expenses budget (Exhibit 23-9) to compute cash payments for operating expenses. April's cash payments for operating expenses consist of four items:

Payment of 50% of March's salary and commissions (from March 31 balance sheet, Exhibit 23-6).	$ 4,250
Payment of 50% of April's salary and commissions (50% × $10,000, Exhibit 23-9).	5,000
Payment of rent expense (Exhibit 23-9).	2,000
Payment of miscellaneous expenses (Exhibit 23-9).	2,500
Total April cash payments for operating expenses	$13,750

Follow April's $13,750 cash payments for operating expenses from Exhibit 23-13 to the cash budget in Exhibit 23-14.

Exhibit 23-13 Budgeted Cash Payments for Operating Expenses

Whitewater Sporting Goods Store No. 18
Budgeted Cash Payments for Operating Expenses

	April	May	June	July	April–July Total
Salary and commissions:					
50% of last month's expenses, from Operating Expenses Budget (Exhibit 23-9).	$ 4,250*	$ 5,000	$ 7,250	$ 5,750	
50% of this month's expenses, from Operating Expenses Budget (Exhibit 23-9).	5,000	7,250	5,750	5,000	
Total salary and commissions	9,250	12,250	13,000	10,750	
Rent expense, from Operating Expenses Budget (Exhibit 23-9).	2,000	2,000	2,000	2,000	
Miscellaneous expenses, from Operating Expenses Budget (Exhibit 23-9)	2,500	4,000	3,000	2,500	
Total payments for operating expenses	$13,750	$18,250	$18,000	$15,250	$65,250

*March 31 salary and commissions payable, Exhibit 23-6.

Why are depreciation expense and insurance expense from the operating expenses budget (Exhibit 23-9) *excluded* from the budgeted cash payments for operating expenses in Exhibit 23-13?

Answer: These expenses do not require cash outlays in the current period. Depreciation is the periodic write-off of the cost of the equipment and fixtures that Whitewater acquired previously. Insurance expense is the expiration of prepaid insurance.

✔ **Starter 23-10**

THE CASH BUDGET To prepare the cash budget in Exhibit 23-14, start with the beginning cash balance and add the budgeted cash collections from Exhibit 23-11 to determine the cash available. Then subtract cash payments for purchases (Exhibit 23-12), operating expenses (Exhibit 23-13), and any capital expenditures. This yields the ending cash balance before financing.

Item 9 (on page 945) states that Whitewater requires a minimum cash balance of $10,000. April's $1,550 budgeted cash balance before financing falls $8,450 short of the minimum required ($10,000 − $1,550). Because Whitewater borrows in $1,000 notes, the company will have to borrow $9,000 to cover April's expected shortfall. The budgeted ending cash balance equals the "ending cash balance before financ-

| Exhibit 23-14 | Cash Budget |

Whitewater Sporting Goods Store No. 18
Cash Budget
Four Months Ending July 31, 20X6

	April	May	June	July
Beginning cash balance	$15,000*	$10,550	$10,410	$18,235
Cash collections (Exhibit 23-11)	46,000	68,000	68,000	54,000
Cash available	$61,000	$78,550	$78,410	$72,235
Cash payments:				
Purchases of inventory (Exhibit 23-12)	$42,700	$48,300	$40,600	$32,900
Operating expenses (Exhibit 23-13)	13,750	18,250	18,000	15,250
Purchase of delivery truck (item 8, page 945)	3,000	—	—	—
Total cash payments	59,450	66,550	58,600	48,150
(1) Ending cash balance before financing	1,550	12,000	19,810	24,085
Less: Minimum cash balance desired	(10,000)	(10,000)	(10,000)	(10,000)
Cash excess (deficiency)	$(8,450)	$ 2,000	$ 9,810	$14,085
Financing of cash deficiency (see notes a–c):				
Borrowing (at end of month)	$ 9,000			
Principal payments (at end of month)		$ (1,500)	$(1,500)	$(1,500)
Interest expense (at 12% annually)		(90)	(75)	(60)
(2) Total effects of financing	9,000	(1,590)	(1,575)	(1,560)
Ending cash balance (1) + (2)	$10,550	$10,410	$18,235	$22,525

*March 31 cash balance, Exhibit 23-6.
Notes
^a Borrowing occurs in multiples of $1,000 and only for the amount needed to maintain a minimum cash balance of $10,000.
^b Monthly principal payments: $9,000 ÷ 6 = $1,500.
^c Interest expense:
  May: $9,000 × (0.12 × 1/12) = $90
  June: ($9,000 – $1,500) × (0.12 × 1/12) = $75
  July: ($9,000 – $1,500 – $1,500) × (0.12 × 1/12) = $60

ing," adjusted for the total effects of the financing (a $9,000 inflow in April). Exhibit 23-14 shows that Whitewater expects to end April with $10,550 of cash ($1,550 + $9,000). The exhibit also shows the cash balance at the end of May, June, and July.

Item 9 states that Whitewater must repay the notes in six equal installments. Thus, May through July show principal repayments of $1,500 ($9,000 ÷ 6) per month. Whitewater also pays interest expense on the outstanding notes payable, at 12% per year. The June interest expense is $75 [($9,000 principal – $1,500 repayment at the end of May) × 12% × 1/12]. Interest expense for the four months totals $225 ($90 + $75 + $60). This interest expense appears on the budgeted income statement in Exhibit 23-10.

The cash balance at the end of July ($22,525) is the cash balance in the July 31 budgeted balance sheet in Exhibit 23-15.

The Budgeted Balance Sheet

To prepare the budgeted balance sheet, project each asset, liability, and owners' equity account based on the plans outlined in the previous exhibits.

Study the budgeted balance sheet in Exhibit 23-15 to make certain you understand the computation of each figure. For example, on the budgeted balance sheet as of July 31, 20X6, budgeted cash equals the ending cash balance from the cash budget in Exhibit 23-14 ($22,525). Accounts receivable as of July 31 equal July's credit sales of $20,000, shown in the sales budget (Exhibit 23-7). July 31 inventory of $42,400 is July's desired ending inventory in the inventory, purchases, and cost of goods sold budget in Exhibit 23-8. Detailed computations for each of the other accounts appear in Exhibit 23-15.

Exhibit 23-15   Budgeted Balance Sheet

Whitewater Sporting Goods Store No. 18
Budgeted Balance Sheet
July 31, 20X6

Assets
Current assets:

Cash (Exhibit 23-14)	$22,525	
Accounts receivable (Sales Budget, Exhibit 23-7)	20,000	
Inventory (Inventory, Purchases, and Cost of Goods Sold Budget, Exhibit 23-8)	42,400	
Prepaid insurance (beginning balance of $1,800 – $800* for four months' expiration; Operating Expenses Budget, Exhibit 23-9)	1,000	
Total current assets		$ 85,925

Plant assets:

Equipment and fixtures (beginning balance of $32,000* + $3,000 truck acquisition; item 8, page 945)	$35,000	
Accumulated depreciation (beginning balance of $12,800* + $2,000 for four months' depreciation; Operating Expenses Budget, Exhibit 23-9)	(14,800)	
Total plant assets		20,200
Total assets		$106,125

Liabilities
Current liabilities:

Accounts payable (0.50 × July purchases of $29,400; Inventory, Purchases, and Cost of Goods Sold Budget, Exhibit 23-8)	$14,700	
Short-term note payable ($9,000 – $4,500 paid back; Exhibit 23-14)	4,500	
Salary and commissions payable (0.50 × July expenses of $10,000; Operating Expenses Budget, Exhibit 23-9)	5,000	
Total liabilities		$ 24,200

Owners' Equity

Owners' equity (beginning balance of $78,950* + $2,975 net income; Exhibit 23-10)		81,925
Total liabilities and owners' equity		$106,125

*March 31, 20X6, Balance Sheet, Exhibit 23-6

The Budgeted Statement of Cash Flows

The final step is preparing the budgeted statement of cash flows. Use the information from the schedules of cash collections and payments, the cash budget, and the beginning balance of cash to project cash flows from operating, investing, and financing activities. Take time to study Exhibit 23-16, and make sure you understand the origin of each figure.

Getting Employees to Accept the Budget

What is the most important part of Whitewater Sporting Goods' budgeting system? Despite all the numbers we have crunched, it is not the mechanics. It is getting managers and employees to accept the budget, so Whitewater can reap the planning, coordination, and control benefits illustrated in Exhibit 23-3.

Few people enjoy having their work monitored and evaluated. So if managers use the budget as a benchmark to evaluate employees' performance, managers must first motivate employees to accept the budget's goals. Here's how they can do it:

- Managers must support the budget themselves, or no one else will.
- Show employees how budgets can help them achieve better results.
- Have employees participate in developing the budget.

Exhibit 23-16

Budgeted Statement of Cash Flows

Whitewater Sporting Goods Store No. 18

Budgeted Statement of Cash Flows
Four Months Ending July 31, 20X6

Cash flows from operating activities:
  Receipts:
    Collections from customers (Exhibit 23-11) . . . . $ 236,000
    Total cash receipts. $236,000
  Payments:
    Purchases of inventory (Exhibit 23-12) . . . . $ (164,500)
    Operating expenses (Exhibit 23-13). . . . .   (65,250)
    Payment of interest expense (Exhibits 23-14 and 23-10). . . . .   (225)
    Total cash payments. . . . .   (229,975)
  Net cash inflow from operating activities.   6,025
Cash flows from investing activities:
  Acquisition of delivery truck (item 8, page 945) . . . . $ (3,000)
  Net cash outflow from investing activities.   (3,000)
Cash flows from financing activities:
  Proceeds from issuance of notes payable (Exhibit 23-14). . . . . $ 9,000
  Payment of notes payable (Exhibit 23-14).   (4,500)
  Net cash inflow from financing activities.   4,500
Net increase in cash . . . . $ 7,525
Cash balance, April 1, 20X6 (Exhibit 23-6 and 23-14)   15,000
Cash balance, July 31, 20X6 (Exhibits 23-14 and 23-15) . . . . $ 22,525

But these principles alone are not enough. As the manager of Store No. 18, your performance is evaluated by comparing actual results to budget. When you develop your store's budget, you may be tempted to build in *slack*. For example, you might want to budget fewer sales and higher purchases than you expect. This increases the chance that actual performance will be better than the budget and that you will receive a good evaluation. But adding slack into the budget makes it less accurate—and less useful for planning and control. When the division manager and the head of the Accounting Department arrive from headquarters next week, they will scour your budget to find any slack you may have inserted.

Student ResourceCD

Enterprise Resource Planning, master budget, sensitivity analysis

Use sensitivity analysis in budgeting

Using Information Technology for Sensitivity Analysis and Rolling Up Unit Budgets

Exhibits 23-7 through 23-16 show that the manager must prepare many calculations to develop the master budget for just one of the retail stores in the Whitewater Sporting Goods merchandising chain. No wonder managers embrace information technology to help prepare budgets! Let's see how advances in information technology make it more cost-effective for managers to:

■ Conduct sensitivity analysis on their own unit's budget

■ Roll up individual unit budgets to create the companywide budget

Sensitivity Analysis

The master budget models the company's *planned* activities. Top management pays special attention to ensure that the results of the budgeted income statement (Exhibit 23-10), the cash budget (Exhibit 23-14), and the budgeted balance sheet (Exhibit 23-15) support key strategies.

But actual results often differ from plans, so management wants to know how budgeted income and cash flows would change if key assumptions turned out to be incorrect. Chapter 22 defined *sensitivity analysis* as a *what-if* technique that asks *what* a result will be *if* a predicted amount is not achieved or *if* an underlying assumption changes. → *What if* the stock market crashes? How will this affect Amazon.com's sales? Will it have to postpone the planned expansion in Asia and Europe? *What* will be Whitewater Store No. 18's cash balance on July 31 *if* the period's sales are 45% cash, not 60% cash? Will Whitewater have to borrow more cash?

Sensitivity analysis is introduced in Chapter 22, page 910.

Most companies use computer spreadsheet programs (or special budget software) to prepare master budget schedules and statements. In fact, one of the earliest spreadsheet programs was developed by graduate business students who realized that computers could take the drudgery out of hand-computed master budget sensitivity analyses. Today, managers answer what-if questions simply by changing a number. At the press of a key, the computer screen flashes a revised budget that includes all the effects of the change.

Technology makes it cost-effective to perform more-comprehensive sensitivity analyses. Armed with a better understanding of how changes in sales and costs are likely to affect the company's bottom line, today's managers can react quickly if key assumptions underlying the master budget (such as sales price or quantity) turn out to be wrong.

Rolling Up Individual Unit Budgets into the Companywide Budget

Whitewater Sporting Goods Store No. 18 is just one of the company's many retail stores. As Exhibit 23-17 shows, Whitewater's headquarters must roll up the budget data from Store No. 18, along with budgets for each of the other stores, to prepare the companywide master budget. This roll-up can be difficult for companies whose units use different spreadsheets to prepare the budgets.

Companies like Sunoco turn to budget-management software to solve this problem. Often designed as a component of the company's Enterprise Resource Planning (ERP) system (or data warehouse), this software helps managers develop and analyze budgets.

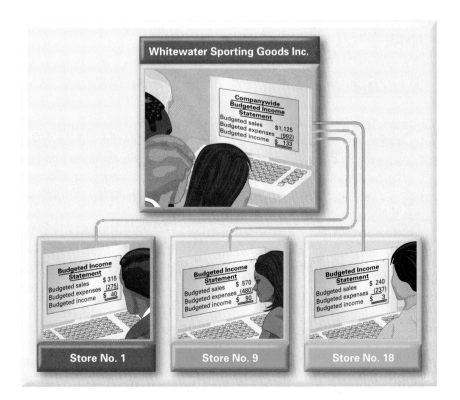

Exhibit 23-17

Rolling Up Individual Unit Budgets into the Companywide Budget

Across the globe, managers sit at their desks, log into the company's budget system, and enter their numbers. The software allows them to conduct sensitivity analyses on their own unit's data. When the manager is satisfied with her budget, she can enter it in the companywide budget with the click of a mouse. Her unit's budget automatically rolls up with budgets from all other units around the world.

Whether at headquarters or on the road, top executives can log into the budget system and conduct their own sensitivity analyses on individual units' budgets or on the companywide budget. Managers can spend less time compiling and summarizing data and more time analyzing it to ensure that the budget leads the company to achieve its key strategic goals.

Consider two budget situations: (1) Whitewater Sporting Goods' marketing analysts produce a near-certain forecast for four-month sales of $4,500,000 for the company's 20 stores. (2) Much uncertainty exists about the period's sales. The most likely amount is $4,500,000, but marketing considers any amount between $3,900,000 and $5,100,000 to be possible. How will the budgeting process differ in these two circumstances?

Answer: Whitewater will prepare a master budget for the expected sales level of $4,500,000 in either case. Because of the uncertainty in situation 2, executives will want a set of budgets covering the entire range of volume rather than a single level. Whitewater's managers may prepare budgets based on sales of, say, $3,900,000, $4,200,000, $4,500,000, $4,800,000, and $5,100,000. These budgets will help managers plan for sales levels throughout the forecasted range.

Accounting.com

Enterprise Resource Planning Keeps Fossil's Budget from Becoming a Fossil

Pioneering companies are shelving their Excel spreadsheets in favor of budgeting and planning software integrated into their Enterprise Resource Planning (ERP) systems. The software, from companies such as Cognos, Inc., and Adaytum, Inc., lets financial managers continuously update revenue and spending forecasts. With the ever-increasing globalization of business, ERP systems help far-flung corporate divisions speak the same financial language. Here are some examples:

- Richardson, Texas, based Fossil, Inc., wants its budgets to be as up-to-the-minute as its watches and accessories. Now, rather than manually consolidating sales and spending forecasts from a host of Excel spreadsheets, the company loads its numbers into a Cognos system, which immediately generates a profit-and-loss forecast. Managers scrutinize the report by product line, department, and distribution channel and spend their time analyzing results.

- AXA Corp., a 2,700-employee financial services corporation based in Paris, owns divisions in Western Europe, North America, Asia, and the Pacific Rim. Before ERP, each division used a different accounting system, and multiple spreadsheets were consolidated by hand. With ERP, AXA has reduced the time it takes to close its books to four days from two weeks, and it processes 350 currencies in a single system.

Based on: Russ Banhan, "Better Budgets," *Journal of Accountancy*, February 2000, pp. 37–40. J. W. Dysart, "Planning for Real-Time Information," *Banking Strategies*, May/June 2000, pp. 6–10. Louisa Wah, "Give ERP a Chance," *Management Review*, March 2000, pp. 20–24. Rick Whiting, "Crystal-Ball Glance into Fiscal Future," *Information Week*, July 22, 2002, p. 37. Jennifer Jaroneczyk, "ERP Streamlines Global Finances," *Internet World*, September 2002, pp. 22–24.

Responsibility Accounting

You've now seen how managers set strategic goals and then develop plans and budget resources for activities that will help reach those goals. Let's look more closely at how managers *use* budgets to control operations.

Each manager is responsible for planning and controlling some part of the firm's activities. A **responsibility center** is a part or subunit of an organization whose manager is accountable for specific activities. Lower-level managers are often responsible for budgeting and controlling costs of a single value-chain function. For example, one manager is responsible for planning and controlling the *production* of Pace picante sauce at the plant, while another is responsible for planning and controlling the *distribution* of the product to customers. Lower-level managers report to higher-level managers, who have broader responsibilities. Managers in charge of production and distribution report to senior managers responsible for profits (revenues minus costs) earned by an entire product line.

Four Types of Responsibility Centers

Responsibility accounting is a system for evaluating the performance of each responsibility center and its manager. Responsibility accounting performance reports compare plans (budgets) with actions (actual results) for each center. Superiors then evaluate how well each manager: (1) used the budgeted resources to achieve the responsibility center's goals and thereby (2) controlled the operations for which he or she was responsible. Exhibit 23-18 illustrates four types of responsibility centers.

 Student Resource CD

responsibility accounting, responsibility center

5 *Prepare performance reports for responsibility centers*

Responsibility Center
A part or subunit of an organization whose manager is accountable for specific activities.

Responsibility Accounting
A system for evaluating the performance of each responsibility center and its manager.

Exhibit 23-18   Four Types of Responsibility Centers

In a **cost center**, such as a production line for Pace picante sauce, managers are responsible for costs.

In a **revenue center**, such as the Midwest sales region, managers are responsible for generating sales revenue.

In a **profit center**, such as a line of products, managers are responsible for generating income.

In an **investment center**, such as Campbell Soups and Sauces division, managers are responsible for income and invested capital.

1. *In a cost center, managers are accountable for costs (expenses) only.* Manufacturing operations like the Pace picante sauce production lines are cost centers. The line foreman controls costs by ensuring that employees work efficiently. The foreman is *not* responsible for generating revenues, because he is not involved in selling the product. The plant manager evaluates the foreman on his ability to control *costs* by comparing actual costs to budgeted costs. All else being equal (for example, holding quality constant), the foreman is likely to receive a more favorable evaluation if actual costs are less than budgeted costs.

✔ **Starter 23-11**

2. *In a revenue center, managers are primarily accountable for revenues.* Examples include the Midwest and Southeast sales regions of businesses like Pace Foods and Reebok. Such managers of revenue centers may also be responsible for the costs of their own sales operations. Revenue center performance reports compare actual with budgeted revenues and may include the costs incurred by the revenue center itself. All else being equal, the manager is likely to receive a more-favorable evaluation if actual revenues exceed the budget.

3. *In a profit center, managers are accountable for both revenues and costs (expenses) and, therefore, profits.* The (higher-level) manager responsible for the entire Pace product line would be accountable for increasing sales revenue *and* controlling costs to achieve the profit goals. Profit center reports include both revenues and expenses to show the profit center's income. Superiors evaluate the manager's performance by comparing actual revenues, expenses, and profits to the budget. All else being equal, the manager is likely to receive a more-favorable evaluation if actual profits exceed the budget.

4. *In an investment center, managers are accountable for investments, revenues, and costs (expenses).* Examples include the Saturn division of General Motors and the North American Sauces and Beverages Division (which includes Pace Foods) of Campbell Soup. Managers of investment centers are responsible for (1) generating sales, (2) controlling expenses, and (3) managing the amount of investment required to earn the income (revenues minus expenses). For example, Bell South Corp considers its information technology (IT) department an investment center. Managers are responsible for keeping IT costs within the budget while using the department's assets to generate revenue from projects such as Bell South's FastAccess DSL service or its e-business operations.

See Chapter 18, p. 721, for discussion of rate of return on total assets. ➡ Top management often evaluates investment center managers based on return on investment (ROI). ⬅ When evaluating a division, the return on investment is often computed as:

$$ROI = \frac{Division's\ operating\ income}{Division's\ average\ total\ assets}$$

All else being equal, the manager will receive a more-favorable evaluation if the division's actual return on investment exceeds the budgeted return on investment.

Responsibility Accounting Performance Reports

Exhibit 23-19 shows how an organization like Campbell Soup Company (the parent company of Pace Foods) may assign responsibility.

At the top level, the CEO oversees each of the four divisions. Division managers generally have broad responsibility, including deciding how to use assets to maximize return on investment. Most companies consider divisions as *investment centers.*

Each division manager supervises all the product lines in that division. Exhibit 23-19 shows that the VP of North American Sauces and Beverages oversees the Prego Italian sauces, Pace Mexican sauces, V8 juice, and Franco-American canned pasta product lines. Product lines are generally considered *profit centers.* Thus, the manager of the Pace product line is responsible for evaluating lower-level managers of both

- *Cost centers* (such as plants that make Pace products) and
- *Revenue centers* (such as managers responsible for selling Pace products).

Exhibit 23-19 Partial Organization Chart

Exhibit 23-20 on the next page illustrates responsibility accounting performance reports for each level of management shown in Exhibit 23-19. Exhibit 23-20 uses assumed numbers to illustrate reports like those

- The CEO may use to evaluate divisions
- The divisional VPs may use to evaluate individual product lines
- The product-line managers may use to evaluate the development, production, marketing, and distribution of their products

At each level, the reports compare actual results with the budget.

Start with the lowest level and move to the top. Follow the $25 million budgeted operating income from the Mexican sauces product-line report to the report of the VP–North American Sauces and Beverages. The VP's report summarizes the budgeted and actual operating incomes for each of the four product lines he supervises.

Now trace the $70 million budgeted operating income from the VP's report to the CEO's report. The CEO's report includes a summary of each division's budgeted and actual profits, as well as the costs incurred by corporate headquarters, which are not assigned to any of the divisions.

MANAGEMENT BY EXCEPTION The variances reported in Exhibit 23-20 aid **management by exception**, which directs executives' attention to important differences between actual and budgeted amounts. Look at the CEO's report. The International Soups and Sauces Division's actual operating income of $34 million is very close to the budgeted $35 million. Unless there are other signs of trouble, the CEO will not waste time investigating such a small variance.

Management by Exception
Directs management's attention to important differences between actual and budgeted amounts.

Exhibit 23-20

Responsibility Accounting Performance Reports

✔ Starter 23-12

✔ Starter 23-13

✔ Starter 23-14

Responsibility Accounting Performance Reports at Various Levels (In Millions of Dollars)

CEO's Quarterly Responsibility Report

Operating Income of Divisions and Corporate Headquarters Expense	Budget	Actual	Variance Favorable/ (Unfavorable)
North American Soups	$218	$209	$ (9)
North American Sauces and Beverages...	70	84	14
Biscuits and Confectionery	79	87	8
International Soups and Sauces	35	34	(1)
Corporate Headquarters Expense	(33)	(29)	4
Operating Income....................	$369	$385	$16

VP—North American Sauces and Beverages, Quarterly Responsibility Report

Operating Income of Product Lines	Budget	Actual	Variance Favorable/ (Unfavorable)
Italian Sauces......................	$20	$18	$ (2)
Mexican Sauces.....................	25	38	13
Vegetable Juices....................	10	15	5
Canned Pastas......................	15	13	(2)
Operating Income...................	$70	$84	$14

Manager—Mexican Sauces Quarterly Responsibility Report

Revenues and Expenses	Budget	Actual	Variance Favorable/ (Unfavorable)
Sales revenue......................	$ 80	$ 84	$ 4
Cost of goods sold	(36)	(30)	6
Gross profit	44	54	10
Marketing expenses	(12)	(9)	3
Research and development expenses	(2)	(3)	(1)
Other expenses	(5)	(4)	1
Operating income...................	$25	$38	$13

In contrast, the North American Sauces and Beverages Division earned much more profit than budgeted. The CEO will want to know why. Suppose the VP of the division believes a national sales promotion was especially effective. That promotion may be repeated or adapted by other divisions. To identify the reason for exceptional results, so that other parts of the organization may benefit, is one reason why managers investigate large favorable variances (not just large unfavorable ones). Another is to ensure that employees are not skimping on ingredients, marketing, or R&D, which could hurt the company's long-term success.

A CEO who received the report at the top of Exhibit 23-20 would likely concentrate on improving the North American Soups Division, because its actual income fell $9 million below budget. The CEO will want to see which product lines caused the shortfall, so that he or she and the VP of the division can work together to correct any problems.

Exhibit 23-20 also shows how summarized data may hide problems. Although the North American Sauces and Beverages Division as a whole performed well, the Italian sauces and canned pasta lines did not. If the CEO received only the condensed report at the top of the exhibit, he or she would rely on division managers to spot and correct problems in individual product lines.

Not a Question of Blame   Responsibility accounting assigns managers responsibility for their unit's actions and provides a way to evaluate both their and the unit's performance. But superiors should not misuse responsibility accounting to find fault or place blame. The question is not "Who is to blame for an unfavorable variance?" Instead, the question is "Who can best explain why a specific variance occurred?" Consider the North American Soups Division in Exhibit 23-20. Suppose a tornado devastated the primary production plant. It may be that the remaining plants operated very efficiently, and this efficiency kept the income variance down to $9 million. If so, the North American Soups Division and its VP may actually have done a good job.

The following Decision Guidelines review budgets and how managers use them in responsibility accounting. Take a moment to study these guidelines before working the summary review problem.

Decision Guidelines

THE MASTER BUDGET AND RESPONSIBILITY ACCOUNTING

Amazon.com's initial strategy was to "get big fast." But without a budget, spending got out of control. So founder and CEO Jeff Bezos added a second strategic goal—to become the world's most cost-efficient high-quality e-tailer. Today, Amazon's managers use budgets to help reach both the growth and cost-efficiency goals. Let's consider some of the decisions Amazon made as it set up its budgeting process.

Decision	Guidelines
What benefits should Amazon.com expect to obtain from developing a budget?	Requires managers to *plan* how to increase sales and how to cut costs
	Promotes *coordination and communication*, such as communicating the importance of the cost-efficiency goal
	Provides a *benchmark* that motivates employees and helps managers evaluate how well employees contributed to the sales growth and cost-efficiency goals
In what order should Amazon's managers prepare the components of the master budget?	Begin with the *operating budget*.
	• Start with the *sales budget*, which feeds into all other budgets.
	• The sales and *ending inventory budgets* determine the *purchases and cost of goods sold budget*.
	• The sales, cost of goods sold, and *operating expense budgets* determine the *budgeted income statement*.
	Next, prepare the *capital expenditures budget*. Finally, prepare the *financial budget*.
	• Start with the *cash budget*.
	• The cash budget provides the ending cash balance for the *budgeted balance sheet* and the details for the *budgeted statement of cash flows*.

Decision Guidelines (continued)

Decision	Guidelines
What extra steps should Amazon take given the uncertainty of Internet-based sales forecasts?	Prepare a *sensitivity analysis* and project budgeted results at different sales levels.

How does Amazon compute budgeted purchases?

$$\frac{\text{Beginning}}{\text{inventory}} + \text{Purchases} - \frac{\text{Ending}}{\text{inventory}} = \frac{\text{Cost of}}{\text{goods sold}}$$

so

$$\text{Purchases} = \frac{\text{Cost of}}{\text{goods sold}} + \frac{\text{Ending}}{\text{inventory}} - \frac{\text{Beginning}}{\text{inventory}}$$

What kind of a responsibility center does each manager supervise?

Cost center: Manager is responsible for costs.
Revenue center: Manager is responsible for revenues.
Profit center: Manager is responsible for both revenues and costs, and therefore profits.
Investment center: Manager is responsible for revenues, costs, and the amount of the investment required to earn the income.

How to evaluate managers?

Compare actual performance with the budget for the manager's responsibility center. *Management by exception* focuses on large differences between budgeted and actual results.

Excel Application Exercise

Goal: Create a spreadsheet to prepare the sales budget and the inventory, purchases, and cost of goods sold budget for a small business.

Scenario: After reading about how **Amazon** uses budgets to help manage its business, you decide that your own business could use them. You estimate the following *total* sales for the coming year: January, $9,000; February, $9,100; March, $8,900; and April, $8,800. Cash sales represent 80% of your business, and your cost of goods sold is 60% of sales revenue. Ending inventory as of December 31 of last year was $1,620, and your desired ending inventory each month is 30% of the next month's cost of goods sold.

When you have completed your worksheet, answer the following questions:

1. What is the total inventory required (e.g., the third line in Exhibit 23-8) in January, in February, and in March?
2. What is the desired ending inventory for March?
3. What happens to purchases each month if February total sales drop to $8,100?

Step-by-Step:

1. Open a new Excel spreadsheet.
2. In column A, create a bold-faced heading as follows:
   a. Chapter 23 Excel Application Exercise
   b. Sales and Inventory, Purchases, and COGS Budgets
   c. Today's Date
3. Two rows down, enter the label, "Total January Sales." In column B, enter the sales amount. Underneath January sales, enter a row for February sales. Do the same for March and April.
4. Two rows down from the sales line items, enter the label "Cash Sales as a Percentage of Total Sales." In column B, enter the percentage given in the scenario. Then, in column A one row down, enter the label, "Cost of Goods Sold Percentage." In column B, enter the percentage. Two rows down, enter the label "Beginning Inventory as of January 1" in column A. Enter the appropriate amount in column B. One row down in column A enter the label, "Desired Ending Inventory Percentage." In column B, enter the percentage given.
5. Move down two rows. Using Exhibit 23-7 as your guide, create a sales budget for your company. All dollar amounts should be formulas. Format as needed.
6. Move down two rows. Using Exhibit 23-8 as your guide, create an inventory, purchases, and COGS budget for your company. Use formulas for all dollar amounts. Format as needed. *Hint:* The desired ending inventory in March requires the use of the April sales figure.
7. Save your worksheet and print a copy for your files.

END-OF-CHAPTER *Summary Problem*

CHECK YOUR RESOURCES

Continue the revised Whitewater Sporting Goods illustration from the mid-chapter summary problem. Now that you think July sales will be $40,000 instead of $50,000, as projected in Exhibit 23-7, how will this affect the financial budget?

Required:

Revise the schedule of budgeted cash collections (Exhibit 23-11), the schedule of budgeted cash payments for purchases (Exhibit 23-12), and the schedule of budgeted cash payments for operating expenses (Exhibit 23-13). Prepare a revised cash budget, a revised budgeted balance sheet at July 31, 20X6, and a revised budgeted statement of cash flows for the four months ended July 31, 20X6. *Note:* You need not repeat the parts of the revised schedule that do not change.

Solution

Although not required, this solution repeats the budgeted amounts for April, May, and June. Revised figures appear in color for emphasis.

Whitewater Sporting Goods Store No. 18

Revised—Budgeted Cash Collections from Customers

	April	May	June	July	Total
Cash sales, from Revised Sales Budget	$30,000	$48,000	$36,000	$24,000	
Collections of last month's credit sales, from Revised Sales Budget	16,000*	20,000	32,000	24,000	
Total collections	$46,000	$68,000	$68,000	$48,000	$230,000

* March 31 accounts receivable, Exhibit 23-6.

Whitewater Sporting Goods Store No. 18

Revised—Budgeted Cash Payments for Purchases

	April	May	June	July	Total
50% of last month's purchases, from Revised Inventory, Purchases, and Cost of Goods Sold Budget	$16,800*	$25,900	$22,400	$15,400	
50% of this month's purchases, from Revised Inventory, Purchases, and Cost of Goods Sold Budget	25,900	22,400	15,400	14,000	
Total payments for purchases	$42,700	$48,300	$37,800	$29,400	$158,200

* March 31 accounts payable, Exhibit 23-6.

Whitewater Sporting Goods Store No. 18

Revised—Budgeted Cash Payments for Operating Expenses

	April	May	June	July	Total
Salary and commissions:					
50% of last month's expenses, from Revised Operating Expenses Budget	$ 4,250*	$ 5,000	$ 7,250	$ 5,750	
50% of this month's expenses, from Revised Operating Expenses Budget	5,000	7,250	5,750	4,250	
Total salary and commissions	9,250	12,250	13,000	10,000	
Rent expense, from Revised Operating Expenses Budget	2,000	2,000	2,000	2,000	
Miscellaneous expenses, from Revised Operating Expenses Budget	2,500	4,000	3,000	2,000	
Total payments for operating expenses	$13,750	$18,250	$18,000	$14,000	$64,000

* March 31 salary and commissions payable, Exhibit 23-6.

Whitewater Sporting Goods Store No. 18

Revised Cash Budget
Four Months Ending July 31, 20X6

	April	May	June	July
Beginning cash balance	$15,000*	$10,550	$10,410	$21,035
Cash collections (Revised Budgeted Cash Collections)	46,000	68,000	68,000	48,000
Cash available	$61,000	$78,550	$78,410	$69,035
Cash payments:				
Purchases of inventory (Revised Budgeted Cash				
Payments for Purchases)	$42,700	$48,300	$37,800	$29,400
Operating expenses (Revised Budgeted Cash				
Payments for Operating Expenses)	13,750	18,250	18,000	14,000
Purchase of delivery truck (item 8, page 945)	3,000	—	—	—
Total cash payments	59,450	66,550	55,800	43,400
(1) Ending cash balance before financing	1,550	12,000	22,610	25,635
Less: Minimum cash balance desired	(10,000)	(10,000)	(10,000)	(10,000)
Cash excess (deficiency)	$(8,450)	$ 2,000	$12,610	$15,635
Financing of cash deficiency (see notes *a–c*):				
Borrowing (at end of month)	$ 9,000			
Principal payments (at end of month)		$(1,500)	$(1,500)	$(1,500)
Interest expense (at 12% annually)		(90)	(75)	(60)
(2) Total effects of financing	9,000	(1,590)	(1,575)	(1,560)
Ending cash balance (1) + (2)	$10,550	$10,410	$21,035	$24,075

* March 31 cash balance, Exhibit 23-6.

Notes

a Borrowing occurs in multiples of $1,000 and only for the amount needed to maintain a minimum cash balance of $10,000.

b Monthly principal payments: $9,000 ÷ 6 = $1,500.

c Interest expense:

  May: $9,000 × (0.12 × 1/12) = $90; June: ($9,000 − $1,500) × (0.12 × 1/12) = $75; July: ($9,000 − $1,500 − $1,500) × (0.12 × 1/12) = $60

Whitewater Sporting Goods Store No. 18

Revised Budgeted Balance Sheet
July 31, 20X6

Assets

Current assets:		
Cash (Revised Cash budget)	$24,075	
Accounts receivable (Revised Sales Budget)	16,000	
Inventory	42,400	
Prepaid insurance	1,000	
Total current assets		$ 83,475
Plant assets:		
Equipment and fixtures	$35,000	
Accumulated depreciation	(14,800)	
Total plant assets		20,200
Total assets		$103,675

Liabilities

Current liabilities:		
Accounts payable (0.50 × July purchases of $28,000;		
Revised Inventory, Purchases, and Cost of Goods		
Sold Budget)	$14,000	
Short-term note payable	4,500	
Salary and commissions payable (0.50 × July expenses		
of $8,500; Revised Operating Expenses Budget) . . .	4,250	
Total liabilities		$ 22,750

Owners' Equity

Owners' equity (beginning balance of $78,950* + $1,975		
net income, Revised Budgeted Income Statement) . . .		80,925
Total liabilities and owners' equity		$103,675

*March 31, 20X6, Balance Sheet, Exhibit 23-6

Whitewater Sporting Goods Store No. 18

Revised Budgeted Statement of Cash Flows
Four Months Ending July 31, 20X6

Cash flows from operating activities:		
Receipts:		
Collections (Revised Budgeted Cash Collections)	$230,000	
Total cash receipts..........................		$230,000
Payments:		
Purchases of inventory (Revised Budgeted Cash Payments for Purchases)..................	(158,200)	
Operating expenses (Revised Budgeted Cash Payments for Operating Expenses).....	(64,000)	
Payment of interest expense.................	(225)	
Total cash payments.......................		(222,425)
Net cash inflow from operating activities........		7,575
Cash flows from investing activities:		
Acquisition of delivery truck..................	$ (3,000)	
Net cash outflow from investing activities........		(3,000)
Cash flows from financing activities:		
Proceeds from issuance of notes payable.........	$ 9,000	
Payment of notes payable....................	(4,500)	
Net cash inflow from financing activities.........		4,500
Net increase in cash...........................		$ 9,075
Cash balance, April 1, 20X6 (Exhibit 23-6)..........		15,000
Cash balance, July 31, 20X6 (Revised Cash Budget)..		$ 24,075

REVIEW *the Master Budget and Responsibility Accounting*

Quick Check

1. **Amazon.com** expected to receive which of the following benefits when it started its budgeting process?
   a. The planning required to develop the budget helps managers foresee and avoid potential problems before they occur.
   b. The budget helps motivate employees to achieve Amazon's sales growth and cost-reduction goals.
   c. The budget provides Amazon's managers with a benchmark against which to compare actual results for performance evaluation.
   d. All of the above.

2. Which of the following is the cornerstone (or most critical element) of the master budget?
   a. The sales budget
   b. The inventory budget
   c. The purchases and cost of goods sold budget
   d. The operating expenses budget

3. The income statement is part of which element of Amazon.com's master budget?
   a. The operating budget
   b. The capital expenditures budget
   c. The financial budget
   d. None of the above

   Use the following information to answer questions 4 through 6. Suppose Amazon.com sells 1 million hardback books a day at an average price of $30 and 1.5 million paperback books a day at an average price of $15. Assume that Amazon's purchase price for the books is 60% of the selling price it charges retail customers. Amazon has no beginning inventory, but it wants to have a three-day supply of ending inventory. Assume that operating expenses are $0.5 million per day.

4. Compute Amazon's budgeted sales for the next (seven-day) week.
   a. $52.5 million
   b. $210 million
   c. $220.5 million
   d. $367.5 million

5. Determine Amazon's budgeted purchases for the next (seven-day) week.
   a. $220.5 million   c. $367.5 million
   b. $315 million   d. $525 million

6. What is Amazon.com's budgeted operating income for a (seven-day) week?
   a. $52.5 million   c. $143.5 million
   b. $56 million   d. $147 million

7. Which of the following expenses would *not* appear in Amazon.com's cash budget?
   a. Depreciation expense   c. Interest expense
   b. Wages expense   d. Marketing expense

8. Information technology has made it easier for Amazon's managers to perform all of the following tasks *except*:
   a. Sensitivity analyses
   b. Rolling up individual units' budgets into the companywide budget
   c. Removing slack from the budget
   d. Preparing responsibility center performance reports that identify variances between actual and budgeted revenues and costs

9. Which of the following managers is at the highest level of the organization?
   a. Cost center manager   c. Profit center manager
   b. Revenue center manager   d. Investment center manager

10. Suppose Amazon.com budgets $5 million for customer service costs but actually spends $4 million.
    a. Because this $1 million variance is favorable, management does not need to investigate further.
    b. Management will investigate this $1 million favorable variance to ensure that the cost savings do not reflect skimping on customer service.
    c. Management will investigate this $1 million unfavorable variance to try to identify and then correct the problem that led to the unfavorable variance.
    d. Management should investigate every variance, especially unfavorable ones.

Accounting Vocabulary

capital expenditures budget (p. 944)
cash budget (p. 950)
financial budget (p. 944)

management by exception (p. 959)
master budget (p. 943)
operating budget (p. 944)

responsibility accounting (p. 957)
responsibility center (p. 957)
statement of budgeted cash receipts and payments (p. 950)

●ASSESS *Your Progress*

See *www.prenhall.com/horngren* for selected Starters, Exercises, and Problems.

Why managers use budgets
(Obj. 1)

Ordering components of the master budget
(Obj. 2, 3)

Starters

S23-1 Consider the budget for your travel itinerary business (page 941). Explain how you benefit from preparing the budget.

S23-2 In what order should you prepare the following components of the master budget?

Budgeted income statement	Operating expense budget	Cash budget
Budgeted statement of cash flows	Purchases and cost of goods sold budget	Capital expenditures budget
Budgeted balance sheet	Sales budget	Inventory budget

Which are components of the operating budget? Which are components of the financial budget?

S23-3 In a series of Starters, you will prepare parts of the master budget for Grippers, which sells its rock-climbing shoes worldwide. We will concentrate on Grippers' budget for January and February.

(continued)

Grippers expects to sell 4,000 pairs of shoes for $185 each in January, and 3,500 pairs of shoes for $220 each in February. All sales are cash only. Prepare the sales budget for January and February.

Preparing a sales budget
(Obj. 2)

S23-4 In Starter 23-3, Grippers expects cost of goods sold to average 65% of sales revenue, and the company expects to sell 4,300 pairs of shoes in March for $240 each. Grippers' target ending inventory is $10,000 plus 50% of the next month's cost of goods sold. Use this information and the sales budget from Starter 23-3 to prepare Grippers' inventory, purchases, and cost of goods sold budget for January and February.

Preparing a purchases, cost of goods sold, and inventory budget
(Obj. 2)

S23-5 Turn to the Whitewater Sporting Goods example on pages 944–954. Suppose June sales are expected to be $40,000 rather than $60,000. Revise Whitewater's sales budget.

What other components of Whitewater's master budget would be affected by this change in the sales budget?

Preparing a sales budget
(Obj. 2, 4)

S23-6 Refer to the original Whitewater Sporting Goods example on pages 944–954. Suppose cost of goods sold averages 75% of sales rather than 70%. Revise Whitewater's inventory, purchases, and cost of goods sold budget for April and May.

What other components of Whitewater's master budget would be affected by the change in the budgeted cost of goods sold?

Preparing a purchases, cost of goods sold, and inventory budget
(Obj. 2, 4)

S23-7 Turn to the original Whitewater Sporting Goods example on pages 944–954. Suppose 70% of sales are cash and 30% are credit. Revise Whitewater's sales budget and budgeted cash collections from customers for April and May.

Preparing a sales budget and cash collections budget
(Obj. 2, 3, 4)

S23-8 Refer to the original Whitewater Sporting Goods example on pages 944–954. Suppose Whitewater pays for 60% of inventory purchases in the month of the purchase and 40% during the next month. Revise Whitewater's budgeted cash payments for purchases of inventory for April and May. (*Hint:* Assume these new percentages also apply to March purchases of $33,600 given in item 5 on page 945).

Preparing a cash payments for purchases budget
(Obj. 3, 4)

S23-9 You prepared Grippers' sales budget in Starter 23-3. Now assume that Grippers' sales are 25% cash and 75% on credit. Grippers' collection history indicates that credit sales are collected as follows:

Budgeting cash collections
(Obj. 3)

| 30% in the month of the sale | 6% two months after the sale |
| 60% in the month after the sale | 4% are never collected |

November sales totaled $391,500 and December sales were $398,250. Prepare a schedule for the budgeted cash collections for January and February.

S23-10 Refer to Starter 23-9. Grippers has $8,300 cash on hand on January 1. The company requires a minimum cash balance of $7,500. January cash collections are $548,330 (as you calculated in Starter 23-9). Total cash payments for January are $583,200. Prepare a cash budget for January. Will Grippers need to borrow cash by the end of January?

Preparing a cash budget
(Obj. 3)

S23-11 Fill in the blanks with the phrase that best completes the sentence.

Distinguishing among different types of responsibility centers
(Obj. 5)

A cost center	A responsibility center	Lower
An investment center	A revenue center	Higher
A profit center		

a. The Maintenance Department at the **San Diego Zoo** is _____.
b. The concession stand at the San Diego Zoo is _____.
c. The Menswear Department at **Bloomingdale's**, which is responsible for buying and selling merchandise, is _____.
d. A production line at a **Palm Pilot** plant is _____.
e. _____ is any segment of the business whose manager is accountable for specific activities.
f. Gatorade, a division of **Quaker Oats**, is _____.
g. The sales manager in charge of **NIKE's** northwest sales territory oversees _____.
h. Managers of cost and revenue centers are at _____ levels of the organization than are managers of profit and investment centers.

*Interpreting a responsibility accounting
performance report*
(Obj. 5)

S23-12 In Exhibit 23-20, the next to last line of the CEO's report consists entirely of expenses. Describe the kinds of expenses that would be included in this category.

*Analyzing a performance report,
management by exception*
(Obj. 5)

S23-13 Look at the performance report in Exhibit 23-20. On which variances should the manager of the Mexican sauces product line focus his efforts, according to the management by exception principle? For these variances, compute the variance as a percent of the budgeted amount, and suggest some questions the manager may want to investigate.

Not a question of blame
(Obj. 5)

S23-14 Exhibit 23-20 shows that the Mexican sauces product line had a favorable marketing expense variance. Does this favorable variance necessarily mean that the manager of the Mexican sauces line is doing a good job? Explain.

Exercises

See *www.prenhall.com/horngren*
for selected Starters, Exercises,
and Problems.

E23-1 Hanna White owns a chain of travel goods stores. Last year, her sales staff sold 10,000 suitcases at an average sale price of $150. Variable expenses were 80% of sales revenue, and the total fixed expense was $100,000. This year the chain sold more-expensive product lines. Sales were 8,000 suitcases at an average price of $200. The variable expense percentage and the total fixed expense were the same both years. White evaluates the chain manager by comparing this year's income with last year's income.

Budgeting and performance evaluation
(Obj. 1)

Prepare a performance report for this year, similar to Exhibit 23-4. How would you improve White's performance evaluation system to better analyze this year's results?

*Budgeting purchases, cost of goods sold,
and inventory*
(Obj. 2)

Student ResourceCD
spreadsheet

E23-2 Leno Inc. sells tire rims. Its sales budget for the nine months ended September 30 follows:

	Quarter Ended			
	March 31	June 30	Sep. 30	Nine-Month Total
Cash sales, 30%	$ 30,000	$ 45,000	$ 37,500	$112,500
Credit sales, 70%	70,000	105,000	87,500	262,500
Total sales, 100%	$100,000	$150,000	$125,000	$375,000

In the past, cost of goods sold has been 60% of total sales. The director of marketing and the financial vice president agree that each quarter's ending inventory should not be below $20,000 plus 10% of cost of goods sold for the following quarter. The marketing director expects sales of $220,000 during the fourth quarter. The January 1 inventory was $19,000.

Prepare an inventory, purchases, and cost of goods sold budget for each of the first three quarters of the year. Compute cost of goods sold for the entire nine-month period. (Use Exhibit 23-8 as a model.)

Budgeting quarterly income for a year
(Obj. 2)

Student ResourceCD
spreadsheet

E23-3 Wheels, Inc., is an exotic car dealership. Suppose that its Miami office projects that 20X7 quarterly sales will increase by 3% in quarter 1, by 4% in quarter 2, by 6% in quarter 3, and by 5% in quarter 4. Management expects operating expenses to be 80% of revenues during each of the first two quarters, 79% of revenues during the third quarter, and 81% during the fourth. The office manager expects to borrow $100,000 on July 1, with quarterly principal payments of $10,000 beginning on September 30 and interest paid at an annual rate of 13%. Assume that fourth-quarter 20X6 sales were $4,000,000.

Prepare a budgeted income statement for each of the four quarters of 20X7 and for the entire year. Present the 20X7 budget as follows:

Quarter 1	Quarter 2	Quarter 3	Quarter 4	Full Year

Computing cash receipts and payments
(Obj. 3)

E23-4 Aqua Pure is a distributor of bottled water. For each of items a through c, compute the amount of cash receipts or payments Aqua Pure will budget for September. The solution to one item may depend on the answer to an earlier item.

(continued)

a. Management expects to sell equipment that cost $14,000 at a gain of $2,000. Accumulated depreciation on this equipment is $7,000.

b. Management expects to sell 7,500 cases of water in August and 9,200 in September. Each case sells for $12. Cash sales average 30% of total sales, and credit sales make up the rest. Three-fourths of credit sales are collected in the month of sale, with the balance collected the following month.

c. The company pays rent and property taxes of $4,200 each month. Commissions and other selling expenses average 25% of sales. Aqua Pure pays two-thirds of commissions and other selling expenses in the month incurred, with the balance paid in the following month.

E23-5 Battery Power, a family-owned battery store, began October with $10,500 cash. Management forecasts that collections from credit customers will be $11,000 in October and $15,000 in November. The store is scheduled to receive $6,000 cash on a business note receivable in October. Projected cash payments include inventory purchases ($13,000 in October and $13,900 in November) and operating expenses ($3,000 each month).

Preparing a cash budget; sensitivity analysis
(Obj. 3, 4)

Student Resource CD

spreadsheet

Battery Power's bank requires a $10,000 minimum balance in the store's checking account. At the end of any month when the account balance dips below $10,000, the bank automatically extends credit to the store in multiples of $1,000. Battery Power borrows as little as possible and pays back loans in quarterly installments of $2,000, plus 4% interest on the entire unpaid principal. The first payment occurs three months after the loan.

Required

1. Prepare Battery Power's cash budget for October and November.

2. How much cash will Battery Power borrow in November if collections from customers that month total $12,000 instead of $15,000?

E23-6 You recently began a job as an accounting intern at Outdoor Adventures Ltd. Your first task was to help prepare the cash budget for February and March. Unfortunately, the computer with the budget file crashed, and you did not have a backup or even a hard copy. You ran a program to salvage bits of data from the budget file. After entering the following data in the budget, you may have just enough information to reconstruct the budget.

Preparing a cash budget
(Obj. 3)

Outdoor Adventures eliminates any cash deficiency by borrowing the exact amount needed from State Street Bank, where the current interest rate is 8%. Outdoor Adventures pays interest on its outstanding debt at the end of each month. The company also repays all borrowed amounts at the end of the month, as cash becomes available.

Complete the following cash budget:

Outdoor Adventures Ltd.
Cash Budget
February and March

	February	March
Beginning cash balance	$ 16,900	$?
Cash collections	?	79,600
Cash from sale of plant assets	0	1,800
Cash available	106,900	?
Cash payments:		
Purchase of inventory	$?	$41,000
Operating expenses	47,200	?
Total payments	98,000	?
(1) Ending cash balance before financing	?	25,100
Minimum cash balance desired	20,000	20,000
Cash excess (deficiency)	$?	$?
Financing of cash deficiency:		
Borrowing (at end of month)	$?	$?
Principal repayments (at end of month)	?	?
Interest expense	?	?
(2) Total effects of financing	?	?
Ending cash balance (1) + (2)	$?	$?

Preparing a budgeted balance sheet
(Obj. 3)

E23-7 Use the following to prepare a budgeted balance sheet for Marine.com at March 31, 20X6. Show computations for the cash and owners' equity amounts.

a. March 31 inventory balance, $15,000
b. March payments for inventory, $4,600
c. March payments of accounts payable and accrued liabilities, $8,200
d. March 31 accounts payable balance, $4,300
e. February 28 furniture and fixtures balance, $34,800; accumulated depreciation balance, $29,870
f. February 28 owners' equity, $26,700

g. March depreciation expense, $600
h. Cost of goods sold, 60% of sales
i. Other March expenses, including income tax, total $5,000; paid in cash
j. February 28 cash balance, $11,400
k. March budgeted sales, $12,200
l. March 31 accounts receivable balance, one-fourth of March sales
m. March cash receipts, $14,300

Identifying different types of responsibility centers
(Obj. 5)

E23-8 Identify each responsibility center as a cost center, a revenue center, a profit center, or an investment center.

a. The bakery department of a **Publix** supermarket reports income for the current year.
b. **Pace Foods** is a subsidiary of **Campbell Soup Company**.
c. The personnel department of **State Farm Insurance Companies** prepares its budget and subsequent performance report on the basis of its expected expenses for the year.
d. The shopping section of **Burpee.com** reports both revenues and expenses.
e. Burpee.com's investor relations Web site provides operating and financial information to investors and other interested parties.
f. The manager of a **BP** service station is evaluated based on the station's revenues and expenses.
g. A charter airline records revenues and expenses for each airplane each month. The airplane's performance report shows its ratio of operating income to average book value.
h. The manager of the southwest sales territory is evaluated based on a comparison of current period sales against budgeted sales.

Using responsibility accounting to evaluate profit centers
(Obj. 5)

E23-9 InTouch is a Seattle company that sells cell phones and PDAs on the Web. InTouch has assistant managers for its digital and video cell phone operations. These assistant managers report to the manager of the total cell phone product line, who with the manager of PDAs reports to the manager for all sales of hand-held devices, Beth Beverly. Beverly received the following data for November operations:

	Cell Phones		
	Digital	**Video**	**PDAs**
Revenues, budget	$204,000	$800,000	$300,000
Expenses, budget	140,000	390,000	225,000
Revenues, actual	214,000	840,000	290,000
Expenses, actual	135,000	400,000	230,000

Arrange the data in a performance report similar to Exhibit 23-20. Show November results, in thousands of dollars, for digital cell phones, for the total cell phone product line, and for all devices. Should Beverly investigate the performance of digital cell phone operations?

Problems

(Group A)

Budgeting income for two months
(Obj. 2)

P23-1A The budget committee of Vinning Office Supply Co. has assembled the following data. As the business manager, you must prepare the budgeted income statements for May and June 20X6.

a. Sales in April were $42,100. You forecast that monthly sales will increase 2.0% in May and 2.4% in June.

(continued)

b. Vinning maintains inventory of $9,000 plus 25% of sales budgeted for the following month. Monthly purchases average 50% of sales revenues in that same month. Actual inventory on April 30 is $14,000. Sales budgeted for July are $42,400.

c. Monthly salaries amount to $4,000. Sales commissions equal 4% of sales for that month. Combine salaries and commissions into a single figure.

d. Other monthly expenses are:

Rent expense............	$3,000, paid as incurred
Depreciation expense....	$ 600
Insurance expense	$ 200, expiration of prepaid amount
Income tax.............	20% of operating income

Prepare Vinning's budgeted income statements for May and June. Show cost of goods sold computations. Round *all* amounts to the nearest $100. (Round amounts ending in $50 or more upward, and amounts ending in less than $50 downward.) For example, budgeted May sales are $42,900 ($42,100 × 1.02), and June sales are $43,900 ($42,900 × 1.024).

P23-2A Refer to Problem 23-1A. Vinning's sales are 70% cash and 30% credit. (Use the rounded sales on the last line of P23-1A.) Credit sales are collected in the month after sale. Inventory purchases are paid 50% in the month of purchase and 50% the following month. Salaries and sales commissions are also paid half in the month earned and half the next month. Income tax is paid at the end of the year.

Budgeting cash receipts and payments **(Obj. 3)**

The April 30, 20X6, balance sheet showed the following balances:

Cash	$11,000
Accounts payable................................	7,400
Salary and commissions payable....................	2,850

Required

1. Prepare schedules of (a) budgeted cash collections, (b) budgeted cash payments for purchases, and (c) budgeted cash payments for operating expenses. Show amounts for each month and totals for May and June. *Round* your computations to the nearest dollar.

2. Prepare a cash budget similar to Exhibit 23-14. If no financing activity took place, what is the budgeted cash balance on June 30, 20X6?

P23-3A Alliance Printing of Baltimore has applied for a loan. Bank of America has requested a budgeted balance sheet at April 30, 20X7, and a budgeted statement of cash flows for April. As Alliance's controller, you have assembled the following information:

Preparing a budgeted balance sheet and budgeted statement of cash flows **(Obj. 3)**

a. March 31 equipment balance, $52,400; accumulated depreciation, $41,300.

b. April capital expenditures of $42,800 budgeted for cash purchase of equipment.

c. April depreciation expense, $900.

d. Cost of goods sold, 60% of sales.

e. Other April operating expenses, including income tax, total $13,200, 25% of which will be paid in cash and the remainder accrued at April 30.

f. March 31 owners' equity, $93,700.

g. March 31 cash balance, $40,600.

h. April budgeted sales, $90,000, 70% of which is for cash. Of the remaining 30%, half will be collected in April and half in May.

i. April cash collections on March sales, $29,700.

j. April cash payments of March 31 liabilities incurred for March purchases of inventory, $17,300.

k. March 31 inventory balance, $29,600.

l. April purchases of inventory, $10,000 for cash and $36,800 on credit. Half of the credit purchases will be paid in April and half in May.

Required

1. Prepare the budgeted balance sheet for Alliance Printing at April 30, 20X7. Show separate computations for cash, inventory, and owners' equity balances.

2. Prepare the budgeted statement of cash flows for April.

3. Suppose that Alliance Printing has become aware of more efficient (and more expensive) equipment than it budgeted for purchase in April. What is the total amount of

(continued)

cash available for equipment purchases in April, before financing, if the minimum desired ending cash balance is $21,000? (For this requirement, disregard the $42,800 initially budgeted for equipment purchases.)

Preparing a budgeted balance sheet; sensitivity analysis
(Obj. 3, 4)

P23-4A Refer to Problem 23-3A. Before granting a loan to Alliance Printing, Bank of America asks for a sensitivity analysis assuming April sales are only $60,000 rather than the $90,000 originally budgeted. (While the cost of goods sold will change, assume that purchases, depreciation, and the other operating expenses will remain the same as in Problem 23-3A.)

Required

1. Prepare a revised budgeted balance sheet for Alliance Printing, showing separate computations for cash, inventory, and owners' equity balances.

2. Suppose Alliance Printing has a minimum desired cash balance of $23,000. Will the company need to borrow cash in April?

3. In this sensitivity analysis, sales declined by $33\frac{1}{3}\%$ ($30,000 ÷ $90,000). Is the decline in expenses and income more or less than $33\frac{1}{3}\%$? Explain why.

Identifying different types of responsibility centers
(Obj. 5)

P23-5A Is each of the following most likely a cost center, a revenue center, a profit center, or an investment center?

a. Shipping department of **Amazon.com**

b. Eastern district of a salesperson's territory

c. Child care department of a church or synagogue

d. Catering operation of **Sonny's BBQ** restaurant

e. Executive headquarters of the **United Way**

f. Accounts payable section of the Accounting Department at **Home Depot**

g. Proposed new office of **Coldwell Banker**, a real-estate firm

h. **Disneyland**

i. The Empire State Building in New York City

j. Branch warehouse of **Dalton Carpets**

k. Information systems department for **Habitat for Humanity**

l. Service Department of Audio Forest stereo shop

m. Investments Department of **Citibank**

n. Assembly-line supervisors at **Dell Computer**

o. American subsidiary of a Japanese manufacturer

p. Surgery unit of a privately owned hospital

q. Research and Development Department of **Cisco Systems**

r. Childrenswear department at a **Target** store

s. Typesetting Department of Northend Press, a printing company

t. Prescription Filling Department of **Drugstore.com**

u. Order-Taking Department at **L.L. Bean**

v. Personnel Department of **Goodyear Tire and Rubber Company**

w. Grounds maintenance department at Augusta National golf course

Preparing a profit center performance report for management by exception; benefits of budgeting
(Obj. 1, 5)

P23-6A Winnie's World operates a chain of pet stores in the Midwest. The manager of each store reports to the region manager, who in turn reports to headquarters in Milwaukee, Wisconsin. The *actual* income statements for the Dayton store, the Ohio region (including the Dayton store) and the company as a whole (including the Ohio region) for July 20X6 are:

	Dayton	Ohio	Companywide
Revenue......................	$148,900	$1,647,000	$4,200,000
Expenses:			
Region manager/			
headquarters office	$ —	$ 60,000	$ 116,000
Cost of materials	81,100	871,900	1,807,000
Salary expense	38,300	415,100	1,119,000
Depreciation expense	7,200	91,000	435,000
Utilities expense..............	4,000	46,200	260,000
Rent expense.................	2,400	34,700	178,000
Total expenses.................	133,000	1,518,900	3,915,000
Operating income	$ 15,900	$ 128,100	$ 285,000

(continued)

Budgeted amounts for July were as follows:

	Dayton	Ohio	Companywide
Revenue	$162,400	$1,769,700	$4,450,000
Expenses:			
Region manager/			
headquarters office	$ —	$ 65,600	$ 118,000
Cost of materials	86,400	963,400	1,972,000
Salary expense	38,800	442,000	1,095,000
Depreciation expense	7,200	87,800	449,000
Utilities expense	4,400	54,400	271,000
Rent expense	3,600	32,300	174,000
Total expenses	140,400	1,645,500	4,079,000
Operating income	$ 22,000	$ 124,200	$ 371,000

Required

1. Prepare a report for July 20X6 that shows the performance of the Dayton store, the Ohio region, and the company as a whole. Follow the format of Exhibit 23-20.

2. As the Ohio region manager, would you investigate the Dayton store on the basis of this report? Why or why not?

3. Briefly discuss the benefits of budgeting. Base your discussion on Winnie's World's performance report.

Problems

(Group B)

P23-1B Representatives of the various departments of Go Sports have assembled the following data. As the business manager, you must prepare the budgeted income statements for August and September 20X7.

Budgeting income for two months
(Obj. 2)

a. Sales in July were $196,000. You forecast that monthly sales will increase 3% in August and 2% in September.

b. Go Sports tries to maintain inventory of $50,000 plus 20% of sales budgeted for the following month. Monthly purchases average 60% of sales revenue in that same month. Actual inventory on July 31 is $90,000. Sales budgeted for October are $220,000.

c. Monthly salaries amount to $15,000. Sales commissions equal 6% of sales for that month. Combine salaries and commissions into a single figure.

d. Other monthly expenses are

Rent expense	$13,000, paid as incurred
Depreciation expense. . . .	$ 4,000
Insurance expense	$ 1,000, expiration of prepaid amount
Income tax	30% of operating income

    Prepare Go Sports' budgeted income statements for August and September. Show cost-of-goods-sold computations. Round *all* amounts to the nearest $1,000. For example, budgeted August sales are $202,000 ($196,000 × 1.03) and September sales are $206,000 ($202,000 × 1.02).

P23-2B Refer to Problem 23-1B. Go Sports' sales are 50% cash and 50% credit. (Use sales on the last two lines of P23-1B.) Credit sales are collected in the month after the sale. Inventory purchases are paid 60% in the month of purchase and 40% the following month. Salaries and sales commissions are paid three-fourths in the month earned and one-fourth the next month. Income tax is paid at the end of the year.

Budgeting cash receipts and payments
(Obj. 3)

    The July 31, 20X7 balance sheet showed the following balances:

Cash	$22,000
Accounts payable	52,000
Salaries and commissions payable	6,750

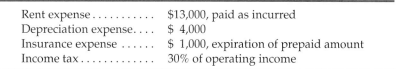

(continued)

Required

1. Prepare schedules of (a) budgeted cash collections from customers, (b) budgeted cash payments for purchases, and (c) budgeted cash payments for operating expenses. Show amounts for each month and totals for August and September. Round your computations to the *nearest dollar*.

2. Prepare a cash budget similar to Exhibit 23-14. If no financing activity took place, what is the budgeted cash balance on September 30, 20X7?

Preparing a budgeted balance sheet and budgeted statement of cash flows
(Obj. 3)

P23-3B The Music Box has applied for a loan. First Central Bank has requested a budgeted balance sheet at June 30, 20X5, and a budgeted statement of cash flows for June. As the controller (chief accounting officer) of The Music Box, you have assembled the following information:

a. May 31 equipment balance, $80,800; accumulated depreciation, $12,400.
b. June capital expenditures of $16,400 budgeted for cash purchase of equipment.
c. June depreciation expense, $400.
d. Cost of goods sold, 50% of sales.
e. Other June operating expenses, including income tax, total $34,000, 75% of which will be paid in cash and the remainder accrued at June 30.
f. May 31 owners' equity, $137,500.
g. May 31 cash balance, $50,200.
h. June budgeted sales, $85,000, 40% of which is for cash. Of the remaining 60%, half will be collected in June and half in July.
i. June cash collections on May sales, $15,300.
j. June cash payments of liabilities for May inventory purchases on credit, $8,300.
k. May 31 inventory balance, $11,900.
l. June purchases of inventory, $11,000 for cash and $37,200 on credit. Half the credit purchases will be paid in June and half in July.

Required

1. Prepare the budgeted balance sheet for The Music Box at June 30, 20X5. Show separate computations for cash, inventory, and owners' equity balances.

2. Prepare the budgeted statement of cash flows for June.

3. On the basis of this data, if you were a First Central Bank loan officer, would you grant The Music Box a loan? Give your reason.

Preparing a budgeted balance sheet; sensitivity analysis
(Obj. 3, 4)

P23-4B Refer to Problem 23-3B. Before granting a loan to The Music Box, First Central Bank asks for a sensitivity analysis, assuming that June sales are only $65,000 rather than the $85,000 originally budgeted. (While cost of goods sold will change, assume that purchases, depreciation, and the other operating expenses will remain the same as in Problem 23-3B.)

Required

1. Prepare a revised budgeted balance sheet for The Music Box, showing separate computations for cash, inventory, and owners' equity balances.

2. Suppose The Music Box has a minimum desired cash balance of $35,000. Will the company borrow cash in June?

3. How would this sensitivity analysis affect First Central's loan decision?

Identifying different types of responsibility centers
(Obj. 5)

P23-5B Is each of the following most likely a cost center, a revenue center, a profit center, or an investment center?

a. Purchasing Department of **Milliken**, a textile manufacturer
b. Quality Control Department of **Mayfield Dairies**
c. European subsidiary of **Coca-Cola**
d. Payroll Department of the University of Wisconsin
e. Lighting Department in a **Sears** store
f. Children's nursery in a church or synagogue
g. Personnel Department of **E* Trade**, the online broker
h. **igourmet.com,** an e-tailer of gourmet cheeses

(continued)

i. Service Department of an automobile dealership
j. Customer Service Department of **Procter & Gamble Co.**
k. Proposed new office of **Deutsche Bank**
l. Southwest region of **Pizza Inns, Inc.**
m. **Delta Air Lines, Inc.**
n. Order-Taking Department at **Lands' End** mail-order company
o. Editorial Department of **The Wall Street Journal**
p. A **Ford Motor Company** production plant
q. Police Department of Boston
r. **Century 21 Real Estate Co.**
s. A small pet grooming business
t. Northeast sales territory for **Boise-Cascade**
u. Different product lines of **Broyhill**, a furniture manufacturer
v. **McDonald's** restaurants under the supervision of a regional manager
w. Job superintendents of a home builder

P23-6B Etown is a chain of home electronics stores. Each store has a manager who answers to a city manager, who in turn reports to a statewide manager. The actual income statements of Store No. 23, all stores in the Dallas area (including Store No. 23), and all stores in the state of Texas (including all Dallas stores) are summarized as follows for April:

Preparing a profit center performance report for management by exception; benefits of budgeting **(Obj. 1, 5)**

	Store No. 23	Dallas	State of Texas
Sales revenue...	$43,300	$486,000	$3,228,500
Expenses:			
City/state manager's office expenses....	$ —	$ 18,000	$ 44,000
Cost of goods sold....	15,000	171,300	1,256,800
Salary expense....	4,000	37,500	409,700
Depreciation expense....	3,700	13,100	320,000
Utilities expense....	1,900	19,300	245,600
Rent expense....	700	16,600	186,000
Total expenses....	25,300	275,800	2,462,100
Operating income....	$18,000	$210,200	$ 766,400

Budgeted amounts for April were as follows:

	Store No. 23	Dallas	State of Texas
Sales revenue...	$39,000	$470,000	$3,129,000
Expenses:			
City/state manager's office expenses....	$ —	$ 19,000	$ 45,000
Cost of goods sold....	12,100	160,800	1,209,000
Salary expense....	6,000	37,900	412,000
Depreciation expense....	3,200	23,400	320,000
Utilities expense....	1,000	15,000	240,000
Rent expense....	700	15,700	181,000
Total expenses....	23,000	271,800	2,407,000
Operating income....	$16,000	$198,200	$ 722,000

Required

1. Prepare a report for April that shows the performance of Store No. 23, all the stores in the Dallas area, and all the stores in Texas. Follow the format of Exhibit 23-20.
2. As the city manager of Dallas, would you investigate Store No. 23 on the basis of this report? Why or why not?
3. Briefly discuss the benefits of budgeting. Base your discussion on Etown's performance report.

APPLY *Your Knowledge*

Decision Cases

Using a budgeted income statement
(Obj. 1)

Case 1. Donna Tse has recently accepted the position of assistant manager at Cycle World, a bicycle store in St. Louis. She has just finished her accounting courses. Cycle World's manager and owner, Jeff Towry, asks Donna to prepare a budgeted income statement for 20X6 based on the information he has collected. Tse's budget follows:

Cycle World		
Budgeted Income Statement		
For the Year Ending July 31, 20X6		
Sales revenue		$244,000
Cost of goods sold...............................		177,000
Gross profit......................................		67,000
Operating expenses:		
Salary and commission expense	$46,000	
Rent expense	8,000	
Depreciation expense	2,000	
Insurance expense..............................	800	
Miscellaneous expenses	12,000	68,800
Operating loss		(1,800)
Interest expense..................................		225
Net loss		$ (2,025)

Required

Tse does not want to give Towry this budget without making constructive suggestions for steps Towry could take to improve expected performance. Write a memo to Towry outlining your suggestions. Your memo should take the following form:

> **Date:** _____
>
> **To:** Mr. Jeff Towry, Manager
>
> Cycle World
>
> **From:** Donna Tse
>
> **Subject:** Cycle World's 20X6 budgeted income statement

Budgeting cash flows and financial statements to analyze alternatives
(Obj. 2, 3)

Case 2. Each autumn, as a hobby, Suzanne De Angelo weaves cotton placemats to sell through a local craft shop. The mats sell for $20 per set of four. The shop charges a 10% commission and remits the net proceeds to De Angelo at the end of December. De Angelo has woven and sold 25 sets each of the last two years. She has enough cotton in inventory to make another 25 sets. She paid $7 per set for the cotton. De Angelo uses a four-harness loom that she purchased for cash exactly two years ago. It is depreciated at the rate of $10 per month. The accounts payable relate to the cotton inventory and are payable by September 30.

De Angelo is considering buying an eight-harness loom so that she can weave more-intricate patterns in linen. The new loom costs $1,000; it would be depreciated at $20 per month. Her bank has agreed to lend her $1,000 at 18% interest, with $200 principal plus accrued interest payable each December 31. De Angelo believes she can weave 15 linen placemat sets in time for the Christmas rush if she does not weave any cotton mats. She predicts that each linen set will sell for $50. Linen costs $18 per set. De Angelo's supplier will sell her linen on credit, payable December 31.

(continued)

De Angelo plans to keep her old loom whether or not she buys the new loom. The balance sheet for her weaving business at August 31, 20X7, is as follows:

Suzanne De Angelo, Weaver			
Balance Sheet			
August 31, 20X7			
Current assets:		Current liabilities:	
Cash	$ 25		
Inventory of cotton.	175	Accounts payable	$ 74
	200		
Fixed assets:			
Loom	500	Owner's equity	386
Accumulated depreciation . .	(240)		
	260	Total liabilities	
Total assets.	$460	and owner's equity.	$460

Required

1. Prepare a cash budget for the four months ending December 31, 20X7, for two alternatives: weaving the placemats in cotton using the existing loom, and weaving the placemats in linen using the new loom. For each alternative, prepare a budgeted income statement for the four months ending December 31, 20X7, and a budgeted balance sheet at December 31, 20X7.

2. On the basis of financial considerations only, what should De Angelo do? Give your reason.

3. What nonfinancial factors might De Angelo consider in her decision?

Ethical Issue

→ *Link Back to Chapter 8, p. 342, for Ethics, Decision Guidelines box.* Residence Suites operates a regional hotel chain. Each hotel is operated by a manager and an assistant manager/controller. Many of the staff who run the front desk, clean the rooms, and prepare the breakfast buffet work part-time or have a second job, so turnover is high.

Budget slack
(Obj. 2, 5)

Assistant manager/controller Terry Dunn asked the new bookkeeper to help prepare the hotel's master budget. The master budget is prepared once a year and submitted to company headquarters for approval. Once approved, the master budget is used to evaluate the hotel's performance. These performance evaluations affect hotel managers' bonuses and they also affect company decisions on which hotels deserve extra funds for capital improvements.

When the budget was almost complete, Dunn asked the bookkeeper to increase amounts budgeted for labor and supplies by 15%. When asked why, Dunn responded that hotel manager Clay Murry told her to do this when she began working at the hotel. Murry explained that this budgetary cushion gave him flexibility in running the hotel. For example, since company headquarters tightly controls capital improvement funds, Murry can use the extra money budgeted for labor and supplies to replace broken televisions or pay "bonuses" to keep valued employees. Dunn initially accepted this explanation because she had observed similar behavior at the hotel where she worked previously.

Put yourself in Dunn's position. Use the ethical judgment decision guidelines in Chapter 8 (page 342) to decide how Dunn should deal with the situation.

Financial Statement Case

Budgets are an important management tool in a large company like **Amazon.com.** Refer to Amazon.com's annual report to answer the following questions:

Budgeting by quarter and segment, types of responsibility centers, performance evaluation
(Obj. 3, 5)

1. When preparing the master budget, would Amazon.com budget approximately the same sales and profit amounts for each quarter? Explain. (*Hint:* Quarterly results appear in footnote 16.)

(continued)

2. **Amazon.com** distinguishes among four segments. Identify these segments. Are these segments cost centers, revenue centers, profit centers, or investment centers? Explain.

3. Prepare a responsibility accounting performance report for 2002 similar to Exhibit 23-20. Show the results, in thousands of dollars, for North America Books, Music, DVD/Video (BMVD); North America; and the company as a whole. (In the report for the company as a whole, combine the two North American segments into a single line item.) Use the 2001 data as the budgeted amounts for 2002. (*Hint:* Business segment data are presented in footnote 15.)

4. CEO Jeff Bezos's 2002 letter to shareholders presents a positive picture of Amazon.com's performance. Does your responsibility accounting performance report support Jeff Bezos's enthusiasm? Explain, considering the results in each level of the responsibility accounting report, starting from the lowest reporting level and working up the organizational hierarchy.

Team Project

Responsibility accounting, return on investment
(Obj. 1, 2, 5)

Xellnet provides e-commerce software for the pharmaceuticals industry. Xellnet is organized into several divisions. A companywide planning committee sets general strategy and goals for the company and its divisions, but each division develops its own budget.

Rick Watson is the new division manager of wireless communications software. His division has two departments: Development and Sales. Carrie Pronai manages the 20 or so programmers and systems specialists typically employed in Development to create and update the division's software applications. Liz Smith manages the sales department.

Xellnet considers the divisions to be investment centers. To earn his bonus next year, Watson must achieve a 30% return on the $3 million invested in his division. Within the Wireless Division, Development is a cost center, while Sales is a revenue center.

Budgeting is in progress. Carrie Pronai met with her staff and is now struggling with two sets of numbers. Alternative A is her best estimate of next year's costs. However, unexpected problems can arise when writing software, and finding competent programmers is an ongoing challenge. She knows that Watson was a programmer before he earned an MBA, so he should be sensitive to this uncertainty. Consequently, she is thinking of increasing her budgeted costs (Alternative B). Her department's bonuses largely depend on whether the department meets its budgeted costs.

Xellnet
Wireless Division
Development Budget 20XX

	Alternative A	Alternative B
Salaries expense (including overtime and part-time)	$2,400,000	$2,640,000
Software expense	120,000	132,000
Travel expense	65,000	71,500
Depreciation expense	255,000	255,000
Miscellaneous expense	100,000	110,000
Total expense	$2,940,000	$3,208,500

Liz Smith is also struggling with her sales budget. Companies have made their initial investments in communications software, so it is harder to win new customers. If things go well, she believes her sales team can maintain the level of growth achieved over the last few years. This is Alternative A in the Sales Budget. However, if Smith is too optimistic, sales may fall short of the budget. If this happens, her team will not receive bonuses. Smith is therefore considering reducing the sales numbers and submitting Alternative B.

(continued)

Xellnet

Wireless Division
Sales Budget 20XX

	Alternative A	Alternative B
Sales revenue	$5,000,000	$4,500,000
Salaries expense	360,000	360,000
Travel expense	240,000	210,500

Split your team into three groups. Each group should meet separately before the entire team meets.

Required

1. The first group plays the role of Development Manager Carrie Pronai. Before meeting with the entire team, determine which set of budget numbers you are going to present to Rick Watson. Write a memo supporting your decision. Use the format shown in Decision Case 1. Give this memo to the third group before the team meeting.

2. The second group plays the role of Sales Manager Liz Smith. Before meeting with the entire team, determine which set of budget numbers you are going to present to Rick Watson. Write a memo supporting your decision. Use the format shown in Decision Case 1. Give this memo to the third group before the team meeting.

3. The third group plays the role of Division Manager Rick Watson. Before meeting with the entire team, use the memos that Pronai and Smith provided you to prepare a division budget based on the sales and development budgets. Your divisional overhead costs (additional costs beyond those incurred by the development and sales departments) are approximately $390,000. Determine whether the Wireless Division can meet its targeted 30% return on assets given the budgeted alternatives submitted by your department managers.

During the meeting of the entire team, the group playing Watson presents the division budget and considers its implications. Each group should take turns discussing its concerns with the proposed budget. The team as a whole should consider whether the division budget must be revised. The team should prepare a report that includes the division budget and a summary of the issues covered in the team meeting.

For Internet Exercises, go to the Web site www.prenhall.com/horngren.

APPENDIX *to Chapter 23*

Departmental Accounting

Responsibility centers are often called *departments*. Consider a retailer such as **Macy's, Lazarus**, or **Nordstrom**. Top managers of a department store want more information than just the net income of the store as a whole. They want to know each department's gross profit (sales minus cost of goods sold). They also usually want to know each department's operating income. These data can help identify the most profitable departments.

It is easy to measure gross profit because each department records sales and cost of goods sold. It is more difficult to measure a department's operating income (gross profit minus operating expenses). Why? Many operating expenses are indirect costs that are not directly traced to the department.

See Chapter 20, pp. 811–813 for a discussion of allocating indirect costs.

Allocating Indirect Costs

Chapter 20 explained how indirect costs are allocated to *products*. ← Indirect costs are allocated to *departments* or responsibility centers using a similar process.

- Choose an allocation base for the indirect cost
- Compute an indirect cost allocation rate:

$$\text{Indirect cost allocation rate} = \frac{\text{Total indirect costs}}{\text{Total quantity of allocation base}}$$

- Allocate the indirect cost to the department:

$$\text{Allocation of indirect costs} = \frac{\text{Quantity of allocation}}{\text{base used by department}} \times \frac{\text{Indirect cost}}{\text{allocation rate}}$$

As we noted in Chapter 20, the ideal cost allocation base is the cost driver. Suppose Macy's decides that its receiving costs are driven by the number of orders placed to purchase inventory. If 15% of the orders are for the Shoe Department and 20% are for the Menswear Department, then Macy's will allocate 15% of the Receiving Department costs to the Shoe Department and 20% to the Menswear Department. (The remaining Receiving Department costs will be allocated to other departments in proportion to the number of orders each issued.)

Exhibit 23A-1 lists common allocation bases for different indirect costs. Managers use their experience and judgment to choose these bases, but there is no single "correct" allocation base for each indirect cost.

✔ **Starter 23A-1**

Exhibit 23A-1

Bases for Allocating Indirect Costs to Departments

Cost or Expense	Base for Allocating Cost
Supervisors' salaries	Time spent, or number of employees, in each department
Equipment depreciation	Separately traced, or hours used by each department
Building depreciation, property taxes	Square feet of space
Janitorial services	Square feet of space
Advertising	Separately traced if possible; otherwise, in proportion to sales
Materials handling	Number or weight of items handled for each department
Personnel Department	Number of employees in each department
Purchasing Department	Number of purchase orders placed for each department

How to Allocate Indirect Costs to Departments: An Example

Exhibit 23A-2 shows a departmental income statement for WorldPC, a retail computer store. Let's see how the company assigns operating expenses to the store's two departments: Hardware and Software.

Salaries and Wages. WorldPC traces salespersons' salaries and department managers' salaries directly to each department.

Rent. WorldPC allocates the $600,000 rent expense based on the square feet each department occupies. The Hardware and Software departments occupy 20,000 square feet and 5,000 square feet, respectively, so WorldPC allocates rent as follows:

Rent for entire store	$600,000
Total square feet (20,000 + 5,000)	÷ 25,000
Rent per square foot..	$ 24

Hardware Department:	20,000 square feet ¥ $24 per square foot = $480,000
Software Department:	5,000 square feet ¥ $24 per square foot = 120,000
Total rent expense	= $600,000

✔ **Starter 23A-2**

WorldPC

Departmental Income Statement
Year Ended December 31, 20X9
(In Thousands)

Exhibit 23A-2

Departmental Income Statement

		Department	
	Total	Hardware	Software
Sales revenue	$10,000	$7,000	$3,000
Cost of goods sold	6,500	4,500	2,000
Gross profit.....................	3,500	2,500	1,000
Operating expenses:			
Salaries and wages expense	1,400	660	740
Rent expense...................	600	480	120
Purchasing department expense ..	48	36	12
Total operating expenses	2,048	1,176	872
Operating income	$ 1,452	$1,324	$ 128

Purchasing Department. WorldPC found that it takes just as long to complete a purchase order for inexpensive modems as for expensive notebook computers. Consequently, the company allocates the $48,000 costs of the Purchasing Department based on the number of purchase orders processed. Hardware had 300 purchase orders, and Software had 100.

Purchasing Department costs..................................	$48,000
Total number of purchase orders (300 + 100)...................	÷ 400
Cost per purchase order	$ 120

Hardware Department:	300 purchase orders × $120 per purchase order	= $36,000
Software Department:	100 purchase orders × $120 per purchase order	= 12,000
Total Purchasing Department cost		= $48,000

WorldPC's top executives can use the departmental income statements in Exhibit 23A-2 to evaluate how well each department and its manager performed in 20X9. Hardware was more profitable than Software. Hardware's profit margin (income divided by sales) was $1,324 ÷ $7,000 = 18.9%, while Software's profit margin was only $128 ÷ $3,000 = 4.3%. However, it is better to compare a department's actual results to its budget rather than to another department's results. For example, if WorldPC has just added the Software Department, performance may have exceeded expectations.

Appendix Assignments
Starters

S23A-1 Listed below are several cost drivers.

Identifying indirect cost allocation bases

Number of loads of materials moved	Number of customer complaints	Number of pages Number of square feet
Number of purchase orders	Number of inches	Number of employees
Number of shipments received	Number of machine hours	

(*continued*)

Which of these is most likely the driver for the following costs?

a. Photocopying Department costs
b. Maintenance Department costs
c. Receiving Department costs
d. Customer Service Department costs
e. Purchasing Department costs

f. Material handling costs
g. Personnel Department costs
h. Building rent and utilities
i. Newspaper advertising costs

Allocating indirect costs to departments

S23A-2 Consider the WorldPC example on page 981. Suppose the Hardware Department occupies 20,000 square feet and the Software Department occupies 10,000 square feet. How much of the $600,000 rent expense would be allocated to each department?

Exercises

Allocating indirect expenses to departments

E23A-1 Scott Manufacturing incurred the following indirect costs in April:

Indirect labor expense..............................	$18,000
Equipment depreciation expense	24,000
Marketing expense	25,200

Data for cost allocations:

	Department		
	Priming	**Welding**	**Custom Orders**
Sales revenue	$60,000	$30,000	$90,000
Indirect labor hours	500	700	300
Machine hours	550	525	125
Building square feet	11,000	3,500	1,000
Marketing expense—allocated to departments in proportion to sales.			

Required

1. Allocate Scott Manufacturing's April indirect expenses to the three departments.
2. Compute total indirect expenses for each department.

Preparing a departmental income statement

E23A-2 Handsong sells chrome and plastic harmonicas. It has two departments: Chrome and Plastic. The company's income statement for 20X6 appears as follows:

Sales revenue	$372,000
Cost of goods sold	154,000
Gross profit	218,000
Operating expenses:	
Salaries expense	$ 78,000
Depreciation expense...........................	40,000
Advertising expense	6,000
Other expenses.................................	12,000
Total operating expenses.......................	136,000
Operating income...............................	$ 82,000

Handsong sales are $206,000 of chrome harmonicas and $166,000 of plastic harmonicas. Cost of goods sold is distributed $68,000 to Chrome and $86,000 to Plastic. Salaries are traced directly to departments: Chrome, $36,000; and Plastic, $42,000. The Chrome Department accounts for 70% of advertising. Depreciation is allocated based on the warehouse square footage occupied by each department: Chrome has 20,000 square feet and Plastic has 30,000 square feet. Other expenses are allocated based on

(*continued*)

the number of employees. Each department currently employs an equal number of employees.

Required

1. Prepare departmental income statements that show revenues, expenses, and operating income for each of the two departments.
2. Which of the expenses in the departmental performance report are the most important for evaluating Handsong department managers? Give your reason.

Problem

P23A-1 The Ritz-Carlton Club, an exclusive "hotel within a hotel," provides an even more luxurious atmosphere than the hotel's regular accommodations. Access is limited to guests residing on the hotel's top floors. The Club's private lounge serves complimentary continental breakfast, afternoon snacks, and evening cocktails and chocolates. The Club has its own concierge staff that provides personal service to Club guests. Guests staying in regular accommodations do not receive complimentary snacks and beverages, nor do they have a private concierge.

Allocating indirect expenses to departments, performance evaluation

Ritz-Carlton Club floors are considered one department, and regular accommodations are considered a separate department.

Suppose the general manager of the new Ritz-Carlton hotel in St. Thomas, an island in the Caribbean, wants to know the costs of her hotel's Club Accommodations Department and Regular Accommodations Department. Housekeeping costs are allocated based on the number of occupied room-nights, utilities are allocated based on the number of cubic feet, and building depreciation is allocated based on the number of square feet. Assume each department reports the following information for March:

	Club Accommodations	Regular Accommodations
Number of occupied room-nights....	540	7,560
Cubic feet	192,000	1,440,000
Square feet.......	16,000	144,000

Required

1. Given the following (assumed) total costs, what are the costs assigned to the Club Accommodations and the Regular Accommodations Departments?

Food and beverage expense........	$ 12,000
Housekeeping expense...........	194,400
Utilities expense..............	97,920
Building depreciation expense........	480,000
Concierge staff salaries..........	15,000
Total.............	$799,320

2. What is the cost per occupied room in Club Accommodations? In Regular Accommodations?
3. Why might the general manager want to know the cost per occupied room for the Club Accommodations and the Regular Accommodations?

CHAPTER 24

Flexible Budgets and Standard Costs

TIPS CHECK YOUR RESOURCES

- Visit the www.prenhall.com/horngren **Web site** for self-study quizzes, video clips, and other resources

- Try the **Quick Check** exercise at the end of the chapter to test your knowledge

- Learn the **key terms**

- Do the **Starter** exercises keyed in the margins

- Work the **mid-** and **end-of-chapter summary problems**

- Use the **Concept Links** to review material in other chapters

- Search the **CD** for review materials by chapter or by key word

- Watch the **tutorial videos** to review key concepts

- Watch the **On Location McDonald's** video for more on flexible budgets.

LEARNING OBJECTIVES

1 Prepare a flexible budget for the income statement

2 Use the flexible budget to show why actual results differ from the static budget

3 Identify the benefits of standard costs and learn how to set standards

4 Compute standard cost variances for direct materials and direct labor

5 Analyze manufacturing overhead in a standard cost system

6 Record transactions at standard cost and prepare a standard cost income statement

How does McDonald's make sure that its 30,000 restaurants deliver quality, service, cleanliness, and value to over 46 million customers worldwide each day? By using budgets, standards, and variances. Managers budget sales for each hour and schedule just enough workers to handle the budgeted level of sales. During the day, the manager computes variances for sales (for example, actual sales minus budgeted sales) and for direct labor. If actual sales fall short of the budget, the manager can send employees home early. This helps control direct labor cost.

McDonald's

McDonald's also sets budgets and standards for direct materials. From Beijing to Miami, the standards for a regular McDonald's hamburger are the same: 1 bun, 1 hamburger patty, 1 pickle slice, 1/8 teaspoon dehydrated onion, 1/8 teaspoon mustard, and 1/3 ounce of ketchup. To control direct materials costs, the manager compares the number of, say, hamburger patties actually used with the number of patties that should have been used, given the store's actual sales.

McDonald's uses budgets, standards, and variances to control costs so prices remain low enough that customers believe McDonald's provides good *value*. McDonald's also uses standards and variances to motivate employees to focus on:

- Quality—sandwiches unsold within 10 minutes are thrown away.
- Service—customers should receive food within 90 seconds of ordering.
- Cleanliness—mystery shoppers score restaurants' cleanliness.

■ Sitemap

- **How Managers Use Flexible Budgets**
- **Actual Results versus Static Budget**
- **Standard Costing**
- **Analyzing Flexible Budget Variance**
- **Manufacturing Overhead Variances**
- **Standard Cost Accounting Systems**

- **How Managers Use Flexible Budgets**
- ☐ Actual Results versus Static Budget
- ☐ Standard Costing
- ☐ Analyzing Flexible Budget Variance
- ☐ Manufacturing Overhead Variances
- ☐ Standard Cost Accounting Systems

Student ResourceCD

flexible budget, static budget, variances

Prepare a flexible budget for the income statement

Static Budget
The budget prepared for only one level of sales volume. Also called the **master budget**.

This chapter builds on your knowledge of budgeting (from Chapter 23) to show how managers use variances to learn *why* actual results differ from budgets. Why is this important? Because you must know *why* actual costs differ from the budget to identify problems and to decide what, if any, action to take.

Suppose you buy soft drinks for a party. Your budget is $30, but you actually spend $35. To know how you can avoid exceeding your budget in the future, you must first know *why* you spent more than the $30 budget.

- If the price per can of soft drinks was higher than the price per can in the budget, then you might:
  - Find a cheaper price at a warehouse club like Costco, or watch for sales and buy soft drinks when they are on special.
  - Buy less-expensive store-brand soft drinks.
- If you bought a larger quantity of soft drinks than you budgeted, why did you need this larger quantity?
  - If more than the planned number of guests attended the party, you could restrict the invitation list.
  - If the expected number of guests attended the party but on average each guest drank more soft drinks than you budgeted, perhaps you could cut per-guest consumption by starting the party later or ending earlier, or by reducing the number of salty snacks served.
- If the budget for soft drinks was unrealistically low, in the future you may have to increase the budget.

In this chapter, you'll learn how you—like managers of companies from McDonald's to Dell Computer—can use flexible budgets, standards, and variances to pinpoint exactly *why* actual results differ from the budget. This is the first step in determining how to correct problems.

How Managers Use Flexible Budgets

Kool-Time Pools installs swimming pools. At the beginning of the year, Kool-Time managers prepared a master budget like the one in Chapter 23 for June. The master budget is a **static budget** that is prepared for *one* level of sales volume. This budget does not change after it is developed.

Exhibit 24-1 shows that Kool-Time's actual operating income is $4,000 higher than expected in the static budget. This is a $4,000 favorable variance in Kool-Time's June operating income. A **variance** is the difference between an actual amount and the budget. The variances in the third column of Exhibit 24-1 are favorable (F) if a higher actual amount increases operating income and unfavorable (U) if a higher actual amount decreases operating income. The variance for the number of pools installed is favorable because higher volume (10 rather than 8 pools) tends to increase income.

Variance
The difference between an actual amount and the budget. A variance is labeled as favorable if it increases operating income and unfavorable if it decreases operating income.

Kool-Time Pools			
Comparison of Actual Results with Static Budget			
Month Ended June 30, 20X5			

Exhibit 24-1

Actual Results versus Static Budget

	Actual Results	Static Budget	Variance
Output units (pools installed).	10	8	2 F
Sales revenue.	$121,000	$96,000	$25,000 F
Expenses	(105,000)	(84,000)	21,000 U
Operating income.	$ 16,000	$12,000	$ 4,000 F

What Is a Flexible Budget?

The report in Exhibit 24-1 is hard to analyze because the static budget is based on 8 pools, but actual results are for 10 pools. Why did the $21,000 unfavorable expense variance occur? Did workers waste materials? Did the cost of materials suddenly increase? How much of the additional expense arose because Kool-Time built 10 rather than 8 pools? Exhibit 24-1's simple comparison of actual results with the static budget does not give managers enough information to answer these questions.

Flexible budgets do answer such questions. Exhibit 24-2 shows that in contrast to the static master budget developed for a single level of sales volume, → **flexible budgets** are summarized budgets that managers can easily compute for several different volume levels.

Flexible Budget
A summarized budget that managers can easily compute for several different volume levels. Flexible budgets separate variable costs from fixed costs; it is the variable costs that put the "flex" in the flexible budget.

← *Chapter 23, pp. 943–954, discusses the master budget process.*

Exhibit 24-2

Static versus Flexible Budgets

Static budget

Flexible budget

(8 Pools) (5 Pools) (8 Pools) (11 Pools)

Expected Output Volume Only

Range of Output Volumes

Exhibit 24-3 uses flexible budgets to show how Kool-Time's revenues and expenses should vary as sales increase from 5 to 8 to 11 pools. The budgeted sale price per pool is $12,000. → The flexible budget formula for total cost is

← *See Chapter 22, pp. 898–899, to review the distinction between variable costs and fixed costs.*

$$\text{Flexible budget total cost} = \left(\begin{array}{c} \text{Number of} \\ \text{output units} \end{array} \times \begin{array}{c} \text{Variable cost} \\ \text{per output unit} \end{array} \right) + \text{Total fixed cost}$$

Exhibit 24-3

Flexible Budget

✔ Starter 24-1

Kool-Time Pools

Flexible Budget
Month Ended June 30, 20X5

	Flexible Budget per Output Unit	Output Units (Pools Installed)		
		5	8	11
Sales revenue	$12,000	$60,000	$96,000	$132,000
Variable expenses.	8,000	40,000	64,000	88,000
Fixed expenses*		20,000	20,000	20,000
Total expenses		60,000	84,000	108,000
Operating income		$ 0	$12,000	$ 24,000

*Fixed expenses are given as a total amount rather than as a cost per unit.

Budgeted total variable costs (such as the cost of materials and labor) increase at the rate of $8,000 per pool installed. It is these variable costs that put the "flex" in the flexible budget because budgeted total monthly fixed costs (such as administrative salaries and depreciation on equipment) remain constant at $20,000 throughout the range of 5 to 11 pools.

Managers develop flexible budgets like Exhibit 24-3 for any number of outputs, using a simple Excel spreadsheet or more-sophisticated Web-based budget management software. However, managers must be wary: *The flexible budget total cost formula applies only to a specific relevant range.* Why? Because total monthly fixed costs and the variable cost per pool change outside this range. Kool-Time's relevant range is 0 to 11 pools. If the company installs 12 pools, it will have to rent additional equipment, so fixed costs will exceed $20,000. Kool-Time will also have to pay workers an overtime premium, so the variable cost per pool will be more than $8,000.

Graphing the Flexible Budget

Exhibit 24-4 shows budgeted total costs for the entire relevant range of 0 to 11 pools. The flexible budget total cost line intersects the vertical axis at the amount of the total fixed cost ($20,000) Kool-Time will incur whether it installs 0 pools or 11 pools. ← The flexible budget's total cost line slopes upward at the rate of $8,000 per pool, which is Kool-Time's variable cost per pool. For example, the cost for one pool is $28,000 [(1 pool × $8,000 variable cost per pool) + $20,000 fixed cost]. But the *extra* cost of installing a second pool is only the additional $8,000 variable cost. The cost to install two pools is therefore $36,000 [(2 pools × $8,000 variable cost per pool) + $20,000 fixed cost].

The flexible budget cost line in Exhibit 24-4 follows the same principles as the cost-volume-profit graph's total cost line in Exhibit 22-7, page 907.

Exhibit 24-4

Kool-Time Pools Monthly Flexible Budget Graph

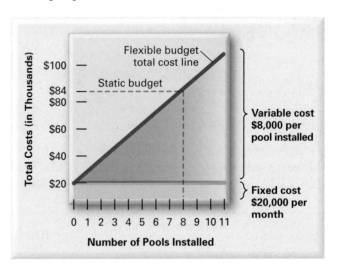

Kool-Time initially expected to install eight pools per month (at a total cost of $84,000). But managers also can use the flexible budget graph in Exhibit 24-4 to *plan costs* for anywhere from 0 to 11 pools.

At the end of the period, managers also can use the flexible budget to help control costs. They plot actual costs on the graph, as shown in Exhibit 24-5. Consider June, when Kool-Time actually installed 10 pools. The flexible budget graphs in Exhibits 24-4 and 24-5 show that *budgeted* total costs for 10 pools are

Variable costs (10 × $8,000)	$ 80,000
Fixed costs	20,000
Total costs	$100,000

June's *actual* costs, or expenses, were $105,000 (Exhibit 24-1). Consequently, Exhibit 24-5 shows that June's actual costs for 10 pools ($105,000) exceed the budget for 10 pools ($100,000). Managers use graphs of actual versus budgeted costs to see at a glance whether actual costs are

- Higher than budgeted for the actual level of output, as in April, June, and August, or
- Lower than budgeted for the actual level of output, as in May and July

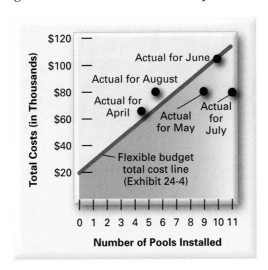

Exhibit 24-5

Kool-Time Pools Graph of Actual and Budgeted Monthly Costs

✔ **Starter 24-2**

Use the graph in Exhibit 24-5 and Kool-Time's flexible budget formula (page 987) to answer the following questions:

1. How many pools did Kool-Time install in July?
2. What were Kool-Time's actual costs in July?
3. Using Kool-Time's flexible budget formula, what is the flexible budget total cost for the month of July?
4. Is Kool-Time's variance for total costs favorable or unfavorable in July?

Answers

1. Exhibit 24-5 shows that Kool-Time installed 11 pools in July.
2. Exhibit 24-5 shows that Kool-Time's actual costs in July were about $80,000.
3. Using Kool-Time's flexible budget total cost formula:

Variable costs (11 × $8,000)	$ 88,000
Fixed costs	20,000
Total costs	$108,000

4. Kool-Time's July variance for total costs is $28,000 ($80,000 − $108,000) favorable, because actual costs are less than the budget.

*Use the flexible budget to show
why actual results differ from the
static budget*

Sales Volume Variance
The difference arising only because the
number of units actually sold differs
from the static budget units. This equals
the difference between a static budget
amount and a flexible budget amount.

The Static Budget Variance, the
Sales Volume Variance, and the
Flexible Budget Variance

Flexible Budget Variance
The difference arising because the
company actually earned more or less
revenue, or incurred more or less cost,
than expected for the actual level of
output. This equals the difference
between the actual amount and a
flexible budget amount.

✔ **Starter 24-3**

🔘 Student ResourceCD

flexible budget, flexible budget variance,
sales volume variance, static budget

Using the Flexible Budget to See Why Actual Results Differ from the Static Budget

Managers must know *why* a variance occurred to pinpoint problems and to identify corrective action. To analyze variances, managers begin by using the *flexible budget for the number of units actually sold* to divide the static budget variance into two broad categories:

■ **Sales volume variance**—arises only because the number of units actually sold differs from the static budget units.

■ **Flexible budget variance**—arises because the company actually earned more or less revenue, or incurred more or less cost, than expected for the actual level of output.

Exhibit 24-6 shows that the sales volume variance is the difference between

1. The *static* (master) budget—for the number of units *expected* to be sold (8 pools, for Kool-Time), and

2. The *flexible* budget—for the number of units *actually* sold (10 pools in June).

Consider Kool-Time Pool's performance report in Exhibit 24-7. The static budget amounts in column 5 are based on the static budget sales forecast developed at the *beginning* of the period—the eight pools Kool-Time *expected* to install. For these eight pools, Kool-Time's

■ Budgeted sales revenue is $96,000 (8 × $12,000).

■ Budgeted variable expenses (costs) are $64,000 (8 × $8,000).

■ Budgeted fixed expenses (costs) are $20,000.

(Note that this is a slightly more detailed version of Kool-Time's static budget for eight pools shown in Exhibit 24-1.)

In contrast to the static budget, which is developed *before* the period, the flexible budget used in the performance report in Exhibit 24-7 is not developed until the *end* of the period. Why? Because *flexible budgets used in performance reports are based on the actual number of outputs, which is not known until the end of the period.* For Kool-Time, the flexible budget used in the performance report (column 3 of Exhibit 24-7) is based on the 10 pools actually installed:

■ Budgeted sales revenue is $120,000 (10 × $12,000).

■ Budgeted variable expenses are $80,000 (10 × $8,000).

■ Budgeted fixed expenses are $20,000.

The only difference between the static and flexible budgets in the performance report is the number of outputs on which the budget is based (8 pools versus 10 pools). Both budgets use the same

■ Budgeted sale price per unit ($12,000 per pool)

■ Budgeted variable cost per unit ($8,000 per pool)

■ Budgeted total fixed costs ($20,000 per month)

Exhibit 24-7

Income Statement Performance Report

Kool-Time Pools
Income Statement Performance Report
Month Ended June 30, 20X5

	(1) Actual Results at Actual Prices	(2) (1)–(3) Flexible Budget Variance	(3) Flexible Budget for Actual Number of Output Units*	(4) (3)–(5) Sales Volume Variance	(5) Static (Master) Budget*
Output units (pools installed) ..	10	–0–	10	2 F	8
Sales revenue	$121,000	$1,000 F	$120,000	$24,000 F	$96,000
Variable expenses	83,000	3,000 U	80,000	16,000 U	64,000
Fixed expenses.	22,000	2,000 U	20,000	–0–	20,000
Total expenses	105,000	5,000 U	100,000	16,000 U	84,000
Operating income	$ 16,000	$4,000 U	$ 20,000	$ 8,000 F	$12,000

Flexible budget variance, $4,000 U

Sales volume variance, $8,000 F

Static budget variance, $4,000 F

*Budgeted sale price is $12,000 per pool, budgeted variable expense is $8,000 per pool, and budgeted total monthly fixed expenses are $20,000.

Holding selling price per unit, variable cost per unit, and total fixed costs constant highlights the effects of differences in sales volume—the variance in column 4. This variance is typically marketing's responsibility. Exhibit 24-7 shows that by installing two more pools than initially expected, Kool-Time's

- Sales revenue should increase from $96,000 (8 × $12,000) to $120,000 (10 × $12,000)—a $24,000 favorable sales volume variance.

- Variable costs should increase from $64,000 (8 × $8,000) to $80,000 (10 × $8,000)—a $16,000 unfavorable sales volume variance.

Budgeted total fixed expenses are unaffected because 8 pools and 10 pools are within the relevant range where fixed expenses total $20,000 (0 to 11 pools). Consequently, installing two more pools should increase operating income by $8,000 ($24,000 F – $16,000 U). So Kool-Time's June sales volume variance is $8,000 F.

Who is responsible for sales volume variance?

Sales Volume
Actual   10
Budgeted 8

Answer: Marketing

When is there a sales volume variance for fixed expenses?

Answer: Only when the number of units actually sold falls within a different relevant range than the static budget sales volume. When actual and expected number of units sold fall in the same relevant range, there is no sales volume variance for fixed expenses.

Stop & Think

✔ Starter 24-4

✔ Starter 24-5

Exhibits 24-6 and 24-7 show that the second piece of the static budget variance is the flexible budget variance—the difference between

- Actual amounts (column 1 in Exhibit 24-7) and
- Flexible budget amounts that should have been incurred *for the actual number of output units* (column 3 in Exhibit 24-7)

Answer: Marketing

Answer: Purchasing, Production, HR

Kool-Time actually incurred $83,000 of variable costs to install the 10 pools. This is $3,000 more than the $80,000 (10 pools × $8,000 per pool) budgeted variable cost for 10 pools. The company also spent $2,000 more than budgeted on fixed expenses ($22,000 – $20,000). Consequently, the flexible budget variance for total expenses is $5,000 unfavorable ($3,000 U + $2,000 U). That is, Kool-Time spent $5,000 more than expected for installing 10 pools.

Exhibit 24-7 shows there is also a flexible budget variance for sales revenue. Kool-Time actually received $121,000 for installing 10 pools, which is $1,000 more than the $120,000 flexible budget sales revenue for 10 pools (10 pools × $12,000). This $1,000 sales revenue price variance means the average sale price was $12,100 per pool ($121,000 ÷ 10 pools), which is $100 higher than the budgeted sale price of $12,000 per pool.

How would Kool-Time's managers use these variances? The favorable sales volume variance reveals that strong sales should have increased Kool-Time's income by $8,000. And the sales staff increased sales without discounting prices: The favorable $1,000 sales revenue flexible budget variance shows that the sale price was on average *higher* than budgeted. These favorable variances on the quantity of pools sold (the $8,000 favorable sales volume variance) and the sale price per pool (the $1,000 favorable sales revenue price variance) suggest that Kool-Time's marketing staff did a better-than-expected job in selling pools and maintaining sales prices.

On the other hand, higher-than-expected expenses offset much of these favorable sales variances. Exhibit 24-7 shows a $5,000 unfavorable flexible budget variance for expenses. Management will want to find out why. The reason might be an uncontrollable increase in the cost of materials. Or higher costs might have resulted from more-controllable factors such as employees wasting materials or working inefficiently. If so, managers can take action to reduce waste or inefficiency. The second half of this chapter explains how Kool-Time's managers probe flexible budget variances to identify the reason for the cost overrun so they can decide what action to take to avoid similar overruns in the future.

Decision Guidelines

FLEXIBLE BUDGETS

You and your roommate have started a business printing T-shirts for special customer requests (for example, including school or student organization logos). How can you use flexible budgets to plan and control your costs?

Decision	Guidelines
How to estimate sales revenues, costs, and profits over the range of likely sales (output) levels?	Prepare a set of flexible budgets for different sales levels.
How to prepare a flexible budget for total costs?	$$\text{Flexible budget total cost} = \left(\text{Number of T-shirts} \times \text{Variable cost per T-shirt} \right) + \text{Fixed cost}$$
How to use budgets to help control costs?	• Graph actual costs versus flexible budget costs, as in Exhibit 24-5. • Prepare an income statement performance report, as in Exhibit 24-7.
On which output level is the budget based?	Static (master) budget—*expected* number of T-shirts, estimated before the period Flexible budget—*actual* number of T-shirts, not known until the end of the period

Decision Guidelines *(continued)*

Decision	Guidelines
Why does your actual income differ from budgeted income?	Prepare an income statement performance report comparing actual results, flexible budget for actual number of T-shirts sold, and static (master) budget, as in Exhibit 24-7.

• How much of the difference is because the actual number of T-shirts sold does not equal budgeted sales?	Compute the sales volume variance (SVV) by comparing the flexible budget with the static budget.
	• Favorable SVV—Income effect if
	   Actual number of T-shirts sold > Expected number of T-shirts sold
	• Unfavorable SVV—Income effect if
	   Actual number of T-shirts sold < Expected number of T-shirts sold

• How much of the difference occurs because actual revenues and costs are not what they should have been for the actual number of T-shirts sold?	Compute the flexible budget variance (FBV) by comparing actual results with the flexible budget.
	• Favorable FBV—Income effect if
	   Actual sales revenue > Flexible budget sales revenue
	   Actual expenses < Flexible budget expenses
	• Unfavorable FBV—Income effect if
	   Actual sales revenue < Flexible budget sales revenue
	   Actual expenses > Flexible budget expenses

What actions can you take to avoid an unfavorable sales volume variance?	• Design more-attractive T-shirts to increase demand. • Provide marketing incentives to increase number of T-shirts sold.
What actions can you take to avoid an unfavorable flexible budget variance?	• Avoid an unfavorable sales revenue price flexible budget variance by maintaining (not discounting) sales prices. • Avoid an unfavorable flexible budget variance for expenses by controlling variable expenses, such as the cost of the plain T-shirts, dye, and labor, and by controlling fixed expenses.

Excel Application Exercise

Goal: Create a spreadsheet and use it to analyze a company's flexible budget.

Scenario: After the first month of operating the T-Shirt Time printing business, you prepare a flexible budget to see how the company did versus your original expectations. When you and your roommate started the business, you expected to sell 1,000 shirts your first month, at $12 each. Your budgeted variable cost per shirt was $6, and budgeted fixed costs were $2,500. At the end of the first month, you had sold 900 shirts at $11 each. Actual variable cost per shirt was $7, and actual fixed expenses were $2,200.

Using Exhibit 24-7 as your guide, prepare an Excel spreadsheet that has two sections: one for budgeted and actual data given above, and one for T-Shirt Time's Income Statement Performance Report. When you have completed your worksheet, answer the following questions:

1. What is T-Shirt Time's sales volume variance? What does this variance mean?
2. What is T-Shirt Time's flexible budget variance? What does this variance mean?
3. How would you and your roommate use these variances?

Step-by-Step:

1. Open a new Excel spreadsheet.

2. In column A, create a bold-faced heading as follows:
   a. Chapter 24 Excel Application Exercise
   b. Flexible Budgets
   c. T-Shirt Time
   d. Today's Date
3. Two rows down, enter "Budgeted Data" in bold. Underneath this heading, create the following four rows:
   a. T-shirts expected to be sold
   b. Budgeted sales price per T-shirt
   c. Budgeted variable cost per T-shirt
   d. Budgeted fixed expenses
4. Two rows down, enter "Actual Data" in bold. Underneath this heading, create the following four rows:
   a. T-shirts actually sold
   b. Actual sales price per T-shirt
   c. Actual variable cost per T-shirt
   d. Actual fixed expenses
5. Across from each description in Budgeted Data and Actual Data, enter the values found in the exercise scenario in column B.
6. Starting two rows down from the Actual Data section, replicate the format of the income statement performance report shown in Exhibit 24-7. Make sure the report consists entirely of formulas based on the budgeted and actual data provided. Format as appropriate.
7. When finished, save your work and print a copy for your files.

CHECK YOUR RESOURCES

Exhibit 24-7 indicates that Kool-Time Pools installed 10 swimming pools during June. Now assume that Kool-Time installed 7 pools (instead of 10) and that the actual sale price averaged $12,500 per pool. Actual variable expenses were $57,400, and actual fixed expenses were $19,000.

Required

1. Prepare a revised income statement performance report using Exhibit 24-7 as a guide.
2. Show that the sum of the flexible budget variance and the sales volume variance for operating income equals the static budget variance for operating income.
3. As the company owner, which employees would you praise or criticize after you analyze this performance report?

Solution

Requirements 1 and 2

Kool-Time Pools

Income Statement Performance Report—Revised
Month Ended June 30, 20X5

	(1)	(2) (1)–(3)	(3)	(4) (3)–(5)	(5)
	Actual Results at Actual Prices	Flexible Budget Variance	Flexible Budget for Actual Number of Output Units	Sales Volume Variance	Static (Master) Budget
Output units................	7	–0–	7	1 U	8
Sales revenue	$87,500	$3,500 F	$84,000	$12,000 U	$96,000
Variable expenses	57,400	1,400 U	56,000	8,000 F	64,000
Fixed expenses..............	19,000	1,000 F	20,000	—	20,000
Total expenses	76,400	400 U	76,000	8,000 F	84,000
Operating income	$11,100	$3,100 F	$ 8,000	$ 4,000 U	$12,000

Flexible budget variance,
$3,100 F

Sales volume variance,
$4,000 U

Static budget variance,
$900 U

Requirement 3

As the company owner, you should determine the *causes* of the variances before deciding who deserves praise or criticism. It is especially important to determine who is responsible for the variance and whether the variance is due to factors the manager can control. For example, the unfavorable sales volume variance could be due to an ineffective sales staff. Or it could be due to an uncontrollable long period of heavy rain that brought work to a standstill. Similarly, the $1,000 favorable flexible budget variance for fixed expenses could be due to an employee finding a lower-cost source of rented equipment. Or the savings might have come from delaying a needed overhaul of equipment that could increase the company's costs in the long run. Smart managers use variances to raise questions and direct attention, not to fix blame.

☐ How Managers Use Flexible Budgets

☐ Actual Results versus Static Budget

■ **Standard Costing**

☐ Analyzing Flexible Budget Variance

☐ Manufacturing Overhead Variances

☐ Standard Cost Accounting Systems

Student ResourceCD

benchmarking, costs, price standard, quantity standard, standard costing

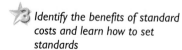

Identify the benefits of standard costs and learn how to set standards

Standard Costing

Most companies use **standard costs** to develop their flexible budgets. Think of a standard cost as a budget for a single unit. For example, Kool-Time Pool's standard variable cost is $8,000 per pool (see Exhibit 24-3). This $8,000 variable cost includes the standard cost of inputs like the direct materials, direct labor, and variable overhead costs necessary to install one pool.

Standard Cost
A budget for a single unit.

In a standard cost system, each input has both a quantity standard and a price standard. McDonald's has a standard for the amount of beef per hamburger and for the price paid per pound of beef. Kool-Time Pools has a standard for the amount of gunite (a concrete derivative) used per pool and for the price it pays per cubic foot of gunite. Let's see how managers set these price and quantity standards.

Price Standards

Accountants help managers set direct material price standards after considering early-payment discounts, freight in, and receiving costs, in addition to base purchase price. World-class businesses expect continuous reductions in direct material standard prices. → For example, Toyota sent its own engineers to one of its bumper suppliers to help the supplier cut costs. Toyota expected the supplier to pass on much of the savings in lower prices. Similarly, suppliers say Dell Computer expects them to push down the prices of their components. When one supplier walked into a meeting carrying cinnamon rolls, Michael Dell reportedly snapped, "Take those back. We don't need food. We want lower prices!"

We discuss continuous improvement in Chapter 19, page 773.

E-commerce helps managers continuously lower direct material price standards. Purchasing managers use the Internet to solicit price quotes from suppliers around the world. Dell uses the Internet to provide its major suppliers with customized virtual windows into Dell's production process. Each supplier sees Dell's production forecast and the inventory of the supplier's parts Dell currently has on hand. The supplier uses this information to decide when to ship more parts to Dell. By sharing information about its operations, Dell helps its suppliers plan their own production, purchasing, and deliveries more precisely, which helps them further cut costs.

For direct labor, accountants work with personnel or human resources managers to determine standard labor rates, taking into account payroll taxes and fringe benefits as well as the hourly wage rate.

For overhead, accountants work with production managers to estimate variable and fixed manufacturing overhead expenses. Production managers then identify an appropriate allocation base that accountants use to compute the standard (predetermined) overhead rates, as you learned in Chapter 20. →

See Chapter 20, pages 810–813, to review the computation of overhead rates.

The manager in charge of purchasing gunite for Kool-Time Pools indicates that the purchase price, net of discounts, is $1.90 per cubic foot of gunite and that delivery, receiving, and inspection costs average $0.10 per cubic foot. Kool-Time's Human Resources Department indicates that the hourly wage rate for workers is $8 and that payroll taxes and fringe benefits total $2.50 per direct labor hour. The production manager estimates that variable and fixed overhead will total $6,400 and $12,000, respectively, and that overhead should be allocated based on 3,200 estimated direct labor hours.

Required: Compute Kool-Time Pools' price standards for direct materials, direct labor, and overhead.

Answer: Direct materials price standard for gunite:

Purchase price, net of discounts	$1.90 per cubic foot
Delivery, receiving, and inspection	0.10 per cubic foot
Total standard cost per cubic foot of gunite . . .	$2.00 per cubic foot

Direct labor price (or rate) standard:

Hourly wage rate	$ 8.00 per direct labor hour
Payroll taxes and fringe benefits	2.50 per direct labor hour
Total standard cost per direct labor hour	$10.50 per direct labor hour

(continued)

Variable overhead price (or rate) standard:

$$\frac{\text{Estimated variable overhead cost}}{\text{Estimated quantity of allocation base}} = \frac{\$6,400}{3,200 \text{ direct labor hours}}$$

$$= \underline{\underline{\$2}} \text{ per direct labor hour}$$

Fixed overhead price (or rate) standard:

$$\frac{\text{Estimated fixed overhead cost}}{\text{Estimated quantity of allocation base}} = \frac{\$12,000}{3,200 \text{ direct labor hours}}$$

$$= \underline{\underline{\$3.75}} \text{ per direct labor hour}$$

Quantity Standards

Engineers and production managers set direct material and direct labor *quantity standards*, usually allowing for unavoidable waste and spoilage. World-class companies often follow the continuous improvement philosophy for setting quantity standards, just as they do for setting price standards. For example, groups of managers and workers in Westinghouse Air Brake's Chicago plant analyzed every moment in the production of the brakes. The goal was to (1) eliminate unnecessary work, (2) reduce the time and effort required for necessary work, and (3) set a time standard for the work.

To eliminate unnecessary work, the company rearranged machines in tight U-shaped cells. Workers no longer had to move parts all over the plant floor. The team conducted time-and-motion studies to streamline the physical demands of various tasks. For example, the plant installed a conveyer at waist height to minimize bending and lifting. The result? Workers slashed the standard time to produce one component by 90%.

Companies from Ritz-Carlton to Federal Express develop quantity standards based on "best practices." This is often called **benchmarking**. The *best practice* may be an internal benchmark from other plants, locations, or divisions within the company or an external benchmark from other companies. Internal benchmarks are easy to obtain, but managers can also purchase external benchmark data. For example, Riverside Hospital in Columbus, Ohio, can compare its cost of performing an appendectomy with the "best practice" cost developed by a consulting firm that compares many different hospitals' costs for the same procedure.

Benchmarking
Using standards based on "best practice." Best practice may be an internal benchmark or an external benchmark from other companies.

Kool-Time Pools' production staff indicate that each pool installed requires 975 cubic feet of gunite and that unavoidable waste and spoilage from hardened, unused gunite averages 25 cubic feet per pool. Each pool should require 400 direct labor hours to install.

Required: Compute Kool-Time's standard quantity of materials (gunite) and labor per pool.

Answer: Direct materials quantity standard:

Gunite required	975 cubic feet per pool
Unavoidable waste and spoilage	25 cubic feet per pool
Total gunite per pool installed	1,000 cubic feet per pool
Direct labor quantity standard	400 direct labor hours per pool

Exhibit 24-8 shows Kool-Time's standard costs for direct materials, direct labor, variable overhead, and fixed overhead.[1]

Exhibit 24-8

Kool-Time's Standard Materials, Labor, and Overhead Costs of Installing One Pool

Why Do Companies Use Standard Costs?

✔ Starter 24-6

U.S. surveys have shown that more than 80% of responding companies use standard costing. International surveys show that over half of responding companies in the United Kingdom, Ireland, Sweden, and Japan use standard costing. Why? Exhibit 24-9 shows five key reasons.

Exhibit 24-9   The Benefits of Standard Costs

Standard cost systems might appear to be expensive. Indeed, the company must invest in developing the standards. But standards can save data-processing costs. It is easier to value all inventories at standard costs rather than at actual costs. With standard costs, accountants avoid the expense of tracking actual unit costs and of making LIFO, FIFO, or average-cost computations.

---

[1]The direct materials ($2,000), direct labor ($4,200), and variable overhead standard costs ($800) sum to $7,000 per pool installed. Exhibit 24-3 showed that the standard variable cost per pool is $8,000. The $1,000 difference is the variable marketing and administrative expense per pool.

Accounting.com

Harley-Davidson, Inc.: Revving Up with Innovation and Cost-Cutting

For Milwaukee-based Harley Davidson, Inc., the 1980s were dark days. The market for heavyweight motorcycles was declining. At one point, the company laid off 40% of its workforce.

Fortunately, CEO and part-owner Jeffrey Bluestein "felt compelled to innovate rather than abdicate." Under Bluestein's stewardship, Harley has enjoyed 16 consecutive years of record revenue and earnings. The key has been involving suppliers in the innovation process.

Harley uses pioneering software, DFM Concurrent Costing 2.0, to investigate the cost impact of alternate manufacturing processes, thus minimizing new-product development costs. For instance, the cost of creating a part by sheet metal bending can be compared with the cost of injection molding the same part. Then Harley and the supplier can work together to cut costs of parts during the design process.

Harley-Davidson uses the software with major suppliers who provide bids accompanied by Concurrent Costing 2.0 reports on new parts based on their specific equipment. The goal is to work with vendors to reduce costs in a way that still allows them to maintain their profit margins. Cheryl Wood, a Harley-Davidson new-products cost analyst, says, "real savings come from helping suppliers reduce the cost of materials and improve the manufacturability of their designs."

Based on: Tim Stevens, "Technologies of the Year: DFM Concurrent Costing Version 2.0," *Industry Week,* December 2002, pp. 64–65. John Teresko, "Fuelled by Innovation," *Industry Week,* December 2002, pp. 52–57. Tim Stevens, "Designs in Sync," http://www.ivvaluechain.com, June 12, 2000.

Student Resource CD

efficiency variance, price variance, standard costing, variances

4 Compute standard cost variances for direct materials and direct labor

How Kool-Time Uses Standard Costing: Analyzing the Flexible Budget Variance

Let's return to our Kool-Time Pools example. Exhibit 24-7 showed that the main cause for concern at Kool-Time is the $5,000 unfavorable flexible budget variance for expenses. The first step in identifying the causes of this variance is to identify the variances in the components of the variable and fixed expenses, as shown in Panel A of Exhibit 24-10.

Study Exhibit 24-10 carefully. Panel B shows how to use the price and quantity standards developed in the Stop & Think on pages 995–996 to compute flexible budget amounts. Panel C shows how to compute actual materials and labor costs. Trace the flexible budget amounts in Panel B and the actual costs in Panel C to the computation of the flexible budget variance in Panel A.

Direct Material Variances

The largest single component of the flexible budget variance in Panel A of Exhibit 24-10 is the $3,100 unfavorable variance in direct materials. Recall that the flexible budget variance is the difference between the actual cost incurred and the flexible budget, as shown in Exhibits 24-6 and 24-7. Exhibit 24-11 on page 1000 shows that Kool-Time computes the direct materials flexible budget variance as the difference between (1) the actual amount paid for gunite and (2) the flexible budget amount (*not the static budget amount!*) that Kool-Time should have spent on gunite for the 10 pools that it actually installed.

Exhibit 24-10

Data for Standard Costing Example

Kool-Time Pools

Data for Standard Costing Example
Month of June 20X5

PANEL A—Comparison of Actual Results with Flexible Budget for 10 Swimming Pools

	Actual Results at Actual Prices	Flexible Budget for 10 Pools	Flexible Budget Variance
Variable expenses:			
Direct materials..............................	$ 23,100*	$ 20,000†	$3,100 U
Direct labor	41,800*	42,000†	200 F
Variable overhead............................	9,000	8,000†	1,000 U
Marketing and administrative expenses.........	9,100	10,000	900 F
Total variable expenses	83,000	80,000	3,000 U
Fixed expenses:			
Fixed overhead	12,300	12,000‡	300 U
Marketing and administrative expenses.........	9,700	8,000	1,700 U
Total fixed expenses........................	22,000	20,000	2,000 U
Total expenses...............................	$105,000	$100,000	$5,000 U

*See Panel C.
†See Panel B.
‡Fixed overhead was budgeted at $12,000 per month (Stop & Think on page 995).

PANEL B—Computation of Flexible Budget for Direct Materials, Direct Labor, and Variable Overhead for 10 Swimming Pools

	(1) Standard Quantity of Inputs Allowed for 10 Pools	(2) Standard Price per Unit of Input	(1) × (2) Flexible Budget for 10 Pools
Direct materials	1,000 cubic feet per pool × 10 pools = 10,000 cubic feet	$ 2.00	$20,000
Direct labor.....................	400 hours per pool × 10 pools = 4,000 hours	10.50	42,000
Variable overhead	400 hours per pool × 10 pools = 4,000 hours	2.00	8,000

PANEL C—Computation of Actual Costs for Direct Materials and Direct Labor for 10 Swimming Pools

	(1) Actual Quantity of Inputs Used for 10 Pools	(2) Actual Price per Unit of Input	(1) × (2) Actual Cost for 10 Pools
Direct materials	11,969 cubic feet actually used	$1.93 actual cost/cubic foot	$23,100
Direct labor.....................	3,800 hours actually used	$11.00 actual cost/hour	41,800

Now that Kool-Time knows it spent $3,100 more than it should have on gunite, the next question is why. Did the $3,100 unfavorable variance arise because Kool-Time:

- Did not meet the price standard because it paid too much for each cubic foot of gunite, or

- Did not meet the quantity standard because workers used more gunite than they should have used to install 10 pools?

Exhibit 24-11

Kool-Time Pools Direct Materials Flexible Budget Variance

To answer this question, Kool-Time's managers separate the flexible budget variance for direct materials into price and efficiency components, as shown in Exhibit 24-12.

Exhibit 24-12

The Relations Among Price, Efficiency, Flexible Budget, Sales Volume, and Static Budget Variances

Exhibit 24-12 emphasizes two points. First, the price and efficiency variances sum to the flexible budget variance. Second, *static budgets like column 5 of Exhibit 24-7 play no role in computing the flexible budget variance or how it is split into price and efficiency variances*. The static budget is used *only* in computing the sales volume variance—never in computing the flexible budget variance or its component price and efficiency variances.

Price Variance
Measures how well the business keeps unit prices of material and labor inputs within standards. This is computed as the difference in prices (actual price per unit minus standard price per unit) of an input multiplied by the actual quantity of the input.

DIRECT MATERIALS PRICE VARIANCE A **price variance** measures how well the business keeps unit prices of material and labor inputs within standards. As the name suggests, the price variance is the *difference in prices* (actual price per unit – standard price per unit) of an input, multiplied by the *actual quantity* of the input:

$$\text{Price variance} = \begin{pmatrix} \text{Difference between} \\ \text{actual and standard} \\ \text{prices per input unit} \end{pmatrix} \times \begin{pmatrix} \text{Actual quantity} \\ \text{of input} \end{pmatrix}$$

$$\text{Price variance} = \begin{pmatrix} \text{Actual} \\ \text{price per} \\ \text{input unit} \end{pmatrix} - \begin{pmatrix} \text{Standard} \\ \text{price per} \\ \text{input unit} \end{pmatrix} \times \begin{pmatrix} \text{Actual quantity} \\ \text{of input} \end{pmatrix}$$

✔ Starter 24-7

✔ Starter 24-8

For Kool-Time, the direct materials price variance for gunite is

$$\begin{aligned} \text{Direct materials} \\ \text{price variance} \end{aligned} = \left(\frac{\$1.93 \text{ per}}{\text{cubic foot}} - \frac{\$2.00 \text{ per}}{\text{cubic foot}} \right) \times 11,969 \text{ cubic feet}$$

$$= (\$0.07 \text{ per cubic foot}) \times 11,969 \text{ cubic feet}$$

$$= \$838 \text{ F (rounded)}$$

The $838 direct materials price variance is *favorable*, because the purchasing manager spent $0.07 *less* per cubic foot of gunite than budgeted ($1.93 actual price – $2.00 standard price).

The purchasing manager is responsible for the price variance on the *actual quantity* of materials he buys, so we multiply the $0.07 favorable price variance per cubic foot by the 11,969 cubic feet of gunite he *actually purchased*. Thus, Kool-Time's June operating income is $838 higher [($1.93 – $2.00) × 11,969] than the flexible budget because the purchasing manager paid less than the standard price for gunite. (Of course, if the purchasing manager had actually paid *more* than the $2.00 per cubic foot standard price, the direct materials price variance would have been *unfavorable*.)

DIRECT MATERIALS EFFICIENCY VARIANCE An **efficiency variance** measures whether the firm meets its quantity standards. In other words, it measures whether the quantity of materials or labor actually used to make the *actual number of outputs* is within the standard allowed for that number of outputs. The efficiency variance is the *difference in quantities* (actual quantity of input used – standard quantity of input allowed for the actual number of outputs) multiplied by the *standard price per unit* of the input.

Who is responsible for direct materials price variance?

Report
Materials Price Variance
<u>Actual</u> <u>Standard</u> <u>Var.</u>
$1.93 – $2.00 = $0.07 F

Answer: Purchasing

Efficiency Variance
Measures whether the quantity of materials or labor used to make the actual number of outputs is within the standard allowed for that number of outputs. This is computed as the difference in quantities (actual quantity of input used minus standard quantity of input allowed for the actual number of outputs) multiplied by the standard price per unit of the input.

$$\text{Efficiency variance} = \begin{pmatrix} \text{Difference between actual quantity of} \\ \text{inputs used and the standard quantity} \\ \text{of inputs that should have been used} \\ \text{for the actual number of outputs} \end{pmatrix} \times \begin{pmatrix} \text{Standard price} \\ \text{per input unit} \end{pmatrix}$$

$$\text{Efficiency variance} = \begin{pmatrix} \text{Actual} & \text{Standard} \\ \text{quantity} & - & \text{quantity} \\ \text{of input} & \text{of input} \end{pmatrix} \times \begin{pmatrix} \text{Standard price} \\ \text{per input unit} \end{pmatrix}$$

The standard quantity of inputs is the *quantity that should have been used*, or the standard quantity of inputs *allowed*, for the actual output. For Kool-Time, the *standard quantity of inputs (gunite) that workers should have used for the actual number of outputs* (10 pools) is

1,000 cubic feet of gunite per pool × 10 pools installed = 10,000 cubic feet of gunite

Thus, the direct materials efficiency variance is

$$\begin{aligned} \text{Direct materials} \atop \text{efficiency variance} &= \begin{pmatrix} 11,969 \\ \text{cubic feet} & - & 10,000 \\ \text{cubic feet} \end{pmatrix} \times \frac{\$2.00 \text{ per}}{\text{cubic foot}} \\ &= (1,969 \text{ cubic feet}) \times \$2.00 \text{ per cubic foot} \\ &= \$3,938 \text{ U} \end{aligned}$$

The $3,938 direct materials efficiency variance is *unfavorable*, because workers actually used 1,969 *more* cubic feet of gunite than they should have used to install 10 pools (11,969 actual cubic feet – 10,000 standard cubic feet).

The manager in charge of installing the pools is responsible for the variance in the quantity of the materials (gunite) used—in this case, the extra 1,969 cubic feet of gunite. However, this manager generally is *not* the person who purchases the gunite. The manager who installs the pools often has no control over the actual price paid for the gunite. Thus, we multiply the extra 1,969 cubic feet of gunite his workers used by the *standard price* of $2.00 per cubic foot to obtain the direct materials efficiency variance. Kool-Time's operating income is $3,938 lower [(11,969 – 10,000) × $2.00] than the flexible budget because workers used more gunite than they should have to install the 10 pools in June. (Of course, if workers had used *less* than the standard 10,000 cubic feet to install the 10 pools, the direct materials efficiency variance would have been *favorable*.)

Who is responsible for direct materials efficiency variance?

Materials Efficiency
Actual – Std. = Var
11,969lb. – 10,000lb. = 1,969lb. U

Answer: Pool Installation Manager

SUMMARY OF DIRECT MATERIAL VARIANCES Exhibit 24-13 summarizes how Kool-Time splits the $3,100 unfavorable direct materials flexible budget variance first identified in Panel A of Exhibit 24-10 into price and efficiency variances.

Exhibit 24-13 | Kool-Time Pools Direct Materials Variances

Kool-Time actually spent $3,100 more than it should have for gunite because:

- A good price for the gunite increased profits by $838, but
- Inefficient use of the gunite reduced profits by $3,938.

Let's review who is responsible for each of these variances and consider why each variance may have occurred.

1. Purchasing managers typically are responsible for direct materials price variances because they should know why the actual price differs from the standard price. Kool-Time's purchasing manager may have negotiated a good price for gunite, or perhaps the supplier did not increase the price of gunite as much as expected when Kool-Time developed its standard cost. In either case, the purchasing manager is in the best position to explain the favorable price variance.

2. Production managers typically are responsible for direct materials efficiency variances because they are responsible for ensuring that workers use materials efficiently and effectively. The manager in charge of installing pools should be able to explain why workers used so much more gunite than they should have used to install the 10 pools. Was the gunite of lower quality? Did workers waste materials? Did their equipment malfunction? Kool-Time's top management needs the answers to these questions to decide what corrective action to take. Should they require purchasing to buy higher quality gunite, train and supervise workers more closely to reduce waste, or improve maintenance of equipment?

Smart managers know that these variances raise questions that can help pinpoint problems. But be careful! A favorable variance does not necessarily mean that a manager did a good job, nor does an unfavorable variance mean that a manager did a bad job. Perhaps Kool-Time's purchasing manager obtained a lower price by purchasing inferior-quality gunite, and this in turn led to waste and spoilage. If so, the purchasing manager's decision hurt the company because the $838 favorable price variance is more than offset by the $3,938 unfavorable efficiency variance. This illustrates why good managers (1) use variances as a guide for investigation rather than as a simple tool to assign blame and (2) investigate favorable as well as unfavorable variances.

Direct Labor Variances

Kool-Time uses a similar approach to analyze the direct labor flexible budget variance. Using the information from Panels B and C of Exhibit 24-10, Exhibit 24-14 shows how Kool-Time computes this variance as the difference between the actual amount paid for direct labor and the flexible budget amount that Kool-Time should have spent on direct labor for 10 pools.

Exhibit 24-14

Kool-Time Pools' Direct Labor Flexible Budget Variance

Why did Kool-Time spend $200 less on labor than it should have to install 10 pools? To answer this question, Kool-Time splits the direct labor flexible budget variance into price and efficiency variances, in exactly the same way as it did for direct materials.

DIRECT LABOR PRICE VARIANCE   The direct labor price variance is computed exactly the same way as the direct materials price variance: ✔ **Starter 24-9**

$$
\text{Price variance} = \left(\begin{matrix} \text{Actual} \\ \text{price per} \\ \text{input unit} \end{matrix} - \begin{matrix} \text{Standard} \\ \text{price per} \\ \text{input unit} \end{matrix} \right) \times \begin{matrix} \text{Actual quantity} \\ \text{of input} \end{matrix}
$$

$$
= \left(\frac{\$11.00 \text{ per}}{\text{hour}} - \frac{\$10.50 \text{ per}}{\text{hour}} \right) \times 3,800 \text{ hours}
$$

$$
= (\$0.50 \text{ per hour}) \times 3,800 \text{ hours}
$$

$$
= \$1,900 \text{ U}
$$

The $1,900 direct labor price variance is *unfavorable* because the Human Resources (or Personnel) Department hired workers at $0.50 *more* per direct labor hour than budgeted ($11.00 actual price – $10.50 standard price).

The human resources manager is responsible for the price variance on the *actual quantity* of labor she hires, so we multiply the $0.50 unfavorable price variance per direct labor hour by the 3,800 hours of labor she *actually purchased*.

DIRECT LABOR EFFICIENCY VARIANCE   The direct labor efficiency variance is computed exactly the same way as the direct materials efficiency variance:

Who is responsible for direct labor price variance?

Labor Price
Actual – Std. = Var
$11.00 – $10.50 = $0.50 U

Answer: HR Department

$$
\text{Efficiency variance} = \left(\begin{matrix} \text{Actual} \\ \text{quantity} \\ \text{of input} \end{matrix} - \begin{matrix} \text{Standard} \\ \text{quantity} \\ \text{of input} \end{matrix} \right) \times \begin{matrix} \text{Standard} \\ \text{price per} \\ \text{input unit} \end{matrix}
$$

For Kool-Time, the *standard quantity of direct labor hours that workers should have used for the actual number of outputs* (10 pools) is

400 direct labor hours per pool × 10 pools installed = 4,000 direct labor hours

Who is responsible for direct labor efficiency variance?

Labor Efficiency
Actual – Std. = Var
3,800hr. – 4,000hr. = 200hr. F

Answer: Pool Installation Manager

Thus, the direct labor efficiency variance is

$$\text{Direct labor efficiency variance} = (3{,}800 \text{ hours} - 4{,}000 \text{ hours}) \times \$10.50 \text{ per hour}$$

$$= (200 \text{ hours}) \times \$10.50 \text{ per hour}$$

$$= \$2{,}100 \text{ F}$$

The \$2,100 direct labor efficiency variance is *favorable* because installers actually worked 200 *fewer* hours than they should have to install 10 pools (3,800 actual hours – 4,000 standard hours).

The manager in charge of installing the pools is responsible for the variance in the quantity of direct labor hours used—in this case, the 200 fewer hours used. Assuming that this manager is not also responsible for setting employees' pay rates (which is usually the responsibility of the human resources or personnel department), the manager in charge of installing the pools has little control over the actual price paid per labor hour. Thus, we multiply the 200 fewer direct labor hours by the *standard price* of \$10.50 per direct labor hour to obtain the direct labor efficiency variance.

SUMMARY OF DIRECT LABOR VARIANCES Exhibit 24-15 summarizes how Kool-Time splits the \$200 favorable direct labor flexible budget variance into price and efficiency variances.

Exhibit 24-15 **Kool-Time Pools Direct Labor Variances**

Actual Cost Incurred:	Standard Cost of Actual Inputs:	Flexible Budget:
Actual quantity of inputs × Actual price per input unit	Actual quantity of inputs × Standard price per input unit	Standard quantity of inputs for actual number of outputs × Standard price per input unit
3,800 × \$11.00 = \$41,800	3,800 × \$10.50 = \$39,900	4,000 × \$10.50 = \$42,000

Price variance, \$1,900 U Efficiency variance, \$2,100 F

Flexible budget variance, \$200 F

Had they looked only at the \$200 favorable direct labor flexible budget variance, Kool-Time's managers might have thought direct labor costs were close to expectations. But this illustrates the danger in ending the analysis after computing only the flexible budget variance. "Peeling the onion" to examine the price and efficiency variances yields more insight:

■ The unfavorable direct labor price variance means that Kool-Time's operating income is \$1,900 lower than expected, because the company paid its employees an average of \$11.00 per hour in June instead of the standard rate of \$10.50. But this unfavorable variance was more than offset by

■ The favorable direct labor efficiency variance. Kool-Time's operating income is \$2,100 higher than expected because workers installed 10 pools in 3,800 hours instead of the budgeted 4,000 hours.

✔ Starter 24-10

Kool-Time's top management will ask the Human Resources Department to explain the unfavorable labor price variance, and they will ask the manager in charge of installing the pools to explain the favorable labor efficiency variance. Once again, there might have been a tradeoff. Kool-Time might have hired more-experienced (and thus more highly paid) workers and traded off an unfavorable price variance for a favorable efficiency variance. If so, the strategy was successful—the overall effect on profits was favorable. This possibility reminds us that managers should be careful in using variances to evaluate performance.

You have now seen how Kool-Time analyzes flexible budget variances for direct materials and direct labor. Variances for variable marketing and administrative expenses could be calculated in the same way, but for simplicity we limit our detailed analysis to the variances in the production element of the value chain. Before leaving this topic, we need to examine three common pitfalls in computing price and efficiency variances.

Price and Efficiency Variances: Three Common Pitfalls

Here are three common pitfalls to avoid in computing price and efficiency variances for direct materials and direct labor:

1. *Static budgets like column 5 of Exhibit 24-7 play no role in computing the flexible budget variance or how it is split into the price and efficiency variances.* Exhibit 24-12 shows that the static budget is used *only* in computing the sales volume variance—never in computing the flexible budget variance or its component price and efficiency variances.

2. In the efficiency variance, the standard quantity is the *standard quantity of inputs allowed for the actual number of outputs*—the basis for the flexible budget. To compute the standard quantity of inputs allowed, first determine the actual number of outputs. For Kool-Time Pools, the actual number of outputs is 10 pools. Next, compute how many inputs should have been used to produce the actual number of outputs (10 pools). For example, each pool should use 400 direct labor hours, so the standard quantity of direct labor hours allowed for 10 pools is 10×400 hours = 4,000 hours.

Notice that the standard quantity of inputs is *not* based on the budgeted number of outputs (8 pools). That number is the basis for the static budget, which is not used to compute price and efficiency variances.

3. In the direct materials price variance, the difference in prices is multiplied by the *actual quantity* of materials. In the direct materials efficiency variance, the difference in quantities is multiplied by the *standard price* of the materials. The following explanation can help you remember this difference.
- The materials price variance is usually the responsibility of purchasing personnel; they purchase the actual quantity used, not just the amount of materials that should have been used (the standard quantity). So the price variance is the difference in prices multiplied by the *actual quantity* of materials purchased.
- The materials efficiency variance is usually the responsibility of production personnel; they have no influence over the actual price paid. So the efficiency variance is computed as the difference in quantities multiplied by the *standard* price (the price that should have been paid).

Similar logic applies to the direct labor price and efficiency variances.

Using Variances

Let's look at some practical tips for using variances.

HOW OFTEN TO COMPUTE VARIANCES?   Many firms monitor sales volume, direct material efficiency, and direct labor efficiency variances day to day or even hour to hour. McDonald's restaurants compute variances for sales and direct labor each hour. Material efficiencies are computed for each shift. The Brass Products Division of Parker Hannafin computes efficiency variances for each job the day after workers finish the job. This allows managers to ask questions about any large variances while the job is still fresh in workers' minds.

Technology like bar coding of materials and even labor (through bar-coded identity cards) and computerized data entry allows McDonald's and Parker

Hannafin to quickly compute efficiency variances. In contrast to efficiency variances, monthly computations of material and labor price variances may be sufficient if long-term contracts with suppliers or labor unions make large price variances unlikely.

USING VARIANCES TO EVALUATE EMPLOYEES' PERFORMANCE Good managers use variances to raise questions, not as simple indicators of whether employees performed well or poorly. Why should you take care in using variances to evaluate performance?

- Some variances are caused by factors managers cannot control. For example, perhaps Kool-Time used more gunite than budgeted because workers had to repair cracked foundations resulting from an earthquake.

- Managers often make trade-offs among variances. Chrysler intentionally accepted a large order for customized Dodge vans because it expected the favorable sales volume variance to more than offset the unfavorable direct labor price variance from the overtime premium and the unfavorable sales revenue price variance from extra rebates offered to the customer. Similarly, managers often trade off price variances against efficiency variances. Purchasing personnel may decide to buy higher-quality (but more expensive) direct materials to reduce waste and spoilage. The unfavorable price variance may be more than offset by a favorable efficiency variance.

- Evaluations based primarily on one variance can encourage managers to take actions that make the variance look good but hurt the company in the long run. For example, Kool-Time's managers could:
  - Purchase low-quality gunite or hire less-experienced labor to get favorable price variances
  - Use less gunite or less labor (resulting in lower-quality installed pools) to get favorable efficiency variances

How can upper management discourage such actions? One approach is to base performance evaluation on *nonfinancial* measures as well, such as quality indicators like variances in the grade of gunite or labor used, or customer satisfaction measures. For example, McDonald's discourages skimping on labor by evaluating nonfinancial measures such as the difference between actual and standard time to serve drive-through customers. If the McDonald's shift manager does not have enough workers, drive-through customers may have to wait too long to get their French fries. They may take their business to Wendy's or Burger King.

Why might an auto assembly plant experience a favorable direct labor efficiency variance? Should managers investigate favorable as well as unfavorable efficiency variances? Why?

Answer:

1. The plant may have redesigned the manufacturing process to avoid wasted motion. For example, a **Dodge** van plant in Canada significantly reduced direct labor by reorganizing production so employees reach for raw materials as needed rather than carrying arm-loads of materials across the plant floor.
2. Employees may have worked harder or more intensely than budgeted.
3. Employees may have rushed through the work and skimped on quality.

There are two reasons why managers should investigate favorable efficiency variances. First, managers want to maximize improvements that increase profits. For example, can managers capitalize on 1 and 2 to further improve labor efficiency at this or other plants? Second, managers want to prevent employees from achieving favorable variances at the expense of long-run profits through strategies like 3.

Manufacturing Overhead Variances

The total manufacturing overhead variance is the difference between:

Actual overhead cost   and   **Standard manufacturing overhead allocated to production**

Exhibit 24-10 shows that Kool-Time actually incurred $21,300 of overhead: $9,000 variable and $12,300 fixed. So the next step is to see how Kool-Time allocates overhead using its standard cost system.

Allocating Overhead in a Standard Cost System

In a standard costing system, the manufacturing overhead allocated to production is

$$\begin{array}{c} \text{Manufacturing overhead} \\ \text{allocated to production} \end{array} = \begin{array}{c} \text{Standard predetermined} \\ \text{manufacturing overhead} \\ \text{rate} \end{array} \times \begin{array}{c} \text{Standard quantity of} \\ \text{the allocation base} \\ \text{allowed for the } \textit{actual} \\ \text{number of outputs} \end{array}$$

Let's begin by computing the first term on the right-hand side, the standard predetermined overhead rate. Kool-Time allocates overhead based on direct labor hours. As explained in Chapter 20 :

$$\begin{array}{c} \text{Standard predetermined} \\ \text{manufacturing overhead rate} \end{array} = \frac{\text{Budgeted manufacturing overhead cost}}{\text{Budgeted quantity of the allocation base}}$$

Managers use predetermined overhead rates because they cannot wait until the end of the year to figure the costs of products. *Predetermined* overhead rates use data that are available at the *beginning* of the year. Thus, most companies base their rates on amounts from the static (master) budget, which is known at the beginning of the year. (The predetermined manufacturing overhead rate cannot be based on the flexible budget for actual production because the actual number of outputs is not known until the end of the year.)

The Stop & Think, pages 995–996, and Exhibit 24-16 show that Kool-Time's standard manufacturing overhead rates are:

Variable: $\dfrac{\$6,400 \text{ static budget variable manufacturing overhead}}{3,200 \text{ static budget direct labor hours}}$

= $\underline{\$2.00}$ per direct labor hour

Fixed: $\dfrac{\$12,000 \text{ static budget fixed manufacturing overhead}}{3,200 \text{ static budget direct labor hours}}$

= $\underline{\$3.75}$ per direct labor hour

Total: $2.00 variable manufacturing overhead per direct labor hour
+ 3.75 fixed manufacturing overhead per direct labor hour
$5.75 total manufacturing overhead per direct labor hour

Now that we have computed the standard predetermined manufacturing overhead rate, the next step is to identify the standard quantity of the allocation base allowed for the *actual* number of outputs. Kool-Time actually installed 10 pools during June. Thus, the standard quantity of the allocation base (direct labor hours) allowed for the actual number of outputs (10 pools) is 4,000 direct labor hours (400 direct labor hours per pool × 10 pools actually installed). Notice that 4,000 direct labor hours is the standard number of direct labor hours for the flexible budget at the actual output level of 10 pools in Exhibit 24-16 and in Exhibit 24-10 (Panel B), and for the direct labor efficiency variance (Exhibit 24-15).

☐ How Managers Use Flexible Budgets
☐ Actual Results versus Static Budget
☐ Standard Costing
☐ Analyzing Flexible Budget Variance
■ **Manufacturing Overhead Variances**
☐ Standard Cost Accounting Systems

Student Resource CD

allocation base, flexible budget variance, manufacturing overhead, production volume variance

 Analyze manufacturing overhead in a standard cost system

To review the computation of the predetermined overhead rate, see Chapter 20, page 812.

✔ **Starter 24-11**

	Kool-Time Pools	
	Budget Data for the Month Ended June 30, 20X5	

	Flexible Budget for Actual Output	**Static Budget** for Expected Output
Output units (pools installed)	10	8
Standard direct labor hours (400 hours per pool).	4,000	3,200
Budgeted manufacturing overhead cost:		
Variable	$ 8,000	$ 6,400
Fixed.	12,000	12,000
Total	$20,000	$18,400
Standard variable manufacturing overhead rate per direct labor hour		$ 6,400 ÷ 3,200 = $2.00
Standard fixed manufacturing overhead rate per direct labor hour		$12,000 ÷ 3,200 = $3.75
Standard total manufacturing overhead rate per direct labor hour		$18,400 ÷ 3,200 = $5.75

Thus, Kool-Time allocates manufacturing overhead as follows:

Kool-Time's total manufacturing overhead variance is the difference between:

Actual overhead cost (Exhibit 24-10)	and	**Standard manufacturing overhead allocated to production**
$21,300		**$23,000**

$1,700 F

Kool-Time actually spent $1,700 less on overhead than it allocated to production. To see why, Kool-Time "drills down" by splitting this total variance into two components:

- The overhead flexible budget variance
- The production volume variance

Overhead Flexible Budget Variance

Overhead Flexible Budget Variance
Shows how well management has controlled overhead costs. It is the difference between the actual overhead cost and the flexible budget overhead for the actual number of outputs.

The **overhead flexible budget variance** shows how well management has controlled overhead costs. It is computed in exactly the same way as the flexible budget variances for direct materials and direct labor. It is the difference between:

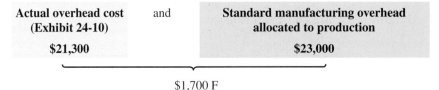

Exhibit 24-10 shows that Kool-Time actually spent $21,300 on overhead items ($9,000 variable + $12,300 fixed) to install the 10 pools. Exhibit 24-16 shows that the flexible budget overhead for the installation of 10 pools is $20,000 ($8,000 variable + $12,000 fixed). So Kool-Time's overhead flexible budget variance is the difference between

Actual overhead cost	**and**	**Flexible budget overhead for the actual number of outputs**
$21,300		$20,000

$1,300 U

Why did Kool-Time spend $1,300 more on overhead items than it should have spent to install the 10 pools in June? You can see from Exhibit 24-17 that $1,000 ($9,000 – $8,000) of the variance is due to higher-than-expected spending on variable overhead items, and the remaining $300 ($12,300 – $12,000) is due to higher spending on fixed overhead items. Kool-Time will investigate the reason for each of these variances.

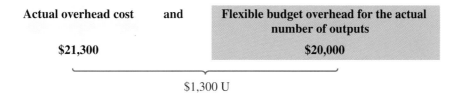 **Exhibit 24-17** | Manufacturing Overhead Variances

Kool-Time Pools

Manufacturing Overhead Variances (For the month ended June 30, 20X5)

	Actual Overhead Cost (Exhibit 24-10)	Flexible Budget Overhead for Actual Number of Outputs (Exhibits 24-10 and 24-16)	Standard Overhead Allocated to Production (Rates from Exhibit 24-16)
Variable overhead.........	$ 9,000	$ 8,000	$2.00 × 4,000 direct labor hours = $ 8,000
Fixed overhead	12,300	12,000	$3.75 × 4,000 direct labor hours = 15,000
Total overhead............	$21,300	$20,000	$5.75 × 4,000 direct labor hours = $23,000

Overhead flexible budget variance, $1,300 U

Production volume variance, $3,000 F

Total manufacturing overhead variance, $1,700 F

Most companies compile actual and budget cost information for the individual component items that make up overhead, such as indirect materials, indirect labor, utilities, and depreciation on plant and equipment. Managers drill down by comparing actual to budgeted costs for each of these individual items. For example, Kool-Time's drill-down analysis might reveal that variable overhead costs were higher than expected because water rates increased or because workers used more water in mixing the gunite than expected for installing 10 pools. Perhaps spending on fixed overhead increased because Kool-Time purchased new equipment and its depreciation expense increased. (Advanced books on cost accounting explain this drill-down variance analysis in more detail.)

✔ **Starter 24-12**

Production Volume Variance

As Exhibit 24-17 shows, the second component of the total manufacturing overhead variance is the **production volume variance**. This variance arises when

Production Volume Variance
Arises when actual production differs from expected production. It is the difference between (1) the manufacturing overhead cost in the flexible budget for actual outputs and (2) the standard overhead allocated to production.

actual production differs from expected production. You can see from Exhibit 24-17 that it is computed as the difference between:

Flexible budget overhead for actual outputs (10 pools)	and	Standard overhead allocated to (actual) production
$20,000 (Exhibits 24-16 and 24-17)		**$23,000** (Exhibit 24-17)

$3,000 F

The production volume variance is favorable whenever actual output (10 pools, for Kool-Time) exceeds expected output (8 pools, Exhibit 24-16). By installing 10 pools instead of 8, Kool-Time used its production capacity more fully than originally planned. If Kool-Time had installed 7 or fewer pools, the production volume variance would have been unfavorable because the company would have used less production capacity than expected.

Exhibit 24-17 reveals that the *variable* overhead cost in the flexible budget for actual outputs is always the same as the standard variable overhead allocated. Both are computed as:

Standard predetermined variable overhead rate	×	Standard quantity of the allocation base allowed for the actual number of outputs

The production volume variance, therefore, is due only to fixed overhead. The $3,000 favorable production volume variance arises because Kool-Time did the following:

- Budgeted fixed overhead of $12,000, but
- Allocated $15,000 of fixed overhead to the 10 pools it installed.

Why did Kool-Time allocate $3,000 more than the budgeted fixed overhead? Exhibit 24-8 shows that the standard fixed overhead cost for each pool is $1,500. Because Kool-Time installed 2 more pools than planned, it allocated $3,000 more fixed overhead (2 pools × $1,500 per pool) than expected when it set the static budget at the beginning of the period.

How did the increase in Kool-Time's "production volume," from 8 pools (the expected static budget amount) to 10 pools (actually installed) affect June's profit? Is this amount equal to the production volume variance?

Answer: Using the contribution margin income statement approach from Chapter 22:

Increase in sales revenue (2 × $12,000)	$24,000
Increase in variable expenses (2 × $8,000)	16,000
Increase in contribution margin	8,000
Increase in fixed expenses	–0–
Increase in operating income	$ 8,000

Installing two more pools increased Kool-Time's profits by $8,000, not by the $3,000 favorable "production volume variance." Thus, the production volume variance does *not* reveal how changes in production volume affect profits. The production volume variance only captures the difference between the flexible budget manufacturing overhead and the allocated manufacturing overhead. Companies use the term *production volume variance* because this variance arises only when actual production differs from expected (static budget) production.

Standard Cost Accounting Systems

Journal Entries

standard costing

Record transactions at standard
cost and prepare a standard cost
income statement

✔ **Starter 24-13**

We use Kool-Time Pools' June transactions to demonstrate standard costing in a job costing context. Because management needs to know about variances in a timely manner so they can correct any problem, Kool-Time recognizes variances from standards as soon as possible. This means that Kool-Time records direct materials price variances when materials are purchased. It also means that Work in Process Inventory is debited (swimming pools are costed) at standard input quantities and standard prices. June's entries follow:

1. Materials Inventory (11,969 × $2.00) 23,938
      Direct Materials Price Variance . . . . | 838
      Accounts Payable (11,969 × $1.93) . . . . | 23,100
      To record purchases of direct materials.

The credit to Accounts Payable is for the *actual quantity* of gunite purchased (11,969 cubic feet) costed at the *actual price* ($1.93 per cubic foot). In contrast, the debit to Materials Inventory is for the *actual quantity* purchased (11,969 cubic feet) costed at the *standard price* ($2 per cubic foot). Maintaining Materials Inventory at the *standard* price ($2.00) allows Kool-Time to record the direct materials price variance at time of purchase. Recall that Kool-Time's direct materials price variance was $838 favorable (page 1000). A favorable variance has a credit balance and is a contra expense, or a reduction in expense. Consequently, the $838 favorable direct materials price variance is a contra expense that increases Kool-Time's June profits.

2. Work in Process Inventory (10,000 × $2.00) . . 20,000
      Direct Materials Efficiency Variance 3,938
        Materials Inventory (11,969 × $2.00) . . . | 23,938
      To record use of direct materials.

Kool-Time's direct materials efficiency variance was $3,938 unfavorable (page 1001). An unfavorable variance has a debit balance, which increases expense. Kool-Time's $3,938 unfavorable direct materials efficiency variance decreases June profits. Kool-Time debits Work in Process Inventory for the *standard price ×
standard quantity* of direct materials that should have been used for the actual output of 10 pools. This maintains Work in Process Inventory at standard cost. Of course, Materials Inventory is credited for the *actual quantity* of materials put into production (11,969 cubic feet) costed at the *standard price* at which journal entry 1 entered them into the Materials Inventory account.

3. Manufacturing Wages (3,800 × $10.50) 39,900
      Direct Labor Price Variance 1,900
        Wages Payable (3,800 × $11.00) . . . . | 41,800
      To record direct labor costs incurred.

By maintaining Manufacturing Wages at the *standard* price for direct labor ($10.50), Kool-Time records the direct labor price variance at the time work is performed. Of course, Wages Payable is credited for the *actual* hours worked at the *actual* wage rate.

4. Work in Process Inventory (4,000 × $10.50) . . 42,000
        Direct Labor Efficiency Variance . . . . . . | 2,100
        Manufacturing Wages (3,800 × $10.50) | 39,900
      To assign direct labor costs.

Kool-Time debits Work in Process Inventory for the standard price × standard quantity of direct labor that should have been used for 10 pools, like direct materials entry 2. This maintains Work in Process Inventory at standard cost.

✔ Starter 24-14

5. Manufacturing Overhead.................. 21,300
      Accounts Payable, Accumulated
        Depreciation, and so on .... | 21,300
   To record actual overhead costs incurred.
   (See Exhibit 24-17.)

6. Work in Process Inventory (4,000 × $5.75)... 23,000
      Manufacturing Overhead............ | 23,000
   To allocate overhead. (See Exhibit 24-17.)

In standard costing, the overhead allocated to Work in Process Inventory is computed as the standard predetermined overhead rate × standard quantity of the allocation base that should have been used for the actual output (10 pools).

✔ Starter 24-15

7. Finished Goods Inventory 85,000
      Work in Process Inventory .... | 85,000
   To record completion of 10 pools ($20,000 of materials +
   $42,000 of labor + $23,000 of manufacturing overhead).

8. Cost of Goods Sold 85,000
      Finished Goods Inventory .... | 85,000
   To record the cost of sales of 10 pools.

9. Manufacturing Overhead................. 1,700
   Overhead Flexible Budget Variance 1,300
      Production Volume Variance .... | 3,000
   To record overhead variances and close the
   Manufacturing Overhead account. (See Exhibit 24-17.)

Entry 9 closes Manufacturing Overhead. Many companies wait until the end of the fiscal year to close this account.

Exhibit 24-18 shows selected Kool-Time accounts after posting these entries.

Standard Cost Income Statement for Management

Exhibit 24-19 shows a standard cost income statement that highlights the variances for Kool-Time's management. The statement shows sales revenue at standard, and then adds the favorable flexible budget sales revenue variance to yield actual sales revenue. Next, the statement shows the cost of goods sold at standard cost. Then the statement separately lists each manufacturing cost variance, followed by the cost of goods sold at actual cost. (Recall that since Kool-Time had no raw materials, work in process, or finished goods inventories, all the variances relate to June's sales.) At the end of the period, all the variance accounts are closed to zero out their balances. The net amount is closed to Income Summary.

The income statement shows that the net effect of all the manufacturing cost variances is $1,200 unfavorable. Thus, June's operating income is $1,200 lower than it would have been if all actual costs had been equal to standard amounts. Management can prepare statements with similar detail for research and development, design, marketing, distribution, and customer service costs, if they are subject to standard cost analysis.

Exhibit 24-18 Kool-Time Pools' Flow of Costs in Standard Costing System

Kool-Time Pools		
Standard Cost Income Statement		
Month Ended June 30, 20X5		
Sales revenue at standard (10 × $12,000)		$120,000
Flexible budget sales revenue variance		$1,000
Sales revenue at actual		121,000
Cost of goods sold at standard cost		85,000
Manufacturing cost variances:		
Direct materials price variance.	$ (838)	
Direct materials efficiency variance	3,938	
Direct labor price variance	1,900	
Direct labor efficiency variance.	(2,100)	
Manufacturing overhead flexible		
budget variance.	1,300	
Production volume variance.	(3,000)	
Total manufacturing variances.		1,200
Cost of goods sold at actual cost		86,200
Gross profit.		34,800
Marketing and administrative expenses*.		(18,800)
Operating income		$16,000

*$9,100 + $9,700 from Exhibit 24-10.

Exhibit 24-19

Standard Cost Income Statement

✔ Starter 24-16

Decision Guidelines

STANDARD COSTS AND VARIANCE ANALYSIS

Now you've seen how managers use standard costs and variances between actual and budgeted costs to identify potential problems. Variances help managers see *why* actual costs differ from the budget. This is the first step in determining how to correct problems.

　　Let's review how Kool-Time Pools made some of the key decisions in setting up and using its standard cost system.

Decision	Guidelines
How to set standards?	Historical performance data Engineering analysis/time-and-motion studies Continuous improvement standards Benchmarking
How to compute a price variance for materials or labor?	$$\text{Price variance} = \left(\begin{array}{c} \text{Actual price} \\ \text{per input unit} \end{array} - \begin{array}{c} \text{Standard price} \\ \text{per input unit} \end{array} \right) \times \begin{array}{c} \text{Actual} \\ \text{quantity of} \\ \text{input} \end{array}$$
How to compute an efficiency variance for materials or labor?	$$\text{Efficiency variance} = \left(\begin{array}{c} \text{Actual} \\ \text{quantity of} \\ \text{input} \end{array} - \begin{array}{c} \text{Standard quantity} \\ \text{of input for actual} \\ \text{number of outputs} \end{array} \right) \times \begin{array}{c} \text{Standard} \\ \text{price per} \\ \text{input unit} \end{array}$$
Who is most likely responsible for: 　Sales volume variance? 　Sales revenue flexible budget variance? 　Direct material price variance? 　Direct material efficiency variance? 　Direct labor price variance? 　Direct labor efficiency variance?	Marketing Department Marketing Department Purchasing Department Production Department Human Resources or Personnel Department Production Department
How to allocate manufacturing overhead in a standard costing system?	$$\begin{array}{c} \text{Manufacturing} \\ \text{overhead} \\ \text{allocated} \end{array} = \left(\begin{array}{c} \text{Standard} \\ \text{predetermined} \\ \text{manufacturing} \\ \text{overhead rate} \end{array} \right) \times \left(\begin{array}{c} \text{Standard quantity of} \\ \text{allocation base allowed} \\ \text{for actual outputs} \end{array} \right)$$
How to analyze over- or underallocated manufacturing overhead?	Split over- or underallocated overhead into $$\text{Flexible budget variance} = \begin{array}{c} \text{Actual} \\ \text{overhead} \end{array} - \begin{array}{c} \text{Flexible budget} \\ \text{overhead} \\ \text{for actual outputs} \end{array}$$ $$\begin{array}{c} \text{Production volume} \\ \text{variance} \end{array} = \begin{array}{c} \text{Flexible budget} \\ \text{overhead} \\ \text{for actual outputs} \end{array} - \begin{array}{c} \text{Standard overhead} \\ \text{allocated to} \\ \text{actual outputs} \end{array}$$
How to record standard costs in the accounts?	Materials Inventory: Actual quantity at standard price Work in Process Inventory (and Finished Goods Inventory and Cost of Goods Sold): Standard quantity of inputs allowed for actual outputs, at standard price of inputs

CHECK YOUR RESOURCES

Exhibit 24-10 indicates that Kool-Time Pools installed 10 swimming pools in June. Suppose Kool-Time had installed 7 pools instead of 10 and that actual expenses were

Direct materials (gunite)	7,400 cubic feet @ $2.00 per cubic foot
Direct labor	2,740 hours @ $10.00 per hour
Variable overhead	$5,400
Fixed overhead	$11,900

Required

1. Given these new data, prepare two exhibits similar to Exhibits 24-10 and 24-16. Ignore marketing and administrative expenses in your first exhibit.
2. Compute price and efficiency variances for direct materials and direct labor.
3. Compute the total variance, the flexible budget variance, and the production volume variance for manufacturing overhead.

Solution

Requirement 1

Kool-Time Pools

Revised Data for Standard Costing Example
Month of June 20X5

**PANEL A—Comparison of Actual Results with Flexible Budget
for 7 Swimming Pools**

	Actual Results at Actual Prices	Flexible Budget for 7 Pools	Flexible Budget Variance
Variable expenses:			
Direct materials	$14,800*	$14,000†	$ 800 U
Direct labor	27,400*	29,400†	2,000 F
Variable overhead	5,400	5,600†	200 F
Total variable expenses	47,600	49,000	1,400 F
Fixed expenses:			
Fixed overhead	11,900	12,000‡	100 F
Total expenses	$59,500	$61,000	$1,500 F

*See Panel C.
†See Panel B.
‡Fixed overhead was budgeted at $12,000 per month.

**PANEL B—Computation of Flexible Budget for Direct Materials,
Direct Labor, and Variable Overhead for 7 Swimming Pools**

	(1) Standard Quantity of Inputs Allowed for 7 Pools	(2) Standard Price per Unit of Input	(1) × (2) Flexible Budget for 7 Pools
Direct materials	1,000 cubic feet per pool × 7 pools = 7,000 cubic feet	$ 2.00	$14,000
Direct labor	400 hours per pool × 7 pools = 2,800 hours	10.50	29,400
Variable overhead	400 hours per pool × 7 pools = 2,800 hours	2.00	5,600

(continued)

Kool-Time Pools (continued)

Revised Data for Standard Costing Example
Month of June, 20X5

PANEL C—Computation of Actual Costs for Direct Materials and Direct
Labor for 7 Swimming Pools

	(1) Actual Quantity of Inputs Used for 7 Pools	(2) Actual Price per Unit of Input	(1) × (2) Actual Cost for 7 Pools
Direct materials.......	7,400 cubic feet actually used	$ 2.00 actual cost/cubic foot	$14,800
Direct labor	2,740 hours actually used	$10.00 actual cost/hour	27,400

Kool-Time Pools

Revised Budget Data for the Month Ended June 30, 20X5

	Flexible Budget for Actual Output	Static Budget for Expected Output
Output units (pools installed)	7	8
Standard direct labor hours (400 hours per pool)....................	2,800	3,200
Budgeted manufacturing overhead cost:		
Variable	$ 5,600*	$ 6,400
Fixed................................	12,000†	12,000
Total	$17,600	$18,400
Standard variable manufacturing overhead rate per direct labor hour.......	$ 6,400 ÷ 3,200 = $2.00	
Standard fixed manufacturing overhead rate per direct labor hour.......	$12,000 ÷ 3,200 = $3.75	
Standard total manufacturing overhead rate per direct labor hour.......	$18,400 ÷ 3,200 = $5.75	

*Flexible budget variable overhead is the standard quantity of the allocation base allowed for
actual outputs (2,800 direct labor hours = 7 pools × 400 direct labor hours per pool) multiplied
by the $2.00 standard variable manufacturing overhead rate per direct labor hour: 2,800 hours
× $2.00 per hour = $5,600.
†Budgeted fixed overhead is *fixed* within the relevant range, so flexible budget fixed overhead
is $12,000, the same as static budget fixed overhead.

Requirement 2

$$\text{Price variance} = \left(\begin{array}{c} \text{Actual price} \\ \text{per input unit} \end{array} - \begin{array}{c} \text{Standard price} \\ \text{per input unit} \end{array} \right) \times \begin{array}{c} \text{Actual} \\ \text{quantity of} \\ \text{input} \end{array}$$

Direct materials:

Price variance = ($2.00 – $2.00) × 7,400 cubic feet = $0

Direct labor:

Price variance = ($10.00 – $10.50) × 2,740 hours = $1,370 F

$$\text{Efficiency variance} = \left(\begin{array}{c} \text{Actual} \\ \text{quantity} \\ \text{of input} \end{array} - \begin{array}{c} \text{Standard} \\ \text{quantity of} \\ \text{input} \end{array} \right) \times \begin{array}{c} \text{Standard} \\ \text{price per} \\ \text{input unit} \end{array}$$

Direct materials:

$$\text{Efficiency variance} = \left(\begin{array}{c} 7,400 \\ \text{cubic feet} \end{array} - \begin{array}{c} 7,000 \\ \text{cubic feet} \end{array} \right) \times \begin{array}{c} \$2.00 \text{ per} \\ \text{cubic foot} \end{array} = \$800 \text{ U}$$

Direct labor:

$$\text{Efficiency variance} = \left(\begin{array}{c} 2,740 \\ \text{hours} \end{array} - \begin{array}{c} 2,800 \\ \text{hours} \end{array} \right) \times \begin{array}{c} \$10.50 \text{ per} \\ \text{hour} \end{array} = \$630 \text{ F}$$

Requirement 3

Total overhead variance:

Actual overhead cost ($5,400 variable + $11,900 fixed)	$17,300
Standard overhead allocated to production	
(2,800 standard direct labor hours × $5.75)	16,100
Total overhead variance	$ 1,200 U

Overhead flexible budget variance:

Actual overhead cost ($5,400 + $11,900).	$17,300
Flexible budget overhead for actual outputs ($5,600 + $12,000) . . .	17,600
Overhead flexible budget variance.	$ 300 F

Production volume variance:

Flexible budget overhead for actual outputs ($5,600 + $12,000) . . .	$17,600
Standard overhead allocated to (actual) production	
(2,800 standard direct labor hours × $5.75)	16,100
Production volume variance	$ 1,500 U

REVIEW *Flexible Budgets and Standard Costing*

Quick Check

Questions 1 through 4 rely on the following data. Digital Systems is a start-up company that makes connectors for high-speed Internet connections. The company has budgeted variable costs of $130 for each connector and fixed costs of $8,000 per month.

Digital's static budget predicted production and sales of 100 connectors in January, but the company actually produced and sold only 75 connectors at a total cost of $23,000.

1. Digital's total flexible budget cost for 75 connectors per month is
   - **a.** $17,750
   - **b.** $13,000
   - **c.** $9,750
   - **d.** $8,130

2. Digital's sales volume variance for total costs is
   - **a.** $3,250 F
   - **b.** $3,250 U
   - **c.** $5,250 F
   - **d.** $5,250 U

3. Digital's flexible budget variance for total costs is
   - **a.** $3,250 F
   - **b.** $3,250 U
   - **c.** $5,250 F
   - **d.** $5,250 U

4. Digital Systems' managers could set direct labor standards based on:
   - **a.** Past actual performance
   - **b.** Continuous improvement
   - **c.** Benchmarking
   - **d.** Time-and-motion studies
   - **e.** Any of the above

Questions 5 through 7 rely on the following data. Digital Systems has budgeted 3 hours of direct labor per connector, at a standard cost of $15 per hour. During January, technicians actually worked 210 hours completing the 75 connectors. Digital paid the technicians $15.50 per hour.

5. What is Digital's direct labor price variance for January?
   - **a.** $37.50 U
   - **b.** $105.00 U
   - **c.** $112.50 U
   - **d.** $120.00 U

6. What is Digital's direct labor efficiency variance for January?
   - **a.** $75.00 F
   - **b.** $225.00 F
   - **c.** $232.50 F
   - **d.** $1,350.00 F

7. The journal entry to record Digital's *use* of direct labor in January is

   a. Manufacturing Wages
      Direct Labor Efficiency Variance
         Work in Process Inventory
   b. Manufacturing Wages
         Direct Labor Efficiency Variance
         Work in Process Inventory
   c. Work in Process Inventory
      Direct Labor Efficiency Variance
         Manufacturing Wages
   d. Work in Process Inventory
         Direct Labor Efficiency Variance
         Manufacturing Wages

8. Digital Systems allocates manufacturing overhead based on machine hours. Each connector should require 10 machine hours. According to the static budget, Digital expected to incur:

   1,000 machine hours per month (100 connectors × 10 machine hours per connector)
   $5,250 in variable manufacturing overhead costs
   $8,000 in fixed manufacturing overhead costs

   During January, Digital actually used 825 machine hours to make the 75 connectors. Digital's predetermined standard *total* manufacturing overhead rate is
   a. $5.25 per machine hour   c. $13.25 per machine hour
   b. $8.00 per machine hour   d. $16.06 per machine hour

9. The total manufacturing overhead variance is composed of:
   a. Price variance and efficiency variance
   b. Price variance and production volume variance
   c. Efficiency variance and production volume variance
   d. Flexible budget variance and production volume variance

10. When Digital *uses* direct materials, the amount of the debit to Work in Process Inventory is based on:
    a. Actual quantity of the materials used × Actual price per unit of the materials
    b. Standard quantity of the materials allowed for the actual production of 75 connectors × Actual price per unit of the materials
    c. Standard quantity of the materials allowed for the actual production of 75 connectors × Standard price per unit of the materials
    d. Actual quantity of the materials used × Standard price per unit of the materials

Accounting Vocabulary

benchmarking (p. 996)
efficiency variance (p. 1001)
flexible budget (p. 987)
flexible budget variance (p. 990)

master budget (p. 986)
overhead flexible budget variance (p. 1008)
price variance (p. 1000)
production volume variance (p. 1009)

sales volume variance (p. 990)
standard cost (p. 994)
static budget (p. 986)
variance (p. 987)

●ASSESS *Your Progress*

See *www.prenhall.com/horngren* for selected Starters, Exercises, and Problems.

Preparing and using flexible budgets
(Obj. 1)

Starters

S24-1 Turn to the Kool-Time Pools example on pages 987 to 988.

1. Using the data from Exhibit 24-3 (page 988), develop flexible budgets for four- and nine-pool levels of output.

2. Would Kool-Time's managers use the flexible budgets you developed in requirement 1 for planning or for controlling? What specific insights can Kool-Time's managers gain from the flexible budgets you prepared in requirement 1?

S24-2 Look at Kool-Time Pools' graph of actual and budgeted monthly costs in Exhibit 24-5 on page 989.

Interpreting flexible budget graph and formula
(Obj. 1)

1. How many pools did Kool-Time install in May?
2. How much were Kool-Time's actual expenses in May?
3. Using Kool-Time's flexible budget formula, what is the flexible budget total cost for May?
4. What is Kool-Time's flexible budget variance for total costs? Is the variance favorable or unfavorable in May?

S24-3 Use your results from Starter 24-2 to explain why the actual results differ from the static budget. Prepare an income statement performance report for Kool-Time Pools for May, using Exhibit 24-7 (page 991) as a guide. Assume that the actual sale price per pool is $12,000, actual variable expenses total $61,000, and actual fixed expenses are $19,000 in May. The static budget number of pools remains eight.

Explaining why actual results differ from the static budget **(Obj. 2)**

    Explain to Kool-Time's management why May's operating income differs from the static budget operating income.

S24-4 Consider the Kool-Time Pools example on pages 986–992.

Role of fixed costs
(Obj. 1, 2)

1. What is the relevant range for the flexible budget total cost formula?
2. Explain whether Kool-Time would have a sales volume variance for fixed expenses in Exhibit 24-7 (page 991) if
   a. Kool-Time installs 14 pools per month.
   b. Kool-Time installs 7 pools per month.

S24-5 Fill in the blank with the phrase that best completes the sentence.

Static budgets and flexible budgets
(Obj. 2)

Actual number of outputs   Beginning of the period   Static budget variance
Expected number of outputs   End of the period
Sales volume variance   Flexible budget variance

a. The static budget is developed at the _____.
b. The flexible budget used in an income statement performance report is based on the

    _____.
c. The master budget is based on the _____.
d. The flexible budget used in an income statement performance report is developed at the _____.
e. The difference between actual costs and the costs that should have been incurred for the actual number of outputs is the _____.

S24-6 **Lladró** is a Spanish manufacturer of porcelain art objects. Raw materials are mixed to form clay, which is shaped into figurines. The pieces are then glazed and fired at high temperatures.

Benefits of standard costs
(Obj. 3)

    Explain how the five benefits of standard costs (Exhibit 24-9) apply to Lladró. Be as specific as possible.

S24-7 In a series of Starters, we will compute variances and record journal entries for Watermate, a manufacturer of ceramic bottles. The company has these standards:

Computing materials variances
(Obj. 4)

Direct materials (clay)............	1 pound per bottle, at a cost of $0.40 per pound
Direct labor.....................	1/5 hour per bottle, at a cost of $14 per hour
Static budget variable overhead ...	$70,000
Static budget fixed overhead......	$30,000
Static budget direct labor hours ...	10,000 hours
Static budget number of bottles ...	50,000

(continued)

Watermate allocates manufacturing overhead to production based on standard direct labor hours. Last month, Watermate reported the following actual results for the production of 70,000 bottles:

Direct materials	1.1 pound per bottle, at a cost of $0.50 per pound
Direct labor	1/4 hour per bottle, at a cost of $13 per hour
Actual variable overhead	$104,000
Actual fixed overhead	$28,000

Compute Watermate's variances for materials.

Computing materials efficiency variances
(Obj. 4)

S24-8 As explained in the chapter opening story, the standard direct materials for a regular **McDonald's** hamburger are:

1 bun	1 pickle slice	1/4 teaspoon mustard
1 hamburger patty	1/8 teaspoon dehydrated onion	1/2 ounce ketchup

Assume that a San Diego, California, McDonald's sold 500 hamburgers yesterday and actually used the following materials:

515 buns	480 pickle slices	140 teaspoons mustard
510 hamburger patties	80 teaspoons dehydrated onion	275 ounces ketchup

Compute the direct materials efficiency variances for each material, using the following standard materials prices (all amounts assumed):

Buns	$0.10 each	Dehydrated onion . .	$0.04 per teaspoon
Hamburger patties . .	0.15 each	Mustard	0.02 per teaspoon
Pickle slices	0.01 per slice	Ketchup	0.04 per ounce

Computing direct labor variances
(Obj. 4)

S24-9 Refer to the Watermate data in Starter 24-7. Compute the direct labor variances.

Interpreting materials and labor variances
(Obj. 4)

S24-10 Refer to Starters 24-7 and 24-9. For each variance, who in Watermate's organization is most likely responsible? Interpret the direct materials and direct labor variances for Watermate's management.

Standard overhead rates
(Obj. 5)

S24-11 Use the Watermate data in Starter 24-7 to compute the standard predetermined variable manufacturing overhead rate and the standard predetermined fixed manufacturing overhead rate.

Computing overhead variances **(Obj. 5)**

S24-12 Refer to the Watermate data in Starters 24-7 and 24-11. Compute the overhead variances. (Use Exhibit 24-17 as a guide.)

Materials and labor journal entries
(Obj. 6)

S24-13 Refer to the information in Starters 24-7 and 24-9. Record Watermate's direct materials and direct labor journal entries.

Overhead journal entries
(Obj. 6)

S24-14 Refer to the information in Starters 24-7 and 24-12. Record Watermate's journal entries for Manufacturing Overhead, including the entry that records the overhead variances and closes the Manufacturing Overhead account.

Journal entries for goods completed and sold
(Obj. 6)

S24-15 Refer to the information in Starters 24-7, 24-9, and 24-12 through 24-14. Watermate sold on account each of the 70,000 bottles at a sale price of $8.00 each. There were no beginning or ending inventories of any kind.

Record the journal entries for the completion and sale of the 70,000 bottles.

Standard cost income statement
(Obj. 6)

S24-16 Use the information from Starters 24-7, 24-9, and 24-12 through 24-15 to prepare a standard cost income statement for Watermate's management, using Exhibit 24-19 as a guide. Actual marketing and administrative expenses were $76,500.

Exercises

E24-1 Logiclik sells its main product, ergonomic mouse pads, for $11 each. Its variable cost is $5 per pad. Fixed expenses are $200,000 per month for volumes up to 60,000 pads. Above 60,000 pads, monthly fixed expenses are $250,000.

Prepare a monthly flexible budget for the product, showing sales, variable expenses, fixed expenses, and operating income or loss for volume levels of 40,000, 50,000, and 70,000 pads.

Preparing a flexible budget for the income statement **(Obj. 1)**

Student Resource CD
spreadsheet

E24-2 → *Link Back to Chapter 22, Exhibit 22-7 (page 907).* Graph the flexible budget total cost line for Logiclik in Exercise 24-1. Show total costs for volume levels of 40,000, 50,000, and 70,000 pads.

Graphing cost behavior **(Obj. 1)**

E24-3 Joe Boxer Company managers received the following incomplete performance report:

Completing a performance report **(Obj. 2)**

Joe Boxer Company

Income Statement Performance Report
Year Ended July 31, 20X7

	Actual Results at Actual Prices	Flexible Budget Variance	Flexible Budget for Actual Number of Output Units	Sales Volume Variance	Static (Master) Budget
Output units............	36,000	____	36,000	4,000 F	____
Sales revenue...........	$216,000	____	$216,000	$24,000 F	____
Variable expenses........	84,000	____	81,000	9,000 U	____
Fixed expenses..........	106,000	____	100,000	–0–	____
Total expenses..........	190,000	____	181,000	9,000 U	____
Operating income........	$ 26,000	____	$ 35,000	$15,000 F	____

Complete the performance report. Identify the employee group that may deserve praise and the group that may be subject to criticism. Give your reasons.

E24-4 Top managers of Manion Industries predicted 20X6 sales of 145,000 units of its product at a unit price of $8. Actual sales for the year were 140,000 units at $9.50 each. Variable expenses were budgeted at $2.20 per unit, and actual variable expenses were $2.30 per unit. Actual fixed expenses of $420,000 exceeded budgeted fixed expenses by $20,000. Prepare Manion's income statement performance report in a format similar to Exercise 24-3. What variance contributed most to the year's favorable results? What caused this variance?

Preparing an income statement performance report **(Obj. 2)**

E24-5 The following direct materials variance computations are incomplete:

Price variance = ($? – $10) × 9,600 pounds = $4,800 U

Efficiency variance = (? – 10,400 pounds) × $10 = ? F

Flexible budget variance = $?

Fill in the missing values, and identify the flexible budget variance as favorable or unfavorable.

Computing price and efficiency variances for direct materials **(Obj. 4)**

E24-6 Dock Guard, which uses a standard cost accounting system, manufactured 200,000 boat fenders during the year, using 1,450,000 feet of extruded vinyl purchased at $1.05 per foot. Production required 4,500 direct labor hours that cost $14.00 per hour. The materials standard was 7 feet of vinyl per fender, at a standard cost of $1.10 per foot. The
(continued)

Price and efficiency variances for materials and labor **(Obj. 4)**

Student Resource CD
spreadsheet

labor standard was 0.025 direct labor hour per fender, at a standard cost of $13.00 per hour. Compute the price and efficiency variances for direct materials and direct labor. Does the pattern of variances suggest Dock Guard's managers have been making trade-offs? Explain.

Journal entries
(Obj. 6)

E24-7 Make the journal entries to record the purchase and use of direct materials and direct labor in Exercise 24-6.

Explaining standard cost variances
(Obj. 4, 5)

E24-8 The managers of Viewx Co., a contract manufacturer of DVD drives, are seeking explanations for the variances in the following report. Explain the meaning of each of Viewx's materials, labor, and overhead variances.

Viewx Co.		
Standard Costing Income Statement		
Year Ended December 31, 20X7		
Sales revenue		$1,200,000
Cost of goods sold at standard cost		700,000
Manufacturing cost variances:		
Direct materials price variance	$ 8,000 F	
Direct materials efficiency variance	32,000 U	
Direct labor price variance.	24,000 F	
Direct labor efficiency variance.	10,000 U	
Manufacturing overhead flexible budget variance . .	28,000 U	
Production volume variance	8,000 F	
Total manufacturing variances		30,000
Cost of goods sold at actual cost.		730,000
Gross profit.		470,000
Marketing and administrative expenses		418,000
Operating income	$	52,000

Computing overhead variances
(Obj. 5)

E24-9 Deelux manufactures paint. The company charges the following standard unit costs to production on the basis of static budget volume of 30,000 gallons of paint per month:

Direct materials	$2.50
Direct labor.	2.00
Manufacturing overhead	1.50
Standard unit cost	$6.00

Deelux allocates overhead based on standard machine hours, and it uses the following monthly flexible budget for overhead:

	Number of Outputs (gallons)		
	27,000	30,000	33,000
Standard machine hours	2,700	3,000	3,300
Budgeted manufacturing overhead cost:			
Variable.	$13,500	$15,000	$16,500
Fixed	30,000	30,000	30,000

Deelux actually produced 33,000 gallons of paint, using 3,100 machine hours. Actual variable overhead was $16,200, and fixed overhead was $32,500. Compute the total overhead variance, the overhead flexible budget variance, and the production volume variance.

E24-10 Western Outfitters, Inc., revenue and expense information for April follows:

Preparing a standard cost income statement for management
(Obj. 6)

Sales revenue	$560,000
Cost of good sold (standard)	342,000
Direct materials price variance	2,000 F
Direct materials efficiency variance	6,000 F
Direct labor price variance	4,000 U
Direct labor efficiency variance	2,000 F
Overhead flexible budget variance	3,500 U
Production volume variance	8,000 F

Prepare a standard cost income statement for management through gross profit. Report all standard cost variances for management's use. Has management done a good or poor job of controlling costs? Explain.

Problems

(Group A)

P24-1A → *Link Back to Chapter 22, Exhibit 22-7 (page 907).* Lasting Bubbles, Inc., produces multicolored bubble solution used for weddings and other events. The company's static budget income statement for August 20X6 follows. It is based on expected sales volume of 55,000 bubble kits.

Preparing a flexible budget income statement and graphing cost behavior
(Obj. 1)

⊙Student Resource CD
spreadsheet

Lasting Bubbles, Inc.	
Static Budget Income Statement	
Month Ended August 31, 20X6	
Sales revenue	$165,000
Variable expenses:	
Cost of goods sold	63,250
Sales commissions	13,750
Utilities expense	6,050
Fixed expenses:	
Salary expense	32,500
Depreciation expense	20,000
Rent expense	11,000
Utilities expense	5,200
Total expenses	151,750
Operating income	$ 13,250

Lasting Bubbles' plant capacity is 62,500 kits. If actual volume exceeds 62,500 kits, the company must expand the plant. In that case, salaries will increase by 10%, depreciation by 15%, and rent by $6,000. Fixed utilities will be unchanged by any volume increase.

Required

1. Prepare flexible budget income statements for the company, showing output levels of 55,000, 60,000, and 65,000 kits.
2. Graph the behavior of the company's total costs.
3. Why might Lasting Bubbles' managers want to see the graph you prepared in requirement 2 as well as the columnar format analysis in requirement 1? What is the disadvantage of the graphic approach?

Preparing an income statement performance report **(Obj. 2)**

P24-2A Refer to Lasting Bubbles, Inc., of Problem 24-1A. The company sold 60,000 bubble kits during August 20X6, and its actual operating income was as follows:

(*continued*)

Lasting Bubbles, Inc.

Income Statement
Month Ended August 31, 20X6

Sales revenue	$185,000
Variable expenses:	
Cost of goods sold	$ 69,500
Sales commissions	18,000
Utilities expense	6,600
Fixed expenses:	
Salary expense	34,000
Depreciation expense	20,000
Rent expense	10,000
Utilities expense	5,200
Total expenses	163,300
Operating income	$ 21,700

Required

1. Prepare an income statement performance report for August 20X6.

2. What accounts for most of the difference between actual operating income and static budget operating income?

3. What is Lasting Bubbles' static budget variance? Explain why the income statement performance report provides Lasting Bubbles' managers with more useful information than the simple static budget variance. What insights can Lasting Bubbles' managers draw from this performance report?

Preparing a flexible budget and computing standard cost variances
(Obj. 1, 3, 4, 5)

P24-3A One System Co. assembles PCs and uses flexible budgeting and a standard cost system. One System allocates overhead based on the number of direct materials parts. The company's performance report includes the following selected data:

	Static Budget (20,000 PCs)	Actual Results (22,000 PCs)
Sales (20,000 PCs × $400)	$8,000,000	
(22,000 PCs × $420)		$9,240,000
Variable manufacturing expenses:		
Direct materials (200,000 parts @ $10.00)	2,000,000	
(214,200 parts @ $9.80)		2,099,160
Direct labor (40,000 hr @ $14.00)	560,000	
(42,500 hr @ $14.60)		620,500
Variable overhead (200,000 parts @ $4.00) . . .	800,000	
(214,200 parts @ $4.10) . . .		878,220
Fixed manufacturing expenses:		
Fixed overhead	900,000	930,000
Total cost of goods sold	4,260,000	4,527,880
Gross profit	$3,740,000	$4,712,120

Required

1. Prepare a flexible budget based on the actual number of PCs sold.

2. Compute the price variance and the efficiency variance for direct materials and for direct labor. For manufacturing overhead, compute the total variance, the flexible budget variance, and the production volume variance.

3. What is the total flexible budget variance for One System's manufacturing costs? Show how the total flexible budget variance is divided into materials, labor, and overhead variances.

4. Have One System's managers done a good job or a poor job controlling material and labor costs? Why?

5. Describe how One System's managers can benefit from the standard costing system.

P24-4A Amanda's Music manufactures harmonicas. Amanda uses standard costs to judge performance. Recently, a clerk mistakenly threw away some of the records, and Amanda has only partial data for October. She knows that the direct labor flexible budget variance for the month was $330 F and that the standard labor price was $10 per hour. A recent pay cut caused a favorable labor price variance of $0.50 per hour. The standard direct labor hours for actual October output were 5,600.

Using incomplete cost and variance information to determine the number of direct labor hours worked
(Obj. 4)

Required

1. Find the actual number of direct labor hours worked during October. First, find the actual direct labor price per hour. Then, determine the actual number of direct labor hours worked by setting up the computation of the direct labor flexible budget variance of $330 F.

2. Compute the direct labor price and efficiency variances. Do these variances suggest the manager may have made any trade-offs? Explain.

P24-5A Avanti manufactures embroidered jackets. The company prepares flexible budgets and uses a standard cost system to control manufacturing costs. The following standard unit cost of a jacket is based on the static budget volume of 14,000 jackets per month:

Computing and journalizing, standard cost variances
(Obj. 4, 5, 6)

Direct materials (3.0 sq. ft @ $4.00 per sq. ft).		$ 12.00
Direct labor (2 hours @ $9.40 per hour)		18.80
Manufacturing overhead:		
Variable (2 hours @ $0.65 per hour)	$1.30	
Fixed (2 hours @ $2.20 per hour).	4.40	5.70
Total cost per jacket.		$36.50

Data for November of the current year include the following:

a. Actual production was 13,600 jackets.
b. Actual direct materials usage was 2.70 square feet per jacket, at an actual cost of $4.15 per square foot.
c. Actual direct labor usage of 24,480 hours cost $235,008.
d. Total actual overhead cost was $79,000.

Required

1. Compute the price and efficiency variances for direct materials and direct labor.

2. Journalize the usage of direct materials and the assignment of direct labor, including the related variances.

3. For manufacturing overhead, compute the total variance, the flexible budget variance, and the production volume variance. (*Hint:* Remember that the total fixed overhead in the flexible budget equals the total fixed overhead in the static budget.)

4. Avanti's management intentionally purchased superior materials for November production. How did this decision affect the other cost variances? Overall, was the decision wise?

P24-6A Happ and Sons, Inc., makes ground covers to prevent weed growth. During May, the company produced and sold 44,000 rolls and recorded the following cost data:

Computing standard cost variances and reporting to management
(Obj. 4, 5, 6)

	Standard Unit Cost	Actual Total Cost
Direct materials:		
Standard (3 lb @ $1.10 per lb)	$3.30	
Actual (136,600 lb @ $1.05 per lb)		$143,430
Direct labor:		
Standard (0.1 hr @ $9.00 per hr)	0.90	
Actual (4,600 hr @ $8.80 per hr).		40,480
		(continued)

(*continued*)

Manufacturing overhead:
  Standard:
    Variable (0.2 machine hr @ $9.00 per hr) $1.80
    Fixed ($96,000 for static budget volume of
        40,000 units and 8,000 machine hours). . . . .   __2.40__   4.20
  Actual   168,800
Total manufacturing costs . . . .   __$8.40__   __$352,710__

Required

1. Compute the price and efficiency variances for direct materials and direct labor.

2. For manufacturing overhead, compute the total variance, the flexible budget variance, and the production volume variance.

3. Prepare a standard cost income statement through gross profit to report all variances to management. Sale price was $10.60 per roll.

4. Happ intentionally purchased cheaper materials during May. Was the decision wise? Discuss the trade-off between the two materials variances.

Problems

(Group B)

Preparing a flexible budget income statement and graphing cost behavior
(Obj. 1)

spreadsheet

P24-1B → *Link Back to Chapter 22, Exhibit 22-7 (page 907).* Digital Technologies manufactures capacitors for cellular base stations and other communications applications. The company's static budget income statement for October 20X7 follows. It is based on expected sales volume of 9,000 units.

Digital Technologies' plant capacity is 9,500 units. If actual volume exceeds 9,500 units, Digital Technologies must rent additional space. In that case, salaries will increase by 15%, rent will double, and insurance expense will increase by $1,000. Depreciation will be unaffected.

Digital Technologies
Static Budget Income Statement
Month Ended October 31, 20X7

Sales revenue	$207,000
Variable expenses:	
Cost of goods sold	90,000
Sales commissions	9,900
Shipping expense.	6,300
Fixed expenses:	
Salary expense	30,500
Depreciation expense	12,750
Rent expense.	11,500
Insurance expense	3,750
Total expenses	164,700
Operating income	$ 42,300

Required

1. Prepare flexible budget income statements for 7,500, 9,000, and 11,000 units.

2. Graph the behavior of the company's total costs.

3. Why might Digital Technologies' managers want to see the graph you prepared in requirement 2 as well as the columnar format analysis in requirement 1? What is the disadvantage of the graphic approach in requirement 2?

P24-2B Refer to Digital Technologies, Problem 24-1B. The company sold 11,000 units during October 20X7, and its actual operating income was as follows:

Preparing an income statement performance report
(Obj. 2)

Digital Technologies	
Income Statement	
Month Ended October 31, 20X7	
Sales revenue	$257,000
Variable expenses:	
Cost of goods sold	112,250
Sales commissions	11,800
Shipping expense.	8,950
Fixed expenses:	
Salary expense	36,650
Depreciation expense	12,750
Rent expense.	22,500
Insurance expense	4,700
Total expenses	209,600
Operating income	$ 47,400

Required

1. Prepare an income statement performance report for October.
2. What was the effect on Digital Technologies' operating income of selling 2,000 units more than the static budget level of sales?
3. What is Digital Technologies' static budget variance? Explain why the income statement performance report provides more useful information to Digital Technologies' managers than the simple static budget variance. What insights can Digital Technologies' managers draw from this performance report?

P24-3B Relax-the-Back manufactures leather recliners and uses flexible budgeting and a standard cost system. Relax-the-Back allocates overhead based on yards of direct materials. The company's performance report includes the following selected data:

Preparing a flexible budget and computing standard cost variances
(Obj. 1, 3, 4, 5)

	Static Budget (1,000 recliners)	Actual Results (980 recliners)
Sales (1,000 recliners × $500)	$500,000	
(980 recliners × $490)		$480,200
Variable manufacturing expenses:		
Direct materials (6,000 yd × $8.90)	53,400	
(6,150 yd × $8.70)		53,505
Direct labor (10,000 hr × $9.00)	90,000	
(9,600 hr × $9.15)		87,840
Variable overhead (6,000 yd × $5.00)	30,000	
(6,150 yd × $6.40)		39,360
Fixed manufacturing expenses:		
Fixed overhead	60,000	66,000
Total cost of goods sold	233,400	246,705
Gross profit	$266,600	$233,495

Required

1. Prepare a flexible budget based on the actual number of recliners sold.
2. Compute the price variance and the efficiency variance for direct materials and for direct labor. For manufacturing overhead, compute the total variance, the flexible budget variance, and the production volume variance.

(continued)

3. What is the total flexible budget variance for Relax-the-Back's manufacturing costs? Show how the total flexible budget variance is divided into materials, labor, and overhead variances.

4. Have Relax-the-Back's managers done a good job or a poor job controlling material and labor costs? Why?

5. Describe how Relax-the-Back's managers can benefit from the standard costing system.

Using incomplete cost and variance information to determine the direct labor hours
(Obj. 4)

P24-4B Adam's Shades manufactures lamp shades. The manager uses standard costs to judge performance. Recently, a clerk mistakenly threw away some of the records, and the manager has only partial data for March. The manager knows that the direct labor flexible budget variance for the month was $1,050 U and that the standard labor price was $9 per hour. The shop experienced an unfavorable labor price variance of $0.50 per hour. The standard direct labor hours for actual March output were 4,000.

Required

1. Find the actual number of direct labor hours worked during March. First, find the actual direct labor price per hour. Then, determine the actual direct labor hours by setting up the computation of the direct labor flexible budget variance of $1,050 U.

2. Compute the direct labor price and efficiency variances. Do these variances suggest the manager may have made any trade-offs? Explain.

Computing and journalizing standard cost variances
(Obj. 4, 5, 6)

P24-5B Alon manufactures paper weights that it sells to other companies for customizing with their own logos. Alon prepares flexible budgets and uses a standard cost system to control manufacturing costs. The standard unit cost of a paper weight is based on static budget volume of 60,000 paper weights per month. The unit cost is computed as follows:

Direct materials (0.2 lb. @ $0.25 per lb.)		$0.05
Direct labor (3 minutes @ $0.12 per minute)		0.36
Manufacturing overhead:		
Variable (3 minutes @ $0.06 per minute)	$0.18	
Fixed (3 minutes @ $0.14 per minute)	0.42	0.60
Total cost per paper weight		$1.01

Transactions during May of the current year included the following:

a. Actual production and sales were 62,700 paper weights.

b. Actual direct materials usage was 0.18 lb. per paper weight, at an actual cost of $0.20 per pound.

c. Actual direct labor usage of 210,000 minutes cost $29,400.

d. Actual overhead cost was $40,800.

Required

1. Compute the price and efficiency variances for direct materials and direct labor.

2. Journalize the usage of direct materials and the assignment of direct labor, including the related variances.

3. For manufacturing overhead, compute the total variance, the flexible budget variance, and the production volume variance. (*Hint:* Remember that the total fixed overhead in the flexible budget equals the total fixed overhead in the static budget.)

4. Alon intentionally hired more skilled workers during May. How did this decision affect the cost variances? Overall, was the decision wise?

Computing standard cost variances and reporting to management
(Obj. 4, 5, 6)

P24-6B Protex Industries manufactures sunglass cases. During August, the company produced and sold 106,000 cases and recorded the following cost data:

(continued)

	Standard Unit Cost	Actual Total Cost
Direct materials:		
Standard (2 parts @ $0.16 per part).....................	$0.32	
Actual (218,000 parts @ $0.20 per part)		$43,600
Direct labor:		
Standard (0.02 hr @ $8.00 per hr)	0.16	
Actual (1,650 hr @ $8.20 per hr)........................		13,530
Manufacturing overhead:		
Standard:		
Variable (0.02 machine hr @ $8.00 per hr)	$0.16	
Fixed ($32,000 for static budget volume of		
100,000 units and 2,000 machine hours).............	0.32 0.48	
Actual		60,500
Total manufacturing costs	$0.96	$117,630

Required

1. Compute the price and efficiency variances for direct materials and direct labor.

2. For manufacturing overhead, compute the total variance, the flexible budget variance, and the production volume variance.

3. Prepare a standard cost income statement through gross profit to report all variances to management. Sale price of the sunglass cases was $1.50 each.

4. Protex's management used more experienced workers during August. Discuss the trade-off between the two direct labor variances.

APPLY *Your Knowledge*

Decision Cases

Case 1. ReelTime, Inc., distributes DVDs to movie retailers, including dot.coms. ReelTime's top management meets monthly to evaluate the company's performance. Controller Terri Lon prepared the following performance report for the meeting.

Preparing a performance report and using it to evaluate performance **(Obj. 1, 2)**

ReelTime, Inc.
Income Statement Performance Report
Month Ended July 31, 2006

	Actual Result	Static Budget	Variance
Sales revenue	$1,640,000	$1,960,000	$320,000 U
Variable expenses:			
Cost of goods sold	773,750	980,000	206,250 F
Sales commissions	77,375	107,800	30,425 F
Shipping expense...........	42,850	53,900	11,050 F
Fixed expenses:			
Salary expense	311,450	300,500	10,950 U
Depreciation expense	208,750	214,000	5,250 F
Rent expense...............	128,250	108,250	20,000 U
Advertising expense	81,100	68,500	12,600 U
Total expenses................	1,623,525	1,832,950	209,425 F
Operating income	$ 16,475	$ 127,050	$110,575 U

    Lon also revealed that the actual sale price of $20 per movie was equal to the budgeted sale price and that there were no changes in inventories for the month.

(continued)

Management is disappointed by the operating income results. CEO Lyle Nesbitt exclaims, "How can actual operating income be roughly 13% of the static budget amount when there are so many favorable variances?"

Required

1. Prepare a more informative performance report. Be sure to include a flexible budget for the actual number of DVDs bought and sold.

2. As a member of ReelTime's management team, which variances would you want investigated? Why?

3. Nesbitt believes that many consumers are postponing purchases of new movies until after the introduction of a new format for recordable DVD players. In light of this information, how would you rate the company's performance?

Efficiency variances and setting standards
(Obj. 4)

Case 2. Assume you manage your local Marble Slab Creamery ice cream parlor. In addition to selling ice cream cones, you make large batches of a few flavors of milk shakes to sell throughout the day. Your parlor is chosen to test the company's "Made-for-You" system. The system allows patrons to customize their milk shakes by choosing different flavors.

Customers like the new system, and your staff appears to be adapting, but you wonder whether this new made-to-order system is as efficient as the old system where you just made a few large batches. Efficiency is a special concern because your performance is evaluated in part on the restaurant's efficient use of materials and labor. Assume that your superiors consider efficiency variances greater than 5% unacceptable.

You decide to look at your sales for a typical day. You find that the parlor used 390 lbs. of ice cream and 72 hours of direct labor to produce and sell 2,000 shakes. Assume that the standard quantity allowed for a shake is 0.2 pound of ice cream and 0.03 hours (1.8 minutes) of direct labor. Further, assume that standard costs are $1.50 per pound for ice cream and $8 an hour for labor.

Required

1. Compute the efficiency variances for direct labor and direct materials.

2. Provide likely explanations for the variances. Do you have reason to be concerned about your performance evaluation? Explain.

3. Write a memo to Marble Slab Creamery's national office explaining your concern and suggesting a remedy. Your memo should take the following form:

Date:	_____
To:	Marble Slab Creamery's National Office
From:	_____
Subject:	"Made-for-You" system

Ethical Issues

Setting standards
(Obj. 3)

Austin Landers is the accountant for Sun Coast, a manufacturer of outdoor furniture that is sold through specialty stores and Internet companies. Annually, Landers is responsible for reviewing the standard costs for the following year. While reviewing the standard costs for the coming year, two ethical issues arise. Use the IMA's ethical guidelines, page 774, to identify the ethical dilemma in each situation. Identify the relevant factors in each situation and suggest what Landers should recommend to the controller.

Issue 1. Landers has been approached by Kara Willis, a former colleague who worked with Landers when they were both employed by a public accounting firm. Willis has recently started her own firm, Willis Benchmarking Associates, which collects and sells data on industry benchmarks. She offers to provide Landers with benchmarks for the outdoor furniture industry free of charge, if he will provide her with the last

(continued)

three years of Sun Coast's standard and actual costs. Willis explains that this is how she obtains most of her firm's benchmarking data. Landers always has a difficult time with the standard-setting process and believes that the benchmark data would be very useful.

Issue 2. Sun Coast's management is starting a continuous improvement policy that requires a 10% reduction in standard costs each year for the next three years. Dan Jones, manufacturing foreman of the Teak furniture line, asks Landers to set loose standard costs this year before the continuous improvement policy is implemented. Jones argues that there is no other way to meet the tightening standards while maintaining the high quality of the Teak line.

Team Project

Setting standards
(Obj. 3, 4)

Pella Corporation is the world's second-largest manufacturer of wood windows and doors. In 1992, Pella entered the national retail market with its ProLine windows and doors, manufactured in Carroll, Iowa. Since then, Pella has introduced many new product lines with manufacturing facilities in several states.

Suppose Pella has been using a standard cost system that bases price and quantity standards on Pella's historical long-run average performance. Assume Pella's controller has engaged your team of management consultants to advise him whether Pella should use some basis other than historical performance for setting standards.

1. List the types of variances you recommend that Pella compute (for example, direct materials price variance for glass). For each variance, what specific standards would Pella need to develop? In addition to cost standards, do you recommend that Pella develop any nonfinancial standards?
2. There are many approaches to setting standards other than simply using long-run average historical prices and quantities.
   a. List three alternative approaches that Pella could use to set standards, and explain how Pella could implement each alternative.
   b. Evaluate each alternative method of setting standards, including the pros and cons of each method.
   c. Write a memo to Pella's controller detailing your recommendations. First, should Pella retain its historical data–based standard cost approach? If not, which of the alternative approaches should it adopt? Use the following format for your memo:

> **Date:** _____
>
> **To:** Controller, Pella Corporation
>
> **From:** _____, Management Consultants
>
> **Subject:** Standard Costs

For Internet Exercises, go to the Web site www.prenhall.com/horngren.

Activity-Based Costing and Other Cost Management Tools

A+

TIPS CHECK YOUR RESOURCES

- Visit the www.prenhall.com/horngren **Web site** for self-study quizzes, video clips, and other resources

- Try the **Quick Check** exercise at the end of the chapter to test your knowledge

- Learn the **key terms**

- Do the **Starter** exercises keyed in the margins

- Work the **mid-** and **end-of-chapter summary problems**

- Use the **Concept Links** to review material in other chapters

- Search the **CD** for review materials by chapter or by key word

- Watch the **tutorial videos** to review key concepts

- Watch the **On Location Dell** video on activity-based costing

LEARNING OBJECTIVES

1 Develop activity-based costs (ABC)

2 Use activity-based management (ABM) to make business decisions, including achieving target costs

3 Decide when ABC is most likely to pass the cost-benefit test

4 Describe a just-in-time (JIT) production system, and record its manufacturing costs

5 Contrast the four types of quality costs and use them to make decisions

After Dell Computer reported its first-ever quarterly loss several years ago, CEO Michael Dell knew he had to focus on the company's most profitable products. But which products were they? The accounting system traced direct materials and direct labor to individual product lines, but it did not do a good job matching indirect costs with the specific products that caused those costs.

Dell needed a more finely tuned cost accounting system: *activity-based costing (ABC)*. Employee teams identified the 10 most important indirect activities—for example, purchases of raw materials, indirect assembly labor, and warranty service. *For each activity*, the teams devel-

Dell Computer

oped a separate indirect cost allocation rate. The goal was to assign the cost of each activity to the product lines that caused that activity's cost. For example:

- Purchasing costs are assigned based on the number of different "part numbers" in a product.

- Indirect assembly labor is assigned based on the number of times the product is "touched."

- Warranty costs are assigned based on the number of service calls for the product line.

ABC assigns costs more accurately than simpler systems that combine the indirect costs of many activities into a single cost pool and then allocate these costs using a single allocation base.

Has ABC worked for Dell? By 2003, Dell was the leader in worldwide PC sales. Given the rapidly changing costs in the computer industry, Dell uses ABC costs for pricing its computers every day. ABC also helps Dell's managers cut costs, especially by highlighting non-value-added activities such as inventory storage. As the controller of Dell Americas Operations says: "Activity-based costing has really allowed Dell to go to the next level of understanding of its profitability for each of the products it sells." ■

■*Sitemap*

- **Refining Cost Systems**
- **Activity-Based Costing**
- **Activity-Based Management**
- **ABC and Cost-Benefit**
- **JIT Systems**
- **Quality Management**

To thrive in a globally competitive market, Dell Computer must deliver value to the customer by providing goods or services at an attractive price, while managing costs so the company still earns a profit. This chapter will show you several methods today's managers use to deliver value to the customer at a profit:

- Activity-based costing
- Activity-based management and target costing
- Just-in-time systems
- Costs of quality

★ *Develop activity-based costs (ABC)*

◉ Student Resource**CD**

cost allocation system, indirect costs

Refining Cost Systems

Why Managers Need More Accurate Cost Systems

Organizations from Dell Computer, to Carolina Power and Light, to the U.S. Marine Corps use refined ABC costing systems. Why? Because simple systems that do not match costs with the consumption of resources can assign costs inequitably. An example shows why.

David Larimer, Matt Sewell, and Marc Bryan are three college friends who share an apartment. They agree to split the following monthly costs equally:

Rent and utilities	$570
Cable TV	50
High-speed Internet access	40
Groceries	240
Total monthly costs	$900

Each roommate's share is $300 ($900/3).

Things go smoothly for the first few months. But then David calls a meeting. "Since I started having dinner at Amy's each night, I shouldn't have to chip in for the groceries." Matt then pipes in: "I'm so busy studying and surfing the Net that I never have time to watch TV. I don't want to pay for the cable TV any more. And Marc, since your friend Jennifer eats here most evenings, you should pay a double share of the grocery bill." Marc retorts, "If that's the way you feel, Matt, then you should pay for the Internet access, since you're the only one around here who uses it!"

What happened? The friends originally agreed to share the costs equally. But they are not participating equally in watching cable TV, surfing the Net, and eating. Splitting these costs equally is not equitable.

The roommates could use an approach that better matches costs with the people who participate in each activity. This means splitting the cable TV costs between David and Marc, assigning the Internet access cost to Matt, and allocating the grocery bill 1/3 to Matt and 2/3 to Marc. Exhibit 25-1 compares the results of this refined system with the original system.

Exhibit 25-1 More-Refined versus Less-Refined Cost Allocation System

	David Larimer	Matt Sewell	Marc Bryan	Total
More-refined cost allocation system:				
Rent and utilities......................................	$190	$190	$190	$570
Cable TV..	25	—	25	50
High-speed Internet access	—	40	—	40
Groceries..	—	80	160	240
Total costs allocated	$215	$310	$375	$900
Less-refined original cost allocation system...............	$300	$300	$300	$900
Difference	$(85)	$ 10	$ 75	$ 0

No wonder David called a meeting! The original system allocated him $300 a month, but the refined system shows that a more-equitable share would be only $215. On the other hand, the new system allocates Marc $375 a month instead of $300. David was paying for resources he did not use (Internet and groceries), while Marc was not paying for all the resources (groceries) he and his guest consumed. David was "overcosted" and Marc was "undercosted."

Total monthly costs are the same ($900) under both systems. The only difference is how that $900 is allocated among the three roommates. The amount by which David is "overcosted" ($85) must exactly equal the amounts by which Matt and Marc are "undercosted" ($10 + $75).

Sharpening the Focus: From Business Functions to Departments to Activities

In today's competitive, globally wired market, Dell needs to know what it costs to assemble and deliver a customized laptop to a buyer in Eugene, Oregon. Why? So Dell can set a price that covers the costs of all the resources required to assemble and deliver that laptop (and provide some profit), yet remain competitive with Gateway and HP prices.

As the chapter-opening story explained, Dell decided it needed to refine its cost system. There is little error in assigning direct costs (like direct materials and direct labor) to computers and servers. So Dell focused on refining the way it allocated *indirect costs*. The goal was to more accurately reflect the cost of the resources each product uses. How? By drilling down from the indirect costs incurred in each of the six functions in the value chain to the indirect costs incurred in each individual department within each value-chain function and, finally, to the indirect costs of the specific activities in each department. Let's look at each step.

The first column of Exhibit 25-2 lists the six value-chain functions: R&D, design, production, marketing, distribution, and customer service. We'll focus on how Dell refined costs in the production element of the value chain, because that is where most companies like Dell and Dow Chemical begin refining their cost systems.

Long ago, when managers could limit their focus to broad business functions, simple cost systems were often good enough. For example, many companies started out with a broad focus on the production function and used a single plantwide indirect cost rate (manufacturing overhead rate), like we did in Chapter 20. ←

As competition increased, managers needed more-accurate estimates of product costs to set prices and to identify the most profitable products. When broad averages like plantwide overhead rates (or like the three roommates splitting their costs equally) are no longer good enough, managers drill down to focus on the indirect costs incurred by each *department* within the function. Exhibit 25-2 shows that Dell's production function includes separate departments (or production lines) for its three main products: servers, desktops, and laptops. The next step in refining its cost system is to establish separate indirect cost rates for each department—one rate for the server department, another for the desktop department, and a third for the laptop department.

See Chapter 20, pp. 811–814, to review the allocation of indirect manufacturing costs (overhead).

To obtain even more accurate estimates of the resources each product uses, managers drill down deeper yet to analyze the indirect costs of each *activity* in a department. Exhibit 25-2 shows the six activities in the desktop production department. Rather than using a single overhead rate for the entire desktop department, Dell develops separate rates for each of these six activities, from kitting to boxing. This is called activity-based costing.

☐ Refining Cost Systems
■ **Activity-Based Costing**
☐ Activity-Based Management
☐ ABC and Cost-Benefit
☐ JIT Systems
☐ Quality Management

Activity-Based Costing

Activity-Based Costing (ABC)
Focuses on *activities* as the fundamental cost objects. The costs of those activities become building blocks for compiling the indirect costs of products, services, and customers.

Activity-based costing (ABC) focuses on *activities* as the fundamental cost objects. The costs of those activities become building blocks for compiling the indirect costs of products, services, and customers. Companies like Allied

Signal, Coca-Cola, and American Express use ABC to more accurately estimate the cost of resources required to produce different products, to render different services, and to serve different customers.

Companies that use ABC trace direct materials and direct labor to cost objects, as described in Chapter 20. → The only difference is that ABC systems make more effort to allocate *indirect costs*—such as manufacturing overhead—to the products, services, or customers that caused those costs. How? By separately estimating the indirect costs of each activity and then allocating those indirect costs based on what caused them.

Each activity's indirect cost has its own (usually unique) cost driver. For example, Dell allocates indirect assembly costs (such as depreciation on the equipment used in the assembly process) based on the number of times workers touch a computer as it moves through assembly. Computers that require more touches are allocated more costs. Exhibit 25-3 illustrates other common activities and related cost drivers.

← *See Chapter 20, pp. 802–808, to review how direct materials and direct labor are traced to cost objects.*

Student Resource CD
activity-based costing, cost allocation rate, cost allocation system, cost driver, manufacturing overhead

Exhibit 25-3 **Activities and Cost Drivers**

Data warehouses and other information technology have made detailed ABC systems easier to use. Optical scanning and bar coding reduce the cost of collecting cost driver information. ERP systems like SAP, Oracle, and Peoplesoft have ABC modules. Managers can also buy specialized ABC software. But Dell began its ABC system simply using Excel spreadsheets!

Developing an Activity-Based Costing System

The main difference between ABC and traditional systems is that ABC systems have separate indirect cost allocation rates for each activity. ABC requires seven steps:

1. Identify the activities.
2. Estimate the total indirect costs of each activity.
3. Identify the allocation base for each activity's indirect costs—this is the primary cost driver.
4. Estimate the total quantity of each allocation base.
5. Compute the cost allocation rate for each activity:

$$\text{Cost allocation rate for activity} = \frac{\text{Estimated total indirect costs of activity}}{\text{Estimated total quantity of cost allocation base}}$$

6. Obtain the actual quantity of each allocation base used by the cost object (for example, the quantity used by a particular product).

7. Allocate the costs to the cost object:

$$\text{Allocated activity cost} \; = \; \frac{\text{Cost allocation rate}}{\text{for activity}} \times \frac{\text{Actual quantity of cost allocation}}{\text{base used by the cost object}}$$

The first step in developing an activity-based costing system is to identify the activities. Analyzing all the activities required to make a product forces managers to think about how each activity might be improved—or whether the activity is necessary at all. Steps 2 through 7 are the same approach used to allocate manufacturing overhead, as explained in Chapter 20. The only difference is that ABC systems repeat steps 2 through 7 for each activity.

Traditional versus Activity-Based Costing Systems: Chemtech

To emphasize the distinctions between ABC systems and traditional costing systems, our example simplifies the process that would occur in a real company, which might identify more than 50 different activities.

Chemtech's Chemical Manufacturing Department produces hundreds of different chemicals. The company has focused on producing mass quantities of "commodity" chemicals for large customers. It also manufactures small quantities of specialty chemicals for individual customers.

Last updated in 1990, the Chemical Manufacturing Department's cost system uses a single indirect cost pool and allocates manufacturing overhead at 200% of direct labor cost. Chemtech's controller, Martha Wise, gathered data for two of the department's many products:

- Aldehyde—a commodity chemical used in producing plastics
- Phenylephrine hydrochloride (PH)—a specialty chemical (A single customer uses PH in blood-pressure medications.)

	Aldehyde	Phenylephrine Hydrochloride (PH)
Number of pounds per year	7,000 lb	5 lb
Direct materials cost per pound	$ 5	$20
Direct labor cost per pound	$ 1	$10
Sale price per pound	$10	$70

Wise used this information to compute each product's gross profit, as shown in Exhibit 25-4.

Exhibit 25-4

Chemtech's Traditional Cost System—Product Cost and Gross Profit

 Starter 25-4

	Aldehyde	PH
Sale price per pound..........................	$10.00	$70.00
Less: Manufacturing cost per pound:		
Direct materials.............................	5.00	20.00
Direct labor	1.00	10.00
Manufacturing overhead		
(at 200% of direct labor cost)................	2.00	20.00
Total manufacturing cost per pound	8.00	50.00
Gross profit per pound.........................	$ 2.00	$20.00

The gross profit for the PH specialty chemical is $20 per pound—10 times as high as the gross profit for the aldehyde commodity chemical ($2). Chemtech CEO Randy Smith is surprised that PH appears so much more profitable (per pound) than aldehyde. He asks Wise to check 50 of the department's other products. Wise confirms that the gross profit per pound is 10 times as high for specialty chemicals as it is for commodity chemicals. Smith wonders whether Chemtech should switch its focus to specialty chemicals.

1. What is the *total* direct labor cost assigned to
   a. Aldehyde?
   b. PH?
2. What is the *total* manufacturing overhead allocated to
   a. Aldehyde?
   b. PH?

Answers

1. Total direct labor cost assigned to aldehyde is 7,000 pounds × $1 per pound = $7,000. Total direct labor cost assigned to PH is 5 pounds × $10 per pound = $50. Thus, Chemtech assigns to aldehyde 140 times as much total direct labor cost as it does to PH ($7,000 ÷ $50 = 140).

2. **Key Point**: Total overhead allocated to aldehyde is 7,000 pounds × $2 per pound = $14,000. Total overhead allocated to PH is 5 pounds × $20 per pound = $100. Thus, because Chemtech uses direct labor cost as its single allocation base, Chemtech also allocates 140 times as much total overhead to aldehyde as to PH ($14,000 ÷ $100). This costing is accurate only if direct labor really is the primary overhead cost driver, and so aldehyde really does cause 140 times as much overhead as PH.

CEO Smith calls a meeting with the department foreman Steve Pronai and controller Wise. Smith is perplexed that the accounting numbers show specialty chemicals are more profitable (on a per-pound basis) than commodity chemicals. He expected the department would be more efficient producing a few commodity chemicals (in a few very large batches) than producing a wide variety of specialty chemicals (in many small batches). Foreman Pronai echoes Smith's concern. Pronai says it takes just as long to mix a small batch of specialty chemicals as a large batch of commodity chemicals. Finally, Smith is puzzled because Chemtech's competitors seem to be earning good profits, even though they usually undercut Chemtech's prices on commodity chemicals.

Wise fears that the problem could be Chemtech's cost accounting system. She suggests that Foreman Pronai and the plant engineer work with her to develop a pilot ABC system. Using a cross-functional team that includes the plant engineer and foreman, as well as the controller, should lead to a more-accurate ABC system because it incorporates a wider variety of perspectives. Also, managers are more likely to believe costs from a system they helped build.

Exhibit 25-5 presents a bird's-eye overview that compares the original direct labor single-allocation-base system (Panel A) to the new ABC system Wise's team developed (Panel B).

Panel B of Exhibit 25-5 shows that Chemtech's ABC team identifies three activities: mixing, processing, and testing. Each activity has its own indirect cost pool and cost driver. But exactly how does this work? The ABC team develops the new system by following the seven steps described earlier. Exhibit 25-6 shows how, with a special focus on computing and assigning the costs of the mixing activity.

Exhibit 25-6 highlights the seven steps in developing Chemtech's ABC system, with a focus on the mixing activity.

| Exhibit 25-5 | Chemtech's Traditional and ABC Systems |

✔ Starter 25-1

✔ Starter 25-7

Follow the details of each step in Exhibit 25-6. Make sure you understand exactly how each ABC step applies to Chemtech's mixing process.

Exhibit 25-7 summarizes the seven steps for all three activities. Study Exhibit 25-7 carefully, following each of the seven steps for the processing and testing activities to make sure you understand how the activity costs are allocated.

Controller Wise then uses the ABC costs allocated to aldehyde and to PH (from column 7 of Exhibit 25-7) to recompute manufacturing overhead costs, as shown in Exhibit 25-8. For each product, Wise adds the total costs of the three activities to obtain the total manufacturing overhead allocated to each product. She then divides each product's total manufacturing overhead cost by the number of pounds Chemtech produced to get the overhead cost per pound.

Compare the overhead cost per pound under the original direct-labor-based system with the ABC costs:

	Overhead Cost per Pound	
	Traditional Direct Labor System (Exhibit 25-4)	**ABC System (Exhibit 25-8)**
Aldehyde	$ 2.00	$ 1.95
PH	20.00	94.00

ABC costs are more accurate because ABC takes into account the resources (mixing costs, machine time, and testing) each product actually uses. Recall that the old direct labor single-allocation-base system allocated 140 times as much overhead to aldehyde as to PH (see the Stop & Think on page 1039).

With more-precise allocations, ABC shifts costs out of aldehyde and into PH, where the costs belong. Why? Exhibit 25-7 shows that aldehyde uses more of each activity's resources than PH, but *not* 140 times as much. Column 6 shows that aldehyde uses 60 times as much mixing, about 15 times as many machine hours (processing costs), and 14 times as much testing as PH.

Step 1: Identify activities: mixing, processing, testing

Chemtech Controller Wise and her team identify three activities in the Chemical Manufacturing Department: mixing, processing , and testing.

Step 2: Estimate total indirect cost of each activity

Foreman Steve Pronai estimates that total mixing costs for all products will be $600,000. Estimated costs for each activity appear in Exhibit 25-7, column 2.

Step 3: Identify allocation base for each activity

The allocation base for each activity should be the primary cost driver. Workers mix ingredients separately for each batch of chemicals, so the number of batches drives mixing costs. Pronai and the plant engineer decide that the number of machine hours is the best allocation base for processing costs, and that number of samples drives testing costs.

Step 4: Estimate total quantity of each allocation base

Wise and Pronai estimate the department will produce a total of 4,000 batches. Estimated quantities of the cost driver allocation bases appear in column 4 of Exhibit 25-7.

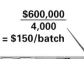

Step 5: Compute allocation rates for each activity

Wise computes the allocation rate for mixing, as follows:

$$\text{Cost allocation rate for mixing} = \frac{\$600,000}{4,000 \text{ batches}} = \$150 \text{ per batch}$$

Column 5 of Exhibit 25-7 shows the cost allocation rate for each activity.

Step 6: Obtain actual quantities of each allocation base used by each product

During the year, Chemtech produces 60 batches of aldehyde and 1 batch of PH. (This total of 61 batches is only a small fraction of the 4,000 total batches Chemtech produces. The remaining batches consist of Chemtech's other chemicals.) Exhibit 25-7, column 6, shows the actual quantities of each activity's allocation base used by aldehyde and PH.

Step 7: Allocate costs to each product

Wise allocates mixing costs as follows:

Aldehyde: 60 batches × $150 per batch = $9,000
PH: 1 batch × $150 per batch = $ 150

Column 7 of Exhibit 25-7 shows the cost allocation for all three activities.

Exhibit 25-7 Summary of Chemtech's Activity-Based Costing System

(1)	(2)	(3)	(4)	(5)	(6) Actual Quantity of Cost Allocation Base Used by:		(7) Allocated Activity Cost	
Activity	Estimated Costs	Cost Allocation Base	Estimated Quantity of Cost Allocation Base	Cost Allocation Rate	Aldehyde	PH	Aldehyde	PH
Mixing	$600,000	# Batches	4,000 batches	$\frac{\$600,000}{4,000} = \$150/\text{batch}$	60 batches	1 batch	$150 × 60 = $9,000	$150 × 1 = $150
Processing	$3,000,000	# Machine hours (MH)	50,000 MH	$\frac{\$3,000,000}{50,000} = \$60/\text{MH}$	30 1/2 MH	2 MH	$60 × 30 1/2 = $1,830	$60 × 2 = $120
Testing	$600,000	# Samples	3,000 samples	$\frac{\$600,000}{3,000} = \$200/\text{sample}$	14 samples	1 sample	$200 × 14 = $2,800	$200 × 1 = $200

Exhibit 25-8

Chemtech's Manufacturing
Overhead Costs Under ABC

Manufacturing Overhead Costs	Aldehyde	PH
Mixing (from Exhibit 25-7).	$ 9,000	$150
Processing (from Exhibit 25-7)	1,830	120
Testing (from Exhibit 25-7).	2,800	200
Total manufacturing overhead	$13,630	$470
Divide by number of pounds	÷ 7,000 lb	÷ 5 lb
Manufacturing overhead per pound	$ 1.95/lb*	$ 94/lb

*Rounded

✔ Starter 25-2

✔ Starter 25-8

✔ Starter 25-9

Allocating overhead based on the actual resources *used* generally increases the costs of low-volume products like PH that are produced in small batches. Why? Because costs like mixing and testing are spread over the small number of units in that batch, which can dramatically increase product costs. For example, although Chemtech made only 5 pounds of PH, column 6 of Exhibit 25-7 shows that this product still required

- Workers to mix a batch, at a mixing cost of $150

- 2 machine hours at $60 per hour

- One sample tested at a cost of $200

Spreading these costs over the 5 pounds of PH yields an overhead cost of $94 per pound, as shown in Exhibit 25-8. This is much higher than the $20-per-pound cost under the original system (Exhibit 25-4).

On the other hand, for high-volume products produced in large batches, such as aldehyde, mixing and testing costs are spread over the larger number of units in the batch. So ABC often assigns *fewer* costs to each unit of high-volume products than do single-allocation-base systems. After implementing ABC, companies often realize they were overcosting high-volume products (Chemtech was overcosting aldehyde) and undercosting low-volume products (Chemtech was undercosting PH).

Now that we know the indirect costs of aldehyde and PH under the refined ABC system, let's see how Chemtech's managers *use* this new cost information to make better pricing and product-mix decisions and to find new ways to cut costs.

☐ Refining Cost Systems
☐ Activity-Based Costing
■ **Activity-Based Management**
☐ ABC and Cost-Benefit
☐ JIT Systems
☐ Quality Management

Use activity-based management (ABM) to make business decisions, including achieving target costs

Student Resource CD

activity-based costing, activity-based management, target cost, target pricing, value engineering

Activity-Based Management
Using activity-based cost information to make decisions that increase profits while satisfying customers' needs.

✔ Starter 25-10

✔ Starter 25-11

Activity-Based Management: Using ABC for Decision Making

Activity-based management (ABM) refers to using activity-based cost information to make decisions that increase profits while satisfying customers' needs. We consider how Chemtech can use ABC information in three kinds of decisions: (1) pricing and product mix, (2) cost cutting, and (3) routine planning and control.

Pricing and Product Mix Decisions

Armed with the ABC manufacturing overhead cost per pound (Exhibit 25-8), Controller Wise recomputes each product's total manufacturing costs and gross profit. Panel A of Exhibit 25-9 shows that the total manufacturing cost per pound of aldehyde is $7.95 under the ABC system. Contrast this with the $8.00 cost per pound under Chemtech's original system, as shown in Panel B. More important, the refined ABC data in Panel A show that specialty chemical PH costs $124 per pound, rather than the $50 per pound indicated by the old system (Panel B). Chemtech has been losing $54 on each pound of PH—and this is *before* nonmanufacturing costs such as R&D, marketing, and distribution! Wise finds that most of Chemtech's other specialty chemicals show similar increases in costs under the ABC system.

PANEL A: Total Manufacturing Cost and Gross Profit Under ABC

	Aldehyde	PH
Sale price per pound	$10.00	$ 70.00
Less: Manufacturing cost per pound:		
Direct materials	$ 5.00	$ 20.00
Direct labor	1.00	10.00
Manufacturing overhead (from Exhibit 25-8)	1.95	94.00
Total manufacturing cost	7.95	124.00
Gross profit (loss) per pound	$ 2.05	$(54.00)

PANEL B: Total Manufacturing Cost and Gross Profit Under Original Cost System (from Exhibit 25-4)

	Aldehyde	PH
Sale price per pound	$10.00	$ 70.00
Less: Manufacturing cost per pound	8.00	50.00
Gross profit per pound	$ 2.00	$ 20.00

Exhibit 25-9

Comparison of Chemtech's Manufacturing Product Costs Under ABC versus Original Systems

✔ **Starter 25-3**

As you'll see in the next section, Chemtech may be able to use the ABC analysis to find ways to cut costs. If it cannot cut costs enough to earn a profit on PH, then it may have to raise the sale price. If customers will not pay more, Chemtech should consider dropping PH. More generally, if the ABC system shows that commodity chemicals are more profitable than Chemtech thought, and specialty chemicals are less profitable, Chemtech may shift its product mix away from specialty chemicals toward commodity chemicals. *This is the exact opposite of the strategy suggested by cost data from the original system.*

Cutting Costs

Most companies adopt ABC to get more-accurate product costs for pricing and product mix decisions. But they often reap even greater benefits by using ABM to pinpoint opportunities to cut costs. For example, farm machinery maker John Deere uses an enterprisewide Web-based system to track cost changes. The system pulls cost data from companywide purchasing, ABC, and forecasting data warehouses. Managers use the system to see how well they are meeting cost-cutting goals for individual products, suppliers, and locations.

ABC can help organizations use value engineering to cut costs. **Value engineering** means reevaluating activities to reduce costs while satisfying customer needs. Value engineering requires cross-functional teams: marketers to identify customer needs, engineers and production personnel to design more efficient processes and products, and accountants to estimate how proposed changes will affect costs.

Why are managers turning to value engineering to cut costs? Companies like Carrier Corporation and General Motors are following Japanese automakers like Toyota and Nissan and setting sale prices based on **target prices**—what customers are willing to pay for the product or service. Instead of starting with the full product cost from all elements of the value chain (as discussed in Chapter 19) and then adding a profit to determine the sale price, Exhibit 25-10 shows that target pricing does just the opposite. Target pricing starts with the price customers are willing to pay and then subtracts the company's desired profit to determine the **target** (or allowable) **cost** to develop, produce, and deliver the product or service. Target costs are usually less than the (current) full cost of the product or service. The target cost is a goal the company must shoot for.

Value Engineering
Reevaluating activities to reduce costs while satisfying customer needs.

Target Price
What customers are willing to pay for the product or service.

Target Cost
Allowable cost to develop, produce, and deliver the product or service. Equals target price minus desired profit.

Exhibit 25-10

**Target Pricing versus Traditional
Cost-Based Pricing**

Let's return to our Chemtech illustration. After seeing the results of the ABC analysis in Exhibit 25-9, CEO Smith decides to focus on commodity chemicals. The marketing department says the market price of aldehyde is likely to fall to $9.50 per pound. Smith wants to earn a profit equal to 20% of the sale price. In addition to the manufacturing costs in Exhibit 25-9, Chemtech incurs a total of $0.50 per pound in nonmanufacturing costs (R&D, design, marketing, distribution, and customer service).

> What is Chemtech's target cost per pound of aldehyde? Do Chemtech's current costs meet this target?
>
> *Answer:*
>
> | | |
> |---|---:|
> | Target sale price per pound of aldehyde .... | $9.50 |
> | Desired profit ($9.50 × 20%) .... | (1.90) |
> | Target cost per pound of aldehyde .... | $7.60 |
>
> Chemtech's current costs do not meet the target cost.
>
> | | |
> |---|---:|
> | Current total manufacturing cost (from Exhibit 25-9) ... | $7.95 |
> | Nonmanufacturing costs .... | 0.50 |
> | Current full product cost per pound of aldehyde .... | $8.45 |

Because Chemtech's current full product costs ($8.45) exceed the target cost of $7.60, Smith assembles a cross-functional value-engineering team to identify opportunities to cut costs. The team includes marketing Manager Liz Smith, plant engineer Edward Michaels, and production foreman Steve Pronai, along with controller Martha Wise. The team analyzes each of Chemtech's three production activities: mixing, processing, and testing. For each activity, the team considers (1) how to cut costs given current production processes and (2) how to redesign the production process to further cut costs.

Of the team's several proposals, Smith chooses three:

1. *Redesign the mixing process to reduce cost per batch mixed.* The proposal is to group raw materials that are used together to reduce time required to assemble them when mixing each batch. Total estimated savings is $150,000, and the plant's total annual number of batches remains unchanged at 4,000.

2. *Redesign the processing activity to reduce the number of machine hours used.* The proposal is to purchase equipment that will cut processing time in half, but it costs $1,000,000. Total machine hours will remain 50,000, but each product will require only half as many hours. (Chemtech will use the extra machine hours to make other profitable products).

3. *Redesign the testing process to reduce* **both** *the cost per sample* **and** *the number of samples.* The recommendation is to improve quality control to reduce the need to test samples of each product. This will cut total testing costs by $375,000 and also will cut the total number of samples tested in half—from 3,000 to just 1,500. Chemtech will now test only 7 rather than 14 samples of aldehyde.

Will these changes allow Chemtech to reach the target cost? Exhibit 25-11 shows how Controller Wise starts with the original data summarized in Exhibit 25-7 and adjusts these data for the value-engineering changes. Wise first recomputes the cost allocation rates for each activity: She incorporates changes in both the numerator (estimated indirect costs of the activity) and the denominator (estimated total quantity of the activity's allocation base). She then uses these new allocation rates to assign the costs of each activity to aldehyde, based on how much of each allocation base aldehyde uses after the value-engineering changes.

Exhibit 25-11 Recomputing Activity Costs for Aldehyde After Value-Engineering Changes

	Mixing	Processing	Testing
Estimated total indirect costs of activity:			
Mixing ($600,000 − $150,000)	$450,000		
Processing ($3,000,000 + $1,000,000)		$4,000,000	
Testing ($600,000 − $375,000)			$225,000
Estimated total quantity of each allocation base	4,000 batches	50,000 MH	1,500 samples
Compute the cost allocation rate for each activity:			
(Divide estimated indirect cost by	$450,000	$4,000,000	$225,000
estimated quantity of the allocation base)	÷ 4,000 batches	÷ 50,000 MH	÷ 1,500 samples
Cost allocation rate for each activity	= $112.50/batch	= $80/MH	= $150/sample
Actual quantity of each allocation base used by aldehyde:			
Mixing	60 batches		
Processing ($30\frac{1}{2} \times 50\%$)		$15\frac{1}{4}$ MH	
Testing			7 samples
Allocate the costs to aldehyde:			
Mixing (60 batches × $112.50)	$6,750		
Processing ($15\frac{1}{4}$ MH × $80)		$1,220	
Testing (7 samples × $150)			$1,050

Exhibit 25-11 shows that value-engineering cuts the total manufacturing overhead costs assigned to aldehyde to $9,020 ($6,750 + $1,220 + $1,050) from $13,630 (in Exhibit 25-8). Spread over 7,000 pounds of aldehyde, this is $1.29 per pound ($9,020 ÷ 7,000, rounded). Now Wise totals the revised cost estimates for aldehyde:

Direct materials (from Exhibit 25-9)	$5.00
Direct labor (from Exhibit 25-9)	1.00
Manufacturing overhead	1.29
Total manufacturing costs	7.29
Nonmanufacturing costs	0.50
Full product cost of aldehyde	$7.79

These changes are quite an improvement from the prior full product cost of $8.45 per pound. But they are *not* enough to meet the $7.60 target cost. Chemtech must conduct more value engineering (or accept less profit) to meet the target sale price.

Routine Planning and Control Decisions

In addition to pricing, product mix, and cost cutting decisions, Chemtech can use ABC in routine planning and control. In activity-based budgeting, managers budget costs of individual activities to build up the indirect cost schedules in the master budget (discussed in Chapter 23). ← Chemtech can also analyze manufacturing overhead variances (presented in Chapter 24) ← in more detail by computing variances for each of the three individual indirect activities (mixing, processing, and testing). Finally, Chemtech's managers can use ABC information to evaluate workers. For example, Foreman Pronai may receive a bonus if he can cut:

- The cost per sample tested (that is, cut the cost allocation rate for the testing activity) or

- The number of samples tested (that is, cut the consumption of the activity) *while maintaining product quality.*

For the master budget, see Chapter 23, pp. 943–954.

Analyzing manufacturing overhead variances; see Chapter 24, pp. 1007–1110.

☐ Refining Cost Systems
☐ Activity-Based Costing
☐ Activity-Based Management
■ ABC and Cost-Benefit
☐ JIT Systems
☐ Quality Management

 Decide when ABC is most likely to pass the cost-benefit test

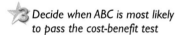tudent Resource**CD**
activity-based costing, cost allocation system, cost-benefit test, indirect costs

When Does ABC Pass the Cost-Benefit Test?

Like all other management tools, ABC must pass the cost-benefit test. The system should be refined enough to provide accurate product costs, but simple enough for managers to understand. In the Chemtech example, ABC triples the number of allocation bases—from the single allocation base (direct labor) in the original system, to three allocation bases (for mixing, processing, and testing) under ABC. ABC systems are even more complex in real-world companies that have many more activities and cost drivers.

The Cost-Benefit Test

Activity-based costing and activity-based management pass the cost-benefit test when the benefits of adopting ABC/ABM exceed the costs. Benefits of adopting ABC/ABM are higher for companies in competitive markets because:

- Accurate product cost information is essential for setting competitive sale prices that still allow the company to earn a profit.

- ABM can pinpoint opportunities for cost savings, which increase the company's profit or are passed on to customers in lower prices.

ABC's benefits are higher when ABC reports different product costs than under the old system. This is likely to happen when:

- The company produces many different products that use different amounts of resources. (If all products use similar amounts of resources, a simple single-allocation-base system works fine.)

- The company has high indirect costs. (If indirect costs are immaterial, it does not matter how they are allocated.)

- The company produces high volumes of some products and low volumes of other products. (Traditional single-allocation-base systems tend to overcost high-volume products and undercost low-volume products.)

The costs of adopting ABC are lower when the company has:

✔ Starter 25-5

✔ Starter 25-6

- Accounting and information system expertise to develop the system
- Information technology like bar coding, optical scanning, or "data warehouse" systems to record and compile cost driver data

Are real-world companies glad they adopted ABC? Usually, but not always. A recent survey has shown that 89% of the companies using ABC data say it was worth the cost.[1] Adoption is on the rise among financial companies like American Express, utilities like Indianapolis Power and Light, and nonprofits like the U.S. Marine Corps. But ABC is not a cure-all. As the controller for one Midwest manufacturer said, "ABC will not reduce cost, it will only help you understand costs better to know what to correct."

Signs That the Cost System May Be Broken

Broken cars or computers simply stop running. But unlike cars and computers, even broken or outdated product cost systems continue to report "product costs." How can you tell whether a cost system needs repair?

Management accounting expert Robin Cooper and others suggest that a company's product cost system may need repair when

Managers don't understand costs and profits:
- In bidding for jobs, managers lose bids they expected to win and win bids they expected to lose.
- Competitors with similar high-volume products price their products below our costs, but still earn good profits.
- Employees do not believe the cost numbers reported by the accounting system.

The cost system is outdated:
- The company uses a single-allocation-base system developed long ago.
- The company has reengineered its production process but has not changed its accounting system.

Review the Chemtech example on pages 1038–1042. List the symptoms that Chemtech's original cost system may be broken.

Answer:

1. The Chemical Manufacturing Department uses a single allocation base (direct labor cost) in a cost system developed over 15 years ago.

2. Competitors that focused on high-volume commodity chemicals earned good profits, despite undercutting Chemtech's sale prices. This was puzzling because Chemtech should be especially efficient at producing large batches of commodity chemicals.

3. Cost numbers reported by the accounting system were inconsistent with employees' intuition.

[1] K. Krumwiede, "ABC: Why It's Tried and How It Succeeds," *Management Accounting* (April 1998), pp. 32–38.

Decision Guidelines

ACTIVITY-BASED COSTING

Several years ago **Dell** decided it needed to refine its cost system. Starting with an Excel spreadsheet, Dell developed a simple ABC system that focused on the 10 most critical activities. Here are some of the decisions Dell faced as it began refining its cost system.

Decision	Guidelines
How to develop an ABC system?	1. Identify the activities. 2. Estimate total indirect costs of each activity. 3. Identify the allocation base (primary cost driver) for each activity's indirect costs. 4. Estimate the total quantity of each allocation base. 5. Compute the cost allocation rate for each activity. 6. Obtain the actual quantity of each allocation base used by cost object. 7. Allocate costs to cost object.
How to compute a cost allocation rate for an activity?	$$\dfrac{\text{Estimated total indirect cost of activity}}{\text{Estimated total quantity of allocation base}}$$
How to allocate an activity's cost to the cost object?	$$\begin{array}{c}\text{Cost allocation}\\\text{rate for}\\\text{activity}\end{array} \times \begin{array}{c}\text{Actual quantity of}\\\text{allocation base used by}\\\text{cost object}\end{array}$$
For what kinds of decisions do managers use ABC?	Managers use ABC data in ABM to make decisions on • Pricing and product mix • Cost cutting • Routine planning and control
How to set target costs?	$$\begin{array}{l}\text{Target sale price (based on market research)}\\\underline{-\text{ minus desired profit}}\\=\text{Target cost}\end{array}$$
How to achieve target costs?	Cross-functional teams use value engineering to cut costs by improving product design or production processes.
What are the main benefits of ABC?	• More-accurate product cost information. • More detailed information on costs of activities and drivers of those costs helps managers control costs.
When is ABC most likely to pass the cost-benefit test?	• Company is in competitive environment and needs accurate product costs. • Company makes different products that use different amounts of resources. • Company has high indirect costs. • Company produces high volumes of some products and lower volumes of other products. • Company has accounting and information technology expertise to implement system. • Old cost system appears "broken."
How to tell when a cost system needs revision?	• Managers lose bids they expected to win and win bids they expected to lose. • Competitors earn profits despite pricing high-volume products below our costs. • Employees do not believe cost numbers. • Company uses a single-allocation-base system developed long ago. • Company has reengineered the production process but not the accounting system.

Excel Application Exercise

Goal: Create a spreadsheet to compare traditional versus activity-based costing.

Scenario: Assume that Circuitech Corporation is one of **Dell's** circuit board suppliers. Circuitech currently uses a traditional costing system that allocates all indirect manufacturing costs based on machine hours, but at Dell's urging, it has decided to move to activity-based costing. You've been asked to compare the two costing methods for the next company board meeting. Your supervisor has given you the following quarterly data for products LP-7310 and PC-33:

	Assembly	*Soldering*	*Inspection*
Total indirect costs for the quarter	$630,000	$270,000	$160,000
Allocation base	Machine Hours	Number of Batches	Testing Hours

	LP-7310	*PC-33*
Direct cost of production (materials, labor)	$162,400	$178,240
Machine hours (assembly)	480	1,080
Number of batches produced (soldering)	60	40
Testing hours (inspection)	6,000	8,000
Number of units per batch	100	100

When you have completed your worksheet, answer the following questions:

1. What is the total manufacturing cost per unit under traditional costing for LP-7310? For PC-33?
2. What is the total manufacturing cost per unit under activity-based costing for LP-7310? For PC-33?
3. What conclusions do you draw from the spreadsheet information?

Step-by-Step:

1. Open a new Excel spreadsheet.
2. In column A, create a bold-faced heading as follows:
   a. Chapter 25 Excel Application Exercise
   b. Traditional vs. Activity-Based Costing
   c. Circuitech Corporation
   d. Today's Date
3. Move down one row. Starting in column C, enter the bold and underlined heading "Assembly." Enter "Soldering" in column D and "Inspection" in column E. In the next row, in column A, enter "Total Indirect Costs for the Quarter." Enter the data from the scenario under each column heading.

4. Two rows under this area, set up three columns: column A for the titles related to the remaining cost data, column D for product LP-7310, and column E for product PC-33. Enter the titles for each data item (from direct costs through the number of units per batch) in column A. Enter the appropriate amounts of each item for LP-7310 and PC-33 in columns D and E, respectively.
5. Two rows down in column A, enter the bold and underlined heading, "Traditional Costing System."
6. Under this heading, enter the description, "Cost Allocation Rate (per machine hour)." In column B, calculate the cost allocation rate.
7. Two rows down, in column A, enter the bold, underlined heading, "Cost per Product." Move over to column D and enter "LP-7310." In column E, enter "PC-33." Make these both bold and underlined.
8. Next, in column A, enter the following descriptions (one per line): "Direct Costs," "Manufacturing Overhead," "Total Manufacturing Cost per Product," "Number of Units," and "Total Manufacturing Cost per Unit." Compute each item for both products.
9. Move down two rows in column A. Enter the bold, underlined heading, "Activity-Based Costing System." In column B, enter the heading, "Cost Allocation Rate." In columns C and D, enter the heading, "Actual Quantity of Cost Allocation Base Used By:." In columns E and F, enter the heading, "Allocated Activity Cost." Make all headings bold.
10. Under the heading "Actual Quantity of Cost Allocation Base Used By:", enter LP-7310 in one column and PC-33 in the next column. Center the heading over the two products.
11. Under the heading "Allocated Activity Cost," enter LP-7310 in one column and PC-33 in the next column. Center the heading over the two products.
12. In column A, list the three activities (assembly, soldering, inspection), one per row. Then, calculate each item for both products.
13. Finally, two rows down, in column A, enter the bold, underlined heading, "Cost per Product." Move over four columns and set up boldfaced and underlined headings for LP-7310 and PC-33. Under the "Cost per Product" heading, enter "Direct Costs," Manufacturing Overhead:," "Assembly," "Soldering," "Inspection," "Total Manufacturing Cost per Product," "Number of Units," and "Total Manufacturing Cost per Unit." Calculate each line item for LP-7310 and PC-33.
14. Save your work and print a copy for your files.

MID-CHAPTER *Summary Problem*

Indianapolis Auto Parts (IAP) has a Seat Manufacturing Department that uses activity-based costing. IAP's system has the following features:

Activity	Allocation Base	Cost Allocation Rate
Purchasing	Number of purchase orders	$60.00 per purchase order
Assembling	Number of parts	0.50 per part
Packaging	Number of finished seats	0.90 per finished seat

TIPS

CHECK YOUR RESOURCES

(continued)

Each seat has 20 parts; direct materials cost per seat is $11. Suppose **Ford** has asked for a bid on 50,000 built-in baby seats that would be installed as an option on some Ford SUVs. IAP will use a total of 200 purchase orders if Ford accepts IAP's bid.

Required

1. Compute the total cost IAP will incur to purchase the needed materials and then assemble and package 50,000 baby seats. Also compute the average cost per seat.
2. For bidding, IAP adds a 30% markup to total cost. What price will the company bid for the Ford order?
3. Suppose that instead of an ABC system, IAP has a traditional product costing system that allocates all costs other than direct materials at the rate of $65 per direct labor hour. The baby-seat order will require 10,000 direct labor hours. What price will IAP bid using this system's total cost?
4. Use your answers to requirements 2 and 3 to explain how ABC can help IAP make a better decision about the bid price it will offer Ford.

Solution

Requirement 1

Total Cost of Order and Average Cost per Seat:

Direct materials, 50,000 × $11.00	$ 550,000
Activity costs:	
Purchasing, 200 × $60.00	12,000
Assembling, 50,000 × 20 × $0.50	500,000
Packaging, 50,000 × $0.90	45,000
Total cost of order............................	$1,107,000
Divide by number of seats	÷ 50,000
Average cost per seat...........................	$ 22.14

Requirement 2

Bid Price (ABC System):

Bid price ($1,107,000 × 130%) $1,439,100

Requirement 3

Bid Price (Traditional System):

Direct materials, 50,000 × $11.00	$ 550,000
Other product costs, 10,000 × $65	650,000
Total cost of order...........................	$1,200,000
Bid price ($1,200,000 × 130%)....................	$1,560,000

Requirement 4

IAP's bid would be $120,900 higher using the direct labor single-allocation-base system than using ABC ($1,560,000 − $1,439,100). Assuming the ABC system more accurately captures the costs caused by the order, the traditional direct labor system overcosts the order. This leads to a higher bid price that reduces IAP's chance of winning the bid. The ABC system shows that IAP can increase its chance of winning the bid by bidding a lower price and still make a profit.

☐ Refining Cost Systems
☐ Activity-Based Costing
☐ Activity-Based Management
☐ ABC and Cost-Benefit
■ JIT Systems
☐ Quality Management

Describe a just-in-time (JIT) production system, and record its manufacturing costs

Traditional versus Just-in-Time Systems

ABC and ABM often reveal the high costs of (1) buying, storing, and moving inventories, and (2) poor-quality products and services. So it is not surprising that a recent study of "best practices" companies revealed most had linked their ABC/ABM systems to just-in-time (JIT) or quality initiatives. For example,

Carrier Corporation's ABC/ABM system's evidence that materials handling was a major cost driver prompted Carrier to adopt JIT. The rest of this chapter expands on Chapter 19's introduction to JIT and quality. →

We begin by contrasting JIT production systems with traditional systems.

← *Chapter 19, p. 771, introduced JIT.*

Student ResourceCD
just-in-time costing, standard costing system

Traditional Systems

Traditional businesses keep large inventories of raw materials, work in process, and finished goods. Why? First, poor-quality raw materials lead companies to buy more than they need. Also, machine breakdowns and production problems *within* departments prompt managers to keep extra work in process *between* departments. Exhibit 25-12 describes the production of drill bits from bar stock (the raw material). Work in process inventory between the grinding and smoothing operations allows smoothing work to continue even if grinding machines break down.

Exhibit 25-12

Sequence of Operations for Drill-Bit Production

A second reason for large inventories is that companies with long setup times often make products in large batches to spread setup costs over many units. A third reason for stocking large inventories is uncertainty in deliveries from suppliers and orders from customers. Large raw material inventories protect against delayed deliveries. Large inventories of finished goods protect against lost sales if customer demand is higher than expected.

Why are large inventories a problem? First, inventories tie up cash. Companies incur interest expense or forgo interest revenue on that cash. Second, inventories often hide quality problems, production bottlenecks, and obsolescence.

Just-in-Time Systems

Workers read orders off a monitor and assemble a Dell desktop every 3 to 5 minutes. Most days, workers finish more than 25,000 computers, which ship directly to customers. But the plant rarely holds more than two *hours* of inventory![2] How does Dell do it? By complete commitment to the just-in-time philosophy.

Companies with JIT systems buy materials and complete finished goods *just in time* for delivery to customers. This reduces waste. Many managers regard JIT as a *general philosophy of waste elimination*. Companies that follow JIT have several common characteristics:

1. ***Production activities in self-contained cells.*** A traditional drill-bit manufacturer would group all the shaping machines in one area, all the grinding machines in another area, and all the smoothing machines in a third area, as illustrated in Panel A of Exhibit 25-13. After switching to JIT, the company would group the machines in self-contained production cells, or production lines, as in Panel B of Exhibit 25-13. The goal is continuous production without interruptions or work in process inventories. Arranging machines in sequential production cells slashes production time. Within six years after adopting JIT, Harley-Davidson reduced the time to produce a motorcycle by 77%.

✔ Starter 25-12

---

[2]*Source:* Kathryn Jones, "The Dell Way," *Business 2.0*, February 2003, www.business2.com.

Exhibit 25-13 Equipment Arrangement in Traditional and JIT Production Systems

PANEL A—Traditional Production System
Each type of machine is grouped together in one area of the plant.

Building A — Cutting Department, Shaping Department, work-in-process

Building B — Grinding Department, Smoothing Department, work-in-process, finished drill bits, finished ratchets

PANEL B—Just-in-Time Production System
Different machines arranged in self-contained production cells.

Building A — Drill Bit Production Line 1: cutting machine, shaping machine, grinding machine, smoothing machine, finished drill bits; Drill Bit Production Line 2: cutting machine, shaping machine, grinding machine, smoothing machine, finished drill bits

Building B — Ratchet Production Line 1: cutting machine, shaping machine, grinding machine, smoothing machine, finished ratchets; Ratchet Production Line 2: cutting machine, shaping machine, grinding machine, smoothing machine, finished ratchets

2. *Short setup times.* JIT companies reduce setup times on machines used for more than one product. Employee training and technology helped Toyota cut setup times from several hours to a few minutes. This increases flexibility in scheduling production to meet customer orders, which in turn increases customer satisfaction and company profits.

3. *Broad employee roles.* Employees in JIT systems do more than operate a single machine. They also conduct maintenance, perform setups, inspect their own work, and operate other machines. This cross-training boosts morale and lowers costs.

4. *Small batches produced just in time.* JIT businesses schedule production in small batches *just in time* to satisfy needs. A customer order triggers manufacturing. The final operation in the production sequence (smoothing, in our drill-bit example) "pulls" parts from the preceding operation (grinding). The grinding-machine operator pulls shaped parts from shaping, and so on. This "demand–pull" system extends back to suppliers of materials. Suppliers make frequent deliveries of defect-free materials *just in time* for production.

Purchasing and producing only what customers demand reduces inventory. Less inventory frees floor space for more productive use. When HP adopted JIT, the company cut its work-in-process inventory by 82% and its production floor space by 40%.

5. *Supply chain management.* Because there are no inventory buffers, JIT requires close coordination with suppliers who guarantee on-time delivery of defect-free materials. ← Chapter 19 defined *supply-chain management* as exchanging information with suppliers and customers to reduce costs, improve quality, and speed delivery of goods and services from the company's suppliers, through the company itself, and on to the company's end customers. Consider the following examples.[3]

See Chapter 19, p. 771, for a discussion of supply-chain management.

---

[3]*Sources:* Gregory L. White, "Chrysler Makes Manufacturing Inroads at Plant in Brazil," *The Wall Street Journal,* Aug. 28, 1998. Emily Nelson, "Wal-Mart Sets Supply Plan as Net Tops Forecasts," *The Wall Street Journal,* Nov. 10, 1999, B12. Joshua Dean, "The Supply Chain's Demands," May 1, 2002. GovExec.com. Joseph Martha, and Sunil Subbakrishna, "When Just-in-Time Becomes Just-in-Case," *The Wall Street Journal,* Oct. 22, 2001, A18.

Chrysler's Brazilian plant, which makes Dakota pickup trucks, buys a partially completed chassis from supplier Dana Corporation's plant 2 miles down the road. Dana assembles 320 parts onto the truck's frame, including axles, brakes, and wheels, within 108 minutes of receiving an electronic order from the Chrysler plant. Dana then delivers each partially complete chassis to the Chrysler production line, in the sequence that Chrysler specifies. Chrysler adds the engines, transmissions, and body to complete each truck.

When Procter & Gamble delivers Crest toothpaste on a just-in-time basis to Wal-Mart's distribution center, Wal-Mart immediately unloads the toothpaste directly onto trucks headed for Wal-Mart stores. On average, the toothpaste is on the Wal-Mart shelf within 4 hours and sold within 24 hours. "It is our objective to sell the merchandise before we pay for it" says a Wal-Mart senior vice president.

Even the U.S. government uses supply-chain management to implement JIT. A flat tire can ground a $20 million jet fighter, and aircraft carriers don't have room to store many spare parts. How does the U.S. Navy ensure that tires and other parts are available when needed? By contracting with Lockheed Martin to manage the supply chain. Sailors simply fill out an online form, and Lockheed Martin must ensure that the Michelin tires are delivered within four days, anywhere in the world.

While companies like Toyota, Carrier, and Dell credit JIT for saving them millions of dollars, the system is not without problems. With no inventory buffers, JIT users are vulnerable when problems strike suppliers or distributors. For example, Ford cut production of its SUVs in response to the tire shortage resulting from the Firestone tire recall. It also had to shut down five of its U.S. plants when engine deliveries from Canadian suppliers were late due to security-related transportation delays in the wake of the World Trade Center attacks.

Continued security-related delays in air, rail, and truck border crossings have stressed DaimlerChrysler's JIT system, which relies on 1,500 daily truckloads of materials crossing the U.S.–Canadian border between Detroit and Windsor, Ontario.

Just-in-Time Costing

After adopting JIT, many companies simplify their accounting systems. **Just-in-time costing**, sometimes called **backflush costing**, is a standard costing system that starts with output completed and then assigns manufacturing costs to units sold and to inventories. There are three major differences between JIT costing and the traditional standard costing system we described in Chapter 24:

Just-in-Time (JIT) Costing
A standard costing system that starts with output completed and then assigns manufacturing costs to units sold and to inventories. Also called **backflush costing**.

1. JIT systems do not track the cost of products from raw materials inventory to work in process inventory to finished goods inventory. Instead, JIT costing systems wait until the units are completed to record the cost of production.

2. Because JIT systems do not track costs attached to units in the production process, JIT systems do not need a separate Work in Process Inventory account. They combine raw materials and work in process inventories into a single account called Raw and In Process Inventory.

3. Under the JIT philosophy, workers perform many tasks. Since little labor is directly traceable to individual finished products, most companies using JIT combine labor and manufacturing overhead costs into an account called Conversion Costs (as we saw in Chapter 21 on process costing). → The Conversion Cost account is a temporary account that works just like the Manufacturing Overhead account described in Chapter 20. Actual conversion costs accumulate as debits in the Conversion Cost account, and the account is credited when conversion costs are allocated to completed units. Accountants close any under- or overallocated conversion costs to Cost of Goods Sold at the end of the year, just like under- or overallocated manufacturing overhead in Chapter 20.

← *Chapter 21, p. 850, introduced conversion costs.*

Accounting.com

Point, Click, Buy, Sell: Businesses Cut Costs by Buying and Selling Online

At Minneapolis-based **3M Company**, processing a single invoice used to cost $120. Thanks to purchasing products online, that cost has dropped to under $40. 3M, **Texas Instruments**, **John Deere**, and **Owens-Corning** are among the hundreds of large U.S. companies who are using e-procurement to achieve incredible cost savings. On average, companies can trim costs by 15 to 20% when they buy online. That's why materials purchased online have ballooned from $75 billion in 2000 to about $3 trillion in 2003.

E-procurement includes: (1) the creation of electronic product catalogs, (2) the exchange of product and purchasing information directly with suppliers via electronic data interchange (EDI), and (3) the use of digital marketplaces or exchanges, such as a "reverse online auction," in which suppliers bid to see who can come in with the lowest price. E-procurement can lead to substantial savings, such as:

- **Mercedes Benz** in Spain has saved between $1.5 million and $3 million, of which 20 to 30% is due to lower transaction-processing costs and the rest due to better price negotiations.
- Toledo, Ohio-based Owens-Corning has cut costs of bottled-water jugs by 60% and stretch wrap by 25%. Overall, the glass and building materials manufacturer has cut 10% on annual purchases of $3.4 billion.
- **HP** cut 30% off the amount it pays for the logos it places on its products.

Yet, these e-procurement success stories do come with some caveats. Most of the companies taking advantage of e-procurement are large companies with at least $750 million in sales. The number of suppliers participating is also limited because they are wary about a technology that cuts their profit margins. For instance, reverse auctions may force suppliers to either bid below their actual costs to get the work or else lose out to competitors. Finally, e-procurement is not just about adopting newfangled software in the purchasing department. All stakeholders—from staff to suppliers—must be convinced of the program's worth and be given the necessary support and training. For some companies, the switch to e-procurement requires a complete organizational change. Yet, judging by the continuing explosion in e-procurement, it's a change many companies find worth making.

Based on: Sarah Perrin, "Business: E-Procurement—Doing It Right," *Accountancy,* September 2002, pp. 59–60. Karen J. Bannan, "The Pulse of the Supply Chain," *Internet World,* January 2003, pp. 22–25. Michael A. Verespej, "E-Procurement Explosion," *Industry Week,* March 2002, pp. 24–28.

Consider Mintel Company, which converts silicon wafers into integrated circuits for computers. Mintel has only one direct manufacturing product cost: silicon wafers, which are labeled "raw." All other manufacturing costs, including labor and various chemicals, are indirect costs of converting the "raw" silicon wafers into the finished integrated circuits. These indirect costs are collected in the "Conversion Costs" account.

Mintel does not use a separate Work in Process Inventory account. Instead, it uses the following two inventory accounts:

- Raw and In Process Inventory, which combines direct materials with work in process
- Finished Goods Inventory

Mintel has $100,000 of Raw and In Process Inventory and $900,000 of Finished ✔ Starter 25-13
Goods Inventory at July 31, and it uses JIT costing to record the August transactions.

1. Mintel purchases $3,020,000 of direct materials (silicon wafers) on account.

Raw and In Process Inventory	3,020,000	
Accounts Payable.		3,020,000

2. Mintel spends $18,540,000 on labor and overhead.

Conversion Costs	18,540,000	
Various Accounts (such as wages payable and accumulated depreciation on property, plant, and equipment.)		18,540,000

3. Mintel completed 3,000,000 circuits. The standard cost of the circuit is $7 ($1 direct materials and $6 conversion cost). The debit (increase) to finished goods is $21,000,000 (3,000,000 completed circuits × $7). There is no work in process inventory in JIT costing, so Mintel credits

- Raw and In Process Inventory, $3,000,000 (3,000,000 completed circuits × $1 standard raw material cost per circuit) for the silicon wafers, and
- Conversion Costs, $18,000,000 (3,000,000 completed circuits × $6 standard conversion cost per completed circuit) for the labor and other indirect costs allocated to the finished circuits.

Finished Goods Inventory	21,000,000	
Raw and In Process Inventory (3,000,000 × $1).		3,000,000
Conversion Costs (3,000,000 × $6). .		18,000,000

This is the essence of JIT costing. The system does not track costs as the circuits move through manufacturing. Instead, *completion* of the circuits triggers the accounting system to go back and pull costs from Raw and In Process Inventory and to allocate conversion costs to the finished products.

4. Mintel sold 2,930,000 circuits (2,930,000 circuits × $7 per circuit = $20,510,000).

Cost of Goods Sold.	20,510,000	
Finished Goods Inventory		20,510,000

Exhibit 25-14 shows Mintel's major accounts. Combining the raw materials inventory with work in process inventory to form the single Raw and In Process Inventory account eliminates detail. Although Mintel tracks the number of physical units in process, the company does not use material requisitions or time records to assign *costs* to circuits as they flow through the production process. Mintel does not assign costs to physical products until the goods are completed.

 Mintel's Major JIT Costing Accounts

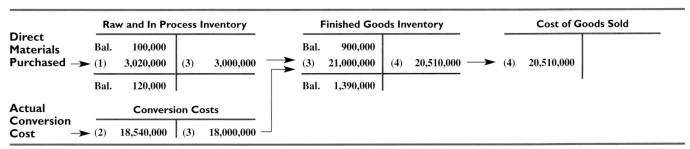

You can see from Exhibit 25-14 that conversion costs are underallocated by $540,000 ($18,540,000 − $18,000,000). Under- and overallocated conversion costs are treated just like under- and overallocated manufacturing overhead and closed to Cost of Goods Sold. ←

See Chapter 20, pp. 815–817, for a → review of under- and overallocated manufacturing overhead.

Cost of Goods Sold	540,000	
Conversion Costs...................		540,000

□ Refining Cost Systems
□ Activity-Based Costing
□ Activity-Based Management
□ ABC and Cost-Benefit
□ JIT Systems
■ Quality Management

⭐ *Contrast the four types of quality costs and use them to make decisions*

 Student Resource CD

quality costs, total quality management

See TQM discussion in Chapter 19, → pp. 772–773.

> Activity-based costing is a detailed costing method that provides more-accurate product costs. Just-in-time costing is simplified and does not track costs through the sequence of manufacturing operations. Are these two costing systems incompatible? Or can they be used together?
>
> *Answer:* ABC and JIT costing can be compatible. Mintel's $6 standard conversion cost per circuit used in JIT costing could be provided by an ABC system.

Continuous Improvement and the Management of Quality

Companies using JIT strive for high-quality production. Because goods are produced only as needed, poor-quality materials or defective manufacturing processes shut down production.

To meet this challenge, many companies adopt *total quality management (TQM)*. ← The goal of TQM is to provide customers with superior products and services. Each business function in the value chain examines its own activities to improve quality and eliminate defects and waste.

Carefully designed products reduce manufacturing time, inspections, rework, and warranty claims. Investing in the front end of the value chain (R&D and design) can generate savings in the back end (production, marketing, and customer service). World-class companies like Toyota and Dell *design* and *build* quality into their products rather than having to *inspect* and *repair* later.

Types of Quality Costs

The four types of quality-related costs include:

Prevention Costs
Costs incurred to *avoid* poor-quality goods or services.

   1. Prevention costs incurred to *avoid* poor-quality goods or services. For example, Michael Dell became convinced that reducing human interaction with critical components was key to improving the quality of Dell computers. So Dell reengineered its assembly process to cut in half the number of times humans touch the hard drive. The result? The hard-drive failure rate dropped 40%.

   Winemaker Robert Mondavi Corporation's prevention costs include the cost of using satellite imaging and Global Positioning Systems in the vineyard to ensure grapes are uniformly ripe at harvest time. Production workers assigned to quality teams at General Motors carry beepers so line workers can page when they spot a problem. The quality team identifies and corrects the cause of the defect (for example, a misaligned robot) right away. The plant does not waste time and materials churning out defective cars.

Appraisal Costs
Costs incurred to *detect* poor-quality goods or services.

   2. Appraisal costs are incurred to *detect* poor-quality goods or services. Intel incurs appraisal costs when it tests its products. One procedure, called burn-in, heats circuits to a high temperature. A circuit that fails the burn-in test is also likely to fail in customer use.

3. Internal failure costs occur when the company detects and corrects poor-quality goods or services *before* delivery to customers. An example is the labor of a BMW mechanic who reworks a faulty brake job after inspection by a supervisor.

4. External failure costs occur when the company does not detect poor-quality goods or services until *after* delivery to customers. If an auto-repair shop does faulty work, the customer will discover the flawed brakes. Then the shop may have to repair the body of the car as well as the brakes. External failures can ruin a company's reputation.

Exhibit 25-15 lists some examples of the four types of quality costs. Most prevention costs occur in the R&D and design stages of the value chain. In contrast, most appraisal and internal failure costs occur in the production element of the value chain. External failure costs occur in the customer-service stage or are opportunity costs of lost sales. Managers make trade-offs among these costs. Many prevention costs are incurred only periodically, while internal and external failure costs are ongoing. One expert estimates that 8¢ spent on prevention saves most manufacturers $1 in failure costs.

Internal Failure Costs
Costs incurred when the company detects and corrects poor-quality goods or services *before* delivery to customers.

External Failure Costs
Costs incurred when the company does not detect poor-quality goods or services until *after* delivery to customers.

✔ **Starter 25-14**

Exhibit 25-15

Four Types of Quality Costs

Prevention Costs	Appraisal Costs
Training personnel	Inspection of incoming materials
Evaluating potential suppliers	Inspection at various stages of production
Improved materials	Inspection of final products or services
Preventive maintenance	Product testing
Improved equipment and processes	

Internal Failure Costs	External Failure Costs
Production loss caused by downtime	Lost profits from lost customers
Rework	Warranty costs
Scrap	Service costs at customer sites
Rejected product units	Sales returns and allowances due to quality problems
Disposal of rejected units	Product liability claims

Deciding Whether to Adopt a New Quality Program

Let's revisit Chemtech. CEO Randy Smith is considering spending the following amounts on a new quality program:

Inspect raw materials	$100,000
Reengineer the production process to improve product quality	750,000
Inspect finished goods	150,000
Supplier screening and certification	25,000
Preventive maintenance of plant and equipment	75,000

Chemtech expects this quality program to reduce costs by the following amounts:

Lost profits from lost sales due to disappointed customers	$800,000
Fewer sales returns to be processed	50,000
Lost profits from lost production time due to rework	250,000
Reduced warranty costs	125,000

Smith asks Controller Wise to

1. Classify each of these costs into one of the four categories (prevention, appraisal, internal failure, external failure) and total the estimated costs in each category.

✔ Starter 25-15

2. Recommend whether Chemtech should undertake the quality program. Wise uses the results in Exhibit 25-16 to analyze Chemtech's two alternatives:
- Incur the prevention and appraisal costs to undertake the quality program
- Do not undertake the quality program and incur the internal and external failure costs

| Exhibit 25-16 | Analysis of Chemtech's Proposed Quality Program |

Undertake the Quality Program		Do Not Undertake the Quality Program	
Prevention		**Internal Failure**	
Reengineer the production process to improve product quality	$ 750,000	Lost profits from lost production time due to rework	$ 250,000
Supplier screening and certification	25,000	Total internal failure costs	$ 250,000
Preventive maintenance of plant and equipment	75,000	**External Failure**	
Total prevention costs	$ 850,000	Lost profits from lost sales due to disappointed customers	$ 800,000
Appraisal		Sales return processing	50,000
Inspect raw materials	$ 100,000	Warranty costs	125,000
Inspect finished goods	150,000	Total external failure costs	$ 975,000
Total appraisal costs	$ 250,000		
Total costs of undertaking the quality program	$1,100,000	**Total costs of not undertaking the** quality program	$1,225,000

Decision: Undertake the Quality Program

These estimates suggest that Chemtech would save $125,000 ($1,225,000 – $1,100,000) by undertaking the quality program.

Quality costs can be hard to measure. For example, design engineers may spend only part of their time on quality. Allocating their salaries to various activities is subjective. It is especially hard to measure external failure costs. The biggest external failure cost—profits lost because unhappy customers never return ($800,000)—does not even appear in the accounting records! So total quality management programs also emphasize nonfinancial measures such as number of customer complaints.

Decision Guidelines

JUST-IN-TIME AND QUALITY COSTS

Dell Computer, the worldwide leader in PC sales, is famous for its complete commitment to both the just-in-time and total quality management philosophies. Following are several decisions Dell's managers made when adopting these two modern management techniques.

Decision	Guidelines	
How to change a traditional production system to a JIT system?	*Traditional*	*JIT*
	Like machines grouped together	Production cells
	Longer setup times	Short setup times
	Larger batches	Smaller batches
	Higher inventories	Lower inventories
	An individual does fewer tasks	An individual does wider range of tasks
	Many suppliers	Fewer, but well-coordinated suppliers

(continued)

Decision Guidelines *(continued)*

Decision	Guidelines
How to simplify costing after adopting JIT?	Use JIT costing.
	1. Summary journal entries are not made until units are completed; costs are not separately tracked as units move through production.
	2. Raw materials and work in process are combined into a single Raw and In Process Inventory account.
	3. Labor and overhead are combined into a Conversion Cost account.
What are the four types of quality costs?	Prevention costs
	Appraisal costs
	Internal failure costs
	External failure costs
How to make trade-offs among the four types of quality costs?	Investment in prevention costs and appraisal costs reduces internal and external failure costs.

END-OF-CHAPTER *Summary Problem*

The Flores Company manufactures cellular telephones. Flores uses JIT costing. The standard unit cost is $37: $24 direct materials and $13 conversion costs. Direct materials purchased on account during June totaled $2,540,000. Actual conversion costs totaled $1,295,000. Flores completed 102,000 telephones in June and sold 98,000.

CHECK YOUR RESOURCES

Required

1. Prepare the June journal entries for these transactions.
2. Make the entry to close the under- or overallocated conversion costs to Cost of Goods Sold.

Solutions

Requirement 1

Raw and In Process Inventory	2,540,000	
Accounts Payable		2,540,000
Conversion Costs	1,295,000	
Various accounts (such as payables and accumulated depreciation). . .		1,295,000
Finished Goods Inventory	3,774,000	
Raw and In Process Inventory (102,000 × $24)		2,448,000
Conversion Costs (102,000 × $13) .		1,326,000
Cost of Goods Sold (98,000 × $37)	3,626,000	
Finished Goods Inventory		3,626,000

Requirement 2

Conversion Costs	31,000	
Cost of Goods Sold		31,000

⬤REVIEW *Activity-Based Costing and Other Cost Management Tools*

Quick Check

1. Which of the following is *false*?
   a. The distinguishing feature of ABC is that it focuses on allocating indirect costs.
   b. Advances in information technology have made it feasible for more companies to adopt ABC.
   c. ABC is primarily for manufacturing firms.
   d. A system that uses ABC is more refined than one that uses departmental overhead rates.

The following data apply to questions 2 through 4. Two of **Dell Computer's** primary production activities are *kitting* (assembling raw materials needed for a particular computer or server in one kit) and *boxing* the completed products for shipment to customers. Assume that Dell spends $5 million a month on the kitting activity and $10 million a month on boxing. It allocates kitting activity costs based on the number of parts used in the product and boxing activity costs based on the cubic feet of space the product requires. Suppose Dell estimates it will use 800 million parts a month and ship products with a total volume of 20 million cubic feet.

Assume that each desktop computer requires 100 parts and has a volume of 5 cubic feet. Assume that each server requires 150 parts and has a volume of 7 cubic feet.

2. What is the activity cost allocation rate for:

	Kitting	Boxing
a.	$0.00625/part	$0.50/cubic foot
b.	$0.0125/part	$0.25/cubic foot
c.	$0.50/part	$40/cubic foot
d.	$160/part	$2/cubic foot

3. What are the kitting and boxing costs assigned to one desktop computer?

	Kitting	Boxing
a.	$0.625	$2.50
b.	$0.9375	$3.50
c.	$1.25	$1.25
d.	$50.00	$200

4. Dell contracts with its suppliers to pre-kit certain component parts before delivering them to Dell. Assume this saves $1.5 million of the kitting activity cost and that it reduces the total number of parts by 400 million (because Dell considers each pre-kit as one part). If a server now uses 80 parts, what is the new kitting cost assigned to one server?
   a. $0.35   c. $0.9375
   b. $0.70   d. $1.00

5. Dell can use ABC information for what decisions?
   a. Pricing   c. Evaluating managers' performance
   b. Cost cutting   d. All of the above

6. Which of the following is *not* a good reason for Dell to use ABC?
   a. The computer industry is highly competitive.
   b. Dell produces many more desktops than servers, and servers are more difficult to assemble.
   c. Most costs are direct; indirect costs are a small proportion of total costs.
   d. Dell has advanced information technology, including bar-coded materials and labor.

7. Dell enjoys many benefits from committing to JIT. Which is *not* a benefit of adopting JIT?
   a. Lower inventory carrying costs
   b. More space available for production
   c. Ability to respond more quickly to changes in customer demand
   d. Ability to continue production despite disruptions in deliveries of raw materials

8. The following account is *not* used in JIT costing:
   a. Raw and in process inventory
   b. Conversion costs
   c. Work in process inventory
   d. Finished goods inventory

9. The cost of lost future sales after a customer finds flaws in a product or service is which of the following quality costs?
   a. External failure cost
   b. Internal failure cost
   c. Appraisal cost
   d. Prevention cost

10. Dell's spending on testing its computers before shipment to customers helps *reduce* which of the following costs?
    a. Prevention cost
    b. Appraisal cost
    c. External failure cost
    d. None of the above

Accounting Vocabulary

activity-based costing (ABC) (p. 1036)
activity-based management (ABM) (p. 1042)
appraisal costs (p. 1056)

backflush costing (p. 1053)
external failure costs (p. 1057)
internal failure costs (p. 1057)
just-in-time (JIT) costing (p. 1053)

prevention costs (p. 1056)
target cost (p. 1043)
target price (p. 1043)
value engineering (p. 1043)

ASSESS *Your Progress* ⬤

Starters

S25-1 Suppose Chemtech's activity-based costing team identifies a fourth activity: machine setup. The foreman estimates that the total setup cost will be $280,000 and that production will require 2,500 setups. (This is less than the 4,000 total batches in Exhibit 25-7. Chemtech often eliminates a setup by running two batches of the same chemical in a row.) Aldehyde will require 30 setups, and PH will require 2 setups.

1. Compute the cost allocation rate for machine setups.
2. Compute the total machine setup costs allocated to aldehyde and to PH.
3. Did Chemtech's original allocation base (200% of direct labor cost) allocate setup costs appropriately? Give your reason.

See *www.prenhall.com/horngren* for selected Starters, Exercises, and Problems.

Developing an activity cost allocation rate
(Obj. I)

S25-2 Consider the Chemtech example on pages 1038–1042 and your analysis in Starter 25-1.

1. Compute the machine setup cost per pound for aldehyde and for PH.
2. Use your answer to requirement 1 to explain why switching from a traditional single-allocation-base system to an ABC system usually shifts costs away from high-volume products toward low-volume products.

Computing activity costs and explaining changes **(Obj. I)**

S25-3 Use the results of Starter 25-1 and the information in Exhibits 25-8 and 25-9 to revise the

1. Manufacturing overhead cost per pound for aldehyde and for PH
2. Gross profit per pound for aldehyde and for PH

Using ABC to allocate indirect costs **(Obj. I)**

S25-4 Starters 25-4 through 25-10 center on Mission, Inc., a technology consulting firm focused on Web site development and integration of Internet business applications. President Susan Nelson's ear is ringing after an unpleasant call from client Jerry Webb.

Allocating indirect costs and computing income **(Obj. I)**

(*continued*)

Webb was irate after opening his bill for Mission's redesign of his company's Web site. Webb said that Nelson's major competitor, Delta Applications, charged much lower fees to another company for which Webb serves on the board of directors.

Nelson is puzzled for two reasons. First, she is confident that her firm knows Web site design and support as well as any of Mission's competitors. Nelson cannot understand how Delta Applications can undercut Mission's rates and still make a profit. But Delta Applications is reputed to be very profitable. Second, just yesterday Nelson received a call from client Keith Greg. Greg was happy with the excellent service and reasonable fees Nelson charged him for adding a database-driven job posting feature to his company's Web site. Nelson was surprised by Greg's compliments because this was an unusual job for Mission that required development of complex database management and control applications, and she had felt a little uneasy accepting it.

Like most consulting firms, Mission traces direct labor to individual engagements (jobs). Mission allocated indirect costs to engagements using a budgeted rate based on direct labor hours. Nelson is happy with this system, which she has used since she established Mission in 1995.

Nelson expects to incur $706,000 of indirect costs this year, and she expects her firm to work 5,000 direct labor hours. Nelson and the other systems consultants earn $350 per hour. Clients are billed at 150% of direct labor cost. Last month Mission's consultants spent 100 hours on Webb's engagement. They also spent 100 hours on Greg's engagement.

1. Compute Mission's indirect cost allocation rate.
2. Compute the total costs assigned to the Webb and Greg engagements.
3. Compute the operating income from the Webb and Greg engagements.

Identifying signals of a broken cost system
(Obj. 3)

S25-5 Review Mission's situation in Starter 25-4. List all the signals or clues that indicate Mission's cost system may be "broken."

Deciding whether ABC will pass cost-benefit test
(Obj. 3)

S25-6 Susan Nelson has employed your consulting firm to help her decide whether to develop an activity-based costing system. After reviewing the information in Starters 25-4 and 25-5, draft a memo to Nelson. Make a recommendation whether her firm should develop an ABC system. Be sure to explain the costs and benefits Nelson could expect from adopting ABC. Use the following format for your memo.

> **Date:** _____
>
> **To:** Ms. Susan Nelson, President, Mission, Inc.
>
> **From:** Student name
>
> **Subject:** Cost system recommendation

Computing ABC allocation rates
(Obj. 1)

S25-7 Susan Nelson from Starter 25-4 suspects that her allocation of indirect costs could be giving misleading results, so she decides to develop an ABC system. She identifies three activities: documentation preparation, information technology support, and training. Nelson figures that documentation costs are driven by the number of pages, information technology support costs are driven by the number of software applications used, and training costs are most closely associated with the number of direct labor hours worked. Estimates of the costs and quantities of the allocation bases follow:

Activity	Estimated Cost	Allocation Base	Estimated Quantity of Cost Driver
Documentation preparation.......	$100,000	Pages	3,125 pages
Information technology support...	156,000	Applications used	780 applications
Training.......................	450,000	Direct labor hours	5,000 hours
Total indirect costs..............	$706,000		

Compute the cost allocation rate for each activity.

S25-8 Refer to Mission, Inc., in Starters 25-4 and 25-7. The Webb and Greg engagements used the following resources last month:

Using ABC to allocate costs and compute profit
(Obj. 1)

Cost Driver	Webb	Greg
Direct labor hours....................	100	100
Pages...............................	50	300
Applications used....................	1	78

1. Compute the cost assigned to the Webb engagement and to the Greg engagement, using the ABC system.
2. Compute the operating income from the Webb engagement and from the Greg engagement, using the ABC system.

S25-9 Write a memo to Susan Nelson comparing the costs of the Webb and Greg jobs using the original direct labor single-allocation-base system (Starter 25-4) and the ABC system (Starter 25-8). Be sure to explain:

Explaining results of ABC analysis
(Obj. 1)

- How have the costs changed under the ABC system?
- Why have the costs changed in the direction they changed, rather than in the opposite direction?
- Do the ABC results solve Nelson's puzzle from Starter 25-4?

Your memo should follow the format outlined in Starter 25-6.

S25-10 Write a memo to Susan Nelson (Starters 25-4 through 25-9) explaining how she can use the ABC information to make decisions about her consulting firm. Consider how she could use ABC information in:

Using ABC information to make decisions
(Obj. 2)

- Setting fees (prices)
- Responding to client concerns about fees
- Controlling costs

Your memo should follow the format outlined in Starter 25-6.

S25-11 The vice president of marketing storms into your office, exclaiming:

Activity-based management, Uses of ABC data
(Obj. 2)

> Activity-based costing is worse than useless. It's endangering the future of our company! Because of your ABC cost "information," the CEO is pressuring us to (1) charge customers higher prices for customized products, (2) shift customers from customized products to standard products, and (3) require customers to accept larger deliveries than they would prefer. This completely violates our motto of "delighting the customer." Worse yet, we are being pressured to drop some of the customers we have spent a great deal of effort cultivating. This stupid ABC system will ruin us all!

Reply to your colleague.

S25-12 Indicate whether each of the following is characteristic of a JIT production system or a traditional production system.

Comparing JIT and traditional production systems
(Obj. 4)

a. Management works with suppliers to ensure defect-free raw materials.
b. Products produced in large batches.
c. Large stocks of finished goods protect against lost sales if customer demand is higher than expected.
d. Suppliers make frequent deliveries of small quantities of raw materials.
e. Long setup times.
f. Employees do a variety of jobs, including maintenance and setups as well as operating machines.

(continued)

g. Machines are grouped into self-contained production cells or production lines.

h. Machines are grouped according to function. For example, all cutting machines are located in one area.

i. Suppliers can access the company's intranet.

j. The final operation in the production sequence "pulls" parts from the preceding operation.

k. Each employee is responsible for inspecting his or her own work.

Recording JIT costing journal entries
(Obj. 4)

S25-13 Hamilton Products uses a JIT system to manufacture trading pins for the 2004 Olympic Games in Athens, Greece. The standard cost per pin is $2 for raw materials and $3 for conversion costs. Last month Hamilton recorded the following data:

Number of pins completed....	4,000 pins	Raw material purchases.........	$ 8,800
Number of pins sold	3,500 pins	Conversion costs..............	$12,660

Use JIT costing to prepare journal entries for the month, including the entry to close the Conversion Cost account.

Giving examples of four types of quality costs
(Obj. 5)

S25-14 Bombardier, Inc., manufactures SeaDoo personal watercraft (jet skis). Give examples of costs Bombardier might incur in each of the four categories of quality costs:

- Prevention costs
- Appraisal costs
- Internal failure costs
- External failure costs

Be as specific as possible.

Classifying and using quality costs in decision making
(Obj. 5)

S25-15 Wharfedale manufactures high-quality speakers. Suppose Wharfedale is considering spending the following amounts on a new quality program:

Additional 20 minutes of testing for each speaker	$ 600,000
Negotiating with and training suppliers to obtain higher quality materials and on-time delivery............................	300,000
Redesigning the speakers to make them easier to manufacture ...	1,400,000

Wharfedale expects this quality program to save costs, as follows:

Reduced warranty repair costs.....................	$200,000
Avoid inspection of raw materials	400,000
Rework avoided because of fewer defective units.....	650,000

It also expects this program to avoid lost profits from:

Lost sales due to disappointed customers............	$850,000
Lost production time due to rework	300,000

1. Classify each of these costs into one of the four categories of quality costs (prevention, appraisal, internal failure, external failure).

2. Should Wharfedale implement the quality program? Give your reasons.

Product costing in an activity-based costing system
(Obj. 1)

Student Resource**CD**

spreadsheet

Exercises

E25-1 Northstar, Inc., uses activity-based costing to account for its chrome wheel manufacturing process. Company managers have identified four manufacturing activities: materials handling, machine setup, insertion of parts, and finishing. The budgeted activity costs for 20X6 and their allocation bases are as follows:

(continued)

Activity	Total Budgeted Cost	Allocation Base
Materials handling	$ 12,000	Number of parts
Machine setup	3,400	Number of setups
Insertion of parts	48,000	Number of parts
Finishing	80,000	Finishing direct labor hours
Total	$143,400	

Northstar, Inc., expects to produce 1,000 chrome wheels during the year. The wheels are expected to use 3,000 parts, require 10 setups, and consume 2,000 hours of finishing time.

Required

1. Compute the cost allocation rate for each activity.
2. Compute the indirect manufacturing cost of each wheel.

E25-2 Several years after reengineering its production process, Enke, Inc., hired a new controller, Natalie Babin. She developed an ABC system very similar to the one used by Enke's chief rival, Northstar, Inc., of Exercise 25-1. Part of the reason Babin developed the ABC system was that Enke's profits had been declining, even though the company had shifted its product mix toward the product that had appeared most profitable under the old system. Before adopting the new ABC system, Enke had used a direct labor hour single-allocation-base system that was developed 20 years ago.

For 20X6, Enke's budgeted ABC allocation rates are

Product costing in ABC and traditional systems
(Obj. 1)

Activity	Allocation Base	Cost Allocation Rate
Materials handling	Number of parts	$ 3.75 per part
Machine setup	Number of setups	300.00 per setup
Insertion of parts	Number of parts	24.00 per part
Finishing	Finishing direct labor hours	50.00 per hour

The number of parts is now a feasible allocation base because Enke recently purchased bar coding technology. Enke produces two wheel models: standard and deluxe. Budgeted data for 20X6 are as follows:

	Standard	Deluxe
Parts per wheel	4.0	6.0
Setups per 1,000 wheels	15.0	15.0
Finishing direct labor hours per wheel	1.0	2.5
Total direct labor hours per wheel	2.0	3.0

The company's managers expect to produce 1,000 units of each model during the year.

Required

1. Compute the total budgeted indirect manufacturing cost for 20X6.
2. Compute the ABC indirect manufacturing cost per unit of each model.
3. Using Enke's old direct labor hour single-allocation-base system, compute the (single) allocation rate based on direct labor hours. Use this rate to determine the indirect manufacturing cost per wheel for each model under the old single-allocation-base method.

E25-3 Refer to Exercise 25-2. For 20X7 Enke's managers have decided to use the same indirect manufacturing costs per wheel that they computed in 20X6. In addition to the unit indirect manufacturing costs, the following data are budgeted for the company's standard and deluxe models for 20X7:

Using activity-based costing to make decisions
(Obj. 2)

	Standard	Deluxe
Sale price.	$300.00	$440.00
Direct materials	30.00	46.00
Direct labor.	45.00	50.00

(continued)

Because of limited machine hour capacity, Enke can produce *either* 2,000 standard wheels or 2,000 deluxe wheels.

Required

1. If the managers rely on the ABC unit cost data computed in Exercise 25-2, which model will they produce? (All nonmanufacturing costs are the same for both models.)
2. If the managers rely on the single-allocation-base cost data, which model will they produce?
3. Which course of action will yield more income for Enke?

Activity-based management and target cost
(Obj. 2)

E25-4 Refer to Exercise 25-2. Controller Natalie Babin is surprised by the increase in cost of the deluxe model under ABC. Market research shows that to remain a viable product while still providing a reasonable profit, Enke will have to meet a target cost of $350 for the deluxe wheel. A value engineering study by Enke's employees suggests that modifications to the finishing process could cut finishing cost from $50 to $40 per hour and reduce the finishing direct labor hours per deluxe wheel from 2.5 hour to 2 hour per wheel. Direct materials would remain unchanged at $46 per wheel, as would direct labor at $50 per wheel. The materials handling, machine setups, and insertion of parts activity costs would remain the same as in Exercise 25-2. Would implementing the value engineering recommendation allow Enke to achieve its target ABC-based cost for the deluxe wheel?

Explaining why ABC passes the cost-benefit test
(Obj. 3)

E25-5 Refer to Exercise 25-2. Why might controller Natalie Babin have expected ABC to pass the cost-benefit test? Were there any warning signs that Enke's old direct-labor-based allocation system was "broken"?

Recording manufacturing costs in a JIT costing system
(Obj. 4)

E25-6 Pixel, Inc., produces flat-screen displays. Pixel uses a JIT costing system. One of the company's products has a standard direct materials cost of $8 per unit and a standard conversion cost of $32 per unit.

During 20X5, Pixel produced 500,000 units and sold 480,000. It purchased $4,400,000 of direct materials and incurred actual conversion costs totaling $15,280,000.

Required

1. Prepare summary journal entries for 20X5.
2. The January 1, 20X5, balance of the Raw and In Process Inventory account was $80,000. Use a T-account to find the December 31, 20X5, balance.
3. Use a T-account to determine whether conversion cost is over- or underallocated for the year. By how much? Give the journal entry to close the Conversion Cost account.

Recording manufacturing costs in a JIT costing system
(Obj. 4)

E25-7 Shutterbug produces digital cameras. Suppose Shutterbug's standard cost per camera is $24 for materials and $32 for conversion costs. The following data apply to July production:

Materials purchased.....................	$6,500,000
Conversion costs incurred................	$7,420,000
Number of cameras completed	200,000 cameras
Number of cameras sold	196,000 cameras

Shutterbug uses JIT costing.

Required

1. Prepare summary journal entries for July, including the entry to close the Conversion Costs account.
2. The beginning balance of Finished Goods Inventory was $100,000. Use a T-account to find the ending balance of Finished Goods Inventory.

E25-8 JIT costing is typically used by businesses that (1) assign standard costs to each product and (2) have low inventories. Explain why each of these conditions makes JIT costing more feasible.

Explaining when JIT costing is most likely to be used
(Obj. 4)

E25-9 Millan & Co. makes electronic components. Mike Millan, the president, recently instructed vice president Steve Bensen to develop a total quality control program. "If we don't at least match the quality improvements our competitors are making," he told Bensen, "we'll soon be out of business." Bensen began by listing various "costs of quality" that Millan incurs. The first six items that came to mind were

Classifying quality costs
(Obj. 5)

a. Costs of electronic components returned by customers
b. Costs incurred by Millan customer representatives traveling to customer sites to repair defective products
c. Lost profits from lost sales due to reputation for less-than-perfect products
d. Costs of inspecting components in one of Millan's production processes
e. Salaries of engineers who are designing components to withstand electrical overloads
f. Costs of reworking defective components after discovery by company inspectors

Required

Classify each item as a prevention cost, an appraisal cost, an internal failure cost, or an external failure cost.

E25-10 Chihooli, Inc., manufactures radiation-shielding glass panels. Suppose Chihooli is considering spending the following amounts on a new total quality management (TQM) program:

Classifying quality costs and using these costs to make decisions
(Obj. 5)

Strength-testing one item from each batch of panels...............	$65,000
Training employees in TQM	30,000
Training suppliers in TQM......................................	40,000
Identifying preferred suppliers who commit to on-time delivery of perfect quality materials	60,000

Chihooli expects the new program would save costs through the following:

Avoid lost profits from lost sales due to disappointed customers....	$90,000
Avoid rework and spoilage	55,000
Avoid inspection of raw materials	45,000
Avoid warranty costs	15,000

Required

1. Classify each item as a prevention cost, an appraisal cost, an internal failure cost, or an external failure cost.
2. Should Chihooli implement the new quality program? Give your reason.

E25-11 Channell Fabricators, Inc., completed two jobs in June 20X6. Channell recorded the following costs assigned to the jobs by the company's activity-based costing system:

Using activity-based costing
(Obj. 1, 2)

		Allocated Cost	
Activity	Allocation Base	Job 409	Job 622
Materials handling	Number of parts	$ 500	$ 1,500
Lathe work	Number of lathe turns	5,000	15,000
Milling	Number of machine hours	4,000	28,000
Grinding	Number of parts	300	1,500
Testing	Number of output units	126	2,700

Job 622 required 3,000 parts, 60,000 lathe turns, and 1,400 machine hours. All 300 of the job's output units were tested. All units of Job 409 were tested.

(continued)

Required

1. How do you know that at least one of the costs recorded for the two jobs is inaccurate?

2. Disregard materials-handling costs. How many parts were used for Job 409? How many lathe turns did Job 409 require? How many machine hours? How many units were produced in Job 409?

3. A nearby company has offered to test all product units for $13 each. On the basis of ABC data, should Channell accept or reject the offer? Give your reason.

Problems

(Group A)

Product costing in an ABC system
(Obj. 1)

P25-1A Narnia Technology's Cell Phone Department, which assembles and tests digital processors, reports the following data regarding processor G27:

Direct materials cost.	$56.00
Activity costs allocated	?
Manufacturing product cost	$?

The activities required to build the processors are as follows:

Activity	Allocation Base	Cost Allocated to Each Board
Start station	Number of processor boards	1 × $ 0.90 = $0.90
Dip insertion	Number of dip insertions	20 × $ 0.25 = ?
Manual insertion	Number of manual insertions	5 × $? = 2.00
Wave solder	Number of processor boards soldered	1 × $ 4.50 = 4.50
Backload	Number of backload insertions	? × $ 0.70 = 2.80
Test	Standard time each processor board is in test activity (hr.)	0.15 × $90.00 = ?
Defect analysis	Standard time for defect analysis and repair (hr.)	0.16 × $? = 8.00
Total		$?

Required

1. Fill in the blanks in both the opening schedule and the list of activities.

2. How is labor cost assigned to products under this product costing system?

3. Why might managers favor this ABC system instead of the older system that allocated all conversion costs on the basis of direct labor?

Product costing in an ABC system
(Obj. 1, 2)

Student Resource CD

spreadsheet

P25-2A Hone's Office Department manufactures computer desks in its Topeka, Kansas, plant. The company uses activity-based costing. Its activities and related data follow.

Activity	Budgeted Cost of Activity	Allocation Base	Cost Allocation Rate
Materials handling	$ 300,000	Number of parts	$ 0.60
Assembling	2,500,000	Direct labor hours	15.00
Painting	170,000	Number of painted desks	5.00

Hone produced two styles of desks in March: The standard desk, and unpainted desk that had fewer parts. Data for each follow:

Product	Total Units Produced	Total Direct Materials Costs	Total Number of Parts	Total Assembling Direct Labor Hours
Standard desk	6,000	$96,000	120,000	6,000
Unpainted desk	1,500	21,000	30,000	900

(continued)

Required

1. Compute the per-unit manufacturing product cost of standard desks and unpainted desks.

2. Premanufacturing activities, such as product design, were assigned to the standard desks at $5 each and to the unpainted desks at $3 each. Similar analyses were conducted of postmanufacturing activities such as distribution, marketing, and customer service. The post-manufacturing costs were $25 per standard and $22 per unpainted desk. Compute the full product costs per desk.

3. Which product costs are reported in the external financial statements? Which costs are used for management decision making? Explain the difference.

4. What price should Hone's managers set for standard desks to earn a $42.00 profit per desk?

P25-3A Xnet, Inc., develops software for Internet applications. The market is very competitive, and Xnet's competitors continue to introduce new products at low prices. Xnet offers a wide variety of different software—from simple programs that enable new users to create personal Web pages, to complex commercial search engines. Like most software companies, Xnet's raw material costs are insignificant.

Comparing costs from ABC versus single-rate systems; clues that ABC passes cost-benefit test
(Obj. 1, 3)

Xnet has just hired Tom Merrell, a recent graduate of State University's accounting program. Merrell asks Software Department manager Jeff Gire to join him in a pilot activity-based costing study. Merrell and Gire identify the following activities, related costs, and cost allocation bases.

Activity	Estimated Indirect Activity Costs	Allocation Base	Estimated Quantity of Allocation Base
Applications development	$1,600,000	New applications	4 new applications
Content production	2,400,000	Lines of code	12 million lines
Testing	288,000	Testing hours	1,800 testing hours
Total indirect costs	$4,288,000		

Xnet is planning to develop the following new applications:

* X-Page—for developing personal Web pages
* X-Secure—commercial security and firewall software

X-Page requires 500,000 lines of code and 100 hours of testing, while X-Secure requires 7.5 million lines of code and 600 hours of testing. Xnet expects to produce and sell 30,000 units of X-Page and 10 units of X-Secure.

Required

1. Compute the cost allocation rate for each activity.

2. Use the activity-based cost allocation rates to compute the activity costs of X-Page and X-Secure. (*Hint:* First compute the total activity costs allocated to each product line, and then compute the cost per unit.)

3. Xnet's original single-allocation-base cost system allocated indirect costs to products at $100 per programmer hour. X-Page requires 10,000 programmer hours, while X-Secure requires 15,000 programmer hours. Compute the total indirect costs allocated to X-Page and X-Secure under the original system. Then compute the indirect cost per unit for each product.

4. Compare the activity-based costs per unit to the costs from the simpler original system. How have the unit costs changed? Explain why the costs changed as they did.

5. What are the clues that Xnet's ABC system is likely to pass the cost-benefit test?

P25-4A Even though Problem 25-3A shows that X-Page's costs are lower under ABC than under the simpler original cost system, Xnet's CEO Jay Wilner is still concerned that the software may be less profitable than expected. Wilner asks Merrell to recommend a sale price that will yield a profit of $8 per unit, after direct production costs of $3 per unit,

Activity-based management, target cost, and value engineering
(Obj. 2)

(continued)

marketing and distribution costs of $5 per unit, and the indirect production costs of $17.20 per unit (from Problem 25-3A). Wilner believes that the sale price must be $30 or less to reach estimated sales of 30,000 units. If Merrell's "cost-plus-based" recommended sale price exceeds $30, Wilner authorizes him to establish a cross-functional value-engineering team to squeeze out cost savings.

Required

1. Determine the sale price that yields a profit of $8 per unit. Will this meet Wilner's target price?

2. Merrell establishes a value-engineering team that finds new software writing routines can cut application development costs for the four new applications from $1.6 million to $1.2 million. This would also save $600,000 in content production and require 10 million instead of 12 million lines of code. Testing would be unaffected. The value-engineering team also finds that improved supply-chain management can cut X-Page's direct production costs from $3 per unit to $2 per unit. However, marketing and distribution costs for X-Page are unchanged.

    Given these cost savings, what are the indirect activity cost allocation rates for application development, content production, and testing?

3. If the value-engineering team's suggestions are implemented, X-Page would require 480,000 lines of code and the same 100 hours of testing. What is the new indirect activity (production) cost per unit (including all three activities) for X-Page?

4. With these changes, can Xnet set a sale price of $30 and still earn a profit of $8 per unit?

Recording manufacturing costs for a JIT costing system
(Obj. 4)

P25-5A Titan produces sports watches. The company has a JIT production system and uses JIT costing.

Titan has two inventory accounts, Raw and In Process Inventory, and Finished Goods Inventory. On August 1, 20X5, the account balances were Raw and In Process Inventory, $12,000; Finished Goods Inventory, $2,000.

Titan's standard cost per watch is $55: $35 direct materials plus $20 conversion costs. The following data pertain to August manufacturing and sales:

Number of watches completed..............	9,000 watches	Raw material purchased	$305,000
Number of watches sold	8,800 watches	Conversion costs incurred	$116,000

Required

1. What are the major features of a JIT production system such as Titan's?

2. Prepare summary journal entries for August. Under- and overallocated conversion costs are closed to Cost of Goods Sold at the end of each month.

3. Use a T-account to determine the August 31, 20X5, balance of Raw and In Process Inventory.

Analyzing costs of quality
(Obj. 5)

P25-6A Real Toys is using a costs-of-quality approach to evaluate design engineering efforts for a new toy robot. The company's senior managers expect the engineering work to reduce appraisal, internal failure, and external failure activities. The predicted reductions in activities over the 2-year life of the toy robot follow. Also shown are the cost allocation rates for each activity.

Activity	Predicted Reduction in Activity Units	Activity Cost Allocation Rate Per Unit
Inspection of incoming materials.......	300	$20
Inspection of finished goods...........	300	30
Number of defective units discovered in-house	3,200	15
Number of defective units discovered by customers	900	35
Lost sales to dissatisfied customers	300	55

(*continued*)

Required

1. Calculate the predicted quality cost savings from the design engineering work.

2. Real Toys spent $60,000 on design engineering for the new toy robot. What is the net benefit of this "preventive" quality activity?

3. What major difficulty would Real Toys' managers have had in implementing this costs-of-quality approach? What alternative approach could they use to measure quality improvement?

Problems

(Group B)

Product costing in an ABC system
(Obj. 1)

P25-1B The Electronics Manufacturing Department of Imagine, Inc., in Austin, Texas, assembles and tests electronic components used in hand-held video phones. Consider the following data regarding component T24:

Direct materials cost	$81.00
Activity costs allocated	?
Manufacturing product cost	$?

The activities required to build the component follow.

Activity	Allocation Base	Cost Allocated to Each Unit		
Start station	Number of raw component chasses	2 × $1.30	=	$ 2.60
Dip insertion	Number of dip insertions	? × $0.40	=	12.00
Manual insertion	Number of manual insertions	12 × $0.80	=	?
Wave solder	Number of components soldered	1 × $1.40	=	1.40
Backload	Number of backload insertions	7 × $?	=	4.20
Test	Standard time each component is in test activity	0.40 × $80.00	=	?
Defect analysis	Standard time for defect analysis and repair	0.10 × $?	=	5.00
Total				$?

Required

1. Fill in the blanks in both the opening schedule and the list of activities.

2. How is labor cost assigned to products under this product costing system?

3. Why might managers favor this ABC system instead of the older system, which allocated all conversion costs on the basis of direct labor?

P25-2B McKinney, Inc., manufactures bookcases and uses an activity-based costing system. McKinney's activity areas and related data follow.

Product costing in an ABC system
(Obj. 1, 2)

Student Resource**CD**

spreadsheet

Activity	Budgeted Cost of Activity	Allocation Base	Cost Allocation Rate
Materials handling	$ 200,000	Number of parts	$ 0.80
Assembling	3,000,000	Direct labor hours	15.00
Finishing	160,000	Number of finished units	3.90

McKinney produced two styles of bookcases in April: the standard bookcase and an unfinished bookcase, which has fewer parts per bookcase and requires no finishing. The totals for quantities, direct materials costs, and other data follow.

Product	Total Units Produced	Total Direct Materials Costs	Total Number of Parts	Total Assembling Direct Labor Hours
Standard bookcase	3,000	$26,000	80,000	3,000
Unfinished bookcase	3,600	27,000	84,000	2,000

(continued)

Required

1. Compute the manufacturing product cost per unit of each type of bookcase.

2. Suppose that premanufacturing activities, such as product design, were assigned to the standard bookcases at $4 each and to the unfinished bookcases at $3 each. Similar analyses were conducted of postmanufacturing activities such as distribution, marketing, and customer service. The postmanufacturing costs were $20 per standard bookcase and $15 per unfinished bookcase. Compute the full product costs per unit.

3. Which product costs are reported in the external financial statements? Which costs are used for management decision making? Explain the difference.

4. What price should McKinney's managers set for unfinished bookcases to earn a unit profit of $16?

Comparing costs from ABC versus single-rate systems; clues that ABC passes cost-benefit test
(Obj. 1, 3)

P25-3B HCI Pharmaceuticals manufactures an over-the-counter allergy medication called Breathe. HCI is trying to win market share from Sudafed and Tylenol. HCI has developed several different Breathe products tailored to specific markets. For example, the company sells large commercial containers of 1,000 capsules to health-care facilities and travel packs of 20 capsules to shops in airports, train stations, and hotels.

HCI's controller Sandra Dean has just returned from a conference on activity-based costing. She asks Keith Yeung, foreman of the Breathe product line, to help her develop an activity-based costing system. Dean and Yeung identify the following activities, related costs, and cost allocation bases:

Activity	Estimated Indirect Activity Costs	Allocation Base	Estimated Quantity of Allocation Base
Materials handling	$190,000	Kilos	19,000 kilos
Packaging	400,000	Machine hours	2,000 hours
Quality assurance	112,500	Samples	1,875 samples
Total indirect costs	$702,500		

The commercial-container Breathe product line had a total weight of 8,000 kilos, used 1,200 machine hours, and required 200 samples. The travel-pack line had a total weight of 6,000 kilos, used 400 machine hours, and required 300 samples. HCI produced 2,500 commercial containers of Breathe and 50,000 travel packs.

Required

1. Compute the cost allocation rate for each activity.

2. Use the activity-based cost allocation rates to compute the activity costs of the commercial containers and the travel packs. (*Hint:* First compute the total activity costs allocated to each product line, and then compute the cost per unit.)

3. HCI's original single-allocation-base cost system allocated indirect costs to products at $300 per machine hour. Compute the total indirect costs allocated to the commercial containers and to the travel packs under the original system. Then compute the indirect cost per unit for each product.

4. Compare the activity-based costs per unit to the costs from the original system. How have the unit costs changed? Explain why the costs changed as they did.

5. What clues indicate that HCI's ABC system is likely to pass the cost-benefit test?

Activity-based management, target cost, and value engineering
(Obj. 2)

P25-4B Continuing Problem 25-3B, HCI controller Sandra Dean is surprised that ABC reports such a higher indirect production cost per travel pack. She wonders whether HCI is making the desired profit of $1.25 per unit on this product. The current sale price is $7.25 per travel pack, direct production costs are $2.15 per pack, marketing and distribution costs are $0.90 per pack, and the indirect production costs are $3.16 per pack (from Problem 25-3B). Dean believes that to reach estimated sales of 50,000 units, the sale price cannot exceed $7.25. If the travel pack is not providing the desired profit of $1.25 per unit,

(*continued*)

Dean decides that the next step should be to establish a cross-functional value-engineering team to identify opportunities for cost savings. If this does not provide the desired profit, Dean doubts it will be possible to increase market share to sales of 50,000 travel packs.

Required

1. Determine the sale price that yields a profit of $1.25 per travel pack. Does this meet the $7.25 target price?

2. Dean establishes a value-engineering team. The value-engineering team finds that improved supply-chain management can cut the travel pack's direct production costs from $2.15 per pack to $2.03 per pack. Further, the team believes it can cut materials-handling costs from $190,000 to $180,500. Changes in the packaging department will save $112,000 in packaging costs and 400 in machine hours. Improvements to quality assurance should reduce costs to $102,000 based on 1,700 samples. Marketing and distribution costs will remain unchanged.

 Given these cost savings, compute the indirect activity cost allocation rates for materials handling, packaging, and quality assurance.

3. If the value-engineering team's suggestions are implemented, the travel pack line would require 6,000 kilos, use 380 machine hours, and require 256 samples. Compute the new indirect production cost per travel pack (including all three activities).

4. With these changes, can HCI set a sale price of $7.25 and still earn a profit of $1.25 per travel pack?

P25-5B North Slope produces fleece jackets. The company uses JIT costing for its JIT production system.

Recording manufacturing costs for a JIT costing system
(Obj. 4)

 North Slope has two inventory accounts: Raw and In Process Inventory and Finished Goods Inventory. On October 1, 20X6, the account balances were Raw and In Process Inventory, $6,000; Finished Goods Inventory, $1,000.

 The standard cost of a jacket is $50—$15 direct materials plus $35 conversion costs. Data for October's activity follow.

Number of jackets completed.....	18,000	Direct materials purchased	$265,000
Number of jackets sold	17,600	Conversion costs incurred	551,000

Required

1. What are the major features of a JIT production system such as North Slope?

2. Prepare summary journal entries for October. Under- or overallocated conversion costs are closed to Cost of Goods Sold monthly.

3. Use a T-account to determine the October 31, 20X6, balance of Raw and In Process Inventory.

P25-6B Big Sky, Inc., is using a costs-of-quality approach to evaluate design engineering efforts for a new wakeboard. Big Sky's senior managers expect the engineering work to reduce appraisal, internal failure, and external failure activities. The predicted reductions in activities over the 2-year life of the wakeboards follow. Also shown are the cost allocation rates for each activity.

Analyzing costs of quality
(Obj. 5)

Activity	Predicted Reduction in Activity Units	Activity Cost Allocation Rate Per Unit
Inspection of incoming materials.......	400	$ 40
Inspection of work in process..........	400	20
Number of defective units discovered in-house	1,100	50
Number of defective units discovered by customers........................	300	70
Lost sales to dissatisfied customers	100	110

(continued)

Required

1. Calculate the predicted quality cost savings from the design engineering work.

2. Big Sky spent $106,000 on design engineering for the new wakeboard. What is the net benefit of this "preventive" quality activity?

3. What major difficulty would Big Sky's managers have in implementing this costs-of-quality approach? What alternative approach could they use to measure quality improvement?

APPLY *Your Knowledge*

Decision Cases

Comparing costs from ABC versus single-rate systems; using these costs to make decisions
(Obj. 1, 2)

Case 1. Axis Systems specializes in servers for workgroup, e-commerce, and ERP applications. The company's original job cost system has two direct cost categories: direct materials and direct labor. Overhead is allocated to jobs at the single rate of $22 per direct labor hour.

A task force headed by Axis's CFO recently designed an ABC system with four activities. The ABC system retains the current system's two direct cost categories. Thus, it budgets only overhead costs for each activity. Pertinent data follow.

Activity	Allocation Base	Cost Allocation Rate
Materials handling	Number of parts	$ 0.85
Machine setup	Number of setups	500.00
Assembling	Assembling hours	80.00
Shipping	Number of shipments	1,500.00

Axis Systems has been awarded two new contracts, which will be produced as Job A and Job B. Budget data relating to the contracts follow.

	Job A	Job B
Number of parts	15,000	2,000
Number of setups	6	4
Number of assembling hours	1,500	200
Number of shipments	1	1
Total direct labor hours	8,000	600
Number of output units......................	100	10
Direct materials cost........................	$210,000	$30,000
Direct labor cost	$160,000	$12,000

Required

1. Compute the product cost per unit for each job, using the original costing system (with two direct cost categories and a single overhead allocation rate).

2. Suppose Axis Systems adopts the ABC system. Compute the product cost per unit for each job using ABC.

3. Which costing system more accurately assigns to jobs the costs of the resources consumed to produce them? Explain.

4. A dependable company has offered to produce both jobs for Axis for $5,400 per output unit. Axis may outsource (buy from the outside company) either Job A only, Job B only, or both jobs. Which course of action will Axis's managers take if they base their decision on (a) the original system? (b) ABC system costs? Which course of action will yield more income? Explain.

Activity-based management, target cost, and value engineering
(Obj. 1, 2)

Case 2. To remain competitive, Axis Systems' management believes the company must produce Job B–type servers (from Decision Case 1) at a target cost of $5,400. Axis Systems

(continued)

has just joined a B2B e-market site that management believes will enable the firm to cut direct material costs by 10%. Axis's management also believes that a value-engineering team can reduce assembly time.

Compute the assembly cost savings per Job B–type server required to meet the $5,400 target cost. (*Hint:* Begin by calculating the direct material, direct labor, and allocated activity cost per server.)

Ethical Issue

Mary Lipe is assistant controller at Stone Packaging, Inc., a manufacturer of cardboard boxes and other packaging materials. Lipe has just returned from a packaging industry conference on activity-based costing. She realizes that ABC may help Stone meet its goal of reducing costs by 5% over each of the next three years.

ABC and ethical decisions
(Obj. 1, 2)

Stone Packaging's Order Department is a likely candidate for ABC. While orders are entered into a computer that updates the accounting records, clerks manually check customers' credit history and hand-deliver orders to shipping. This process occurs whether the sales order is for a dozen specialty boxes worth $80, or 10,000 basic boxes worth $8,000.

Lipe believes that identifying the cost of processing a sales order would justify (1) further computerization of the order process and (2) changing the way the company processes small orders. However, the significant cost savings would arise from elimination of two positions in the Order Department. The company's sales order clerks have been with the company many years. Lipe is uncomfortable with the prospect of proposing a change that will likely result in terminating these employees.

Required

Use the IMA's ethical standards (Exhibit 19-14) to consider Lipe's responsibility when cost savings come at the expense of employees' jobs.

Financial Statement Case

In his annual letter to shareholders, Jeff Bezos, founder and chief executive officer of **Amazon.com,** discusses the three pillars of Amazon.com's success: selection, convenience, and lower prices. Bezos and his management team need ABC information to continuously improve Amazon.com's customer experience. They need this information to make decisions like whether to improve selection by increasing the available items in Amazon.com's Electronics Store or by additional alliances with affiliates such as **Circuit City.**

Identifying activities and cost drivers at Amazon.com
(Obj. 1)

Many of Amazon.com's activities and cost drivers are the same as those for retailers like **Wal-Mart** and **Best Buy,** but others are unique to e-tailers. Before answering the following questions, read Jeff Bezos' Letter to Shareholders and Amazon.com's annual report.

Required

1. Activities like purchasing books and DVDs from suppliers, and the associated cost drivers (number of orders), are common to all retailers, including Amazon.com and Best Buy. Identify four other activities and their cost drivers that would be the same for Amazon.com and Best Buy.
2. Other activities are unique to e-tailers. Suppose Amazon.com managers have identified the following 12 specific activities. Because it would be too expensive to track each activity with a separate cost driver, management has identified four general activities (also listed below). Assign each of the 12 specific activities to one of the four general activities.

Specific Activities

- Maintain hardware and software to process customer orders
- Upload and remove images from Web site
- Improve the Web site's design
- Track affiliate sales from Amazon.com's Web site
- Research new hardware and software products

(*continued*)

- Select product images for the Web site
- Obtain approval to scan and put products on Web site
- Create product information and product reviews for each product
- Maintain the Web site and telephone system for processing customers' orders
- Prepare and maintain affiliate links on the Web site
- Contact Internet businesses to promote new affiliate marketing opportunities
- Research and test new Web site features

General Activities

- Electronic customer-order processing
- Inventory selection and management
- Web site optimization
- Affiliate marketing

3. Identify a cost driver for each of the four general activities.

Team Project

Developing an ABC system; explaining how ABC changes costs; signs of a broken cost system
(Obj. 1, 2, 3)

Lahana Shrimp Farms in Kihei Hawaii, has a Processing Department that processes raw shrimp into two products:

- Headless shrimp
- Peeled and deveined shrimp

Lahana recently submitted bids for two orders: (1) headless shrimp for a cruise line and (2) peeled and deveined shrimp for a restaurant chain. Lahana won the first bid, but lost the second. The production and sales managers are upset. They believe that Lahana's state-of-the-art equipment should have given the company an edge in the peeled and deveined market. Consequently, production managers are starting to keep their own sets of product cost records.

Lahana is reexamining both its production process and its cost system. The company is considering changing its cost accounting system, which has been in place since 1991. The existing system allocates all indirect costs based on direct labor hours. Lahana is considering adopting activity-based costing. Controller Heather Barefield and a team of production managers performed a preliminary study. The team identified six activities, with the following (departmentwide) estimated indirect costs and cost drivers:

Activity	Total Estimated Cost of Activity	Allocation Base
Redesign of production process (costs of changing process and equipment)........	$ 5,000	Number of design changes
Production scheduling (production scheduler's salary)	6,000	Number of batches
Chilling (depreciation on refrigerators)........	1,500	Weight (in pounds)
Processing (utilities and depreciation on equipment)............................	21,000	Number of cuts
Packaging (indirect labor and depreciation on equipment)	1,425	Cubic feet of surface exposed
Order filling (order-takers' and shipping clerks' wages)...........................	7,000	Number of orders
Total indirect costs for the entire department...	$41,925	

The raw shrimp are chilled and then cut. For headless shrimp, employees remove the heads, then rinse the shrimp. For peeled and deveined shrimp, the headless shrimp are further processed—the shells are removed and the backs are slit for deveining. Both headless shrimp and peeled and deveined shrimp are packaged in foam trays and covered with shrink wrap. The Order-Filling Department assembles orders of headless shrimp as well as peeled and deveined shrimp.

(continued)

Barefield estimates that Lahana will produce 10,000 packages of headless shrimp and 50,000 packages of peeled and deveined shrimp. The two products incur the following costs per package:

	Costs per Package	
	Headless Shrimp	**Peeled and Deveined Shrimp**
Shrimp	$3.50	$4.50
Foam trays	$0.05	$0.05
Shrink wrap	$0.05	$0.02
Number of cuts	12 cuts	48 cuts
Cubic feet of exposed surface	1 cubic foot	0.75 cubic foot
Weight (in pounds)	2.5 pounds	1 pound
Direct labor hours	0.01 hour	0.05 hour

Lahana pays direct laborers $20 per hour. Barefield estimates that each product line will also require the following *total* resources:

	Headless Shrimp			**Peeled and Deveined Shrimp**		
Design changes	1 change	}	for all	4 changes	}	for all
Batches	40 batches		10,000	20 batches		50,000
Sales orders	90 orders		packages	110 orders		packages

Required

Form groups of four students. All group members should work together to develop the group's answers to the four requirements. However, the first two students have primary responsibility for writing up the final responses to requirements 1 and 4, while the other two students have primary responsibility for writing up the responses to requirements 2 and 3. (Carry all computations at least four decimal places.)

1. List the clues that Lahana's original cost system may be broken.

2. Using the original cost system with the single indirect cost allocation base (direct labor hours), compute the *total budgeted cost per package* for the headless shrimp and then for the peeled and deveined shrimp. (*Hint:* First compute the indirect cost allocation rate—that is, the predetermined overhead rate. Then compute the total budgeted cost per package for each product.)

3. Use activity-based costing to recompute the *total budgeted cost per package* for the headless shrimp and then for the peeled and deveined shrimp. (*Hint:* First, calculate the budgeted cost allocation rate for each activity. Then calculate the total indirect costs of (a) the entire headless shrimp product line and (b) the entire peeled and deveined shrimp product line. Next compute the indirect cost per package of each product. Finally, calculate the total cost per package of each product.)

4. Write a memo to Lahana CEO Gary Pololu explaining the results of the ABC study. Compare the costs reported by the ABC system with the costs reported by the original system. Point out whether the ABC system shifted costs toward headless shrimp or toward peeled and deveined shrimp, and explain why. Finally, explain whether Pololu should feel more comfortable making decisions using cost data from the original system or from the new ABC system. Use the memo format outlined in Starter 25-6.

For Internet Exercises, go to the Web site www.prenhall.com/horngren.

CHAPTER 26

Special Business Decisions and Capital Budgeting

TIPS CHECK YOUR RESOURCES

- Visit the www.prenhall.com/horngren **Web site** for self-study quizzes, video clips, and other resources
- Try the **Quick Check** exercise at the end of the chapter to test your knowledge
- Learn the **key terms**
- Do the **Starter** exercises keyed in the margins
- Work the **mid-** and **end-of-chapter summary problems**
- Use the **Concept Links** to review material in other chapters
- Search the **CD** for review materials by chapter or by key word
- Watch the **tutorial videos** to review key concepts
- Watch the **On Location Deer Valley** video to see how the company handles capital budgeting

LEARNING OBJECTIVES

1. Identify the relevant information for a special business decision

2. Make five types of short-term special business decisions

3. Use payback and accounting rate of return models to make longer-term capital budgeting decisions

4. Use discounted cash flow models to make longer-term capital budgeting decisions

5. Compare and contrast the four capital budgeting methods

On the slopes of Deer Valley Ski Resort in Park Valley, Utah—site of the 2002 Winter Olympics slalom competition—management accounting seems a world away. But the counter where you rent your skis, the chairlift that whisks you up the mountain, and the restaurant that serves you dinner are all part of the resort's recent expansion. How did Deer Valley's developers decide to spend $13 million to expand Snow Park Lodge?

Director of Finance Jim Madsen explains that when the resort reaches a target number of skiers per day and a target level of profit, the owners expand. But each expansion must meet two requirements. First, the project must be profitable. Second, Deer Valley must expect to get its money back on the investment in a relatively short time. To figure out which projects

Deer Valley Ski Resort

meet these requirements, Deer Valley's managers compare the amount of the investment needed to expand the resort with the additional revenues expected from expansion. Managers make this comparison using two *capital budgeting* techniques:

- *Net present value*—to predict whether the investment will be profitable
- *Payback period*—to predict how long it will take to "get the money back" ■

In this chapter, we'll see how companies like Deer Valley use net present value, payback period, and other capital budgeting techniques to decide which long-term capital investments to make. Deer Valley's capital expansion project is a *long-term* special decision because it will tie up the company's resources for years. We'll tackle these long-term special decisions in the second half of this chapter. First, we consider *short-term* special decisions.

Relevant Information

In this chapter, you'll see how managers use financial information to guide important decisions about how to maximize profits.

How Managers Make Decisions

Exhibit 26-1 illustrates how managers make decisions among alternative courses of action. Management accountants help with the third step: gathering and analyzing *relevant information* to compare alternatives. The key is to focus on information that is *relevant* to the decision at hand.

Exhibit 26-1 How Managers Make Decisions

 Identify the relevant information for a special business decision

✔ **Starter 26-1**

Relevant Information
Expected future data that differs among alternatives.

What Information Is Relevant to a Special Business Decision?

Exhibit 26-2 shows that **relevant information** is expected future data that differs among alternatives.

Suppose you are deciding whether to buy a Toyota or a Saturn car. The cost of the car, the insurance premium on this car, and the cost to maintain the car are all relevant because these costs

- Will be incurred in the *future* (after you decide to buy the car), and
- Will *differ between alternatives* (each car has a different cost, and maintenance and insurance costs will also differ)

Exhibit 26-2

Relevant Information

These costs are *relevant* because they can affect your decision of which car to purchase. Costs that were incurred in the past and costs that do not differ between alternatives are *irrelevant* because they do not affect your decision. For example, a campus parking sticker costs the same whether you buy the Toyota or the Saturn, so that cost is irrelevant to your decision.

The same distinction applies to all situations—*only relevant data affect decisions.* Let's consider another application of this general principle.

Suppose Pendleton Woolen Mills is deciding whether to use pure wool or a wool blend in a new line of sweaters. Assume Pendleton predicts the following costs under the two alternatives:

| | Expected Materials and Labor Cost per Sweater | | |
	Wool	Wool Blend	Cost Difference
Direct materials.............................	$10	$6	$4
Direct labor	2	2	0
Total cost of direct materials and direct labor ..	$12	$8	$4

The cost of direct materials is relevant because this cost differs between alternatives (the wool costs $4 more than the wool blend). The labor cost is irrelevant because that cost is the same for both.

Managers base their decisions on expected future data rather than on historical data. Historical data supplied by the accounting system are useful guides for predictions. However, historical data by themselves are irrelevant for making decisions about the future.

You are considering replacing your Pentium IV computer with the latest model. Is the $1,500 you spent (in 2003) on the Pentium relevant to your decision about buying the new model?

Answer: The $1,500 cost of your Pentium is irrelevant. The $1,500 is a *past* (sunk) cost that has already been incurred, so it is the same whether or not you buy the new computer.

How to Make Short-Term Special Decisions

Our approach to making short-term special decisions is called the *relevant information approach,* or the *incremental analysis approach.* We'll consider five kinds of decisions:

- Special sales orders
- Dropping products, departments, and territories

 Make five types of short-term special business decisions

- Product mix
- Outsourcing (make or buy)
- Selling as is or processing further

Student Resource**CD**

absorption costing, contribution margin, outsourcing, opportunity cost, relevant information approach, sunk cost

As you study these decisions, keep in mind the two keys in analyzing short-term special business decisions shown in Exhibit 26-3. We'll use these two keys in each decision.

Exhibit 26-3

Two Keys to Making Short-Term Special Decisions

When to Accept a Special Sales Order

Suppose ACDelco sells oil filters for $3.20 each. Assume that a mail-order company has offered ACDelco $35,000 for 20,000 oil filters, or $1.75 per filter ($35,000 ÷ 20,000 = $1.75). This sale will not affect regular business, and it:

- Will not change fixed costs
- Will not require any additional variable nonmanufacturing expenses
- Will use manufacturing capacity that would otherwise be idle

Suppose ACDelco made and sold 250,000 oil filters before considering the special order. Using the conventional (absorption costing) income statement on the left-hand side of Exhibit 26-4, the manufacturing cost per unit is $2 ($500,000 ÷ 250,000). This suggests that ACDelco should *not* accept the special order at a sale price of $1.75, because each oil filter costs $2 to manufacture. But appearances can be deceiving!

Exhibit 26-4 Conventional (Absorption Costing) Format and Contribution Margin Format Income Statements

Income Statement
Year Ended December 31, 20X5

Conventional (Absorption Costing) Format		Contribution Margin Format		
Sales revenue............................	$800,000	Sales revenue..............		$800,000
Less manufacturing cost of goods sold.....	500,000	Less variable expenses:		
Gross profit	300,000	Manufacturing	$300,000	
Less marketing and administrative		Marketing and		
expenses............................	200,000	administrative.........	75,000	375,000
		Contribution margin		425,000
		Less fixed expenses:		
		Manufacturing	$200,000	
		Marketing and		
		administrative.........	125,000	325,000
Operating income.....................	$100,000	Operating income..........		$100,000

The right-hand side of Exhibit 26-4 shows the contribution margin income statement that separates variable expenses from fixed expenses. → Managers find this format more useful because it shows how sales volume affects costs and income. The contribution margin income statement allows us to see that the *variable* manufacturing cost per unit is only $1.20 ($300,000 ÷ 250,000).

Now let's reconsider the key question facing ACDelco: How would the special sale affect the company's operating income? The correct analysis in Exhibit 26-5 is an incremental approach that follows the two key guidelines:

Chapter 22, page 903, explains that contribution margin equals revenues minus all variable expenses. Chapter 22 also compares conventional and contribution margin income statements.

1. Focus on relevant revenues, costs, and profits.
2. Use a contribution margin approach.

Exhibit 26-5 shows that this special sale increases revenues by $35,000 (20,000 × $1.75). The only cost that will differ between the alternatives is the variable manufacturing cost, which is expected to increase by $24,000 (20,000 × $1.20). The other costs are irrelevant. Variable marketing and administrative expenses will be the same whether or not ACDelco accepts the special order, because no special efforts were made to get this sale. Fixed expenses are unchanged because ACDelco has enough idle capacity to produce 20,000 extra oil filters without requiring additional facilities.

Expected increase in revenues—	
sale of 20,000 oil filters × $1.75 each.	$35,000
Expected increase in expenses—variable manufacturing costs:	
20,000 oil filters × $1.20 each.	(24,000)
Expected increase in operating income.	$11,000

Exhibit 26-5

Incremental Analysis of Special Sales Order

ACDelco compares the additional (incremental) revenues with the additional (incremental) expenses. If the increase in revenues exceeds the increase in expenses, the sale contributes to profits. Management predicts that the order will increase operating income by $11,000, as shown in Exhibit 26-5, so ACDelco should accept the special order.

Thus, the decision rule is:

✔ **Starter 26-2**

DECISION RULE: Accept special order?

If expected increase in revenues exceeds expected increase in variable and fixed costs	If expected increase in revenues is less than expected increase in variable and fixed costs
Accept the special order	**Reject** the special order

The absorption costing income statement on the left-hand side of Exhibit 26-4 shows that the total cost of manufacturing 250,000 filters is $500,000. What is the flaw in reasoning that ACDelco should accept special orders only if the sale price exceeds $2 each?

Answer: The flaw in this analysis arises from treating a fixed cost as though it changes in total like a variable cost does. Manufacturing one extra oil filter will only cost $1.20—the variable manufacturing cost. *Fixed expenses are irrelevant because ACDelco will incur $200,000 of fixed manufacturing overhead expenses whether or not the company accepts the special order.* Producing 20,000 more oil filters will not increase *total* fixed expenses, so manufacturing costs increase at the rate of $1.20 per unit, not $2.00 per unit.

Our special sales order analysis focused on the short-term expected effect on operating income. We must also consider long-term factors. Will accepting the order at $1.75 hurt ACDelco's ability to sell the oil filter at the regular price of $3.20? Will regular customers find out about the special price and balk at paying more? How will competitors react? Will this sale start a price war?

If the sales manager believes these disadvantages outweigh the extra $11,000 in profit from accepting the order, he will reject the order. The company is better off passing up $11,000 now to protect its long-term market position and customer relations. Rejecting the special sales order may be an $11,000 "investment" in the company's long-term future.

We will use this same approach of analyzing changes in revenues and costs among the different alternatives for the remaining short-term special decisions.

When to Drop Products, Departments, or Territories

Assume that ACDelco is operating at the 270,000-unit level, as shown in Exhibit 26-6. Suppose the company is now considering *dropping* the air cleaner product line with $35,000 (20,000 units) in sales and total variable costs per unit of $1.50. Exhibit 26-6 shows contribution margin income statements by product line.

Exhibit 26-6

Contribution Margin Income Statements by Product Line

	Total (270,000 units)	Product Line Oil Filters (250,000 units)	Air Cleaners (20,000 units)
Sales revenue	$835,000	$800,000	$ 35,000
Variable expenses.	405,000	375,000	30,000
Contribution margin	430,000	425,000	5,000
Fixed expenses:			
Manufacturing	200,000	185,185*	14,815*
Marketing and administrative.	125,000	115,741†	9,259†
Total fixed expenses.	325,000	300,926	24,074
Operating income (loss)	$105,000	$124,074	$(19,074)

* $200,000 ÷ 270,000 units = $0.74074 per unit; 250,000 units × $0.74074 = $185,185; 20,000 units × $0.74074 = $14,815

† $125,000 ÷ 270,000 units = $0.462963 per unit; 250,000 units × $0.462963 = $115,741; 20,000 units × $0.462963 = $9,259

Suppose ACDelco allocates fixed expenses in proportion to the number of units sold. Dividing the fixed manufacturing expense of $200,000 by 270,000 total units yields a fixed manufacturing cost of $0.74074 per unit. Allocating this unit cost to the 250,000 oil filters assigns fixed manufacturing cost of $185,185 to this product. The same procedure allocates $14,815 to air cleaners. Fixed marketing and administrative expenses are allocated in the same manner.

The result is an operating loss of $19,074 for air cleaners. Should ACDelco drop the air cleaner product line? The answer depends on whether or not fixed costs change.

✔ **Starter 26-3**

FIXED COSTS DO NOT CHANGE As in the special sales order example, we follow the two key guidelines for special business decisions: (1) focus on relevant data items, and (2) use a contribution margin approach. The relevant items are still the changes in revenues and expenses, but now we are considering a *decrease* in volume rather than an increase. If fixed costs remain the same whether or not the air cleaner product line is dropped, the fixed costs are not relevant to the decision. Only the revenues and variable expenses are relevant.

Exhibit 26-6 shows that the air cleaner product line has a positive contribution margin of $5,000. If this product line is dropped, the company will forgo this $5,000. Exhibit 26-7 verifies that expected revenue decreases by $35,000, and expected variable expenses decrease by $30,000, a net $5,000 decrease in operating income (since fixed costs are unaffected). This analysis suggests that management should *not* drop air cleaners.

Expected decrease in revenues:	
Sale of air cleaners (20,000 × $1.75)............................	$35,000
Expected decrease in expenses:	
Variable manufacturing expenses (20,000 × $1.50)...............	30,000
Expected decrease in operating income.........................	$ 5,000

Exhibit 26-7

Incremental Analysis for Dropping a Product—Fixed Costs Do Not Change

FIXED COSTS CHANGE   Don't jump to the conclusion that fixed costs never change and are always irrelevant. Suppose ACDelco employed a part-time foreman to oversee the air cleaner product line. The foreman's $13,000 salary can be avoided if the company stops producing air cleaners.

Exhibit 26-8 shows that in this situation, operating income will increase by $8,000 if ACDelco drops air cleaners. A "fixed" cost *is* relevant, so managers must consider the change in the cost.

✔ **Starter 26-4**

Expected decrease in revenues:		
Sale of air cleaners (20,000 × $1.75)		$35,000
Expected decrease in expenses:		
Variable manufacturing expenses (20,000 × $1.50)	$30,000	
Fixed expenses—foreman's salary...................	13,000	
Expected decrease in total expenses		43,000
Expected increase in operating income................		$ 8,000

Exhibit 26-8

Incremental Analysis for Dropping a Product—Fixed Costs Change

Special decisions should take into account all costs affected by the choice of action. Managers must ask: What total costs—variable *and* fixed—will change? As Exhibits 26-7 and 26-8 show, the key to deciding whether to drop products, departments, or territories is to compare the lost revenue against the costs that can be saved from dropping. The decision rule is:

Product Mix—Which Product to Emphasize?

Companies do not have unlimited resources. **Constraints** that restrict production or sale of a product vary from company to company. For example, Dell Computer has limited production capacity. For a manufacturer, the production constraint may be labor hours, machine hours, or available materials. For a merchandiser like Wal-Mart, the primary constraint is cubic feet of display space.

Constraint
A factor that restricts production or sale of a product.

Other companies are constrained by sales. Competition may be stiff, and the company may be able to sell only so many units.

Consider Chazz, a manufacturer of shirts and slacks. The following data suggest that shirts are more profitable than slacks:

	Per Unit	
	Shirts	**Slacks**
Sale price	$30	$60
Variable expenses	12	48
Contribution margin	$18	$12
Contribution margin ratio:		
Shirts—$18 ÷ $30.	60%	
Slacks—$12 ÷ $60		20%

However, an important piece of information is missing—the time it takes to manufacture each product. Chazz can produce either 20 pairs of slacks *or* 10 shirts per machine hour. The company can sell all the shirts and slacks it produces. The company has 2,000 machine hours of capacity. Which product should it emphasize?

To maximize profits, follow the decision rule:

Chazz can sell all the slacks and shirts it makes, so production (machine hours) is the constraint. Thus, Chazz should produce the product with the highest contribution margin per machine hour. Exhibit 26-9 determines the contribution margin per machine hour for each product. Slacks have a higher contribution margin per machine hour ($240 = 20 pairs of slacks × $12 per pair) than shirts ($180 = 10 shirts × $18 per shirt). Chazz will earn more profit by producing slacks. Why? Because even though slacks have a lower contribution margin *per unit*, Chazz can make twice as many slacks as shirts in the available machine hours. Exhibit 26-9 proves that Chazz earns more total profit by making slacks. Multiplying the contribution margin per machine hour by the available number of machine hours shows that Chazz can earn $480,000 of contribution margin by producing slacks, but only $360,000 by producing shirts.

Exhibit 26-9

Product Mix—Which Product to Emphasize

	Shirts	**Slacks**
(1) Units that can be produced each hour	10	20
(2) Contribution margin per unit	× $18	× $12
Contribution margin per hour (1) × (2)	$180	$240
Capacity—number of hours.	× 2,000	× 2,000
Total contribution margin at full capacity	$360,000	$480,000

✔ **Starter 26-5**

Notice that the analysis again follows the two guidelines for special business decisions: (1) Focus on relevant data (contribution margin in this example, because only sales revenue and variable costs are relevant), and (2) use a contribution margin approach.

> Why are Chazz's fixed expenses irrelevant in the decision to produce slacks or shirts?
>
> *Answer:* Chazz will use the same property, plant, and equipment to make either slacks or shirts. The fixed expenses will be the same whether the company makes slacks or shirts, so the fixed expenses are irrelevant.

When to Outsource

IBM, the company that invented the dominant type of personal computer, has decided to outsource (or buy from a supplier) most of its desktop models. Cisco Systems buys most of its products from low-cost technology manufacturing specialists in Asia. On the other hand, Nokia has become the cost leader in cell phone manufacturing using its own plants in high-cost areas like Finland, the United States, and Germany.[1] Make-or-buy decisions are often called **outsourcing** decisions, because managers must decide whether to buy a component product or service or produce it in-house. The heart of these decisions is *how best to use available facilities.*

Outsourcing
A make-or-buy decision: managers decide whether to buy a component product or service or produce it in-house.

Let's see how managers make outsourcing decisions. DefTone, a manufacturer of music CDs, is deciding whether to make the paper liners for the CD jewel boxes in-house or whether to outsource them to Mūz-Art, a company that specializes in producing paper liners. DefTone's cost to produce 250,000 liners is:

	Total Cost (250,000 liners)
Direct materials	$ 40,000
Direct labor.	20,000
Variable overhead	15,000
Fixed overhead	50,000
Total manufacturing cost	$125,000
Cost per liner ($125,000 ÷ 250,000)	$0.50

Mūz-Art offers to sell DefTone the liners for $0.37 each. Should DefTone make the liners or buy them from Mūz-Art? DefTone's $0.50 cost per unit to make the liner is $0.13 higher than the cost of buying it from Mūz-Art. It appears that DefTone should outsource the liners. But the correct answer is not so simple.

To make the best decision, you must compare the difference in expected future costs between the alternatives. Which costs will differ depending on whether DefTone makes or buys the liners?

By purchasing the liners, DefTone can avoid all variable manufacturing costs and reduce its fixed overhead cost by $10,000. (Fixed overhead will decrease to $40,000.) Exhibit 26-10 shows the differences in costs between the make and buy alternatives.

Liner Costs	Make Liners	Buy Liners	Difference
Direct materials	$ 40,000	—	$40,000
Direct labor.	20,000	—	20,000
Variable overhead	15,000	—	15,000
Fixed overhead	50,000	$ 40,000	10,000
Purchase cost from Mūz-Art			
(250,000 × $0.37).	—	92,500	(92,500)
Total cost of liners	$125,000	$132,500	$(7,500)
Cost per unit—Divide by 250,000 liners	$0.50	$0.53	$(0.03)

Exhibit 26-10

Incremental Analysis for Outsourcing Decision

✔ **Starter 26-6**

✔ **Starter 26-7**

---

[1]*Source*: David Pringle, "How Nokia Thrives by Breaking the Rules," *The Wall Street Journal*, Jan. 3, 2003, A7.

The decision rule is:

Exhibit 26-10 shows that it would cost DefTone less to make the liners than to buy them from Mūz-Art. The net savings from making 250,000 liners is $7,500, which works out to $0.03 each.

This example shows that *fixed costs are relevant to a special decision when those fixed costs differ between alternatives.* Exhibit 26-10 also shows that outsourcing decisions follow our two guidelines for special business decisions: (1) Focus on relevant data (variable and fixed manufacturing costs in this case), and (2) use a contribution margin approach that separates variable costs from fixed costs. They help answer the fundamental question: What difference does the proposed change make?

The analysis in Exhibit 26-10 assumes there is no other use for the production facilities freed up if DefTone buys the liners from Mūz-Art. But suppose DefTone has an opportunity to use its freed-up facilities to make more CDs, which have an expected profit of $18,000. Now DefTone must consider its **opportunity cost**—the benefit forgone by not choosing an alternative course of action. In this case, DefTone's opportunity cost of making the liners is the $18,000 profit it forgoes if it does not free its production facilities to make the additional CDs.

Let's see how DefTone's managers decide among three alternatives:

1. Use the facilities to make the liners.
2. Buy the liners and leave facilities idle.
3. Buy the liners and use facilities to make more CDs.

The alternative with the lowest *net* cost is the best use of DefTone's facilities. Exhibit 26-11 compares the three alternatives.

Opportunity Cost
The benefit forgone by not choosing an alternative course of action.

Exhibit 26-11

Best Use of Facilities, Given Opportunity Costs

		Buy Liners	
	Make Liners	Facilities Idle	Make Additional CDs
Expected cost of obtaining 250,000 liners (from Exhibit 26-10).....................	$125,000	$132,500	$132,500
Expected profit from additional CDs.........	—	—	(18,000)
Expected net cost of obtaining 250,000 liners ..	$125,000	$132,500	$114,500

DefTone should buy the liners from Mūz-Art and use the vacated facilities to make more CDs. If DefTone makes the liners, or if it buys the liners from Mūz-Art but leaves its production facilities idle, it will forgo the opportunity to earn $18,000.

DefTone's managers should consider qualitative factors as well as revenue and cost differences in making their final decision. For example, DefTone managers may believe they can better control quality by making the liners themselves. This argues for making the liners.

Outsourcing decisions are increasingly important in today's globally wired economy. In the past, make-or-buy decisions often ended up as "make" because coordination, information exchange, and paperwork problems made buying from suppliers too inconvenient. Now companies can use the Web to tap into information systems of suppliers and customers located around the world. Paperwork vanishes, and information required to satisfy the strictest just-in-time delivery schedule is available in real time. As a result, companies are focusing on their core competencies and outsourcing more and more other functions.

Like Cisco Systems and Nike, many world-class competitors have discovered that their core competency lies not in manufacturing, but in research and development and in brand marketing. Such companies outsource much of their manufacturing to contract manufacturers like Flextronics and Yue Yuen Industrial Holdings, which operate huge plants in Mexico and Taiwan, where labor is less expensive.

Cisco makes its most sophisticated components, but outside suppliers directly fill many of Cisco's customers' orders. Hewlett-Packard (HP) is a leader in laser printers, but it outsources production of the laser mechanisms to Canon.

Outsourcing doesn't stop at production. Many companies outsource computing and software needs instead of developing information technology in-house. Application service providers, or ASPs, install and maintain software

We Brand It, You Make It: The Outsourcing Trend

Here's a riddle for our times: What makes an IBM computer an IBM computer? Do IBM employees have to assemble the computer, or just design and service it? Increasingly, companies like IBM and Motorola are outsourcing the manufacture of their products to off-shore contract manufacturers. In 2003, IBM signed a $3.6 billion deal with Sanmina-SCI Corp. to manufacture servers and desktop PCs in Guadalajara, Mexico.

The deal with Sanmina is part of IBM's continuing quest to reduce its total supply-chain costs. According to a *Purchasing* magazine survey, 81% of electronics manufacturers cited cost as their reason for outsourcing everything from motherboards and set-top boxes to entire products. Contract manufacturers can produce products more cheaply because orders from multiple clients keep them busy around the clock and cover overhead costs.

Outsourcing manufacturing also allows IBM to concentrate on other activities where it adds more value. As Meta Group analyst Steve Kleyhan puts it, outsourcing "lets IBM focus on design and customer service instead of the bits, bytes, and bolts of making the box, where IBM has no competitive advantage." Yet outsourcing cuts into activities once thought of as core capabilities, such as product development and technical support. The outsourcing of knowledge work has already begun in China, India, eastern Europe, and other countries with an educated white-collar workforce that will do the work for less than their U.S. counterparts. For instance, engineers in India and China who once wrote code for chips designed in the U.S. now develop devices for Texas Instruments, Intel, and others. The savings are considerable: The Indian engineers—with master's degrees and five years' experience—make $1,000 a month. Their U.S. counterparts make $7,000.

Based on: Jeffrey Burt, "Sanmina to Build IBM eServers, IntelliStations," *eWeek,* January 13, 2002, p. 23. Steve Lohr, "IBM in Deal to Farm Out Some PC Jobs," *The New York Times,* January 8, 2003, p. C4. Pete Engardio, Aaron Bernstein, and Manjeet Kripalani, "Is Your Job Next?" *Business Week,* February 3, 2003, pp. 50–60. James Carbone, "What Buyers Look For in Contract Manufacturers," *Purchasing,* March 23, 2000, pp. 32–38.

Accounting.com

ranging from budgeting and activity-based costing applications to e-mail and supply-chain management. The ASP then charges its client companies to access this software through the Internet. The fee charged depends on the time the client is logged on and the specific features of the software that the client uses.

Companies are even outsourcing telemarketing and customer service. GE, American Express, and IBM were among the first to outsource such work to "business process outsourcing" firms, largely located in India. Now half the Fortune 500, including Microsoft and Dell, send work to India. So chances are that the last time you phoned a customer help desk, the voice on the line was in New Delhi![2]

Many outsourcing decisions are short-term but Cisco's decision to subcontract most of its manufacturing is a long-term one. When making decisions with long-term consequences, managers identify and analyze the relevant costs and benefits of different alternatives, as DefTone did in Exhibits 26-10 and 26-11. The only difference is that these cost and benefit calculations may extend many years into the future. Managers discount these costs and benefits to their *present values*, as we explain in the second half of the chapter.

Sell As Is or Process Further?

After processing crude oil into regular gasoline, should Chevron sell the regular gas as is, or should it spend more to process the gas into premium grade? Suppose Chevron spent $48,000 to produce 50,000 gallons of regular gasoline, as shown in Exhibit 26-12. Assume Chevron can sell this regular gasoline for $1.20 per gallon, for a total of $60,000 (50,000 × $1.20). Alternatively Chevron could further process this regular gasoline into premium-grade gas. Suppose the additional cost to process the gas further is $0.11 per gallon, for an additional cost of $5,500 (50,000 gallons × $0.11). Assume the sale price of premium gasoline is $1.40 per gallon, for a total of $70,000 (50,000 × $1.40).

Exhibit 26-12

Sell As Is or Process Further Decision

Which items are relevant to the sell-or-process-further decision? The $48,000 cost of producing the 50,000 gallons of regular gasoline is *not* relevant. It is a **sunk cost**—a past cost that cannot be changed regardless of which future action is taken. The $48,000 has been incurred whether Chevron sells the regular gasoline as is or processes it further into premium.

Exhibits 26-12 and 26-13 show that the relevant items that differ between Chevron's (1) sell as is and (2) process further alternatives are

■ Expected revenues   ■ Expected costs of processing further

Sunk Cost
A past cost that cannot be changed regardless of which future action is taken.

✔ **Starter 26-8**

The $10,000 extra revenue ($70,000 − $60,000) outweighs the $5,500 cost of the extra processing, so Chevron should process the gasoline into the premium grade.

---

[2]Mary Carmichael, "Help from Far Away," *Newsweek*, May 12, 2003, pp. E16–E17.

Exhibit 26-13 | Incremental Analysis for Sell As Is or Process Further Decision

	Sell As Is	Process Further	Difference
Expected revenue from selling 50,000 gallons of regular gasoline at $1.20 per gallon	$60,000		
Expected revenue from selling 50,000 gallons of premium gasoline at $1.40 per gallon		$70,000	$10,000
Additional costs of $0.11 per gallon to convert 50,000 gallons of regular gasoline into premium gasoline		(5,500)	(5,500)
Total net revenue	$60,000	$64,500	
Difference in net revenue			$ 4,500

Thus, the decision rule is:

Suppose one of **Chevron's** customers wants to buy the 50,000 gallons, but in the form of regular gasoline, not premium. The customer is willing to pay more than $1.20 a gallon for the regular gas. What is the minimum price Chevron should charge?

Answer: Exhibit 26-13 shows that if Chevron does not process the gas into premium grade, it would give up $64,500 ($70,000 revenues given up – $5,500 further processing cost not incurred). To obtain the same income from selling the gas as regular grade, Chevron must sell the regular gas for at least $1.29 per gallon ($64,500 revenue required ÷ 50,000 gallons of regular gas). If the customer offers to pay more than $1.29 per gallon, Chevron will be better off selling regular gas to this customer. If the customer offers less than $1.29, Chevron will be better off further processing the gas into premium grade.

How Do Short-Term and Long-Term Special Decisions Differ?

The special decisions we reviewed pertain to short periods of time, such as a year. In this time frame:

- Many costs are fixed and do not vary with the volume of goods or services produced. This is why short-term special business decisions use the contribution margin approach, which distinguishes variable from fixed costs.
- There is no need to worry about the time value of money. Managers do not bother computing present values of revenues and expenses for short-term decisions.

In the next half of the chapter, we turn to longer-term special decisions, like Deer Valley's decision to expand Snow Park Lodge. For long-term decisions:

- Few if any costs are fixed.
- Managers often take into account the time value of money.

The approach to long-term decisions will reflect these differences.

But before moving on to long-term special decisions, stop for a moment to review the Decision Guidelines that summarize key points from our discussion of short-term decisions. Then work the mid-chapter summary problems.

Decision Guidelines

SHORT-TERM SPECIAL BUSINESS DECISIONS

Amazon.com has confronted most of the special business decisions we've covered. Of course, Amazon's managers consider qualitative factors as they make each decision, but a quantitative analysis of the decision's immediate effect on profits is a good starting point. Here are key guidelines Amazon.com's managers follow in making their decisions.

Decision	Guideline
What information is relevant to a short-term special business decision?	Relevant data: 1. Are expected *future* data 2. *Differ* between alternatives
What are two key guidelines in making short-term special business decisions?	Key guidelines: 1. Focus on *relevant* data 2. Use a *contribution margin* approach that separates variable costs from fixed costs
Should Amazon.com accept a lower sale price for a large order from a customer in São Paulo, Brazil?	If the revenue from the order exceeds the extra variable and fixed costs incurred to fill the order, then accepting the order will increase operating income.
Should Amazon.com drop its electronics product line?	If the cost savings exceed the lost revenues from dropping the electronics product line, then dropping will increase operating income.
Given limited warehouse space, which products should Amazon.com focus on selling?	Amazon should focus on selling the products with the highest contribution margin per unit of the constraint, which is cubic feet of warehouse space.
Should Amazon.com outsource its warehousing operations?	If the incremental costs of operating its own warehouses exceed the costs of outsourcing, then outsourcing will increase operating income.
How to decide whether to sell a product as is or process further?	Process further only if the extra sales revenue (from processing further) exceeds the extra costs of additional processing.

● MID-CHAPTER *Summary Problems*

CHECK YOUR RESOURCES

Problem 1

Aziz, Inc., produces standard and deluxe sunglasses:

	Per Pair	
	Standard	Deluxe
Sale price	$20	$30
Variable expenses	16	21

(continued)

The company has 15,000 machine hours available. In one machine hour, Aziz can produce either 70 pairs of the standard model or 30 pairs of the deluxe model. Which should Aziz emphasize?

Problem 2

Just Do It! incurs the following costs for 20,000 pairs of its high-tech hiking socks:

Direct materials	$ 20,000
Direct labor	80,000
Variable overhead	40,000
Fixed overhead	80,000
Total manufacturing cost	$220,000
Cost per pair ($220,000 ÷ 20,000)	$11

Another manufacturer has offered to sell Just Do It! similar socks for $10, a total purchase cost of $200,000. If Just Do It! outsources *and* leaves its plant idle, it can save $50,000 of fixed overhead cost. Or, the company can use the released facilities to make other products that will contribute $70,000 to profits. Identify and analyze the alternatives. What is the best course of action?

Solutions:

Problem 1

	Style of Sunglasses	
	Standard	Deluxe
Sale price per pair	$ 20	$ 30
Variable expense per pair	(16)	(21)
Contribution margin per pair	$ 4	$ 9
Units produced each machine hour	× 70	× 30
Contribution margin per machine hour	$ 280	$ 270
Capacity—number of machine hours	× 15,000	× 15,000
Total contribution margin at full capacity	$4,200,000	$4,050,000

Decision: Emphasize the standard model because it has the higher contribution margin per unit of the constraint—machine hours.

Problem 2

		Buy Socks	
	Make Socks	Facilities Idle	Make Other Products
Relevant costs:			
Direct materials	$ 20,000	—	
Direct labor	80,000	—	
Variable overhead	40,000	—	
Fixed overhead	80,000	$ 30,000	$ 80,000
Purchase cost from outsider (20,000 × $10)	—	200,000	200,000
Total cost of obtaining socks	220,000	230,000	280,000
Profit from other products	—	—	(70,000)
Net cost of obtaining 20,000 pairs of socks	$220,000	$230,000	$210,000

Decision: Just Do It! should buy the socks from the outside supplier and use the released facilities to make other products.

Use payback and accounting rate of return models to make longer-term capital budgeting decisions.

Student ResourceCD

accounting rate of return, capital budgeting, payback period, residual value

Capital Budgeting
Budgeting for the acquisition of capital assets—assets used for a long period of time.

We discussed cash flows from operating activities, often the primary source of cash, in Chapter 17, page 659.

Payback
The length of time it takes to recover, in net cash inflows, the dollars of a capital outlay.

✔ **Starter 26-9**

✔ **Starter 26-10**

Using Payback and Accounting Rate of Return to Make Capital Budgeting Decisions

Think back to the chapter-opening story. The Deer Valley owners' decision to spend $13 million to expand Snow Park Lodge will tie up resources for years to come. So will Amazon.com's decision to build several highly automated warehouses at over $20 million each. How did management decide that these expansions would be a good investment? By using capital budgeting analysis.

Capital budgeting is budgeting for the acquisition of *capital assets*—assets used for a long period of time. Capital budgeting decisions include expanding the Deer Valley resort, building a new plant, or developing a major commercial Web site.

Capital budgeting is not an exact science. Although the calculations may appear precise, remember that they are based on predictions about an uncertain future. These predictions must consider many unknown factors, such as changing consumer preferences, competition, and government regulations. The further into the future the decision extends, the more likely that actual results will differ from predictions. Long-term decisions are thus riskier than short-term decisions.

We now discuss four popular capital budgeting decision models (or decision methods): payback, accounting rate of return, net present value, and internal rate of return. Three of these models compare the *net cash inflows from operations* each alternative generates. ← Generally accepted accounting principles are based on accrual accounting, but capital budgeting focuses on cash flows. The desirability of a capital asset depends on its ability to generate net cash inflows—that is, inflows in excess of outflows—over the asset's useful life.

Payback Period

Payback is the length of time it takes to recover, in net cash inflows, the dollars of a capital outlay. The payback model measures how quickly managers expect to recover their investment dollars. The shorter the payback period, the more attractive the asset, all else being equal.

Tierra Firma, which makes camping gear, is considering investing $240,000 in hardware and software to develop a portal, or interface, with a business-to-business (B2B) electronic market. Employees throughout the company will use the portal to enter the electronic market of certified suppliers to purchase goods and services appropriate to their jobs. The portal will limit the kinds of goods and services each employee can buy. Accountants will be able to buy office supplies, and maintenance workers will be able to buy parts. Tierra Firma expects the portal to save $60,000 a year for the six years of its useful life. The savings will arise from reducing the number of purchasing personnel the company employs and from lower prices on the goods and services purchased.

When net cash inflows are equal each year, managers compute the payback period as follows:

$$\text{Payback period} = \frac{\text{Amount invested}}{\text{Expected annual net cash inflow}}$$

Net cash inflows arise from an increase in revenues, a decrease in expenses, or both. In Tierra's case, the net cash inflows result from lower expenses. Tierra computes the investment's payback as follows:

$$\text{Payback period for B2B portal} = \frac{\$240,000}{\$60,000} = 4 \text{ years}$$

Exhibit 26-14 verifies that Tierra expects to recoup the $240,000 investment in the B2B portal by the end of year 4, when the accumulated cash inflows (savings) total $240,000.

Tierra Firma is also considering investing $240,000 to develop a Web site. The company expects the Web site to generate $80,000 in cash inflows each year of its three-year life. The payback period is computed as follows:

$$\text{Payback period for Web site development} = \frac{\$240,000}{\$80,000} = 3 \text{ years}$$

Exhibit 26-14 verifies that Tierra Firma will recoup the $240,000 investment for Web site development by the end of year 3, when the accumulated net cash inflows total $240,000. The payback model favors Web site development because it recovers the investment more quickly.

Exhibit 26-14

Payback—Equal Annual Net Cash Inflows

| | | Net Cash Inflows | | | |
| | | B2B Portal | | Web Site Development | |
Year	Amount Invested	Annual	Accumulated	Annual	Accumulated
0	$240,000	—	—	—	
1	—	$60,000	$ 60,000	$80,000	$ 80,000
2	—	60,000	120,000	80,000	160,000
3	—	60,000	180,000	80,000	240,000
4	—	60,000	240,000		
5	—	60,000	300,000		
6	—	60,000	360,000		

Given the fast pace of advances in technology, information technology managers find payback's emphasis on the short term to be useful. For example, Amazon.com considers its software to have a useful life of only two years!

But using the payback method alone can lead to unwise decisions, because payback focuses only on time; it does not consider profitability. The asset's payback period must be shorter than its useful life to provide any profit. In Tierra Firma's decision about developing a B2B portal or Web site, Exhibit 26-14 shows that the Web site's useful life is the same as its payback period—three years. The Web site will merely cover its cost and provide no profit. On the other hand, the B2B portal has a useful life of six years. It will continue to generate net cash inflows for two years after its payback period. This will give the company an additional net cash inflow of $120,000 ($60,000 × 2 years). Unlike the Web site, the B2B portal will be profitable. After considering the assets' useful lives, the B2B portal appears to be the better investment. The key point is that the investment with the shortest payback period is best *only if all other factors are the same.*

This leads to the following decision rule:

DECISION RULE: Payback Period

Invest only if payback is shorter than the asset's useful life.

Investments with shorter payback periods are more desirable, *all else being equal.*

Managers at Deer Valley Resort use the payback method to eliminate proposals that are too risky—those with long payback periods. But they rarely use payback alone, because it ignores profitability.

Accounting Rate of Return

✔ Starter 26-11

Accounting Rate of Return
A measure of profitability computed by dividing the average annual operating income from an asset by the average amount invested in the asset.

Companies are in business to earn profits. One measure of profitability is the **accounting rate of return** on an asset:

$$\frac{\text{Accounting}}{\text{rate of return}} = \frac{\text{Average annual operating income from asset}}{\text{Average amount invested in asset}}$$

The accounting rate of return focuses on the operating income an asset generates. Operating income from an asset can be computed as net cash inflow from the asset minus depreciation on the asset. Exhibit 26-15 computes the accounting rate of return for Tierra Firma's B2B portal in the original payback example. Recall that Tierra expects the portal to generate annual net cash inflows of $60,000. The portal's development costs $240,000, and it has a useful life of six years with no residual value. Annual straight-line depreciation is $40,000 ($240,000 ÷ 6 years). ← Exhibit 26-15 shows that Tierra expects the portal to generate average annual operating income of $20,000 ($60,000 – $40,000).

Recall from Chapter 10, page 405, *that straight-line depreciation assigns an equal amount of depreciation expense to each year of an asset's life.*

Exhibit 26-15

Accounting Rate of Return

$$\frac{\text{Accounting}}{\text{rate of return}} = \frac{\text{Average annual operating income from asset *}}{\text{Average amount invested in asset}}$$

$$= \frac{\text{Annual net cash inflow} - \text{Annual depreciation}}{\text{from asset} \qquad \text{on asset}}{(\text{Amount invested in asset} + \text{Residual value}) / 2}$$

$$= \frac{\$60,000 - \$40,000^\dagger}{(\$240,000 + \$0)/2}$$

$$= \frac{\$20,000}{\$120,000} = 0.167 = 16.7\%$$

*Operating income can also be computed as revenues minus operating expenses.

$\dagger\$40,000 = \dfrac{\$240,000}{6 \text{ years}}$

The accounting rate of return measures the *average* rate of return over the asset's entire life. First, consider the average annual operating income in the numerator. If operating income varies by year, compute the *total* operating income over the asset's life. Then divide the total by the number of years of life to find the *average* annual operating income from the asset.

Second, consider the average amount invested. The book value of the asset decreases as it is used and depreciated. Thus, the company's investment in the asset declines over time. The *average* amount invested is the amount invested halfway through the asset's useful life. To find the average amount invested, we divide by 2. If the asset's residual value is zero, the average investment is half the asset's cost. Exhibit 26-15 shows that the average amount invested in Tierra's B2B portal from the original payback example is $120,000 ($240,000 ÷ 2).

If the asset's residual value is not zero, the average amount invested is greater than half the asset's cost. For example, assume the residual value of the portal's technology is $30,000. Then annual depreciation declines to $35,000 [($240,000 − $30,000)/6]. The accounting rate of return is

$$\text{Accounting rate of return} = \frac{\$60,000 - \$35,000}{(\$240,000 + \$30,000)/2} = \frac{\$25,000}{\$135,000} = 0.185 = 18.5\%$$

Companies that use the accounting rate of return model set a minimum required rate of return. The decision rule is:

If Tierra Firma requires a rate of return of at least 20%, then its managers would not approve an investment in the B2B portal in Exhibit 26-15, because the average annual return is less than 20%.

Using Discounted Cash-Flow Models to Make Capital Budgeting Decisions

A dollar received today is worth more than a dollar to be received in the future. Why? Because you can invest today's dollar and earn extra income. If you receive $1 today and deposit it in a bank that pays 6% interest, a year from today you will have $1.06 (the original $1 plus $0.06 interest). Presumably, you would rather receive the $1 now, which will grow to $1.06 a year from today, rather than receive $1 a year from today. The fact that money can be invested to earn income over time is called the **time value of money**, and this explains why we would prefer to receive cash sooner rather than later.

The time value of money → means that the timing of capital investments' net cash flows is important. Consider two $10,000 investments that both promise future cash inflows of $11,000. Investment 1 will bring in cash of $5,500 at the end of each of the next two years. Investment 2 will return the full $11,000 at the end of the second year. Which investment is better? Investment 1, because it brings in cash sooner. Its $5,500 net cash inflow at the end of the first year can be reinvested right away to earn additional returns.

Neither the payback period nor the accounting rate of return recognizes the time value of money. That is, these models fail to consider the *timing* of the net cash flows an asset generates. *Discounted cash-flow models*— the net present value and the internal rate of return—overcome this weakness. Over 85% of large industrial firms in the United States use discounted cash-flow methods to make capital budgeting decisions. Companies that provide services, like Deer Valley Resort, also use these models.

Net Present Value

Allegra is considering producing CD players and VCRs. The products require different specialized machines that each cost $1 million. Each machine has a five-

Use discounted cash flow models to make longer-term capital budgeting decisions

Student Resource**CD**

annuity, cash flows, cost of capital, discount rate, internal rate of return, present value, required rate of return, sensitivity analysis, time value of money

Time Value of Money
The fact that money can be invested to earn income over time.

← *The time value of money is discussed in the Chapter 15 appendix, page 616.*

year life and zero residual value. The two products have different patterns of predicted net cash inflows:

	Annual Net Cash Inflows	
Year	CD Players	VCRs
1	$ 305,450	$ 500,000
2	305,450	350,000
3	305,450	300,000
4	305,450	250,000
5	305,450	40,000
Total	$1,527,250	$1,440,000

Net Present Value (NPV)
The decision model that brings cash inflows and outflows back to a common time period by discounting these expected future cash flows to their present value, using a minimum desired rate of return.

Discount Rate
Management's minimum desired rate of return on an investment. Also called the **hurdle rate, required rate of return**, and **cost of capital**.

Annuity
A stream of equal periodic cash flows.

The CD-player project generates more net cash inflows. But the VCR project brings in cash sooner. To decide which investment is better, we use **net present value (NPV)** to bring cash inflows and outflows back to a common time period. We *discount* these expected future cash flows to their present value, using Allegra's minimum desired rate of return on the investment, which is also called the **discount rate**. Synonyms are **hurdle rate, required rate of return**, and **cost of capital**. The discount rate depends on the riskiness of investments. The higher the risk, the higher the discount rate. Allegra's discount rate for these investments is 14%.

NET PRESENT VALUE WITH EQUAL PERIODIC CASH FLOWS (ANNUITY)

Allegra expects the CD-player project to generate $305,450 of new cash inflows each year. This stream of equal periodic cash flows is an **annuity**. The present value of an annuity is:

Periodic Cash Flow × Present Value of an Annuity of $1
(Exhibit 26-16 and Appendix C-2)

Exhibit 26-16 shows the present value of annuity factors for various interest rates and numbers of periods. (This is an excerpt from the more-comprehensive table in Appendix C-2.) The present value of an annuity of $1 received each year for five years, discounted at 14% per year, is $3.433. That is, the value today of receiving $1 at the end of each year for the next five years, discounted at 14%, is $3.433. Another way to think about this is that if Allegra invested $3.433 today at a 14% annual interest rate, there would be just enough money to pay out $1 at the end of each year for the next five years.

Exhibit 26-16

Present Value of Annuity of $1

	Present Value of Annuity of $1						
Period	4%	6%	8%	10%	12%	14%	16%
1	0.962	0.943	0.926	0.909	0.893	0.877	0.862
2	1.886	1.833	1.783	1.736	1.690	1.647	1.605
3	2.775	2.673	2.577	2.487	2.402	2.322	2.246
4	3.630	3.465	3.312	3.170	3.037	2.914	2.798
5	4.452	4.212	3.993	3.791	3.605	3.433	3.274
6	5.242	4.917	4.623	4.355	4.111	3.889	3.685
7	6.002	5.582	5.206	4.868	4.564	4.288	4.039
8	6.733	6.210	5.747	5.335	4.968	4.639	4.344
9	7.435	6.802	6.247	5.759	5.328	4.946	4.607
10	8.111	7.360	6.710	6.145	5.650	5.216	4.833

Appendix C-2 provides a more-comprehensive table for the present value of an annuity of $1.

The present value of the cash inflows from Allegra's CD-player project is:

Present Value = Periodic Cash Flow × Present Value of an Annuity of $1

= $305,450   × 3.433

= $1,048,610

After subtracting the $1,000,000 investment, the net present value of the CD-player project is $48,610, as shown in Exhibit 26-17.

	Present Value at 14%	Net Cash Inflow	Total Present Value
Present value of annuity of equal annual net cash inflows for 5 years at 14%........	3.433* × $305,450 per year =		$1,048,610
Investment..............................			(1,000,000)
Net present value of the CD-player project ..			$ 48,610

*Present value of an annuity of $1 for 5 years at 14%.

Exhibit 26-17

Net Present Value with Equal Cash Flows—CD-Player Project

A positive net present value means that the project earns more than the required rate of return. A negative net present value means that the project fails to earn the required rate of return. This leads to the following decision rule:

✔ Starter 26-12

In Allegra's case, the $48,610 positive net present value means that the CD-player project earns more than the target 14% rate of return. The project is an attractive investment.

NET PRESENT VALUE WITH UNEQUAL PERIODIC CASH FLOWS   In contrast to the CD-player project, the net cash inflows of the VCR project are unequal—$500,000 in year 1, $350,000 in year 2, and so on. Because these amounts vary by year, Allegra's managers cannot use the annuity table in Exhibit 26-16 to compute the present value of the VCR project. They must compute the present value of each individual year's cash flows separately, using the present value of $1 table in Exhibit 26-18 (which is an excerpt from the more-comprehensive table in Appendix C-1).

Period	4%	6%	8%	10%	12%	14%	16%
			Present Value of $1				
1	0.962	0.943	0.926	0.909	0.893	0.877	0.862
2	0.925	0.890	0.857	0.826	0.797	0.769	0.743
3	0.889	0.840	0.794	0.751	0.712	0.675	0.641
4	0.855	0.792	0.735	0.683	0.636	0.592	0.552
5	0.822	0.747	0.681	0.621	0.567	0.519	0.476
6	0.790	0.705	0.630	0.564	0.507	0.456	0.410
7	0.760	0.665	0.583	0.513	0.452	0.400	0.354
8	0.731	0.627	0.540	0.467	0.404	0.351	0.305
9	0.703	0.592	0.500	0.424	0.361	0.308	0.263
10	0.676	0.558	0.463	0.386	0.322	0.270	0.227

Appendix C-1 provides a more-comprehensive table for the present value of $1.

Exhibit 26-18

Present Value of $1

Exhibit 26-19 shows that the total present value of the VCR project's net cash inflows is $1,078,910. After subtracting the $1,000,000 investment, the VCR project has a total net present value of $78,910. Allegra expects the VCR project to earn more than the 14% target rate of return, so this is an attractive investment.

| Exhibit 26-19 | Net Present Value with Unequal Cash Flows—VCR Project |

	Present Value of $1 from Exhibit 26-18, 14% Column		Net Cash Inflow		Present Value of Net Cash Inflow
Present value of each year's net cash inflows discounted at 14%:					
Year 1.....................................	0.877†	×	$500,000	=	$ 438,500
Year 2.....................................	0.769	×	350,000	=	269,150
Year 3.....................................	0.675	×	300,000	=	202,500
Year 4.....................................	0.592	×	250,000	=	148,000
Year 5.....................................	0.519	×	40,000	=	20,760
Total present value of net cash inflows					1,078,910
Investment					(1,000,000)
Net present value of the VCR project.............					$ 78,910

†Present value of $1 in 1 year, 2 years, 3 years, and so on, at 14%, Exhibit 26-18.

Use the present value of $1 table in Exhibit 26-18 to find the present value of an *annuity* of $1 for five years, discounted at 14%. Compare the result to the present value of an annuity of $1 factor from the table in Exhibit 26-16.

Answer: Exhibit 26-18 shows that at a 14% discount rate, the present value of $1 received:

In one year is	$0.877
In two years is	0.769
In three years is	0.675
In four years is	0.592
In five years is	0.519
Total present value of $1 received at the end of each year for five years, discounted at 14% is	$3.432

Except for a slight rounding error, this sum ($3.432) equals the present value of an annuity of $1 for five years discounted at 14%, shown in Exhibit 26-16 ($3.433). This shows how entries in the present value of an annuity table (Exhibit 26-16) are the sums of the present value of $1 factors from Exhibit 26-18.

Exhibits 26-17 and 26-19 show that both projects have positive net present values. Therefore, both are attractive investments. If Allegra wants to pursue only one of the projects, the net present value analysis favors the VCR. This project should earn an additional $78,910 beyond the 14% required rate of return, while the CD-player project returns only an additional $48,610.

This example illustrates an important point. The CD-player project promises more *total* net cash inflows. But the *timing* of the VCR cash flows—loaded near the beginning of the project—gives the VCR investment a higher net present value. The VCR project is more attractive because of the time value of money. Its dollars, which are received sooner, are worth more now than the more-distant dollars of the CD-player project.

SENSITIVITY ANALYSIS   Capital budgeting decisions affect cash flows far into the future. Allegra's managers might want to know whether their decision would be affected by any of their major assumptions. For example:

- Changing the discount rate from 14% to 12% or to 16%
- Changing the net cash flows by 10%

After entering the basic information for net present value analysis into spreadsheet software, managers perform sensitivity analyses with just a few keystrokes. The software quickly recalculates and displays the results.

Suppose Allegra uses a 6% discount rate rather than the 14% rate. Would the net present value of the CD-player project using the 6% rate be higher or lower than the original 14% rate? Why?

Answer: The smaller the discount rate, the higher the present value (today) of dollars to be received in the future. Thus, discounting the cash flows at 6% rather than 14% *increases* the net present value of the CD-player project, as follows:

CD-Player Project	Present Value at 6%	Net Cash Inflow	Total Present Value
Present value of annuity of equal annual net cash inflows for 5 years...........................	4.212* ×	$305,450 =	$1,286,555
Investment...			(1,000,000)
Net present value at 6%...................................			286,555
Net present value at 14% (from Ex. 26-17).....			(48,610)
Difference...			$ 237,945

*Present value of an annuity of $1 for 5 years at 6%, Exhibit 26-16.

Internal Rate of Return

Another discounted cash-flow model for capital budgeting is the internal rate of return. The **internal rate of return (IRR)** is the rate of return (based on discounted cash flows) a company can expect to earn by investing in the project. It is the discount rate that makes the net present value of the project's cash flows equal to zero. The higher the IRR, the more desirable the project.

For projects with equal cash flows each period, like Allegra's CD-player project, use the following three steps to compute the IRR:

1. Identify the expected net cash inflows ($305,450 each year for five years) exactly as in calculating the net present value.
2. Find the discount rate that makes the total present value of the cash inflows equal to the present value of the cash outflows. Work backward to find the discount rate that makes the present value of the annuity of cash inflows equal to the amount of the investment by solving the following equation for the annuity present value (PV) factor:

Internal Rate of Return (IRR)
The rate of return (based on discounted cash flows) that a company can expect to earn by investing in the project. The discount rate that makes the net present value of the project's cash flows equal to zero.

✔ **Starter 26-13**

$$\text{Investment} = \text{Expected annual net cash flow} \times \text{Annuity PV factor}$$

$$\text{Annuity PV factor} = \frac{\text{Investment}}{\text{Expected annual net cash flow}}$$

$$= \frac{\$1,000,000}{\$305,450}$$

$$= 3.274$$

3. Turn to the table presenting the present value of an annuity of $1 (Exhibit 26-16). Scan the row corresponding to the project's expected life—period 5, in our example. Choose the column with the number closest to the annuity PV factor you calculated in step 2. The 3.274 annuity factor is in the 16% column. Therefore, the IRR of the CD-player project is 16%. Allegra expects the project to earn an annual rate of return of 16% over its life. Exhibit 26-20 confirms this result.

Exhibit 26-20 **Internal Rate of Return, CD-Player Project**

	Present Value at 16%		Net Cash Inflow		Total Present Value
Present value of annuity of equal annual net cash inflows for 5 years at 16%.............	3.274*	×	$305,450	=	$1,000,000†
Investment..................................					(1,000,000)
Net present value of the CD-player project.........					$0‡

*Present value of annuity of $1 for 5 years at 16%, Exhibit 26-16.
†Slight rounding error.
‡The zero difference proves that the IRR is 16%.

To decide whether the project is acceptable, compare the IRR with the minimum desired rate of return. The decision rule is:

If CD players were the only investment under consideration, Allegra would invest in CD players because their 16% IRR exceeds the 14% discount rate. But recall that the VCR project has a higher net present value. The VCR investment also has a higher IRR. Because the VCR project has unequal cash inflows, however, computation of the VCR's IRR requires a trial-and-error procedure that is covered in more-advanced courses. (Spreadsheet software and even calculators can perform these computations.)

□ Relevant Information
□ Short-Term Special Decisions
□ Using Payback and ARR
□ Using Discounted Cash-Flow Models
■ Comparing Capital Budgeting Methods

 Compare and contrast the four capital budgeting methods

 Student Resource CD

internal rate of return, payback period, present value

Comparing Capital Budgeting Methods

Payback period, net present value, and internal rate of return are all based on *cash inflows and outflows*. Only the accounting rate of return is based on accrual accounting *revenues and expenses*. Payback is the simplest to compute, but it ignores profitability and the time value of money. The accounting rate of return considers profitability, but it also ignores the time value of money. Only net present value and internal rate of return consider the time value of money.

How do the net present value and IRR approaches compare? Net present value indicates the amount of the excess (or deficiency) of a project's present value of net cash inflows over (or under) its cost—at a specified discount rate.

But net present value does not show the project's unique rate of return. The internal rate of return shows the project's rate but does not indicate the dollar difference between the project's present value and its investment cost. In many cases, the two discounted cash-flow methods lead to the same investment decision.

✔ Starter 26-14

The discounted cash-flow methods are superior because they consider both the time value of money and profitability. The time value of money enters the analysis through the discounting of future dollars to present value. Profitability is built into the discounted cash-flow methods because they consider all cash inflows and outflows over the project's life. The payback model considers only the cash flows necessary to recover the initial cash invested.

Exhibit 26-21 summarizes the strengths and weaknesses of payback, accounting rate of return, and the discounted cash-flow methods. Managers often use more than one method to gain different perspectives on risks and returns. For example, Deer Valley's owners could decide to pursue capital projects with positive net present values, provided that those projects have a payback of four years or less.

Method	Strengths	Weaknesses
Payback	Easy to understand Based on cash flows Highlights risks	Ignores profitability and the time value of money
Accounting rate of return	Based on profitability	Ignores the time value of money
Discounted cash flow: Net present value Internal rate of return	Based on cash flows, profitability, and the time value of money	Difficult to determine discount rate

Exhibit 26-21

Capital Budgeting Methods

A pharmaceutical company is considering two research projects. Project A has a net present value of $232,000 and a 3-year payback period. Project B has a net present value of $237,000 and a payback period of 4.5 years. Which project would you choose?

Answer: Many managers would choose project A. Net present value is a better guide to decision making than payback period. But managers would consider the 2.2% [($237,000 − $232,000)/$232,000] difference between the net present values to be insignificant. In contrast, the 50% [(4.5 years − 3.0 years)/3.0 years] difference between payback periods *is* significant. The uncertainty of receiving operating cash flows increases with each passing year. Managers often forgo small differences in expected cash inflows to decrease the risk of investments.

Decision Guidelines

CAPITAL BUDGETING

Amazon.com started as a virtual retailer. It held no inventory. Instead, it bought books and CDs only as needed to fill customer orders. As the company grew, its managers decided to invest in their own warehouse facilities. Why? Owning warehouse facilities allows Amazon to save money by buying in bulk. Also, shipping all items in the customer's order in one package, from one location, saves shipping costs. Here are some of the guidelines Amazon.com's managers used as they made the major capital budgeting decision to invest in building warehouses.

Decision Guidelines (*continued*)

Decision	Guideline

Should we make a long-term investment in warehouse facilities?	Investment in warehouse facilities may be worthwhile if:
	• Payback period is shorter than warehouse's useful life.
	• Expected accounting rate of return on warehouse exceeds required rate of return.
	• Discounted cash-flow methods:
	  Net present value (NPV) is positive.
	  Internal rate of return (IRR) exceeds required rate of return.

How to compute the payback period?	$$\text{Payback period} = \frac{\text{Amount invested in warehouse}}{\text{Expected annual net cash inflow (from cost savings)}}$$
How to compute the accounting rate of return?	$$\frac{\text{Accounting rate of return}}{} = \frac{\text{Average annual operating income (cost savings) from warehouse}}{\text{Average amount invested in warehouse}}$$ $$= \frac{\text{Average annual net cash inflow from warehouse} - \text{Annual depreciation on warehouse}}{(\text{Amount invested in warehouse} + \text{Residual value})/2}$$
How to compute net present value with • Equal annual cash flows?	$$\begin{matrix}\text{Present value of}\\ \textit{annuity} \text{ of \$1}\\ \text{(Exhibit 26-16)}\end{matrix} \times \begin{matrix}\text{Annual net cash}\\ \text{inflow or outflow}\end{matrix}$$
• Unequal annual cash flows?	Compute the present value of each year's net cash inflow or outflow (present value of \$1 from Exhibit 26-18 × net cash inflow or outflow) and add up yearly present values.
How to compute internal rate of return with • Equal annual cash flows?	$$\begin{matrix}\text{Annuity PV factor}\\ \text{(Use Exhibit 26-16)}\end{matrix} = \frac{\text{Investment in warehouse}}{\text{Expected annual net cash inflow}}$$
• Unequal annual cash flows?	Trial and error, spreadsheet software, or calculator
Which capital budgeting methods are best?	Discounted cash-flow methods (net present value and IRR) are best because they incorporate both profitability and the time value of money.

Excel Application Exercise

Goal: Create a spreadsheet to compute payback period, accounting rate of return, and net present value of a machine.

Scenario: Suppose **Amazon** is considering the purchase of a new bar-coding machine for one of its warehouses. You are asked to prepare a simple analysis to determine whether the machine should be purchased. The summary problem for review at the end of the chapter provides a good outline for completing your analysis.

The bar-coding machine costs \$60,000. It has a five-year useful life with no salvage value. The estimated annual net cash flow from the machine is \$16,000. Assume Amazon's required rate of return is 12%.

When you have completed your worksheet, answer the following questions:

1. What is the machine's payback period?
2. What is the machine's accounting rate of return?
3. What is the machine's net present value (NPV)?
4. Should Amazon purchase the machine? Why or why not?

Step-by-Step:
1. Open a new Excel spreadsheet.
2. In column A, create a bold-faced heading as follows:
   a. Chapter 26 Excel Application Exercise
   b. Capital Budgeting Decision
   c. Amazon
   d. Today's Date

(*continued*)

3. Two rows down, create a bold-faced and underlined heading titled "Data Section." Enter the data and descriptions provided in the problem under this heading in your spreadsheet.

4. At the end of the Data Section, add a row for "Annual Depreciation on Asset." Use the "SLN" financial function to compute depreciation.

5. Move down two rows. In column A, enter the description "Payback Period (years)." Compute the payback period in column B.

6. Move down one row. In column A, enter the description "Accounting Rate of Return." Compute the accounting rate of return in column B.

7. Move down two rows, and enter "Net Present Value" as a bold-faced and underlined heading.

8. Underneath the heading, use the textbook's Summary Problem format (listed as Requirement 3 on page 1106) to compute net present value. Use the "PV" financial function for the present value of an annuity.

9. Save your file to disk, and print a copy for your files.

END-OF-CHAPTER *Summary Problem*

Zetamax is considering buying a new bar-coding machine for its Austin, Texas, plant. The data for the machine follow:

Cost of machine	$48,000
Estimated residual value	$ 0
Estimated annual net cash inflow (each year for 5 years)	$13,000
Estimated useful life	5 years
Required rate of return	16%

CHECK YOUR RESOURCES

Required

1. Compute the bar-coding machine's payback period.
2. Compute the bar-coding machine's accounting rate of return.
3. Compute the bar-coding machine's net present value.
4. Would you buy the bar-coding machine? Why?

Solution

Requirement 1

$$\text{Payback period} = \frac{\text{Amount invested}}{\text{Expected annual net cash inflow}} = \frac{\$48,000}{\$13,000} = 3.7 \text{ years (rounded)}$$

Requirement 2

$$\text{Accounting rate of return} = \frac{\text{Average annual operating income from asset}}{\text{Average amount invested in asset}}$$

$$= \frac{\substack{\text{Average annual net cash} \\ \text{inflow from asset}} - \substack{\text{Annual} \\ \text{depreciation on asset}}}{(\text{Amount invested in asset} + \text{Residual value})/2}$$

$$= \frac{\$13,000 - \$9,600*}{(\$48,000 + \$0)/2}$$

$$= \frac{\$3,400}{\$24,000}$$

$$= 0.142 \text{ (rounded)}$$

$$= 14.2\%$$

$$* \frac{\$48,000}{5 \text{ years}} = \$9,600$$

Requirement 3

Present value of annuity of equal annual net cash inflows at 16% ($13,000 × 3.274†)	$42,562
Investment	(48,000)
Net present value	$(5,438)

†Present value of annuity of $1 for 5 years at 16%, Exhibit 26-16.

Requirement 4

Decision: Do not buy the bar-coding machine because it has a negative net present value. The net present value model considers profitability and the time value of money. The other models ignore at least one of those factors.

REVIEW *Special Business Decisions and Capital Budgeting*

Quick Check

1. In making short-term special decisions, you should:
   a. Focus on total costs
   b. Separate variable from fixed costs
   c. Use a conventional absorption costing approach
   d. Discount cash flows to their present values

2. Which of the following is relevant to **Amazon.com's** decision to accept a special order at a lower sale price from a large customer in China?
   a. The cost of Amazon's warehouses in the United States
   b. Amazon's investment in its Web site
   c. The cost of shipping the order to the customer
   d. Founder Jeff Bezos's salary

3. In deciding whether to drop its electronics product line, Amazon.com would consider:
   a. The costs it could save by dropping the product line
   b. The revenues it would lose from dropping the product line
   c. How dropping the electronics product line would affect sales of its other products like CDs
   d. All of the above

4. In deciding which product lines to emphasize, Amazon.com should focus on the product line that has the highest:
   a. Profit per unit of product
   b. Contribution margin per unit of product
   c. Contribution margin ratio
   d. Contribution margin per unit of the constraining factor

5. Suppose **Deer Valley** is considering whether to (1) bake bread for all its restaurants in-house or (2) buy the bread from a local bakery. The chef estimates that variable costs for each loaf include $0.50 of ingredients and $1.00 of direct labor for kneading and forming the loaves. Allocating fixed overhead (depreciation on the kitchen equipment and building) based on direct labor assigns $1.00 of fixed overhead per loaf. The local bakery charges $1.75 per loaf. Should Deer Valley bake the bread in-house or buy from the local bakery?
   a. There is a $0.25 per loaf advantage to baking the bread in-house.
   b. There is a $1.25 per loaf advantage to baking the bread in-house.
   c. There is a $0.25 per loaf advantage to buying the bread from the local bakery.
   d. There is a $0.75 per loaf advantage to buying the bread from the local bakery.

6. In computing the accounting rate of return on the Snow Park Lodge expansion, Deer Valley would consider all of the following *except*:
   a. Predicted cash inflows over the life of the expansion
   b. The cost of the expansion
   c. Depreciation on the assets built in the expansion
   d. Present value factors

7. Suppose Deer Valley is deciding whether to purchase new accounting software. The payback period for the $30,000 software package is 4 years, and the software's expected life is 6 years. What are the expected annual cash savings from the new software?
   a. $7,500   c. $200
   b. $5,000   d. $130

8. In computing the net present value of the Snow Park Lodge expansion, Deer Valley would consider all of the following *except*:
   a. Predicted cash inflows over the life of the expansion
   b. The cost of the expansion
   c. Depreciation on the assets built in the expansion
   d. The company's required rate of return on investments

9. Suppose Amazon.com is considering investing in warehouse-management software that costs $500,000 and should lead to cost savings of $120,000 a year for its 5-year life. If Amazon has a 12% required rate of return, what is the net present value of the software investment?
   a. ($88,040)   c. $411,960
   b. ($67,400)   d. $432,600

10. Which of the following is the most reliable method for making capital budgeting decisions?
    a. Net present value method   c. Payback method
    b. Accounting rate of return method   d. Incremental method

Accounting Vocabulary

accounting rate of return (p. 1096)
annuity (p. 1098)
capital budgeting (p. 1094)
constraint (p. 1085)
cost of capital (p. 1098)
discount rate (p. 1098)

hurdle rate (p. 1098)
internal rate of return (IRR) (p. 1101)
net present value (NPV) (p. 1098)
opportunity cost (p. 1088)
outsourcing (p. 1087)

payback (p. 1094)
relevant information (p. 1080)
required rate of return (p. 1098)
sunk cost (p. 1090)
time value of money (p. 1097)

ASSESS *Your Progress*

Starters

S26-1 You are trying to decide whether to trade in your inkjet printer for a more-recent model. Your usage pattern will remain unchanged, but the old and new printers use different ink cartridges. Are the following items relevant or irrelevant to your decision?

a. The price of the new printer
b. The price you paid for the old printer
c. The trade-in value of the old printer
d. Paper costs
e. The difference between ink cartridges' costs

S26-2 Consider the **ACDelco** special sales order example on pages 1082–1084. Suppose that:

a. ACDelco's variable manufacturing cost is $1.35 per oil filter (instead of $1.20).
b. ACDelco would have to buy a special stamping machine that costs $9,000 to mark the customer's logo on the special-order oil filters. The machine would be scrapped when the special order is complete.

Would you recommend that ACDelco accept the special order under these conditions?

See *www.prenhall.com/horngren* for selected Starters, Exercises, and Problems.

Identifying relevant data
(Obj. 1)

Accepting or rejecting a special sales order
(Obj. 2)

Dropping a department
(Obj. 2)

S26-3 Knight Fashion in New York operates three departments: Men's, Women's, and Accessories. Knight Fashion allocates fixed expenses (building depreciation and utilities) based on the square feet occupied by each department. Departmental operating income data for the third quarter of 20X7 are as follows:

| | Department | | | |
	Men's	Women's	Accessories	Total
Sales revenue..................	$105,000	$54,000	$100,000	$259,000
Variable expenses..............	60,000	30,000	80,000	170,000
Fixed expenses	25,000	20,000	25,000	70,000
Total expenses.................	85,000	50,000	105,000	240,000
Operating income (loss).........	$ 20,000	$ 4,000	$ (5,000)	$ 19,000

Should Knight Fashion drop any of the departments? Give your reason. (The store will remain in the same building regardless of the decision.)

Dropping a department
(Obj. 2)

S26-4 Consider Knight Fashion from Starter 26-3. Assume that the fixed expenses assigned to each department include only:

- Salary of the department's manager
- Cost of advertising directly related to that department

Knight Fashion will not incur these fixed expenses if the department is dropped. Under these circumstances, should Knight Fashion drop any of the departments? Give your reason.

Determining product mix
(Obj. 1, 2)

S26-5 Lifemaster, Inc., produces two types of exercise treadmills: Regular and Deluxe.

The exercise craze is such that Lifemaster could use all its available machine hours producing either model. The two models are processed through the same production departments.

What is the constraint? Which model should Lifemaster produce? If both models should be produced, compute the mix that will maximize operating income.

| | Per Unit | |
	Deluxe	Regular
Sale price	$1,000	$550
Costs:		
Direct materials.......................	$ 290	$100
Direct labor	80	180
Variable manufacturing overhead*	240	80
Fixed manufacturing overhead*..........	120	40
Variable operating expenses	115	65
Total cost.............................	845	465
Operating income.......................	$ 155	$ 85

* Allocated on the basis of machine hours.

Outsourcing decision for services
(Obj. 1, 2)

S26-6 U.S. Food Corp. in Lexington, Kentucky, manufactures and markets snack foods. Betsy Gonzalez manages the company's fleet of 200 delivery trucks. Gonzalez has been charged with "reengineering" the fleet-management function. She has an important decision to make.

- Should she continue to manage the fleet in-house with the five employees reporting to her? To do so, she will have to acquire new fleet-management software to streamline U.S. Food's fleet-management process.
- Should she outsource the fleet-management function to Fleet Management Services, a company that specializes in managing fleets of trucks for other companies? Fleet Management Services would take over the maintenance, repair, and scheduling of U.S. Food's fleet (but U.S. Food would retain ownership). This

(continued)

alternative would require Gonzalez to lay off her five employees. However, her own job would be secure as she would be U.S. Food's liaison with Fleet Management Services.

Assume that Gonzalez's records show the following data concerning U.S. Food's fleet:

Book value of U.S. Food's trucks, with an estimated 5-year life....	$3,500,000
Annual leasing fee for new fleet-management software..........	8,000
Annual maintenance of trucks...............................	145,500
Fleet Supervisor Gonzalez's annual salary.....................	60,000
Total annual salaries of U.S. Food's five other fleet-management employees...	150,000

Suppose that Fleet Management Services offers to manage U.S. Food's fleet for an annual fee of $290,000.

Which alternative will maximize U.S. Food's short-term operating income?

S26-7 Refer to U.S. Food Corp. in Starter 26-6. What qualitative factors should Gonzalez consider before making a final decision?

Outsourcing decision for services
(Obj. 2)

S26-8 Auto Components, Inc., has an inventory of 500 obsolete remote entry keys that are carried in inventory at a manufacturing cost of $80,000. Production Supervisor Terri Smith must decide whether to:

- Process the inventory further at a cost of $20,000, with the expectation of selling it for $28,000, or
- Scrap the inventory for a sale price of $6,000

Deciding whether to sell as is or process further **(Obj. 1, 2)**

What should Smith do? Present figures to support your decision.

S26-9 Starters 26-9 through 26-14 consider how **Deer Valley Resort** (from the chapter-opening story) could use capital budgeting methods to decide whether the $13 million Snow Park Lodge expansion would be a good investment.

Computing net cash inflow from project **(Obj. 3)**

Assume Deer Valley's managers developed the following estimates concerning the expansion (all numbers assumed):

Number of additional skiers per day........................	120
Average number of days per year that weather conditions allow skiing at Deer Valley....................	150
Useful life of expansion (in years).........................	10
Average cash spent by each skier per day....................	$245
Average variable cost of serving each skier per day..........	$85
Cost of expansion	$13,000,000
Discount rate	12%

Assume that Deer Valley uses the straight-line depreciation method and expects the lodge expansion to have a residual value of $1 million at the end of its 10-year life.

Compute the average annual net cash inflow from the expansion.

S26-10 Refer to the Deer Valley Snow Park Lodge expansion project in Starter 26-9. Compute the payback period for the expansion project.

Computing payback period **(Obj. 3)**

S26-11 Refer to the Deer Valley Snow Park Lodge expansion project in Starter 26-9. What is the accounting rate of return?

Computing accounting rate of return **(Obj. 3)**

S26-12 ← *Link Back to Chapter 15 (Present-Value Concepts).* Refer to Starter 26-9. *Assume the expansion has zero residual value.* What is the project's net present value?

Computing net present value **(Obj. 4)**

Computing internal rate of return
(Obj. 4)

S26-13 Refer to Starter 26-9. *Assume the expansion has zero residual value.* What is the project's internal rate of return?

Evaluating results of different capital budgeting methods
(Obj. 5)

S26-14 Use your results from Starters 26-9 through 26-13 to write a memo to Deer Valley Director of Finance Jim Madsen, recommending whether Deer Valley should undertake the expansion. Cover the strengths and weaknesses of each capital budgeting method cited in your memo. Use the following format:

Date: _____	
To:	Mr. Jim Madsen, Director of Finance
From: _____	
Subject: _____	

Accepting or rejecting a special sales order
(Obj. 1, 2)

Student Resource CD

spreadsheet

Exercises

E26-1 Suppose the **Baseball Hall of Fame** in Cooperstown, New York, has approached Sports-Cardz, Inc., with a special order. The Hall of Fame wishes to purchase 50,000 baseball card packs for a special promotional campaign and offers $0.40 per pack, a total of $20,000. Sports-Cardz's, total production cost is $0.60 per pack, as follows:

Variable costs:	
Direct materials....................................	$0.14
Direct labor	0.08
Variable overhead................................	0.13
Fixed overhead	0.25
Total cost	$0.60

Sports-Cardz has enough excess capacity to handle the special order.

Required

1. Prepare an incremental analysis to determine whether Sports-Cardz should accept the special sales order.

2. Now assume that the Hall of Fame wants special hologram baseball cards. Sports-Cardz will spend $5,000 to develop this hologram, which will be useless after the special order is completed. Should Sports-Cardz accept the special order under these circumstances?

Deciding on a special sales order
(Obj. 1, 2)

E26-2 Maui Jane sunglasses sell for about $150 per pair. Suppose that the company incurs the following average costs per pair:

Direct materials......................................	$40
Direct labor	12
Variable manufacturing overhead	8
Variable marketing expenses	4
Fixed manufacturing overhead	20*
Total costs..	$84

* $2,000,000 total fixed manufacturing overhead
     100,000 pairs of sunglasses

Maui Jane has enough idle capacity to accept a one-time-only special order from Lenscrafters for 20,000 pairs of sunglasses at $76 per pair. Maui Jane will not incur any additional variable marketing expenses for the order.

Required

1. How would accepting the order affect Maui Jane's operating income? In addition to the special order's effect on profits, what other (longer-term qualitative) factors should Maui Jane's managers consider in deciding whether to accept the order?

(continued)

2. Maui Jane's marketing manager, Jim Revo, argues against accepting the special order because the offer price of $76 is less than Maui Jane's $84 cost to make the sunglasses. Revo asks you, as one of Maui Jane's staff accountants, to write a memo explaining whether his analysis is correct. Use the format from S26-14.

E26-3 Top managers of Video Avenue are alarmed about their operating losses. They are considering dropping the VCR-tape product line. Company accountants have prepared the following analysis to help make this decision:

Keeping or dropping a product line (fixed costs unchanged)
(Obj. 1, 2)

	Total	DVD Discs	VCR Tapes
Sales revenue	$420,000	$300,000	$120,000
Variable expenses.	230,000	150,000	80,000
Contribution margin	190,000	150,000	40,000
Fixed expenses:			
Manufacturing	125,000	70,000	55,000
Marketing and administrative.	70,000	55,000	15,000
Total fixed expenses.	195,000	125,000	70,000
Operating income (loss)	$ (5,000)	$ 25,000	$ (30,000)

Total fixed costs will not change if the company stops selling VCR tapes.

    Prepare an incremental analysis to show whether Video Avenue should drop the VCR-tape product line. Will dropping VCR tapes add $30,000 to operating income? Explain.

E26-4 Refer to Exercise 26-3. Assume that Video Avenue can avoid $30,000 of fixed expenses by dropping the VCR-tape product line. Prepare an incremental analysis to show whether Video Avenue should stop selling VCR tapes.

Keeping or dropping a product line (fixed costs change) **(Obj. 1, 2)**

E26-5 Vivace sells both designer and moderately priced fashion accessories. Top management is deciding which product line to emphasize. Accountants have provided the following data:

Determining product mix
(Obj. 1, 2)

	Per Item	
	Designer	Moderately Priced
Average sale price	$200	$84
Average variable expenses	85	24
Average contribution margin	115	60
Average fixed expenses (allocated)	20	10
Average operating income	$ 95	$50

    The Vivace store in Reno, Nevada, has 10,000 square feet of floor space. If it emphasizes moderately priced goods, 650 items can be displayed in the store. If it emphasizes designer wear, only 300 designer items can be displayed. These numbers are also the average monthly sales in units.

    Prepare an analysis to show which product to emphasize.

E26-6 Fiber Systems manufactures an optical switch that it uses in its final product. The switch has the following manufacturing costs per unit:

Outsourcing decision
(Obj. 1, 2)

Direct materials	$ 9.00
Direct labor	1.50
Variable overhead	2.00
Fixed overhead	6.50
Manufacturing product cost.	$19.00

Student Resource CD

spreadsheet

    Another company has offered to sell Fiber Systems the switch for $14 per unit. If Fiber Systems buys the switch from the outside supplier, the manufacturing facilities that will be idled cannot be used for any other purpose. Should Fiber Systems make or buy the switch?

Determining best use of facilities
(Obj. 1, 2)

*Student Resource*CD
spreadsheet

Sell or process further
(Obj. 1, 2)

Computing payback
(Obj. 3)

Determining accounting rate of return
(Obj. 3)

Computing net present value
(Obj. 4)

*Student Resource*CD
spreadsheet

Computing internal rate of return
(Obj. 4)

Determining product mix
(Obj. 2)

E26-7 Refer to Exercise 26-6. Fiber Systems needs 80,000 optical switches. By outsourcing them, Fiber Systems can use its idle facilities to manufacture another product that will contribute $220,000 to operating income. Identify the *incremental* costs that Fiber Systems will incur to acquire 80,000 switches under three alternative plans. Which plan makes the best use of Fiber System's facilities? Support your answer.

E26-8 Concert Sounds has damaged some custom speakers that cost the company $10,000 to manufacture. Owner Jim Buffett is considering two options for disposing of this inventory. One plan is to sell the speakers as damaged inventory for $2,500. The alternative is to spend an additional $500 to repair the damage and expect to sell the speakers for $3,100. What should Buffett do? Support your answer with an analysis that shows expected net revenue under each alternative.

E26-9 Quiksilver Co. is considering acquiring a manufacturing plant. The purchase price is $1,236,100. The owners believe the plant will generate net cash inflows of $309,025 annually. It will have to be replaced in 8 years. Use the payback method to determine whether Quiksilver should purchase this plant.

E26-10 Engineered Products is shopping for new equipment. Managers are considering two investments. Equipment manufactured by Atlas, Inc., costs $1,000,000 and will last for five years, with no residual value. The Atlas equipment is expected to generate annual operating income of $160,000. Equipment manufactured by Veras Co. is priced at $1,200,000 and will remain useful for six years. It promises annual operating income of $240,500, and its expected residual value is $100,000.

Which equipment offers the higher accounting rate of return?

E26-11 ← *Link Back to Chapter 15 (Present-Value Concepts).* Use the net present value method to determine whether Salon Products should invest in the following projects:

- *Project A*: Costs $272,000 and offers eight annual net cash inflows of $60,000. Salon Products requires an annual return of 14% on projects like A.
- *Project B*: Costs $380,000 and offers nine annual net cash inflows of $70,000. Salon Products demands an annual return of 12% on investments of this nature.

What is the net present value of each project? What is the maximum acceptable price to pay for each project?

E26-12 Refer to Exercise 26-11. Compute the internal rate of return of each project, and use this information to identify the better investment.

E26-13 Each morning, Max Imery stocks the drink case at Max's Beach Hut in Myrtle Beach, South Carolina. Max's has 100 linear feet of refrigerated display space for cold drinks. Each linear foot can hold either six 12-ounce cans or four 20-ounce plastic or glass bottles. Max's sells three types of cold drinks:

- Coca-Cola in 12-oz. cans, for $1.50 per can
- Coca-Cola in 20-oz. plastic bottles, for $1.75 per bottle
- SoBe in 20-oz. glass bottles, for $2.20 per bottle

Max's pays its suppliers:

- $0.25 per 12-oz. can of Coca-Cola
- $0.40 per 20-oz. bottle of Coca-Cola
- $0.75 per 20-oz. bottle of SoBe

Max's monthly fixed expenses include:

Hut rental	$ 375
Refrigerator rental	75
Max's salary	1,550
Total fixed expenses	$2,000

(continued)

Max's can sell all the drinks stocked in the display case each morning.

1. What is Max's constraining factor? What should Imery stock to maximize profits?
2. Suppose Max's refuses to devote more than 60 linear feet to any individual product. Under this condition, how many linear feet of each drink should Imery stock? How many units of each product will be available for sale each day?

Problems

(Group A)

P26-1A Buoy, Inc. manufactures flotation vests in Tampa, Florida. Buoy's contribution-margin income statement for the most recent month contains the following data:

Accepting or rejecting a special sales order
(Obj. 1, 2)

Sales in units	31,000
Sales revenue.	$434,000
Variable expenses:	
Manufacturing	$ 93,000
Marketing and administrative	107,000
Total variable expenses	200,000
Contribution margin	234,000
Fixed expenses:	
Manufacturing	126,000
Marketing and administrative	90,000
Total fixed expenses.	216,000
Operating income.	$ 18,000

Suppose Overton's wishes to buy 5,000 vests from Buoy. Acceptance of the order will not increase any of Buoy's marketing and administrative expenses. The Buoy plant has enough unused capacity to manufacture the additional vests. Overton's has offered $10.00 per vest, which is below the normal sale price of $14.

Required

1. Prepare an incremental analysis to determine whether Buoy should accept this special sales order.
2. Identify long-term factors Buoy should consider in deciding whether to accept the special sales order.

P26-2A Members of the board of directors of Security Systems, Inc., have received the following operating income data for the year just ended.

Keeping or dropping a product line
(Obj. 1, 2)

	Product Line		
	Industrial Systems	Household Systems	Total
Sales revenue	$300,000	$310,000	$610,000
Cost of goods sold:			
Variable.	$ 38,000	$ 42,000	$ 80,000
Fixed	210,000	69,000	279,000
Total cost of goods sold	248,000	111,000	359,000
Gross profit.	52,000	199,000	251,000
Marketing and administrative expenses:			
Variable.	66,000	71,000	137,000
Fixed	40,000	22,000	62,000
Total marketing and administrative expenses	106,000	93,000	199,000
Operating income (loss)	$(54,000)	$106,000	$ 52,000

Members of the board are surprised that the industrial-systems product line is losing money. They commission a study to determine whether the company should drop the line. Company accountants estimate that dropping industrial systems will decrease fixed cost of goods sold by $80,000 and decrease fixed marketing and administrative expenses by $12,000.

Required

1. Prepare an incremental analysis to show whether Security Systems should drop the industrial-systems product line.

2. Prepare contribution margin income statements to show Security Systems' total operating income under the two alternatives: (a) with the industrial systems line, and (b) without the line. Compare the *difference* between the two alternatives' income numbers to your answer to Requirement 1. What have you learned from this comparison?

Determining product mix
(Obj. 1, 2)

P26-3A Brun Corp., located in St. Cloud, Minnesota, produces two lines of electric toothbrushes: deluxe and standard. Because Brun can sell all the toothbrushes it can produce, the owners are expanding the plant. They are deciding which product line to emphasize. To make this decision, they assemble the following data.

	Per Unit	
	Deluxe Toothbrush	Standard Toothbrush
Sale price.....................	$80	$48
Variable expenses.............	20	18
Contribution margin...........	$60	$30
Contribution margin ratio	75%	62.5%

After expansion, the factory will have a production capacity of 4,500 machine hours per month. The plant can manufacture either 60 standard electric toothbrushes or 24 deluxe electric toothbrushes per machine hour.

Required

1. Identify the constraining factor for Brun Corp.

2. Prepare an analysis to show which product line to emphasize.

Outsourcing; best use of facilities
(Obj. 1, 2)

P26-4A X-Perience manufactures snow boards. Its cost of making 1,800 bindings is

Direct materials....................................	$17,520
Direct labor.......................................	3,100
Variable overhead.................................	2,080
Fixed overhead	6,800
Total manufacturing costs for 1,800 bindings..........	$29,500

Suppose O'Brien will sell bindings to X-Perience for $14 each. X-Perience would pay $1 per unit to transport the bindings to its manufacturing plant, where it would add its own logo at a cost of $0.20 per binding.

Required

1. X-Perience's accountants predict that purchasing the bindings from O'Brien will enable the company to avoid $2,200 of fixed overhead. Prepare an analysis to show whether X-Perience should make or buy the bindings.

2. The facilities freed by purchasing bindings from O'Brien can be used to manufacture another product that will contribute $3,100 to profit. Total fixed costs will be the same as if X-Perience had produced the bindings. Show which alternative makes the best use of X-Perience's facilities: (a) make bindings, (b) buy bindings and leave facilities idle, or (c) buy bindings and make another product.

P26-5A Vision Chemical Corporation has spent $240,000 to refine 72,000 gallons of acetone, which can be sold for $2.16 a gallon. Alternatively, Vision can process the acetone further. This processing will yield a total of 60,000 gallons of lacquer thinner that can be sold for $3.20 a gallon. The additional processing will cost $0.62 per gallon of lacquer thinner. To sell the lacquer thinner, Vision must pay shipping of $0.22 a gallon and administrative expenses of $0.10 a gallon on the thinner.

Deciding whether to sell as is or process further
(Obj. 1, 2)

Required

1. Diagram Vision's decision, using Exhibit 26-12 as a guide.

2. Identify the sunk cost. Is the sunk cost relevant to Vision's decision?

3. Should Vision sell the acetone or process it into lacquer thinner? Show the expected net revenue difference between the two alternatives.

P26-6A Water World, Inc. is considering purchasing a water park in San Antonio, Texas, for $1,850,000. The new facility will generate annual net cash inflows of $520,000 for eight years. Engineers estimate that the facility will remain useful for eight years and have no residual value. The company uses straight-line depreciation, and its stockholders demand an annual return of 12% on investments of this nature.

Capital budgeting
(Obj. 3, 4, 5)

Required

1. Compute the payback period, the accounting rate of return, and the net present value of this investment.

2. Make a recommendation whether the company should invest in this project.

P26-7A Locos operates a chain of sandwich shops. The company is considering two possible expansion plans. Plan A would open eight smaller shops at a cost of $8,440,000. Expected annual net cash inflows are $1,600,000, with zero residual value at the end of 10 years. Under plan B, Locos would open three larger shops at a cost of $8,340,000. This plan is expected to generate net cash inflows of $1,100,000 per year for 10 years, the estimated life of the properties. Estimated residual value is $1,000,000. Locos uses straight-line depreciation and requires an annual return of 8%

Capital budgeting
(Obj. 3, 4, 5)

Required

1. Compute the payback period, the accounting rate of return, and the net present value of these two plans. Use the residual value when calculating the accounting rate of return, but *assume a residual value of zero when calculating net present values.* What are the strengths and weaknesses of these capital budgeting models?

2. Which expansion plan should Locos choose? Why?

3. Estimate plan A's internal rate of return (IRR). How does the IRR compare with the company's required rate of return?

Problems

(Group B)

P26-1B United Packaging Co.'s contribution margin income statement follows:

Accepting or rejecting a special sales order
(Obj. 1, 2)

Sales in units	360,000
Sales revenue.	$432,000
Variable expenses:	
Manufacturing	$108,000
Marketing and administrative	53,000
Total variable expenses	161,000
Contribution margin	271,000
Fixed expenses:	
Manufacturing	156,000
Marketing and administrative	40,000
Total fixed expenses.	196,000
Operating income.	$ 75,000

(*continued*)

Wallace Farms wants to buy 5,000 produce boxes from United. Acceptance of the order will not increase any of United's marketing and administrative expenses. United's plant has enough unused capacity to manufacture the additional boxes. Wallace Farms has offered $0.80 per box, which is considerably below the normal sale price of $1.20.

Required

1. Prepare an incremental analysis to determine whether United Packaging should accept this special sales order.

2. Identify long-term factors that United Packaging should consider in deciding whether to accept the special sales order.

Keeping or dropping a product line
(Obj. 1, 2)

P26-2B The following operating income data of Abalone Seafood highlight the losses of the fresh seafood product line:

| | | Product Line | |
| | | Fresh | Frozen |
	Total	Seafood	Seafood
Sales revenue	$730,500	$190,500	$540,000
Cost of goods sold:			
Variable.	$138,000	$ 44,000	$ 94,000
Fixed	61,000	20,000	41,000
Total cost of goods sold	199,000	64,000	135,000
Gross profit.	531,500	126,500	405,000
Marketing and administrative expenses:			
Variable.	223,000	98,000	125,000
Fixed	93,000	38,000	55,000
Total marketing and administrative expenses	316,000	136,000	180,000
Operating income (loss).	$215,500	$ (9,500)	$225,000

Abalone is considering discontinuing the fresh seafood product line. The company's accountants estimate that dropping the fresh seafood line will decrease fixed cost of goods sold by $16,000 and decrease fixed marketing and administrative expenses by $10,000.

Required

1. Prepare an incremental analysis to show whether Abalone should drop the fresh seafood product line.

2. Prepare contribution margin income statements to compare Abalone's total operating income (a) with the fresh seafood product line, and (b) without it. Compare the *difference* between the two alternatives' income numbers to your answer to Requirement 1. What have you learned from this comparison?

Determining product mix
(Obj. 1, 2)

P26-3B Easy Living of Charlotte, North Carolina, specializes in outdoor furniture and spas. Owner Linda Spring is expanding the store. She is deciding which product line to emphasize. To make this decision, she assembles the following data:

| | Per Unit | |
	Spas	Patio Sets
Sale price.	$1,000	$800
Variable expenses.	480	440
Contribution margin	$ 520	$360
Contribution margin ratio	52%	45%

(*continued*)

After renovation, the store will have 8,000 square feet of floor space. By devoting the new floor space to patio sets, Easy Living can display 60 patio sets. Alternatively, Easy Living could display 30 spas. Spring expects monthly sales to equal the maximum number of units displayed.

Required

1. Identify the constraining factor for Easy Living.

2. Prepare an analysis to show which product line to emphasize.

P26-4B Morning Grain, Inc., makes organic cereal. Cost data for producing 140,000 boxes of cereal each year are as follows:

Outsourcing; best use of facilities
(Obj. 1, 2)

Direct materials	$220,000
Direct labor.	140,000
Variable overhead	60,000
Fixed overhead	440,000
Total manufacturing costs	$860,000

Suppose Kellogg will sell Morning Grain the cereal for $4 a box. Morning Grain would also pay $0.19 a box to transport the cereal to its warehouse.

Required

1. Morning Grain's accountants predict that purchasing the cereal from Kellogg will enable the company to avoid $140,000 of fixed overhead. Prepare an analysis to show whether Morning Grain should make or buy the cereal.

2. Assume that the Morning Grain facilities freed up by purchasing the cereal from Kellogg can be used to manufacture snack bars that will contribute $180,000 to profit. Total fixed costs will be the same as if Morning Grain used the plant to make cereal. Prepare an analysis to show which alternative makes the best use of Morning Grain's facilities: (a) make cereal, (b) buy cereal and leave facilities idle, or (c) buy cereal and make snack bars.

P26-5B Acme Petroleum has spent $200,000 to refine 60,000 gallons of petroleum distillate. Suppose Acme can sell the distillate for $6 a gallon. Alternatively, it can process the distillate further and produce cleaner fluid. The additional processing will cost another $1.75 a gallon and the cleaner can be sold for $8.50 a gallon. To sell cleaner fluid, Acme must pay a sales commission of $0.10 a gallon and a transportation charge of $0.15 a gallon.

Deciding whether to sell as is or process further
(Obj. 1, 2)

Required

1. Diagram Acme's alternatives, using Exhibit 26-12 as a guide.

2. Identify the sunk cost. Is the sunk cost relevant to Acme's decision?

3. Prepare an analysis to indicate whether Acme should sell the distillate or process it into cleaner. Show the expected net revenue difference between the two alternatives.

P26-6B Zippi Co. manufactures motorized scooters in Oakland, California. The company is considering an expansion. The plan calls for a construction cost of $5,200,000. The expansion will generate annual net cash inflows of $675,000 for 10 years. Engineers estimate that the new facilities will remain useful for 10 years and have no residual value. The company uses straight-line depreciation, and its stockholders demand an annual return of 10% on investments of this nature.

Capital budgeting
(Obj. 3, 4, 5)

Required

1. Compute the payback period, the accounting rate of return, and the net present value of this investment.

2. Make a recommendation whether the company should invest in this project.

P26-7B Java Café is considering two possible expansion plans. Plan A is to open 8 cafés at a cost of $4,180,000. Expected annual net cash inflows are $780,000, with residual value of $820,000 at the end of seven years. Under plan B, Java Café would open 12 cafés at a cost of $4,200,000. This investment is expected to generate net cash inflows of $994,000 each year for seven years, which is the estimated useful life of the properties. Estimated residual value of the plan B cafés is zero. Java Café uses straight-line depreciation and requires an annual return of 14%.

Required

1. Compute the payback period, the accounting rate of return, and the net present value of each plan. Use the residual value when calculating the accounting rate of return, but *assume a zero residual value when calculating the net present values*. What are the strengths and weaknesses of these capital budgeting models?
2. Which expansion plan should Java Café adopt? Why?
3. Estimate the internal rate of return (IRR) for plan B. How does plan B's IRR compare with Java Café's required rate of return?

●APPLY *Your Knowledge*

Decision Cases

Case 1. BKFin.com provides banks access to sophisticated financial information and analysis systems over the Web. The company combines these tools with benchmarking data access, including e-mail and wireless communications, so that banks can instantly evaluate individual loan applications and entire loan portfolios.

BKFin.com's CEO Jon Wise is happy with the company's growth. To better focus on client service, Wise is considering outsourcing some functions. CFO Jenny Lee suggests that the company's e-mail may be the place to start. She recently attended a conference and learned that companies like **Continental Airlines, DellNet, GTE**, and **NBC** were outsourcing their e-mail function. Wise asks Lee to identify costs related to BKFin.com's in-house **Microsoft** Exchange mail application, which has 2,300 mailboxes. This information follows:

Variable costs:	
E-mail license	$7 per mailbox per month
Virus protection license	$1 per mailbox per month
Other variable costs	$8 per mailbox per month
Fixed costs:	
Computer hardware costs	$94,300 per month
$8,050 monthly salary for two information technology staff members who work only on e-mail	$16,100 per month

Required

1. Compute the *total cost* per mailbox per month of BKFin.com's current e-mail function.
2. Suppose **Mail.com**, a leading provider of Internet messaging outsourcing services, offers to host BKFin.com's e-mail function for $9 per mailbox per month. If BKFin.com outsources its e-mail to Mail.com, BKFin.com will still need the virus protection software, its computer hardware, and one information technology staff member, who would be responsible for maintaining virus protection, quarantining suspicious e-mail, and managing content (e.g., screening e-mail for objectionable content). Should CEO Wise accept Mail.com's offer?

(continued)

3. Suppose for an additional $5 per mailbox per month, Mail.com will also provide virus protection, quarantine, and content-management services. Outsourcing these additional functions would mean that BKFin.com would not need either an e-mail information technology staff member or the separate virus protection license. Should CEO Wise outsource these extra services to Mail.com?

Case 2. Ted Christensen, a second-year business student at the University of Utah, will graduate in two years with an accounting major and a Spanish minor. Christensen is trying to decide where to work this summer. He has two choices: work full-time for a bottling plant or work part-time in the Accounting Department of a meat-packing plant. He probably will work at the same place next summer as well. He is able to work 12 weeks during the summer.

Analyzing relevant factors in an employment decision
(Obj. 1, 4)

The bottling plant will pay Christensen $380 per week this year and 7% more next year. At the meat-packing plant, he could work 20 hours per week at $8.75 per hour. By working only part-time, he could take two accounting courses this summer. Tuition is $225 per hour for each of the four-hour courses. Christensen believes that the experience he gains this summer will qualify him for a full-time accounting position with the meat-packing plant next year. That position will pay $550 per week.

Christensen sees two additional benefits of working part-time this summer. First, he could reduce his workload during the fall and spring semesters by one course each term. Second, he would have the time to work as a grader in the university's Accounting Department during the 15-week fall term. Grading pays $50 per week.

Required

1. Suppose that Ted Christensen ignores the time value of money in decisions that cover this short a time period. Suppose also that his sole goal is to make as much money as possible between now and the end of next summer. What should he do? What would *you* do if you were faced with these alternatives?

2. Now suppose that Christensen considers the time value of money for all cash flows that he expects to receive one year or more in the future. Which alternative does this consideration favor? Why?

Ethical Issue

→ *Link Back to the IMA Ethical Guidelines in Chapter 19.* Mary Tan is the controller for Duck Associates, a property management company in Portland, Oregon. Each year Tan and payroll clerk Toby Stock meet with the external auditors about payroll accounting. This year, the auditors suggest that Tan consider outsourcing Duck Associates' payroll accounting to a company specializing in payroll processing services. This would allow Tan and her staff to focus on their primary responsibility: accounting for the properties under management. At present, payroll requires 1.5 employee positions—payroll clerk Toby Stock and a bookkeeper who spends half her time entering payroll data in the system.

Make or buy decision
(Obj. 1, 2)

Tan considers this suggestion, and she lists the following items relating to outsourcing payroll accounting:

a. The current payroll software that was purchased for $4,000 three years ago would not be needed if payroll processing were outsourced.

b. Duck's bookkeeper would spend half her time preparing the weekly payroll input form that is given to the payroll processing service. She is paid $450 a week.

c. Duck Associates would no longer need payroll clerk Toby Stock, whose annual salary is $42,000.

d. The payroll processing service would charge $2,000 a month.

Required

1. Would outsourcing the payroll function increase or decrease Duck Associates' operating income?

(continued)

2. Tan believes that outsourcing payroll would simplify her job, but she does not like the prospect of having to lay off Toby Stock, who has become a close personal friend. She does not believe there is another position available for Stock at his current salary. Can you think of other factors that might support keeping Stock, rather than outsourcing payroll processing? How should each of the factors affect Tan's decision if she wants to do what is best for Duck and act ethically?

Financial Statement Case

Computing payback period and NPV of investments
(Obj. 3, 4)

In creating **Amazon.com**, CEO Jeff Bezos realized the importance of investing in technology. Brick and mortar retailers rely on convenient store location to attract shoppers. Bezos saw that technology could create the same competitive edge for Internet shopping. He invested heavily in technology to make Amazon.com a leader in both: (1) Web site design to facilitate customers' purchases, and (2) warehouse operations to deliver those purchases quickly.

Required

1. Notes to the Consolidated Financial Statements in Amazon.com's 2002 Annual Report (in Appendix A of this book) describe the company's accounting policies. Look at notes 1 and 3.
   a. What depreciation method does Amazon.com use?
   b. What is the range of useful lives over which Amazon.com depreciates its fixed assets?
   c. Identify the types of assets Amazon.com includes in fixed assets. For each type of asset, would the useful life fall toward the shorter or longer end of the range?
2. Amazon.com's 2002 Consolidated Financial Statements indicate a cash outflow of $39,163,000 for investment in fixed assets. Assume that these investments have an average useful life of four years and that Amazon.com requires a 14% rate of return on such investments. Compute the minimum average annual net cash inflow that would justify this investment.
3. For the investment of $39,163,000, and using the average annual net cash inflows calculated in Requirement 2, determine the investment's (a) payback period and (b) accounting rate of return. Assume a zero residual value.
4. Compare the average payback period calculated in Requirement 3 to the estimated useful lives of the different assets identified in Requirement 1. When different assets have very different estimated useful lives, what are the implications for using the payback model to make investment decisions?

Team Project

Identifying relevant data, outsourcing, capital budgeting
(Obj. 1, 2, 3, 4)

John Menard is the founder and sole owner of **Menards, Inc.**. Analysts have estimated that his chain of home improvement stores scattered around nine midwestern states generate about $3 billion in annual sales. But how can Menards compete with giant **Home Depot**?

Suppose Menard is trying to decide whether to invest $45 million in a state-of-the-art manufacturing plant in Eau Claire, Wisconsin. Menard expects the plant would operate for 15 years, after which it would have no residual value. The plant would produce Menards' own line of Formica countertops, cabinets, and picnic tables.

Suppose Menards would incur the following unit costs in producing its own product lines:

	Per Unit		
	Countertops	**Cabinets**	**Picnic Tables**
Direct materials.	$15	$10	$25
Direct labor	10	5	15
Variable manufacturing overhead . .	5	2	6

(continued)

Rather than making these products, assume Menards could buy them from outside suppliers. Suppliers would charge Menards $40 per countertop, $25 per cabinet, and $65 per picnic table.

Whether Menard makes or buys these products, assume that he expects the following annual sales:

- Countertops—487,200 at $130 each
- Picnic tables—100,000 at $225 each
- Cabinets—150,000 at $75 each

If "making" is sufficiently more profitable than outsourcing, Menard will build the new plant. John Menard has asked your consulting group for a recommendation. Menard uses a 14% discount rate and the straight-line depreciation method.

Required

1. Are the following items relevant or irrelevant in Menard's decision to build a new plant that will manufacture his own products?
   a. The unit sale prices of the countertops, cabinets, and picnic tables (the sale prices that Menards charges its customers)
   b. The prices outside suppliers would charge Menards for the three products, if Menards decides to outsource the products rather than make them
   c. The $45 million to build the new plant
   d. The direct materials, direct labor, and variable overhead Menards would incur to manufacture the three product lines
   e. Menard's salary

2. Determine whether Menards should make or outsource the countertops, cabinets, and picnic tables, *assuming that the company has already built the plant and therefore has the manufacturing capacity to produce these products.* In other words, what is the annual difference in cash flows if Menards decides to make rather than outsource each of these three products?

3. In requirement 2, you computed the annual difference in cash flows if Menards decides to make rather than buy the three products. To analyze the investment in the plant relative to the alternative of outsourcing the products, use this *difference* in annual cash flows to compute the following for the investment in the new plant:
   a. Payback period   c. Net present value
   b. Accounting rate of return d. Internal rate of return
   (*Hint*: Base the benefit side of your computations on the *difference* in annual cash flows you computed in requirement 2, *not* the total expected cash flows from building the plant. Use the present value tables in Appendix C.)

4. Write a memo giving your recommendation to John Menard. The memo should clearly state your recommendation, along with a brief summary of the reasons for your recommendation. Use the memo format outlined in Starter 26-14.

For Internet exercises, go to the Web site www.prenhall.com/horngren.

2 0 0 2

ANNUAL REPORT (EXCERPTED)

amazon.com.

To our shareholders:

In many ways, Amazon.com is not a normal store. We have deep selection that is unconstrained by shelf space. We turn our inventory 19 times in a year. We personalize the store for each and every customer. We trade real estate for technology (which gets cheaper and more capable every year). We display customer reviews critical of our products. You can make a purchase with a few seconds and one click. We put used products next to new ones so you can choose. We share our prime real estate—our product detail pages—with third parties, and, if they can offer better value, we let them.

One of our most exciting peculiarities is poorly understood. People see that we're determined to offer both world-leading customer experience *and* the lowest possible prices, but to some this dual goal seems paradoxical if not downright quixotic. Traditional stores face a time-tested tradeoff between offering high-touch customer experience on the one hand and the lowest possible prices on the other. How can Amazon.com be trying to do both?

The answer is that we transform much of customer experience—such as unmatched selection, extensive product information, personalized recommendations, and other new software features—into largely a fixed expense. With customer experience costs largely fixed (more like a publishing model than a retailing model), our costs as a percentage of sales can shrink rapidly as we grow our business. Moreover, customer experience costs that remain variable—such as the variable portion of fulfillment costs—improve in our model as we reduce defects. Eliminating defects improves costs and leads to better customer experience.

We believe our ability to lower prices and simultaneously drive customer experience is a big deal, and this past year offers evidence that the strategy is working.

First, we do continue to drive customer experience. The holiday season this year is one example. While delivering a record number of units to customers, we also delivered our best-ever experience. Cycle time, the amount of time taken by our fulfillment centers to process an order, improved 17% compared with last year. And our most sensitive measure of customer satisfaction, contacts per order, saw a 13% improvement.

Inside existing product categories, we've worked hard to increase selection. Electronics selection is up over 40% in the U.S. alone over the prior year, and we now offer 10 times the selection of a typical big box electronics store. Even in U.S. books, where we've been working for 8 years, we increased selection by 15%, mostly in harder-to-find and out-of-print titles. And, of course, we've added new categories. Our Apparel and Accessories store has more than 500 top clothing brands, and in its first 60 days, customers bought 153,000 shirts, 106,000 pairs of pants, and 31,000 pairs of underwear.

In this year's American Customer Satisfaction Index, the most authoritative study of customer satisfaction, Amazon.com scored an 88, the highest score ever recorded—not just online, not just in retailing—but the highest score ever recorded in any service industry. In ACSI's words:

"Amazon.com continues to show remarkably high levels of customer satisfaction. With a score of 88 (up 5%), it is generating satisfaction at a level unheard of in the service industry.... Can customer satisfaction for Amazon climb more? The latest ACSI data suggest that it is indeed possible. Both service and the value proposition offered by Amazon have increased at a steep rate."

Second, while focused on customer experience, we've also been lowering price substantially. We've been doing so broadly across product categories, from books to electronics, and we've eliminated shipping fees with our 365 day-per-year Free Super Saver Shipping on orders over $25. We've been taking similar actions in every country in which we do business.

Our pricing objective is not to discount a small number of products for a limited period of time, but to offer low prices everyday and apply them broadly across our entire product range. To illustrate this point, we recently did a price comparison versus a major well-known chain of book superstores. We did not hand pick a choice group of books against which we wanted to compare. Instead, we used their published list of their 100 bestsellers for 2002. It was a good representation of the kinds of books people buy most, consisting of 45 hardcover titles and 55 paperbacks across many different categories, including Literature, Romance, Mystery and Thrillers, Nonfiction, Children's, Self-Help, and so on.

We priced all 100 titles by visiting their superstores in both Seattle and New York City. It took us six hours in four of their different superstores to find all 100 books on their list. When we added up everything we spent, we discovered that:

- At their stores, these 100 bestselling books cost $1,561. At Amazon.com, the same books cost $1,195 for a total savings of $366, or 23%.

- For 72 of the 100 books, our price was cheaper. On 25 of the books, our price was the same. On 3 of the 100, their prices were better (we subsequently reduced our prices on these three books).

- In these physical-world superstores, only 15 of their 100 titles were discounted—they were selling the other 85 at full list price. At Amazon.com, 76 of the 100 were discounted and 24 were sold at list price.

To be sure, you may find reasons to shop in the physical world—for instance, if you need something immediately—but, if you do so, you'll be paying a premium. If you want to save money and time, you'll do better by shopping at Amazon.com.

Third, our determination to deliver low price *and* customer experience is generating financial results. Net sales this year increased 26% to a record $3.9 billion, and unit sales grew at an even faster 34%. Free cash flow—our most important financial measure—reached $135 million, a $305 million improvement over the prior year.[1]

In short, what's good for customers is good for shareholders.

Once again this year, I attach a copy of our original 1997 letter and encourage current and prospective shareowners to take a look at it. Given how much we've grown and how much the Internet has evolved, it's notable that the fundamentals of how we do business remain the same.

As always, we at Amazon.com are grateful to our customers for their business and trust, to each other for our hard work, and to our shareholders for their support and encouragement.

Jeffrey P. Bezos
Founder and Chief Executive Officer
Amazon.com, Inc.

---

[1] Free cash flow for 2002 of $135 million is net cash provided by operating activities of $174 million less purchases of fixed assets of $39 million. Free cash flow for 2001 of negative $170 million is net cash used in operating activities of $120 million less purchases of fixed assets of $50 million.

REPORT OF ERNST & YOUNG LLP, INDEPENDENT AUDITORS

The Board of Directors and Stockholders
Amazon.com, Inc.

We have audited the accompanying consolidated balance sheets of Amazon.com, Inc. as of December 31, 2002 and 2001, and the related consolidated statements of operations, stockholders' equity (deficit) and cash flows for each of the three years in the period ended December 31, 2002. Our audits also included the financial statement schedule listed at Item 15(a)(2). These financial statements and schedule are the responsibility of the Company's management. Our responsibility is to express an opinion on these financial statements and schedule based on our audits.

We conducted our audits in accordance with auditing standards generally accepted in the United States. Those standards require that we plan and perform the audit to obtain reasonable assurance about whether the financial statements are free of material misstatement. An audit includes examining, on a test basis, evidence supporting the amounts and disclosures in the financial statements. An audit also includes assessing the accounting principles used and significant estimates made by management, as well as evaluating the overall financial statement presentation. We believe that our audits provide a reasonable basis for our opinion.

In our opinion, the financial statements referred to above present fairly, in all material respects, the consolidated financial position of Amazon.com, Inc. at December 31, 2002 and 2001, and the consolidated results of its operations and its cash flows for each of the three years in the period ended December 31, 2002, in conformity with accounting principles generally accepted in the United States. Also, in our opinion, the related financial statement schedule, when considered in relation to the basic financial statements taken as a whole, presents fairly in all material respects the information set forth therein.

As discussed in Note 1 to the consolidated financial statements, the Company adopted the full provisions of Statement of Financial Accounting Standards No. 141, Business Combinations, and No. 142, Goodwill and Other Intangible Assets, effective January 1, 2002. The Company also adopted Statement of Financial Accounting Standards No. 133, Accounting for Derivative Instruments and Hedging Activities, effective January 1, 2001. In addition, as discussed in Note 1 to the consolidated financial statements, effective January 1, 2002, the Company prospectively changed its inventory costing method to the first-in first-out method of accounting.

/s/ ERNST & YOUNG LLP

Seattle, Washington
January 17, 2003

1997 LETTER TO SHAREHOLDERS
(Reprinted from the 1997 Annual Report)

To our shareholders:

Amazon.com passed many milestones in 1997: by year-end, we had served more than 1.5 million customers, yielding 838% revenue growth to $147.8 million, and extended our market leadership despite aggressive competitive entry.

But this is Day 1 for the Internet and, if we execute well, for Amazon.com. Today, online commerce saves customers money and precious time. Tomorrow, through personalization, online commerce will accelerate the very process of discovery. Amazon.com uses the Internet to create real value for its customers and, by doing so, hopes to create an enduring franchise, even in established and large markets.

We have a window of opportunity as larger players marshal the resources to pursue the online opportunity and as customers, new to purchasing online, are receptive to forming new relationships. The competitive landscape has continued to evolve at a fast pace. Many large players have moved online with credible offerings and have devoted substantial energy and resources to building awareness, traffic, and sales. Our goal is to move quickly to solidify and extend our current position while we begin to pursue the online commerce opportunities in other areas. We see substantial opportunity in the large markets we are targeting. This strategy is not without risk: it requires serious investment and crisp execution against established franchise leaders.

It's All About the Long Term

We believe that a fundamental measure of our success will be the shareholder value we create over the *long term*. This value will be a direct result of our ability to extend and solidify our current market leadership position. The stronger our market leadership, the more powerful our economic model. Market leadership can translate directly to higher revenue, higher profitability, greater capital velocity, and correspondingly stronger returns on invested capital.

Our decisions have consistently reflected this focus. We first measure ourselves in terms of the metrics most indicative of our market leadership: customer and revenue growth, the degree to which our customers continue to purchase from us on a repeat basis, and the strength of our brand. We have invested and will continue to invest aggressively to expand and leverage our customer base, brand, and infrastructure as we move to establish an enduring franchise.

Because of our emphasis on the long term, we may make decisions and weigh tradeoffs differently than some companies. Accordingly, we want to share with you our fundamental management and decision-making approach so that you, our shareholders, may confirm that it is consistent with your investment philosophy:

- We will continue to focus relentlessly on our customers.

- We will continue to make investment decisions in light of long-term market leadership considerations rather than short-term profitability considerations or short-term Wall Street reactions.

- We will continue to measure our programs and the effectiveness of our investments analytically, to jettison those that do not provide acceptable returns, and to step up our investment in those that work best. We will continue to learn from both our successes and our failures.

- We will make bold rather than timid investment decisions where we see a sufficient probability of gaining market leadership advantages. Some of these investments will pay off, others will not, and we will have learned another valuable lesson in either case.

- When forced to choose between optimizing the appearance of our GAAP accounting and maximizing the present value of future cash flows, we'll take the cash flows.

- We will share our strategic thought processes with you when we make bold choices (to the extent competitive pressures allow), so that you may evaluate for yourselves whether we are making rational long-term leadership investments.

- We will work hard to spend wisely and maintain our lean culture. We understand the importance of continually reinforcing a cost-conscious culture, particularly in a business incurring net losses.

- We will balance our focus on growth with emphasis on long-term profitability and capital management. At this stage, we choose to prioritize growth because we believe that scale is central to achieving the potential of our business model.

- We will continue to focus on hiring and retaining versatile and talented employees, and continue to weight their compensation to stock options rather than cash. We know our success will be largely affected by our ability to attract and retain a motivated employee base, each of whom must think like, and therefore must actually be, an owner.

We aren't so bold as to claim that the above is the "right" investment philosophy, but it's ours, and we would be remiss if we weren't clear in the approach we have taken and will continue to take.

With this foundation, we would like to turn to a review of our business focus, our progress in 1997, and our outlook for the future.

Obsess Over Customers

From the beginning, our focus has been on offering our customers compelling value. We realized that the Web was, and still is, the World Wide Wait. Therefore, we set out to offer customers something they simply could not get any other way, and began serving them with books. We brought them much more selection than was possible in a physical store (our store would now occupy 6 football fields), and presented it in a useful, easy-to-search, and easy-to-browse format in a store open 365 days a year, 24 hours a day. We maintained a dogged focus on improving the shopping experience, and in 1997 substantially enhanced our store. We now offer customers gift certificates, 1-Click^{SM} shopping, and vastly more reviews, content, browsing options, and recommendation features. We dramatically lowered prices, further increasing customer value. Word of mouth remains the most powerful customer acquisition tool we have, and we are grateful for the trust our customers have placed in us. Repeat purchases and word of mouth have combined to make Amazon.com the market leader in online bookselling.

By many measures, Amazon.com came a long way in 1997:

- Sales grew from $15.7 million in 1996 to $147.8 million—an 838% increase.

- Cumulative customer accounts grew from 180,000 to 1,510,000—a 738% increase.

- The percentage of orders from repeat customers grew from over 46% in the fourth quarter of 1996 to over 58% in the same period in 1997.

- In terms of audience reach, per Media Metrix, our Web site went from a rank of 90th to within the top 20.

- We established long-term relationships with many important strategic partners, including America Online, Yahoo!, Excite, Netscape, GeoCities, AltaVista, @Home, and Prodigy.

Infrastructure

During 1997, we worked hard to expand our business infrastructure to support these greatly increased traffic, sales, and service levels:

- Amazon.com's employee base grew from 158 to 614, and we significantly strengthened our management team.

- Distribution center capacity grew from 50,000 to 285,000 square feet, including a 70% expansion of our Seattle facilities and the launch of our second distribution center in Delaware in November.

- Inventories rose to over 200,000 titles at year-end, enabling us to improve availability for our customers.

- Our cash and investment balances at year-end were $125 million, thanks to our initial public offering in May 1997 and our $75 million loan, affording us substantial strategic flexibility.

Our Employees

The past year's success is the product of a talented, smart, hard-working group, and I take great pride in being a part of this team. Setting the bar high in our approach to hiring has been, and will continue to be, the single most important element of Amazon.com's success.

It's not easy to work here (when I interview people I tell them, "You can work long, hard, or smart, but at Amazon.com you can't choose two out of three"), but we are working to build something important, something that matters to our customers, something that we can all tell our grandchildren about. Such things aren't meant to be easy. We are incredibly fortunate to have this group of dedicated employees whose sacrifices and passion build Amazon.com.

Goals for 1998

We are still in the early stages of learning how to bring new value to our customers through Internet commerce and merchandising. Our goal remains to continue to solidify and extend our brand and customer base. This requires sustained investment in systems and infrastructure to support outstanding customer convenience, selection, and service while we grow. We are planning to add music to our product offering, and over time we believe that other products may be prudent investments. We also believe there are significant opportunities to better serve our customers overseas, such as reducing delivery times and better tailoring the customer experience. To be certain, a big part of the challenge for us will lie not in finding new ways to expand our business, but in prioritizing our investments.

We now know vastly more about online commerce than when Amazon.com was founded, but we still have so much to learn. Though we are optimistic, we must remain vigilant and maintain a sense of urgency. The challenges and hurdles we will face to make our long-term vision for Amazon.com a reality are several: aggressive, capable, well-funded competition; considerable growth challenges and execution risk; the risks of product and geographic expansion; and the need for large continuing investments to meet an expanding market opportunity. However, as we've long said, online bookselling, and online commerce in general, should prove to be a very large market, and it's likely that a number of companies will see significant benefit. We feel good about what we've done, and even more excited about what we want to do.

1997 was indeed an incredible year. We at Amazon.com are grateful to our customers for their business and trust, to each other for our hard work, and to our shareholders for their support and encouragement.

Jeffrey P. Bezos
Founder and Chief Executive Officer
Amazon.com, Inc.

AMAZON.COM, INC.

CONSOLIDATED BALANCE SHEETS

	December 31, 2002	December 31, 2001
	(In thousands, except per share data)	

ASSETS

Current assets:		
Cash and cash equivalents	$ 738,254	$ 540,282
Marketable securities	562,715	456,303
Inventories	202,425	143,722
Accounts receivable, net and other current assets	112,282	67,613
Total current assets	1,615,676	1,207,920
Fixed assets, net	239,398	271,751
Goodwill, net	70,811	45,367
Other intangibles, net	3,460	34,382
Other equity investments	15,442	28,359
Other assets	45,662	49,768
Total assets	$ 1,990,449	$ 1,637,547

LIABILITIES AND STOCKHOLDERS' DEFICIT

Current liabilities:		
Accounts payable	$ 618,128	$ 444,748
Accrued expenses and other current liabilities	314,935	305,064
Unearned revenue	47,916	87,978
Interest payable	71,661	68,632
Current portion of long-term debt and other	13,318	14,992
Total current liabilities	1,065,958	921,414
Long-term debt and other	2,277,305	2,156,133
Commitments and contingencies		
Stockholders' deficit:		
Preferred stock, $0.01 par value:		
Authorized shares — 500,000		
Issued and outstanding shares — none	—	—
Common stock, $0.01 par value:		
Authorized shares — 5,000,000		
Issued and outstanding shares — 387,906 and 373,218 shares, respectively	3,879	3,732
Additional paid-in capital	1,649,946	1,462,769
Deferred stock-based compensation	(6,591)	(9,853)
Accumulated other comprehensive income (loss)	9,662	(36,070)
Accumulated deficit	(3,009,710)	(2,860,578)
Total stockholders' deficit	(1,352,814)	(1,440,000)
Total liabilities and stockholders' deficit	$ 1,990,449	$ 1,637,547

See accompanying notes to consolidated financial statements.

AMAZON.COM, INC.

CONSOLIDATED STATEMENTS OF OPERATIONS (Adapted)

	Years Ended December 31,		
	2002	2001	2000
	(In thousands, except per share data)		
Net sales	$3,932,936	$3,122,433	$ 2,761,983
Cost of sales	2,940,318	2,323,875	2,106,206
Gross profit	992,618	798,558	655,777
Operating expenses:			
Fulfillment	392,467	374,250	414,509
Marketing	125,383	138,283	179,980
Technology and content	215,617	241,165	269,326
General and administrative	79,049	89,862	108,962
Stock-based compensation	68,927	4,637	24,797
Amortization of goodwill and other intangibles	5,478	181,033	321,772
Restructuring-related and other	41,573	181,585	200,311
Total operating expenses	928,494	1,210,815	1,519,657
Income (loss) from operations	64,124	(412,257)	(863,880)
Interest income	23,687	29,103	40,821
Interest expense	(142,925)	(139,232)	(130,921)
Other income (expense), net	5,623	(1,900)	(10,058)
Other gains (losses), net	(96,273)	(2,141)	(142,639)
Total non-operating expenses, net	(209,888)	(114,170)	(242,797)
Loss before equity in losses of equity-method investees	(145,764)	(526,427)	(1,106,677)
Equity in losses of equity-method investees, net	(4,169)	(30,327)	(304,596)
Loss before change in accounting principle	(149,933)	(556,754)	(1,411,273)
Cumulative effect of change in accounting principle	801	(10,523)	—
Net loss	$ (149,132)	$ (567,277)	$(1,411,273)
Basic and diluted loss per share:			
Prior to cumulative effect of change in accounting principle	$ (0.40)	$ (1.53)	$ (4.02)
Cumulative effect of change in accounting principle	0.01	(0.03)	—
	$ (0.39)	$ (1.56)	$ (4.02)
Shares used in computation of loss per share:			
Basic and diluted	378,363	364,211	350,873

•   •   •

See accompanying notes to consolidated financial statements.

AMAZON.COM, INC.

CONSOLIDATED STATEMENTS OF CASH FLOWS

	Years Ended December 31,		
	2002	**2001**	**2000**
		(In thousands)	
CASH AND CASH EQUIVALENTS, BEGINNING OF PERIOD	$ 540,282	$ 822,435	$ 133,309
OPERATING ACTIVITIES:			
Net loss	(149,132)	(567,277)	(1,411,273)
Adjustments to reconcile net loss to net cash provided by (used in) operating activities:			
Depreciation of fixed assets and other amortization	82,274	84,709	84,460
Stock-based compensation	68,927	4,637	24,797
Equity in losses of equity-method investees, net	4,169	30,327	304,596
Amortization of goodwill and other intangibles	5,478	181,033	321,772
Non-cash restructuring-related and other	3,470	73,293	200,311
Gain on sale of marketable securities, net	(5,700)	(1,335)	(280)
Other losses (gains), net	96,273	2,141	142,639
Non-cash interest expense and other	29,586	26,629	24,766
Cumulative effect of change in accounting principle	(801)	10,523	—
Changes in operating assets and liabilities:			
Inventories	(51,303)	30,628	46,083
Accounts receivable, net and other current assets	(32,948)	20,732	(8,585)
Accounts payable	156,542	(44,438)	22,357
Accrued expenses and other current liabilities	4,491	50,031	93,967
Unearned revenue	95,404	114,738	97,818
Amortization of previously unearned revenue	(135,466)	(135,808)	(108,211)
Interest payable	3,027	(345)	34,341
Net cash provided by (used in) operating activities	174,291	(119,782)	(130,442)
INVESTING ACTIVITIES:			
Sales and maturities of marketable securities and other investments	553,289	370,377	545,724
Purchases of marketable securities	(635,810)	(567,152)	(184,455)
Purchases of fixed assets, including internal-use software and Web site development	(39,163)	(50,321)	(134,758)
Investments in equity-method investees and other investments . . .	—	(6,198)	(62,533)
Net cash provided by (used in) investing activities	(121,684)	(253,294)	163,978
FINANCING ACTIVITIES:			
Proceeds from exercise of stock options and other	121,689	16,625	44,697
Proceeds from issuance of common stock, net of issuance costs . .	—	99,831	—
Proceeds from long-term debt and other	—	10,000	681,499
Repayment of capital lease obligations and other	(14,795)	(19,575)	(16,927)
Financing costs	—	—	(16,122)
Net cash provided by financing activities	106,894	106,881	693,147
Effect of exchange-rate changes on cash and cash equivalents . . .	38,471	(15,958)	(37,557)
Net increase (decrease) in cash and cash equivalents	197,972	(282,153)	689,126
CASH AND CASH EQUIVALENTS, END OF PERIOD	$ 738,254	$ 540,282	$ 822,435
SUPPLEMENTAL CASH FLOW INFORMATION:			
Fixed assets acquired under capital leases and other financing arrangements	$ 3,023	$ 5,597	$ 9,303
Equity securities received for commercial agreements	—	331	106,848
Stock issued in connection with business acquisitions and minority investments	—	5,000	32,130
Cash paid for interest	111,589	112,184	67,252

See accompanying notes to consolidated financial statements.

AMAZON.COM, INC.

CONSOLIDATED STATEMENTS OF STOCKHOLDERS' EQUITY (DEFICIT)

	Common Stock		Additional Paid-In Capital	Deferred Stock-Based Compensation	Accumulated Other Comprehensive Income (Loss)	Accumulated Deficit	Total Stockholders' Equity (Deficit)
	Shares	Amount					
				(In thousands)			
Balance at December 31, 1999	345,155	$3,452	$1,194,369	$(47,806)	$ (1,709)	$ (882,028)	$ 266,278
Net loss	—	—	—	—	—	(1,411,273)	(1,411,273)
Foreign currency translation losses, net..................	—	—	—	—	(364)	—	(364)
Change in unrealized gain (loss) on available-for-sale securities, net...	—	—	—	—	(303)	—	(303)
Comprehensive loss	—	—	—	—	—	—	(1,411,940)
Issuance of capital stock, net of issuance costs	866	8	30,977	—	—	—	30,985
Exercise of common stock options, net.....................	11,119	111	41,995	—	—	—	42,106
Public offering of equity-method investee	—	—	76,898	—	—	—	76,898
Note receivable for common stock ..	—	—	27	—	—	—	27
Deferred stock-based compensation, net of adjustments	—	—	(5,963)	2,528	—	—	(3,435)
Amortization of deferred stock-based compensation.................	—	—	—	31,830	—	—	31,830
Balance at December 31, 2000	357,140	3,571	1,338,303	(13,448)	(2,376)	(2,293,301)	(967,251)
Net loss	—	—	—	—	—	(567,277)	(567,277)
Foreign currency translation losses, net..................	—	—	—	—	(1,257)	—	(1,257)
Change in unrealized gain (loss) on available-for-sale securities, net...	—	—	—	—	7,005	—	7,005
Net unrealized losses on Euro-based currency swap	—	—	—	—	(17,337)	—	(17,337)
Reclassification of currency gains on 6.875% PEACS...............	—	—	—	—	(9,811)	—	(9,811)
Cumulative effect of change in accounting principle	—	—	—	—	(12,294)	—	(12,294)
Comprehensive loss	—	—	—	—	—	—	(600,971)
Issuance of capital stock, net of issuance costs	8,989	90	98,716	—	—	—	98,806
Exercise of common stock options, net.....................	6,089	61	14,989	—	—	—	15,050
Repayments of note receivable for common stock	—	—	1,130	—	—	—	1,130
Deferred stock-based compensation, net of adjustments	1,000	10	9,631	(4,797)	—	—	4,844
Amortization of deferred stock-based compensation.................	—	—	—	8,392	—	—	8,392
Balance at December 31, 2001	373,218	3,732	1,462,769	(9,853)	(36,070)	(2,860,578)	(1,440,000)
Net loss	—	—	—	—	—	(149,132)	(149,132)
Foreign currency translation gains, net..................	—	—	—	—	16,910	—	16,910
Change in unrealized gain (loss) on available-for-sale securities, net...	—	—	—	—	20,294	—	20,294
Net unrealized gains on Euro-based currency swap	—	—	—	—	8,528	—	8,528
Comprehensive loss	—	—	—	—	—	—	(103,400)
Exercise of common stock options, net.....................	14,728	147	121,542	—	—	—	121,689
Deferred stock-based compensation, net of adjustments	(40)	—	1,592	(2,828)	—	—	(1,236)
Amortization of deferred stock-based compensation.................	—	—	—	6,090	—	—	6,090
Variable accounting and other stock compensation amortization	—	—	64,043	—	—	—	64,043
Balance at December 31, 2002	387,906	$3,879	$1,649,946	$ (6,591)	$ 9,662	$(3,009,710)	$(1,352,814)

See accompanying notes to consolidated financial statements.

AMAZON.COM, INC.

NOTES TO CONSOLIDATED FINANCIAL STATEMENTS (Excerpts; Adapted)

Note 1 — Description of Business and Accounting Policies (Partial)

Description of Business

Amazon.com, Inc., a Fortune 500 company, commenced operations on the World Wide Web in July 1995. The Company seeks to offer Earth's Biggest Selection and to be Earth's most customer-centric company, where customers can find and discover anything they may want to buy online. The Company and its sellers list new, used and collectible items in categories such as apparel and accessories, electronics, computers, kitchen and housewares, books, music, DVDs, videos, cameras and photo items, office products, toys, baby items and baby registry, software, computer and video games, cell phones and service, tools and hardware, travel services, magazine subscriptions and outdoor living items. Through Amazon Marketplace, the Merchants@ program, zShops and Auctions, participating businesses or individuals can sell their products to Amazon.com's customers.

The Company operates six global Web sites: *www.amazon.com, www.amazon.co.uk, www.amazon.de, www.amazon.fr, www.amazon.co.jp* and *www.amazon.ca*. The Company also owns and operates the Internet Movie Database at *www.imdb.com* ("IMDb"), which is a source of information on movie and entertainment titles and cast and crew members. IMDb offers IMDb Pro, a subscription service designed for the entertainment industry.

Principles of Consolidation

The consolidated financial statements include the accounts of the Company and its wholly owned subsidiaries. All intercompany balances and transactions have been eliminated.

Use of Estimates

The preparation of financial statements in conformity with accounting principles generally accepted in the United States requires estimates and assumptions that affect the reported amounts of assets and liabilities, revenues and expenses, and related disclosures of contingent assets and liabilities in the consolidated financial statements and accompanying notes. Estimates are used for, but not limited to, inventory valuation, depreciable lives, sales returns, receivables valuation, restructuring-related liabilities, incentive discount offers, valuation of investments, taxes and contingencies. Actual results could differ materially from those estimates.

Business Combinations

For business combinations that have been accounted for under the purchase method of accounting, the Company includes the results of operations of the acquired business from the date of acquisition. Net assets of the companies acquired are recorded at their fair value at the date of acquisition. The excess of the purchase price over the fair value of tangible and identifiable intangible net assets acquired is included in goodwill on the accompanying consolidated balance sheets.

Cash and Cash Equivalents

The Company classifies all highly liquid instruments with an original maturity of three months or less at the time of purchase as cash equivalents.

Inventories

Inventories, consisting of products available for sale, are valued at the lower of cost or market value. The Company makes judgments, based on currently-available information, about the likely method of disposition (whether through sales to individual customers, returns to product vendors or liquidations), and expected recoverable values of each disposition category. Based on this evaluation, which is applied consistently from period to period, the Company records a valuation allowance to adjust the carrying amount of its inventories to lower of cost or market value.

Accounting Changes

Inventories

Effective January 1, 2002, the Company prospectively changed its inventory costing method to the first-in first-out ("FIFO") method of accounting. This change resulted in a cumulative increase in inventory of $0.8 million, with a corresponding amount recorded to "Cumulative effect of change in accounting principle" on the consolidated statements of operations. The Company evaluated the effect of the change on each quarter of 2001 and determined such effect to be less than $1.2 million individually and in the aggregate. The Company determined this change to be preferable under accounting principles generally accepted in the United States since, among other reasons, it facilitates the Company's record keeping process, significantly improves its ability to provide cost-efficient fulfillment services to third-party companies as part of its services offering and results in increased consistency with others in the industry. The Company received a letter of preferability for this change in inventory costing from its independent auditors.

• • •

Fixed Assets

Fixed assets are stated at cost less accumulated depreciation, which includes the amortization of assets recorded under capital leases. Fixed assets, including assets purchased under capital leases, are depreciated on a straight-line basis over the estimated useful lives of the assets (generally two to ten years).

Included in fixed assets is the cost of internal-use software, including software used to upgrade and enhance the Company's Web sites. The Company expenses all costs related to the development of internal-use software other than those incurred during the application development stage. Costs incurred during the application development stage are capitalized and amortized over the estimated useful life of the software (generally two years).

• • •

Cost of Sales

Cost of sales consists of the purchase price of consumer products sold by the Company, inbound and outbound shipping charges, packaging supplies and certain costs associated with service revenues. Costs associated with service revenues classified as cost of services generally include direct and allocated indirect fulfillment-related costs to ship products on behalf of third-party sellers, costs to provide customer service, credit card fees and other related costs.

Outbound shipping charges and the cost of tangible supplies used to package products for shipment to customers totaled $404 million, $376 million, and $340 million in 2002, 2001 and 2000, respectively.

Fulfillment

Fulfillment costs represent those costs incurred in operating and staffing the Company's fulfillment and customer service centers, including costs attributable to: receiving, inspecting and warehousing inventories; picking, packaging and preparing customers' orders for shipment; credit card fees and bad debt costs; and responding to inquiries from customers. Fulfillment costs also include amounts paid to third-party co-sourcers that assist the Company in fulfillment and customer service operations. Certain Services segment fulfillment-related costs incurred on behalf of other businesses are classified as cost of sales rather than fulfillment.

Marketing

Marketing expenses consist of advertising, promotional, and public relations expenditures, and payroll and related expenses for personnel engaged in marketing and selling activities. The Company expenses general media advertising costs as incurred. The Company enters into certain online promotional agreements with third parties to increase traffic to its Web sites. Costs associated with these promotional agreements consist of fixed payments, variable activity-based payments, or a combination of the two. Fixed payments are amortized ratably over the corresponding agreement term and variable payments are expensed in the period incurred. The Company receives reimbursements from vendors for certain general media and other advertising costs. Such reimbursements are recorded as a reduction of expense. Advertising expense and other promotional costs were $114 million, $125 million and $172 million in 2002, 2001 and 2000, respectively. Prepaid advertising costs were $1 million and $2 million at December 31, 2002 and 2001, respectively.

Technology and Content

Technology and content expenses consist principally of payroll and related expenses for development, editorial, systems, and telecommunications operations personnel; and systems and telecommunications infrastructure.

Technology and content costs are expensed as incurred, except for certain costs relating to the development of internal-use software, including upgrades and enhancements to the Company's Web sites, that are capitalized and depreciated over two years. Fixed assets associated with capitalized internal-use software, net of accumulated depreciation, was $23 million and $24 million at December 31, 2002 and 2001, respectively. Costs capitalized during the application development stage for internal-use software, offset by corresponding amortization, was a net expense of $1 million in 2002, and net deferrals of $3 million and $14 million in 2001 and 2000, respectively.

• • •

Note 2 — Cash, Cash Equivalents and Marketable Securities

The following tables summarize, by major security type, the Company's cash and marketable securities (in thousands):

| | December 31, 2002 | | | |
	Cost or Amortized Cost	Gross Unrealized Gains	Gross Unrealized Losses	Estimated Fair Value
Cash....................................	$ 302,964	$ —	$ —	$ 302,964
Commercial paper and short-term obligations	429,943	5,347	—	435,290
Cash and cash equivalents...............	732,907	5,347	—	738,254
Certificates of deposit	19,494	2,832	—	22,326
Commercial paper and short-term obligations	2,073	—	—	2,073
Corporate notes and bonds	42,586	355	—	42,941
Asset-backed and agency securities	309,549	7,166	—	316,715
U.S. Treasury notes and bonds.............	172,145	2,616	(35)	174,726
Equity securities	3,934	—	—	3,934
Marketable securities	549,781	12,969	(35)	562,715
Total	$1,282,688	$18,316	$(35)	$1,300,969

• • •

Note 3 — Fixed Assets

Fixed assets, at cost, consist of the following (in thousands):

| | December 31, | |
	2002	2001
Furniture, fixtures and leasehold improvements	$ 112,943	$ 109,227
Technology infrastructure and other computer equipment	57,086	58,140
Software purchased or developed for internal use	94,561	70,944
Equipment and other fixed assets acquired under capital leases	218,146	199,832
	482,736	438,143
Less accumulated depreciation..................................	(243,338)	(166,392)
Fixed assets, net...	$ 239,398	$ 271,751

Depreciation expense on fixed assets was $77 million, $83 million and $83 million, which includes amortization of fixed assets acquired under capital lease obligations of $7 million, $9 million and $11 million for 2002, 2001 and 2000, respectively.

• • •

Note 6 — Long-Term Debt and Other

The Company's long-term debt and other long-term liabilities are summarized as follows (in thousands):

| | December 31, | |
	2002	2001
4.75% Convertible Subordinated Notes	$1,249,807	$1,249,807
6.875% PEACS	724,500	608,787
Senior Discount Notes	255,597	231,830
Long-term restructuring liabilities	31,614	20,640
Euro currency swap	12,159	33,265
Capital lease obligations	8,491	16,415
Other long-term debt......................................	8,456	10,381
	2,290,624	2,171,125
Less current portion of capital lease obligations....................	(7,506)	(9,922)
Less current portion of other long-term debt	(5,813)	(5,070)
	$2,277,305	$2,156,133

• • •

Note 15 — Segment Information

The Company presents information to its chief operating decision maker in four segments: North America Books, Music, and DVD/Video ("BMVD"); North America Electronics, Tools, and Kitchen ("ETK"); International; and Services. Accordingly, the Company discloses its segment financial information along these lines.

• • •

BMVD Segment

The BMVD segment includes retail sales from *www.amazon.com* and *www.amazon.ca* of books, music and DVD/video products and magazine subscription commissions. This segment also includes commissions from sales of these products, new, used or collectible, through Amazon Marketplace, amounts earned from sales of these products by other businesses through the Merchants@ program and product revenues from stores offering these products through the Syndicated Stores program.

ETK Segment

The ETK segment includes *www.amazon.com* retail sales of electronics, home improvement and home and garden products, as well as our mail-order catalog sales. This segment also includes commissions from sales of these products, new, used or collectible, through Amazon Marketplace and amounts earned from sales of these products by other businesses through the Merchants@ program, such as with Office Depot, and will include revenues from stores offering these products, if any, through the Syndicated Stores program.

International Segment

The International segment includes all retail sales of the following internationally-focused Web sites: *www.amazon.co.uk, www.amazon.de, www.amazon.fr* and *www.amazon.co.jp*. These international sites share a common Amazon.com experience, but are localized in terms of language, products, customer service and fulfillment. To the extent available on these sites, this segment includes commissions and other amounts earned from sales of products through Amazon Marketplace and revenues from stores offering products through the Syndicated Stores program, such as *www.waterstones.co.uk* and *www.virginmega.co.jp,* and amounts earned from sales of products by other businesses through the Merchants@ program. The International segment includes export sales from *www.amazon.co.uk, www.amazon.de, www.amazon.fr* and *www.amazon.co.jp* (including export sales from these sites to customers in the U.S. and Canada), but excludes export sales from *www.amazon.com* and *www.amazon.ca*. Operating results for the International segment are affected by movements in foreign exchange rates. During 2002, International segment revenues improved $47 million, and operating results improved $4 million in comparison to the prior year due to changes in foreign exchange rates.

Services Segment

The Services segment consists of commissions, fees and other amounts earned from the services business, including the Merchant.com program (such as *www.target.com*), and to the extent full product categories are not also offered by the Company through its online retail stores, the Merchants@ program, such as the apparel store, Toysrus.com and Babiesrus.com stores, and portions of the Target store at *www.amazon.com,* as well as the commercial agreement with America Online, Inc. This segment also includes Auctions, zShops, Amazon Payments and miscellaneous marketing and promotional agreements.

Included in Services segment revenues are equity-based service revenues of $13 million, $27 million and $79 million for 2002, 2001 and 2000, respectively.

The Company measures the results of operations of its reportable segments using a pro forma measure. Pro forma results from operations, which exclude stock-based compensation, amortization of goodwill and other intangibles, and restructuring-related and other charges, are not in conformity with accounting principles generally accepted in the United States. Stock-based compensation, amortization of goodwill and other intangibles, and restructuring-related and other costs are not allocated to segment results. All other centrally-incurred operating costs are fully allocated to segment results. There are no internal transactions between the Company's reporting segments.

Information on reportable segments and reconciliation to consolidated net loss is as follows (in thousands):

Year Ended 2002:

	North America					
	Books, Music and DVD/Video	Electronics, Tools and Kitchen	Total	International	Services	Consolidated
Net sales	$1,873,291	$645,031	$2,518,322	$1,168,935	$245,679	$3,932,936
Gross profit	527,542	89,863	617,405	249,089	126,124	992,618
Pro forma income (loss) from operations...................	211,363	(73,220)	138,143	(640)	42,599	180,102
Stock-based compensation						(68,927)
Amortization of other intangibles						(5,478)
Restructuring-related and other.......						(41,573)
Total non-operating expenses, net						(209,888)
Equity in losses of equity-method investees, net						(4,169)
Cumulative effect of change in accounting principle						801
Net loss						$ (149,132)

Year Ended 2001:

	North America					
	Books. Music and DVD/Video	Electronics, Tools and Kitchen	Total	International	Services	Consolidated
Net sales.........................	$1,688,752	$ 547,190	$2,235,942	$ 661,374	$225,117	$3,122,433
Gross profit......................	453,129	78,384	531,513	140,606	126,439	798,558
Pro forma income (loss) from operations	156,753	(140,685)	16,068	(103,112)	42,042	(45,002)
Stock-based compensation						(4,637)
Amortization of goodwill and other intangibles.....................						(181,033)
Restructuring-related and other						(181,585)
Total non-operating expenses, net						(114,170)
Equity in losses of equity-method investees, net						(30,327)
Cumulative effect of change in accounting principle..............						(10,523)
Net loss.........................						$ (567,277)

Year Ended 2000:

| | North America | | | | | |
	Books, Music and DVD/Video	Electronics, Tools and Kitchen	Total	International	Services	Consolidated
Net sales	$1,698,266	$ 484,151	$2,182,417	$ 381,075	$198,491	$ 2,761,983
Gross profit	417,452	44,655	462,107	77,436	116,234	655,777
Pro forma income (loss) from operations......................	71,441	(269,890)	(198,449)	(145,070)	26,519	(317,000)
Stock-based compensation..........						(24,797)
Amortization of goodwill and other intangibles						(321,772)
Restructuring-related and other						(200,311)
Total non-operating expenses, net.....						(242,797)
Equity in losses of equity-method investees, net..................						(304,596)
Net loss						$(1,411,273)

Net sales to customers outside of the U.S. represented approximately 35%, 29% and 22% of net sales for 2002, 2001 and 2000, respectively. Other than sales into the United Kingdom, which represents approximately 11% of total net sales in 2002, no individual foreign country, geographical area or customer accounted for more than 10% of net sales in any of the periods presented.

Depreciation expense, by segment, was as follows (in thousands):

| | North America | | | | | |
Year Ended December 31,	Books, Music and DVD/Video	Electronics, Tools and Kitchen	Total	Services	International	Consolidated
2002	$25,774	$19,051	$44,825	$7,339	$21,194	$73,358
2001	29,317	21,670	50,987	8,349	24,108	83,444
2000	29,501	26,818	56,319	7,649	18,970	82,938

At December 31, 2002 and 2001, fixed assets, net totaled $196 million and $228 million in the United States, respectively, and $43 million and $44 million in other countries, respectively.

Note 16 — Quarterly Results (Unaudited)

The following tables contain selected unaudited statement of operations information for each quarter of 2002, 2001 and 2000. The Company believes that the following information reflects all normal recurring adjustments necessary for a fair presentation of the information for the periods presented. The operating results for any quarter are not necessarily indicative of results for any future period. Unaudited quarterly results were as follows (in thousands, except per share data):

	Year Ended December 31, 2002			
	Fourth Quarter	Third Quarter	Second Quarter	First Quarter
Net sales	$1,428,610	$851,299	$805,605	$847,422
Gross profit	335,159	216,167	218,167	223,125
Income (loss) before change in accounting principle	2,651	(35,080)	(93,553)	(23,951)
Cumulative effect of change in accounting principle	—	—	—	801
Net income (loss)	2,651	(35,080)	(93,553)	(23,150)
Basic income (loss) per share(1):				
Prior to cumulative effect of change in accounting principle	$ 0.01	$ (0.09)	$ (0.25)	$ (0.06)
Cumulative effect of change in accounting principle	—	—	—	—
	$ 0.01	$ (0.09)	$ (0.25)	$ (0.06)
Diluted income (loss) per share(1):				
Prior to cumulative effect of change in accounting principle	$ 0.01	$ (0.09)	$ (0.25)	$ (0.06)
Cumulative effect of change in accounting principle	—	—	—	—
	$ 0.01	$ (0.09)	$ (0.25)	$ (0.06)
Shares used in computation of income (loss) per share:				
Basic	383,702	379,650	376,937	373,031
Diluted	407,056	379,650	376,937	373,031

	Year Ended December 31, 2001			
	Fourth Quarter	Third Quarter	Second Quarter	First Quarter
Net sales	$1,115,171	$ 639,281	$ 667,625	$ 700,356
Gross profit	274,049	162,192	179,720	182,597
Income (loss) before change in accounting principle	5,087	(169,874)	(168,359)	(223,608)
Cumulative effect of change in accounting principle	—	—	—	(10,523)
Net income (loss)	5,087	(169,874)	(168,359)	(234,131)

	Year Ended December 31, 2001			
	Fourth Quarter	Third Quarter	Second Quarter	First Quarter
Basic and diluted income (loss) per share(1):				
Prior to cumulative effect of change in accounting principle	$ 0.01	$ (0.46)	$ (0.47)	$ (0.63)
Cumulative effect of change in accounting principle	—	—	—	(0.03)
	$ 0.01	$ (0.46)	$ (0.47)	$ (0.66)
Shares used in computation of basic income (loss) per share.....................	371,420	368,052	359,752	357,424
Shares used in computation of diluted income (loss) per share	384,045	368,052	359,752	357,424

	Year Ended December 31, 2000			
	Fourth Quarter	Third Quarter	Second Quarter	First Quarter
Net sales	$ 972,360	$ 637,858	$ 577,876	$ 573,889
Gross profit	224,300	167,279	136,064	128,134
Net loss	(545,140)	(240,524)	(317,184)	(308,425)
Basic and diluted loss per share(1)	$ (1.53)	$ (0.68)	$ (0.91)	$ (0.90)
Shares used in computation of basic and diluted loss per share	355,681	353,954	349,886	343,884

(1) The sum of quarterly per share amounts may not equal per share amounts reported for year-to-date periods. This is due to changes in the number of weighted-average shares outstanding and the effects of rounding for each period.

■ Appendix B

(For Businesses Discussed in Chapters 1–12)

Service Proprietorship

Assets	Liabilities	Owner's Equity
Cash	Accounts Payable	Owner, Capital
Accounts Receivable	Notes Payable, Short-Term	Owner, Withdrawals
Allowance for Uncollectible Accounts	Salary Payable	**Revenues and Gains**
Notes Receivable, Short-Term	Wage Payable	Service Revenue
Interest Receivable	Employee Income Tax Payable	Interest Revenue
Supplies	FICA Tax Payable	Gain on Sale of Land (or Furniture,
Prepaid Rent	State Unemployment Tax Payable	Equipment, or Building)
Prepaid Insurance	Federal Unemployment Tax Payable	**Expenses and Losses**
Notes Receivable, Long-Term	Employee Benefits Payable	Salary Expense
Land	Interest Payable	Payroll Tax Expense
Furniture	Unearned Service Revenue	Rent Expense
Accumulated Depreciation—Furniture	Notes Payable, Long-Term	Insurance Expense
Equipment		Supplies Expense
Accumulated Depreciation—Equipment		Uncollectible-Account Expense
Building		Depreciation Expense—Furniture
Accumulated Depreciation—Building		Depreciation Expense—Equipment
		Depreciation Expense—Building
		Property Tax Expense
		Interest Expense
		Miscellaneous Expense
		Loss on Sale of Land (Furniture,
		Equipment, or Building)

Service Partnership

Same as Service Proprietorship, except for Owners' Equity:

Owners' Equity

Partner 1, Capital
Partner 2, Capital
Partner N, Capital

Partner 1, Drawing
Partner 2, Drawing
Partner N, Drawing

(For Businesses Discussed in Chapters 13–26)

Merchandising Corporation

Assets	Liabilities	Stockholder's Equity
Cash	Accounts Payable	Preferred Stock
Short-Term Investments (Trading Securities)	Notes Payable, Short-Term	Paid-in Capital in Excess of Par—Preferred
Accounts Receivable	Current Portion of Bonds Payable	Common Stock
Allowance for Uncollectible Accounts	Salary Payable	Paid-in Capital in Excess of Par—Common
Notes Receivable, Short-Term	Wage Payable	Paid-in Capital from Treasury Stock Transactions
Interest Receivable	Employee Income Tax Payable	Paid-in Capital from Retirement of Stock
Inventory	FICA Tax Payable	Retained Earnings
Supplies	State Unemployment Tax Payable	Foreign Currency Translation Adjustment
Prepaid Rent	Federal Unemployment Tax Payable	Treasury Stock
Prepaid Insurance	Employee Benefits Payable	
Notes Receivable, Long-Term	Interest Payable	
Investments in Stock (Available-for-Sale Securities)	Income Tax Payable	
Investments in Bonds (Held-to-Maturity Securities)	Unearned Sales Revenue	
Other Receivables, Long-Term	Notes Payable, Long-Term	
Land	Bonds Payable	

Stockholder's Equity (continued)

Revenues and Gains	Expenses and Losses
Sales Revenue	Cost of Goods Sold
Interest Revenue	Salary Expense
Dividend Revenue	Wage Expense
Equity-Method Investment Revenue	Commission Expense
Unrealized Gain on Investments	Payroll Tax Expense
Gain on Sale of Investments	Rent Expense
Gain on Sale of Land (Furniture and Fixtures, Equipment, or Buildings)	Insurance Expense
Discontinued Operations—Gain	Supplies Expense
Extraordinary Gains	Uncollectible-Account Expense

Assets (continued):
Land Improvements
Furniture and Fixtures
Accumulated Depreciation—Furniture and Fixtures
Equipment
Accumulated Depreciation—Equipment
Buildings
Accumulated Depreciation—Buildings
Franchises
Patents
Leaseholds
Goodwill

Expenses and Losses (continued):
Depreciation Expense—Land Improvements
Depreciation Expense—Furniture and Fixtures
Depreciation Expense—Equipment
Depreciation Expense—Buildings
Amortization Expense—Franchises
Amortization Expense—Leaseholds
Loss on Goodwill
Income Tax Expense
Unrealized Loss on Investments
Loss on Sale of Investments
Loss on Sale of Land (Furniture and Fixtures, Equipment, or Buildings)
Discontinued Operations—Loss
Extraordinary Losses

Manufacturing Corporation

Same as Merchandising Corporation, except for Assets and Expenses:

Assets	Expenses (Contra Expenses If Credit Balance)
Inventories:	Direct Materials Price Variance
Materials Inventory	Direct Materials Efficiency Variance
Work in Process Inventory	Direct Labor Price Variance
Finished Goods Inventory	Direct Labor Efficiency Variance
	Manufacturing Overhead Flexible Budget Variance
	Manufacturing Overhead Production Volume Variance

■ A p p e n d i x   C

Present Value Tables and Future Value Tables

This appendix provides present value tables and future value tables (more complete than those in the Chapter 15 appendix and in Chapter 26).

Present Value of $1

Present Value

Periods	1%	2%	3%	4%	5%	6%	7%	8%	9%	10%	12%
1	0.990	0.980	0.971	0.962	0.952	0.943	0.935	0.926	0.917	0.909	0.893
2	0.980	0.961	0.943	0.925	0.907	0.890	0.873	0.857	0.842	0.826	0.797
3	0.971	0.942	0.915	0.889	0.864	0.840	0.816	0.794	0.772	0.751	0.712
4	0.961	0.924	0.888	0.855	0.823	0.792	0.763	0.735	0.708	0.683	0.636
5	0.951	0.906	0.883	0.822	0.784	0.747	0.713	0.681	0.650	0.621	0.567
6	0.942	0.888	0.837	0.790	0.746	0.705	0.666	0.630	0.596	0.564	0.507
7	0.933	0.871	0.813	0.760	0.711	0.665	0.623	0.583	0.547	0.513	0.452
8	0.923	0.853	0.789	0.731	0.677	0.627	0.582	0.540	0.502	0.467	0.404
9	0.914	0.837	0.766	0.703	0.645	0.592	0.544	0.500	0.460	0.424	0.361
10	0.905	0.820	0.744	0.676	0.614	0.558	0.508	0.463	0.422	0.386	0.322
11	0.896	0.804	0.722	0.650	0.585	0.527	0.475	0.429	0.388	0.350	0.287
12	0.887	0.788	0.701	0.625	0.557	0.497	0.444	0.397	0.356	0.319	0.257
13	0.879	0.773	0.681	0.601	0.530	0.469	0.415	0.368	0.326	0.290	0.229
14	0.870	0.758	0.661	0.577	0.505	0.442	0.388	0.340	0.299	0.263	0.205
15	0.861	0.743	0.642	0.555	0.481	0.417	0.362	0.315	0.275	0.239	0.183
16	0.853	0.728	0.623	0.534	0.458	0.394	0.339	0.292	0.252	0.218	0.163
17	0.844	0.714	0.605	0.513	0.436	0.371	0.317	0.270	0.231	0.198	0.146
18	0.836	0.700	0.587	0.494	0.416	0.350	0.296	0.250	0.212	0.180	0.130
19	0.828	0.686	0.570	0.475	0.396	0.331	0.277	0.232	0.194	0.164	0.116
20	0.820	0.673	0.554	0.456	0.377	0.312	0.258	0.215	0.178	0.149	0.104
21	0.811	0.660	0.538	0.439	0.359	0.294	0.242	0.199	0.164	0.135	0.093
22	0.803	0.647	0.522	0.422	0.342	0.278	0.226	0.184	0.150	0.123	0.083
23	0.795	0.634	0.507	0.406	0.326	0.262	0.211	0.170	0.138	0.112	0.074
24	0.788	0.622	0.492	0.390	0.310	0.247	0.197	0.158	0.126	0.102	0.066
25	0.780	0.610	0.478	0.375	0.295	0.233	0.184	0.146	0.116	0.092	0.059
26	0.772	0.598	0.464	0.361	0.281	0.220	0.172	0.135	0.106	0.084	0.053
27	0.764	0.586	0.450	0.347	0.268	0.207	0.161	0.125	0.098	0.076	0.047
28	0.757	0.574	0.437	0.333	0.255	0.196	0.150	0.116	0.090	0.069	0.042
29	0.749	0.563	0.424	0.321	0.243	0.185	0.141	0.107	0.082	0.063	0.037
30	0.742	0.552	0.412	0.308	0.231	0.174	0.131	0.099	0.075	0.057	0.033
40	0.672	0.453	0.307	0.208	0.142	0.097	0.067	0.046	0.032	0.022	0.011
50	0.608	0.372	0.228	0.141	0.087	0.054	0.034	0.021	0.013	0.009	0.003

Exhibit C-1

(cont'd)

Present Value

14%	15%	16%	18%	20%	25%	30%	35%	40%	45%	50%	Periods
0.877	0.870	0.862	0.847	0.833	0.800	0.769	0.741	0.714	0.690	0.667	1
0.769	0.756	0.743	0.718	0.694	0.640	0.592	0.549	0.510	0.476	0.444	2
0.675	0.658	0.641	0.609	0.579	0.512	0.455	0.406	0.364	0.328	0.296	3
0.592	0.572	0.552	0.516	0.482	0.410	0.350	0.301	0.260	0.226	0.198	4
0.519	0.497	0.476	0.437	0.402	0.328	0.269	0.223	0.186	0.156	0.132	5
0.456	0.432	0.410	0.370	0.335	0.262	0.207	0.165	0.133	0.108	0.088	6
0.400	0.376	0.354	0.314	0.279	0.210	0.159	0.122	0.095	0.074	0.059	7
0.351	0.327	0.305	0.266	0.233	0.168	0.123	0.091	0.068	0.051	0.039	8
0.308	0.284	0.263	0.225	0.194	0.134	0.094	0.067	0.048	0.035	0.026	9
0.270	0.247	0.227	0.191	0.162	0.107	0.073	0.050	0.035	0.024	0.017	10
0.237	0.215	0.195	0.162	0.135	0.086	0.056	0.037	0.025	0.017	0.012	11
0.208	0.187	0.168	0.137	0.112	0.069	0.043	0.027	0.018	0.012	0.008	12
0.182	0.163	0.145	0.116	0.093	0.055	0.033	0.020	0.013	0.008	0.005	13
0.160	0.141	0.125	0.099	0.078	0.044	0.025	0.015	0.009	0.006	0.003	14
0.140	0.123	0.108	0.084	0.065	0.035	0.020	0.011	0.006	0.004	0.002	15
0.123	0.107	0.093	0.071	0.054	0.028	0.015	0.008	0.005	0.003	0.002	16
0.108	0.093	0.080	0.060	0.045	0.023	0.012	0.006	0.003	0.002	0.001	17
0.095	0.081	0.069	0.051	0.038	0.018	0.009	0.005	0.002	0.001	0.001	18
0.083	0.070	0.060	0.043	0.031	0.014	0.007	0.003	0.002	0.001		19
0.073	0.061	0.051	0.037	0.026	0.012	0.005	0.002	0.001	0.001		20
0.064	0.053	0.044	0.031	0.022	0.009	0.004	0.002	0.001			21
0.056	0.046	0.038	0.026	0.018	0.007	0.003	0.001	0.001			22
0.049	0.040	0.033	0.022	0.015	0.006	0.002	0.001				23
0.043	0.035	0.028	0.019	0.013	0.005	0.002	0.001				24
0.038	0.030	0.024	0.016	0.010	0.004	0.001	0.001				25
0.033	0.026	0.021	0.014	0.009	0.003	0.001					26
0.029	0.023	0.018	0.011	0.007	0.002	0.001					27
0.026	0.020	0.016	0.010	0.006	0.002	0.001					28
0.022	0.017	0.014	0.008	0.005	0.002						29
0.020	0.015	0.012	0.007	0.004	0.001						30
0.005	0.004	0.003	0.001	0.001							40
0.001	0.001	0.001									50

Exhibit C-2

Present Value of Annuity of $1

						Present Value					
Periods	1%	2%	3%	4%	5%	6%	7%	8%	9%	10%	12%
1	0.990	0.980	0.971	0.962	0.952	0.943	0.935	0.926	0.917	0.909	0.893
2	1.970	1.942	1.913	1.886	1.859	1.833	1.808	1.783	1.759	1.736	1.690
3	2.941	2.884	2.829	2.775	2.723	2.673	2.624	2.577	2.531	2.487	2.402
4	3.902	3.808	3.717	3.630	3.546	3.465	3.387	3.312	3.240	3.170	3.037
5	4.853	4.713	4.580	4.452	4.329	4.212	4.100	3.993	3.890	3.791	3.605
6	5.795	5.601	5.417	5.242	5.076	4.917	4.767	4.623	4.486	4.355	4.111
7	6.728	6.472	6.230	6.002	5.786	5.582	5.389	5.206	5.033	4.868	4.564
8	7.652	7.325	7.020	6.733	6.463	6.210	5.971	5.747	5.535	5.335	4.968
9	8.566	8.162	7.786	7.435	7.108	6.802	6.515	6.247	5.995	5.759	5.328
10	9.471	8.983	8.530	8.111	7.722	7.360	7.024	6.710	6.418	6.145	5.650
11	10.368	9.787	9.253	8.760	8.306	7.887	7.499	7.139	6.805	6.495	5.938
12	11.255	10.575	9.954	9.385	8.863	8.384	7.943	7.536	7.161	6.814	6.194
13	12.134	11.348	10.635	9.986	9.394	8.853	8.358	7.904	7.487	7.103	6.424
14	13.004	12.106	11.296	10.563	9.899	9.295	8.745	8.244	7.786	7.367	6.628
15	13.865	12.849	11.938	11.118	10.380	9.712	9.108	8.559	8.061	7.606	6.811
16	14.718	13.578	12.561	11.652	10.838	10.106	9.447	8.851	8.313	7.824	6.974
17	15.562	14.292	13.166	12.166	11.274	10.477	9.763	9.122	8.544	8.022	7.120
18	16.398	14.992	13.754	12.659	11.690	10.828	10.059	9.372	8.756	8.201	7.250
19	17.226	15.678	14.324	13.134	12.085	11.158	10.336	9.604	8.950	8.365	7.366
20	18.046	16.351	14.878	13.590	12.462	11.470	10.594	9.818	9.129	8.514	7.469
21	18.857	17.011	15.415	14.029	12.821	11.764	10.836	10.017	9.292	8.649	7.562
22	19.660	17.658	15.937	14.451	13.163	12.042	11.061	10.201	9.442	8.772	7.645
23	20.456	18.292	16.444	14.857	13.489	12.303	11.272	10.371	9.580	8.883	7.718
24	21.243	18.914	16.936	15.247	13.799	12.550	11.469	10.529	9.707	8.985	7.784
25	22.023	19.523	17.413	15.622	14.094	12.783	11.654	10.675	9.823	9.077	7.843
26	22.795	20.121	17.877	15.983	14.375	13.003	11.826	10.810	9.929	9.161	7.896
27	23.560	20.707	18.327	16.330	14.643	13.211	11.987	10.935	10.027	9.237	7.943
28	24.316	21.281	18.764	16.663	14.898	13.406	12.137	11.051	10.116	9.307	7.984
29	25.066	21.844	19.189	16.984	15.141	13.591	12.278	11.158	10.198	9.370	8.022
30	25.808	22.396	19.600	17.292	15.373	13.765	12.409	11.258	10.274	9.427	8.055
40	32.835	27.355	23.115	19.793	17.159	15.046	13.332	11.925	10.757	9.779	8.244
50	39.196	31.424	25.730	21.482	18.256	15.762	13.801	12.234	10.962	9.915	8.305

Exhibit C-2
(cont'd)

Present Value

14%	15%	16%	18%	20%	25%	30%	35%	40%	45%	50%	Periods
0.877	0.870	0.862	0.847	0.833	0.800	0.769	0.741	0.714	0.690	0.667	1
1.647	1.626	1.605	1.566	1.528	1.440	1.361	1.289	1.224	1.165	1.111	2
2.322	2.283	2.246	2.174	2.106	1.952	1.816	1.696	1.589	1.493	1.407	3
2.914	2.855	2.798	2.690	2.589	2.362	2.166	1.997	1.849	1.720	1.605	4
3.433	3.352	3.274	3.127	2.991	2.689	2.436	2.220	2.035	1.876	1.737	5
3.889	3.784	3.685	3.498	3.326	2.951	2.643	2.385	2.168	1.983	1.824	6
4.288	4.160	4.039	3.812	3.605	3.161	2.802	2.508	2.263	2.057	1.883	7
4.639	4.487	4.344	4.078	3.837	3.329	2.925	2.598	2.331	2.109	1.922	8
4.946	4.772	4.607	4.303	4.031	3.463	3.019	2.665	2.379	2.144	1.948	9
5.216	5.019	4.833	4.494	4.192	3.571	3.092	2.715	2.414	2.168	1.965	10
5.553	5.234	5.029	4.656	4.327	3.656	3.147	2.752	2.438	2.185	1.977	11
5.660	5.421	5.197	4.793	4.439	3.725	3.190	2.779	2.456	2.197	1.985	12
5.842	5.583	5.342	4.910	4.533	3.780	3.223	2.799	2.469	2.204	1.990	13
6.002	5.724	5.468	5.008	4.611	3.824	3.249	2.814	2.478	2.210	1.993	14
6.142	5.847	5.575	5.092	4.675	3.859	3.268	2.825	2.484	2.214	1.995	15
6.265	5.954	5.669	5.162	4.730	3.887	3.283	2.834	2.489	2.216	1.997	16
6.373	6.047	5.749	5.222	4.775	3.910	3.295	2.840	2.492	2.218	1.998	17
6.467	6.128	5.818	5.273	4.812	3.928	3.304	2.844	2.494	2.219	1.999	18
6.550	6.198	5.877	5.316	4.844	3.942	3.311	2.848	2.496	2.220	1.999	19
6.623	6.259	5.929	5.353	4.870	3.954	3.316	2.850	2.497	2.221	1.999	20
6.687	6.312	5.973	5.384	4.891	3.963	3.320	2.852	2.498	2.221	2.000	21
6.743	6.359	6.011	5.410	4.909	3.970	3.323	2.853	2.498	2.222	2.000	22
6.792	6.399	6.044	5.432	4.925	3.976	3.325	2.854	2.499	2.222	2.000	23
6.835	6.434	6.073	5.451	4.937	3.981	3.327	2.855	2.499	2.222	2.000	24
6.873	6.464	6.097	5.467	4.948	3.985	3.329	2.856	2.499	2.222	2.000	25
6.906	6.491	6.118	5.480	4.956	3.988	3.330	2.856	2.500	2.222	2.000	26
6.935	6.514	6.136	5.492	4.964	3.990	3.331	2.856	2.500	2.222	2.000	27
6.961	6.534	6.152	5.502	4.970	3.992	3.331	2.857	2.500	2.222	2.000	28
6.983	6.551	6.166	5.510	4.975	3.994	3.332	2.857	2.500	2.222	2.000	29
7.003	6.566	6.177	5.517	4.979	3.995	3.332	2.857	2.500	2.222	2.000	30
7.105	6.642	6.234	5.548	4.997	3.999	3.333	2.857	2.500	2.222	2.000	40
7.133	6.661	6.246	5.554	4.999	4.000	3.333	2.857	2.500	2.222	2.000	50

Exhibit C-3

Future Value of $1

Future Value

Periods	1%	2%	3%	4%	5%	6%	7%	8%	9%	10%	12%	14%	15%
1	1.010	1.020	1.030	1.040	1.050	1.060	1.070	1.080	1.090	1.100	1.120	1.140	1.150
2	1.020	1.040	1.061	1.082	1.103	1.124	1.145	1.166	1.188	1.210	1.254	1.300	1.323
3	1.030	1.061	1.093	1.125	1.158	1.191	1.225	1.260	1.295	1.331	1.405	1.482	1.521
4	1.041	1.082	1.126	1.170	1.216	1.262	1.311	1.360	1.412	1.464	1.574	1.689	1.749
5	1.051	1.104	1.159	1.217	1.276	1.338	1.403	1.469	1.539	1.611	1.762	1.925	2.011
6	1.062	1.126	1.194	1.265	1.340	1.419	1.501	1.587	1.677	1.772	1.974	2.195	2.313
7	1.072	1.149	1.230	1.316	1.407	1.504	1.606	1.714	1.828	1.949	2.211	2.502	2.660
8	1.083	1.172	1.267	1.369	1.477	1.594	1.718	1.851	1.993	2.144	2.476	2.853	3.059
9	1.094	1.195	1.305	1.423	1.551	1.689	1.838	1.999	2.172	2.358	2.773	3.252	3.518
10	1.105	1.219	1.344	1.480	1.629	1.791	1.967	2.159	2.367	2.594	3.106	3.707	4.046
11	1.116	1.243	1.384	1.539	1.710	1.898	2.105	2.332	2.580	2.853	3.479	4.226	4.652
12	1.127	1.268	1.426	1.601	1.796	2.012	2.252	2.518	2.813	3.138	3.896	4.818	5.350
13	1.138	1.294	1.469	1.665	1.886	2.133	2.410	2.720	3.066	3.452	4.363	5.492	6.153
14	1.149	1.319	1.513	1.732	1.980	2.261	2.579	2.937	3.342	3.798	4.887	6.261	7.076
15	1.161	1.346	1.558	1.801	2.079	2.397	2.759	3.172	3.642	4.177	5.474	7.138	8.137
16	1.173	1.373	1.605	1.873	2.183	2.540	2.952	3.426	3.970	4.595	6.130	8.137	9.358
17	1.184	1.400	1.653	1.948	2.292	2.693	3.159	3.700	4.328	5.054	6.866	9.276	10.76
18	1.196	1.428	1.702	2.026	2.407	2.854	3.380	3.996	4.717	5.560	7.690	10.58	12.38
19	1.208	1.457	1.754	2.107	2.527	3.026	3.617	4.316	5.142	6.116	8.613	12.06	14.23
20	1.220	1.486	1.806	2.191	2.653	3.207	3.870	4.661	5.604	6.728	9.646	13.74	16.37
21	1.232	1.516	1.860	2.279	2.786	3.400	4.141	5.034	6.109	7.400	10.80	15.67	18.82
22	1.245	1.546	1.916	2.370	2.925	3.604	4.430	5.437	6.659	8.140	12.10	17.86	21.64
23	1.257	1.577	1.974	2.465	3.072	3.820	4.741	5.871	7.258	8.954	13.55	20.36	24.89
24	1.270	1.608	2.033	2.563	3.225	4.049	5.072	6.341	7.911	9.850	15.18	23.21	28.63
25	1.282	1.641	2.094	2.666	3.386	4.292	5.427	6.848	8.623	10.83	17.00	26.46	32.92
26	1.295	1.673	2.157	2.772	3.556	4.549	5.807	7.396	9.399	11.92	19.04	30.17	37.86
27	1.308	1.707	2.221	2.883	3.733	4.822	6.214	7.988	10.25	13.11	21.32	34.39	43.54
28	1.321	1.741	2.288	2.999	3.920	5.112	6.649	8.627	11.17	14.42	23.88	39.20	50.07
29	1.335	1.776	2.357	3.119	4.116	5.418	7.114	9.317	12.17	15.86	26.75	44.69	57.58
30	1.348	1.811	2.427	3.243	4.322	5.743	7.612	10.06	13.27	17.45	29.96	50.95	66.21
40	1.489	2.208	3.262	4.801	7.040	10.29	14.97	21.72	31.41	45.26	93.05	188.9	267.9
50	1.645	2.692	4.384	7.107	11.47	18.42	29.46	46.90	74.36	117.4	289.0	700.2	1,084

Exhibit C-4

Future Value of Annuity $1

						Future Value							
Periods	1%	2%	3%	4%	5%	6%	7%	8%	9%	10%	12%	14%	15%
1	1.000	1.000	1.000	1.000	1.000	1.000	1.000	1.000	1.000	1.000	1.000	1.000	1.000
2	2.010	2.020	2.030	2.040	2.050	2.060	2.070	2.080	2.090	2.100	2.120	2.140	2.150
3	3.030	3.060	3.091	3.122	3.153	3.184	3.215	3.246	3.278	3.310	3.374	3.440	3.473
4	4.060	4.122	4.184	4.246	4.310	4.375	4.440	4.506	4.573	4.641	4.779	4.921	4.993
5	5.101	5.204	5.309	5.416	5.526	5.637	5.751	5.867	5.985	6.105	6.353	6.610	6.742
6	6.152	6.308	6.468	6.633	6.802	6.975	7.153	7.336	7.523	7.716	8.115	8.536	8.754
7	7.214	7.434	7.662	7.898	8.142	8.394	8.654	8.923	9.200	9.487	10.09	10.73	11.07
8	8.286	8.583	8.892	9.214	9.549	9.897	10.26	10.64	11.03	11.44	12.30	13.23	13.73
9	9.369	9.755	10.16	10.58	11.03	11.49	11.98	12.49	13.02	13.58	14.78	16.09	16.79
10	10.46	10.95	11.46	12.01	12.58	13.18	13.82	14.49	15.19	15.94	17.55	19.34	20.30
11	11.57	12.17	12.81	13.49	14.21	14.97	15.78	16.65	17.56	18.53	20.65	23.04	24.35
12	12.68	13.41	14.19	15.03	15.92	16.87	17.89	18.98	20.14	21.38	24.13	27.27	29.00
13	13.81	14.68	15.62	16.63	17.71	18.88	20.14	21.50	22.95	24.52	28.03	32.09	34.35
14	14.95	15.97	17.09	18.29	19.60	21.02	22.55	24.21	26.02	27.98	32.39	37.58	40.50
15	16.10	17.29	18.60	20.02	21.58	23.28	25.13	27.15	29.36	31.77	37.28	43.84	47.58
16	17.26	18.64	20.16	21.82	23.66	25.67	27.89	30.32	33.00	35.95	42.75	50.98	55.72
17	18.43	20.01	21.76	23.70	25.84	28.21	30.84	33.75	36.97	40.54	48.88	59.12	65.08
18	19.61	21.41	23.41	25.65	28.13	30.91	34.00	37.45	41.30	45.60	55.75	68.39	75.84
19	20.81	22.84	25.12	27.67	30.54	33.76	37.38	41.45	46.02	51.16	63.44	78.97	88.21
20	22.02	24.30	26.87	29.78	33.07	36.79	41.00	45.76	51.16	57.28	72.05	91.02	102.4
21	23.24	25.78	28.68	31.97	35.72	39.99	44.87	50.42	56.76	64.00	81.70	104.8	118.8
22	24.47	27.30	30.54	34.25	38.51	43.39	49.01	55.46	62.87	71.40	92.50	120.4	137.6
23	25.72	28.85	32.45	36.62	41.43	47.00	53.44	60.89	69.53	79.54	104.6	138.3	159.3
24	26.97	30.42	34.43	39.08	44.50	50.82	58.18	66.76	76.79	88.50	118.2	158.7	184.2
25	28.24	32.03	36.46	41.65	47.73	54.86	63.25	73.11	84.70	98.35	133.3	181.9	212.8
26	29.53	33.67	38.55	44.31	51.11	59.16	68.68	79.95	93.32	109.2	150.3	208.3	245.7
27	30.82	35.34	40.71	47.08	54.67	63.71	74.48	87.35	102.7	121.1	169.4	238.5	283.6
28	32.13	37.05	42.93	49.97	58.40	68.53	80.70	95.34	113.0	134.2	190.7	272.9	327.1
29	33.45	38.79	45.22	52.97	62.32	73.64	87.35	104.0	124.1	148.6	214.6	312.1	377.2
30	34.78	40.57	47.58	56.08	66.44	79.06	94.46	113.3	136.3	164.5	241.3	356.8	434.7
40	48.89	60.40	75.40	95.03	120.8	154.8	199.6	259.1	337.9	442.6	767.1	1,342	1,779
50	64.46	84.58	112.8	152.7	209.3	290.3	406.5	573.8	815.1	1,164	2,400	4,995	7,218

■ A p p e n d i x   D

*Check Figures**

Chapter 1

Quick Check   1 b; 2 c; 3 b; 4 d; 5 a; 6 d;
    7 c; 8 c; 9 a; 10 d
S1-1   NCF
S1-2   NCF
S1-3   NCF
S1-4   NCF
S1-5   Owner, Capital $10,000
S1-6   Briggs, Capital $3,000
S1-7   NCF
S1-8   Gillen, Capital $34,000
S1-9   NCF
S1-10   Owner, Capital:
    (a) $10,000 (b) −$6,000
S1-11   Net income $5,200
    Total assets $35,400
S1-12   NCF
S1-13   Net income $40,000
S1-14   Owner, capital, Dec. 31, 20X8
    $17,000
S1-15   Total assets $25,000
E1-1   NCF
E1-2   NCF
E1-3   NCF
E1-4   NCF
E1-5   Amy's Hallmark Owner's
    Equity $22,900
E1-6   1. Increase in equity $3,000
E1-7   1. Net income $13,000
    3. Net loss $1,000
E1-8   NCF
E1-9   Total assets $64,800
E1-10   2. Net income $1,000
E1-11   2. Total assets $25,000
E1-12   1. Net income $65,200
    2. Capital, ending $27,100
E1-13   1. Net income $0.6 billion
    2. Owner equity, ending $5.9
    billion
E1-14   Net income $45,000
P1-1A   2. a. Total assets $100,600
    d. Net income $1,100
P1-2A   1. Total assets $38,320
    2. Net income $4,240
P1-3A   NCF
P1-4A   a. Net income $37,000
    b. L. Collins, capital $71,000
    c. Total assets $89,000
P1-5A   1. Net income $47,000
    2. Matthew Vail, capital $58,000
    3. Total assets $102,000
P1-6A   1. Total assets $105,000
P1-7A   1. Total assets $50,000
P1-1B   2. a. Total assets $81,000
    d. Net income $4,000
P1-2B   1. Total assets $29,850
    2. Net income $2,100

P1-3B   NCF
P1-4B   a. Net income $46,000
    b. J. Robinson, capital $52,000
    c. Total assets $88,000
P1-5B   1. Net income $64,000
    2. Brian Sartor, capital $174,000
    3. Total assets $279,000
P1-6B   1. Total assets $145,000
P1-7B   1. Total assets $88,000
Case 1 2. Total assets $500,000
Case 2 NCF
Financial Statement Case   2. Total
    assets Dec. 31, 2002
    $1,990,449,000
    4. Net sales increased
    $810,503,000

Chapter 2

Quick Check   1 c; 2 a; 3 d; 4 c; 5 b; 6 b;
    7 c; 8 d; 9 a; 10 a
S2-1   NCF
S2-2   NCF
S2-3   NCF
S2-4   NCF
S2-5   NCF
S2-6   NCF
S2-7   NCF
S2-8   NCF
S2-9   3. a. Earned $6,000
    b. Total assets $6,000
S2-10   3. Trial bal. total $45,000
S2-11   Trial bal. total $74 mil.
S2-12   Incorrect Trial bal. total debits
    $24,200
S2-13   Incorrect Trial bal. total debits
    $13,300
S2-14   Total debits $180,000
E2-1   NCF
E2-2   1. Owners' equity $11 bil.
    2. Net income $4 bil.
E2-3   NCF
E2-4   Total debits $180,600
E2-5   NCF
E2-6   2. Trial bal. total $74,700
E2-7   4. Trial bal. total $47,600
E2-8   NCF
E2-9   Trial bal. total $59,400
E2-10   Trial bal. total $184,100
E2-11   Trial bal. total $74,600
E2-12   Cash bal. $4,300
E2-13   Trial bal. total $22,300
E2-14   3. Total debits $53,000
E2-15   NCF
E2-16   b. Cash paid $75,000
    c. Cash collected $88,000
E2-17   4. Trial bal. total $20,400

P2-1A   1. Total assets $268,000
    Net income $45,000
P2-2A   NCF
P2-3A   3. Trial bal. total $35,500
P2-4A   3. Trial bal. total $33,500
P2-5A   1. Trial bal. total $85,100
    2. Net income $10,140
P2-6A   3. Trial bal. total $61,200
P2-7A   1. Net income $400
    2. Vince Serrano, capital Jan. 31,
    20X7 $28,800
    3. Total assets $54,900
P2-1B   1. Total assets $106,000
    Net income $57,000
P2-2B   NCF
P2-3B   3. Trial bal. total $27,300
P2-4B   3. Trial bal. total $42,000
P2-5B   1. Trial bal. total $200,500
    2. Net income $6,370
P2-6B   3. Trial bal. total $93,600
P2-7B   1. Net income $2,800
    2. Christie Clinton, capital Dec.
    31, 20X3 $50,300
    3. Total assets $82,200
Case 1 3. Trial bal. total $17,500
    4. Net income $5,550
Case 2 NCF
Financial Statement Case   Dec. 5 Debit
    Cash $110,000; Credit Sales
    Revenue $110,000

Chapter 3

Quick Check   1 d; 2 a; 3 b; 4 c; 5 a; 6 c;
    7 a; 8 b; 9 d; 10 c
S3-1   Service revenue:
    Cash basis $900;
    Accrual basis $1,200
S3-2   NCF
S3-3   2. Revenue $375,000
S3-4   Expense $140,000
S3-5   1. Prepaid Rent bal. $2,500
    Rent Expense bal. $500
S3-6   3. Book value $23,000
S3-7   2. Interest Payable at Dec. 31
    $900
S3-8   2. Interest Receivable at Dec. 31
    $900
S3-9   NCF
S3-10   Supplies to report on balance
    sheet $400
S3-11   Income statement reports ser-
    vice revenue $7,400
S3-12   1. Total assets $45,925
    Total liabilities $14,350
S3-13   1. Net income $3,525
E3-1   NCF

*(NCF = No check figure)

D-1

E3-2	NCF
E3-3	NCF
E3-4	A. Rent Expense $1,500
	B. Total to account for $1,300
E3-5	NCF
E3-6	Overall, net income is overstated by $7,000
E3-7	NCF
E3-8	Service Revenue bal. $6,900
E3-9	Adjusted trial bal. total $54,400
E3-10	NCF
E3-11	Net income $7,100; S. Perdue, capital $28,400; Total assets $29,300
E3-12	1. Net income $68,500
E3-13	1. Kent Black, capital Dec. 31, 20X5 $126,000
E3-14	Supplies expense $7,800 Salary expense $84,000 Service revenue $182,300
E3-15	7. Net income $1,690; Marsha Walker, capital $14,090; Total assets $18,790
P3-1A	2. Net income $9,150
P3-2A	NCF
P3-3A	a. Insurance Expense $1,800 d. Supplies Expense $6,600
P3-4A	Rental Revenue $700; Interest Revenue $300; Wage Expense $300
P3-5A	3. Adjusted trial bal. total $450,000
P3-6A	1. Net income $40,900; Cindy Sorrel, capital Dec. 31, 20X6 $37,900; Total assets $43,000
P3-7A	2. Net income $10,800; Pat Patillo, capital, July 31, 20X6 $45,900; Total assets $49,500
P3-1B	2. Net income $3,750
P3-2B	NCF
P3-3B	a. Salary Expense $4,000 d. Supplies Expense $6,400
P3-4B	Commission Revenue $8,000; Supplies Expense $900; Salary Expense $1,000
P3-5B	3. Adjusted trial bal. total $62,300
P3-6B	1. Net income $83,470; D. Brooks, capital Dec. 31, 20X8 $67,850; Total assets $134,030
P3-7B	2. Net income $5,400; Jack Dicorte, capital, Oct. 31, 20X7 $132,800; Total assets $136,000
Case 1	1. Your highest price $167,500 2. Wayne's lowest price $139,100
Case 2	Net income $33,540
Financial Statement Case	3. Account balances—all credits: Accum. Depr. $243,338,000; Interest Payable $71,661,000; Unearned Revenue $47,916,000
E3A-1	Supplies bal. $860
E3A-2	Unearned Service Revenue bal. $3,700

E3A-1	Prepaid Rent bal. $2,250; Unearned Service Revenue bal. $2,400

Chapter 4

Quick Check   1 a; 2 a; 3 d; 4 b; 5 b; 6 c; 7 d; 8 b; 9 b; 10 d

S4-1	NCF
S4-2	NCF
S4-3	NCF
S4-4	1. d. Close $3,525 2. Gay Gillen, Capital $31,575
S4-5	1. Gay Gillen, Capital $31,575
S4-6	NCF
S4-7	Income Summary Credit bal. $2,496 mil.
S4-8	Trial bal. total $7,260 mil.
S4-9	NCF
S4-10	c. $826 mil. d. $5,658 mil. e. $1,322 mil.
S4-11	Current ratio 1.71 Debt ratio 0.67
S4-12	1. $1.79 2. 49%
E4-1	Net income $2,200
E4-2	Sep. 30 Close net income of $2,200 to Gail Pfeiffer, Capital
E4-3	Gail Pfeiffer, Capital bal. $36,200
E4-4	Trial bal. total $42,200
E4-5	2. b. Insurance Expense $4,600
E4-6	Ending balances of Insurance Expense and Service Revenue are zero
E4-7	Park Daewoo, Capital bal. $59,800
E4-8	Felix Rohr, Capital bal. $72,700
E4-9	Alvin Chang, Capital, Dec. 31, 20X2 $235,000
E4-10	2. Net income $9,300
E4-11	1. Total assets $61,700 2. Current ratio of current year 1.99
E4-12	Net income $52,300
E4-13	1. Marsha Walker, Capital bal. $14,090; 2. Total assets $18,790 3. Net income $1,690
P4-1A	Net income $15,000
P4-2A	1. Net income $117,000 2. Ross Reagan, capital $104,000; Total assets $164,000
P4-3A	2. Close net income of $33,300
P4-4A	Net income $33,300
P4-5A	2. Net income $12,670 3. Total assets $45,460 5. Postclosing trial bal. total $49,110
P4-6A	1. Total assets $81,400 2. Debt ratio 20X3 0.53
P4-7A	a. Overall, net income is understated by $2,520
P4-1B	Net income $16,400

P4-2B	1. Net income $90,000 2. Betsy Willis, Capital $64,000; Total assets $131,000
P4-3B	2. Close net income of $85,100
P4-4B	Net income $85,100
P4-5B	2. Net income $21,000 3. Total assets $99,320 5. Postclosing trial bal. total $141,220
P4-6B	1. Total assets $124,600 2. Debt ratio 20X6 0.46
P4-7B	a. Overall, net income is understated by $1,060
Case 1	Net income $55,440
Case 2	NCF
Financial Statement Case	3. Current ratio at Dec. 31, 2002 1.52 5. Book value $239,398,000
Team Project	1. Net income $2,750 2. Total assets $2,950
P4A-1	All balances are the same both without and with reversing entries.

Chapter 5

Quick Check   1 d; 2 b; 3 c; 4 a; 5 a; 6 c; 7 d; 8 c; 9 b; 10 d

S5-1	NCF
S5-2	a. $100,000 b. $97,000
S5-3	c. Credit Cash for $97,000
S5-4	Cost of inventory $137,200
S5-5	c. Debit Cash for $137,200
S5-6	Gross profit $6,030
S5-7	b. Gross profit $315,360
S5-8	NCF
S5-9	C. Earnest, Capital bal. $25,650
S5-10	NCF
S5-11	Net income $1,666 mil.
S5-12	Total assets $11,471 mil.
S5-13	Gross profit % 20.7% Invy. turnover 56.4 times
S5-14	b. Excess of collections over payments $641 mil.
E5-1	May 22 Credit Cash for $464.75
E5-2	June 14 Credit Cash for $6,858
E5-3	May 14 Debit Cash for $6,790
E5-4	Sept. 23 Debit Cash for $2,231
E5-5	b. Net income for 2001 $13.7 bil.
E5-6	2. Gross profit for 20X1 $3,541 mil.
E5-7	f. $115,100 g. $112,100
E5-8	2. Owner Capital bal. $10,805 mil.
E5-9	Net income $80,760
E5-10	Net income $80,760
E5-11	1. Net income $31,300 2. Invy. turnover—current year 4.9 times
E5-12	Net income $31,300 Gross profit %—current year 48%

E5-13	Gross profit % 40%
	Invy. turnover 6.6 times
E5-14	3. Net income $4,900
P5-1A	NCF
P5-2A	NCF
P5-3A	2. Receivable $2,200
P5-4A	1. Net income $52,500
P5-5A	Net income $35,000
P5-6A	2. Elaine Lorens, Capital bal. $61,820
P5-7A	1. Net income $10,300
	2. Total assets $374,100
P5-8A	1. Net income $10,300
	2. Total assets $374,100
P5-9A	1. Net income $42,760
	2. Invy. turnover for 20X9 8.5 times
P5-1B	NCF
P5-2B	NCF
P5-3B	2. Belmont was $70 better off as a result of borrowing.
P5-4B	1. Net income $24,200
P5-5B	Net income $48,190
P5-6B	2. Jacob Xiang, Capital bal. $64,560
P5-7B	1. Net income $56,400
	2. Total assets $200,900
P5-8B	1. Net income $56,400
	2. Total assets $200,900
P5-9B	1. Net income $57,310
	2. Invy. turnover for 20X4 2.03 times
Case 1	Net income: Sever's plan $97,000
	Hagins' plan $102,000
Case 2	2. Net income $78,380
	Total assets $104,590
Financial Statement Case	Dec. 31 Credit Income Summary for total revenues of $3,963,047,000. Then debit Income Summary for total expenses of $4,112,179,000. Finally, credit Income Summary for net loss of $149,132,000.

Chapter 5 Appendix

E5A-1	June 23 Debit Cash for $2,352
E5A-2	May 22 Credit Cash for $469.54
E5A-3	May 14 Credit Cash for $6,790
	June 14 Credit Cash for $6,858
E5A-4	May 14 Debit Cash for $6,790
P5A-1	Nov. 27 Walgreen credits Cash for $2,300. Providence debits Cash for $2,300.
P5A-2	May 26 Credit Cash for $3,920.
	May 28 Debit Cash for $2,940.
P5A-3	1. Net income $88,850
	3. Ben Latham, Capital bal. $195,590
	4. Total assets $218,110

Chapter 6

Quick Check	1 a; 2 b; 3 d; 4 c; 5 d; 6 c; 7 a; 8 d; 9 b; 10 a
S6-1	a. COGS $160
	b. Inventory $310
S6-2	COGS $400
S6-3	Inventory $267
S6-4	Inventory bal. $100
S6-5	NCF
S6-6	NCF
S6-7	Gross profit: FIFO $260; LIFO $230
S6-8	COGS $338
S6-9	Report Inventory at $90
S6-10	NCF
S6-11	COGS understated by $100 mil.
S6-12	COGS overstated by $100 mil.
S6-13	Ending invy. $150,000
S6-14	Estimated cost of ending invy. $30,000
E6-1	End. invy. $240; COGS $910
E6-2	May 17 COGS $300
E6-3	End. invy. $220; COGS $930
E6-4	COGS $915; May 31 Invy. $235
E6-5	2. Gross profit $1,574 thou.
E6-6	End. invy.: FIFO $110; LIFO $102
E6-7	COGS: FIFO $420; LIFO $428
E6-8	Gross profit: FIFO $4,500; LIFO $3,700; Avg. $4,071
E6-9	COGS: Avg. $3,320; FIFO $3,270; LIFO $3,368
E6-10	a. $64,800; c. $24,350; d. $30,200; f. $34,700
E6-11	Gross profit $110,567
E6-12	Gross profit $68,000; End. invy. $18,300
E6-13	Gross profit is $70,000 with invy. overstated; $76,000 with invy. understated
E6-14	Net income: 20X2 $41,100; 20X1 $27,300
E6-15	Estimated cost of invy. destroyed $250,000
E6-16	Estimated cost of end. invy. $49,100
P6-1A	1. COGS $6,000; End. invy. $800
P6-2A	1. COGS $6,016; End. invy. $784
	2. Net income $2,484
P6-3A	1. COGS $1,365; End. invy. $225
	3. Gross profit $1,315
P6-4A	2. Gross profit: Avg. $34,293; FIFO $35,484; LIFO $33,092
P6-5A	1. Sales revenue $310,000
	2. COGS $195,000
P6-6A	NCF
P6-7A	1. Net income: 20X3 $11,000; 20X2 $9,000; 20X1 $27,000
P6-8A	1. Estimated cost of end. invy. $672,000
	2. Gross profit $2,592,000
P6-1B	1. COGS $7,750; End. invy. $300
P6-2B	1. COGS $7,705; End. invy. $345
	2. Net income $945

P6-3B	1. COGS $4,640; End. invy. $1,840
	3. Gross profit $3,270
P6-4B	2. Gross profit: Avg. $7,555; FIFO $7,833: LIFO $7,242
P6-5B	1. Sales revenue $378,000
	2. COGS $155,000
P6-6B	NCF
P6-7B	1. Net income: 20X3 $61,000; 20X2 $59,000; 20X1 $15,000
P6-8B	1. Estimated cost of end. invy. $275,000
	2. Gross profit $2,562,000
Case 1	NCF
Case 2	NCF
Financial Statement Case	3. Purchases $2,999,021,000

Chapter 7

Quick Check	1 c; 2 e; 3 a; 4 b; 5 c; 6 a; 7 b; 8 d; 9 d; 10 b
S7-1	NCF
S7-2	NCF
S7-3	NCF
S7-4	NCF
S7-5	NCF
S7-6	NCF
S7-7	NCF
S7-8	NCF
S7-9	2. Decrease in Accounts Receivable $1,235
S7-10	2. Credit Cash $2,876
S7-11	1. Increase in Accounts Payable $2,876
S7-12	2. Net sales revenue $7,456
E7-1	NCF
E7-2	Total assets $107,000
E7-3	NCF
E7-4	NCF
E7-5	Total debit to Cash $450
E7-6	NCF
E7-7	NCF
E7-8	Purchases journal: Total credit to Accounts Payable $18,265
E7-9	3. Total Accounts Payable $3,300
E7-10	Total credit to Cash $11,697
E7-11	Kendrick: Credit Cash for $1,151
E7-12	Gross profit $3,935
P7-1A	NCF
P7-2A	1. Cash receipts journal: Total debit to Cash $53,748
P7-3A	3. Corrected cash receipts journal: Total debit to Cash $24,302
P7-4A	1. Cash payments journal: Total credit to Cash $15,109
P7-5A	6. Total Accounts Receivable $560
	Total Accounts Payable $2,925
P7-1B	NCF
P7-2B	1. Cash receipts journal: Total debit to Cash $35,345

P7-3B	3. Corrected cash receipts journal: Total debit to Cash $10,830
P7-4B	1. Cash payments journal: Total credit to Cash $17,237
P7-5B	6. Total Accounts Receivable $496 Total Accounts Payable $2,692
Case 1	Cash receipts journal: Total debit to Cash $7,749
Case 2	NCF

Chapter 8

Quick Check   1 d; 2 a; 3 b; 4 d; 5 b; 6 d; 7 c; 8 c; 9 a; 10 c

S8-1	NCF
S8-2	NCF
S8-3	NCF
S8-4	NCF
S8-5	NCF
S8-6	Adjusted balance $2,900
S8-7	NCF
S8-8	NCF
S8-9	NCF
S8-10	NCF
S8-11	April 30 Credit Cash for $181
S8-12	NCF
E8-1	NCF
E8-2	NCF
E8-3	NCF
E8-4	NCF
E8-5	Adjusted balance $1,581
E8-6	Adjusted balance $3,371
E8-7	NCF
E8-8	NCF
E8-9	NCF
E8-10	1. Credit Cash in Bank for $209
E8-11	3. Petty Cash balance $400
E8-12	NCF
P8-1A	NCF
P8-2A	NCF
P8-3A	Adjusted balance $14,679
P8-4A	1. Adjusted balance $6,046.33
P8-5A	NCF
P8-6A	3. June 30 Credit Cash in Bank for $303
P8-7A	NCF
P8-1B	NCF
P8-2B	NCF
P8-3B	Adjusted balance $15,670
P8-4B	1. Adjusted balance $19,047.77
P8-5B	NCF
P8-6B	3. April 30 Credit Cash in Bank for $376
P8-7B	NCF
Case 1	NCF
Case 2	Cashier stole $1,000
Financial Statement Case	5. Cash increased by $197,972,000

Chapter 9

Quick Check   1 d; 2 c; 3 b; 4 a; 5 b; 6 d; 7 c; 8 b; 9 a; 10 c

S9-1	NCF
S9-2	NCF
S9-3	Accts. Rec., net $80,000
S9-4	Uncollectible-Account Expenses $14,000
S9-5	Allowance for Uncollectible Accts. bal. $5,000
S9-6	Uncollectible-Account Expense $2,300
S9-7	June 30 Accts. Rec. bal. $5,000
S9-8	Debit Cash for $7,760
S9-9	Note 1 $4,000 Note 2 $375
S9-10	a. Credit Cash for $100,000 b. Debit Cash for $102,000
S9-11	b. Debit Interest Receivable for $22.50
S9-12	1. Net income $1,184 mil. 2. Accts. Rec., net $2,464 mil.
S9-13	a. 1.01 b. 35 days
S9-14	a. 1.48 c. 0.38 b. 0.47 d. 6.9 times
E9-1	NCF
E9-2	2. Accts. Rec., net $54,600
E9-3	2. Accts. Rec. bal. $56,800
E9-4	2. Accts. Rec., net $289,300
E9-5	Accts. Rec., net $125,900
E9-6	1. Interest for: 20X7 $6,000 20X8 $3,000
E9-7	June 30 Debit Interest Receivable for $420
E9-8	May 1, 20X9 Debit Cash for $22,400
E9-9	Dec. 31 Debit Cash for $10,150
E9-10	1. 20X9 0.95 2. 32 days
E9-11	1. 27 days
E9-12	Net income: Without bankcards $75,000; With bankcards $94,300
P9-1A	NCF
P9-2A	Uncollectible-Acct. Expense: 1. $11,200 2. $8,900
P9-3A	3. Accts. Rec., net $159,300
P9-4A	3. Accts. Rec., net $134,400
P9-5A	1. Note 1 $14,170; Note 2 $12,720; Note 3 $9,075 3. Debit Cash for $14,170
P9-6A	Feb. 17, 20X5 Debit Cash for $3,060 Dec. 1, 20X5 Debit Cash for $10,550
P9-7A	Dec. 31, 20X6 Debit Uncollectible-Acct. Expense for $14,800
P9-8A	1. Ratios for 20X6: a. 1.37 c. 18 days b. 0.70
P9-1B	NCF
P9-2B	Uncollectible-Acct. Expense: 1. $8,900; 2. $3,500
P9-3B	3. Accts. rec., net $244,500
P9-4B	3. Accts. rec., net $160,100
P9-5B	1. Note 1 $13,080; Note 2 $11,330; Note 3 $15,250 3. Debit Cash for $13,080

P9-6B	Jan. 20, 20X7 Debit Cash for $2,823 Dec. 14, 20X7 Debit Cash for $6,195
P9-7B	Dec. 31, 20X4 Debit Uncollectible-Acct. Expense for $15,700
P9-8B	1. Ratios for 20X8: a. 1.88 c. 20 days b. 0.67
Case 1	2. Expected amount to collect $16,200
Case 2	1. Net income: 20X6 $106,600; 20X5 $85,550
Financial Statement Case	2. b. Expect to collect $112,282,000 c. Expect not to collect $5,718,000 3. Acid-test ratio for 2002 1.33

Chapter 10

Quick Check   1 b; 2 a; 3 d; 4 c; 5 a; 6 d; 7 b; 8 a; 9 c; 10 d

S10-1	NCF
S10-2	Land $60,000; Building $45,000; Equipment $15,000
S10-3	2. Net income overstated by $800,000
S10-4	2. Book value $34,800,000
S10-5	2nd-year depreciation: b. UOP $9,000,000; DDB $10,080,000
S10-6	2. Extra tax deduction with DDB $9,600,000
S10-7	$5,400,000
S10-8	Depreciation Expense $10,000
S10-9	Gain on Sale $3,000
S10-10	2. Depletion Expense $6.0 bil.
S10-11	Goodwill $500,000
S10-12	Net income $200,000
E10-1	Land $210,000; Land improvements $67,400; Building $800,000
E10-2	1. Cost of building $954,000
E10-3	Bed 1 $2,500; Bed 2 $4,170; Bed 3 $3,330
E10-4	NCF
E10-5	NCF
E10-6	20X9 Depreciation: SL $3,000; UOP $2,400; DDB $375
E10-7	Extra depreciation with DDB $38,388
E10-8	Depreciation for Year 16 $20,000
E10-9	Gain on sale $800
E10-10	Cost of new truck $300,000
E10-11	c. Depletion Expense $92,000
E10-12	Part 2. Amortization Expense for year 5 $250,000
E10-13	Goodwill $6,000,000
E10-14	Year 5: Equipment is correct; Net income is overstated by 1 million euros
E10-15	Gain on sale $458 mil.

P10-1A 2. Depreciation: Land Improvements $2,480; Building $16,500; Furniture $9,108

P10-2A Dec. 31 Depreciation Expense: Motor-Carrier Equip. $18,000; Buildings $750

P10-3A NCF

P10-4A 1. Book value at Dec. 31, 20X7: SL $64,000; UOP $53,000; DDB $31,104

P10-5A Part 1. Goodwill $2,500,000 Part 2. Net income $134,000

P10-6A 1. Book value $5.9 bil.; 2. Owners' equity $11.8 bil.; 3. Net income $3.1 bil.

P10-1B 2. Depreciation: Land Improvements $3,975; Building $30,621; Furniture $11,681

P10-2B Dec. 31 Depreciation Expense: Comm. Equip. $9,600; Televideo Equip. $1,067; Office Equip. $4,167

P10-3B NCF

P10-4B 1. Book value at Dec. 31, 20X8: SL $23,500; UOP $22,012; DDB $14,200

P10-5B Part 1. Goodwill $500,000 Part 2. Net income $95,000

P10-6B 1. Book value $29.0 bil.; 2. Owners' equity $12.6 bil.; 3. Net loss $1.4 bil.

Case 1 1. Net income: Stewart $164,000; Jordan $126,700

Case 2 NCF

Financial Statement Case
2. Depreciation expense $77 mil.
3. Purchases of fixed assets $39,613,000

Chapter 11

Quick Check   1 a; 2 c; 3 d; 4 c; 5 b; 6 a; 7 d; 8 a; 9 c; 10 d

S11-1 b. Credit Cash for $8,800

S11-2 Interest Expense $400

S11-3 2. Estimated Warranty Payable bal. $5,000

S11-4 NCF

S11-5 NCF

S11-6 2. Net pay $676.50

S11-7 Total expense $1,000.40

S11-8 a. Salary Payable $676.50

S11-9 Net pay $5,640

S11-10 1. Total salary expense $14,654; 2. Net pay $10,269.30

S11-11 NCF

S11-12 Total current liabilities $60,726

E11-1 Mar. 31 Debit Cash for $208,000

E11-2 Unearned subscription revenue bal. $120

E11-3 2. Estimated Warranty Payable bal. $5,000

E11-4 May 1, 20X3 Credit Cash for $15,900

E11-5 Net pay $7,430

E11-6 a. Net pay $462.50

E11-7 Payroll Tax Expense $7,630

E11-8 Salary expense $600,000; Salary payable $4,000

E11-9 20X1: Current portion of long-term note payable $1,000,000; Interest payable $270,000

E11-10 Total current liabilities $86,400

E11-11 Ratios for 20X2: Current 1.24; Debt 0.702

E11-12 NCF

P11-1A NCF

P11-2A 1. c. $83,693

P11-3A 1. Net pay $68,483 2. Total cost $101,574

P11-4A 3. Total liabilities $200,390

P11-5A 1. Total net pay $2,334 3. Credit Cash for $2,334 4. Debit Payroll Tax Expense for $181

P11-6A NCF

P11-1B NCF

P11-2B 1. c. $23,949

P11-3B 1. Net pay $68,993

P11-4B 2. Total cost $102,264 3. Total liabilities $331,440

P11-5B 1. Total net pay $3,412 3. Credit Cash for $3,412 4. Debit Payroll Tax Expense for $127

P11-6B NCF

Case 1 NCF

Case 2 NCF

Financial Statement Case
1. Debit Accounts Payable for $618,128,000; Credit Cash for $618,128,000
2. Total long-term debt $2,290,623,000

Chapter 12

Quick Check   1 b; 2 d; 3 b; 4 a; 5 c; 6 b; 7 d; 8 c; 9 d; 10 a

S12-1 NCF

S12-2 Debit Land for $400,000

S12-3 1. Total equity $23 mil.

S12-4 2. Benz, Capital $460,000 Hanna, Capital $95,000

S12-5 Lawson $38,000; Martinez $22,000; Norris $50,000

S12-6 NCF

S12-7 Teal, Capital $80,000

S12-8 Credit Page, Capital $6,667; Franco, Capital $3,333; Neely, Capital $130,000

S12-9 NCF

S12-10 a. Credit Green, Capital $10,000; Henry, Capital $20,000; Isaac, Capital $10,000

S12-11 Pay Akers $37,000; Bloch $19,000; Crane $9,000

S12-12 Final entry: Debit Akers, Capital $37,000; Bloch, Capital $19,000; Crane, Capital $9,000

S12-13 Green, capital $64,000; Henry, capital $63,000

S12-14 Net income: Frost $63,000; Martin $42,000

E12-1 NCF

E12-2 Credit Monteros, Capital for $76,700

E12-3 c. Coe $33,000; Price $65,000

E12-4 Partnership capital increased by $8,000

E12-5 c. Tse, capital $44,000; Graham, capital $108,000; Ott, capital $68,000

E12-6 c. Credit Tse, Capital for $44,000; Graham, Capital for $8,000; Ott, Capital for $8,000

E12-7 1. Echols receives $50,000; 2. Scheffer's equity $60,000

E12-8 b. Debit Augustine, Capital for $46,000; Rye, Capital for $8,400; Bermuda, Capital for $5,600

E12-9 2. Grant gets $20,000, Harris $17,000, and Isbell $8,000

E12-10 Pay Park $26,000, Quade $19,500, Ross $15,500

E12-11 Selling for $140,000: West, Capital $15,500; Young, Capital $43,300; Zeno, Capital $10,200

E12-12 Total assets $283,200; Klatt, capital $90,700; Stover, capital $93,100

P12-1A NCF

P12-2A 2. Total assets $102,100; Ogden, capital $41,500; Croyle, capital $41,500

P12-3A Carter's capital: 2. $60,000 3. $95,000

P12-4A 1. b. Net income to: Lake $79,750 Wood $63,500 Parks $66,750

P12-5A 3. Debit McNut, Capital for $50,000; Black, Capital for $13,548; Tate, Capital for $16,452

P12-6A 1. Pay Parr $19,700, Johnston $35,100, Rake $30,200

P12-7A 2. Capital balances: Vela $27,000 Thomas $16,000 Prago $9,000

P12-1B NCF

P12-2B 2. Total assets $124,740; Dalton, capital $51,220; Sperry, capital $51,220

P12-3B Milano's capital: 2. $50,000 3. $31,250

P12-4B 1. b. Net income to: Trump $33,667 Rivers $28,667 Jetta $23,666

P12-5B 3. Debit Tracy, Capital for $38,000; Mertz, Capital for $1,143; Brucks, Capital for $857

P12-6B 1. Pay Jackson $20,700; Pierce $52,800; Fenner $11,500

P12-7B 2. Capital balances:
Alberts $10,250
Beech $12,750
Sumner $17,000

Case 1 NCF

Case 2 NCF

Chapter 13

Quick Check   1 d; 2 b; 3 a; 4 b; 5 c; 6 a;
7 c; 8 d; 9 c; 10 a

S13-1 NCF

S13-2 NCF

S13-3 NCF

S13-4 Balances: Building $500,000;
Equip. $200,000

S13-5 1. Paid-in Capital in Excess of
Par $3,855

S13-6 1. Total increase in paid-in capital $337 mil.

S13-7 a. Paid-in Capital in Excess—
Common $49,000

S13-8 Total stockholders' equity
$736,000

S13-9 a. Net income $80,000; c. Total
assets $924,000

S13-10 NCF

S13-11 4. Preferred gets $6,000; common gets $3,000

S13-12 Book value per share of common $40.80

S13-13 NCF

S13-14 NCF

S13-15 ROA 13.8%
ROE 26.3%

S13-16 2. Net income $60,000

E13-1 NCF

E13-2 2. Total paid-in capital $59,500

E13-3 2. Total stockholders' equity
$86,000

E13-4 Both plans result in total paid-in capital of $50,000

E13-5 Total stockholders' equity
$206,000

E13-6 Total paid-in capital $400,000

E13-7 Total stockholders' equity
$400,000

E13-8 20X2: Preferred gets $17,000;
common gets $33,000

E13-9 Preferred gets $40,000;
Common gets $110,000

E13-10 Book value per share of common $22.20

E13-11 Book value per share of common $22.11

E13-12 ROA 0.063
ROE 0.111

E13-13 2. Net income $96 mil.
Deferred tax liability $24 mil.

E13-14 d. Close net income of $8 mil.
to Retained Earnings

P13-1A NCF

P13-2A 2. Total stockholders' equity
$266,000

P13-3A 5. Total stockholders' equity
$152,000

P13-4A Total stockholders' equity:
Seville $799,000; Madrid
$399,000

P13-5A 3. Dividends Payable: Preferred
$12 mil.; Common $38 mil.

P13-6A 1. Total assets $387,000; Total
S/E $309,000
2. ROA 0.144; ROE 0.198

P13-7A 1. b. 20X2: Preferred gets
$70,000; Common gets $30,000

P13-8A 6. Book value per share of common $11.80

P13-9A 3. Net income $126,000

P13-1B NCF

P13-2B 2. Total stockholders' equity
$272,000

P13-3B 5. Total stockholders' equity
$263,000

P13-4B Total stockholders' equity:
Yurman $430,000; Northern
$622,900

P13-5B 3. Dividends Payable: Preferred
$100 mil.; Common $400 mil.

P13-6B 1. Total assets $574,000; Total
S/E $419,000
2. ROA 0.104; ROE 0.120

P13-7B 1. b. 20X2: Preferred gets
$3,500; common gets $11,500

P13-8B 5. Book value per share of common $9.74

P13-9B 3. Net income $149,500

Case 1 3. Total stockholders' equity:
Plan 1 $420,000; Plan 2 $400,000

Case 2 NCF

Financial Statement Case 3. At Dec.
31, 2002, Common shares
issued 387,906,000; Common
Stock balance $3,879,000

Chapter 14

Quick Check   1 d; 2 d; 3 a; 4 c; 5 c; 6 b; 7
a; 8 b; 9 a; 10 c

S14-1 Paid-in Capital in Excess of Par
$75,000

S14-2 NCF

S14-3 1. Total stockholders' equity
$590,000

S14-4 Balance sheet reports Treasury
stock $(5,000)

S14-5 NCF

S14-6 NCF

S14-7 NCF

S14-8 Net income $21,000

S14-9 EPS for net income $1.80

S14-10 NCF

S14-11 Comprehensive income $17,000

S14-12 Retained earnings Dec. 31,
20X8 $460,000

S14-13 2. $80,000
3. Sold treasury stock for
$15,000

E14-1 2. Total stockholders' equity
$570,000

E14-2 NCF

E14-3 Total stockholders' equity
$800,000

E14-4 d. Increase stockholders' equity
by $3,000

E14-5 Aug. 22 Credit Paid-in Capital
from Treasury Stock
Transactions for $3,600

E14-6 Total stockholders' equity
$870,000

E14-7 b. Total stockholders' equity
$750,000

E14-8 Net income $42,000

E14-9 EPS $1.40

E14-10 EPS for net income $2.94

E14-11 Retained earnings Dec. 31,
20X3 $470 mil.

E14-12 Retained earnings Dec. 31,
20X7 $460 mil.

E14-13 1. Comprehensive income
$114,000
2. EPS $5.85

E14-14 Total stockholders' equity Dec.
31, 20X7 $1,465,000

E14-15 2. Total stockholders' equity
Dec. 31, 20X5 $17,000,000

P14-1A Dec. 22 Credit Paid-in Capital
from Treasury Stock
Transactions for $1,000

P14-2A 2. Total stockholders' equity
$568,000

P14-3A NCF

P14-4A 3. Total stockholders' equity
$552,700

P14-5A Net income $62,000; EPS for
net income $2.80

P14-6A Retained earnings June 30,
20X4 $277,000; EPS for net
income $4.15

P14-7A EPS for net income $3.10

P14-8A 1. Par value $1.80
2. Price per share $11.00
3. Increase in equity $16,000

P14-1B Nov. 8 Credit Paid-in Capital
from Treasury Stock
Transactions for $3,000

P14-2B 2. Total stockholders' equity
$414,000

P14-3B NCF

P14-4B 3. Total stockholders' equity
$710,680

P14-5B Net income $64,000; EPS for
net income $2.25

P14-6B Retained earnings Dec. 31,
20X3 $444,200; EPS for net
income $1.80

P14-7B 1. EPS for net income $2.25

P14-8B 1. Par value $2
2. Price per share $6.40
3. Increase in equity $28,000

Case 1 NCF

Case 2 NCF

Financial Statement Case 2. Basic EPS
(loss per share) $(0.39)
3. Accumulated Deficit balance—debit of $3,009,710,000

Chapter 15

Quick Check 1 a; 2 c; 3 d; 4 c; 5 b; 6 a;
7 b; 8 c; 9 b; 10 d
S15-1 c. $77,750
d. $110,375
S15-2 a. $4,825
c. $162.50
S15-3 NCF
S15-4 NCF
S15-5 NCF
S15-6 July 1, 2000 Interest Expense
$188
S15-7 July 1, 2000 Interest Expense
$138
S15-8 Dec. 31, 2000 Interest Expense
$188
S15-9 LT liabilities: Bonds payable,
net $4,550
S15-10 2. Bond carrying amount. Mar.
31, 20X4 $546,749
S15-11 2. Bond carrying amount May
31, 20X6 $217,158
S15-12 Interest Expense July 1, 2000
$54.17
S15-13 Gain on retirement of bonds
$6,872
S15-14 2. Paid-in Capital in Excess of
Par $820,000
S15-15 Total current liabilities $26,000;
LT bonds payable, net $344,000
S15-16 EPS: Plan A $5.78; Plan B $3.15
E15-1 c. Dec. 31 Interest Expense
$10,000
E15-2 July 1 Interest Expense $4,050
E15-3 At July 1:
b. Credit Discount for $250
c. Debit Premium for $250
E15-4 NCF
E15-5 1. Bond carrying amount
1-2-X5 $280,995
E15-6 1. Bond carrying amount
3-31-X3 $219,390
E15-7 Bond carrying amount
12-31-X5 $500,000
E15-8 Total cash received $510,000
E15-9 b. Oct. 31 Interest Expense
$10,000
E15-10 Oct. 1 Loss on Retirement of
Bonds $12,750
E15-11 2. Bond carrying amount July
31, 20X9 $691,600
E15-12 2. Oct. 1 Credit Paid-in Capital
in Excess of Par for $144,000
E15-13 NCF
E15-14 EPS: Plan A $7.98; Plan B $4.26
E15-15 4. Interest expense $40,575,000
5. Bond carrying amount Mar.
31, 2001 $295,717
6. Interest expense $40,343,000
E15-16 2. a. $295,725
b. $295,950
P15-1A 2. Interest Expense Jan. 31,
20X4 $4,500; 3. Interest expense
for 20X3 $49,500; Interest
payable $22,500

P15-2A 3. d. Interest Expense Mar. 31,
20X7 $7,900
P15-3A Interest Expense:
Dec. 31, 2009 $14,600
Dec. 31, 2018 $14,600
P15-4A 2. Bond carrying amount Sep.
30, Year 3 $148,095
P15-5A 1. d. Interest Expense Mar. 31,
20X5 $67,500
2. Interest payable at Dec. 31,
20X4 $67,500
P15-6A 3. Convertible bonds payable,
net $569,903
P15-7A Total current liabilities $152,000
Total LT liabilities $383,000
P15-8A NCF
P15-1B 2. Interest Expense, Apr. 30,
20X6 $13,333
3. Interest expense $26,667;
Interest payable $6,667
P15-2B 3. d. Interest Expense Feb. 28,
20X5 $5,633
P15-3B Interest Expense:
Dec. 31, 2005 $38,400
Dec. 31, 2014 $38,400
P15-4B 2. Bond carrying amount Sep.
30, Year 3 $167,263
P15-5B 1. d. Interest Expense May 31,
20X6 $233,333
2. Interest payable at Dec. 31,
20X5 $46,667
P15-6B 3. Convertible bonds payable,
net $423,327
P15-7B Total current liabilities $100,000
Total LT liabilities $289,000
P15-8B NCF
Case 1 EPS: Plan A $6.24; Plan B $5.30;
Plan C $6.00
Case 2 NCF
Financial Statement Case
3. Annual interest $59,366,000

Chapter 15 Appendix

P15A-1 Future value:
Plan A $15,432
Plan B $15,870
P15A-2 Present value:
GE $216,300
Westinghouse $226,800
P15A-3 1. Invest $5,580 today
P15A-4 Present value of bonds:
a. $88,018
b. $78,640
c. $98,975
P15A-5 Interest expense for bonds
issued at:
12% $5,280
14% $5,748
10% $4,731
P15A-6 2. Bond carrying amount
12-31-X2 $380,838
3. Interest expense Dec. 31,
20X2 $15,205

Chapter 16

Quick Check 1 a; 2 c; 3 b; 4 d; 5 c; 6 c;
7 b; 8 a; 9 b; 10 d
S16-1 a. $3,314
b. $38,304
S16-2 NCF
S16-3 2. Jan. 27, 20X5 Loss on Sale
$3,000
S16-4 2. Jan. 16, 20X7 Gain on Sale
$1,750
S16-5 2. Gain on sale $1,000
S16-6 2. Unrealized loss $435
S16-7 1. Gain on Sale $510
S16-8 3. LT Equity-Method
Investment bal. $104 mil.
S16-9 NCF
S16-10 4. Annual interest revenue
$78,000
S16-11 b. Interest Revenue $70,000
c. Interest Revenue $8,000
S16-12 Overall foreign-currency gain
$1,000
E16-1 1. Jan. 14, 20X9 Gain on Sale
$6,000
E16-2 d. Gain on Sale $800
E16-3 Dec. 4 Loss on Sale $550
E16-4 3. LT available-for-sale invest-
ments $205,030; Unrealized
loss $15,500
E16-5 b. Equity-Method Investment
Revenue $156,000
E16-6 Gain on sale $444,000
E16-7 2. LT Equity-Method
Investment bal. $169,000
E16-8 3. LT investment in bonds $27,840
E16-9 Dec. 16 Foreign-Currency Loss
$160
Dec. 30 Foreign-Currency Gain
$2,400
E16-10 1. Cost $274 mil.
2. Loss on sale $15 mil.
P16-1A 1. Dec. 31 Loss on Trading
Investment $3,500
P16-2A 3. LT available-for-sale invest-
ments $26,800; LT equity-
method investments $431,500
P16-3A LT Equity-Method Investment
bal. $832,000; Unrealized gain
$1,100
P16-4A 2. LT investment in bonds
$409,600
P16-5A Investment carrying amount
12-31-X6 $488,051
P16-6A Income statement reports
Foreign-currency loss, net $2,400
P16-1B 1. Dec. 31 Loss on Trading
Investment $4,500
P16-2B 3. LT available-for-sale invest-
ment $44,100; LT equity-
method investments $724,000
P16-3B LT Equity-Method Investment
bal. $920,000; Unrealized loss
$2,500
P16-4B 2. LT investment in bonds
$744,000

P16-5B Investment carrying amount
12-31-X7 $388,355
P16-6B Income statement reports
Foreign-currency loss, net $600
Case 1 NCF
Case 2 NCF
Financial Statement Case 1.a. Market
value $562,715,000

Chapter 17

Quick Check 1 b; 2 d; 3 c; 4 a; 5 d; 6 c;
7 a; 8 a; 9 d; 10 b
S17-1 NCF
S17-2 NCF
S17-3 NCF
S17-4 Net cash from operating
$48,000
S17-5 Net cash from operating
$40,000
S17-6 Net cash from operating
$40,000; Net increase in cash
$39,000
S17-7 Acquisitions of plant assets
$100,000
S17-8 a. $2,000 c. $84,000
b. $3,000
S17-9 Net cash from operating
$180,000; Cash balance ending
$94,000
S17-10 Net cash from operating
$50,000
S17-11 Net cash from operating
$50,000; Net increase in cash
$54,000
S17-12 a. $704,000
b. $331,000
E17-1 NCF
E17-2 NCF
E17-3 NCF
E17-4 Net cash used for operating
$(8,000)
E17-5 Net cash from operating $79,000
E17-6 1. Net cash from operating
$80,000; investing ($77,000);
financing $4,000
E17-7 a. $34,000
b. $6,000
E17-8 NCF
E17-9 NCF
E17-10 Net cash used for operating
$(8,000)
E17-11 NCF
E17-12 Net cash from operating
$80,000; investing ($77,000);
financing $4,000
E17-13 a. $85,000
b. $89,000
E17-14 a. $24,440 mil.
b. $18,516 mil.
c. $4,793 mil.
d. $1,186 mil.
e. $14 mil.
f. $230 mil.
g. $143 mil.

P17-1A NCF
P17-2A 1. Net income $35,000
2. Total assets $588,000
3. Net cash used for operating
$(71,000); Cash bal., Dec. 31,
20X8 $268,000
P17-3A Net cash from operating
$87,000; investing $(67,000);
financing $43,000; Total non-
cash investing and financing
$65,000
P17-4A 1. Net cash from operating
$96,900; investing $(125,700);
financing $31,000
P17-5A 1. Net cash from operating
$69,100; investing $(37,000);
financing $(30,600)
P17-6A Net cash from operating
$115,700; investing $(37,000);
financing $(70,800)
P17-7A 1. Net income $35,000; 2. Total
assets $588,000; 3. Net cash
used for operating $(71,000);
Cash balance Dec. 31, 20X8
$268,000
P17-8A 1. Net cash from operating
$69,100; investing $(37,100);
financing $(30,600)
P17-9A Net cash from operating
$67,800; investing $(10,200);
financing $(47,600)
P17-1B NCF
P17-2B 1. Net income $80,000 2. Total
assets $345,000 3. Net cash
from operating $85,000; Cash
bal., Dec. 31, 20X6 $195,000
P17-3B Net cash from operating
$80,000; investing $(69,000);
financing $11,000; Total non-
cash investing and financing
$118,000
P17-4B 1. Net cash from operating
$49,000; investing $(179,000);
financing $120,000
P17-5B 1. Net cash from operating
$79,800; investing $(47,600);
financing $(29,900)
P17-6B Net cash from operating
$(30,000); investing $(40,300);
financing $91,700
P17-7B 1. Net income $80,000 2. Total
assets $345,000 3. Net cash
from operating $85,000; Cash
bal., Dec. 31, 20X6 $195,000
P17-8B 1. Net cash from operating
$79,800; investing $(47,600);
financing $(29,900)
P17-9B Net cash from operating
$77,200; investing $(51,500);
financing $(30,300)
Case 1 1. Net cash from operating
$140,000; investing $(141,000);
financing $(37,000)
Case 2 NCF

Financial Statement Case 3. a.
Collections $3,888,267,000
b. Payments $2,825,641,000

Chapter 17 Appendix

P17A-1 Column totals:
Dec. 31, 20X7 $255,400
Dec. 31, 20X8 $287,800
17A-2 Column totals:
Dec. 31, 20X7 $255,400
Dec. 31, 20X8 $287,800

Chapter 18

Quick Check 1 a; 2 b; 3 d; 4 c; 5 b; 6 c;
7 c; 8 a; 9 d; 10 d
S18-1 2002 Gross profit increase 5.0%
S18-2 1. Trend % for 2002 revenue
113%
S18-3 20X6 Cash 20.9% of total assets
S18-4 Net income % of sales: Nike
6.2%; Home Depot 4.8%
S18-5 1. Current ratio for 2002 1.21
S18-6 a. 3.9 times
b. 70 days
S18-7 1. Debt ratio 0.64
S18-8 a. 11.4% c. 22.9%
b. 9.4%
S18-9 1. $0.48
2. 56 times
S18-10 d. $698 mil.
S18-11 a. $631 mil.
c. $1,581 mil.
f. $6,315 mil.
S18-12 1. EVA® $1,858 mil.
E18-1 2006 Increase in working capi-
tal 14.3%
E18-2 Total revenue increased 15.3%;
Net income increased 58.8%
E18-3 Trend % for Year 5:
Total revenue 136%
Net income 155%
E18-4 Total current assets 13.0%;
Long-term debt 33.3%
E18-5 % for 2005: COGS 47.0%; Net
income 18.8%
E18-6 a. 1.41 c. 4.01 times
b. 0.70 d. 55 days
E18-7 Ratios for 20X4:
a. 1.56 c. 0.59
b. 0.69 d. 3.44 times
E18-8 Ratios for 20X6:
a. 0.103 c. 0.162
b. 0.137 d. $0.75
E18-9 Ratios for 20X4:
a. 20 c. $4.75
b. 0.022
E18-10 EVA®: Oracle $1,598 mil.; Wells
Fargo −$986 mil.
E18-11 Total assets $19,565 mil.;
Current liabilities $6,752 mil.

P18-1A 1. Trend % for 20X8: Net sales 127%; Net income 161%; Total assets 145%
2. Return on sales for 20X8 0.081

P18-2A 1. Gross profit 31.9%; Net income 9.2%; Current assets 77.1%; Stockholders' equity 39.4%

P18-3A 2. a. Current ratio 2.23; Debt ratio 0.49; EPS no effect

P18-4A 1. Ratios for 20X6:
a. 2.10   d. 0.253
b. 1.18   e. $4.47
c. 2.81   f. 8.2

P18-5A 1. Blues ratios:
a. 0.66   d. 0.68
b. 2.30   e. $0.37
c. 94 days   f. 21.6
2. Blues EVA® $25,000

P18-6A NCF

P18-1B 1. Trend % for 2008: Net revenues 118%; Net income 106%; Common stockholders' equity 124%
2. ROE for 2008 0.142

P18-2B 1. Gross profit 36.4%; Net income 14.7%; Current assets 77.8%; Stockholders' equity 40.2%

P18-3B 2. a. Current ratio 1.35; Debt ratio 0.61; EPS No effect

P18-4B 1. Ratios for 20X9:
a. 1.80   d. 0.357
b. 1.48   e. $5.00
c. 8.82   f. 10.6

P18-5B 1. Caremark ratios:
a. 0.78   d. 0.41
b. 2.32   e. $4.80
c. 40 days   f. 10.6
2. Caremark EVA® $29,000

P18-6B NCF
Case 1 NCF
Case 2 NCF
Financial Statement Case NCF

Chapter 19

Quick Check   1 d; 2 a; 3 b; 4 b; 5 d; 6 c; 7 d; 8 a; 9 a; 10 c
S19-1 NCF
S19-2 NCF
S19-3 NCF
S19-4 NCF
S19-5 NCF
S19-6 CGS $41,000
S19-7 CGM $35,000
S19-8 Total MOH $15,275
S19-9 DM used $19,700
S19-10 NCF
S19-11 NCF
S19-12 Total expected benefits $199 million
S19-13 NCF
S19-14 NCF

E19-1 NCF
E19-2 Total inventoriable product costs $142
E19-3 Total inventoriable product costs $33,000
E19-4 NCF
E19-5 Total current assets $214,000
E19-6 CGM $213,000
E19-7 NI $49,000
E19-8 a. CGS $15,000
b. Beg. Materials inv. $2,000
c. End. FG inv. $5,100
E19-9 NCF
E19-10 Expected benefits exceed costs by $84,500
E19-11 NCF
P19-1A Total MOH $4,775
Total inventoriable product costs $34,575
P19-2A Part One: Hannah's Pets Op. Inc. $13,500
Part Two: Best Friends Manufacturing CGM $67,655; Op. Inc. $35,545
Part Three: Best Friends' Manufacturing total inventories $15,695
P19-3A Direct labor $71,000; CGM $162,000; Op. Inc. $100,000
P19-4A *Req 1:* Total benefits if project succeeds $830,000
Req 2: Expected value of the benefits exceed cost by $109,000
P19-5A *Req 2:* Expected value of the benefits falls short of costs by $57,000
P19-6A Present value of benefits exceeds costs by $227,000
P19-7A *Req 1:* Present value of expected benefits $1,102,600
Req 2: Expected value of benefits falls short of costs by $27,400
P19-8A NCF
P19-1B Total MOH $415
Total inventoriable product costs $12,145
P19-2B Part One: Precious Memories Op. Inc. $33,750
Part Two: Forever Manufacturing CGM $72,750; Op. Inc. $44,000
Part Three: Forever Manufacturing total inventories $11,500
P19-3B Manufacturing overhead $40,000; Beg. FG inv. $124,000
P19-4B *Req 1:* Total benefits if project succeeds $470,500
Req 2: Expected value of the benefits exceeds cost by $78,850
P19-5B NCF
P19-6B Present value of benefits exceeds costs by $3,200

P19-7B *Req 1:* Expected value of benefits from additional business $49,560
Req 2: Present value of expected benefits exceeds cost by $9,560
P19-8B NCF
Case 1 End. Materials inv $143,000; End. WIP inv. $239,000; End FG inv. $150,000
Case 2 NCF
Ethical Issue NCF
Financial Statement Case NCF
Team Project NCF

Chapter 20

Quick Check   1 b; 2 d; 3 c; 4 d; 5 a; 6 a; 7 c; 8 b; 9 d; 10 a
S20-1 NCF
S20-2 NCF
S20-3 Ending Materials Inv., $43,500
S20-4 DM, $200
S20-5 NCF
S20-6 Total MOH, $65,000
S20-7 Total cost, $1,180
S20-8 Indirect materials used, $2,000
S20-9 MOH is $1,000 underallocated
S20-10 MOH is $25,000 underallocated
S20-11 NCF
S20-12 DL for Client 367, $770
S20-13 Indirect cost for Client 367, $350
E20-1 NCF
E20-2 WIP Inv., $8,400
E20-3 MOH allocated, $21,000
E20-4 Item f is closing underallocated MOH
E20-5 1. End. WIP Inv., $11,000
4. GP on G-65, $8,000
E20-6 2. MOH allocated, $102,240
3. Underallocated MOH, $2,360
E20-7 2. MOH allocated, $440,000
3. Underallocated MOH, $70,000
E20-8 1. Overallocated MOH, $10,000
3. Adjusted CGS, $590,000
E20-9 1. b. Indirect cost allocation rate, 70%
2. Total predicted cost, $58,718
E20-10 1. MH used, 20,250
2. Underallocated overhead, $243,000
P20-1A 1. c. March CGS, $3,000
April CGS, $2,900
4. GP for Job 5, $900
P20-2A 2. End. WIP Inv., $102,400
FG Inv., $92,820
5. GP for Chalet 13, $34,220
P20-3A 1. MOH allocated, $1,134
Total job cost, $4,504
P20-4A 1. PMOHR, $25/MH
3. Underallocated MOH, $22,000

P20-5A 2. End. WIP Inv., $99,090
FG Inv., $60,550
4. CGM, $63,200

P20-6A 2. GoVacation.com, $74,890
3. Port Armour, $5,950

P20-1B 1. c. Nov. CGS, $1,400
Dec. CGS, $3,650
2. Transferred to FG in Nov., $3,300
Transferred to FG in Dec., $3,850

P20-2B 2. End. WIP Inv., $272,900
FG Inv., $117,620
5. GP for House 304, $51,340

P20-3B 1. MOH allocated, $648
Total job cost, $2,373

P20-4B 1. PMOHR, $7/MH
3. Underallocated MOH, $49,750

P20-5B 2. End. WIP Inv., $38,080
FG Inv., $21,280
4. CGM, $49,160

P20-6B 2. Organic Foods, $128,500
3. SunNow.com, $9,575

Case 1 NCF
Case 2 NCF
Ethical Issue NCF
Team Project 1. Delta's profit per flight 1247, $1,004.79
2. JetBlue's profit per flight 53, $2,659.55

Chapter 21

Quick Check 1 b; 2 c; 3 d; 4 a; 5 c; 6 a; 7 d; 8 d; 9 b; 10 d

S21-1 NCF
S21-2 2. Cost per liter, $0.84
S21-3 2. EU of DM, 200,000
EU of CC, 192,000
S21-4 EU of DM, 50,000
EU of CC, 43,000
S21-5 CC/EU, $1.90
S21-6 DM/EU, $0.60; CC/EU, $0.25
S21-7 2. End. WIP Inv., $32,000
S21-8 End. WIP Inv., $32,000
S21-9 2. EU of TI costs, 168,000
EU of DM, 154,000
EU of CC, 163,800
S21-10 TI cost/EU, $0.82; DM/EU, $0.20; CC/EU, $0.35
S21-11 End. WIP Inv., $14,910
S21-12 End. WIP Inv., $14,910
E21-1 NCF
E21-2 NCF
E21-3 2. EU of DM, 8,000
3. End. WIP Inv., $1,440
E21-4 2. End. WIP Inv., $1,440
3. Avg. Cost/gal. CTO, $1.00
E21-5 1. EU of DM 18,000
2. CC/EU, $1.40
3. End. WIP Inv., $10,610
E21-6 2. EU of CC, 7,710
3. End. WIP Inv., $3,146.50
E21-7 3. Avg. Cost/gal. CTO, $2.35

E21-8 Costs transferred out, $392,400
E21-9 2. Mixing Dep't. EU of TI costs, 90,000
Heating Dep't. EU of TI costs, 86,000
E21-10 2. EU of TI, 35,000
3. End. WIP Inv., $75,996
P21-1A 2. EU of DM, 20,400
CC/EU, $0.25
3b. End. WIP Inv., $1,560
P21-2A 2. EU of CC, 11,700
CC/EU, $25
3b. End. WIP Inv., $172,500
P21-3A 2. EU of CC, 14,160
3. CC/EU, $1
3b. End. WIP Inv., $3,570
P21-4A 2. EU of CC, 2,900
TI cost/EU, $15; CC/EU, $24
3. Costs transferred out, $110,000
P21-5A 2. EU of CC, 19,800
3. TI cost/EU, $0.14
3b. End. WIP Inv., $3,078
P21-1B 2. EU of CC, 90,560
CC/EU, $3.05
3b. End. WIP Inv., $131,688
P21-2B 2. EU of CC, 4,600
CC/EU, $0.90
3b. End. WIP Inv., $210
P21-3B 2. EU of CC, 2,370
3. CC/EU, $0.80
3b. End. WIP Inv., $1,281
P21-4B 2. EU of CC, 608
TI cost/EU, $40; CC/EU, $93
3. Costs transferred out, $77,000
P21-5B 2. EU of CC, 6,000
3. TI cost/EU, $85
3. b. End. WIP Inv., $447,000
Case 3. Op. Inc., $1,800
5. Selling price per box, $12.93
Ethical Issue NCF
Team Project 1. Max. TI cost/lb., $0.23
2. Cutting Dep't. cost/lb., $0.17

Chapter 21 Appendix

S21A-1 2. EU of TI, 160,000
EU of CC, 160,600
S21A-2 DM/EU, $0.20
S21A-3 End. WIP Inv., $15,330
E21A-1 1a. 40%, 25%
2. Mixing Dep't. EU of DM 75,000
Cooking Dep't. EU of CC 76,700
E21A-2 2. EU of CC, 25,900
3. b. End. WIP Inv., $79,200
P21A-1 2. EU of DM, 3,100
DM/EU, $8; CC/EU, $16
3. Costs transferred out, $123,140
P21A-2 2. EU of CC, 17,700
CC/EU, $0.11
3b. End. WIP Inv., $3,648
P21A-3 2. EU of DM, 2,200
TI cost/EU, $12; DM/EU, $11
3. Costs transferred out, $116,300

Chapter 22

Quick Check 1 b; 2 d; 3 a; 4 b; 5 b; 6 a; 7 b; 8 a; 9 a; 10 c

S22-1 NCF
S22-2 1c. Total cost, $33
S22-3 a. BEP, 6,875 tickets
S22-4 1. CM ratio, 0.66667
S22-5 7,875 tickets
S22-6 NCF
S22-7 B is the total expense line
S22-8 1. 9,167 tickets
2. 6,111 tickets
S22-9 1. BEP, 5,000 tickets
S22-10 a. Margin of safety, 125 tickets
c. Margin of safety, 1.79%
S22-11 b. Margin of safety, $10,500
S22-12 VC Op. Inc., $106,500
S22-13 1. AC Op. Inc., $101,500
S22-14 NCF
E22-1 NCF
E22-2 Op. Loss when sales are $250,000 = $20,000
BEP, $283,333
E22-3 1. CM ratio, 50%
2. BEP, 100,000 packages
E22-4 1. BEP, $12,000
2. Sales required to earn target income, $24,500
E22-5 2. Op. Loss when sales are $500,000 = $240,000
E22-6 3. BEP, 500 students, $50,000
E22-7 2. BEP, 1,200,000 tickets
E22-8 1. Margin of safety, $40,000
E22-9 1. AC Op. Inc., $675,000
VC Op. Inc., $525,000
3. Increase in Op. Inc., $75,000
P22-1A NCF
P22-2A CM ratio:
Q 0.70
S 0.60
T 0.711
P22-3A 1. VE per show, $15,200
2. BEP, 38 shows
3. Target shows, 96 shows
P22-4A 1. BEP, 150,000 cartons
2. Target sales, $2,000,000
3. Op. Inc., $2,070,000
4. BEP, $2,535,750
P22-5A 1. BEP, 24 trades
2. Target sales, $14,400
4. BEP, 32 trades
P22-6A 1. AC product cost/meal
Jan., $4.50
Feb., $4.70
2. a. AC Op. Inc.
Jan., $900
Feb., $1,040
P22-1B NCF
P22-2B A CM ratio, 0.550
B CM per unit, $3.75
C CM ratio, 0.491
P22-3B 1. VE per show, $27,200
2. BEP, 9 shows
3. Target shows, 139 shows

P22-4B 1. BEP, 87,000 flags
2. Target sales, $1,094,000
3. Op. Loss, $132,600
4. BEP, 108,576 flags

P22-5B 1. BEP, 40 trades
2. Target sales, $42,000
4. BEP, 50 trades

P22-6B 1. AC product cost/game
Oct., $19
Nov., $20
2. a. AC Op. Inc.
Oct., $17,000
Nov., $17,900

Case 1 BEP, 4,800 meals
To earn target Op. Inc., 7,500 meals

Case 2 NCF

Ethical Issue NCF

Financial Statement Case
3. 2002 CM, $899,769
4. 2002 CM ratio, 0.22878
5. 2002 BEP, $3,652,614

Team Project 1. Op. Loss in 20X6, $1.5 million
2. Adopting ad campaign will increase Op. Inc. by $1.5 million

Chapter 22 Appendix

S22A-1 WA CM/unit, $66.91
S22A-2 a. 3,737 total tickets
E22A-1 BEP, 264 standard and 176 chrome
E22A-2 WA CM/unit, $125;
CM per Classic, $300
P22A-1 1. BEP, 12,000 small and 4,000 large
3. Op. Inc., $31,750

Chapter 23

Quick Check 1 d; 2 a; 3 a; 4 d; 5 b; 6 c; 7 a; 8 c; 9 d; 10 b
S23-1 NCF
S23-2 NCF
S23-3 Feb. sales, $770,000
S23-4 Jan. purchases, $490,750
Feb. purchases, $585,650
S23-5 June cash sales, $24,000
S23-6 May purchases, $48,000
S23-7 May cash collections, $71,000
S23-8 May cash payments for purchases, $47,600
S23-9 January cash collections, $548,330
S23-10 Grippers must borrow $34,070
S23-11 NCF
S23-12 NCF
S23-13 NCF
S23-14 NCF

E23-1 NI this year, $220,000
E23-2 Purchases, qtr. ended June 30, $88,500
Purchases, qtr. ended Sept. 30, $80,700
E23-3 Qtr. 2 NI, $856,960
Qtr. 3 NI, $950,546
E23-4 b. Sept. cash receipts from customers, $106,830
E23-5 1. Nov. borrowing, $1,000
E23-6 Feb. borrowing, $11,100
March interest paid, $74
E23-7 Total assets, $30,280
Owners' Equity, $25,980
E23-8 NCF
E23-9 Total cell phone Op. Inc. Var., $45,000 F
P23-1A May CGS, $15,500
May NI, $14,300
June NI, $9,500
P23-2A 1a. May cash collections, $42,660
b. May cash payments for purchases, $18,125
c. May cash payments for op. expenses, $8,708
2. May ending cash balance, $26,827
June ending cash balance, $39,991
P23-3A 1. Ending cash balance, $55,000
Total Assets, $143,900
Owners' Equity, $115,600
2. Net increase in cash, $14,400
3. Cash available, $76,800
P23-4A 1. Ending cash balance, $29,500
Total Assets, $131,900
Owners' Equity, $103,600
P23-5A NCF
P23-6A 1. Dayton Op. Inc. Var., $6,100U
Other Ohio stores Op. Inc. Var., $4,400 F
Companywide Op. Inc. Var., $86,000 U
P23-1B Aug. CGS, $120,000
Aug. NI, $26,000
Sept. NI, $28,000
P23-2B 1a. Aug. cash collections, $199,000
b. Aug. cash payments for purchases, $124,720
c. Aug. cash payments for op. expenses, $40,090
2. Aug. ending cash balance, $56,190
Sept. ending cash balance, $97,250
P23-3B 1. Ending cash balance, $45,200
Total Assets, $172,700
Owners' Equity, $145,600
2. Net decrease in cash, $5,000
P23-4B 1. Ending cash balance, $31,200
Total Assets, $162,700
Owners' Equity, $135,600
P23-5B NCF

P23-6B 1. Store No. 23 Op. Inc. Var., $2,000 F
Other Dallas stores Op. Inc. Var., $9,000 F
Texas Op. Inc. Var., $44,400 F
Case 1 NCF
Case 2 1. NI cotton mats, $235
NI linen mats, $225
Ethical Issue NCF
Financial Statement Case
3. Company-wide total Op. Inc. Var., $225,104 F
North American Books, Music, DVD/Video Op. Inc. Var., $54,610 F
Team Project NCF

Chapter 23 Appendix

S23A-1 NCF
S23A-2 Software Dep't., $200,000
E23A-1 Marketing cost allocated to Welding, $4,200
Total indirect costs allocated to Priming, $25,400
E23A-2 1. Chrome Op. Inc., $75,800
P23-A1 1. Housekeeping cost, $24/room
Total Club expense, $99,480
2. Club cost $184.22/room
Regular cost $92.57/room

Chapter 24

Quick Check 1 a; 2 a; 3 d; 4 e; 5 b; 6 b; 7 d; 8 c; 9 d; 10 c
S24-1 1. 4-Pool Op. Loss, $4,000
S24-2 2. Actual expenses, $80,000
4. FB Var., $12,000F
S24-3 Total FB Var., $12,000F; Total SVV, $4,000F
S24-4 1. Relevant range, 0–11 pools
S24-5 NCF
S24-6 NCF
S24-7 DM Eff. Var., $2,800U
S24-8 DM Eff. Var. for onion, $0.70U
S24-9 DL Price Var., $17,500F
S24-10 NCF
S24-11 VMOHR = $7/DLH
S24-12 FB Var., $4,000U; PVV, $12,000F
S24-13 NCF
S24-14 NCF
S24-15 CGS, $364,000
S24-16 Op. Inc., $85,500
E24-1 Op. Inc. at 70,000 units, $170,000
E24-2 NCF
E24-3 Total FB Var., $9,000U;
Static Budget Op. Inc., $20,000
E24-4 Sales Revenue FB Var., $210,000F; Static Budget Op. Inc., $441,000
E24-5 Actual price, $10.50/lb.
E24-6 DM Price Var., $72,500F;
DL Eff. Var., $6,500F
E24-7 NCF
E24-8 NCF

E24-9 MOH FB Var., $2,200U; PVV, $3,000F

E24-10 GP, $228,500

P24-1A 1. 60,000 units: SR, $180,000; CGS, $69,000; Op. Inc., $20,700

P24-2A 1. Total Exp. FB Var., $4,000U; Total Exp. SVV, $7,550U

P24-3A 1. FB Gross Profit, $4,204,000
2. DM Price Var., $42,840F; DM Eff. Var., $58,000F; MOH FB Var., $28,220U
3. Total FB Var., $68,120F

P24-4A 1. DL hrs. worked, 5,860 hrs.
2. DL Price Var., $2,930F

P24-5A 1. DL Price Var., $4,896U; DL Eff. Var., $25,568F
3. PVV, $1,760U

P24-6A 1. DL Price Var., $920F
2. MOH FB Var., $6,400F
3. Total Man. Cost Variances, $16,890F

P24-1B 1. 11,000 units: SR, $253,000; CGS, $110,000; Op. Inc., $47,625

P24-2B 1. Total Exp. FB Var., $4,225U; Total Exp. SVV, $40,675U

P24-3B 1. FB Gross Profit, $260,068
2. DM Price Var., $1,230F; DM Eff. Var., $2,403U; MOH FB Var., $15,960U
3. Total FB Var., $16,773U

P24-4B 1. DL hrs. worked, 3,900 hrs.
2. DL Price Var., $1,950U

P24-5B 1. DL Price Var., $4,200U; DL Eff. Var., $2,628U
3. PVV, $1,134F

P24-6B 1. DL Price Var., $330U
2. MOH FB Var., $11,540U
3. Total Man. Cost Variances, $15,870U

Case 1 Total FB Var., $23,025 F Total SVV, $133,600U

Case 2 DL Eff. Var., $96U

Ethical Issue NCF

Team Project NCF

Chapter 25

Quick Check 1 c; 2 a; 3 a; 4 b; 5 d; 6 c; 7 d; 8 c; 9 a; 10 c

S25-1 2. Aldehyde, $3,360

S25-2 1. Setup cost/lb. of PH, $44.80

S25-3 1. MOH/lb. of PH, $138.80
2. GP/lb. of aldehyde, $1.57

S25-4 2. TC of Webb, $49,120
3. Op. Inc. of Greg, $3,380

S25-5 NCF

S25-6 NCF

S25-7 Doc. Prep., $32/page

S25-8 1. TC of Webb, $45,800
2. Op. Loss of Greg, $16,700

S25-9 NCF

S25-10 NCF

S25-11 NCF

S25-12 NCF

S25-13 CC are $660 underallocated

S25-14 NCF

S25-15 2. Net advantage to implementing quality program, $100,000

E25-1 1. Mat. Handling, $4/part
2. Ind. mfg. cost/wheel, $143.40

E25-2 1. Total budgeted indirect mfg. costs, $461,500
2. ABC indirect cost/Deluxe wheel, $296
3. Original system indirect cost/Deluxe wheel, $276.90

E25-3 1. ABC GP for Standard, $59.50
2. Original system GP for Standard, $40.40

E25-4 Total cost of Deluxe, $347

E25-5 NCF

E25-6 2. EB RIP, $480,000
3. CC, $720,000 overallocated

E25-7 1. CC, $1,020,000 underallocated
2. EB FG, $324,000

E25-8 NCF

E25-9 NCF

E25-10 2. Net advantage to undertaking TQM, $10,000

E25-11 2. Job 409 Lathe turns, 20,000

P25-1A Mfg. product cost, $92.70

P25-2A 1. Total mfg. cost of Standard, $288,000
2. Full product cost of Standard, $78/unit
4. Sale price, $120

P25-3A 2. X-Secure indirect cost, $199,600/unit
3. X-Page indirect cost, $33.33/unit

P25-4A 1. Total cost, $25.20/unit
3. Indirect cost, $13.41/unit

P25-5A 2. CC, $64,000 overallocated
3. EB RIP, $2,000

P25-6A 2. Net benefit, $51,000

P25-1B Mfg. product cost, $147.80

P25-2B 1. Total mfg. cost of Standard, $146,700
2. Full product cost of Standard, $72.90/unit
4. Sale price, $68.50

P25-3B 2. Commercial indirect cost, $132.80/unit
3. Travel pack indirect cost, $2.40/unit

P25-4B 1. Total cost, $6.21/unit
3. Indirect cost, $2.82/unit

P25-5B 2. CC, $79,000 overallocated
3. EB RIP, $1,000

P25-6B 2. Net benefit, $5,000

Case 1 1. Original system cost/unit of Job A, $5,460
2. ABC cost/unit of Job A, $5,072.50

Case 2 Savings required, $620

Ethical Issue NCF

Financial Statement Case NCF

Team Project 2. Ind. cost allocation rate, $16.125/DLH; Total cost/lb. of Headless shrimp, $3.96125
3. Scheduling, $100/batch; Chilling, $0.02/lb.; Total indirect cost/lb. of Headless shrimp, $0.995; Total cost/lb. of Headless shrimp, $4.795

Chapter 26

Quick Check 1 b; 2 c; 3 d; 4 d; 5 a; 6 d; 7 a; 8 c; 9 b; 10 a

S26-1 NCF

S26-2 Expected decrease in Op. Inc., $1,000

S26-3 NCF

S26-4 NCF

S26-5 Regular CM/unit, $125

S26-6 Advantage to outsourcing, $13,500

S26-7 NCF

S26-8 Advantage to processing further, $2,000

S26-9 Average annual net cash inflow, $2,880,000

S26-10 Payback period, 4.51 years

S26-11 ARR, 24%

S26-12 NPV, $3,272,000

S26-13 IRR, over 16%

S26-14 NCF

E26-1 1. Increase in Op. Inc., $2,500
2. Decrease in Op. Inc., $2,500

E26-2 1. Increase in Op. Inc., $320,000

E26-3 Decrease in Op. Inc., $40,000

E26-4 Decrease in Op. Inc., $10,000

E26-5 Total CM of moderately priced line, $39,000

E26-6 Advantage to making switch, $1.50/unit

E26-7 Advantage to buying and using facilities for other product, $100,000

E26-8 Advantage to processing further, $100

E26-9 Payback period, 4 years

E26-10 ARR Veras, 37%

E26-11 NPV Project B, $(7,040)

E26-12 IRR Project A, between 14% and 16%

E26-13 1. 12 oz. cans of Coca-Cola, CM/linear foot, $7.50
2. 360 12 oz. cans of Coca-Cola

P26-1A 1. Increase in Op. Inc., $35,000

P26-2A 1. Decrease in Op. Inc., $104,000
2b. Operating loss, $52,000

P26-3A 2. Deluxe: CM, $1,440 / MH; Total CM at capacity, $6,480,000

P26-4A 1. Advantage to making, $2,460
2. Net cost to buy and make another product, $31,060

P26-5A 1. Cost of further processing, $56,400
3. Advantage to selling as is, $19,920
P26-6A 1. ARR, 31.2%; NPV, $733,360
P26-7A 1. Plan B's ARR, 7.8% Plan B's NPV, $(959,000)
3. IRR, 12%–14%
P26-1B 1. Increase in Op. Inc., $2,500
P26-2B 1. Decrease in Op. Inc., $22,500
2b. Op. Inc. $193,000
P26-3B 2. Spas: CM, $1.95/sq. ft.; Total CM at capacity, $15,600
P26-4B 1. Advantage to making, $26,600
2. Net cost to buy and make snack bars, $846,600

P26-5B 1. Cost of further processing, $120,000
3. Advantage to process further, $30,000
P26-6B 1. ARR, 6%; NPV, $(1,052,125)
P26-7B 1. Plan A's ARR, 12% Plan A's NPV, $(835,360)
3. IRR, 14%–16%
Case 1 1. Total cost/mailbox per month, $64
2. Total advantage to outsourcing, $21,850
3. Advantage to insourcing extra services, $1,150

Case 2 1. Total earnings if he chooses the meat packing plant, $9,450
Ethical Issue Advantage to outsourcing, $18,000/year
Financial Statement Case 2. Annual net cash inflow, $13,439,602
3.b. ARR, 18.6%
Team Project 2. Annual cash inflow advantage to insourcing, $7,972,000
3.b. ARR, 22.1%
c. NPV, $3,964,024

Glossary

Absorption Costing. The costing method that assigns both variable and fixed manufacturing costs to products.

Accelerated Depreciation Method. A depreciation method that writes off more of the asset's cost near the start of its useful life than the straight-line method does.

Account. The detailed record of the changes in a particular asset, liability, or owner's equity during a period. The basic summary device of accounting.

Account Payable. A liability backed by the general reputation and credit standing of the debtor.

Account Receivable. A promise to receive cash from customers to whom the business has sold goods or for whom the business has performed services.

Accounting. The information system that measures business activities, processes that information into reports, and communicates the results to decision makers.

Accounting Cycle. Process by which companies produce their financial statements for a specific period.

Accounting Equation. The basic tool of accounting, measuring the resources of the business and the claims to those resources: Assets = Liabilities + Owner's Equity.

Accounting Information System. The combination of personnel, records, and procedures that a business uses to provide financial data.

Accounting Rate of Return. A measure of profitability computed by dividing the average annual operating income from an asset by the average amount invested in the asset.

Accounts Receivable Turnover. Measures a company's ability to collect cash from credit customers. To compute accounts receivable turnover, divide net credit sales by average net accounts receivable.

Accrual Accounting. Accounting that records the impact of a business event as it occurs, regardless of whether the transaction affected cash.

Accrued Expense. An expense that the business has not yet paid. Also called **accrued liability**.

Accrued Revenue. A revenue that has been earned but not yet collected in cash.

Accumulated Depreciation. The cumulative sum of all depreciation expense recorded for an asset.

Acid-Test Ratio. Ratio of the sum of cash plus short-term investments plus net current receivables, to total current liabilities.

Tells whether the entity could pay all its current liabilities if they came due immediately. Also called the **quick ratio**.

Activity-Based Costing (ABC). Focuses on *activities* as the fundamental cost objects. The costs of those activities become building blocks for compiling the indirect costs of products, services, and customers.

Activity-Based Management. Using activity-based cost information to make decisions that increase profits while satisfying customers' needs.

Additional Paid-In Capital. The paid-in capital in excess of par, common plus other accounts combined for reporting on the balance sheet.

Adjusted Trial Balance. A list of all the accounts with their adjusted balances.

Adjusting Entry. Entry made at the end of the period to assign revenues to the period in which they are earned and expenses to the period in which they are incurred. Adjusting entries help measure the period's income and bring the related asset and liability accounts to correct balances for the financial statements.

Aging-of-Accounts Method. A way to estimate bad debts by analyzing individual accounts receivable according to the length of time they have been receivable from the customer. Also called the **balance-sheet approach**.

Allocation base. A common denominator that links indirect costs to cost objects. Ideally, the allocation base is the primary cost driver of the indirect cost.

Allowance for Uncollectible Accounts. A contra account, related to accounts receivable, that holds the estimated amount of collection losses. Also called **Allowance for Doubtful Accounts**.

Allowance Method. A method of recording collection losses on the basis of estimates, instead of waiting to see which customers the company will not collect from.

Amortization. Systematic reduction of the asset's carrying value on the books. Expense that applies to intangibles in the same way depreciation applies to plant assets and depletion to natural resources.

Annuity. A stream of equal periodic cash flows.

Appraisal Costs. Costs incurred to *detect* poor-quality goods or services.

Appropriation of Retained Earnings. Restriction of retained earnings that is recorded by a formal journal entry.

Asset. An economic resource that is expected to be of benefit in the future.

Audit. An examination of a company's financial statements and the accounting system.

Authorization of Stock. Provision in a corporate charter that gives the state's permission for the corporation to issue—that is, to sell—a certain number of shares of stock.

Available-for-Sale Investments. All less-than-20% investments other than trading securities.

Average-Cost Method. Inventory costing method based on the average cost of inventory during the period. Average cost is determined by dividing the cost of goods available for sale by the number of units available.

Balance Sheet. An entity's assets, liabilities, and owner's equity as of a specific date. Also called the **statement of financial position**.

Bank Collection. Collection of money by the bank on behalf of a depositor.

Bank Reconciliation. Document explaining the reasons for the difference between a depositor's cash records and the depositor's cash balance in its bank account.

Bank Statement. Document the bank uses to report what it did with the depositor's cash. Shows the bank account's beginning and ending balances and lists the month's cash transactions conducted through the bank.

Batch Processing. Computerized accounting for similar transactions in a group or batch.

Benchmarking. The practice of comparing a company with other companies that are leaders.

Board of Directors. Group elected by the stockholders to set policy and to appoint the officers.

Bonds Payable. Groups of notes payable issued to multiple lenders called bondholders.

Book Value. Amount of owners' equity on the company's books for each share of its stock.

Book Value (of a Plant Asset). The asset's cost minus accumulated depreciation.

Book Value per Share of Common Stock. Common stockholders' equity divided by the number of shares of common stock outstanding. The recorded amount for each share of common stock outstanding.

Breakeven Point. The sales level at which operating income is zero: Total revenues equal total expenses.

Budget. Quantitative expression of a plan that helps managers coordinate and implement the plan.

Bylaws. Constitution for governing a corporation.

Callable Bonds. Bonds that the issuer may call or pay off at a specified price whenever the issuer wants.

Capital Budgeting. Budgeting for the acquisition of capital assets—assets used for a long period of time.

Capital Charge. The amount that stockholders and lenders charge a company for the use of their money. Calculated as (Notes payable + Loans payable + Long-term debt + Stockholders' equity)

Capital Expenditure. Expenditure that increases the capacity or efficiency of an asset or extends its useful life. Capital expenditures are debited to an asset account.

Capital Expenditures Budget. A company's plan for purchases of property, plant, equipment, and other long-term assets.

Capital Lease. Lease agreement that meets any one of four criteria: (1) The lease transfers title of the leased asset to the lessee. (2) The lease contains a bargain purchase option. (3) The lease term is 75% or more of the estimated useful life of the leased asset. (4) The present value of the lease payments is 90% or more of the market value of the leased asset.

Cash Budget. Details how the business expects to go from the beginning cash balance to the desired ending balance. Also called the **statement of budgeted cash receipts and payments**.

Cash Equivalents. Highly liquid short-term investments that can be readily converted into cash.

Cash Flows. Cash receipts and cash payments.

Cash Payments Journal. Special journal used to record cash payments by check. Also called the **check register** or **cash disbursements journal**.

Cash Receipts Journal. Special journal used to record cash receipts.

Cash-Basis Accounting. Accounting that records transactions only when cash is received or paid.

Certified Management Accountant (CMA). A licensed accountant who works for a single company.

Certified Public Accountant (CPA). A licensed accountant who serves the general public rather than one particular company.

Chairperson. Elected by a corporation's board of directors, the most powerful person in the corporation.

Chart of Accounts. List of all the accounts and their account numbers in the ledger.

Charter. Document that gives the state's permission to form a corporation.

Check. Document that instructs a bank to pay the designated person or business a specified amount of money.

Closing Entries. Entries that transfer the revenue, expense, and owner withdrawal balances to the capital account.

Closing the Accounts. Step in the accounting cycle at the end of the period. Closing the accounts consists of journalizing and posting the closing entries to set the balances of the revenue, expense, and withdrawal accounts to zero for the next period.

Common Stock. The basic form of capital stock. In a corporation, the common stockholders are the owners of the business.

Common-Size Statement. A financial statement that reports only percentages (no dollar amounts).

Comprehensive Income. Company's change in total stockholders' equity from all sources other than from the owners.

Computer Virus. A malicious program that (a) reproduces itself, (b) enters program code without consent, and (c) performs destructive actions.

Conservatism. Reporting the least favorable figures in the financial statements.

Consistency Principle. A business should use the same accounting methods and procedures from period to period.

Consolidated Statements. Financial statements of the parent company plus those of majority-owned subsidiaries as if the combination were a single legal entity.

Constraint. A factor that restricts production or sale of a product.

Continuous Improvement. A philosophy requiring employees to continually look for ways to improve performance.

Contra Account. An account that always has a companion account and whose normal balance is opposite that of the companion account.

Contribution Margin. Sales revenue minus variable expenses.

Contribution Margin Income Statement. Income statement that groups costs by behavior —variable costs or fixed costs— and highlights the contribution margin.

Contribution Margin Ratio. Ratio of contribution margin to sales revenue.

Control Account. An account whose balance equals the sum of the balances in a group of related accounts in a subsidiary ledger.

Controller. The chief accounting officer of a company.

Controlling. Evaluating the results of business operations by comparing the actual results to the plan.

Controlling Interest. Ownership of more than 50% of an investee company's voting stock. Also called **majority interest**.

Conversion Costs. Direct labor plus manufacturing overhead.

Convertible Bonds. Bonds that may be converted into the common stock of the issuing company at the option of the investor.

Copyright. Exclusive right to reproduce and sell a book, musical composition, film, other work of art, or computer program. Issued by the federal government, copyrights extend 70 years beyond the author's life.

Corporation. A business owned by stockholders; it begins when the state approves its articles of incorporation. A corporation is a legal entity, an "artificial person," in the eyes of the law.

Cost Allocation. Assigning indirect costs (such as manufacturing overhead) to cost objects (such as jobs or production processes).

Cost Assignment. A general term that refers to both tracing direct costs and allocating indirect costs to cost objects.

Cost Behavior. Describes how costs change as volume changes.

Cost Driver. The primary factor that causes a cost.

Cost Object. Anything for which managers want a separate measurement of costs.

Cost of Capital. A weighted average of the returns demanded by the company's stockholders and lenders.

Cost of Goods Manufactured. The manufacturing (or plant-related) cost of the goods that finished the production process this period.

Cost of Goods Sold. The cost of the inventory that the business has sold to customers. Also called **cost of sales**.

Cost Tracing. Assigning direct costs (such as direct materials and direct labor) to cost objects (such as jobs or production processes) that used those costs.

Cost-Benefit Analysis. Weighing costs against benefits to help make decisions.

Cost-Volume-Profit (CVP) Analysis. Expresses the relationships among costs, volume, and profit or loss.

Credit. The right side of an account.

Credit Memorandum or Credit Memo. A document issued by a seller to credit a customer account for returned merchandise.

Creditor. The party to a credit transaction who sells goods or a service and obtains a receivable.

Cumulative Preferred Stock. Preferred stock whose owners must receive all dividends in arrears before the corporation pays dividends to the common stockholders.

Current Asset. An asset that is expected to be converted to cash, sold, or consumed during the next 12 months, or within the business's normal operating cycle if the cycle is longer than a year.

Current Liability. A debt due to be paid with cash or with goods and services within one year or within the entity's operating cycle if the cycle is longer than a year.

Current Portion of Long-Term Debt. Amount of the principal that is payable within one year. Also called **current maturity**.

Current Ratio. Current assets divided by current liabilities. Measures the company's ability to pay current liabilities from current assets.

Customer Service. Support provided for customers after the sale.

Data Warehouse. A very large database holding data for a number of years and used for analysis rather than for transaction processing.

Database. A computerized storehouse of information.

Days' Sales in Receivables. Ratio of average net accounts receivable to one day's sales. Indicates how many days' sales it takes to collect the average level of receivables. Also called the **collection period**.

Debentures. Unsecured bonds backed only by the good faith of the borrower.

Debit. The left side of an account.

Debit Memorandum or Debit Memo. A document issued by a buyer when returning merchandise. The memo informs the seller that the buyer no longer owes the seller for the amount of the returned purchases.

Debt Ratio. Ratio of total liabilities to total assets. Shows the proportion of a company's assets that it has financed with debt.

Debtor. The party to a credit transaction who makes a purchase and has a payable.

Deficit. Debit balance in the Retained Earnings account.

Depletion Expense. Portion of a natural resource's cost used up in a particular period. Computed in the same way as units-of-production depreciation.

Deposit in Transit. A deposit recorded by the company but not yet by its bank.

Depreciable Cost. The cost of a plant asset minus its estimated residual value.

Depreciation. The allocation of a plant asset's cost to expense over its useful life.

Design. Detailed engineering of products and services, or processes for producing them.

Direct Cost. A cost that can be specifically traced to a cost object.

Direct Labor. The compensation of employees who physically convert materials into the company's products; labor costs that are directly traceable to finished products.

Direct Materials. Materials that become a physical part of a finished product and whose costs are traceable to the finished product.

Direct Method. Format of the operating activities section of the statement of cash flows; lists the major categories of operating cash receipts and cash payments.

Direct Write-Off Method. A method of accounting for uncollectible receivables, in which the company waits until the credit department decides that a customer's account receivable is uncollectible, and then debits Uncollectible-Account Expense and credits the customer's Account Receivable.

Disclosure Principle. A business's financial statements must report enough information for outsiders to make knowledgeable decisions about the company.

Discount (on a Bond). Excess of a bond's maturity value over its issue price. Also called a **bond discount**.

Discount Rate. Management's minimum desired rate of return on an investment. Also called the **hurdle rate, required rate of return**, and **cost of capital**.

Discounting a Note Receivable. Selling a note receivable before its maturity date.

Dishonor of a Note. Failure of a note's maker to pay a note receivable at maturity. Also called **default on a note**.

Dissolution. Ending of a partnership.

Distribution. Delivery of products or services to customers.

Dividend Yield. Ratio of dividends per share of stock to the stock's market price per share. Tells the percentage of a stock's market value that the company returns to stockholders annually as dividends.

Dividends. Distributions by a corporation to its stockholders.

Double Taxation. Corporations pay their own income taxes on corporate income. Then, the stockholders pay personal income tax on the cash dividends they receive from corporations.

Double-Declining-Balance (DDB) Depreciation Method. An accelerated depreciation method that computes annual depreciation by multiplying the asset's decreasing book value by a constant percent that is two times the straight-line rate.

Earnings Per Share (EPS). Amount of a company's net income for each share of its outstanding common stock.

Economic Value Added (EVA). EVA = Net income + Interest expense − Capital charge. Used to evaluate a company's operating performance.

Efficiency Variance. Measures whether the quantity of materials or labor used to make the actual number of outputs is within the standard allowed for that number of outputs. This is computed as the difference in quantities (actual quantity of input used minus standard quantity of input allowed for the actual number of outputs) multiplied by the standard price per unit of the input.

Electronic Funds Transfer (EFT). System that transfers cash by electronic communication rather than by paper documents.

Encryption. Rearranging plain-text messages by a mathematical process; the primary method of achieving confidentiality in e-commerce.

Entity. An organization or a section of an organization that, for accounting purposes, stands apart from other organizations and individuals as a separate economic unit.

Equity Method. Method used to account for investments in which the investor has 20% to 50% of the investee's voting stock and can significantly influence the decisions of the investee.

Equivalent Units. Express the amount of work done during a period in terms of fully complete units of output.

Enterprise Resource Planning (ERP). Software systems that can integrate all of a company's worldwide functions, departments, and data into a single system.

Estimated Residual Value. Expected cash value of an asset at the end of its useful life. Also called **salvage value**.

Estimated Useful Life. Length of the service period expected from an asset. May be expressed in years, units of output, miles, or another measure.

Expense. Decrease in owner's equity that occurs from using assets or increasing liabilities in the course of delivering goods or services to customers.

External Failure Costs. Costs incurred when the company does not detect poor-quality goods or services until *after* delivery to customers.

Extraordinary Gains and Losses. A gain or loss that is both unusual for the company and infrequent. Also called **extraordinary items**.

Extraordinary Repair. Repair work that generates a capital expenditure.

Financial Accounting. The branch of accounting that focuses on information for people outside the firm.

Financial Accounting Standards Board (FASB). The private organization that determines how accounting is practiced in the United States.

Financial Budget. The case budget (cash inflows and outflows), the budgeted period-end balance sheet, and the budgeted statement of cash flows.

Financial Statements. Documents that report on a business in monetary amounts, providing information to help people make informed business decisions.

Financing Activities. Activities that obtain the cash needed to launch and sustain the business; a section of the statement of cash flows.

Finished Goods Inventory. Completed goods that have not yet been sold.

Firewalls. Devices that enable members of a local network to access the Internet but keep nonmembers out of the network.

First-In, First-Out (FIFO) Inventory Costing Method. Inventory costing method: the first costs into inventory are the first costs out to cost of goods sold. Ending inventory is based on the costs of the most recent purchases.

First-In, First-Out (FIFO) Process Costing Method. A process costing method that values each equivalent unit of work at the cost per equivalent unit in effect during the period the work is done.

Flexible Budget. A summarized budget that managers can easily compute for several different volume levels. Flexible budgets separate variable costs from fixed costs; it is the variable costs that put the "flex" in the flexible budget.

Flexible Budget Variance. The difference arising because the company actually earned more or less revenue, or incurred more or less cost, than expected for the actual level of output. This equals the difference between the actual amount and a flexible budget amount.

Foreign-Currency Exchange Rate. The measure of one currency against another currency.

Franchises, Licenses. Privileges granted by a private business or a government to sell a product or service under specified conditions.

Full Product Costs. The costs of all resources used throughout the value chain for a product.

General Ledger. Ledger of accounts that are reported in the financial statements.

General Partnership. A form of partnership in which each partner is an owner of the business, with all the privileges and risks of ownership.

Generally Accepted Accounting Principles (GAAP). Accounting guidelines, formulated by the Financial Accounting Standards Board, that govern how accountants measure, process, and communicate financial information.

Goodwill. Excess of the cost of an acquired company over the sum of the market values of its net assets (assets minus liabilities).

Gross Pay. Total amount of salary, wages, commissions, or any other employee compensation before taxes and other deductions.

Gross Profit. Excess of net sales revenue over cost of goods sold. Also called **gross margin**.

Gross Profit Method. A way to estimate inventory on the basis of the cost-of-goods-sold model: Beginning inventory + Net purchases = Cost of goods available for sale. Cost of goods available for sale − Cost of goods sold = Ending inventory.

Gross Profit Percentage. Gross profit divided by net sales revenue. A measure of profitability. Also called **gross margin percentage**.

Hardware. Electronic equipment that includes computers, disk drives, monitors, printers, and the network that connects them.

Hedging. Protecting oneself from losing money in one transaction by engaging in a counterbalancing transaction.

Held-to-Maturity Investments. Investment in bonds, notes, and other debt securities that the investor expects to hold until their maturity date.

Horizontal Analysis. Study of percentage changes in comparative financial statements.

Imprest System. A way to account for petty cash by maintaining a constant balance in the petty cash account, supported by the fund (cash plus payment tickets) totaling the same amount.

Income Statement. Summary of an entity's revenues, expenses, and net income or net loss for a specific period. Also called the **statement of earnings** or the **statement of operations**.

Income Summary. A temporary "holding tank" account into which revenues and expenses are transferred prior to their final transfer to the capital account.

Indirect Cost. A cost that cannot be specifically traced to a cost object.

Indirect Labor. Labor costs that are difficult to trace to specific products.

Indirect Materials. Materials whose costs cannot conveniently be directly traced to particular finished products.

Indirect Method. Format of the operating activities section of the statement of cash flows; starts with net income and reconciles to net cash provided by operating activities.

Intangibles. Assets with no physical form. Valuable because of the special rights they carry. Examples are patents and copyrights.

Interest. The revenue to the payee for loaning money; the expense to the debtor.

Interest period. The period of time during which interest is computed. It extends from the original date of the note to the maturity date. Also called **note term**, or simply **time**.

Interest rate. The percentage rate of interest specified by the note. Interest rates are almost always stated for a period of one year. A 9% note means that the amount of interest for one year is 9% of the note's principal amount.

Internal Control. Organizational plan and all the related measures adopted by an entity to safeguard assets, encourage employees to follow company policies, promote operational efficiency, and ensure accurate and reliable accounting records.

Internal Failure Costs. Costs incurred when the company detects and corrects poor-quality goods or services *before* delivery to customers.

Internal Rate of Return (IRR). The rate of return (based on discounted cash flows) that a company can expect to earn by investing in the project. The discount rate that makes the net present value of the project's cash flows equal to zero.

Inventoriable Product Costs. All costs of a product that GAAP requires companies to treat as an asset for external financial reporting. These costs are not expensed until the product is sold.

Inventory. All the goods that the company owns and expects to sell in the normal course of operations.

Inventory Turnover. Ratio of cost of goods sold to average inventory. Measures the number of times a company sells its average level of inventory during a year.

Investing Activities. Activities that increase or decrease long-term assets; a section of the statement of cash flows.

Invoice. A seller's request for cash from the purchaser.

Job Cost Record. Document that accumulates the direct materials, direct labor, and manufacturing overhead costs assigned to each individual job.

Job Costing. System for assigning costs to a specific unit or to a small batch of products or services that (1) pass through production steps as a distinct identifiable job and (2) can vary considerably in materials, labor, and overhead costs.

Journal. The chronological accounting record of an entity's transactions.

Just-in-Time (JIT). A system in which a company produces just in time to satisfy needs. Suppliers deliver materials just in time to begin production, and finished units are completed just in time for delivery to customers.

Just-in-Time (JIT) Costing. A standard costing system that starts with output completed and then assigns manufacturing costs to units sold and to inventories. Also called **backflush costing**.

Labor Time Record. Identifies the employee, the amount of time spent on a particular job, and the labor cost charged to the job; a record used to assign direct labor cost to specific jobs.

Last-In, Last-Out (LIFO) Inventory Costing Method. Inventory costing method: the last costs into inventory are the first costs out to cost of goods sold. Leaves the oldest costs—those of beginning inventory and the earliest purchases of the period—in ending inventory.

Lease. Rental agreement in which the tenant (lessee) agrees to make rent payments to the property owner (lessor) to obtain the use of the asset.

Ledger. The record holding all the accounts.

Legal Capital. The portion of stockholders' equity that cannot be used for dividends.

Lessee. Tenant in a lease agreement.

Lessor. Property owner in a lease agreement.

Leverage. Earning more income on borrowed money than the related interest expense, thereby increasing the earnings for the owners of the business.

Liability. An economic obligation (a debt) payable to an individual or an organization outside the business.

Limited Liability. No personal obligation of a stockholder for corporation debts. A stockholder can lose no more on an investment in a corporation's stock than the cost of the investment.

Limited Liability Partnership. A form of partnership in which each partner's personal liability for the business's debts is limited to a certain amount. Also called **LLPs**.

Limited Partnership. A partnership with at least two classes of partners: a general partner and limited partners.

Liquidation. The process of going out of business by selling the entity's assets and paying its liabilities. The final step in liquidation is the distribution of any remaining cash to the owner(s).

Liquidity. Measure of how quickly an item can be converted to cash.

Long-Term Asset. An asset other than a current asset.

Long-Term Investment. A noncurrent asset; a separate asset category reported on the balance sheet between current assets and plant assets.

Long-Term Liability. A liability other than a current liability.

Lower-of-Cost-or-Market (LCM) Rule. Rule that an asset should be reported in the financial statements at whichever is lower—its historical cost or its market value.

Maker of a Note. The person or business that signs the note and promises to pay the amount required by the note agreement; the debtor.

Management Accounting. The branch of accounting that focuses on information for internal decision makers of a business.

Management by Exception. Directs management's attention to important differences between actual and budgeted amounts.

Manufacturing Company. A company that uses labor, plant, and equipment to convert raw materials into new finished products.

Manufacturing Overhead. All manufacturing costs other than direct materials and direct labor. Also called **factory overhead** or **indirect manufacturing cost**.

Margin of Safety. Excess of expected sales over breakeven sales. Drop in sales a company can absorb without incurring an operating loss.

Market Interest Rate. Interest rate that investors demand in order to loan their money. Also called the **effective interest rate**.

Market Value. Price for which a person could buy or sell a share of stock.

Marketing. Promotion of products or services.

Market-Value Method. Used to account for all trading investments. These investments are reported at their current market value.

Master Budget. The set of budgeted financial statements and supporting schedules for the entire organization. Includes the operating budget, the capital expenditures budget, and the financial budget.

Matching Principle. Guide to accounting for expenses. Identify all expenses incurred during the period, measure the expenses, and match them against the revenues earned during that same time period.

Materiality Concept. A company must perform strictly proper accounting only for items that are significant to the business's financial statements.

Materials Inventory. Raw materials for use in manufacturing.

Materials Requisition. Request for the transfer of materials to the production floor, prepared by the production team.

Maturity Date. The date when final payment of the note is due. Also called the **due date**.

Maturity Value. The sum of the principal plus interest due at maturity.

Menu. A list of options for choosing computer functions.

Merchandising Company. A company that resells products previously bought from suppliers.

Minority Interest. A subsidiary company's equity that is held by stockholders other than the parent company.

Mixed Costs. Costs that have both variable and fixed components.

Module. Separate compatible units of an accounting package that are integrated to function together.

Mortgage. Borrower's promise to transfer the legal title to certain assets to the lender if the debt is not paid on schedule.

Multi-Step Income Statement. Format that contains subtotals to highlight significant relationships. In addition to net income, it reports gross profit and operating income.

Mutual Agency. Every partner can bind the business to a contract within the scope of the partnership's regular business operations.

Net Income. Excess of total revenues over total expenses. Also called **net earnings** or **net profit**.

Net Loss. Excess of total expenses over total revenues.

Net Pay. Gross pay minus all deductions. The amount of compensation that the employee actually takes home.

Net Present Value (NPV). The decision model that brings cash inflows and outflows back to a common time period by discounting these expected future cash flows to their present value, using a minimum desired rate of return.

Net Purchases. Purchases less purchase discounts and purchase returns and allowances.

Net Sales Revenue. Sales revenue less sales discounts and sales returns and allowances.

Network. The system of electronic linkages that allows different computers to share the same information.

Nonsufficient Funds (NSF) Check. A "hot" check, one for which the maker's bank account has insufficient money to pay the check.

Normal Balance. The balance that appears on the side of an account—debit or credit—where we record increases.

Note Payable. A written promise of future payment.

Note Receivable. A written promise for future collection of cash.

Online Processing. Computerized processing of related functions, such as the recording and posting of transactions, on a continuous basis.

Operating Activities. Activities that create revenue or expense in the entity's major line of business; a section of the statement of cash flows. Operating activities affect the income statement.

Operating Budget. Projects sales revenue, cost of goods sold, and operating expenses, leading to the budgeted income statement that projects operating income for the period.

Operating Cycle. Time span during which cash is paid for goods and services, which are then sold to customers from whom the business collects cash.

Operating Expenses. Expenses, other than cost of goods sold, that are incurred in the entity's major line of business. Examples include rent, depreciation, salaries, wages, utilities, and supplies expense.

Operating Income. Gross profit minus operating expenses plus any other operating revenues. Also called **income from operations**.

Operating Lease. Usually a short-term or cancelable rental agreement.

Opportunity Cost. The benefit forgone by not choosing an alternative course of action.

Ordinary Repair. Repair work that is debited to an expense account.

Other Expense. Expense that is outside the main operations of a business, such as a loss on the sale of plant assets.

Other Revenue. Revenue that is outside the main operations of a business, such as a gain on the sale of plant assets.

Outsourcing. A make-or-buy decision: managers decide whether to buy a component product or service or produce it in-house.

Outstanding Check. A check issued by the company and recorded on its books but not yet paid by its bank.

Outstanding Stock. Stock in the hands of stockholders.

Overallocated (Manufacturing) Overhead. The manufacturing overhead allocated to Work in Process Inventory is more than the amount of manufacturing overhead costs actually incurred.

Overhead Flexible Budget Variance. Shows how well management has controlled overhead costs. It is the difference between the actual overhead cost and the flexible budget overhead for the actual number of outputs.

Owner Withdrawals. Amounts removed from the business by an owner.

Owner's Equity. The claim of a business owner to the assets of the business. Also called **capital**.

Paid-in Capital. Capital from investments by the stockholders. Also called **contributed capital**.

Par Value. Arbitrary amount assigned to a share of stock.

Parent Company. An investor company that owns more than 50% of the voting stock of a subsidiary company.

Partnership. An association of two or more persons who co-own a business for profit.

Partnership Agreement. The contract between partners that specifies such items as the name, location, and nature of the business; the name, capital investment, and duties of each partner; and the method of sharing profits and losses among the partners. Also called **articles of partnership**.

Patent. A federal government grant giving the holder the exclusive right to produce and sell an invention for 20 years.

Payback. The length of time it takes to recover, in net cash inflows, the dollars of a capital outlay.

Payee of a Note. The person or business to whom the maker of a note promises future payment; the creditor.

Payroll. A major expense. Also called **employee compensation**.

Percent-of-Sales Method. A method of estimating uncollectible receivables that calculates uncollectible-account expense. Also called the **income-statement approach**.

Period Costs. Operating costs that are expensed in the period in which they are incurred.

Periodic Inventory System. A system in which the business does not keep a continuous record of inventory on hand. At the end of the period, it makes a physical count of on-hand inventory and uses this information to prepare the financial statements.

Permanent Accounts. Accounts that are *not* closed at the end of the period—the asset, liability, and capital accounts.

Perpetual Inventory System. The accounting inventory system in which the business keeps a running record of inventory and cost of goods sold.

Petty Cash. Fund containing a small amount of cash that is used to pay for minor expenditures.

Planning. Choosing goals and deciding how to achieve them.

Plant Assets. Long-lived tangible assets, such as land, buildings, and equipment, used to operate a business.

Plant or Fixed Asset. Another name for property, plant, and equipment.

Postclosing Trial Balance. List of the accounts and their balances at the end of the period after journalizing and posting the closing entries. This last step of the accounting cycle ensures that the ledger is in balance to start the next accounting period.

Posting. Copying amounts from the journal to the ledger.

Predetermined Manufacturing Overhead Rate. Estimated manufacturing overhead allocation rate computed at the beginning of the year, calculated as the total estimated manufacturing overhead costs divided by the total estimated quantity of the manufacturing overhead allocation base. Also called the **budgeted manufacturing overhead rate**.

Preferred Stock. Stock that gives its owners certain advantages over common stockholders, such as the right to receive dividends before the common stockholders and the right to receive assets before the common stockholders if the corporation liquidates.

Premium. Excess of a bond's issue price over its maturity value. Also called **bond premium**.

Prepaid Expense. Advance payments of expenses. Examples include prepaid rent, prepaid insurance, and supplies.

Present Value. Amount a person would invest now to receive a greater amount in the future.

President. Chief operating officer in charge of managing the day-to-day operations of a corporation.

Prevention Costs. Costs incurred to *avoid* poor-quality goods or services.

Price Variance. Measures how well the business keeps unit prices of material and labor inputs within standards. This is computed as the difference in prices (actual price per unit minus standard price per unit) of an input multiplied by the actual quantity of the input.

Price/Earnings Ratio. Ratio of the market price of a share of common stock to the company's earnings per share. Measures the value that the stock market places on $1 of a company's earnings.

Principal Amount, or Principal. The amount loaned out by the payee and borrowed by the maker of the note.

Prior-Period Adjustment. A correction to retained earnings for an error of an earlier period.

Process Costing. System for assigning costs to large numbers of identical units that usually proceed in a continuous fash-

ion through a series of uniform production steps or processes.

Production Cost Report. Summarizes a processing department's operations for a period.

Production or Purchases. Resources used to produce a product or service, or to purchase finished merchandise.

Production Volume Variance. Arises when actual production differs from expected production. It is the difference between (1) the manufacturing overhead cost in the flexible budget for actual outputs and (2) the standard overhead allocated to production.

Promissory note. A written promise to pay a specified amount of money at a particular future date.

Proprietorship. A business with a single owner.

Purchases Journal. Special journal used to record all purchases of inventory, supplies, and other assets on account.

Rate of Return on Common Stockholders' Equity. Net income minus preferred dividends, divided by average common stockholders' equity. A measure of profitability. Also called **return on equity**.

Rate of Return on Net Sales. Ratio of net income to net sales. A measure of profitability. Also called **return on sales**.

Rate of Return on Total Assets. Net income plus interest expense, divided by average total assets. Measures the success a company has in using its assets to earn income for those financing the business. Also called **return on assets**.

Receivables. Monetary claims against a business or an individual.

Relevant Information. Expected future data that differs among alternatives.

Relevant Range. The band of volume where total fixed costs remain constant and where the variable cost per unit remains constant.

Research and Development (R&D). Researching and developing new or improved products or services, or the processes for producing them.

Responsibility Accounting. A system for evaluating the performance of each responsibility center and its manager.

Responsibility Center. A part or subunit of an organization whose manager is accountable for specific activities.

Retained Earnings. Capital earned through profitable operation of the business.

Revenue. Amounts earned by delivering goods or services to customers. Revenues increase owner's equity.

Revenue Principle. The basis for recording revenues; tells accountants when to record revenue and the amount of revenue to record.

Reversing Entries. Special journal entries that ease the burden of accounting for transactions in the next period.

S Corporation. A corporation taxed in the same way as a partnership.

Sales Discount. Reduction in the amount receivable from a customer, offered by the seller as an incentive for the customer to pay promptly. A contra account to Sales Revenue.

Sales Journal. Special journal used to record credit sales.

Sales Mix. Combination of products that make up total sales.

Sales Returns and Allowances. Decreases in the seller's receivable from a customer's return of merchandise or from granting the customer an allowance from the amount owed to the seller. A contra account to Sales Revenue.

Sales Revenue. The amount that a merchandiser earns from selling its inventory. Also called **sales**.

Sales Volume Variance. The difference arising only because the number of units actually sold differs from the static budget units. This equals the difference between a static budget amount and a flexible budget amount.

Segment of the Business. One of various separate divisions of a company.

Sensitivity Analysis. A "what if" technique that asks what results will be if actual prices or costs change, or if an underlying assumption changes.

Serial Bonds. Bonds that mature in installments over a period of time.

Server. The main computer in a network, where the program and data are stored.

Service Company. A company that sells intangible services, rather than tangible products.

Short-Term Investment. A current asset; an investment that is readily convertible to cash and that the investor intends either to convert to cash within one year or use to pay a current liability. Also called a **marketable security**.

Short-Term Note Payable. Promissory note payable due within one year, a common form of financing.

Single-Step Income Statement. Format that groups all revenues together and then lists and deducts all expenses together without drawing any subtotals.

Social Security Tax. Federal Insurance Contributions Act (FICA) tax, which is withheld from employees' pay. Also called **FICA tax**.

Software. Set of programs or instructions that drive the computer to perform the work desired.

Specific-Unit-Cost Method. Inventory cost method based on the specific cost of particular units of inventory. Also called the **specific-identification method**.

Spreadsheet. A computer program that links data by means of formulas and functions; an electronic work sheet.

Standard Cost. A budget for a single unit.

Stated Interest Rate. Interest rate that determines the amount of cash interest the borrower pays and the investor receives each year.

Stated Value. An arbitrary amount that accountants treat as though it were par value.

Statement of Cash Flows. Reports cash receipts and cash payments during a period.

Statement of Owner's Equity. Summary of the changes in an entity's owner's equity during a specific period.

Statement of Stockholders' Equity. Reports the changes in all categories of stockholders' equity during the period.

Static Budget. The budget prepared for only one level of sales volume. Also called the **master budget**.

Stock. Shares into which the owners' equity of a corporation is divided.

Stock Dividend. A distribution by a corporation of its own stock to its stockholders.

Stock Split. An increase in the number of outstanding shares of stock coupled with a proportionate reduction in the par value of the stock.

Stockholder. A person who owns the stock of a corporation. Also called **shareholder**.

Stockholders' Equity. Owners' equity of a corporation.

Straight-Line (SL) Depreciation Method. Depreciation method in which an equal amount of depreciation expense is assigned to each year of asset use.

Strong Currency. A currency that is rising relative to other nations' currencies.

Subsidiary Company. A company in which a parent company owns more than 50% of the voting stock.

Subsidiary Ledger. Record of accounts that provides supporting details on individual balances, the total of which appears in a general ledger account.

Sunk Cost. A past cost that cannot be changed regardless of which future action is taken.

Supply-Chain Management. Exchange of information with suppliers and customers to reduce costs, improve quality, and speed delivery of goods and services from suppliers, through the company itself, and on to customers.

Target Cost. Allowable cost to develop, produce, and deliver the product or service. Equals target price minus desired profit.

Target Price. What customers are willing to pay for the product or service.

Temporary Accounts. The revenue and expense accounts that relate to a particular accounting period and are closed at the end of the period. For a proprietorship, the owner withdrawal account is also temporary.

Term Bonds. Bonds that all mature at the same time for a particular issue.

Throughput Time. The time between buying raw materials and selling finished products.

Time Record. Source document used to trace direct labor to specific jobs.

Time Value of Money. The fact that money can be invested to earn income over time.

Time-Period Concept. Ensures that information is reported at regular intervals.

Times-Interest-Earned Ratio. Ratio of income from operations to interest expense. Measures the number of times that operating income can cover interest expense. Also called the **interest-coverage ratio**.

Total Fixed Costs. Costs that do not change in total despite wide changes in volume.

Total Quality Management (TQM). A philosophy of delighting customers by providing them with superior products and services. Requires improving quality and eliminating defects and waste throughout the value chain.

Total Variable Costs. Costs that change in total in direct proportion to changes in volume.

Trademarks, Trade Names, or Brand Names. Assets that represent distinctive identifications of a product or service.

Trading Investments. Investments that are to be sold in the very near future with the intent of generating profits on price changes.

Trading on the Equity. Earning more income on borrowed money than the related interest expense, thereby increasing the earnings for the owners of the business. Also called **leverage**.

Transaction. An event that affects the financial position of a particular entity and can be recorded reliably.

Transferred-in Costs. Costs incurred in a previous process that are carried forward as part of the product's cost when it moves to the next process.

Treasury Stock. A corporation's own stock that it has issued and later reacquired.

Trend Percentages. A form of horizontal analysis in which percentages are computed by selecting a base year as 100% and expressing amounts for following years as a percentage of the base amount.

Trial Balance. A list of all the accounts with their balances.

Trojan Horse. A malicious program that works like a virus but does not reproduce.

Uncollectible-Account Expense. Cost to the seller of extending credit. Arises from the failure to collect from credit customers. Also called **doubtful-account expense**, or **bad-debt expense**.

Underallocated (Manufacturing) Overhead. The manufacturing overhead allocated to Work in Process Inventory is less than the amount of manufacturing overhead costs actually incurred.

Unearned Revenue. A liability created when a business collects cash from customers in advance of doing work. Also called **deferred revenue**.

Unemployment Compensation Tax. Payroll tax paid by employers to the government, which uses the money to pay unemployment benefits to people who are out of work.

Units-of-Production (UOP) Depreciation Method. Depreciation method by which a fixed amount of depreciation is assigned to each unit of output produced by an asset.

Unlimited Personal Liability. When a partnership (or a proprietorship) cannot pay its debts with business assets, the partners (or the proprietor) must use personal assets to meet the debt.

Value Chain. The activities that add value to a firm's products and services. Includes R&D, design, production or purchases, marketing, distribution, and customer service.

Value Engineering. Reevaluating activities to reduce costs while satisfying customer needs.

Variable Costing. The costing method that assigns only variable manufacturing costs to products.

Variance. The difference between an actual amount and the budget. A variance is labeled as favorable if it increases operating income and unfavorable if it decreases operating income.

Vertical Analysis. Analysis of a financial statement that reveals the relationship of each statement item to a specified base, which is the 100% figure.

Voucher. Instrument authorizing a cash payment.

Weak Currency. A currency that is falling relative to other nations' currencies.

Weighted-Average Process Costing Method. A process costing method that costs all equivalent units of work with a weighted average of the previous period's and the current period's cost per equivalent unit.

Withheld Income Tax. Income tax deducted from employees' gross pay.

Work in Process Inventory. Goods that are partway through the manufacturing process but not yet complete.

Work Sheet. A columnar document designed to help move data from the trial balance to the financial statements.

Working Capital. Current assets minus current liabilities; measures a business's ability to meet its short-term obligations with its current assets.

Company Index

■Subject Index

SINGLE PC LICENSE AGREEMENT AND LIMITED WARRANTY

READ THIS LICENSE CAREFULLY BEFORE USING THIS PACKAGE. BY USING THIS PACKAGE, YOU ARE AGREEING TO THE TERMS AND CONDITIONS OF THIS LICENSE. IF YOU DO NOT AGREE, DO NOT USE THE PACKAGE. PROMPTLY RETURN THE UNUSED PACKAGE AND ALL ACCOMPANYING ITEMS TO THE PLACE YOU OBTAINED THEM. **THESE TERMS APPLY TO ALL LICENSED SOFTWARE ON THE DISK EXCEPT THAT THE TERMS FOR USE OF ANY SHAREWARE OR FREEWARE ON THE DISKETTES ARE AS SET FORTH IN THE ELECTRONIC LICENSE LOCATED ON THE DISK:**

1.   **GRANT OF LICENSE and OWNERSHIP:**   The enclosed computer programs and data ("Software") are licensed, not sold, to you by Pearson Education, Inc. (publishing as "We" or the "Company") and in of your purchase or adoption of the accompanying Company textbooks and/or other materials, and your agreement to these terms. We reserve any rights not granted to you. You own only the disk(s) but we and/or our licensors own the Software itself.   This license allows you to use and display your copy of the Software on a single computer (i.e., with a single CPU) at a single location for academic use only, so long as you comply with the terms of this Agreement. You may make one copy for back up, or transfer your copy to another CPU, provided that the Software is usable on only one computer.

2.   **RESTRICTIONS:**   You may not transfer or distribute the Software or documentation to anyone else. Except for backup, you may not copy the documentation or the Software. You may not network the Software or otherwise use it on more than one computer or computer terminal at the same time. You may not reverse engineer, disassemble, decompile, modify, adapt, translate, or create derivative works based on the Software or the Documentation. You may be held legally responsible for any copying or copyright infringement that is caused by your failure to abide by the terms of these restrictions.

3.   **TERMINATION:**   This license is effective until terminated. This license will terminate automatically without notice from the Company if you fail to comply with any provisions or limitations of this license. Upon termination, you shall destroy the Documentation and all copies of the Software. All provisions of this Agreement as to limitation and disclaimer of warranties, limitation of liability, remedies or damages, and our ownership rights shall survive termination.

4.   **LIMITED WARRANTY AND DISCLAIMER OF WARRANTY:**   Company warrants that for a period of 60 days from the date you purchase this SOFTWARE (or purchase or adopt the accompanying textbook), the Software, when properly installed and used in accordance with the Documentation, will operate in substantial conformity with the description of the Software set forth in the Documentation, and that for a period of 30 days the disk(s) on which the Software is delivered shall be free from defects in materials and workmanship under normal use. The Company does not warrant that the Software will meet your requirements or that the operation of the Software will be uninterrupted or error-free. Your only remedy and the Company's only obligation under these limited warranties is, at the Company's option, return of the disk for a refund of any amounts paid for it by you or replacement of the disk. THIS LIMITED WARRANTY IS THE ONLY WARRANTY PROVIDED BY THE COMPANY AND ITS LICENSORS, AND THE COMPANY AND ITS LICENSORS DISCLAIM ALL OTHER WARRANTIES, EXPRESS OR IMPLIED, INCLUDING WITHOUT LIMITATION, THE IMPLIED WARRANTIES OF MERCHANTABILITY AND FITNESS FOR A PARTICULAR PURPOSE. THE COMPANY DOES NOT WARRANT, GUARANTEE OR MAKE ANY REPRESENTATION REGARDING THE ACCURACY, RELIABILITY, CURRENTNESS, USE, OR RESULTS OF USE, OF THE SOFTWARE.

5.   **LIMITATION OF REMEDIES AND DAMAGES:**   IN NO EVENT, SHALL THE COMPANY OR ITS EMPLOYEES, AGENTS, LICENSORS, OR CONTRACTORS BE LIABLE FOR ANY INCIDENTAL, INDIRECT, SPECIAL, OR CONSEQUENTIAL DAMAGES ARISING OUT OF OR IN CONNECTION WITH THIS LICENSE OR THE SOFTWARE, INCLUDING FOR LOSS OF USE, LOSS OF DATA, LOSS OF INCOME OR PROFIT, OR OTHER LOSSES, SUSTAINED AS A RESULT OF INJURY TO ANY PERSON, OR LOSS OF OR DAMAGE TO PROPERTY, OR CLAIMS OF THIRD PARTIES, EVEN IF THE COMPANY OR AN AUTHORIZED REPRESENTATIVE OF THE COMPANY HAS BEEN ADVISED OF THE POSSIBILITY OF SUCH DAMAGES. IN NO EVENT SHALL THE LIABILITY OF THE COMPANY FOR DAMAGES WITH RESPECT TO THE SOFTWARE EXCEED THE AMOUNTS ACTUALLY PAID BY YOU, IF ANY, FOR THE SOFTWARE OR THE ACCOMPANYING TEXTBOOK. BECAUSE SOME JURISDICTIONS DO NOT ALLOW THE LIMITATION OF LIABILITY IN CERTAIN CIRCUMSTANCES, THE ABOVE LIMITATIONS MAY NOT ALWAYS APPLY TO YOU.

6.   **GENERAL:**   THIS AGREEMENT SHALL BE CONSTRUED IN ACCORDANCE WITH THE LAWS OF THE UNITED STATES OF AMERICA AND THE STATE OF NEW YORK, APPLICABLE TO CONTRACTS MADE IN NEW YORK, AND SHALL BENEFIT THE COMPANY, ITS AFFILIATES AND ASSIGNEES. HIS AGREEMENT IS THE COMPLETE AND EXCLUSIVE STATEMENT OF THE AGREEMENT BETWEEN YOU AND THE COMPANY AND SUPERSEDES ALL PROPOSALS OR PRIOR AGREEMENTS, ORAL, OR WRITTEN, AND ANY OTHER COMMUNICATIONS BETWEEN YOU AND THE COMPANY OR ANY REPRESENTATIVE OF THE COMPANY RELATING TO THE SUBJECT MATTER OF THIS AGREEMENT. If you are a U.S. Government user, this Software is licensed with "restricted rights" as set forth in subparagraphs (a)-(d) of the Commercial Computer-Restricted Rights clause at FAR 52.227-19 or in subparagraphs (c)(1)(ii) of the Rights in Technical Data and Computer Software clause at DFARS 252.227-7013, and similar clauses, as applicable.

Should you have any questions concerning this agreement or if you wish to contact the Company for any reason, please contact in writing:
Director, Media Production
Prentice Hall Business Publishing
1 Lake Street
Upper Saddle River, New Jersey 07458